CIVIC WORSHIP

The GOOD BOOK

 Compiled by Patricia H. Bean.

This publication is simply the opinions of many contributors
and the entity will not be held liable in any way for its contents.
About 250 volunteer readers contributed to this publication.

CIVIC WORSHIP & Infinity Bible are the same book.

1st edition.

Many of the scriptures have been shortened due to page length
of the book.

This book is an attempt to provide a historical and religious
perspective of faiths and lives, and how we treat each other.

CE means Current Era
BCE means Before Current Era

Books of the CIVIC

FAITH

1. Rejoice, O Follower of God, for there is none like the Lord, who has knowledge of all things. Sing praises to the Lord, for the Lord has done excellent things; let this be known to all the Earth. The Lord is the Everlasting God who governs the universe and who leads the people in strength. The Lord is Almighty and Powerful and will reign forever and ever. God is perfect in wisdom and understanding. Behold, the Great One! All the people of the Earth recognize the hand of the Lord as mighty and will revere the Lord forever! You are great, O Lord; there is none like you. You have established yourself to your people forever. Your name shall be magnified forever.

2. Let the heavens be glad and let the earth rejoice; and let people say among themselves, the Lord reigns! Let the sea roar, let the fields rejoice, and all things in it! Let the lights of the universe brighten, let the trees of the woods sing out for joy before the Lord, for the Lord is the One who balances the clouds and shines the rainbows, makes the lightening for the rain, and brings forth the wind to cause the vapors to ascend to the ends of the Earth. The Lord made the Universe by Holy Power. In the inner peace of the Lord, we find everlasting happiness.

3. The Lord is the taste in water, the light in the moon and the sun, the syllables of love that we speak, the sound in air, the fragrance of the earth, the life in the living, the wisdom of those who follow good ways, the brilliance of the fire, the heat of the sun, and unselfishness. The Lord can hold back rain and release it. The Lord is life and death, and all that is and is not.

The Lord is the father and mother of the universe, the essence and goal of all knowledge, the beginning and the end, origin and dissolution, refuge, home, true lover, womb and imperishable seed.

4. The Lord established the universe by divine understanding. God judges and governs the Earth.
The Lord reigns under the heavens to the ends of the universe, as far as the east is from the west, the north is from the south, and as far as all zenith above to all nadir below. The Lord knows all of the azimuth angle measurement degrees.

5. Let us worship the Lord, Our Maker, for the Lord is our God and we are all God's people, for God shows no partiality.
Worship the Lord in the beauty of holiness; let the whole Earth stand in awe of Our Creator. We are believers and humble servants who hear your calling, O Lord, and we will follow You all the days of our lives with perfect faith. We pray for peace and guidance from the Spirit to fill our hearts and minds for our good and for the good of all people. Lord, fill us with Your Presence. You are our Living Home. Praise be to God when your heart is engaged in commemoration of God and your soul is gladdened and absorbed in prayer, asking for the Lord's guidance.

Let God's beloved, each and every one, be the essence of purity, the very life of holiness and sanctified, humble before the Lord. This is the station of the sincere; this is the way of the loyal; this is the brightness that shines on the face of those near God. Prophets and saints are bridges to God.

Wherefore must the friends of God, with utter sanctity, with one accord, rise up in spirit, in unity with one another to become one being and one soul to achieve one spiritual union.

Let us dwell in unity and individually be bringers of joy, even as the angels and spirits.

Let not selfish motives drag you away from the Cause of the Holiness, to unite all people in peace and love. The center of love of all religions is a divine one.

Be like a lighthouse of hope and healing to others.

As for the doers of mischief, their works are like the vapour in a desert which the thirsty dream to be water, a mirage until when they come unto it, they find nothing. O you loved ones of God! Be committed to holiness and serve the Lord, being servants even to each other. Save yourself and save poor lost souls and dedicate your life to follow the Lord. Strive with your heart and soul to make this world a mirror-image of the Divine Realm. Friends of God should stand strong together to engage with love and joy to spread the good news of the Lord and hear the word of the Lord.

May divine teachings reach the peoples of the world and be set forth with brilliance and eloquence in the spiritual assemblages of humanity, for the good of the whole world. Spirit of God, Your presence is welcomed here.

6. Meditate in Self, let go of conflict, and find the enlightenment of nirvana, where you embrace all of the universal energy as connected; then you will know the Creator in a state of balance. As a lamp sheltered from the wind does not flicker, compare this to a person of yoga when the mind has become serene and the unruly senses of the mind have been restrained, and the focus is on the Creator of the Cosmos and the elemental unity of all beings in the Akasha Realm of universal energy.

7. Be praised, adored, and thanked, O Lord, forever and ever. Yours, O Lord, is the greatness behind all power and glory and all victory and majesty. All that is in the heavens and earth is Yours. The universe is Your Realm, O Lord, and Yours it is to be exalted as Head Over All.

8. The Lord is the Holy of Holies. I will rejoice in the divine wisdom of the Lord.

9. Give thanks to the Lord, call on God's name; make known God's doings among the peoples. Let your decree cry out for the Spirit! Believe with perfect faith that all creation reveals the Lord's Majesty!

10. Glory to The Holy Names; let the hearts of those who seek the Lord rejoice

11. Seek the eternal life-giving, honey-sweet ways of the Spirit; this Holy Ghost is the unseen and unknown God, the Spirit that is called by many names.

Humankind must renounce the own self of inordinate desires and selfish purposes, and seek the guidance of the Spirit, and follow the yearnings of the Buddha Higher Self, with thy heart fixed upon the Beauty of God.

12. The clear signs of presence are shown to us from our Lord, that is the whole universe, and whatever has come to be, and the vital breaths of life and rhythms that are established in the space outside of a human and in the space inside of a human, and the light which shines beyond the heavens, and on to the back of all things, and every single thing, in the highest and most exalted worlds, that is indeed the same heat and light felt, seen or heard within all people and life.

13. The Unknown One is in my Self within the heart, smaller than a grain of rice or a mustard seed and yet in every cell of my body, and encompasses all works, all desires, all scents, all tastes, all light and sound, and all knowledge and matter of the universe and does not speak; when we depart from hence shall we merge into it.

14. And when the end approaches, a life is something that cannot be destroyed and can never fall or fail, but is only quickened by the breath of life into the highest light and is given to the Plans of the Unknown God. God is our beginning and our end.

15. And the secret doctrine of the Holy Spirit never sets and it never rests but the truth is always in the midst, and faith continues through time.

16. Praise the Lord our God, Who rules the Cosmos. The Lord has established

the Holy Firmament forever. There is no Rock like our God Who is a strong Fortress and a shield for those who trust; the Lord is our refuge and rest. God is our Deliverer from hopelessness and despair, our Strength to show us the way.

17. The scriptures and the world call the Holy Spirit the Ultimate Person, the highest Self. The Spirit is the source of all memory and knowledge and future, all life-giving power and all elements.

18. Sing to the Lord, all the Earth; show forth from day to day the work of Holy Salvation. Declare glorious and holy works among the people, for great is the Lord and greatly to be praised. Let everything that hath breath praise the Lord.

19. The Lord is perfect and the Lord's ways are perfect. The Lord has perfect timing and has complete knowledge of all things seen and unseen.
The Holy Spirit is the Divine Testament of the Messengers.

O sons and daughters of the Universe, thanks to the teachings and loving acts of faithful ones who lived before us, Teachers of God who are now songsters in the meadows of truth and have soared beyond to the realm of glory and are now Angels and Saints of the Heavens, so let the breaths of the Spirit blow upon you; wherefore, with great gladness, engage in praise and glorification of the Lord at every moment, and pray a myriad of thanks for the Lord's abounding favor, exceeding grace, and energy.
All of the great Teachers of God are like Blessed Trees with arms of love and strength stretched forth
from the Lord! So let your yourself be a great teacher for the Blessed Beautiful Lord!

20. You are the God Who does mysterious works; You are the Mysterious Wonder. You have demonstrated Your Power among the people. You, O Lord, are enthroned forever; and the fame of Your Names endures to all generations.

CREATION

1. Even before the beginning of all time, Our Creator was the source of all origin. The question of who God is is a very old question.
No one knows if God is male, female, in human-form or another, or Spirit only. It may be that female characteristics of God exist in women, male characteristics of God exist in men, and other characteristics exist in other elements. People have different philosophies about the origin of the universe and humankind.
2. From Divine Treasures of Mighty Power, God created the elements of the whole universe, but whether creation was commanded in silence, by divine syllable, or by a golden egg arising from a lotus flower - it is not known.
In the beginning God created the chemistry of atoms such as hydrogen, helium, lithium, gold, copper, iron, carbon, oxygen and others. Each of the basic elements of the universe have their own unique number of positively charged protons in the nucleus, negatively charged electrons around the nucleus, atomic weight, density, atomic radius, and crystal structure; these attributes give the elements their own unique properties. There are 92 naturally occurring elements that scientists have identified, and elements 93 thru 118 have been produced in nuclear reactors. Elements may be solids, liquids, gases, and possibly plasmas in intersetellar space.

Billions of molecules are needed to make a speck visible to the naked eye, even to see a single dot on this page.

God put two hydrogen atoms together with one oxygen atom and created water. The Lord is the Master Scientist.

The Lord also created the anti-matter; it is identical to matter except that it is composed of particles whose electric charges are opposite to those found in normal matter. But there is an asymmetry of matter and antimatter in the visible universe; this is a great unsolved problem in physics.

Scientists believe the universe was created between 8 and 14 billion years ago. Our solar system with one star and planets was created 4 billion years ago. An exoplanet is a planet in another solar system.

The story of Adam and Eve, the first man and woman in the Garden of Eden, was told in religions originating from the Middle East around the Mediterranean Sea. The Japanese Tenrikyo religion tells that the first two humans were created by God at a pillar called Jiba at Nihon in Japan.
3. The complexities in the design of the universe are beyond human knowledge. The order in which God created the universe is unknown, and only God of Infinite Wisdom knows the order of all origin.

4. God created light and darkness and sound, and the speed of light and the speed of sound and the

totality of everything in existence including all space, time, matter, energy, planets, stars, comets, and galaxies. God created the sound of silence.

5. In the vastness of celestial universe, the Lord created many solar systems and galaxies. Outer space is not a perfect vacuum and contains charged particles, electromagnetic fields, stars and other matter; but there may be perfect vacuums between galaxies. Only the Lord knows the boundaries and shape of the universe and which direction is truly up, down or sideways; scientists believe the universe is curved or flat because they have been studying math and observing what goes on in particle accelerators. Scientists have been known to say the energy that created the universe and all elements is of divine nature. Only God knows the center of the universe. Only God knows the significance of all creation.

Cosmologists believe a Big Bang Theory could explain how our universe and even our solar system were formed from one point in a huge cloud of dust and gas. Gravity caused the cloud to collapse inward and begin to rotate. At the center, the temperature rose to a point where hydrogen fused to form helium and the Sun was born. Away from the sun the dust particles were drawn together by electrostatic forces, sunlight, and other forces, and gradually rocks were formed which collided together to form planets. The four planets nearest the Sun – Mercury, Venus, Earth, and Mars - are made up largely of solid rocky material. The planets farther away – Jupiter, Saturn, Uranus, and Neptune - are made of gas. Pluto is the planet that is the ninth one out; it is a solitary ice ball. Pluto is so far out that if you were on Pluto, the sun would appear in the sky as a tiny dot. A rocket launched in 2006 CE reached Pluto in 2014 and then kept on going out further into the Universe.

It takes sunlight 8 minutes to reach the earth and 5.5 years to reach Pluto. The equation used to calculate how long it takes sunlight to reach earth: sunlight travels 150,000,000 km divided by 300,000 km/sec = 500 seconds. 500 seconds divided by 60 seconds is approximately 8 minutes.

Moonlight reaches the earth in 1.26 seconds.

As the universe expanded, it created space; but it is not known if this space exists inside of another space. Some scientists thought the whole universe was created from one mass, but others think there was an inflationary reaction. Some scientists think the universe was created in 3 minutes. No one knows exactly how the universe was created, but people hope that one day the Lord will reveal the knowledge.

It is believed that in recent centuries, fewer stars and galaxies are forming. There is much dark matter and dark energy that fill the void of space which are a type of

anti-gravity causing the expansion of the universe to speed up. Will the anti-gravity overpower gravity, causing the universe to contract back in, causing a Big Crunch? Or will gravity win over anti-gravity and leave the universe intact? Or will the universe simply continue to expand forever after all the stars have died?
Or will a Big Rip occur in the universe, shredding all galaxies and atoms? At the center of the galaxy is a black hole that emanates 511 keV gamma rays; the black hole totally annihilates incoming particles and nothing is left. All neutrons are crushed to nothing.

Asteroid and comet belts exist between planets and such rocks may hit the earth once in a million years; such occurrences are hard to detect until six months in advance, which would not give people enough time on earth to prepare for a hit. Currently there are no rockets on earth or missiles ready in space that could destroy such asteroids well in advance before they may hit the earth. Scientists around the earth are uniting in space efforts to protect the planet from asteroid hits and other dangers to the global atmosphere. The gravity of Jupiter captured some asteroids that could have hit earth.

Scientists believe that most species on earth only survive for about 4 million years due
to events that happen on earth. Modern humans have only existed for around 50,000 years as of 2000CE.

Cosmologists have heard the sounds emitted by photons of cosmic radiation leftover from the Big Bang and it can be visibly seen 90 billion trillion miles away from the planet earth.

The nearest star is called Proxima Centauri. The next nearest star is called Sirius. The average distance between stars is 20 million million miles.

The Earth is part of the Milky Way galaxy. The next nearest galaxy is called Andromeda.
The two galaxies are expected to collide because of gravitational attraction, but this will be in billions of years. There are about 30 galaxies in our cluster of galaxies.
Investigators think our sun is getting hotter and hotter and in 500,000 million years animal and plant life will not exist on our planet.

In the northern hemisphere, Polaris is the North Star. The North Star is over the North Pole. To visually locate the North Star, find the Big Dipper Constellation which looks like a cup with a long handle. There are two stars that form the side of the cup not attached to the handle. To the right of those stars should be the bright North Star.

6. When God created the universe and all processes of evolution with divine energy, the planets were

made to spin and comets travel, the Earth was made to revolve around the sun, and the moon to revolve around the Earth, although no one is sure of the order. Some cosmologists think the moon might have been an asteroid or another planet that hit the earth and either bounced off of the earth and ended up in the orbit of the earth or pieces of the earth's crust broke up and orbited the earth and coalesced to form the Moon. The impact collision theory explains the 23-degree tilt angle of the earth from a perpendicular axis with the Sun which is
the reason for the seasons.
Without the tilt and no seasons, day length all over the world would be the same all year round, and scientists believe the poles would be much colder and extend farther, there would be no wet and dry seasons in subtropical regions, the deserts would be more extensive, and animals would not have a reason to migrate due to effects of seasonal changes like temperature and food availability. Scientists believe the moon's gravity stabilizes the tilt of the earth; without the moon the tilt of the earth might vary, which could even cause the earth's poles to tilt toward the sun, melting the ice caps totally.

The days in between seasons may be partially warm and partially cold.

If the tides stopped, the top layer of the ocean could become stagnant; the results are uncertain.

The tides of the oceans are key to understanding how the moon got out to where it is today and why the day is 24 hours long. Scientists believe the earth was closer to the sun millions of years ago and a day was 6 hours long because earth rotated faster. The Sun and the Moon are vital to life as we know it on Earth.
Scientists have been studying the moon for a long time, and with the help of laser instruments, they have determined that the moon is slowly moving away from the earth. With the aid of atomic clocks, scientists have determined that the rotation or spin of the earth is slowing down by a few nanoseconds each year.

If someone struck a match on the moon in the year 2000CE, astronomers could see the flare with a telescope, such is the great progress that is being made in the world by good humans who are seeking knowledge.

Scientists believe there was no oxygen in the Earth's atmosphere in the beginning of the creation of the earth, but mostly only hydrogen, hydrogen sulfide, and carbon dioxide. Asteroids that were still hitting the earth may have brought the first primitive carbon compounds onto the surface of the earth. These earliest organisms may have emitted oxygen, which gradually formed a part of the atmosphere.

Scientists know that water is two hydrogen atoms and one oxygen atom, and there is also heavy water which is HDO, or Deuterium protium oxide.

7. God created beautiful sunrises, sunsets, rainbows, sunbeams, moonbeams, and nighttime skies sparkling with stars, the crescent phases of the moon, the full moon, and the new moon, the eclipses of the sun, the auroras at the poles. During a solar eclipse, the pupils of your eyes dilate when the sky darkens, and it is dangerous to look at the eclipse because solar rays could cause retinal damage.

A laser is a man-made rainbow and lasers can be dangerous.

8. Upon the Earth, the Lord created the land, the sky, the wind, the gravity known as 10 to the 38 power, the waters, the weather of hot, cold, medium, rainy, dry, windy, humid, misty, foggy, clear, cloudy, and the seasons. God created the sound of the ocean surf, the swish of the wind, the sounds of animals, the boom of thunder, the cooling of rainfall, the heat of lightening and fire, and the genetic evolution of all life.

Acid rain or poison rain is rain that is high in acid content caused emissions of sulfur dioxide and nitrogen oxide.
9. The Lord created the breath of life, animal and plant divisions, mineral divisions, and intellect and interrelationships.

10. The Lord created genetics and the Lord is the Master Geneticist. Genetics is the complex code for each organism. If you are reading this, you are a miracle that you exist as a result of all genetic life that has evolved since the first protoplasmic primordial atomic globule millions of years ago; you are special. Humans live about 650,000 hours or 74 years. Chimera genetics changes the genes of God's evolution and involves mixing human genes with the genes of animals; it is controversial.

11. The Lord created the calmness and stillness of a dormant time to sleep and rest. The bears hibernate through a winter season.The Lord created a springtime of renewal and energy. The alternating forces of rest and energy are seen in humans, animals, and nature. Even while dormant, cells are alive, and this is a divine mystery and one of the holy laws.

12. All energy comes from the domain of the Divine Realm. The universe was created from divine power that is unbeknownst. The energy of Our Creator, angels, saints, and the energies of animals, plants, mineral rocks, matter, and humans are all part of universal energy.

Many believe the celestial energy of the divine angels is all around us, doing the Lord's work. No one knows for sure.

Nobody knows why humans have to experience natural disasters and personal disasters or bad things such as tornadoes, hurricances, cyclones, hail storms, droughts, floods, dust storms, epidemics of diseases, personal illnesses, fires, mental breakdowns, abuse and hatred, self-hatred, divorces, or fraud and injustices but life goes on, we can seek help and help each other to make the world a better place. Some things can be rebuilt from nothing. Some things cannot be fixed but must be learned to cope with.

The synergy of all human beings on the planet working together as a team is good for the planet. For as in one physical body, we have many parts and all the parts do not have the same function, such as ears, eyes, hands, and legs. So, numerous as we are, one with the Spirit, yet individually we are parts of another. We all have gifts, faculties, talents, and qualities that differ according to the grace given us. Humans need each other and we are all a part of the same synergy. We are all a part of universal energy that was created by the Divine Unknown.

And what we do in this life reverberates throughout the halls of heaven for all of eternity.

13. The Lord created life and universe for all generations past, present, and future.

14. God stands for goodness (righteousness, dharma, ren, yi, and li).

15. Many believe the ways and purposes of the Lord are perfect. The Lord has perfect timing (godspeed) and complete knowledge of all things. The Spirit is the supreme judge and administrator of the universe.

16. With providence, the Spirit of the Lord rules the angels who are the heavenly beings and the saints who are the souls of the deceased.

17. Our Creator is beyond comprehension and imagination. Only the Lord knows the true meaning of everything that was, is, and is yet to come. God is greater than great. The knowledge that God has of all things is supreme and perfect.
The work of the Divine encompasses all dimensions of time, space, and matter and is unbeknownst to humanity.
Many believe that the Lord gives humans divine knowledge or inspiration to create things.

18. Through eras of time, God's works have been for a divine purpose that only God knows, a reasoning that surpasses human logic.

AFFIRMATIONS

CHAPTER 1
Religious Rituals

1. The Lord is at the center of all religions. God knows the truth of all things. The beatific vision of God is the finest destiny that anyone can hope for.

Humble servants seek the love and guidance of God, the divine unknown mysterious wonder. We are subservient to the Lord, who is over us.
God is ultimately unique. God is reserved and set apart, different from everything else.
We can do all things through the love of the Lord, who strengthens us!

Religions are man-made philosophies but many feel the religions were inspired by God. The Lord exists for all.
It is acknowledged that peoples and cultures have created names, words of instructions, songs, and customs that have been passed from generation to generation for the glory of Our Creator and to establish images of the sacred. A purpose of religions is for healing, not hatred and destruction.

At the end of prayers, words are said to verify the truths of religious beliefs.

'Gloria!' is Latin and means 'Glory to you who has shown us the light.'

'Kyrie eleison' is Greek and means 'Give thanks to the Lord who is good, whose mercy endures forever.'

'Baruch ata Adonai' is Hebrew and means 'Blessed are you Lord Our God, Creator of the Universe.'

'Om' is Sanskrit and means 'that which is sounded loudly from everywhere in the Universe and in human hearts.'

'Alleluia' is Hebrew and means 'Praise God.'

'Amen' is a Hebrew, Greek, Arabic, and Christian word that means 'Truly' or 'Verily'.

'Selah' is a Hebrew word that means 'Listen and know it is forever.'

'Shalom' is Hebrew and means 'peace'.

'Namaste' is a Hindu greeting that means 'I bow to the divine in you.'

'Nam myo-ho renge kyo' is a Buddhist mantra that means 'attain perfect and complete awakening, a devotion to the mystic Law of the Lotus Sutra.'

'Siyahamba' is South African Zulu language and means 'We are marching in the light of God.'

'Bwana Awabariki' is Swahili for 'May God grant you a blessing.'

'Kumbaya' is African for 'We join hands in agreement.'

'Hehewuti' in Native American Hopi means 'warrrior mother spirit.' 'Heammawihio' means 'wise one above' in Cheyenne. 'Wicapi' means 'holy star.' 'Kwanita' means 'God is Gracious' in Zuni. 'Dakota' means friend.

Pa Makha De Kha means May your journey be safe and happy in Pashtunwali language in Afghanistan and Pakistan.

Kuila i ka nu'u is a Hawaiian proverb that means 'Strive for the highest.'

Adebimpe means the crown is complete in Yoruba.

Chanting to drumbeats or singing hymns solo or by a choir (a chorus of people) accompanied by musical instruments such as stringed instruments, organs, and pianos has existed for thousands of years. Songs sung a capello or acapella means with out music. A capello is an Italian term that means 'in the style of the chapel' without music. Southern gospel music consists of two to four people harmonizing melodies together with or without music. Modern religious music may be played by rock and roll bands, on electronic keyboards, and more.

2. The Lord is all things to all people. To those needing compassion, the Lord is compassionate. To those needing strength, the Lord is a strengthener. To those needing counseling, the Lord is listening. To those needing love and security, the Lord is there for us. The Lord may not answer our prayers and concerns immediately, but in God's time according to divine plans.

3. Bless the hearts of those who seek the Lord. Bless the hearts of those who are hurting or suffering. Bless the hearts of those who are trying to achieve and do good things. Bless the hearts of those who know not that they are being taken advantage of by evil ones. Bless the hearts of those who are trying their best but are being ridiculed.

4. Faith is the assurance of the things we hope for, being the proof of things we do not see and the conviction of their reality. By faith we understand that all creation is fashioned and equipped for their intended purposes of God.

5. God is mysterious but many think the Lord works for good purposes only and could include the works of the spirits of angels, jinns, kami.
In Judaism, angels were spirits doing God's works.
In Islam, Jinns were spirits that granted a person's wish but may cause the wish to be gotten in evil ways. In Shintoism, kami were elemental spirits of the universe that may have been ancestors.

6. We should not have unrealistic expectations of God and expect miracles to happen all of the time, because only Our Unique Creator knows what is going on in the great master plan.

7. Inspired people who teach peace, goodness, and holiness on the earth are called by human-made titles such as patriarch, preacher, monk, rabbi, priest, pope, nun, imam, ulama, caliph, sheikh, mullah, maulvi, guru, evangelist, revivalist, pentecostal, bishop, deacon, missionary, minister, elder, pastor, parson, cardinal, crusader, prophet,

prophetess, messiah, oracle, disciple, apostle, reverend, sufi, cleric, vicar, rector, mu, kangshinmu, seseummu.

8. Some people believe that everybody on earth is a prophet and we all have our own testimony to tell about our relationship with Our Creator. Ordinary people are filled with the inspiration of God to do good works and inspire others. Humans are working hard upon the earth; they are work-day heroes.

9. People should not expect perfection from others who are trying to help. Humans are not perfect in things they do or say, but many people are trying to help, serve, and love others while living their own lives at the same time.

10. Religious rituals include:

external signs of gestures such as kneeling, prostration, bowing down, lifting the hands up, looking up, laying of hands on, blessing yourself or another by indicating the four points of the cross

missions to help others

95 prayer beads (19X5) for Baha'i

99 or 33 misbaha beads for Islam

50 rosary beads (5X10), 54 + 4, 100, or 33 for Catholic

108 japa mala beads (27X4) for Buddhist, Hindu, Sikh

komboloi worry beads for Greek relaxation and enjoyment

prayers, mantras, testimonies, chanting, speaking in tongues

ceremony

pilgrimages represent the soul's journey to God

declaring food or water to be holy

divining

dancing

singing, writing songs of devotion and praise, playing music with instruments, ringing hand bells, cathedral bells, playing morsing

sprinkling with holy water

individual worship

giving thanks

breaking bread together in communion

fellowship dinners

creating holy symbols and emblems

creating holy books

creating holy statues and artifacts, and artwork

creating holy buildings

creating holy cities

burning incense & candles

anointing, dedicating, affirming, or christening with oils or water

libation of pouring wine, oil, or ghee

confessing bad actions and repenting

asceticism such as fasting, austerity, and celibacy

washing the body

flower offerings

rules about clothing, tattoos, jewelry, length of hair, head coverings, body piercing

rules about medical care and medicine

rules about tobacco inhalation

rules about food

inhaling or ingesting herbs or opiates for a spiritual connection.

11. Holy dwellings or structures are:
ashrams,
basilicas,
cathedrals,
chapels,
churches,
congregations,
convent,
coven,
grotto,
gurdwara,
hospital inter-faith room,
houses,
inter-faith worship center,
kamidana,
mandir,
monasteries,
mosques,
pagoda,
prayer circles outdoors,
prayer walls,
shrines,
synagogues,
temples,
tents and more.

12. Some worshippers think they must have the same chair, pew, seat, floor mat, or table each week during worship service or the religious school, or the same parking spot in the parking lot, or the same bicycle slot in the bicycle rack, but be considerate of others and do not argue over this matter. And when the service has ended, be considerate of each other when leaving the worship hall or driving out of the parking lot, or the bicycle court. Also, the music in worship services should not be so loud that it can damage eardrums. Prayers of thanksgiving may be said before sharing fellowship dinners. Prayer requires more of the heart than the tongue. Don't just be nice during a worship service; be nice all week.

13. There are many philosophies about God.

Deists believe in a Divine Character by reason or nature without supernatural revelation. Atheists do not believe in a Divine Character.

Many people just believe in good ethics and not religions.

Gnostics shunned the material world and lived spiritually. Agnostics believe the existence of a Divine Character is unknown or unknowable.

Theists believe in a god. Polytheists believe in many gods. A demigod is a lesser god.

Some people believe in a pantheon of gods such as a god of the sun, god of the earth, god of the sky, god of the dead, goddess of childbirth, goddess of love and beauty, goddess of wisdom and courage, god of harvest, gods of the universe. Many people just believe in spirituality and spirits.

Martyrs are people who willingly sacrifice their own selfish needs to help others.

14. Religious beliefs have been the basis of many wars and oppressions for thousands of years.

A long time ago before modern civilization, empires fought for (1) power and control over lands, territories, food sources, and people (2) disagreements over the name of the Spirit and religious customs, and (3) disagreements about the belief of whether the earth was flat or round.

Many human beings who were trying to make progress in the world were put to death as martyrs in their causes; for example, some astronomers and scientists were put to death just for teaching that the earth was round. Some people were burned at the stake for saying the flaming chalice is for everyone to light and not just priests. Many human civil rights leaders were jailed. Prophets were killed or jailed for trying to teach against tyranny and oppression of human beings.

15. Some religions shun a person who leaves a religion and the person who left is labeled as an outcast and a *heretic*. A *bigot* is the person who will not tolerate any belief that is different from his own.

16. *Heresy* is speaking against the traditional doctrine.

17. *Iconoclasm* is the deliberate destruction within a culture of the culture's own religious icons. *Iconolatry* is reveration or veneration of religious symbols or images.

18. *Apocalypse* is the religious belief that there will be a world ending, but originally meant a revelation of God's will. *Armageddon* is also a term that means the end of the world and varies in interpretations.

19. *Blasphemy* is unholy words or action concerning God or sacred things.

20. *Hypocrisy* is the professing of publicly approved beliefs, qualities, or feelings that one does not really possess.

21. A *cult* is a group of people bound together by extremist ideologies that most people do not believe and members of the group are usually threatened emotionally or physically if they want to leave the group.

22. God's mercy withholds in forgiveness the punishment we often deserve, while God's grace gives us what we often don't deserve. Many believe if we stray from the path of God, we will be welcomed back with love. Some believe that God will test our faith or chasten us.

23. History has shown that humans have chosen good as the right way to go and the right thing to do through the dispensations (eras, epochs, or ages) of time. We should rebuke all evil.

Good is to alleviate the suffering of others, to strive for peace, to nurture humans and animals so they can be at their best, to try to progress for the better, to achieve things we think are worthwhile, to educate ourselves to improve the world, to respect each other.

If you fail to do good for others, you fail to do it for the Great Creator God. Love each other for the love of God.

24. Some think all humans are born with a spiritual debt or sin that is inherited from ancestors before us; some think not.

25. Humans have made all kinds of rules about religions, civilizations, and cultures. It is a diverse world with many opinions. There are many religions and many forms of worship and spirituality.

Spirituality is the feelings of a person's heart and soul, the core of our innermost being.

Humans created religions but many feel the religions were inspired by God. God exists for all. If you take away the religions, clothing, and money, we are all the same naked; therefore make a choice for peace and friendship instead of fighting.

Religions have helped to create order out of chaos, to fashion morals, to promote peace and love, to satisfy our questions about our origin, to remind us to be thankful for what we have, and to give us hope and guidance. There is always something to be thankful for.

26. Some people have experienced sensations known as déjà-vu or which is a feeling like you've done something before, or clairvoyant moments, as knowing something in advance. People have wondered if these instances are divine revelation of the akasha realm or heaven.

27. People have had dreams or near-death experiences of the afterlife in paradise heaven which was known as a glorious place of light, or of nirvana which is perfect balance.

28. Many *believers* praise a Divine Unknown, saying I believe in the Creator of the Universe.

CHAPTER 2
Revelations

1. Revelations are experiences where a human feels like they were revealed divine or worldly knowledge.

2. People have suddenly turned themselves to God and became a believer in the unseen Lord and their soul was saved, when previously they did not know a spiritual realm.

3. Mathematicians realized that the number Pi has no ending.
It is the ratio of a circle's circumference to its diameter; it never ends and it never settles into a permanent repeating pattern. People usually express the Pi mathematical constant as 3.14. In Berlin, Germany there is a mosaic representation of this mystery.

4. People see miraculous changes. Miracles have occurred when people suddenly stop a bad habit and become strong with a new refreshed attitude and start over.

5. Some say that with God, it isn't who you *were* that matters; it's who you are *becoming*.

6. People share testimonies to demonstrate the 'before and after' power of knowing the Lord. Stories of how God has changed lives aren't intended to focus on the sins but are meant to glorify God's saving grace; therefore, let go of labels that have defined people in the past and focus on who the person is now.

7. There have been mysterious instances reported such as stone statues have cried tears, doors have opened and no one knew who opened them, rocking chairs have started rocking by themselves, and images have been seen in mirrors; people believe such instances could have been caused by a spirit.

The will of the Spirit has been witnessed in mysterious and unexplainable ways and actions. Angels may have been sent to do divine work. No one knows what angels look like. And there is nothing that God cannot do!

8. People have believed their loved ones have revisited them in spirit.

Eva was a woman who was thinking about her mother while she was cooking in her kitchen. Suddenly she accidentally dropped a cooking utensil between the counter and the refrigerator and had to move the refrigerator to retrieve the cooking utensil. When she moved the refrigerator, she found one of her mother's earrings that her sister was wearing at a holiday party and had lost a year earlier.

There was a tale of a family in which several family members smelled the aroma of a freshly baked apple pie, although the oven had not even been turned on. The grandmother who had lived with them prior to her passing liked to bake apple pies. The family had reported the aromas at several different times at different occasions so all the family members assumed it could have only been the spirit of Grandma Ethel.

Raymundo was a teen who was driving in his car and saw a vision in his rearview mirror of his cousin Jose sitting in the back seat of his car. Jose was a teen who had sadly lost his life to cancer. Raymundo quietly said a prayer for his lost cousin, who was also his friend.

9. Aamori was an African woman who taught children. The name 'Aamori' means *good*. For an activity each year, she let the children make a colorful painted handprint of their hand or a footprint of their foot on a thick sheet of paper to give as a gift to their family. Handprints or footprints between years revealed that the children's bodies were growing strong and healthy.

10. People all around the world experience unexplainable happenings that many attribute to God's 'blaze of glory' or God's glorious light. People have found lost wallets and letters that were returned to the rightful owners many years later.

11. Boutros was a young adult who was sitting on his bicycle when a white dove ascended upon the handlebars.
It brought him a peaceful feeling and near to God for the rest of his life.

12. Yue Yue reached for a picture of her sister Sasha that was on her dresser when suddenly the telephone rang. It was her sister Sasha. 'Hi, Sister Yue Yue, would you like to meet for lunch?' Was it telepathy, divine guidance, or just a coincidence?

13. Some people have revelations about instances when they are being scammed.

Make sure a cashier gives you back your correct change when making a purchase.

Do not buy real estate that does not exist or stolen property.

Do not marry a person who says they are single but they are already married.

Many think that huge lotteries could have better prizes. For example, when a person has to pick 5 numbers out of 50 numbers to be a winner, some think that picking 3 numbers out of 5 should return a payout of $1000 instead of $10. There are different theories about the payouts. In most lottos, if there is no ticket with 5 winning numbers, all of the money carries over to the next play. But some think that only a percentage of the money should be carried over to the next play and that would enable bigger payouts for tickets with 4 or 3 winning numbers. For the hopeful people who invest $1 in a lottery play, a winning of $1000 could change their life! It might be the amount of money they need to pay off a tax lien, a downpayment for an item needed, an insurance payment, or payment to a dentist to have a tooth cavity fixed.

Footprints in the Sand

14. One night a man had a dream. He dreamed he was walking along the beach with the Lord. Across the sky flashed scenes of his life. He noticed footprints in the sand, one for himself and one for the Lord. During some sad times in his life, he noticed only one set of footprints in the sand. He questioned the Lord about it – was God not with him during the sad times? The Lord said 'My precious child, I love you and I would never leave you. During your times of sadness, trials, and sufferings, when you saw only one set of footprints in the sand, it was then that I was carrying you. As I carried you, my people should carry each other and keep your souls alive.'

15. Irony is like using a toothpick to remove food particles between your teeth and a piece of the toothpick breaks off and gets stuck in the teeth. Irony is like looking for a spoon but finding many forks instead.

16. Fate is circumstances in life or things that happened that we cannot control.

CHAPTER 3
Absolutes

1. We will do good unto others as we would do good unto ourselves.
2. We will honor mothers, fathers, guardians, counselors, family, friends, teachers, caregivers, those doing us a service, and respect our neighbors.
3. We will act responsibly as good human beings, be accountable for our actions, and admit our mistakes. We will be in control of ourselves, and interact with others in peaceful ways.
4. We will bring up children in the way of goodness and keep them safe from harm. Love your children; protect them and defend them like a lion or a bear defends its cubs!
5. Being a parent, a caretaker for another, and hectic work schedules can cause a human to get stressed or fatigued; if you need help ask someone for help.
6. Rebuke all evil such as the devil, uncontrolled emotions, murder, violence, wickedness, thievery, trickery, dishonesty, slavery, kidnapping, adultery, fornication, foolishness, slander, lying, greediness, bribery, jealousy, covetousness, racism, death threats, incest, rape, injustice, misjudgment, misguidance, mishandling, misrepresentation, cheating, defrauding, illegal computer hacking, counterfeiting, conspiracy, fraud, blackmail, abuse of humans or animals, shenanigans, terrorism, extortion, racketeering, money laundering, entrapment, robbery, gossip, poisoning humans or animals, bullying, hazing, contriving evil, torture, treason, evil espionage, adult slave labor, child slave labor, crimes against humanity, illegal drug trade or consumption,

plagiarism, dropping heavy items from bridge overpasses onto passing vehicles, operating machinery or vehicles while impaired, distracted, or fatigued.

7. We will not contrive evil. We will not follow a crowd to do evil or to prevent justice. Do not desire to be with evil people. Be the true soul you seek.
8. We will not withhold good from those to whom it is due, when it is in our power to do it.
9. We will consider good reasoning, justice, gentleness, and calmness to prevent great offenses. Execute true judgment and show mercy and kindness and tender compassion, every person to another.
10. Do not make hasty and premature judgments. We will be temperate and well-balanced. Do not malign and accuse before getting the facts. Be alert and aware of what is going on.
11. We will not steal money from our religious organization. Law enforcement should not steal money from drug confiscations.
12. You should not cause a little fender bender car wreck or stop a car and give them a ticket just to see who is driving the car or to delay them. You should not create havoc for no reason.
13. We will not spy on people in the privacy of their homes. We will not hack information in computer data bases, car engines, or create false news. We will not spy on a person by hacking their cell phone, computer, laptop, or tablet.
14. A spy may be a secret agent to secure their country. To be a double agent and betray your country by selling secrets to an enemy is evil; such betrayal is treason.
15. It has been said that once you commit violence, it is easier to do it again, because you become desensitized to the negative feelings after repeated exposure. This is also true when experiencing positive things.
16. We will not use vulgar and lewd language. Some put a coin in a jar as the penalty for each time a curse word in said.
17. Do not bring a frivolous lawsuit just to get money, gain a competitive advantage, or drive a company out of business.
18. It is a sin to steal another artist's or inventor's creative idea and pitch is as your own.
19. If you have declared bankruptcy because of frivolous consumer spending habits and have been given another chance, it is wrong to be frivolous again in spending habits when you could be repaying back the creditors that you declared bankruptcy on. If you declared bankruptcy because you lost your job or incurred severe hardship, then your bankruptcy is more justified.
20. Hit and runs when denting someone's car or hitting a human are evil. Stop and give insurance information or explain why the accidental hit occurred.

CHAPTER 4
Actions

1. Many believe that it is honorable to try to leave things in a better condition than when you found it. Try to improve things and make things better. It is better to be productive than destructive.

2. Some people may change their focus in life during different times of their life while other people may have a more steady focus in their lives. Some think growth hormones, loss of hormones, or chemicals in the brain are causes of behavior, some think all behavior is learned, some think behavior can be reactive to circumstances, some think behavior can be caused by spiritual causes or the Spirit, some think the powerful energy of love and passion causes behavior, some think people's behaviors are combinations of all different things. Some people might feel very spiritual in their lives at times, and not spiritual at other times.

Human behavior can be very complex. Often people change careers, move to new places, go visit places, do things, change things, and they don't have any answer except for feelings they had, so such feelings need to be monitored by the person them self so nothing will lead to a bad consequence.

3. There was a story of a woman who told her family and friends that she was intensely drawn over and over again to go take walks at a local park. The woman one day was struck dead by lightening, the odds of which are slim. Some people feel that her case was divine.

4. Some people turn to each other at the exact same moment and say the exact same thing.

5. A prayer sheet or prayer cloth may contain names of those that need prayers, guidance, help, and love. The clothes may have been prayed over to invoke blessings and miracles of God.

6. Parents and guardians should watch over their children carefully and be good role models through good actions to benefit, nurture, praise, and encourage their children. If you love your child, you will not hurt your child physically or emotionally. If you discipline your child, make sure your child understands why he or she is being disciplined to avoid confusion in the child's mind.

7. Many feel that families and friends should try to help each other live the best life we can by being physically or emotionally available to each other. We all have hard or difficult times when we need help. We can each try to help ourselves individually be the best we can be emotionally and physically.

8. Our individual strength and happiness is in our control; we should not make our happiness or well-being contingent on someone else if we have the capability to do for ourselves.

9. Random acts of kindness are benevolent acts to help and assist others. Thank others for their kindness in return; kindness is much appreciated.

Paying it forward is doing something in advance with the hope of receiving something in return at a later time.

Agape love is giving without expecting anything back. Some say it is a miracle when someone gives something to another who needs something.

10. Giving respect to others is a noble action; all life is given by the Spirit and the Earth exists for all.

11. Do your actions match your words? Do you think before you speak? Can you do self-analysis and improve your behavior? Have you done a spiritual growth assessment of yourself? Do you make promises you cannot keep? God's promises are like the stars – the stars shine brightly in the dark sky and the stars are still in the sky during the daytime but we cannot see them. Sometimes we can't see God's promises, but they are still there!

12. Sometimes we may have to act (put on a pretense) to hide our real emotions. Do we want to reveal our every thought every moment, like wearing your heart on your sleeve, to show our whole soul?

Do we really want to say something mean, or can we let it pass for the moment? Can we restructure what we want to say in a better way? Sometimes our feelings get hurt or we get angry, but we act like we are not bothered and do not react, when at other times we may express our feelings. Human emotions are very complex. The important thing is to be aware of our feelings and control them; control your feelings and do not let your feelings control you. It is better to think before you speak and control your tongue and what you say. Harsh words hurt. Before you strike out with harsh words, think about who you are talking to and what that person has lived through and be fair in what you say to them or back to them. It is hard to think in a moment of anger, but be a champion and be fair in your speech.

Sometimes you may reveal all of your innermost feelings while other times you may be more selective about what you will say.

13. If we act foolishly or take foolish risks, then trouble may follow and we may have guilt, shame and regrets. If we act wisely, we have a better chance of staying out of trouble and out of harm's way.

14. Many agree that humans are not perfect and are bound to make mistakes. Many agree that those people who are intentionally wicked over and over again by hurting others and plotting evil schemes are not good people.

15. Some think if we talk to ourselves and coach our selves, it will help us to act better. It has been said that if we talk to ourselves and hear ourselves, it might help us to use better reasoning and logic. Talk to yourself in positive ways. Act in control of yourself. Take control of your spirit. Your spirit is the soul of who you are.

16. Some have said that actions speak louder than words because sometimes words can be unfulfilled promises.

Our actions can affect other people's lives. Our thoughts and what we say to other people can shape their personality, beliefs, and self-image.

If you see someone who needs help or some love, can you do something for the person?

If you are a parent and brought a life into the world, are you being a good parent to your children?

Can you play with toys or building blocks or read a book to a child if they need companionship? Are you keeping your home clean and safe and being good to your children?

If you are in a relationship are you committed to the terms of the relationship and honoring the terms?

Can you open a door for a person who needs help?

Can you give goods, a service, or a small amount of money to help someone without expecting repayment? Or, if you have received goods, money, or services on loan, will you repay them in a honest manner? Some can afford to give donations to help others and do not expect repayment, but others can only afford to loan and need to be repaid.

17. Agape is Greek for 'love', as the flowing happiness of communion in the abundance of liberating and sustaining energy that is the clear light freedom ground of every universe.

18. Sacrifices are times you give up things voluntarily or may be forced to prioritize.

(1) to help others without expecting anything in return, giving with agape love.

(2) Two people might be trying to get one parking spot from two different directions and are actually entitled to it because they both saw it at the same time; one person has to give it up and the person who gives it up might have another opportunity opened by the Lord at some other time in their life.

(3) In a divorce involving children, usually one person will be granted physical custody so that the children will have a permanent place to call home because it is a comforting thought, so one parent will have to sacrifice or give up physical custody of the children and agree to visitation; this should not be a problem and both parents should work together so the children can enjoy time with both parents. The children were born to both parents and it is evil of one parent to think a child only belongs to them. It is the duty of parents to teach children good ways, to help their child have a good life, and keep them safe until they are grown. Children have busy schedules, so it may stress a child to have to pack luggage or a backpack every week to visit the non-custodial parent. Three solutions are: the parents could help pack the luggage or backpacks; the visits wouldn't always have to involve sleepovers; clothes, toiletries, and toys could be at both parental locations so no packing of luggage or backpacks is necessary.

If a parent was not given visits to children because of abuse to the child or unusual circumstances, supervised visits may be arranged; judges should consider actual facts of a divorce case since some custodial parents may tell lies about the other parent's behavior simply to gain full custody.

Parents should not brainwash children against the other parent.

The children are having to adjust to the divorce as well as the parents; it is not necessary for lives to be ruined simply because the dissolution of a marriage.

(4) Persons serving in the military defense of a country are often killed in action or go missing in action, sacrificing their lives for their countries. A nation should not forget its defenders of peace, justice and human rights.

Some countries have rules that if several members of a family are in the military at one time, that not all of them are stationed at one place. It was said that during WW II, five brothers from the same family were on the same boat during a war, and the boat was hit by a tornado and sank. Sir Winston Churchill (b. 1874) was Prime Minster of England during WW II. Churchill told the people 'This is a time to stand together and hold firm.'

(5) Some people will give as a sacrifice a human organ donation to help others who need a vital organ to live.

(6) Some think there are times that good quality is sacrificed for time, quantity, or money.

(7) Sometimes people will not speak, and words are sacrificed for peace.

(8) Sometimes relaxation, rest, sleep, and fun are sacrificed to focus on work.

19. Some people want to help others all the time, but others think one shouldn't meddle in everyone's affairs.

Some people don't help enough, and others think these people should do more.

20. Many pray for divine guidance each day. Follow the good ways of the Lord in all of your actions and stay on the right path with God.

21. Many people believe that you can make a decree of divine restoration or divine release and make things happen through positive divine energy. People have said 'We declare forgiveness in this situation and to be renewed and restored to our good divine plan' and it has actually changed their lives. Or 'We declare that our neighbors put aside their bitterness and to be restored to joy' and their neighbors became calm and peaceful.

22. A person's wealth may go from being a beggar with a bag to a basket with just enough, to a barrel with enough plus a little extra, to a barn or storehouse with wealth enough to share with their community or the world.

23. Parents and teachers educate children to benefit the next generation of workers.

Fujihira was a Japanese potter who taught children that clay had to be exactly centered on a potter's wheel as it spun or the clay would fly off the wheel and splatter things.

Children have to be taught everything; a baby has to learn to eat and use the toilet. Good teachers must have patience when teaching.

Humans never stop learning. New skills and new hobbies can bring joy.

24. Revivals and religious education help keep our faith strong.

25. If conditions get bad on earth, we may have to learn how to migrate to another planet. Engineers, physicists, mathematicians, nutritionists, botanists, chemists, medical teams, pilots, entertainers, psychologists, cooks, custodians, and many other professionals will be needed if humans go to another planet.

CHAPTER 5
Traditions

1. Customs and traditions are held all over the world for religious beliefs, for superstitions, to honor the living and deceased, because it was a tradition that was simply passed down from a previous generation, for health reasons, for a new idea, and more. Traditions create memories that stay with us and bond us together as family and friends.
2. The spirit of the Winter Festival & Holiday season is peace, joy, hope, love, goodwill and compassion, thinking of others, being with family and friends, and praising Our Creator, although in different parts of the world Our Creator is called by different names.

Customs may include festive decorations such as lanterns, decorated trees, candy canes, decorating halls with boughs of holly, poinsettias, jingle bells, parades, colorful displays of lights and candles, gift-giving, parties and feasts, autumn hay-rides, holiday songs and music, holiday foods, cookies, and goodies, toasting marshmallows over an open fire, and worship services. Holiday cheer and festivities help us get through the cold winter months. Warm drinks, warm soup, warm blankets help also.

Holiday times can be hectic and busy, and traffic can be bad, on holiday eves, so be patient and try not to stress; remember to cherish the meanings of the holidays – peace, love, and thanksgiving to God. Santa has become a worldwide mythological figure who keeps a list of naughty and nice children and brings presents to the nice children in the middle of a midwinter night or on Dec. 31. The naughty children may not get a present. Santa Claus and Mrs. Claus live at the North Pole where elves help them make toys and gifts in a barn. Santa puts the toys in great bags and loads them onto a sleigh led by nine reindeer (Dasher, Dancer, Prancer, Vixen, Comet, Cupid, Dunder, Blixem, and Rudolph the red-nosed reindeer) that is flown through nighttime skies of the world to deliver the gifts to children that are on Santa's good list. Some families leave a snack of milk and cookies for Santa and carrots for the reindeer.

The winter celebrations may have derived from festivals called Yule, or Yuletide, the celebration of the winter solstice in ancient European cultures.

Saint Nicholas was a Greek bishop that lived in the years 270-346CE. He had miracles associated with his acts of kindness which included secret gift-giving.

Candy canes were created in the 17th-century in Germany to quiet restless children during winter holiday religious services.

During major holidays, it is nice if people share holiday time so loved ones and children can visit with both parents, relatives, and friends.

A COLD WINTER NIGHT

'Twas a cold winter's night
When all through the house
Not a creature was stirring
Not even a mouse
The stockings were hung by the
chimney with care
In hopes that St. Nicholas soon would
be there

The children were all nestled and
snug in their beds
While visions of sugar plums
danced in their heads
And Ma in her kerchief and I
In my cap
Had just settled down for a
long winter's nap

When out on the lawn there
arose such a clutter
I sprang from my bed to see what
was the matter
Away to the window I flew like a flash
Tore open the shutters, and threw up
the sash

The moon on the breast of the
new fallen snow
Gave the lustre of mid-day to
objects below
When, what to my wondering
eyes should appear
But a miniature sleigh and
eight tiny reindeer

With a little old driver so lively
and quick
I knew in a moment it must be
St. Nick
More rapid than eagles his
coursers they came
And he whistled and shouted
And called them by name

Now Dasher Now Dancer
Now Prancer Now Vixen !
On Comet On Cupid
On Dunder On Blixem !
To the top of the porce
To the top of the wall
Now Dash away Dash away
Dash away all !

As dry leaves before the wild
hurricane fly
When they meet with an
obstacle, mount to the sky,
So up to the house-top the coursers
they flew
With the sleigh full of toys
And St. Nicholas too

And then in a twinkling I heard
on the roof
The prancing and pawing of each
little hoof.
As I drew in my head and was
turning around,
Down the chimney St. Nicholas
came with a bound

He was dressed all in fur from
his head to his foot
And his clothes were all tarnished
with ashes and soot
A bundle of toys was flung on
his back
And he looked just like a peddler
just opening his pack

His eyes – how they twinkled !
His dimples – how merry!
His droll little mouth drawn up
like a bow
And the beard of his chin was as
white as the snow

The stump of a pipe he held
tight in this teeth
And the smoke – it encircled his
head like a wreath
He had a broad face, and a little
round belly
That shook when he laughed
like a bowl full of jelly

He was chubby and plump, a right
jolly old elf
And I laughed when I saw him
in spite of myself
A wink of his eye and a twist
of his head
Soon gave me to know
I had nothing to dread

He spoke not a word but went
straight to his work
And laying his finger aside of his nose
And, giving a nod, up the chimney
he rose

He sprang to his sleigh
To his team gave a whistle
And away they all flew like the
down of a thistle
But I heard him exclain
as they drove out of sight
Happy Winter to all
And to all a good night!

3. Hannukah, or Chanukah is an 8-day holiday for Jews consisting of a festival of lights on the nine-branched menorah candelabrum and commemorates the rededication of the Holy Temple. Eating latkes (potato pancakes) fried in oil during Hannukah is done to commemorate the 'miracle of the oil' that kept a menorah lit for eight nights when there was only enough oil left for one night.
Yom Kippur is the holiest holiday for Jews and is a 25-hr period of fasting and prayer.

Some famous Hannukah songs:
Dreidel Dreidel, Hannukah Oh Hannukah, Shir La La Chanukah, Happy Joyous Hannukah, Hanukkah Dance, Candlelight, 8 Days of Hannukah, The Chanukah Song

4. Christmas holidays are celebrated in December or January, depending on various churches. Christmas is an annual commemoration of the birth of Jesus for Christians, Amish, and Mormons. A manger scene with Mary, Jesus, Joseph, barn animals, and the Three Wise Men are displayed. Twelve Days of Christmas is a song about gift-giving.

Some famous Christmas carols are:
Rudolph the Red-Nose Reindeer, Silver Bells, We Wish You A Merry Christmas, Winter Wonderland about sleigh bells ringing, The Christmas Song about chestnuts roasting on an open fire,

Silent Night about Jesus and Mary, his mother. **Famous Christmas book**: 'TWAS THE NIGHT BEFORE CHRISTMAS By: Clement C. Moore 1823)

5. Epiphany is the celebration of the Magi, the Three Wise Men who traveled to see the baby Jesus when he was born. Epiphany is also called Three Kings Day.
6. Mardi Gras is a carnival that is observed by followers of Jesus. Mardi Gras (Fat Tuesday) is celebrated to eat hearty food before the beginning of Lent, a period of fasting or self-denial.
7. Pentecost is the descension of the Holy Spirit upon Apostles of God.
8. Ramadan is a month of religious worship of increased prayer offerings and recitation of the Koran for Muslims.

The end of Ramadan is celebrated by the festivity called Eid ul-Fitr which is celebrated with food, colorful lights and lanterns.

Day of Ashura is the 10th day of Muharram, day of New Year in Islam. Sunni Muslims celebrate the freedom of the Israelites from Egyptian bondage and believe Moses fasted on this day; Shiia Muslims remember the Battle of Karbala in which Mohammad's grandson Husayn and other supporters were killed in religious fighting.

9. Zoroastrians celebrate a midwinter festival called Sadeh or Adar-Jashan 100 days before New Year's.
10. Bahai's observe a nineteen-day period each year during the month of March dedicated to God from sunrise to sunset.

The Festival of Ridvan is a twelve day festival that is celebrated in the Baha'i faith to celebrate Baha'ullah's announcement of prophethood. It is referred to as the 'Most Great Festival'.

11. At the end of July the Rastafari Festival at Judah Square in Knysna celebrates the birthday of Haile Selassie with Nyabingi drumming, dancing, and singing. Hot chocolate and bread may be served.
12. Kwanzaa is a week-long celebration of feast and gift-giving for African people. Kinara candles represent people, struggle, future and hope. The lights of Kwanzaa proclaim that when we share our inner flame and nurture each other with pride, we will harvest peace and love.
13. Diwali, the Hindu Festival of Lights symbolizes that good triumphs over evil and is celebrated with small clay lamps filled with oil.
14. Dussera is a Hindu celebration to commemorate victory of the god Rama over the devil Ravana.
15. Navrati is the Nine-Day Festival for goddess Durga.
16. Vesak is the celebration of Buddha's enlightenment, birthday, and death and is a major festival for Buddhists.
17. Duanwu Festival, or Dragon Boat Festival is celebrated in China in June. The festival is celebrated to honor Qu Yuan (278-340BCE) and Wu Zixu (died 484BCE), leaders who jumped into the river to avoid

enemies and were sought after by local people in dragon boats to rescue them. The people dropped rice into the water so the fish would eat the rice instead of the men. In modern times the festival is a celebration of 'People's Day.' Activities include preparing and eating sticky rice (zongzi) and realgar wine and racing dragon boats.

The sun and Chinese dragon represent masculine energy. The moon and phoenix represent feminine energy.

18. Tanabata is a Japanese star festival on July 7 to celebrate the meeting of Orihime and Hikobushi.

19. The Dogon religion celebrates a Sigui ceremony that takes place every 60 years and can last for several years

20. Mulids are festivals held in Egypt to celebrate the saint of a particular church and includes music and artwork.

21. Jameson's Finches are songbirds that symbolize good luck in Egypt and have been found mummified in the tombs of pharaohs.

22. Spring Festivals and religious festivals are held worldwide to celebrate the springtime renewal of the earth.

Easter, Ostara, or Pascha was created as a festival to honor the Germanic goddess of the dawn Eostre and the Norse god of light Austri, which symbolized radiant dawns, spirits of light, and fertility. Woven baskets filled with candy, flower and vegetable seeds, and decorated eggs symbolized regrowth.

The Kangelaris Easter Dance is of great splendor in Papadates, Greece during the 3 days following the resurrection of Jesus.

The Springtime Bunny has become a worldwide mythological figure who brings gifts in the Spring.

The Egyptian goddess of fertility was Isis (Al-Uzza).

The Roman goddess of fertility was Aurora.

The Indian goddess of fertility was Ushas.

The tradition of carrying a rabbit's foot for luck began because rabbits burrow underground and are fertile creatures; therefore, rabbits were believed to ward off bad luck and bring on good luck.

Easter springtime celebration is often combined with Trinity Sunday for Catholics and Protestant Christians.

Prayer for Spring Festivals:
'Praise the divine realities, the wildflowers and grasses, spring buds of green, the honeybees, bumblebees and butterflies, the baby birds in their nests, that have come forth from the Lord's bestowal of spring, spreading seeds upon the winds to set forth and sustain the Earth! Praise the Lord!'

23. All saints day, all souls day, day of the dead, and day are established holidays in many countries of the world to honor and remember deceased loved ones.

The day is dedicated to remembering the spirits of the deceased souls.
Some will display a picture of deceased love one in a prominent place for the day. Do not say things about a deceased person that are not true because the dead cannot speak to defend themselves.
The day is called Halloween in some places, and is celebrated with costume parties, candied-apples, jack-o-lantern pumpkins.
Trick-or-treat is a custom of knocking on neighbors' doors to receive a gift of candy. In Japan, Obon or Bon is the Ghost Festival to honor ancestor spirits.
24. Native American Indians celebrate the sun as a life giving power in a festival called Inti Raymi on June 21 the winter solstice of the southern hemisphere.
25. New Year's Day is celebrated around the world to celebrate the start of a new year; new year resolutions (commitments) are made focusing on goals and things to achieve. The singing of Auld Lang Syne on New Years's Eve comes from an ancient custom of ending parties with a song. Auld Lang Syne is Scots dialect for 'old long since' or the good old days.
26. Thanksgiving Day is a day to give thanks for all that we have and is often celebrated with a huge feast of food and fellowship. Macy's in New York has sponsored a huge Thanksgiving Day Parade since 1948.
27. Individual birthdays and wedding anniversaries are celebrated by people around the world with cakes, gifts, parties, dinners, confetti, and greeting cards. Hugs are great gifts.
Some people prefer simple and quiet celebrations while others prefer magnificent extravaganzas. Some think it is better to snuff out candles on cakes by fanning instead of blowing to avoid passing germs.
28. Saying prayers before meals gives thanks for food and is believed to help you digest the meal.
29. Clinking glasses after a toast of honor began in the olden days of frequent poisonings; drinkers would pour a little wine into each other's cup to ensure that neither had it in for the other; hence, the touching of the rims of glasses today.
30. In 200 BCE, if Druid enemies met under a tree where mistletoe grew, they were required to lay down their weapons and differences for the day. The Celts believed mistletoe could heal injuries, boost fertility, and initiate friendship. It became a tradition to shake hands, hug, or kiss under the mistletoe.
31. Many nations have a special holiday to honor their nation and leaders.
32. Earth Day is April 22, for conservation of our planet.
Recycling glass, cans, plastics, and cardboard will reduce trash. Trash piles that are buried in the ground produce methane gas but compost piles that receive oxygen produce CO2. Biodegradable paper cups and plates are better for the earth than foam and plastics that are not biodegradable.
33. Mother's Day and Father's Day is to honor parents.

34. Family Traditions can be passed-down recipes, religious books, photographs, furniture, houses, sutras or family sayings, family emblems, family reunions.
35. Obituaries are public announcements describing the lives of our deceased loved ones and tell how they lived their lives; obituaries can make us realize what humans are capable of achieving in our short lives. Some write their own obituary. *In Loving Memory* cards may be passed out to friends that contain a picture and/or details of the desceased's life.
Funerary works are done involving the remains of the dead for cremation or burial. Remains are buried on land or at sea, cryo-frozen, ashes scattered, or bodies given to the earth creatures in ossuary pits. A pine box is biodegradable. It is wrong to vandalize graves. Some people donate their corpse to science.
A cenotaph is an empty tomb or a monument built to honor the persons who have left the world.
Bardo is the Buddhist tradition of chanting mantras for 49 days to ease the dead toward happiness in their next state.
Respectful services are held and prayers and invocations are recited to insure the highest degree of glory in the afterlife for our dearly deceased loved ones. When dying, things may take on new meaning or less meaning, depending on your point of view. Some people may want to have a gathering with friends or family to say goodbye before they die. Some people with terminal illness opt to end their life prematurely (euthanasia).

Prayer for loss of a loved one

Dear Lord, we ask that you watch over this family in this sad time. Watch over our departed loved one as they make their journey to cross over into your glorious light in the Great Beyond. We thank thee, O Lord, that we are able to join together in fellowship at this time to pay tribute and share memories of their life. We recognize now more than ever the power and joy of family and friends. May the love of friends and family comfort you in difficult times. Love lives on forever in each memory and thought of those who shaped our lives and all the happiness they've brought. Love lives on forever – it will never fade away – for, in our hearts, our loved ones are with us each and every day. Amen.

CHAPTER 6
Beliefs

1. A person's belief system is often simply the beliefs that a person has been taught since birth or in their lifetime such as spirituality, politics, manners of etiquette of social conduct, art, professions, food, dress, customs.

Many times people do not even question their beliefs, simply because they never thought to question them.
2. If you half-believe, you only believe half of something or you

only believe it half-way in your mind.
3. It is best to substantiate facts before making an opinion in order to find truths and avoid rumors.
4. We all have our own comfort zones; sometimes we may have to think out of our comfort zone to do something different and expand our horizons.
5. Become aware of realities; when you understand realizations then you can consciously make plans to take control of your life to make the changes or goals.
6. Mythological unicorns with magic tusks, leprechauns bringing gold, elves, fairies with magic wands, nymphs (maiden inhabiting rivers and woods), genies in bottles that grant wishes, mermaids (half-fish, half-woman), centaurus (half-horse, half-man), vampires, trolls, gnomes, and cornucopias bringing unending food are not real.

CHAPTER 7
Symbols

1. An ankh is an ancient Egyptian spiritual symbol of life that consists of a cross with a loop at the top.
2. A Star of David or a Menorah represent the God of Israel in Judaism.
3. A crucifix with Jesus signifies the death of Jesus. A fish symbol represents to be a follower of Jesus.
4. A starfish represents Mary the Blessed Mother of Jesus. Stella Maris in Latin means Our Lady, Star of the Sea.
5. A smiling sunshine represents that God loves us.
6. A cross of life represents faith in the Holy Spirit who is the giver of life, the provider of sustenance for all life whose divine works will endure for all eternity.
A cross can symbolize a vertical relationship with God and a horizontal relationship with all other things.
7. A nine pointed star and ringstone represent Bahai.
8. A wheel of dharma, lotus flower, and zen rocks represent Buddhism.
9. The Angel Moroni represents the Mormon faith.
10. The Pentacle and Tripple Goddess represent Wiccan.
11. The Eckankar Symbol represents Eckankar.
12. The lotus flower and pranava represent Hinduism.
13. The Crescent and Star represent Islam.
14. The ahimsa hand represents Jainism. Open palms is a reminder to stop and consider all actions, ahimsa is the principle of non-violence, and the wheel is the symbol of the cycle of death and rebirth.
15. The Khanda and Ik Onkar represents Sikhism.
16. The Torii represents Shintoism.
17. The Yin & Yang Taiji represents Taoism or Daoism.
18. The flaming chalice represents the glowing love of Unitarian Universalists.
19. The faravahar represents Zoroastrianism.
20. The Yoonir or Ndut represents Serer.
21. A Sacred Hoop called a dreamcatcher and the waterbird are

symbols of Native American spiritualism.
22. The Imperial Lion is the Symbol of the Rastafarians.
23. The left eye of God representing yang strength balanced by the yin nurturing of Mother Goddess is the symbol of Cao Daism.
24. The 8-pointed cross represents Scientology.
25. The unicursal hexagram is the symbol for Thelema.
26. The Korean Taegeuk (Taeguk) symbolizes the interactions of two energies as in Daoism. It can also symbolize heaven and earth. A tricolored taegeuk symbolizes humanity, heaven, and earth.
27. The symbol of the circle is known worldwide as representing a never-ending circle of love.
28. Some people wear shark's teeth or shell necklaces for the love of the oceans.
29. A butterfly has long been a symbol of rebirth and renewal.
30. Praying hands symbolize hope and faith.
31. The heart symbol represents love.
32. A phoenix is a symbol in Greek mythology that represented a phoenix rising out of the ashes for continual unending existence.
33. The peace symbol opposes nuclear arms and promotes peace on earth.
34. Many people believe a horse shoe can bring good luck, because the horse shoe resembles a crescent moon, which is a symbol of luck.
35. The leaves of the rare four-leaf clover symbolize hope, faith, love, and luck. The three-leaf shamrock is a symbol of Ireland and the Christian Holy Trinity.
36. The figure-eight loop represents the infinity and eternity of God. Infinity and eternity mean forever.
37. An ancient symbol of the Norse god Thor is the Mjolnir hammer.
38. The seal of The Lamb of God (Agnus Dei in Latin) symbolizes the Moravian Church. The Latin inscription says 'Our lamb has conquered, let us follow Him.' (Vicit egnus noster, eum sequamur in Latin.)
39. The circled dot was used by Pythagoreans and Greeks to represent the first metaphysical being, the Monad, or The Absolute.

RELIGIONS

Divine Male god spirit

Judaism, Orthodox Judaism	Holy Spirit, Elohim, Adonai, Lord God, Jehovah, Yahweh

Ancient Eastern Orthodox - (Coptic Egyptian, Ethiopian, Oriental, Eritrean, Syriac, Malankara Syrian)
Eastern Orthodox - (Greek, Russian, Armenian Apostolic)
Catholic-(Roman, Coptic)

Christian	Jesus, Jehovah, Yahweh, God, Lord
Islam	Allah (Arabic), Khudai (Pashto), God, Lord
Egyptian God	Amun-Ra, Heh, Geb
Chinese God	Shangdi
Korean God	Dangun,Sansin
Vietnamese God	Duc Cao Dai
Norse God	Tyr
Arabian Gods	Hubal, Allah
African Igbo God	Chukwu
African Serer Faith	Roog
Yoruba Faith	Olorun
Dogon God	Amma, Lebe Serou
Santeria	More than 400 Gods
Rastafari	Jah, Jehovah
Sioux, Hopi Native American	Wakan Tanka or Great Spirit
Cahuilla Native American	Umnaah or Our Creator
Rapa Nui God	Makemake
Shinto God	Kunitokotachi
Buddhism	Buddha, Brahma, Dharmakaya
Hindu Gods	Krishna, Vishnu, Mahesh, Shiva, Shakti (Deva)
Daoism	Jade Emperor

Jainism Buddha	Yaksha
Zoroastrian God	Ahura Mazda
Sikhism God	God
Scientology God, Eckankar God	Holy Spirit, God
Wiccan God	Horned God
Thelema Gods	Egyptian Gods
Confucianism	Focus on family and current world
Tenrikyo	Tenri-O-no-Mikoto, Tsukihi
Falun Dafa	Many gods and spirits
Theosophy	God
Bahai Faith, Unitarian Universalist, Cao Dai, New Age, New Thought, Spiritual, Druze	Many Beliefs Welcomed
Raelians	Extraterrestrial God

Divine Female god spirit

Christian Orthodox, Roman Catholic, Coptic Goddess	Mary Mother of Jesus
Greek Goddess	Gaia,Hera
Arabian Goddess	Allat
African Goddess	Ani, Gleti
Spanish Goddess	Mari, Lurbira
Egyptian Goddess	Neith
Korean Goddess	Sungmo, Jamo, Daemo, Sinmo, Nogo
Vietnamest Goddess	Duc Phat Mau
Roman Goddess	Diana
Norse Goddess	Sjofn
Sumerian Goddess	Inanna
Shinto Goddess	Amaterasu
Buddhist Bodhisattva	Arya Tara
Hindu Devi	Lakshmi, Saraswati,

	Kali,Durga, Parvati
Jainism Bodhisattva	Yakshi
Wiccan Goddess	Triple Goddess

Heaven

Heaven	Abrahamic Religions of Judaism, Christianity, Mormon
Jannah, Paradise	Abrahamic Religion of Islam
Nirvana, Moksa	Dharmic Religions of Hinduism
Deva Loka	Jainism Religion
Paradise	Greek Religion
Tian	Taoism Religion
Akasha	Theosophy

Angels

Aggelos	Greek Religion
Farishta, Firishta,Fereshteh	Persian Religions
Spirits, Messengers, Hosts,	
Malaikah, Angels	- Abrahamic Religions
Maids of Heaven	Bahai Faith, Sikhism, Taoism
Angel of Light	Hinduism Religions

Saints

Saints	Christianity
Wali	Arabic, Muslim Religions
Tzadik	Judaism Religion
Sant, bhakta, mahatma	Hinduism, Sikhism
Arhat	Buddhism
Irunmole, Orisa	Yoruba Religion

Hell

Hell, Gehenna	-Greek, Hebrew, Judeo-Christian Religions, Mormonism
Jahannam	- Islam Religion
Naraka	Hinduism, Buddhism, Jainism, Sikhism
Kalichi	-Indian
Metnal, Xibalba	Aztec, Mayan
Tartarus	- Greek
Kuzimu	-African
Uffern	-Celtic
Tuonela	-Finnish

Hades

Sheoul, Place of the Dead	Greek, Judeo-Christian Religions
Jaaniw, Sacred Dwelling of the Soul	African Serer Religions
Yomi	- Shintoism

Evil

Satan	- Hebrew, Christian, Mormon Religions
Shaita	- Arab Christians and Muslim Religions
Devil, Diabolus	- Greek Religions
Iblis, Shaytan	- Islam Religions
Kroni, Asuras	- Hinduism
Susanoo	- Shintoism
Angra Mainyu	Zoroastrianism
Beelzebub	- Greek, Judaism
Ekwensu, Esu, Elegbara	- African
Set	- Egyptian
Ahriman	- Middle Persian
Maya (illusions)	Sikh

History of Religions

Earliest religions in history included spiritual paganism and shamanisn to acknowledge Unseen Creator Spirit with idols, cave drawings, etchings on metal or wooden or stone plates, or statues because books and scrolls had not been invented.

Earliest religious worship included ancient Native Egyptian, Arabian, Greek, Roman, Indian, Chinese, Japanese, Spanish, Nordic, Mexican, African, American, British Columbian, Asian, Eskimo, Australian Aborigine religions in which statues, idols, and artifacts have been found and embrace a great variety of beliefs such as gods, nature and the earth. The North American Delaware Lenape Indians that migrated to the north American continent from Alaska from Asia wrote of their journey in the Red Record (Wallam Olum).

Hinduism, Buddhism, Jainism, and Sikhism originated in India. Hinduism, Buddhism, and Jainism are polytheistic religions with beliefs in many gods. Sikhism is a combination of Hinduism and Islam and is a monotheistic religion with a belief in one god. Tibetan Buddhism differs from ancient Buddhism in that Tibetan Buddhism has the essence of the experience of real Buddhas dwelling on the earth.

Taoism, Confucianism originated in China. Taoism, also called Daoism is a philosophical and religious tradition that emphasizes living in harmony with the Tao, also called Dao, which is the ineffable, the source and driving force behind everything else. The Tao is not a supreme being; it is a cosmic principle of all aspects of creation.

Confucianism focuses on humanism, or ren, and the focus of spiritual concern is this world and family, not on gods or the afterlife. In Confucianism, women were considered to be inferior to men, but both men and women are important to the world as yin & yang. Ren, or humaneness, means kindness, love, altruism, goodness, compassion, and benevolence. Confucianism emphasizes the importance of learning and life passage rituals from childhood to adulthood.
Confucianism ethics are ren, yi, and li. Ren is obligation to altruism and humaneness for individuals. Yi is upholding of morals to do good, Li is a system of norms and propriety that determines good behavior in society.

Falun Dafa is a meditative practice involving qigong exercises which aim to rebuild or rebalance *qi* which is the essential life force or energy to put practitioners in touch with the cosmic energy of the universe.

In Vietnam, Ngo Van Chieu started Cao Dai (a unity religion) in 1920CE and Huynh Phu So started Hoa Hao (Buddhism) in 1939CE.

In Korea, both men and women shaman-priests can be intermediaries between God, Gods of Nature, and humanity.

Shintoism is the native polytheistic religion of Japan. Shinto means 'way of the gods'. Shintoism is regarded as a way of life rather than a religion. Tenrikyo is a Japanese religion started in 1838 by a woman named Nakayama Miki (Oyasama) after a revelation during a Buddhist ritual.

Judaism originated in the Middle East around 3000BCE;
Jews believe in one supreme creator god who was the God of Abraham of the middle-east. The God of Abraham is called Jehovah or Yahweh in the Torah and King James Bible and earlier Bibles.

Religions with origins from Judaism with Jesus as the Saviour Messiah are Essenes, Roman Catholic, Coptic Catholic, Christian Orthodox (Greek, Coptic Egyptian, Ethiopian, and Russian), Mormon, Baha'i Faith, Church of England (and Anglican denominations such as Lutheran, Episcopalian, Presbyterian, Quakers, Shakers), and Christian denominations such as Methodist, Baptist, Seventh-Day Adventist, Church of God, Church of Christ, Jehovah's Witness, Amish, and Christian Scientist.

The God of Abraham is called Allah in the Koran in Islam. It was written in 700CE by Ibn Ishak that the tribal descendents of a son of Abraham named Ismail in the Jewish Torah formed the Islam religion around 600 CE (600AD) but some Muslim scholars dispute this claim and have said that
Mohammad was not a descendent of Ismail (Ismael). Even if Mohammed was not a descendent of Ismail, Mohammed included stories of Jews and Christians in the Koran, leaving an open door for a path of peace.

Zoroastrianism started around 600BCE in Persia (Iran) which borders the middle-east and the east.

Wiccans revere the natural world as a living, breathing organism and revere people as 'gods' and 'goddesses'. They often consider the supreme deity to be a nature goddess.

Baha'i Faith, Unitarian, Druze, Cao Dai and other religions encourage respect of spiritual beliefs and spiritual growth for all and recognize that Our Creator is known by many names all over the world. All people are welcome in Sikh temples. The Baha'i faith teaches the oneness of God, the oneness of religion, the oneness of humankind; harmony between science and religion; divine revelation is continuous and progress to promote the peace of God.

Religions that originated in Africa include Igbo Mythology, Serer Faith, and Yoruba Religion. The Yoruba Religion believes in The Supreme God that has three manifestations: Olodumare (The Creator), Olorun (Ruler of Heavens), and Olofi (Conduit between Heaven and Earth). The Vodou Religions share theology taken from beliefs of the Yoruba.
The Serer Faith believes in God Roog. In Igbo Mythology, Chuckwu is God. Santeria is a religion that combines traditional African religion with Catholicism; Santeria was believed to have been formed by slaves on the sugar plantations in Cuba. Igbo has been combined with Judaism, Christianity, Catholicism, and Islam.

Rastafari movement originated in Jamaica in the 1930s. Emperor Haile Selassie I of Ethiopia was born Ras Tafari Makonnen. (Ras is a title of nobility). Tafari was a member of the Ethiopian Orthodox Church. The people believed Ras Tafari was a messiah or savior (the lion of Judah) that was prophesized in the Old Testament of the King James Bible for a new Zion in Africa. Some Rastafarians believe that Ras Tafari was the Second Coming of Jesus or an incarnation of God Jah.

The New Thought Movement was begun by Phineas Quimby (1802-1866CE) who emphasized that spirituality is shared by all people on earth.

Raelians believe in world peace, sharing democracy, and nonviolence. They believe life on earth was created by a species of extraterrestrials, in intelligent design. Raelians believe in messengers or prophets that inform humans in eras of history.

Scientology was formed in 1954 by L. Ron Hubbard. It uses Dianetics to remove the 'reactive mind' that prevents people from being happy, aware, and more ethical. Auditors ask a person questions that help them obtain a spiritual healing and good mental health.

Eckankar was formed in 1965 by Paul Twitchell. The leader of the non-profit is called the Mahanta or the Living ECK Master. Eckankar helps people find God through spiritual experiences.

Prophets or Human Messengers of the Religions

Moses for the Jews,
Jesus Christ for the Christians,
Jesus Christ, Mormon, Joseph Smith, and Brigham Young for the Mormons,
Mohammad for the Muslims,
Bab and Baha'ullah for the Baha'i,
Mirza Ghulam Ahmad for the Ahmadiyya,
Zoroaster for the Zoroastrians,
Mohammad and Jesus Christ for the Yazidi,
Sultan Sahak and Mithra for the Yarsan,
Moses, Mohammad, Nashtakin ad-Darazi, and Jethro for the Druze,
Guru Nanak for the Sikh,
Siddhartha Gautama Buddha for the Hindus and Buddhists,
Veda Vyasa for the Hindus and Buddhists,
Nasadiya Sukta for the Hindus and Buddhists,
Krishna and Sai Baba for the Hindus,
Mohandas Gandhi for the Hindus,
Mahavira for the Jain,
Laozi (Lao-Tze) for the Daoists,
Confucius for the Confucians,
Nakayama Miki (Oyasama) for the Tenrikyans,
Ngo Van Chieu for the Cao Dai,
Huynh Phu So for the Hoa Haoi,
Jesus Christ and Anne Lee for the Shakers,
Jesus Christ, Ras Tafari Haile Selasie, Athlyi, Marcus Garvey for Rastafari,
Onowutok, and Tamanend for the Lenape Native American Indians,
Phineas Quimby for the New Thought Movement,
Aleister Crowley for the Thelema,
Ron Hubbard for Scientology,
Paul Twitchell for Eckankar.

Verses

Hindu Mantra from Mandukya Upanishad
It is not outer awareness
It is not inner awareness
Nor is it suspension of awareness
It is not knowing
It is not unknowing
Nor is it knowingness itself
It can neither be seen nor understood
It cannot be given boundaries
It is ineffable and beyond thought
It is indefinable
It is known only through becoming it.
Who knows this knows the Self (atman).

Hindu Mantra from Rig-Veda
United your resolve,
united your hearts,
may your spirits be at one,
that you may long together dwell
in unity and concord.

Buddhist Sutra The Dhammapada
We are what we think
All that we are arises with our thoughts.
With our thoughts we make the world.
Speak or act with an impure mind
and trouble will follow you,
As the wheel follows the ox that draws the cart.
Speak or act with a pure mind
and happiness will follow you.
As your shadow, unshakeable.

The Sacredness of This Moment
Chogyam Trungpa Ripoche
The way to experience nowness is to realize that this very moment, this very point in your life, is always the occasion. So the consideration of where you are and what you are, on the spot, is very important. That is one reason that your family situation, your domestic everyday life, is so important. You should regard your home as sacred, as a golden opportunity to experience nowness. Appreciating

sacredness begins very simply by taking an interest in all the details of your life.

Jewish Prayer

Throughout all generations we will render
thanks unto Thee
And declare Thy praise evening, morning, and noon,
For our lives which are in Thy care,
For our souls which are in Thy keeping
For thy miracles which we witness daily,
And for Thy wondrous deeds and blessings
Toward us at all times.

Jewish Prayer

I believe in the sun even when it is not shining.
I believe in love even when feeling it not.
I believe in God even when he is silent.

Christian Prayer

May the road rise to meet you,
may the wind be always at your back,
may the sun shine warm on your feet,
the rain fall softly on your fields;
and until we meet again,
may God hold you in the palm of his hand.

Christian Prayer

O God, we cannot do your will unless you guide us.
Send the Holy Spirit into our lives to show us how to live.

White Eagle Native American Prayer

Let us lay aside all thought of the material world
and seek to make contact with the Source of life.
O gracious Spirit, all-enfolding love, light and life,
we come before thee in humility and tranquility of heart and mind. May nothing in us prevent us from steeping forward into the light; and when sorrow and trouble come may we willingly surrender to thy love and wisdom; knowing that underneath are thine everlasting arms: for thou art merciful and just and all-loving. May our hearts be open and minds subdued, waiting to receive the beauty of thy light of thy Divine Loop.
O Father Mother God, we thank thee for thy infinite love. May these thy children go their way in peace, filled with thy holy spirit. Bless them, bless them, O Spirit.

Native American Spiritualist Proverb
Oh, what beautiful dreams we may weave
When we simply give our hearts the power to believe.

Arabic Prayer
It is Glory enough for me
That I should be Your servant.
It is grace enough for me
That You should be my Lord.

Prayer for Guidance
God be with me in my heart,
my mind, and in my understanding;
God be in my speaking,
And in my actions;
And in my thinking;
God be at my end,
And at my departing.

Love Each Other Now
Love each other now,
So each can know,
The sweet and tender feelings,
Which from affection flow.
Love each other now,
While you are living,
Do not wait until tomorrow,
Love each other today,
So you can treasure it.

Bravery of a Buddhist Bodhisattva – Ngulchu Thogme
If you have not tamed the enemy of your own anger
Combating outer opponents will only make them multiply
Therefore, with an army of loving-kindness and compassion,
To tame your own mind is the practice of a Bodhisattva.

Islamic Prayer
O God,
You are Peace.
From You comes Peace,
To You returns Peace.
Revive us with a salutation of Peace,
and lead us to your abode of Peace.

An article of Mormon faith
We claim the privilege of worshipping Almighty
God according to the dictates of our own
conscience, and allow all men the same privilege,
let them worship how, where, or what they may.

Baha'i Prayer
O God, O thou Most Generous Lord! We are thy radiant
servants asking to drink from thy cup of guidance that
brimmeth over with Thy measureless grace. Light up
our hearts to disclose among all thy bounteous favour.
Assist us to understand Thy divine mysteries. Verily, thou art the Mighty,
the Powerful, the Protector, the Beneficent, and
the Lord of all mercies.

Shinto Prayer
O Most High, help to bring thy light into the darkened conditions of the world! Be gracious to us thy humble servants and bless us with illumination as to that which is Divinely relevant to the fulfillment of thy will!

O Most High, inspire thy servants throughout the world to further efforts toward leading thy children who are led astray to the right way, and to live and act on the faith of what has been taught by the great founders of the religions!

Bless all spiritual leaders with thy power and enable them to give help, joy, comfort, and reassurance to those suffering, to whom they minister!

Sikh Prayer
May the hearts of believers
be humble, may their wisdom be high,
and may they be guided in their
wisdom by the Lord.

Jaina Prayer
Lead me from Death to Life,
from Falsehood to Truth.
Lead me from Despair to Hope,
from Fear to Trust.
Lead me from Hate to Love,
from War to Peace.
Let Peace fill our Heart,

our World, our Universe.

Hindu Mantra
Attach thy mind to Me,
those of faith.

Islamic Prayer
By the Moon and the Night
By the Sun and the Day
The Lord is the One
I choose to follow and to hold my soul.

Islam Prayer
So by the soul, and the order of understanding given to it,
the enlightenment as to its wrong and its right,
truly one succeeds who purifies it,
and truly one fails who corrupts it.

Muslim Sufi Prayer
Where the path of love begins
Greet the hue of day
Out of the fog of darkness
Let God into your heart and mind
Now is the time!
Magnificent are the signs of God!

Baha'i Prayer
O Lord! We are gathered together with intent hearts
spellbound to be carried away by Thy Love.
Weak though we be, we await the revelations of Thy Might and Power. Poor though we be, we take riches from the Treasures of the Treasures of Thy Heaven.

O Thou Provider! Send down thine aid, that each one
gathered in Your Great Names may become a lighted
candle, each one a summoner to Thy Heavenly Realm,
till at last we make this world a mirror image of Thy
Paradise Heaven.

Zoroastrian Prayer
God is love, understanding, wisdom, and virtue.
Let us love one another, let us practice mercy and forgiveness, let us have peace.

Let my joy be of altruistic living, of doing good to others. Happiness is unto him from who happiness proceeds to any other human being.

International Spiritual Liberation Prayer
The cosmic laughter of Spirit bathes my soul in joy.
I see with clear seeing, and all that I do is from the pure
joy of being. I love life and I love living. I love being me
as I am me.

African Prayer
Earth, while I am yet alive,
It is upon you that I put my trust
Earth who nourishes and receives my body
I am addressing you,
And you will understand.

African American Spiritual
Hold to the God's hand,
the unchanging hand!
Build your hopes on things eternal!
Hold to God's unchanging hand!
We join hands in agreement (Kumbaya).

Young Bull (Pawnee Native American Wisdom)
Our people were made by the stars.
When the time comes for all things to end,
our people will turn into small stars.

Tao Te Ching Virtue
Knowing others is wisdom
Knowing the self is enlightenment
Mastering others requires force
Mastering the self requires strength
He who knows he has enough is rich
Perseverance is a sign of will power
To die but not to perish is to be eternal

Bhagavad Gita
For men whose minds are forever
focused on me, whose love has grown
deep through meditation,
I am easy to reach.

Wiccan Spell for Protection and Peace

(With candle and incense)
Mother of all, Protecting Lady,
Goddess of all things,
Of grey waters and bright stars
And the brown fruitful earth,
Here is your favor
And the protection you give.

Sweetness Prayer of Mother Theresa
Lord, the very thought of thee
Fills us with sweetness
All the world reveres the Lord, Our Maker.
Spread love everywhere you go. Let no one ever come to you without leaving happier.

Family Prayer of Mother Theresa
The family that prays together stays together.

Serenity Prayer of Saint Francis
God grant me the serenity to accept the things I cannot change; the courage to change the things I can; and the wisdom to know the difference.

Desideratum
There is no place where God is not,
Wherever I go, there God is.
Now and always, God upholds me
with divine power and keeps me safe with love.
Lord, Who art the way, the truth and the life,
We pray thee
not to suffer us to stray from thee, Who art the way,
not to distrust thee, Who art the truth,
nor to rest on any other than thee, Who art the life.
Teach us to believe, what to do, and wherein to take our rest.

Bhagavad-Gita
The Blessed Lord (as Krishna in human form) said:

When a man has become unattached
to objects of sense or to actions,
renouncing his own selfish will,
then he is mature in yoga and has climbed the heights of spiritual exercise.
He should lift up the self by the Self,
Let not the self droop down;

For self's friend is self indeed,
So too is self self's enemy.

Constantly mastering his mind,
the man of yoga grows peaceful,
attains that supreme peace which has nirvana
as its end and which subsists in Me.

Herein there is no doubt,
Hard is the mind to curb and fickle;
But by untiring effort and by transcending passion
It can be held in check.

He who finds peace and joy
and radiance within himself -
That man becomes one with God
and knows God's bliss

He who controls his mind
and has concern for the welfare of others
realizes the Self; he knows
that God is near.

Bhagavad-Gita
The Blessed Lord (as Krishna in human form) said:
The worship of all gods with love (bhakta),
full filled with faith, do worship ME,
though the rites differ between the acts -
I am the Recipient Lord of All.
Know me as I am and do not fall from good ways.

Baha'i Prayer
O Thou Loving Provider! These souls have hearkened
to the summons of the Divine Essence. They have risen
upward to the call of love; they are enamoured of Thy
Nature, and they worship Thy beauty. Unto Thee they have
gathered together, seeking out Thy heavenly realm.
Thou art the Giver, the Bestower, the Ever-Loving.
Thou art the Universal Mind.

Baha'i Prayer
O God, my God! This is thy radiant servant, who hath drawn nigh unto Thee
and approached Thy presence,
acknowledging Thy Names among all peoples. Lord,

give us to drink from Thy cup of Guidance, Forgiveness, and Grace. Assist your servants under all conditions, cause your servants to learn your mysteries and realities of all things.

Christian Prayer
All ye peoples bless the Lord in one accord
All the earth proclaim the power of the Lord
Hearts to heaven and voices raise
Sing to God a hymn of gladness and praise
Of joy and triumph everlasting

Christian Kyrie Eleison Prayer
Great is what God has done, is doing, and will continue to do.

Prayer for All People
I said a prayer for you today
And know God must have heard
I felt the answer in my heart
Although God spoke no word
I didn't ask for wealth or fame
I knew you wouldn't mind
I asked God to send treasures
Of a far more lasting kind!
I asked that God be near you
At the start of each new day
To grant you health and blessings
And friends to share your way!
I asked for happiness for you
In all things great and small
But it was for God's loving care
I prayed the most of all!

Unitarian Universalist Belief
We believe great teachers of many faiths have emphasized the worth and dignity of every person, the relatedness of all people and encouragement for spiritual growth, ethical behavior, living in harmony with nature, and peace, liberty, justice, and compassion for all.

Back to Earth Prayer
As my eyes wander thru the trees
I see the beauty of the leaves
I am reminded of the Source
I am a part of the Good Earth

From where we came
And where we shall return

Spiritual Prayer

We celebrate one world, one heart, and many paths to God. One with Spirit, together we create a global community centered in peace, love and joy.

Praise the Divine Spirit, unseen but known by many names. Let all the world unite for peace and goodwill.
May you feel the glory of God, wherever you are.

International Embodiment Prayer

I consciously choose happiness as a way of life. I fill my mind with joy, the joy that comes from within; it informs my thoughts and emotions and acts through me. My prayer today is for holy guidance. I thank God for being real.

Confucianism Thought

The ether of earth ascends,
the ether of heaven descends;
the Yin & Yang interact,
the forces of heaven and earth co-operate.
They are drummed on by thunder,
stirred by wind and rain,
kept in motion by the four seasons,
warmed by the sun and moon;
from all this the innumerable
transformations arise.
This being so, music is the harmony
of heaven and earth.

Cao Dai Five Vows

We pray that the wisdom the Great Tao be widely spread on Earth,
May peaceful existence manifest
for all creatures of Nature's birth.
May all humanity be redeemed
and our whole world know peace.
And may the places we meet to
worship You be granted safety's lease.

Tenrikyo Ofudesaki Scripture

Whatever marvels you may see,
they are none other than the workings of God.
Never take it as a trivial matter.

The intention of Heaven is profound.
If only the Service is done without error,
The Gift of Heaven, also will be given without fail.
This path is a path of true sincerity and is difficult to follow.
Everyone must ponder well
and wipe mental dusts from their mind.
There may be no one at all who knows the true workings of God.
Everything depends on the pure hearts of all humankind.

Prayer for a Guardian Angel
Angel of God, my guardian here,
To Whom God's love commits me here,
Ever this day be at my side,
And in my heart to light and guide.

Akasha Realm Prayer
O, Thou Creator of the Universe
Realm of consciousness of All Great Names
Realm of angels, saints, and good souls
Fill us with guidance and knowledge this day
To follow the divine plan
Help lift the burdens of life
Fill us with peace, love and hope
In Your Divine Greatness Do We Trust.

4 Candle Spiritual Practice
Today I will light four candles to help the world.
The first candle will be for the healing of sick people
and animals.
The second candle will be for hope for the hopeless
or abandoned.
The third candle will be for help for dreams,
hopes, and desires.
The fourth candle will be to spread love in the world.
Some days I might only light one candle,
but I pray it will send helpful energy along the way.

Rastafari Motto
Our motto is peace. Our standard is doing Right. Our hopes are salvation.
He that liveth a productive life in God, seeketh and shall obtain heaven terrestrial and heaven eternal.

Thelema

Love is the law.

The Prayer Before A Prayer (African Bishop Tutu)

I want to be willing to forgive
I am not yet ready
God grant me the will to want to forgive
Can I even form the words to forgive the hurt
that I have caused and have been given?
Is there a place in the middle where we can meet?
Where you are right and I am right too
And both of us are wrong and wronged
And look for the place
Where the path begins on forgiveness and peace

The Common Quest

In creed we may differ, yet we are dedicated to one august destiny and share a common quest for an eternal verity (truth). We may build different altars, but we are children of one great love, united in our one eternal family. We all have holy yearning and offer prayers.

Thank You Prayer

Lord, Thank you for good humans who are working hard and doing good things for others. Thank you for good humans who produce clean water, clean food, and energy sources so we can be warm in cold weather and cool in hot weather. Keep safe good humans who are emergency responders, police officers, firefighters, EMT medical responders, construction crew, volunteers, and any workers who put their lives in jeopardy during the course of their work. Thank for you humans who are studying sciences and math to make further progress for the world. Thank you for our family and friends. Thank you for the scriptures, the saviors and prophets, and the organization of the religious entities. Thank you for the good diligence of any human who is doing good things and not causing evil. Thank you for watching over the Universe and being our guiding force. Thank you for happiness, love, and forgiveness.

Each Person Matters

There is a dignity and worth of every person in the relatedness of all of God's people. All lives matter.

THE GOLDEN RULE

Baha'i Faith – Lay not on any soul a load that you would not wish to be laid upon you, and desire not for anyone the things you would not desire for yourself.

Buddhism – Treat not others in ways that you yourself would find hurtful.

Christianity – In everything, do to others as you would have them do to you: for this is the law and the prophets.

Confucianism – One word which sums up the basis of all good Conduct...loving-kindness. Do not do to others what you do not want done to yourself.

Hinduism – This is the sum of duty: Do not do to others what would cause pain if done to you.

Islam – Not one of you truly believes until you wish for others what you wish for yourself.

Jainism – One should treat all creatures in the world as one would like to be treated.

Judaism – What is hateful to you, do not do to your neighbor. This is the whole Torah; all the rest is commentary. Go and learn it.

Native Spirituality – We are as much alive as we keep earth alive.

Sikhism – I am a stranger to no one; and no one is a stranger to me. Indeed, I am a friend to all. God is within everyone.

Taoism – Regard your neighbor's gain as your own gain and your neighbor's loss as your own loss.

Tenrikyo - All human beings in this world are the children of God.

Unitarianism – We affirm and promote respect for the interdependent web of all existence of which we are a part.

Thelema, Wicca – If it harms none, do what you will.

Zoroastrianism – Do not do unto others whatever is injurious to yourself.

SCRIPTURES

This book of Scriptures contains information about how religions have progressed over the past 3000 years.

CHAPTER 1
A very long time ago

1. Statues, buildings, hieroglyphic symbols, and paintings on cave walls were evidence of spirituality in humanity because there was no paper.
Marvelous paintings of animals on cavern walls in Altamira, Spain and Lascaux, France date back to 30,000BCE. The purpose of the paintings could have been in hope to promote plentiful hunting, to teach ways of hunting, or to tell stories by flickering firelight deep inside the caves.
Mysterious etchings in the desert Nazca plains of Peru date to 1CE or before; they are forty square miles of animals, insects, flora and geometric patterns, some miles long with straight lines. It is unknown how the etchings were made or who made them.

The Rosetta Stone found in Memphis, Egypt contains text dated 196 BCE issued on behalf of King Ptolemy V.

In 1446 CE a stone was placed in the Blarney Castle in Ireland; it is believed if you kiss the stone you will be granted the gift of eloquent speaking.

3. In 2400 BCE two Gods of Egypt were Horus and Set. They decided to have a boat race to see who would be God of Egypt. Horus won. Horus made his boat out of wood and Set made his boat out of stone. Set's boat sunk but Horus' boat floated so Horus won the boat race.
Because Set lost, it is said that he became evil.
Horus was the son of the Queen Isis and Osiris. Osiris was killed by Set and the weeping of Isis caused the land to become dried up; Isis cried out 'A man should seek to rule his own heart, not a land or people.' Osiris was resurrected from the dead briefly by Isis, who enfolded him in the fanning of her wings, and that is when Horus was conceived.

4. There was an Egyptian god named Amun-Ra. Amun represented the essential and hidden. Ra represented divinity and the sun. The sun rose from a mound of pyramidal of earth or from a lotus flower or in the form of a beetle, falcon, heron or human child.
Amun-Ra was the champion of the poor or troubled and was central to personal piety. It is believed the 'Amen' that was later used after prayer affirmations in Judaism, Christianity, Mormonism, and Christian Orthodoxy comes from the Egyptian god Amun.
The Egyptian goddess Sekhmet (also spelled Sakhmet or Sakhet) was a goddess of healing and power. It was an urban legend that her breath formed the desert. Sekhmet was sometimes depicted as a lioness for her power.

5. Hathor was a cow goddess in Egypt by 8,000 BC or 8,000 BCE. Cows were believed to have been domesticated at that time.

In India, cows are considered sacred even in the year 2013 CE. (Current Era). Cows may roam freely and the populations of people exist among the sacred cows.

6. Heh was an Egyptian God of Eternity.

7. An Egyptian creation myth is inscribed in stone by ancient priests of Egypt which say that divine thoughts come into existence by the thought of the heart and the commandment of the tongue. It is the heart that brings forth every issue, and the tongue repeats the thought of the heart. Thus were fashioned all the gods, from Atum, the first diety, whose presence was inscripted from tombs dated 2350 BCE. Atum brought forth two children, Shu and Tenut. Shu and Tenut united and created twins, Geb and Nut.
Geb was an Egyptian God of the Earth and he lay stretched upon his back, while his twin sister, Nut, showed herself in a bridge of stars in the sky.

8. The Arabian gods that were pre-Islamic were Hubal and Allah. The Arabian goddesses were Allat, Manat, and Al-Uzza who were three daughters of Allah. Artifacts date to 100CE which is the same as 100 AD.

9. The Phoenicians (1200-539 BCE) worshipped gods Baal and Ashtoreth (Astarte); incense was lighted alongside the molten image idols. It is believed that human sacrifices and human child sacrifices were offered and ritual sex was part of worship.

10. The Greeks worshipped 12 major divine deities. The pantheon of the 12 Greek Olympians lived on Mount Olympus and they were all related to Zeus in some way.
The male gods were Zeus, Poseidon, Hestia, Apollo, Ares, Hephaestus, and Hermes. The female goddesses were Hera, Demeter, Athena, Artemis, and Aphrodite. The Greek gods overthrew the Titans, who overthrew Uranus. The Parthenon was a temple to Athena built in 447 BCE at the Acropolis in Athens, Greece. In 500 CE Current Era or 500 AD (after the death of Christ) the Parthenon was converted to a Christian church. It was a mosque in 1460 during the Ottoman conquest. In 1800 the British took marble carvings from the Parthenon and put them in the British Museum. In 1832 Greece gained back its independence. The Greeks have asked the British to return the artifacts to Greece.

11. The Romans worshipped 12 major divine deities. The pantheon of Roman gods were called the Dii Consentes and included six pairs of male gods and female goddesses:

god Jupiter with goddess Juno,
god Neptune with goddess Minerva,
god Mars with goddess Venus,
god Apollo with goddess Diana,
god Vulcan with goddess
Vesta,
god Mercury with goddess
Ceres.
Three of the deities formed the Capitoline Triad and they were Jupiter, Juno, and Minerva. A lectisternium was a banquet for the Gods in 217BCE.

12. *Greek Gods were often paired with equivalent Roman Gods*:
Zeus and Jupiter were called the King of Gods, the gods of storm, air, and sky.

Hera and Juno were called the Queen of Gods, the goddesses of marriage and family.

Poseidon and Neptune were the gods of the sea, earthquakes, tidal waves, and horses.

Demeter and Ceres were gods of fertility and the harvest, agriculture, nature and seasons.

Dionysus and Bacchus were the gods of wine, ecstasy, celebrations, and theatre.

Apollo was a Greek and a Roman god and was the god of poetry, music, oracles, light, knowledge, healing.

Artemis and Diana were goddesses of hunt, archery, fertility, moon, animals, and childbirth.

Hermes and Mercury were gods of commerce and games.

Athena and Minerva were goddesses of wisdom, handicrafts, defense, strategic warfare.

Ares and Mars were gods of war, violence, and bloodshed.

Aphrodite and Venus were goddesses of love, beauty, and desire.

Hephaestus and Vulcan were gods of blacksmith, craftsman, fire, and the iron forge.

Vesta was a Roman goddess of hearth and sacred fire.

There are Greek and Roman statues of nudes believed to be Venus and David.

Hades guarded the entrance to the place of the dead with a 3-headed monster Cerberus who had a face resembling a dog, a serpent's tail, and lions claws.

13. The 12 Hittite gods were all male.

14. The Roman god Janus is the god of beginnings, transitions, and endings. The Roman god of the doorway, Janus is said to have two faces with which he looks into the past and future simultaneously.
The month of January is named after Janus.

15. The Roman god of men was Mars and the Roman goddess of women was Venus.

16. In 1500 BCE the Hindu god Indra, trembling in fear, went against the monstrous dragon Vittra, who had swallowed all sacred waters, to set the waters free again.

17. In 100 CE in ancient Buddhism, the sun was born from the egg of the sun bird. The eternally unborn, Brahma, in deep concentration, took up the two halves of the egg shell and sang seven holy verses, giving fashion to the elephant Airavata, the mount for the god Indra (God of Productive Great Forces), King of the Gods. After Airavata emerged came seven more noble elephants for the gods.

18. The savior god Ioskeha,
of the Huron Indians saved our planet from dying up by throwing a coconut at the belly of a frog who had swallowed up all water on earth, and waters were released from the frog's mouth into all streams, rivers, and channels again.

19. A story of Andaman Islanders is of a woodpecker that was eating honey from an abandoned bee's nest high up in the trees. A frog was resting at the foot of the tree, looking up, hoping to share in the feast. The woodpecker suggested to the frog to grasp hold of a creeper vine hanging from the tree, and the woodpecker promised to haul the frog up and they could feast together. While the vine was being raised, it broke and the frog tumbled to the ground and he was bruised and his feelings were hurt. The frog decided to swallow all of the water on earth to make all plants and animals thirsty. The animals decided to try to make the frog laugh to spill forth all of the water. Finally, a dancing wriggling eel made the frog laugh so

hard that all waters spilled forth from the frog back into all pools, ponds, lakes, and streams.

20. The Greek God of the sky named Zeus carried a thunderbolt in his raised right hand and was seated in majesty. His sacred bird was a golden eagle. Zeus drank nectar. Hera was his second wife and she wore a crown. Kronos (Time) was the father of Zeus of Olympia.

Atlas was a mythological wise philosopher, mathematician, and astronomer who made the first celestial globe. Atlas was ordered by the Greek god Zeus and to stand at the western edge of Gaia (Earth) and hold Uranus (the sky) on his shoulders; this was because Atlas and his brother Menoetius were Titans and were defeated in a war against the Olympian gods, which was when Zeus punished Atlas and made his bear the globe on his shoulder.
Atlas was paired with the goddess Phoebe who governed the moon.

Prometheus was a Titan in Greek mythology who was creative and original and sometimes a trickster and rebelled against what everyone else was doing. Prometheus gave the idea that humans were formed from clay and he stole fire from the gods and gave it to humanity for progress.

Midas was the Greek God who turned everything into gold that he touched.

Narcissus was the Greek God who fell in love with his own reflection by the pond and drowned trying to get a closer look.

21. Apollo was the God of light, knowledge, music, poetry, prophecy, and archery. Apollo was a Greek god and a Roman god. Apollo gave a lyre as a gift to Orpheus, who became an accomplished singer and musician. When Orpheus played music, even animals gathered to hear the music and even the trees of the earth swayed in harmony.

22. Eros was a Greek god of sensual love and beauty.
In myth, Eros was the first creature to leap out of the World Egg when it split in two. Eros was golden-winged and double-sexed, and the seed of all gods.

23. Cupid was the Roman equivalent of Eros. Cupid carried a bow and arrow, a lyre, dolphins, roses, and torches.

24. Aphrodite was the Greek goddess of love, beauty, and sensuality. Some of her symbols were myrtles, doves, sparrows, mirrors, and swans. Aphrodite was born from the ocean. Soft breezes wafted her ashore the island of Cyprus. She appeared nude and smiling, riding on a scallop shell, but although she appeared to be defenseless she was a actually mighty deity. Mirrors can give optical illusions.

Pandora was the Greek goddess who opened a box of evils tht might plague all of humanity.

25. Makemake was the god of the Rapa Nui on the Easter Islands in the South Pacific.

26. An Inca ruler had been taught to worship the sun. But the king began doubting his faith in the sun, as he observed the sun must be obeying strict laws of motion each day. Therefore, the king concluded that there was a higher power than the sun. The king ordered a temple to be built and kept empty, dedicating it to 'THE UNKNOWN GOD'.

27. The Norse God Thor of Thunder was a good friend to the common people. Once he was visiting a poor peasant family who had not one bite to eat. For supper that night, God Thor offered his two goats for dinner and they enjoyed a succulent roast. The youngest son of the family accidentally sliced a bone with a

knife as he was cutting the meat. The next morning when god Thor arose he lifted his hammer, Mjollnir (which also could produce a thunderbolt) and his two goats sprang to life, ready to pull his chariot. But one of the goats had a slight limp.
God Thor's hammer, Mjollnir, was the shape of a heavy iron cross and acted like a boomerang which could return to where it was thrown from. Thor was the strongest of northern gods and would try anything once. He dared to wrestle with death and old age for humanity's benefit, but was defeated in the contest. Thor defeated a giant named Hrungnir and released his prisoner in jail who was named Orwandill.

In Sweden there are runestones left from 900CE that may have marked burial sites or were shrines marked with inscriptions to Norse gods such as Odin.

The Storkyrkan or The Great Church is also called the Sankt Nikolaikyrka or The Church of Saint Nicholas and was built by Birger Jarl. The Church of Sweden in Stockholm 1279 was Catholic until in became Lutheran Protestant.

28. Freja (Freyja) was the Norse Goddess of love, beauty, fertility,
Loki was the Norse Trickster God. Odin was the Norse Father of Gods. Tane was a forest God.

Heimdallr was Norse Guardian of the Bifrost – rainbow bridge that connected the world of god and the world of humans. Heimdallr will blow the Gjallerhorn, a horn that predicts the end of the world. In Norse mythology, the end of the world ends with a bang, an epic battle between gods when the entire world will sink beneath waves except 2 humans: Liv and Livtrasir, who will come up from the underworld to repopulate the world.

29. One African god is Chukwu. But African supreme gods can have many names. In Ghana, the Akan people believe that God interacted with humans, but after being continually struck by the pestle of an old woman pounding fufu, a traditional Ghanaian food, God moved far up into the sky.

Native Spiritualism

30. Native Spiritualism was evidenced by ancient shamanism in North America, Netherlands, and Asia (1000BCE).

Lenape Native Indians from Asia came to North America over the Bering Strait to Alaska and onto the continent about 15,000 years ago.

The Klamath tribe of Native American Spiritualism believed the sky god Skell and the god of the underworld Llao engaged in battle that formed Crater Lake in Oregon. The sacred lake has no rivers flowing into it or out of it. Crater Lake is a sacred site to the Klamath tribe of Indians.

The Pawnee Native American tribes believed that at the end of time, people will turn into stars, since all people were made by the stars.

Track Rock Gap is an archaeological area in the Chattahoochee National Forest in Georgia, USA which contains preserved petroglyphs of ancient Native Americans in six soapstone boulders dated to 1,000 BCE.

The petroglyphs resemble animal and bird tracks, crosses, circles, and human footprints. The area of forest is 52-acres or 210,00 m^2.
The Arkaquah Trail that starts at Brasstown Bald in Georgia, USA is a hiking trail that is 5.5 mi (8.25 km) in length and ends at Track Rock Gap. Brasstown Bald is known to Cherokee, Mohican, and Muscogee (Creek) people as Enotah; the mountain is the highest point in Georgia, USA. The Coharie and Lumbee tribes are in North Carolina.

The Armuchee is a land named after the Cherokee word *armuchee* which means corn hominy grits or land of the flowers.

The Green Corn Ceremony of the Cherokee is celebrated at harvest by carrying woven baskets of vegetables and corn. The Hopi corn mother is Chochmingwu.

The Etowah mounds of the Muscogee in Bartow County, Georgia, were used as speaking, mortuary, house, temple, and dance platforms at pow wow gatherings.
The Appalachian trail goes from Maine to Georgia.
The League of Six Nations of Iroquois were Seneca, Cayuga, Mohawk, Onondaga, Oneida, and Lenape around areas of New York, USA and were called the Mahongwi (Mengwe). The league was admired by the Founding Fathers of the U.S. who used the league as a model to establish the federal government.
The Iroquois and Mohawk are in New York, USA.
The Huron were Iroquois in NY.
The Mohican are around Massachusetts.
The Menominee are a tribe in Wisconsin.
The Chippewa are at Lake Superior in Michigan.
The Blackfoot emigrated from the Great Lakes area to the Northwest.
The Ponca and Omaha are in Nebraska.
The Cheyenne, Crow, Comanche, Osage, and Chickasaw are in Oklahoma and Montana.
The Sioux, Santee, and Lakota are near North and South Dakota, Minnesota, and Iowa.
The Pueblo, Coyotero, Chaco, and Manataka live in Arizona or New Mexico.
The Yosemite and Miwok are in California.
The Talega, Alligewi, and Natchez live in Mississippi.
The Pequot live in Connecticut. The Lenape live in Delaware.
The Tappacola, Pensacola, Choctaw, Apalachee, and Muskogee lived in Florida.
The Inuit Eskimo of the ancient Lenape live in Alaska and Canada.
The Powhatan were in Virginia.
The Assiniboine were in Montana.

Chief Redstone of the Assiniboine in Wolf Point, Montana, carved peace pipes from Native American Indian sacred red stone found in Montana and Minnesota. wood. The European colonists and the Native Americans Indians used tomahawk axes to cut wood. Tomahawk is a Powhatan word.
The Ojibwe (Chippewa) made a Sacred Hoop called a dreamcatcher which hung on walls over beds to catch bad dreams and keep them from light of day. The Mohicans could run miles through the woods without being heard.

Cheyenne dancers wear a buffalo headress to perform a healing ceremony called the massaum.

The Navajo Nation and related Apachee, Hopi, Pima, Chiricahua, Mescalero, Jicarilla, and Lipan tribes are in SouthWest USA and are known for sand painting, turquoise and silver jewelry crafting, pottery, wool and grain production, moccasins for the feet, and sheep and cattle herding. Geronimo was a great tribal brave leader for the Bendonkohe Apache. A brave is a male, a squaw sachem is a female chief, and a papoose is a baby or small child.

The Native Americans sent smoke signals up into the air as a form of communication to other native tribes. Natives invented dwellings such as the Navajo hogan, the Apache wickiup, the Pueblo adobe hut, the Seminole Chickee, the Ojibwa wigwam, and the Lakota tipi. Natives worked fields to grow corn, squash and beans; invented pipes to smoke tobacco; and were expert trackers of animals and people.

The Tsimshian and Tlingit Native British Columbian tribes of Canada beat drums at reservation meetings by the Skeena River and built totem sculptures with carvings of animals and characters that symbolized beliefs, clan lineages, or events for their culture.

The Wolastoqiyik or Maliseet natives lived near New Brunswick and Quebec, Canada and Maine near the St. John River. Wolastoq means 'Beautiful River.' The natives believed that animals had special gifts, such as healing powers especially if an animal looked at you a certain way.

The Kuna Indians are a tribe in San Blas Archipelago on the Atlantic side of the Republic of Panama.

CHAPTER 2

Papyrus & Bamboo Paper

1. When papyrus was invented as the earliest paper *4000 years BCE*, the writings of philosophers and sacred writings of religions became popular.
Papyrus was also used for boats, mattresses, mats, ropes, sandals, and baskets in the middle-east.
Bamboo paper was made in Asia.
Stone paper and sugar cane paper have been produced in the 21st century.

2. The Dead Sea Scrolls are dated 500 BCE and contain texts written in Hebrew, Aramaic, Greek, and Nabataean.

3. Earliest sacred writings of Hebrew text for the Torah or Greek Septuigant (later the Old Testament of Bible) date to 2200 BCE.

The Talmud is a collection of Jewish writings that is composed of the Mishnah (200CE) and Gemara (500CE). The Mishnah are writings of Oral Torah that were not in the Torah (5 books of Moses) of the Tanakh (The Hebrew Bible) .
The Gemara contains writings concerning Halakha (law), Jewish ethics, philosophy, customs, history, lore, and other.

Rabbi Yochanan ben Zakkai began working on the Hebrew Bible at the Council of Jamnia in Yavneh in 90 CE.

4. Earliest sacred writings or surahs of Koran date 632 CE.

5. Earliest sacred writings of Mormons are dated 692 BCE.

6. The Ordnung is a sacred Amish book dated 1700 CE.

7. The Vedas, Upanishads, and the Gita are sacred scriptures or poems (shruti) in Hinduism dated 1500BCE. Sanskrit is the ancient Indian language of Hindu literature.

8. The Kojiki is the sacred foundation of written Shintoism history in Japan dated 711CE. It was written by O no Yasumaro.

9. Tenrikyo is a religion of Japan based on sacred scriptures of the Ofudesaki dated 1882 CE.

10. The 12 religious sacred scriptures of the ancient Aztec Mayans are known as the Florentine Codex and cite gods, humanity, and natural history. The Florentine Codex is written in Nahuatl and Spanish dated 1590CE. Ancient Mayans of Central America may have migrated to north America in 900CE. Viracocha Pachamac was an Incan leader who cracked codes hidden in Mayan carvings.

11. The Book of Shadows is a sacred book of Wicca dated 1950CE.

12. The Avesta is a sacred book of Zoroastrianism dated 559BC.

13. The Aqdas is a sacred book of Bahai dated 1873CE.

14. The adi Granth is a sacred book of Sikhism. The Guru Granth Sahib is a sacred book of the eleventh guru and the earliest texts are dated 1469CE.

15. The Tripitaka is a sacred book of Buddhism dated 416CE. Tripitaka means Three Baskets and contains canons of scriptures.

16. The sacred Tao Te Ching (the Laozi) was written in 300BC by the sage Laozi (Lao Tzu 'Old Master') on bamboo papers tied together with rope. The name of the title translates to 'the way' and 'virtue, integrity, personal character.'

17. The holy book Liber AL vel Legis of the Thelema religion is based on ideas of will, choice, inclination, desire, pleasure, yoga, and mysticism and is based on Egyptian gods. It was started by the prophet Aleister Crowley in 1904Ad (1904CE).
A motto is 'Love is the law.'

18. The Holy Piby of Rastafari was written by Shepherd Athlyi in 1924CE.

19. The Dianetics is the sacred book of Scientology dated 1950CE.

20. Around 2000 CE holy scriptures were read online on computer internet.

21. The CIVIC was written in 2011CE near Rubes Creek in Ga., USA. and contained modern translations of religious scriptures

in one book. 'Civic' means the affairs of the community, all citizens living among each other with respect, peace, and cooperation in a refined, advanced society that values life, progress, and conservation of our planet.

22. Homer Socrates, Plato, Diogenes, and Aristotle were Greek philosophers who established writings around 450BC of philosophies of humane reasoning and religion.
Homer said 'All men have need of the gods.' Plato was a student of Socrates, and Aristotle was a student of Plato. Diogenes walked around with a lamp looking for an honest man.They wrote about ethics, aesthetics, logic, rhetoric, knowledge, religion, science, mathematics, politics, metaphysics, and philosophy.
Euclid was a significant mathemetician who wrote a book about fundamental geometry, aritmetics, and axioms.
Plato was the founder of the Academy, the first institution of higher learning; it was located on a plot of land in the Grove of Hecademus in Athens that was once the property of a citizen of Athens who was named Academus.
Socrates was put to death because some thought he did not believe in the Greek gods. Socrates was put on trial and he said that he did believe in the gods, but questioned their abilities.
Socrates said there are two lives to be had, either a divinely happy one, or a godless, miserable one.
Plato advocated for the belief in the immortality of the soul.
Aristotle said out of wonder comes wisdom.
Aristotle (384-322CE) noted in 200BCE that the moon marked the boundary between the earth and the stars. Aristotle and Pling the Elder argued that the full moon induced insanity, believing the moon, with power over ocean tides, could also affect the waters of the cells in the brain and body.

The Boy Who Cried 'WOLF'

A famous fable written by Aesop was of a boy named Peter who cried WOLF too many times as a bluff or a lie in order to make townspeople run toward the sheep herd. When the people arrived, Peter laughed at them out of boredom. Then, in an emergency when there was a wolf, no one came. There were many dead sheep and Peter had climbed a tree to survive.

23. Seleucus of Selencia noted in 200BCE that the tides of the ocean were connected to the moon.

24. Confucious was an Asian philosopher of wisdom. Mencus was a philosopher who followed Confucious. Four Books of Confucian philosophy are: Confucian Analects, Book of Mencius, Great Learning, and Doctrine of the Mean.

25. Anaxagores was a Greek philosopher in 428BCE who reasoned the sun and the moon were both spheres of rocks and theorized the moon reflected light

from the earth (now we know it is reflected sunlight).

26. Pythagoras (570BCE-495BCE) and Euclid (300BCE) were Greek mathematicians and philosophers who devised theories used in geometry.

27. A Chinese astronomer named Jing Fang (78-37BCE) noted sphericity of the moon.

28. In 499CE, in India, an astronomer named Aryabhata mentioned that the reflected sunlight caused the shining of the moon.

29. Omar Khayyam (1050-1123CE) was an Arab mathematician whose work was fundamental in Algebra. One source said he lived from 1048-1131CE and was born in Persia in Khorasan (Iran).

30. Dante Alighieri (1308-1321CE) was an Italian Christian who wrote a poem called the Divine Comedy which describes an encounter in hell, a vision of the afterlife, and a soul's journey to God. Virgil the Roman poet (70-19 BCE) was the guide through hell in Dante' work. Giordano Brun in 1600CE was put to death for teaching the earth moved around the sun; Galileo the astronomer escaped the same fate a few years later when he was teaching the same scientific discovery.

31. Michel Eyquem de Montaigne (1533-1592CE) was a French writer who was known to combine casual anecdotes with serious intellectual ideas. The phrase 'What do I know?' is attributed to him when he doubted his own intellect. Montaigne influenced writers such as Descartes and Shakespeare. Montaigne said: 'The testimonies of a good conscience are pleasant; and such a natural pleasure is very beneficial to us; it is the only payment that can never fail.'

32. Rene Descartes (1596-1650CE) was a French philosopher, writer, and mathematician who lived most of his life in the Dutch Republic. His books on 'Meditations on First Philosophy' and 'Passions of the Soul' were widely read. He wrote about emotions and rationalism (logical truths in reasoning). Descartes is famous for saying 'I think, therefore I am.' It was an answer to the question of 'Is there anything I know with certainty?'
Three hundred years later, another philosopher named Jean-Paul Sartre (1905-1980) questioned Descartes' statement 'I think, therefore I am' and said "The consciousness that says 'I am' is not the consciousness that thinks." This means that when you are aware that you are thinking, that awareness is not part of thinking. It is a different dimension of consciousness. And it is that awareness that says 'I am'. Compare a dreamer who doesn't know he is dreaming to a dreamer that is aware that he is dreaming. When you know that you are dreaming, you are awake within the dream and that is the 'I am', the ego, the unconsciousness of repetitive and persistent thoughts, emotions, and reactive patterns that you identify with most strongly.

33. Baruch Spinoza was a Dutch philosopher who lived in Holland (1632-1677CE) and was considered to be a rational thinker; Spinoza was shunned by the Jewish and Catholic priests because he told others that God must exist everywhere in the universe. Spinoza recognized no absolute divide between science and philosophy of

religion. Spinoza questioned why does anything exist since Time Zero and what are humans in the scheme of things. Modern philosophers have said it was a wonder that Spinoza lived in a country that allowed freedom of thought to be expressed.

34. Isaac Newton (1642-1727CE) and Gottfried Wilhelm Leibniz (1646-1716CE) were philosophers and mathematicians whose work was fundamental in Calculus.

35. The seven sages of ancient Greece (620-530BCE) traditionally represented an aspect of worldly wisdom which sometimes varied. The seven sages were:

(1) Cleobulus of Lindos: 'Moderation is the best thing.' He governed as tyrant of Lindos, in the Greek island of Rhodes around 600BCE.

(2) Solon of Athens: 'Keep everything in moderation (discussion).' He was a famous legislator and reformer, writing laws to shape democracy around 638-655 BCE.

(3) Chilon of Sparta: 'You should not desire the impossible.' Chilon was a politician in 6th century BCE.

(4) Bias of Priene: 'All people are essentially the same and all want a good life.' Bias was a politician and legislator of the 6th century BCE.

(5) Thales of Miletus: 'Know thyself.' Thales was a philosopher and mathematician in 546-624BC and his saying was engraved on the front façade of the Oracle of Apollo in Delphi. Thales also studied static electricity.

(6) Pittacus of Mytilene:'You should consider which opportunities to choose.' Pittacus governed Mytilene and Myrsilus and recognized the popular classes in addition to nobility. This was in 568-640 BCE.

(7) Periander of Corinth: 'Be farsighted with everything.' He was the tyrant of Corinth in the 6th and 7th centuries BCE. During his rule, Corinth knew a golden age of stability.

36. George Ivanovich Gurdjieff (1866CD) was an Armenian Greek spiritual philosopher who taught The Fourth Way. Instead of focusing on body (hatha yoga), emotions (monasticism), or mind (raja yoga) to transform oneself, utilize the Fourth Way which is to use all three at the same time while dealing with life's opportunities and challenges to achieve harmony and balance. Famous spiritual philosophers of the late 1800's were Pyotr Ouspenski of Russia, Rajneesh of India, Thomas de Hartmann of Russia, Jeanne de Salzmann of France, Jiddu Kishnamurti of India, Maurice Nicoll of UK, John G. Bennett of London, and Helena Blavatsky of Russia.

37. William James (1842, New York, USA) was a philosopher who said one could justify a belief in a god by what the belief brings to one's life.

CHAPTER 3
Middle-Eastern Religions

Jewish Religion

1. The written scriptures of the Abrahamic religions originated from The Torah of Judaism dated 2200 BCE.

The Jewish God Jehovah made promises known as covenants with Jews on the earth and gave moral commandments such as The Ten Commandments given to the Jewish prophet Moses by God Jehavah to guide humankind. *Faith* is believing in the redemption of soul (salvation), *mercy* (forgiveness), *grace* (generosity), blessings, and divine ways of the Lord.

The Torah includes Genesis (Story of Creation), Garden of Eden, Noah, Abraham, Gideon, Sodom and Gomorrah, Lot, Joseph, Exodus (the journey of the Jews from Egypt from slave bondage back to the land of the Israelites), the story of Moses and the Ark of the Covenant of the Ten Commandments, the story of King David and King Solomon and the building of the Two Jewish Temples, the angel Gabriel, *Nevi'm*: the Jewish prophets Isaiah, Ezekiel, Elijah, Elisha and others, *Ketuvim*: the stories of Samuel, Ruth, Joshua, Job, Book of Life, Jonah, Satan (the angel who was cast from heaven into Hell).

Some of the ideas in Judaism such as resurrections are believed to have been taken from old Egyptian religions.

2. Pharoah Siamun was the 6th pharaoh of Egypt during the 21st Dynasty; it is believe Pharoah Siamun lived 986BCE-967BCE). In 1999CE, an archaeologist named Chris Bennett made a good case from an inscription at the Temple of Semna that Pahroah Saimun might have been married to Queen Karimala, who was the daughter of Osorkon the Elder, who reigned before Saimun.

Some believe the Israeli King Solomon's temple could have been an Assyrian King or Egyptian Pharoah Siamun's Temple; no one is sure because the languages and markings on the excavated items are hard to translate. Also, it could have been that there were 2 different temples at 2 different locations.

Archaelologists have been digging since the late 1800's CE in the middle-east to gain knowledge about what happened in ancient empires but no one is exactly certain about what happened during the times of Moses, Jesus, Mohammad, and Mormon; the Neolithic period (8500BCE-4300BCE) of Syria, Israel, and Lebanon was when agriculture was first practiced. An archaeologist named Dorothy Garrod in 1928CE found tools from the Neolithic period. The Bronze Age was from 3330BCE-1200BCE. The Iron Age was from 1200BCE-540BCE. The Persian and Hellenistic Periods followed the Iron Age. The Roman Age is dated from 63BCE-330CE. The Byzantine Period is dated 330BCE-638CE. Excavators in 1985CE, led by Lawrence Stager, dug in the seaport town of Ashkelon in Israel because its history dates back to the Neolithic Age and has been ruled by Canaanites, Philistines, Egyptians, Israelites, Assyrians, Babylonians, Greeks, Phoenicians, Hasmoneans, Hellenistic, Romans, Byzantine, Islamic, Persians, Arabs, and Crusaders, until Ashkelon was destroyed by the Mamluks in 1270CE. A bronze vault and a

silvered bronze statue of a bull calf have been found.
Ahmed Kamal Bey Pasha (1851-1923CE) was an excavator in Egypt.

3. Mormon, Roman Catholic, Coptic, Christian Orthodox, Anglican Church of England, Christian Protestant, Baptist, Muslim, Baha'i, and Ras Tafari religions all have heritage (beginnings or history) from Judaism.

John the Baptist

4. John the Baptist
anointed believers of God by dipping them in the river.

Baptism and dedication ceremonies point to an important truth of new beginnings; a miracle is celebrated of a new life where there once was none. A child or an adult who has found new faith gives us hope for a better world with new ways of understanding and new beginnings.

The dedications include spiritual souls of the family and community who acknowledge that they will help the spiritual and ethical development of others to help them grow in mind, body, and spirit.

Christian Apostle Religions

5. The Gospels described the life and teachings of Jesus and testimonies to God Jehovah.

Mormon, Catholic, Coptic, Christian Orthodox, Anglican Church of England, Christian Protestant, Baptist, Muslim, Baha'i and Ras Tafari religions all have heritage (beginnings or history) from Judaism.

Orthodox Egyptian traditions spoke of Jesus' family traveling through Egypt.

Jesus preached doctrines of love, peace, and forgiveness.
Jesus told the people to pray for lepers, beggars, orphans, widows, and enemies.

At that time in history of Jesus, leprosy was rampant and lepers were sent to leper colonies because there was no cure and the bacteria which causes leprosy can cause damage to skin, nerves, limbs, and eyes.

In the years 1980-2000CE, 16 million people who had leprosy were cured of the disease but the bacterial ailment is still present in the world. Leprosy is also called Hansen's disease, named after the physician Gerhard Hansen who studied leprosy. Vaccines are biological preparations of a small amount of a disease-causing micro-organism that stimulate the body's immune system to destroy it. Vaccinations against smallpox were studied in China in the 10th century. Jonas Edward Salk (1914-1995) made a vaccine for polio.

Jesus told the people that they could eat anything that was safe to eat, different grains could be mixed together, and the food did not have to be blessed by a Jewish rabbi priest before the food could be eaten. Jesus picked spikes of grain on the Jewish Sabbath but the Pharisees told Jesus that no one was permitted to pick grain on the Sabbath, but Jesus called them hypocrites and also said Woe to you, scribes and Pharisees, for ye pay tithe of mint, anise, and cumin, and have omitted the weightier matters of the law, judgment, mercy, and faith: these ought ye to have done, and not to leave the other undone.

Jesus, John the Baptist, and their Disciples started their own ministry; but some of the Jewish rabbi priests of the Sanhedrin Council were angry that they were disregarding the rules of the Sanhedrin Council so they conspired to kill John the Baptist and Jesus. Nicodemus was a Pharisee and a member of the Sanhedrin who reminded the Sanhedrin priests that the law required a person to be heard before being judged.

Gospels were written by disciples named Matthew, Mark, Luke, John, Thomas, and Andrew.

The teachings of Jesus were written in gospels that are claimed by several groups of people. One group was called the Essenes who were followers of Jesus; the Essenes buried gospel scrolls near the Dead Sea in jars which a shepherd traveling through the desert found many years later. The gospels were in written in Aramaic and were dated 70AD or 70CE. The gospels were then translated into Hebrew, Greek, and Latin.

The Dead Sea Scrolls also contained the writings of the first five books of the Torah which were the stories of Adam and Eve, Noah, Moses, and others. It is believed that the Hebrew Torah was translated into Greek as The Septuigant.

Some believe Jesus was a prophet, saint, or an actual Son of God filled with God's wisdom and direction to bring 'light' to the world of the evil oppression that was occurring in organized religions at that time in history, to remind people of loving-kindness, forgiveness for human imperfections, and that God was more than just the God of the Israelites;
Jesus realized that organized religions were being too controlling, oppressive and violent, that is why Jesus took a stand against the evil Sanhedrin council; Jesus risked his life and he was murdered. Some thought Jesus was a mystic because sometimes he spoke in thought-provoking parables.

Jesus' birthday was thought to have been in the spring but it was celebrated on the pagan holiday of the winter solstice, the time when the time of daylight starts getting longer. Yule, or Yuletide, was the celebration of the winter solstice in ancient European cultures; Yuletide also became known as a Christmas winter celebration for Christians. Christianity was forced upon the pagan cultures by Emperor

Constantine around 300CE. The city Constantinople (current city of Istanbul) was the capital of the Byzantine Empire.

The Vulgate was an early Catholic Bible that was translated into Latin from Hebrew by Saint Jerome in 382CE. The Bible included the Old Testament which was the Jewish Torah and the New Testament which were the Gospels of Jesus.

Trinity Concept

6. Trinity Sunday was established by the Catholic church in 325CE in Rome, Italy. 'Trinity' in Catholicism means Father, Son, and Holy Spirit.
Saint Athanasius of Alexandria was an Egyptian leader of the Coptic Egyptian Church (296-373CE) who was a defender of the Trinity so the trinity is also described as Athansian doctrine.

The Arian belief put forth by Arius (250-336CE) of Alexandria, Egypt is that Jesus Christ is a Son of God but is subordinate to God.

Followers of Jesus who believe in the Trinity concept celebrate Forty Days of Lent, which is a period of fasting and penitence for forty days from Ash Wednesday, Good Friday, and until the Resurrection of Jesus on Trinity Sunday.

A person can only get married once in a Catholic Church. Catholics do not believe in divorce.

Saint Patrick symbolized the trinity with a green 3-leaf clover called the shamrock: one leaf for hope, one leaf for faith, one for love.

Easter springtime celebration is often combined with Trinity Sunday for Catholics and Protestant Christians.

The Apostle Luke wrote that Jesus referred to a Threefold Glory as God of Heaven, Jesus, and the Holy Angels.

Some think Trinity could be One's Self, Creator, and Universe.

Some Christians did not believe in a Trinity concept and believed simply that Jesus was divine; these were early Coptic Christians.

Some believe Jesus was a human being guided by God.

A messiah Baha'ullah (1863CE) wrote that a meaning of Trinity is union, harmony, and affection.

A trinity of the earth is land, air, and sea; and the creatures thereof.

An investigator in 2000CE believed the concept of triage (Trinity) was divinely put forth to help the human mind think in new dimensions to discover the components of atoms (nucleus, proton, and electron) and molecules thousands of years later.

Coptic and Christian Orthodox

7. The Orthodox Churches and Coptic Churches were formed in Armenia, Syria, Egypt, Ethiopia, Turkey, and Russia.
The Cappadocian Fathers were holy men in Persia of Mount Taurus and Mount Erciyes who spread good messages about the Lord and promoted the idea of the trinity.
They were Basil (330-379CE) who was bishop of Caesarea, Gregory (332-395CE) who was bishop of Nyssa, and Gregory (329-389CE) who was bishop of Nazianzus.

Antony the Great

8. Antony the Great was a monk in Upper Egypt in 300CE. He lived for 80 years in the desert and taught other monks how to live an angelic life. He followed the teachings of Jesus and gave up everything he owned before he headed for the desert.
Ammon was also another great Egyptian monk at the same time who settled in the desert of Nitria, west of the Nile Delta. Soon after, there were 5000 monks living in the desert; some died of starvation. The leaders of the monks in the desert were called 'abba' which meant father. Some called Jesus 'Abba' or 'Gevurah' which means 'from the mouth of the Spirit' in Greek.

Catholic Religion

9. King Constantine (272-337CE) of the Roman Empire saw a cross in the sky when he was going into battle, and it changed the feelings of his heart. He stopped religious persecution under his reign. This is how the Catholic church began in Rome.

Around 225CE the original Christian Orthodox church split into the Eastern Orthodox church and the Roman Catholic Western Orthodox church because there were disputes over the Nicene Creed and linguistics (Greek language or Roman language).
The Catholic church was formed with unity in mind. Catholic means 'universal'. Canon law are the laws and legal principles governing the Catholic church and its mission.

Jewish prophets, Jesus, saints, and angels are remembered in the Mass Worship as well as worshipping God.
Priests break bread and reenact the Last Supper of Jesus in Communion with the parishioners (the members of the congregation).

Jewish and Christian scriptures were combined into the Vulgate, an early Catholic Bible, leaving an open door for peace between fighting Jews and Christians.
The Vulgate was an early Catholic Bible that was translated into Latin from Hebrew by Saint Jerome in 382CE when the Protestant Reformation began and there were schisms in the faith of believers. The Bible included the Old Testament which was the Jewish Torah and the New Testament which were the Gospels of Jesus.

Catholic women wore a mantilla scarf (lace or silk veil) around or on head and a shawl on their shoulders to attend church.

Sins were confessed to priests.

Attila the Hun (406-453) of the Hunnic Empire was an enemy of the Western and Eastern Romans. Attila tried to conquer Persia but was unable to take Constantinople. He crossed the Danube River twice and destroyed areas of the Balkans. Attila even tried to conquer France but was defeated at the Battle of Catalaunlan Plains when he tried to conquer Orleans after crossing the Rhine River. After Attila died, Ardaric of the Gepids led a Germanic revolt against the Hunnic Empire and the empire collapsed.

Francis Bernadone, a Catholic of Assisi, Italy (1181-1226 CE) moved worms off of the road so they wouldn't get run over by rolling carts.

Thomas Aquinas, a Catholic of Assisi, Italy (1274-1225 CE) said that God's nature is perfect and absolute love, and the final vision of God is the Beatific

Vision and what we will see when we die.

Rosary beads were made by Queen Gwendolen who rolled rose petals into balls as she meditated while sitting in her garden. Then she got the idea to string them together in the certain order that she recited different prayers.

Jesuit Order of Catholic priests was founded in Paris, France in 1540 by St. Ignatius Loyola and St. Francis Xavier of Spain, and others.

Around 225 CE (225 AD)
'AD' signifies after death of Jesus

It is believed the members of the Church of St. Peter near Antakya, Turkey called themselves Christians or Roman Catholics.

The early believers of Jesus split into different organizations because they had different beliefs about whether Jesus was a prophet or a messiah, and had different language preferences for the verses of Order of the Mass.

The schisms after the Council of Chalcedon (451CE) defining the Trinity

The traditions of the first apostolic churches split into 3 divisions:

The Eastern Orthodox and Catholic Church believe Jesus is divine and human of 2 natures (Chalcedonian)

(1) Christian Eastern Orthodox of which Constantinople is the center. The Eastern Orthodox church is comprised of 16 main churches in Constantinople, Alexandria, Antioch, Jerusalem, Georgia, Cyprus, Bulgaria, Serbia, Russia, Greece, Poland, Romania, Albania, Czech, Slovakia, and America.

(2) Roman Catholic Western churches of which Rome is the center.

(3) Coptic Eastern Catholic churches of which Cairo is the center.

The ancient Coptic Orthodox Egyptian Church and Oriental Orthodox churches believe Jesus is of one divine nature (non-Chalcedonian)

The Coptic Orthodox Church of Alexandria, Egypt is the center of the Oriental Orthodox churches.

Other orthodox churches are Ethiopian, Eritrean, Syriac, Malankara Syriac (Indian Orthodox), Armenian Apostolic, and Tewahedo.

The East-West Schism of 1054CE concerning unleavened vs. leavened bread at communion.

The Roman Catholic church mandated that unleavened bread was to be used at communion, but the Eastern Orthodox church did not believe in the mandate.

Today the two divisions send a representative to the others' celebration of patron saints: Saint Peter and Paul for Rome (29 June) and Saint Andrew (30 Nov) for Constantinople.

The Marionite Eastern Catholic Church began around 400CE. The Marionites are Syriac Christians that were driven out to the plains of Syria and to Lebanon by Muslim invasions around 685CE. The first Patriarch was Saint John Maron who was a Syrian monk. The Maronites are Chalcedonian. The coat of arms of the

Marionites includes a cross that has 3 cross beams.

LITURGY

The verses recited in the Coptic, Christian Orthodox, and Catholic churches have remained similar for nearly two thousand years, since 225 CE. The litany are prayers that are led by the priest who says one verse and the congregation responds together with another verse. Confession is telling your wrongdoings to a priest. Jesus is present in the adoration chapel.

10. Around 1535CE, the Christian Reformation began. The Church of England split away from the Roman Catholic Church.
Since that time, many different sects of Christianity have been formed; many of them have dropped the verses of the Order of the Mass and the Celebration of the Eucharist of Holy Communion (the breaking of bread in remembrance of the Last Supper of Jesus).

TWO MEN ACCUSED OF HERESY

Augustine

11. Augustine (354-430CE) of Hippo (present day Algeria in Arica) and his contemporary Jerome were gnostics who taught about the grace and salvation of God. Augustine practiced the Manichaeism religion before he practiced Christianity. Mani described himself as possible reincarnations from different religions such as Buddha, Lord Krishna, Zoroaster, and Jesus. Manichaeism also put emphasis on making a choice between good and evil.

Augustine said that man does not have free will, that God commands impossibilities because man cannot quit sinning, and the Roman Catholic Church is the supreme authority. Some Christians called Augustine a heretic.

Chinese emperors and Islamic caliphs killed thousands of followers of the Manichaeism religion in the years between 700 and 800CE and Christian Crusaders also killed thousands to gain control of middle-eastern regions. The Mongols took Kiev from the Slavic people in 1240.

Peter of Bruys

Peter of Bruys 1117-1131 France protested crosses by burning them. He was a religious teacher in France and opposed infant baptism, churches, and crosses. The Catholic church called him a heretic.

The Cup Jesus drank from at the Last Supper

12. A quest was started to find the Holy Grail of Jesus, which was the cup he drank from at the Last Supper. Some believed the Holy Grail went to Ethiopia and was kept for 2,000 years in a Monastery made of Obsidian. King Arthur was a member of the British Knights of the Round Table who went in search of the Holy Grail; it was legend that at Camelot, Perceval, and Gawain found the Grail Castle in Glastonbury and the grail was returned to Jerusalem; then the grail was taken from Jerusalem to Egypt and then finally to the monastery in Ethiopia. But many thought that certainly the cup used at the last supper was washed and stored with the other drinking vessels and the cup that Jesus drank from could never have been identified.

The Hagia Sophia

13. The Hagia Sophia (Holy Wisdom) is a Greek Orthodox Church that was built in Istanbul, Turkey in 537CE by Byzantine Emperor Justinian; it was the third church as the first and second church

were destroyed by rioters. From 537-1453CE it was a Christian Orthodox cathedral under Patriarchate Constantinople, except from 1204-1261CE when it was a Catholic Church under the Latin Empire. Then the building was a mosque from 1453-1931CE under Turks in the Ottoman Empire under Sultan Muhmed II. Constantinople was renamed Istanbul in 1930. In 1935CE, it was opened as a museum by the Republic of Turkey. The Hagia Sophia has survived a fire and several earthquakes.

Temple of Artemis

Ephesus was a large city south of Constantinople on the coast of the region called Ionia. Ephesus had an Artemesium, Library of Celsus, medical school, and a theatre for 25,000 spectators.

There is a structure in Ephesus that is believed by excavators to have been at first a Greek temple to Artemis the goddess of wildland and animals, then a Church of St. John during Roman rule, and then the Isa Bey Mosque under Ottoman rule. Ephesus was destroyed by East Germanic Goths in 263 and an earthquake of 614.

Excavators have found ruins of houses that had mosaic floors, frescoes on walls, open-air courtyards, atriums, terraces, water reservoirs, clay piping and bench seats with slits in them that must have served as toilets, and buildings that must have been public baths. A church of St. Mary built by Byzantines was also at Ephesus.

The people in the Middle East have been fighting for over 3000 years.

Derinkuyu is a subterranean city in Turkey that protected ancient cultures from opposing forces in war. There are 36 underground cities near Cappadocia, Turkey.

Along the Bosphorus strait in Istanbul, yali (magnificent summer houses) were built for viziers
(wazir) a high-ranking policial advisor of caliphs.

The Temple Mount

14. The Temple Mount (*Har HaBayit* or *Har HaMoriya* in Hebrew and *Haram al-Sharif* in Arabic) is the site where the First Jewish Temple and later the Second Jewish Temple stood in 516 BCE for God Jehovah before the Second was destroyed in 70CE by Romans who built a Temple to Jupiter, who was the King of Gods, God of Sky & Thunder in the Roman Religion. Jupiter is the equivalent of the Greek God Zeus.

The Dome of the Rock in the center of the Temple Mount in the Old City of Jerusalem, Israel, is the site of the shrine where Mohammad the Islam prophet rode a horse named Buraq to heaven to speak with (God) Allah; Muslims seized the land from the Jews in 637CE. Caliph Abd al-Malik built the Dome of the Rock shrine in 691CE. It is hard to determine who exactly owned the lands around Jerusalem in the hundreds of years before this.

This site of land is also significant to Christians, because it is the site where Jesus went into the Jewish Temple and overturned the tables of merchants; Jesus said the Temple was a place of prayer and they should not be exchanging money in the temple. Christians Crusaded in 1095CE to fight for access to Jerusalem. Religious fighting in Jerusalem has caused many deaths.

Much fighting is occurring in East Jerusalem, West Bank, and Gaza.

The Shatt al-Arab River is formed by convergence of the Tigris and Euphrates Rivers in Iraq and has caused conflicts in Iraq and Iran.

There is a 32 foot tall (9.75 meters) mesquite tree in Bahrain known as the Tree of Life that is 400 years old.

The Kotel

The Western Wall is a holy site for Jews to offer prayers.

Jesus Christ Statues

15. A statue of Jesus, Christ the Redeemer was erected on Corcovado Mountain in Rio de Janeiro, Brazil. The statue stands 125 feet tall and was completed in 1931CE. Christ of the Ozarks statue stands 67 feet tall in Arkansas.

Images of Mary

Italian artist Raphael painted Madonna and Child on the Colonna altarpiece in Rome in 1504. Madonna means My Lady in Italian. Italian artist Michelangelo painted fresco (plaster) religious scenes depicting Judgment Day on the ceiling of the Sistine Chapel inside the Vatican between 1508-1512 during the Italian Renaissance period. Michelangelo also painted nudes and was quoted as saying 'the foot is more beautiful than the shoe and the skin is more beautiful that the garment'. The paintings were done with oil paints or tempera (pigments mixed with egg yolk, gum, Arabic or animal glue.
In 1806 Russian artist Alexander Ivanov painted a gigantic scene of the appearance of Christ to the people.
Later etchings (drawings) and paintings were done by artists with colored pencils, chalks, translucent watercolors (pigments binded in natural gum Arabic or synthetic glycol), giclee (digital prints), encaustic wax paints, gouache (opaque watercolors).

Gounod and Bach composed music for Ave Maria in 1853 in C Major. Beethoven composed religious music for the Catholic church in 1770. In 1791 Mozart composed Requiem in D minor to remember the souls of the dead. In 1740 Handel composed The Messiah in 3 parts ending with Hallelujah chorus in D chord. Concertos were solo instruments such as piano, violin, flute, or cello accompanied by a symphony orchestra. The music compositions were in keys such as A Minor, C Major, C Minor, D Major, E Flat Major, E Minor, G Major, and G Minor. Changes can be made to a room or concert hall by sound engineers to improve acoustic clarity of soundwaves for listeners.

AVE MARIA (Holy Mary)
Originally in Latin and translated to English:

Hail Mary, Full of Grace, the Lord is with thee. Blessed art thou among women, and blessed is the fruit of thy womb, Jesus. Holy Mary, Mother of God, pray for us sinners, now and at the hour of our death. Amen.

Catholics in 1803 began to say Holy Mackeral instead of Holy Mother of God as a figure of speech while swearing when under stress.

The Medieval or Middle Ages are defined as years 476-1500 when the Roman Empire fell and feudalism prevailed as kings ruled. The Renaissance is defined as a period of classical and inductive learning, diplomacy, art, architecture, politics, and literature, invention of concrete and movable type.

Niccoli di Bernado dei Machiavelli (b. 1469 during the Renaissance) was an Italian philosopher and diplomat who wrote about devious and deceitful practices being used by politicians. From 1618-1648 was the Thirty Year wars between Catholics of Italy, Spain, Austria, Hungary, Poland, Russia versus Protestants in England, Sweden, Denmark but Denmark switched sides later on. From 1562-1598 there was fighting in France between Roman Catholics and Huguenots (Reformed Calvinist Protestants), The Ottomans took the Ukraine from the Polish in 1669. The Treaty of Perpetual Peace of 1686 gave Left-Bank Ukraine and Kiev to Russia and the Right-Bank Ukraine to Poland.

The Industrial Revolution in 1760-1800 marked the beginning of the modern period.

In 1968CE, an image of Virgin Mary, the mother of Jesus, appeared in Egypt above the domes of a church at Zaytun in greater Cairo, Egypt. A Christian pilgrimage is held each year where people flock to the church to pray for her divine presence or apparitions.

In the late 1990's CE, an image of Mary, the mother of Jesus appeared to a woman named Mary Fowler in Conyers, Georgia, U.S.A., in Rockdale County.

In December 2015, an image of Mary appeared at Transfiguration Catholic Church in Marietta, Ga.

Monastery of the Holy Spirit

16. There is a Roman Catholic Church, a monastery, and an open burial ground at the Honey Creek Woodlands in Conyers, Ga., U.S.A.

Islam Religion

17. At Jerusalem around 632CE, the angel Gabriel directed the holy prophet Mohammad to recite the surahs of the holy Koran in the name of Allah, the Most Gracious, Most Merciful.
The angel held Mohammad in a tight embrace 3 times before Mohammad was convinced. It was said that the Prophet Mohammad hid under a blanket for 2 days after Allah's voice spoke to him. It is said that Mohammad only recited the surahs during his lifetime from memory, and it was many years after his death that the surahs were written in the book called the Holy Q'uran (Koran).

The Sunni', the Shia's, and the Sufi's are the biggest Muslim sects of Islam. The Ibadi (700CE), the Ahmadiyya (1889CE), and the Sufi are other sects.

The Sunni's are people of the tradition of Mohammad the Prophet and agree on the Ummah (nation) and the sayings and actions of Mohammad the Prophet as recorded in the Hadith (Hadeeth).
Mohammad said in the Hadith that Allah said 'My mercy prevails over my wrath'. There are 25 prophets in Islam. The Day of Judgment will be on a Friday.
Sunni Muslims believe that Abu Bakr, Companion and father-in-law of Mohammad, should succeed the Prophet Mohammad as the caliph (successor). *Sunnah* is the way of

life prescribed for Muslims on the basis of the teachings and practices of Mohammad.

The Shia's believe that Mohammad's descendants are the only true Imams, beginning with his son-in-law and cousin, Ali ibi abi Talib.

They believe Mohammad had nominated his cousin Ali to be the caliphs to lead Islam. Mohammad's descendants through his daughter Fatima are known as Sharifs, Syeds, Sayyids, and are regarded highly by Shias.

There is a branch of Islam that recognized Twelve-Imam Shia. There is another branch of Shias that are called the Seveners; they do not recognize the last five Imams. Shia Muslims believe in a Mahdi, a redeemer (messenger, messiah) who remains hidden and is predicted to come at the end of the world.

Sunnis and Shias believe:
Allah is in the 7 Heavens with angels and Mohammad was the Holy Prophet for the Muslim people. Muslims must pray 5 times a day facing Mecca, which is a holy city for Muslims. Charity must be practiced. Fasting and pilgrimage to Mecca once a year is mandatory. The Koran was revealed to Mohammad by Allah. There will be a Day of Judgment. Righteous souls are resurrected to be with Allah.

The Sufi's have a more broadened scope in their viewpoint of Islam. Mystic poems, trancelike experiences, and whirling dervish dancers are a part of religious services. Sufis seek to find divine love through direct personal experience with (God) Allah. Rumi was a sufi who sang about love. Rumi said 'Fortunate is he who does not walk with envy in his heart for envy is not a good companion.'
The term 'sufi' originated with the coarse wool cloak that wandering mystics wore.

In 941CE Mohammad al-Mahdi, the Twelth Imam of Shia said he was a descendant of Mohammad to restore the religion.

In 1121CE Mohammad ibn Tumart from Morocco claimed to be the Mahdi (Guided One, A Redeemer) but his claim was challenged. His father was a lamp-lighter in the mosque they attended.

Ismailism is a sect of Shia Islam that began after there was a conflict over who should succeed Jaafer al-Sadiq as the sixth imam.

The Mansour Mosque in Morocco was meant to be the largest mosque in the world but construction stopped when Sultan Yacoub-al-Mansour died.

The Gnawam Tribe

The Gnawa tribe of Morocco, Algeria, the Sahara desert, and parts of Libya originated from West Africa.

The Alawite

18. The Alawite or Alawis of the Syrian coast are Shia Muslims. Khidr (Elijah) is a primary prophet. Humans are lights from heaven and may be reincarnated before returning to heaven.

The Alevi

19. The Alevi are Shia or Suffi Muslims in Turkey living among Balkans and Kurds. They hold services in cemevi halls and the services include music, wine, and dancing as well as prayers.

The Druze

20. The Druze (1000CE) is a small sect in Lebanon, Syria, and Israel; it is a sect from Ismailism. Drueze highlights the role of the human mind and truthfulness, elements from Abrahamic religions of Islam, Judaism, and Christianity, Gnosticism, Neoplatoism, Pythagoreanism, Hinduism,and promotes ideas of unity. Neoplatoism was influenced by ideas of Plato; developing the soul through Henosis, which is union with the One, the Source, the Monad which is a circle with a dot in the middle (God), The Absolute. The soul is united with the Cosmic Mind. The religion takes its name from Muhammad bin Ismail Nashtakin ad-Darazi, an early preacher. Jethro of Midian is the prophet of the Druze. Many Druze communities exist near Jabal al-Druze, a volcanic mountain in southern Syria.

The Kurds

21. The Kurds are descendants of Noah and have 12 tribes of Kurdish people in the Kurdistan region around Iran, Iraq, Syria, and Turkey. Kurds can be Sunni, Shia, or Sufi Muslims, Yarsans, Yazidis, Zoroastrians, Jews, or Christians.
The keffiyeh is a woven checkered scarf that has been worn by Arabs living in Arabia, Jordan, and Iraq for over 100 years.

The Zoroastrian Religion

22. The Parsi are Iranians who fled to India after a Muslim Arab conquest in 700CE or 900CE.

The *Qissa-i Sanjan* is a book
that is the story of the journey of the Parsis to India after they fled for reasons of religious freedom and were allowed to live in India thanks to a Hindu prince.

The sacred text Avesta was composed over several centuries beginning around 559BC by 31 kings and began translation in 51AD (51CE) by King Volgash.

Zoroaster was a prophet and composed the Gathas, a sacred hymn for his followers.

Ahura Mazda is the one God who represents good, but dualism is embraced.
Angra Mainyu represents evil.

The Yarsan Religion

23. The Yarsan religion rejects caste, class, and accepts the idea of reincarnation. The Kalam-e Saranam is the sacred text of Yarsan. The Yarsan religion was started by Sultan Sahak around 1300BCE, who was given birth by Rezbar, a Kurdish woman; Rezbar was sleeping under a pomegranate tree and a kernel of fruit fell into her mouth after being pecked by a bird, and divine conception led to the birth of the (Saviour) Saoshyant.

The Yazidism Religion

24. In the Yazidism, God created the world but left it in the care of a heptad of holy beings or angels. The most prominent angel is Melek Taus (Kurdish: Tawuse Melek), the Peacock Angel, God's representative on earth. Yazidis believe in the periodic reincarnation of the seven holy beings in human form. Their holiest shrine and the tomb of the faith's founder is located in Lalish, in northern Iraq.

The Pashtunwali

25. The Pashtunwali of Afghanistan and Pakistan have a non-written Code of Honor Conduct and system of law since the year 900 to protect an individual against his enemies. The Pastunwali do not want outside cultural influences from the west or the east. Some of the Code of Honor Conduct are:

1. Jirga is the decision to wage war or to settle peacefully.
2. Badal is retaliation.
3. Nanawatay is asylum to fugitives.
4. Melmastia is hospitality to a guest.
5. Tor is death to adulterers.

Pa Khair Ossey means May you be safe. Pa Makha De Kha means May your journey be safe and happy.

CHAPTER 4
Reformation of Middle-Eastern religions

1. In the 1500s CE, many new sects of the Abrahamic religions evolved and some people believed in reforming or changing the old Jewish religious ideas such as:

it was not necessary to bring animal sacrifices to an altar,

that both men and women could preach about God,

that men and women did not have to be separated in the synagogues or temples,

that religious persons could marry and have personal lives as well as serving God,

that fasting (abstaining from food for a period of time) was not necessary as an offering to God,

that pilgrimages to holy sites were not necessary in order to go to heaven,

that eating certain foods was not forbidden nor a sin,

that it was not a sin to plant two different kinds of herb seeds side by side in the same garden,

that it is not right to own another human being as a slave,

that wearing clothes woven from two different kinds of yarn is not a sin,

that men and women could both wear tunics or pants,

that body tattoos are not a sin,

that sex aside from procreation is not a sin,

that God will not bring bad weather such as floods, earthquakes, and tornados in wrath because of the wickedness of the people or to wash away the bad things we said that resound in the air

that angels cannot protect you from dangerous lions or cobra serpents,

that it is not right to kill in the name of God,

that a person does not have to confess a sin publicly to another for God to hear,

that mutilating human body parts is not necessary to honor God,

that no one knows if God is a man or a woman or even the image of a human person.

2. *Jewish Reformations*

Jews who accepted Jesus formed their own congregations. 'Yeshua' is the Hebrew name for Jesus. Many Jews stopped pilgrimages and animal sacrificing.

Sephardic Judaism (1492CE)referred to Jews in Iberia (Portugal and Spain) but after the Christian conquest the Jews fled to France, England, Netherlands, Italy, and North Africa. There are differences in diet, holidays, prayer, and worship.

Hasidic Judaism (1740CE) refers to a branch of Orthodox Judaism that emphasizes a mystical relationship with God and involves meditating, praying, and studying the Torah.

Neoorthodox Judaism adapts to the demands of the modern world. Jews are encouraged to engage in life activities with non-Jews.

Reform Judaism accepts woman rabbis and many old dietary laws have been dropped.

Jewish Science (1920CE) was founded by Alfred G. Moses, Morris Lichtenstein, and Tehilla Lichtenstein. God is seen as an energy force that permeates the universe and as a restorer of health. Physical health and spiritual health are promoted. Medical treatment is allowed.

Reconstructionist Judaism follow a Sabbath Prayer Book that includes no mention of a coming Messiah.

Humanistic Judaism was founded by Rabbi Sherwin T. Wine in the US in 1963CE. The philosophy is of a secular perspective; adherents are encouraged to focus on self-determination, self-help, participation in cultures of Jews and non-Jews, and there is no mention of God.

Jewish synagogues were first established in China in 25-220 during the Han, Tang and Song dynasties. Qingzhen Si is the name an old synagogue.

3. *Muslim Reformations*

Muslim mosques were established in China around 700-900 during the Tang, Song, Yuan, Ming, and Qing dynasties. The Huaisheng Mosque is the oldest mosque and believed to have been built by Muhammed's uncle.

The Baha'i Religion

In 1844CE, Siyyid Ali Mohammad Shirazi claimed to be the Mahdi of Shia Islam. He adopted the title of Bab.
Bab was a chosen Teacher of the Holy Spirit in the Middle East and heralded the coming of Baha'ullah. Bab has been compared to John the Baptist, who heralded a divine teacher who was to come later. The Bab had 18 disciples. He pilgrimaged to Mecca in 1844 CE and openly declared that He was a Reformer of Divine Religions and claimed he was

the Mahdi (the redeemer predicted) and he was imprisoned.

Baha'ullah was persecuted and imprisoned for 24
years in Akka, Palestine. Upon his release from prison, he lived at a Mansion called Bahji, which was purchased from a Christian family called Jamal. Baha'ullah died in 1892CE and buried at the Mansion at Bahji; his resting place is a Qiblih (a direction of prayer energy) to Bahai's.

While he was in prison, Baha'ullah wrote letters to Pope Pius IX of the Catholics, to Queen Victoria in England, to Napoleon III in France, and to many others to encourage the unity of diversity of all religions and races (peoples).

The Baha'i Aqdas

The Aqdas holy book contains themes of worship, societal relations, administrative organization, and governance of the Baha'i religion.

The Ahmadiyya Religion

The Ahmadiyya (1889CE) was founded by a Sunni Muslim named Mirza Ghulam Ahmad (1835-1908CE) in Qadian, India, who claimed to be a messiah figure and divinely inspired as the Mahdi; he said he was a spiritual successor of Jesus. He claimed that maybe Jesus did not die on the cross but traveled to another country. Ahmadiyya Muslims desire to share the message of worship to both Muslims and non-Muslims.

Mohammad Abduh
Tariq Ramaden (1960CE) is an Islamic scholar from Egypt who expresses that it is possible to be a Muslim and a citizen of another country at the same time; that Muslims can adhere to Islam and follow the laws of the host country that they live in, wherever they are in the world, promoting good and equity.

Salafism is a modern Sunni Islam movement. Adherents uphold the precedence of sharia law and the literal truth of the Quran.

The Nation of Islam (1930CE) was formed in the US by W. Fard Mohammad, to whom some have ascribed divinity as the messiah predicted by the Torah and the Quran. It upholds a strict code of ethics and spreads ideas about faith and equality for all people.
Malcolm X was an American Muslim minister who left the Nation of Islam religion and embraced Sunni Islam in 1964 CE, but it is believed that the Nation of Islam murdered him.
Louis Farrakhan who was born in 1933 in Bronx, New York is the leader of the Nation of Islam and a civil rights leader. He has spoken at mosques in Harlem, New York and Boston, Massachusetts.

The country of Malaysia is a federal constitutional monarchy is Southeast Asia. Islam is the official religion of the country stated in the constitution but religious freedom is allowed for non-Muslims.

4. *Christian Reformations*

The Church of England was formed separately from the Roman Catholic Church in 1534CE in London, England by Augustine of Canterbury.

Anglican and Episcopalian Churches formed and the *Anglican Book of Common Prayer* written for Morning Prayer, Evening Prayer, Litany 'Kyrie Eleison' Prayer for Mass, Baptisms, and more.

The Plymouth Brethren (1831CE) was formed in Plymouth, England.

Methodist preacher William Booth founded the Salvation Army in London in 1865CE.

Martin Luther, a German monk, established the Lutheran Church (1520CE).

French theologian John Calvin (1535CE) and John Knox formed the Presbyterian Church.

English theologian John Wesley formed the Methodist Church (1720CE). Wesley said "My jubilee is my testament. Let us come together and share God's grace and love. Testify how God is working in your life. With God's presence there is fullness of joy and pleasures evermore. Praise Jesus, for Jesus opened God's community to people of all faiths, creeds, and races."

Thomas Helwys and John Smyth formed the Baptist Church (1612CE) in the Netherlands and England. Annie Armstong (b. 1850 Baltimore, Maryland USA) started a woman's missionary union for the Southern Baptist.

George Fox formed the Quakers (1650CE) in Great Britain.

In 1736 a reforming synod took place at Mount Lebanon for the Marionite Church.

Many Catholic and Protestant churches and basilicas were established in China in 635 but were banned during certain dynasties. Wang Yi founded the Protestant Early Rain Reformed Church in 2005 in Chengdu province of Sichuan. Wansui is immortal life. Other protestant churches are Lisu Church and Three-Self Church.

Wangfujing Cathedral in Beijing is dedicated to St. Joseph. St. Theresa's Cathedral is in Changchun. The Chinese Patriotic Catholic Church was established in 1957.

Church of Hawaii

The Church of Hawaii was established in 1862 by Kamehameha IV of Hawaii and Queen Emma of Hawaii. The Church of Hawaii was Anglican Episcopal. Queen Victoria of England helped Hawaii establish independence in 1852 after a French invasion because Catholics were being persecuted. The United States annexed Hawaii in 1898. Princess Kaiulani tried to stop the annexation but was unsuccessful. Princess Kaiulani died at age 23 of pneumonia.

Mennonites

Dutch preacher Menno Simons formed the Mennonites (1540CE). The Mennonites are neither Catholic or Protestant. They believe in Jesus Christ, a triune God of Father, Son, and Holy Spirit, and family values.

Amish

Jacob (Jakob) Amman formed the Amish (1690CE) in Switzerland. The Amish were a group that derived from the Mennonites.
The Ordnung contains the law of the Amish people and include prohibitions and limitations on the use of power-line electricity, telephones, automobiles, and regulations on clothing.
The Amish do not believe in divorce.
The Amish believe in the seasons of life such as childhood, courtship, marriage, raising kids, family life, retirement, and death.
Anything that promotes sloth, luxury, or vanity is prohibited.

The Ordnung moral code addresses:
1) acceptable behavior,
2) esteemed behavior,

3) frowned-upon behavior,
4) forbidden behavior.

The Ordnung is not set in concrete and may be clarified, developed, and modified at special meetings twice a year.
Two key concepts in the Amish religion are rejection of HOCHMUT (pride, arrogance, haughtiness),
and high-values placed on DEMUT (humility).
and
GELASSENHEIT (calmness, composure, placidity).
Amish community life is gathered around potluck dinners, weddings, fundraisers, farewells, and other events.
Amish restaurants and markets may sell pies, preserves, bread mixes, pickled produce, desserts, and canned goods.

Nikolaus von Zinzendorf formed the Moravian Brethren (1722CE) in Germany.

Charles Parham formed the Pentecostals (1900CE) USA.

Mary Baker Eddy formed the Church of Christ Scientist (1879CE) in the USA.

William Miller formed the Seventh-Day Adventist Church (1863CE) in the USA.

Simon Kimbangu formed the Kimbanguist African Christians (1921CE).

Reverend Richard Allen formed the A.M.E. African Methodist Episcopal Church in 1816 in Philadelphia, Pennsylvania, USA.

Samuel Bilehou Joseph Oschoffa formed the Celestial Church of Christ of Africa (1947CE) in Nigeria and Benin.

The Kenyan American Community Church in Marietta, Georgia, was pioneered by Reverend Dr. G. G. Gitahi.

Anne Lee, who claimed she was Jesus Christ's female counterpart, formed Shakers in 1758CE in Great Britain.

John Thomas formed Christadelphianism (1848CE) in the USA.

Charles Taze Russell and Joseph Franklin Rutherford formed the Jehovah's Witness (1872CE) in the USA.
Jehovah's Witnesses teach that united and happy families are originated from an intelligent God.
They direct that marriage partners should value each other's opinions, listen to each other, be faithful to each other, and treat each other with concern, respect, and love. They also direct marriage partners to give time and attention to children and teach children right principles, and children should listen and obey parents. Some children are starving for love and attention.

Jehovah's Witnesses also preach to be determined to avoid the bad temptations of the world.

Christian Scientist is a religion that believes in the absolute faith of God and an absolute rejection of modern medical procedures. They do not believe in the Trinity. It was founded by Mary Baker Eddy in 1879CE.

Quakers believe in Jesus, prayer, personal integrity, stewardship, marriage and family, lifelong commitments, regard for mind & body, peace, non-violence, human equality, and the ministry of both men and women.

Unitarian Quakers understand and accept that there are many paths to God and world peace benefits all.

Joan of Arc of France was murdered by some radical Catholics in Rouen, France, in 1431CE; she was burned at the stake. One reason Joan was hated was for wearing pants, which was considered to be only men's clothing. But the Catholic church apologized in 1920CE and recognized Joan as a saint. Katherine Hepburn, an artist who worked as an actress and businesswoman in the movie industry, started wearing pants in the U.S. in the 1960's.

Reformer Jan Hus was murdered in 1415CE in Bohemia of the Czech lands; he was burned at the stake. Petr Chelcicky and Jan Hus founded the Moravian Brethren.

Many religions appointed deceased people who were exceptionally holy as saints.
Saint Andrew is a patron saint of Scotland. Saint David is a patron saint of Wales.
Saint Patrick is the patron saint of Ireland. Saint George is the patron saint of England. Saint Francis is a Catholic saint of all God's creatures.

In the 1960s CE, many Catholic dioceses did not require women to wear the mantilla scarves on their heads. Catholic deacons in the church could marry a spouse. Some orders of nuns did not require traditional habits of gowns and head coverings.

In the poor sections of many cities, the Catholic church will share the church building with other religions so the faithful may conduct worship services.

The Gyosei is an international Japanese Roman Catholic school.

It is a tradition in many Baptist and Methodist Christian churches in the United States to have Wednesday night suppers or a brief Wednesday night worship service.

Catholic Bible, Christian Bible

The Vulgate was an early Catholic Bible that was translated into Latin from Hebrew by Saint Jerome in 382CE when the Protestant Reformation began and there were schisms in the faith of believers. The Old Testament of the Bible included the Jewish Torah (Genesis - the Story of Creation, Garden of Eden, Noah, Abraham, Gideon, Sodom and Gomorrah, Lot, Joseph; Exodus - the journey of the Jews from Egypt where some were kept in bondage as slaves back to the land of the Israelites; the story of Moses and the Ark of the Covenant of the Ten Commandments; the story of King David and King Solomon and the building of the Two Jewish Temples; the angel Gabriel and others; the prophets Isaiah and Ezekiel and others; Joshua; Job; Book of Life; Jonah; Satan - the angel who was cast from heaven and became ruler of Hell; and more.)
The New Testament included the Affirmations of John the Baptist, Gospels of Jesus, the Apostles of the Good News, and the Revelations of the End of Time and a description of Heaven.

John Wycliffe published the first major Protestant translation of the Bible in 1382CE in Western Europe.

The Gutenberg Bible was printed by Johannes Gutenberg in Mainz, Germany in the 1450sCE; it was the first book published by movable type which made easy distribution.

In England, The Great Bible was printed under King Henry VIII of England in 1535CE, the Bishop's Bible in 1568CE, and the King James Bible is the English translation of 1604-1611CE.

It is believed that as missionaries traveled around the world and spread the message of love and distributed religious scriptures, it helped to stop cannibalism that took place in remote parts of the world.

In 1690CE there was a war in Ireland between the Catholic King James II of England and the Protestant King William II of England and II of Scotland.
The Catholic King James had been overturned by the Protestants in 1688 for declaring religious freedom in England and Scotland; the Williamites only wanted Protestant and English rule in Ireland. The Williamites defeated the Jacobites who supported King James. Then Catholics were oppressed in England; they were forbidden to vote and Protestants were told to not marry Catholics. In 2000CE Roman Catholics are the largest Christian denomination in Ireland.

EUROPEAN SETTLERS
emigrated to a new world to the west

After explorers such as Christopher Columbus from Italy and Ferdinand Magellan from Portugal, who sailed for the Spanish Empire, discovered the Americas in 1492CE, people emigrated to North America, some to escape from tyranny or religious persecution that occurred in some world empires. At first, the explorers thought they had reached the country of India, so they called the Native Americans 'Indians.' Amerigo Vespucci was an Italian who explored North Ameica in 1500. Richard ap Merke also spelled Amerike was an Englishman who explore America in the 1400s. Giovanni John Cabot from Venice arrived in North America in 1497.

When the British Empire colonized North America in 1607 CE, Jamestown, Virginia was the first colony. It is believed that diseases brought from Europe to North America caused many deaths of Native Indians and that many Europeans died from diseases of the Native Indians. Pedro Menendez de Aviles founded St. Augustine, Florida in 1574.

A fleet of 500 Chinese junks (ships) sailed by Admiral Zheng of Ming Dynasty Emperor Zhu Di reached North America in 1421 but did not leave settlers.

Danish explorer Vitus J. Bering explored the Bering Strait between Russia and Alaska in 1741 funded by Russian Empress Anna.

Greenland was settled by a Norseman named Erik the Red in the 980s CE. Erik the Red had a son named Leif Erickson who was born in Greenland and led voyages for the Vikings. Some people think Leif Erickson reached the shores of North America in a region called Vinland in the early 1000s.

King Louis of France sent expeditions to the new lands in 1534. Jacques Cartier sailed to the North America and established the areas called Quebec in Canada and New Orleans in the United States. Giovanni, an Italian man, also sailed funded by France.

In 1605 King Christian and King Frederick of Denmark sent expeditions to Greenland where Luthran and Moravian ministries were established.

The French, Spanish, Scandanavian, and English fought each other and fought against the Native Americans for territories in North America during the years 1400-1800s.
Some people were killed by black bears, wolves, snakes. disease, starvation, or tornadoes.

William Penn, an American Quaker Society of Friends, helped to establish peaceful relationships between white

Europeans (paleface) and Native American Indians, whose skin had reddish-brown pigments (redskin). Tamanend, a Delaware Lenni Lanape native chief, enjoined in a successful colonial relationship based on peace, respect, and equal justice. Tamanend called William Penn by the name of Mikwon which means feather of the quill pen.

From 1526-1827, slaves were brought from West Africa to South America, the Caribbean, Europe, India, and North America by traders who exchanged money or goods with West African leaders for African people who had brown-skin (nigeri means 'of Nigerian region').

Daniel Boone was a Kentucky frontiersman in 1750 who explored the territories into Tennessee and North Carolina. Boone and his fellow hunter Benjamin Cutbirth were captured by the Shawnee Indian warriors and Chief Blackfish who confiscated Boone and Cutbirth's animal meat and skins. John John James Audubon (b. 1785) was a naturalist painter who studied birds for many years.

The European colonists protested high taxes on tea shipments imposed by the British Parliament, so the colonists rebelled by disguising themselves as Mohawk Indians, jumping aboard three British ships, and dumping the tea into the harbor. The raid became known as the Boston Tea Party. When the United States of America fought the British Empire for independence in 1776CE in the Revolutionary War, the forefathers founded a nation for civil liberties, dignity, and justice for all human lives. The forefathers were of Judeo-Christian heritage but believed in freedom to express and practice personal religious beliefs. The USA is a federal republic and was designed for the constitution and freedoms to be protected; there are checks and balances that allow the majority opinion of democracy to be heard and the establishment of the republic of states to be protected by a constitution.

The first president of the United States was George Washington who was the son of a tobacco farmer. The forefathers did not believe in genocide or oppression of humans, but indentured servitude was allowed as a custom of the empires. Lenape Chief White Eyes was a friend of George Washington and served as a Colonel in the Revolutionary War.
In 1838 Native American tribes were forced west of the Mississippi River in what is called the Trail of Tears; they drummed a sacred beat. The Middle West of America contains fertile farmlands. Many Native American tribes formed new tribal nations; some stayed near the new colonies and taught the colonists how to eat and grow corn. Some natives became plantation owners. Thomas Jefferson, the Caucasian third president and the principal author of the Declaration of Independence, wrote that people should have the right to bear arms (have guns) to protect themselves against tyranny in the government. Benjamin Banneker was a free African, son of a former slave, who corresponded with Thomas Jefferson on topics of abolishing slavery and racial equality. He was a surveyor, farmer, and almanac author who helped Major Andrew Elliott to survey the borders of and lay out the land of the District of Columbia where slaves helped build many government buildings. Eli Whitney from New Haven, Connecticut, was a Caucasian engineer who designed a cotton gin in 1825 which processed cotton that was picked by African slaves on cotton plantations. Frederick Augustus Douglas was an African American slave who escaped from slavery in Maryland and fled to Massachusetts and New York and became an abolitionist. Victoria Woodhull from Homerr, Ohio, a

Caucasian leader of the women's suffrage voting rights movement, ran for president in 1872 and asked Frederick Douglas to be her vice-presidential running mate.
Abraham Lincoln, a Caucasian lawyer and the 16th president of the US, abolished slavery in 1863CE in America. Harriet Tubman was a woman slave who helped free slaves.
Booker Taliaferro Washington from Tuskegee, Alabama, was an African advisor to presidents between 1890-1915.
John Fitzgerald Kennedy, the Caucasian 35th president, said 'Ask not what your country can do for you. Ask what you can do for your country." Jimmy Carter, the Caucasian 39th president said that peace is more than absence of war. He said that inner peace comes from human rights issues to voice opinions, feed your family, raise healthy children, and choose the leaders of your country. Barack Obama, the 44th president, became the first president with African family history. There were several outbreaks of typhoid fever in the United States in the 1800s.

The Prophet Joseph Smith

The Mormon prophet Joseph Smith received scriptures on golden metal plates from the angel Moroni, who was the prophet Mormon's son, at Hill Cumorah in the western land in 1823CE. The angel Moroni said do not condemn the records because of imperfections because the same shall know of greater things than these.

The Book of Mormon

The Book of Moroni in the Book of Mormon says the Holy Spirit is the Comforter that fills one with hope and perfect love. The eleven witnesses to the plates of Nephi and the testimony of Joseph Smith were the disciples Oliver Cowdery, David Whitmer, Martin Harris, Christian Whitmer, Jacob Whitmer, Peter Whitmer, John Whitmer, Hiram Page, Joseph Smith, Senior, Hyrum Smith, and Samuel H.Smith. Brigham Young was also a prophet in the latter-days for the Mormons. Brigham Young led the saints into the Salt Lake Valley where the Mormon Temple was built for the Mormons. Mormon temples were established in China in 1997.

Unity School

In1889, Charles and Myrtle Fillmore started the Unity School of Christianity which taught that God is loving, kind, and benevolent instead of revengeful and reproachful.

Ras Tafari the Savior

Ras Tafari of Ethiopian nobility was a devout member of the Ethiopian Orthodox Church who proclaimed to be a savior and a second-coming of Jesus. The religion takes its roots from the Coptic Church of Alexandria in originally founded by St. Mark in 42CE.

Mother Theresa

Mother Theresa of Albania, a follower of Jesus, was a winner of the Nobel Prize. She was a self-less servant to the poor and dying in India. She said to smile at someone you have contention with for the sake of peace. She said to take time out of a busy day for your family. She was a Catholic sister.

Unification Church

The *Unification Church* was started by Sun Myung Moon in South Korea in 1954CE. Moon's family converted from Confucianism to Christianity when he was ten years old. Sun Myung Moon married Hak Ja Han in 1960CE and good marriages and rededications are encouraged. Mass weddings are held where many couples are married in one ceremony.

5. ***Mega-Crowd Ministry***

Christian Evangelists

A Caucasian man named Billy Graham, his son Franklin, and his grandson Will are evangelist missionaries who preach to nondenominational megacongregations that began in 1950. John Hagee, Benny Hinn, Jimmy Swaggart, Jerry Falwell, Jack van Impe, Hal Lindsey, Chuck Missler, John Hager, Tim La Haye preached about Jesus.. Rex Humbard was a Pentecostal from Arkansas in 1950 who preached to many. A man named James Bakker and his wife Tamara Faye from Michigan and a man named Marion (Pat) Robertson from Virginia established worldwide ministries. There are many mega-evangelists. A man named Oral Roberts and his wife Evelyn, his son Richard Roberts and his wife Lindsay have a ministry in Oklahoma. A man named Joel Osteen his wife Victoria are televangelists from Texas. A woman named Joyce Meyer and her husband Dave have a ministry that feeds the poor in many countries around the globe. Creflo Dollar of Georgia, T.D. Jakes of West Virginia, Charles Stanley of Georgia and his son Andrew, Jentezen Franklin, Kenneth Copeland, David Jeremiah, and Benny Hinn were megacrowd evangelists. Small-time pastors are just as influential as big-time pastors.

An African American man named Martin Luther King, Jr. began an evangelical ministry is Atlanta, Georgia around 1940 and a man named Raphael Warnock preaches in the same church today. A man named Howard Thurman was an influential Baptist minister who was ordained in Virginia and preached in several states. A man named Arthur Price is a mega-evangelist in Alabama. A woman named Vashti Murphy McKenzie is the first Bishop of the African Methodist Episcopal Church. A woman named Trillia Newbell from Tennessee is preaching God's word. Reverend Al Sharpton preaches in NY and Calvin O. Butts preaches in Harlem, New York. A man named Arman Kirbyjon Caldwell is a mega-evangelist in Houston, Texas. Reverend Ike was from Detroit. Juanita Bynum Thomas was a gospel female singer and preacher from Chicago. Bishop Dale Bronner, Nathaniel Bronner, and Arthur Bronner preached in Atlanta. Jesse Jackson was a Baptist minister in S. Carolina. Colton Burpo from Imperial, Nebraska, is one of several human beings who experienced a visit to heaven.

A Hispanic man named Pastor Choco Wilfredo De Jesus and a man named Noel Castellanos preach to crowds in Chicago, Illinois. A man named D.A. Horton preaches in Atlanta, Ga. A man named Sam Rodriguez and a woman named Bishop Minerva G. Carcano and a man named Archbisop Jose Gomez preach in Los Angeles, California.

Joseph Prince is a preacher from Singapore. TB Joshua is a prophet of the Synagogue Church of All Nations in Nigeria who can remove bad voodoo. An Apostle in Nigeria named David O. Oyedepo preaches about the supernatural root of faith.

Jewish Rabbis

Rabbi Rigoberto Vinas is a Hispanic Jew in New York.

Muslim Imams

Mujahid Fletcher is a Hispanic Muslim preaching in Texas.

Spiritual Healer

Vicki Jamison-Peterson felt the Lord guide her to heal others with singing and laughter.

CHAPTER 5
Sikhism

Sikhism began in 1469CE by Guru Nanak, who taught that if you worship god Ram or god Allah, it is the same Holy Spirit.
'Sikh' is from the Sanskrit word for 'learner' or 'disciple'.
Sikhism combines beliefs of the Muslim and Hindu faiths.

CHAPTER 6
Religions of India

Hinduism and Buddhism

1. Hinduism and Buddhism both teach pure thoughts of heart and mind, unity, concord.

2. Hindus and Buddhists say the way to truth is to be self-controlled in mind and body, have concern for others in the world, and then the self will know the unknown spirit and truth. God dwells within you as you.

3. A concept of heaven in Hinduism is moksha is when you have achieved a place of balance, when bliss is natural and permanent. The secret of joy is a personal choice - a person must choose heaven over hell - on a daily basis when they first wake up. Misery is a choice. A person must choose to be happy. Hindu woman wear a bindi or a red dot on their forehead that represents divine sight.

4. Great spiritual leaders in the eastern countries were Gautama Buddha (Siddhartha Gautama) for Dharmakaya, and Veda Vyasa and Nasadiya Sukta for Brahma.

Sankara was the greatest of the monistic commentators on the sacred texts of The Upanishads and Bhagavad-Gita.

'Upanishad' means to 'sit up close' to your guru, or religious teacher, and listen and pay attention.

5. In the Rig-Veda of Hinduism, the gods created the first primordial man (Purusha) to create the heavens and universe.
Three-quarters of the Man rose up on high, and a quarter of him came to be again down here: from this he spread in all directions, into all that eats and does not eat. In the beginning, from the gods and the first primordial man came the fashioning of horses, cattle, goats, sheep, all creatures, the Veda scriptures, the Brahman, the moon, fire, wind, sky, earth, seven enclosing sticks and thrice seven fuel-sticks, and religious rites.
The spirit of the Universe Keeper entered the souls of the simple creatures.

6. In Hinduism, the
Golden Embryo evolved with god Prajapati, who is the giver of life and strength, who all and all gods must obey, who created the earth, gave birth to the waters, purification of air, vegetables, brought forth all creatures, snowy peaks, seas, rain, firmament, and sun.

The Great Controller is the generator of all things - all evolves from the Great Controller.

7. Another teaching is that the sun is Brahman which developed into an egg. After the measure of a year, it split in two. The two egg shells became silver (the earth) and gold (the sky). When the sun was born, shouts and cries of joy rose up, so this is the teaching to give praise for the Brahman, and to follow and encourage him.

8. The Bhagavad Gita means 'The Blessed One' and is a poem of the battle at Mahabharata. The Gita tells of the story

of war between the two clans of a royal family in northern India. One clan is the Pandavas, led by Arjuna and his four brothers. The opposing clan is the Kauravas, their evil cousins who are of King Dhritarashtra. On a battlefield, Arjuna and Krishna go into the open space between the two armies with their chariots to survey the combatants. But Arjuna is overwhelmed by the loss of so many lives and drops his weapons and refuses to fight, which is when Krishna, who is God Vishnu incarnate, begins to preach about life and death, duty, nonattachment, the Self, love, spiritual practice, and the inconceivable depths of reality. The essence of the teaching is to let go of desire and ideas about reality, and focus on Self in freedom, which can be achieved through karma yoga (the path of action), jnana yoga (the path of knowledge or wisdom), raja yoga (the path of meditation), and bhakti yoga (the path of devotion, love, and true worship).

9. Mohandas Gandhi was a spiritual leader in India who lived from 1869-1948CE). He expressed his beliefs of tolerance for all creeds and religions. The people called Gandhi the Mahatma (Great Soul). He believed in truth and nonviolence, lived a simple life, and thought it was wrong to kill animals for food or clothing.
One purpose Gandhi worked for was to stop fighting among Hindu, Muslim, and other groups.
He was assassinated by a Hindu fanatic who opposed Gandhi's program for tolerance for all creeds and religions. Gandhi said 'Religions are not for separating men from one another; they are meant to bind them.' Gandhi also said to live as if you were to die tomorrow, but learn as if you were to live forever.

Gandhi and his troops walked for 25 days and 241 miles as revolutionaries to the Arabian sea to defy an unjust British law prohibiting the collection of salt from its colony.

Gandhi established the Gujarat Vidyapith Indian school as an alternative school to the British education.

10. Rajiv Gandhi (no relation to Mohandas Gandhi) was a prime minister in India from 1984-1989CE who promoted economic development, population control, and the reduction of tension between India's ethnic and religious groups.

11. Buddhism and Hinduism say that it is not important to know exactly about the beginnings of time.

12. The 7 Chakras of Buddhism and Hinduism are:

1. Root Chakra or Base of Spine, feeling of being grounded.
2. Sacred Chakra or Abdomen, accept others and new experiences.
3. Solar Plexus Chakra, confidence and in control of our lives.
4. Heart Chakra, love.
5. Throat Chakra, communication.
6. Brow or Third Eye Chakra, focus and see the big-picture.
7. Crown or Tip of Head Chakra, connect spirituality.

The Chakras are the energy centers in our body in which energy flows through. The Chakras maintain metabolic balance.

13. India and Pakistan have been fighting over the Kashmir region since 1947CE when Muslim tribal militias tried to take over Pakistan. Pakistan asked India for help to stop the Muslim militia and agreed to give India rule of Kashmir in 1947CE.

Jainism Religion

Jainism (550BCE) prescribes a path of non-violence for all living beings. Jainism is one of the oldest religions in the world and originated in India by the teacher Mahavira (599-527BCE).

CHAPTER 7
Hindu Reformation

Some Hindu reformers believe it is not necessary that cows should be allowed to roam among the populations of people or that celebrations with elephants trains are a necessary holy ritual.

Vaishnavism focus on the worship of Vishnu as the one supreme god; Vishnu is the preserver of the universe.

Shaivism holds that Shiva is the supreme god because Shiva embodies the coming together of opposites like no other diety and Shiva embraces many dualities.

Shaktism is the devotion to Shakti, the goddess of the divine power that creates and sustains all of creation.

Darshanas follow several sects inclusing Vaishnavism, Shaivism, Shaktism, and the ultimate of the Brahman.

Smartism is an orthodox Hindu sect that uphold the rules of ancient texts and worship the supreme god as Shiva, Shakti, Vishnu, Ganesha, or Virya.

Lingayatism take their name from the linga, emblem of the god Shiva. They reject the Brahmin caste and promote a message of social equality and reform.

Swaminarayan Sampraday was founded by the religious reformer Swami Narayan in the 1800sCE in response to corruption among other Hindu sects.

Brahmoism (1828CE) was founded by Ram Mohan Roy in Calcutta, India. It rejects the sole authority of the Vedas, accepts avatars (incarnations of dieties or appearances of dieties on earth), and promotes social reform and equality for all people.

Arya Samaj (1875CE) was founded by Swami Dayananda, who sought to reaffirm the authority of the Vedas. The sect is opposed to the caste system. The sect is not accepting of other faiths besides Hinduism.

Sai Baba of Shirdi (1838-1918CE) was a spiritual master who is regarded as a saint, fakir, avatar (reincarnation), or sadguru of God. Sai baba taught a moral code of love, forgiveness, helping others, charity, helping others, inner peace, and devotion to God; he gave no distinction to religions or caste of people.
He combined elements of Hinduism and Islam. At the Shirdi shrine of Sai Baba, 20,000 meals a day are cooked for pilgrims visiting the temple. It is said that Sai Baba has a never-ending casserole dish.

Satyat Sai Baba Society (1950CE) was founded after Sathyanarayana Rajuin (b. 1926CE) was thought to have performed miracles. At age 14 he was bit by a scorpion and went into a trance. On waking he claimed to be a reincarnation of the guru Shirdi Sai Baba, and was known as Satya Sai Baba. His fame spread and his followers are guided by four principles: truth (satya), duty (dharma), peace (shanti), and divine love (prema). Satya Sai Baba said all social classes are equal.

The International Society of Krishna Consciousness was founded by spiritual leader Mukunda Goswami, who was born as Michael Grant in Portland Oregon, USA in 1942CE.

The gurus of the Sant Mat in Northern India oppose the caste system and religious distinctions; the religious services of the Sant Mat are open to all people. The Sant Mat believes in equality for all people.

The Hindu deity Khandoba is a god of select warrior, farming, herding, and Brahmin castes. Khandoba is worshipped with turmeric, bel fruit-leaves, onions and vegetables in western India in the Deccan plateau in the states of Maharashta and Karnataka.

CHAPTER 8
Buddhist Reformation

Reformation also occurred in Buddhism, where the idea of essentially reaching the balance of the Buddha personally within oneself upon the earth was desired as much as revering the ways of the unseen Lord Brahma, because to become in control of one self's own actions and to conduct one self's behavior in good ways is to know the way of the Lords.

Theravada Buddhism (600BCE) is closest to the original teachings of Buddha.

Mahayan Buddhism (300BCE) believes that Buddha has remained eternally present in the world and other people can become buddhas of enlightenment.

Pure Land Buddhism(600CE) is a sect that is devoted to Amitabha, the Buddha of Infinite Light, said to rule a paradise known as the Pure Land. The faithful may avoid the cycle of death and rebirth and go to dwell with Amitabha in the Pure Land, and thereafter receive enlightenment.

Tibetan Buddhism (600CE)has an order of monks and its own religious practices and a devotion to a guru, a spiritual leader. Succession is by reincarnation, and when a lama is at the end of his life, he gives clues to the identity of his next incarnation. Chinese Chairman Mao Zedong overtook Tibet in 1949 and destroyed Buddhist temples.

Tantric Buddhism (600CE) takes its name from the texts known as Tantras. Tantrics revere many Buddhas and believe a person can realize their Buddha nature more quickly using all states and emotions.

Zen Buddhism (1100CE) is the Chinese version and emphasizes meditation, enlightenment, and the value of experience over scriptures, the belief that humans are identical with the cosmos and all that is in it. Zen pervades everyday life – physical, intellectual, and spiritual. Composing poetry and rock gardens are Zen activities.

Nichiren Buddhism (1200CE) was founded by the Japanese monk Nichiren and is based on the passionate faith in the supreme spiritual power of the Lotus Sutra, a collection of Buddhist teachings.

Soka Gakkai (1937CE) was founded by two Japanese reformers, Tsunesaburo Makiguchi and Josei Toda. They were inspired by Nichiren. It has a strong emphasis on the Lotus Sutra and also on ritual chanting.

Triratna Buddhist Community (1967CE) United Kingdom, is a Western Buddhist Community founded by English-born Buddhist monk Sangharakshita. Members do not have to be ordained monks. Core principles include taking Triple Refuge in the Buddha and study and devotion to moral precepts.

CHAPTER 9
Asian Philosophies

Daoism/ Taoism

1. Daoism (550BCE), or Taoism, is a religious tradition that emphasizes living in harmony with the Dao, or Tao, which is the ineffable, the source and driving force behind everything else.

A Daoist sage Laozi wrote the Daodejing (Tao Te Ching) in 600BCE with many authors.

Taoism teaches that one should act as if one was in the presence of gods all the time, never permitting your heart to contain wicked or jealous feelings.

In the Tao Te Ching:
The way that can be told of is not an unvarying way. The names that can be named are not unvarying names. It was from the Nameless that Heaven and Earth sprang; the named is but the mother that rears

the ten thousand creatures, each after its kind.

The Valley Spirit never dies.
It is named the Mysterious Female.
It is the base from which Heaven and Earth sprang;
It is there within us all the while;
Draw upon it as you will, it never runs dry.

Eternal return is the continual return of the myriad of creatures to the cosmic principle from which they arose. The ten thousand creatures and all plants and trees while they are alive are supple and soft, but when dead they become brittle and dry. This is returning to the beginning of things.

The Taoist philosopher Chang Tao-ling once led three hundred disciples to the highest peak of Yun-T'ai. They saw a blue abyss on the far side of the mountain, and a peach tree grew out of a rock some 30 feet down into the abyss. Chang challenged which one of the disciples would dare to pluck a peach. A young man named Chao climbed down and gathered enough peaches for every one of the disciples, tossing the peaches up to the disciples and to Master Chang. Then, the Master Chang stretched his arm out 30 feet down to help Chao climb safely up again, saying 'Chao has showed courage.'

Daoists agree that the highest value is life, so the highest practice is the art of nurturing life. We should not let life slip away by not living it fully, or not living it for long.

Daoists value the natural environments and landscapes of the earth.

Individualism is valued.

The practice of feng shui 'wind and water' is a consideration of energy placement that is used in modern architecture and interior design. Feng shui was used in ancient times along with Yin 'shady' and Yang 'sunny' to position graves on cemetery hills.

Martial arts help humans to learn about concepts such as qi (chi) which is energy.

One must preserve and circulate qi, to balance our yin and our yang. Techniques used to nurture life include
'sitting and forgetting', 'fasting of the mind', 'free and easy wandering', dietary regimens, breath control, visualization exercises, purification rites, sexual practices, mediation techniques, physical exercises like bear strides and bird stretches, elixirs, and incense.

Three Treasures of TAO:
compassion, moderation,
and humility.

The three treasures of the human body are:
Qi is vital energy, jing is sexual energy, and shen is spirit.

'Biospiritual' exercises in breathing are called qigong.

Daoists absorb new ideas into their traditions instead of simply rejecting; saying 'I want to hear an idea for a Daoist.'

Daoists value traditions, changes, progress, bodily exercises, supernatural stories, philosophical observations, moral guidelines, medicinal theories, longevity techniques, funerary rites, holy books, and humor.
Daoists value sacred mountains and landscapes,
pilgrimages, festivals, wine, incense, hymns, sexual practices, alternative medicine, martial arts, meandering conversations, and immortals who 'wander in the mists' or 'dance in the Infinite.'

In Taoism, a Zhenren or chen-jen saint is one who has reached attainment of passionate unity with the divine absolute.

If a person knows the Eternal Supreme One, who is pure and tranquil, yet powerful and mighty, and deep and unfathomable, they are enlightened and wise.
The Eternal God existed before all heavens and earth existed, and the Eternal changes not.
All things depend on the Great Source for life. The Supreme sustains the universe and sustains it all.
How the Supreme perfects, guides, and directs is a mystery. Those who aspire to greatness must learn to humble themselves, work hard and achieve self-control.

A Dun Wu is a revelation of spiritual or worldly truth.

Shen is the soul.

Mantras are said for Seven Soul Houses of body energy using body power, soul power, mind power, and sound power.

A Mi Tuo Fo is a greeting or mantra for a Buddha.

The Yin & Yang are complementary opposites and though they oppose each other, they are not in opposition to each other but work together to seek a natural balance. When a seed grows it is Yang, but when fully grown and breaks down, it is Yin.
Yin is dark, feminine, slow, and soft. Yang is light, masculine, fast, and hard.

Other concepts of yin & yang are light and dark, daytime and nighttime, cold and hot, and low and high.

Confucianism

2. Confucianism (600BCE) focuses on humanism, the focus of spiritual concern is this world and family, not gods and the afterlife. Human beings are teachable and improvable through cultivation of virtues and ethics. Confucianism ethics are ren, yi, and li. Ren is obligation to altruism and humaneness for individuals. Yi is upholding of

morals to do good, Li is a system of norms and propriety that determines good behavior in society. Zhi is knowledge, lifebreath, and will.
Xin is integrity (heart and mind).
So, the five constants in Confucianism are ren, yi, li, zhi, and xin.

Confucious was an Asian philosopher of wisdom. Mencus was a philosopher who followed Confucious. Four Books of Confucian philosophy are: Confucian Analects, Book of Mencius, Great Learning, and Doctrine of the Mean.

Four Chinese virtues (sizi) are Zhong which is loyalty, Yiao (filial priority), Jie (constancy), and Yi (righteousness).

Qi is the natural energy or breath, the power of energy flow.

To be 'Gung Ho' is to be enthusiastic about something.

Yan Hui was the most outstanding student of Confucius. Confucius told Yan that 'one should see nothing improper, hear nothing improper, say nothing improper, do nothing improper'. Confucius said Ren is 'wishing to establish oneself and establish others for good things. Ren is not far off; he who seeks it has already found it. Ren is close to man and never leaves him.'
Zisi was the grandson of Confucius; Zisi was also a Chinese philosopher.

Zigong was a disciple of Confucious who said that Tian (God) set the master on the path to become a wise man. Confucious said Tian gave him life and from that he developed virtue (de).

Confucianism is grouped today alongside Daoism and Buddhism as one of China's 'Three Teachings'.
A popular Chinese saying is 'Every Chinese wears a Confucian cap, a Daoist robe, and Buddhist sandals.'
Another saying is every Chinese is a Confucian at work, a Daoist at leisure, and Buddhists at death.

In China, the three teachings of Confucianism, Daoism, and Buddhism mix quite well in society. The Daoist teaching of 'individual creative flow and flow of nature', the formal virtues of Confucianism, and the 'Awakening' of Buddhism are three philosophies that are considered.
In China, it is believed that if you polled a person at random and asked them what their religion was, they would most likely say they were a combination of religions instead of just one.

Chinese imperialist rule included 4,000 years of dynasties:
XIA, Shang, Chou (Zhou) 770 BCE, Qin 221 BCE, Han 206 BCE, Six dynasties of Wu, Dong Jin, Liu Song, Nan Qi, Nan Liang, Nan Chen 222 CE – 589 CE, Sui 590 CE, Tang 907 CE, Five dynasties of Later Liang, Later Tang, Later Jin, Later Han, Later Zhou 907 CE– 960 CE, Song 979 CE, Yuan (Mongol ruled), Ming (finished

Great Wall and defeated Mongols), Qing.

The dynasties ended when the Republic of China ruled from 1912-1949. The People's Republic of China recognizes 5 religious organizations: Buddhist Association, Chinese Taoist Association, Islamic Association, Three-Self Patriotic Movement, and Chinese Patriotic Catholic Association.

In Confucianism, saintliness is achieved through ideal ethical good conduct. Saints are humans who have 'pure souls' more than other humans.

Stand in awe of our divine ancestors, that we may achieve the majesty of the divine light.

Confess your errors and make quick amends. Stand near to the truth of things. Good deeds will have rewards. The superior person is given to self-adjustment, self-improvement, and then will be free from anxiety and fear.

Let compassion be a part of all punishment.

CHAPTER 10
Japanese Religions

Shinto Religion

1. Shinto, or Shintoism, is the native religion of Japan, a system of nature and ancestor worship and the way of the Gods, but some regard Shinto as a way of life. 'Shinto' means 'way of the gods'. The Emperor of Japan in 680 CE was a direct descendant of Amaterasu so the peasants bowed to him.

Tenrikyo Religion

2. The Tenrikyo religion of Japan contains 1,711 worship poems in the sacred scripture book Ofudesaki that are intended to return the human mind to original pristine condition, a mind like clear water, a mind that is appropriate to time, place, and spiritual maturity of all human beings. The Tenrikyo religion was started by a Japanese peasant woman named Nakayama Miki (Oyasama) following revelations to her from Tenri-O-no-Mikoto, God the Parent, Tsukihi (Moon-Sun), during a Buddhist ritual in 1838.

Jiba is where the first 2 humans were conceived; it is marked by the Kanrodai pillar. The Kagura Service teaches profound truths.

3. Masaoka Shiki (1867-1912CE) was a Japanese poet who established the tanka (also called haiku or hokku) short poem which consists of 5 units. The choka is the long poem.

4. Tatemae is the Japanese word that means 'the way things are', the way a person is in public and the behavior acceptable to society. Honne is the Japanese word that means 'the way things really are', the way a person is in private and their private desires.

5. The Ainu islanders are people of Mongoloid descent who believe that

everything in nature has a kamuy (spirit on the inside_. The god of the bear is Kim-un Kamuy. The goddess of hearth is Kamuy Fuchi. The god of the sea, fishing, and marine animals is Repun Kamuy. Ceremonies include prayers, libations of sake, offering willow sticks. The Ainu give thanks before eating and pray to the diety of fire in time of sickness. The Ainu can be Buddhist, Shinto, and Russian Orthodox.

CHAPTER 11
Korean Tradition

In Korean traditional religion, Mudang (female priest) and Baksu (male priest) are intermediaries between the first God, gods of nature, and humanity. Sungmo 'Holy Mother', Daemo 'Great Mother', Jamo 'Benevolent Mother', Sinmo 'Divine Mother', and Nogo 'Ancient Lady' are names for Goddess and the origin of a mother goddess is linked to a mountain.

Dangun is the name of the Sandlewood King, the heavenly king and initiator of the Korean nation. Dangun is also called Sansin 'God of the Mountain'.

The mu is an ancient word meaning magician, medicine man, mystic, and poet. Kangshinmu are chosen priests and seseummu are hereditary priests who have obtained the position through families.

Some Korean traditions have been blended with Christian Western traditions.

CHAPTER 12
African Religions

Yoruba Religion

1. In Southwestern Nigeria and parts of Benin, Togo, Brazil, Cuba, Puerto Rico, and Trinidad, the religious practice is Yoruba.

Yoruba is part of Itan, which is the total complexity of songs, histories, songs, and culture of Yoruba society.

The Supreme God has three manifestations: Olodumare - The Creator, Olorun - Ruler of Heavens, and Olofi – conduit between Heaven and Earth.

Each person attempts to achieve transcendence and find their destiny in Orun-Rere (the spiritual realm of those who do good and beneficial things).

The prayer or *Petition For Divine Support* is called adura.

Dogon Religion

2. The Dogon people live in a plateau region of Mali in western Africa. There is a mighty sandstone cliff in the region and the Niger River is near. The Dogon religion embraces many aspects of nature. A Sigui ceremony takes place every 60 years and can last for several years.

The ancient Dogon people had astronomical knowledge about the stars Sirius (Star of the Sigui) *sigi tolo*, and 2 companion stars: Digitaria *po tolo* and Sorghum *emme ya tolo*. The orbit cycle of the 2 companion stars is 50 years.

Sects of the Dogon religion are:
(1) The Amma sect worships the Creator God Amma.
A celebration once a years consists of offering boiled millet on an Amma altar
(2) The Lebe sect worships Lebe Serou, the first mortal being, who was transformed into a snake.
(3) The Binou sect uses totems; common totems for the village and individual totems for the priests. A totem animal such as a buffalo, panther, or crocodile, is worshipped on an altar. It is believed that one will not be harmed by and one cannot eat the animal of their totem.
(4)The twin sect believes that twin births are good luck.
(5) The mono sect have altars at the entrance of each village. Once a year unmarried men carry fire torches around the altar while singing and chanting.

Igbo Religion

3. The ancient Igbo religion is known as Odinani and the god is Chuckwu.

The Nsude Pyramids in Abaja in northern Igboland are ten pyramidal structures built of clay of mud, temples for the God Ala / Uto.

Many Igbo people are Christians, Catholic, Jews and Muslims.

CHAPTER 13
Shamanism

A *shaman* is an intermediary or messenger between the human world and the spirit world. The shaman can enter the supernatural realm or dimension to obtain solutions to problems afflicting individuals or community. The shaman in ancient times were monks in North Asia or Korea, or Natives of America or Africa who could spend time in a dangerous forest and spend a lot of time hunting for food and connecting to the spiritual world.

Shaman practices can be:
1. Divination rituals in which diviners ascertain interpretations, such as reading the results of throwing down sticks or rocks, how a crab moves about in a of traywater, randomly opening a holy book and pointing to a passage and interpreting the meaning.
2. Animism is which non-human entities such as animals, plants, and objects are believed to possess a spiritual essence.
3. Fetishism is objects like idols and charms are believed to have superpowers, such as beaded necklaces.

4. Initiation rituals such as the diksha mantras of Buddhism, Hinduism, and Jainism; the baptisms and confirmations of Christianity; the bar and bat mitzvahs of Judaism.

5. 'Mana' is the supernatural power of God.
6. Ceremonies that include rituals, magic, sorcery, or symbols to connect with supernatural forces.
7. Spiritual healing practices to cure illness or raindancing to make rain.
8. Astronomy readings to mark supernatural times.
9. Totem poles or object to represent a spiritual being or an emblem of a family or tribe.

CHAPTER 14
Theosophy

Theosophy is the philosophy that describes the cosmos as a Divine Hierarchy. Centered at the top of the Cosmic Logos or God is a Trinity of Creator, Preserver, and Destroyer, and under which seven Planetary Logoi rule every star in the universe. Our own sun and solar system are under the jurisdiction of the Solar Logos who is humanity's God. There are seven logoi beneath the Solar Logos who are associated with angelic beings known as devas. Linking humanity and the divine bureaucracy are the mahatmas or masters, men and women who assist the rest of humanity. Theosophy includes the truths of karma, reincarnation, akashic records and ascended masters, meditation and yoga.

Akasha

Akasha is a reputed etheric compendium of pictorial records or 'memories' of all events, thoughts and feelings that have occurred since the beginning of time, a reservoir of occult power that transmits the energy waves of human willpower, thought, emotion and imagination. It is through this ocean of unconsciousness that allegedly links everyone that prophecy, clairvoyance, déjà vu, and ESP (extrasensory perception) are believed to become possible.

CHAPTER 15
The Spiritual Movement

The New Thought Movement was begun by Phineas Quimby (1802-1866CE), an American clockmaker, inventor and philosopher who lived in New Hampshire but moved to Maine. Quimby taught that infinite intelligence (God) is everywhere and divinity dwells within each person, that good mental thinking and caring for each other can be manifested and become our experience in daily living.

The ***Unitarian Universalist Association of Congregations*** began in 1825CE and has seven principles to affirm and promote:

(1) The inherent worth and dignity of every person;
(2) Justice, equity and compassion in human relations;
(3) Acceptance of one another and encouragement to spiritual growth in our congregations;
(4) A free and responsible search for truth and meaning;
(5) The right of conscience and the use of the democratic process with

the Unitarian congregations and in society at large;
(6) The goal of world community with peace, liberty, and justice for all;
(7) Respect for the interdependent web of all existence of which we are a part.

The New Age or New Era Movement is a spiritual movement of the 1970s CE that has a holistic view of the cosmos with an emphasis on self-spirituality and motivational self-help. The New Age Movement is infused with influences from the zodiac, wisdom from philosophers, and traditions from various religions.

Cao Dai

In Vietnam in 1920, a civil servant named Ngo Van Chieu stated that a Surpreme Being said to unite all religions.

Hoahaoism

Hoahaoism was founded in 1939 CE by the Vietnamese prophet Huynh Phu So.

The Shriners

The Shriners was established in 1870CE by Walter M. Fleming, M.D. and William J. Florence to be an appendant body to Freemasonry. The original name of the organization was the Ancient Arabic Order of the Nobles of the Mystic Shrine. The fraternity (brotherhood) is based on fun, fellowship, charity, and Masonic principles of brotherly love. Money is raised for children's hospitals. Members wear red fezzes on their head when collecting donated monies. The group has a middle-eastern theme and meet in Masonic Temples. There are approximately 195 temples in the United States, Canada, Brazil, Mexico, Republic of Panama, Philippines, Puerto Rico, Europe, and Australia.
The Freemasons have opened their organization to both men and women.

Divine Matrix

Japanese American physicist Michio Kaku of City College in New York proposed that we live in a universe matrix made by rules created by an intelligence. Everything in the universe is planned and governed; nothing is out of place. The string theory says that there is a symphony of vibrating strings emanating from the mind of God resonating through an 11-dimensional hyperspace.

Pantheism

Pantheism is the belief that God is equal to the forces and laws of the universe.

Kabalarian Philosophy

Kabalarian Philosophy is the study of who we are, healthful living, harmonious talking, spiritual ideas, personal growth, and logic, reason and fact. It was started by Alfred J. Parker in 1930 in Cananda.

CHAPTER 16

Astrology and Numerology

The *Zodiac* in astrology and astronomy is a circle of 12 thirty-degree divisions of celestial longitude that are centered upon the path of the Sun of the Earth's Solar System over the course of a year. The twelve Zodiac signs are Aries, Taurus, Gemini, Cancer, Leo,Virgo, Libra, Scorpio, Sagittarius, Capricorn, Aquarius, and Pisces. The twelve *Chinese Zodiac* signs are Rat, Ox, Tiger, Rabbit, Dragon, Snake, Horse, Goat, Monkey, Rooster, Dog, and Pig.

Numerology is the belief that there is a divine and mystical relationship between numbers, words, names, and ideas.

CHAPTER 17
The Earth

1. Humans used to think the earth was flat. An astronomer named Giordano Brun (1600CE) was put to death for suggesting that the earth revolved around the sun; the astronomer Galileo almost had the same fate but avoided death by talking himself out of the situation. Guards came to Galileo's house in the middle of the night, the house that he shared with Martina, his mistress; they took him away and put him in a cage on wheels drawn by a horse. Galileo was thrown into a (jail) prison for several weeks before he was taken before the court. The judges accused Galilieo of teaching that universal changes had occurred throughout milleniums of time which was heresy against what the church preaced – that God had created everything and put everything in its place. But Galileo begged the judges not to kill him; he said he was simply studying theories with another scientist named Luigi Martinelli in another country; that they were not a threat to the church, so the judges let Galileo go.

2. In modern times, an atlas contains maps of all places on Earth. Early cartographers, also called mapmakers, agreed on the convention of naming the Arctic Circle the North Pole and Antarctica the South Pole. Also, cartographers agreed on the convention of naming the Greenwich Meridian as the 0 degree meridian so flat maps of the Earth usually show the Atlantic Ocean in the middle of the map with the left being called west and the right being called east. For this reason, the text herein refers to areas of the world as the west, middle-east, or east.

Before cartographers had agreed upon standard map conventions, some explorers had Africa and Australia and the Antarctica in the top-half of the globe and the Americas, Europe, Middle-East and Asia in the bottom-half of the globe and vice-versa. Because of the star-mapping of Galileo, the cartographers decided to standardize maps of the world with the Americas, Europe, Middle-East, and Asia in the top-half of the globe. The magnetic poles of the earth reverse over the millennia.

Beautiful atlases of the world have been compiled for our browsing pleasure. Cartographers have also put forth much effort to compile local map books that map not only land and water, but streets, schools, religious buildings, fire stations, police stations, park reserves, and other significant places.

The first picture of Earth that was sent back from space by the astronauts and cosmonauts was considered to be upside-down and was rotated to be in sync with the maps that most humans are familiar with that showed the Atlantic Ocean in the middle.

Only the Lord knows actually which way in the Universe is up, because only the Lord knows the ends of the universe.

In 2010CE most locations on earth and in the universe could be located with electronic GPS global positioning systems.

Green cars may look like trees from space. Blue roofs may look like water from space.

3. Scientists have different theories about how our planet was formed and how life began on earth. Many think all life started with a single organism that may have emerged out of a rock, either on earth or from an asteroid. Then the organism evolved perhaps out of the sea to a crawling organism and over billions of years and dramatic changes that occurred to earth's atmosphere and crust, evolved into humans.

Scientists have learned that viruses, bacteria, nuclear radiation, and pollution can be spread around the earth. It is believed that when the earliest explorers sailed around the world on ships, they both brought bacteria and viruses to new regions, and brought back with them to their native home lands new bacteria and viruses. The bacteria and viruses are transmitted by humans, vegetation, animals and insects, and through the air currents.

There was a bubonic plague called black plague in Europe in 1346-1353 caused by the bacteria Yersinia pestis transmitted by fleas and thousands of people died. In 1848-1850 There was a cholera epidemic or plague in Europe which was carried to the United States and thousands of people died. Cholera is caused by eating foods or drinking water that is contaminated with human feces.

A scientist named Roald Hoffmann wrote: To see a world in a grain of sand, And a heaven in a wild flower: Hold infinity in the palm of your hand, And eternity in an hour.

CHAPTER 18
Work, Progress, Knowledge & Everyday Heroes

1. Humans have served the Lord and other human beings as spiritual leaders and in other significant ways to make progress in the world.

Explorers went to new lands. Astronomers studied the universe. Mathematicians invented numbers. Engineers invented methods of transportation and manufacturing. Scientists studied the earth elements. Inventions were made to continually improve medicine, technology, food science, communication, transportation, education, clothing, and recreation. Humans gained information for other humans to use as references, some even died in their quests.

Ferdinand Magellan was a Portuguese explorer who lived from 1480-1521CE; he led part of the first expedition around the world. There is a telescope in Chile named after him.

Aelius Claudius Galenus, or Galen, lived in 129CE; he was a Greek physician, surgeon, and philosopher who did much research to establish the various disciplines of medicine such as:
anatomy (human body), physiology (cells of plants and animals), pathology (diagnosis of disease), pharmacology (remedies), neurology (nervous system).

Robert Hooke was the scientist who described a cell in a living organism. Carl Linne of Sweden, Charles Darwin and Alfred Russel Wallace were scientists who classified life systems upon the earth. Mendel was the scientist who discovered genetics.

In his book *Principia,* Isaac Newton wrote down laws of motion and gravity, and calculus from his work
at Cambridge University in England. Newton suggested the earth was not a perfect sphere but slightly oblate, bulging at the equator and more flat at the poles. Isaac Newton and Charles Darwin are both buried at Westminster Abbey, London. Scientists worked for over half a century to measure the earth.

Edmond Halley was a British astronomer who recognized the comet he saw in 1682CE was the same one that others
saw in 240BCE (recorded by Chinese, Babylonian, and European chroniclers), 1456, 1531, and 1607CE so it was named Halley's comet. It will reappear in 2061CE.

The sundial was the earliest method of keeping time; the sundial told time from the position of the sun in the sky by casting a shadow on the ground from its surface. Next, the hourglass is believed to have been invented in Europe in the 8th century, in the 700 AD or 700 CE. The hourglass was used for over a thousand years. The hourglass contained sand, ground eggshells, or water. The water hourglasses didn't
work as well because the condensation interfered. Hourglasses today are still used in Australia for certain timing procedures. Modern day uses for the hourglass are egg-timers or in board games. Then mechanical clocks were invented that contained gears. Cuckoo clocks made in Germany make a small cuckoo bird announce the hours. Grandfather clocks are in tall cabinets with a pendulum inside. Later clocks used electricity.

Over 2400 years, the work of philosophers, naturalists, scientists, and chemists led to the discovery and harnessment of electricity. Thales of Miletus of Greece studied static electricity in 600BCE.
It is believed that gold and silver plated pottery could have been used as batteries in tunnels in Persia (what is now Baghdad, Iraq) in 275BCE. William Gilbert (1544-1600CE), Thomas Browne

(1646CE), and Stephen Gray (1666-1736CE) from England, Otto von Guericke (1686CE) from Germany, Robert Boyle (1627-1691CE) from Ireland, C.F. du Fay (1698-1739CE) from France, and Benjamin Franklin (1785-1788CE) from America worked to invent ways to harness electricity. Benjamin Franklin flew kites in lightning storms to study electricity.

It took 22 inventors over a period of 75 years to make a long-lasting light bulb. The first bulb was invented in 1802 by Humphry Davy with a platinum strip but it was not bright enough. In 1879CE, Thomas A. Edison invented a bulb that could last 13.5 hours with a carbon-filament. Eventually the bulb was improved to last 1200 hours.

One of Thomas A. Edison's famous quotations was "If I find 10,000 ways something won't work, I haven't failed. I am not discouraged; every wrong attempt discarded is another step forward."

It was his way of saying that we can learn from failures in order to reach success.

Do not give up on yourself. We all make mistakes and have turbulence in our lives. Keep working for improvements to make progress.

Nikola Tesla (b. July 1856) was a Serbian Austrian-American from the area that is now Croatia. Tesla invented the alternating current AC electrical generation which used 240 volts as opposed to Thomas Edison who used 110 volts in direct current DC. 50 or 60 HZ are common frequencies.

Richard Norwood was an English mathematician who worked for years to measure the earth, invented trigonometry, and published his findings in 1637CE in a book called *The Seaman's Practice.* French astronomers named Jean Picard, Giovanni and Jacques Cassini, Bouguer, and La Condamine also measured the earth. British astronomer Nevil Maskelyne, Charles Mason, and Jeremiah Dixon all worked for years to measure the earth.

In the 1940s CE at the University of Chicago, Willard Libby and Tim Flannery worked on carbon dating methods to date living organisms that had died. In 1999 the frozen body of a 15-yr old Inca maiden was found on a volcano in Argentina and was estimated to be 500 years old.

Scientists worked for over 200 years to estimate the age of the earth. In the 1920s CE Arthur Holmes was a geologist at Durham University who worked on dating rocks and suggested to measure the decay rate of uranium into lead to calculate the age of rocks, and thus the earth.

The work was a continuation of the work after Lord Kelvin and George Becker who were trying to determine the age of the earth. In 1904CE Ernest Rutherford of New Zealand worked with radioactive materials and determined the age of the earth. In the 1940s an Iowa farm boy named Clair Patterson tried to date the earth with a lead isotope but the work was contaminated due to lead pollutants in the air caused by gasoline additives to reduce engine knock, lead solders in the cans of food and water tanks – many people died before it was realized that lead is poisonous to humans. Clair Cameron Patterson continued working to calculate an age of the earth, studying meteorites, using a spectrograph capable of detecting and measuring quantities of uranium and lead locked up in ancient crystals; in 1950 he came up with an estimate that the earth was at least 4.550 billion years old, plus or minus 70 million years.

In 1906CE, a French physicist named Bernard Brunhes found that earth's magnetic field reverses itself time to time, and the record of these reversals can be found permanently in certain rocks at the time of their birth.

Geologists including Patrick Blackett and S. K. Runcorn worked in the 1950s to study the magnetic patterns in rocks of North America and Europe to conclude that the magnetic patterns fit together neatly. Geophysicsts like Drummond Matthews and Fred Vine of Cambridge University and a Canadian geologist named Lawrence Morley used magnetic studies to prove an ocean floor was spreading.

In the 1940s, a Princeton mineralogist named Harry Hess worked to discover a mountain range that extends under the oceans for 46,600 miles that extends from Iceland down the center of the Atlantic Ocean, around the bottom of Africa, across the Indian and Southern Oceans, below Australia, angled across the Pacific and extending up the west coast of the United States to Alaska. In 1960CE core samples were taken from different parts of the Atlantic Ocean floor which suggested that new ocean crust was being formed in the middle, moving both west and east; at the same time the crust was being forced under the edges of the continents.

In the 1970s CE Harold Jeffreys insisted that plate tectonics was impossible. In the 1980s John McPhee noted that one in eight geologists did not believe in plate tectonics. But in 2000 CE some geologists believed there were eight to twelve big plates moving on the earth that can cause earthquakes.

Scientists have written that Denver and South Africa are lands that have risen recently in the last millions of years, but Australia and Indonesia are sinking recently in the last millions of years.

Richard Owen was a British man who invented the concept of museums.

Reginald Daly of Harvard University put forth the idea that the moon was created from an impact of another body slamming into the earth and bouncing off earth crust that formed into the moon.

Albert Einstein, born in Germany (1879-1955CE), put forth the theory of relativity that the universe must be contracting or expanding.
A quote by Einstein was 'God does not play dice with the Universe'.

An astronomer named Vesto Slipher at the Lowell Observatory in Arizona suggested that the stars appeared to be moving away from us. Edwin Hubble was born in

1889CE in Missouri and worked with two women named Henrietta Swan Leavitt and Annie Jump Cannon at Harvard University Observatory to measure the universe and concluded that the universe was expanding evenly in all directions.

Khedive Ismail Pasha (1863-1879CE) of Egypt, grandson of Mohammad Ali, abolished slavery, established schools, established a sugar trade, built the Suez Canal, and helped to bring modern progress to Egypt and Sudan.

In 1863CE in the United States of America, President Abraham Lincoln issued the Emancipation Proclamation which led to the outlaw of slavery of human beings in the US. Harriet Tubman was a woman slave who helped free slaves. In the USA in the 1960s Martin Luther King, who was a civil rights activist, President John Kennedy and President Lyndon B. Johnson helped to have civil rights laws enacted in the US. Both Martin Luther King and President John Kennedy were killed by radical extremists.

In 1859CE Henry Dunant from Switzerland called for an international relief organization to bring aid to the war-injured.

Disaster relief organizations such as Red Cross, Red Crescent, Red Lion, Red Star of David, Red Crystal, Salvation Army, Samaritan's Purse, United Methodist Committee on Relief, Catholic Relief Services, Southern Baptist Disaster Relief, Islamic Relief, and Tenrikyo Disaster Relief are humanitarian organizations that were founded to protect human life and health and promote dignity and respect for all human beings on earth. Humanitarian organizations work for peaceful causes and have provided medical care, food, water, clothing, and shelter for soldiers and civilians (non-combatants) who were injured in wars or natural disasters such as earthquakes, tornadoes, hurricanes, tsunamis, and famines. Many think that looting after disasters is wrong.

Mao Zedong, or Mao Tse-Tung (Dec. 26, 1893-Sept. 9, 1976CE), also known as Chairman Mao was a Chinese Communist Revolutionary who built China into a world power called the Republic of China; it was the end of the Chinese Empire dynasties. Chairman Mao promoted the status of women, established ties with other countries, improved education and healthcare, and established the idea of communes where people in the a community help each other for the benefit of everyone in the community.

Hippocrates of Kos was a Greek physician (460-370BCE) who established a school of medicine and wrote an oath of integrity for doctors.

Hippocratic Oath

I swear by Apollo the physician, and Aesculapius the surgeon, likewise Hygeia and Panacea, and call all the gods and goddesses to witness, that I will observe and keep this underwritten oath, to the utmost of my power and judgment.

I will reverence my master who taught me the art. Equally with my parents, will I allow him things necessary for his support, and will consider his sons as brothers. I will teach them my art without reward or agreement; and I will impart all my acquirement, instructions, and whatever I know, to my master's children, as to my own; and likewise to all my pupils, who shall bind and tie themselves by a professional oath, but to none else.

With regard to healing the sick, I will devise and order for them the best diet, according to my judgment and means; and

I will take care that they suffer no hurt or damage.

Nor shall any man's entreaty prevail upon me to administer poison to anyone; neither will I counsel any man to do so. Moreover, I will give no sort of medicine to any pregnant woman, with a view to destroy the child.

Further, I will comport myself and use my knowledge in a godly manner.

I will not cut for the stone, but will commit that affair entirely to the surgeons.

Whatsoever house I may enter, my visit shall be for the convenience and advantage of the patient; and I will willingly refrain from doing any injury or wrong from falsehood, and (in an especial manner) from acts of an amorous nature, whatever may be the rank of those who it may be my duty to cure, whether mistress or servant, bond or free.

Whatever, in the course of my practice, I may see or hear (even when not invited), whatever I may happen to obtain knowledge of, if it be not proper to repeat it, I will keep sacred and secret within my own breast.

If I faithfully observe this oath, may I thrive and prosper in my fortune and profession, and live in the estimation of posterity; or on breach thereof, may the reverse be my fate!

Hippocrates also prescribed patients to chew on white willow bark to ingest salicin to reduce fever and inflammation. Aspirin is a synthetic form of salicin.

LAW ENFORCEMENT OATH

In many countries police officers and peace officers take an oath of integrity and bravery to uphold laws and peace in their community and nation.

JOURNALIST CREED

Walter Williams of Missouri School of Journalism, U.S.A., published a creed in 1914 for news reporting journalists. Main points of the creed: It is a responsibility of journalists to accurately report true facts and not take bribes to report lies. News should not be suppressed because people have a right to know news that affects the general welfare of all people. Journalists should be unmoved by pride or greed but be respectful to the reading audience. News items or opinions should be reported in good manners.

LINGUISTICS CREED

SIL (Summer Institute of Languages) is a worldwide Christian based institute that promotes the respect and study of languages. The creed notes that language is an important gift from God and has enabled cultures and civilization to develop. The language that a person speaks is part of their self-identity. Languages deserve to be preserved for a culture. The different languages may cause complications in communications between people of different cultures.

Translators who translate information between cultures should translate accurately and honestly.

Some World Progress

Francisco Romero, Dominique Jean Larrey, Henry Dalton, and Daniel Hale Williams began studying heart surgery in the late 1800s.

On Sept. 4, 1895, Dr. Axel Cappelen in Oslo, Norway, performed one of the first heart surgeries to try to save the life of a 24-yr old man who had been stabbed in the left heart.

There is a picture on a stone slate of a Chinese man in a wheelchair in 1680CE believed to be Confucius.

There is a child's bed with wheels painted on a Greek vase dated 600BCE.

In Bath, England (1760CE) a wheelchair was invented that had 2 side wheels and 1 wheel on the front.

Harry Jennings and Herbert Everest were mechanical engineers who invented the first lightweight, collapsible wheelchair in 1933CE. Everest had broken his back in a mining accident.

Wheelchairs that go in snow and sand have wider wheels to distribute weight over a larger area. The electric-powered wheelchair was invented by George Klein in Canada in 1953CE; it had a captain's chair. Standing wheelchairs support a person in a nearly standing-up position.

The windshield wiper for vehicles was invented around 1903CE by inventors Mary Anderson, Robert Douglas, and John Apjohn.

Carl Jung (1875CE-1961CE) of Switzerland studied the possibilities of the mind. He believed that life has a spiritual purpose beyond material goals. Our main task is to discover our individual potentials, to find self and the divine, which is at the heart of all religions. Every individual has a personal unconscious which is a personal reservoir of experience unique to them and a collective unconscious which collects personal experiences that are inherited from pre-existent forms. Jung traveled to London, USA, East Africa to Mount Elgon, and India. Carl Jung was married to Emma Rauschenbach of Switzerland and they had five children.

The Vanderbilt family immigrated to the U.S.A. from Denmark around 1880 and helped build railroads and factories in North America. They attended the Moravian Church and later the Episcopalian Church. They built some grand mansions including the Biltmore House in Ashville, North Carolina and The Breakers in Newport, Rhode Island. There are ski resorts near the Biltmore called Wolf Ridge, Cataloochee, Beech, and Sugar Mountain with snowboarding. The time of great industrial expansion in the U.S.A. happened from 1860-1890 and was called the Gilded Age. It was after the civil war and coincided with the Victorian age in England when Queen Victoria ruled from 1837-1901.

In 1994, after the dismantling of apartheid in South Africa, Nelson Mandela became the first dark skin toned President of South Africa. Nelson Mandela suffered great oppression and was imprisoned for many years for his cause; he never gave up hope. Apartheid was cultural segregation of races by skin tone color.

"Action without vision is only passing time, vision without action is merely day dreaming, but vision with action can change the world." Nelson Mandela

Nelson shared a prize, the first Sakharov Prize for Freedom of Thought which was established by the European Union in 1988 CE and named after Andrei Sakharov. The other recipient of the first Sakharov Prize was posthumously awarded to Anatoly Marchenko, a Russian who campaigned for human rights, was put in prison several times, and died in prison.

Archbishop Desmond Tutu and his daughter Reverend MPHO Tuto, an Anglican priest, also worked to abolish injustices in South Africa.

Alhaji Ahmad Tejan Kabbah (1932-2014CE) was an international servant and president of Sierra Leone in W. Africa who promoted peace.

In the early 1900s, Mohandas Ghandi was a lawyer and a spiritual Hindu who also believed in non-violence and fought for civil rights for people against apartheid. Ghandi was killed by a Hindu radical extremist.

A wall that divided the people in the city of Berlin, Germany from 1961-1989CE finally came down in 1992CE. The wall divided the people because they believed in different theories of government.

The Shang, Ming, Qin, Han and other Dynasties of China built a great wall to mark its borders, keep out lions and enemies, and to impose tariffs on goods being moved along the Silk Route or Silk Road from 2600-200BCE. Astronauts and cosmonauts have seen the Great Wall of China from space. The Genghis Khan dynasty ruled Mongolia when the Silk Route was built. The Silk Route connected the Mediterranean and Far East Asia.

Earth Day is April 22. Earth Day was the brainchild of Senator Gaylord Nelson of Wisconsin, United States, who believed in clean water and conservation of natural resources of our planet.

International Peace Day is Sept. 21.

World Health Day is April 7.

An Outer Space Treaty has been signed among nations that says space is 'free to all nations to explore for peaceful purposes.'

An award called Nobel Peace Prize is given each December 10 in Norway to a recipient that has done the best work for fraternity among nations and peace. The five prizes, which began in 1901 and given by the Swedish industrialist and inventor Alfred Nobel, are awarded in Chemistry, Physics, Physiology or Medicine, Literature, and Peace.

The Mahatma Gandhi International Award for Peace and Reconciliation is given by the Government of India honoring the ideals of Mahatma Gandhi.

The Order of the Sacred Treasure is a Japanese Order 1888 by Emperor Meiji; it is a distinguished achievement in research, business, healthcare, social work, government, or improvement for the needy.

Shigeru Ban is an international architect from Tokyo, Japan who has won awards, including the Pritzker Architecture Prize, for his innovative humanitarian work with recycled cardboard; his efforts included constructing temporary structures and shelters out of cardboard to help people after major disasters like earthquakes and hurricanes.

The International Olympic Games are sporting events featuring winter and summer game competitions; they are games of fraternity among nations. A refugee team was established for athletes that have left their countries that are ravaged by wars.
As of 2013CE, more than 200 nations and thousands of athletes participate in 33 different sports and 400 events. The prizes awarded are a gold medal for 1st place, a silver medal for 2nd place, and a bronze medal for 3rd place. The Summer Olympics began in 1896CE and are held every four years such as 2008, 2012, 2016, 2020. The Winter Olympics began in 1924 and are held every four years such as 2010, 2014, 2018, 2022. The Paralympic Games are held for athletes with disabilities. The Youth Olympic Games are held for teenage athletes. The Senior Olympics are for people of older ages. The Olympics takes it name from ancient Greek Olympic games. The five Olympic rings symbolize the five continents of Olympic athletes. All competitors from first place to last place are honorable because the intentions of the games is fraternity among nations.

Invictus Games for soldiers who incurred injuries was founded by Prince Harry of England in 2015. Harry and his brother William are the sons of Prince Charles who is a son of Queen Elizabeth who began reigning over Great Britain in 1952.

Special Olympics are held in some cities for athletes with intellectual challenges.

Everyday Heros

In 2006 a young Amish girl named Marian gave her life to protect other young girls from being killed by a crazed gunman in America. She told the gunman 'Shoot me first' in order to spare the others. She was 13 years old. The gunman killed a total of five children.

Soldiers, firefighters, police officers, coast guard, rescuers, emergency responders, tow truckers, taxi and bus drivers, airplane crew, infrastructure engineers and ditch diggers, road pavers, electricians, political leaders, religious leaders, coal miners, journalists, bank tellers, retail workers, medical professionals, any job working with the public or for public works, astronauts and cosmonauts, and many others are professions that may involve personal endangerment (professionals that risk their own lives or health when helping or protecting others).

Humans and animals have been rescued from wells and underground mines by humans who were heroes.Heroes are those who do epic actions to help others.

A mother named Stephanie had her arms tightly wrapped around her two young children in the basement of their house trying to survive a tornado in Indiana, USA; the two children were not harmed.

Heroes can be teachers and sages who are dedicated to helping students master the topics of study.

Some professions require humans to work in extreme weather conditions, with dangerous materials, in emotionally-challenging situations, jobs with long hours. Humans are working hard upon the earth; they are work-day heroes.

Good people traveling on highways have stopped to help stranded motorists on roads by helping to change flat tires and have lost their lives being hit by cars.

Human Invention

Scientists, engineers, chefs and food professionals have worked hard to create manufacturing plants, delicious food products, and ways to increase food production.

Inventors have invented toys for kids and pets, gym and recreation equipment, TV, movies, poetry, books, weather forecasting, radios, machinery, factories.

Educators have devised ways to make learning fun.

Musicians create beautiful music and songs lyrics. Visual artists create lovely paintings and abstract art, murals, and fabrics. Sculptors mold and shape forms into art.

Advertisers create interesting ads for goods offered by retailers in lovely stores.

Share the happiness!

Beautiful songs, hymns, and poems have been written by humans around the world to honor Our Creator, to promote world peace and for humanitarian causes.

Ideas

No idea is stupid. *Ideas are possibilities* that may or may not happen. *The good news is that someone tried* something new and inventive. There is beauty in success or failure, simplicity or complexity.

Oliver Wendell Holmes (1809-1984CE) said 'A mind once expanded by a new idea never returns to its original dimension.'

Ordinary people in all walks of life do little things to help others.

An American Catholic philosopher, journalist, novelist, and diplomat named Michael Novak, in 1983, wrote: 'Unity in diversity is the highest possible attainment of a civilization, a testimony to the most noble possibilities of the human race. The attainment is made possible through passionate concern for choice, in an atmosphere of social trust.'

In 2010 current era Coleman G. Howard, a motivational speaker, said: When we love each other, the whole world wins.

The European Union, EU, a union of European nations, took as their motto 'United in Diversity' and are working together for peace and prosperity, realizing that many different cultures, cultural heritages or traditions, and languages are a positive asset for their continent. The countries of Indonesia, Papua New Guinea, and South Africa have also declared mottos of being United in Diversity.

CHAPTER 19

Coexistence of Religions

1. Spiritual beliefs cannot be proved; so humans should coexist in peace with regard to religions. No one knows exactly who God is. No one can speak for God.
2. Some people just believe in good ethics not spiritualality.
3. There are billions of people on the planet who have been taught different beliefs.

All people must cooperate for there to be global peace; which will make the world a better place. We can have different religious opinions without wars.

4. Some countries want government and religions separated, some countries want religions to rule the country, some countries want no religions.
5. Different countries in the world offer different freedoms, such as freedom of religion, work occupation, opportunity to serve in the government, and more.
6. Anarchy is absence of government, chaos, and utter confusion. Some forms of government are totalitarianism, communism, democracy, monarchy, oligarchy, republic, and more. No government is perfect.

Governments and parliaments that are good to the people are the best ones.

7. Humans who hurt other humans without cause are enemies and may be banned from a country.

We can be our own enemy, because we fail to use wisdom or principles of love.

We can discuss issues around a table and hopefully be able to compromise and come to an agreement, concensus, or solution.

8. Let all the world's oceans be joined together in peace.

CHILD STORY

1. Pray each day to fill your heart and mind with love and wisdom.

2. Be happy and hopeful because you only live one life on earth, so make it a good life. Stay out of trouble.

STORIES

1. *Tobi the Donkey And His Friends*

Once there were three donkeys who were eating grass in a field by a stream of water. It was a beautiful day; the sky was blue with white clouds and the grass was green. The temperature of the air was not too hot and not too cold.

The donkey named Tobi decided to walk into an olive garden. In the olive garden a bird flew down and landed on Tobi's back. 'Can I ride on your back?' asked the bird. 'Yes, you can,' replied Tobi . Then Tobi the donkey walked to the stream to get a drink of water. At the stream, a butterfly landed on his back. 'Can I ride on your back?' asked the butterfly. 'Yes,' replied Tobi. So now there was a bird and a butterfly riding on the donkey's back. Then, Tobi trodded back to the field to join the other donkeys. This time a dragonfly landed on his back. 'Can I ride on your back?' asked the dragonfly. 'Yes, you can,' laughed Tobi. So, there was a bird, a butterfly, and a dragonfly all riding on the donkey's back. Tobi said 'It's a beautiful day and a beautiful world!' Then, Astor the farmer came to the field and rang the bell. He said 'Time to come home to the barn.' So the three donkeys made their way back to the barn. And the bird, the butterfly, and the dragonfly all flew back to their homes in the trees. 'Thanks for the fun, friends' is what they all said to each other. And this is the story of Tobi the donkey and the day he gave a ride on his back to a bird, a butterfly, and a dragonfly. The friends were nice to each other.

2. *The Family Who Loved and Helped Each Other*

Back in the day when there were many small family farms, there was a boy named Carlos who lived with his grandmother and grandfather who had been married for 57 years. The family lived in a farmhouse. There were blackberry vines along the fence and his grandmother made blackberry cobbler with the blackberries. There was a peach tree on the property also and a small

lake. Wild onions grew in some fields.
When Carlos woke up in the morning when he heard the rooster crow, he spent a few minutes thinking about God and his coming day. Carlos said a prayer to thank God for his family, for food, and for a nice bed to sleep in. He smelled the delicious scent of blueberry muffins from the oven and got out of bed to go eat breakfast. His eyes were puffy from sleep.
'Good Morning, Everyone!', Carlos said to his grandparents. 'Good Morning!', they replied.
They ate a wonderful nutritious breakfast cooked by his grandmother. But sometimes his grandfather would make breakfast, too.
Then, Carlos asked his grandfather: 'May I help feed the chickens?'
'Yes, I would like your help', said the grandfather.
So Carlos and his grandfather went out to feed grain to the chickens. And after that, they sat on the swing on the big porch.
Then his grandmother came out of the house with a waterpot. 'Would you like to help me water the flowers, Carlos?' asked grandmother. So Carlos helped to water the flowers in the flower pots.

3. *The Playground Tree*

Once there was a school in a small village. All of the children had to go to one school. The children were playing on the playground on a beautiful day when they sky was blue. They were having fun on the swings, slides, playing in the sandbox, jumping rope, and playing tag. With supervision from the teacher, the children held a stick and swung at a piñata filled with candy to celebrate the last day of school. Piñatas originated in China, Mexico, and Europe. There were all the bells and whistles for the celebration.
There was a big apple tree at the corner of the schoolyard.
Suddenly a voice called from the apple tree 'Help, help! Get Francesca to help me, please!'
The children ran to the bottom of the apple tree and looked up.
Gil was a boy who had climbed up the apple tree but couldn't get back down.
'Help! I can't climb down!'
So, Cara, one of the girls, and Won, one of the boys, ran to get the teacher; her name was Francesca.
The teacher ran to the apple tree and put out both of her arms and lifted Gil down from the apple tree.
Francesca told the children later on that they needed to think carefully before they did things to stay out of trouble. 'Think first!', she said.

4. *The Baby Eagles*

Once upon a time there was a nest of baby eagles. The baby eagles loved their nest, which their mother and father had built safely in the branches of a big magnolia tree. The large leaves of the magnolia tree protected the nest from the rain.
When the baby eagles had grown big enough to leave the nest, they were nudged on their backs by their mother as she said 'Today I will teach you how to fly.' So, baby eagles fluttered their wings and took

to the sky. 'Hooray!' they exclaimed, as they flew through the beautiful blue sky and felt the nice warm sun on their backs.
But a few of the baby eagles' wings were not strong enough, and they began to falter a little, but the mother eagle and the father eagle quickly flew under their wings and lifted them back up again. Finally, after several practices, the baby eagles could fly on their own.

Engineers studied how birds fly in order to create airplanes and studied sea sponges in order to create artificial sponges, because science matters.

5. The Sleepy Princess

Once upon a time there was a princess who lived in a big castle. One morning she woke up in her big bed but she felt very sleepy. She rang the bell to let her chamber maids know that she was awake. "Good Morning," the princess said to her chamber maids, Mia, Rona, and Kimmie. The princess yawned a big yawn and her eyes looked very sleepy.

"Good Morning, Princess Fiona", replied the chambermaids. "How did you sleep?"

"I am still very sleepy,"replied the princess. "I feel that my bed is lumpy."

That day the chambermaids took all of the sheets and the coverlet off of the princess' bed, smoothed down the mattress, fluffed up the pillows, and remade the bed with fresh clean sheets.

The next morning the same thing happened. Princess Fiona awoke, yawning more than ever and eyelids were drooping; she could hardly stay awake. "I am so sleepy," said the princess.

That day Mia, Rona, and Kimmie lifted up the bed and found a small pebble under the bedpost. They had no idea how a small pebble had gotten there but they removed it.

And the princess slept very well that night because there was no pebble under the bedpost.

"Thank you for helping me," the princess said to the chambermaids. "I feel better now that I slept good."

GAMES & RECREATION

Children enjoy outdoor recreation such as flying kites, tossing a ball, riding bikes, and playgrounds. Indoor games are reading books, matching card games, crayons and coloring books, action figures, Mr. Potato Head, building blocks, toy cars and trucks, and dolls. Russian matryoshkas are dolls within a doll. Hopscotch was invented in Britain, where children draw squares in chalk on pavements and skip from square to square in different sequences. You can make up your own games.

HISTORY

Scientists believe the earth was closer to the sun billions of years ago (before 2010CE) and that originally there was only one land mass on the earth which eventually broke apart.

Scientists believe the earth has gone through several alternating periods of ice ages and global warming.

Scientists think that modern humans have only existed for around 50,000 years but the earth is 600 million years old.

Archeologists have found artifacts that were left behind from humans who lived thousands of years ago; some artifacts are believed to have been religious items or household items from many different cultures that existed 5000 years BCE.

Human Ingenuity

The first humans learned how to create fire from the friction of rubbing sticks together. Scientists have said that memory is what has allowed languages and cognitive functions to evolve.

The first humans invented the wheel, probably modeled after fallen tree logs that could roll, which was a major achievement that would enable progress for humans. The first humans probably lived in caves, because caves have been discovered containing markings and etchings.

Humans saw a 'man in the moon' because the side of the moon that faces earth can resemble a face.

For much of the past 50,000 years humans have lived in agrarian societies, meaning that field and farmers, and small villages were a way of life, which meant there were small cultural villages around the globe. The farmers and their wives had many children; many hands and people were needed to do the farm work, gather berries, milk goats or cows, fetch water, grind corn and wheat on the millstone, and gather firewood in order to survive. They were up out of their beds at the crack of dawn in order to do all of the work. Oxen pulled the plows. Oxen and horses were worked hard. If there were no fences, a cow bell was placed around a cow's neck so it could be found if it wandered off. Humans used a dirt hole or pot as a toilet.

People were amazed at the inventions of candles, sugar, salt, clean boiled water, vinegar, olive oil, butter, toothbrushes and hairbrushes, eating utensils and pottery, and fabrics woven by hand on the loom.

It took many centuries for humans to agree on how to measure time; finally the science behind the solar calendar was agreed upon by many nations in 1582CE.

Mathematical concepts have allowed bridges and buildings to be built and much more.

Math has many concepts such as Basic Math, Algebra, Geometry, Trigonometry, Statistics, Calculus, Series, Theorems, rational numbers, irrational numbers, prime numbers, complex numbers, perfect numbers, fractions, fractals, equations, Origami, Wonders of Math, music, sports ratios and much more.

Global Industrial Age

It was only around 1760CE in the Industrial Revolution in Europe that real changes in societies started, with the invention of steel mills, the marked acceleration in the output of industrial goods due to power-driven machinery which enabled a decline in human manual labor. Many inventions were the result of the free enterprise system. Worker labor unions were formed in some parts of the world to protect working conditions and establish fair pay guidelines. The labor unions and the companies need to debate fairly.

The first railroad and steam locomotive was built in 1804 in the U.K. by Richard Trevithick, an English engineer from Cornwall to satisfy a bet from an iron master named Samuel Honfray. By 1830, there were railroads in Liverpool and Machester, England.

After the train, airplane, cars, and electricity were invented, world cultures began sharing more trade goods such as food, spices, sugars, plants, animals, clothing, candles, inventions, and ideas.

The invention of the car

The first car was invented in 1886 by Karl Benz in Germany. Karl Benz and Gottlieb Daimler produced the Mercedes automobile in 1901. The Volkswagen Beetle was an economy car produced in Germany by Ferdinand Porsche under German leader Adolf Hitler.

Henry Ford (1863-1947) of America helped created the first assembly line to mass produce cars. The first car engines were very loud until mufflers were invented. The first cars had no seatbelts, until people died in car wrecks and then seatbelts were invented. Charles Goodyear of Connecticut, USA is credited with developing a pliable rubber for tires by treating rubber with sulfur in the late 1800's.

Shea butter is a moisturizer made from the African shea tree and is put into cosmetics and hand lotions. Many parts of the whale are used for making oils, foods, and other products.

The WTO (World Trade Organization) is an intergovernmental organization that regulates international trade. In 2015CE, 247 countries or territories are established in the world.

In earlier millenniums, great empires existed to Britain, Japan, China, Portugal, Spain, France, Netherlands, Denmark, Belgium, Germany, Italy, Russia, Turkey, Romans, Greece and more. Some were religious empires. Some empires imposed huge taxes and servitude upon the people, causing many to be homeless or imprisoned in dungeons because they could not pay the taxes. Peasants could be bought and sold as property. People could be held against their will for no good reason. Evil tyranny took away personal freedoms of many people, both poor and rich. In the 1500s Russian Communists and Muslims of the Ottoman Empire from the Mediterranean or North African regions had white slaves that were Slavish or Turkish people. In the 1800s European Jews and Christians had white and dark-skinned slaves from Europe and Africa called indentured servants.

Starting in 1802CE, it took over 75 years, until 1879CE, for the electric light bulb to be invented as a feasible source of light, and even then the light bulb only lasted for thirteen hours.

From 1760-2010CE, a period of about 250 years, life and methods of work dramatically changed and progressed for humans.

Methods of farming and preparing foods have improved, indoor plumbing and electricity have been incorporated into dwellings to give human beings the most comfortable life-styles that humans have ever enjoyed before in the entire history of the world. Elaborate furniture, furnishings, and electrical appliances have been invented and designed by scientists, artists, craftsmen, and engineers.

The food that is available to humans in beautiful grocery stores is astounding and of great variety. Food preparation is quicker and easier than in past history when butter had to be churned each day, vegetables had to be gathered or animals hunted each day, and water had to be lifted from wells.

The variety of clothing that is available in the world is vastly different from the clothing humans wore 3,000 years ago – parkas have been invented with material that will keep humans so warm they can hike to the tops of mountains or travel to the earth poles and be kept warm; fabrics and plastics have been invented that allow humans to dive to the bottom of lakes and shallow seas, or walk through marshes and forests with protection of limbs; spacesuits allow humans to spend time in space, even in space walks; slip-resistant shoes with rubber tread like tires on automobiles help to prevent falls on slippery floors. Coco Chanel of France made vast changes to women's attire in Europe in the late 1880's by simplifying designs.

Some people are in between sizes of clothing or shoes, so that the clothing doesn't fit quite perfectly.
'One size fits all' label is a paradox because despite the acceptable premise it can be senseless or self-contradictory to expectations.

Mail and packages are now delivered to your mailbox or even to your door by mail carriers, whereas 100 or 200 years ago, letters and mail were delivered on horseback or by homing pigeons.

Improvements in medicine have increased life expectancies dramatically in the past 100 years since 1900CE, and have even more dramatically improved them in the past 25 years since 2000CE. Clean water, antibiotics, vaccines, anti-venoms, anesthesia, vinegar, sliced bread, dishes and eating utensils, toothbrushes, toothpaste, cameras, phonographs to record sounds, umbrellas, light bulbs, batteries, telephones, balloons, airplanes, mattresses, indoor plumbing, cotton swabs, zinc oxide and ultra-violet skin protectants, sandpaper for furniture and feet, computers and printers, 3D printers, wireless technology, LASIK Eye surgery, hair transplant and restoral, were some of the phenomenal inventions – there were millions more! Cell phones made phone booths practically obsolete.

Humans have discovered nutrition, gravity, radiation, physics, music.

Humans invented cars, balloons, airplanes, trains, ships, the news media, being organized, dictionaries, yellow pages, diapers, music boxes and musical mobile, toys for kids, reference books, art, entertainment, photography, wheel chairs, hearing aids, x-rays and MRIs, 3D, microwave ovens, recipes, menus, poetry, telescopes,cell phones, stairs, furniture, pencils and pens, gardens, magnifying glass, eyeglasses, holidays, sliced bread, sandwiches, ice cream, rehab, lava lamps, incense, perfume, cologne, sports, candles, light bulbs, mazes, puzzles, kaleidoscopes, straws, backscratchers, and much more. Many things have been used as backscratchers.

Humans created or recognized the concepts of respect, tact, education, conservation, giving and taking, parties, leaders and followers, unconditional love, random acts of kindness, helping other human beings, willpower, déjà vu, luck, taking thing for granted, surprises, secrets, governments, insurance, time measurement, measurements for volume, mass, length, and area, religions and spiritualty, leash laws for animals.

Appreciate the human efforts and divine inspiration behind all creations. God will lead the way. God is the inspiration behind all creation.

At one time, humans thought the world was flat until other humans proved that the world was a sphere. (Some people were even put to death for saying the earth was not flat; this is an example of 'old civilization and old beliefs' in contrast to 'modern civilization and modern beliefs'.)

Appreciate the progress that humans have made to civilize the world and are searching for answers to unknowns.

In life, many think you should consider yourself fortunate if you are warm, safe, dry, fed, have clean water and air, and are free from oppression and injustice.

Humans have explored earth, sent men to circle and land on the moon, and have put into orbit communications satellites and an international space station. Now scientists from many nations are working on a joint effort to send humans to the planet Mars.

In 2014, the European Space Agency successfully landed a spacecraft named Rosetta on a comet named 67P or Churyumov Gerasimenko. Due to gravitational pulls and mathematical calculations, scientists created a slingshot effect that enabled Rosetta to speed to 34,500 mph to reach the comet. A lander named Philae will fall 14 miles from Rosetta to land on top of the comet and begin studying the composition of the comet, transmitting the information back to Earth. The mission was a ten-year effort. New Horizons is a NASA space probe that flew past Pluto in 2015.

Since 1998CE, methods of communication greatly improved due to internet computers and satellites, which enable better global communication than was ever known in the entire history of the world.

There are more opportunities now for the human race than ever before. People have learned that education, stable family situations, healthy bodies and minds, and personal dedication can lead to good lives and personal successes. Communication was very poor 2000 years BCE and world cultures were very separated with their own distinct languages, religions, diet preferences, customs, governments, and physical genetic characteristics because the continents were separated by oceans; it is distance that has separated humans and caused distinct cultural differences. Now God is bringing the cultures together again with modern transportation and communication.

There are differences of skin tones in humans ranging from dark brown to medium tan to very white. Some skin tones may have yellow or red tints. The differences in human traits of the human races are believed to have resulted from the earth being very close to the sun thousands of years ago. Some people want all races to blend together and produce human beings that all look the same, but many want to stay in their own race and continue the heritage of their race; people should respect both opinions because all humans are beautiful people.

If all flowers were blended into one kind of flower, there would only be one kind of flower.

A rainbow has many colors. It is a symbol of diversity.

Global Community and The Information Age

The invention of the computer

Thanks to good humans who invented computer technology, computers and the internet transformed the world by speeding up communication and business transactions. You can order flowers over the internet and have them delivered to someone in a foreign country the next day. The internet has helped law enforcement to have more knowledge about criminals and has helped doctors to share medical information quickly. Family genealogy computer apps can show a person's genetic history or family relatives. The first computer was called Colossus and was invented by Thomas Flowers in the 1940's in London England.

In the early mainframe computers, programs were read in by punch cards until computer monitors with cathode ray tubes were invented. Early TVs had cathode ray tubes. Storage mediums for computers were magnetic for floppy disks, cassette and VHS tapes. CDs and DVDs are optical storage and are read with lasers. Plasma screens display electronically charged ionized gases called plasma. HDTV are high definition screens with more resolution which means they have more pixels than standard tvs.

A crypto or bitcoin is a unit of currency on the internet. Some have said that the bitcoin computer is not hackable. Satoshi

Nakamoto claimed to invent the bitcoin in 2008 but later revealed his name was Craig Wright from Australia. Many believe paper money or gold ingot kilobars will always be a form of currency because of the dangers of computers controlling the world.

A problem with the internet computer empire is that privacy is being invaded; computer hackers and programmers can hack into cell phones, computers, car engines, and wireless medical implants. Jammers are devices that block cell signals for a fifty-yard radius, rendering cell phones or garage doors useless. Some think the internet should be optional in phones, computers, tvs, and vehicle engines. Protest if the government puts a computer chip under our scalp.

Artificial Intelligence

Dest top computers, laptop computers, smart phones (cell phone with computer) became world popular around 2000. Around 2020, the artificial information revolution is expected to be a successful technology. Scientists have been putting millions of picture images into computers so computers can make decisions that humans once could only make. For example, a computer could read a medical image scan and make a diagnosis that previously only a doctor could have made by studying x-rays or medical imaging. Another example is computers can identify a person from a photographs, which Facebook is already doing. In 2016, a truck drove itself 1000 miles to make a delivery.

We were all born naked

If there were no clothing, no languages, no money, and no professions, and no religions – we would have less diversity and we would all be the same. We were all born naked into this world.

Now, with improvements in travel and communication due to satellites and the internet, the world is becoming a more global culture. People are now realizing how very much alike all humans on the planet are. We are celebrating our similarities instead of letting our differences alienate us from each other.

Some people are world travelers while others prefer to stay local.

Pollution & Recycling

Although humans have made great progress to bring humanity to where we are today, there are problems resulting from the industrial revolution that need to be addressed such as controlling pollution on earth and in space. Trash landfills are filling up. People are dumping toxins into the waters; medicines should not be flushed down drains. Some think it is helpful to wash cars on grassy areas with natural citrus-based formulas which can be absorbed into the ground instead of soapy water being washed down concrete driveways into the public water systems. Burning less fossil fuels will reduce the carbon emissions being emitted into the atmosphere.

Scientists are looking for ways to create renewable energy from the sun, winds, and biofuels to sustain us; if the earth population keeps increasing there may not be enough food to feed everybody. Some think God already knows about our problems.

In the year 2000 CE there is an environmental movement to save the earth because the earth's natural resources such as virgin lands and forests, and whales and fishes are being depleted and the delicate balance of earth microorganisms in the soils, bacteria, fungi, and the chemistry of the earth's atmosphere, and ocean waters are being compromised; scientists said that all life systems on the earth were in decline due to global warming caused by the burning of fossil fuels.

The ocean is absorbing carbon. If the upper layer of the ocean is too warm and kills many life forms or if weather patterns change and the tides or wave patterns in the oceans stop and the oceans become stagnant, it may be the end of life on earth for humans and other species. The environmentalists said there has to be a spiritual consciousness in all humanity to love the earth and universe to reverse the damages that were the result of the industrial age. Humans can make a choice to respond to problems in our lives and make corrections in our actions to make things better. 'Green' manufacturing which includes processes that use clean energy and emits zero waste can replace old manufacturing methods.

Some scientists think the earth may change its orbit around the sun over centuries of time, causing the earth to go into and out of ice ages.

The human attitude must change to recycle plastics, metals, glass, paper, cardboard and foam. About 500 million plastic drinking straws are thrown away each day. Donate good discard items instead of trashing them. Precious metals like gold, silver, and titanium and diamonds and gemstones can be recycled. Conserve energy. People could live near their work location for shorter commutes. Some think that in some cultures, people are working too hard to pay for things that they really do not need; for example, people think they have to go out and buy all new things when in reality they could buy used things that are good and functional. Environmentalists say the human attitude needs to change from the belief that humans need to produce more and more things; now humans need to refocus their energies to recycle, reuse, and simplify life. A flat round plastic cookie cake tray container that has a small rim could be filled with water for turtles or birds in your yard.

There are some places on earth where humans do not have clean drinking water.

One tree can distill 57,000 gallons of water in its lifetime. Trees are vital to the earth's health because they make oxygen, sequester carbon, provide habitat to hundreds of species, accrue solar energy to make complex sugars, create microclimates, and can self-replicate.

Genetic Engineering

The ethics of genetic engineering is being debated. Some think changing genetics is going against the will of the Creator while others think not. It has been written that scientists have implanted false memories in the brains of mice. Fruits, vegetables, flowers, and plants have been genetically altered and scientifically hybridized in cross-pollination. Blue roses are not natural but are genetically engineered. Green and orange cauliflower were scientifically created while white cauliflower is natural. Purple carrots were scientifically created while orange carrots are natural.

Wars in the World

Religious fighting about 'who God is' has been occurring for about 3000 years.

Wars have been fought since the beginning of human civilization over issues such as power and control of land, people, slaves, and religions.

After World War I and World War II in 1949CE in which ten million people were killed, the Geneva Convention was held in Switzerland that resulted in treaties international laws for humanitarian treatment of war and defined protection for citizens who were non-combatants. The treaties also led to the establishment of disaster relief organizations such as the Red Cross, Red Crescent, Red Lion, Red Star of David, Red Crystal which are humanitarian organizations that were founded to protect human life and health and promote dignity and respect for all. Atrocities and genocides have been committed by humans in many cultures all over the world throughout history.

WW I was caused by the assassination of Archduke Franz Ferdinand of Austria by a Serbian nationalist in Yugoslavia named Gavrilo Princip in response to the Austria-Hungary annexation of Bosnia. WW II started in 1939 when Germany invaded Poland; then Britain and France declared war on Germany because they had treaties with Poland. German leader Hitler killed millions of Jews, Catholics and nomad gypsies in the 1930-40s in a holocaust (gas chambers, starvation, or with guns). Hitler invaded 12 countries in Europe (Czechoslovakia, Austria, Poland, Denmark, Norway, France, Belgium, Netherlands, France, Britain, Soviet Union, Italy). Russian leader Stalin killed millions of Ukrainians in the 1930s in a holodomar (starving them to death by taking away all livestock, seeds, and farm equipment). The Vietnam War lasted from 1955 to 1975 and ended when Saigon also called Ho Chi Minh was liberated from the communists of North Vietnam. The Korean War lasted from 1950-1953 when North Korea invaded South Korea. African leaders committed tribal genocides in the 1980s-2000s. Historians have concluded from documented evidence and artifacts that innocent peoples were killed as great empires spread throughout Asia and the Middle East 3000 years ago and as early as 15,000 years ago. The Japanese killed 150,000 Christians in 1612 in Japan. Humans have mutilated body parts as culture rituals. Peasants living on the lands of kings and queens of great empires around the world lived at the mercy of the kings and queens for food, shelter, and medical care. Humans cultures in many parts of the world have taken other humans into slavery and denied them personal freedoms. In some ancient cultures people were thrown into dungeons (jails) if they could not pay their taxes. Good humans have died in wars to fight against the atrocities and genocides. In some modern cultures humans were allowed to own their own houses, businesses, stock in the stock market to earn dividends, or holdings in investment portfolios that gain interest. Humans left their native countries and empires (1) to seek better lives or more freedoms, (2) were forced to leave their country because a ruler forced them to leave, or a force of nature changed the land (3) there was human desire for knowledge, curiosity, and the quest for unknowns.

Some people are seeking solutions to problems and are trying to advance progress in the world for everyone. Some people are simply trying to force their values on others and bringing harm to the world. Some claim there is a conspiracy of one group of people trying to control the whole world. It is correct for people to analyze all aspects of all situation or critical thinking.

In 2015, the Kuwait dinar had the highest currency exchange rate in the world because of oil reserves.

Geneva, Switzerland has become a worldwide center for international diplomacy since 1864CE.

Most people who believe in God believe that it is possible to live peacefully on our planet without killing each other over religion.

Humans have evolved to a life where we now have to make choices about how we want human life to progress on our planet. We should try to do our best and be safe in all of our endeavors be it our work, inventions, recreation, sports competitions, transportation, partying, health, explorations, hobbies, conversations, communications, responsibilities, daily routines and behaviors, and all things.

Most people want peace and they do good things.

NATIVE AMERICAN INDIAN

Scientists believe the early natives came to North America over the Bering Strait from Asia to Alaska and onto the continent about 15,000 years ago. Historians have classified the native Americans into Paleoindians of 15,000 years ago, Cloxis of 9500 years ago, Folsom of 8000 years ago, and Plano of 6000 years ago. Palynologists who study ancient plant pollen and spores in stratified sediments to reconstruct past environments believe that the upper half of North America was covered by an ice glacier until about 10,000 years ago.

Some of these early peoples may have migrated further down to South America. Palenque is an ancient Mayan culture dated 226 BCE in Chiapas, Mexico. Artifacts have been excavacted in the United States that indicate some Mayans may have migrated to the southeastern United States.

Artifacts of the early natives include tools like projectile and fluted points that were most likely tied to throwing sticks to make spears to kill deer, buffalo, squirrel, turkey, rabbits, or fish for food and to kill mountain lions and bears.

Other artifacts that have been recovered include bone pins made from bones, antler tip points, stone knives, pottery vessels, smoking pipes, items that look like scrapers, fossils, and remains of extinct animals such as mammoth bones and antlers. Some of these items have been radio carbon-14 dated to 9000 years ago. Javelin-sticks were buried with bones of large woolly mammoth animals that had fluted points stuck between ribs.

Bearskins were dried and used as clothing and blankets. Carvings with symbols have been found on bearskins.

Excavated human bones have been dated to 1400 BCE (almost 3500 years ago) and were buried with headdresses made with eagle and turkey feathers or buffalo heads.

Stones were used to grind grains like wheat and corn. Spoons were made from bison horns. Clay figures were effigies of birds and owls.

EUROPEAN SETTLERS

emigrated to a new world to the west

After explorers such as Christopher Columbus from Italy and Ferdinand Magellan from Portugal, who sailed for the Spanish Empire, discovered the Americas in 1492CE, people emigrated to North America, some to escape from tyranny or religious persecution that occurred in some world empires. At first, the explorers thought they had reached the country of India, so they called the Native Americans 'Indians.' Amerigo Vespucci was an Italian who explored North Ameica in 1500. Richard ap Merke also spelled Amerike was an Englishman who explore America in the 1400s. Giovanni John Cabot from Venice arrived in North America in 1497.
When the British Empire colonized North America in 1607 CE, Jamestown, Virginia was the first colony. It is believed that diseases brought from Europe to North America caused many deaths of Native Indians and that many Europeans died from diseases of the Native Indians. Pedro Menendez de Aviles founded St. Augustine, Florida in 1574.

A fleet of 500 Chinese junks (ships) sailed by Admiral Zheng of Ming Dynasty Emperor Zhu Di reached North America in 1421 but did not leave settlers.

Danish explorer Vitus J. Bering explored the Bering Strait between Russia and Alaska in 1741 funded by Russian Empress Anna.

Greenland was settled by a Norseman named Erik the Red in the 980s CE. Erik the Red had a son named Leif Erickson who was born in Greenland and led voyages for the Vikings. Some people think Leif Erickson reached the shores of North America in a region called Vinland in the early 1000s.

King Louis of France sent expeditions to the new lands in 1534. Jacques Cartier sailed to the North America and established the areas called Quebec in Canada and New Orleans in the United States. Giovanni, an Italian man, also sailed funded by France.

In 1605 King Christian and King Frederick of Denmark sent expeditions to Greenland where Luthran and Moravian ministries were established.

The French, Spanish, Scandanavian, and English fought each other and fought against the Native Americans for territories in North America during the years 1400-1800s.

Some people were killed by black bears, wolves, snakes. disease, starvation, or tornadoes.

William Penn, an American Quaker Society of Friends, helped to establish peaceful relationships between white Europeans (paleface) and Native American Indians, whose skin had reddish-brown pigments (redskin). Tamanend, a Delaware Lenni Lanape native chief, enjoined in a successful colonial relationship based on peace, respect, and equal justice. Tamanend called William Penn by the name of Mikwon which means feather of the quill pen.

From 1526-1827, slaves were brought from West Africa to South America, the Caribbean, Europe, India, and North America by traders who exchanged money or goods with West African leaders for African people who had brown-skin (nigeri means 'of Nigerian region').

Daniel Boone was a Kentucky frontiersman in 1750 who explored the territories into Tennessee and North Carolina. Boone and his fellow hunter Benjamin Cutbirth were captured by the Shawnee Indian warriors and Chief Blackfish who confiscated Boone and Cutbirth's animal meat and skins. John James Audubon (b. 1785) was a naturalist painter who studied birds for many years.

The European colonists protested high taxes on tea shipments imposed by the British Parliament, so the colonists rebelled by disguising themselves as Mohawk Indians, jumping aboard three British ships, and dumping the tea into the harbor. The raid became known as the Boston Tea Party. When the United States of America fought the British Empire for independence in 1776CE in the Revolutionary War, the forefathers founded a nation for civil liberties, dignity, and justice for all human lives. The forefathers were of Judeo-Christian heritage but believed in freedom to express and practice personal religious beliefs. The USA is a federal republic and was designed for the constitution and freedoms to be protected; there are checks and balances that allow the majority opinion of democracy to be heard and the establishment of the republic of states to be protected by a constitution.

The first president of the United States was George Washington who was the son of a tobacco farmer. The forefathers did not believe in genocide or oppression of humans, but indentured servitude was allowed as a custom of the empires. Lenape Chief White Eyes was a friend of George Washington and served as a Colonel in the Revolutionary War.

In 1838 Native American tribes were forced west of the Mississippi River in

what is called the Trail of Tears; they drummed a sacred beat. The Middle West of America contains fertile farmlands. Many Native American tribes formed new tribal nations; some stayed near the new colonies and taught the colonists how to eat and grow corn. Some natives became plantation owners. Thomas Jefferson, the Caucasian third president and the principal author of the Declaration of Independence, wrote that people should have the right to bear arms (have guns) to protect themselves against tyranny in the government. Benjamin Banneker was a free African, son of a former slave, who corresponded with Thomas Jefferson on topics of abolishing slavery and racial equality. He was a surveyor, farmer, and almanac author who helped Major Andrew Elliott to survey the borders of and lay out the land of the District of Columbia where slaves helped build many government buildings. Eli Whitney from New Haven, Connecticut, was a Caucasian engineer who designed a cotton gin in 1825 which processed cotton that was picked by African slaves on cotton plantations. Frederick Augustus Douglas was an African American slave who escaped from slavery in Maryland and fled to Massachusetts and New York and became an abolitionist. Victoria Woodhull from Homerr, Ohio, a Caucasian leader of the women's suffrage voting rights movement, ran for president in 1872 and asked Frederick Douglas to be her vice-presidential running mate.
Abraham Lincoln, a Caucasian lawyer and the 16th president of the US, abolished slavery in 1863CE in America. Harriet Tubman was a woman slave who helped free slaves. Booker Taliaferro Washington from Tuskegee, Alabama, was an African advisor to presidents between 1890-1915.
John Fitzgerald Kennedy, the Caucasian 35th president, said 'Ask not what your country can do for you. Ask what you can do for your country." Jimmy Carter, the Caucasian 39th president said that peace is more than absence of war. He said that inner peace comes from human rights issues to voice opinions, feed your family, raise healthy children, and choose the leaders of your country. Barack Obama, the 44th president, became the first president with African family history.

Many conflicts occurred between the white European settlers and the Native American Indians. It is believed that negotiations or payments made for lands were misunderstood by the Native Americans which caused anger. Language barriers caused confusion. Men, women, and children were abducted or killed on both sides. An area near Niagra Falls was a recognized neutral zone and was used for mediations, intertribal trade, and festivals.
Nancy Ward negotiated a peace treaty in Tennessee in 1781
It is said that a white light arose from the body of Nancy Ward when she died; the light fluttered around the room and flew out the door toward her town of Chota.

Lenape Chief Sassoonan kept Wampum records and signed a peace treaty with William Penn in 1718.
Many lands, rivers, and lakes are named after the Native American Indian tribes.
The name for the island of Manhattan is taken from the Lenape name Manahachtanienk.
There were civil wars among the Indian tribes for territories.
In an encounter with the Iroquois, a Lenape ambassador named Mottschujinga which means Little Grizzly Bear carried a black wampum belt in one hand which meant a declaration of war and a pipe of peace in the other hand when he went to meet

them, fearless and partially nude in a bearskin loin cloth in the manner of the Lenape, and waited for the Iroquois to make a choice. The pipe of peace wafted the feelings of the heart out to blend with those of the other smokers, and up to the watching spirits of the universe.

In 2016, there are 567 tribes on 326 Native American Indian Reservations in the United States.

The Klamath tribe believed the sky god Skell and the god of the underworld Llao engaged in battle that formed Crater Lake in Oregon. The sacred lake has no rivers flowing into it or out of it. Crater Lake is a sacred site to the Klamath tribe of Indians.

The Pawnee Native American tribes believed that at the end of time, people will turn into stars, since all people were made by the stars.

Track Rock Gap is an archaeological area in the Chattahoochee National Forest in Georgia, USA which contains preserved petroglyphs of ancient Native Americans in six soapstone boulders dated to 1,000 BCE (3000 years ago).
The petroglyphs resemble animal and bird tracks, crosses, circles, and human footprints. The area of forest is 52-acres or 210,00 m^2.
The Arkaquah Trail that starts at Brasstown Bald in Georgia, USA is a hiking trail that is 5.5 mi (8.25 km) in length and ends at Track Rock Gap. Brasstown Bald is known to Cherokee, Choctaw, and Muscogee (Creek) people as Enotah; the mountain is the highest point in Georgia, USA. The Coharie and Lumbee tribes are in North Carolina.

The Armuchee is a land named after the Cherokee word *armuchee* which means corn hominy grits or land of the flowers.

The Green Corn Ceremony of the Cherokee is celebrated at harvest by carrying woven baskets of vegetables and corn. The Hopi corn mother is Chochmingwu.

The Etowah mounds of the Muscogee in Bartow County, Georgia, were used as speaking, mortuary, house, temple, and dance platforms at pow wow gatherings.
The Appalachian trail goes from Maine to Georgia.
The League of Six Nations of Iroquois were Seneca, Cayuga, Mohawk, Onondaga, Oneida, and Lenape around areas of New York, USA and were called the Mahongwi (Mengwe). The league was admired by the Founding Fathers of the U.S. who used the league as a model to establish the federal government.
The Iroquois and Mohawk are in New York, USA.
The Huron were Iroquois in NY.
The Mohican are around Massachusetts.
The Menominee are a tribe in Wisconsin.
The Chippewa are at Lake Superior in Michigan.
The Blackfoot emigrated from the Great Lakes area to the Northwest.
The Ponca and Omaha are in Nebraska.
The Cheyenne, Crow, Comanche, Osage, and Chickasaw are in Oklahoma and Montana.
The Sioux, Santee, and Lakota are near North and South Dakota, Minnesota, and Iowa.
The Pueblo, Coyotero, Chaco, and Manataka live in Arizona or New Mexico.
The Yosemite and Miwok are in California.
The Talega, Alligewi, and Natchez live in Mississippi.
The Pequot live in Connecticut. The Lenape live in Delaware.
The Tappacola, Pensacola, Choctaw, Apalachee, and Muskogee lived in Florida.
The Inuit Eskimo of the ancient Lenape live in Alaska and Canada.
The Powhatan were in Virginia.

The Assiniboine were in Montana.

Chief Redstone of the Assiniboine in Wolf Point, Montana, carved peace pipes from Native American Indian sacred red stone found in Montana and Minnesota. wood. The European colonists and the Native Americans Indians used tomahawk axes to cut wood. Tomahawk is a Powhatan word.

The Ojibwe (Chippewa) made a Sacred Hoop called a dreamcatcher which hung on walls over beds to catch bad dreams and keep them from light of day.
The Mohicans could run miles through the woods without being heard.

Cheyenne dancers wear a buffalo headress to perform a healing ceremony called the massaum.

The Navajo Nation and related Apachee, Hopi, Pima, Chiricahua, Mescalero, Jicarilla, and Lipan tribes are in SouthWest USA and are known for sand painting, turquoise and silver jewelry crafting, pottery, wool and grain production, and sheep and cattle herding. Geronimo was a great tribal brave leader for the Bendonkohe Apache. A brave is a male, a squaw sachem is a female chief, and a papoose is a baby or small child. The artistry of wool weavings reflect Navajo principles of balance and harmony.

A sun dance celebrates the coming of summer. A corn grinding dance celebrates harvest. The Kiowa hold a Gourd Dance to renew tribal spirits. The Yurok, Hupa, and Karok of California hold an acorn feast. Hupa shaman get powers from dancing and dreaming. Pueblo shamans believe in kachinas spirits that perform functions at festivals.

The Native Americans sent smoke signals up into the air as a form of communication to other tribes. Natives invented dwellings such as the Navajo hogan, the Apache wickiup, the Pueblo adobe hut, the Seminole Chickee, the Ojibwa wigwam, and the Lakota tipi. Natives worked fields to grow corn, squash and beans; invented pipes to smoke tobacco; and were expert trackers of animals and people. Spies and scouts were sent ahead on expeditions.

The Tsimshian and Tlingit Native British Columbian tribes of Canada beat drums at reservation meetings by the Skeena River and built totem sculptures with carvings of animals and characters that symbolized beliefs, clan lineages, or events for their culture. The Salish are in the northwest America.

A Salish and Kootenal Flathead reservation includes a Buddhist garden and a Catholic church. In Arizona there is a Mormon Temple on a Native Indian Reservation.
The Wolastoqiyik or Maliseet natives live near New Brunswick and Quebec, Canada and Maine near the St. John River. Wolastoq means 'Beautiful River.' The natives believed that animals had special gifts, such as healing powers especially if an animal looked at you a certain way. The Kuna Indians are a tribe in San Blas Archipelago on the Atlantic side of the Republic of Panama. The Montagnais, Naskapi, live in the upper St. Lawrence River valley of Northeast Canada. The Cree and Algonkins live in Canada also.

Sacajawea was a Shoshone Indian born in 1788 who married Quebec trapper Toussaint Charbonneau; they assisted during the travel expeditions of Meriwether Lewis and William Clark. Medicine Snake Woman, wife of a Blood Indian chief, assisted Americans to select a practical land route for a railroad from the Mississippi River to the Pacific Ocean in 1853. Pocahontas was a Powhatan woman who married John Rolfe and helped the English Jamestown settlers of Virginia.

Governor Sam Houston secured Texas in the Battle of San Jacinto in 1836 which lasted 18 minutes against Mexico. Male settlers who built ranches in the midwest and herded cattle were called *cowboys* in 1866.

The Zunis in southwest North America survived on grasses until the Sun sent them six corn maidens who transformed the fields into maize (corn).

The Papago Indians of the Sonoran Desert make wine from the fruit of the Saguaro cactus plant. Sonoma is a town in California famous for its wines. Sonoma is a Native American name for Valley of the Moon.

A Lakota story is that a beautiful maiden appeared to natives on the Great Plains with a pipe and a stone. She told the Lakota that the pipe bowl represented the earth and the wood stem symbolized all growing things and that the buffalo carved on the bowl stood for all animals and the pipe's 12 feathers signified all winged creatures. Whoever prayed with this pipe would be in harmony with the universe. Seven circles carved on the stone represented 7 holy rites that were to be observed by the Lakota people forever. After disclosing these mysteries to the Lakota, the maiden transformed into a buffalo calf and disappeared into a large herd of buffalo, leaving behind the pipe and stones of the medicine bundle and sacred teachings with the people.

Annie Jarvis and Essie Parrish were prophet woman and spiritual leaders for the Kashaya Pomos in California. Essie Parrish also included the Bible in her teachings and visited a Mormon church. The Native American Church was established and sermons about the Great Spirit of God are given. God may deal with humans through the spirits of the waterbird and the thunderbird. The fruit of the peyote cactus which contains mescaline (an alkaloid drug) may be eaten to induce hallucinogenic effects to commune with God or spirits, receive guidance, reproof, and healing.

Some Native American Indian Chiefs

Red Jacket Seneca (1760),
Black Hoof Shawnee (1760),
Chief Pontiac Ottawa (1740),
Teedyuscung (1740) and his son Chief Bull, Mangas Coloradas Apache (1810),
Chief Seattle Duwamish (1800), Cinon Mataweer Kumeyaay (1800), Tecumseh Shawnee (1800), American Horse Sioux (1820), Osceola Seminole (1820),
Benito Juarez Zapoteca (1820),
Chief Manuelito Navajo (1830), Hatam Kumeyaay (1830),
Conchise Apache (1830),
Geronimo (1850),
Sitting Bull Lakota (1850),
Red Cloud Lakota (1840),
Standing Bear Ponca (1850),
Joseph Nez Perce (1860),
Crazy Horse Lakota (1860),
Captain Jack Modoc (1860),
Charles Curtis Kaw (1880),
Quanah Parker (1900),
Adam Castillo Cahuilla (1900),
Chief Dan George Tsleil-Waututh (1920),
Russell Means Oglala Lakota (1950),Anna Prieto Sandovel Kumeyaay (1950), Henry Chee Dodge Navajo(1940), Richard Milanovich Cahuilla (1960).

Wilma Mankiller became the first woman sachem chief for the Cherokee in 1985.

A sachem chief is a first among equals. A Cahuilla Chief named John Tortes Meyers was a catcher in major league baseball.

Feather headresses are reserved for elders or indians who earned them.

The Moravian United Brethren of Protestants living among the Delaware Lenape Native Indians from 1740 to 1808 kept records of the symbols of the Delaware tribe. Chief Teedyuscung joined the Moravian Church for a time and was baptized a Christian. Constantine Rafinesque who was born in 1787 of French and German parents in Constantinople (the city founded by ancient Greeks in 600 which has been ruled by Greeks, Roman Byzantines, and Muslim Ottomans and is now called Istanbul, Turkey) translated the symbols into 687 words and 183 symbols called the Red Record or Wallam Olum. Rafinesque was a botanist, an archaeologist, managed a savings bank and invented the coupon bond, and studied fifty languages. The Fragment is a history of the Lenape after the 1620s written by John Burns most likely in the late 1880s when many historians researched Indians after the Trail of Tears.

The Red Record
(Wallam Olum) 400–1620 CE

BOOK 1

Lenape Delaware Words	English Words
1. Sayewitalli	At the beginning,
Wemiguma	The sea everywhere
Wokgetaki	Covered the earth.
2. Hackung-kwelik	Above extended
Owanaku	A swirling cloud,
Wak yutali	And within it,
Kitanitowit-essop	The Great Spirit moved.
3. Sayewis	Primordial,
Hallemewis	Everlasting,
Nolemewi	Invisible,
Elemamik	Omnipresent –
Kitanitowit-essop	The Great Spirit moved.
4. Sohalawak	Bringing forth
Kwelik	The sky
Hakik	The earth,
Owak	The clouds,
Awasagamak	The heavens.
5. Gishuk	The day,
Nipahum	The night,
Alankwak	The stars.
6. Wemi-sohalawak	Bring forth all
Yulik	Of these
Yuch-aan	to move in harmony.
9. Kitanitowit	The Great Spirit

Manito	Created
Manitoak	The creator spirits,
10. Owiniwak	Living beings,
Angelatawiwak	Immortals,
Chichankwak	The Souls
Wemiwak	Everything.
11. Wrenkmanito	Then the Spirit
Jinwis	Ancestor
Lennowak	Grandfather
Mukom	Of Men
12. Milap	Gave
Netami-gaho	The First Mother
Owini-gaho	Mother of Life
13. Namesik milap	(who) gave the fish
Tulpewik milap	gave the turtles
Awesik milap	gave the beasts
Cholensak milap	gave the birds.
14. Makimani-shak	But the bad spirit
Sohalawak	brought forth
Makowini	bad creatures –
N'akowak	The snakes and
Amangamek	sea monsters,
15. Uchewak	flies,
Pungusak	mosquitoes.
16. Nitisak	Friends were
Wemi owini	all living things
W'delsinewuap	with each other.
17. Kiwis Wunand	The Benefactor
Wishimanitowak	and the helpful spirits
Essopak	were busy.
18. Nijini	Those ancestors,
Netami lennowak	The first men,
Nigoha	were alone.
Netami okwewi	The first women
Nantinewak	who brought them.
19. Gattamin	Hungry for
Netami mitzi	The first food,
Nijini	Those ancestors
Nantine	gathered it.
20. Wemi wingi-namenap	All were delighted.
Wemi ksin-elendamep	All were carefree.
Wemi wullatemanuwi	All were happy.
21. Shukand	But then
Eli-kemi	Very secretly

Mekenikink	at the end
Wakon	an evil snake
Powako	a sorceror
Initako	came to the earth.
22. Mattalogas	Wickedness
Pallalogas	Wrongfulness
Maktaten owagan	Criminal acts
Payat-chik yutali	these came here.
23. Wihillan payat	Sickness came
Mboagan payat	Death came
24. Wonwemi	All of this
Wiwunch	was long ago
Kamik atak	in the land beyond
Kitahikan	The great flood
Netamaki	The first world
Epit	There was.

BOOK 2

1. Wulamo	Long ago
Maskanako-anup	in the time of the mighty serpent
Lennowak	were the men and
Makowini essopak	evil beings.
2. Maskanako	The Mighty Serpent or Dragon
Shigalusit	was an enemy to
Nijini essopak	those ancestors there,
Shawelendamep	who soon grew
Eken shingalan	to hate it.
3. Nishawi palliton	They both fought
Nishawi machiton	They both did wrong
Nishawi matta lungundowin	They both had no peace.
4. Mattapewi wiki	Homes were destroyed
Nihantuwit	by murderers.
Mekwazoan	And bloodshed.
5. Maskanako	The Mighty Serpent or Dragon
6. Nakowa petonep	brought the snakes
Amangam petonep	brought the sea monsters
7. Pahella pahella	flooding and flooding
8. Tulapit menapit	at Turtle Island
Nanaboush	was Nenabush
Maskaboush	The great hare
Owinimokom	Grandfather to Life
Linowimokom	Grandfather of humanity.
9. Tulagishatten-lohxin	The Turtle went to the rescue.
10. Owini linowi	Living things and people

Wemoltin	All went forth through
Pehella gahani	the rapids and shallows,
Pommixin nahiwi	struggling downstream
Tatalli tulapin	to where the turtle was.
12. Manito-dasin	The Spirit daughter
Mokol-wichemap	helped with a boat.
16. Kshipehelen penkwihilen	The Great Flood dried.
Palliwi	It was over.

It has been suggested that the Turtle People left the area of China, Mongolia, and Russia around 2600 BCE around the time of the Shang Dynasty when the Great Wall of China was built. They crossed the Bering Strait to the Yukon valley in Alaska. Excavations in Alaska have supported the theory. The turtle is the symbol for the north in Chinese tradition.
Around 6000 BCE, farming communities existed along the Hwang Ho River.

BOOK 3

1. Lennapewi	The Lenape, the True Men
Tulapewini	The Turtle People,
Psakwiken	were crowded together
Woliwikgun wittanktalli	living in cave shelters.
2. Topan-akpinep	Their home was icy.
Wineu-akpinep	Their home was snowy.
Kshakan-akpinep	Their home was windy.
Thupin-akpinep	Their home was freezing.
3. Lowankwamink	To the north slope
Wulaton Wtakan tihill	To have less cold
Kelik meshautang	Many big-game
Siliewak	Herds went.
4. Chitanes-sin	To be strong
Powalessin	To be rich
Elowichik	The Hunters
Pokwihil	Broke away
6. Lowaniwi	Northern
Wapaniwi	Eastern
Shawaniwi	Southern
Wunkeniwi	Western
Apakichik	The Explorers.
11. Nihillapewin	The free men
Lowaniwi wemiten	all went northward
Chihillen	spreading across
Winiaken	the snowy country.
12. Namesuagipek	By the dark fish sea,
Guneunga Waplanewa ouken	settled the White Eagle clan
Waptumewi ouken	and the White Wolf clan.

13. Amokolen nallahemen	Rowing, crossing the water,
Agunouken pawasinep	For long they gloried
Wapasinep	In the eastern light
Akomenep	In the land of Akomen (Alaska).
14. Wihlamok	Beaver Head and
Kicholen	Great Bird
Luchundi wematam	They said, "Let us go!"
Akomen luchundi	"to Akomen!" they said.
16. Nguttichin Iowaniwi	The northerners agreed,
Ngutticin wapaniwi	The easterners agreed,
Agamunk topanpek	Across the icy ocean
Wulliton epannek	was a better place to be.
17. Wulelemil w'shakuppek	on a wondrous sheet of ice
Wemopannek hakhsinipek	all crossed the frozen sea
Kitahikan	at low tide in the
Pokhakhopek	narrows of theocean.
18. Tellenchen kittapakki	Ten times a thousand,
Nillawi	they crossed;
Wemoltin gutikuni	all went forth in a night.
Wemiwi olini	Everyone together.

Verse 16: the Lenape left Asia because of conflict or to seek better living conditions.

BOOK 4

1. Wulamo	Long ago,
Linapioken	The ancient Lenape
Manup	Came to
Shinaking	The evergreen land.
2. Wapallanewa	The White Eagle
Sittamaganat	Had been the path-maker
5. Wemilo	All declared
Kolawil	Kolawil, Noble Elder
Sakima Lissilma	Thou art sachem here.
8. Wrenkolawil	After Kolawil
Sakimanep	The sachem was
Wapagokhos	The White Owl.
9. Wtenknekama	After him
Sakimanep	The sachem was
Janotowi	Constantly
Enolowin	On Guard.
10. Wtenknekama	After him
Sakimanep	The sachem was
Chilili	Chilili the Snow Bird
Shawaniluen	Who spoke of the south.

11. Wokenapi	That our people
Nitaton	would be able
Wullaton	to grow and
Apakchikton	spread there.
12. Shawaniwaen	Southward we went
Wapaniwaen	Eastward we went
Tamakwi	The Beaver
13. Shawanaki	southern country
Kitshinaki	tall pine country
Shabiyaki	seashore country
14. Wapanaki	to eastern country
Namesaki	fishing country
Pemapaki	mountain country
Sisilaki	game herd country
15. Wtenkchilili	After Chilili
Sakimanep	The sachem was
Ayamek	Ayamek, The Seizer
Weminilluk	He slew enemies.
27. Sakimawtenk Penkwonwi	The next sachem was Drought.
28. Attasokelan	There was no rain,
Attaminin	No food to gather;
Wapaniwaen	Eastward they went
Italissipek	to where there was water.
34. Wisawana	By the Yellow River
Lapppiwittank	they settled again.
35. Weminitis Tamenend	Everyone's Friend, Tamanend.
39. Wingenund Sakimanep	The Willing One was the sachem,
Powatanep Gentikalanop	was the shaman at the festivals.
48. Wapagishik	To the Rising Sun
Makelohok	Many were those
Wapaneken	Who eastward went.
54. Talamatan	The Iroquois
Nitilowan	Their northern friends
Payatchik	Then arrived
Wemiten	to join them.
60. Wingelendam	Jubilant were
Wemilennowak	All of the people.
61. Shawanipekis	South of the Great Lakes
Gunehungind	We lit our fires
Lowanipekis	North of the Lakes were
Talamatanitis	our Wyandot friends. (Iroquois)
62. Attalechinitis	But they were not true friends.
63. Linniwulamen Sakimanep	Truthful Man was the sachem
Pallitonep Talamatan	Who fought against the Iroquois.

Shawnee legends tell of long canoe journey, salmon migrations inland from the ocean, and tall evergreens of the northwest.
After Ayamek, other sachem kings were: The Peaceful One, The Blameless One, Constant Love, House Maker, Chastely Loving, Long Lineage, Big Teeth, History Man, Frozen One, Hominy Man, Subdivider, Shriveled Man, Drought, Exhaustion, The Hardened One, The Denouncer, The Beloved One, Tamanend, Mighty Bison, The Great Owl, White Crane, The Willing One, Rich Again, Painted Red, White Chick, Mighty Wolf, Whole-Hearted, Strong is Good, Poor One, East Looking. Lodge Man, Strong Ally, Sharp One, Stirring, Breaking Open, The Crusher, Having Possession, Long in the Woods, Truthful Man, Righteous.
Tamanend the First (v.35) brought the Lenape together in harmony.

BOOK 5

1. Wemilangundo	All was peaceful,
Wulamotalli Talegaking	Long ago, there in Talega country. (Ohio)
2. Tamaganend Sakimanep	The Path Maker was the sachem
Wapalaneng	beside the Shining Stream.
3. Wapashuwi Sakimanep	White Lynx was the sachem
Kelilgeman	growing great crops.
4. Wulitshinik Sakimanep	Fine Forests was the sachem
Makelpannik	the people were many.
5. Lekhihitin Sakimanep	The Author was the sachem
Wallamolumin	Writing the Red Record.
6. Kolachuisen Sakimanep	Pretty Bluebird was the sachem
Makeliming	there were great harvests.
7. Pematallli Sakimanep	Always There was the sachem
Makelinik	the towns were many.
8. Pepomahemen Sakimanep	Navigator was the sachem
Makelaning	along many streams.
9. Tankawon Sakimanep	Little Cloud was the sachem
Makeleyachik	many were those who left.
10. Nentegowi	The Nanticokes and
Shawanowi	The Shawnee
Shawanaking	went to the south land.
11. Kichitamak Sakimanep	Great Beaver was the sachem
Wapahoning	at the White Salt Lick.
12. Onowutok Awolagan	The Prophet, seer of heaven,
Wunkenahep	went westward.
13. Wunkiwikwotank	west, visiting all there.
32. Lappitamenend	Tamanend the Second,
Sakimanepit	Then was the sachem
Wemilangundit	making peace with all.
33. Weminitis	Befriending all,
Wemitakwieken	United them all,
Sakimakichwon	was this great sachem.
40. Wonwihil	For at this time,
Wapekunchi	From the Dawn Sea,
Wapsipayat	The White people appeared.

60. Langomuwak Kitohatewa Ewenikiktit? — Friendly people in great ships Who are they?

The Nanticokes found their way through the Cumberland Gap into Virginia and Maryland. The Shawnee traveled into the South along the valley of the Appalachian Mountains. Other sachems were: Rich Turtle, Traveler, Canoe Master, Hunter in Snow, The Beholder, Eastern Home, Trail Blazer, River Loving, Near Fulfilled, Red Arrow, Good Inscribed, Good Fighter, Tamanend the Second, Great Beaver, Dawn Ground, Harmonizer, Mistaken, Much Honored, Well Praised, White Otter, White Horn, Friend Coming, Cranberry Eating, North Walker, Quite Ready, Calling Retreat, Kindred, Saluted, and White Crab.

In 1610 Captain Samuel Argall called the River of the Lenape the 'Delaware' after the governor of Jamestown, Sir Thomas West, Lord de la Warr. Verse 60 could be referring to a ship of Swedish colonists who sailed the river in 1638.

The FRAGMENT

The Wallamolum was written by Lekhibit to record the glory of the Lenape.

We have had many Sachem Chiefs since that unhappy time when the white men invaded our lands. There were 3 chiefs till the friend of Mikwon (William Penn) came. The first was Mattanikum when the Winakoli (Swedes) came to Winaki (Pennsylvania). The second was Nahumen (Raccoon) when the Hopocani Senalwi (Dutch) came. The third was Palkinap or Ikwahon (Sharp-fighter for Women) when the Yankwis (English) came with Mikwon soon after and his friends. They (Mikon and his friends) were all well received and fed with Corn, but no land was ever sold, we never sold any. They were allowed to live with us, to build houses and plant Corn, as our friends and ally. Because they were hungry and thought Children of Sunland and not Snakes or children of Snakes.

But then the traders came, bringing from Europe fine new iron tools, weapons, cloth and glass beads, which we exchanged Skins, Furs, and wampums (shell beads). We liked the white traders and thought some of their baubles and trinkets were good, made by Children of Sunland. But some of our crafts were better.

After Mikon the children of Dolojo Sakima (King George) came who more land more land we must have, and no limts could be put to their steps and increase.

In the North were the children of Lowi-Sakima (King Louis) and they were our good friends, allies of our allies, foes of our foes, yet Dolojo always wanted to war with them.

We had 3 Sachem Chiefs after Mikwon. 1. Skalichi (Last Tamanend). 2. Sassunam Wikwikhon (Our Uncle Builder). 3. Tatami (Beaver Taker). The last was killed by a Yankwako English Snake, and we vowed revenge.

Netawatwis became chief of all nations in the West, again at Talligewink (Ohio) on the R. Cayahaga, with our old allies the Talamatans (Hurons or Guyandots) and calls all from the East.

Tadescung was chief at the East at Mahoning and bribed by the Yankwis. Tadescung was killed and robbed.

We joined our friend Lowi in war against the Yankwis, but they were strong and took Lowanaki (North land) from Lowi, and came to us in Talegawink when peace was made; and we called them Bigknives, Kichikani (areas around Ohio, Kentucky, and Virginia).

Then Alimi (Whiteeyes) who was also called Coquetakeghton (That Which is Near the Head) and Gelelenund (Buck-killer) were chiefs and all the Indian Nations near us were allies under us or our grandchildren again.

Alimi or Allemewi may have been a sachem who attended Christian services of Moravian missionaires who renamed Alimi 'Solomon'.

Gelelemund and Unaniwi (Turtle Clan chief) were killed and our brothers on Muskingum and Hopokan of the Wolf tribe was made chief and made War on the Kichikani Yankwis rather choosing Dolojo for ally as he was so Strong.

Some thought Whiteyes died of smallpox but some thought he was murdered.

The Delaware wampum records and deeds were stolen by Americans.

We went to Wapahani (White R.) to be farther away, but they follow everywhere. We made peace and settle limits, and our next Chief was Hakhingpomskan (Hard Walker) who was good and peaceful. He would not join our Brother allies Shawanis & Ottawas nor Dolojo in the new war.

After the last peace, the Yankwis came in crowds all around us, and they want again our lands of Wapahani.

Kithtithund and Lapanibi (White Water) were the chiefs of our 2 tribes, when we resolved to exchange our lands and return beyond the Mississippi near to our Ancient Seat.

The Delaware Native American Indians moved west to the James Fork of the White River in Missouri in 1820.

We shall be near our foes the Wakon (Ozages) but they are better than the Yankwiakhon (English Snakers) who want to possess the whole Big Island.

Shall we be free and happy there? At the New Wapahani, We want rest and peace and Wisdom.

JEWISH

Jewish Bible Scriptures derived from the Jewish Torah and Talmud.

The Tanakh (Mikra) is the Hebrew Bible that consists of the Torah (5 books of Moses: Genesis, Exodus, Leviticus, Numbers and Deuteronomy), the Nevi'm (Prophets), and Ketuvim (Writings).

Kabbalah is the mystical Jewish knowledge of trying to understand the relationship between God's creation of the finite universe and humans, and time that is endless and forever. Kabbalah is to appreciate the nature of the universe and life and to wonder about the purpose of all existence.

The word 'God' has been substituted for Jehovah or Yahweh in many verses. 'Jew' means 'Judah' in Hebrew.

The Torah
2200 BCE
Book of GENESIS

In the beginning, God Jehovah created the heavens and the earth. The earth was without form and an empty waste, and darkness was upon the face of the very great deep. The Spirit of God Jehovah moved (hovered) over the face of the waters.

And God said, Let there be light; and there was light.
And God saw that the light was good and gave approval; and God separated the light from the darkness, calling the light Day and the darkness Night. And there was evening and there was morning, one day.

And God said, Let there be a firmament (expanse of sky) in the midst of the waters, and let it separate the waters above from the waters below. And it was so. And God called the firmament Heavens. And there was evening and morning, a second day.

And God said, Let the waters under the heavens be collected into one place and let the dry land appear. And it was so.

God called the dry land Earth, and the accumulated waters were called Seas. And God saw this was good (fitting, admirable) and it was approved.

And God said, Let the earth put forth (tender, manifest) vegetation: plants yielding seed and fruit trees yielding fruit whose seed is in itself, each according to its kind, upon the earth. And it was so.

And God saw the vegetation was good and varied and it was approved. And there was evening and there was morning, a third day.

And God said, Let there be lights in the expanse of the heavens to separate the day from the night, and let them be signs and tokens (of God's provident care) and to mark seasons, days, and years. And let the lights in the expanse of the sky give light upon the earth. And it was so.

And God made the two great lights - the greater light (the sun) to rule the day and the lesser light (the moon) to rule the night. And God made the stars.

And God saw that the lights were good and pleasant and they were approved. And there was evening and morning, a fourth day.

And God said, Let the waters bring forth abundantly and swarm with living creatures, and let birds fly over the earth in the open expanse of the heavens. And God saw it was good and suitable and the creatures were approved.

And God blessed them, the sea creatures and every kind of fowl, and they were fruitful and multiplied upon the earth. And there was evening and morning, a fifth day.

And God said, Let the dry earth bring forth living creatures according to their kinds: livestock, creeping things, wild beasts, and domestic animals according to their kinds. And it was so.

And God saw that it was good and fitting and gave approval.

And God created man in His own image, in the image and likeness of God He created male and female.

And God blessed them and said to them, Be fruitful, multiply and fill the earth, and have dominion over the fish of the sea, the birds of the are, and over every living creature that moves upon the earth.

And God approved of the creatures upon the earth, and there was evening and morning, a sixth day.

Thus the heavens and the earth were finished, and all the host of them.

And on the seventh day, the Spirit of God rested from all work and the creation that was done, and the Lord saw that rest was good, and the Lord blessed and hallowed the part put aside for rest.

This is the history of the heavens and the earth when they were created.

In the day that the Lord made the earth, when no plant or herb had sprung up yet, for the Lord has not caused it to rain yet and there was no man to till the ground.

And there went up a mist (fog, vapor) from the land and watered the whole surface of the ground.

And the Spirit of God formed man from the dust of the ground and breathed into his nostrils the breath or spirit of life, and man became a living soul.

Garden of Eden

And God planted a garden eastward called Eden (delight) and there was put the man that was formed. And out of the ground, every tree was made to grow that was pleasant to the sight or to be desired for food; the tree of life also in the center of the garden, the tree of knowledge subsisting of the difference between good and evil and blessing and calamity.

And a river went out of Eden to water the garden; and from there it divided and became four rivers of four areas: the first was named Pishon; it was the one that flowed around the land of Havilah where there was gold. The gold was of high quality; pearls and onyx stone were there.

The second river was named Gihon; it flowed around the whole land of Cush.

The third river was named Hiddekel (the Tigris); it was the one that flowed east of Assyria. And the fourth river was the Euphrates.

And the Lord told the man in the garden to tend to it and guard and keep it, saying, You will be called Adam which means the earth, and you may eat freely of every tree of the garden, but not of the tree in the center, for that is my tree.

Next the Spirit of the Lord caused a deep sleep to fall upon Adam; and while he slept, the Lord took one of his ribs or a part of his side and closed up the part with flesh.

And the rib or a part of his side was built up into a woman, and her nostrils were also filled with the breath of life, and the Lord's Spirit guided the woman to Adam.

And the Spirit of the Lord came upon Adam and he said, This woman is now bone of my bones and flesh of my flesh, and she shall be called woman because she was taken out of man. Therefore shall a man leave his father and his mother and shall cleave unto his wife, and they shall be one flesh.

And the man and his woman were both naked and were not embarrassed or ashamed in each other's presence.

And so Adam was a man and Eve was a woman, and the two loved each other. The Lord told them to eat of all the fruits of the earth, but not to eat the forbidden fruit of the tree of knowledge.

Then the serpent was more subtle than any beast the Lord had made. The serpent who was Satan in disguise tempted Eve to eat from the tree of knowledge; and Eve was weak of spirit to resist and she was beguiled by the serpent. She ate of the fruit of knowledge and gave some to her husband Adam and he ate also.

They soon realized they were naked and covered their bodies with fig leaves. They heard the voice of the Lord walking in the garden in the cool of the day and they hid themselves among the trees.

And the Lord called upon Adam: Where art thou?

Adam said: I heard thy voice in the garden and because I was naked, I hid.

And God said Who told thee that thou was naked? Has thou eaten of the tree that I forbad thee to eat?

And the man said, The woman whom thou gavest to be with me, she gave me of the tree, and I did eat.

And the Lord God said unto the woman, What is this that thou hast done? And the woman said, The serpent beguiled me and I did eat.

And the Lord said to the serpent You are cursed above all cattle and every beast of the field, and upon thy belly thou shalt go and dust shalt thou eat all the days of your life.

God said I will put enmity between the serpent and the woman, and between thy seed and her seed; thou shall bruise thy head, and thou shalt bruise his heel. Unto thy woman God said In sorrow shall you bring forth your children, and thy desire shall be to your husband, and he shall rule over thee.

And unto Adam God said: Because thou has hearkened unto the voice of thy wife, and has eaten of the tree of which I commanded thee not to eat of, cursed is the ground for thy sake, in sorrow shalt thou eat of it all the days of thy life. Thorns, thistles, and herbs will the ground bring. In the sweat of thy face shalt thou eat bread, till thou return unto the ground, for out of it was thou taken; for dust thou art and unto dust shalt thou return. And Adam called his wife Eve which means mother of all living. Unto Adam and Eve the Lord made coats of skins and clothed them. The Lord said, Behold the man has become like us, knowing good from evil, and now, lest he put forth his hand, and take of the tree of life, and eat, and live forever.

Therefore the Lord sent him from the garden of Eden to till the ground from whence he came. Then God placed at the east of the garden of Eden Cherubims and a flaming sword which turned every way to keep the way of the tree of life.

Lucifer Satan dwelled in heaven for more than five hundred thousand years before God expelled him because Satan was rebellious and wanted to overthrow God; Satan would not accept the reality of the heavenly Lord. Then Satan dwelled in Hell, a God forsakened (abandoned) place.

Adam and Eve had three sons and called them Cain, Abel, and Seth. The three sons loved each other and only wanted the best for each other. The Lord loved

Cain, Abel, and Seth equally, even though the three were talented in different ways. Cain like to work the fields and plant crops, Abel was interested in milking the cows, making cheese and tending to goats, and Seth was interested in woodworking and building houses. An angel of the Lord Jehovah spoke a revelation unto Cain, Abel, and Seth saying: 'My precious children, I love all of you equally. I have given each of you special uniqueness and life. Follow Me and you will have eternal life, for all good souls are a part of Me.' And Adam lived 930 years.

In the Nephilim theory, the interpretation is that Eve had sex with Satan and Cain was born. Cain made a cereal offering of sacrifice to Jehovah and Abel offered fatty meats; then Jehovah told Cain that Abel's sacrifice was greater, so Cain killed Abel out of jealousy. But Cain had a conscience and he was grieved; God said that no one should hurt Cain. Cain's children became the seedline of Satan; the daughters of men of Cain's line mated with the sons of God of Seth's line and the Nephilim race was produced; the Nephilim were giants who inhabited Canaan.

And the Jews celebrated Rosh Hashanah each year (also called Yom Teruah) to celebrate the creation of Adam and Eve. A shofar (ram's horn) was blown so it is also called the Feast of the Trumpets. And honey was eaten on apples to hope for a 'sweet new year'. 'Shalom' means peace.

Noah and the Flood

This is the story of the genealogy leading up to the life of Noah.

Seth was the father of Enosh, and Seth had other sons and daughters.

Enosh was the father of Kenan, and Enosh had other sons and daughters.

Kenan was the father of Mahalalel, and Kenan had other sons and daughters.

Mahalalel was the father of Jared, and Mahalalel had other sons and daughters.

Jared was the father of Enoch, and Jared had other sons and daughters.

Enoch was the father of Methuselah, and Enoch walked with God and had other sons and daughters. Then God took Enoch away.

Methuselah was the father of Lamech, and Lamech had other sons and daughters.

Methuselah lived 969 years.

And Lamech was the father of Noah, and Noah was the father of Shem, Ham, and Japheth.

There was going to be a great deluge, a flood upon the Earth and it would rain for 40 days and 40 nights, so God told Noah, who was a descendant of Adam, that Noah would help preserve life for future generations.

God told Noah when Noah was 600 years old to build an ark and fill it with every living thing in pairs because a flood was coming.

Noah filled the ark with his family and friends, and pairs of animals, male and female. When they finally boarded the ark and closed the gate, they prayed to God to be delivered from the mighty scourge. They lived in the ark for one year and 10 days. A giraffe stepped on the foot of Noah's wife, who was called Nell, when she was feeding the animals in the ark, and her foot hurt. Noah gave her a stick so she could balance herself when she stood until her foot healed.

Then Noah sent forth from the ark a raven that flew back and forth but returned to the ark. Then Noah sent forth a dove named Columba, and the dove came back also. Noah waited seven days and sent forth the dove again. The dove came back to Noah with a newly sprouted and freshly plucked olive branch so Noah knew the waters had subsided. Noah waited seven more days and sent forth the dove again. The dove did not return to him again, so Noah knew it was time to release the animals from the ark.

The ark came to rest upon a mountain called Mount Ararat and Noah opened the doors of the ark and lowered the ramp. The animals came out of the boat vessel and down the ramp and multiplied upon the Earth. Noah was 600 years old when the flood of waters came upon the earth or land.

God told Noah that the bow in the sky (the rainbow) would be a sign of a covenant with the people on earth to remind them that God is real and watches over the earth.

Noah planted a seed from the Garden of Eden that his grandfather Methuselah gave him before the flood. And Noah built a vineyard. He harvested the grapes and made grape juice for children and wine for adults. Noah also built a tower called Babel, so decrees could be called out to all in the land. It was said that God called out from the Tower of Babel to confound the languages of the earth so that no nation could become stronger than God.

One time Noah was drunk and his children found him naked, so his sons Shem and Japhth covered up Noah's nakedness; when Noah woke up he was embarrassed when his sons told him what they had seen.

Some told accounts of Noah's brother who was called Jed; Jed ventured on the ark to help Noah continue life on earth after the flood.

Noah lived after the flood 350 years. All the days of Noah were 950 years, and he died.

The origin of the Noah and the flood account is uncertain. Some people thought the great flood broke the one giant continent on the earth into the seven continents, dispersing the people of the earth which would separate them for thousands of years until humans figured out how to build boats which would enable explorations.

Scientists concluded that over thousands of years, humans developed genetic dominances of human traits in different temperature zones of the earth and different languages on various parts of the earth.

Abraham 2166-1991 BCE

This is an account of only some of the things that happened.

Terah was a descendant eight generations from Shem in the middle-eastern lands of Arabia. Terah's children were Abraham, Nahor, and Haran; they all went forth together from the city of commerce called Ur of the Chaldees and ventured into the land of Canaan. There were 20 generations from Adam to Abraham. Abraham had a spirit of discontent and thought he was created for more; he thought this is not what God intended me to do and Abraham sought a place of yonder, where the Lord would guide him; the Lord appeared to him 7 times and the Lord saved Abraham (also called Abram) from a life of destruction.

The Lord said to Abram, 'Go from your country, your people and your father's household, to the land I will show you. I will make you into a great nation, and I will bless you. I will make your name great, and you will be a blessing.'

Abraham sojourned through the land and pitched his tent on a mountain; the mountain was east of Bethel and west of Ai.

Abraham loved the Lord and built an altar; then Abraham placed a lighted candle on the altar in affirmation of the Lord. Abraham called the name of the altar The Lord Will Provide. And it is said to this day, on the mount of the

Lord that it will be provided. Melchizedek king of Salem brought out bread and wine; he was the priest of God Most High. He blessed Abraham and said, 'Blessed be Abram by God Most High, Possessor and Maker of heaven and earth. The Lord said there is no peace for the wicked; the sins of humans will withhold the good things from them. Those who seek the Lord will inherit the earth and find peace. Love your neighbor as yourself and whatsoever you hate - do to no one. Love each other as I love my children.
The path of the just is as a shining light which shines more and more until the perfect day. Those who turn to righteousness, let them return to me, and I will have mercy on them.' From thirty years old and upward, even to the age of 50, Melchizedek priests served in the tent of the meeting.

And Melchizedek missionaries ventured to Persia, Egypt, India, China and other parts of the world to teach about the Lord. The Lord Jehovah told Abraham 'I am your Shield and abundant compensation, and your reward shall be exceedingly great. I will multiply the Jewish people on the earth like the stars of the heavens and like the sand on the seashores.'

Isaac and Ishmael (Ismail)
2066-1886 BCE

Abraham's first wife was named Sarai, who could not conceive a child at first. So, then Sarai gave Abraham her mistress who was named Hagar, so that Abraham could have a child. Abraham knew Hagar, an Egyptian bondwoman who was Sarai's maid, and a son named Ishmael was born; this was when Abraham was 86 years old.

Sarai and Hagar had jealousy between them after Hagar conceived, and their bond was broken, and Hagar fled.

Hagar was by the well called Beer-lahai-roi between Kadesh and Bered. The name of the well means A Well to the Living One Who sees me. An angel of the Lord told Hagar that both Hagar and Sarai would have sons and both would be blessed with descendants as multiple as the stars in the universe.

Years later Sarai and Abraham did have a son of their own named Isaac which means Laughter; Sarai was 90 years old and Abraham was 100 years old when Isaac was born. The Lord told Abraham to change Sarai's name to Sarah. Then, Sarah told Abraham that Ishmael would not be counted in the tribes for inheritances and only Isaac would be an heir in their region which was called Canaan.

Now Hagar was dismayed that Ishmael her son was not to be included in the inheritance of Abraham's tribe (because Hagar was not Abraham's wife), but the angel of the Lord reassured Hagar that Ishmael would be blessed in another land. And, then Hagar, the mother of Ishmael (Ismail), prayed for water in the wilderness of Beersheba and found water at the Zamzam spring by the hills of Safa and Marwah near the city of Makkah (Mecca). Abraham planted a tamarisk tree at the well.

Lot (son of Haran)

Abraham and his nephew Lot were herding their sheep when Lot was captured by enemy war kings, but Abraham's forces went and fought against the enemy forces and were able to rescue Lot.

Sodom and Gomorrah Destroyed

Sodom and Gomorrah were cities that became filled with sin and wicked ways; many avoided the cities like they avoided the plague. The people were committing crimes and fornication was rampant; there was murder and disease. The citizens were not taking care of their cities and there was chaos and confusion and no civility, and then Sodom and Gomorrah burned down, some thought in a drunken brawl when candles were overturned in the tavern and a fire started.

Lot and his 2 daughters escaped the fire, but Lot's wife looked back as she was escaping, and she was turned into a pillar of salt.

Lot and his 2 daughters stayed in a cave after Sodom and Gomorrah burned down.

Then Lot's two daughters slept with their father when he was drunk on two different nights and both conceived; they bore sons.

There was great chaos in the lands after Sodom and Gomorrah burned down when God destroyed them.

Sarai buried at Cave Machpelah

Sarai died at the age of 127 in Kiriatharba, that is Hebron, in the land of Canaan.

Ephron sold a field and a cave to Abraham for 400 shekels in order that Abraham would have a place to bury Sarai. And Abraham buried her in the cave called Machpelah.

Then Abraham took as a wife Ketorah, and she bore him Zimran, Jokshan, Medan, Midian, Ishbak, and Shuah.

Gideon

Gideon also loved the Holy Spirit of Jehovah and offered prayers and fleece wool offerings shaved from his sheep upon the altar.

Gideon was a judge, military leader, and prophet of the region where he lived and he also grew wheat. Gideon named his first son Jether which means 'abundance and prosperity'.

Gideon was the son of Joash from the Abiezite clan in the tribe of

Manasseh who lived in Ephra (Ophrah).

An angel caused Gideon to become aware of his nearness to the Holy Spirit after the destruction of Sodom and Gomorrah, and spoke to him and gave him sacred knowledge, thus said Gideon to the people when he spoke from the heights of the Tower of Babel so all below could hear: 'Just as one threshes the wheat to separate the grain from the chaff, separate thyself from all ways that are not of faithfulness, diligence and integrity in every way. This is a spiritual principle.' Gideon also had a son named Abimelech by a maid servant.

Bramble Bush Parable

When Gideon died, the people forgot to worship the Lord of Israel and they began to worship the Philistine god Baal and goddess Ashtaroth. Abimelech murdered 70 of his brothers because he wanted to be king but Jotham escaped. His brother Jotham told a parable of the low bramble bush. They said, the olive tree did not want to leave its fatness, the fig tree did not want to leave its sweetness, the grapevine did not want to leave its new wine, but Gideon, our father, was a bramble bush who served the people – he fought for you and led you because he is your kinsmen – but now you have forgotten to take refuge in the shade of the Lord.

The Twelve Tribes of Ishmael became the Muslim religion around 632CE

The twelve sons of Ismael who were called the twelve princes according to their tribes of Nebaioth, Kedar, Adbeel, Mibsam, Mishma, Dumah, Massa, Hadad, Tema, Jetur, Naphish, and Kedemah. The daughter of Ishmael was called Mahalath. The twelve princes lived in lands before Egypt in the direction of Assyria. Ismael became an archer in the wilderness near Mount Paran and his wife was Egyptian.

When Abraham died at the age of 175, Isaac and Ismael buried him in the cave called Machpelah where his first wife, Sarai, was buried.

And Ismael lived 137 years.

Isaac marries Rebekah; Twelve Tribes of Israel are derived from their son Jacob to form the Jewish religion

Abraham had directed his servant to find a wife for his son Isaac, and the servant took ten of his master's camels and journeyed, taking some of his master's treasures with him. That evening, he made his camels to kneel down outside the city by a well of water at the time of the evening that the women went to draw water.

And the servant prayed let it be that the maiden that offers me a little water to drink that she be

the one to be the wife for Isaac. So Rebekah came with her water jar on her shoulder and offered him a drink of water and his camels a drink also.
Rebekah was beautiful and attractive, chaste and modest, and unmarried; she was the daughter of Bethuel who was the son of Milcah. Milcah was the wife of Nahor who was the brother of Abraham. Rebekah was the cousin of Isaac. The servant blessed the God of Abraham who led him to his master's brother's grand-daughter to be Isaac's wife, and he placed earrings on her ears and bracelets on her arms. Now Bethuel told the servant that he could not speak on the matter for his daughter, but Rebekah should speak for herself. So Rebekah said she would go to be Isaac's wife.

And the servant Eliezer brought out jewels of silver and gold, and garments and gave them to Rebekah for her ransom (mohar). He also gave precious things to her brother and her mother. The servant also gave Rebekah a veil (scarf, mantle) that she could wear around her head if a whirlwind (sandstorm) should stir up the desert sands, then the cloth would keep the sand out of her eyes, nose, mouth, and ears.

And Isaac and his wife named Rebekah loved each other inside of their tent; and their two sons were Jacob and Esau.

Esau married Judith, Basemath, and Mahalath.
Mahalath was Ishmael's daughter.
Esau also married
Adah, and Oholibamah. The descendants of Esau were called Edomites.

Jacob 2006-1859 BCE

Jacob had a dream of a ladder that reached to heaven, and the angels of the Lord were ascending and descending on it; and the Lord told Jacob that all the families of the earth would multiply and be blessed.
And Jacob arose in the morning and took the stone that he had put under his head as a pillow to sleep on, and he poured oil on its top. He named the altar place Bethel and made a vow, saying, If God will be with me and will keep me in this way that I go and will give me food to eat and clothing to wear, so that I may live in peace, I set this stone up as a sacred place for all that the Lord gives me and I will give back. The Lord told Jacob that his new name was Israel.

Then Jacob traveled 400 miles to the east, where he met Leah and Rachel,the daughters of Laban, his mother's brother, who was a descendant of Nahor, who was Abraham's brother. And Jacob took his two cousins Leah and Rachel as his wives, but he loved Rachel more. Leban said, It is not permitted in our country to give the younger in marriage before the elder. Finish the week of the wedding feast for Leah. Then we will give you Rachel, and you shall work for me yet seven years more. And Laban showed Jacob how to separate their flocks with rods at the watering trough because they did not want the white sheep to breed and conceive with the black sheep or the speckled sheep because the rug weavers wanted white wool to color the fibers with fruit juice and rock pigment. Jacob told Laban that he was willing to be paid in speckled or black sheep.

A pillar of peace called a mizpah was built by Jacob and his father-in-law, Laban, as a witness of peace between them. Laban said that the Lord would watch as a witness between them when they were absent from one another and the Lord would know their actions.

At first, Rachel was barren and was not conceiving a child, so she gave her maid Bilhah to Jacob to conceive a child.Bilhah gave birth to sons Dan and Naphtali. For Jacob, Leah gave birth to sons Reuben, Simeon, Levi, Judah, Zebulun, and Dinah, a daughter. Leah's maid named Zilpah was given to Jacob and their sons were Gad, Asher, and Issacher. Then, Rachel conceived and gave birth to sons Joseph and Benjamin.

Joseph sold into slavery

Joseph told his brothers a dream he had about their work in the fields binding sheaves; he told his brothers that their sheaves bowed down to his. His brothers asked Joseph 'What is the meaning of your dream, shall you rule over us?' And they hated Joseph for his dream.

And one day in the fields they noticed a string of camels coming toward them, a company of Ishmaelites from Gilead bearing spicery and balm and myrrh, carrying it down to Egypt. And the older brothers sold Joseph as a slave to Potiphar of the Ishmaelites for 20 pieces of silver and he was taken to Egypt, but Reuben was the good brother who tried to stop the sale. The brothers told Jacob their father, who was also called Israel, that a beast had eaten Joseph. Jacob mourned for the profound loss of his son.

Judah was a brother of Joseph; Judah married Tamar. Tamar had twins; when the babies were born, the midwife put a scarlet ribbon around the wrist of the firstborn who was called Zerah so the birth of the oldest would be known; the oldest had the birthright to the family inheritance. Perez was born second.

Joseph was treated well by the Egyptian Pharoah and given the Pharoah's daughter Asenath to be his wife; their sons were Ephraim and Manasseh. Joseph acquired wealth while living in Egypt and was made a governor.

Joseph interpreted a dream that the Pharoah had about 7 good grains of corn and 7 bad grains of corn to be there would be 7 years of plentiful crops and then 7 years of famine, so the Pharoah knew to set aside grain during the 7 plentiful years so there would be food during the 7 years of famine. There were plagues of locusts and sometimes frogs. During a time of seven years of famine in Israel, Jacob sent his sons to Egypt to buy food. The brothers came upon the fields of Joseph but did not recognize their brother, but Joseph recognized them. Joseph was glad to see his brother Benjamin and wept, and the brothers hugged each other.

Joseph sent to his father by way of his brothers ten donkeys loaded with the good things of Egypt, grain, bread, and nourishing food.

When the brothers told their father Jacob that they had found Joseph alive and prosperous, Jacob said 'It is enough! Joseph my son is alive and well. I will go see him before I die.'

So Jacob who was called Israel made his journey to Egypt with the Israelites because it was the time of famine; the Israelites were seventy in number those who went to dwell in Egypt. And Joseph presented his father Jacob to the Pharoah, who welcomed Jacob and gave them the best of the land of Goshen to dwell in, and Jacob blessed the Pharoah. Jacob told his son Joseph,

'I had not thought I would see your face again, but see, the Lord has shown me your offspring also.'

And Joseph provided for and supported his brothers and their offspring, and his father.

During a time of famine and drought, when the ravens had flown away to find water because smaller streams had dried up, Joseph took corn from his grain storehouse and put the corn in baskets and let them float down the river to help feed others.

Now when Jacob was about to die, he begged Joseph to take his body back to Canaan to be buried, and so he did bury Jacob in the cave at Machpelah. Joseph did return back to Egypt.

Then Joseph's brethren saw that their father was dead and said, Perhaps now Joseph will pay us back for all the evil we did to him.

And his brothers went before him and bowed down to Joseph, saying, 'We are your slaves! Forgive us our trespasses.' But Joseph wept and said to them, 'Fear not, for the Holy Spirit of the Lord is watching over us.' And Joseph did not take revenge on his brothers but said 'Good came out of it as many of us were kept alive from the famine.' Joseph became known as a mensch for he had brains, heart, integrity, and bravery.

Joseph told his brethren, I am going to die. But God will bring you out of this land back to the land of Abraham, Isaac, and Jacob who was called Israel.

Book of EXODUS

Moses 1526 BCE

Amram was a man of the house of Levi who took as his wife Jochebed, who was a daughter of the tribe of Levi.
Now Jochebed was fishing in the river, when she realized her baby's cradle had drifted away and floated down the river.
So Moses was a Jewish infant boy that was found floating in a river by the daughter of an Egyptian pharoah king; she was bathing in the river. The daughter of the pharaoh kindly returned Moses to his mother, Jochebed, who frantically travelled the road along the river to find Moses her infant child. Jochebed came across the women Judith and Tamaria who went with her. Along the path they came across Balak and his donkey Balaam; the donkey spoke saying 'keep looking.' Finally, they came to the place where the pharaoh's daughter was sitting outside the palace holding the baby; she was pleased that Jochebed had found Moses. Moses had a brother Aaron and a sister Miriam. In one version the pharaoh's daughter raised Moses.

The Israelites' Exodus from Egypt to the land of Canaan 1446-1406 BCE

Now the Israelites were in Egypt to avoid a time of famine, but 430 years later Moses and the Israelites journeyed back to the land of Israel in an exodus. About 600,000 Israelites journeyed on foot from Rameses to Succoth, mixed with a multitude of livestock, both flocks and herds, carrying baskets of unleavened bread on their shoulders.
Some of the Israelites had been slaves for the Egyptians. On the first night after the Passover from Egypt, they baked matzo which are unleavened cakes of dough which they brought from Egypt; it was unleavened because they had left with no time to delay; they also ate a paschal lamb and bitter herbs. On the second night they ate barley also. They built a sukkah (a walled booth structure covered with leafy plants and palm leaves) as their dwelling in the desert wilderness.
The menorah, a seven-branched lampstand in which olive oil was burned, provided light at night in the desert.

So, the Israelites passed over from Egypt back to the land of the Canaanites of Israel. And the Lord led them during the day in a pillar of cloud and at night by a pillar of fire, all the way back to Canaan. And along the way Moses and the people sang a song, saying The Lord is My Strength and My Song, My Salvation, this is my God, and I will praise the Lord.

Pharaoh Thothmes of Memphis, Egypt (around 1540 BCE) did not want the descendants of Ephraim and Manasseh, sons of the Pharaoh's daughter Asenath and Joseph (son of Jacob), to leave the land of Egypt because he would

miss them; he said 'I do not want to let my people go away from me!' Moses and Pharaoh Rameses prayed together in unity before Moses left Egypt to go back to the land of the Israelites. At Mount Horeb,
God made a covenant for a safe return to Israel.

But Moses led the people back to the land of Israel and even through a shallow part of Red Sea, the waters parted by the command of God spoken through Moses so his people who were the Hebrews could cross over the bottom of the river to the other shore of dry land. The Israelites called him 'Holy Moses'.

The people encamped in the wilderness; the Israelites had no food along the way but they remembered the fish, cucumbers, melons, leeks, onions, garlic, coriander seed, and cakes made with fish oil or meat that were plentiful in Egypt. Scouts were sent out from the encampments to find lands of milk and honey; this is its fruit. The Israelites cried to Moses 'Our souls are drying up'. Moses led the Israelites in prayer because they had no food, and God miraculously brought forth manna in the field for food to sustain them; the manna glistened on top of the ground like the dew in the early morning. Once the Israelites made an altar in the middle of the wilderness and made a burnt offering of an animal sacrifice of a ram and a lamb to the Lord; they prayed before they ate the meat.
And in the wilderness Moses and the people tried to keep to ways of cleanliness. Some Israelites complained about the harshness of the wilderness and the Lord sent snakes to bite them.
Moses killed a vagabond wayfarer who tried to harm his people.

Moses marries Zipporah

When Moses and the Israelites left Egypt and dwelled in the land of Midian, he met Jethro the priest.
Jethro had seven daughters and he gave Zipporah, one of his daughters to Moses.
Moses had two sons with Zipporah; she bore him two sons named Gershom and Eliezer.

God's voice speaks to Moses

They journeyed 52 days from the land of Goshen past the towns of Succoth, Marah, Elim, Rephidim to Mount Sinai.
Moses was tending the flock of Jethro and led it across the wilderness near Horeb or Sinai, the mountain of God when the Angel of the Lord appeared to Moses in a flame of fire out of the midst of a bush; and Moses looked but behold the bush was burning but was not consumed; there was a voice but no form. And the Lord God Jehovah said 'Moses, I am the Lord of Abraham. I have chosen you to lead my people. I AM WHO I AM. I

AM THE HOLY SPIRIT. Know my commandments; bind them on your hearts with a seal, for they are a covenant with my people for all ages. The Lord your God will bring you into the land which he swore to your forefathers Abraham, Isaac, and Jacob for their inheritance. Hear, Israel, the Lord is your God and you must love your God with all your heart and with all your soul and with all your strength. You are the children of the Lord your God. I will take you to Me for a people, and I will be to you a God; and you shall know that it is I, the Lord your God, who will give you the land of Canaan as heritage and a holy land.'

' Teach these commandments (mitzvot) to your children also, and it will be a blessing for you if you follow them.'

The Mosaic Decalogue
The Ten Commandments:

(1) I am your God Jehovah; there shall be no other gods before Me.
(2) Love your neighbor as yourself.
(3) Thou shall not take the name of the Lord in vain.
(4) Keep holy the Sabbath, a rest day.
(5) Honor your mother and father.
(6) Thou shall not kill.
(7) Thou shall not commit adultery.
(8) Thou shall not steal or act slyly.
(9) Thou shall not bear false witness against your neighbor.
(10) Thou shall not covet thy neighbor's goods, servants, wife or husband.

If you listen diligently to the voice of the Lord your God, being watchful to do all the commandments, the Lord your God will set you high above the earth. If you do not follow the commandments your soul will find rest in Sheoul. Cursed is the one who does not support and uphold good laws; Jews who follow the good laws are God's chosen ones.

And all blessings shall come upon you and overtake you if you heed the good ways of the Lord.

Blessed shall you be in the city and blessed shall you be in the field.

Blessed shall be the fruit of your body and the fruit of your ground and the fruit of your beasts, the increase of your cattle and the young of your flock.

Blessed shall be your basket and your kneading trough.

Blessed shall you be when you come in and blessed shall you be when you go out.

Cursed is the person who moves back his neighbor's line.

Cursed is the person who misleads a blind man the wrong way.

Cursed is the person who dishonors an innocent one or takes a bribe to slay him.

Cursed is the man who lies with his sister, his half-sister, his mother, his children, or another man's wife.

Cursed is the woman who lies with her brother, her half-brother, her father, her children, or another woman's husband.

Whoever kidnaps a man, whether he sells him or is found in his possession, shall surely be put to death.

Whoever curses his mother or father or strikes his servant shall be punished.

If a servant is injured so that an eye or a tooth is injured, then the servant shall be set free.

If men contend with each other and a pregnant woman injured in the circumstance and she has a miscarriage, the man who hurt her shall be punished with a fine paid to the woman's husband, as much as the judges determine.

If a man leaves a pit open and does not cover it and an ox or a donkey falls into it, the owner of the pit shall make it good and shall give shekels (money) to the animal's owner if the ox or donkey cannot be taken out of the pit.

If a thief steals money and is found, he shall pay double.

If you lend money to My people with you who is poor, you shall not be to him as a creditor charging interest.

If you take your neighbor's garment or plow as a pledge, you shall return it by sundown.

You shall do no evil nor shall you follow a crowd to do evil.

You shall not bear false witness at a trial to pervert justice.

Do not be a schmuck (a foolish person) but be wise and have good behavior.

Be strong, courageous, and firm; fear not nor be in terror before the world, for it is the Lord your God Who goes with you; God will not fail you or forsake you.

God is the Rock and the work of all perfection and justice and has many Names.

NAMES for JEHOVAH

Yahweh – The Lord
Elohim – The Lord is good
Elyon – The Lord God Most High
El-Shaddai – The Almighty God
Jireh – The Lord will provide
Repheka – The Lord is healer
Tsidqenu – The Lord is our righteousness
Tsebaoth – The Lord of Hosts
Nissi – The Lord is conqueror
Shalom – The Lord is peace
Shamah – The Lord is there

Remember the days of old; consider the years of many generations of those before you. Your elders will tell you about the goodness of the Lord, so you tell your children.

There is none like God. Your God goes with you wherever you go, God is even in your heart and mind, that all people of the earth may know that the hand of the lord is mighty and strong and that you may revere the Lord your God forever. May peace go with you in your hearts. And

Moses wrote these things in the Book of the Covenant to read to the people.
Aaron gathered gold from the people; they gave Aaron the gold rings from their hands and ears and Aaron melted the gold and fashioned a molten calf to be placed on an altar, but Moses destroyed the molten calf; Moses melted it and said it was sinful because God cannot be seen.

Once when there was no water, Moses and the Israelites prayed to God Jehovah for water; Moses struck a rock and water gushed forth for the people to drink. This was in the area near Kadesh Barnea. Kadesh means 'holy' and Barnea means 'desert wandering place'. Twelve spies were sent out to spy near Paran and the land of Canaan.

Book of LEVITICUS

Tent of the Meeting

And a Tent of the Meeting was put up for Testimony for the Lord. And an Angel of the Lord appeared in a pillar of a cloud at the Tent Door before Moses, Aaron, and Miriam, saying: 'Hear My Words; if there will be a prophet among you, I the Lord will make Myself known to him in a vision and speak to him in a dream.' After that, Miriam became white as snow and was set aside for 7 days until she could recover from hearing the Voice of God. And so a prophet was a dreamer of dreams who gives signs and wonders.

Thenafter, Moses wore a veil (scarf) before praying to Jehovah.

The Jewish Pentecost or Shavuot will be a feast to celebrate the Law that was given on Mount Sinai.

Bezalel and Aholiab prepared curtains of goat's hair with loops and golden clasps. Clasps of bronze coupled the tent covering that was made from ram skins tanned red and also dolphin and porpoise skins.
Boards of acacia wood were made for the ark of the commandments. Blue, purple, and scarlet veils were made to screen the doors of the Ark and the entrance to the Tent of the Meeting. Gold, silver, and bronze artistic designs were devised. Onyx stones, oil, fragrant spices, and incenses were set. A perpetual burning oil was lit. Angel cherubims, beings that had human faces but had wings like eagles and who sit on thrones in heaven, were made from gold for both sides of the mercy seat of the Rabbi.

Garments were made for Aaron the priest consisting of long white robes with a shawl containing tassels and blue stripes. Turbans and yarmulke (kippah, kipa prayer caps) were made for the head with the inscription Holy To The Lord. A crown of jewels was made and attached to the turban. Wearing caps outside of the synagogue became a custom (ritual). Black boxes containing scrolls of prayers were strapped to the foreheads of the holy Jewish men of Israel. Rituals of the priest were performed behind a veil curtain. Pomegranates and bells were sewn to the bottom of the priestly robes, and a rope was tied to the priest's ankles in case the priest fainted or died and had to be drawn out from behind the veil curtain. A test of fidelity was performed by a priest who stirred dust into holy water behind the veil curtain; a person was required to drink the dusty water and if their body swelled, they were guilty of the iniquity of sin.

The women and men should be separated when they came to the Tent of the Meeting. The women were not permitted to look the men in the eye.

Those who were 20 years or older were to bring sacrifices of silver, gold, bronze, cereal, honey, or fruit for sins, peace, thanks, or worship offerings. Every cereal offering was to be seasoned with salt, a sign of preservation, and the salt of the covenant of God Jehovah was not to be lacking. The offerings were for Jehovah; do not rob Jehovah.

A trumpet was to be blown at the tabernacle of the tent when the service started and at the giving of the offerings.

Some brought animal sacrifices but Moses said it was not necessary, that animal sacrifices were only to be for food. The ancient rite of animal sacrifice was replaced with gifts of personal sacrifice such as offering oils, fruits, grains, coins, time, and labor.

For hundreds of years the two stone tablets of The Decalogue were kept in a box made from acacia wood called the Ark of the Testament which was sometimes carried to different cities on poles during times of war. The Levites were the tribe of Israel that guarded the Ark for the Jewish religion.

Eventually the Ark was put on wheels to make it easier to transport it around to religious services. There was a time when a bystander reached out to steady the Ark as it was going over a bump on the dirt road to prevent the Ark from falling over; the person was trying to help; it was written that he was killed by the Holy Spirit just for touching the Ark. So David was afraid of the Ark of the Covenant and left the Ark for 3 months in the house of Obed the Gittite who was born in Gath.

There were assemblages of the Israelites at Mizpah in Ephraim, from Dan to Beersheba, Adora, and Hebron, including the land of Gilead, the land of Reuben, the land of Issachar to the north, and as far north as Tyre in the land of Asher.

The Ten Commandments were later written into a book called the Holy Torah. The priest Eleazor led assemblages at Mt. Pisgah and Mt. Peor.

The Acts of Jewish Devotion included 3 opening benedictions of praise (1-3 below), 13 petition blessings (4-16), and 3 concluding benedictions of Thanksgiving.

Acts of Devotion

(1) Avot: God of our Father
(2) Gevurot: the Mighty God
(3) Qedushat Hashem: the sanctification of God
(4) Binah: for understanding
(5) Teshuvah: for repentance
(6) Selihah: for forgiveness
(7) Ge'ulah: for redemption
(8) Refu'ah: for healing
(9) Hashanim: for natural abundance
(10) Qibbuts Galuyot: for the ingathering of the Exile
(11) Mishpat: for the establishment of justice
(12) Haminim: for the destruction of the oppression
(13) Tzaddikim: for the righteous
(14) Yerushalayim: for the rebuilding of Jerusalem
(15) David: for the advent of the Messiah
(16) Tefilah: that our prayer will be heard
(17) Avodah: for the restoration of the temple
(18) Hoda'ah: our expression of gratitude
(19) Kohanim: the prayer for peace

Amidah: the devotion par excellence

If a man or woman is brought before the priest with a sore or a scab on their skin, then after the seventh day, if the scab is still there the man or woman may be quarantined. But after seven more days, if the scab is still there and has spread, the person is unclean and shall live alone outside the camp and their house will be declared unclean and shut up.

But if it is pronounced by the priest that the person is clean and has healed and may return to the camp, the priest shall command for two living clean birds and cedar wood and scarlet cloth and hyssop mint to be gathered. Then one of the birds may be killed over an earthen vessel (jar) over fresh water. And the living bird, the cedar wood, the scarlet cloth, and the hyssop mint shall be dipped in the vessel. The person who has been healed of the scabs may be sprinkled with the blood; then shall let go the living bird free to fly into the open field. Then the house of the lepor may be examined; if there is no disease of dark green or red spots in the plaster of the wall then sprinkle the inside of the house with the blood seven times. But if there are dark green or red spots in the plaster of the house, the house is unclean and should be torn down and carried away outside the city.

If a woman bears a male child, she is unclean for seven days. If a woman bears a female child, she is unclean for fourteen days. She shall bring an oil or grain offering and then she shall be clean.

On her monthly discomfort, she shall be separated until she is clean again.

Anyone who touches a dead animal or person or blood is unclean and must be washed with holy water; then they are unclean until sundown.

Book of NUMBERS
Population Numbers of Twelve Tribes of Israel

Moses counted twelve tribes of Jacob's (Israel) family as: Reuben, Simeon, Judah, Gad, Issacher, Zebulun, Naphtali, Benjamin, Dan, Asher, and Joseph's half-Egyptian sons Ephraim and Manasseh. Dinah, the daughter, was not given her own tribe. Levi was to be the tribe of the Jewish religion. The twelve tribes were the Mosaic tribes of the Jews and 12 rods were put into the Ark of the Testimony; Aaron's rod blossomed.

Moses told the sons of one tribe who could not agree on how to divide their work; Sons of Israel, to my right hand are the ones who will water the sheep and to my left hand are the ones who will bring in the sheaves; but tomorrow it will be that those who watered the sheep today will gather the sheaves and those who gathered the sheaves today will water the sheep.

The twelve tribes of Israel could not marry outside of the tribes and their inheritances were to stay within the tribes; this was because the family of Zelophehad came to Moses with a concern: if the daughters married outside the tribe they would take family inheritance away from the family and it would be added to tribes outside of the tribes of Israel. So Moses said: Let the daughters of Zelophehad marry who they wish, but let them marry within the tribes of Israel.

But, a thousand years later an angel of the God of Israel told the priests to tell the people it was better to marry outside of the family tribes because inbreeding was causing diseases and marrying outside of family tribes would enable genetics to make the people stronger, and so incest was recognized as bad and was outlawed or discouraged. The knowledge of science was helping to eliminate some commonly inherited genetic ailments, and this was a good thing; it was progress being made for all of humanity, and human beings began to realize the value of 'knowledge'.

Moses did not count the son of Abraham and Hagar who was Ishmael into the tribes, because Ishmael was Hagar's son and not Sarai's, but Ishmael was blessed and prosperous in the land of the Philistines that became the land of the Muslims.

Mosaic Laws & Customs

Moses repeated The Ten Commandments and gave ordinances of secondary-law (deuteronomy) in the plains of Moab by the Jordan River. Moses instructed the Levites to take care of the Ark containing the Ten Commandments. Moses said to the Levites: wash four chalices with rainwater and then put the four chalices upon the altar and bless them with love first. Then fill the chalices with wine, unleavened matzo bread, cheese, and nuts such as sunflower seeds or cranberries. Then follow with chant to the Holy Spirit with the rabbi at the front of the Tent of the Meeting at the beginning of each month; Moses and Aaron and his sons were to encamp at sunrise to keep charge of the rites of the sanctuary. A chest was laid outside the gate to collect the tax that Moses had laid upon the people. Let the rabbi priests wear robes of velvet with tassels, turbans, and caps. Let all of the people Passover all of the chalice offerings at the altar to each other and share in the goodness of the gifts.

There was no more animal sacrificing at the altar.
The showbread signified the presence of the Holy Spirit, and the Passover became the Feast Of the Unleavened Bread. God Jehovah is the only god of the Jews. The Lord bless you and keep you.

Moses preached about the manna and the showbread: 'Man shall not live and be sustained by bread alone, but by every word and expression of God.' It is forbidden to break bread with a foreigner.

Laws of Equality were made such as 'An eye for an eye, a tooth for a tooth, a life for life.'

It was the custom in the land that if a man died, his brother married his wife in order to carry on his inheritance. There was a brother who did not want to marry the wife of his deceased brother, so the woman slapped the brother because she was rejected; the brother cut off her hand. When the priest Eleazar heard about it, he said it was unfair and unequal. Eleazar was the son of Aaron.

Jubilee

Jubilee was celebrated every 7 years; then debts were forgiven for fellow-countrymen but not foreigners, inheritances were given, the poor ate free, slaves were set free unless they wanted to remain with their master. Feasts were celebrated with grapes, pears, plums, squash, promegranates, cheese, beans, melons, olives, flatbread, lentils, figs, eggs, fowl, fish, soup, and wine.

The mystical powers of wine made some of the people sing and dance; but some fell asleep after drinking it.

Every three years, the full tithe from the produce for that year was given to the Levites to sustain them because they had no holding of ancestral land.

The Israelites were allowed to eat ox, sheep, goat, buck, gazelle, deer, and antelope but were forbidden to eat camel, hare, badger, and pig. All things in the water with fins and scales were allowed to be eaten except the creatures on the ocean floor that ate sludge. Winged creatures could be eaten except these were forbidden: vulture, kite, falcon, crow, owl, hawk, osprey, stork, cormorant, hoopoe, and bat. You must not eat anything that has died already. The hands were to be washed before eating.

Do not mix grains in the same bread, for it will not be pure.

Fasting (refrain from eating for a period of time) could be a sacrificial offering to God Jehovah.

Moses told the people to set aside a tithe portion of all produce year by year in case it needed to be converted to money.

Prostitution was forbidden to the Israelites, women or men.

Gladiator fighting is forbidden, for it is not right to kill.

It is forbidden to castrate humans or animals. Male circumcision may be practiced for cleanliness.

Should you see a fellow-countryman's ox or sheep straying, do not ignore it; you must take it back to him.

Should you see a fellow countryman's donkey lying down, do not ignore it; you must help to raise it to its feet. You are permitted to rescue your donkey on the Sabbath, but no work must be done, for Sabbath was made for the man, not man for the Sabbath.

When traveling through the desert, make sure you bring saddlebags of water on the camels until you make it to the oasis.

When your children are rebellious, take them aside and sit down and speak with them.

The child that is firstborn has the first rights of the inheritance laws.

During the course of war, do not destroy the fruit trees and the water wells, because they will provide you with food and water.

Put a railing around your roof so you will not fall off. To celebrate springtime, plant flowers by the gate.

Men should wear the clothing of men. Women should wear the clothing of women.

Your valuation of a male from 20 to 60 years old shall be 50 shekels of silver and your valuation of a female 30 shekels. The priest will determine the value of a beast, human, house, or field.

Tattoos are a sin because your body is a holy vessel of the Lord.

It you are ill, poor, or a victim of pestilence or whirlwind or injustice, it is because you have sinned before Jehovah your God.

If a man and woman enter into marriage together, they will be blessed by the rabbi at the altar of the Lord. If they do not find favour with each other, a certificate of divorce will be written.

Do not charge interest on anything lended to a fellow countryman; only to a foreigner.

There were to be 6 cities of refuge; 3 east of the Jordan River and 3 in the land of Canaan. If a person was accidentally killed by an ax when they were chopping brush or trees with other people, a person who was accused of murder even though it was unintentional could retreat to the city of refuge. Those who intentionally committed crimes such as blasphemy, murder, thievery, or worked on the Sabbath could be put to death by stoning or crucifixion.

You must not keep back the wages of a man who has performed good work for you, whether the man is a fellow countryman or a foreign alien working in your country on one of your settlements.

When you harvest the olives trees or the grape trees from the gardens, do not glean afterwards but leave what is left for the orphans, the fatherless, the aliens, and the widows. Keep in mind that some of you were slaves in other lands; that is why I command you to do this.

Blessed are those who follow the Ten Commandments, and cursed are those who do not.

You cannot drink the Lord's cup and the demon's cup. You cannot partake of the Lord's table and the demon's table. Whoever cleanses himself and separates himself from corruptness will be a vessel set apart and useful for honorable and noble purposes.

Your body is the temple, the very sanctuary of the Spirit, Who lives within you. You are not your own but God's creation.

The soul that sins shall bear the sin. A son shall not bear and be punished for the iniquity of his father; neither shall the father bear and be punished for the iniquity of the son. The righteousness of the righteous shall be upon the righteous, and the wickedness of the wicked shall be upon the wicked.

When the Israelites were encamped in the plains of Moab, on the east side of the Jordan River, the king of Moab was Balak. Balak was terrified of the many Israelites in his land. Balak asked the foreteller (oracle) Balaam if the Israelites should be forced out of the land. Balaam said to Balak, 'Build seven altars and prepare a bull and a ram as as a sacrifice on each altar. Then stand by your burnt offering while I go to meet the Lord yonder.'

And when Balaam struck his donkey to move, the Lord put the words out of the donkey's mouth and she said 'What have I done that you should strike me?' Then the Lord told Balaam that the Israelites were to be blessed, saying 'A star and a scepter shall rise from Israel to make peace for all people.'

Aaron

All of the men aged twenty years and older were to help Aaron (brother of Moses) in the service of the house of the Lord, caring for the courts, the chambers, the cleansing of all the holy things, any work of the service of the Lord's house, including the showbread also, which was the fine flour for a cereal offering, whether unleavened wafers or what is baked on the griddle in oil. They were to start every morning with hark and praise for the Lord. They were in charge of cereal, fruit, and wine that were worship offerings of sacrifice and sin offerings of sacrifice that were given to the Lord on Sabbaths, New Moon festivals and feast days. They were also in charge of Tent Meetings, the Holy Place, and attending to kinsmen. Shiloah was to be Jerusalem's perennial fountain and a water gate was built. The priests of Aaronic Priesthood were called kohanim.

Aaron was a great peace maker. When some of the men were quarreling among each other and then would not speak to each other, he spoke to them and many times brought back friendship among them, saying that friendship was a gift from the Lord.

There was a rabbi priest who was arguing with a merchant that he did not want to pay full shekels for a small donkey, saying the tent of his synagogue had given oil lanterns to some needy so they did not have enough money to pay full price for both the donkey and new oil lanterns.

Aaron died on Mount Hor in 1407BCE when he was 123 years old; it was the fortieth year after the Israelites came out of Egypt. They mourned the loss of Aaron for 30 days. Aaron's son Eleazer took over as Second Kohen Gadol (High Priest). Miriam died at Kadesh which was renamed Petra by the Nabataeans.

Book of DEUTERONOMY

Moses repeated the Ten Commandments and gave ordinances of secondary law (deuteronomy) in the plains of Moab by the Jordan River.

And you shall do what is right and good in the sight of the Lord, that it may go right with you.

If you obey the commandments of the Lord, the Lord will set you high; blessed shall you be in the city and blessed shall you shall be in the field. The eternal God is thy refuge, and underneath are the everlasting arms.

The secret things are known by God, and the Lord will reveal knowledge in ways only known by God.

The Lord makes poor and the Lord makes rich. The Lord brings low and lifts up high.

The pillars of the earth are the Lord's, who has set the world upon them.

Moses told the people that God Jehovah instructed that six days were for work, but the seventh day was a day of rest called Sabbath, which was a covenant with Jewish people.

Miracles would provide oil to keep lamps lit for seven days and more. Hannukah was a time for the Jewish people to celebrate the God Jehovah.

Moses went up from the plains of Moab to Mount Nebo, to the top of Pisgah, and the Lord showed to him all the lands and said, This is the land I gave to Abraham, Isaac, and Jacob. My doctrines shall drop as the rain. My speech shall distill as the dew. The earth shall hear the words of my mouth. Remember the days of old, live the present day, and consider the many years and generations to come. Keep the way of the tree of life.

Even when the Lord found Moses wandering in the howling wilderness, He kept him as the apple of his eye and let him know there was no strange god beside him except Jehovah. And Moses died when he was 120 years old; his sight was not dim. They mourned the loss of Moses for 30 days.

There never was risen in Israel a prophet like Moses, whom the Lord knew face to face; remember the strong hand of Moses and the awesome deeds which he did in the sight of all the people. Be aware of false prophets who teach evil things or tell you that a snake will not bite you if you have faith in the Lord.

Joshua the high priest (a high priest is also called kohen gadol) succeeds Moses

When Moses died, God Jehovah instructed Joshua to take over as leader of the covenant of the Ten Commandments because of his wholehearted devotion to the Holy Spirit. Joshua, a high priest, said 'The Lord is with you wherever you go. As for me and my house, we will follow the ways of the Lord.'

Once after a battle with an enemy, the Israelites set aside and consecrated gold, silver, bronze, and iron for the Lord; it was from the booty they collected from an enemy; the rest was set for destruction. But some of the Israelites looted the part that was set aside. Joshua found out and told them that they had transgressed, sinned, and trespassed against the laws of Moses. Joshua said that God was a jealous god and would not tolerate foreign gods. Joshua told the parable of the bramble bush.

A long time after that, Joshua summoned all Israel, their elders, heads, judges, and officers, and said to them, I am old and advanced in years. I have allotted inheritances to the tribes and seen over the affairs but now I will step down. Joshua died when he was 110 years old.
And Caleb of the tribe of Judah led the Israelites after that. The Lord gave Caleb the land of Hebron because of his faithfulness and Caleb gave his daughter Achsah a spring of water as a present.

Jewish Judges
1375-1050 BCE

The judges were to relieve military pressure and deliver the people from oppression of foreign nations. The judges were Othniel (40 years), Ehud (80 years), Shamgar, Deborah (40+ years), Gideon (40 years), Tola (23 years), Jair (22 years), Jephthah (6 years), Ibzan (7 years), Elon (10 years), Abdon (8 years), Samson (2 years).

Deborah was a woman who was a prophetess and a judge. Deborah and Yael, who was the wife of Heber, and Barak, son of Abinoam from Kadesh in Naphtali, defeated Sisera and his army of 900 iron-clad chariots. Yael told Sisera of the Ten Commandments in a tentside meeting; and Sisera turned back his army.

The judges were to inquire diligently about the facts of the cases. False witnesses (those who gave false testimonies and lied) were to be done according as they intended to do to their brother.

One witness would not prevail against a person for a crime; two or three witnesses had to be established.

Judges shall do no injustice judging a case and shall not show preference for the rich.

Elijah was a prophet of the Lord who told a rabbi about the righteousness of two men who were in the marketplace at the bazaar;

Elijah gave merit to the two men because when they saw people quarreling, the two men helped to settle disputes and bring friendship among the men again.

Jewish Prophets Elijah and Elisha

Elijah and Elisha were men of God who were sojourning from Gilgal to Bethel and to Jericho and the two stopped by the side of the Jordan River. And Elijah took his mantle and rolled it up and struck the waters and they divided, so that the two of them went over dry ground.

And when they had gone over, Elijah asked Elisha, Ask what I can do for you before I am taken from you. And Elisha said I pray you, let a double portion of your spirit be upon me. Elijah replied, You have asked a hard thing. However, if you see me when I am taken from you, it shall be so for you, but if not, it shall not be so. And behold, a chariot of fire and horses parted the two, and Elijah went up by a whirlwind into heaven. And Elisha cried out 'Elijah, o prophet!' and took the mantle that had fallen from Elijah; he rolled it up and struck the waters, and the waters parted so that Elisha could cross to dry ground. Now fifty sons of the prophets were watching and they sought for three days for Elijah and found him not.

Then Elisha cast salt into the spring of waters that were near, and the waters were healed unto this day.

While a minstrel was playing music, the hand and power of the Lord came upon the prophet Elisha, who was a man. Now, the wife of a son of the prophets cried to Elisha that a creditor was coming to take her two sons away as slaves. Elisha said to her, What shall I do for you? Tell me, what have you in the house to be sold? She said, I have nothing in the house except a jar of oil. Then Elisha said, Go around and borrow vessels from all your neighbors - empty vessels - and not a few. And when you come in, shut the doors upon you and your sons. Then pour out the oil into all those vessels, setting aside each one when it is full. So she went from him and shut the door upon herself and her sons who brought to her the vessels as she poured the oil.

When the vessels were all full, she said to her son, bring me another vessel. And he said to her, There is not a one left. Then the oil stopped multiplying. Then she went to Mount Carmel and told the man of God, who was Elisha. He said, Go, sell the oil and pay the debt, and you and your sons live on the rest. So the prophet Elisha did provide the miracle of the oil so the woman's sons were not carried into slavery.

Fighting for conquest of lands and religions

Now in this age of times, kings and queens, pharaohs, emperors, empresses, and tribal leaders were fighting amongst each other over lands and the powers to behold. It is believed that humans were taken as slave labor against their will, even to build great pyramids and aquaducts. The pyramids were the tombs of the Egyptian pharaohs. Some seers and sages were interested in the ways of science and the unknowns of the earth, and the seers and sages were killed just for thinking, talking and philosophizing. Many people were fighting and killing over different religions, the ideas of the Unknown. Sages were killed for thinking the earth was round and not flat.
Some religions were peaceful, but some of the religions were forced upon people; this was happening in the entire world, not just the mideast. There was fighting among the twelve tribes of Israel and the Levites. Jews fought Jews over religious principles. Some Jews got angry with other Jews for worshipping the gods Baal and Ashtoreth of the Pagan Gentiles in addition to going into the Tent of the Testimony that contained the Ark of the Ten Commandments.
Many people were killed just because they called the Holy Spirit by a different name than someone else did. Some kings destroyed religious buildings, idols and statues, while other kings created religious buildings, idols, and statues of gods and goddesses. Many people were afraid because of religious fighting and persecution. The Holy Spirit was watching all from the heavens, wondering when the people would live in peace and enjoy the earth.

Story of Samson

An angel of the Lord said to Manoah and his wife who was barren and unable to conceive that Samson, a male Jewish child, would be born. The Lord told the woman to drink no wine or eat no forbidden food while carrying the child in her womb. The woman's husband was Manoah who was of the tribe of Dan. The woman and her husband both fell on their faces in thankfulness to the Lord. Samson had long hair and his great strength came from his hair.

Samson married a Philistine woman because she was beautiful and he fell in love with her. But she felt that Samson did not love her, so they separated. Then, Samson went away to Ashkelon. When he came back, Samson's wife had been given away to his best friend. Samson was angry.

Then Samson left to go to Gaza. Delilah, who was a woman of the valley of Sorek, spied on Samson and determined that his hair was his strength. Delilah was a temptress of an enemy to Samson and he loved her. Delilah told an enemy to cut off Samson's hair, Samson lost his strength and was put in prison. But when his hair grew back, he regained his strength. When Samson was summoned out of prison, he was made to stand in front of a house between two pillars. But he pulled on both pillars, one with each arm, and pulled the pillars together, and brought the roof down and killed 3000 people, including himself.

Ruth

Naomi and her husband Elimech left Bethlehem of Judea because of famine and went to sojourn in the land of Moab. Their two sons took Orpah and Ruth as their wives. But all three men died. Naomi and her daughter-in-law Ruth decided to return to Judea, but the other daughter-in-law Orpah wanted to stay.

Then the widow Ruth met her second husband, Boaz, and he went in to her, and the Lord caused her to conceive, and she bore a son named Obed who was the father of Jesse, who was the father of David; it is believed that David lived from 1040BCE-970BCE).

Samuel

Elkanah had 2 wives: Hannah and Peninnah. Samuel was the son of Hannah.

God found favor with Samuel and was delighted with his ways, so Samuel was a prophet. Then Samuel was a king who judged Israel all his days. From year to year he went on a circuit roundabout to Bethel, Gilgal, and Mizpah, and was a judge in all those places.

The Israelites and the Philistines had a battle and the Philistines took the Jewish Ark of the Covenant. But then they returned the Ark to the Israelites, apologized with guilt offerings.

God told Samuel to appoint Saul a king, but Saul made an incorrect judgment, so Samuel appointed David a king. Saul's son was Jonathan.

King David

King David won a battle against a giant named Goliath in the Valley of Elah.

There was a long war between the house of Saul and the house of David; Saul was jealous of David and tried to kill David but David kept escaping.

Sons were born to David in Hebron; Amnon, by Ahinoam the Jezreelitess; Chileab, by Abigail, widow of Nabal of Carmel;

Absalom by Maacah the daughter of Talmai king of Geshur; Adonijah by Haggith; and Shephatiah by Abital.

David married Saul's daughter Michal; once, Michal helped David to escape Saul when he had intention to harm him.

One time David had no food to eat and he received holy bread to eat from the priest Ahimelech who said all of the women had gone on a journey and so there was no one to bake bread. So Ahimelech gave the showbread of the priests for David to eat. He also gave David the sword of Goliath which he had wrapped in a cloth and stored in a box. Jonathan was an assistant to David; Jonathan gave him a robe and armor for defense against Saul.

But when David had a chance to kill Saul at the Cave at the Rock of the Wild Goats, he didn't; but David tore Saul's skirt. David and Saul made peace. Abigail became David's wife. Ahinoam became David's wife also. David's first wife, Michal, was given to Phalti, after David and Michal were divorced.

But David requested to see Michal again 14 years later and they worshipped God Jehovah together when the Ark of the Lord came to stay at the house of Obededom for three months. David distributed among the people of Israel, both to men and women, a cake of bread, a portion of meat, and a cake of raisins. David took off his kingly robes after worship service and was singing and dancing to music with the servants. Michal later told David that she was upset that he had humbled himself before the servants, but David told her that he would humble himself even lower in his own sight, and he considered it an honor. David had a son named Solomon; Solomon's mother was Bathsheba.

The area of northern Samaria became the lands of ten tribes of Israel and the land to the south was Judea. The northern monarchy was destroyed by the Assyrians around 700BCE and the Ten Tribes dispersed. The land of Judea came to an end and was destroyed in 586BCE by the Babylonians who destroyed the first Jewish Temple. Seventy years later, after Persia defeated the Babylonians, the Jews returned to Palestine and rebuilt the Temple. Then the Greeks defeated the Persians and the Romans defeated the Greeks. The Romans destroyed the 2nd Temple in 70CE.

The First Jewish Temple

The Lord spoke to the prophet Nathan saying: Go and tell My Servant David, Thus says the Lord: Shall you build Me a house in which to dwell. In accordance with these words and all this vision Nathan spoke to David. And so King David planned to construct a temple of worship Mount Moriah.

King David was making preparations to build the first house unto the Lord God Jehovah. He paid 600 shekels of gold by weight to Ornan for the site of land.

David had a vision of an angel of the Lord carrying a sword between heaven and earth; David and the elders, clothed in sackcloth, fell upon their faces. And the angel directed David to build an altar for the Lord.

The temple was to be for prayer, singing songs, burning incense, and giving offerings to the unseen God Jehovah who resided in a heaven that is filled with angels, gates, bright glorious lights, and streets of gold.

David prepared iron in abundance for nails for the doors and gates and couplings. Cedar trees were cut down in Lebanon, and food, drink, and money was given to transport cedar timber to the seaport of Joppa. The cedar was then transported to Zion (Israel) the City of David which would later be transported to Jerusalem by King Solomon.

Money was given to masons and carpenters to build towers at the corner gates of Jerusalem.

Ironsmiths used chisels, sharpeners, and hammers and worked over coals to forge nails.

The prophet Isaiah told David to make the way of the road to the temple straight and level; to clear the way to the Lord with a safe highway. As when the field is leveled, does he not sow caraway and scatter cumin. Does he not plant wheat, barley, and spelt in its field?

The prophet Nathan told David that the Lord is everywhere, not just in a house of cedar (temple) or in an ark of a testimony.

King David commanded all the princes to help Solomon his son and set their hearts and minds on building a sanctuary to the Lord for the ark of the Ten Commandments that were etched on the two stone tablets.

The Prophet Isaiah

The prophet Isaiah, son of Amoz, proclaimed 'The Spirit of the Lord God is upon me, because the Lord has anointed and qualified me to preach the Gospel of good tidings to those who behold the Lord and the Lord shall call them holy people. And, later, Isaiah told the people that God Jehovah did not require animal holocaust sacrifices, that God wanted sacrifices of our hearts concerning love rather than sacrifices of animals. Isaiah said also that God did not require new moon festivals, Sabbaths, the calling of assemblies, or the burning of incense; Isaiah said that God wanted the people to do right by caring for the orphans, the widowed, the poor, the needy, and seeking justice for the oppressed. The prophet said that foreigners from far away lands who came to the middle-east were helping the Jews with new ideas; that the foreigners wanted the middle-eastern people to be

happy and prosperous, so it was time to change Moses' law that Jews should not break bread with foreigners.
Isaiah said it was time to remove the veil off all nations
so the whole world will know the Divine Creator together. Forget the former things and do not dwell on the past, said Isaiah. Isaiah told the people that God said the silver had lost its shine and the wine was mixed with water, that the people had become too materialistic with customs, silver and gold, treasures, horses, chariots, headbands, ankle chains, trinkets, perfume boxes, amulets and charms, signet rings and nose rings, festal robes, cloaks, stoles and shawls, handbags, hand mirrors, fine linens, turbans, and veils. Isaiah said if the people did not stop being too materialistic it shall come to pass that instead of sweet odor of spices there shall be the stench of rottenness and the people would be like dry bones of the dead. Instead of feeling joy the people would lament. The prophet Isaiah said 'All things are full of weariness. A man cannot utter it. And the Lord will do the thing the Lord hath promised and believers will survive with the help of angels.' Isaiah said 'Those who put their hope in the Lord will renew their strength; they will mount up and soar on wings like eagles and will not grow weary, the Lord will put the wind beneath their wings. When you go through deep waters, God will be with you. He gives strength to the weary and increases the power of the weak. Every weapon raised against you will not prosper but will weaken. Every tongue raised in judgement against you will be shown to be in the wrong. The green grass dries up and the blossom withers, but the word of our God endures forever. For my hand made all things that came into being. To him who walks in faith is humble and contrite of spirit, and who trembles at My Word." And God told Isaiah: 'Fear not, for I have heard your words, seen your tears, and I am with you.'

In the days when King Hezekiah became deadly ill, the prophet Isaiah said to him: Thus says the Lord: Set your house and affairs in order, for you shall die; you shall not recover.
Then Hezekiah turned his face to the wall and prayed to the Lord: I beseech You, O Lord, to remember me now, how I have walked in faithfulness and truth and with a whole heart (entirely devoted to you) and have done what is good in Your Sight. And Hezekiah wept bitterly.
Before Isaiah had gone out of the middle court, the word of the Lord came to him:
Turn back and tell Hezekiah that I have heard your prayer and have seen your tears; behold, I will heal you and I am with you. On the third day you will go up to the house of the Lord. I will add to your life fifteen years and deliver you from this affliction.

Hezekiah said to Isaiah: What shall be the sign that the Lord will heal me and that I shall go up into the house of the Lord on the third day?
And Isaiah said: This is the sign to you from the Lord that the Lord will do the thing that was promised: shall the shadow of the sundial go forward ten steps or go back ten steps?
Hezekiah answered: It is an easy matter for the shadow to go forward ten steps; so let the shadow go back ten steps.
So Isaiah the prophet cried to the Lord, and the Lord brought the shadow the ten steps backward by which it had gone down on the sundial of Ahaz.
Then Hezekiah said to Isaiah: The word of the Lord you have spoken is good and true.
Hezekiah finished his acts with all his might to build the pool and canals which brought water into the city of Jerusalem.

The prophet Isaiah told the people of Israel of King David near Mount Zion that there shall come forth a shoot out of the stock of Jesse (David's father), and a Branch out of his roots shall grow and bear fruit,
and the wolf shall dwell with the lamb, the cow and the bear shall feed side by side, and the root of Jesse shall stand as a signal for all peoples; all nations will seek knowledge and His dwelling shall be glory.
For unto us a child was born, unto us a son was given; and his name shall be called Wonderful Counselor, The Mighty God, The Everlasting Father, the Prince of Peace. They shall call His name Emmanuel which means God with us.

In that day the Lord shall recover the remnant of His people which is left, from Assyria, from Lower Egypt, from Pathros, from Ethiopia, from Elam in Persia, from Shinar (Babylonia), from Hamath in upper Syria, and from the countries bordering the Mediterranean Sea. All evil will be stricken. There shall be a highway from Assyria for the remnant left of His people, as there was for Israel when they came up out of the land of Egypt.
A messiah called wonderful would be born in the future who was to be called Immanuel which means God With Us; the voice of one crying in the wilderness: Prepare the way for the Lord!' A star would come forth out of Jacob and a scepter would rise out of Israel. The scepter or leadership would not depart from Judah until Shiloh (the Messiah, the peaceful One) comes.

Isaiah said: 'Hear a voice of one who cries: Comfort, comfort My people, says your God. Speak tenderly to the heart of Jerusalem, and the glory of the Lord shall be revealed. O you who bring good tidings to Jerusalem, lift up your voice in strength, lift it up and trust in the Lord. Your reward is with the Lord. God will feed His flock like a shepherd: He will gather the lambs in His arm.

He will carry them in His bosom and will gently lead the people. Behold, the nations are like drops from a bucket and are counted as small dust on the grand scale of the universe. It is God Who sits above the circle (horizon) of the earth and stretches out the heavens. Tell everyone,
the everlasting God, the Lord, the Creator of the ends of the earth, does not faint or grow weary.
Wait for and look for the Lord. The Lord will renew the strength and hope of the weary; they shall lift their wings and mount up (soar) as eagles, and they will not faint or become tired. I am the Lord, and there is no one else; there is no God besides Me.
That you may know from the rising of the sun in the east to the setting of the sun in the west that there is no God besides Me. I am the Lord, and no one else is.
Delight yourself in the Lord, and I will make you to ride on the high places of the earth, and I will feed you with the heritage of Jacob your father.
But your iniquities will make a separation between you and your God, so remain in righteousness with the Lord and do not stray from good ways.
The evil bring mischief and their thoughts are on iniquities; desolation and destruction are in their paths and highways; their feet run to evil and they shed innocent blood. They trust in emptiness, worthlessness and futility, and they speak lies! The way of peace they know not, and there is no justice or right in their doings.
Do not rebel against or deny God. Do not speak oppression and revolt. Do not speak words of falsehood. Thou wilt keep him in perfect peace, whose mind is stayed on God; because he trusteth in thee.
For the Lord put on a breastplate of righteousness and speak the truth. Write the words of the Lord upon your heart, and My Words which I have put in your mouth shall not depart out of your mouth, or out of the mouths of your children, or out of the mouths of your children's children, says the Lord, from henceforth and forever.

Then said Hezekiah to Isaiah, The word of the Lord which you have spoken is good, for there will be peace and faithfulness to the Lord in my days.

King Solomon

It is believed Solomon (son of David) lived from 970BCE-931BCE.

Two woman and a baby

Two women who had become mothers out of wedlock stood before King Solomon at Jerusalem.
And one woman said, O my lord, I and this woman dwell in one house; and I was delivered of a child with her in the house.
And the third day after I was delivered, this woman also was

delivered. And we were together; no stranger was with us, just we two in the house. And this woman's child died in the night because she lay on him. And she arose at midnight and took my son from beside me while I slept and laid him in her bosom and laid her dead child in my bosom. And when I rose to nurse my child, behold, he was dead. But when I had considered him in the morning, behold, it was not the son I had borne.
But the other woman said No! But the living one is my son, and the dead one is your son. And this one said, No! But the dead son is your son, and the living is my son. Thus they spoke before the king. The king Solomon said, Bring me a sword. And they brought him a sword. The king said, Divide the child in two and give half to the one and half to the other. The real mother cried 'Do not hurt the baby!' Then King Solomon knew who the real mother was because she did not want the baby to be hurt. And all of the people in the land heard of the judgment of the king, who had a keen discerning wisdom, and they stood in awe that the wisdom of God was in him to do justice.

After seven years King Solomon finished the first temple unto the Lord at Jerusalem for Jews; it took twenty years to build the temple and his own house. Solomon prayed and consecrated the temple. Solomon prayed, "Lord, thank you for the Blessings You bestow on Your Faithful Followers of Israel, for You return beauty for ashes, pay back double, with all things working together for our good and the good of all people." And he built the Forest of Lebanon House with cedar pillars, a Hall of Pillars, and a Porch of Judgement in his own house, from where he was to judge.
The temple was complete with priests, singers, musicians and gatekeepers. King Solomon wrote two beautiful psalms and proverbs to the Lord.
David, Asaph, the Sons of Korah, Moses, Heman the Ezrahite, and Ethan the Ezrahite, wrote most of the psalms.

The ark that contained the two tablets of stone containing the ten commandments were brought from the city of Zion, the city of David.
There was an altar of bronze, a round ring of molten metal; under it were figures of oxen encircling it.
The son of a woman of the daughters of Dan; he was a trained worker in gold, silver, bronze, iron, stone, and wood; he helped women secure the linens of purple, blue, and crimson colors for the sanctuary.
Engravers designed cherub angels for the walls.
Also, ten golden lampstands, ten tables, a priests' court, and the great court and doors for the court, the doors overlaid with bronze. Huram made the pots, shovels, and basins. Lampstands, basins, dishes for incense, and

snuffers made out of pure gold were made for the temple entry. The smoke of the incense and herbs filled the temple. There were 400 pomegranates to cover the capitals of the pillars. Workmen were paid to make vessels of gold and silver for offerings. When the temple was finished and the services were held, the people listened to the Word of God being taught to them by the priests; they listened eagerly and attentively, with focus and attention.

Solomon imported horses from Egypt and timber from Lebanon. Solomon gave King Hiram of Tyre twenty cities of land in exchange for timber of cedar and cypress and gold. Solomon built a fleet of ships which Hiram helped to command and every three years the fleet brought gold, silver, ivory, spices, and peacocks. King Solomon married a Pharaoh of Egypt's daughter.

The Queen of Sheba visited King Solomon. She came to Jerusalem with a train of camels, bearing spices, gold, and precious stones.

She delivered a scroll from a merchant to King Solomon regarding trade goods.

She experienced the food on his table, the seating of his officials, the standing at attention of his servants, their apparel, his cupbearers, his ascent by which he went up to the house of the Lord, and she was breathless and overcome. The Queen of Sheba told King Solomon that it was true what she had heard about him and that she did not believe it until she had seen it with her own eyes and that half was not told her. She said Solomon added wisdom and goodness exceeding the fame she heard. She saw how happy his army and servants were. She communed with Solomon about everything that was on her mind and Solomon answered all of her questions. Sheba returned to her own country. Solomon continued in wealth and built an ivory and gold throne with a canopy and arm rests, and two lions stood beside the armrests.

In one year Solomon received 666 talents of gold. He had 1400 chariots and 12,000 horsemen and drinking vessels of silver and gold. A chariot could be brought out of Egypt for a price of 600 shekels of silver, and a horse for 150.

King Solomon had a vineyard with keepers, a cottage with gardens of flowers, grapes, fruits, and cucumbers, horses, and ships. There was a problem with the foxes in the grape vineyards. Take us the foxes, the little foxes, that spoil the vines; for our vines have tender grapes yet the foxes ruin the entire vine.

It was rumored many years later that the Queen of Sheba had a son by King Solomon and her child was called Menelik; the Menelik dynasty ruled in Ethiopia until 1974CE. It was said that the Ark of the Covenant was brought to a monastery on Lake Tana which feeds its waters into the Blue Nile because Muslims tried to capture the Ark. After Menelik died, Ezana became the new emperor.

King Solomon had 700 wives and also built worship places near Jerusalem for Ashtoreth (Goddess of the Sidonians), Chemosh (God of the Moabites), and Milcom (God of Ammonites); but King Josiah destroyed all of these.

A bride of Solomon told her companions that the wedding guests were in the cottage and she was looking forward to the groom's arrival when they would drink spiced wine and pomegranate juice, embrace and kiss, and their bodies would be like gardens to each other. The bride wanted the groom to put a seal of love on his heart for her, and she would put a seal of love on her heart for him. The bride also told that King Solomon said that her love was more beautiful than wine, that her lips dropped honey as the honeycomb, that she was a fountain in a garden, and that his bride was a garden enclosed for his enjoyment. You are like a lovely orchard bearing precious fruit, with the rarest of perfumes, nard and saffron, calamus, cinnamon, and perfume from every other incense tree, as well as myrrh and aloes, and every other spice. You are a garden fountain, a well of living water, refreshing as the streams from the Lebanon mountains. The bride told King Solomon that his eyes were like those of doves, that he was to her like a cluster of henna flowers in the vineyards of fragrant shrubs, and that he was beautiful. The bride said she was only a little rose or a lily of the valley but Solomon said that his bride was a lily among thorns. Solomon said his bride was like an apple tree in the middle of the trees of the woods. The king said her body was like the stature of a palm tree and her breasts were like clusters of dates.

When the lovers were separated, the bride addressed her absent groom to herself and told him to run like a gazelle or a young hart as he covered the grounds and mountains that separated them until they could once be together again.

When Solomon died, his son Rehoboam became king. The region divided in two; Israel to the north and Judah to the south. When King Rehoboam died, his son Abijam ruled. When King Abijam died, his son Asa reigned. There was a war between King Asa of Judah and King Baasha of Israel. After King Baasha died, King Ahab reigned and married Jezebel.

Queen Jezebel and Elijah fight over religions

Queen Jezebel, a Sidonian, was a pagan idol Baal worshipper who was married to King Ahab of Israel. Jezebel wore eye makeup. Ahab did worship both Jehovah and Baal. Baal was a golden calf idol.

Jezebel was involved in a dispute with the Jewish Prophet Elijah of the Israelites; about 450 prophets were killed on each side.

Queen Jezebel was tricked by King Jehu who was an enemy when they were having conversation on her balcony; she was thrown over the railing and then run over by a chariot of King Jehu.

Then kings and queens were surrounded by bodyguards during meetings with rivals to reach peace accords.

Solomon's Proverbs

The parables and proverbs are truths obscurely expressed.

PROVERB 1

Thou people, receive knowledge and instruction in wise dealing.

Know the discipline of wise thoughtfulness, justice, righteousness, and integrity; remember good knowledge and follow godly wisdom.

Understand a proverb and enigmas, with their interpretations.

Solomon said, "Be like Isaiah who was a prophet like Moses."

Hear the instruction of thy mother and father; keep hold their good teachings.

Withhold not discipline from a child or they may be brought to shame. It was said 'Ye shall strike them with a rod and deliver them from Sheol' but to strike a child is not necessary if you can reason with their mind to correct them.

If sinners entice you, do not consent.

Whoso hearkens to wisdom shall dwell securely and in confident trust and shall be without fear or dread of evil.

PROVERB 2

If you cry out for insight and raise your voice for understanding, if you seek wisdom, then you will understand.

PROVERB 3

Happy is the man who finds wisdom, for the gaining of it is better than the gaining of silver, and the profit of it better than fine gold. Skillful and godly wisdom is more precious than rubies or pearls. She (wisdom) is a tree of life to those who lay hold on her, and happy is everyone who holds her fast and dear to heart. When you are secure with wisdom and confident in the lord, your sleep shall be sweet.

Do not contrive evil against your neighbor. Contend not with a man for no reason – when he has done you no wrong.

Do not be resentfully envy or jealous.

PROVERB 4

David said to Solomon: 'Let your heart hold fast to my words. Keep the commandments and live righteously. Get wisdom and understanding, and take firm hold and do not let go, and you shall not stumble off the good path.

Guard your heart, put away dishonest speech, let your gaze be straight before you, and you will avoid trouble and enjoy the springs of life. Remove your foot from evil.

Hear, O my son, and receive my sayings, and the years of thy life shall be many.

PROVERB 5

Avoid any temptation to go astray with loose women or men, the harlots, who may lead you as dogs are enticed by food. The harlots will entice you to delight yourselves with love until morning on cushions of tapestry and sheets of fine linen, scented with perfumes like myrrh, aloes, and cinnamon. Whoever commits adultery lacks heart and understanding and destroys his own life; he shall not be innocent but will be *disgraced.*

But confine yourself to your own wife or husband and your children. Let your fountain of life be blessed with the rewards of a loving family.

PROVERB 6

There are 7 things the Lord hates indeed: a proud look that makes one overestimate himself and underestimate others, a lying tongue, hands that shed innocent blood, a heart that manufactures wicked thoughts and plans, feet that are swift in running to evil, a false witness that breathes out lies, one who sows discord among brethren, adultery and harlots.

Beauty is vain but the one who fears the Lord shall be praised.

My son, keep God's commandments and forsake not the law of God. Bind them continually upon your heart.

Give not unnecessary sleep to your eyes; be like a gazelle escaping from the hand of the hunter. Go to the ant, you sluggard, and consider her ways and be wise.

PROVERB 7

My son, keep the Words of Wisdom, the laws and teachings of wisdom as the apple (the pupil) of your eye.

Say to Wisdom, you are my sister.

PROVERB 8

I (Wisdom) walk in the way of moral upright in the midst of the paths of justice. I love those who love me, and those who seek me early and diligently shall find me, and I shall fill their treasures.

The Lord formed and brought me (Wisdom) forth at the beginning of the divine creation. For whoever finds me (Wisdom) finds a peaceful life and obtains favor from the Lord. But the one who dismisses me shall find chaos.

PROVERB 9

Wisdom has built her house and set up her pillars; come, eat of my bread and wine, and walk in the way of good insight and fine understanding. Stay on the good path that I (Wisdom) have laid out for you. For whoever is led astray will be invited to share stolen waters; the shades of the dead are there haunting the scene from the depths of Sheol, the lower world, Hades, the place of the dead.

PROVERB 10

The proverbs of Solomon: a wise son or daughter makes a glad parent but a foolish son or daughter is the grief of his father and mother.

Treasures of wickedness profit nothing, but righteousness delivers from chaos, grief and destruction.

He who heeds instruction and correction is wise in the way of life. He who neglects or refuses reproof (correction of mistakes) goes astray, causes err, and is a path toward ruin for others.

He who hides hatred is of lying lips, and he who utters slander is an over-confindent fool.

He who restrains his lips is prudent and wise.

Those who are wicked and out of harmony with God's good commandments are of little value. He who walks in integrity walks securely.

PROVERB 11

Sins and unrighteous dealings are offensive to God. Much arrogance leads to emptiness; the humble have more wisdom.

Where no wise guidance is, the people fall, but in the multitude of counselors there is safety.

A good and gracious woman wins honor, but a woman who hates righteousness sits on a throne of dishonor.

He who waters shall himself be watered.

The people curse him who holds back grain, but a blessing is upon the head of him who sells it.

He who trusts in riches shall fall, but the righteous who trust in good ways and do right things shall flourish like a green bough.

PROVERB 12

Whoever loves instruction and correction loves knowledge, but he who hates reproof (correction) is like a brute beast, stupid and indiscriminating.

Better is he who is lightly esteemed but works for his own support than he who assumes honor for himself and lacks bread.

Anxiety in a man's heart weighs it down, but an encouraging word makes it glad.

The righteous man is a guide to his neighbor, but the way of the wicked causes others to go astray.

PROVERB 13

A wise son heeds his father's instruction and correction, but a scoffer listens not to rebuke. A scoffer will not listen to good knowledge.

The appetite of the sluggard craves and gets nothing, but the appetite of the diligent is abundantly supplied.

One man considers himself rich, yet has nothing to keep permanently; another man considers himself poor, yet has great and indestructible riches because his soul is clean.

The light of the righteous grows brighter, but the lamp of the wicked shall be put out shortly.

He who disciplines his son fairly loves him.

PROVERB 14

Every wise woman builds her house, but the foolish one tears it down.

Even in laughter a heart may be sorrowful.

The simpleton believes every word he hears, but the prudent man looks and considers well where he is going.

A wise man pays attention and avoids danger.

Fools acquire folly, but the prudent are crowned with knowledge.

In all labor there is profit, but idle talk leads only to poverty.

A calm and undisturbed mind and heart are the life and health of the body, but envy, jealousy, and wrath are like rottenness of the bones.

He who oppresses the poor insults his Maker, but he who is kind andmerciful to the needy honors the Lord.

Uprightness and good standing with God elevate a nation, but sin is a reproach to any people.

PROVERB 15

A soft answer turns away wrath, but grievous harsh words stir up anger.

To make an apt answer is a joy and a word in season.

The tongue of the wise utters knowledge rightly, but the mouth of the fool pours out folly.

The eyes of the Lord are in every place, keeping watch upon the evil and the good.

The words of a gentle tongue with its healing power are a tree of life, but the words of a harsh tongue break down the spirit.

PROVERB 16

Divinely directed decisions are on the lips of one who seeks guidance from the Lord.

A just balance and scales are the Lord's; all the weights of the bag are God's work.

It is an abomination to God for kings or queens to commit wickedness, for a throne is established and made secure by righteousness.

How much better it is to get skillful and godly Wisdom than gold!

A worthless man devises mischief, but the wise in heart have understanding that is a well-spring of life.

Gracious words are like a honeycomb.

PROVERB 17

Better is a dry morsel with quietness than a house full of feasting with strife.

The refining pot is for silver and the furnace for gold, but the heart is the safeplace for the Lord's good precepts.

A happy heart is good medicine and a cheerful mind works healing, but a broken spirit dries up the bones.

PROVERB 18

He who willfully separates and estranges himself from God and man is lost.

A fool has no delight in understanding others, but is only interested in revealing his personal opinions.

The words of a discreet man are like deep waters.

Wisdom is like a gushing stream - sparkling, fresh, pure, and life-giving.

The name of the Lord is a strong tower.

A brother offended is harder to be won over than a strong city, and their contentions separate them like the bars of a castle.

A man's moral self is filled by the fruit of his mouth and the self-instruction of his own mind.

The one who finds a true husband or wife finds a good thing.

The man of many friends is stretched thin, but there is a friend who sticks closer than a brother.

PROVERB 19

Better is a poor man who walks in good integrity than a rich man who is perverse in his speech or actions.

Desire without knowledge is not good, and to be overhasty is to sin and miss the mark.

Wealth makes many friends, but a poor man is avoided.

Good sense makes a man restrain his anger, and it is his glory to overlook a transgression or an offense.

The king's wrath is as terrifying as the roaring of a lion, but his favor is as refreshing as dew upon the grass.

The contentions of a wife are like a continual dripping of water through a chunk in the roof.

Houses and riches are the inheritance from fathers, but a wise, understanding, and prudent nature is from God.

Many plans are in a man's mind, but it is the Lord's purpose for him that will stand.

He who does violence to another causes shame and destroys his own life.

PROVERB 20

Wine is a mocker, strong drink a riotous brawler; and whoever errs or reels because of it is not wise.

Many a man proclaims his own loving-kindness and goodness, but a faithful man will put forth the effort and act.

The righteous man walks in his integrity and has a heart that is pure and clean.

Whoever curses his good father or good mother should search his own heart.

Loving-kindness and mercy, and truth and faithfulness preserve a king and his throne is upheld by loyalty.

The glory of young men is their strength, and the beauty of old men is their gray hair, suggesting wisdom and experience.

PROVERB 21

Every way of a man is right in his own eyes, but the Lord weighs and tries the hearts.

Whoever does not listen to the cry of the poor will one day cry out himself and not be heard.

The horse is prepared for battle, but deliverance and victory are for the Lord.

PROVERB 22

A good name is to be chosen than great riches, and loving favor rather than silver and gold.

The rich and the poor meet together; the Lord is the Maker of them all.

Train up a child in the good way they should go, and when they get older they will remember it and will not depart from it.

The rich rule over the poor, and the borrower is servant to the lender.

Rob not the poor or the rich.

Try to turn a man away from his anger and lead him back to the peace of the Lord.

A prudent man sees danger and takes refuge, but the simple keep going and suffer for it.

PROVERB 23

As one thinks in his heart, so is he.

Say to your son: If your heart is wise, my heart will be glad. Yes, my heart will rejoice when your lips speak right things.

Let not your heart envy sinners, but continue in the good ways of the Lord.

Do not associate with the evil ones who are scheming to do evil things.

Seek the truth and only the truth. Do not bribe a brother to change the truth.

PROVERB 24

Be not envious, but live your own life.

A wise man is strong and stronger than a strong man.

My son, eat honey, for it is good, and the drippings of the honeycomb are sweet to your taste.

I went by the field of the lazy man, and by the vineyard of the man void of understanding; and behold, it was overgrown with thorns and its stone wall was broken down.

So, shall poverty come as a robber to those who do not care.

PROVERB 25

These are also the proverbs of Solomon, which the men of Hezekiah king of Judah copied: It is the glory of God to conceal a thing, but the glory of kings is to search out a thing.

Hearts and minds are unsearchable.

Take away the dross from the silver, and there shall come forth a beautiful vessel.

Be not forward in the presence of a king or queen, until told to come up there. You should be put lower in their presence.

Argue (discuss) your cause with your neighbor without anger; let calmness prevail.

Let your foot be in your neighbor's house when invited, lest he become tired of you.

He who sings songs to a heavy heart is like putting on a garment in cold weather or putting kindle on a warm fire.

Like cold water to a thirsty soul, so is good news from a far country (home).

PROVERB 26

Like the sparrow in her wandering, like the swallow in her flying, the causeless curse does not alight.

How can I curse those the Lord has not cursed? How can I

denounce those the Lord has not denounced?

PROVERB 27

Do not boast of tomorrow, for you know not what tomorrow may bring forth.

Let another man be the first to praise you, and not your own mouth.

Like a bird that wanders from the nest, so is a man who strays from his home.

Oil and perfume rejoice the heart; so does the sweetness of a friend's counsel that comes from the heart.

Iron sharpens iron; so a man sharpens the countenance of his friend.

Whoever tends the fig tree shall eat its fruit.

As water reflects face, so does the heart reflect the man.

Be diligent to know the state of your flocks, and look well to your herds.

When the hay is gone, the tender grass shows itself, and the herbs of the mountain are gathered in.

The lambs will be for your clothing, and the goats will furnish you the price of a field. And there will be goats' milk enough for your food, for the food of your household, and for the maintenance of your maids.

PROVERB 28

A poor man who oppresses the poor is like a sweeping rain flood which leaves no food.

Some do not despise a thief if he steals to feed his family.

Whoever robs his father or mother is no better than a lawless robber.

He who puts his trust in the Lord shall be enriched and blessed.

PROVERB 29

When the righteous are in authority, the people rejoice, but when the wicked man rules, the people mourn, groan and sigh.

A king by justice establishes the land, and evil are those who transgress boundaries to do harm to a righteous people.

If a ruler listens to a falsehood, all of his officials will become wicked.

The king or queen who faithfully judges the people will have their thrown established continuously.

He who pampers his servant from childhood will have him expecting the rights of a son afterward.

Whoever is partnered in evil hates his own life; but he who loves his life avoids sin.

PROVERB 30

The words of Agur, son of Jakeh of Massa: The man says to Ithiel, to Ithiel and to Ucal:

Every word of God is tried and purified. God is our refuge and our strength.

Remove far from me falsehood and lies; give me neither poverty nor riches; feed me with the food that is needful for me.

Do not accuse another without just cause.

There is a class of people who curse their fathers and do not bless their mothers.

There is a class of people who are pure in their own eyes (their own image) but are not washed from their own filth.

There is a class of people whose teeth are like fangs and sharpened knives, to devour the poor and needy.

There is a class of people who are like leeches - give to me, give to me!

There is a class of people who desire to follow the Lord, shunning all evil and making a commitment to good ways.

There are four things that are little on the earth, but they are exceedingly wise:

The ants are a people not strong, yet they work together to lay up food and build houses.

The birds are but a feeble folk, yet they make their houses in trees and rocks.

The locusts have no king, yet they go forth all of them by bands.

The lizard you can seize with your hands, yet it is in king's palaces.

The lion, the war horse, the male goat also are three who are stately in their step.

If you have done foolishly in exalting yourself, or if you have thought evil, lay your hand upon your mouth and sin no more.

PROVERB 31

The words of Lemuel, king of Massa, which his mother taught him:

What, son of my womb, shall I advise you, son of my vows and my dedication to God?

Give not your strength to loose women, nor your ways to those who ruin and destroy kings.

It is not for kings, O Lemuel, it is not for kings to drink wine, or for rulers to desire strong drink. Lest they drink and forget the law and what it decrees, and pervert the justice due any of the afflicted.

Lest they drink and cannot defend the city from evil enemies.

Give strong drink to him as medicine to him who is ready to pass away. Give a little wine to him in bitter distress of heart.

Open your mouth and speak up for the dumb and for the rights of all who are left desolate and defenseless.

Open your mouth to judge righteously and administer justice for the poor and the needy.

A capable, intelligent, and virtuous woman - she is far more precious than jewels and her value is far above rubies and pearls.

The heart of her husband trusts in her confidently and relies on and believes in her securely, so that he has no lack of gain or need of spoil.

She comforts, encourages, and does him good as long as there is life within her.

She seeks out wool and flax and works with willing hands to develop it.

She is like the merchant ships loaded with foodstuffs; she brings her household's food from afar.

She rises while it is still night and gets food for her household and assigns her maids their tasks.

She considers a new field before she buys or accepts it and she plants fruitful vines in her vineyard.

She girds herself with spiritual, physical, and mental strength.

She knows the gain from her work is good; her lamp goes not out, but burns continually through the night of work.

She lays her hands to the spindle and her thoughts are good ones.

She opens her hands to the poor; she reaches out to the needy in body, mind, or spirit.

She fears not the snow for her family, for they have warm clothing.

She makes for her home coverlets, cushions, rugs of tapestry, and linen garments of clothing; others may buy them. She delivers up girdles and sashes to the merchants. Her position is strong and secure; she rejoices over the future. She open her mouth in skillful and godly Wisdom, and on her tongue is the law of kindness. She looks well to see how things go in her household, and the bread of idleness she will not eat.

Her children rise up and call her blessed and honored, and her husband praises, loves, and adores her. We are thankful for godly mothers and fathers.

A woman or man who reverently and worshipfully fears and loves the Lord, they shall be praised! Give them the fruit of their hands, and let their good works be praised within the gates of the city!

Prophet Zechariah slain

One time the sons of Queen Athaliah broke into the Temple of God and used it for Baal and Asherim worship.

But King Johoiada of Israel sent officers to tear down the images of Baal to pieces; Johoiada was a priest for Lord Jehovah. Mattan, the priest of Baal, was slain before the altars. Queen Athaliah was also slain. Then King Johoiada become old and died; he was 130 years old.

Joash was a repairman for the temple who became king after Johoiada died.

Zechariah who was also called Zack objected to the violence and killing and told King Joash that the priests were not following the Ten Commandments and to stop killing people just because they worshipped other images of God. Zechariah also told the priests that fasting for long periods of time was not necessary.

But Joash did not remember the kindness of Johoiada, and Joash conspired against Zechariah and had him stoned in the court of the Lord's house!

Nebuchadnezzar

During the reign of King Zedekiah who was King of Judah, King Nebuchadnezzar of the Babylonians destroyed Solomon's temple, looted it, and distributed much of artifacts and Moses' people, called Jews, were exiled to Egypt. King Zedekiah was captured in the plains of Jericho and was taken to Babylon. The Nabataeans moved into areas that the Edomites left. The Nabataeans worshipped the sun god Dushara and goddess Allat.

The Jewish Prophet Jeremiah

The Jewish prophet Jeremiah weeped and warned that the temple would be destroyed because of sinfulness. Jeremiah pleaded with the Lord in the name of the people that it was not in the way of a man to direct his own steps. The Lord knew Jeremiah and had set him apart to be a prophet even before the Lord formed him in the womb. Jeremiah did tell what God Jehovah revealed to him, saying 'I, the Lord, search the mind and heart of every person. I know the ways and doings of every person and no one can hide from Me. I have plans to prosper you and not harm you, and plans to give you a future. Stand at the crossroads and look; ask for the ancient paths, ask where the good way is and walk in it, and you will find rest for your souls. Then you will call on Me and come and pray to me, and I will listen to you. You will seek Me and find Me when you seek Me with all of your heart.'

King Nebuchadnezzar also destroyed Egyptian temples that were built to worship Egyptian gods.

Two prophets had a dispute

The prophet Hananiah said that within 2 years, the Lord would bring back all of the silver and gold vessels that Nebuchadnezzar's army had carried off to Babylon when they destroyed Solomon's temple. The prophet Jeremiah told other people at the hearing that Hananiah would only be a true prophet when his prophecy came true and to not believe in a lie; then Hananiah took the yoke bar off the prophet Jeremiah's neck and smashed it and said that he was not a false prophet. The priest Zephaniah tried to make peace between the two prophets.

Prophet Ezekiel and the parable of the cedar twig

The Spirit spoke to Ezekiel saying: 'Son of man, open your mouth and eat what I give you.' And behold, it was a scroll of a book with words of mourning and lamentation. 'The rebellious house of Israel are stubborn of heart and will not listen to Me.' So Ezekiel opened his mouth and ate the scroll; it was as sweet as honey.

Again the word of the Lord Yahweh, who was also called God

Jehovah, came to Ezekiel, saying: 'Son of man, cause Jerusalem to know, understand and realize that the fighting is an abomination and detestable to me. The Israelites and the Philistines will not quit fighting and it is detestable to me. For I desire peace unto all the world. And I, the Lord, will judge those who shed blood. I myself will take a twig from the lofty top of a cedar and will set it out, that it may bring forth boughs and bear fruit and be a noble cedar, and under it shall dwell all birds of every feather; in the shade of its branches they shall nestle and find rest. And all the trees of the field shall know that I the Lord have spoken, and I will do it.'

Ezekiel was a man of God, a prophet, and the word of the Lord came to Ezekiel, saying: 'Son of man, put forth this riddle and speak a parable to the Israelites:'

'A great eagle with great wings and long pinions, rich in feathers of various colors, came down in a field and took the top of a cedar tree. The eagle broke off the topmost twigs and carried it into a land of trade and set it in a city of merchants. Zedekiah, a member of a royal family, took of the seedlings and planted them in fertile soil and a fruitful field; he placed it beside abundant waters and set it as a willow tree. And it grew and became a spreading vine of low stature, whose branches turned toward him, and its roots remained under and subject to him, so it became a vine and brought forth branches and shot forth leafy twigs. There was also another great eagle with great wings and many feathers that took the top of Zedekiah's first vine and carried it away and left it in a new city, and, behold, this vine shot forth its branches for water. The parable is this:

Though a vine was planted in good soil where water was plentiful for it to produce leaves and to bear fruit, it was transplanted, that it might become a splendid vine throughout many places. Likewise, the work of the Spirit is done throughout the world in all lands.'

Ezekiel said: 'We are of this world but the Lord is not of this world. The Lord is the vine and we are the branches. And God hath power over all things.'

And the Lord spoke a message about the seaport of Tyre: O merchant center of the world; your sailors come from cities afar with all their goods to barter for trade; wrought iron, cassia, cinnamon, sweet cane, bronze dishes, fine linen, jewelry of coral and agate, honey oil, balm, choice fabrics of linens, embroidery, carpets bound with chords. Son of dust, be not too boastful that you have used wisdom to get great wealth. A man will not be saved by wealth but by living by what is fair and just.'

The vision of dry bones

And the prophet Ezekiel told of vision he received from the Lord in which the Lord put sinews of muscle and flesh back onto dry human bones that were left in a valley, breathed life into them, and the life became new. Ezekiel prophesized that this meant to have hope in the Lord, that God said 'I will put a new heart and spirit in you. This day is a new beginning to renew your sense of purpose.'

The vision of a temple

Ezekiel had a vision from the Lord Jehovah of a future temple; Ezekiel said: 'I saw cherub angels sitting on thrones in heaven with the Lord, and there were gates to the Temple, each ten cubits in width, on the north, south, east, and west sides; and there was an altar measured in cubits of one cubit plus a handbreadth; its base was a cubit high and a cubit wide; the ledge all around it: one span; the hearth of the altar was square and twelve cubits by twelve cubits and rested upon the base with a ledge all round of half a cubit. The steps to the altar were on the east side. There was an inner court and an outer court, and an outer wall. There were two leaves which made up one door, each leaf on hinges. There were carved cherubs and palm trees on the doors.
The east gate is only for the priests. Holy water was sprinkled on those who believed. The Lord spoke from a halo that resembled a rainbow to angels that were working and their construction was like a wheel within a wheel. And I saw that the Lord Jehovah also carried a sword to protect heaven from Satan.'

Belshazzar and the writing on the wall

King Belshazzar was a descendant of King Nebuchadnezzar. Belshazzer was feasting on wine in silver and gold vessels that his father Nebuchadnezzar had taken from the temple that he had destroyed. Suddenly there appeared fingers of a man's hand that wrote on the plaster of the wall opposite the candlestick; the king's face immediately changed to astonishment and alarmed him. The king cried to bring in the enchanters and soothsayers and astrologers. The king said 'Whoever can read this writing and show me the interpretation of it will be clothed in purple and have a chain of gold put around his neck'. The wise men could not interpret it. Then Daniel was brought before the king and the king said to him 'I have been told that you can make interpretations out of knotty problems. Now, if you can read this writing and interpret it you will be clothed in purple and I will put a chain of gold around your neck.' Then Daniel answered before the king, 'Let your gifts be

for yourself and give your rewards to another.
Your father Nebuchadnezzar had a kingdom of glory and greatness and majesty, but then he was hardened and he lost his glory. Belshazzaar, the message on the wall says that the days of your kingship will be brought to an end.' Then King Darius took control of the kingdom.

Daniel

Now Daniel, a Jew, would get down on his knees three times a day to worship the God of Israel, the Ancient of Days. The angel Gabriel gave him understandings to his prayers. Daniel ate only vegetables and fruits. Some men saw him praying when the windows to his chambers were opened; it was forbidden to pray to anyone except the king.
The men brought Daniel before the king and Daniel was thrown into a den of lions, but the lions did not hurt him. Then the king commanded that Daniel should be taken up out of the den of lions. Then King Darius wrote all the nations that dwelt on earth to decree that they should fear the God of Daniel, for He is the living God, enduring and steadfast forever, and His Realm shall never be destroyed and His Dominion should be to the end of the world. Daniel had a night vision, and behold, on the clouds of the heavens came One like a Son of Man, and He came to the Ancient of Days, and there was given to Him (the Messiah) dominion and glory, and the God of heaven will set up a kingdom that will never be destroyed.

Hosea the Jewish Minister

Hosea was a Jew and a minister for God's message. Hosea had 3 children by Gomer; a son called Jezreel, a daughter called Lo-ruhamah, and a son called Lo-Ammi. The Lord said to Hosea 'I will betroth My people to me forever in stability and in faithfulness and they shall know the Lord forever in steadfast love. I will pour down rain from the heavens, and the earth will respond in grain and oil and living creatures. You are my people and they will say 'You are my God!' Hosea's wife was unfaithful to him once, so Hosea was deeply hurt and embittered, but the Lord told Hosea to forgive her. Gomer was given a second chance and their life was refashioned and recreated for the better. Hosea and Gomer reaffirmed their love for each other; they reconfirmed their marriage.

The Jewish Prophet Joel

Joel in 830BCE did say 'Tell your children about the Lord, and let your children tell their children, and their children another generation.
And you shall eat in plenty and be satisfied and praise the name of the Lord, your God.'

The Jewish herder Amos

Amos was a Jewish herder of sheep who grew figs and sycamore trees in Tekoa, southeast of Bethlehem. Amos declared to the people 'hate evil and love good. Seek the Maker of the constellations Pleiades and Orion. Turn to the One who calls for the waters of the sea and pours them out upon the face of the earth - the Lord!'

The Jewish Prophet Obadiah

Obadiah was a prophet and servant of the Lord who told the people of Edom 'Do not let the pride of your heart deceive you. Say in your heart, 'I belong to the Lord and I will always state the truth and do the righteousness of the Lord.'

The Jewish Prophet Micah

The prophet Micah did say to the people 'Let the Lord be witness among you for righteousness. Let the Lord be the conqueror of all evil. The Lord will hold all people together like sheep, like a flock in the midst of the pasture, the Lord at their head.'

'The promise of restoration provides hope for those who put their trust in the Lord.'

The Peace Parable

And Isaiah and Micah knew the parable of the vine and the fig tree which told that one day everyone beneath a vine and fig tree shall live in peace, and shall plow shares in turn, unafraid, and nations shall learn war no more.

The Jewish Prophet Nahum

Nahum did say the Lord was slow to anger and great in power. Nahum said 'The Lord is good, a Strength and Stronghold in the day of troubles or calm. The Lord brings healing. The Lord unceasingly and continually gathers the people together that are scattered. And those who bring good tidings and peace will celebrate feasts with the Lord.'

The Jewish Prophet Habakkuk

The Lord told Habakkuk that divine plans were being put in place to promote righteousness and justice forever upon the earth; the Lord said 'Evilness and slayings will be abolished, and the righteous will live by faith and faithfulness. Woe to those who do wickedness.' And Habakkuk put to music the words 'The Lord God is my personal bravery and my invincible guide!' And Habakkuk did say that the Lord is in the holy temple and the earth should be quiet before the Lord.

The Jewish Prophet Zephaniah

Zephaniah did tell the people to make the Lord the foremost necessity of your life, never ceasing to pray and reflect upon the goodness of the Lord.

The Jewish Prophet Haggai

Haggai did tell the Israelites: Who is left among you who saw the temple in its former glory?

The work of your hands has been focused on your mansions; the temple is being neglected.
So the time came when the people restored the temple to all of its beauty and majesty.

The Jewish Prophet Zechariah

Zechariah had visions given to him from the Lord that reassured the people that the Lord cares. Zeckariah protected his sheep from the wolves with a staff, or cane, of a carved wooden stick. The Lord told Zechariah that all people are under a covenant of divine guidance, just as Zechariah protected his flock of sheep, so God is protecting all people on earth. Zechariah and Haggai were both prophets who told the Israelites to not be dismayed but to rebuild the temple to the Lord; Zechariah said an angel of the Lord told him that God's people would be prosperous again. Zechariah said the Feast of the Booths (Sukkot) or the Feast of the Tabernacle would last 7 days to celebrate pilgrimages to the temple and to remember the sukkot that housed the Jews during the exodus in the wilderness. A sukkah is a walled structure (booth) covered with leafy plants and palm leaves.

In a vision Joshua the high priest was clothed in dirty garments, but Zechariah told Joshua to put a clean turban upon his head and clothe himself in clean garments. Then an angel of the Lord said 'This is a sign that iniquity is passed from you and you are clothed anew and clean of sin.'
And the angel of the Lord told Zechariah to behold a vision of a lampstand of all gold, with its bowl for oil on the top of it, with seven pipes to each of the seven lamps upon it. And there are two olive trees by it, one on the right and one on the left; and both olive trees feed it continuously with oil so it is never without oil.

Rejoice greatly, Daughter Zion! I will take away the chariots and warhorses from Jerusalem, and the battle bow will be broken. A king will come to you riding on a donkey and He will proclaim peace to the nations.

The Last Jewish Prophet – Malachi

Malachi told the Israelites to always love the Lord and never forget God's presence and love. Malachi said that the Lord said: I am the Lord, I do not change, and that is why the generations of people continue throughout all ages of time, and all nations will be happy and blessed. Towidah is Hebrew for generations.

I will send Elijah the prophet before the day the Lord comes, and he will reconcile the heart of ungodly back to Me.

Behold, I send My messenger, and he shall prepare the way before Me. And the Lord whom you seek, will suddenly come to the Temple, the Messenger or Angel of the covenant, Whom you desire, behold, he shall come, says the Lord.

Ecclesiastes the Jewish preacher

Ecclesiastes wrote:
To everything there is a season, and a time for every matter or purpose under heaven: a time to be born and a time to die,
a time to plant and a time to harvest,
a time to kill and a time to heal,
a time to break down and a time to build up,
a time to weep and a time to laugh,
a time to mourn and a time to dance,
a time to cast away stones and a time to gather stones together,
a time to embrace and a time to refrain from embracing,
a time to get and a time to lose,
a time to keep and a time to cast away,
a time to rend and a time to sew,
a time to keep silence and a time to speak,
a time to love and a time to hate,
a time for war and a time for peace,
a time to preserve and a time to change.
What profit remains for the worker from his toil? I have seem painful labor and exertion and miserable business that God has given to men and women to keep them busy. God has made everything beautiful in its time. God has planted eternity in people's hearts and minds, a divinely implanted sense of a purpose working through the ages which nothing under the sun but God Elohim alone can satisfy, yet so people cannot find out what God has done from the beginning to the end.
I know that there is nothing better for them than to be glad and to get and do good as long as they live; and also that every person should eat and drink and enjoy the good of all their labor – it is the gift of God. And there is no person who has power over the Spirit to retain the breath of life, neither have they power over the day of death. Fear God and obey the good commands, for this is the duty of humankind.

The Second JewishTemple

King Cyrus of Persia declared that he would build a second temple to the Lord in Jerusalem and it was completed.
Then there was a fire and the gates of Jerusalem were destroyed. When King Artaxerxes made Nehemiah governor, Nehemiah tried to repair the walls and gates of Jerusalem with the priest Ezra. They had help. The gates repaired were the Fish Gate, Old Gate, Valley Gate, Dung Gate, Fountain Gate, Horse Gate, Water Gate,
East Gate, Muster Gate, Sheep Gate. The gates were built and set to stand up with bolts and the bars were set. They repaired the Broad Wall and the Tower. Nehemiah said 'The joy of the Lord is my strength.'

Hannukkah

In 165 BCE, Judah Maccabee and Mattathias ben Johanan of the Hasmoneans led a revolt against king Antiochus IV of the Selecid Empire who tried to abolish Judaism for a

Hellenistic religion. The uprising ended Greek rule and the Hanukkah festival is named for the Maccabean victory and commemorates the rededication of the Jewish Temple. Hanukkah is a festival that lasts 8 days from the 25th day of Kislev (in December) which is the 9th month in Judaism and called the month of dreams. Lighting the Menorah with 8 candles and eating potato latkes and applesauce are traditions of Hanukkah. When the Menashe family of the Jews were starving during a cold winter, their dog dug up some potatoes in the snow and found some apples, saving the family. King Antiochus also forbade the Jews to read the Torah but they studied it silently. If the Jews heard enemy soldier footsteps, they hid the Torah and played the game of dreidel. The dreidel is a spinning top with 4 letters on its sides with a double meaning. To begin the game, about 10-15 objects are gathered (such as nuts, raisins, pennies, or rocks) and put into the middle pot. A player spins the dreidel. If the dreidel says N they get nothing. If the dreidel says G the get the entire pot. If the dreidel says H they get half of what is in the pot (plus one, if there is an odd number left). If the dreidel says SH they have to put two objects into the pot. When only one object or none is left in the pot, every player adds one. When one person has everything, they win the game.
The letters of the dreidel also stand for Nes Gadol Haya Sham wich means A Great Miracle Happened Here.

Mattathias was a Kohen (a Jewish priest). The Maccabees were of the Sadducees who were a priestly class of Jews in charge of the Temple. The Pharisees were a rabbinic class of Jews. The Pharisees did not include the Maccabees in the Hebrew Bible because of political rivalry with Sadducees. Mattathias was a son of John and a grandson of Simeon. Mattathias moved his family from Jerusalem to Modein. The sons of Mattathias were John also called Gadd, Simon also called Thassi, Judas also called Maccabeus, Eleazar also called Avaran, and Jonathan also called Apphus.

Jewish leader Simon Bar Kokhba revolted again in 132 CE but was defeated by the Romans.

King Ahasuerus and Queen Vashti got a divorce.

Then King Ahasuerus took Esther, daughter of Abihail, from a harem of maidens and she obtained grace and favor in his sight so he made her a queen and placed a crown upon her head and royal robes upon her shoulders. And the older queen taught the young maidens how to be ladylike in verse, and the proper way to stand and sit. Queen Esther liked to worship the Jehovah Spirit with the Jews and Egyptians, and she spent time with maids Amantha and Natasha weaving cotton mats and blankets for orphans and widows, but King Ahasuerus called it unnecessary of the queen. Esther told him that her hands could not rest all the time. Ahasuerus called Esther a Queen of Mercy.
Queen Esther and King Ahasuerus held a banquet and guests were invited, and Amantha and Natasha brought mint leaves and figs.

Book of Job

And there was Job, a righteous Jewish man who was blameless and of great wealth; he abstained from and shunned all evil.
Job had seven sons and three daughters.
He possessed 7,000 sheep, 3,000 camels, 500 yoke of oxen, 500 donkeys, and a very great body of servants, so that he had much.

Then Job came upon many troubles; robbers stole some of his herds, a bolt of lightning burned up a portion of his property, and some of his family were killed when a dust whirlwind from the desert collapsed the four corners of the house, but he had great faith in the Holy Spirit, although he questioned God: 'Surely, O God, you have worn me out; why was I born? What is the purpose of my life? Why am I living in misery and why is my life bitter to the soul? For my sighing and groaning comes before you, poured out like water. I was not or am not at ease, nor had I or have not rest, nor was I or am quiet, yet trouble came and still comes upon me.'

Eliphaz, a friend of Job ventured to converse with him 'Job, will you be offended if I speak?'
'Your own good words have before held firm many who were falling, and now you are distressed and grieved and your confidence in God has been shaken, but I beg you to keep the faith in God. Seek God who does great and marvelous things and maintain hope in the Holy Spirit. This is what I have searched out and it is true.'

And Job answered 'If my grief and impatience could be weighed on a balance against all hope, my grief would be heavier that the sand of the sea. Man is appointed a hard labor upon earth and my soul is afflicted in my suffering; I am looking for my reward but I am allotted only futile suffering and misery. When I lie down at night, I am full of tossing to and fro till the dawning of the day. I know that my life is but a swift breath in passing, yet my bitterness will not comfort me this day; I am speaking with the anguish of my spirit.'

Then the friend Bildad did say to Job, 'How long will you say these things? The words from your mouth are like a mighty wind. Know that our fathers of former age also searched out the strength to hold fast to God. Surely you will be filled with laughter and joyful shouting once again. If we do not keep faith maybe the Lord will inflict us with punishment in our lives.'

Then Job answered, 'Hold your peace and let me speak! I do appeal for mercy from the Lord, although I know it is true that God may not answer all questions of the thousands. But I loathe the workings of my life at present. It exists in gloom.'

Then Zophar replied to Job, 'God's wisdom is as high as the heights of heaven and longer in measure than the

Earth. Lift your face to the Lord and set your heart aright and stretch out your hands to God, and you shall forget your misery and you will not be afraid. I do not think the Lord inflicted a punishment on Job – I think it was just evil men who stole his herds. As for the whirlwind which killed his family, that is knowledge for the Lord.'

Job answered; 'No doubt you are wise yourself and have understanding. I have become a laughingstock to my friends. With the aged comes wisdom and with the length of days comes understanding. Behold, my ear has heard and understood your words. Your memorable sayings are as proverbs. Still I do beg for the Lord to listen to the pleadings of my lips.'

Then Eliphaz answered Job: 'Among us are both the gray-haired and aged and you have uttered such as a wise man. Do not let the feelings of your heart carry you away and control you in torment, but turn your spirit to God and be filled with hope.'

Job said; 'My face has been red and swollen with weeping. I am withered and my spirit has broken. Who is there that will give security to me? I have lost much.'

Bildad suggested: 'The Lord is working your situation and will place the branches of powers where they will be.'

Job begged: 'Have pity on me! O you my friends! I know my God my Redeemer lives yet I have been destroyed.'

Zophar then replied: 'It is of my understanding and my spirit that answers that from of old times before man has reached unto the heavens. Your heart should be filled with the spirits of your friends here beside you who wish you well.'

Job replied; 'You have comforted me with your words.'

Eliphaz spoke: 'Be profitable to God - give to others who are also weary – water to drink and bread to the hungry. It is not a gain to God to make only your own ways perfect. There are many among us that suffer.'

Job said: 'My complaint today is rebellious and bitter, but I lay my cause before God and fill my mouth with arguments. I seek to learn that God will answer me. But I do go forward in righteousness and my foot has held fast to the Lord's steps. I have not gone back from the commandments that were brought forth by Moses. Though am I troubled and terrified, my innermost heart has not been broken and I will not be cut off from the Lord. I am not a liar, wrongdoer, or murderer.'

Bildad said; 'The Lord has dominion over everything and will make peace. All people get frustrated with this life on earth.'

Job was gladdened and said: 'Your counsel of assistance is plentiful in knowledge. It is with the Lord's spirit that you have uttered these words. Who can

contemplate the magnificent whispers of the voice of the True Spirit?
As long as my life is still whole within me and the breath of God is in my nostrils, my lips shall not speak untruth, nor shall my tongue utter deceit. I pray that those who have taken away my right and denied my justice, who have vexed and embittered my life, will be reproached. I hope that God will hear my cry and I will hold to the delight in the Almighty. God causes men to clap their hands at good times and hiss out in bad times with regard to Faith. I remember the days when I was in my prime, surrounded by my children and the rock poured out streams of oil! But those were days of old. Terrors turned upon me and my confidence was torn apart and I am living in days of affliction. I am stretching out my hand for a second look in a heap of calamity. My heart is troubled and it does not rest. I am a brother to the howling jackals and a companion to screaming ostriches. I have not walked falsehood and vanity.
Does God see my ways and count all my ways and all my steps?
Oh, let me be weighed on a just balance. Oh, for a hearing and an answer from the Almighty!
My Redeemer liveth, and although my flesh be weak, yet shall I be healed, and I shall behold the Lord.
I would proudly bear on my shoulder my scroll for the Lord and the number of steps that I have taken to approach the presence of the Holy Spirit when my life is over.'

So the three men and Job ceased counsel, but there was a fifth man also – Elihu, son of Barachel.

Elihu said: 'Hear my words also, for the ear tries words as the palate tastes food. I will bring my knowledge.
Multitudes of the oppressed cry for help because of the violence of the mighty, the pride of evil men. Bear with me for I still have something to say. Let not the greatness
of suffering turn you aside. Take heed; turn not to complaining against God.
For God may have allowed you out of the mouth of distress into a broad place where there is no situation of perplexity or privation; and that which would be set on your table would be full.
So let not wrath entice you into scorning chastisements
and let not suffering turn you aside from God. God spreads the lightening in the sky but shines the blue skies also. With rich moisture in the clouds and an icy breath, the Lord sends the snowstorms and the rainstorms.
If the Lord changes the weather maybe that is why the Lord changes our lives – no one knows and that is why we must keep our faith.'

So Job and his friends had profound conversations discussing God Jehovah and the mysteries of divine intervention and divine works. The Holy Spirit

spoke to Job in a revelation, saying:
'There are things on earth that are not understood that only I understand. Those who seek my way seek love and righteousness for all. Life is hard so be servants to each other in love so all can have radiant, good lives. Those who think they know everything do not. Do not believe evil and do not commit evil. Do not judge another, for only I know the true intentions of everything. Do not think that you alone are limited to divine wisdom, for that is only for God.'

Job prayed; 'Teach me Lord and I will hold my peace. I am of small account and vile! I lay my hand on my mouth.'

Job's life was restored after much hard work and the support of his family and friends. It was Job's season of peace and prosperity, his season of Shalom. Job believed the Holy Spirit visited him because his herds were magnified to 14,000 sheep, 6,000 camels, 1.000 yoke of oxen, and 1,000 donkeys. Job lived 140 years and died. Job never lost his faith in the Holy Spirit and Job never lost his good spirit despite all of the obstacles that he faced.

The Book of Life

Some of the Jews thought God was keeping records and if your name was written in the Book of Life, your soul will be saved and there was a record of sinners, but many servants of God did not believe in such a book; they said God could keep records without a book.

The Jewish Prophet Jonah

The Lord told Jonah to go tell some people that they were sinning. Jonah did not obey and went wayward instead. Jonah was in a boat and there was a raging storm in the sea. Other men in the boat thought that Jonah was causing the storm because the Lord was mad at Jonah for disobeying His order. The men tossed Jonah overboard and Jonah was swallowed by a fish. Jonah prayed for His Creator to *redeem* him (save him) from the belly of the fish and he was vomited out after three days, recovered, and lived on.

Jonah went to Nineveh and preached the word of God.

The king of Nineveh arose from his throne, laid his robe aside, put on his sackcloth and sat in ashes to humble himself. The king decreed and made a proclamation for all people to cover themselves in sackcloth and fast for a time; Let everyone turn from their evil ways and from the violence that is at hand, he said.

The Lord forgave the sinners for their wickedness but Jonah was angry at the Most High for forgiving them. The Most High explained to Jonah that the people did not know their left hand from their right hand and for Jonah to not be angry.

The psalms were praise songs with the accompaniment of musical instruments. Most of them were written by David, but some are attributed to Asaph, sons of Korah, Moses, Heman the Ezrahite, Etham the Ezrahite, and a few to Solomon. The 150 psalms have been reduced of redundancy and have been condensed into 45 psalms.

PSALM 1

God Jehovah is Good

A psalm of David

1. Blessed and happy is the one who does not take the counsel of the wicked for a guide, or follow the path that sinners walk, or take his seat in the company of the scornful.
2. His delight is in the law of the God Jehovah; it is his meditation day and night.
3. He is like a tree planted beside water channels; it yields its fruit in season and its foliage never fades. So he too prospers in all he does.
4. The wicked – those who knowingly do evil - are not like this; rather they are like chaff driven by wind.
5. When judgement comes, therefore, the wicked and sinners will not stand firm in the assembly of the righteous.
6. For God Jehovah knows and is fully acquainted with the way of the righteous and the sinners and will judge both accordingly to the Lord's will.
7. Know and understand that the Lord is God! It is God who made us, not we ourselves.
8. The Lord is resplendent with lightband glorious and excellent, more majestic than the everlasting mountains.
9. We are God's people and the sheep of God's pasture. Jehovah is constantly thinking about us and He will bless the people of Israel and the priests of Aaron.
10. The Lord is good and the Lord's love endures forever; the Lord's everlasting loving-kindness and truth endure to all generations. Blessed is Jehovah's name forever and forever. Praise Him from sunrise to sunset!

PSALM 2

God is Our Leader

A psalm of Solomon

1. Why are the nations in turmoil?
Why do the peoples plan their futile plots?
2. He who sits as God Jehovah enthroned in the heavens declares: be mindful, you earthly rulers, worship God with reverence,
tremble and pay glad homage to Your Creator, for I Am the Only Ruler and the Leader of All.
3. Magistrates and judges defend the afflicted among the people, save the children of the needy, and demand justice from the oppressor.
4. May the leaders and judges honor You, O Lord, as all the earth gives tribute to You.

5. May leaders be as good as the showers that water the earth.
6. We will pray for our leaders, who save the oppressed from fraud and violence, and help the needy and the poor.
7. A corrupt throne cannot be allied with You, O Lord. A corrupt throne brings on misery by its own decrees.
8. Blessed and happy are all who find refuge in the Lord, who is the mighty counsel from on High. God Jehovah is our light.
9. The Lord decreed a statute of righteousness, and our forefathers followed the statute.
10. I will behave myself wisely and be careful to live a blameless life. I will walk in my house in integrity and with an innocent heart. I will calm my heart and soul and enjoy the peace of God.
11. I hate the deeds of wicked people, of those who turn aside from the good path; it shall not grasp me.
12. Whoever slanders his neighbor to spread lies, I will have no part. Whoever has a boastful heart where undue, I will not endure.
13. My time will be spent with the faithful in the land, that they may dwell with me; he whose walk is blameless will minister to me.
14. He who practices deceit shall not dwell in my house; no one who speaks falsely will stand in my presence.
15. Oh, do not deliver the life of your turtledove to the wild beast; forget not the lives of your afflicted people forever.
16. Morning after morning I will reaffirm my resistance to all evil in the land; I will recommit myself to the Lord.
17. God is our hope and strength, a very present help in trouble. Therefore will we not fear, though the earth be moved and though the hills be carried into the midst of the sea;
Though the waters thereof rage and swell, and though the mountains shake,
18. God is in the midst of us, therefore shall we not be moved.
19. God maketh wars to cease in all the world; God breaketh the bow, and knappeth the spear in sunder, and burneth the chariots in the fire.
20. Be still then, and know that I am God. I will be exalted among the nations, and I will be exalted in the earth.
21. The Lord of hosts is with us; the God of Jacob is our refuge. Trust and rely on the Lord who led Moses, Aaron, and Jacob.
22. The Lord reigns, let all the earth be glad; let the distant shores, the multitude of isles and coastlands rejoice!

PSALM 3

God is Victor over Enemies

1. Lord, how numerous are my enemies!
2. How many there are against me, how many who say of me "He will not find safety in God!"
3. But you, Lord, are a

shield to cover me: you are my
glory, you raise my head high.
4. As often as I cry aloud to the
Lord, the Lord answers from the
heavens.
5. I lie down and sleep,
and I wake again, for the Lord
upholds me.
6. I shall not fear their myriad
forces ranged against me on
every side.
7. Arise, Lord; save me from my
enemies, my God!
8. Frustrate and divide evil
counsels, Lord!
I have seen violence and strife in
the city;
9. day and night they encircle it;
all along the walls,
it is filled with trouble and
mischief,
10. there is much destruction;
its public square is never free
from oppression and deceit.
11. One time it was no enemy
that taunted me, or I should have
avoided him. It was a man of my
own sort, a comrade of my own.
12. Evening and morning and at
noonday
I will make my complaint and
groan.
13. The Lord will hear my cry
and deliver me and give me
security so that none attack me,
for many are hostile to me; they
outnumber the hairs on my head.
14. I am worn out crying for
help; my throat is parched. I am
forced to restore what I did not
steal.
15. Such evil men do violence to
those at peace with them and
break their solemn word;
they have no respect for an oath,
nor any fear of God.
16. Their speech is smooth, but
their thoughts are at war.
17. Requite evil-doers for their
devious works and their evil
deeds,
18. You have established a
bulwark of strength against your
adversaries to restrain the enemy
and the avenger.
19. Yours is the victory, Lord;
your blessing will rest on your
people.
20. In my day of fear, I put my
trust in You, The Most High.
21. in God, whose promise is my
boast, in God I trust and shall not
be afraid;
what can mortals do to me?
22. Innocent though I am, they
rush to oppose me.
But You, O God of angelic hosts,
arouse yourself to come to me
and keep watch.
23. Have no mercy on the
treacherous evildoers
24. who come out at nightfall,
snarling like dogs as they prowl
about the city.
25. God, hear my cry; listen to my
prayer
26. From the end of the earth I
call to you with fainting heart;
lift me up and set me high on a
rock.
27. For you have been my shelter,
a tower of strength against
hopelessness.
28. The Lord will scatter evil and
break it apart.
29. The evil flee at your reproach

30. but the good are like doves with wings of silver and platinum and feathers of gold and bronze.
31. The wicked shall lick the dust.
32. Truly my soul finds rest in God who gives me salvation. Restore to me the joy of your salvation, and uphold me with a willing spirit.

PSALM 4

Trust in the Lord

A psalm of Asaph

1. Answer me when I call, O God, the upholder of my righteousness!
When I was in distress you set me free; have mercy on me and hear my prayer.
2. O men, how long will you turn my glory and honor into shame? How long will you seek after lies?
3. The Lord knows a loyal servant; the Lord hears when I call to Him.
4. offer your due of sacrifice, and put your trust in the Lord.
5. There are many who say, 'If we might see good times! Let the light of your face shine on us. Lord.'
6. Today, if you hear the Lord's voice,
7. harden not your hearts,
8. and wait in patience with the Lord
9. and do not let your hearts go astray, but know the good ways of the Lord.
10. The Lord has put into my heart a greater happiness than others had from grain and wine in plenty.
11. From the rising of the sun to its setting, and as far as the east is from the west, I put my trust in You, O Lord.
12. For You are my hope, O God. You have been my hope since my youth.
13. From birth I have relied on You, for You brought me from my mother's womb. You made me hope and trust when I was on my mother's breasts.
You have been my benefactor from that day. My praise is continually of You, and I will ever praise you.
14. Now in peace I shall lie down and sleep;
for it is you alone, Lord, who lets me live in safety and confident trust.

PSALM 5

Have Faith in the Lord

A psalm of Asaph

1. Listen to my words, Lord, consider my inmost thoughts;
2. heed my cry for help, Dear God,
3. When I pray to you , Lord, in the morning and lay my requests before you, I wait in expectation that you will hear me.
4. You are not a God who welcomes wickedness; evil can be no guest of yours.
5. You will make an end of liars. The Lord abhors those who are violent and deceitful.
6. But through Your great love I may come into Your House, and at Your holy temple bow down in awe.

7. Lead me and protect me, Lord, because I am beset by enemies; give me a straight path to follow Your way.
8. Nothing they say is true; they are bent on complete destruction and slander; their smooth talk runs off their tongues.
9. God, they have defied you and Your desire for goodness.
10. But let all who take refuge in You rejoice, and
let them forever shout for joy; shelter those who love Your name, that they may exult in You.
11. For You, Lord, will bless the righteous; You will surround them with favour as with a shield.
12. There is great assembly in the congregation to praise the Lord. Let the daughters and sons of Mount Zion be glad!
13. Your ways are seen, O Lord, even your procession into the holy sanctuary. The procession is festive all the way to the decorated altar to the Lord.
14. In front are singers, musicians, and dancers.
15. O, Spirit of all creation, the people adore You.
16. In the course of my life, my Lord has been the source of my strength; in times of weakness, affliction, troubles, and joy.
17. As a father or mother has compassion for their children, so the Lord has compassion on those who worship God.

PSALM 6

Praise the Lord

A psalm of Moses

1. Lord, you have been our dwelling place throughout all generations.
2. Before the mountains were brought forth or before the earth was formed, from everlasting to everlasting You are God.
3. You turn men back to dust;
4. for a thousand years in your sight are like a day that has just gone by, or like a watch in the night;
5. you cut mortals off and they are asleep in death.
They are like grass which shoots up;
6. though in the morning it flourishes and shoots up,
by evening it droops and withers.
7. He that dwelleth in the secret place of the Most High
shall abide under the shadow of the Almighty. I will say of the Lord, the Lord is my refuge and my fortress. My God, in Him will I trust.
8. Lord, do not be angry at us or punish us but uphold us in the light of your presence.
Forgive our iniquities, our secret heart and its sins.
9. The days pass by and turn into years
10. Seventy years is the span of our life,
eighty if our strength holds;
at their best they are but toil and sorrow,
for they pass quickly and we fly away to vanish.
11. Who knows the power of your wisdom, O God? Your wisdom is as great as the honor that is due you.

12. Teach us to number our days aright, that we may gain a heart of wisdom.
13. O Lord, how long will it be? Have compassion now on your servants.
14. O satisfy us with Your mercy and loving-kindness in this morning, before we get older, that we may rejoice and be glad all our days.
15. Make us glad for as many days as you have humbled us,
for as many years as we have known misfortune.
16. Let Your work be revealed to Your servants, and Your glorious majesty to their children.
17. And may the delight of the Lord our God rest upon us; confirm and establish the work of our hands for us – yes, the work of our hands, confirm and establish it.
18. The Lord on High is mightier and more glorious than the noise of many waters, yes, than the mighty thunders and waves of the sea.
19. Holiness adorns your house for all eternity, O Lord.
Your statutes and testimonies will stand firm for all time.
20. How good it is that brothers dwell in unity. Praise the Lord.

PSALM 7

The Lord is my savior

A psalm of the sons of Korah
1. Lord, my God, in You I find refuge and put my trust; rescue me from all my pursuers and save me
2. before they tear at my life like a lion and drag me off beyond hope of rescue.
3. Lord my God, if I have done any of these things –if I have stained my hands with guilt,
4. if I have done evil to a friend or robbed an enemy –
5. then let the enemy trample my life and then lay my honour in the dust.
6. Decree your justice and order justice done, O, Lord.
7. Let the assembly of the people be gathered about You, and let the Lord rule over them from on high.
8. The Lord judges the people. Judge me, Lord, according to the integrity that is in me.
9. O, righteous Lord, who searches minds and hearts, let the wicked do no more harm, and make the righteous secure.
10. My defense and shield is God Most High, who saves the honest of heart.
11. God is a just judge,
constant in his righteous directions.
12. I shall praise the Lord for divine righteousness and sing to the name of the Lord Most High.
13. Let my heart be sound in Your good statutes, that I may not be put to shame.
14. Be merciful to those who desire to follow your good ways.
15. Let your compassion and merciful forgiveness come to me that I may live delightfully.
16. I thank you for the graceful blessings that you bestow upon me.

17. Protect my life according to Your love and keep me from the snarls of evil.
18. Direct my footsteps according to Your will; let no sin rule over me.
19. I will pray to you at dawn and at midnight; I will pray to You continually all day long.
20. I cry out to You for help; I have put my hope in You,
My beautiful God.
21. Quiet and calm my soul, O Lord, like a weaned child with its mother or a governing father.
22. Lord, put me where you want me and make me to flourish as you wish; You are my keen and firm strength.
23. The Lord's laws comes first to my mind.
24. Your statutes are my heritage forever; they are the joy of my heart.
25. I have inclined my heart to perform your statutes forever, even to the end.
26. I hate the thoughts of evil, but I love your laws. I confess when I have done wrong.
27. I am small and insignificant in the great scheme of things, but I do not forget You, God.
28. Long ago I learned of Your statutes, and for a long time I have known tht You have established them forever.
29. How shall a man or woman keep their way pure?
By living according to Your Word. Praise the Lord.
30. Thus will I bless God while I live; I will lift up my hands in thy Name.

PSALM 8

The Majestic Earth

1. O Lord our Lord,
how glorious is Your name throughout the earth!
Your majesty is praised as high as the heavens,
2. even from the mouths of babes and infants at the breast.
3. When I look up at your heavens, the work of your fingers, at the moon and the stars you have set in place,
4. God's lightning lights up the world
5. light is shed upon and strewn along pathways
6. what is a frail mortal, that you should be mindful of him, a human being, that you should take notice of him?
7. Yet you have made him little less than a heavenly being,
8. You make him master over all that you have made, putting everything in subjection under his feet:
9. all sheep and oxen, all the wild animals,
10. the birds in the air, the fish in the sea, and everything that moves along ocean paths.
11. The meadows are clothed in flocks, the valleys are covered with grain; they shout for joy and sing together.
12. You send abundant showers and warm sunlight to refresh our weary heritage;
13. the trees were watered and filled with sap, the cedars that were planted.

14. The high mountains are for the wild goats; the rocks as refuge for the badgers.
15. The moon knows its phases and the sun knows its settings.
16. You bring darkness, it becomes night, and all the night beasts of the forest prowl.
17. The young lions roar after their prey and seek their food from God.
18. When the sun rises, they withdraw themselves and lie down in their dens.
19. The people go forth out to work and remain at task until evening when the sun goes down.
20. O Lord, how many and varied are Your works! In wisdom have You made them all; the earth is full of Your riches and Your creatures.
21. Your people flourished From Your bounty and goodness.
22. There is the sea, vast and wide, in which are innumerable creatures, both great and small.
23. There go the ships of the sea, and the sea monster; which You have formed to frolic there.
24. These all wait and are dependent upon You, that You may give them their food in due season, their nourishment at the proper time.
25. You sent Your Spirit and gave them breath, and You replenish the earth.
26. O Lord our sovereign,
how glorious are Your works and how glorious is Your name throughout the world!
27. As for man, his days are like grass; he flourishes like a flower; the wind blows over it and it is gone, and its place shall know it no more.

PSALM 9

God is a Tower of Strength

1. I shall give praise to you, Lord, with my whole heart, I shall recount all your marvelous deeds.
2. I shall rejoice and be glad in You, the Most High; I shall sing praise to your name.
3. For seated on Your Throne forever, You are a righteous judge.
4. The evil are finished, and ruined forever.
You have overthrown the evil; all memory of them is lost.
5. The Lord will judge the world with justice, and will try the cause of peoples with equity.
6. May the Lord be a tower of strength for the oppressed,
a tower of strength in time of trouble.
7. Those who acknowledge Your Name will trust in You, for you, Lord, do not abandon those who seek you.
8. Sing to the Lord and proclaim his deeds among the nations.
9. The poor will not be unheeded, nor the hope of the destitute be forgotten.
10. The nations have plunged into a pit of their own making; their feet are entangled in the net they have hidden.
11. Arise, Lord, restrain the power of mortals;
let the nations be judged in the presence of Your Spirit.

PSALM 10

When the Lord is silent

1. Why do You stand far off, Lord? Why hide away in times of trouble?
2. The wicked in their arrogance hunt down the afflicted; but let them be taken in their own crafty schemes.
3. The wicked boast of the desires they harbour: in their greed they curse and revile the Lord.
4. The wicked in their pride do not seek God; there is no place for God in any of their schemes.
5. Their ways are always devious;
Your judgements are beyond their grasp, and they scoff at all their adversaries.
6. Because they escape misfortune, they think they will never be shaken.
7. The wicked person's mouth is full of
cursing, deceit, and violence;
mischief and wickedness are under his tongue.
8. He lurks in ambush in hiding places and murders the innocent by stealth.
9. He lies in wait like a lion, he lies in wait to seize the poor; he seizes the poor into his net.
10. The helpless fall by his toils.
11. He says to himself, 'God has forgotten;
he has hidden his face and seen nothing.'
12. Arise, Lord, set your hand to the task;
God, do not forget the afflicted and the humble.
13. Why have the wicked rejected you, God,
and said that you will not call them to account?
14. You see that mischief are their companions;
you take the matter into your own hands.
The hapless victim commits himself to you;
in you the victims find a helper.
15. Break the power of the wicked;
hunt out wickedness until you can find no more.
16. Lord, you have heard the lament and grief of the humble;
you strengthen and direct their hearts, you give heed to them,
17. bringing justice to the hopeless and the oppressed,
so that no one on earth may terror them again.
18. Lord, bring joy to the hearts of the grieving.
19. Show favour and mercy to me,
Lord, for my strength fails;
Lord, heal me, for my body is racked with pain;
20. I am utterly distraught and for how long? When will you act, Lord?
21. Return, Lord, deliver me;
save me, for your love is steadfast.
22. Lord, I want to praise you
all the days of my life.
23. I am wearied with my groaning; all night long my pillow is wet with tears, I drench my bed with weeping and drench my couch with tears.

24. Sorrow and grief dims my
eyes; they are worn out because
of all my adversaries.
25. Leave me alone, you workers
of evil, for the Lord has heard my
weeping!
26. The Lord has heard my
entreaty; the Lord will accept my
prayer.
27. All of my enemies will be
ashamed, stricken with terror;
they will turn away in sudden
disgrace.

PSALM 11

God is the holy foundation

A psalm of Solomon

1. In the Lord I take refuge. How
can you say to me,
'Flee like a bird to the
mountains?;
2. For see, the wicked are aiming;
they make ready their evil and in
darkness may ruin the upright in
heart.'
3. If the foundations are
destroyed,
what can the righteous do, or
what has he accomplished?
My faith is in the Lord.
4. The Lord is in the holy temple;
the Lord's throne is in the
paradise of heaven.
The gaze of the Lord is upon
mankind. I will worship toward
the holy temple and praise thy
Name because of they loving-
kindness and truth, for thou has
magnified thy Name and thy
word, above all things.
5. All kings of the earth shall
praise thee, O Lord. For they have
heard your glorious words.
6. The Lord weighs just and
unjust, and he hates the wicked
and hates violence.
For the Lord is righteous and
loves righteous deeds. The Lord
beholds the upright. The Lord is
gracious, righteous, and full of
compassion. The Lord protects
the unwary. When I was brought
low, He saved me.
7. How lovely is Your dwelling
place, O Lord Almighty!
8. My soul yearns, even faints for
the courts of the Lord;
My heart and my flesh cry out for
the living God.
9. Even as sparrows and
swallows find nests for
themselves, I find my place next
to you, O Lord, my God.
10. Blessed are those who dwell
in your house;
they are ever praising You.
11. Blessed are those whose
strength is in You,
Who have set their hearts on
following your good ways.
12. Hear my prayer, O Lord God
Almighty; listen to me, O God.
13. Look with favor upon your
anointed one and help us to
diligently obey you and follow
your ways.
14. Better is one day in your
courts than a thousand
elsewhere;
I would rather be a doorkeeper in
the house of my God than dwell
in the tents of the wicked.
15. For the Lord God is a sun and
a shield; the Lord bestows favor
and honor;

no good thing does he withhold
from those whose walk is
blameless.
16. O Lord Almighty, blessed is
the man who trusts in You.
17. Praise the Lord of my soul!
18. You are the one who covers
Yourself with light as with a
garment, Who stretches out the
heavens like a curtain or tent
19. and lays the beams of the
heavens on the waters.
20. Who makes the clouds a
chariot and rides on the wings of
the wind.
21. You make the wind Your
messenger and flames of fire
your ministers.
22. You set the earth on its
foundations; that is shall not be
moved forever.
23. At your command the waters
rise and fall, mountains rose,
valleys sank to the place You
appointed for them.
24. You set the boundaries that
the waters cannot pass.
25. You make springs pour water
into the valleys; their waters run
among the mountains.
26. and give drink to the beasts of
the fields; the wild donkeys
quench their thirst there.
27. Beside them the birds of the
air have their nests; they sing
among the branches;
as for the stork, the fir trees are
its home.
28. You water the mountains
from heaven; the earth is
satisfied and abounds with the
fruit of the Lord's works.
29. The Lord makes grass to grow
for the cattle and plants for man
to cultivate – bringing forth food
from the earth.
30. wine that gladdens the heart
of man and softens the skin, and
makes his face shine like oil upon
it, and bread that sustains his
heart.
31. All my springs are in you, O
Lord.

PSALM 12

The Lord's word is pure

1. Help, Lord! Some are
principled and godly people but
some are no more; there are
lands where good faith between
people has vanished.
2. To his neighbor each one
speaks words without worth or
truth; with smooth words and
deceit in their hearts they speak.
3. May the Lord make an end of
such smooth words and the
tongue that talks so boastfully!
4. They say 'By our tongues we
shall prevail. Our words are our
own command. Who is lord and
master over us?'
5. 'Now I will arise,' says the Lord
'because the poor are oppressed,
because of the groans of the
needy;
I will set them in safety and in the
salvation for which they long.'
6. The words and promises of the
Lord are pure and flawless, like
silver refined in a clay furnace
and like pure gold.
7. O Lord, you will keep
us safe and protect us from such
people forever, the wicked who
honor vileness.
8. The wicked lay crafty schemes
against Your people and consult

together against those you cherish. Save us, Lord, redeem us from the evil ones.
9. All our fountains are in You, O Lord.
10. The power of Your awesome works pour forth like a pure fountain, giving fame to Your name.

PSALM 13

Lord, I need help

To the Chief Musician set to the tune of Aijeleth Hashshahar
A psalm of David

1. My God, My God, why have you forsaken Me? Why are you so far from helping me?
2. How long will you forget me, O Lord? Forever?
3. How long must I have torment and have sorrow in my heart? How long will my enemy triumph over me?
4. Consider and answer me, O Lord my God, lighten my faith lest I will sleep in death,
5. and my enemy will say he has prevailed over me and my foes will rejoice when I am shaken and fall.
6. In return for my love, they attacked me without cause.
7. They repaid me with evil although I did good for them.
8. But I trust in your unfailing and merciful love; my heart shall rejoice and be in high spirits in Your salvation.
9. I will sing to the Lord, for He has been good to me.
10. Surely and truly God is good to the pure in heart.

PSALM 14

God restores

1. The pure in heart follow good ways; yet even the pure in heart fall short, for only the Lord is purely awesome.
2. The Lord Jehovah looks down from heaven upon all people and knows the actions of both wise and foolish.
3. As for me, my feet had almost slipped, I had nearly lost my foothold; I was envious when I saw the prosperity of one who had no struggles of the common man; but facts were that deceit was their garment.
4. Lord, restore our callous hearts and wash our hands in innocence. Restore our honor, O God. I entrust my God to show me the way I should go.
5. The evildoers frustrate the plans of the poor, but the poor take refuge in the Lord.
6. Like a bad dream, you want to forget the wicked.
7. God is in the assembly of the righteous.
8. The Lord will restore the baskets of righteous doers and lift our burdens.
9. I will reaffirm every morning that I desire to follow God.
10. I did not fully understand about the salvation of God until I entered the sanctuary of God; then I understood about our final destiny.
11. I will praise you with the harp for your greatness, O Lord.
I will sing praise to you with the lyre, O Holy Lord.

PSALM 15

God loves truth

1. Lord, who may dwell in your holy sanctuary?
2. He whose walk is blameless and who speaks the truth,
3. has no slander on his tongue, who does his neighbor no wrong and casts no slur on his fellow man,
4. who despises a vile man, but honors those who follow the Lord, who keeps his oath even when it hurts,
5. who lends money without usury and does not accept a bribe to hurt the innocent.
He who does these things will never be shaken.
6. We swear an oath to the Lord and make a vow to the Mighty One, Our Creator:
7. We will allow no slumber to our eyes till we find a place for the Lord in our heart.

PSALM 16

The Lord is our Lord

1. Keep me safe, O God, for in you I take refuge, and in You do I put my trust and hide myself.
2. I say to the Lord 'You are my Lord, I have no good apart from You.'
3. As for the godly who are in the land, they are the excellent, the noble, and the glorious, in whom is all my delight.
4. The Lord is my chosen portion and my cup, my blessed assurance. The Holy Spirit is my hold and makes me secure; you maintain my boundaries.
5. I will praise the Lord who counsels me in my heart.
6. I have set the Lord always before me.
7. My heart is glad and my soul rejoices; my body shall rest and confidently dwell in safety.
8. You will show me the path of life.
9.Your presence is fullness of joy and eternal pleasures.
10. Lord, how awesome are Your Works because of your great power.
11. All the earth will worship You, Jehovah, Lord of all creation.
12. Our descendants will know Your Great Name, Lord.

PSALM 17

The Lord's path is good

1. Hear my righteous and honest plea, O Lord, hear my cry.
2. Give ear to my prayer, and judge it in righteousness.
3. Examine my heart and mind and you will find that I have resolved not to sin and there is no malice in me.
4. Because you stand for all good and holiness,
I have avoided the ways of the violent;
5. my steps have held to your paths, my feet have not slipped.
6. I have called upon You, O God, for You will hear me.
7. Show Your marvelous unfailing loving-kindness, O You Who save those who trust and take refuge in You.
8. Keep and guard me as the pupil in Your eye;

9. hide me in the shadow of Your wings from the wicked who oppress me and surround me like hungry lions for prey.
10. They are enclosed in their own prosperity and have shut up their callous hearts to pit; with their mouths they make exorbitant claims and speak proudly and arrogantly.
11. Rise up, O Lord, confront the wicked and bring them down. Deliver me from the wicked. By Your hand save me from such men who are idle and vain. The good servants rise up against evil doers.
12. I will store my wealth in You and may my children and their children store their wealth in You.
13. I will continue to behold in You and be satisfied.

PSALM 18

The Lord is perfect

1. This is the day which the Lord has made; Let us rejoice and be glad in it. I love you fervently and devotedly, O Lord, my strength.
2. The Lord is my Rock, my Fortress, and my Deliverer; my God is my rock, in whom I take refuge, my shield, my salvation, my stronghold.
3. I will call upon the Lord, Who is to be praised; so I shall be saved from my sorrows.
4. In my distress I called to the Lord for help and the Lord heard my cry for help.
5. Does the Lord make the earth shake and bring storms?
6. The Lord was my support; God rescued me when distress surrounded me.
7. I have kept to the good ways of the Lord, I have not turned from my God to wickedness, ever to keep myself free from sin and guilt.
8. You, O Lord, keep my lamp burning; my God turns my darkness into light.
9. As for God, the way of the Lord is perfect! The Lord is a refuge for all who take shield in God.
10. Who is God but God?
11. It is God who arms me with strength and makes my way perfect.
12. Lord, You have held me up in hope; in You I take refuge.
13. The Lord lives! Blessed be my Rock; and let the God of my salvation be exalted.
14. I will give thanks unto thee, O Lord, with my whole heart and sing praise unto thee. I will give thanks to the Lord for He is good, and sing praises to Your Name.

PSALM 19

The knowledge of the Lord

1. The heavens declare the glory of God; the skies proclaim the work of God's hands,
2. day after day and night after night they display the knowledge of the Lord,
3. without speaking, their voice goes out to all the earth.
4. Their voice goes out into all the earth, their words to the ends of the world.
In the heavens the Lord has pitched a tent for the sun,

5. which is like a bridegroom
coming forth from his pavilion,
like a champion rejoicing to run
his course.
6. It rises as one end of the
heavens and makes it circuit to
the other; nothing is hidden from
its heat.
7. The law of the Lord is perfect
and revives the soul.
The statutes of the Lord are
trustworthy. The Lord's
instruction never fails.
8.The precepts of the Lord are
right, giving joy to the heart.
9. The commands of the Lord are
radiant and pure, enduring
forever.
The Lord's judgements are true
and righteous, every one of them.
10. They are more precious than
gold, they are sweeter than
honey.
11. It is through them that your
servant is warned; in keeping
them there is great reward.
12. Who is aware of his
unwitting sins? Forgive me of my
hidden faults.
13. Keep your servant also from
willful sins;
may they not rule over me. Then I
will be blameless and innocent of
great transgression.
14. May the words of my mouth
and the meditation of my heart
be acceptable to you, Lord, my
Rock and my Redeemer.
May the thoughts of my mind be
pleasing in your sight, O Lord.

PSALM 20

May the Lord fulfill our petitions

A psalm of the sons of Korah
1. May the Lord answer you in
time of trouble or distress; may
the name of God protect you.
2. May the Lord send you help
from the heavenly sanctuary.
3. May the Lord remember your
good deeds and faith.
4. May the Lord give you your
heart's desire, and grant success
to all your plans.
5. Followers will shout for joy in
victory and lift up banners in the
name of God.
May the Lord grant all your
requests.
6.The Lord saves the anointed;
God answers them from the holy
heavens with saving power.
7. Some trust in and boast of their
chariots and horses, but we will
trust in the name of the Lord.
8. We trust in the name of the
Lord our God.
9. O Lord, answer us when we
call.

PSALM 21

The Lord's Power

1. Lord, we rejoice in your
strength and rejoice in your
victories.
2. You have answered our
prayers and have granted our
requests.
3. You have provided us with
blessings through your unfailing
love.
4. You gave life to us in length of
days, for ever and ever.
5. We glory because of Your aid.
6. You make us glad with the joy
of Your presence.

7.Your loving care keeps us
confident.
8. The Lord will take care of the
wicked; they cannot succeed.
9. We sing a psalm of praise to
the power at Your hand.
10. Seven times a day I praise you
and I do not forget your
commandments.

PSALM 22

Our forefathers had faith in the Lord Jehovah

A psalm of David

1. Lord, You are the Holy One and
praised by all.
2. In You our forefathers put their
trust; they trusted and You
delivered them.
3. They cried to you and were
saved; in You they trusted and
were not disappointed.
4. We will declare Your Name to
our brothers and praise you at
congregation.
5. All descendants will revere the
Lord.
6. For the Lord hears our cry and
will come to our aid.
7. The poor will eat and be
satisfied; they who seek the Lord
will praise God!
8. Future generations will be told
about the Lord; they will
proclaim God's righteousness to a
people yet unborn – for God has
done it.
9. The Lord remembers the
commandment of righteousness;
it is imprinted on the tablet of the
Lord's heart.
10. The Lord's word is an
everlasting covenant He made
with and swore to Abraham who
lived before us; he gave the land
of Canaan as a possession and
inheritance
11. and Jehovah confirmed it as a
promise to Jacob and to Israel
which He commanded and
established for a thousand
generations.
12. In the beginning, there were
but few people, who wandered
from nation to nation;
now the people have increased in
multitude.
13. The Lord is above all the
kings and queens, who are the
sons and daughters of God.
14. The Lord is above all angels
and saints.
15. The word of the Lord is the
truth and it will be proven, that
righteousness will blot out all evil
from the lands.
16. Lord, make us stronger than
our oppressors.
17. Lord, show us signs of
miracles and wonder in the lands.
18. Help us to protect the
innocent and the needy.
19. Stand before us and lead us in
Your dear ways; Jehovah,
20. keep your people together.

PSALM 23

The Lord is my shepherd

A psalm of David

1. The Lord is my shepherd, I
shall not want;
2. The Lord makes me lie down in
green pastures, and leads me
beside quiet waters,
3. the Lord restores my soul and
revives my spirit.

God guides me in the paths of righteousness for the sake of the Lord.
4. Even though I walk through the valley of the deepest shadows, I will fear no evil, for God is with me; Your shepherd's staff, they comfort me.
5. Lord, You spread a table before me in the presence of my enemies, You anoint my head with oil, and my cup overflows.
6. Surely goodness and love unfailing will follow me all the days of my life, and I shall dwell in the house of the Lord forever.

PSALM 24

The Lord made the Earth

1. The earth is the Lord's and everything in it, the world and all its inhabitants,
2. for the Lord founded it upon the seas.
3. Who will stand holy with the Lord?
4. Followers with clean hands and pure hearts will receive blessings from the Lord; all generations with clean hands and pure hearts that seek the Lord will receive blessings.
5. God brought our forefathers to a place where they founded cities to settle;
6. they sowed fields and planted vineyards and grains that yielded fruitful harvests;
their herds did not diminish.
7. The Lord blessed them, and their numbers greatly increased, and the Lord did not let their hearts diminish despite the floods, plagues, calamity of wars, and sorrows;
8. the people maintained their steadfast hope in the plans of the Lord.
9. The people prayed for relief from their troubles; they rolled up their sleeves and went to work; the people survived.
10. Lift up your heads,
that the glory of God
may come in.
11. Who is the Lord of glory? The Lord in Heaven is the Lord of glory. Amen.
12. Why do unbelievers say 'Where is their God?'
13. The Lord is mighty and strong. The Lord Almighty is the Lord of glory.
14. All people will declare the work of God, for they will wisely consider and acknowledge that it is what God has brought about.
15. When I am overwhelmed, I call on the name of the Lord.
16. Open the gates of righteousness; I will enter through them. I will enter the gate of the Lord at the temple.
17. Blessed is he who comes in the name of the Lord; and from the house of the Lord, we bless you. The Lord 's name is written on the cornerstone.

PSALM 25

I give my soul to God

1. To you, O Lord, I lift up my soul; in you I trust, O my God.
2. No one whose hope is in You will ever be put to shame, but they will be put to shame who are treacherous without cause.

3. Make your paths known to me, O God.
Teach me your good ways.
4. Guide me in your truth, for you are my God and Saviour, my hope is in you all day long.
5. Remember, Lord, your tender care and love unfailing, for they are from of old.
6. Remember not the sins of my youth and my rebellious ways; in accordance to Your love remember me, for you are good, O Lord.
7. Good and upright is the Lord;
8. The Lord guides the humble in right conduct and teaches them a good way.
9. All the ways of the Lord are loving and faithful.
10. Who, then, is the man who fears the Lord?
The Lord will instruct him in the way chosen for him.
11. and he will prosper and be blessed by the Lord.
12. My soul is satisfied as with a rich feast, and my lips shall praise you with joyful words.
Your praise will ever be on my lips.
13. How can a man attach silver and gold to his soul?
14. Awake, O People, idolize the Lord and not silver and gold.

PSALM 26

The Lord's love is constant

1. Lord, uphold my cause, for I have led a blameless life and have put unfaltering trust in You.
2. Test my mind and heart for my faith in You, O Lord;
for Your constant love is before my eyes, and I live by your faithfulness.
3. I have not sat among the worthless, nor do I associate with hypocrites;
4. I detest the company of evildoers,
nor shall I sit among the ungodly.
5. I wash my hands free from guilt to go in procession before you,
6. Lord, recounting your marvelous deeds, making them known with thankful voice.
7. Lord, I love the earth where you dwell, the place where your glory resides.
8. Do not sweep me away with sinners, nor cast me out with those who thirst for evil,
9. whose fingers are active in mischief, who hands are full of bribes.
10. But I lead a blameless life; deliver me and show me your favour.
11. My feet are planted on firm ground; I shall bless the Lord in the full assembly.
12. Though I walk in the midst of trouble or temptations, You revive me.
13. You stretch forth Your hand and guide me.

PSALM 27

The Lord is my stronghold

1. The Lord is my light and my salvation; whom shall I fear?
The Lord is the stronghold of my life; Of whom then should I go in dread? I am never alone.

2. My heart will have no fear; I will not be dismayed.
3. One thing I ask of the Lord, it is the one thing I seek; that I may dwell in the house of the Lord all the days of my life, to gaze on the beauty of the Lord in the holy temple.
4. For the Lord will hide me in shelter in the day of misfortune; The Lord will conceal me under cover of the holy tent, set me high on a rock.
5. Now my head will be raised high above the enemy all about me;
and I will sing a psalm of praise to the Lord.
6. Well I remain confident of this: I know that I shall see the goodness of the Lord in the land of the living.
7. Wait for the Lord; be strong and brave, and put your hope in the Lord.
8. I love the Lord, because the Lord inclined and heard my voice; the Lord heard my cry for mercy.
9. Because the Lord heard my prayer; therefore will I call upon the Lord for as long as I live.
10. I called upon the name of the Lord: 'O Lord, I beseech You, save my life and deliver me!' The Lord will adopt me as His child.
11. Gracious is the Lord and righteous; yes, Our God is merciful and full of compassion.
12. The Lord protects the simple hearted and chaste; I was brought low, and the Lord helped and saved me.
13. Be at rest, O my soul, for the Lord is good.
14. How can I repay the Lord for all the blessings the Lord has given to me?
15. I will lift up the cup of salvation and call on the name of the Lord,
16. I will fulfill my vows to the Lord, yes, in the presence of the Lord's people.
17. Precious in the sight of the Lord are the saints.
18. O Lord, truly I am your servant; I am your servant and You are my maker.
19. I will offer to You thanks and praise and call on You all day long.
20. Let the house of the Lord say: The Lord's love endures Forever.

PSALM 28

I seek the Lord's guidance

1. To You, Lord, I call; if you answer me with silence,
I become like those who go down to the abyss.
2. Hear my voice as I plead for mercy, as I call to you for help with my hands uplifted towards your holy shrine. I have gone astray like a lost sheep.
3. Do not drag me away with the ungodly, with evildoers who speak civilized and cordially to their fellows, though with malice in their hearts.
4. I will worship you in congregation with my brethren, seeking your good ways.
5. Lord, according to Your will, for You are the only Judge.

6. Blessed be the Lord,
for the Lord has heard my voice
as I plead for mercy.
7. The Lord is my strength and
my shield;
in the Lord my heart trusts.
I am sustained, and my heart
leaps for joy,
and with my song I praise the
Lord.
8. The Lord is strength to all
people,
a safe refuge for all of the
anointed.
9. Save your people and bless
those who belong to You,
shepherd them and carry them
forever.

PSALM 29

The works of the Lord

A psalm for the Sabbath Day
1. Ascribe to the Lord, all
people, ascribe to the Lord glory
and might.
2. Ascribe to the Lord the glory
due to the Lord's name; in holy
attire worship the Lord.
3. The voice of the Lord echoes
over the waters;
the God of glory
shines over all the earth;
the Lord thunders over
the mighty waters,
the voice of the Lord is
powerful,
the voice of the Lord is
majestic.
The Lord has taken the
royal throne forever.
4. The Lord will give strength to
all people; the Lord Jehovah will
bless people with peace.
5. I give thanks to God all day
long and find my rest in the hope
of the Lord.
6. The fear, reverence, and
respect of the Lord is the
beginning of all wisdom.

PSALM 30

In hard times

A psalm of Heman the Ezrahite
1. I shall exalt you, Lord;
and give thanks to Your
Holy name.
2. Tears may linger at nightfall,
but rejoicing comes in the
morning. In good times and hard
times we trust in the Lord.
3. I felt secure and said,
'I can never be shaken.'
In the times I am afraid, I will
trust in thee, Lord.
4. Lord, by your favour you made
my mountain strong;
when you hid your face, I was
struck with dismay.
5. To you, Lord, I called and
pleaded with you for mercy;
do not be far off.
6. 'What profit is there in my
death, in my going down to the
pit?
Can the dust praise you?
Can it proclaim your truth?
7. Hear, Lord, and be gracious to
me; Lord, be my helper.'
8. You have turned my laments
into dancing;
you have stripped off my
sackcloth and clothed me with
joy; no evil shall befall my tent.
9. that I may sing psalms to you
without ceasing, Lord my God, I
shall praise you for ever.

PSALM 31

Commit your spirit to God

1. In you, Lord, I have found
refuge; let me never be put to
shame. By your saving power
deliver me,
2. Be gracious to me, Lord, for I
am in distress and my eyes are
dimmed with grief.
3. My life is worn away with
sorrow and my years with
sighing;
4. Into your hand I commit my
spirit.
You have delivered me, Lord, you
are a God of truth.
5. I hate all who worship evil, for
I put all my trust in the Lord.
6. I shall rejoice and be glad in
your unfailing love,
for you have seen my affliction
and have cared for me in my
distress,
7. You will not abandon me;
beside Your presence I am in a
good place.
8. I am scorned by all my
enemies,
my neighbors find me
burdensome,
my friends shudder at me; when
they see me on the street they
turn away quickly,
9. Like the dead I have passed
out of mind;
I have become like broken
pottery thrown away.
10. For I hear many
whispering threats from
every side, conspiring together
against me and
scheming to take my life.
11. But in you, Lord, I put my
trust;
I say, 'You are my God.'
12. My times are in your hand;
rescue me from the power of my
enemies and those who
persecute me.
13. Let your face shine on your
servant; save me in your unfailing
love.
14. May lying lips be silenced,
lips speaking with contempt
against the righteous
in pride and arrogance.
15. How great is your goodness,
stored up for those who fear you,
made manifest before mortal
eyes, for all who turn to you for
shelter.
16. Blessed be the Lord, whose
unfailing love infuses our soul
when we call for help.
17. Be strong and faithful, let
your heart take courage, all you
whose hope is in the Lord.

PSALM 32

I will not sin

1. Happy is he whose offence is
forgiven, whose sin is blotted out!
2. Happy is he to whom the Lord
imputes no fault,
in whose spirit there is no deceit.
3. While I refused to speak, my
body wasted away
with day-long moaning.
4. For day and night
Your hand was heavy upon me;
the sap in me dried up as in
summer drought.
5. I am a worm and scorned but
when I acknowledged my sin to
you, when I no longer concealed

my guilt, but said 'I shall confess my offence to the Lord,'
then you for your part remitted the penalty of my sin. Selah.
6. So let every faithful heart pray to you in the hour of anxiety;
7. You are a hiding-place for me from distress;
You guard me and enfold me in salvation with shouts and songs of deliverance. Selah.
8. The Lord shall teach you and guide you in the way you should go.
The Lord shall keep you under the Lord's eye.
9. Do not behave like a horse or a mule, unreasoning creatures whose mettle must be curbed with bit and bridle or they will not come to you.
10. Many are the woes of the wicked and the torments of the ungodly; but unfailing love enfolds him who trusts in the Lord.
11. Rejoice in the Lord and be glad, you righteous;
and sing aloud, all you who are upright in heart. Selah.
12. The righteous will say to the evil 'You strayed from the path of goodness and did not make God your strength.'
13. But I am like an olive tree flourishing in the house of the Lord; I will trust and delight myself in Your commandments, which I love.
14. I will follow and meditate on Your statues, O Lord.
15. Remember the word and promise to Your servants, in which we hope.
16. You are our comfort and consolation in our suffering; it is Your Word that has revived us and gives us life.
17. We walk at liberty and ease, for we have sought out and follow your precepts.
18. We will speak of your statutes before kings and queens and will not be put to shame, for your ways are just.
19. Lord, you are the author of all that is good in the conscience of man; you abhor all evil and reject wickedness.
20. We will make haste and follow your commandments.
21. I am a friend to all who revere and worship the Lord.

PSALM 33

Play music and sing for the Lord

To the chief musician on stringed instruments
A psalm of David

1. Shout for joy before the Lord, you who are righteous;
it is fitting for the upright to praise the Lord.
2. Give thanks to the Lord on the harp; sing the Lord psalms on the ten-stringed lyre.
3. Sing for joy to God our strength; blow the ram's horn at the moon to celebrate.
4. Sing the Lord a new song, Who has done marvelous things; celebrate with skillful art and shout in triumph.
5. for the word of the Lord holds true, and all of the Lord's work endures.

6. The Lord loves righteousness and justice;
the earth is full of the Lord's unfailing love.
7. By the word of the Lord the heavens were made,
all the host of heaven was made by the Lord's command.
8. God gathered the sea like water in jars;
God laid up the deep in storehouses.
9. Let the whole world fear the Lord and all men on earth stand in awe of God.
10. For the Lord spoke, and it came to be;
the Lord commanded, and it stood firm.
11. The Lord brings the plans of nations to nothing;
God makes the purposes of the peoples and their plans of no effect.
12. But the Lord's own plans shall stand for ever,
the purposes of his heart endure through all generations.
13. Happy is the nation whose God is the Lord,
the people will have the Lord's good inheritance.
14. The Lord looks out from Heaven and sees the whole mankind of men and women;
15. the Lord surveys all inhabitants of the earth from the holy dwelling place.
16. It is the Lord who fashions the hearts of all people, who considers
everything they do.
17. No king or queen is saved by the size of the royal army, nor a warrior delivered by great strength.
18. A man cannot trust his horse to save him, nor can it deliver him for all its strength.
19. But the eyes of the Lord are on those who fear and hope in the Lord; the unfailing love of the Lord
20. to deliver them from death, to keep them alive in famine.
21. We have awaited eagerly for the Lord; the Lord is our help and our shield.
22. For in the Lord our hearts rejoice and are glad; we trust in the holy name of the Lord.
23. May your unfailing love rest upon us, O Lord, even as we put our hope in you.
24. Blessed is the nation whose God is the Lord, whose people he has chosen as his own. The Lord gazes down upon humanity from where he lives. He has made their hearts and closely watches everything they do.

PSALM 34

Angels

A psalm of Ethan the Ezrahite

1. I will honor the Lord continually; to praise the Lord will always be on my lips.
2. My soul will boast in the Lord; the humble shall hear and be glad.
3. Glorify the Lord with me; let us exalt the name of the Lord together.
4. I sought the Lord and the Lord heard me; the Lord delivered me from all my fears.

5. Look to the Lord and shine
with joy;
no longer hang your head in
shame.
6. Here was a poor wretch who
cried to the Lord; and the Lord
heard him and saved him from
his troubles.
7. Hear us, O Mighty Shepherd,
who leads us like a flock, you who
sits enthroned between the
cherubim, shine forth
8. The angel of the Lord
encamps around those
who fear the Lord, and rescues
them.
9. See that the Lord is good;
happy is the man or woman who
finds refuge in the Lord!
10. Fear the Lord, all you holy
followers, for those who fear the
Lord lack nothing.
Unbelievers suffer want and go
hungry, but those who seek the
Lord lack no good thing. Your
seed I will establish forever.
11. All children should listen and
learn of the Lord;
12. whoever of you loves life and
desires to see many good days,
13. should keep your tongue
from evil and your lips from
uttering lies.
14. Turn from evil and pursue the
straight way.
15. The eyes of the Lord are upon
the righteous and the ears of the
Lord are open to their cries.
16. The face of the Lord is
against those who do evil, to blot
out their memory from the earth.
17. When the righteous cry out
for help, the Lord hears them.
18. The Lord is close to those
whose courage is broken, the
brokenhearted,
and the Lord saves those whose
spirit is crushed.
19. For the Lord will command
the angels concerning you to
accompany and defend and
preserve you in all your ways;
20. they will lift you up in their
hands so that you will not strike
your foot against a stone, and
21. you will tread upon the lion
and the cobra;
22. 'Because he has set his love
upon Me,' says the Lord, 'I will
rescue him and protect him, for
he acknowledges and
understands My name.'

PSALM 35

God's love is unfailing

1. Contend, O Lord, with those
who contend with me; fight
against those who fight against
me.
2. Take up shield and buckler;
arise and come to my aid.
3. Hold back those who pursue
me. Say to my soul,
'I am your salvation.'
4. May shame and disgrace be on
those who seek my life;
may those who plot my ruin be
turned back in dismay.
5. May they be like chaff before
the wind,
with the angel of the Lord driving
them away;
6. may their path be dark and
slippery, with the angel of the
Lord pursuing them.

7. Since they hid their net for me
without cause and without cause
dug a pit for me,
8. may ruin overtake them by
surprise – may the net they hid
entangle them, may they fall into
their own pit, to their ruin. But,
only you, O Lord, can reward.
9. I shall rejoice in the Lord of my
salvation.
10. My whole being will exclaim,
'Who is like you, O Lord?
You rescue the poor from those
too strong for them, the poor and
needy from those who rob them.'
11. Malicious witnesses step
forward; they question me on
matters of which I know nothing.
12. They repay me evil for good
and leave my soul forlorn.
13. Yet when they were ill, I put
on sackcloth and humbled myself
with fasting and prayer.
14. I went about mourning as
though weeping for a brother or
friend. I bowed my head in grief
as though weeping for my mother
or father.
15. But when I stumbled, they
gathered in glee;
nameless smiters jeered
at me and they slandered me
without ceasing.
16. Like the ungodly, they
maliciously mocked.
17. O Lord, how long will you
look on those who hate me for no
reason?
Rescue me out of their cruel grip,
my precious life, from these
attackers?
18. Then I will give you thanks
and praise before a great
assembly;
I will extol you where many
people meet.
19. Let no treacherous enemy
gloat over me without cause, nor
leer at me in triumph. No friendly
greeting do they give to
peaceable folk.
20. They devise false
accusations, they invent lie after
lie, against those
who live quietly in the land.
21. They gape at me and say
'Hurrah!' in their joy, feasting
their eye on me.
22. O Lord, you have seen this?
be not silent.
O Lord, be not far from me.
23. Awake, and rise to my
defense! Contend for me, my God
and my Lord.
24. Judge me Lord and vindicate
me in your righteousness, O Lord
my God; do not let them gloat
over me.
25. Do not let them say 'Hurrah!
We have swallowed him up at one
gulp.'
26. May all who gloat over my
distress be put to shame and
confusion; let them be covered
with disgrace.
27. May those who delight in my
vindication shout for joy and
gladness;
let them cry continually,
'All glory to the Lord who would
see this servant thrive!'
28. My tongue will speak of your
righteousness and of your praises
all day long.
29. But your love, O Lord,
reaches to the heavens,
your faithfulness to the skies.

30. Your righteousness is like the lofty mountains, your justice like the great deep.
O Lord, you save both man and beast;
31. how precious is your unfailing love!
32. Both high and low among men find refuge in the shadow of your wing.
33. They feast on the abundance of your house;
You give them drink from your river of delights.
For with You is the fountain of life; in Your
light we see light.
34. Continue your love to those who know you,
your righteousness to the men of honest heart.
35. Let not the foot of the pride overtake me, nor the hand of the wicked drive me away.

PSALM 36

Commit your ways to the Lord

1. Deep in his heart, sin whispers to the wicked man who does not fear God.
2. Do not fret because of evil men or be envious of those who do evil;
for like the grass they will soon wither, and fade like the green of spring.
3. Trust in the Lord and do good; so you shall dwell in the land and enjoy safe pastures.
4. Delight yourself in the Lord; depend upon the Lord, for the Lord knows the desires and the secret petitions of your heart.
5. The Lord will make your righteousness shine clear like the dawn, the justice of your cause like the noonday sun.
6. Be still before the Lord and wait patiently; those who hope in the Lord will inherit the earth.
7. The meek will inherit the earth and enjoy great peace and untold prosperity.
8. The wicked plot against the righteous and gnash their teeth at them;
9. but the Lord laughs at the wicked, for the Lord knows their day is coming.
10. Their contriving will hurt their own hearts, and their power will be broken.
11. The wicked man borrows and does not repay, but the righteous give generously;
12. though the righteous stumble, he will not fall, for the Lord upholds him by hand.
13. The Lord is an everlasting provider, and his children are a blessing.
14. I shall sing of Your strength and acclaim your love, for you have been my strong tower and a refuge in my day of trouble.
15. I shall raise a psalm to my gracious God.
16. O Lord of heavenly hosts, arouse yourself to come to me and keep watch.

PSALM 37

God's creations

1. O Lord, You have searched me and You know me.
2. You know when I sit and when I rise;

You know and understand my
thoughts.
3. You know the path I walk and
my lying down;
You are acquainted with all my
ways.
4. For there is not a word on my
tongue that You know it
altogether.
5. You put me where you want
me; You have laid Your hand upon
me.
6. Your knowledge is too
wonderful for me; it is high above
me, I cannot reach it.
7. Where can I go from your
Spirit? Where could I flee from
Your presence?
8. If I go up to the heavens, You
are there;
if I make my bed in the depths of
Sheoul, You are there.
9. If I rise on the wings of dawn,
if I settle on the far side of the
sea,
10. even there shall Your hand
lead me, and Your hands shall
hold me.
11. If I say, surely the darkness
shall cover me and the night shall
be the only light about me,
12. even the darkness hides
nothing from You, but the night
will shine like day,
for darkness and the light
are both alike to You.
13. For You created my innermost
being; You knit me together in my
mother's womb.
14. I will confess and praise You
for You are fearful and wonderful
and you fill me with awe. I praise
You for the awesome wonder of
my birth! Your works are
wonderful, I know that full well.
15. My frame was not hidden
from You when I was made in the
secret place.
When I was woven together in
the depths of the earth
16. Your eyes saw my unformed
substance, and in Your book all
the days of my life were written
before ever they took shape,
when as yet there was none of
them.
17. How precious to me are your
thoughts, O God!
How vast is the sum of them!
18. If I could count them, they
would be more in number than
the grains of sand. When I
finished counting, I would still be
with You.
19. Search me, O God, and know
my heart. Try me and know my
thoughts!
20. And see if there is any wicked
or hurtful way in me, and lead me
in the way everlasting.
21. The Lord sends a command to
earth; and that command runs
swiftly.
22. The Lord spreads the snow
like a blanket of wool and hurls
down hail like crumbs; who can
withstand the icy blast?
23. The Lord melts the ice and
snow, causes wind to blow, and
waters to flow.
24. The Lord gives food to beasts
and ravens for which they cry.
25. Sing to the Lord with
thanksgiving, make music to our
God on the harp,
26. Who covers the heavens with
clouds, Who prepares rain for the

earth, Who makes grass to grow on the mountains.
27. The Lord determines the number of stars and calls them each by name.
28. The Lord decreed sea monsters and creatures of the deep.
29. Lightning, hail, fog, and frost, and stormy winds all work at the Lord's order.
30. You mountains and hills, fruitful trees and cedars!
31. beasts and all cattle, creeping things and flying birds,
32. This is My resting place forever, says the Lord; here I will dwell, for I have desired it.
33. Here I will make a horn grown for my people and set up a lamp for my anointed ones.
34. The Lord has done this for all nations.

PSALM 38

Keep our thoughts pure

1. Lord, I call upon You; come quickly to me. Hear my voice when I cry to You.
2. Let my prayer be set before you like incense, the lifting up of my hands as praise.
3. Set a guard, O Lord, before my mouth; keep watch at the door of my lips.
4. Let not my heart be drawn to what is evil or to take part in wicked ways with evildoers;
let me not eat of their delicacies.
5. Let a righteous man correct me – it is a kindness. Let a righteous man correct me – it is oil on my head. My head will not refuse it.
6. Let the wicked know that You are Lord; let my slanderers know that my words were sweet.
7. Correct the ways of the wicked; turn them to good.
8. But my eyes are toward You, O God the Lord; in You do I trust and take refuge; protect me from death by the evildoer;
9. Let me pass safely by the nets of the wicked,
let me pass and not snared.
10. Trust in God at all times, you people; pour out your
Hearts before the Lord; God is our shelter.
11. Evil people are a sham.
12. Put no trust in extortion, no false confidence in robbery; though wealth increases, do not set your heart on it.
13. All power belongs to God; unfailing love is yours, Lord;
You reward everyone according to what he has done.

PSALM 39

I lift my voice to the Lord

1. I cry to the Lord with my voice for mercy.
2. I pour out my complaint before the Lord; I tell the Lord my troubles.
3. When my spirit grows faint within me,
it is You who knows my way.
4. No one is concerned for me. I have no refuge; no one cares for my life.
5. I cry to You, O Lord; I say, 'You are my refuge, and my need in the land of the living.'
6. Listen to my cry, for I am brought very low.

7. Hear my prayer, O Lord, listen to my request! In your faithfulness come to my relief.
8. May I not be judged by You, for in Your sight no one living is perfectly righteous before you.
9. My spirit is overwhelmed and wrapped in gloom.
10. Save my life, O Lord, for Your name's sake; in your righteousness, bring me out of distress and trouble.
11. Save me, O Lord, for I am Your servant who follows the commands of Jehovah.

PSALM 40

Revive us

1. Praise be to the Lord, my Rock, my keen and firm strength.
2. The Lord is my loving God and my fortress, my stronghold and my deliverer, my shield, in whom I take refuge, who will watch over me.
3. Lord, your people and the sons and daughters of your people are like breaths;
4. our days are like fleeting shadows.
5. Part your heavens, O Lord, and come down; touch the mountains, so they blossom.
6. Send forth lightning and rain; scatter enemies and
7. reach down Your hand from on high and revive us; deliver me from enemies
8. whose mouths are full of lies,
9. I will sing a new song to you, O God; on the ten-stringed lyre harp I will make music to You,
10. to the One who saves.
11. Let our children be like well-nurtured plants or pillars carved to adorn a palace.
12. Let our barns be filled with every kind of provision. Let our sheep multiply. Let our oxen be strong.
13. And when there are no invaders, no besiegers, no murders, and no outcrys in our streets;
14. Happy and blessed will be the people of whom this is true;
15. blessed are the people whose God is the Lord.
16. Have mercy upon me, O God; according to Your steadfast love, according to the multitude of Your loving-kind works.
17. Wash me thoroughly from my iniquity and guilt and cleanse me and make me wholly pure from my sin!
18. For I am conscious of my transgressions and I acknowledge them; my sin is ever before me.
19. Behold, I am a mere human and not perfect and subject to sinning.
20. Behold, you desire truth in the inner being; make me therefore to know wisdom in my inner-most heart.
21. Make me to hear joy and gladness; restore my broken spirit and bones;
and let me rejoice.
22. Create in me a clean heart, O God, renew a right, preserving, and steadfast spirit in me.
23. Purify me with hyssop mint, and I shall be cleaner than snow;

Make me to hear joy and gladness;
24. Then I will teach transgressors Your Ways, and sinner will be converted and return to You.
25. If you, O Lord, kept a record of sins, who could be in good standing with You?
26. But with You there is forgiveness; therefore You are revered.
27. Save me from doing evil and from death, O God, the God of my salvation, and my tongue shall sing aloud of your righteousness.
28. Revive us again, that your people may rejoice in You.
29. You take notice of the sacrifices of the humble
30. and those with a contrite heart. You do not despise the penitent.
31. In Your pleasure, uphold me, O Lord; keep me safe under your arms.
32. When I am filled with fear and trembling and my whole body shudders, I say: 'Oh, that I had wings of a dove to fly away and find rest!'
33. I would escape far away to the safety of the Lord's wings.
34. Soon I would find myself a shelter from raging wind and tempest.
35. Lord, acknowledge me in Your record as pure and clean.
36. Will you remember me when I die?
37. For mortals return to the earth when their breaths leave them; on that very day their thoughts, plans, and purposes perish from earth's walk.
38. Do not cast me from your presence or take your spirit from me.
39. With God, we are like a bird escaped from the snare of fowlers; the snare is broken, and we have escaped.

PSALM 41

The Lord's Dominion Will Endure Forever

1. I will exalt you, O Lord;
I will praise your name forever and ever.
2. Every day will I bless You, affectionately and gratefully praise You forever and ever.
3. Great is the Lord and most worthy of praise;
the greatness of the Lord is so great that no one can fathom.
4. One generation will praise Your works to another;
and shall tell of Your mighty acts.
5. They will speak of the glorious splendor of your majesty,
and I will meditate on your wonderful works.
6. Your heaven is an everlasting heaven, and your dominion endures through all generations.
7. Let the heavens be glad and let the earth rejoice; and let men say among nations, The Lord reigns!
8. Let the sea roar, and all the things that fill it; let the fields rejoice, and all that is in them.
9, Then shall the trees of the wood sing out for joy before the Lord. Sing to the Lord and give thanks and praise.

10. Honor and majesty are found in His Presence. Glory is His Holy name Jehovah. Peace be upon Israel.

PSALM 42

I will praise God all the days of my life

1. Praise the Lord! Hallelujah! Praise the Lord, O my soul.
2. I will praise the Lord all my life; I will sing praise to my God as long as I live.
3. Put not your trust in mortals, but only in God.
4. Blessed is the one whose help and hope is in the Lord,
5. the Maker of heaven and earth, the sea, and everything in them – the Lord, who remains faithful forever.
6. There is no strength but in thee, O Lord, thou art my mother and father.
7. Because Your loving-kindness is better than life; my lips will praise You.
8. I lift my hands in Your Name.
9. Your life is a blessing from the Lord.
10. For the Lord's purposes you will live all the days of your life.
11. Unless the Lord builds the house, its builders labor in vain.
12. Unless the Lord watches over the city; the watchman stand guard in vain.
13. In vain you rise early and stay up late, toiling for food to eat – unless you live for the Lord.
14. The Lord will watch your coming and going both now and forevermore.
15. I lift my eyes to the hills – I pray to my Lord, the Lord of all people on earth.
16. My help comes from the Lord, the Maker of heaven and earth.
17. The Lord has compassion for all people.

PSALM 43

The Lord is the Maker of All

1. Praise the Lord! For it is good to sing praises to our God, the God is gracious and lovely; praise is becoming and appropriate.
2. The Lord builds up all nations on earth.
3. The Lord heals the brokenhearted and binds up their wounds.
4. The Lord determines the number of the stars and calls them each by name.
5. Great is our Lord and mighty in power; God's understanding has no limit.
6. Sing to the Lord with thanksgiving; make music to our God on the harp,
7. Who covers the heavens with clouds, Who prepares rain for the earth, Who makes grass to grow on the mountains
8. Who gives to the beast his food, and to the young ravens that for which they cry.
9. God delights not in the strength of the horse,
nor in the legs of a man;
10. the Lord delights in those who revere the Lord,
who put their hope in the unfailing love of the Lord.
11. Praise the Lord, all the earth! Praise Your God, Our Maker.

12. The Lord will satisfy you with the finest of wheat.
13. The Lord sends a command to earth; and that command runs swiftly.
14. The Lord spreads the snow like a blanket of wool and scatters the frost like ashes.
15. The Lord hurls down hail like crumbs; who can withstand his icy blast?
16. The Lord melts the ice and snow, causes wind to blow, and waters to flow.
17. Praise the Lord from the heavens, Praise the Lord from the heights, you waters above skies.
18. Praise all angels, the heavenly hosts.
18. Praise the Lord, sun and moon, praise the Lord, all you stars of light!
20. Praise the Lord, you highest heavens.
21. Let them praise the name of the Lord, for the Lord commanded and they were created.
22. The Lord established them forever and ever; the Lord made a decree which shall not pass away.
23. Praise the Lord from the earth, you sea monsters and all deeps!
24. You lightning, hail, fog, and frost, you stormy wind that work at the Lord's order!
25. You mountains and all hills, fruitful trees and cedars,
beasts and all cattle, creeping things and flying birds,
26. kings, queens, and all peoples, princes, princesses, and all rulers and judges of the earth!
27. both young men and young maidens, old men and women, and children;
28. Let them praise the name of the Lord, for the Lord's name alone is exalted; the splendor of the Lord is above the earth and the heavens.
29. The Lord has lifted up a horn for all people, a song of praise for the saints of the Lord, the people close to the heart of the Lord. Praise the Lord. Selah.

PSALM 44

Let the whole earth rejoice

1. Sing to the Lord a new song in chorus and choir,
2. praise the Lord in the assembly of the saints.
3. Let the whole earth rejoice in their Maker; let the people be glad in their God.
4. Praise the Lord! Hallelujah!
5. Praise the Lord in holy sanctuary; praise the Lord of the mighty heavens.
6. Praise the Lord for mighty and wonderful works; praise the Lord for abundance.
7. Praise the Lord with trumpet sound; praise the Lord with lute and harp.
8. Praise the Lord with tambourine and dance; praise the Lord with stringed and wind instruments or flutes,
And resounding cymbals!
9. Praise the Lord for things seen and unseen.
10. Look to things unseen, for they are eternal.

11. Silver and gold we take not with us, but the soul is beholden to the Lord.
12. Do not be overawed when a man grows rich, when the splendor of his house increases; for he will take nothing with him when he dies, his splendor will not go with him.
14. Though in his lifetime he counted himself happy and was raised in prosperity, he will go to join the company of his forefathers, who will never see again light on earth.

PSALM 45

God is the author of Peace

1. O Lord, let the light of Your presence guide us, for in Your light do we see light.
2. Make peaceable for us our steps, Jehovah, O Lord, our Lord who has no Lord.
3. Have hope that there will be a happy end for the blameless man and the innocent child.
4. It is my desire to do Your Will, Lord, and your law of goodness is in my heart.
5. As a deer longs for running streams, so do I long for you, O God.
6. With my whole being I thirst for God, the living God. When can I go and meet with God?
7. As I pour out my soul, I remember how I used to go with many in procession to the house of God, with shouts of joy and thanksgiving, the clamour of the faithful.
8. But my heart is stirred by a noble theme as I recite verses for the Lord; my tongue is a pen of a skillful writer.
9. The Mighty One, God, the Lord, speaks and summons the earth from the rising of the sin to its setting.
10. God shines forth the earth in perfect beauty.
11. Our God comes and does not keep silent; Our God is alive and the heavens proclaim the Lord's righteousness, saying
12. Now consider this, I am God.

TALMUD

The Talmud is 63 tractates or 6200 pages in the canon of 35 volumes. It was written in tannaitic Hebrew and Aramic. It has Halaka (law), ethics, philosophy, customs, and history.

1. The Torah speaks in the tongue of men inspired by the Lord our God.
2. The atonement for any wrong that one man has done to another begins with repairing the injury in full and then hoping for God's absolution.
3. Pay outstanding debts.
4. Do not waste your life on evil. 5. Confession in Judaism is a whisper of the entire congregation at once. This same confession seals the individual in his privacy with God but draws him into a communal world.
6. Repentance, prayer, and good works can dissolve the evil decree.
7. Husbands and wives may sleep in twin beds so they can sleep apart for a time during the menses of a woman or if a man labors hard for a day and cannot bathe.
8. And you shall do what is right and good in the wisdom of the Lord, that it may go well with you.
9. The first law is that Jehovah God made a covenant with the people that God will be there for us; the second laws were given to Moses in the Ten Commandments.
10. Jews will pray 3 times a day; morning, noon, and night. The grace blessing after meals is birkat hamazon. Foods blessed by a rabbi are kosher.
11. Jews should not eat with non-Jews or marry non-Jews. Jews should not

eat with Akum (worshippers of the stars).
12. Talmud scholars should not eat with Jews who do not study the Talmud.

Sh'ma

The Creed and the Service

Hear, O Israel, the Lord Our God,the Lord is One.

And you shall love the Lord your God with all your heart, and with all your soul, and with all your might. And these words which I command you today shall be upon your heart. And you shall teach them to your children and celebrate a bar-mitzvah for the young men and a bas-mitzvah for the young women to initiate them into religious responsibility. And you shall bind them for a sign upon your hand and mind between your eyes. And you shall write them upon the door posts of your house, and upon your gates.

And I will give grass in your field for your cattle, and you shall eat and be satisfied.

And the Lord spoke to Moses, saying, Speak to the children of Israel, and tell them to make a fringe upon the corners of their garments down the generations, and they will put a thread of blue on the fringe of each corner. And it will be a fringe for you, that you may see it, and remember all the commands of God and do them, that you remember and be holy to your God. I am the Lord your God.

18 Benedictions

1. Avot - God of our father Abraham
2. Gevurot - A mighty God
3. Qedushat Hashem - You are the most holy God, Selah!
4. Binah - Grant us Your Wisdom
5. Teshuvah - Our Lord delights in repentance
6. Selihah -Lord, we beg for Your forgiveness
7. Ge'ulah - Lord, You are Our Redeemer (Savior)
8. Refu'ah - Lord, heal your sick and hopeless people
9. Hashanim - Blessed are you, O Lord, who bless the years.
10. Qibbuts Galuyot - You are the Lord who gathers the people of Israel
11. Mishpat - Lord, restore justice in judgment.
12. Haminin - Lord, banish violence, injustice, and slander.
13. Tzaddikim - Lord, grant a good reward for Your righteous and trustworthy believers.
14. Yerushalayim - Blessed are you, O Lord, who make the glory of salvation flower.
15. Tefiah - Blessed are You, O Lord, You hear our prayers, Amen.
16. Avodah - Lord, bless our temples.
17. Hoda'ah - Lord, unto You it is fitting to give thanks, Selah!
18. Kohanim - Lord, bless all people with peace.

Amidah - The devotion par excellence.

SHABBAT SYNAGOGUE SONGS

Songs Sung or Chanted

At the Opening of the Ark :

Va Yehi Binsoa

Gadlu

Echod Elokeinu

L'Choh Hashem Hagedula

Modeh Ani (It's Another Wonderful Morning)

CHRISTIAN

Bible Scriptures derived from the Christian New Testament of the King James Bible and Anglican Book of Common Prayer

The story of Jesus was told in the Four Gospels of Matthew, Mark, Luke, and John in the New Testament of the King James Bible.

The word 'God' has been substituted for Jehovah or Yahweh in many verses.

The Ministry of Jesus

1. The book of the ancestry of Jesus Christ, the son of David, the son of Abraham.

Abraham, was the father of Isaac, Isaac the father of Jacob, Jacob the father of Judah and his brothers,

Judah, the father of Perez and Zerah, whose mother was Tamar. Perez was the father of Hezron, Hezron the father of Aram,

Aram the father of Aminadab, Aminadab the father of Nahshon, Nahshon the father of Salmon,

Salmon the father of Boaz, whose mother was Rahab, Boaz the father of Obed, whose mother was Ruth, Obed the father of Jesse,

Jesse, the father of King David, King David the father of Solomon, whose mother had been the wife of Uriah,

Solomon the father of Rehoboam, Rehoboam the father of Abijah, Abijah the father of Asa,

Asa the father of Jehoshaphat, Jehoshaphat the father of Joram (Jehoram), Joram the father of Uzziah,

Uzziah the father of Jotham, Jotham the father of Ahaz, Ahaz the father of Hezekiah,

Hezekiah the father of Manasseh, Manasseh the father of Amon, Amon the father of Josiah,

And Josiah became the father of Jeconiah (also called Coniah and Jehoiachin) and his brothers about the time of the removal to Babylon.

After the exile to Babylon, Jeconiah became the father of Shealtiel (Salathiel), Shealtiel the father of Zerubbabel,

Zerubbabel the father of Abiud, Abiud the father of Eliakim, Eliakim the father of Azor,

Azor the father of Sadoc, Sadoc the father of Achim,
Achim the father of Eliud,

Eliud the father of Eleazar, Eleazar the father of Matthan,
Matthan the father of Jacob,
Jacob the father of Joseph, the husband of Mary, of whom was born Jesus (Joshua), Who is called the Christ.

So all generations from Abraham to David are fourteen, from David to the Babylonian exile are fourteen generations, from the Babylonian exile to the Christ fourteen generations.

Mary and Joseph

2. Mary became engaged to a carpenter named Joseph, but before the wedding she realized that she

would bear a child, and she was afraid.
And, behold, an angel of the Lord named Gabriel appeared to Mary saying, Mary do not fear, for you will bear a son who will save the people from their sins. You and Joseph are chosen because you both are sinless and have committed no evil, you and Joseph have pure souls and are true believers of the good ways of the Lord. I will fill your son with My Divine Guidance to save the people and lead them to righteousness, and you shall call him Jesus (Greek form of the Hebrew name Joshua). Anne of David's line was Mary's mother and Joachim was Mary's father.

The angel of the Lord appeared to Joseph, who was a descendant of David, who was the son of Jesse, in a dream, saying, your wife will bear a son that will save the people from their sins. You will be a good father to Jesus because you are pure in soul and you have committed no evil, and Joseph agreed to marry her. And it was said Mary was a virgin who would give birth to a child of God.

Jesus was born in a manger

3. Mary and Joseph journeyed forth to be counted in the census, and the time came for the child to be born. All of the inns were filled but Joseph was offered a barn for the night. And so Jesus was born in Bethlehem; and she wrapped Him in swaddling clothes and laid Him in a manger, because there was no room for them in the inn.

And behold, an angel of the Lord stood by them, and the glory of the Lord flashed and shone all about them, and the angel said: Do not be afraid, for behold, I bring you tidings of great joy which will come to all people. For unto you is born this day in the city of David a Savior who will be a symbol of love. And he was called Christ the Lord. And cherub angels sang all around. Three wise men who were astrologers and were called the Magi had an epiphany of a divine one that had been born; they were ecstatic to see the star in the east and followed it to find the baby. They brought gifts of gold to symbolize royalty, frankincense to symbolize divinity, and myrrh to symbolize immortality. The wise men also said they had followed the sounds of childbirth to find the manger could offer their assistance if needed. The three wise men said that King Herod heard some say that the Jewish messiah had been born; the three wise men decided to avoid King Herod because they were not sure of the king's intentions, so the three wise men decided to go to another land and not their home land. The three wise men told Mary and Joseph to go to Egypt to avoid King Herod and the famine that was occurring in the region.

4. *Jesus' Family went to Egypt*

In Egypt, there was oral tradition that was spoken of three years and some months that Joseph, Mary, and Jesus lived in Egypt. They left Nazareth during the night when Jesus was an infant. The Holy Family entered Egypt riding on a donkey along the coastal road that led to the eastern delta lands of the Nile River. Salome, the family's maidservant journeyed with the family because she was much needed and appreciated. When the family arrived in the city of Sakha, north of Cairo, they were thirsty but there was no water. Then the child Jesus touched a stone with his foot, water spouted forth, and his foot left an imprint; this stone has been called Bikha Isous and was discovered in April 1984CE; it was said 'Allah' was etched on the back.

Sometimes during the journey Joseph would carry the baby Jesus on his back.

At the city of Musturud, the infant Jesus brought forth a spring of water.

A sycamore tree sheltered the holy family at Matariya. Mary bathed Jesus, and after bathing him, she poured the water out on the ground – a balsam tree sprang forth and grew with a beautiful scent.

Some say the holy family ventured west to the area of Wadi al-Natrun; it became a blessed place for monks. The wadi is the valley of a riverbed that may contain water.

While traveling south on the Nile near Gabal al-Tayr (mountain of the birds) and Gabal al-Kaff (mountain of the palm), a mountain peak bowed as the Christ Child bowed; Jesus extended his hand and the mountain returned to its original position. A date palm bowed to the holy family when they were hungry; they picked the fruit and ate it. The palm returned to its original position after the holy family passed by the palm tree.

At the city Al-Ashmunayn the Christ Child left a handprint and another blessed tree.

A handprint was found on a stone in 1986CE showing fingers and a palm tree which said 'This is a handprint of Jesus according to Coptic tradition' but Bishop Yu'annis of Gharbia said it could not be proven that it was actually a handprint of Jesus.

When the holy family was in the city of Cusae living in a house in the countryside, an angel of the Lord told Joseph to take the family back to the land of Israel. Then, beside the Nile, Mary prayed to the Lord and made the sign of a cross across the Nile, and a boat appeared which was the beginning of the sojourn back to Nazareth.

Some said that the holy family also stayed in a cave near a quarry at Durunka in southern Egypt. Some said there was an altar that was blessed by the presence of the holy family and the Christ Child.

Jesus' family returned to Nazareth from Egypt

The holy family went back to Galilee around Nazareth instead of to Bethlehem of Judea, which was near Jerusalem because Herod's son Archelaus was ruling in place of his father Herod.

5. In Galilee was a town called Nazareth which means 'Branch, Separated One'.

When Jesus was twelve years in Jerusalem; he spent time with the priests and rabbis at a Jewish Passover Feast in the Temple and even preached among them. Jesus loved all people. Jesus was separated from his parents; it took them three days to find him.

6. Jesus, his brother James, his half-brother Jude, and his parents did gather among Jews, Egyptians, Philistines, and Assyrians along the river with food, music, dance, and sometimes magicians. Jesus listened and was grieved to learn that people were persecuting and killing each other over religions or religious rules.
People were getting killed for no good reason.

7. Then Mary remained with Elizabeth her cousin for 3 months and returned to her home. Elizabeth gave birth to a son named John, whose tongue was speaking praise for the Lord at a young age; this was discussed throughout the hill country of Judea.

8. A tradition said that his great uncle (his mother's father's brother), a merchant in the copper and spice trade, told Jesus about or took him to several other cities in England, India, and Africa when he had visited on business trips.
Food ideas and languages from different cultures were being shared.
There were people in Africa with darker skin tone than in the middle-east. There were people in England with lighter skin tone than in the middle-east. There were oriental people visiting from Asia with medium tan skin with a yellow tone.

9. The Nabataeans were Arab nomads who brought spices from India and China to the lands around the Mediterranean Sea. Their capital city was Petra.

Ministry of Jesus

10. Jesus was a carpenter like his father Joseph. When Joseph died, Jesus began his ministry of teaching to others about good ways . He was thirty years old when he started his ministry.
And Jesus increased in wisdom and in stature and in years, and in favor with God and other people.
11. In those days, John the Baptist was preaching in the wilderness desert of Judea.
The practice of baptism for the repentance of sins was being conferred by John the Baptist, son of the father Zachariah who owned a vineyard and mother Elizabeth. John said in baptism: 'Repent, for the divine realm of heaven is at hand. Change your mind and sin no more.'
John was preaching to followers about salvation.
John did instruct: 'Bear works that are deserving and consistent with your repentance (conduct of a heart changed from doing sin). Bring forth fruit that is consistent with repentance.
(Let your lives show your change of heart from evil back to good ways.)
If you have two tunics, may you

share one tunic with another who has none; if you have food, may you share with another who has none.'

And people were in suspense and enamored by John and wondered if John was a messiah predicted by Isaiah –'an anointed one, a christ', such was the meaning of the word in those times.

But John answered the people: 'I baptized you with water; but it is Yahweh (God) Who is mightier than I.' So with many other appeals and questions John preached the good news of the Lord to the people.

John said 'He who is coming after me is mightier than I, whose sandals I am not worthy or fit to carry'.

And Jesus went from Galilee to the Jordan River to be baptized by John, but John protested, saying, 'It is I who needs to be baptized by You, and You come to me?'

But Jesus replied to John: 'This is a fitting way for both of us to fulfill all righteousness.' And so Jesus was baptized by John; water from the river was poured over Jesus and John saw the Holy Spirit descended upon Jesus like a dove.

And behold, there came a voice from heaven that said:

'This is my son, in whom I delight and am well pleased.'

Many in Jerusalem and Judea and the country around the Jordan were baptized by him and confessed their sins.

And some Pharisees and Sadducees came to be baptized, but John refused to baptize them but called them hypocrites. He told them to change their evil ways first.

In that region of the land, there was concern because evilness was being conducted by some evil priests in the Sanhedrin Council; some priests were ordering people to be killed for working on the Sabbath or for not worshipping Jehovah.

But not all of the rabbi priests were evil, and the Lord knew the hearts and minds of the priests who were the true followers of God.

And then John the Baptist was arrested put in prison.

12. When Jesus heard that John the Baptist had been put in prison, Jesus left Nazareth and went down to Capernaum by the sea in the country of Zebulon and Naphtali. As he was walking by the sea, he told people to repent or they could not enter Heaven.

He noticed two brothers , Simon (who was called Peter) and Andrew his brother who were throwing a dragnet into the sea; they were fishermen. He said to them: 'Come after Me, follow Me, and I will make you fishers of men!' And they left their nets and became his disciples.

And James and John who were Galilean fishermen were in a boat with their father Zebedee mending their nets, and they also left to follow Jesus. John was the son of Salome, the sister of Mary the mother of Jesus.

And he came across Matthew ben Alphaeus (Levi), who was a tax collector and said: Join me, as my attendant, and Matthew followed him.

Then Jesus walked along the seashore and then up into the hills, preaching and performing miracles everywhere he went about Galilee; Jesus cured people from blindness and leprosy.

Jesus summoned 12 disciples by saying: 'If you would be perfect, go sell what you have and give it to the poor, and you will have riches in heaven, and come and be my disciple.'
The names of these apostles were Simon, who is called Peter, and Andrew his brother; James, son of Zebedee and John his brother; Phillip and Bartholomew; Thomas and Matthew the tax collector; James son of Alphaeus, and Thaddaeus also called Judas, Simon the Cananaean, and Judas Iscariot. Jesus said 'I am sending you out like sheep in the midst of wolves to teach the good news; be wary and wise as a fox and innocent as a dove. Do not be anxious about what to speak, for what you are to say will be given to you by God.' And Jesus gave them power and authority to cure diseases, weaknesses, and infirmity.

Jesus said 'I tell you and I speak the truth, anyone who doesn't receive the kingdom of heaven like a child will never enter it.' Let the children come to me. A child named Ignatius sat on Jesus' lap; Jesus hugged the child and blessed him.

Jesus and the Apostles went to cities and villages, synagogues, temples, houses, tents, and outdoor gatherings to proclaim the good news of the Lord and life eternal, helping others wherever they could. And Pharisees gave alms to the poor and spoke of resurrection.

There was a crowd of people who had followed Jesus for three days and had not eaten.
Jesus miraculously multiplied 7 loaves of bread and a few small fish so those who follow a crowd of 4,000 people could eat.

Jesus said if a man has a hundred sheep, and one of them has gone astray, will not the man rejoice to find the one that is lost.

And if a brother wrongs you, go and discuss this fault, between you and him privately. If he listens to you, then you have won back your brother.

A group of men dragged a woman who was a harlot, a sinner before Jesus for judgment, but Jesus said let the one among them who had never sinned speak first, and all of them were ashamed.
Jesus said: Why do you say that I perfect like God? None of us are perfect except for God.

Jesus said: Do not think I have come to do away with the Law or the Prophets; I have come not to do away with but to complete and fulfill them.
Whoever teaches and practices the commandments shall be called great in heaven.

Jesus told the people that they could eat anything that was safe to eat and the food did not have to be blessed by a Jewish rabbi priest before the food could be eaten.
Jesus picked spikes of grain on the Sabbath but the Pharisees told Jesus that no one was permitted to pick grain on the Sabbath, but Jesus called them hypocrites.

So Jesus, John, and their Disciples started their own ministry; but some of the Jewish rabbi priests of the Sanhedrin Council were angry that Jesus was disregarding the rules of the Sanhedrin Council so they conspired to kill him. Nicodemus was a Pharisee and a member of the Sanhedrin who reminded the Sanhedrin priests that the law required a person to be heard before being judged.

Jesus told the people to pray for lepers, beggars, and the downtrodden, saying 'Whoever fails to do for the least of these, fails to do for me.'

Jesus raised a man who had died back to life; the man was laying on his funeral bier and being carried away when his mother begged Jesus to bring her son back to life, and the son sat up and was awake. Jesus also raised a daughter back to life for a man and a woman who were her parents; he did this in the presence of Peter, James, and John and a crown of flute players was heard. Jesus told her parents "Weep not. She is not dead but only sleeping.' And Jesus touched her arm and her spirit returned and the child raised to life. Jesus ordered that some food be given to her and to not tell others what had happened.

At Capernaum, Jesus restored a servant boy of a centurion back to health. Jesus cured lepers, cast out demons, and restored sight to a blind man by spitting saliva in the dirt and smearing the clay on the man's forehead. Jesus restored an injured hand of a man back to normal, and commanded a paralyzed man to walk again; he told the paralyzed man to get up off of his sleeping pad, pack it up, and go home. A woman who was bent over and could not stand up straight was cured. A hemophiliac who was bleeding from a wound that would not heal was healed after she touched Jesus' garment. Jesus cured a girl who was possessed by a demon. Peter's mother-in-law had a fever, and her fever left her body after Jesus touched her with his hand. A woman pleaded with Jesus to help her daughter who was miserable, but Jesus said he was sent only to the lost sheep of the house of Israel. The woman begged for Jesus to help her child, saying: Even the little pups eat the crumbs (table scraps) that fall from their masters' table. And so Jesus healed her daughter; she was cured that moment.

Jesus said special prayers for the lives of precious children, for their safety and guidance and said Let the children come to me.

Jesus, Peter, James, and John were on a mountain. When Jesus was praying, the disciples saw his countenance change and become radiant. They saw a vision of Moses and Elijah and a transfiguration, and heard the voice of God telling them 'You are my sons, in whom I am well pleased. Spread the good news of the Lord, and keep to good ways, shunning all evil.'

Jesus and the Disciples were out on the boat; Jesus was sleeping but he was awakened by the disciples who were afraid of a storm that was

rocking the boat. Jesus walked on water, showing his disciples to have faith, and Jesus calmed the waters. And Peter said: Lord, if it is You, command me to come to You on the water.
Jesus said: Come! So Peter got out of the boat and walked on the water and came toward Jesus. He was frightened and began to sink, and cried out, Lord, save me! Instantly, Jesus reached out His hand and caught and held Peter up, saying: have faith and do not doubt the power of God. So they crossed to the other side and went ashore at Gennesaret.

Jesus asked the lawyers and Pharisees: Is it lawful to do work on the Sabbath? And they were silent. Jesus told the people that it was acceptable to do work on the Sabbath; he said 'Who among you would not rescue a donkey, goat, or sheep that accidentally fell over a wall?
So if I perform miracles on the Sabbath to heal another,
should that be unlawful?
Moses is your accuser, not me.'
Jesus told this to the people because some evil rabbi priests were killing people who were gathering sticks on the Sabbath. (The Sabbath was the 7th day on which the Jewish God Jehovah who was also called Yahweh rested from work after He had worked for 6 days to create the universe, earth, and all creatures on earth.)

Jesus told the people that they could eat anything that was safe to eat and the food did not have to be blessed by a rabbi priest before the food could be eaten. Jesus picked spikes of grain on the Sabbath but the Pharisees told Jesus that no one was permitted to pick grain on the Sabbath. When the Sanhedrin Council heard that Jesus was performing miracles and working on the Sabbath, they were enraged and sought to kill him.
Jesus said the Pharisees were hypocrites and said Woe to you, scribes and Pharisees, for ye pay tithe of mint, anise, and cumin, and have omitted the weightier matters of the law, judgment, mercy, and faith: these ought ye to have done, and not to leave the other undone.

Jesus miraculously multiplied loaves of bread and fish so a crowd of starving people could eat. Jesus fed 5,000 people with 5 loaves of barley bread. When the people were finished eating, the scraps of bread filled 12 baskets with the leftovers.

He turned water into wine when the wine ran out at a wedding; he told the attendants to fill the stone pots up to the brimwith water, but when they drank the water it was wine.

He told the crowds that people can outwardly seem to be just and upright but inside they are full of pretense, lawlessness, hostility, and iniquity.

Once Jesus' mother and brothers came to see him while he was preaching. When a disciple told him that his family was there, Jesus said that whoever does the good will of God is his family.

Jesus arrived in Bethany six days before the Passover Feast.

A woman washed Jesus' feet with her tears and dried them with her hair, and anointed Jesus' feet with perfume. She was humbled to be in his presence and begged forgiveness for her sins and Jesus told her that all of her sins were forgiven; her name was Mary Magdalene.

Jesus raised Lazarus, a friend, from the dead.
Lazarus lived in Bethany, the village where Mary Magdalene and her sister, Martha lived. Lazarus had been in the tomb for four days. Thomas went also and said to his fellow disciples: 'Let us go, too, that we may die along with Him.' Jesus told Martha not to worry, that she would see her brother Lazarus again. Jesus said: 'Whoever so believes in the Lord as the Lord is in Me, shall live forever.' And Jesus said: 'Where have you lain him?' And they took Jesus to the tomb of Lazarus and Jesus told them to take away the rock at the entrance and said 'Lazarus, come out', and Lazarus was raised from the dead and walked out of the tomb.

Now, when the Pharisees and the Sanhedrin Council of the chief priests heard of the teachings and miracles of Jesus, they were concerned that the followers of Jesus were increasing in number, so they plotted to kill Jesus and Lazarus.

An elder paid Judas Iscariot, one of Jesus' 12 Disciples, thirty pieces of silver to tell Pilate where Jesus was staying.

And King Herod killed and beheaded John the Baptist around this time, because John the Baptist accused Herod of adultery. (King Herod had killed his own brother so that he could take his brother's wife as his own.)

On the way to the Passover Feast of the Unleavened Bread, Jesus rode a donkey to Jerusalem. His followers exalted him with branches of palm trees shouting as he rode by: 'Hosanna! Blessed is Jesus who serves in the name of the Lord!' The great crowd was also hoping to see Lazarus, who Jesus had raised from the dead.

When Jesus entered the temple, he overturned tables and drove out those who were selling, telling them It is written that My house shall be a house of prayer but you have made it into a cave of robbers. And he continued to teach in the porches and courts of the temple. The chief priests and scribes were angered but people were in awe of the words of Jesus.

Jesus ate with the sinners and preached by the lake, by the fig trees, and on the Mount of Olives across from the First Jewish Temple. Jesus said to forgive and show mercy, because the Holy Spirit in Heaven forgives us. 'From your heart, forgive your brother his offenses.' After the Sermon on the mount, the crowds were astonished, overwhelmed, and bewildered at his teachings. His fame spread throughout the region; some said 'I want to be like Jesus and follow his loving-kindness.'

Zacchaeus was a rich tax collector who climbed up into a tree to see Jesus, because he could not see Jesus through the crowd of people. Jesus told Zacchaeus to come down from the tree and that he needed to stay at Zacchaeus' house that day.

So, Zacchaeus and Jesus talked, and Zacchaeus declared that he had given half of his goods to the poor and he did not cheat anyone out of anything. And Jesus said; Today is messianic and spiritual, for salvation has come to this house, not all tax collectors are sinners.

John wrote that Jesus got up from the Passover supper, poured water into a basin and washed the disciples' feet and wiped them dry with a servant's towel.

He asked the disciples: Do you understand what I have just done? You call me the Teacher and the Lord, so if I then, Your Lord and Teacher, have washed your feet, you should wash one another's feet. And you are clean but not all of you.

The disciples kept looking at one another, puzzled as to whom Jesus could mean.

Jesus answered: It is the one whom I am going to give this morsel of food after I have dipped it. So he gave the morsel of food to Judas, who was Simon Iscariot's son. And he told Judas to do quickly what he must do. So Judas left and the other disciples thought that Judas went to buy something for the Festival or to give something to the poor.

And Jesus told his disciples: I will only be with you a little longer, so I tell you now, you are not able to go where I am going.

I give you a new commandment: that you should love one another. Just as I have loved you, so you too should love one another.

Jesus arose to go into the garden and Peter asked to follow him. Jesus answered: You are not able to follow me but you will follow me afterward.

Peter said to Jesus: Lord, why cannot I follow You now? I will lay down my life for You.

Jesus answered, Will you lay down your life for me? I assure you, most solemnly I tell you, before a rooster crows, you will deny Me three times.

Then Thomas asked Jesus: Lord, we do not know where You are going, so how can we know the way?

Jesus said: 'Follow me and I will be with you in spirit; by me shall you reach the Father.'

Philip said to Jesus: 'Show us the Father Yahweh (God), then we shall be satisfied.'

Jesus said to Philip: 'Do you not believe that I am the Father Yahweh (God), and that Father (God) is in me? What I am telling you I do not say on My own accord, but my words are from the Father who lives continually in Me and does the works of miracles and deeds of powers.

If you love me, you will keep my commandments. I will not leave you desolate and alone as orphans; I will ask the Father to give you another Comforter, that God will remain with you forever. Peace I leave with you; my own peace I now give to you. Not as the world gives do I give to you. In this world there will be trouble, but do not let your hearts be troubled, neither let them be afraid,

for I am always with you, until the end. In the end I will wipe every tear away for the final time. I will not talk with you much more, for Satan the evil genius is coming but Satan has nothing in common with me; there is nothing in Me that belongs to him, and he has not power over Me.
I only do what God the Father has instructed me to do.

I am the Vine; you are the branches. Whoever lives in Me and I in them bears much fruit. Apart from God who is the Vinedresser, you can do nothing, for you would be like a withered branch.

I still have much to say, but you are not able to bear them or to take them upon you or to grasp them now.
But the Spirit of Truth will guide you into the Truth by speaking a message that has been given to one who will announce and declare to you the things that are to come. The one will honor and glorify me, taking what is Mine and revealing it to you.

I assure you, most solemnly I tell you, that you shall weep and grieve, but the world will rejoice. You will be sorrowful, but your sorrow will be turned to joy.

A woman, when she gives birth to a child, has agony of pain, but when she has delivered the child, she no longer remembers her pain because she is so glad that a child has been born into the world.

So for the present you are also in sorrow, but I will see you again and then your hearts will rejoice, and no one can take from you your joy.

Now, I came from God and I am leaving the world and going back to God.

In this world you have tribulation and trials and distress and frustration, but be of good cheer, be confident, certain, and undaunted. For I will be with you in spirit, and the Father God will listen to your prayers.'

And then Jesus prayed to heaven: 'Lord, the hour has come. Glorify Your Son, so that Your Son may glorify You. I have spoken the words that You gave me to speak on earth. Holy Father, keep in Your Knowledge those whom You have given Me, that they may be one as We are one. I have revealed Your character and Your very Self and have made known that the love which You have bestowed on Me may be in them, and that I myself may be in them.

Philip and Andrew were approached by some Greeks who were wanting to speak with Jesus, and they took them to Jesus, and they praised Him.

Jesus broke bread and drank wine with his disciples, telling them to remember and desire for the Lord even as you eat; he said 'Man shall not live and be sustained by bread alone, but by every word and expression of God.'

Now as they were eating, Jesus took bread and, praising God, gave thanks and asked God to bless it to their use, and when He had broken it, He gave it to the disciples and said, Take, eat; this is My body.
And He took a cup, and when He had given thanks, He gave it to them, saying, Drink of it, all of you: For this

is My blood of the new covenant, which is being poured out for many for the forgiveness of sins.
Do this in remembrance of me.

I say to you, I shall not drink again of this fruit of the vine until that day when I drink it with you new and of superior quality in My Father's heaven.

And when they had sung a hymn, they went out to the Mount of Olives.

Jesus told the disciples to follow him always and be not scattered from Him. Peter told Jesus he would never fall away, but Jesus told him, solemnly I tell you, this very night, before a single rooster crows, you will deny me three times.

Peter said: No, I would never deny you.

And Judas betrayed Jesus by revealing to Pontius Pilate's men the location of Jesus, the place where he often retired to. Luke wrote that Judas went up to Jesus and kissed him; that is how the Pharisees knew which man was Jesus.

Jesus and his disciples were praying in the Garden of Gethsemane at night; the disciples were gathered around Jesus in a circle; they prayed 'Abba' which means 'Everything is possible for you, Lord.' And then
Jesus the Nazarene was arrested by the Pharisees and Governor Pilate's men, who were also looking to arrest Lazarus, but he was not found.
The chief priests and elders of the Sanhedrin were jealous of Jesus because Jesus was acquiring followers, believers of the Holy Spirit to pray with him, but the Sanhedrin Council of the high priests wanted the people to only worship with the Levites before the ark of the Ten Commandments at the First Temple to the Lord; this was religious persecution.

Jesus was first taken before Annas, the father-in-law of Caiaphas, who was the high priest that year.

And a servant of a high priest asked Peter who was standing in the doorway: You are also a disciple of this Man? But Peter said: I am not!

The high priest asked Jesus about His disciples and His teachings.

Jesus answered him: 'I have spoken openly to the world. I have always taught in a synagogue and in the temple where the Jews congregate and I have spoken nothing secretly. Why do you ask me?
Ask those who have heard me, what I said to them.
I have said nothing evil; I have only spoken rightly and properly. Why do you strike me?'

Then Annas sent Jesus bound to Caiaphas the high priest.

Now Peter was standing and was warming himself around a fire of coals that the servants had made, and a servant asked him: Are you not a disciple of Jesus? But Peter said No.
Next, a relative of the high priest inquired to Peter: 'Did I not see you in the garden with him?'

And again Peter denied it.
And immediately a rooster crowed.

Pilate pardoned a prisoner each year. When Pilate asked the people who to pardon, they chose Barabass instead of Jesus. Pilate said he would not be responsible for Jesus' death because Jesus was a righteous man.

When Jesus was asked under what authority he had to do the things like performing work on the Sabbath, Jesus answered that he would not tell them by what power of authority that he did the things he did.

Jesus was crucified to death on a cross alongside two other prisoners; they made him carry his own cross; it was a Friday. Luke wrote that one of the prisoners asked Jesus 'Are you not the Christ Messiah? Rescue Yourself and us from death!'

Jesus said 'My God, my God, forgive them, for they know not what they are doing. Into your hands do I commit my Spirit.'
When Jesus died, many said there was a flash of lightening in the sky and the earth shook, as Jesus said: 'Eli, Eli, lama sabachthani? – that is, My God, My God, why have You abandoned me in my need?' ('Why have you forsaken me?') And some bystanders said: 'This man is calling for the prophet Elijah.'
And some of the wicked put vinegar on a sponge and lifted it up for Jesus to drink.
And Jesus cried again with a loud voice and gave up his spirit. Jesus had been ministering for 3 ½ years when he was crucified upon the cross.
And Joseph, a Jew from the city of Arimathea who was a disciple of Jesus, took Jesus' body off the crucifix. And Nicodemus, who had first come to see Jesus that night, also came with a mixture of myrrh and aloes, weighing several pounds. They rolled the body of Jesus up in a clean linen cloth used for swathing dead bodies and carried it into a cave and rolled a big boulder over the entrance and went away.

Pilate ordered that the door of the tomb should be guarded since there was much an uproar of perceptions among the people of the nature of the crucified prisoner, Jesus.

Resurrection of Jesus

On the third day Mary (the mother) of James, Mary Magdalene, and Salome who was the sister of Mary, the mother of Jesus, went to the tomb of Jesus so they might anoint Jesus' body. But when they rolled back the stone, the tomb was empty except for the linen cloths of Jesus, and they wept. A young man who was sitting by the tomb said to them: 'Do not be amazed or terrified, you are looking for Jesus, who was crucified but has risen. He is not here.'
Many thought Jesus was raised to heaven. It was also written by some that Jesus first descended to hell and then ascended to heaven.

When Judas Iscariot learned what happened to Jesus, he brought the thirty pieces of silver back to the priests and threw them on the ground, saying that they had caused the shed of innocent blood. Then he hanged himself. The priests buried the silver in a potter's field.

The Disciples met in the Upper Room and proposed two men to replace Judas: Joseph called

Barsabbas or Matthias. The two men drew lots and the lot fell to Matthias.

Gospels were written by disciples named Matthew, Mark, Luke, John, Thomas, and Andrew.

There were different versions of the Gospels and the Bible, and translations differed.

The Apostle Matthew wrote that when Jesus died and gave up his spirit, the curtain of the sanctuary of the temple was torn in two from top to bottom, the earth shook and rocks were split, tombs were opened and many bodies of the saints who had died were raised to life. The saints went into the holy city and appeared to people, who were frightened and filled with awe, saying 'Truly this was God's Son!' An angel robed in white sat upon the boulder that was rolled back from the entrance to the tomb and told the women – Mary of Magdalene and the other Mary – 'I know you are looking for Jesus, Who was crucified, but He is not here, He has risen. He is going before you in Galilee; there you will see Him. Behold, I have told you.'

And as they went, Jesus met them and said: 'Hail, (greetings)'. And the women went to Him, clasped His feet and worshipped Him.

And some of the guards of the tomb went into the city and reported to chief priests and elders all that had happened; they consulted and a sufficient amount of money was given to the soldiers and said: 'Tell people His disciples came at night and stole Him away while we were sleeping.' And if the governor hears of it, we will appease him and make you safe and free from trouble. So they took the money and did as they were instructed; and this story has been current among the Jews to the present day.

The eleven disciples then went to the mountain on Galilee and saw Jesus, fell down in worship, but some doubted. And Jesus said to them: 'Go teach others of the good commandments and know that I will be with you all the days to the very consummation of the ages. Amen. (so let it be).'

The Apostle Mark wrote that Jesus appeared to Mary Magdalene, who went and told others.

Afterward, Jesus appeared to Eleven of the disciples who did not betray him. They reclined at a table together; Jesus said: 'Go into all the world and preach the Good News of the Lord to all.'

The Apostle Luke wrote that Jesus spoke to Peter and Cleopas on a street in the village of Emmaus on the third day after the tomb was found empty saying: 'Believe what the prophets have spoken! The Lord is the Way, the Truth, and the Guidance!' Peter and Cleopas were startled, they thought they saw a spirit. They saw Jesus take a loaf of bread, say thanks, break it, give it to them to eat, and then they opened their eyes and Jesus vanished.

The Apostle John wrote that Jesus was buried in a new tomb in a garden in the place where he was crucified. And when Mary Magdalene saw that the tomb was empty, she ran to find Peter and

another disciple, and they ran to the empty tomb but they went back home after they saw it was empty, and left Mary Magdalene alone, crying.
Then two angels appeared to her, one near where the head of Jesus had lain, and the other near where the feet of Jesus had rested. And the angels said to her: 'Why are you sobbing?' She told them: 'Because they have taken away my Lord, and I do not know where they have lain Him.' After saying this, she turned around and Jesus was standing there, but she did not know it was Jesus. He said: 'Woman, why are you crying? For whom are you looking?' And Mary Magdalene replied: "If you are the gardener, tell me where you have put Him.' Then Jesus said: 'Mary!' And she realized it was Jesus and said in Hebrew: 'Rabboni – which means Teacher or Master.' Then Jesus said to her: 'Do not cling to Me, but go tell the others that I am ascending to My God and Your God.' So Mary Magdalene brought the disciples the news. And Jesus appeared to the disciples behind closed doors and said 'Peace to you! Just as God sent me forth, I am sending you.' And Jesus breathed on them and said: 'Receive the Holy Spirit.' But Thomas did not believe. Eight days later
Jesus did appear to Thomas and said: 'Reach out your fingers into the marks made by the nails, so you will believe.' And so Thomas did feel the marks of the nails and had faith and believed, saying: 'My Lord and my God!'
And Jesus said: 'Blessed are those who believe in the Lord yet have never seen.'
After this, Jesus appeared to His Disciples a third time as they were fishing from their boats not far from shore. There was a fire of coals on the shore, fish were cooking, and there was bread. Jesus said: 'Come and have breakfast.' So Peter and the other disciples dragged up the net and there were 153 fish. And Jesus said to Peter and the other disciples: 'Follow me! Feed my lambs for all eternity.'

Jesus is revered by some as a sacrificial lamb from God to set humanity free from sins (redemption) to allow atonement (reconciliation) with God; some believe that Jesus died so that we may live (justification of his death), that the blood of the lamb of Jesus washed away the sins of humanity before Jesus reconciled with God. Some have said four words represent the two upright and the two transverse pieces of the crucifix: atonement, redemption, justification, and reconciliation.

Some thought Jesus' body was raised (resurrected) from the dead, but others believed a fact was misinterpreted and that his spirit was raised (resurrected).
Some believe his body was stolen. The historians have said the translations of early texts from papyrus were uncertain. Some believe that Jesus and his disciples saved the gentiles and set them free from the evil members of the Sanhedrin Council who were killing people for working on the Sabbath

Day or who wouldn't convert to Judaism.

Affirmations of being saved through Jesus include:
a belief with your whole heart to trust and have confidence in Jesus, a justification to believe in Jesus since he preached righteousness, making amends for past wrong deeds, and making a personal commitment to follow good ways - then your soul will be saved and your spirit is reborn and you are a new person with God through Jesus Christ who then becomes your personal savior. Jesus is the Way, the
Truth and the Life, and no one gets to the Lord except through Jesus. When you are 'reborn' and saved, you are alive! O, Happy Day, is the day I came to Jesus and washed my heart clean from sin.

Some people were fighting over whether to worship to Jesus or the Lord Jehovah and the Ark of the Covenant of the Jews that contained the Ten Commandments, and a Greek judge named Gallio said that the Holy Spirit existed in both. Gallio refused to decide and said the people should decide their individual religion.

A council of Jewish leaders called the Sanhedrin did not approve of the teachings of the disciples following the Apostles of Jesus, the Sanhedrin council only endorsed the Jewish Temple; this was religious persecution. But not all of the Jewish leaders were oppressive of other religions; some Jewish leaders were accepting of the teachings of Jesus or the pagan followers; some Jewish leaders said 'God is an unknown spirit.'

A certain Pharisee in the Sanhedrin Council was named Gamaliel; he was a teacher of the Law and highly esteemed. Gamaliel told the Sanhedrins to let the apostles go and not to harm them; he said 'If it is God, you will not be able to stop or overthrow or destroy them; you might even be found fighting against God.' So some of the apostles were let go and were not harmed.

King Herod was a Roman leader who was responsible for the death of James, the brother of Jesus and John, and Peter.

A disciple named Stephen was brought before the Sanhedrin council and made to speak, for he was accused of bearing false witness. Stephen recanted the history of the forefathers from Abraham to Moses; how they worshipped the Lord and kept the Mosaic Laws. The function of the Mosaic Laws were to make humans recognize and be conscious of sin. It was said he had the appearance of the face of an angel. Stephen proclaimed that Jesus was a messiah. Stephen told the Jewish rabbi priest Ananias that he was breaking Moses' law that said 'Do not kill' when he killed people for working on the Sabbath. This comment angered the Sanhedrin Council and Stephen was stoned to death. As they were stoning him, he prayed 'Lord Jesus, receive and accept and welcome my spirit!' He fell on his knees and cried out loudly, 'Lord, forgive them and fix not this sin upon them,' and he died. Stephen was later proclaimed to be a saint.

Apostles of Jesus 33 - 70CE

The Holy Spirit descended upon the Twelve Apostles of Jesus in a Pentecost; they continued preaching the ways of Jesus; the apostles were messengers of the faith. Paul was a Benjamite Jew who first persecuted Christians. But Jesus spoke to him from heaven; after that Paul believed in both the teachings of Jesus and Mosaic Law and traveled about the middle-east and Mediterranean Sea areas teaching the religion of Christianity; Timothy, Artemas, Silvanus, and Tychicus went with him. Paul was chosen by God to be a messenger and a missionary for Jesus Christ, as was Timothy and the other apostles. Paul was a tentmaker. Paul spoke to a man who was a master of deception and wickedness, saying to him: 'you are the son of the devil, an enemy of everything that is upright and good and are making crooked the straight paths of the Lord and plotting against the Lord's good purposes.' But then the man believed and reformed his evil ways back to good, and true love grew out of sincere devotion to God.

Paul said to baptize people in the name of Jesus Christ with anointment of oil or water instead of baptizing for repentance of sins; and he baptized Apollos. The word 'christo' is a greek word that meant 'annointed one' and was used for people dedicating themselves to an official position. Paul thanked the people in the churches who supported their mission, and he sent greetings from people in one church to the other churches. Paul preached to the people 'I don't want your money; I want you to turn to God and practice good ways. I commit you to God, who is able to make you strong and steady in the Lord. This is God's plan of salvation for all the world, to bring people under His Wing. Praise the Lord of all people, who is wise and to be glorified forever. When you are baptized before the Lord in the name of Jesus Christ, you will see your evil nature die and you will be filled with a new nature and a new life because you trusted the Word of the Almighty God. We are saved by grace through faith. Jesus practiced tenderhearted mercy and kindness to others because Jesus was filled with love and concern for others so be convinced of this Good News. Jesus rescued us from Satan's kingdom and brought us to the Lord's kingdom.'

The high priest Ananias and Tertullus brought evidence against Paul that he was a pest, an agitator, and a source of disturbance to the Sanhedrin Council, so Paul and Timothy served prison terms for teaching their faith in Jesus. But Festus, who was a good Jew, was a witness who went before King Agrippa and spoke on their behalf, saying that they had done nothing that deserved for them to have been put in prison. King Agrippa heard the case and send Paul to Rome to stand before Caesar.

Zenas the lawyer and Apollos helped them. When Caesar heard the case, he also agreed that Paul and Timothy had committed no crime and were simply expressing their viewpoint of the Unknown God, and Caesar let them go free. Caesar said to let them worship God as they wished.

Paul (who was also called Saul) wrote letters to his assistants Timothy, Titus, and Luke and are dated approximately 55AD or 55CE.

Paul may have wrote the letters to his workers who were men named Archippus, Clement, Mark, Luke, Aristarchus, Demas, Origen,and a woman named Apphia. In the letter he said he was returning Onesimus back to Philemon, who was probably his wife. Onesimus was a slave who had escaped from Philemon and had traveled to find Paul. Paul also requested for someone to prepare a guest room for him because he was expecting to arrive back home after his prison term.

James, Peter, Jude, and John also wrote letters to Christian churches honoring the Holy Spirit and giving Christians good directives.

A LETTER OF PAUL TO TITUS

From Paul, servant of God and apostle of Jesus Christ, marked as such by faith and knowledge and hope – the faith of God's chosen people, knowledge of the truth as our religion has it, and the hope of eternal life. Yes, it is eternal life that God, who cannot lie, promised long ages ago, and now in his own good time he has openly declared himself in the proclamation which was entrusted to me by ordinance of God our Savior.

To Titus, my true-born son in the faith which we share, grace and peace from God our Father and Christ Jesus our Savior who became wisdom from God.

My intention to you is to institute elders in each town that are men of impeccable character, faithful to his one wife and his children, be no brawler, no money-grubber, or short-tempered. He must be of good judgment, devout, and self-controlled.

He who unites himself to a prostitute is one with her, for it is said they become one flesh, Flee from sexual immorality. Your body is a holy temple.

Some of the Jewish converts are out of control and talking wildly about marrying poor women or rich women.

Tell slaves to respect their masters.

Remind the people to be submissive to their governments and to obey authorities. Our people must be taught to be honest in their employment to produce the necessities of life.

Be not slaves to passions and pleasures of every kind. Do not pick quick quarrels. Live like you have been rescued. Jesus is our lifeline from heaven to earth.

Feel secure in the Lord. Now is the day of salvation.

Such are the points I wish you to insist on.

When I send Artemas to you, or Tychicus, make haste to join me at Nicopolis, for that is where I will spend the winter.

All who are with me send greetings. My greetings to those who are our friends in truth. Grace be with you all!

Christian Churches

Christian churches were established at Corinth, Galatia, Antioch, Iconium, Lystra, Derbe, Ephesus, Philippia, Colosse, Thessalonica, and throughout Greece and Italy. At Philippia, church was held in the home of a woman named Lydia. Epaphroditus of the Philippians worked with Paul. Philemon led a church meeting at her house. Acquilla and Priscilla were women who held church service in their homes, saying to their wee little ones, the children 'Be thou quieter than a church mouse and listen to the sermon.' Archippus led a church meeting at his house. Simeon (Niger), Manaen, and Lucius of Cyrene were prophets and teachers at the church in Antioch. Phoebe was a woman deacon and helper of Paul. Tychicus was a pastor and fellow worker of Paul. Paul did say to Timothy that a little wine occasionally may be good for health. Some disciples from Caesarea went with Paul to the house of Mnason, a man from Cyprus, and lodged there on the way to Jerusalem to see James. They all joined together constantly in prayer.

Some early followers of Jesus were called Essenes, Nazarenes or Apostolics.

The Philippians cried out 'The saints salute you, O Lord! We can do all things through God who gives us strength.'

Paul told the Philippians: 'My genuine yokefellow, help spread the good news of the Gospel, as Clement and the rest of my fellow workers whose names are in the Book of Life. Do not fret or have anxiety about anything, but in every circumstance by prayer and petition, with thanksgiving, continue to make your wants known to God. And make God's peace yours, the tranquil state of the soul, assured of its salvation through Jesus Christ. Any virtue or excellence, anything worthy of praise; fix your mind on these things. Be stars in the dark world. Be compassionate people and be genuine in friendship without murmuring or bickering and without blemish, for this is a dishonest, crooked and twisted generation. Live with spiritual abundance instead of spiritual poverty. Love God more than your desires. God blesses us more than we deserve. Let Christ be your example of virtue and humility. Say 'I can do all this through him who gives me strength'.

The Colossians taught that the fruit of the lips was to praise God, to give God the glory all day everyday, and told of the importance of prayer, to ask God to fill you with knowledge and spiritual understanding, to produce good works, to pray for others' needs as well as your own. Epaphras told this good news: 'Let the word of Christ dwell in you richly, teaching and admonishing one another in wisdom, singing psalms and hymns and spiritual songs, with thankfulness in your hearts to God.'

The Romans said Hope is for things unseen; for all have sinned and come short of the glory of God but whosoever shall call upon the name of the Lord shall be saved. The wages of sin is eternal separation from God but the gift of God is eternal life. The plans that God has directed, the same God will carry out. Never be lacking in zeal but keep your spiritual fervor, serving the Lord. Find hope in the comfort of the scriptures. Do not conform to the pattern of this world but be transformed by the renewing of your minds and discern what is good and acceptable. Live according to God's good, pleasing, and perfect will. God is real hope for the future.

Paul told them in the letters that he wrote in prison while he was often chained to a Roman guard: My faith is strong, stronger than my fear. Through each heartache, pain and tragedy in my life, God has always revealed a purpose. This journey will be no different. I am covered with many prayers and with His feathers.

Be wanting for nothing, but in every thing by prayer and supplication with thanksgiving let your requests be made known to God. Have patience in all things, as Antioch and Corinth were not built in a day. And the peace of God, which passeth all understanding, shall keep your hearts and minds through Christ Jesus.

May the God of hope fill you with all joy and peace as you trust in Him, so that you may overflow with hope by the power of the Holy Spirit. And the God of peace will soon crush Satan for all time. Salute Urbanus, Tryphaena, and Tryphosa, our fellow workers in Christ. Greet my tribal kinsman Herodion. Greet Persis, Asynchritus, Phlegon, Hermes, Patrobas, Hermas, Philolgus, Julia, Nereus, Olympas, and all the saints with them. Remember me to Rufus. Timothy, my fellow worker, wishes to be remembered to you, as do Lucius, Jason, and Sosipater, my tribal kinsman. Gaius, who is host to me and to the whole church here, greets you. So do Erastus, the city treasurer, and our brother Quartus. Aristarchus, who was with me as a prisoner, sends his love. Jesus Justus also sends his love. Greet one another with a holy kiss. I rejoice in my fellow Christians and encourage peace and unity among church members All the

churches of Christ wish to be remembered to you.
The grace of our Lord Jesus Christ (the Messiah) be with you.

The Hebrews said If you will only hear the Lord's voice, Harden not your hearts, Faith is the substance of things hoped for. Whom the Lord loveth, the Lord chastens so that afterward it yieldeth fruit. God is the anchor of our soul. And another said Let us throw off everything that hinders and the sin that so easily entangles. And let us run with perseverance the race marked out for us. Do not neglect to do good and to share what you have with others.

A LETTER OF PAUL TO
Ephesians, Romans, Galatians, Thessalonians, Corinthians, Colossians, Philippinans, Hebrews

Paul, summoned by the will and purpose of God to be an apostle of Christ Jesus, and with Sosthenes, Silvanus, and Timothy to the assembly of the church.

Praise God who has blessed us with all blessings from heaven, to speak the Word of Truth, to not lose heart but keep faith, to have good morals, be firm-footed in stability, to seek good purposes and let them be done by reason of purity of heart and life.

My prayer for you is to produce good fruit and get rid of feelings of hatred. Away then with sinful sexual and evil desires. Do not steal from each other and do not steal from the Lord. Control your tongue and speak good things. Each one of us will have burdens and sorrows and joy. Fathers, do not provoke your children to anger but bring them up in the discipline and instruction of the Lord or they may be brought to shame. God loves us, so it is discipline that we have to endure, and we must be zealous and repent.

If one is ill, put oil upon his forehead and call upon the Lord to save him. Let everyone do try their best at good causes. Cheer each other up and help each other. Let love guide your life and the church will stay in perfect harmony. Forget the past and look to the future.

Moses was an earthly messenger and God spoke through Moses from heaven but do not listen to all of the strict rules of the Jews; it is alright to save a sheep on the Sabbath and it is alright to eat pork and shellfish. Do not worship the Jewish angels but worship God. Humans are lower than angels, but if we are filled with the holy Spirit, we can do God's work. Be good and just to your slaves. Before you Gentiles knew good, you were slaves to wordly sins. This is my work; I do it because Christ's mighty energy is at work within me. I thank my God at all times for you because of the grace (spiritual blessing) of God which was bestowed on you in Christ Jesus. God is the source of affection, goodwill, love, benevolence, and the author and promoter of peace, and the rhythm of our hearts. It is by God's free gift of grace that we are saved through our faith. God's work was recreated in Jesus Christ, that we may do good works and enjoy peace. For it is Jesus Christ who preached the glad tidings of peace and love to you who were far off and to those who were near. Jesus Christ made a peace bond of unity and harmony between both Jew and Gentile and has broken down the hostile dividing wall between us. Praise Jesus Christ's holy name.

A LETTER OF PAUL TO
Ephesians, Romans, Galatians, Thessalonians, Corinthians, Colossians, Philippinans, Hebrews

To each one is given a manifestation of the Holy Spirit: a message of wisdom, the extraordinary powers of healing, the workings of miracles, prophetic insight, and the ability to discern between true

spirits and false spirits, various kinds of tongues. All of these gifts are brought to pass by the Holy Spirit Who as to apportions to each person individually as He chooses. To those who are called is the wisdom of God.
For just as the body is a unity and has many parts, though many, form one body, we are all collectively one body in Christ, each part distinct in its own function.

The person who is united to the Lord becomes one spirit with God. Do you not know that your body is the temple of the Lord and a gift from God? You are not your own.

Let each person scrutinize and examine his own conduct. Each must bear his own faults.

Jesus is our peace. He is both Jew and Gentile. Jesus is our example of humility. Jesus is the same yesterday, today, and tomorrow.

Do everything for God, and nothing for selfish motives. Give thanks to the Father who has made us to be qualified and share in the inheritance of the saints, God's holy people of the Light.

May the Lord direct your hearts to the love of God. Remember the poor. Love the loveless and save lost souls.

The purpose of our instruction is to love, which stems from a pure heart and a clear conscience and sincere faith.

Timothy is being released from prison soon and will be with us.

Greetings and grace be with you. Amen.

Paul was a learned man who could read and write and an interpreter who spoke various kinds of tongues which were the different languages. Very few people spoke multiple languages and the ones speaking in other tongues were called 'barbarians.' There was little papyrus for people to use to record and write their thoughts or accounting budgets; most communication was done by speaking. Hearing foreign tongues was like hearing the call of the trumpet but not knowing its meaning.

On one visit Paul told the Christians that Apollos could not visit this time but that he sent his regards and would accompany Paul on the next visit.

Paul told them when they were shipwrecked at the island of Malta, he was bitten by a snake when he gathered sticks and put them on a fire. The heat drove out the viper. But he was healed.

Paul tried to end the bickering between two women saying, the two women Euodiast and Syntyche should quit quarreling and be friends again.

The Corinthians devoutly believed in Jesus who was raised from the dead, our Saviour Messiah. They proclaimed 'Blessed be God, even the Father of our Lord Jesus Christ, the Father of mercies, and the God of all comfort; who comforteth us in all our tribulation. Leaven thy bread with sincerity and truth and not the leaven of malice and wickedness.

If any should not work, neither should they eat. Thanks be to God for His unspeakable gifts. We are ambassadors for Christ, God making his appeal through us. We implore you on behalf of Christ to be reconciled to God. God is a prize to be reached like athletes competing in a race. In a letter (an epistle) to the Corinthinans, Paul wrote: Love endures long and is patient and kind, love is never envious or jealous, is not boastful or vainglorious, does not display itself
haughtily. Love is not conceited, rude, does not act unbecomingly, is not self-seeking, is not resentful, is forgiving. Love does not rejoice at injustice and unrighteousness, but rejoices when right and truth prevail. Love bears up under anything and everything that comes, is

ever ready to believe the best of every person, its hopes are fadeless under circumstances, and it endures everything.
Love never fails. We know in part and prophecy in part. When that which is perfect comes, that which is in part will fade away., I talked like a child, I thought like a child, I reasoned like a child; now that I have become an adult, I am done with childish ways and have put them aside. Faith, hope, and love abide, but the greatest of these is love.

Paul, Silvanus (Silas) and Timothy to the Thessalonians: We were bereft of you, brethren, for a little while because Satan hindered and impeded us. What is our hope or happiness or our victor's wreath of exaltant triumph when we stand in the presence of our Lord Jesus at His Coming? Is it not you? For you who believe in love and became imitators of the assemblies of God in Christ Jesus which are in Judea, and have suffered persecution, being forbidden to speak to the Gentiles that they may be saved, are indeed our glory and our joy! For I am not ashamed of the gospel, because it is the power of God that brings salvation to everyone who believes, first to the Jew, then to the Gentile.
We sent Timothy who is our brother and God's servant to spread the good news to encourage your faith, that no one should be disturbed and beguiled and led astray by afflictions, stress, and crushing difficulties. Be filled with comfort and cheer because of your faith. Give complete trust and confidence to the Lord God. We really live if we stand firm in the Lord. Continue to pray with intense earnestness (unction) night and day and pray for us. Continue in baptism and anointing by oil with unction. Now may God and our Messiah Jesus Christ guide our steps to increase and excel and overflow in love for one another and for all people, just as we do for you. May the Lord strengthen and confirm and establish your hearts to be faultlessly pure and unblamable in holiness in the sight of God. The wisdom from above is pure and peace-loving. Thank God in everything every day and thank the human hands doing good works. Now may the Lord of Peace give you peace at all times and in every way. The Lord be with all of you during another day on earth or in the afterlife when we pass or if our bones are raised up from dust. Never stop praying.

A Thessalonian said 'When we rise to meet the Lord in the air, we shall ever be with the Lord. Comfort each other with these words.' One said: Jesus is a live man instead of a golden idol. Jesus is revealed from heaven.
Paul tried to teach Christianity to Asian people who were not interested because they practiced Hinduism and Buddhism. Epaenetus was the first Christian in Asia. Sandeep was a Buddhist who told Paul that for one to be wise and self-controlled was to be like the Lord Buddha. A believer said that when a human dies, the energy from the body will fly the universe.

The Ephesians proclaimed One God Spirit, One Faith, and One Baptism; wherever you are in the world, tell people about the goodness of the Lord. God gave some to be apostles, some prophets with revelations, some evangelists with psalms, some pastors and teachers with interpretations, for the equipping of the saints for the work of God's ministry. Let all things be done for edification (spiritual enlightenment) for the followers of the body of Christ. Come as you are to God and renounce your wicked ways. Do not bow down to lies, but worship only the truth. For by grace are ye saved through faith; and that not of yourselves: it is the gift of

God: not of works, lest any man should boast.

Paul said to the Ephesians: Take unto you the armor of God, take the shield of faith, the helmet of salvation, the sword of the spirit which is the Word of God, that ye may be able to withstand evil and quench all the fiery darts of the wicked antichrists. When angry, do not let your fury last until the sun goes down. Be imitators of God. Walk in love. I have learned to control my emotions, especially excessive anger. Do not get drunk. Love your neighbors as you love yourself. Children, obey your parents.

The Galatians said: The works of the carnal flesh are good or bad, depending on the purity of heart, mind, and spirit. Let us not become weary of doing good. Paul said: Be not deceived. God is not mocked. For whatsoever a man soweth, that he shall also reap. For he that soweth to his flesh shall of the flesh reap corruption; but he that soweth to the Spirit shall of the Spirit reap life everlasting. God gave a covenant to Abraham and the law of Moses was given 430 years later. Now God's promise is fulfilled in Jesus. I have been crucified with Christ and I no longer live, but Christ lives in me. The life I live in my body, it is Christ who lives in me. I live by faith in the Son of God who died for us, loved us, and gave himself for us. Therefore, if anyone is in Christ, the new creation has come: The old has gone, the new one is here!

Paul taught: It was best to have only one wife in marriage. Women are subservient to their husbands and must take a secondary place to them. The husband is the head of the wife, as Christ is the head of the church; Christ gave himself up for the Church. Women are supposed to be quiet in church.

Paul said the women should wear head coverings in the church, but the men should not wear head coverings in the church. Paul was against male circumcision.

For one to make it obvious that they follow the Holy Spirit one does not need ink writings or etchings on tablets of stone, but by writing it on their heart. By following the Holy Spirit, we are reborn anew with a fresh spirit.
The object and purpose of disciples of Jesus was to instruct to love, which springs from a pure heart, a good conscience, and sincere faith of Holy Spirit. We came into the world with nothing, and we will leave the world with nothing, and money is the root of all evil. Christians should help their own relatives. Young widows should remarry so others will have no reason to slander. Only a man knows himself what is in his own mind. Every man will receive his commendation from God. All will be judged at the last trumpet. The person who is united to the Lord becomes one spirit with Him.
The person who is united to the Lord becomes one spirit with Him.
The Apostle Paul performed miracles in the name of God. People were healed from sickness after touching a cloth Paul had touched. During their evangelical mission Paul, Aristarchus, and Epaphras were imprisoned. Paul was beheaded for his faith.

The Apostle Peter wrote a letter to the churches in 63AD or 63CE that stated that the *good news of the Lord endures forever*.
Peter raised a girl named Tabitha from the dead and healed a man named Aeneas completely from paralysis and other ailments. When Peter was hungry, he prayed for food, and the Spirit lowered a sheet down from Heaven filled with food.

Peter taught:
Be holy in all your conduct and manner of living.
Be a Blessed Tree like Jesus Christ. Be a stone of the spiritual house like the Cornerstone. Be patient.
Beauty is in the heart.
Never return evil for evil or insult for insult.
Each person has received gifts from the Holy Spirit, so use them for the good of all as a grace. Peter was arrested by King Herod and crucified.
Believers of the Spirit later proclaimed Peter as a Saint at the entrance gate to heaven.

The Apostle John wrote letters and his gospel has been dated to 85AD or 85CE:
Do not hate others.
Earthly things are not from Heaven.
We should love one another.
Let us not love in theory or in speech, but in deed and in truth.
God knows everything.
Let us love one another, for love is from God.
The Spirit is the Truth.
God listens to and hears us.
Be born again and you will know the kingdom of God; God is within you.
Accept and believe in Jesus and you will find salvation through Christ who said 'I will come to you and comfort you. I will never leave you.'

The Apostle James, who was the brother of Jesus, said Jesus preached
'Love your neighbor as you love yourself.'
The gospel of James is dated 48AD (48CE).

Jude, the half-brother of Jesus, said the archangel Michael rebukes Satan and all fallen angels. Jude said the wicked corrupt themselves for the sake of gain and their own desires and passions, and scoffers who seek to gratify unholy desires and agitators who cause trouble are devoid of the Holy Spirit and destitute of any higher spiritual life.

Mary Magdalene, Joanna, Salome, Susanna, Thomas, and Philip were also disciples of Jesus.

A certain Joseph, a Levite and a native of Cyprus who was surnamed Barnabas by the apostles, which interpreted means Sons of Encouragement; this Joseph sold a field which belonged to him and brought the sum of money at the feet of the apostles for their mission for he was Jewish and believed in the teachings of Moses but also believed in the teachings of Jesus.

A certain man named Arlan with his wife Sapphira sold a piece of property, held back a portion for their personal needs, and donated the rest to the apostles for the mission of the church of Christ, so Peter did bow his head in prayer of thanksgiving for the generosity of Arlan and Sapphira. And Peter did give greetings to other believers and workers for the Lord when he came upon them or went to see them.

And Phoebe, a woman of the church, said 'To those who are called to God, they could be of any faith and religion, but they will know the Power of God and the Wisdom of God.' And Cush and Asaph were musicians in the church who stood under the covered walkway to the church called Solomon's Porch and sang a song 'Come together at the gate and seek the Lord'. They said 'May your day be good' at the end of the service.

An angel of the Lord said to Philip to proceed southward on the road that led from Jerusalem to Gaza. Thereupon did Philip depart and behold he came upon an Ethiopian man of great authority under Candace the queen of the

Ethiopians who was in charge of all her treasure. He had come to Jerusalem to worship and was sitting on his chariot reading the book of the prophet Isaiah. And Philip told the Ethiopian about the gospels of Jesus. Then the Ethiopian requested to be baptized and Philip baptized him.

Philip the disciple did say 'Live in harmony and be in the same mind and one in purpose for the accord of love. Let this same mind be in you that was in Christ Jesus; he was of the same mind of God and stripped himself of privileges to assume the guise of a servant; Jesus humbled himself and stood low to exalt the name of the Holy Spirit above all else. So you should also realize that it is not your own strength that is at work in you but it is the power and desire of the Holy Spirit. Knowing the Lord is having a possession of priceless privilege. Seek to have knowledge of the Lord and become intimately acquainted with the Holy Spirit to attain the perfect ideal. Whoeverso will seek the Holy Spirit will be fashioned to conform to the glory of the Most High, as did Christ Jesus, the Apostles, Mary, and those in the future who will worship the Holy Spirit. When we pass from this world, there will still be people worshipping in this very temple after we are gone.'

GOSPELS of JESUS

GOSPEL OF MATTHEW

1. Once Jesus was led to the desert; he did not eat for forty days and forty nights, and he was hungry. Satan tempted Jesus by saying: 'If You are God's Son, command these stones to be made loaves of bread.' Jesus replied: 'Man shall not live by bread alone but by every word of God (Yahweh). Be gone, Satan!' And the devil departed. And angels came and ministered to Jesus.
Satan tempted Jesus a second time: 'If you are God's Son, throw yourself down so the angels will take charge over you.'
Jesus replied: 'Do not tempt or test the Lord your God.'

Satan tempted Jesus a third time. Satan pointed out all of the skies, mountains, valleys, lakes, and deserts, saying to Jesus: 'If you will prostrate yourself before me and do homage and worship me, I will give you all that you see before you.'
Jesus replied: 'Be gone, Satan!
For it has been written you shall worship the Lord your God, and God alone shall you serve.' And the devil took Jesus to Jerusalem and set him on a gable of the temple and said to him, 'If you are the Son of God, cast yourself down from there.' But Jesus replied, 'You should not tempt your Lord.' And the devil stood off from Him.

2. Jesus ate with the sinners saying, 'Let all come to the table. Come join the sinners who have been redeemed. Take your place beside the Savior. Sit down and be set free.' He preached by the lake, by the fig trees, and on the Mount of Olives across from the First Jewish Temple. Jesus said to forgive each other, because the Holy Spirit in Heaven forgives us. 'From your heart, forgive your brother his offenses.'
Jesus taught that if a person sins, solemnly tell them and if they repent, forgive them. Keep forgiving them, up to 7 times each day if they repent to you each of the 7 times.

Jesus said to love your enemies. Go after and save the unbeliever.
Jesus said the last will be first and the first will be last in heaven. Jesus said to not be gloomy when fasting but to perfume your head and wash your face, and the Holy Spirit knows when you are fasting. Jesus taught that if a person divorces and remarries, it is adulterous. A marriage started at the beginning when a man and a woman became one flesh and a marriage should be for all eternity. Put away your pride; pride goes before destruction.
Jesus said you had to give up all of your possessions and even give up your family if you wanted to follow him.

3. It is better to be charitable, self-sacrificing, giving, and loving than to receive only and guard riches. With men, this is impossible, but with God all things are possible. Peter asked Jesus: We have become Your Disciples, what then shall we receive? Jesus said to them: In the new age when the Son of Man shall sit on the throne of glory, you who have become my disciples will also sit on twelve thrones and judge the twelve tribes of Israel.

4. Jesus said that those who worked hard to have good harvests deserved more than people who did not work hard to have good harvest. Sow your seeds in good soil so they will bear good fruit.
Do not sow seeds in rocky soil, as the sun will parch the plant when it grows and it will die because it is thirsty. Do not sow seeds by the roadside, where birds will eat the seeds up. Do not sow seeds in weeds, where the weeds will choke out the plant.

5. Jesus told a parable about a nobleman who gave his bond servants minas (money) to invest in a bank while he went off on a journey. When the nobleman came back, the servants all had made additional minas by buying and selling, except one servant who had not made any additional minas because he was afraid of the risk of losing the minas he had. Jesus said there are consequences to the risks you take, but one should remember, do not risk to gain the whole world and yet lose they soul.

6. Jesus said if you give a banquet, invite poor people to the banquet as well as rich people.

7. Jesus told this parable; whoever tries to preserve his life will lose it, but whoever loses his life will preserve it.

8. Jesus said one who is faithful in a little will be faithful in much, and one who is dishonest in a little will be dishonest in much.

9. Jesus said no one is perfect except for God.

10. Once Jesus was sitting in a boat and the crowds of people were gathered along the shore listening to him. Jesus told a parable about planting seeds.
The seed represented the word of God. A sower went to plant seed. As he sowed, some seed fell along the footpath, where the birds ate it up. Some seed fell on rock and, after sprouting, it withered for lack of moisture. Some seed fell among thistles, where the thistles grew up with the seedling and choked it. But

the seed that was planted in good soil grew and yielded a hundredfold. The parable meant that seed along the footpath represented those who hear the word of God and then the devil comes and carries off the word from their hearts, that they may not be saved and believers of God. The seeds on rock represent those who receive the word with joy when they hear it, but have no root; that is they believe for a while but in times of trial they fall away. The seeds among thistles represent those who hear, but their growth is choked by cares and pleasures of life and their fruit does not ripen to maturity. But the seeds in good soil represent those who bring a good and honest heart to the hearing of the word, hold it fast in a just and noble heart and, with perseverance, steadily bring forth fruit with patience.

11. Jesus told the people wherever there were 2 or 3 people gathered in the name of God and agreed upon a thing to ask God, it would come to pass and be done for them by Our Creator in Heaven. Jesus said wherever 2 or 3 people are gathered in the midst of prayer, that the Holy Spirit would be with them. Jesus said: 'Except that ye shall keep the commandments, ye shall not enter into heaven'.

Blessed are ye when ye are righteous and good yet ye are persecuted in the name of the Holy Spirit. Let your good deeds shine before all people, so that they may glorify your Lord who is in heaven.

12. Think not that I have come to destroy the law of the prophets but to complete and fulfill it. I came to save the lost sheep of Israel who have strayed. Keep the commandments of God on the tablet of your heart.

13. Love the Lord God with your whole heart, soul, mind, and strength.

14. Love your neighbor as yourself. There is no other commandment greater than this.

15. Whoever wishes to be the greatest among you shall be your servant. Pray that it is the Holy Spirit that is working within you, guiding your thoughts, words, and actions.

16. The Pharisees also with the Sadducees came, and tempting, desired Jesus that he would show them a sign from heaven. He answered and said unto them: When it is evening, ye say, it will be fair weather for the sky is red and lowering. O ye hypocrites, ye can discern the face of the sky; but can ye not discern the signs of the times? A wicked and adulterous generations seeketh after a sign; and there shall no sign be given unto it, but the sign of the prophet Jonas. And he left them, and departed. And when his disciples were come to the other side, they had forgotten to take bread. Then Jesus said unto them, Take heed and beware of the leaven of the Pharisees and of the Sadducees. And they reasoned among themselves and realized that Jesus was not talking about bread, but of their doctrines. When Jesus came into the coasts of Caesarea Philippi, he asked his disciples, saying, Whom do men say that I am the Son of Man? And they said, Some say that thou art John the Baptist; some say Elias or Jeremias, or one of the prophets. He saith unto them, But whom say ye that I am? And Simon Peter answered and said, Thous art the Christ, the Son of the living

God. And Jesus answered and said to them, Blessed art thou, Simon Barjona: Flesh and blood hath not revealed it unto thee, but my father which is in heaven. And I say also unto thee, That thou art Peter, and upon this rock I will build my church; and the gates of hell shall not prevail against it. And I will give unto thee the keys of the kingdom of heaven: and whatsoever thou shalt bind on earth shall be bound in heaven; and whatsoever thou shalt loose on earth shall be loosed in heaven.

17. Do not judge, criticize, and condemn others, so that you may not be judged, criticized, or condemned.

The Lord's Prayer

18. And Jesus went up the mountain and when he was seated, his disciples came to him and he opened his mouth and taught them, saying:

Pray this to the Lord: 'Our Father, who art in heaven, hallowed (holy) be Thy Name, Thy Kingdom come,Thy Will be done on earth as it is in heaven. Give us this day, our daily bread, and forgive us our trespasses as we forgive those who trespass against us. Lead us not into temptation but deliver us from evil and grant us peace in our days. For Thine is the Kingdom, the Power and the Glory Forever.' Amen.

19. Jesus said it is easier for a camel to go through the eye of a needle than it was for a rich man to go to heaven.

And Jesus continued speaking *Beatitudes*:

Blessed are the poor in spirit, for they may be born again.

Blessed are those who mourn, for they shall be comforted.

Blessed are the meek, for they shall find confidence.

Blessed are those who seek God, for they shall be completely satisfied.

Blessed are those who are merciful, for they shall obtain mercy.

Blessed are those who are pure in heart and follow the good commandments, for they shall see God.

Blessed are the peacemakers and those who are maintainers or peace, for they shall be called sons and daughters of God.

Blessed are those who have been persecuted for doing the right thing, for their souls shall obtain heaven.

Blessed are those who are a shining beacon of light, an inspiration and a helper to others, for they know God and are true lovers of God.

Blessed be the tie that binds my heart to God; God's word declares it so.

Love your enemies and pray for them.

If you love only those who love you, what gain do you have, for do not even tax collectors do that?

The Lord will separate the kind-hearted from the ones with stones for hearts, saying 'I was hungry and you gave me food, I was thirsty and you gave me water, I was a stranger and you welcomed me, I was naked and you clothed me. Whoever does these works for a brethren does the good works for Me.'

But the Lord will say to those who won't help, 'Be gone from me because if you fail to help one in need, you fail to do it for Me.'

You must be of perfect godliness in mind and character, as is written of your heavenly Father.

Do not harm or molest children for they are heavenly.

And the crowds were bewildered and amazed at his teachings.

20. Heaven and earth may pass away, but the Lord will exist forever. And where are you going? Follow the Lord.

21. Do not worry or be anxious, for the Lord knows well all that you need. Seek the Lord and all these things together will be given you. Do not worry about tomorrow, tomorrow will have its own worries and anxieties of its own. Sufficient for each day is its own trouble.

22. Do not gather and heap us and store for yourselves treasures on the earth, rather gather up for yourselves treasures on your soul for heaven.

23. Jesus said: Come to me, all you who labor and are heavy-laden and overburdened, and I will give you rest. Take my yoke upon you and learn of Me, for I am gentle and humble in heart, and you will find rest for your souls. My yoke is wholesome and righteous, My burden is light and easy to bear.

24. Do not be like those who seem to be just and upright but on the inside they are full of evil thoughts, pretense, lawlessness, and iniquities.

25. Do not throw your pearls to the hogs, lest they will trample them.

26. Whatever you desire that others would do to you and for you, even so do also to and for them, for this sums up the Law and the Prophets.

27. Anyone who hears My Words and doesn't follow them is like one who builds a house upon sand – there is no firm foundation and the house may crumble.

28. If someone strikes you on the cheek, offer them the other cheek. If they take your garment, give them another.

29. Do not boast about your gifts of charity, but give quietly. God, who sees in secret, sees what you do.

Do not blow a trumpet before you give to the poor or when you fast.

When you fast, perfume your head and wash your face; do not look gloomy when fasting.

30. On the Day of Judgment, every person will be accountable for every word spoken and every action.

31. You cannot serve two masters. You cannot serve God and mammon (material wealth). Love God and Me before anything else.

32. Be aware of the evil ones. You recognize people by their fruits; the good figs are kept but the bad figs are tossed aside.

33. If you follow my words, it is like a wise man who built his house upon a rock.

34. I call repentance to those who need to set their ways aright.

35. The disciples of John came to Jesus and asked him: Why do we have to fast as disciples of John but Your disciples do not fast? Jesus replied 'No one puts new wine into old wineskins.'

36. Jesus said no one is perfect except for God.

37. Who among you would give your son a stone to eat when he asks for bread? Who among you would deny your neighbor a loaf of bread if he asks for one? Therfore, be bearers of good gifts for one another.

38. The narrow gate is the way to heaven but wide is the gate for error; therefore do not go astray from the good path and help your neighbor along the same way.

39. Jesus said: Follow Me, for Whoever welcomes Me welcomes the One who sent Me.

40. Angels will separate good and evil souls, and God will try to reform the evil souls before giving up on them.

41. Have good thoughts in your mind to lead your speech.

42. Whatever two or more agree upon and ask of the Holy Spirit in Heaven, it will come to pass.

43. When a man and woman are united in marriage, the two become one flesh; what therefore God has joined in marriage let no one put asunder.

44. Moses commanded a divorce certificate because of the hardness of your hearts; divorce should only be as a last hope.

45. Sell all of your possessions and give your money to the poor and follow me; then you will be My True Disciples.

46. Jesus said to Peter: Go put the hook in the water and the first fish in the water that you pull out will have a shekel in its mouth; then use the shekel to pay the required temple tax.

47. All things are possible with God.

48. Behold, there was a Canaanite woman who begged Jesus to save her daughter who was possessed of a demon. But Jesus told her, I was sent only to the lost sheep of Israel; it is not right to give bread to gentiles. But she begged him, saying, 'Lord, please help her.' Jesus replied 'Great is your faith' and he healed her daughter and she was cured.

GOSPEL OF MARK

1. Jesus said that whoever gives another a cup of water to drink because you belong to and bear the name of Christ will by no means fail to get his reward in heaven.

2. Jesus said that a good person will not cause another person to stumble.

Why do you see the speck of sawdust that is in your brother's eye but do not notice or consider the dust in your own eye? Or, how can you say to your brother, Brother, allow me to take out the speck that is in your eye, when you yourself do not see the beam in your own eye? First, take the beam out of your own eye, then you will see clearly to take out the speck that is in your brother's eye. For in posing as a judge and passing sentence on another, you condemn yourself, because you who judge habitually practice the very same things. But the judgment of God falls justly and in accordance with truth upon those who practice judgment. The judgment of God falls equally upon all people.

How can you teach others if you do not teach yourself?

3. Many who are first now will be last in Heaven.

Jesus said 'Whoever is bent on saving their life for this world will lose it; whoever loses his life for God will have everlasting life.'

4. Before you pray in the temple or offer gifts, if you have anything against anyone, go and forgive them first and make peace, then come back into the temple to pray and offer gifts, or you might have to suffer the consequences from the Sanhedrin Council if your accuser turns you over for judgement.

5. Jesus said: Love God with your whole heart and love your neighbor; there are no commandments greater than these.

6. Jesus taught: Do not be overly anxious or worried, for it will not add a moment of time to your life. Your Lord in Heaven knows what you need before you ask. If God grows lilies and grass in the field, will not God clothe you? And if God

feeds the birds, will not God feed you?
If you clutter your mind with little things, will there be any room left for big things?
Solomon in all of his magnificence was not arrayed as beautiful as the lilies and grass in the field.

7. Jesus said: Pay to Caesar what is due Caesar; pay to God what is due God.

8. John the Baptist wore clothing of camel's hair and a leather girdle around his loins; ate locusts and wild honey.

9. Once some men cut a hole in the roof of a house where Jesus and the Disciples were staying because the house was so crowded that there was room for no more. They lowered a paralyzed man on a stretcher through the roof so that Jesus could cure him, and Jesus did.

10. We told Jesus that we saw apostles performing miracles in the name of Jesus, but we did not recognize the men. Jesus said that if they were not against us, they were with us.

11. With God, all things are possible. Move the mountain with faith.

12. At Jericho, a blind man named Bartimaeus, son of Timaeus, was sitting by the roadside and he reached out, trying to touch Jesus' robe. Jesus laid his hand upon him and his sight returned.

13. There was a crowd of people who had followed Jesus for three days and had not eaten.
Jesus miraculously multiplied 7 loaves of bread and a few small fish so a crowd of 4,000 people could eat.

14. Jesus said if a man has a hundred sheep, and one of them has gone astray, will not the man rejoice to find the one that is lost.

15. And if a brother wrongs you, go and discuss this fault, between you and him privately. If he listens to you, then you have won back your brother. Forgive a person seventy times seven.

16. Jesus said the sun will darken and the moon will have no light when he comes back in the clouds. Keep awake and be on your watch; be ready, because of when I will return, only I know. Sky and earth will pass away, but my words will not pass away.

GOSPEL OF LUKE

1. Luke wrote that Jesus said heaven was like a mustard seed, a small seed that became a large garden herb tree with branches that provided shelter for wild birds that roosted and nested in its branches.
Heaven was like leaven, which like a woman adds to 3 measures of wheat flour or meal until it is leavened.
After the resurrection, everyone that is saved will be like an angel; Pray you will be accounted worthy to stand in the presence of God and the Son of Man.
Love is caring for others, the desire to do good for others, and to serve God. I pray not only for my disciples but for all people.
Glory to God in the highest, and on earth peace, good will toward men.

a house divided will not stand.

2. Luke wrote about the prophetess Anna, the daughter of Phanuel, of the tribe of Asher, who worshipped faithfully at the temple with fasting and prayer. The prophetess knew about Pagan, Roman, Greek, Spanish, Egyptian, Persian, Jewish, African, and Asian religions. Anna said 'There is a Divine Creator in all religions.' Anna was at the temple when Simeon blessed the baby Jesus; then there was a gathering at her house with barley cakes and olive oil, and fish.

3. Luke wrote that Jesus said he would come back on a cloud. Luke wrote that Jesus said for every two people, one would be taken and one would be left, but it was not clear what he meant; people say this will be a happening at the end of time called Rapture, when the dead and the living will meet the Lord.

4. The Pharisees and their scribes were grumbling why Jesus and his disciples were eating and drinking with tax collectors and sinners? And Jesus replied to them; 'It is not those who are healthy who need a physician, but those who are sick.'

5. Give away to everyone who begs of you, and do not demand or require them back again. But for those who are able, the borrower should return what they have borrowed.

6. No one who lights a lamp them puts it under the table; they put it on a lampstand, that those who come in may see the light. And there is nothing hidden that shall not be disclosed, nor anything secret that shall not be known and come out into the open.

7. Be careful how you listen and what you speak.

8. Repent and change your mind for the better or you will perish and be lost eternally.

9. Jesus said when you are invited by anyone to a marriage feast, do not recline on the chief seat (the place of honor), lest a more distinguished person than you has been invited. And then he who invited both of you will come to you and say who will have the seat. This is to show your humbleness.

10. Those who believe in a prophet will receive a prophet's reward. Those who accept a righteous man will receive a righteous man's reward.
Those who care for children, widows, orphans and the needy will receive a most high place in heaven. For those who believe in Me, Trust in Me, and Follow Me, I will testify for them in the Threefold Glory of the Father, Myself, and the Holy Angels.

11. Some were saying that John had a demon! Some said that Jesus had a demon, too! Some said that John the Baptist was a messenger predicted by Malachi – the spirit of the prophet Elijah. Happy are those hearing the word of God and keeping it.

12. It was heard that King Herod said that Jesus was filled with the spirit of John the Baptist after John the Baptist was killed, or that Jesus was filled with the spirit of the prophet Elijah.

13. Jesus chose 70 others and sent them out in pairs, two by two, into every town and place to preach the good news, to thank the Lord of heaven and earth. Gracious is the Lord's will and choice and good pleasures.

14. Everything secret will be revealed.

15. Jesus said you can lambast (speak against) the prophets or the Son of Man, but do not speak against or blaspheme the Holy Spirit.

16. Blessed is the servant in the household who is set over to supply them their allowance of food.

17. He who sends an envoy forward to ask terms of peace of another king who is still a great way off is My Disciple.

18. Some who are last now will be first in heaven, and some who are first now will be last in heaven.

19. When some Pharisees told Jesus that King Herod was out to get him (meaning Jesus), Jesus said to go tell that fox that he would perform miracles on the Sabbath and the next day and the day after.

20. Temptations are sure to come, but blessed are those who can resist for their own good.

21. Those who hurt innocent children are evil. Love the precious little ones and teach them well in their childhood.

22. There was a prodigal son who went away from his father and came upon hard times, partly because of his own wastefulness. He came back to his father starving. His father welcomed him with open arms and prepared a feast for his son. Jesus said if one sheep is lost and is found, it is like heaven.

23. If someone is sinning, reprove them (tell them) so they can repent and be saved.

24. Forgive someone 7 times in a day. And seventy times seven.

25. The apostles asked Jesus to increase their faith; their Lord answered: even if you have the faith of a tiny mustard seed, things may be done by our God in heaven.

26. Those who lose faith should take heed that they do not lose their way. The faithless are like the dead; wherever a dead body is, there will be vultures gathered overhead.

27. A pupil is not superior to his teacher, but everyone completely trained will be like his teacher.

28. Humble yourselves before God and admit you are not perfect and have made mistakes. Ask forgiveness. Then you may ask God for other things and receive God's blessings.

29. Jesus said; Why do you say I am good and perfect? None of us are perfect except God. Only God is perfect.

30. For like the lightening, that flashes up and lights the sky from one end to another, so will the Son of Man be in His own day. . Jesus can calm a raging sea.

31. Jesus said: God will send prophets and messengers required of this age and the generations to come. Woe to those who shed innocent blood, like the time the people of King Joash slew the prophet Zechariah between the altar and the sanctuary just for asking the people why they transgressed

against the commandments. They stoned Zechariah to death for no good reason!

32. In the town of Bethany, Martha invited and welcomed Jesus into her home and her sister Mary seated herself at the Lord's feet and listened to His teaching. Martha served them food but the words of Jesus was the good portion; good words that would not be taken away.

33. Blessed are those who keep the Word of God, obey it, and practice it.

GOSPEL OF JOHN

1. In the beginning was the Word, and the Word was divine, and the Word was God.
All things came into existence through God. God is life, and life is the soul and spirit of the people.

There came a man sent from God, whose name was John the Baptist; this man came to witness that he might testify of God, that all people might trust in the Lord, the Holy Spirit.

John said to give praise to God for the gifts which are given to us. You are witnesses to the Anointed One, Christ Jesus. Jesus must increase now and I must decrease. Jesus speaks the language of heaven, but others speak the languages of the earth. God has sent Jesus to speak the words of God's message.
Believe in the one He has sent. Accept Jesus and you will find salvation.
The Word became flesh among us, through the law of prophets like Moses and the truth of Jesus Christ, who was the Son of Man.

The Jews sent the priests to ask Jesus: Are you Elijah? Are you the prophet? And he answered 'No! I am the voice of one crying in the wilderness – prepare the way of the Lord, as the prophet Isaiah said!'

John gave evidence: I have seen The Spirit descending as a dove out of heaven and it dwelt on Jesus. And this is my testimony that Jesus is the Son of God!

2. Once, Jesus was tired on a sojourn and rested beside a well. And there was a woman at the well who was a Samaritan; she had had five husbands. And Jesus asked her for a drink of water, and she asked him: How is it that you ask me, a Samaritan, for a cup of water? For Jews have nothing to do with Samaritans. Our forefathers told us that Mount Gerizim is holy but the Jews say you have to come to Jerusalem.

And Jesus told her that if she asked, he would tell her about water that would quench her thirst forever. Jesus answered her: If you had recognized who is asking you for water, you would have received living water.

The woman asked Jesus: Are you greater than our ancestor Jacob, who gave us this well for his sons and his cattle?

And Jesus replied: All who drink from this well will be thirsty again. But whoever takes a drink of the water I give them shall never be thirsty any longer. . Whoever believes in Me, as scripture as said, rivers of living water
will flow from within them.

And John wrote later that when a person has faith in God, the water the Lord gives you to quench your thirst will become in you like a spring of water in eternal life. Jesus did say 'Come, whoever is thirsty, and whoever wishes; let him take the free gift of the water of life.'

3. John wrote that when Jesus had finished his earth life, that Jesus had so revealed the Master inside himself that Jesus could truly say:

1) I am the bread of life.
2) I am the living water.
3) I am the light of the world. Whoever follows me will not despair but will have the light of life and hope.
4) I am the desire of all ages.
5) I am the open door to eternal salvation.
6) I am the reality of endless life.
7) I am the good shepherd.
8) I am the pathway of infinite perfection.
9) I am the resurrection and the life.
10) I am the secret of eternal survival.
11) I am the infinite Father of my finite children.
12) I am the true vine; you are the branches.
13) I am the hope of all who know the living truth.
14) I am the living bridge from one world to another.
15) I am the living link between time and eternity.
(16) Jesus said to Thomas:
'I am the Way and the Truth and the Life; no one gets to the Father except by Me.

And John said 'For God so loved the world, that He gave his only begotten Son, that whosoever believeth in Him shall not perish, but have eternal life.'

John also testified:

17) Makes plans to prosper and not to harm, so we can enjoy future reward.

Keep the faith in Jesus Christ who said 'I am not teaching you my own thoughts, but those of God who sent me. If any of you really want to do God's will, then you will certainly know whether my teaching is from God or is merely my own. The Sanhedrin who are trying to kill me, they are mad at me for healing a man on the Sabbath, but why are they condemning me for it? Think this through and you will see that I am right. I know God because I was with Him and He sent me to you. I am in Him and You are in Me. I have come to do the Father's Will.'

18) Where possible, actions can speak louder than words.

4. Jesus said 'The world may hate Me because I denounce wicked works and evilness.'

5. Jesus told a parable: 'I am the Door for the sheep; anyone who enter in through Me will be saved. He will come in and he will go out freely and will find pasture.

6. I am the Good Shepherd. The Good Shepherd risks and lays down His own life for the sheep.

7. There are other sheep not of this fold. I must bring and impel those also; they will listen to My voice and heed My call, and there will be one flock under one Shepherd.'

8. Jesus turned water into wine at a wedding feast; it was a miracle witnessed by the guests. Jesus told

the servants who brought the waterpots of stone: Fill them to the brim with water. Then he said: Draw some out, and the water was wine.

9. Nicodemus, a Pharisee and an esteemed teacher of the Sanhedrin, came to Jesus and said: You come from God as a Teacher, for, Rabbi, no one can perform these wonderworks that you do unless God is with a person.

10. Jesus said to be renewed in the Spirit, find your faith in God and stay in good ways.

Talking about being baptized and being reborn and renewed in the Spirit, Jesus said 'Truly, truly I say to you, unless one is born again, he cannot see the kingdom of God.' Nicedemus said to Jesus, 'How can a man be born when he is old? He cannot enter a second time into his mother's womb and be born, can he?' Jesus answered, 'Truly, truly I say to you, unless one is born of water and the Spirit, he cannot enter into the kingdom of God. That which is born of the flesh is flesh, and that which is born of the Spirit is spirit. Do not marvel that I said to you, You must be born again.'

Jesus said: God sent me so the world might find salvation and rest, and be made safe. I came not to judge. Have you asked for salvation; are you going to heaven?

The thief comes only to steal and kill and destroy; I have come that they may have life, and have it to the full.

11. Be content with the gifts that are given to you from God; there is no other source.

12. Some people love evil more than good – wrongdoers hate! But the people who practices truth and good works comes into the Realm of God.

13. Jesus has put a seal on the testimony that God is true. God is real; whoever has faith will have eternal life.

14. God is a Spirit and those who worship should worship God in spirit and truth. I will work for Jesus and God; will you?

15. In Jerusalem, there is a pool near the Sheep Gate called Bethesda; and there are five porches nearby.

At this pool, the blind and the lame were put into it, and they were healed. Some were cured on the Sabbath, and the Jews were angry that Jesus was violating the law that no work was to be done on the Sabbath.

16. Jesus said: The Son of man is able to do nothing by Himself – but he is able to do only what He sees the Father doing! Yahweh (God) raises the dead and cures the blind – not Me – it is the One who sent Me that raises the dead and cures the blind.

I am able to do nothing on my own accord, but only as I am taught by God. I mention all things in order that you may be saved. John the Baptist was another prophet who testified for God, and you delighted in John the Baptist.

I came to do God's will, not my own.

Whoever commits sin is a slave to the sin.

No one has greater love than to lay down his life for his friends.

17. At the Jewish Feast of the Tabernacle when Jews made the pilgrimage to the Temple, Jesus told his disciples: the world hates me because I denounce their wicked ways; I fear my time is up. But many said 'Jesus is good!'

18. When some Jews were astonished at the teachings of Jesus, he said: My teaching is not my own, but God who sent me is speaking through me. Be from above; do not be from this world!

19. Accept and believe in Jesus and you will find salvation through Christ who said 'I will come to you and comfort you. I will never leave you.'

20. Know that love and knowledge, food, and helping each other can be spread around the world; this is the Good News.

21. Be a light to the world, for a city set on a hill cannot be hidden. Likewise, put your lamp on a lamp stand so it can give light to all in the house. Let your light shine before others that they may see your moral excellence and your praiseworthy nobleness and good deeds. For God Who said, let light shine out of darkness, has shined in our hearts so as to beam forth the Light for the illumination and knowledge of the majesty and glory of God. We possess this treasure to show that the power of God is from God, and not from ourselves. Walk in faith with trust and holy fervor. Consider and look not to things that are seen but to the things that are unseen. Recognize and honor and praise and glorify our Maker.

22. What one has, one ought to use; and whatever one does, one should do with all his might.

23. He who works sparingly and grudgingly will reap sparingly and grudgingly; he who works generously will reap generously.

24. I have no demon in Me, for I honor my Father. These things I have spoken unto you, that in me ye might have peace. In the world ye shall have tribulation, but be of good cheer; I have overcome the world.

25. When we are blind to our sins, God will open our eyes so we can see anew and we feel guilt. Jesus is a Man from God who has opened our eyes.

26. And many believers trusted and relied on Jesus.

TESTAMENT OF JAMES

1. James , the brother of Jesus, said Ask God for wisdom.
2. Let every man be quick to hear, slow to speak, slow to take offense and get angry. For the anger of man does not produce the righteousness of God.
3. Care for orphans and the poor. If you indeed fulfill the royal law in accordance with the Scripture, you shall love your neighbor as yourself, and you do well.
4. Good works should accompany faith.
5. Pray to be near to God, and God will be near to you. Cleanse yourself of sins and purify your hearts.
6. Say 'If the Lord is willing' it will happen.
7. Confess to one another and pray for one another.

8. Elijah prayed for no rain and Elijah prayed for rain.
9. One who seeks God must be unwavering in faith, and one who wavers in faith is like the billowing surge out at sea that is blown hither and tither and tossed by the wind.
10. The humbled may be shown riches, but the rich may be humbled and shown their human frailty.
11. The tongue can be a restless evil.

TESTAMENT OF JUDE

1. Jude, a brother of James and a half-brother of Jesus, said Those who commit evil and complain and grumble, going after their own desires, are the impious ungodly ones. The evil are like Satan, who was cast off from God because Satan abandoned properness to wickedness. The archangel Michael (In Hebrew Michael means *Who is like God*) contends with Satan. Michael is the supreme enemy of Satan and all fallen angels. The Lord is sovereign over Satan.
2. Build your faith on a higher edifice, praying in the Holy Spirit. Guard and keep yourselves in the love of God.
3. Strive to save others from all pollution of the mind and flesh.

TESTAMENT OF PETER

1. Like newborn babies, you should crave the pure spiritual milk, that by it you may be nurtured and grow into salvation with God.
2. By obedience to Truth, you will purify your hearts.
3. All believers of God should be holy in conduct and in all manner of living. God welcomes all nations. When you put sin behind you, it doesn't mean that you won't sin again, since we are imperfect humans. When you avoid sin, you may endure suffering for the glory of our Creator. Just as Christ suffered in the flesh, so we may suffer in the flesh, too, rather than fail to please God. For the time is past for doing what the Gentiles like to do in shameless wantonness, in lustful desires, in slander, drunkenness, lawless idolatries. The lost souls are astonished and think it queer that you do not run hand in hand with them in the same excesses. But they will have to give account to God at their end. This is why the good news of the Gospel is preached, as to our ancestors, so that though judged in flesh bodies as humans, they might live in the spirit as God does. Be focused on living a righteous life. Do not sin and have intense and unfailing love for one another and do so without grumbling. Guard your hearts from the fiery darts of the wicked. Be clear-minded and disciplined, wise, and in control of emotions and stay in tune with God. We all have spiritual gifts so speak as God would speak, with grace and love.
4. Be honest in all your conduct of living.
5. Beauty is in the heart.
6. Never return evil for evil.
7. The devil roams like a lion, ready to seize upon and devour anyone.
8. Christian qualities are virtue, knowledge, self-control,

steadfastness, godliness, and friendship.

Now for a season, if need be, ye are in heaviness through manifold temptations: that the trial of your faith, being much more precious than of gold that perisheth, though it be tried with fire, might be found unto praise and honor and glory at the appearing of Jesus Christ.

9. The Christ Messiah is not a cleverly-devised story; they heard a voice from heaven saying 'This is my Beloved Son is Whom I am well-pleased and delight.'

10. Jesus drove an evil spirit out of a man and commanded the spirit to go into swine. Then the swine went over a cliff and the swine were killed.

11. In the region of Caesarea Philippi, Jesus asked: Who do people say the Son of Man is?

And the disciples replied: Some say John the Baptist, others say Elijah, Jeremiah, or one of the prophets. But Peter told Jesus that he was the Son of God. And Jesus said to Peter ('Peter' means a large piece of rock in Greek 'petros') 'I will build my church upon this rock, you, Peter.'

12. Saul (Paul), a Jew from Tarsus in Cilicia, requested letters to the Jewish synagogues at Damascus authorizing any Christians to be bound in chains and brought to Jerusalem. But as he traveled on a road near Damascus, suddenly a light from heaven flashed around him, and he fell to the ground.

Paul heard a voice saying 'Saul, Saul, why are you persecuting me?' And Paul said 'Who are You, Lord?'

And the voice said 'I am Jesus, whom you are persecuting. It will turn out badly for you to harm others and fight God.'

Paul was trembling and astonished and asked the Lord "What do you want me to do?' The Lord said to him 'Arise and go into the city and you will be told what to do.' So Paul got up from the ground but he could not see because he had been blinded by the light; he was led to Ananias of Damascus. Ananias had heard bad things about Paul; that Paul was arresting Christians and sending them to be imprisoned. But the Lord said to Ananias 'Paul is a chosen instrument of Mine to bear My name before the gentiles and kings and the descendants of Israel.' So Ananias laid his hands on Brother Saul, and instantly Paul's sight was restored and he could see again and increased in strength.

But after considerable time, the Jews conspired to slay Paul because Paul believed in the power of Jesus Christ.

But Barnabas took him to the apostles and explained how Paul preached confidently in the name of Jesus.

So then the brethren brought Paul down to Caesarea and sent him off to Tarsus, which was Paul's home town.

Paul spoke to a man who was a master of deception and wickedness , saying to him: 'you are the son of the devil, an enemy of everything that is upright and good and are making crooked the straight paths of the Lord and plotting against the Lord's good purposes.' But then the man believed and reformed his evil ways back to good, and true love grew out of sincere devotion to God.

The churches throughout the whole of Judea, Galilee, and Samaria had peace and continued to increase and were multiplied.

And I, Peter, went to the saints who lived at Lydda and found a man named Aeneas, who had been bedfast and paralyzed for eight years. And I told Aeneas to get out of the bed in the name of Jesus Christ, and Aeneas stood up.

13. Now living at Caesarea there was a man whose name was Cornelius, a centurion of what was known as the Italian Regiment. Cornelius was a devout man who venerated (loved and respected) God and gave charitable alms to the people and prayed continually to God.

About mid-afternoon of a day he saw a vision of an angel of God who said to him "Send men to Joppa and have them call a certain Simon whose surname is Peter, and invite him to your home.'

So Simon Peter did travel to see Cornelius. On the way he was hungry and prayed to God for food, and a sheet was lowered by four corners from Heaven that containted all kinds of beasts, and he ate and was satisfied. And then the sheet was taken back up to heaven.

And when Simon whose surname was Peter reached the home of Cornelius, he was greeted by relatives and friends of Cornelius.

And when the day of Pentecost had come and they were assembled together in one place, and the free gift of the Holy Spirit came upon the people and they began speaking in tongues (different dialects), and Peter opened his mouth and said: God shows no partiality to people and in any nation those who revere God are acceptable to Him.

And whereto Peter preached the messages of love and the miracles of Jesus. And 3,000 souls were baptized in the name of Jesus, and they begged for Peter to stay on there for some days.

TESTAMENT OF PAUL

1. Comfort each other as God comforts us.
2. The spirit of God is written on the tablet of the human heart of good men.
3. Forgive each other. 'Vengeance is mine' saith the Lord.
4. In Jesus Christ, we are a new creation; the old person is passed away; we are reborn.
5. We must keep Satan from getting the advantage over us.
6. We are frail human vessels on the earth, but we possess the precious treasure of Divine Guidance.

How we praise God, who has blessed us with every blessing in heaven. If God is for us, who can be against us?

7. Jesus said: I am coming back and for the time of my concern, there will be no end.
8. Be of the mind of Jesus Christ: serve people, sacrifice for others and put them first, love each other, gather the believers for the holy works of the Lord, be ready to

forgive others, make plans to move progress forward for the future, rejoice in the Lord for evermore and forever.
9. Do not forget to show hospitality to strangers, for by doing so some people have shown hospitality to angels without knowing it.

TESTAMENT OF TIMOTHY

1. Do not give importance to legends, fables, and myths which foster useless speculations and questionings; rather accept faith in God's administration and have confidence and trust in the Lord. Be eager and do not be ashamed to do your utmost to present your best self to God. Finish the race and fight the good fight of testifying the good news of God's grace.
2. Hold fast to faith and the glorious grace of God. Have a good clear conscience and stay clear of evil doings. Look well into your own heart as to your own teaching, for by doing so you will save both yourself and those who hear you. The purpose of our instruction should be love, which springs from a pure heart, clear conscience, and sincere faith.
4. The love of money is a root of all evils.
5. The Lord strengthens me, so that I may spread good messages. All good scripture is inspired by God.

TESTAMENT OF STEPHEN

1. The God of our forefathers (Abraham and Moses) made all things. The Lord sent the Commandments to teach the people good from evil.
2. Our forefathers set up the Tent of the Witnesses for the Lord in the wilderness and carried it from city to city along with the Tabernacle, the Ark of the Ten Commandments.
3. Whoever is full of the Holy Spirit will be filled with the glory and splendor of God, and Jesus stands with God. Jesus said to set your affection on things above and not on earthly matters. One day Jesus is coming back with his army and the wicked will be no more.

TESTAMENT OF TITUS

1. To the pure in heart and mind, all things are pure; they commit not corruption or pollution in their minds. According to God's mercy we are saved, by the washing of regeneration and renewing of the Holy Ghost. Slander and abuse no one.
2. The home should be a good and chaste place where all go for rest.
3. The messages of scriptures should bring good news. Avoid stupid and foolish controversies, disputes about genealogies, dissensions, and wrangling about the Law of Moses. Go forth among the people and tell them that Jesus preached.

TESTAMENT OF PHILLIP

1. God's peace is a tranquil state of the soul.
2. Practice good ways of living and model your way of living after Jesus.
3. Bless the fish or bread you eat on Friday to remember the work of Jesus. Let us break bread together in prayer.
4. God's living water of truth and wisdom comes from the mouth of Jesus. Cast

your burdens unto Jesus, he cares for you.

LOST GOSPELS

There were lost gospels that were not included in the King James Bible.

UNAUTHORED TESTAMENT

1. The sacrifices of humans, animals, or cereals is powerless to take sins away.
2. It is not fair that only the Levi descendants can collect tithes at the Lord's Tent.
3. Discipline and hard work seem painful and grievous but bring joy and rewards.
4. God will never leave you and the way to Heaven is
by the grace of God.
5. You can eat whatever is safe; it does not have to be blessed by a rabbi priest.
6. Non-violence is the weapon of the strong.
7. Jesus is our good example.
8. Pray this to the Good Lord: Holy Lord, whose desire is peace and love and all good things, the faith of eons of generations on earth, thank you for your grace of bounteous blessings and your mercy that comforts us in times of sorrow. Keep us safe from all harm and evil. Forgive us our mistakes as we forgive others. Guide us to have loving and caring hearts, to respect thy brother and all of thy creation. Thy will be done, for thine is the everlasting God, the Power and Glory of Love and Hope. Amen.

GNOSTIC TESTAMENT
Of One Named Judas

1. Jesus picked Judas to betray him because he knew that Judas understood the meaning of his sacrifice.
2. Heaven on earth is under the stars and in the sunrise when the birds call out to each other, heralding the dawn.

TESTAMENT OF THOMAS

1. A student is not better than his teacher. It is enough for a student to be like his teacher.
2. A good man produces good things; an evil man produces evil things.
3. Jesus was a sage and a mystic.
4. Don't be afraid of those who can kill the body but can't kill the soul.
5. Shame on you, Pharisees! You are scrupulous about giving a tithe of mint and dill and cumin to the priests, but you neglect justice and helping the needy, which is the love of God.
6. You clean the outside of the cup, but inside you are full of greed; clean the inside, too!
7. You love front seats in the assembly, but you hide things in your hearts.
8. Someone asked Jesus, 'Teacher, tell my brother to divide the inheritance of my father with me. Jesus said 'Who made me your judge or lawyer?' Then he told them the parable of the land of a rich man who produced in abundance; the man stored his grain in many barns so he reasoned to himself that he could relax, eat, drink, and be merry.' But God said 'This very night you will give your soul to Me; the things you produced, whose will they be? What happens to the one who stores up treasure for himself is not rich in the sight of God.'

Book of Revelation

John, a disciple and apostle for Jesus, also had a vision, a Revelation of a time of Tribulation of hard times and an Apocalypse (describing the end of time) while he was banished to the island of Patmos, off the coast of Greece. He was imprisoned for preaching about Jesus.

In his vision, John was told by the Lord to write down his vision and address it to seven churches in Asia that were called Ephesus, Smyrna, Pergamum, Thyatira, Sardis, Philadelphia, and Laodicea.
John said there would be a period of tribulation of 7 years of hardships and suffering before the angels would trumpet to signal the end of the time on earth.
In John's vision, heaven had 12 gate entrances made of pearl and illumination that was of holiness and not from the sun or moon, a square city that had walls built of jasper but the foundation of the walls were ornamented with stones of sapphire, white agate, emerald, onyx, sardius, chrysolite, beryl, topaz, chrysoprase, jacinth, and amethyst . The city itself was built of pure gold, clear and transparent like glass. A river flowed from the throne of God thru the middle of the city; on either side of the river was the tree of life with twelve varieties of fruit. There were 24 thrones for the elders of the Jewish Sanhedrin. Lions were guarding the thrones.
Angels were sitting on thrones with trumpets. Then the Jewish priests prostrated themselves in worship to revere Jehovah the Omnipotent God. The head angel Raphael was blowing a trumpet signaling the end of time and Judgement Day. Angels were gathering grapes from the earth to make wine, and an angel flying in midair telling *eternal good news* to inhabitants of every race, tribe, language, and people.
There was an angel sitting on a cloud saying: Blessed and happy to be envied are the dead, for now they may rest from their labors on earth and now their good deeds will follow them to heaven.
And there were angels with harps that sang the song of Moses the servant of God, 'Mighty and Marvelous are Your Works, O Lord!'

There was a single angel stationed in the sun's light and with a mighty voice, he shouted to all the birds that fly across the sky: Come, gather yourselves together for the great supper of God.
And there was one angel holding a key and a chain to the Abyss, a desolate and lonely place.
All angels rejoiced and shouted Hallelujah in praise to the Lord and some bowed in prostration to the Lord.
And I fell prostrate before the feet of Jesus to worship and pay divine honors to him, but he said 'Refrain! You must not do that for I am only another servant to you and your brethren and your sisters who accepted my testimony. Worship God!
For the substance and essence of truth revealed by Jesus is of The Spirit, of all prophecy and good works. Jesus said: Whoever overcomes evil, I will make him a pillar in the sanctuary of my God; these are the words of the Amen, the True Witness, the Origin and Beginning and the Author of All Creation.
Then a heaven opened and a luminous horse of many colors appeared upon which The One rode with a sign attached to a garment robe that said LORD OF LORDS. The Lord slew a wild beast with seven heads and ten horns with 666 as the mark of the beast that rose from the sea. Then there appeared to be a battle at Armageddon between the Lord and Satan, and Satan and all who had the mark of the beast were cast out and sealed out of existence forever; evil was blotted out of existence forever and only love and peace remained.
The Lord said 'I am the Alpha and the Omega.' To the thirsty and those who wish, God will give water without price from the Fountain Spring of the Water of Life. The righteous who have been recorded in the Book of Life will inherit all good things and they will be called the Children of God. But the souls who went astray from good ways will be counseled

according to their cases; the Abyss is for the evil souls who wish to serve Satan. And whoever affirms and testifies to the tree of life and the city of holiness and lived a righteous life are God's holy people, and the day that the Lord will come will come swiftly, so watch and be on your guard, watch and pray, and be ready. Whoever cancels or takes away from the words of the Lord or the prophecy of Christ's Kingdom, God will take away their share of the Tree of Life and city of holiness. Amen.

Scriptures derived from the Nicene Creed and traditions of the first apostolic churches – Christian Orthodox which split into Greek, Russian Orthodox, Ethiopian Orthodox, Egyptian Coptic, Armenian Apostolic and Roman
CATHOLIC CHURCHES.

Around 225 CE (225 AD)
'AD' signifies after death of Jesus

It is believed the members of the Church of St. Peter near Antakya, Turkey called themselves Christians or Catholics; these early apostolic churches have the tradition of reciting the same holy verses for two thousand years.

Some Verses of the Liturgal Mass of Coptic, Christian Orthodox, and Catholic Churches

Priest: Holy Lord of all creation.

People: God of power and might!

Priest: O, God of all good things, we pray for our needs.

Penitential Act

People: God, hear our prayers!

I confess to almighty God and to my brothers and sisters,
that I have sinned in my thoughts and in my words,
in what I have done and in what I have failed to do,
and I ask God to grant me forgiveness for intentional and unintentional mistakes of an imperfect human. I ask Jesus, the ever blessed Mary and all the angels and saints, and you, my brothers and sisters, to pray for me to the Lord our God. Have mercy on us!

Priest: Fill our hearts and minds with righteousness.

People: Fill our hearts with love and hope. We entrust all things and loved ones dear to us to your loving care, knowing well that you have plans for all things.

All: We pray through Jesus Christ and all saints, who liveth and reigneth with thee in the unity of the Spirit, forever with thee, world without end. Amen.

Holy, Holy, Holy Sanctus

Holy, holy, holy Lord,
God of Heaven and earth,
Heaven and earth are full of your glory,
Hosanna in the highest,
Blessed are those who proclaim the name of the Lord.
Hosanna in the highest!
Deliver us, Lord, we pray, from every evil
And grant us peace in our days, that,
By the help of your mercy,
We may always be free from sin.
And safe from all harm,
As we praise our Lord.
Hosanna in the highest!

Act of Contrition

O my God, I am heartily sorry for having offended Thee,

and I detest all my sins because they offend Thee, my God,
Who art all good and deserving of all my love.
I firmly resolve, with the help of Thy grace, to confess my sins, to do penance, avoid evil,
and to amend my life. Amen.

Act of Contrition

Lord have mercy on me,
Have mercy on my soul.
I am sorry for what I have done wrong and for failing to do good.
Do not look upon my sins and
Mistakes but take away my guilt and wrong desires. Create in me a clean heart and renew within me an upright spirit. Amen.

Gloria

Glory to God in the highest, and peace to all people on Earth.Lord God, Divine Creator, We worship you, we give you thanks, We praise You for Your glory. Lord, take away the sins of the world, and have mercy on us.
Lord, protect us from anxieties, and receive our prayers.
For You alone are the Holy One, You alone are the Lord, You alone are the Most High,The glory of God the Almighty.
Amen.

The Lord's Nicene Creed (Apostles' Creed)

We believe in God, Maker of Heaven and Earth, and of all things seen and unseen,
We believe in the wisdom of Our Creator, the one in existence before all the ages and who will have no end,
true God of light,
thru whom all things were made and
thru whom all things are possible, the giver of life.
We believe in the grace and mercy of the Lord,
We believe in Jesus Christ, Mary, and all of angels and saints who went before us. We believe in the Holy Spirit,
The communion of saints,
The forgiveness of sins, the resurrection, and of life everlasting.
Let us give thanks to the Lord, for God is good; God's mercy and ever-loving kindness endure forever.
God is the One of Glory and the Lord of Angels. Amen.

Universal Prayer

Blessed be your name, Lord,
and peace to your people on earth.
Amen.

The Lord's Prayer (modern)

Our Father, Who art in Heaven, Hallowed be thy Name, thy Spirit come, thy Will be done, on earth, as it is in Heaven, Give us this day, Our daily bread, and forgive us our trespasses, as we forgive those who trespass against us, and lead us not into temptation, but deliver us from evil, as it was in the beginning, is now, and ever shall be, world without end. Amen.

ANGLICAN CHURCH

Around 1535CE, the Christian Reformation began. The Church of England split away from the Roman Catholic Church. In 1558CE the Church of England decreed it was both Catholic and Protestant.
The Anglican Communion includes the Church Of England, The Episcopal Church in the United States, and other member churches. The 1662CE Book of Common Prayer is used for Matins and Evensong. The liturgy of the Church of England included Gloria, the Apostles' Nicene Creed, the Lord's Prayer and the Trinity Athansian view.

The Collect

To collect the intentions of the faithful

Almighty God, unto whom all hearts are open, all desires known, and from whom no secrets are hid; Cleanse the thoughts of our hearts by the inspiration of thy Holy Spirit, that we may perfectly love thee, and worthily magnify thy Holy Name; through Christ our Lord. Amen.

Anglican General Confession

ALMIGHTY and most merciful Father;
We have erred, and strayed from thy ways like lost sheep. We have followed too much the devices and desires of our own hearts. We have offended against thy holy laws. We have left undone those things which we ought to have done;
And we have done those things which we ought not to have done;
And there is less hope in us.
But thou, O Lord, have mercy upon us, miserable offenders.
Spare thou them, O God, which confess their faults. Restore thou them that are penitent; According to thy promises declared unto mankind in Christ Jesus our Lord. And grant, O most merciful Father, for his sake; That we may hereafter live a godly, righteous, and sober life, To the glory of thy holy Name. Amen.

Anglican Prayers for the World

O God, who would fold both heaven and earth in a single peace:
let the design of thy great love
lighten upon the waste of our wraths and sorrows:
and give peace to thy Church,
peace among nations,
peace in our dwellings,
and peace in our hearts:
through thy Son our Saviour Jesus Christ.
Amen.

O Lord our God,
source of all goodness and love,
accept the fervent prayers of your people; in the multitude of your mercies look with compassion upon all who turn to you for help; for you are gracious, O lover of souls, and to you we give glory, Father, Son, and Holy Spirit, now and for ever.
God of love, turn our hearts to your ways; and give us peace. Amen.

Verses From BAPTIST WORSHIP

Celebration and Hymnal Book

Worship Leader: Blessed be God Who has blessed us with spiritual blessing. See the wonderful works of the Lord.

Everyone: We rejoice with thanksgiving, for from God and through God are all these things. Give thanks to the Lord who satisfies the longing soul and fills the hungry soul with goodness.

Worship Leader: O God, you are my God. Earnestly we seek You. You are Our Help. We behold Your Power and Glory. We sing in the shadow of Your Wings

Everyone: You, O Lord, are strong and loving. You are our strength and our salvation.

Worship Leader: The Lord is good and God's love endures forever. If we confess our sins God will forgive us and cleanse our hearts from evil. We will pray to the Lord Who is great in mercy and love and God will grace us with the gift of salvation. We will be renewed in the Holy Spirit. We will be washed in regeneration and renewed and baptized in the hope of eternal life.

Everyone: The faithfulness and love of the Lord endures forever through all generations. We will serve the Lord with gladness! Create in me a pure heart, O Lord.

Worship Leader: in God's hands is the universe and the words of the holy laws. The Lord's lovingkindness and comfort is everlasting. Let the heart of those who seek the Lord be glad. You shall love your neighbor as you love yourself. There is no other commandment greater than this. Honor all people.

Everyone: Love does no harm to a neighbor; therefore love is the fulfillment of the law. Love the Lord God with all your heart, soul, mind,and strength.

Worship Leader: The Lord is our God. Go in peace to serve each other for the glory of our God, in the name of Jesus Christ.

Verses From METHODIST WORSHIP
Service and Hymnal Book

A Methodist Modern Affirmation

Leader: This is the good news in which we stand, and by which we have received, and by which we are saved.
Great indeed is the mystery of God.

Leader and People:
Where the Spirit of the Lord is, there is one true church, apostolic and universal, whose holy faith let us now declare.
We are the people of God, we believe in the Holy Spirit, infinite in wisdom, power, and love. We ask the divine presence to be present in our lives. We believe in the example of the blessed Jesus Christ and the Apostles who gave the gifts of God's love and hope. We believe in faith, in the service of love, so that peace may come upon the earth.
We will tend to the poor, sick, hungry, and lonely. We will care for our family and friends.
We believe in God, Creator of the World and of all people, and in Jesus Christ, incarnate among us, who died and rose again, and we believe in the Holy Spirit, present and with us to guide, strengthen, and comfort. We rejoice in every sign of God, in the upholding of human dignity and community, in every expression of love, justice, and reconciliation, in each act of self-giving to others, in the abundance of God's gifts and the stewardship entrusted to us that all may have enough, in all responsible use of the earth's resources. Glory be to God on high, and on earth, peace.

We confess our sins, by our silence or action, misuse of power, abuse of technology, any action or thought which endangers life on earth.
Lord, have mercy.
We commit ourselves to the way of Christ. We take up the cross for faith, hope, and love, praying for the love and peace of God's community.

Lord, we have heard your calling and we will hold your people in our hearts. Amen.

Methodist Service Closing Prayer:
The time has come Oh Lord for us to leave this place, Guide us and protect us and lead us in thy grace. Whereever life may take us, as we go our separate ways, Help us share with others the things we shared today. May the peace of God the Father, and the love of Christ His Son, Guide us in the days ahead and strengthen us, each one. May the blessings of the spirit, fill us from within. God bless us and return us to this fellowship once again. Amen. Amen!

SOME CHRISTIAN HYMNS

Praise God From Whom All Blessings Flow Doxology 1709 Anglican Bishop Thomas Ken

Shall We Gather At The River by Robert Lowry 1861

Go Tell It On The Mountain by John Wesley Work, Jr. 1865

Holy, Holy, Holy by Reginald Heber 1861

Let Us Break Bread Together by John Rosamond Johnson 1873 African American

Jesus Loves Me by Anna & Susan Warner 1827

This Little Light of Mine (African Spiritual)

Amazing Grace by John Newton 1725 an Anglican

O Guide Me Great Redeemer by William Williams 1762 of Wales

How Great Thou Art by Carl Boberg 1859 of Sweden

Blessed Assurance by Fanny Crosby 1873

What a Friend We Have in Jesus by Josesph Scriven 1855

It Is Well With My Soul by Horacio Spafford 1873

Be Thou My Vision Irish Hymn

Come Thou Font of Every Blessing by John Wyeth Nettleton 1757

Crown Him With Many Crowns by Matthew Bridges and Godfrey Thring 1852 in Baptist, Methodist, and Presbyterian hymnals. The song is **Diademat**a by Sir George Job Elvey 1868 of U.K. in Anglican hymnals. Diademata means 'crown' Greek.

The Lord's Prayer by Albert Hay Malotte 1935

Let There Be Peace On Earth by Jill Jackson-Miller and Sy Miller 1955

Sent Forth By God's Blessing by Omer Westenderf 1964

Here I Am, Lord by Dan Schutte 1981

A Mighty Fortress is Our God
Christ the Lord is Risen Today
Hark! The Herald Angels Sing
I Surrender All
Faith of Our Fathers
Morning Has Broken
O Come All Ye Faithful
O Holy Night
O Little Town of Bethlehem
Just As I Am
In the Sweet By and By
Precious Lord Take My Hand
We Three Kings
O Mary, Our Mother

In Christ Alone by Keith Getty and Stuart Townend 2001
God of This City by Chris Tomlin 2011
Your Great Name by Krissy Nordhoff and Michael Neale 2012
Shackles Praise You by Mandisa 1999 African American
Jesus, You're Beautiful by CeCe Winans

Trust in Jesus by Third Day

You Are Not Alone by Kari Jobe
10,000 Reasons Bless the Lord Matt Redman

Who Am I? Casting Crowns

You Raise Me Up Selah

Our God is An Awesome God Michael W. Smith, Rich Mullins Hillsong United

The Gospel by Ryan Stevenson

Some Christian churches hold traditional services with choirs and hymns and modern services with rock and roll bands or modern music.

The Church of Jesus Christ of Latter-day Saints MORMON

Mormon Christian Scriptures derived from the Book Of Mormon

The word 'God' has been substituted for Jehovah or Yahweh in many verses.

We invite all people everywhere to read the Book of Mormon, to ponder in their hearts the message it contains, and then to ask God, the Eternal Father, in the name of Christ, if the book is true. Those who pursue this course and ask in faith will gain a testimony of its truth and divinity by the power of the Holy Ghost.

The Jaredite Mormons depart for a new land after God confounded languages at Jewish Tower of Babel 2200BCE

Now Jared and his brother, who would become the Jaredites, cried unto the Lord for guidance, and the Lord told them to gather together flocks, female and male, of every kind, and also of the seed of the earth of every kind, and thy families and friends, and prepare supplies and build barges to cross the sea to the new promised land. The Lord appeared to Jared and gave him two stones, the Urim and the Thummim, which would magnify to the eyes of men the writings of the plates. The Lord told Jared and his brother to write down for the people to exercise faith in the Lord, and the Lord will show them greater knowledge, nothing that is withheld because of unbelief.
The Lord said when you rend the unbelief which causes wickedness and hardness of heart, great and marvelous things which have been hid up from the foundation of the world from you, will be revealed and cause you a contrite spirit and a heart filled with hope and love, a covenant of the Lord with those who are righteous. Blessed is the one who is found faithful unto the Lord and shall enjoy an everlasting life with the Lord. Jared had four sons who were Jacom, Gilgah, Mahah, and Orihah. And the eight Jaredite barges were driven to the winds to the promised land; it took 344 days to reach the shore. where kings succeeded kings, and there were wars and dissensions, and wickedness, and many tears were shed. Twenty-two friends of Jared and his brothers crossed the ocean to the a new promised land. The brother of Jared had such great faith that he removed a mountain just by saying 'Remove'.
The Lord told the brother of Jared: Ye shall be as a whale in the midst of the sea; for the waves will dash upon you. Nevertheless, I will bring you across the depths of the sea and prepare the way for you.'
And twenty-four plates of Jared and Jaredite history were written by Ether, who was a descendant of

Coriantor, who was the son of
Moron, who was the son of Ethem,
who was the son of Ahah,
who was the son of Seth,
who was the son of Shiblon,
who was the son of Com,
who was the son of Coriantum,
who was the son of
Amnigaddah,
who was the son of Aaron,
who was a descendant of Heth, who
was the son of
Hearthom,
who was the son of Lib,
who was the son of Kish,
who was the son of Corom,
who was the son of Levi,
who was the son of Kim,
who was the son of Morianton,
who was a descendant of
Riplakish,
who was the son of Shez,
who was the son of Heth,
who was the son of Com,
who was the son of Coriantum,
who was the son of Emer,
who was the son of Omer,
who was the son of Shule,
who was the son of Kib,
who was the son of Orihah,
who was the son of Jared.

The prophet Ether came forth in the days of Coriantumr and began to prophesy unto the people, for he could not be restrained because of the Spirit of the Lord which was in him. For Ether did cry from the morning, even until the going down of the sun, exhorting the people to believe in God unto repentance lest they should be lost, saying, wherefore, whoso believeth in God might with surety hope for a better world, and hope cometh of faith, maketh an anchor to the souls of men, which would make them sure and steadfast, always abounding in good works, being led to glorify God. And Ether did prophesy great that those will have hope and be partakers of the gift, if they would but have faith. The Lord came to Ether that he should prophesize unto Coriantumr to cease wars with Shared and Shiz. The wars did not cease and they sought to kill Ether, but he escaped, Coriantumr and Shiz fought in a battle and Coriantumr killed Shiz with a sword.
Concerning the house of Israel, Ether wrote about Jerusalem from whence Lehi should come; after it is destroyed it should be built up again, a holy city unto the Lord to save souls from destruction, a New Jerusalem should be built in the new land unto the remnant of the seed of Joseph whose Father went to Egypt to see him.
Ether hid the twenty-four plates in a manner that the people of Limhi could find them.

Lehi of the Mormons sails for the promised land after destruction of Solomon's temple

Lehi of the Nephites was descended from Manasseh who was descended from Joseph, the same Joseph who was sold into slavery in Egypt.
Lehi and his wife Sariah, and their four sons, Laman, Lemuel, Sam, and Nephi left Jerusalem because of the destruction of Solomon's temple, so the Nephite people came out of

Jerusalem at the time of Zedekiah, when Jerusalem was destroyed. Lehi decided to leave for the new promised land just as his ancestor Jared had before the time of Moses.

Nephi and his brothers and also Zoram took the daughters of Ishmael of Shazer who was later buried at Nathom, as wives, and sojourned into the wilderness for eight years toward Bountiful, a land of fruit and wild honey,
near the sea called Irreantum, where they pitched tents by the seashore. Nephi was told by the Holy Spirit to build a ship and sail to a new promised land to the west where later they would be called the Mormons. On the ship there was singing and dancing, and the Nephites stood at the railings of the ship looking at the beautiful waters and skies. The ship that sailed the Nephites reached the land in the west, which was called Zamaria, the people multiplied, and a temple for the Lord was built.
Lehi and Sariah had two more sons, Jacob and Joseph.

Plates of Brass

Nephi and his people recorded Plates of Brass that contained all of the teachings of Moses and a history of the Jews to the reign of Zedekiah; this was in 600BCE, and the
story Adam and Eve, who ate of the tree of knowledge which resulted in all humanity having knowledge of nakedness, guilt, and uncleanness.

Nephi had a vision of the future coming of Jesus, a messiah who would be born to a mother, named Mary, and the need for righteousness and baptism in humanity, and recorded it onto the Plates of Nephi. The prophet Zenos told the Nepites to remember they were a remnant of the house of Israel and God Jehovah was their Redeemer.
Before his death, Lehi told his descendants to put on armor of righteousness and observe the statues of the Lord, to awake from deep sleep, come forth from obscurity, and shake off chains which bind children of men and women in misery and woe.
Nephi told the people Satan would be overcome and righteousness would be preserved. Nephi told the people to continually pray and ask for guidance from the Holy Spirit; that angels speak by the power of the Holy Spirit. Nephi said he was harshly against sin and for the plainness of truth, and that he had charity for Jews and Gentiles. Nephi prayed for those whose hearts were hardened against the Holy Spirit, that lost hearts would turn toward righteousness. Nephi said to believe in the great day that Christ would come.

Plates of Nephi

Fifty-five years after Lehi left Jerusalem, Joseph and Jacob read large engraven plates of brass left to them of the Nephites telling of faith in Holy Spirit, of denouncing concubines, teaching for men to have only one wife in marriage, and condoning chastity for men and women. The prophet Zenos told that a vine of the olive tree would be plucked off and be transplanted, and young and tender branches would shoot forth so the vine would perish not but may be preserved for the Lord's purposes. And Enos, son of Jacob, taught righteous of the Holy Spirit and prayed for the Lord God to end fighting among Nephites and Lamanites. Enos wrestled with sins and received remission after he kneeled down before his Maker and cried hungrily in mighty prayer and supplication for his soul.

And Jarom, son of Enos, after two hundred years more, wrote on small plates so his genealogy may be kept, that the prophets, priests, and teachers did diligently work to preserve the law of Moses and the intent for which it was given and to look forward to the Messiah. And Omni, son of Jarom, kept records and passed the plates to his son Amaron. Amaron wrote a few things in 279 BCE and did pass the plates to his brother Chemish. Chemish passed the plates to his son, Abinadom. The son of Abinadom was Amaleki, who recorded actions of Mosiah, who was made king over the land of Zarahemia.

In the land of Zarahemia, the new promised land, King Benjamin had three sons; Mosiah, Helorum, and Helaman. King Benjamin told his sons to remember the teaching of the plates of Moses and the plates of Nephi, which were the teachings since their forefathers left Jerusalem until the present. At first the families pitched their tents round about the temple, with each his door open towards the temple, that thereby they might remain in their tents and hear the words king Benjamin spoke, but when the masses of people became so great, King Benjamin built a tower and spoke to the people from the tower. King Benjamin said he was a mere human with infirmities of body and mind, and he was not boasting but wanted the people to know that he was in the service of God.

Benjamin told the people he wished them good things and he wanted to serve them, and he reminded them not to murder, steal, commit adultery, be wicked, or make slaves of each other. Benjamin told the people to render thanks and praise with their whole soul to the God that created them and walk with a clear conscience before God and do not be rebellious to God or an enemy to righteousness but be steadfast and immovable in good works. And King Benjamin took and recorded the names of those who wanted to enter into a covenant with God to live a righteous life; King Benjamin was a holy man.

King Benjamin retired and appointed his son Mosiah to replace him as king, and it was 124BCE. King Benjamin also appointed priests to teach the people that they might know the commandments of God.

A decree by Judge Helaman caused contention between Lamanites and Nephites but Moronihah established peace.

Now Zeniff was a Nephite who led a prosperous people who built buildings and walls, and planted all manner of seeds, seeds of corn, wheat, barley, and fruit; and the people under King Laman tried to undermine those of Zeniff who was a spy, but Zeniff was delivered and did not fall into the hands of enemies. Zeniff also refused to engage in battle with the enemies; Zeniff wanted no bloodshed; instead Zeniff made a treaty with the enemies. King Mosiah sent sixteen strong men to sojourn to the land of Lehi-Nephi in the land of Shilom to find lost brethren. Among the sixteen men was Ammon; they ventured for forty days and came to a rest at a hill north of Shilom where they pitched tent. Then Ammon took three men who were Amaleki, Helem, and Hem and they went down into the valley at Nephi, where they were surrounded and put in prison for two days and then King Limhi released them.
Limhi showed the twenty-four Plates of Ether of the Jaredites engraved of pure gold and requested of Ammon if he could translate the ancient language from 2500BCE because Limhi said they could learn knowledge from an ancient people, but Ammon could not but told of Daniel, who was a translator of ancient languages back in the land of the Israelites.

Abinadi was a Mormon prophet who taught the Ten Commandments and told the people to not be carnal and devilish. Abinadi testified that those who sow filthiness reap the whirlwind.

Alma was a descendant of Nephi who began setting forth the covenant of baptism at the waters of Mormon, which was a fountain of pure water near a thicket of small trees.
Alma baptized Helam saying, Helam, I baptize you under authority of the Almighty God, as a testimony that you have entered a covenant to serve the Lord all the days of your life, and may the Holy Spirit who has prepared the foundation of the world be poured out upon you and grant you eternal life.
Alma was offered to be a king but declined; Alma only wanted to be a High Priest and organized the Church of God. Alma said to love your neighbor as yourself, that there should be no contention among them.

And King Mosiah sent a proclamation throughout the land that there should be no persecutions among believers of the Holy Spirit; that there should be an equality among all men; that no pride or haughtiness should disturb their peace; that every person should esteem his neighbor as himself, laboring with their own hands for their own support.
And there began to be much peace in the land, peace in the valley and there was no contention; and the people began to be very numerous, and began to scatter abroad upon the face of the earth, on the north

and on the south, on the east and on the west, building large cities and villages in all quarters of the land. And the Lord did visit them and prosper them, and they became a large and wealthy people.

Samuel the Lamanite was a prophet of the Lord in the land of America who predicted a new star would appear at Christ messiah's birth and told the Nephites the Lord would bless those who are steadfast enlightened believers. Jesus Christ sent Samuel the Lamanite in 5 BCE to foretell of his birth. Prophet Samuel reminded them that Prophet Zenos said that the Lord would work toward restoration of unbelieving brethren, such is the promise of the Lord.

TESTAMENT OF MORMON

In 34CE Jesus appeared to the Nephite people who were the Mormons in the land and the people did cry out with one accord, saying: Hosanna! Blessed be the name of the Most High!
Jesus appeared in a white robe and his voice was heard 3 times to the Nephite Mormon people in a land in the west. Jesus appointed twelve disciples who were named Nephi, Timothy, Jonas, Mathoni, Mathonihah, Kumen, Kumenonhi, Jeremiah, Shemnon, Jonas, Zedekiah, and Isaiah. And the disciples did teach the words that Jesus spoke.

Jesus said: 'Think not that I am come to destroy the law of Moses or the prophets; I am not come to destroy but to fulfill; I did not come to condemn the world, but to save it, and I have given you the commandments and have asked that you repent of your sins and believe in me, that you shall enter into the divine realm of heaven. Mormon will be a great prophet unto you as a guiding candle.'

Jesus told the people to repent and be like little children, and to commit themselves to the Holy Spirit; saying I am never alone; God is in me. Jesus said 'I tell you the truth, anyone who doesn't receive the kingdom of God like a child will never enter it. The kingdom of God is within your heart; it is of the Spirit and among us.'
The Nephites were to be excited and joyous learners, anxious to learn more about embracing good ways and a strong faith in the Lord, who is the sweetest of loves and fills us with the glory of goodness.

Jesus said blessed are the peacemakers for they shall be called children of God,
blessed are those who mourn for they shall be comforted, blessed are the meek for they shall inherit the earth, blessed are those who thirst for righteousness for they shall be filled with the Holy Spirit, blessed are the merciful for they shall obtain mercy, blessed are the pure in heart for they shall see God. Jesus said a person should be like a light unto the world, set upon a hill.
Jesus said to deny oneself of lust and greed, pray for your enemies, to

give to those who ask, and do not judge each other.
If you are angry with a brother, reconcile with him, and then come unto me with full purpose of heart, and I will receive you.
If you don't know what to say, just say 'Jesus.'

The Lord's Prayer

Jesus said to pray secretly to the Holy Spirit in Heaven instead of loudly in synagogues and on street corners. Jesus taught the people to pray 'Our Father, Who art in Heaven, Hallowed be thy Name, thy kingdom come, thy Will be done, on earth, as it is in Heaven, Give us this day, Our daily bread, and forgive us our trespasses, as we forgive those who trespass against us, and lead us not into temptation, but deliver us from evil.'
Jesus told the believers that treasures are in heaven and not upon the earth. And Jesus provided bread and wine to the people saying that the soul of the one who hungers and thirsts for the Holy Spirit shall be filled. Jesus said verily, verily, I say unto you, it is a covenant that whoever is filled with the Holy Spirit will be set high.

Behold what the scriptures say – man shall not smite, neither shall he judge, for judgment is mine saith the Lord. The eternal work and purposes of the Lord shall roll on, until all his promises shall be fulfilled. The Lord knoweth our prayers, and the prayers said in behalf of our brothers and sisters, and our faith.

There are some who love money and substance and fine apparel, and the adorning of buildings more than they love the poor, the needy, the sick, and the afflicted.
Why do you adorn yourselves with that which has no life, and yet suffer the hungry, and the needy, and the naked, and the sick and the afflicted to pass by you, and notice them not?
Why do you think that greater is the value of an endless happiness than that misery which never dies?

Be wise in the days of your life; strip yourselves of all uncleanness; ask not that you may consume it on your lusts, but ask with a firmness unshaken, that you will yield to no temptation, but that you will serve the true and living God, and do it in the name of Jesus Christ.

The Plates of Mormon abridged to Plates of Nephi

So from Nephi to his son, Amos, and from Amos to his brother Ammaron, the plates of records of the Nephites were given to Mormon with sacred engravings on the borders of Zarahemia by the waters of Sidon and also Angola. Mormon received the plates when he was but a mere youth of ten years old, because he was a sober child who had a learned tongue and was quick to observe.

THE PROPHET MORMON

Thus the prophet Mormon delivered a record unto the plates of Nephi as a testament to Jesus. The plates of

Mormon were abridged to the plates of Nephi and the Plates of Brass.

Plates of Ether

Moroni, son of Mormon, was angry with Amalickiah who conspired to be king because Amamlickiah said cunning and flattering things to the brethren which lead them to do wicked things away from God. And Moroni fastened on his headplate and breastplate and armor shields the title of liberty and went forth among the people, waving the rent part of his garment in the air, that all might see the writing which he had written, crying in a loud voice: 'Behold, whosoever will maintain this title upon the land, let them come forth in the strength of the Lord, and enter into a covenant that they will maintain their rights and their religion, that the Lord God may bless them. Do not follow the evil teachings of Amalickiah or anyone else who leads you away from good ways.'

The Lord spoke to the Prophet Ether to prophesy to Sharad, Coriantumr, Gilead, Lib, and Shiz to cease their iniquities and repent before their wickedness led to everlasting destruction in their land.

And Moroni did record the words of the Prophet Ether upon plates and hid them in the land of Cumorah in a hill, abridged to the plates of Brass, the plates of Nephi, and the plates of Mormon. It was when there was a period of war in the years 400CE and all Nephites were killed except Moroni.

Prophet Moroni said: Pray with a sincere heart, with real intent, having faith in Jesus Christ and God.

A man being evil cannot do that which is good. A bitter fountain cannot bring forth good water.

All things which are good cometh of God; and that which is evil cometh of the devil; for the devil is the enemy of God. Fight against the devil continually, and inviteth and enticeth not to sin.

But behold that which is of God inviteth and enticeth to do good continually; do good and love God is to serve God and be inspired by God.

Teach little children about the good ways of God. God loves little children with a perfect love; little children are innocent so they do not need to repent in baptism. Pray for children and anoint them in the faith of the Lord.

Moroni did this in the name of Christians who were peaceful and kept the commandments of God. Moroni beheld that Jesus and the disciples did minister unto them, and he said that whoso received the records, they shall not condemn them because of imperfections in them; the same shall know of greater things than these. He said 'Behold, I am Moroni; and were it possible, I would make all things known unto you. And I am the same who hideth up this record unto the Lord; the plates thereof are of no worth, because of the commandment of the Lord. For the Lord truly saith that no one shall have them to get gain; but the record thereof is of great worth; and whoso shall bring it to light, him the Lord will bless. For none can have power to reveal it except to whom God gives power to reveal it, and this is a long dispersed covenant with the people of the Lord. And it shall come to the knowledge of the people and shine forth, and it will be done by the power of the Lord.' And furthermore, Moroni said 'Behold what the scriptures says - man shall not smite, neither shall he judge, for judgment is mine saith the Lord. The eternal work and purposes of the Lord shall roll on, until all his promises shall be fulfilled. The Lord knoweth our prayers, and the prayers said in behalf of our brothers, and our faith.

After Jesus Christ visited the people on the American continent, the people lived in peace for 170 years.

Moroni told the people:
John the Apostle testified that Jesus said: 'I am the way, the truth, and the life.'

Jesus Christ said: Other sheep I have, which are not of this fold; them also I must bring, and they shall hear my voice; and there shall be one fold and I will be their shepherd.

Nephi, who was the son of Helaman, did write the words of Jesus Christ:
Arise and come forth unto me that ye may thrust your hands into my side and that ye may feel the prints of the nails in my hands and feed, that ye may know that I am God and have been slain for the sins of the world.
If ye shall believe in Christ, ye will believe that the words of Christ teach all people that they should do good.
Jesus Christ is our Divine Redeemer and that by living according to His Gospel, we can find peace in this life and eternal happiness in the life to come.
Jesus did say to his disciples to go into all the world and preach the gospel of peace to every creature.

Nephi said: For God is the same yesterday, today, and forever; and the way is prepared for all people from the foundation of the world, if it so be that they repent and seek God. For he that diligently seeketh shall find; and the mysteries of God shall be unfolded unto them, by the power of the Holy Spirit, as well in these times as in times of old, and as well in times of old as in times to come; wherefore, the course of the Lord is one eternal round. And the Holy Spirit giveth authority that I should speak these things, and deny them not.

Divine Words for All Nations

And behold, the Lord has delivered divine words that are sealed up in the books of many religions. Know ye that there are many nations and God created all people and the isles of the sea and the lands. God rules the heavens above and the earth below. The Lord has delivered words to all nations and the testimonies of all nations shall run together. Suppose ye have a Bible, then ye may not assume that all words have been delivered unto the Bible. So it may come to pass that many books shall be inspired by the Divine One. The Nephites will have the words of the Jews, and the Jews will have the words of the Nephites, so Mormons believe that the Covenants of the Lord will be with all people.

The Prophet Zenos said:
The Lord said: 'I will gather to me all people from the four quarters of the earth and they will dwell in peace and be joyful.'
All of the earth shall see the salvation of the Lord; every nation, kindred, tongue, and people shall be blessed; their distress lightened. And I am speaking unto all people, so it will be that they obtain these good things.

Prophet Alma said 'God is mindful of every people. All the earth and its motion and all the planets which move in regular form do witness that there is a Supreme Creator.' Alma was also a priest and a judge who also taught that every man should love his neighbor as himself, that there should be no contention among them. And Alma was a founder of a church; he refused to be king when he was offered the chance. Gideon and Helaman were men of the church with Alma. Gideon was instrumental in helping the people to soften their hearts when their hearts had become hardened, for wickedness came among them.

Prophet Lehi: 'We can be encircled about eternally in the arms of God's love. I, Lehi, prophesy according to the workings of the Spirit which is in me, that there shall none come into this land of liberty except those that shall be brought by the hand of the Lord.'
And Lehi said to prepare your souls for that glorious day when justice shall be administered to the righteous, that you may not shrink with awful fear in remembering your guilt and transgressions when the devil obtained you as prey to his awful misery.
Lehi also said: Do not spend money for that which is of no worth, nor your labor for that which cannot satisfy. Remember the words of the Lord God and feast upon that which perisheth not, neither can be corrupted, and let your soul delight in the goodness of the Lord. Pray to God continually by day and by night and give thanks unto the Holy Name. Let your hearts rejoice. Amen.
Remember when the Lord saved you in the exodus when you walked in darkness and dwelled in shadow; the Lord sent his word unto you and you rejoiced and trusted in the Lord God Jehovah. And the Lord performed divine work upon Mount Zion and upon Jersusalem. The Lord became your strength and song, and also your salvation.

For unto us a child was born, unto us a son was given; and his name shall be called Wonderful Counselor, The Mighty God, The Everlasting Father, the Prince of Peace, who is Jesus Christ. They shall call His name Emmanuel which means God with us.

THE PROPHET
Joseph Smith

Because the Christian church went through a period of dark ages and many Christians were disagreeing on issues and there was much quarreling, Jesus Christ came to Joseph Smith.
In 1820CE, when Joseph Smith was 14 years old, he was called by God to restore the Church of Jesus Christ on earth, allowing everyone to receive the joy and blessings that come from living it. So, Joseph Smith was in the woods in a Sacred Grove in Manchester, New York; God and Jesus Christ appeared to him to commence restoral of faith. The testament of Joseph Smith said:
"I saw a pillar of light over my head and a voice did say 'This is My Beloved Son – hear Him!'
Surely the Lord God will reveal secrets to servants the prophets."
In 1823CE Joseph Smith was visited by a heavenly angelic messenger Moroni, who was the prophet Mormon's son. Moroni told Joseph the record of ancient inhabitants and the gospel of Jesus Christ were translated and recorded on thin sheets of gold and were buried at Hill Cumorah in the western land. The angel Moroni said do not condemn the records because of imperfections because the same shall know of greater things than these. Moroni said the Holy Spirit is the Comforter that fills one with hope and perfect love. Moroni instructed Joseph Smith about the Book of Mormon coming forth and that the Spirit of Elijah the prophet would reveal God's truth as it had been revealed by the mouths of prophets since the world began.
The time arrived for obtaining the golden plates, the two stones called the Urim and the Thummim, and the breastplate. On the 22nd day of September, 1827, the heavenly messenger delivered them to Joseph Smith and told him to be responsible for them and to use all efforts to preserve them and protect them, and that after the work was done that was required of Joseph, the angel would call for the items to be taken back. So the items remained safe in the hands of Joseph Smith; he translated the writings on the golden plates into the Book of Mormon which was an instrument of God to sweep the Earth and after he had accomplished what was required at his hands, the messenger did call for them, and Joseph did deliver the items back into the hands of the angel on the 2nd day of May, 1838, and the angel has them in divine charge to this day.
The eleven witnesses to the plates of Nephi and the testimony of Joseph Smith were the disciples Oliver Cowdery, David Whitmer, Martin Harris, Christian Whitmer, Jacob Whitmer, Peter Whitmer, John

Whitmer, Hiram Page, Joseph Smith, Senior, Hyrum Smith, and Samuel H.Smith.
Joseph Smith received the Melchizedek priesthood authority at the hands of John the Baptist, Peter, James, and John; they appeared as angels and bestowed the priesthood on him. Joseph Smith was chosen by God to be a prophet, seer, revelator, and translator to restore the teachings of Jesus Christ. Joseph Smith said "I was ordained by the Grand Council of Heaven before this world was, as all prophets were." Moses and the spirit of Elijah also guided Joseph Smith.
Aaronic priesthood is given to young men ages 12-18. Duties of priests in the Mormon church include preparing, blessing, and administering sacraments, collecting offerings, performing church and community services, and assisting or performing baptisms. Baptism is for remission of sins, for membership in the church, for entrance to the celestial kingdom, doorway to personal sanctification, dedicating your heart and actions to the Lord.
In 1830, The Book or Mormon was printed and distributed in Palmyra, New York.
Joseph Smith and his followers established settlements in Ohio, Missouri, and Illinois, USA. Joseph Smith called the area a new Zion.
The first Mormon Temple was built in Kirtland Ohio in 1836CE. It was destroyed by a mob and a fire by people who disagreed with Mormons. The Nauvoo Temple was built to replace it on the same site in 1937CE.
In 1830CE, Joseph Smith restored the Church of Jesus Christ of Latter Day Saints. The Prophet Joseph Smith had a wife named Emma but was also reported to have wed Rhoda, Emily, Olive, Eliza, Mary, Zina, Louisa, Helen, Sarah, Flora, Nancy, and Fanny but there is conflicting information about the names and numbers Joseph Smith was martyred in 1844CE.
The Pearl of the Great Price contains scriptures for Mormons, including stories taken from the Jewish Torah. The Quorum of Twelve Apostles was established in 1835 and is a governing body for the church. The Seventy is a priesthood from several Mormon churches.

Elder Bruce R. McConkie wrote "Transfiguration is a special change in appearance and nature which is wrought upon a person or thing by the power of God. This divine transformation is from a lower to a higher state and results in a more exalted, impressive, and glorious condition. By the power of the Holy Ghost many prophets have been transfigured so as to stand in the presence of God and view the visions of eternity. We have agency to choose between good and evil."

Elder Boyd K. Packer wrote in 1984 "Immortality is to live forever in the resurrected state with God. This thing is certain; no one will ever ascend above God; no one will ever replace God. He is Elohim, the Father. We revere Our Father; we worship our God."

Elder James E. Talmage wrote "Moses acknowledged that man is nothing is perspective to all of God's creations. Humans are God's greatest miracles." Towidah is the Hebrew word for the accounting story of the generations of people.

Elder Spencer W. Kimball wrote "Jesus positively and promptly rejected Satan and the devil leaveth him. Do not give Satan a chance. Bind Satan so he cannot tempt any human. Prevent sin rather than having to cure it."

President Joseph Fielding Smith wrote "All prophets had the holy ghost. All humans who became servants of God will have immortality."

Enoch and Elijah were taken directly to heaven without dying; their place of habitat is in the presence of God and is the terrestrial order which is reserved for ministering angels unto many planets.

President Herbert C. Kimball wrote "6 days of creation is a mere term- it does not matter if 6 days, 6 months, 6 years or 6000 years."

President David O. McKay wrote "God gave man power of choice."

Elder Marion G. Romney wrote "Jesus Christ was chosen to put into operation throughout the universe God Elohim's great plan to pass eternal life to man. The gospel of Jesus Christ is the only way."

Elder John A. Widtsoe wrote "The earth came into being by the will and power of the mind of God. Chance is ruled out."

Elder Neal A. Maxwell wrote in 1985 "Moses was assigned to write about the earth. Moses saw the bitterness of hell. Being in constant rebellion toward God is a living hell. Perdition is hell, loss, and destruction. God does not live in the only dimension of time as do we. God has knowledge of the past, present, and future. Man cannot know the future."

Elder Russell M. Nelson wrote "The plan of salvation is the plan of happiness, redemption, restoration, the plan of mercy, deliverance, and the everlasting gospel."

Elder John Taylor wrote "God is light, the light of the sun and stars and the power thereof."

Elder Marion D. Hanks, a member of the Seventy, wrote "Trangress is to sin. When God saw and foresaw the suffering that follows self-willed rebellious courses of sin, God wept."

Elder Mark E. Peterson wrote "Noah was a great servant, a ministering angel."

Elder Dallin H. Oaks wrote "The Sabbath was blessed and sanctified as a holy day of rest for a purpose, that man should pursue his own pleasure."

Elder Henry D. Taylor wrote "We are our brothers' keepers – we should help each other. The prophet Alma said God is mindful of every people."

THE PROPHET Brigham Young

Brigham Young (1801-1897CE) was the second president of the church. Brigham Young led the saints into the Salt Lake Valley where the Mormon Temple was built for the Mormons. Thomas S. Monson is the next authorized successor of the church.

Mormons believe in God and angels, talking with their kids about God, playing with their kids and teaching their kids good values, running their churches well, and having good morals. Women wear dresses and men wear suits to church. The marital triangle is God, man, and woman. The spouses are equally yoked. Either spouse may be an offender; an offender should repent to keep the triangle intact.

Sins of commission are evils acts that are intentional such as theft, murder, rape, adultery, physical or mental abuse, and lying. Sins of omission are sins such as failing to take care of your family, failing to help others, failing to pray or be thankful.

God is real; whoever has faith will have eternal life. Faith is actions and agency to obey God and to do good things.

The church meets together to pray, sing hymns, and partake communion of bread and wine in remembrance of Jesus. Hymns can be sung joyfully, solemnly, fervrently, reverently, prayfully, calmly, with dignity, and energetically.

An elder or priest shall administer bread and in this manner shall he call upon the Father in solemn prayer, saying:

O God, the eternal Father, we ask thee in the name of thy Son, Jesus Christ, to bless and sanctify this bread to the souls of all who partake of it, that they may eat in remembrance of the body of thy Son, and witness unto thee, O God, the eternal Father, that they are willing to take upon them the name of thy Son, and always remember him, and keep his commandments which he had given them, that they may always have his Spirit to be with them. Amen.

In the manner of administering the wine, he shall take the cup also, and say:

O God, the Eternal Father, we ask thee in the name of thy Son, Jesus Christ, to bless and sanctify this wine to the souls of all who drink of it, that they may do it in remembrance of the blood of thy Son, which was shed for them; that they may witness unto thee, O God, the Eternal Father, that they do always remember him, that they may have his Spirit to be with them. Amen.

Align yourselves with the spirit of God. God cares about our eternal progression. Look forward to what God has in store for us. God know what worries us, when we need peace, when we need to grow and learn and change, when we need to be comforted.

Whoever follows Jesus Christ will never be thirsty again. The spirit of Jesus is eternal.

By obedience to Truth, you will purify your hearts. Believers of God should be holy in conduct and in all manner of living. Christian qualities are virtue, knowledge, self-control, steadfastness, godliness, and brotherly affection. Church is the best place to be. Avoid natural man; seek God.

Spread the Good News of the Lord around the world.

MUSLIM

Because of language barriers, the word 'God' has been substituted for 'Allah' in several places.

Ishmael (Ismail) of the Jewish Torah 2200 BCE

Hagar, the mother of Ishmael (Ismail), prayed for water in the wilderness of Beersheba and found water at the Zamzam spring by the hills of Safa and Marwah near the city of Makkah (Mecca). Abraham, who was Ishmael's father, planted a tamarisk tree at the well.

So Abraham worshipped at the Jewish tent with Isaac, and at the Philistine tent with Ismael. When Abraham died at the age of 175, Isaac and Ismael buried him in the cave called Machpelah where Abraham's first wife, Sarai, was buried.

The twelve sons of Ismael who were called the twelve princes according to their tribes of Nebaioth, Kedar, Adbeel, Mibsam, Mishma, Dumah, Massa, Hadad, Tema, Jetur, Naphish, and Kedemah. The daughter of Ishmael was called Mahalath. The twelve princes lived in lands before Egypt in the direction of Assyria. Ismael became an archer in the wilderness near Mount Paran and his wife was Egyptian. And Ismael lived 137 years.

The Twelve Tribes of Ishmael formed Islam around 632CE

Abraham and his son Ismael (Ismail) by the mother named Hagar built a sacred mosque called Kabah in the land of Saudi Arabia at Makkah (Mecca). The mosque was for prayer to Allah.

The angels made a covenant with Abraham and Ismail to sanctify the House and use it as a retreat, or bow and prostrate themselves therein in prayer. And Abraham prayed: 'Our Lord! Accept this service from us, for thou art the All-Hearing, the All-Knowing. Make us Muslims, and a progeny of our people bowing to Thy Will. Show us our places for the celebration of rites; and turn us in mercy, for Thou art the Oft-Returning Most Merciful.'

The Holy Prophet of Islam Mohammad 632 CE

Mohammad received the first divine revelation on Jabal al Nur, the Mountain of Light (Mount of Hira). And the first Qiblah, the direction of prayer, was Jerusalem. But the Qiblah of Islam religion was later changed to be Makkah instead of Jerusalem.

Celebrations of praise to Allah at the Sacred Monument near Mount Arafat could continue, but the pilgrimage was changed to Makkah instead of to Jerusalem. The mother of Mohammad was Aminah; Mohammad's father died a few months before he was born. Mohammad was born in 570CE. His mother, Aminah, died in 576CE.

After Aminah died, Mohammad stayed with his grandfather until he turned 8 years old; that was when his grandfather died. Mohammad had three uncles: Abu-Talib, the most generous; Abu-Harith, the least wealthy; and Abu-Abbus, the wealthy. Abu-Talib offered to take care of Mohammad and they had a good relationship.

When Mohammad received his divine revelation at age forty and began preaching, there were unbelievers who wished him harm because they did not believe in his teachings. His uncle Abu Lahab had a fiery temper and did not approve of Mohammad's work. Abu Lahab's wife, who was wicked, laid out ropes of thorns so Mohammad would step on them on dark nights, and persecutors threw stones at Mohammad's head,
but the spirit of the Holy Prophet was not broken by sticks, stones, thorns, or harsh words.

Mohammad escaped from Mecca (Makkah) and performed his Hijrah to Madinah with his companion Abu Bakr. They concealed themselves in the cave Thaur for three days at one point, hiding from enemies. The cave was three miles from Madinah. Mohammad had previously sent his followers to Madinah ahead of him. 'We are but two' said Abu Bakr who was afraid they would be attacked; but Mohammad replied: 'Nay, for Allah is with us.' Faith gave their minds peace and rest, and Allah gave them safety; they reached Madinah safely.

'The second of two' became Abu Bakr's proud title.

The Muhajirs forsook their homes in Makkah and followed Mohammad al Mustafa in exile to Madinah. The Anars were the Madinah people who received them with honour and hospitality into their city. Poor people traded pomegranates and pearls to get what they needed.

Mohammad married Khadijah in 595CE and they were married for 25 years; she was a holy woman of great faith who practiced great charity. Khadijah was also a camel-train merchant; Khadijah was very wealthy. Their children were daughters Ruqayyah, Umm Kulthum, Zainab, and Fatima, and grandsons were Al Hasan and Al Husayn. Mohammad had two sons who died in childhood.

Now Abu-Talib (Mohammad's uncle) lived about 80 years and died around 619CE.
Khadijah died when Mohammad was 50 years old; Khadijah died within a month after Abu-Talib died, so it was called the Year of Sorrow.

Mohammad did remarry.
Then his wives were Sawdah who needed protection, Aishah who was clever and learned on the life of Mohammad, Zaynab who was devoted to the poor and was called 'Mother of the Poor'; Zaynab was the daughter of Khuzaymah. He also married Zaynab who was skilled in leather work and worked for the poor; this Zaynab was the daughter of Jahsh. So Mohammad's wives were four after Khadijah. One time all four wives were quarreling; Mohammad threatened to divorce the society of his wives, all four of

them, and marry new wives. One source listed 12 wives.

Mohammad preached to believers under a tree. The great ceremony of the Fealty (Loyalty) of Allah's Good Pleasure took place while Mohammad sat under a tree in the plain of Hudaybiyah.
The Lord sent Mohammad as a bringer of glad tidings with the good messages to celebrate the holy spirit with praises at morning, evening, and during the day. Then the Lord will send tranquility of peace and calm into the hearts of believers, that they may add faith to faith, so good men and good women may be admitted to the Gardens of Bliss on their day of resurrection.
The Holy Prophet Mohammad was very busy guiding the Muslims in good instruction and the verses of the Q'uran. One time a poor blind man who wanted to learn interrupted Mohammad and Mohammad show impatience; but Mohammad quickly realized his impatience and apologized, held counsel with the man, and forever held the poor man in high regard. Afterward Mohammad taught that giving spiritual food to others is just as important as giving them actual earthly food and water. Mohammad also taught about self-restraint and showed people how to be more patient with others. He banned the felling of trees in the desert and established protected areas for conservation and wildlife.
Mohammad said that even a lizard doesn't leap to the next branch until it is sure of its stability.

His wife Aisha (Aishah) told a story of Mohammad.
While walking to his house one night, he was overcome with sleep and lay down in a doorway near the Kaaba in Mekkah (Mecca). The angel Gabriel appeared and purified the Prophet's heart and Gabriel pointed to a winged beast at the end of the street that was in the form of a donkey. Calling the creature Buraq, the angel bade the Prophet Mohammad to mount it, and the steed flew Mohammad to Jerusalem where he visioned a mosque. Then Buraq flew Mohammad to heaven where he spoke with Abraham, Moses, and Jesus, and Allah. Allah told Mohammad for the people to pray 50 times a day. Mohammad then told Moses what Allah had instructed, but Moses said that 50 times a day was too much and to go seek the Lord once again and ask to reconsider. So Mohammad returned to the Lord and the Lord granted the request to reduce prayers for the faithful to only 5 times each day. So Mohammad told all of this revelation to Aisha (Aishah) his wife. When Aisha told this story later, she added 'We do not need Buraq to reach God, our steed is the soul. Allabu Akbar (God is great).'

Adhan is the call to prayer. The muezzin is the servant of the mosque chosen for his good character who recites the call to prayer.
The 5 Muslim prayers are Fajr at dawn, Duha (extra prayer 15 minutes after sunrise), Dhuhr (noon), Asr (afternoon), Maghrib

(after sunset til dusk), Isha (before midnite). Dhikr is repeating short prayers silently or aloud.

There was a group of scribes who were responsible for writing down the revelations of the surahs as they were given to Mohammad; Zayd ibn Thabit was one of Prophet Mohammad's companions who produced the manuscript of the Koran (Qur'an) which was presented to Hafsah, one of Mohammad's wives.
Uthman ibn Affan was another one of Mohammad's companions who translated another version of the Qur'an.

The guidance of the Muslim Koran

The guidance of the Koran to the Muslims says Praise be to Allah, the Cherisher and Sustainer of the Worlds; Master of the Day of Judgment. Thee do we worship and thine aid we seek. Show us the straight (good) way, The way of those on whom thou hast bestowed Thy Grace, Those whose portion is not wrath, and who go not astray. Those who believe in the Unseen are steadfast in prayer.
Those who believe in Revelation sent to them,
have the assurance of the Hereafter. They are on true guidance from their Lord and they will prosper. Allah has set a seal on their hearts to make not mischief on the earth. O ye people! Adore your Guardian Lord Who created you, and those who came before you, That ye may become righteous. Who has made the earth your couch and the heavens your canopy; and sent down rain from the heavens; And brought forth fruits for your sustenance. Allah gave you life and then Allah will cause you to die and again to the Lord will ye return. The Lord created for you all things on earth and made heaven with velvet couches, plates of fruit, drinking goblets of silver, gold and crystal, blissful gardens, and flowing streams, carpets of heavy brocade, bracelets of silver and pearls, garments of green silk.
In heaven there is a fountain of Kafur, where camphor is added to wine, there is a fountain of Zanjabil of the essence of ginger, there is a fountain of Salsabil to seek the way. The righteous may also drink Tasnim (Nectar) in heaven. One may eat and drink to thy heart's contentment at the divine banquets in heaven, and there are 7 gates to heaven.
And of all things the Lord hath perfect knowledge. Allah is not unmindful of what we do. Be steadfast in prayer and regular in charity: And whatever good ye send forth for your souls before you, ye shall find it with Lord Allah.
And Muslims believe in the inspiration and revelation given to Noah, Abraham, Ismail (Ismael), Isaac, Jacob, Joseph, David, Saul, Solomon, Moses and the Criterion, the prophet Elisha, Elias(Elijah), Aaron the priest, Ezekiel (Dhu al Kifl), Idris (a man of constancy and patience), Jonah(Dhu al Nun), Job, Jesus and Mary.

Jesus was to direct the people to righteousness and to avoid the evilness of Satan. The Koran says Jesus is a messenger from Allah and Jesus taught love, forgiveness, and non-violence. (Allah is an unseen holy spirit.)
David slew a giant named Goliath who had evil intentions. David and Saul fought over differences.
To each is a goal to which Allah turns him; then strive together towards all that is good. Seek help with patience and perseverance. When afflicted with calamity, say 'we belong to Allah to Him is our return'. In the creation of the heavens and the earth, of the night and day, in the sailing of ships through the ocean, in the rain which Allah sends down from the skies, in the beasts of all kinds, in the change of the winds, and the clouds which trail - indeed are signs for a people that are wise. Eat good things that are provided for you, be grateful, and do not waste.

Ramadan is a month for guidance and judgment and to glorify our Lord. Taking short fasts from eating can be healthy and respectful to Allah's goodness of providing sustenance. During Ramadan, fast from eating fish for a day until sundown and remember to recite beautiful prayers to the Lord Allah. Allah will send down a clear message of spiritual wisdom during a blessed night during the month of Ramadan, for the Lord sends revelations and knows all things; the Lord is the Lord of the Heavens and the Earth and all between them, if ye have assured faith.

Friday Jumu'ah prayer:
When the call is proclaimed to prayer on Friday - Day of Assembly - it is common public prayer, preceeded by a khutbah, in which the Imam leader reviews the week's spiritual life and offers advice.
Say prayers to the Lord and when prayers are finished, disperse to the house or to conduct thy business.

Each person prays 5 times a day and at the ids every year, large area meeting.
Once in a lifetime, go to Mecca for the pilgrimage.
Say prayers to the Lord and when prayers are finished, disperse to the house or to conduct thy business.
Women wear *hijab* (head covering scarf) outside of the home. Some Muslim women cover their entire face with *burqa*, *chadri* or *paranja*.
Men wear a prayer cap called *taqiyah* in Saudi Arabia, *topi* in Pakistan and India, and *kufi* in US and Britain.
Prayer beads contain 99 beads, for the 99 names of Allah.
Shahadah is the creed of Muslims; salat are the daily prayers; zakah is charity; fasting is Ramadan; hajj is pilgrimage to Mecca; and *jihad* is to strive for moral perfection and practice good ways, promote peace, to defend homes and mosques from enemies.

The five pillars of Islam are:
(1) shahada - profession of faith
(2) salat (prayer)
(3) almsgiving (tithes) zakat or zakah (charity)
(4) fasting (sawm)
(5) hajj-pilgrimage to Mecca

Three dimensions of Islam are: Islam - what one should do, Iman - why one should do, and Ihsan - to do beautiful things.
Ihan is the inner dimension of religion or spirituality.
Ehsan or shariah is the external practice of religion or spirituality.

The Lord has sent Messengers in eras of time to remind the people the Clear Signs of the Lord,
and to Sanctify the Signs, and to instruct them in Scripture and Wisdom.

Be fair and equitable when husbands and wives divorce and take care of your children. Care for the widowed and the orphaned. No soul shall have a burden laid on it greater than it can bear. If a husband and wife have discord, try counseling with arbiters from both sides of the family. Restore orphans their property. Do not engage in incest. When dividing property of the deceased, be fair to relatives.
Do not covet others' goods.
Whoever helps a good cause becomes a therein; whoever helps an evil cause shares in its burden. If you are travelling, you are permitted to shorten your prayers. If you put a sin on an innocent soul, it is falsehood and a flagrant sin.
An act of charity or justice or conciliation between men to seek the good pleasure of Allah shall receive a reward. Allah is an unseen god. Satan creates false desires and false promises. Allah promises truth. Men and women who do deeds of righteousness will enter Heaven and not the least injustice will be done to them. Allah did take Abraham for a friend. To Allah belongs all things; Allah could destroy us if it was Thy Will, and create another race of mankind, for Allah has the power to do this. Stand firmly for justice and follow not the lusts of your heart.

There were religious battles called the battle of Badr and the battle of Uhad in which
Muslims fought Muslims over religious principles; humans were dying because of religious fighting over the unseen Holy Spirit. Abu Jahl was an unbeliever who forbid prayers or devotions to the Lord; Abu Jahl fought against the people of Mohammad, but Abu Jahl met his end in the Battle of Badr.

Mohammad said that Abraham lived a long time ago and no one could be sure who his sons and daughters were, so after a long time had passed, many are now sons and daughters of Abraham. Mohammad said that humanity could benefit by making trade alliances with each other, no matter what religion a person practiced.

There was the Battle of Trenches at Medinah - where Jewish tribes and confederates fought against the Muslims. It was a big war. And even some of the Quraysh (Mohammad's family tribe)fought against the Muslims. We, the angels, have been instructed to tell people to stop religious fighting - only fight to defend your mosque or if you are put out from your houses because of your religion.

Abrahah Ashram was an Abyssinian ruler who attacked Makkah (Mecca) intending to destroy the Kaaba. He rode forth with an elephant train.

Tarek was a Muslim youth who drummed a djembe in song.

The Kaaba is the Sacred Cube inside the mosque at Mecca. The Quraysh were the tribe that had custody of the Kaaba.

Allah sent 3,000 angels and then 5,000 angels to help stop all of the fighting, but the people were still fighting over religions, and Allah sat on the High Throne and was distraught, for Allah loveth all the people on earth and wanted the fighting to stop. Allah is an advocate for peace among all people.

Seven youths who were companions were afraid because they worshipped the Lord of the heavens and there was religious fighting over the name of the Holy Spirit, so they hid in a cave and fell asleep for 309 years. The angels turned them on their right and left sides when they were sleeping and took care of their dog.

A traveler smashed in the cave wall and the companions in the cave woke up. One of the youths had money and gave it to one of them to go into town to get food. Their case was known to the people that the Lord Allah protected them from religious persecution while sleeping in the cave for 309 years and while they were unaware of anything happening in the outside world.

King Dhu al Qarnayn was given power on earth and the ways and means to establish justice and righteousness. Dhu al Qarnayn left alone the people who were living simple lives bothering no one, warned those who were doing mischief to stop, and ended fighting among two groups of people by building a wall barrier between them with blocks of iron; the wall would come down when both sides of people return to the Lord.

Luqman was a wise old sage who said earnest seekers of righteousness will receive guidance from Allah and Gardens of bliss, and that wisdom consists in moderation. Luqman said the Lord has more wisdom than if all the trees on earth were made to be pens and more wisdom than all of the world's oceans multiplied by seven times over.

In a garden near Mekka, there were the people who were resolved to gather the fruits of their labor in the early morning, before indigents awoke, so the indigents could not share the best of the harvest. But a visit from the Lord during the night swept the fruit away, so as morning broke, as the people went in secret tones to gather the best fruit, but found none, their revelation unto themselves was 'We have surely lost our way and have sinned to the poor, now the Lord has shut us out of our own labor! Verily we have been doing wrong!'

And the people offered prayer in repentance and said: 'Let us hope the Lord will give us in exchange a favorable garden, for we have turned our souls in repentance!'

Ifrit was a Jinn who could be trusted to help; Ifrit was in good standing with the Lord.

Abraham said: 'I do indeed worship only the Lord who made me and will certainly guide me!' And this is left as a word to those who came after him, that they may turn to the Lord. And the Lord Allah said: 'I have given the good things of this life to the people and their ancestors before them, and the messengers, that they will know the Truth, yet some will reject righteousness and choose the evil way of life. Those who choose evil go deeper and deeper to do more evil. Evil doth not pleaseth the Lord Allah. Turn away from the unbelievers of righteousness and say Peace!'

The Lord records all affairs in the Clear Record. The Record of the Righteous is preserved in Illiyin (Illiyun).
The Record of the Wicked is preserved in Sijjin.

Muslim saints (wali) should be remembered for good deeds and following Allah's good ways.

Mohammed is the Last Prophet for Muslims and the Koran says that Islam is not to be divided into sects.

In 600 CE in Arabia, Muslims of the Ottoman Empire had defeated the Byzantines (Romans) and Persians (Zoroastrians) for lands. The Q'uran (Koran) and Islam (the word *Islam* means *Peace*) was not forced on the *dhimmis* (people of other faiths); if the dhimmis or a dhimmi did not convert to Islam they were required to pay a yearly penalty tax called a jizya. The pagan idol worshippers of al-Lat were given a chance to convert to Islam or they were put in prison. Mohammed destroyed the shrine to al-Lat (Allat) in Taif; Mohammed said there would be no pagan worshippers in Muslim lands.

Muslim surahs derived from the Holy Q'uran

The Holy Koran

SURAH 1
The Opening

In the name of Allah, Most Gracious, Most Merciful. Praise be to Allah, the Cherisher and Sustainer of the Worlds;
Most Gracious, Most Merciful.
Master of the Day of Judgement.
Thee do we worship, and Thine aid we seek. Show us the straight way, the way of those on whom thou hast bestowed Thy Grace, Those whose portion is not wrath, and who go not astray.

SURAH 2
The Cow

Those who are on true guidance from the Lord are those who are steadfast in prayer, enjoin in good conduct, practice charity, and stay out of mischief.
Adore the Guardian Lord Who created you and those that came before you, that you may become righteous,
who has made the earth your couch and the heavens your canopy

and sent down rain and brought forth fruit for
your sustenance.
The Lord comes first before anything else in your life.

Give glad tidings to
those who believe and work righteousness; they will have warm memories and companions who are pure and holy.

The parable of those who reject Faith is as if one shouts out to things that listen to nothing, but calls and calls – they are void of wisdom.

Seek Allah's help with patient perseverance and prayer and know with certainty that all will meet the Lord.

All of Allah's creation has meaning from the lowest as well as the highest. It is Allah who brings you to life, and to Allah you will return.

Those who do mischief on the earth will cause loss to themselves.

Do not sell your souls for this material world but draw thyselves to heaven.
Those who do mischief on the earth will cause loss to
themselves.

We believe that Satan did make Adam and Eve slip from felicity. (happiness)

We believe in the religion of Abraham.

And we believe in the
inspiration and revelation given to Adam, Noah, Abraham, Ismail, Isaac, Jacob and the Tribes, David, Solomon, Moses and the book of Moses and the Criterion of the Old Testament of the Bible, the prophet Elisha, Elias (Elijah), Lot (nephew of Abraham) who was saved from among the wicked people, Aaron the priest, Jonah, Job, Jesus and his mother Mary, the Apostles and Disciples,
the Ark of the Covenant, and we make no distinction between one and another of them, and to the Spirit do we bow our will.

And the Lord made the shade of clouds, manna, and quails, garlic, onions, lentils, cucumbers, and pot-herbs, cows, and sheep, abundant fruits, saying:
'Eat of the good things that are provided for you on the earth'.
Do not eat dead animals that have died unto themselves.

Imran was the father of Moses and Aaron, and from them came a woman named Mary, the mother of Jesus. The Lord commended her and her offspring Jesus to protect the righteous from the Evil One. The men cast arrows to see who would take care of Mary; Zakariya was chosen and the Lord made Mary grow in purity and beauty.
While Zakariya was standing in prayer in his chamber, praying to have a child, the angels called unto him: 'Allah doth give thee glad tidings of Yahya who will be a prophet of the goodly company of

the righteous.' Yahya will be the son of Zakariya.
Yahya was John the Baptist and was the herald of prophet Jesus. Jesus was strengthened by the Holy Spirit and the gospels of Jesus reveal the miracles of the Lord.

And the angels Gabriel and Michael brought the message to Mohammad Al Mustafa, and the Holy Prophet Mohammad wrote the Holy Quran (Holy Koran) for the Muslims.

Ismail and Abraham raised the foundations of the House at Mecca, the City of Peace; this is the Sacred Mosque. And the Lord said that Abraham would be an imam for the people.
Qiblah is the direction of prayer for Muslims, which is the direction of the mosque.

Treat with kindness your parents and kindred, and orphans, and those in need and for wayfarers, and speak fairly to others.

A person's speech about this world's life may dazzle others, but Allah knows what is in a person's heart. There is the type of person of this world, and there is the type of person of the Lord.
Allah knows what a person conceals and what they reveal.

Those whose work is righteousness shall have their reward with their Lord.

The parable of the rock is that the hearts of sinners are as hard as stone.

Those who have faith are companions of the Garden and therein they shall abide forever.

Whoever submits to Allah
and is a doer of good –
will get their reward with their Lord.

And your God is One God;
There is no God but the Lord.

Divorce is permitted, and a 4-month period is required before divorcing to insure that the woman is not pregnant.
Be fair in divorces when dividing up properties, and let each other go in kindness, for Allah is understanding in these matters. If you choose to stay together, Allah is understanding, forgiving, and merciful.
Mothers and fathers should both be treated fairly in matters of children. Mothers and fathers should both help to take care of and provide for children. If a foster parent is appointed to take care of children, the foster parent should be equitably compensated.

Jihad means to strive for perfection of morals and behavior. Another meaning protects righteous believers from enemies if enemies try to harm the faithful or invade a mosque.

Jews, Christians, and Muslims will not quit fighting and quarreling but the Holy Spirit belongs to all people, and all people will be judged on Judgement Day.

Judgement Day will be on a Friday.

The enemy of righteousness is Satan.

Treat with kindness parents and kindred, orphans, and those in need. Practice regular charity from what you are given.

To orphans restore their property. Do not substitute your worthless things for their good ones.

The Law of Equality is prescribed to you in cases of murder; a life for a life.
But if any remission is made by the family of the slain, then grant any reasonable demand and compensate them with handsome gratitude; this is a concession of mercy from Your Lord.
When dividing property of the deceased, be fair to relatives and orphans.
A widow must wait 4 months before remarrying to make sure she is not pregnant. Bequeath to your family or make financial plans to maintain them in case you cannot work or in case you die.

Be plain and honest in your words, and speak not ambiguous words.

Believers of Faith guard themselves from all evil; do not turn back to infidelity.
Shed no blood amongst you, for Allah is mindful of what you do.

The Middle Prayer in the middle of the day reminds us that Allah is with us in the midst of our lives in worldly affairs.
Allah is full of bounty to humanity but most are ungrateful.
Whoever rejects evil and believes in Allah hath grasped the most trustworthy handhold that never breaks. Allah heareth and knoweth all things. Allah is the Protector of those who have faith. Allah is the unseen Holy Spirit to whom is due the primal origin of the heavens and the earth.

Do nothing to be ashamed of, for Allah knows the secrets of your hearts.

To each is a goal which Allah turns him. Then strive together towards all that is good wheresoever ye are.

If you remember the Holy Spirit, the Holy Spirit will remember you. Be grateful to Allah, the Cherisher and Most Holy Spirit.

Do not follow the steps of the Evil One to do mischief, for he is an avowed enemy.

Believe in righteousness and the Messengers, and do not turn your face from the truth of God.
To Allah do all questions go back for decisions.

I listen to the prayer of every suppliant who calls
on me, and I am indeed close to them.

And if you will learn self-restraint from violence, these believers will walk in the straight (good) and right way.

The sacred symbols of Allah are Safa and Marwa, Kabah, and Arafat.

Ramadan

During the month of Ramadan, the Hajj and the Umrah are pilgrimages as a symbol of service and worship, and the ihran is the pilgrimage garment renouncing the vanities of the world. Let there be no obscenity, wickedness, or wrangling in the pilgrimage; the best provision is right conduct.

When you pour down from Mount Aarafat, celebrate the praises of Allah at the Sacred Monument with your heart and soul but pass quickly because there are many believers who follow a crowd who need to pass by the Sacred Monument.

There should be no fighting at the Sacred Mosque, unless an enemy starts the fighting there, but if they stop fighting - let the hostility stop.

And if you will learn self-restraint against vanities and worldly greed, then you will walk in the straight and right way.

Follow Good Criterion

In excessive gambling and intoxicants is great sin, for
Satan's plan is to make you forget about the Lord and prayer.

And if you will learn self-restraint from overeating, these believers will walk in the right way. Eat, drink, and spousal relations are to be enjoyed at night after a day of fast.

In hoarding riches is great sin. Spend out of bounties that are given to you to employ good works, physically and mentally.

Usury is great sin and is forbidden.

If a debtor is in difficulty,
grant the debtor time to repay. But if you forgive payment by charity, it is best.

Whenever you make a commercial contract verbally or in writing, have 2 witnesses. Let no harm come to scribe or witnesses. If the party is mentally
deficient or weak or unable, let his guardian dictate faithfully.

A pledge of possession may serve the purpose where one person deposits a thing on trust with another; let the trustee faithfully conduct his trust and return the pledge at the right time.

Conceal not evidence, for concealing evidence is sin.

Allah knows everything in your heart and mind, whether you try to conceal it or not.

Allah has full knowledge of those who do wrong.

To disclose acts of charity is well, but if you conceal it in silence, Allah is well-acquainted with the good deed that you did.

Allah will forgive those who desist (stop) from sinning but will judge those who repeat evil.

Do not marry unbelievers who have not faith.

Stay away from your wives during their courses, for they need to rest.

The Lord loveth not the transgressors who contribute to destruction with their own hands, but Allah is with those who restrain themselves.

Let there be no hostility to an opposite party who is not oppressing you.

The Day of Judgement

On the Day of Judgement there will be no bargaining but each will receive the reward from their Lord.

If you reject all evil you will be admitted on the Day of Judgement to a gate of great honor where there will be a garden of bliss with date palms, vines, streams overflowing, fruit, velvet couches, and drinking goblets.

Time, life, and death are in Allah's command. For Allah caused one to die for 100 years and raised him back to life; his donkey lay beside him in bones; the food and drink showed no signs of age. When this was shown to Ezekiel, he said: 'God hath power over all things.'

The parable of the corn

The parable of those who spend their substance in the way of the Lord is that of a grain of corn that growth seven ears and each ear hath a hundred grains; Allah giveth manifold increase to whom he pleases. And Allah careth for all and knoweth all things.

Charity

Spending time or money for God's Causes such as charity for the poor, or maintenance of the mosque is a beautiful loan, and Allah will multiply it back to you.

All the gold on earth will not help you if you reject the faith of the Lord.

Praise Allah standing, sitting, or lying on the side.

Ye who believe let there be among you traffic and trade by mutual good will, and do not kill yourselves, for verily Allah hath been to you Most Merciful!

Do not covet the goods of others.

Be happy with what the Lord has provided for you, and spend out of this bounty; do not go into financial debt.

If you work for the cause of the Spirit and righteousness, the angels will give you great reward, so fight against friends of Satan.

Short is the enjoyment of this world, and the hereafter is the best.

Whoever helps a good cause becomes a party therein. Whoever helps an evil cause shares in it burden.

When a courteous greeting is offered you, meet it with a greeting still more courteous, or of equal courtesy.

If someone is peaceful, do not harm them, because Allah the Lord has opened a way for peace.
Allah will forgive real weakness, but not excuses.

If anyone sins and does evil, it goes against your soul. If you put a sin on an innocent soul, it is a falsehood and a flagrant sin. Satan creates false desires and promises, but the Lord promises truths.
The Evil One bids you to conduct unseemly (bad conduct), but the Lord will protect you from the Evil One (Satan).
Men and women of righteousness will enter Heaven. Stand firmly for justice and do not follow the lusts of your hearts.
Pray 'Our Lord! Lay not on us a burden greater than we have strength to bear.
Blot out our sins, and grant us forgiveness. Have mercy on us. Thou art our Protector; help protect us from those who stand against Faith and Believers of God.'

SURAH 3

The Family of Imran

Allah is the Exalted in Might, the Wise.
Allah desires good for all righteous people, and no harm or mischief should be done for the cause of Allah.
Allah knoweth all things and searcheth your heart for good things.
No one knows the meanings of all things except the Lord Allah.
Let our hearts not deviate from the good guidance of the Lord, but grant us mercy from thine own presence, for thou art the grantor of bounties without measure.
Humans covet gold, silver, bronze, horses, cars, people, and possessions of this world, but the Lord Allah will give you glad tidings far better. The righteous will have gardens with rivers flowing and companions that are pure and holy.

Allah sent down the surahs.

Those who show patience, firmness, self-control, worship devotedly, and pray for forgiveness are righteous to Allah.
Those who believe and understand the Lord say 'O Lord! Thou art the Holy Spirit that will gather all humankind together
against a Day about which there is no doubt. Do not let the righteous be vanquished, for we have resisted Satan and we have been charitable and loving to others.' This was taught before to the people of Imran, the father of Moses who led the Jews.
Among the People of the Book are those who, entrusted with a hoard of gold will pay it back; others, who, if entrusted with a single silver coin will not repay it, saying 'There is no call on us to keep Faith.' But this is a lie against Allah and they know it.
But Allah loves those who act aright (in righteous good ways).
Worship the Lord in a way that is straight; do not be led astray on a crooked path;

Do not stray from good ways.

By no means shall you obtain righteousness unless you give freely of that which you love, and whatever you give, of a truth the Lord Allah knoweth it well.

All ye believers, hold fast together, by the rope of mutual support, which the Spirit stretches out for you, and be not divided among yourselves, but remember the gratitude of the Lord's favour on you, and fear your enemy Satan.

Join your hearts in love,
so that by the grace of the
Spirit, you become
brethren, people together, inviting
all that is good;
forbidding what is wrong;
this is a clear sign that you may be
guided by the Lord,
and will attain felicity (happiness).

Be not like those who are divided amongst themselves and fall into disputations and are filled with hatred, for they will have trouble.

The best people evolved in humankind are those who enjoin what is right and reject what is wrong.

Not all people are alike; the believers are righteous but the mischief makers cause trouble. The Lord God knoweth well those who do good.

Those who are filled with rage and hate against you want you to perish: If good prevails you, it grieves them; but if some misfortune overtakes you, they rejoice at it. But if you are constant and do right, their evil cunning will not hurt you, for the Lord Allah is Compassionate and Wise, and Allah knoweth what the evil do.

To Lord Allah belongeth all that is in the heavens and on earth, and Allah is Oft-Forgiving, Most Merciful.
To Allah do all questions go back for decisions.
Who can forgive sins except the Lord Allah?

To adhere to righteousness during
prosperity or adversity,
to not lose heart,
to not fall into despair,
this is to gain mastery
of true Faith.

For the family of Imran, who was the father of Moses, the Old Law of Equality taught a wound for a wound, a life for a life, a tooth for a tooth, a slave for a slave, but if any remission of charity is made by the family of the slain, then grant any reasonable demand and compensate them with handsome gratitude. This is a concession of mercy from your Lord and this is the teaching of Jesus and Mohammad, to forgive is to not retaliate.

Mohammad is a Messenger who was given Scripture and Wisdom, like many who were the messengers who passed away before him. Mohammad led good examples and promoted peace and love.

No soul can die except by Allah's leave.
And Allah loveth those who do good and will reward the Prophets.
Pray for Lord Allah to purge evil from your hearts, for it was Satan who caused you to fail.

Pray to the Lord for forgiveness and mercy.

Only the Lord knows the judgment of the unbelievers, those who reject the Messengers and the Books of Enlightenment.
Allah took a Covenant with the righteous believers who will see Gardens of Bliss, fruit, flowing streams, and holy companions of men and women. Some said there would be virgin maidens.

'Our Lord! We have heard the call to Faith and we have believed in the Lord Our Lord! Forgive us our sins, blot out from us our
Iniquities, and take to Thyself our souls in the
company of the righteous.

'Our Lord! Grant us What Thou didst promise
Unto us through Thy
Messengers,
And save us from shame On the Day of Judgement;
For Thou never breakest
Thy promise.'
The Lord spoke: Never will I forget the work of any of you, be a male or female; you are from one another. Those who work for the cause of the Holy Spirit will be admitted to the Gardens in the Hereafter, with rivers flowing beneath.

A reward from God is the best of rewards.

Bow in humility and praise to Allah and reject Satan, and strengthen each other that ye may prosper.

SURAH 4
The Women

O humankind! Revere Your Guardian-Lord, Who
created you, for Allah ever watches over you.

Treat family and orphans fairly. Do good to parents and kinfolk, orphans, those in need, neighbors, strangers, the wayfarer, and the Companion by your side. Allah loveth deeds of service and kindness.

When orphans reach adulthood, release their property to them; but consume it not wastefully nor in haste while they are growing up to adulthood.
If the guardian is well-off (wealthy) let them claim no remuneration, but if the guardian is poor, let them have what is just and reasonable. When you release property back to the orphans, take witnesses in their presence. But all-sufficient Allah is taking account.

Bequeath what is left by parents or relatives (who have died) to designated beneficiaries. Let those disposing of an estate give the beneficiaries their due and just portions; let the
disposers have the same
fairness in their minds as they would have for their own families if they had left a helpless family behind after their own deaths.

Allah accepts the repentance of those who do evil in ignorance, but of no effect is those who continue to do evil yet know it is wrong.

It is forbidden to marry your relatives.

It is forbidden to marry those who are already married.

Seek marriage for chastity and love, not for lust. Seek not paramours when you are in wedlock.

Reject lewdness and evil.

The Lord Allah doth wish to lighten your difficulties.

O ye who believe!
Eat not up your property
among yourselves in
vanities; but let there be amongst
you traffic and
trade by mutual good will:
Nor kill or destroy
Yourselves.

If you rid of evil in yourself, you will be admitted to a Gate of Great Honour in Heaven.

In nowise covet the gifts of others, but the Lord Allah hath bestowed gifts on all and hath full knowledge of all things.

Whoever recommends and helps a good cause becomes a partner therein;
and whoever recommends and helps an evil cause shares in its burden.

When a courteous greeting is offered you, meet it with a greeting still more courteous or at least of equal courteous.

Fight not against those who are peaceful towards you.

Never should a believer kill a believer.

A believer who works for the cause of the Holy Spirit Allah against the evil of Satan is granted a higher grade from Allah.

Some of the evil say 'We were weak and oppressed on the earth.' But is the earth spacious enough for you to move yourselves away from the evil? Have hope and direct yourselves to a refuge away from evil.

If you are traveling the earth, it is permissible to shorten your prayers.

If you are praying with others who you have not yet prayed (strangers), take precautions and bear arms (weapons) to avoid an assault from an Evil One. Put away your arms (weapons) when you trust your Companion in Prayer.

Establish regular prayers and practice regular charity.

If you are suffering hardships, remember that there are others who are suffering hardships.
If anyone does evil or wrongs their own soul, seek Allah's forgiveness against your own soul.

If anyone throws a fault or sin on an innocent soul, that person throws it on their own soul as a flagrant sin.

Whoever takes Satan for a friend hath of a surety suffered a loss that is manifest, for Satan makes false promises and deceptions.

But those who believe and do deeds of righteousness will be admitted into the Gardens, with rivers flowing beneath, to dwell therein forever, Allah's promise is the truth. Be they male or female, those who do deeds of righteousness will enter Heaven and not the least
injustice will be done to them.

The women who bear
children will extend the line of the family to the next generation.

Do not be swayed by greed, and practice self-restraint.

To Allah belongs all things in the heavens and the earth.

O ye who believe! Take not for friends those who make mischief. It is better to have friends who are believers in order to avoid scandals of evil, and to continue in the inspiration of righteousness.

SURAH 5
The Goal

O ye who believe!
Fulfill all of your obligations in honesty!

Eschew sins and lies;
Eschew all iniquities.

Recognize those with justice in their hearts - those who are sincere and humble.

To those who believe
and do good deeds of righteousness hath Allah promised forgiveness and a great reward.

Lawful unto you to eat are all things good and pure: do not eat dead meat or meat which has been partly eaten by an animal.
Do not be thoughtless about the life taken to eat but be solemn and thankful to the Lord for the food, to which we render the life back.

When ye prepare to eat, wash ye hands.

Do not eat in excess, for Allah loveth you to have good health.

The Lord did send down a table to Jesus, Mary, and the Disciples for a festival.
Jesus Christ was a Messenger and Mary was a woman of truth. Jesus made a figure of a bird out of clay and breathed life into it, and it became a bird.
Jesus and Mohammad both taught that remitting retaliation by way of laws of justice or charity is better than the old laws of Moses that said 'An eye for an eye' or 'A tooth for a tooth' or 'wound for a wound', and that to forgive others is an act of atonement that the Lord will find favorable on your soul.

For Allah forgiveth whom Allah forgiveth,
punisheth whom Allah punisheth, and pleaseth whom Allah pleaseth.

When ye prepare to pray, wash ye hands, faces, elbows, heads, and feet. Wash your whole body if you are in a state of ceremonial impurity. If ye cannot find clean water, rub your bodies with clean sand or earth.
The Lord Allah guideth all who seek the good pleasure of the Lord to ways of peace and safety, and leadeth them out of evil to a path that is straight and good.

Take only righteous believers as friends.

Marriage partners should be pure and good to each other.

When believers hear revelations from messengers, their eyes wilt overflow with tears, for they recognize the truth of the Holy Spirit and they pray: 'Our Lord! We believe; write us down among the witnesses.'

Those who are rebellious and commit evil are people without understanding of God.

Satan's plan is to excite enmity and hatred between believers, so cast Satan aside and take care of one another. Guard yourselves from evil. Guard your own souls; if ye follow right guidance, no hurt can come to you from those who stray.

The goal of you all is the Lord who will show you the truth of matters that ye dispute, who will show you peace and love for each other.

SURAH 6
The Cattle

The Lord created you from clay, and then decreed a stated term for your life.
The Lord created heavens, earth, darkness, and light.
There is not an animal on the earth, nor a being that flies, that will be omitted but gathered back to their Lord in the end.
Those who accept the Lord and listen in truth will be returned to the Lord in the end.
Do not let your hearts become hardened by suffering or Satan will make sinful acts seem alluring. Do not forget the Lord Allah, the Cherisher of the Worlds.

Say: 'I will not follow vain desires; If I did, I would disobey my Lord and stray from the path.'

Say: 'For me, I work on a clear sign from my Lord, but if ye reject Faith, what ye would see hastened is not in my power. The Command rests with none but the Lord who declares Truth, and the Lord is the best of judges.'

With the Lord are the keys to the seen and unseen treasures. The Lord knoweth whatever is on the earth and in the seas. The Lord produces the wind and rain and the clouds, and the stars as beacons in

the skies. Not a leaf doth fall but with the Lord's knowledge. There is not a grain of earth, nor anything fresh green or dry withered that is not recorded in the Record Clear.
The Lord takes your souls by night when you are asleep, and hath knowledge of all that ye have done day by day when the Lord raises you up again in the morning. In the end unto the Lord ye shall return. Then the Lord will show you the truth of all that ye did.
The Lord is irresistible from above over the worshippers and sets guardians over you. When death approaches, an angel will take your soul and they never fail in their duty.

Those who have lost their souls are the unbelievers.
The souls are returned unto the Lord Allah, their True Protector, surely the Lord is the Command and is the Swiftest in taking account.

It is the Lord Allah who created the heavens and earth; and the Lord will be the dominion the day the trumpet will be blown. The Lord knoweth the Unseen and the Seen, for the Lord is Wise and Well-Acquainted.
It is the Lord who produced you and the earth is a place of sojourn and departure. The Lord produces rain and vegetation of all kinds: grains, fruits, date palms,
gardens of grapes, and olives, and pomegranates,
each similar yet different. When they begin to bear fruit, feast your eyes with the fruit, and the ripeness thereof, and this is a sign for the people thereof.

And the invisible forces of the spirits of Jinn were created by the Lord Allah.
The jinns are not equal to Allah.
The Lord is above all Comprehension, yet is acquainted with all things.

Talk to the ones who are lost in their trespasses and wandering in distraction, and turn them toward the guidance of the Lord, so that they may dwell in the Hereafter.

When the night covered him over, Abraham saw a star he said; 'This is my Lord.'
When he saw a moon rising in splendor, he said: 'This is my Lord.'
When he saw the sun he said: 'This is also my Lord.'
And Abraham and his father Azar set their faces firmly and truly towards their Lord , the Perfect-Creator.

Every Messenger has evil enemies, but the Word of the Lord doth find its fufilment in truth and justice. Do not be mislead by evil jinns.

God's plan is all that hath been and all that will be.

For the righteous there will be a Home Of Peace in the presence of the Lord: the Lord will be their friend, because they practiced good deeds and kept the way of the Truth.

It is the Lord who produces the gardens and fruits for the day of the

harvest. Eat of the fruits of the season, but render the dues that are proper on the day the harvest is gathered.
Waste not by excess, for Allah loveth not the wasters. For meat, there are camels, cows, goats, ox, sheep, and fish with gills ad fins.

Say:
'Be good to your parents.
Kill not your children.
Come not to shameful deeds, whether open or secret.
Learn ye wisdom.
Guard the orphan's property until the age they are of full strength.
Speak justly.
Place no burden on any soul, but only that which it can bear.'

There are those who break up religion into sects, but fight ye not, for every soul draws the need for the Lord.

SURAH 7
The Heights

Say: The things that my Lord hath indeed forbidden are: shameful deeds, whether open or secret; sins and trespasses against truth or reason.

Follow the revelation given unto you from your Lord.
Each person has the term of their life, and then the Lord Allah will take you back. When the person's term is reached, there is no delay and there is no advance anticipation of the hour of their death.

To those who reject faith, the gates of Heaven may not open. But for the righteous, there will be Companions in the Garden of those who passed before you, and beneath them will be rivers flowing, to dwell in supreme felicity.

Pray for the Messengers to bring good tidings to us to prevent lost souls.
The Lord can turn suffering into prosperity.
Those who are near to the Lord, forget not to worship; celebrate praises and bow down before the Lord.
Let Satan not seduce you against truth and good reason.
Hold to forgiveness, charity,
Command what is right,
But turn away from ignorance and evil.
The Most Beautiful Names belong to Allah.

SURAH 8
The Spoils of War

When you need help, Lord Allah will assist you with a thousand
angels if need be – this is a message of hope and assurance to your hearts.
God is exalted in Power.

Remember the Lord
inspired the angels with:
'I am with you. Give hope and firmness to believers.'

Give your response to Allah when the Lord calleth you. And know that the Lord will cometh in between a person and their heart, and that is how ye shall be gathered.

The Lord accomplishes all matters, and to the Lord do all questions go back for decisions.

Fall into no disputes, lest ye lose heart and your power depart; be patient and persevering, for the Lord is with those who are patient and persevere.

The spoils of war bring things to ruin, so prevent wars with peace treaties if at all possible.

The only men who can guard the Sacred Mosque are the righteous.

In the end, those who do not believe in God may have sighs and regrets.

Allah loves the pure of heart.

There prevails justice and
faith in Allah;
Allah is your Protector –
The Best to Protect
And the Best to help.

Call on the Lord much and often that ye may succeed and prosper.
Allah will never change grace bestowed.

Let not the Unbelievers
think that they can
get the better of the godly;
they will never frustrate them.

Make ready your strength against enemies, but if an enemy inclines towards peace, do thou also incline towards peace.

SURAH 9

The Repentance

Fulfill obligations that ye have entered into that the alliance hath not failed you nor aided anyone against you, for Allah love the righteous.
As long as Pagans of other religions stand true to a treaty made with you, stand ye true to them, for Allah love the righteous who fulfill obligations.

Allah should be dearer to you than any earthly ties or comforts.

Little is the comfort of this life, as compared with the Hereafter.

Zakah is charity; charitable gifts for the poor and needy, and for those employed to administer the gifts to help those in bondage, slavery, or strangers that may be lost, or those who have recently returned to Faith and need help.
Allah doth receive repentance from rotaries and gifts of charity; Allah will observe your work.
Allah is the knower of what is hidden and open, and will show you the truth of all that ye did on the Day of Judgement.
The Believers, men and women, are protectors, one of another; they
enjoin what is just, and
forbid what is evil: they
observe regular prayers,
practice regular charity,
and obey the Lord.

Believers lay their foundation on piety to Allah instead of building their foundation on sand,
which may crumble to pieces -
Which then is best?

Hypocrites are those who enjoin evil and forbid what is just; they have forgotten Allah's path of goodness.
Allah is Ever-Loving.
On Allah is my trust - Allah is the Lord of the Throne Supreme!

SURAH 10
Jonah

Remember verses of good wisdom.

Nothing is hidden from the Lord, not even the weight of an atom. All things and all life depend on God for its sustenance; all things are recorded in a Clear Record.

Those who receive guidance from the Lord do so for their own souls; those who stray, do so to their own loss - this is The Criterion between right and wrong.
The Lord enables you to transgress through winds and sea, even when you board a ship and are being overwhelmed with winds and waves; or as Jonah who was swallowed by the whale; you offer to the Lord: 'If thou will deliver us from this, we shall truly show our gratitude' but when Allah delivereth them, they forget about Allah because their enjoyment of life is only of the present, but you must remember that your goal is eternal life with the Lord. There is the likeness of the life of the present, by night or by day, and we make it, but Allah doth call us to the Home of Peace; Allah doth guide whom Allah pleaseth to a way that is good, which is the way to the Eternal Home with Allah.
Follow thou the inspiration sent unto thee, and be patient and constant, and thou will follow the straight good way.
Those who have earned evil will receive a reward of evil, this is a path to Satan.

A whole lifetime did Mohammad al Mustafa live in purity and virtue amongst his people, pleading with them to avoid sin and wrongdoing.

The people are scattered on different continents and have different piety and religions, but it still reverts back to the same ultimate Divine Reality.

SURAH 11
Prophet Hud

The prophet Hud taught:
Seek ye the forgiveness of your Lord. Turn to the Lord in repentance; that the Lord Allah may grant you enjoyment and bounties, and bestow abounding grace on all who abound in merit!

Say: 'I seek no wealth; my reward is from the Unseen Lord who created me.'

SURAH 12
Prophet Joseph (Yusuf in Arabic)

The prophet Joseph did say that the human soul is prone to evil, but strive to be true and virtuous, and constant in righteousness.
Joseph (Yusuf) the Israelite was sold into slavery by his brothers to an Egyptian pharaoh, but Joseph did forgive his brothers.

Rely on Allah (God).

The home of the Hereafter is best, for those who do right. Will ye not understand?

Angels will assist Messengers to help deliver the people to safety.

SURAH 13
The Thunder

The Lord is the Throne of Authority Who holds the heavens in place with no pillars. The sun and moon are subjected to the Lord's authority.

The Lord regulates all affairs, the night and the day, even the rain and thunderbolts, the pollinating winds, and all flowers, grains, vines, plants, and all animal pairs. Some plants are more excellent to eat than others.

The Lord knows what the female womb doth bear.

The Lord knows the Seen and Unseen.

The Lord knows when you conceal speech or declare it openly.

The Lord shows you the lightening, by way of fear or hope.
Behold! Verily in these things are signs for those who understand that the Lord regulates all affairs so ye may believe with certainty in the meeting with your Lord.

Angels surround each person and the angels are commanded by the Lord Allah.

Heaven will be perpetual for the righteous, a Beautiful Place of Return,
Where you will be among your mother, father, spouse, children, friends, ancestors, and angels.

Unbelievers will never have peace in their hearts but only unrest.

With Allah is the mother of the surahs.

SURAH 14
Abraham

Those who love the life of this world more than the Hereafter and seek evil and dishonest ways upon the earth are astray from righteousness by a long distance.

Teach those who have strayed to remember the favours that the Lord has bestowed on them. Teach all to be grateful for what has been given to them.

Let there be no doubt that the Lord is the Creator of heavens and earth; believe as Abraham did. Abraham lived 175 years and Sarah lived 127 years; they were both believers.

We are human and the Lord is our Authority so we should put our trust in Allah.

The works of the evil are ashes, and they have strayed far from the goals of the Lord.
Do not follow Satan.

The parable of the goodly tree
The parable of the goodly word is like a goodly tree, whose roots are firmly planted, and its branches reach to Heaven.

And the parable of the evil word is of a tree that has no stability.

If you tried to count the favours that the Lord has done for you, you would be unable to count them.
'O My Lord! Make me One who establishes regular prayer and also among my offspring establish regular prayer.'
'O our Lord! Cover us with Thy Forgiveness – me, my parents, and all believers, on the Day of Reckoning.'

SURAH 15
The Gates of Heaven

Adore thy Lord, the Sources of All Treasures are with Allah, the Creator and Sustainer of the Worlds. When the time comes of the Certain Hour, let a gate of Heaven be opened so that all Believers can ascend, one by one, to the Irresistible Lord and the endless Treasures, and there are seven gates.

The Lord set out the Zodiac signs in the heavens and made them beautiful to behold, and the earth is like a carpet, mountains grand, and produced all things in balance.

The Lord sends down in due and ascertainable measures our needs, but the Lord's powers and treasures are inexhaustible and endless.

The Lord created humans from clay and mud molded into shape and gave humans a spirit.

Verily, the Lord is the Master-Creator, Knowing all things.

Iblis, also called Satan, was cast out of Heaven for being rebellious against the Lord.

The righteous will be amid garden and fountains, and pleasant rivers. Their greeting will be: 'Enter ye here in Peace & Security.'
Any injuries will be removed from their hearts. Believers will face each other on thrones of dignity. No sense of fatigue shall touch them, nor shall they ever be asked to leave glad tidings that will be given to them openly.

SURAH 16
The Bees

The Lord sends angels with inspirations from the Lord. The angel Gabriel brings revelations.

The Lord created humans, who forget the Creator at times.
The Lord gave humans the animals to help them carry heavy loads to lands that they could not.
The Lord created horses, mules, donkeys for humans to ride and use for show.
The Lord created camels and goats, the fur of which is used to make garments, blankets, and tents to keep humans warm. The milk of female goats and cattle is good to drink. Some eat the flesh of such animals.
The Lord gave vegetation to eat such as corn, olives, date palms, and grapes, and every kind of fruit, and ye may get wholesome drink from the milk of cows and from the drink of fruits. And the Lord taught the Bee how to build Beehives and make Honey.

These are Signs for those who give thought.

The Lord made seas to travel and the fish to swim and eat thereof, and mountains to climb, rivers and roads to travel.

Who can create like the Lord?

To the righteous, Gardens of Eternity they will enter.
But they do not know when they will be raised up.
And the angels will say 'Peace be on you, enter the Garden, because of the good which ye did in the world.'

Allah has made for you mates of your own nature, and made for you, out of them, sons and daughters, and grandchildren.
To the Lord belongeth the Mystery to all things.

Whoever works righteousness, whether man or woman, and has Faith, verily, they will have a good and pure reward.

There is the parable of two men; one dumb and a wearisome burden to his master, and one who commands justice and is on the good way.

At one time male babies were preferred to female babies – this was evil.

If Allah were to punish humans for their sins and wrongdoing, there would not be a single human left on the earth.

Allah preaches the Clear Message to stay on the good path and to put your trust in the Lord and revere the Lord.
Love the Lord more than the life of this world.

Allah is with those who restrain themselves, those who do good, and those who show gratitude.
Allah forbids shameful deeds and injustice.

SURAH 17

The Most Beautiful Names

On the Day of Judgement the angels will bring out a scroll for every person to see of thine own record.

The Lord is the Only Supreme Judge at that time.
The bounties of thy Lord
are not closed to anyone
but only thy Lord has knowledge of those who receive bounties.

Follow Good Criterion

Worship the Lord and be kind to parents; when thy parents attain old age in thy life, say not to them a word of contempt, nor repel them, but address them in terms of honour.
And, out of kindness, lower to thy parents a wing of humility, and say:
'My Lord! Bestow on them Thy
Mercy even as they
Cherished me in childhood.'

Your Lord knoweth best what is in your hearts: If ye do deeds of righteousness, verily the Lord is Most Forgiving to those who turn to the Lord again and again.

And render to kindred their due rights, and it is kind to help thy kindred and those in want.
And even if thou hast to turn away from them, speak to them a word of easy kindness.

Kill not your children; verily the killing of them is a great sin.
Sons and daughters are both to be cherished.

Nor come nigh to unlawful sex for it is a shameful deed and an evil.

Nor take life – which is given by the Lord – except for just cause according to the laws of 'a life for a life' – for if anyone is slain wrongfully, then it is wrong.

Do not take advantage of orphans, only try to improve their situation until they attain the age of
full strength.

Do not take advantage of anyone to diminish them in any way.

Give full measure when ye measure, and weigh with a balance that is straight:
that is the most fitting
and the most advantageous
in the final determination.

Pursue not that of which thou hast no need to know, to avoid trouble.

Nor walk on the earth with insolence or arrogance, but walk a steady walk.

Of all such things the evil
is hateful in the sight of the Lord.

These are among the precepts of wisdom of thy Lord that humans have discerned.

Say to the Lord's servants that they should only say these things that are best.
As for servants of the Lord, Satan shall have no authority over them - enough is the Lord for a disposer of affairs.

Call upon the Lord when the ship sails smoothly or in distress.

Satan sows dissensions among people, and Satan is to humans an avowed enemy.

Establish regular prayers – at the sun's decline till the darkness of the night, and the morning prayer and reading: for the prayer
and reading in the morning carry their testimony.

And pray in the small watches of the morning:
An additional prayer for thee: soon will thy Lord raise thee to a Station Of Praise and Glory!

Say: 'O My Lord!
Let my entry be
By the Gate of Truth
And Honour, and likewise
My exit by the Gate
Of Truth and Honour;
And grant me
From Thy Presence
An authority to aid me.

And say: 'Truth as arrived,
And Falsehood perished':
For Falsehood is
bound to perish.

Do not give up to despair, for the Lord is thy help.
When ye are happy, realize
it is from the Lord;
Be thankful for the Lord's favours.

Everyone acts according to their own disposition, but the best guidance is from
your Lord, so hold fast to God.

Concerning The Spirit of Inspiration,
Say: 'The Spirit cometh
by command of my Lord:
of knowledge it is only
a little that is communicated to men and women on earth.'

There are some who shall not believe in God until God causeth for them a spring of water to gush forth or a garden of date trees to grow, or a house adorned with gold, or a book to be read, or until Allah and the angels are before them face to face. Say to them: 'Enough is the Lord's creation of the heavens and the earth, and all animals, plants, and humankind – for me these are signs that serve as a witness between me and you to believe in my Lord.'
Can the unbelievers not understand and believe?
Do not the unbelievers see the glorious works of the Lord in all creation?

By whatever name ye call upon the Lord it is well, for to the Lord belong the Most Beautiful Names.

Call upon Allah or call upon Al Rahman which means 'Grace and Mercy'; by whatever name you call the Lord, it is well.
Magnify the Lord
for the Lord's greatness and glory.

SURAH 18
The Cave

Praise Allah, who brings *good news.*

The earth is but a glittering show
that is a test for human conduct;
what is on the earth is dust.

Seven youths who were companions were afraid because they worshipped the Lord of the heavens and there was religious fighting over the name of the Spirit, so they hid in a cave and fell asleep for 309 years. The angels turned them on their right and left sides when they were sleeping and took care of their dog. A traveler smashed in the cave wall and the companions of the cave woke up. They all had different opinions about how long they had been there, but one of the youths had money and gave it to one of them to go into town to get food. Their case was known to the people that the Lord Allah protected them from religious persecution while sleeping in the cave for 309 years and while they were unaware of anything happening in the outside world.

As to those who believe and work righteousness
the reward for them
will be Gardens Of Eternity; beneath them Rivers will flow: they will be adorned therein
With bracelets of gold and pearls,
And they will wear
Green garments of fine silk
And heavy brocade;
They will recline therein
on raised thrones.
How good the recompense!
How beautiful a couch
to recline on!

There is the parable of two men who both had gardens of grapes surrounded by date palms with cornfields and a river therein also. The man who was more wealthy boasted to the other of his wealth and power, but the other reminded him of the power of the Lord Allah, who giveth all things and said 'Dost thou see me less than thee in wealth, but there is no power except from the Lord. It may be that my Lord will give me something better than thy garden.' And when the garden of the wealthy one was tumbled to pieces, he said 'Woe is me! I should have put my hope in the Lord instead of my wealth.' Because the allurements of the life of the world do not endure, but the things
that endure are the foundation of hope in the Lord and Good Deeds.

Evil is the exchange for those who bow down to Iblis.

On the day when the trumpet will be blown, we shall be collected together and the promise of the Lord will be true as to each our reward,
On the Day of Judgment all people will appear before the Lord in the appointment to meet us; and the Book of Deeds will be placed before you – it leaves out nothing, but takes account thereof your entire life, - and the Lord will call on those thought to be Partners with the Lord.
Those who believe and work righteousness deeds will have Gardens of Paradise, but those who

reject Faith and are wicked will be judged by the Lord.

Say: 'I am but a man or woman like yourselves, the inspiration has come to me, that Your God is One God; whoever expects to meet his Lord, let him or her work righteousness, and in the worship of thy Lord, let nothing lead him or her astray.'

Say: 'If the ocean were ink wherewith to write out the words of my Lord, sooner would the ocean be exhausted than would the words of my Lord, even if we added another ocean like it for its aid.'

SURAH 19

Mary (Mariam in Arabic)

Mary (Mariam) gave birth to Jesus at the base of a palm tree in a tent when she and Joseph (Yusuf) were on a sojourn.

Jesus said: 'I am indeed a servant of the Lord who gave me revelation. The Lord made me blessed wheresoever I be, and hath enjoined on me prayer and charity as long as I live. The Lord made me kind to my mother, Mary and my father, Joseph, (Yusuf) not overbearing and miserable. So peace is on me the day I was born, the day that I die, and when my spirit is resurrected.'

The Gardens will be the inheritances of those who guard against evil; this is known only by Allah.

The angels say: 'We descend not but by the command of thy Lord: to the Lord belongeth what is before us, and what is behind us, and what is between; and the Lord never doth forget. -
Lord of the Heavens and of the earth, and of all that is between them,
so worship the Lord, and be constant and patient; there is none of the same Name as the Lord!'

The Lord created everything from nothing, such is the power of the Lord, the Originator of All Creation.

The Lord will gather the believers, but the wrongdoers will be humbled to their knees.

If anyone go astray, Allah the Most Gracious extends the rope to them to advance them in guidance.
Allah doth advance in guidance those who seek Guidance; and the things
that endure are Good Deeds, are best.
Let not evil ones incite the good ones with fury, but let the righteous continue in the good ways of God.

It may be for those who serve Satan, a penalty will be afflicted by Lord Allah.

Let all believers hasten to the Lord into the realm of safety and righteousness; avoid the bridge to the seven gates of hell.
Of Mashhat (Judgement Day), On the day the angels will gather the righteous, they will be put before Allah like a band presented before a king for honours.

SURAH 20

O, Humanity!

O, men and women!

Even the magicians at the Day of the Festival believe in the power of the Lord; the magic of magicians is but what they have faked in tricks but the power of the Lord is the truth.

Allah hath given to you all sustenance for spiritual and physical survival, do not take this for granted or use this for evil purposes.

Celebrate constantly the
praises of thy Lord before the rising
of the sun, and before its setting,
and during the day and night,
that thou mayest have joy;
just as through a fire
Moses spoke to the Lord;
the Lord told Moses:
'I have chosen thee to inspiration to
establish prayer and goodness
among the people.'

Ask the Lord for guidance to follow Thy Signs before we are humbled and put to shame.

Say: 'Each is praying and waiting to know who it is that is on the straight even way, and who it is that has received guidance.'

The angels sent down the surahs to establish a revelation between humans and the Lord, To Whom belongs beautiful names.

The Caller is the angel whose voice will call all people and direct them to the Lord's presence o Judgement Day.

Be patient with what you say and do, and celebrate Allah constantly. A human is a creature of haste, so be patient in order that you may be safe by day and night.

SURAH 21

The Prophets

Seek the Blessed Messages of the Holy Prophet and the Criterion of the Lord, that thee will follow good ways.

The Good Criterion was given to all of the prophets: Moses, Aaron, Abraham, Noah, David who sought justice, Ezekiel (Dhu al Kifl), Solomon, Job, Ismail, Idris, Jonah (Dhu al Nun) who turned to God after a misunderstanding, Zakariya, Mary, and all men and women of patience and constancy.

Idris was a man of truth, sincere, and a prophet who had a high position among the people; he kept to truth and piety.

The wrongdoers conceal private counsels for evil causes, but the righteous follow the good messages. The Lord knoweth all words spoken and knoweth all things.

Say: 'My Lord knoweth every word spoken in the heavens and on earth. The Lord is the One that heareth and knoweth all things.'

The Lord of the Throne cannot be questioned for divine actions.
The Lord hath made the mountains and the highways in between so we can pass through the mountains, like guidance.
The Lord hath made the heavens as a canopy, the breath of life, the sun, and the moon, the night and the day, the hills, trees, animals, birds, wind, rain, and humankind; these are the Signs which point to the Lord. The Lord Allah doth protect you, and this is also a Sign for you. Do not the unbelievers see these signs of God?

Say: 'The Lord is the Lord of the Heavens and Earth. The Lord created all things, and I am a witness to this truth.'

The scales of justice will be set for the Day of Judgement. Not a soul will be dealt with unjustly in the least. Nor more than a mustard seed will be brought into account.

No good deed is fruitless; the good will multiply.

Whoever works any act of righteousness and faith – his or her endeavor will not be rejected: the angels will record it in their favour.

Those who stay in good ways are admitted to mercy and unity of believers. Generations before you, now, and after you are under the guidance of the Lord.

The Lord knows what is open in speech and what you hide in your hearts.

Say: 'O my Lord! Judge Thou in truth! Our Lord Most Gracious is the One Whose assistance should be sought against blasphemies that we utter.'

SURAH 22

The Pilgrimage

O humankind! Know your Lord! Follow the good ways of the Lord. There will be a Judgment Day when the good souls will be separated from the evil souls.

It is decreed that whoever turns to the Evil One (Iblis) (Satan) will be led astray.

But whoever follows the Spirit of the Divine Reality,
The Lord who created all things and gives life and universe, will have eternal life in Heaven.
If ye have a doubt about your resurrection, consider that Lord Allah has created you out of dust to your manifest as babes, then to full strength, then to the feebleness of old age when you are called to die and sent back. And, as you can see, this is true about life such as animals in pairs and plants. This is so, because Allah is the Reality who gives life and has power over all things.
Holy Books of Enlightenment comfort and guide humans to stay close to the Holy Spirit; do not let Satan lead you astray to mischief.
There are some people who love God if good befalls them, they are therewith well content; but if hardship comes to them, they turn

their faces and lose faith - they lose both this world and the Hereafter - this loss is straying from the way of the good.
Seest thou to worship and honor Allah for all things in heaven and earth - the symbols of the sun, moon, stars, hills, trees, animals, plants, and people.
Those who believe and work righteous deeds will be admitted to Heavenly Gardens of Delight of beneath which rivers flow; they shall be adorned with bracelets of gold and pearls, garments of silk, feasting on fruit, and relaxing on couches among other believers.

Allah is just to those who serve thy Lord.
Those who work righteous deeds have been guided to the Path of the Lord Who is Worthy of all Praise.
Those who reject the good ways of the Lord will suffer a most grievous penalty.

Your God is One God; submit then your wills to the Lord and give thou the good news to those who humble themselves, for Allah giveth sustenance to you.
Celebrate the name of Allah over the sustenance given for human survival. Give this good news to others. Allah loveth those who show gratitude in thanks.

The camels and cattle that ye sacrifice to eat are among the Symbols from Allah that are good for you, and beg with humility that Allah has made the animals subject to you, that ye may be grateful.

The camels are used for mounts to carry burdens,
the goats for milk, the sheep for hair and wool, the camel's hair for cloth.

Permission is given to fight only in self-defense or if you are wronged, such as being put out of your homes unjustly.

Permission is given to fight to defend mosques and houses that are commemorated for prayer to Allah.
Do not destroy monasteries, churches, synagogues, or temples of other religions.

Establish prayer and charity, enjoin the right and forbid the wrong, and travel through the lands to learn wisdom.
Take care of wells and castles - make sure they are well built.

A day in the sight of the Lord is like a thousand years of your reckoning.

Allah will cancel any vanity that Satan throws to prophets or messengers.

Those who believe and work righteousness, for them is forgiveness and a sustenance Most generous.
The Day of Dominion will be the day the Lord has conquered Satan forever and all evil will be gone.

Allah is the Lord who understands the finest mysteries.
Allah merges day into night and night into day,

And sends spring rain after winter
to clothe the earth in green again.
Allah is the Spirit of all things.
Allah is free of all wants because
everything belongs to the Lord; the
Lord is worthy of all praise.

Allah chooses Messengers from angels and humans for Allah's work.

Bow down, prostrate yourselves, or stand, and adore your Lord; and do good;
make a pilgrimage to the mosque,
that ye spirit may prosper.
Establish regular prayer,
Give regular charity,
And host fast to Allah!
Allah is your Protector –
The best to protect you and the Best to help you!

SURAH 23
The Believers

Those who humble themselves in prayer,
Who establish regular prayer,
Who avoid vain talk,
Who are active in deeds of charity,
Who do good works,
Who care for orphans,
Who care for the poor,
Who help the lost,
Who love their family and friends,
Who do no evil,
Who abstain from sex except with those joined in the marriage bond,
Are free from blame,
And will be heirs who will inherit Paradise forever.
But those whose desires exceed these limits are transgressors.

The Lord created a human to grow from a sperm cell and an ovum that hath joined together. Then the Lord breathed the Holy Spirit into you and all animals and plants.

On the Day of Judgement, ye will be judged.

The Lord grows for you benefits like gardens of date palms, vines, abundant fruits, and olives; the Lord sends water and sunlight; the Lord created cattle, sheep, goats – from their bodies within, the Lord gives milk to drink and meat to eat and, on the animals ye ride as well as in ships.

The Lord sent before you in previous generations a long line of prophets to give you guidance such as Noah, Moses and his brother Aaron, Jesus, and Mohammad.

And messengers for the Lord Allah who dispense their charity with their hearts and hasten every good work will enjoy all things good and pure, and verily the Believers follow the Lord and Cherisher.

Revenge is not the way to go; two evils do not make a good. Do what is lawful.
Repel evil with what is best – leave it to Allah.
Say: 'I seek refuge with Thee and repel the suggestions of the evil ones or lest they should come near me!'

Those whose balance of good deeds is heavy, they will attain salvation in the seven heavens.

Do you think the Lord has created you in jest, and that you will not be brought back to be accountable for ye actions? Verily, the Lord knows all of your actions and there will be a day of reckoning.

Say: 'O My Lord! Grant thou forgiveness and mercy, for Thou art the best of those who show Mercy.'

Believers have left their affair of unity and have divided into sects; each party is rejoicing only in that which is itself - this is confused ignorance - those who believe in the Holy Spirit should be united in harmony.
The recompense of the Lord is best: Allah is the best of those who give sustenance.

Those who disperse charity with good hearts and hasten to do good works will return to their Lord. On no soul will the Lord place a burden greater than it can bear, for Lord knows everything.
But verily thou callest all to the Straight Way (the Good Way).

It is Allah Who created you and gave you faculties of hearing, sight, and feeling, and understanding. And Allah has multiplied you upon the earth, and Allah will gather you Back, for Allah giveth life and death.

SURAH 24
The Light

Believers of the Lord do not tell lies but speak the light and purity of truth. Slander and lies are evil and a serious matter in the concern of Allah.

Men and women should honour their marriage.

Witnesses should speak the truth.

Allah loveth not a liar.

Allah is full of knowledge,
Wisdom, truth, kindness, and mercy; and these are the Signs of Allah.

O you who believe! Follow not Satan's footsteps. If any follow Satan they will only command what is shameful and wrong.

Allah loveth what is pure and just, and Allah loveth the truth.

The Holy Spirit is the Truth that makes all things manifest.

Enter not houses other than your own, until ye have asked permission and saluted those in them: that is best for you, in order that ye may heed respect.
If ye find no one in the house, enter not until permission is given to you; if ye are asked to go back, go back; that makes for greater purity for yourselves, and Allah knows all that ye do.

Say to believing men and women that they should lower their gaze and guard their modesty, for chastity and purity of heart are

virtues to behold in the goods of this life;
Moderation and self-restraint keep believers in the good way.

In a household, men and women of age should dress modestly and be pure in conduct.

Children should ask permission to seniors of the household rules.

All should ask for permission to enter a room before the morning prayer, after the evening prayer, and when clothes are taken off for sleep.

Force not slavery, prostitution, scandalous conduct, false witness, mischief, or lies.
Those who perform wicked acts are unbelievers.

Believers of holy laws are on right guidance and work righteous deeds.

Eat in your own houses or those of your father, mother, brother, sister, father's brother, father's sister, mother's brother, mother's sister, the houses of friends, or the houses of which the keys are in your possession.
No blame on you, whether ye eat in company or by yourself separately.

SURAH 25
The Criterion

Blessed is the Lord who sent the Criterion of wrong and right to Messengers, to Whom belongs the dominion of the Heavens and Earth and Universe, who created all things in due proportions.

If the believers follow the revelation of the Good Criterion, they will find Gardens of Bliss on the Day of the Trumpet.
Blessed is the believer who, if they could, would give thee better things than even the Treasures of the Eternal Garden.

Say: 'Of good or evil, which is best? For the good ways, the promised eternal Garden is a reward as well as a goal.

For the righteous, in the eternal Garden will be all that they wish for, a promise to be prayed for from thy Lord.'
The Day the Lord will gather all the together, the righteous will be asked, 'Why did my other servants go astray?'

The righteous will say: 'Glory to Thee! We sought the protection of our Lord but They forgot the good messages and were a people who went lost.'

And the Lord will say: 'I will never lose patience in gathering to me all of my lost sheep.'

The Day of Judgment will be joyful for the good ones; they will be among the angels and the Companions of the Gardens of Bliss, and all will be well in the Dominion of Truth.

The Lord will deal with those who have rejected faith and the ways of the good ones.
The Lord could prolong a shadow if it was the Lord's will; the Lord's will is what keeps the sun shining and the earth revolving. The Lord made sleep as a repose and the awakening as a resurrection.
The Lord made the sweet waters and the salt waters.

The Holy Spirit is distributed over all, that all may celebrate praise; yet some are averse with ingratitude and are not
making Heaven their goal.

Listen not to the wicked, but join the ranks of the righteous, who bring good deeds and glad tidings to others.

Say: 'I beg of thee to take a good path to the Lord, the one who created the heaven and earth. No reward do I ask of you for this good message; my reward is only from the Lord.'

Blessed is the Creator who made constellations in the skies and placed therein the lamp of the sun and the moon of reflective light, and the day and night which follow each other, like conscious and sleep.

Adore thy Lord!

If thy balance be heavy on the good side, then thou shall be honourable to Allah.

SURAH 26

Moses

The verses of the Holy Books make it clear that the Lord is Exalted in Might, the Most Merciful, the Lord and Cherisher of the Worlds.

There are some Jews, Egyptians, Christians, Greeks, Romans, Syrians, and Muslims who were still fighting over differences even though a long time had passed.

Say: 'My desire is that My Lord will forgive my faults as I become a believer.

The Lord and Cherisher of the Worlds created me, guides me, gives me food and drink, cures me when I am ill, will cause me to die, and then to live again. And who, I hope, will forgive my faults at my resurrection.'

And Moses parted the sea when he led the Israelite Jews who were the Hebrews back from Egypt, and the waters closed when they reached the far side.
And Moses and his attendant were traveling to reach the junction of the Gulf of Agabah and the Gulf of Suez at the Sinai Peninsula and came upon the servant Khidr who was bestowed with knowledge from the Divine. Moses said: 'May I follow you, Khidr, so that you may teach me something?' And Khidr said: 'Only if you do not ask any questions and be patient with me.'
So they came upon a boat,
and Khidr did scuttle (sink) the boat. And Moses did not speak but

thought 'Surely that is a strange thing to scuttle the boat.'
Next they came upon a wall which had fallen, and Khidr did put up the wall without asking for recompense. And Moses did not speak but thought 'That was generous of him to fix the wall without asking for payment.'
Then Khidr said: 'Now I will tell thee the interpretation of those things which I asked of thou patience. As for the boat, it belonged to a certain man in dire need, yet it was seized, stolen and docked by a certain king of force. As for the wall, I happen to know of a buried treasure that belongs to two orphans to which they are entitled and now they can find it – their father was a righteous man.'
And Moses also said:
'O my Lord! Bestow wisdom on me and join me with the righteous.
Grant me honourable mention in the words of truth among my generation.
Make me one of the inheritors of the Garden of Bliss;
Do not let me be in disgrace on the Day of Judgment.'

The day that the Lord will draw the Garden near for the righteous,
the gates will be shut to the wicked.

The Lord gave you to enjoy, gardens and springs,
cornfields, date palms, fruit, houses, caves,
animals, mates, friends –
will you not enjoy your life and give remembrance
of these things to the Lord?

Touch a camel not with harm, for the camel has a right to watering just as you have a right.

Lut (Lot) loves the marriage of a man and woman so keep the union sacred.

Give just measure, weigh with scales true and upright.

Cause no loss to others by fraud.

Withhold not things justly due to men or women, orphans, or widows.

Do no evil or mischief.

Let thy revelations to Thy Hearts and Minds be the Spirit of Faith and Truth.
Without a doubt, the Holy Spirit is pure and good. Lower thy wing, O Lord, to the Believers who follow Thee.

SURAH 27

The Ants

Those who establish regular prayer and give in regular charity will have a blessed assurance of the hereafter. Those who do not believe may wander in distraction, pray that the Lord may direct the lost back to the good way.

Reject evil so thy soul will not be corrupt.

Queen Bilquis (Sheba) (952-992BCE) came from Yemen, her son was Menyelek; she visited Solomon's region.

One of the ants said: 'O ye ants, get into your underground habitations, lest Solomon's army will crush you under foot without knowing it.'

Say: 'O my Lord. Order me that I may be grateful for Thy Favours which Thou has bestowed on me and my parents and friends, and that I may work righteousness that will please thee, and to share my abundance with others. Then admit me, by Thy Grace, to the ranks of Thy Righteous Servants.'

Who listens to the soul distressed when it calls, relieves its suffering, and makes humans inheritors of the earth? – none other than God!

Who guides you, sends angels who are heralds of glad tidings, originated all creation, and gives humans sustenance? – none other than God!

There is nothing seen or unseen that isn't recorded in a clear record kept by God.

Thou seest the mountains, valleys, and clouds, but they may change and pass away – such is the artistry of Allah.

Ifrit was a jinn who could be trusted by the Lord.

SURAH 28
The Narrations

The verses of the Holy Koran make things clear.

Moses and the Pharaoh
prayed together by the river before Moses departed from Egypt to lead the Jews back to the land of the Israelites.

Hearken not to follow the lusts of your heart, instead follow God.

When believers hear vain talks, turn away and say: 'To us our deeds, and to you, yours. Peace be to you.'

Allah will guide those who believe in righteousness.
Spiritual goods are better than material goods.

A person is what they are,
not what they have.

For those who return from wicked ways to good ways, they will achieve salvation for their souls.

If any one does good, the reward is better than the deed. If any does evil, it is punished to the extent of the law. The Lord hath a Clear Record of all things.

SURAH 29
The Spider

God is free from needs, since God created everything.

Enjoin kindness on your parents.

Allah (God) knoweth the believers from the hypocrites.

On the Day of Judgment, all people will receive just rewards or just burdens.

Allah originated all creation and Allah will produce later creations, for Allah has power over all things.

Allah directed Noah to build the Ark before the flood, and Allah did give Abraham, Isaac, Ismael, Jacob, and Lut (Lot) divine wisdom.

The parable of the spider web is to know of the wisdom of Allah, for Allah giveth the knowledge to the spider to construct the radiating threads of silk from the central point. The web looks flimsy, but an insect caught will cause vibrations to occur throughout the web to alert the spider of the prey; the revelation to the spider of his sustenance. The spider web is a Clear Sign of the Work of the Lord.

The Lord knows everything that is in the Universe, in Heaven, and on the Earth; The Lord is the Cherisher Of All Creation.

When you embark on a boat, or on your feet to walk – call on Allah Your Lord to deliver you safely to your destination.

SURAH 30
The Eternal

The Lord is in the Past, in the Future, and in the Present.
The Lord will not depart from the Earth.

On the hour of the day that believers are summoned, believers will dwell in tranquility with Companions of the Garden.

Set thy face steadily and firmly in good faith with the Lord. Cry to the Lord in prayer in times of trouble, and the Lord will receive your cry for help.
The Lord is merciful and kind, and will send angels and jinn to help thee to strength and prosperity.

From your own wealth, give to family, the needy, and the stranger if they need help; and Allah will multiply your recompense.

Those who reject faith suffer a loss but those who work righteousness will see rewards, for the Lord loveth righteous good deeds.

It is the Lord who creates you as a babe and weak, then gives you strength in adulthood, then brings you to the feebleness of old age; and then brings you back to heaven; such stages in life is the Lord's will and promise.

SURAH 31
LUQMAN the Wise

There are those people who will prefer idle tales to realities to mislead from the path of Allah, announce to them that Allah will judge them on Judgment Day.
But enjoin them back onto the good path so they will dwell with the Lord who created them.

The Lord set heavens and mountains firm, without any pillars to hold them up, and scattered creatures of all kinds in pairs and some creatures not in pairs, set rains to fall from the sky, such are the Creations of the Lord.

The divine wisdom bestowed in Luqman was:
'showing thy gratitude to Allah will profit thy own soul,'

'showing thy gratitude to thy parents and treating them good is righteous.'

'O my son!' said Luqman
'If there be but the weight of a tiny mustard seed hidden in a rock, or anywhere on earth or in the heavens, the Lord will bring it forth, for Allah understands the finer mysteries and is well-acquainted with them.'

'O my son!'
'Establish regular prayer, enjoin what is just, and forbid what is wrong; and bear with patient constancy whatever betide thee, for this is firmness of purpose in the conduct of affairs. Be moderate in thy pace and in thy voice.'

Walk not in pride and insolence through the earth, for Allah loveth not any arrogant boastings.

Do you not see that Allah will use all things, seen and unseen, in the heavens and on earth to bestow bounties to you in exceeding measures both seen and unseen? This is a revelation from Allah.

Whoever submits their whole self to the Lord and is a doer of good, has grasped indeed the most trustworthy handhold; and with the Lord rests the End, the final goal, and Decision of All Affairs.

Every soul will return to the Lord for its reckoning.
The Lord will know the souls of the good doers and the souls of the evil doers.

Each person's individual creation and resurrection is of knowledge to God.

The sun and moon, and night and day, are subject to Allah's law.

Our Creator is the Divine Reality.

Do your good duties to your Lord.

The day of Account is coming when no parent can avail aught for his child, nor can a child avail aught for his parent.
Keep to the promise of the Lord, and let not the Chief Deceiver Iblis (Satan) deceive you.

Only the Lord knows what will happen tomorrow.

SURAH 32
The Angels

We, the Angels, bring forth truth and divine works from the Lord Allah.

Allah created the heavens in six days.

The Lord rules from the heavens, and to the Lord one day is like a thousand years of earth days, because the Lord's time is eternal in past, present, and future generations.

The Lord has fashioned the human in due proportion and breathed into the human the spirit of life. Give thanks for the abilities to hear, see, taste, and feel. Give thanks for thy mind, so that thy reason may be good.

You may hear the message of the Lord, have inner vision, and feel the love and have understandings of life, and taste of the sustenance – the salty, the sweet, the bitter.

There are skeptics who do not believe in a life hereafter and deny the meeting with their Lord but say to them 'The Angel Death doth take your soul back to your Lord.'

The will of the Lord will come true.
The Lord will judge humans and jinns.
Jinn spirits should not tempt humans.

Believe in the Lord,
Adore the Lord,
Call on the Lord,
With hope,
And spend in charity –
For those who do good and those who are rebellious and wicked are not equal.

The Lord has given guidance to previous generations through Moses, Jesus, and Mohammad.

The Lord Allah commands the rain to moisten the parched soil and therewith to produce crops for the cattle and the people;
How can the unbelievers not believe in the Lord?
There will be a Day of Decision when the Lord will grant the Believers respite, but the unbelievers will have no respite.

SURAH 33
Khadijah

Allah is full of knowledge and wisdom. Put thy trust is Allah, and enough is Allah as a Disposer of Affairs.
Allah has not made for any one two hearts in one body; therefore when you have two hearts, seek Allah for the good decision of wisdom of the way to go.
What counts to the Lord Allah is the intentions of your heart.

The Prophet Mohammad is closer to the Believers than their own selves. The Prophet's wife, Khadijah, is like a mother to others, administering charity and kindness.

Blood-relations among each other have close personal ties. Adopted-relatives are to be treated as brothers and sisters in faith and to be treated kindly.

Do what is right and just to your closest friends.

We, the angels, gave instruction to the Prophets for the Covenants and Holy Guides; we gave instruction to Noah, Abraham, Moses, Jesus the son of Mary, and Mohammad the son of Aminah.

The prophets were sent to witness about the Spirit of
Holiness, to bear glad tidings, to warn about the Day of Judgment, to lead people to good, to spread righteousness throughout the world.

Believers are true to the Covenants and Holy Guides.

Believers of the Lord are custodians of Truth and Kindness.

Remember the Grace of the Lord Allah, for Allah sees clearly all that ye do.
The faith of believers may be shaken to the test, but the angels will assist you in a beautiful pattern of conduct for any one whose hope is in Allah.

The evil ones who are wicked and do mischief will gain no advantage, for the Lord Allah will enforce righteousness.

We, the angels, have been instructed to tell people to stop religious fighting - only fight to defend your mosque or if you are put out from your houses because of your religion.
The best inheritance will be from the Lord on Day of Judgment.
O consorts of the Prophet!
Be not ye like those who seek only the glitter life of this world, but be of works of righteousness and of speech that is just.

Allah decrees no unhappy wedlock, fear not to dissolve an unhappy marriage, but provide what is right and just for husband and wife when they part, for Allah watches goodly conduct among all people.

In the former times of ignorance there was abomination among people, now make it pure and spotless among members of the family of believers, that all should establish regular prayer, charity and practice good deeds.

Enter not a friend's house without permission. If you are invited to dinner, arrive when expected and do not stay too long after the dinner for a lengthy visit may annoy the host or hostess.

O believers! Allah and Allah's angels send blessings on the Prophet Mohammad and salute him with all respect.

Moses was also honorable in Allah's sight.

To those who falsely accuse others or spread false rumors it is a sin.

The believing women of Islam should wear outer garments over their persons for protection against being molested.

O ye who believe! Always say words directed to the truth, that your conduct will be whole and sound!

Whoever follows the Lord has already attained the highest achievement, the highest Salvation with the Lord.

The Lord Allah offers us The Trust and believers accept it with free will, but the unbelievers refuse it.

SURAH 34
Sheba

Praise be to the Lord to Whom belongs all things in the heavens and on earth:
Praise be to the Lord in the Hereafter:
The Lord is full of wisdom, Acquainted with all things.

The Lord knows all that goes into the earth, and all that comes out thereof;
All that comes down from
the sky and all that ascends thereto; the seen and unseen.
The least little atom is not hidden from Our Creator
but everything is recorded in the Clear Record.
Those who work deeds of righteousness are on the path of divine guidance and are worthy of all praise.
The Exalted Lord bestows revelations and blessings to guide believers to good things,
and thy Lord doth watch over all things.

Allah released a flood and saved Noah and his family and pairs of animals.

The Lord produced fruits, tamarisk trees, and small shrubs.

Repel Satan, who does gather followers.

We, the angels, brought the psalms to David (Zabur) and the surahs to Mohammad. We brought mighty armour, iron chains, and wealth to David and Solomon, and Queen Bilqu (Sheba). And when we decreed Solomon's death, he was standing holding his cane. Even the jinns thought Solomon was alive. But God made a small worm eat part of his cane and weaken it so that Solomon;s body fell to the ground.

It is not your wealth that will bring you nearer to the Divine Creator, but those who believe and work righteousness – these are the ones for whom there is a Multiplied Reward for their good deeds;
While secure they will reside in the Dwellings on High!

Say: 'Verily my Lord bestows sustenance and revelations, and burdens also, to whom the Lord pleases and the Lord gathers all souls back to the Beloved Creator.'

Say: 'No reward do I ask to tell you to follow good ways and stand before the Lord; my reward is from the Lord who is witness to all things.'

Say: 'If I am astray from the path of righteousness, I only stray to the loss of my own soul; but if I receive guidance, it is because of the inspiration of my Lord to me. It is God who hears all things, and is always near.'

Those who reject Faith and good ways and continue in slanders and wickedness are practicers of Falsehood.

SURAH 35

The Originator of Creation

Praise be to the Holy Spirit of Allah, Who created the heavens and earth out of nothing,
Who created the angels - messengers with wings .

Let not the present life or the Chief Deceiver Satan deceive you about Allah; let thy soul follow only the promise of thy Good Lord.

If any do seek for glory and power - to the Holy Spirit of Allah belong all glory and praise.

To the Lord raise words of purity: it is the Lord who exalts each deed of righteousness.

The Lord created females to conceive a male's sperm drop with the ovum to bring forth new life among men and women, all cattle, and crawling creatures.

The Lord Allah decrees the length of our lives.

The Lord created two bodies of water, one sweet and pleasant to drink, and the other salty - and you extract food, pearls, and coral from the sea,
and there are ornaments that you make from gold.

The Lord created the rains, skies with beautiful hues of colors blue, pink, and orange - with white clouds,
mountains with tracts of white, brown, green, and red - intense in hue, orchards with date palms and vines - with succulent fruits and olives.

The Lord merges night into day, and day into night, and subjects the sun and moon - each one to run its course for a term appointed;

All of Creation,
All of this is easy for Allah.

Each soul bears its own sins and its own good deeds.

Verily the Lord sends those of truth as bearers of glad tidings and as warners to others reminding them of their goal of the Heaven of Gardens, where there will be no sense of weariness or toil but only good fruits, good companions, and comfort.

Wrongdoers promise each other nothing but delusions; they are damaging their own souls with wicked deeds.

Those who plot evil, can they not see what was the end of those who plotted evil before them? No change wilt thou find in the Lord's way of dealing with them, for verily the Lord is All-Knowing and to all things do go back to the Lord for decisions.

If the Lord Allah were to punish men and women according to what they deserve, there would not be left on earth a single living creature, but the Lord gives them respite for a stated term and then their soul will return to Allah for judgment, forgiveness, and rewards most generous of the Lord.

SURAH 36

Mohammad the Messenger

By the Koran (Quran),
Full of Wisdom,
Mohammad was one of the Messengers,
A Revelation sent down from the Exalted to tell of the good tidings.

The Lord records all accounts in a Clear Book Of Evidence.

Mohammad did say:
'O My People,'
'It would not be reasonable in me if I did not serve Allah who created me and to Whom ye shall all be brought back.'

'It is my duty to proclaim the Clear Message of the Holy Lord Who knoweth All things and direct Thy Servants to the Good Path.'
'For me I have faith in the Lord Allah. Listen, then, to me!'

Except by way of mercy are humans here to serve for a time on earth.

Say: 'O Lord, guide my soul by the ways of thy Holy Spirit of Allah and not by words of men or women. '

Say: 'The way of the Lord Allah is good and pure, and the souls of all people are property of the Lord Allah, to whom goes back all decisions.'

Ask that ye may receive the Lord's mercy for all that is in past and future.

On the Day of the Trumpet, the Judgment Seat of the Lord and the exalted assemblage of the Angels will be brought before us, and all will be judged according to our deeds;
Those who are righteous will enjoy Heavenly Gardens of Bliss, thrones of dignity, and every fruit for enjoyment.
But sinners may face a penalty from the Lord.

If it were the Lord's will, humans could have been transformed to remain in their places, unable to move about. But the nature of human life is that it changes from babe to strength to old age and feebleness, this is a clear message of life and change.

The Lord is well-versed in every kind of creation. The Lord is the Creator Supreme of skill and knowledge, who intends a thing with a command of 'Be' and it is!

So glory to the Lord who holds the Dominion of All Things, and to the Lord who all things be brought back.

SURAH 37

Those ranged in Ranks

By those who range
Themselves in ranks,
And so are strong in repelling evil,
And thus proclaim the Message of the Lord,
Verily, your God is the absolute divine unity of the Creator.
For beauty and for guard against all rebellious evil spirits and sinners.
The Day of Judgment will be a day of Sorting Out,
And the Truthful will be gathered together for the Heavenly Gardens of Bliss, and the Lord will deal with both the righteous and the sinners.

Sincere and devoted servants of the Lord Allah, for them is a sustenance determined, fruits, honour, and dignity.
In Gardens of Felicity, facing each other on thrones, round will be passed to them a cup from a clear-flowing fountain of crystal white water, of a taste delicious to those who drink thereof.

The Tree Zaqqum of Hell puts forth a bitter fruit.

Noah was a believing servant and was strong in the great calamity of the flood – Noah and his family were not overwhelmed by the waters. Peace and salutations to Noah among the nations!

Abraham was 86 years old when Ismail was born, and they did build a sacred mosque to the Lord. Peace and salutations to Abraham and Ismail!
We, the angels, did bestow knowledge and direction to Isaac the Prophet, who
was one of the Righteous, and to Elias (Elijah).
Peace and salutations to
Isaac and Elias!
We, the angels, did bestow favor from the Lord on Moses and his brother Aaron. Peace and salutations to Moses and Aaron!
We, the angels did bestow favor on Lut and Jonah. Peace and salutations to Lut and Jonah!

Jinns are spirits created out of the fire; jinns may believe or disbelieve.
Jinns may find a way into a human to make hidden qualities or capacities.
Jinns can be animals. Humans can possibly manipulate jinns.
Jinns accept or reject guidance – they are a hidden force or spirit which can have some free will. Jinns can be visible or invisible.
Jinns will be called to account on Judgment Day.
Some say jinns are the hidden jungle folk in hills or forest, or hiding behind rocks.

Those ranged in ranks say:
'We are all appointed before the Lord and we are verily those who declare the Lord's glory and the words of truth!'

Glory to thy Lord and Cherisher of the Worlds!
The Lord of Honour and Power!
And Peace on the Messengers.

SURAH 38
Messengers

Without measure are
The Treasures of the Mercy of the Lord,
The Exalted in Power,
The Grantor of Bounties
And All Blessings.

We, the Angels, do commemorate Our Servants Noah, Abraham, Isaac, Ismail, and Jacob, Moses, David, Solomon, Jesus, Mary, Mohammad, and Khadijah who were Possessors of Power and Vision, and who Exalted the Glory of the Lord; we gave them knowledge and wisdom out of Our Treasures of the Beyond World.
They enjoyed a beautiful approach to the angels and a glorious final return.

The servants of the Lord are possessors of power and vision; they were chosen to proclaim the Message of the Hereafter. The servants are of the Company of the Elect and Good.
For the righteous is a beautiful place of Return.

Gardens of eternity whose doors will be open to them; therein will they recline and call for fruit and drink with companions of God.

Say: 'Truly am I a Messenger: God is Supreme and Irresistible, the Lord of the heavens and earth, exalted in might, enforcing divine will, forgiving again and again. No knowledge have I on high except to reveal the Lord's bounty
plainly and publicly.'

To Adam the Lord gave names to all things, and the angels bowed to Adam.
But Iblis (Satan)was cast out from Heaven because he would not bow down before Adam as God instructed.

Say: 'No reward do I ask of you for this good message – seek the Lord and you shall know love and truth.'

SURAH 39
Souls

Say: 'O Servants who believe! Good is the reward for the souls who do good in this world.
Those in loss are those who lose their souls to wickedness.'

The Lord will deliver the righteous to their place of Salvation, no evil shall touch them nor shall they grieve.

Allah put forth a parable – A man belonging to many partners at variance with each other, and a man belonging to entirely one partner; are these two equal in comparison? Praise be to Allah!

Who, then, doth more wrong than one who utters a lie against the

Lord? Those who bring the Truth and confirm it, such are those who do right;
they shall have all that they wish for in the presence of their Lord, such is the reward of those who do good.

Allah takes souls at death and during the sleep. Those souls on whom death is not decreed are returned from sleep to live until their term appointed.
To Allah belongs the keys of the heavens and the earth. Worship Allah and be of those who give thanks.

The Trumpet will be sounded and all will hear, then will a second one be sounded and all will be standing and looking on! The Earth will shine with the glory of the Lord. The Record of Deeds will be opened, the prophets and witnesses will be brought forward; and to every soul will just decision be pronounced of its deeds, and the Lord knoweth best for True Judgment all that they do, unlike the judges on earth in the earthly court that did not know all that the Lord did.

SURAH 40
The Believer

Say: 'O my people! This life is nothing but temporary convenience. It is the hereafter that is the Home that will last. I will lead you to the Path of Right Salvation.'

The Lord is the Living Unity; Call upon the Lord with sincere devotion.

The Believer said: 'Soon will ye remember what I say to you. My own affair I commit to the Lord, for the Lord watches over the Servants.'

The Lord created the sky as a canopy and has made beautiful sunrise and sunsets, shapes of mountains and valleys, and has provided sustenance, cattle, and ships.
The Lord created humans from a sperm-drop and an egg, from childhood to full strength to an old age for a term appointed; it is the Lord who gives life and death.

SURAH 41
The Expounded

The world was created in 6 days with 7 heavens.

Goodness and evil are not equal; repel evil and hatred, then there will be more friendship and intimacy, such goodness is granted to those who exercise patience and self-restraint – persons of the greatest nature!

Celebrate the praises of the Lord, by night and by day.

The Lord is the One Full of Wisdom.

Whoever works righteousness benefits their soul; whoever works evil, it is against their own soul.

Men and women do not weary of asking for good things, but if ill touches them they give up all hope and give in to despair; when they

are given mercy they forget the good bounty was from Allah but praise themself instead - this is far from the Truth –
all revelations and blessings are from Allah, so do not forget Thy-Bountiful Lord!

SURAH 42
Consultation

Allah does send inspiration to thee as to those before thee.

Whatever it is that you differ, whatever it be wherein you differ, thereof is with Allah, in God I trust and to God I turn.

The Lord is the Creator of Heavens and Earth, and all animal and plant life. To the Lord belong the keys of all existence and the keys of all sustenance; the Lord knows full well all things.

Allah has enjoined on you the same religion as Noah, Abraham, Moses, and Jesus who came before Mohammad. Allah does desire that a gospel of unity should be the goal – the Holy Spirit of Allah goes forth from the Heavens throughout the Universe. All religions that stand for peace, love, and good works are acceptable to Allah, who is Ever-Loving, the Cherisher of All People. For Allah wants a good
life for every man, woman, and child; for Allah is the Supreme Protector and will protect us from Satan.

The Lord sends Truth and Balance; those who believe in the Lord hold the Spirit in awe, and know it is the Truth. Gracious is the Holy Spirit of Allah!
Those who believe and work righteous deeds will be in luxuriant meadows of the Heavenly Gardens; they will have the magnificent bounty of Lord Allah. The Lord will direct the believers and the unbelievers to their station of reward in the Heavenly Gardens.

Say; 'No reward do I ask for except the love of the Lord and those near of kin!'

The Lords knows well the secrets of all hearts and knows all that ye do.
The Lord listens to those who believe and do deeds of righteousness.
The Lord listens to those who have gone astray but then turn their face and ways back to the Lord.
The Lords sends provisions and mercy as the Lord pleases. The Holy Spirit of Allah sends rain even after you have given up all hope.
There are consequences for your own actions, so let your work be just.
Among the Lord's signs are the ships, smooth-sailing through the ocean, If the Lord Allah wanted to still the waters of the ocean and still the wind, the ships would become motionless – this is in the Lord's power.
Through the Lord's power, humans have invented ships.

Why do unbelievers dispute the powerful signs of the Lord's existence?

Life on earth is but a quick convenience, but life with Allah is better and more lasting; it is for those who
have *Keys Of Understanding*:
1) believe,
2) put their trust in the Lord,
3) avoid crimes, violence,
and shameful deeds,
4) forgive others when they are angry,
5) are thankful for the creations and sustenance of the Lord,
6) offer prayer and praise,
7) conduct affairs by mutual consultation and agreements,
8) practice charity of helping others out of sustenance the Lord has given them,
9) help and defend themselves – their human rights, the rights of kin, community rights.
10) be truthful and honest,
sincere, and speak words that are not ambiguous.

The recompense for loss of a life is loss of a life, but if a person forgives and makes reconciliation, they will win the pleasure of Lord Allah, for Lord Allah loveth not those who do wrong.

Jesus preached to offer the other cheek to someone who has slapped you, but Jesus should have spoken up and said that it is wrong to hurt another.
So, indeed, if any do help and defend themselves after a wrong to them, against such there is no cause to them.
But do what is lawful from what the majority of the people have lawfully established in goodness.

The blame is only against the evil oppressors who wrongfully and insolently transgress beyond bounds through the lands, defying right and justice, violating human rights; Allah loveth not those who do wrong.

Mohammad became a Holy Prophet at age 40, who had known not before his revelation; the Mohammad led the people as a Messenger of God to establish righteousness and love among the people.

SURAH 43
The Gold Adornments

Say: 'Glory to the Lord of All Creation, for we could never have accomplished This by ourselves. Surely we must keep our Faith.'

Celebrate ye no false glitter on the earth, for it will not last, but hold fast to the real glory of Truth and Revelations from thy Lord!

The mercy and presence of the Lord is better than any wealth of silver and gold.

The evil may have to face Malik, who guards hell; hell is not a good place.

Hold fast to the good revelation sent down to thee from thy divine Lord.

Blessed are the messengers Jesus and Mohammad who preached the Gospel of Unity; they were witness to The Truth.

SURAH 44

The Smoke

Allah doth send down clear messages of spiritual wisdom to save all people; there is no obscurity. Good is good, and evil is evil.

Messengers are sent to explain things clearly and to clear the smoke so that the truth is plainly visible.

Appetites of evil may eventually feed upon a bitter tree in Hell called the Tree of Zaqqum; this tree is food for the sinful and the wicked ones. The drink for the evil will be the bitter Dari.

SURAH 45

The Kneeling Down

All creation in the heavens and earth are signs for those of assured faith in the Lord. Men, women, children, animals, alteration of night and day, Rain, sunlight, winds, the sea, the mountains, the valleys: such are the Signs of the Lord Allah.
Woe to those who reject good ways.

Seek the Lord and be grateful for the bountiful gifts of thy Lord.

If one does good, it benefits their soul; if one does evil, it works against their soul.

Every one will bow at the knee at the Hour of Judgment before the Divine One and will be called accountable for their Record Clear; in the end all will be brought back to your Lord.

SURAH 46

Winding Sand-Tracts

The prophet Hud told
the people to watch the yellow streaks on the winding sand-tracts of camel trains carrying the weight of goods and people; they were a Sign of the Lord, a beautiful sign to behold. Some of the camel trains are 1,000 camels long.

All Messengers are filled with divine inspiration to bring good messages to the believers, and to turn the unbelievers back to the Holy Spirit. Allah sent the Jinns to listen to the Holy Quran to give the good news to the Muslims.

SURAH 47

Mohammad

The Holy Prophet Mohammad said: 'Blessed are those who spend out of sustenance for good causes, charity, and for the Lord Allah.'

The Lord is the Protector of those who believe, but those who do not believe do not have a Protector.

It is not necessary to kill yourself or others over the cause of religions, for the Cause of God will not fail, but people and time will uphold the Cause of the Holiness for future generations. Life is to be lived until the Lord takes us back. The only way to the Lord is when we are taken to heaven.

SURAH 48

The Victorious

It is in the Gospel of Jesus, that sowing a seed will fill the sowers with wonder and delight.

And Moses and Aaron in the Torah, they fell in prayer to God with all praise.

Believers who love the Holy Spirit are strong in compassion and help for each other; they are good servants to each other; they are victorious in good spirit and have avoided all bad conduct.

Enter the Sacred Mosque with minds and hearts secure in the righteous ways of the Lord.

SURAH 49

The Chambers

Raise not your voices above the voice of the prophet.

Lower your voice in the presence of the prophet.
Raise not your voice to thee from outside the chambers of a spiritual prophet.

If a wicked person comes to you with any news, ascertain the truth, lest ye harm people unwittingly and unnecessarily, and afterwards become full of repentance and remorse for what ye have done.

If believers fall into a quarrel, make ye peace with one another but do not harm each other.

The believers are but a single unity, that ye may know the love and mercy of the holy spirit, a brotherhood of brothers and a sisterhood of sisters.

Let not some among you laugh at others to ridicule; it may be that the latter are better than the former in righteousness of heart.
Nor defame nor be sarcastic to each other, nor call each other by offensive nicknames; this is wickedness.

Avoid suspicion as much as possible, and spy not on each other, nor speak ill of each other behind their backs.

The Lord made you into nations and tribes that ye may know each other; the most righteous of you are those with faith and goodness in their hearts.
Embrace Islam and you will accept guidance from Allah.

SURAH 50

The Matter has been Decreed

A full account of the Soul's doings is recorded in the Lord's Record Book, for the Lord knows all things.

The Lord created man and woman and the Lord gave them two guardian angels, one on the right and one on the left, and the sentinel is recording all words.

On the Day of Judgment the righteous will be brought to peace and serenity, but the wicked will be directed by the Lord.

Celebrate the praises of the Lord by prayers of the rosary beads before the rising and setting of the sun.

SURAH 51
The Winds that Scatter

By the winds of angels that scatter dust, seeds, and rain, and lift and bear heavy clouds, flow with gentle clouds for smooth sailing, by the commands of God, do the works of the Lord come to pass.
Take joy in the things the Lord has done. On earth such are the signs for those of Faith.

As for your own selves, will ye not see? The Lord of the heavens and earth is the Very Truth, that ye can speak intelligently to each other.

The Lord created Abraham and his wife, Moses, Pharaoh, Noah's people, Jesus, Mohammad, and all people. The Lord created all animals and plants. The Lord is the Lord of All Creation; this is the Very Truth.

SURAH 52
The Mount

Mount Sinai was for Moses,
Mount of Olives was for
Jesus,
Mount of Hira was for
Mohammad, -
mountains upon which revelation descended from the divine realm.

By divine revelation,
By a decree inscribed
in a scroll unfolded,
By the much-frequented
houses of worship,
By Heaven & Earth,
will the righteousness
of God prevail over evil.
The Lord doth seek good ways, but repels all evil.

And those who believe and whose families follow in faith – to them shall be joined with families and companions in Heavenly Gardens of Bliss, and shall be bestowed with fruit and anything they shall desire, and they shall exchange a loving cup with one another and engage with each other in mutual pleasant conversation.
But for the wicked, the Day of the Trumpet is when their plotting will avail them nothing and no help shall be given to them except advice from the Lord. Will the Lord give them another chance?

SURAH 53
The Star

By the Sun, when it goes down and rises back up again, have ye seen a sign of the Lord!

Mohammad was taught by the angel Gabriel, who was mighty in Power, at the Mountain of Light and Mohammad was endued with wisdom. So did the Lord Allah convey the inspiration to Mohammad the servant.

Mohammad saw the angel Gabriel at a second descent near the Lote-Tree, shrouded in mystery, near the Garden of Abode which means 'Souls of Believers'.

Some Arab Pagans worship the goddess Manat.

It is to God that the End and the Beginning of all things belong.

Desire not the vanities from the life of this world, but let the fruit of thy striving be thy Holy Spirit of God.

Each soul will bear its own sins and good deeds, and each soul will be judged and rewarded.

Let the Lord be thy goal.

The Lord granteth laughter and tears, life and death,
wealth and no wealth;
the Lord granteth satisfaction that is not of this world.

SURAH 54

The Moon

The bright light of the moon and the twinkling of the stars are a sure Sign of the Lord - will thou not believe?

And the courses that the moon follows is exactly created. And the Lord created the Balance of the Universe.

SURAH 55

The Most Gracious

The Most Gracious, the Lord Allah, created the heavens and the earth, and all that is Between.

God created man and woman, and Jinns from Fire,

the animals and plants,
the fruit of date palms and pomegranates, corn, and sweet-smelling plants,
sweet water and salt water,
and pearls and coral,
ships to sail the seas,
colorful skies,
now then, which of the
favours of your Lord will
ye deny?

For those whose goal is Heaven, there will be a time to stand before the Lord in Garden containing all delights and companions. There will be 4 gardens and 2 water springs,
Allah's chamber,
7 heavens, carpets of rich brocade, fruits, dates, & pomegranates.
Heaven will be a good reward for a good soul.

The Day of the Caller will summon believers forth to the gates of Heaven for protectin and recompense of a fruitful reward.

Those who rejected faith and committed evil and mischief will be turned back from the Gate of Good and be directed for further counsel from the Lord because they did not follow the Sacred Path.

Let not the mischief makers follow Satan's evil path! Let the evil turn to the Assemblage of Truth and Love, and set the goal for the Presence of the Sovereign Omnipotent!

Blessed be the Name of God, full of Majesty, Bounty, & Honours.

SURAH 56

The Inevitable

When the Event Inevitable, the Hour of Judgment cometh to pass, no soul can deny the time,
the good souls will be directed to the Good Gate, but the wicked will be directed to the Wicked Gate.

The good souls will be on thrones encrusted with gold and precious pearls, rubies, garnets, sapphires, emeralds, and diamonds,
reclining on them with goblets, beakers, and cups filled with clear water. A selection of fruits and fowl will be available, Friendly companions will be available for conversation.
There will be flowers piled one above another, with both shade long-extended and warm areas of sunlight for their comfort and satisfaction. But the evil souls will be denied this comfort.

Now, do you not want to testify to the Truth of God?

It is God who created everything!

Why then not celebrate praise to God?

God created the seed that ye grow in the ground, even the human seed, so life can be recreated.
God created the rain, to replenish moisture in the soils, seas, and all life.
God kindles the fires, which provide warmth, and the guidance of light to those traveling in darkness; this is the parable of the fire.

Remember the Lord and celebrate praises to the Supreme!

SURAH 57

Iron

The Lord is the First and the Last,
The Evident and the Hidden.

The heritage of the Universe belongs to the Lord.

Your cause should be to believe in the Good Ways of the Lord, if ye are men and women of faith.
Say prayers at morning, evening, and even during the day as a memorial to the Lord. Even as ye gather rocks of iron or milk the cows, celebrate the Lord in all ye works of the day.

The prophets brought forth the good messages, the Balance between Right and Wrong,
which was the Criterion,
but the monasteries were invented by the believers.

One day shalt thou see how light runs forward before the believers,
men and women of faith,
who say in greeting:

'Good news for you this day!'
The righteous call out in warning:
'Do not let the Deceiver deceive you!'
As a gateway to safety,
repel the abode with Iblis .
Say to your friends: 'Do not be led to the Satan and the temptation of evil and ruin. Do not be a rebellious transgressor but be a sincere Lover of Truth and testify for the Lord!'

Let no people think they have control over the will, power, and grace of the Lord; what the Lord wills will be.

SURAH 58

Those Who Plead

Whenever a man or a woman carries their pleads and concerns in prayer to Allah, Allah hears all arguments between all sides and Allah know the truths of all things. And Allah knoweth all of your needs and desires.

Allah hath reckoned the value of each soul, and Allah is a witness to all things.

Love your family and friends, and love your own life until Allah takes back your soul.

When divorcing, conduct this event fairly.

When making a treaty, do so in honesty, fairness and sincerity, and honour the obligation.

Conduct business with honesty and sincerity, and honour your contracts and obligations.

There is not a secret conduct between three, but Allah makes the fourth among them –
nor between five but Allah makes six between them;
Allah is with them wheresoever they may be; in the end Allah will remind them of the truth of their conduct.

Turnest thou not thy sight to secret counsels that are for iniquity, hostility, or evil purposes.

Salute thee sincerely as Lord Allah salutes, not in trickery.

When ye hold secret counsel, do it not for iniquity, hostility, or evil things, but do it for righteousness and self-restraint, and good causes and put thy trust in the timing of the Lord.

When ye are asked to make room in the assemblies, spread out and make room for your friends: ample room will the Lord make for you. When ye are asked to stand up in the assemblies, stand up.

When ye consult with the messenger in private, spend something in charity before your private consultation. If ye cannot spend a sum before your private consultation, then at least establish a prayer or practice a charity (Zakah).

Turn away from those who knowingly do evil; truly it is the Party of the Evil One that will perish on Judgment Day!

But the Party of Believers will achieve Felicity of Happiness and Bliss.

SURAH 59
The Mustering

Those who gather together in Unity, Faith, and Truth are fortified in wisdom and mustered in strength.

Those who save themselves from coveting only their own soul – they are the ones who achieve true prosperity.

Let every soul seek what the Lord will provide in the next life, a holy providence.

Those who lend a helping hand do it for love and crave no reward, nor feel the least envy or jealousy.

Not equal are companions of the Lord and companions of Iblis.

The Lord is the Source of Peace, the Creator, the Evolver, the Origin, the Preserver of Love, the Sovereign, the Most Holy Spirit.
To the Lord belong the Most Beautiful Names.

SURAH 60
That Which Examines

Seek protection from enemies who wish you evil or have evil causes.

But deal kindly and justly with all people; it may be that those who hated you now love you.

The Torah was written 2000 years before the Koran. But the holy angels sent divine inspiration
for the the books to be written.
There is much religious fighting. It may be that the Lord will grant love and friendship between you and those whom ye now hold as enemies.

O ye who believe! Those who drive ye out of your houses for your faith are not your friends!

When there come to you refugees who are believers
and practice good ways, do not turn them back to unbelievers.

O ye who believe!
Say with assurance that ye will not steal;
ye will not commit
adultery or fornication;
ye will not injure or kill
your children;
ye will not injure or kill
other men or women;
ye will not utter slander;
ye will not forge falsehoods;
ye will not prevent justice.
But take every care to keep your society free and pure,
repel injustice and evil doings from civilization among you.

SURAH 61
The Battle Array

Jesus spoke of Comforters and Advocates of the Holy Spirit that would come after Him; Mohammad is such a Holy Prophet.

O ye who believe! Why say ye are just and righteous, yet ye act not and commit evil acts?

It is wrong to create evil while promoting unity and harmony for the Lord.

It is Satan's intention to extinguish the truth of the Lord, but warriors of the Lord will protect righteousness and love in battle array. So let all believers of righteousness join together to promote the love and good ways of the Lord.

The love of the Lord Allah is like a good bargain (tijarah - give little but get a lot) – we believe in the Lord and strive in good ways, but in return we get forgiveness, the promise of Allah in a beautiful eternity, and divine assistance – we got more than we gave!

As Jesus and Mohammad said to Disciples, if ye
promote unity, harmony,
faith and trust for the Lord, then you will be as a true messenger.

SURAH 62
Friday

The Prophet Isaiah said:
'The God of Abraham and the God of David said that it will come to pass that believers will survive with the help of angels. The Lord said: I have heard your prayers, I have seen your tears, and I am with you.'

'The Lord will do the things the Lord hath promised. The Lord will comfort you and provide you with love and sustenance.'

When the call is proclaimed to prayer on Friday – Day of Assembly – it is common public prayer, preceeded by a khutbah, in which the Imam leader reviews the week's spiritual life and offers advice.
Each person prays 5 times a day and at the ids every year, large area meeting.
Once in a lifetime, go to Mecca for the pilgrimage.

Say prayers to the Lord and when prayers are finished, disperse to the house or to conduct thy business.

The Lord has sent Messengers in eras of time to remind the people the Clear Signs of the Lord,
and to Sanctify the Signs, and to instruct them in Scripture and Wisdom.

SURAH 63
The Hypocrites

Hypocrites are those who turn away from the Lord, reject faith and truth, and do evil deeds, yet they boast of their own greatness and they boast of the evil deeds. Their hearts are sealed with evil instead of love. Their exterior looks may please you, but they speak deceit; they are like rotten timber and will crumble.

They will not seek repentance or forgiveness or righteousness; the hypocrites have no understanding of The Treasures of Heaven.
They will not provide charity or kindness to others.
Hypocrites becomes companions of Iblis.

Let nothing divert you from the remembrance of Lord Allah, and service to Lord Allah in brotherhood and sisterhood; this includes every act of good service, every thought of kindness, every motive and deed that is pure and right.

SURAH 64
The Mutual Loss and Gain

The same Allah (God) created all things and all men, women, and children.

When ye commit evil, it is a loss on your soul, and a loss to God.

When ye commit good acts, it is a benefit on your soul, and a gain to God.

For God gathers believers together, as many as can be mustered, an assemblage of the righteous.
So, therefore, all in one family should hold each other to the guidance of the Good Way, trusting in each other and treating each other with charity and love.

Let your spirit grow for the Lord.

SURAH 65
Divorce

Try to reconcile a marriage before divorcing, for a marriage knot is sacred.
Keep the marriage sacred, but where it must be dissolved, use all means to ensure justice to both parties and protect the interests of the children.
Lies and falsehoods against each other is forbidden for both parties in the divorce.
Put your trust in the Lord to guide you, for the Lord knows the burdens and questions of your heart.

SURAH 66
Prohibition

Turn to the Lord with sincere repentance and ask that the Lord protect you from all evil; all evil is prohibited.

The angels will back you with divine protection and prohibit any weakness or folly from gaining power.

SURAH 67
The Dominion

The Lord has dominion
over all creation in the universe, heavens, and earth and no want of proportion wilt thou see;
turn thy vision even twice and thou wilt see no flaws but only order and beauty.
And even there is Perfection in the Invisible World where the angels dwell.

The lowest heaven is
filled with lamps of stars,

some that shoot across the sky, and even those studying the skies with telescopes will confess themselves defeated in trying to explain the ultimate mysteries. The fire in the stars draw in of its breath as it blazes forth and it can be heard.

And the Lord knows what is good in your hearts, and what is bad in your hearts, so let your hearts shine forth with only the good. The Lord has full knowledge of the secrets of all hearts. So then let your hearts be guided by the good ways of the Lord.

The Lord has made the earth manageable for you, to traverse through its tracts of deserts and mountains, to follow the course of streams and rivers, to gather up rocks to build, to toil seed into the ground to grow corn.

Why does the One in Heaven swallow up the earth in earthquakes or bring showers of ice in tornados and typhoons?

Observe the birds above spreading their wings and flying in formation, and Allah doth uplift them, and truly Allah watches over all things.

Who is there that can provide sustenance if God were to withhold provision to you?

So be ye guided evenly in the straight way – the way of good – and on the path of the Lord, for the Lord created you and all souls go back to the Lord one day.

The Lord gave you the faculties of hearing, seeing, feeling, tasting, smelling, and understanding – and use your faculties to serve the Lord and in charity for others.

As to the knowledge of time, it is with the Lord alone; and Allah is Most Gracious.

Say: 'Say ye? – If your stream be some morning lost in the underground earth, who then can supply you with clear-flowing water?' Such is like the Lord, who is the only one who can save your soul.

SURAH 68

The Pen

By the Pen and by the Record which the Messengers did write, they were not mad or possessed – by the grace of thy Lord, and verily for thee are Records Unfailing.

Which of you is afflicted with madness? Verily it is the Lord that knoweth best what is in the hearts of souls, which one of ye have strayed from the Lord's path.

In a garden near Mekka, there were the people who were resolved to gather the fruits of their labor in the early morning, before indigents awoke, so the indigents could not share the best of the harvest. But a visit from the Lord during the night swept the fruit away, so as morning broke, as the people departed in secret tones to gather the best fruit, but found none, their revelation unto themselves was 'We have

surely lost our way and have sinned to the poor, now the Lord has shut us out of our own labor! Verily we have been doing wrong!'
And the people offered prayer in repentance and said: 'Let us hope the Lord will give us in exchange a favorable garden, for we have turned our souls in repentance!'

So hearken not to those who deny Truth; their desire is thou shouldst be pliant with evil causes, violence, and slander – Heed not this type of despicable person, ready with oaths that are lies, habitually hindering all good, transgressors beyond good bounds, deep in sin, violence and cruelty, and a companion of Iblis.

Ye People of Faith have Covenants with the Holy Spirit on oath from the Unseen so it was written down. So wait with patience for the command and the grace of thy Lord to reach you.

And the unbelievers would almost trip thee up with their eyes when they hear the Message of a good person, and they say: 'Surely this Messenger is possessed!' But is nothing less than a Good Message to all the worlds.

SURAH 69
The Sure Reality

The prophet Salih, a brethren, put forth a she-camel as a symbol of the rights of the poor, that they should have drinking water as well as the rich. The prophet Hud, a brethren, was a messenger to the people of Ad who was fourth generation from Noah, being son of Aus, son of Aram, son of Sam, son of Noah.
What is the Sure Reality?
The Sure Reality is on the Day when the Great Event will come to pass – when thy soul will pass to come before thy Lord , and the Angels of Ascent will be on all sides; no acts of your own will be hidden but your record will be Read.

And I, Mohammad, do call to witness what ye see and what ye see not – that this is verily the word of an honourable messenger.

Glorify the name of thy Lord Most High, for verily it is Truth of Assured Certainty.

SURAH 70
The Ways of Ascent

Thou do hold a patience of beautiful contentment for thy day of ascension as far-off, yet the angels and the Lord see it as near, for a day to thou is as the measure of a thousand of years to the Lord.

So turn thyself to the Lord and remain steadfast in patience, that thou may reach Allah, Lord of the Ways of Ascent.
And guard the sacredness of worship, such will be the honoured ones in Heaven.

The messengers call to witness the Lord of all points north, south, east, and west, above and below, and the Angels of the Ascent.

SURAH 71
Noah

The Lord directed Noah to build a mighty ship called the Ark that would sail upon the waters. Then the Lord said to fill the ark with pairs of animals, one male and one female. Noah's family ascended into the ark.

And the Lord saved Noah, Noah's family, and pairs of animals from perishing in the Great Flood that lasted forty days and forty nights. Noah and his family prayed and worshipped the Lord every day, they were faithful people; that is why the Lord chose Noah for the time upon the Ark.

SURAH 72
The Jinns

A company of Jinns (Spirits) said: 'We have heard wonderful revelations from Allah, the One exalted in Majesty. Let no one say untruths against the Lord; the Lord is good.'

O, believers! Say ! -
'We understand not whether hard times are intended for those on earth, but since we have listened to and seek the guidance from the Messengers, among us are some that submit our wills to the Lord and lean to good ways of conduct and justice. '

Say! –
'It is not in my power to cause you harm, or to bring you to practice good conduct. I only seek to find refuge in my Lord and deliver to you the good news of the love & mercy of the Holy Spirit.'

Say! –
'I can only convey the message from my Lord that God knows the Unseen and the Seen and is acquainted with all mysteries. The Lord will choose messengers and angels, and will make a band of watchers march before the messenger and behind the messenger. And the Lord's work will be. The Lord takes account of every single thing.'

SURAH 73
The Enfolded One

O thou folded in garments,
thy garments protect thy body but thy soul stands simple before God.

Govern thy soul with prayer and a word of praise and thanks.

There is prolonged occupation with manifold engagements to keep thy life abreast, but keep in remembrance the names of thy Holy Spirit of the Lord and devote thyself to holiness and goodness wholeheartedly.

Let the Lord deal with the unbelievers who cause mischief.

Whatever good ye send forth from your souls, ye shall find it in Lord Allah's presence in the End.

SURAH 74
The One Wrapped Up

O seer! O prophet!
Arise and deliver thy good message about thy Lord,
Do thou glorify and keep thy soul free from stain!
And all abomination shun!
Nor expect, in giving, any increase for thyself!
But, for the Lord's cause,
Be patient and constant!

O seer! O prophet!
Spread the revelation thou hast received from the divine
Lord – 'Follow good conduct in all affairs and make thy Lord thy goal when thy soul departs.'

When the Day of the Trumpet comes, it will be easy for the righteous but for the wayward it will be a Day of Distress – the Lord will deal with the creatures of all creation as the Lord wills.
As the Lord will, it will be.

Say: 'By the light of the moon and the night, By the dawn of the sun and the day, The Lord is but the One I choose to follow and to hold my soul.'

SURAH 75
The Resurrection

Call to witness thy own soul to rebuke the tendency for evil.

The Day of Account will come and your own conscience will bear witness to thy deeds of good or evil; there will be no excuses.

Woe to the soul who practices evil.

In all deeds will one will evidence to their own self.

SURAH 76
The Time

Kronos (Time) was the father of the Greek god Zeus himself.

Time was deified also by Pagan Arabs.

Has there not been a long period of time of nothing before man and woman were mentioned?

The Creator has brought us forth and now we have a will, to follow the path of righteousness to drink a cup at the fountain of purity in Heaven or to join Iblis in Hell and Hell is not filled with pleasure.

Use your time on earth to perform your vows and to feed with the love of God the orphan, the indigent, captives of war, and animals under thy subjection.

Say: 'We feed you for the sake of Allah alone. No reward do we desire from you, nor thanks. We only fear a Day of Judgment when we stand ourselves alone before the Lord.'

Love not this fleeting time on earth, but put before thee thy eternal life.

SURAH 77
Those Sent Forth

Do not hold thy creation fluids or parts as despicable, thy gestation period in thy womb is just as thou gestation period outside the womb in the world, for all thy souls will return to the Lord after this life, and thy body will return to dust.

And the Lord is the Best to Determine the period of time and need for all things and the destination of thy soul.

SURAH 78
The Great News

Concerning what they are disputing - concerning about the Great News about which they cannot agree -

Verily, they should know that the Good News is the Lord, the Cherisher of the Worlds!

The Creator giveth order and perfection to all constructed in the heavens and earth. The Creator made the earth a wide expanse with mountains and waters, plants and animals, man and woman, sleep for rest, work for sustenance, clouds for water abundance - that corn and vegetables and fruits may be produced, thunder with streaks of lightning to look as yellow camels streaking across the sand desert.

If thy soul is abandoned on the Day of Spiritual Destiny, thou will have no recompense from thy Lord, so woe to thy soul that strayed from the good ways.

SURAH 79
The Resurrection Angels

On the Day that one shall be Reminded of all thy hath done, the wicked would not even depart from their body upon death, but their will is futile - the angels take both the souls of the righteous and the souls of the wicked; the angels of death may have to tear out the souls of the wicked because the wicked will be afraid to leave this world.

The Lord appoints time with declarations thereof, with the Lord the Limits fixed therefore are but divine.

SURAH 80
He Frowned

The Lord provides water for you to drink and to provide moisture for the earth, food for you to eat - corn, grapes, nutritious plants, olives, dates, gardens dense with lofty trees, fruits, and fodder for your cattle, camels, and goats.

Now, see that thou messengers give spiritual food for your soul and for your moral conduct.

Everyone makes mistakes, for we are only human.

Even Mohammad himself apologized one time for showing impatience to a man who wanted to speak with him so be like Mohammad and follow his good ways.

Now, see thou the importance of thy spiritual food from thy messengers.

SURAH 81
The Folding Up

If the sun with is spacious light should be folded up in cataclysm, there will be only the smaller lights. Then wither go ye?

Then the she-camel, ten months with young , will be unattended as the shepherd seeks shelter from the cold.

Then when the scrolls are laid open, it will be the Time of the Calling. Verily, this is no less than a Message to all.

SURAH 82
The Cleaving Asunder

The day must come when Discord must finally cease, and the Peace of God abounds.

Verily over you are angels to protect you – they know and understand all that ye do.

But the Lord who fashioned you in due proportion, giving you great capacities and destinies, also gave a you bias of your own free will.

Use thy gifts of mind and spirit to guide thy soul to the Final Goal of Thy Lord Allah.

SURAH 83
The Dealers in Fraud

Woe to those that deal in fraud.

Those who, when have to receive by measure from men or women, exact full measure. But when they have to give by measure or weight to men or women, give less than due.

Those in sin laugh at those who believe, but the sinners are the people truly astray!

SURAH 84
The Rendering Asunder

Say: 'I do call to witness the ruddy glow of the Sunset, it changes every moment as it vanishes in twilight.
And the
Night and its Moon that travels from stage to stage; these are Clear Signs of Our Lord, so announce this to
All people.

SURAH 85
The Constellations

To God belongs the dominion of the heavens and earth, and the sky filled with constellations and stars telling the Zodiac signs.

SURAH 86
The Day Star

By the day sky with the star of piercing brightness, that allows the earth to sprout vegetation and gush out springs and pour down rain, now let people think from what they are created!
And every soul has a protector over it.
And the Lord is making divine plans.

SURAH 87

The Most High

Glorify the name of thy Guardian Lord, Most High, who hath ordained order and proportion to all things in the universe.

The Lord is the Maker of All Divine Plans, the Originator of All Things.

SURAH 88

The Overwhelming Event

Say: 'Has the story reached thee of the Overwhelming Event, the Day of Judgment?
The righteous will dwell in a garden on high with a bubbly spring with goblets, cushions, and rich carpets all spread out.

Say: 'Do you not look at the camels, the sky, mountains, oceans, the earth, and all of the people?'

But thou art not one to manage the affairs of men and women – they must follow Lord Allah on their own.

SURAH 89

The Dawn

By the Break of Day and the Setting into Night,
By the Even Numbers and the Odd Numbers,
Is there not in these evidence for those who understand?

Now, as for men and women, when the Lord giveth them honour and rights then they saith 'My Lord has honoured me.'
But when their sustenance is restricted then they saith 'My Lord has humiliated me.'
And yet some do not honour the orphans or feed the poor, but only devour inheritance with greed, and love wealth with inordinate love!
So, to thy soul keep to the Lord in good and bad times so Devotees may enter thou into Heaven.

SURAH 90

The City

There are two highways of life – the one of virtue and the one of vice and rejection of faith and good ways.
Those who give food and help to the poor, the indigent, and the orphan; and those who enjoin patience and self-restraint, and enjoin deeds of kindness and compassion are on the path of good virtue.

SURAH 91

The Sun

Prophet Salih wanted clean water for the camels, just as clean water is needed for the people. Clean water is pure and good.
So by the soul, and the order of understanding given to it,
the enlightenment as to its wrong and its right,
truly one succeeds who purifies it,
and truly one fails who corrupts it.

SURAH 92

The Night

These who in all sincerity and truthfulness testify to the best will indeed make smooth for the self the path to bliss.
But those who give the lie and falsehood to the best will indeed make smooth for themselves the path to misery.
By the calm of the night pray ye to stay in the ways of righteousness.

SURAH 93
The Glorious Morning Light

By the glorious morning light and the stillness of the night, the Lord is with thee and is pleased with thee. The Lord will give thee guidance and spiritual riches, and the Lord will hear all petitions asked.

SURAH 94
The Expansion of the Breast

Thy Lord will expand thy breast and remove thy burden to raise thy esteem.
So verily, with every difficulty, there is relief.
Therefore when thou art free from burden, still labour hard. And to thy Lord turn all thy attention.

SURAH 95
The Fig

The parable of the Fig Tree is that some of the figs will be good but some will be rotten.

Thy good figs must be separated from the rotten ones.

By the fig, a most delicious and fine fruit, and wholesome,
By the olive of a blessed tree, of an oil delicious in flavour,
and of purity in colour,
Conduct thy life in good and fruitful ways, and pleasing to the Lord.
For Allah doest create man and woman from the best of moulds, but ye can fall to low depths of evil unless ye seek to live a good life of righteousness.

SURAH 96
Read!

Proclaim! In the name of the Lord Most Bountiful who taught man and woman that which they knew not, who bestows talents, gifts, and knowledge on all men, women, and children.
Yet some looketh upon themselves as self-sufficient, but, verily, to the Lord give thanks.
Study and read to educate thyself in knowledge, for knowledge is power to the mind.
And, verily, give thanks to the Lord for the eternal principles of Right which lay deep in the hearts of the believers, thy devotees of Love and Peace; thy faithful votaries will not turn away from their Lord.
Say: 'Heed not unbelievers: But bow down in adoration and bring thyself closer to the Lord of the Unseen Spirit.'

SURAH 97
The Night of Power or Honour

Blessed are the revelations from the Lord that come to thy heart and soul!
A power from the Lord in a moment's time is better than the time of a thousand months!
For the angels and the Spirit bring peace on every errand. So thou may rest in Spiritual Glory.

SURAH 98
The Clear Evidence

If a polytheist or a pagan is peaceful to you, be
peaceful to them,
for Allah doth loveth peace.
The Spirit is known by many names in many religions.
A religion that is right and good offers no more than this;
Love thyAllah (Love thy God) with a pure heart and practice charity for others - to do aught else is to fall from grace.
The righteous will dwell in the heavenly Gardens of Eternity, with the mutual soul of the Lord, but the mischief makers will be hold accountable
If no religions had been invented, all would have faith in the same Unknown.

SURAH 99
The Earthquake

In the final end, anyone who has done an atom's weight of good, see it! In this world, good and evil are mixed in degrees - but thy must repel the evil to stay in the right way.

SURAH 100
Those That Run

In the midst of thy labours and wealth of thy days, acquaint thy soul with the blessings from thy Lord.
Do not let clouds of dust keep you from the Lord.
Remember thy Lord who makes all things manifest.
And all wealth that is acquired on earth will be lost and scatter at the time of resurrection and the grave.

SURAH 101
The Great Calamity

The day of Noise and Clamour is the Day of Judgment. Men and women will be like moths scattered about. Mountains will not be solid but like flakes of wool.

On your Day of Account before the Lord let your Balance of Justice be heavy on the side of good deeds and light on the side of bad deeds.

For the good deeds will be rewarded with the Lord's grace. The bad deeds are a matter of humiliation and guilt, and the Lord will direct the way of the rebellious.

SURAH 102
The Piling Up

O believers! Learn the serious issues of higher life instead of desiring to accumulate wealth and thy material possessions!

There are 3 kinds of knowledge:
1) Ilm al-yaqin is man's power of judgment and reasoning, inference.

2) Ayn al-yaqin is seeing is believing, certainty by personal inspection.

3) Haqq al-yaqin is the absolute truth, as with ancillary aids such as microscopes.

The three yaqeen, the three certainties, are the pathway to walaya, which is the pathway of Saints. Divine knowledge is given to a person by the Lord; knowledge given to true messengers.

SURAH 103
Time Through the Ages

By time throughout the ages,
men and women are at loss,
so waste not your short life,
and remember thy holy scriptures
for righteousness, so that thou have
layers and layers of meaning and
guidance.

In the late afternoon, as the day passes into the night, remember thy day and the quick passing of thy day, and do establish thou work for good causes.

SURAH 104
The Scandal Monger

Woe to every kind of scandal monger who creates lies. Woe to the back biter, even if ye speak a truth, for taint is the nature.
Woe to those who are misers when it comes to charitable purpose.
Only pure souls will be enjoined with the Soul of Sovereign.

SURAH 105
The Elephant

The souls of Prophets and believers are greater than worship buildings, for worship buildings may crumble, but souls are for eternity.

The ruler Abrahah Ashram who came with an elephant train to destroy the mosque was an evil one.

The Lord is with thee in Spirit wheresoever ye may be.

SURAH 106
The Tribe of Quraysh

The tribe of the Holy Prophet Mohammad was Quraysh. But some of the Quraysh did not believe in the teachings of Mohammad.

Let all adore the Lord, who provides food against hunger and security against fear.

SURAH 107
The Neighborly Assistance

Woe to worshippers who make great show and wish to be seen, but refuse to occasionally supply even neighborly needs to those in want.

Vain is worship without heart, soul, and charity.

SURAH 108
The Abundance

O believers, you are blessed with a Fountain of Spirituality for your thirst, therefore turn to thy Lord in adoration and devotion. And practice not hatred, which destroys hope of the present and future.

SURAH 109
Those Who Reject Faith

There are those who reject faith and cling to worldly interests. There are those who call the Holy Spirit by different names.
Say: 'I worship not that which ye worship, Nor will ye worship that which I worship.
To you be your way
And mine to mine.
And peace to all people.'

SURAH 110
The Help

For that which is right and good, the help of the Holy Spirit is ever near. When the spirit of people is stirred by a good cause, they are welcomed by the Lord and the angels, so celebrate thy praises to the Heavenly Realm.

SURAH 111
The Plaited Rope

A wicked woman laid out ropes of thorns so Mohammad would step on them on dark nights, and persecutors threw stones at Mohammad's head,
but the spirit of the Holy Prophet was not broken by sticks, stones, thorns, or harsh words.
And, the spirits of the souls who are truly faithful to the Lord Allah cannot be broken by sticks, stones, thorns, or harsh words.

SURAH 112
The Purity of Faith

Say: 'Allah is Eternal and Absolute.' And there is none like the Spirit of Allah.

SURAH 113
The Daybreak

Say: 'I seek refuge with
the Lord,
the Lord of the Dawn and Dusk,
the Lord of the Day and Night.
I seek refuge from the mischief of slander, rumours, and secret plottings, perverted wants, danger, fear, superstition, and ignorance.
And from the mischief of the envious one who practices envy and jealousy.
I will put my hope in the Lord Allah and no disturbance can affect the happiness of the fortress of my inmost soul.'

SURAH 114
Humanity

Say: 'I seek refuge with the Lord and Cherisher of All Creation.
I reject those who whisper evil among jinns and humankind,
and I reject the evil whispers even from my own heart.
The Lord is my sure shield and protection against mischief, for Lord Allah doth care to protect and cherish me. Allah is the sure goal to which all souls return.'
Say: 'I reject mischief and will seek the comfort and joy in the Grace Divine!'
We, the angels, did give Mohammad these beautiful surahs for eternity.

HADITH

Mohammad said:
1. Seek knowledge from the cradle to the grave.
2. The ink of the scholar is more sacred than the blood of the martyr.
3. The best action is the striving (mujahadat) of Allah's servants against their idle desires.
4. When God decreed the Creation He pledged by writing in His book: My mercy prevails over My wrath.

BAHAI

In 1844CE, Siyyid Ali Mohammad Shirazi claimed to be the Mahdi of Shia Islam.
He adopted the title of Bab.
Bab heralded the coming of Baha'ullah. Bab has been compared to John the Baptist, who heralded a divine teacher who was to come later. The Bab had 18 disciples. He pilgrimaged to Mecca in 1844 CE and openly declared that He was a Reformer of Divine Religions and claimed he was the Mahdi (the redeemer predicted) and he was imprisoned. Bab was a good soul who tried to institute a new religion which produced good effects on the thoughts, no oppression because of religious beliefs, good morals, good customs, and improvements on the conditions in Persia.

Tahirih (Tahere), 'the pure one', is short for Fatimah Baraghami (1814-1852 CE).
Tahirih was a young woman poet and theologian of the Babi Faith who was killed for her religious belief and following the Bab.

Bab was killed in 1850 because some people did not believe He was divinely inspired. In 1852 thousands of Babis were killed for their religious beliefs. Bab is buried at Mount Carmel. The Day of Judgment is the Day by acceptance or rejection of those who know the voice and ways of the Good Shepherd and follow the Lord and obtain entrance to Heaven for life everlasting. Followers of Bab practiced love and courtesy to others, engaged in arts, sciences, technology, and education. Men and women were considered to be equal with equal freedoms. The poor people and orphans were provided for out of a common treasury. The guiding motive of Babis was pure love and selfless giving, without hope of reward, to know and love God, and mirror forth the attributes of the good and holy God.

The Messiah Baha'ullah

In 1863CE Mirza Husayn Ali Nuri called himself Baha'ullah which means 'Glory of God' or the 'Promised One' and claimed he was a messiah messenger and a fulfiller of prophecies just as Moses, Buddha, Jesus, Krishna, and Mohammad.
He said he was not actually God because God would not descend to the human world because 'GOD IS A HOLY SPIRIT', but that he was speaking with the attributes of God and that God told him that religions should stop fighting. Baha'ullah taught that humanity is one single race and the age has come for its unification in global society. Baha'i Faith followers believe in the progression of divine leaders from the beginning of time.
Baha'ullah said one of faith should live their whole life as it were a prayer; all actions should be holy.

It is more important to be a spiritual person than to adhere to strict rules of human-created religions.

Baptism with water is not necessary; a change of heart and intent of mind is needed.

All humanity is one family; men and women are equal.

All prejudices of race, religion, national, or economic - are destructive and must be overcome.

All truths and facts should be investigated with preconceptions.

Science and the divine realm are in harmony.

Spiritual people who created religions for good purposes and who preach good things are filled with the Spirit of God. World peace benefits all.

The Reality of Divinity is the Essence of essences, the Truth of truths, the Mystery of mysteries. The Reality of the Divinity is hidden from all comprehension, and religions help humans to understand that plane of existence.

Happy are those who seek to gain knowledge and truth.
Woe to those who have fallen into the lowest depths of foolishness, ignorance, and evilness.

A meaning of trinity is union, harmony, and affection.

A Pentecost is when the Holy Spirit descends upon Apostles and they teach the Cause of God.

Knowledge is 2 kinds: (1) perceptible to our human physical senses (2) intellectual realities such as emotions, happiness, sadness, divine revelations.

A *testimony* is to deliver a divine message promoting the good ways of God so that the light of the virtues of the world of humanity might shine forth.

The fez was a hat for men that started in Egypt in 1873 CE and was a modern symbol for religion outside of religions.

Baha'i Apostles 1863CE

Baha'ullah had 19 Apostles, and the names of the Apostles were: Mirza Musa,
Badi, Sultanush-Shuhada, Haji Amin, Mirza Abul-Fadl,
Varqa, Mirza Mahmud, Haji Akhund, Nabil-i-Akbar, Vakilu'd-Dawlih, Ibn-i-Abhar, Nabil-i-Azam, Kazim-i-Samandar, Mirza Mustafa, Mishkin-Qalam, Adib, Shaykh Mohammad-Ali, Zaynu'l-Muquarrabin, Ibn-i-Asdaq.
Baha'ullah closest Apostle was Samandar.

The 19 Apostles were entrusted with the teachings of the Tablets of Baha'ullah.

Badi (1852-1869CE) was tortured and killed for following the teachings of the Bab and Baha'ullah; Badi was only 17 years old.

Some Muslims in the Ottoman Empire did not agree with the teachings of Baha'ullah, and the Messiah
Baha'ullah was persecuted and imprisoned for 24
years in Akka, Palestine. Upon his release from prison, he lived at a Mansion called Bahji, which was purchased from a Christian family called Jamal. Baha'ullah died in 1892CE and buried at the Mansion at Bahji; his resting place is a Qiblih (a direction of prayer energy) to Bahai's.

While he was in prison, Baha'ullah wrote letters to Pope Pius IX of the Catholics,
to Queen Victoria in England, to Napoleon III in France, and to many others to encourage the unity of diversity of all religions and races (peoples).

The Baha'i Aqdas

The Aqdas holy book contains themes of worship, societal relations, administrative organization, and governance of the Baha'i religion. Bahai's observe a 19-day period from sunset to sunrise each spring dedicated to God. The faith of the Baha'is is not to be enforced upon anyone who does not desire to follow it or hear its messages. The Bahai Faith prohibits congregational prayers except for at funerals; prayer is to be private from the heart but gatherings at the Baha'i Centers allow gatherings for spiritual sharing. Tyranny and oppression is forbidden.
Reformation of economic conditions so poverty will disappear is a good consideration. Leaders of religions are encouraged to speak in each other's different religious dwellings. Hell is simply deprivation of that knowledge of God with consequent failure to attain divine perfection and loss of Eternal Favour.

Before Baha'ullah died, he appointed his son, Abdul-Baha as his successor. Abdul-Baha was born in Tehran in 1844 and led the mission of the Baha'i Faith until his death in 1921CE. Abdu'l-Baha traveled from Akka to Haifa, to Alexandria, London, Paris, New York, and cities in Egypt to spread the Baha'i messages that the same holy spirit is in all religions.
Abdul-Baha wrote a concept of Trinity is union, harmony, and affection.
Before he died, Abdul-Baha appointed his grandson Shoghi Effendi as the head of the Baha'i Faith and he published the AQDAS in 1890CE. Shoghi Effendi died in England in 1957CE.

Martha Louis Root (1872-1939 CE), daughter of Timothy and Nancy Root of the United States of America, was a teacher of the Baha'i Faith and the writings of Baha'ullah and his successor (who was his son) Abdul-Baha. She traveled worldwide to spread the *good news* of the Baha'i Faith.

Martha had 2 brothers, Clarence and Claude.
Her father Timothy was a dairy farmer in Ohio.

Martha Louis Root shared the writings of the Baha'i Faith with Queen Marie of Romanie, and Queen Marie accepted Baha'ullah as a Teacher of the Lord.

Kitabi means 'from the ancient laws of our forefathers' and Aqdas means 'purity'.

Verses derived from:

Kitabi - I - AQDAS (IQAN) 1873 CE By Baha'u'llah

The well-being of mankind, its peace and security, are attainable if unity is established.

Rules for the Baha'i Faith prohibit congregational prayer except for the dead, fixes the Qiblih as He Who God will make manifest for Baha'i, establishes laws of inheritances, establishes the Nineteen Day Feast and Baha'I Festivals, prohibits slavery, prohibits asceticism, penance, and kissing of hands. Monogamy (one wife) is encouraged and divorce is discouraged. There is a ban on the use of opium, intoxicating liquors, and gambling. There are punishments for crimes such as murder, arson, adultery, and theft. Baha'u'llah stresses the importance of education for all children and the engagement in a trade of work for adults. Each person should write their own will and testament and obey one's government. Followers of Baha'i Faith should be friends with humans of all religions.
Baha'u'llah discourages fanaticism, sedition (coup to overthrow a government), pride, and violence. Dispute and contention should be discussed among mankind and differences should be referred to God. Salat are obligatory prayers said by an individual in private to God. The prohibition that banned ordinary people from wearing silk was lifted.

The AQDAS is a holy book of heaven which we have adorned with the stars of Our Commandments and prohibitions, and we ponder the verses sent down in it by God, the Lord of Power, the Almighty. Blessed is the man who reads holy verses that are sent to amaze the minds of humans. Blessed is the palate that savors sweetness (kindness, goodness), the mind that recognizes the treasures of the holy verses, and the heart that seeks the God that is among revelations, allusions, and mysteries. Blessed are those who ponder God.

IN THE NAME OF GOD WHO IS THE SUPREME RULER OVER ALL THAT HATH BEEN AND ALL THAT IS TO BE

1. The first duty prescribed by God is recognition of Divine Revelations and Fountains of God's Laws and Gifts of Treasures. The second duty

is to follow the Ordinances of God. These twin duties are inseparable.

2. Those that turn away from God's good ways and submit to evil passions and corrupt desires are foolish.

3. O ye peoples of the world! Know assuredly that My Commandments are the lamps of My Loving Providence among My Servants and the keep of My Mercy for My Creatures. The will of Your Lord gives sweetness to words and truth to commandments.

4. The Lord's omnipotent glory and grace is like a perfume of fine fragrance.

5. By pens of revelation, the Lord and the Lord's code of laws have been unsealed like choice Wine.

6. Prayers (salat) can be offered in the morning, at noon, and at night.

7. Everything that hath come to be has been through the Lord's irrestible decrees.

8. The details for the salat obligatory prayers and fasts are written in another Tablet. Prostrate once and then you can sit.

9. You are free to wear your hair as you please. You are free to wear the fur of the beaver, the squirrel, and other animals, as you please.

10. We have removed the obligation to prostrate on a clean surface, for God hath knowledge of that whereof ye know naught.

11. The Prayer of the Signs for earthquakes and sandstorms is annulled.

12. Repeat 'Allah'u'Abha' 6 times which means God is Most Glorious. Then repeat 19 times the following verses:
'We all, verily, worship God. We all, verily, bow down before God. We all, verily, are devoted unto God.
We all, verily, give praise to God.
We all, verily, give thanks unto God.
We all, verily, are patient to God.'

13. Women in their courses, the ill and the weak are exempt from fasting.

14. When traveling, stop in a safe spot to pray.

19. Ye are forbidden to commit murder, adultery, theft, slander, arson, or slander to God.

20. Divide inheritances into seven categories: children, mother, father, brothers, sisters, teachers, and the unborn.

30. In every city shall be a House of Justice for the people of Baha'i.

31. Build ye houses of worship.

33. Engage in an occupation or craft.

34. Kissing of hands is forbidden.

36. Leave your sandals by the door.

40. Rejoice not in the things ye possess; all will perish and tomorrow others will possess them.

42. Gifts made to charity revert to God.

43. Seek ye the Middle Way which is the remembrance of Me.

44. Shave not your heads.

45. Prison is for the thief and place a mark upon his brow on the third offence.

48. Parents must educate their child in the art of reading and writing. The House of Justice is a shelter for the poor and the needy. He who hath brought up a son or the son of another, it is as though he hath brought up a child of Mine. The age of maturity is 15 for male and

female. Old age is 70 for male and female.
49. Adulterers must pay a fine to the House of Justice of 9 mithquals of gold.
51. It is lawful for you to listen to music and sing.
53. Should differences arise amongst you, refer it to God.
55. Be ye thankful for My showers of Bounty that pour down from the heaven of My Loving-Kindness.
58. Beware lest desires of flesh and corrupt inclinations will bring ruin. Be ye as fingers of one hand for the good work of the Lord.
60. If ye hunt beasts and birds of prey, hunt not to excess.
61. Do not steal from the property of others.
62. Those who commit arson or murder shall also be put to death. Follow God and abandon the ways of the ignorant.
65. Marriage is the consent of both parties.
66. Marriage is conditioned on payment of a dowry from the man which is 19 mithqals of pure gold for city-dwellers and 19 mithqals of silver for village-dwellers.
67. If a husband travels, he should tell his wife when he will return. If he does not return within one year, the wife is free to remarry.
70. Divorce is allowed, but God loveth union and harmony.
72. Slavery is forbidden.
77. It is permitted to read about the sciences and to comprehend them.
84. Detach yourselves from all else but Me, Your Lord. The Crimson Ark has been prepared for the people of Baha'i.
103. The verses of the Mother Book and the Burning Bush at the Mount above the Holy Land proclaim: 'The Lord is Sovereign of All, the All-Powerful, the Loving!"
106. Pare (cut) your nails and bathe yourselves each week.
107. Do not marry the wives of your father.
109. All should write a will and testament.
116. Those who recite holy verses are blessed.
124. Regard humans as a flock of sheep that need a shepherd for their protection.
128. The dead should be buried in coffins made of crystal, stone, or wood. 130. The dead should be buried enfolded in sheets of silk or cotton.
137. The Qiblih is Him who God will make manifest.
144. Consort with all religions with amity and concord.
145. Take heed ye enter no house in the absence of its owner.
148. Ye are forbidden to engage in contention and conflict and strike another. Wish not for others what ye wish not for yourselves.
150. Teach your children verses from the heaven in the alcoves within the Mashriqu'l Adhkars.
152. Wash your feet every day in summer and every 3 days in winter.
153. Respond to anger with gentleness.
154. Ye have been prohibited from making use of pulpits. Whoso wisheth to recite unto you the verses of his Lord, let him sit on a chair placed upon a dais (platform), that he may make mention of God. It

is pleasing to God that ye should seat yourselves on chairs and benches as a mark of honour to hear about the love ye bear for God.
155. Gambling and opium are forbidden.
156. If invited to a banquet or festivity, respond with joy and gladness.
159. You are forbidden to carry arms unless essential.
163. Infidels distract the soul of the believer who is steadfast in the Lord. Infidels suggest evilness.
166. Call to mind the shaykh (Islamic scholar) whose name was Muhammad-Hasan, who was one of the most learned divines of his day. Some rejected him, while a sifter of wheat and barley accepted him and turned unto the Lord.
178. Religion is not a Cause to be made a plaything for fantasies. God is an arena for love, truth and upliftment.
187. Do not burden an animal with more than it can bear.
188. Should anyone unintentionally take another's life, it is incumbent upon him to render to the family of the deceased an indemnity of 100 mithquals of gold.
189. Select a language for the world and it may bring peace.

Baha'i Scriptures derived from Selections of the Baha'i Writings of the Bab, Baha'ullah, and Abdul-baha

The purities were reduced of redundancy from over 200 to 123.

The messiahs Bab and then Baha'ullah preached that the Holy Spirit sent them to tell the world to break down religious barriers.

The Holy Spirit has worked thru humanity since the beginnings of time. The divine work of the holy spirit was known in all of the prophets since the beginning of time who have preached about the Holy Spirit.

All major religions come from God.

World peace benefits all.

PURITY 1

God's faith is Peace and Love

O, peoples of the world! The Sun of Truth hath risen to illumine the whole earth, and to spiritualize the community of humanity. Praiseworthy are the results and the fruits thereof, abundant the holy evidences deriving from this grace. This is mercy and bounty in pure form; it is light for the world and all its peoples; it is harmony and fellowship, and love and solidarity; indeed it is compassion and unity, and the end of foreignness; it is the being at one, in complete dignity, integrity and freedom, with all on earth.

The Blessed Beauty said: 'You are all the fruits of one tree, the leaves of one branch.' Thus God hath likened this world of being to a single tree, and all its peoples to the leaves thereof, and the blossoms and fruits. It is needful for the bough to blossom, and leaf and fruit to flourish, and there is an interconnection of all parts of the world-tree. For this reason must all human beings powerfully sustain one another and seek for everlasting life. For this reason must the lovers of God in this world become the mercies and blessings sent forth by the Unseen God.

We are all a part of one humankind as leaves and blossoms and fruits of the tree of being. Let all people at all times concern themselves with doing a kindly thing for another person, offering love, consideration, or thoughtful help.

The one favored at the Threshold of the Lord is the one who hands round the cup of faithfulness; who bestows, even upon his enemies, the jewel of bounty, and lends, even to his fallen oppressor, a helping hand; it is the one who will, even to the fiercest foe, be a loving friend. These are the Teachings of the Blessed Beauty, these are the counsels of the Most Great Name.

O ye dear friends! When there are wars and the hate has taken over, the good faith is blotted out. People sharpen their tongues and claws, hurling themselves one against the other; destroying the foundation of the human race. In wars thousands of human beings are killed on dusty battlefields; their life and joy gone from them. But the generals of the armies boast of their violence and aggression towards other people or nations – it is censuring love, righteousness, harmony, and devotion to the truth of God.

The Faith of the Blessed Beauty is summoning humankind to safety and love, to amity and peace, and directs its call to all nations. Wherefore, O you who are God's lovers, know the value of precious Faith, walk in this road that is drawn straight, and show this way to the people. Lift up your voices and sing out the song of the Loving Lord, so that this world will change into a better world for all, so that all souls will seek immortality with the holy Lord.

All humans die, soon will your swiftly-passing days be over, and the fame, riches, comforts, joys, and sorrows will be gone without a trace. Summon the people to God, and invite humanity to follow the example of the Company On High. Be loving to the orphan, a refuge for the helpless, a treasury for the poor, and a cure for the ailing. Be helpers for every victim of oppression, the patrons of the disadvantaged. Think at all times of rendering some service to every member of the human race. Pay no heed to disdain, hostility, and injustice: act in the opposite way. Be sincerely kind, not in appearance only. Let each one of God's loved ones center his or her attention on this: to be the Lord's mercy to another; to be the Lord's grace to another. Let him or her do some good to every person whose path is crossed with his or her own, and be of some benefit to each other. Improve the character of each other and reorient the minds of each other; guide each other to stay on the good path. In this way, the light of divine guidance will shine forth, and the blessings of God will cradle all humankind. O friends of God! That the hidden Mystery may stand revealed, and the secret essence of all things may be disclosed, strive to banish all evils and hatred for ever and ever.

PURITY 2

Divine Essence

O my Lord! I draw near to Thee, confiding in Thee with my heart, trembling with joy at the sweet scents that blow from Thy Realm, the All-Glorious, calling unto Thee, saying: O my Lord, no words do I find to adequately glorify Thee; Thy very being is beyond the praises offered Thee by the people that Thou hast created.

Thou art exalted above all understanding! Forever will Thou remain enwrapped within the holiness of Thine own reality, unmatched by anything.

O God, my God! How can I glorify or describe Thee inaccessible as Thou art; immeasurably high and sanctified art Thou above every description and praise. Thou are high and low; Thou exists everywhere.

O God, my God! Have mercy upon my helpless state, my poverty, my misery, my humbleness. Give me to drink from the generous cup of Thy grace and forgiveness, stir me with the sweet scents of Thy love, gladden my bosom with the light of Thy knowledge, purify my soul with the mysteries of Thy oneness, raise me to life with the gentle breezes that come from the gardens of Thy mercy. I will hold fast to the hem of Thy garment of Grandeur and consign to oblivion all that is not Thee. Let me be companioned by Thy sweet breathings that waft, and may I attain unto faithfulness at Thy Threshold.

O God, my God! I beg of Thee by the dawning of the light of Thy Beauty and the compassion of Thy Divine Essence – to help the faithful who love you, O God.

O loved ones of God! When the Sun of Reality spread its endless bounties from the Dawning Point of all beginnings, with such intensity did the earth of dust become a sphere of the supernatural realm. The gentle breeze of holiness blew over it; the winds of heaven from the Source wafted fruitful airs over the world, so that all creation came forth, bringing immortal blooms, fresh greenery, gardens of holiness, and everlasting life. Then came forth flowers of mystic learning bespeaking the knowledge of God. The world displays God's bounties and reflect glories of divine realm. Divine summon was proclaimed, the tablet of Eternal Covenant was readied, the cup of the Testament was passed from hand to hand, and the universe was sent forth. God's word is clear in the spiritual visions and words of Moses and Elias on Mount Tabor and all the great messengers of the Spirit worldwide in all religions. Lovers of the Holy Spirit were illuminated by the light of grace and were united on the path of joy. People of the world carry candles for the Covenant of Unity. God will give guidance with divine bestowal, for many are called, but few are chosen.

Yet alas, the neglectful and foolish who have strayed should be offered the sweet winds or honey-dew that perfume the earth.
Train your soul and refine your character and ask for bestowal of guidance back to good ways and truth, for the sake of everlasting glory.

Remind yourselves to purify your character and conduct to goodness. The lovers of God reflect good qualities and perform good actions, such as to be a blessed individual, to free yourself from disdain, to adorn thyself with good qualities.
The foul – those who knowingly do evil - should learn that there is a realm of purity.

The reality of the inner self of humankind should seek divine guidance in order to sanctify Thy own self;
wherefore, O beloved of the Lord, strive with your heart and soul to receive a share of holy attributes and take a portion of holy bounties – that you may become tokens of unity, the standards of singleness, and seek out the meaning of Oneness; that you may, in this garden of God, lift up your voices and sing the blissful anthems of spirit; become as the birds who offer the Lord their thanks or as the blossoms who offer the Lord their beauty; chant such melodies as will dazzle the minds of those who seek the Lord. Raise a banner on the highest peaks of the world, a flag of God's favor to ripple and wave in the winds of divinity; plant trees, flowers and fruits that will yield freshness.

The Holy One is our Divine Teacher. Swear by the True Teacher that if you will act in accord with the good ways of God, holiness will mirror forth. Praise be to the Lord, the unseen Sun of Truth! Know the value of the Lord. Stay entirely clear of the evils of the world, and become known by the good attributes in Heaven. Then shall you see how intense is the glory of the tokens of glory of the invisible realm.

PURITY 3

Eternal God

O you beloved of God! The holiness of the Celestial Concourse is the truth, beauteous, and unique.

God is the Alpha and the Omega.

God gives to the thirsty the fountain of the water of life and bestows upon the sick the remedy of true salvation. He or she that receives the most glorious heritage from the Divine Essence receives grace.
Rejoice, then, O lovers of the Lord, for you are the children of God and you are God's people; raise your voices to praise and magnify the Lord, the Most High, whose power beams forth light and has scattered pearls on every shore.

PURITY 4

Judgement Day

Praise be to the Lord who hath made the invisible world to appear visible, yet the lost men and women still wander and stray.

The trumpet will be sounded on the Judgement Day, the Balance will be set up, and the Ever-Forgiving Lord will judge each accordingly from the Realm on High.

The splendours of the Lord will be manifest for all to see, standing as proof of Divine Presence, demonstrating perfection.

PURITY 5

Believe in the Lord

O you beloved of the Lord! Beware lest you hesitate and waver. Let not fear fall upon you, neither be troubled or dismayed. Take good heed lest this calamitous day slacken the flames of ardour, and quench your tender hopes. Today is the day for steadfastness and consistency.

Blessed are they that stand firm and immovable as the rock and brave the storm and stress of this tempestuous hour. They, verily, shall be the recipients of God's grace; they, verily, shall receive divine assistance, and shall be truly victorious. They shall shine amidst humankind with a radiance which the dwellers of the Pavilion of Glory laud and magnify. When the beauty of the instructed ones is withdrawn and their utterance is stilled, do not be dismayed, for there is yet another day-star appointed by God to further the cause of holiness and righteousness, and the angels shall behold from the realm of glory to exalt God's Word among all people.

PURITY 6

Give Thanks to God

O you people of the Holy Spirit! Long for thy soul to expend all its span of life in worship! Thank God for setting upon your heads the crown of glory everlasting, for granting you immeasurable grace. As a thank-offering for this bestowal, you should grow in faith and constancy as day follows day, and should draw ever nearer to the Lord, your God, becoming magnetized to such a degree, and so aflame, that your holy melodies in praise of the Beloved will reach upward to the Company on High; and that each one of you, even as a nightingale in this rose garden of God, will glorify the Lord of Angels, and become a teacher of righteousness to all who dwell on earth.

PURITY 7

Universal Fellowship

O you spiritual friends, let your hearts dance for joy and fill your souls with an ecstasy of love and rapture. So intensely hath the glory of Divine Unity penetrated souls and hearts that all are now bound one to another with heavenly ties, and all are even as a single heart, a single soul.

Wherefore reflections of spirit and impressions of the Divine are now mirrored from one humankind. May God strengthen these spiritual bonds as day follows day, and make this mystic oneness to shine ever more brightly, until at last all shall be gathered together beneath the banner of the Covenant of Unity within the shelter of the Word of God; that all may strive with all their might until universal fellowship, close and warm, and pure love and spiritual relationships will connect all the hearts in the world. Then will conflict and dissension vanish from the face of the earth, then will all humankind be cradled in love with the All-Glorious Holy Spirit. Discord will change to accord, dissension to unison. The roots of malevolence will be torn out, the basis of aggression destroyed. The bright rays of union will obliterate the darkness of limitations, and the splendours of heaven will make the human heart rich with the love of God.

O God, the Most Great Name! Aid Thou thy trusted servants to have loving and tender hearts. Help them to spread the light of guidance and joy that cometh from the Lord, Who is the Ancient Beauty.

PURITY 8

God's Family

O Lord! Clear the heads of the unmindful, that they may perceive the sweet spirit of the Most Bountiful. The righteous taste the honey of reunion in the congregation of the Lord. The Holy Writings say that we must be at one with every people - behold no person is different from yourselves - see all people as friends in love and unity.

All creatures are a sign of God, and it was by the power and grace of the Lord that each did step into the world; therefore they are not strangers, but in the family; not aliens, but friends, and to be treated as such.

PURITY 9

Follow the Lord's Covenants

O thou whose heart overflows with love for the Lord! The hearts of those who believeth in God's oneness are raised on summits of bliss, thus the Lord will make these believers a sign for every seeker of the truth.

Hold fast to the Covenants of thy Lord, and as the days go by, increase thy store of love in thy hearts for the work of thy Lord, the All-Merciful, that thou may hoist the sail of love upon the ark of peace that moves across the seas of life. Let nothing grieve you, and be angered at none.

It behoveth thee to be content with the Will of God, and be a true and loving and trusted friend to all the peoples of the earth, without any exceptions whatever. This is the quality of the sincere, the way of the saints, the emblem of those who believe in the unity of God, and the raiment of the people of Bahá. Verily is the Holy Spirit Ever-Bestowing, Loving, and Tender.

PURITY 10

The Guidance of the Holy Spirit

Believe thou in God, and keep thy mind fixed upon Heaven and good ways.

Stand firm in the Covenant; yearn thou to ascend into the Heaven of the Universal Light. Be thou set apart from this world and reborn through the sweet scents of holiness that blow from the realm of the All-Highest. Be thou a summoner to love, and be thou kind to all the human race. Love thou all children, men, and women and share all their sorrows and joys. Be thou of those who foster peace. Offer thy friendship and be worthy of trust. Recite the verses of guidance and praise. Be engaged in the worship of thy Lord, and rise up to lead the people aright. Loosen thy tongue to teach the love of God, and let thy face be bright with the fire of God's love. Thus may thou become a sign and a symbol of love, by the grace of the Holy Spirit.

PURITY 11

Kindness and Helping Others

Service to friends is service to God.

Consideration shown to the poor is one of the greatest teachings of God.

PURITY 12

Love is heaven's kindly light, the Holy Spirit's eternal breath that vivifies the human soul and gives life to all things. Love is the cause of God's revelation unto man, the vital bond inherent, in accordance with divine creation, in the realities of things. Love inspires felicity in the heart. Love is the light that guides, the link that unites God with humankind, that assures progress of every illuminated soul. Love is the most great law that rules this mighty and heavenly cycle, the unique power that binds together all the diverse elements of this material world and the entire universe, the supreme magnetic force that directs the movements of the spheres in the celestial realms.

Love reveals with unfailing and limitless power the mysteries latent in the universe.

Love is the spirit of life unto the adorned body of humankind, the establisher of true civilization in this mortal world, the shedder of imperishable glory upon every high-aiming race and nation.

Whatsoever people is graciously favoured therewith by the Holy Spirit, thy people shall surely be magnified and extolled by the Concourse from on High, by the company of angels, to spread the Covenant and remind the people to stay on the good path of life and avoid all evil.

PURITY 13

Baha'i Conduct

O believers of the Lord! Serve the oneness of the world of humanity, show love to all religions and be kind to all people. The divine religions must be the cause of oneness among all people, and the means of unity and love; they must promote universal peace, free the minds of people from prejudices, bestow joy and gladness, and exercise kindness to all people. Just as Baha'ullah addressed the world of humanity saying: 'O people! Ye are the fruits of one tree and the leaves of one branch. At most it is this, that some souls are ignorant and must be educated; some are sick and must be healed; some are still of tender age and must be helped to attain maturity, and the utmost kindness must be shown to them. This is the conduct of the people of Bahá. I hope that thy brothers and sisters will all become the well-wishers of the world of humankind.'

PURITY 14

Human will to think and act

O ye blessed souls! Investigate the truth and be freed from limitations and superstitions, that ye observe with your own eyes and not with those of others, hearken your ears and not with the ears of others, and discover mysteries with the help of ye own consciences and not with those of others; ye hath a will of your own.

The path of life will have bumps and twists, but leads thy way only to the Realm of the Holy Spirit.

PURITY 15

Unity

To be a lover of the Holy Spirit is to embody every excellence there is to the highest degree of certitude and faith, having no doubt of thy covenant with the Holy Spirit.

May the many rivers, each flowing along in diverse and separated beds, all find their way back to the sea of oneness; the unity of truth of the one Holy Spirit that exists for all religions. If unity be gained, other problems will disappear. People can achieve peace if they desire.

For a single purpose were the Prophets of all religions, each and all, sent down to earth; that the world of humans should become the world of the Holy Spirit, which is called by many names – and unity, fellowship, and love be won for the whole human race and the discord be destroyed, so that life and grace everlasting should become the harvest of humanity.

When thou dost consider all phenomena, thou wilt see that everything has come into being through the mingling of many elements, and this harmony of components has brought forth unity and mutual attraction, to promote life and progress.

In cycles gone by, unity of all humans was not achieved because continents were widely divided and interchange of thought was poor. In this day, however, means of communication have multiplied and now it is easy to travel to any land and exchange views with other people, and read the thoughts of other people through written publications and speeches before thy countenance. All members of the human family whether people or governments, cities or villages, have become increasingly interdependent. Between nations, the bonds of trade, industry, agriculture, education, science, communication, medicine, and humanitarian causes are being strengthened every day.

It is the wonders of this glorious century, this wondrous age, that past ages were deprived of, but, due to progress and knowledge and

time, this century is endowed with greater illumination.
Eventually even more progress will be made in the world.

Seven Candles can be lit for peace or unity in global issues.
The first candle is for peace in the political realm. The second candle is thoughts of world goals. The third candle is for freedoms. The fourth candle is for respect of all religions. The fifth candle is for nations, causing people to regard themselves as good citizens of the world. The sixth candle is for humans with disregard to race. The seventh candle is for language and standards of measurement, so that all people may converse and understand together.

The realm of the Holy Spirit is the foundation of the entire universe and is recognized in all religions.

PURITY 16

O ye illuminated loved ones! Somber night skies are filled with the moon and stars, and bright morning dawns light up the eastern skies. The morning and evening horizons are glorified in colors. The sun mounts to high noon shining it glorious light to heat up the earth. At dusk, the sun sets beneath the western horizon, when ye shall need a candle for illumination. So far as you are able, ignite a candle of love in every meeting, and with tenderness, rejoice and cheer ye every heart.

Act in accordance with the counsels of the Lord: that is: each day light a candle of love. Plant flowers or a tree in the name of a loved one.

PURITY 17

Praise the Lord of Angels!
Thank and praise God of infinite bestowals who sent divine heralds from the realm above through acts and verses of humankind known as the saints, prophets, and messiahs, and holy tablets. May each one of you be even as a candle casting its light or as a bed of flowers shedding sweet scents.

Lift up your voices and sing out the songs of the Divine Reality. Quench the fires of war, lift high the banners of peace, work for the oneness of humanity and remember that religions are the channel of love unto all peoples. The children of men and women are sheep of God and God is their loving Shepherd, the Lord cares tenderly for all the sheep and makes them to feed in green pastures and to drink from the wellspring of life. The Lord's precepts is the oneness of humanity.

The inexhaustible blessings of the Lord are a sign of celestial grace. The Blessed Tree casts its shade over all the earth, making unity for all. The counsels of 'Abdu'l-Baha' hope that all hearts on earth will be united in spirit with bonds of love, out of the bounties and bestowals of the Beloved, with tears I pray to the Lord and implore the Lord to rain down blessings upon all of you, gladden all hearts, make blissful all souls, and grant all of you exceeding joy and heavenly delights.

PURITY 18

Be attached to heavenly teachings

O thou possessor of a seeing heart! Thy heart sees and thy spirit hears more than material subjects, which assuredly will be ultimately lost at the end of our lives. O loved one, you know more importance should be attached to heavenly teachings and the love of God; it discerneth and discovereth the divine realm which is everlasting and eternal. Praise God, therefore, that the sight of thy heart is illumined and the hearing of thy mind responsive to the good ways of the Lord.

PURITY 19

God and Jesus

Praise the Promised One of the seen and unseen worlds! Salutations, blessings, and welcome to that Universal Reality, that Perfect Word, the Guide to all nations, that Splendour that dawns in the highest heaven, the grace of all creation. The bestowals of thy Lord encompasses all things; may glory rest upon them. Praise be to the Lord who fashions eras of times.

It was said by Jesus Christ that he was God's Son and the unbelievers hanged him on a cross to die; it was their ignorance of the inner core of divine mysteries that they disregarded, the splendours of the Holy Spirit, and ignored the utterances of Jesus Christ; the unbelievers did not have to kill Jesus but they did it out of evilness.

Jesus Christ caused love among Romans, Greeks, Syrians, Egyptians, Phoenicians, Israelites, and other peoples of Europe, Asia, and Africa; a dove did descent upon Jesus once.

Know the Divine Essence, which is called the Invisible of the Invisibles, which is well beyond the reach of mind that intellect can never grasp it, which has created a universe like a scroll that discloses divine secrets. All atoms of the universe and all creatures reveal the glory of the Divine Essence that is spread upon all things and shining within them, telling of the splendours and mysteries manifested by them. Look upon the trees, blossoms, fruits, and even the stones, therein like a mirror, reflect the beauty of Our Creator. Those who cannot see and hear the beauty of God's work do not understand the signs of divine essence.

PURITY 20

Reformation

Some rules of the Torah are outdated; it is not needed that whoever breaks the rule of working on Sabbath should be put to death. The Jews believe when the Holy Spirit comes to earth the lion and the gazelle will dwell in one pasture, the snake and the mouse will share one hole in the ground, the eagle and the partridge will share one lake in peace.

The meanings of the signs, or revelations, from the Spirit of God were manifest in the prophets and in the messiahs and in the sages.

For Bahai's say the sovereignty of the Holy Being is everlasting and is being exalted throughout all ages.

PURITY 21
Believers

The Reality of the Divinity encompasseth all creation and the planes of all things - minerals, vegetables, animals, humans - but how could it be possible for humans to understand the true nature of the Pre-Existent Essence, the Genuine Divine Being?

All created things are connected one to another by a linkage complete and perfect, even, for example, as are the parts of the human body.

Look into the endless universe; a universal power, led by a Director, carrieth out its functions in perfect order, every separate part of it performing its own task with complete reliability. Thus it is clear that a Universal Power existeth, directing and regulating the universe.

Life on the earth is dependent on the bounty of the sun which giveth light to vegetation so the vegetation will grow. To sum it up, of this is the existence of the phenomenal universal Reality of God.

PURITY 22
The Lord's will

Ask whatsoever thou wishest of the Lord; seek whatsoever thou seekest from the Lord - but the Lord doeth as the Lord doeth, and what recourse have we? The Lord carrieth out the Lord's will and ordaineth whatsoever the Lord pleaseth. Then better for thee to bow down thy head in submission, and put thy trust in the All-Merciful Lord.

With a glance and a nod the Lord granteth hopes, healeth incurable ills, layeth balm on wounds, and freeth hearts from grief.

PURITY 23
One World

The religions of God have been made manifest for one to follow another, each reviving humankind to enlightenment, education, and happiness; but ultimately the religions of God are one.

Thoughts change, ways of life are improved, sciences and art invigorate, discoveries, inventions, perceptions are made, but humans for centuries have remained steadfast to a belief in a Divine Reality, which urges high thoughts upon the mind, refine our character, and lay the foundation for human integrity and honour. This power in none other than the breathings of the Holy Spirit and the mighty inflow of the Word of God. This power above and beyond all powers is what ends resentment, malice, hate, wrangles, wars, grudges, and spites - and changes that into fellowship and love amongst all peoples of the earth.

PURITY 24

O spiritual people! Praise thou God that thou hast pictured in the realm of the mind, whose core of inner mystery hath been made known unto thee. The Essence of Essences, the Invisible of Invisibles – the Fashioner of all that is – is sanctified above all human speculation and of that realm no understanding is known with certainty.

Philosophers like Socrates and Hippocrates - and learned doctors - have tried to learn about the Essence, but one needs a greater power more than humankind to fully comprehend the state and inner mystery of the Essence of the Essences.

PURITY 25

Death

O spiritual people! The spirit leaves the body upon death, returning to the Essence of the Universe which is maintained by the Unseeable Divine Reality.

PURITY 26

O thou seekers of Heaven! The Holy manifestations of God may be spiritual or physical. The Divine Educators will teach by words and deeds to reveal the pathway of truth; such is the servant of Baha (Abdul-Baha, son of Baha'ullah), a visible expression of servitude to the Threshold of Beauty.

PURITY 27

Ask for divine guidance

O lovers of God! Make thou an effort to be a manifestation of the divine Spirit and direct thy efforts to assist others.

PURITY 28

O leaf upon the Tree of Life! The gates of Heaven are opened wide, for favoured souls to seat at the banquet table of the Lord.

Praise be to God, thou too art present to share of the bounties. Strive with all thy might to guide all people to the Holy Reality.

For Baha'ullah is of the Tree of Life – as all humankind are – and thank thou God that thou has become related to that Tree, and that thou art flourishing and fresh. For Moses and Jesus Christ said whoever eateth of the bread that hath come down from heaven shall live forever.

PURITY 29

Abdul-Baha hopes for love and peace

O thou who art captivated
by the truth and heaven! It is the hope of Abdul-Baha that high ideals, noble intentions of the heart, and tidings of heaven shalt become so luminous that all ages of humanity shall glorify the light of thy love for God.

Humanity will look upon the Tablet of Existence as a scroll endlessly unfolding,
and every atom of the universe will be witnessed as being of the oneness of the realm of the Holy Spirit. The dispensations of past ages are connected with those that follow them, the world groweth to a world of humanity of full beauty of

unity and diversity that dazzles the mind.

For this reason did Jesus Christ say: ' I have yet many things to say unto you, matters needing to be told, but ye cannot bear to hear them now '
and Baha'ullah did say 'The Holy Spirit doth make progression throughout all ages'.

Therefore, in this age of splendours, teachings once limited to the few are made available to all, that the mercy of the Lord may embrace both east and west, that the oneness of the world of humanity may appear in its full beauty, and that the dazzling rays of reality may enlighten minds.

Read thy holy tablets and holy books which contain heavenly teachings that are a remedy for a sick and suffering world – they are the spirit of life, the ark of salvation, the magnet for eternal glory, the dynamic power to motivate the Inner Self of humans –
the tablets and books were written down by humans and have been translated over and again many times – the godly people write of the good ways of the Good Spirit and not of hatred, killing, violence, and deceptions. Do not be misled to do evil.

PURITY 30

Existence is of two kinds:

The first one is the existence of God which is beyond the comprehension of humankind; the Holy Spirit is Invisible, the Lofty and the Incomprehensible.

The second existence is everything else of life and matter: human existence, mineral existence, vegetable existence, and animal existence.

PURITY 31
Universal God

The Holy Spirit is universal law which is at work in all things. Ponder thou the shelter and all-protecting shade of the Spirit. Compare the present with the past, and see how great is the difference; humankind has worked hard to improve life.

The difference among the religions of the world are due to the varying types of minds and opinions which differ from another.

The differing opinions of all religions– do merge into a spiritual harmony and oneness for an invisible Spiritual Realm of Divine Reality.

Observe that after you follow the teachings of Prophets and Messiahs and Brahmas - that spiritual emotions are calmed and love becomes great and that love is the main thing. Love's power is far greater than all people and love is the ground of all things.

The essence of Baha'ullah's Teaching is all-embracing love, for love includeth every excellence of humankind. It causeth every soul to go forward.

PURITY 32

Future ages and generations shall behold the radiance and the manifestations of the Lord!

The cause of God is love.

PURITY 33

O servant of God! All humankind can be empowered to deliver divine revelations from the Blessed Beautiful Lord!

And one year for humankind may be like one day to the Lord.

PURITY 34

United Diversity and Friendship

It is appropriate in the age of progress for all humankind to serve each other.

It is called being a good steward or a good servant to other people.

It is called being friends in fellowship.

It is called being united in diversity.

Every imperfect soul is self-centered and thinketh only of his own good. But as a person's thoughts expand then the person will begin to think of the welfare and comfort of their family and friends - and even the whole world; the person will then be the well-wisher of all people and the seeker of the prosperity of all lands - this is perfection.

The divine Manifestations of God have been wide and all-inclusive. Therefore, ye must be thinking of everyone.

Love ye all religions and all people with a love that is true and sincere and show that love through deeds and not through the tongue only by speaking.

PURITY 35

West, Middle, and East

Eating healthy, sensibly, and in moderation is a symbol of self-restraint and demonstrates spiritual wisdom. Short-term fasting is a religious symbol of self-restraint.

It is the hope of Baha'ullah that the west and the east will become one in love and peace, a united harmony.

O, people of the Holy Spirit! Arise with aims of purified of self and follow the Teachings of God, to make this world a Mirror of Heaven, to cause all humankind to adopt the ways of righteousness.

All followers of Baha'i Faith should become known for sincerity, faithfulness, love, honesty, fidelity, truthfulness, and loving-kindness towards all the peoples of the world, so that others may say: 'This person is unquestionably a Baha'i, for their manners, their behavior, their conduct, their morals, their nature, and their disposition all reflect the good attributes of the Baha'is.'

Baha'ullah desires for all religions to adopt only good attributes.

It is the era of the oneness of all religions.

Whenever ye behold a person who, with pure intent, is rendering service for the Cause of God; whose behavior has not the slightest trace of egotism or private motives, who wandereth in love, who drinketh from the cup of knowledge of God, who is engrossed in spreading the sweet savours of God – know ye that this individual will be supported and reinforced by heaven.

To set humankind free, Jesus Christ, and Baha'ullah hath all said: Ye are the fruits of one tree and the leaves of one branch; be ye compassionate and kind to all the human race.

Deal ye with strangers the same as with friends, cherish ye others just as ye would your own. See foes as friends. Be ye a refuge to the fearful. Bring ye rest and peace to the disturbed. Make ye a provision for the destitute. Be a treasury of riches for the poor. Help to alleviate the suffering of those who suffer pain or those who are ailing. Promote friendship, honour, conciliation, and devotion to God. Nurture altruistic aims and plans for the well-being of ye fellow humankind.

The Bab gave up His life, possessions, and kindred for the Cause of God, yet He was imprisoned and chained because He foretold of the coming of Baha'ullah.

O army of God! Pray ye for all people on the great big earth; ask ye that all be blessed, all be forgiven. Do not seek vengeance, even against one who is thirsting for your blood. Do not offend the feelings of another, even though they be an evil-doer, and they wish you evil.

When calamity striketh, be ye patient and composed. However afflictive your sufferings may be, stay ye undisturbed, and with perfect confidence in the abounding grace of God, brave ye the tempest of tribulations.

O Thou Provider! Unite all the world unto Thyself as to behold the friends of far east, middle, and far west in close embrace; to see all the members of human society gathered with love in a single great assemblage, even as individual drops of water collected in one mighty sea; to behold them all as birds in one garden, as pearls of one ocean, as leaves of one tree, as rays of one sun.

PURITY 36

How good it is if all friends be as close as sheaves of light, if they stand together side by side, firmly unbroken; united in adoration as worshippers, in a wide-spreading shelter for all peoples gathered together;
all souls become as one soul, and all hearts as one heart.
Let all be set free from the multiple identities that were born of passion and desire, and in the oneness of their love for God find a new way of life.

PURITY 37

Let all friends raise a banner of guidance to exalt God's Word, spread God's sweet savours, educate the souls of all people.

Spiritual friends should stay connected.

PURITY 38

We are all God's people

In the sight of Abdu'l-Baha, women and men of all skin colors are accounted equally, as is the spiritual viewpoint of God, there is no difference between them.

PURITY 39

Angels

Angels are heavenly blessed beings who are revealers of God's abounding grace.

Dire events in this world take place: these are cups that yieldeth bitter wine. But the angels pass around only sweet savours for all.

PURITY 40

Spiritual assemblies have for their defender, their supporter, their helper, their inspirer, - the omnipotent Lord.

Now shall come to pass greater things, for this is the summons of the Lord of Hosts, this is the trumpet-call of the Living Lord, this is the anthem of world peace, this is the standard of righteousness, trust and understanding raised up among all people of the globe; this is the holiness of the Spirit of God.

O ye loved ones of God, offer up thanks to God! Blessed are ye to receive gifts, glad tidings, and abounding grace; such assemblies are supported by Abdu'l-Baha with great joy.

Look ye upon the seed, look ye upon the tree, and its blossoms, and its leaves
and its fruits.

Consider what shall come to pass are greater things for the good of all people on earth. Consider the days before when a small few did desire to follow a crowd for the
Spirit of God; then observe what a mighty Tree that seed became, behold ye all today at the Footage of the Tree of the Lord.

PURITY 41

Spiritual assemblies are instruments for establishing unity and harmony. Make this world a mirror of the unity of God. When all lovers of God unite, then will the whole world be one native land, its diverse peoples one single kind, the nations of the world one household; this is a vision of beauty.

PURITY 42

The Lord is a refuge of peace in your hearts.

PURITY 43

Purity

The prime requisites for the lovers of God are purity of motive, radiance of spirit, detachment from all else except God, attraction to Divine Goodness, humility and lowliness (putting God above all things), patience and servitude to God.

PURITY 44
Peace

All people should have freedom to express an opinion and argument; but if, the Lord forbid, differences of opinion should arise, a peaceful solution must be sought.
No human should be physically or emotionally hurt for expressing their opinion.

PURITY 45

Lovers of God are waves of one sea, drops of one river, stars of one heaven, rays of one sun, trees of one orchard, flowers of one garden. The earth is a fleck of dust.
—Absolute love and harmony must exist amongst members of an assembly of lovers of God.
If there is much discord, the assemblage should be dispersed and that assembly be brought to naught.

When a majority of opinions prevails to make a decision, the matter may still be discussed in the future with new knowledge and opinions.

There must be freedom to express thoughts and it is not wise to belittle or scorn the thought of another but in moderation (discussion) the truth set forth.

PURITY 46
Bahi Messengers

I, Abdu'l-Baha, along with the Bab, Baha'ullah,
and good spiritual leaders - we are all constantly engaged with those who are devoted to God and the holy laws of love and unity – to them these Devotees of God are whole-heartedly attached and with them they are linked by everlasting ties in the spiritual realm; thus correspondence to them is sincere, constant, and uninterrupted.

PURITY 47

O ye true friends! Whatsoever gatherings is arranged with the utmost love, and where those who attend are turning towards God and where the discourse (talk, speeches) is the good teachings of God – that gathering is the Lord's, and that festive table hath come down from heaven.

For a world continually in turmoil and conflict, such gatherings may help misunderstandings among the world's peoples to vanish away the turmoils; then, will all nations come to peace with one another.

It is your duty to be kind to every human being and to wish them well, to work for the upliftment of society, and to bring humankind to God.

PURITY 48

O ye loyal servants of the Ancient Beauty! Gatherings are held to worship and glorify God,
where the holy verses, the heavenly odes and laudations are intoned, and the heart is quickened and enlightened, and carried away from itself. Spiritual delights are present, so the body may mirror the spiritual world, to keep the friends of God alert and heedful, and bringing them peace of mind, and joy.

PURITY 49

May the breathings of the Holy Spirit make each person present in assemblages eloquent in tongue (speech) and love of heart to acclaim the glory of God.

PURITY 50

The Baha'i feast is held every month to foster comradeship and love, to call God to mind with contrite hearts, and to encourage benevolent pursuits. The friends of God dwell upon God, read prayers and holy verses, and treat one another with the utmost affection and love.

PURITY 51

Houses of Worship

When friends gather to glorify God, they will find themselves spiritually restored and endued with a power that is not of this world.

It befitteth and behoveth friends to hold gatherings where they shall glorify God and fix their hearts upon the Lord, and read and recite Holy Writings for the Blessed Beauty.

Build ye Houses of Worship for glorification of God to forge bonds of unity from heart to heart; a collective center for your souls.

The righteous draw nearer to Thy Sacred Threshold.

Pray to God day and night and beg for forgiveness and pardon. Pray that God will help to solve every difficulty.

Strive with heart and soul that ye may become renowned in character and knowledge.

PURITY 52

Thanksgiving

Loved ones of God are found in every land, and all are underneath the shadow of the Tree of Life and under the protection of God's good providence.

We should give thanks for the Lord's blessings and ask for abundance of grace and divine assistance. There should be a spirit of true friendship, fellowship, and loving communion amongst the friends.

Remember the saying:
'Of all pilgrimages the greatest is to praise the Lord.'

PURITY 53

The Good News

Consecrate thyself to service in the Cause of God. Beg thou God to make thee a lighted candle such as the prophets and messiahs are, so that thou mayest guide a great multitude of humans to the Holy Spirit.

The Cause of God is to bring about the oneness of humankind and the tabernacle of unity; the banners of love and universality of all humankind will be unfurled on the earth to teach good news to all people.

PURITY 54

The bounties and joyful tidings of Baha'ullah shall be imparted unto thee and ye shalt be filled with the Spirit.

Praise be the Lord, the Cause of God hath been proclaimed throughout the world. Many have given for the Cause of God;
one man gave a thousand camels, one gave half his sustenance, and still another offered all that he had, and a woman stricken in years gave her sole possession, a handful of dates, a humble contribution.

The lovers of God evince a great spirit of self-sacrifice.

PURITY 55

O thou who hast sought illumination from the light of guidance! Pray that thou mayest ever grow in faith and assurance, to bestow on others Thy guidance.

Whenever an assemblage of the friends of God is gathered, the Holy Spirit is yet present in spirit and in soul.

Distance prevents not the association of two souls that are closely attached in heart even though they may be in two different countries, so make the Lord thy close companion, attuned and in harmony with thy soul.

PURITY 56

God centers around union and harmony among friends; so that this unity and concord may be the cause of the promulgation of the oneness of the world of humanity.

Do not worship yourselves!

Worship the divine reality!

Do not be captives of the world but be aware of the divine.

Peter was a fisherman and Mary Magdalene a peasant, but they were favoured with the blessings of Jesus Christ, and to the present day they are shining from everlasting glory.

PURITY 57

I, Abdu'l-Baha, through the bounties of Baha'ullah, am teaching the divine words of Baha'ullah in my travels throughout the world.

PURITY 58

Those with a pure and sanctified purpose wish for nothing except the good pleasure of God and are engaged in the promulgation of divine teachings and the explanation of abstruse metaphysical problems.

The Tablets of Baha'ullah are:
1) Investigation of truth,
2) The oneness of humankind,
3) Universal peace,
4) Conformity between science and divine revelation,
5) Abandonment of racial, religious, worldly, and political prejudices, which are prejudices that destroy the foundation of humanity.
6) Righteousness and justice,
7) The betterment of morals and heavenly education,
8) The equality of men and women,
9) The diffusion of knowledge and education,
10) Economic questions.

The teachings of Baha'ullah lay the foundation of the oneness of the world of humanity and promulgate universal friendship; the teachings are founded upon unity of science and religion and upon investigation of truth; the teachings uphold the principle that religion should be a cause of amity, union and harmony among humankind; the teachings establish the equality of men and women and propound economic principles which are for the happiness of individuals; the teachings diffuse universal education, that every soul may as much as possible have a share of knowledge; the teachings abrogate and nullify prejudices in religions, races, politics, patriotism, and economics. Whoever promulgates the teachings of Baha will verily be assisted by the Divine Realm of Providence.

PURITY 59

Science

Sciences are bridges to reality and a means of access to God.

It is incumbent upon thee to acquire various branches of knowledge, and to turn thee toward the beauty and guidance of God, that thou mayest be a sign of saving guidance amongst the peoples of the world.

PURITY 60

Progress

See how powerful is the influence exerted by God upon the inner essence of all created things!

Glory has spread so that the accumulated product of our recent times is more than that of a hundred years gone before. For example, the sum total of all books written in our current time (around1870 CE) far exceed the total number of volumes that were written in all previous ages.

PURITY 61

O bird that singeth sweetly of the Creator's Beauty! The musician's and painter's arts who recount the good blessings are worthy of the highest praise.

To study and excel in sciences, craftsmanship, and arts should be considered as an act of worship to God.

PURITY 62

Respect overcometh all prejudices of race or nation; only hearts are considered. Praise be to God, the hearts of friends are united and linked together, whether they be from east or west, from north or south, or whether the skin is light, darker, yellow, or brown.

PURITY 63

The Teachings of Baha'ullah advocate voluntary sharing, the freely-chosen expending of one's substance for the comfort and peace of others.

PURITY 64

Disaster Relief

The souls who serve in the Red Cross, the disaster relief organization that helps humans ravaged from wars or natural disasters - are of the workings of God.

PURITY 65

Marriage

Among the people of Baha'i, marriage is a union of the body and the spirit to form a bond that will abide forever, so that throughout every phase of life and in all the worlds of God, their union will endure, for this oneness is a gleaming out of the love of God.

When any souls grow to be true believers and attain spiritual relationships with other true believers, they will attain a union and tenderness which is not of this world; such souls have detached themselves from the chains of the world and are focused on the spiritual realm.

Baha'i marriage is the commitment of the two people one to the other, and their mutual attachment of mind and heart. Each must exercise utmost care to become acquainted with the character of the other, to become a loving companion, and one with each other for time and eternity. True Baha'i marriage is that husband and wife should be united physically and spiritually, that they may ever improve the spirituality of each other, and may enjoy everlasting unity throughout all the worlds of God.

Through the union of marriage the primal oneness of God is made to appear; thus is laid the foundation of love in the spirit.

Wherefore do we offer felicitations and pray for blessings from God upon you to make your wedding feast a joy to all.

May two united in marriage become as one tree, which may blossom and grow, and yield fruit, so that your line may eternally endure. Upon ye be the Glory of Most Glorious.

In a marriage, be firm and steadfast and do not be shaken by tests and trials but the husband and wife should have patience with each other.

Make the husband and wife to have knowledge of God in their hearts and minds; make them one of thy angels whose feet walk upon this earth even as their souls are connected to the high heavens, cause them to become a brilliant lamp, shining out with the light of Thy Wisdom in the midst of Thy People.

O Thou marriage couples who pray to God! Blessed art thou, for the beauty of God hath enraptured thy heart, and the light of inner wisdom hath filled thy mind, to reflect the glory of the Holy Spirit.

The Lord hath made woman and man to abide with each other in the closest relationship, and to be even as a single soul. They are two helpmates, two intimate friends, who should be concerned about the welfare of each other. Strive as two doves in the nest to live in contentment and peace.

PURITY 66

Regarding marriage, one must choose one who is pleasing to thee, and then the mother and father are told of thy marriage plans.
Before thou makest thy choice, the parents have no right to interfere.

PURITY 67

Believers of God spread sweet savours of Holy Teachings to children, women, and men, even teachings of good behavior, good morals, good conduct, good character, and good physical and mental health.

PURITY 68
Children

It is incumbent upon parents to raise their children to have good character, good morals, and good virtues, to prevent development of behavior that would be worthy of blame ,and to foster them in the embrace of the knowledge of God and God's love. Then the children will grow and flourish, learn perseverance and progress, and purity of life. Parents should praise and applaud when they seeth that their child hath done well to cheer the child's heart. If an undesirable action should manifest, counsel the child with verbal counsel based on reason. It is not permissible to strike a child or vilify a child, for the child's character may become totally distraught if the child is subjected to physical or verbal abuse.

Raise your children from infancy in a way of life that conforms to divine teachings so that their inmost heart and very nature will be strong in following God.

From the beginning, children must continually be reminded to remember their Creator, who is God. Let the love of God pervade their inmost being, co-mingled with the nourishment of their mother's milk.

Parents are the first educators of their children and can help determine happiness, success, learning, judgement, understanding, and faith of their little ones.

May divine love be with a new-born at the beginning and until the final breath at the end of life.

Spiritual assemblies should encourage parents to raise children well so the children will grow and flourish and know God's love.

To worship God is to raise and educate your children well, for children are precious.

Do not hurt your child physically or emotionally.

May all children be granted a happy outcome.

PURITY 69

O ye who have peace of soul! There are certain pillars which have been established as the unshakeable supports of the Faith of God. The mightiest of these is learning and the use of the mind, the expansion of consciousness, and insight into the realities of the universe and the mysteries of Almighty God.

To promote knowledge is thus an inescapable duty imposed on everyone of the friends of God. It is incumbent upon assemblages of God to exert every effort to educate humankind to know the ways of God, even from infancy.

PURITY 70

Were there no educator, all souls might remain savage or ignorant creatures.

PURITY 71

To know God is to rejoice in thy heart, human happiness, and can help in times of sorrows and troubles.

PURITY 72

Among the Divine Tablets and Holy Books is this: It is incumbent upon the father and mother to help educate their children both in good conduct and the study of books so that no child will remain illiterate. If the parents cannot perform this duty, the House of Justice should take over the education of a child; in no case should a child be left without an education.

PURITY 73

O true companions! All humankind are as children in a school, and the Dawning-Points of Light, the sources of divine revelation, are the wondrous teachers.
Let the children share in every new wondrous craft and art. Bring them up to work and strive, and accustom them to diligence. Teach them to dedicate their lives to matters of great importance, and inspire them to undertake studies and tasks that will benefit humanity.

PURITY 74
Spiritual Nourishment

Education is the indispensable foundation of human excellence. If a child be trained from infancy in excellent ways, the child will, through the loving care of the Holy Gardener, drink in crystal waters of the spirit, like a young tree amid the flowing brooks. From infancy, the child must be trained in the spirit of God's love and nurtured in the embrace of God's good ways, that the child may grow in spiritually, be filled with wisdom and knowledge, and take on holy characteristics of the angelic host.

PURITY 75
God Loves All People

O loved ones of God! No one hath any superiority over another before God. All souls are equal to begin with; variation among minds and differing degrees of perceptions and opinions are due to differences in education, genetics, training, and culture. Education bringeth forth the capacities capable of an individual. All individuals have unique gifts.

PURITY 76

There is a big difference between material civilization and divine civilization. Divine civilization trains every member of society so that no one will commit a crime but that all will acquire the good virtues of humankind to further human progress and spread prosperity across the world.

PURITY 77

Secular worldly education

Help thy children to grow like pearls of divine bounty in the shell of education. Help thy children to develop natures like unto the sweet airs that blow across the gardens of the All-Glorious, Beloved Spirit.

Ye should consider goodly character as of the first importance. It is incumbent upon every father and mother to counsel their children over a long period of time, and guide them unto those things which lead to everlasting honour.

Encourage your children to deliver speeches of high quality, to express themselves with clarity and eloquence of good utterance.

Glances of heavenly grace from the Company on High will be given to those who educate a child in good ways.

Schools should be clean and a place of discipline and order. Students and teachers should be clean.

All should be taught that it is not desirable to be rude, unwashed, and ill-natured. A person who conducts themself well is a benefit to others.

If a person can be trained to be both learned in education and good in conduct, the result is light upon light.

Children will grow up in whatever way ye train them. Take the utmost care to give high ideals and goals so they will cast their beams like brilliant candles on the world, and will not be defiled by lusts and passions in the way of animals, heedless and unaware, but instead will set their hearts on achieving everlasting honour and acquiring all the excellences of humankind.

PURITY 78

The root cause of wrongdoing is ignorance, we must therefore hold fast to the tools of knowledge and perception.

Good character must be taught so all may acquire the heavenly characteristics of spirit, and see for themselves that there is no fiercer hell than to possess a character that is evil and unsound, showing qualities which deserve to be condemned.

It followeth that a school must be a place of utmost discipline and order, highest ethics and learning, so that a moral foundation – a structure of holiness of character – will be raised up in the very essence of the child; in early childhood it is good to establish good morals and habits.

PURITY 79

Spiritual education

An individual should be educated in spirituality that they have no desire to tell a lie or commit a crime or hurt another person. Thus will be kindled a sense of human dignity and pride, to burn away the reapings of lustful desires. Then will a person shine of God's love with qualities of the spirit as if a bright moon or sun, and the relationship of each to God will not be illusory but real, as a very foundation of a building, not some embellishment on its façade.

An outline of the fundamental principles underlying all religions is good information for all humankind. Attending services at different religions can do no harm.

PURITY 80

The greatest consideration must be given to orphans to help them attain the age of maturity as true servants of the world of humanity and as bright candles in the assemblages of humankind.

PURITY 81

Whatever a person speaketh, then let the person prove by their deeds (acts). If a person claimeth to be a believer of God, then let the person act according to the precepts of God, which are thought to be of righteousness and goodness.

PURITY 82

Serve the Lord and one another.

PURITY 83

O dear one of Abdu'l-Baha! Be one of the Holy Tree. Be one of soul and heart and not only of water and clay.

PURITY 84

Let each person become a leader in wisdom.

Let all people in the world achieve intellectual attainments.

For growth and development of the individual, depend on your powers of intellect and reason, render thanks unto the Lord for this wondrous gift.

PURITY 85

According to the teachings of Baha'ullah, may each person become a lighted candle in the world of humanity, devoted to the service of all humankind, giving up rest and comfort, and become the cause of tranquility in the world. May each person become the cause of joy and gladness to all on earth.

PURITY 86
Dedication and Commitment

Perseverance is steadfastness and firmness in an activity to lead to good results, with importance attached to it, so that day by day it will grow and be quickened with the breaths of the Holy Spirit.

PURITY 87
Work

Let all humankind pursue their professions so that their efforts may produce that which will manifest the greatest beauty and perfection before all.

May thou be protected and assisted under the providence of the True One and be occupied always in mentioning the Lord and display effort to complete thy profession;

striving for perfection. Whilst thou art occupied with thy profession, thou canst remember the True One.

PURITY 88

Purity

Be pure and holy in all things; just as the Q'uran saith that pure water was poured down from heaven, the Gospel saith to be baptized with the holy water of the Spirit, the Torah said to Passover the gifts and share, and the Gita saith we are all a part of one universe.

In every aspect of life, purity and holiness, and cleanliness and refinement exalt the human condition and further the development of one's inner reality. The Bab prohibited smoking tobacco; it can become a noxious addiction and a waste of time and money, renouncing it will make it possible to have a fresh mouth and unstained fingers, and hair that is free of a foul and unpleasant smell. Opium is foul and accursed; according to the texts of the Holy Books, it is forbidden and its use is utterly condemned. Reason showeth that smoking opium is a kind of insanity, and experience attesteth that the user is completely cut off from humankind.

May God protect all against the perpetration of an act so hideous as smoking opium, an act which layeth in ruins the very foundation of what it is to be human, and which causeth the user to be dispossessed for ever and ever. For opium fastens on the soul, so the user's conscience dieth, his mind is blotted away, his perceptions are eroded; Fortunate are they who never even speak the name of it; then think how wretched is the user. The use of opium must be prevented by any means whatsoever.

O ye lovers of God! Violence and force, constraint, and oppression are all condemned. O Divine Providence! Save the people from committing any repugnant act or evil habit. Deliver them from intoxicating drinks, tobacco, and opium that bringeth on madness; instead may they enjoy the sweet savours of holiness and drink from the mystic cup of heavenly love and know the rapture of being drawn ever closer unto the Realm of God; instead may they be conduceth to health and vigour, keenness of mind and bodily strength. May the Lord free humankind from the enslavement of intoxicating liquor, tobacco, and opium and fill thy people with self-control, knowledge, health, and love so they shall be pure, free, and wise.

PURITY 89

Medical Community

Praise be to God for distinguished physicians to undertake physical healing and spiritual healing. Matters related to a person's spirit have a great effect on their bodily condition. For instance, thou should impart gladness to thy patient, give them comfort and joy; how often hath it occurred that this hath caused early recovery. Therefore, treat thou the sick with both powers.

When giving medical treatment or at the bedside of a patient, cheer and gladden their heart and spirit through celestial power of prayer.

Ill health is hard to bear. The bounty of good health is the greatest of all gifts.

God hath revealed to humankind and made manifest medical science so human servants may profit from treatment. Physical and spiritual treatments may both produce marvelous effects.

PURITY 90

Healthy Human Body

The human body has a natural equilibrium of components and if the essential balance of a component is disturbed, disease or sickness may occur; for instance, the salt component must be present to a given amount, and the sugar to a given amount – so long as each remaineth in its natural proportion to the whole, there is no cause for concern of sickness. When, however, these constituents vary as to their natural amounts – that is, when they are either augmented or diminished – it may cause disease or illness.

Illnesses may also be caused by genetics.

And highly-skilled physicians are investigating this matter about foods. Natural healthy foods may improve the general health of humankind.

PURITY 91

Even if the patient is a physician, the patient should consult with another physician for advice in order to maintain health.

PURITY 92

The Lord giveth healing.

PURITY 93

Food chains

Some do express astonishment at the hunting of innocent animals, creatures who are guilty of no wrong.

But reflect upon the realities of the universe, the inner-relationships in the physical realm where all things are eaters and eaten: the plant drinketh in the mineral, the animal doth eat the plant, humankind doth feed upon plants and animals. Whensoever thou dost examine, through a microscope, the water man drinketh, the air he doth breathe, thou wilt see that with every breath of air, man taketh in an abundance of animal life, and with every draught of water, he also swalloweth down a great variety of animals. These workings of the fabric of life are the laws of God!

PURITY 94

Baha'i faith encourages believers of God to treat all humankind and animals with mercy and loving compassion.

Caution should be taken with tyrants, deceivers, thieves, blood-thirsty wolves, and poisonous snakes, for these harm innocent humans and sheep.

And yet in truth, there is no difference between physical harm to a human or a beast. If a human is injured, he hath a language and can have recourse to the authorities. But a beast cannot take its case to the authorities in court. Therefore, it is essential that ye show forth the utmost consideration of the animal as to your fellow man.
Train your children from earliest days to be loving to animals; if an animal be sick, try to heal it; if it be hungry, then feed it; if it be thirsty, let them quench its thirst; if weary, let them see that it rests. Train your children to stay away from the dangerous animals.

PURITY 95

O servant of God! The human spirit possesseth wondrous powers, but it should be reinforced by the Holy Spirit. Ariseth thy soul with qualities essential to bear the heavenly glad tidings; turn thy heart fully to the Holy Spirit, and invite others to do the same; then shall ye witness wonderful results. All the members and parts of the universe are very strongly linked together in that space, and this connection produces a reciprocity of material effects.

O believers of God! Recite prayers for both physical and spiritual healing, to heal both the body and the soul.

PURITY 96

Disciples of the Holy Spirit have experienced divine transfiguration through spiritual discovery.

PURITY 97
Faith

O thou lovers of God, those who remain staunch in faith! For those sincere in the Cause of God, hard times should maketh not the souls to waver, but to remain fixed and unshakeable in their love for the Holy Creator.

In the Jewish Torah, Job made a statement that
'My Redeemer liveth, and although my flesh be weak, yet shall I be healed, and I shall behold the Lord': this did Job say after his friends had reproached him, when he was lamenting about his tribulations and the harm they had wreaked upon him and his soul.

Convey thou this message to the believers that in such tests they must stand unmoved and faithful in love for God. After the storms, the calm brings the birds that trill out upon the branches their songs for joy, and sermonize in lilting tones from the pulpits of the trees.

I, Abdu'l-Baha, beg of God to bestow upon thee a spiritual soul and the life of Heaven, and to make thee a leaf verdant (green)and flourishing on the Tree of Life, that thou may serve the Lord with spirituality and cheer.

Thy generous Lord will cause thee to labour in the Holy Vineyard and cause thee to be a means of spreading the spirit of unity among humankind. Verily, the Lord is Forgiving, Compassionate, and of Immeasureable Grace.

PURITY 98

Springs of wisdom will well up within believers, and jet forth even as fountains that leapeth from their own original sources. The wisdom of a dispensation (era of time) will reach heights to far transcend dispensations gone before; then know how much progress has been gained by divine law.

PURITY 99

The Holy Spirit is a fine and delicate essence. Open thee the gates of thy soul that thou mayest become informed of the divine mysteries.

PURITY 100
No human is perfect

It is incumbent upon us, when we direct our gaze toward other people, to see where they excel, rather than where they fail.

PURITY 101
Progress

The spirit of humankind is a power that encompasseth the realities of all things. Wondrous products of human workmanship, inventions, discoveries, and like evidences – each one of these was once a secret hidden away in the realm of the unknown. The human spirit laid that secret bare, and drew it forth from the unseen into the visible world. There is, for example, the power of steam, photograph, phonograph, wireless technology, advances in mathematics, each and every one of these was once a mystery, a closely guarded secret, yet the human spirit unravelled these secrets and brought them out of the invisible to reality in the light of day.

The divine spirit doth unveil divine realities and divine mysteries that lie within the spiritual world. It is my hope that thou wilst attain unto this divine spirit, so that thou mayest uncover the secrets of the other world.

PURITY 102

O thou servant of God! Divest thyself of all attachment to this world, and put on the vesture of holiness; thou will limit all thy thoughts and all thy words to the remembrance and praise of God, to spread the sweet savours of the Lord, and perform righteous acts to help others.

Pray thou:
' O God, my God! Fill up for me the cup of detachment from all things, and in the assembly of Thy Splendours and Bestowals, rejoice me with loving Thee. Free me from the assaults of passions and desires, break off from me the shackles of this world, draw me with rapture unto Thy Supernatural Realm, and refresh me with the breathings of Thy Holiness, that I may proclaim Thy Cause, promote Thy Love.'

As to the fundamentals of teaching the Faith: know thou that delivering the Good Messages of God can be accomplished only through goodly deeds and spiritual attributes to exalt the Word of the Lord.

Once the Lord hath enabled thee to attain sincerity in faith, be thou assured that the Holy Spirit will inspire thee with words of truth and will cause thee to speak through the breathings of the Holy Spirit.

PURITY 103

Reflect upon past events to understand present events.

PURITY 104

O ye sons and daughters of the Holy Spirit, thanks to the teachings of Moses, Jesus, Mohammad, Baha'ullah, Zoroaster, Krishna, Buddha, Ramana Marhasi, and Gandhi – they summoned all humankind to amity and peace - are ye now songsters in the meadows of truth and have soared upward to the heights of glory. All humans are the sheep of God and God is the shepherd, as Moses did say. All prejudices in race, religion, wealth, and politics should be set aside for peace.

Love is the remedy for all people, this was established through divine teachings; even through etchings and statues of the religions before papyrus was invented for the writings.

Many inspired souls radiate heavenly gladness from the heart, as a bright candle in every assembly of faith, and beam forth as twinkling stars in the nighttime sky.

PURITY 105

O thou who is born in the spirit! May your perception be open, may your soul hearken (hear), may all truths be made plain and clear, then veils will fall away and all things will be made clear, for in this garden of God every plant exerts its own influence and hath its own properties and fragrance. Although the pages of a book know nothing of the word and the meanings, even so, friends pass them reverently from hand to hand. This connection, furthermore, is purest beauty.

PURITY 106

Human life will pass

Grieve thou not over the troubles and hardships of this world, nor be thou glad in times of ease and comfort, for both shall pass away.

This present life is even as a swelling wave, or a mirage, or drifting shadows. Wide is the difference between fancy of imagination and fact. The realm of the Lord is real, but this world is only a shadow, and a shadow hath no life of its own. Rely upon God. Trust in God. Praise God. Call God continually to mind. The Lord turneth trouble into ease, sorrow into solace, and toil into peace. The Lord hath dominion over all things.

Release thyself from the fetters of whatsoever cometh to pass. Nay rather, under all conditions, thank thou Thy Loving Lord, and yield up thine affairs unto God's will that worketh as the Lord pleaseth – this is better for thee than all else in either worlds.

PURITY 107

O thou believer in the oneness of God! Know thou that nothing profiteth a soul or lifteth a heart save (except) the splendor and love of the Lord.

Forsake thou every other concern, let oblivion overtake the memory of all else, and confine thy thoughts to whatever will lift up the human soul to the paradise of heavenly grace.

PURITY 108

As to the question regarding the soul of a murderer, only the Lord knows what the station of the murder's soul will be.

PURITY 109

O thou lover of God! In this day, to thank God for bounties consisteth in possessing a radiant heart, and a soul open to the promptings of the Spirit. This is the essence of thanksgiving, the imitations of the Spirit, these emanations from the deep recess of the heart. On the Day of Grace, while justice is allotted to each whatever is their due, look thou at the boundless favour of the Holy Spirit.

PURITY 110
God's Love

When the love of the Lord is near, every bitterness turneth sweet.

PURITY 111
The Soul

Nearness to God is verily of the soul, not of the body; and the help that is sought and the help that cometh, is not material but of the Spirit; the bounties of God will verily encompass a sanctified soul even as the sun's light doth the moon and stars, be thou assured of this.

PURITY 112
Reincarnation

The belief in reincarnation of the soul goeth far back into ancient history of almost all peoples and was held even by philosophers of Greece, the Roman sages, the ancient Egyptians, and the great Assyrians.

The major argument for reincarnation is that according to the justice of God, each must receive their due until nirvana is reached; the spirit of a person may pass into a new living creature for another life until perfect balance is reached. Only the Lord knoweth as the Lord doeth, for the Lord possesseth invisible realms which human intellect can never hope to fathom (understand).

Another return is meant the return of the qualities, conditions, efforts, perfections, and inner realities of the lights which recur in every dispensation; this reference is not to individual souls.

PURITY 113
Deceased Loved Ones

Grieve not over the beloved who hath risen unto the Lord in death, for thy beloved is now a bird of

Heaven, thou hast quit the earthly nest and soared away to a garden of eternal holiness, a station of light. Thy beloved has quit this earthly world and risen upward unto the grace of the invisible realm and unto the threshold of the Lord.
Thou loved one hast left the lamp that was thy body here; the glass that was thy human form, thy earthly elements, the way of life on earth. Thou hast lit a flame within the lamp of the Company on High, thou hast set foot in Paradise, and found a shelter in the Shadow of the Blessed Tree, thou hast attained thy Meeting in the haven of Heaven.

Thy song is even as birdsong now, thou pourest forth verses as to the mercy and goodness of the Lord, who forgiveth ever and loveth ever, thou wert a thankful servant, wherefore hast thou entered into exceeding bliss. The Lord hath made thee to enter the garden of the Lord's close companions – the angels. Thou hast won eternal life, and the bounty that faileth never, and a life to please thee well, and plenteous grace.

Mortal beauty shall fade away and be no more, but the Beauty of the True One will endureth eternally and the glory of the Lord lasts forever. The countenance that reflects the Light of the Lord hast acquired the pearl of true knowledge.
Be not grieved at the death of thy respected companion, for thy departed hath attained Thy Meeting with the Lord at the Seat of Truth.

May God draw thee loved one ever closer, and rejoice thou heart with nearness to God's presence, to fill thee with hope, beauty, and glory at all times, for thee deceased loved one be called to mind and shall never be forgotten.
Pray for thy beloved by day, by night. See them plain before ye, as if in open day, to remember thy beloved of past.

PURITY 114

Only the Lord knoweth the stations the souls occupy after their release from the body.

PURITY 115
Spiritual Knowledge

O sincere lover of the Lord! Whensoever thou dost find an opportunity, use thy tongue to guide the human race to the Lord! Read thou the Books and Tablets of God that were written by believers. Ask thou of God that the magnet of Divine Love should draw unto thee the knowledge of the Lord that thy soul becometh holy in all things.

Baha'ullah is with you in Spirit always, like all of the Great Lovers of God!
The ascension of the blessed soul on Sept. 30, 1912CE should be respected and praised for the attributes of Abdu'l-Baha.

PURITY 116
The question of Free Will

Regarding fate, predestination, and God's will. Fate and predestination are placed in the realities through the power of creation and every incident of fate is a consequence of the predestined relationships.

God's Will is an active force which controls these relationships and these incidents.

The question of the Free Will of Humankind is a mystery but pray for God's Will to keep thee all people in good ways.

PURITY 117

Messengers in Different Dispensations of Time

O thou lover of Safe Havens and Heaven!

Praise thou God in the age of dispensation when Baha'ullah saith to unite the oneness of humankind.

Praise thou Moses in the age of dispensation when he spoke the Ten Commandments.

Praise thou the blessed ones before Moses who felt the Spirit!

Praise thou God in the age of dispensation when Jesus Christ saith humankind should forgive and love one another.

Praise the current Teachers of God and may God guide you in every word and action for thy gathering of the holy believers!

May you grasp an opportunity to ignite a candle that shall never be extinguished and which shall pour out its light eternally illuminating the world of all humanity!

PURITY 118

The essence of purity

Let God's beloved, each and every one, be the essence of purity, the very life of holiness and sanctified, humble before the Lord. This is the station of the sincere; this is the way of the loyal; this is the brightness that shineth on the face of those near God.

Wherefore must the friends of God, with utter sanctity, with one accord, rise up in spirit, in unity with one another to become one spiritual union.

Let your own thoughts dwell on your own spiritual development, yet let thee dwell in unity. Be the bringers of joy, even as the angels.

Humankind must renounce the own self, meaning to renounce inordinate desires, passions, and selfish purposes, and seek the guidance of the Holy Spirit.

PURITY 119

The Unity of Humanity

O friends of God! Turn your faces to the promulgation of the oneness of the world of humanity, to promote unity among humankind. Mischief makers have many strategies to instill doubts among friends, so friends of God must be aware that such strategies are not the faith covenant of the Lord.

Baha'i unity is to uphold the Cause of God for the oneness of all people. Those who are doing evil and hurting others are not true believers of the Cause of God.

Let not selfish motives drag ye away from the Cause of the Holy Spirit, to unite all peoples in peace and love. The center of love of all religions is the Spirit.

PURITY 120

Baha'ullah the Messiah

Baha'ullah, a Blessed Beautiful Messiah, did ascend unto Heaven in Spirit with Promise that a host of angels will assist Servants of God from the Realm of Glory.

Free yourselves from selfishness and follow the pathway of service for the realm of God, the divine universal mind.

O my Lord, wing those who are oppressed with victory that they may soar upward to salvation in Thy Threshold of Holiness.

Believers of the Divine God spread the equality of every member of the human race.

The Lord of all humankind hath fashioned a garden of Eden, an earthly paradise, for the human realm.

It must find its way to harmony and peace; it is a place of manifold blessings and unending delights. Remember how a quarrel did break out between Adam and Eve, and Satan, which led to a bitter loss. And this was meant as a warning to the human race to keep thy soul with God and that conflicts and disputes are not allowable. Even with such a lesson, still do we see war in the world – this world would become another world if humankind would take heed and cease from fighting and violence!

PURITY 121

Peace

May God grant the promise of peace and enable this distinguished assemblage to conclude a fair treaty and establish a just covenant to bless all humankind forever, across the unborn reaches of time.

Where unity existeth in a family, the affairs and progress of the family may lead to prosperity. Their concerns are in order, they enjoy comfort and tranquility, they are secure, their position respected by all. Such a family is of honorable stature, as day succeedeth day. And if we widen out the sphere to include inhabitants of the village who seek to be loving and united, who associate with and are kind to one another, what advances they will be seen to make, how secure and protected they will be. Then let us widen out the sphere a little more, to enable progress and unity in a great city. And if the sphere be widened still further out, inhabitants of a nation may develop peaceable hearts cooperating with one another in unity. Then, peace will it have and plenty, and vast wealth of friendship. If all nations would open their arms to one another and establish a world council for assemblage and peaceful discussion, there is no doubt that progress could unite the hearts of those with Faith.

PURITY 122

To every human being be kind, for we are all drops of one ocean and foliage of the Holy Tree.
Such is the counsel of Abdu'l-Baha, this hapless servant who was wrongly chained and put in prison.

God's love was manifest through prophets, messiahs, and sages. Take ye good heed, O People of Insight! Is real unity possible to be revealed and in perfect accord among humans?

The answer is that there are differences of two kinds in people: there are differences of mentality, and there are differences in physical appearance.

The first is that there are mental differences of:
thought (logic), temperament (anger),
and morals (ideas of good character).
Some people are peaceful and some are hateful mischief-makers.

The second is differences in physical appearance – consider the flowers of a garden: though differing in kind, colour, form and shape, and fragrance, they all need water and the rays of the sun. The diversity of the human body in form and shape and hues of skin, body size, hair, and eyes are under the influence of the power of the soul. So the power of the soul may pervade the body and mind to reinforce harmony, love, and unity among all humanity.

When the meetings are held adorned with souls from various nations of the world, one would be amazed and suppose that all were from one nation, one community, one thought, one belief, one opinion, and one world. The need for love, food, water, air, shelter, and clothing is for all to be concerned.
It is hoped that the power of God will establish a peace that will remain effective and secure.

Many people, governments, and nations have become tired of war, of the loss of life, of the affliction and oppression of humankind, of human slavery, of the number of orphans and the homeless – and these good souls are driven by a desire for peace and the oneness of humankind.

Wars are destruction while peace is construction; war is death while peace is life; war is an appurtenance (subordinate)of the world of nature while peace is at the foundation of the religions of God; war is the destroyer of humankind while peace is a preserver of humankind; war is like a devouring wolf while peace is like heavenly angels; war is the struggle for existence while peace is mutual aid and co-operation among peoples of the world and the Cause of God.

When the minds of humankind become united, important matters can be accomplished. At present, universal peace is a matter of great importance, but unity of conscience is essential for a secure foundation in the establishment of peace.

Baha'ullah expounded the question of universal peace and He was wronged and imprisoned in the fortress of Akka because nations displayed the utmost enmity and hatred towards each other.

Good people of different nations and various religions gathered together for one pathway; they embraced many teachings to support universal peace. Among the teachings were:
1) the independent investigation of reality and truths,
2) the oneness of the world of humanity, because God created us all,
3) religion is a cause of fellowship and love; religion should be a remedy and not cause problems of hatred,
4) religion should not exclude the truths of science and reason,
5) prejudices in religion, race, politics, economics, and patriotism destroy humanity.

For 6,000 years, the world of humanity has not been free from war, strife, murder, and blood-thirstiness. For peace to happen, prejudices must be abandoned and acquisition of good morals and education must be attained.

All humankind are of one tree of God and all nations are like branches, while the individuals of humanity are like leaves, blossoms, and fruits thereof. Religion should be a cause of fellowship and peace; otherwise it is not necessary and it is fruitless.

The surface of the earth is one native land. Everyone can choose to live in any spot on the globe, but we are born in only one location which is called our birth location. The boundaries have been devised by humans. In the creation, such boundaries were not assigned. The continents are Europe, Asia, Africa, Australia, North America, South America, the islands, and the two icecaps of Antarctica and the Arctic Circle.
In the beginning of the first centuries of civilization, selfish souls assigned boundaries for their own interests and this led to intense hatred and bloodshed. But the progress of humanity has led to limited areas which we call our native countries that we regard as our motherlands, where the terrestrial globe is the motherland for all. The native countries exist for the welfare of the peoples living within the boundaries (borders) of that country and the boundaries exist to prevent chaos and confusion. Most leaders are not greedy and selfish. The native countries should respect each other's boundaries as humans should respect each other's existence and share food and resources.

Consider a dove from the east, a dove from the west, a dove from the north, and a dove from the south chance to arrive, at the same time, in one spot, - they immediately associate in harmony. So it is with the blessed birds.

But the ferocious animals will attack and fight each other and tear each other to pieces and it is impossible for them to live peaceably together in one spot; they are unsociable and fierce, savage, and combative fighters.

Nations are being strengthened by the exchange of commodities, and universal benefits result.
A long time ago, the idea of universal peace was considered to be impossible, but events are taking place where humankind is showing one another courtesy and negotiation.

One language for all people on earth may eliminate misunderstandings among humans.

Men and women are equal. The world of humanity has two wings – one is women and one is men. Not until both wings are equally developed can the bird fly.

Voluntary sharing of one's property with other humans is greater than equality. To sacrifice one's property to help others who need help; this is done among the Baha'is.

Every human should be free from captivity.

Religion is a mighty bulwark (a defense wall, a line of protection) and prevents commotion and chaos, for religion is a safeguard that prevents humankind from wrongdoing to others.

Laws punish criminals but religion may prevent the manifest of crime because religion educates humankind in morals and promotes felicity (happiness and bliss).

Material civilization hath produced guns, rifles, dynamite, submarines, torpedoes, armed aircraft, bombers, bombs – these are weapons of war to hurt others. Spiritual civilization would never have produced these fiery weapons; rather, human energy and efforts would have been wholly devoted to useful inventions and praiseworthy discoveries.
Material civilization is like the body but spiritual civilization is like the spirit of holiness in all souls.
Humankind is in need of the Spirit.
Holiness may convert the animal instinct in humans
to holiness.

It is impossible and impractical to enforce laws of ancient religious texts – the teachings of Baha'ullah which pertain to freedoms and virtues of humankind and welfare for the peace and good of the whole world are better because they are more realistic to the current ways of civilization. (For example, humankind no longer offer animal sacrifice at the altar for the favour of God, this is a principle of the Torah.) Some religions will not allow automobiles to be driven, and this is a rule of the religion and not from God.
Therefore, some of the teachings of the past, such as those of the Torah, Bible, and Q'uran cannot be carried out at the present day – the writings

say that if you do not follow the rules of the book you are not of faith, which is not true. The ancient teachings must be revised. The purpose of each religion should be to promote peace and love among all.

PURITY 123

O God, my God! Graciously look upon Thy Servant and strengthen me in my servitude of Thee. Release me from distracting thoughts, deliver your divine message with an eloquent speech, adorn your assemblages with praise and strength of the divine, till bounty encompasses the world.

Help me to be selfless and detached from all things in the material world, as dust in the pathway, except to be a servant to others and to be guided by your holy ways.

Thou, Lord art the Universal Mind.

RAS TAFARI

The Rastafarian religion began in Jamaica in the 1920s CE. The religion is an originator of reggae music.

Rastafarians also live in the United States, Canada, Australia, New Zealand, South Africa, and many European countries.

Jah is God after Jahweh or Yahweh.

Ras Tafari was of Ethiopian nobility and was a devout member of the Ethiopian Orthodox Church. He was also called Haile Selassie which means 'Might of the Trinity'.
Ras Tafari was proclaimed to be a savior and a second-coming of Jesus, but Ras Tafari did not claim this.

Ras Tafari said 'The Lion of Judah has risen in Zion Africa'.

Marcus Garvey is an apostle and a prophet;
In 1924 Garvey urged all people of African descent to return to Africa. But in 1975CE, Rastafarians dropped this belief.

The religion takes its roots from the Coptic Church of Alexandria in originally founded by St. Mark in 42CE.

Modern rastafari way of life may include hair dreadlocks, enjoying a smoking pipe called a chalice (a practice of the Old Testament of the Bible), and a Nyahbinghi drumming rhythm.

Sects of Rastafari are called Mansions of Rastafari because the Bible New Testament says 'In My father's House are Many Mansions.' Sects include Nyahbinghi, Bobo Ashanti based on Asante ancestors, Twelve Tribes, African Unity, Covenant Rastafari, Messianic Dreads, and Selassian Church.

Rastafari Scripures derived from the Holy Piby

The Holy Piby
1924CE

Shepherd Athlyi

The souls of Ethiopian mothers weeped for their suffering generations, and behold two angels of the Lord resembling two saints of Ethiopia appeared before Robert Athlyi Rogers in 1918CE in Newark, New Jersey for the source of The Holy Piby and for the establishment of the Rastafari tradition; one of the angels was named Douglas. The angel who had less to say lifted her eyes to the heaven and cried, Blessed be thou Ethiopia, glory be the father, thou Elijah, Hosanna, Hosanna to Jehovah, praise ye Douglas the convention have triumph.
His Divine Highness Jesus Christ, Prince of the Kingdom of God,

appeared to Athlyi and said quickly Behold the messengers of my Father. At this saying Athlyi turned to the angels of the Lord and said, thy will be done, O God of Ethiopia, but how can I be a shepherd when I am but a twig before the eyes of man?
And the angels of the Lord answered him saying, a twig that is made by the Holy Spirit, an instrument to lead men, is great in the sight of God, over which the armies of the earth or the hosts of hell shall not prevail.
And it came to pass that a committee from among them (Sister Rachel Hamilton, Rev. James Barber, Sister Gilby Rose, Brother C.E. Harris, and Brother James Reed) confirmed the Shepherd Athlyi and decorated him in a robe of four colors (blue, black, red, and green) and committed to him a staff so as to confirm the authority confirmed upon him by the heavenly officials. Athlyi was anointed by prayer and the Athlyians shouted with great joy and cried 'Lead on, Shepherd of the Athlyians.'
There appeared a beautiful light on earth and when the light flashed Athlyi looked toward the heaven, and behold the heaven was open and there was a great host of saints robed in blue, millions of millions as far as his eyes could see there was a mighty host.
And Ethiopia was anointed on earth; the messengers said 'Blessed be Ethiopia for this day thou art anointed, thou are blest with a blessing, be ye forever united and stand up, let the world know your God.'
And when the two angels of the Lord neared the multitude the whole host roared with a thunder of joy that shook the earth like a mighty earthquake.
And it came to pass that an angel robed in four colors came forward to receive them and the whole celestial multitude stood and quietly formed an aisle. And when the two messenger angels appeared before the heavenly host they bowed to the multitude and turned themselves around and also bowed to the earth. Then came forward the mighty Angel robed in four colors and placed a gold ring upon their heads, and came forward also two mothers of Ethiopia, each with a star in their hand, and pinned them on the breast of the two messengers of the Lord.

There was great rejoicing in Heaven and singing hosanna to Elijah; praise ye Angel Douglas; blessed be thou Ethiopia forever and forever; the people at the end of the known world, and world unknown, shall look for coming of they children with food and blessings. An angel said: 'Mothers of Ethiopia, your cries of sorrow have awakened the people of the earth, saying prepare ye the way for a redeemer.'
And the Shepherd Athlyi and the house of Athlyi is founded by the holy spirit to purify the children of Ethiopia and to administer the holy law commanded to them by the Lord God of all mercies, and in the end they shall be ushered in the kingdom of his Divine Majesty by faith through consecration in love,

justice and by the pledging of life's loyalty to a prolific and defensive cause for the welfare of mankind.

The Holy Commandments for Ethiopia

1. Love ye one another, O children of Ethiopia, for by no other way can ye love the Lord your God.

2. Be thou industrious, thrifty and fruitful, O offsprings of Ethiopia, for by no other way can ye show gratitude to the Lord your God, for the many blessings he has bestowed upon earth free to all mankind.

3. Be ye concretized with water and ever united, for by the power of unity ye shall demand respect of the nations.

4. Work ye willingly with all thy heart with all thy soul and with all thy strength to relieve suffering and oppressed humanity, for by no other way can ye render integral service to the Lord your God.

5. Be thou clean and pleasant, O generation of Ethiopia, for thou art anointed, moreover the angels of the Lord dwelleth with thee.

6. Be thou punctual, honest and truthful that ye gain favor in the sight of the Lord your God, and that your pathway be prosperous.

7. Let no people take away that which the Lord thy God giveth thee, for the Lord shall inquire of it and if ye shall say some one hath taken it, ye shall in no wise escape punishment, for he that dieth in retreat of his enemy the Lord shall not hold him guiltless, but a people who dieth in pursuit of their enemy for the protection of that which the Lord God giveth them, shall receive a reward in the kingdom of their Father.

8. Thou shalt first bind up the wound of thy brother and correct the mistakes in thine own household before ye can see the sore on the body of your friend, or the error in the household of thy neighbor.

9. O generation of Ethiopia, shed not the blood of thine own for the welfare of others for such is the pathway to destruction and contempt.

10. Be ye not contented in the vineyard or household of others, for ye know not the day or the hour when denial shall appear, prepare ye rather for yourselves a foundation, for by no other way can man manifest love for the offsprings of the womb.

11. Athlyi, Athlyi, thou shepherd of the holy law and of the children of Ethiopia, establish ye upon the Law a Holy temple for the Lord according to thy name and there shall all the children of Ethiopia worship the Lord their God, and there shall the apostles of the shepherd administer the law and receive pledges thereto and concretize within the Law. Verily he that is concretized within

the Law shall be a follower and a defender thereof, more-over the generations born of him that is concretized within the law are also of the law.

12. O generation of Ethiopia, thou shalt have no other God but the Creator of Heaven and Earth and the things thereof. Sing ye praises and shout Hosanna to the Lord your God, while for a foundation ye sacrifice on earth for His Divine Majesty the Lord our Lord in six days created, the heaven and earth and rested the seventh; ye also shall hallow the seventh day, for it is blessed by the Lord, therefore on this day thou shall do no manner of work or any within thy gates.

The Shepherd's Prayer By Athlyi

O God of Ethiopia, thy divine majesty; thy spirit come in our hearts to dwell in the path of righteousness, lead us, help us to forgive that we may be forgiven, teach us love and loyalty on earth as it is in Heaven, endow us with wisdom and understanding to do thy will, thy blessing to us that the hungry be fed, the naked clothed, the sick nourished, the aged protected and the infants cared for. Deliver us from the hands of our enemies that we prove fruitful, then in the last day when life is o'er, our bodies in the clay, or in the depths of the sea, or in the belly of a beast, O give our souls a place in thy kingdom forever and forever. Amen.

And Shepherd Athlyi first went about the city of Newark, New Jersey, USA, telling of the Law and preaching concretation, saying, I come not only to baptize but to concretize with water, for verily I say unto you, first seek ye righteousness toward humanity and all things will be added unto you, even in the kingdom of God.
And there came to him many to be concretized with water, and the names of his stars were: Rev. J.H. Harris, Sister R.J. Hamilton, Brother J. Reid, Rev. and Mrs. J. Barber, Brother C.C. Harris, Sister Leila Best, Sister Thurston, Brother H. Pope, Rev. and Mrs. Flanagan, Brother Charles McLaurin, Sister Letica Johnson, Brother and Sister Adam Costly, Brother and Sister W. D. Sullivan, Sister Sarah Johnson, Brother G.W. Roberts, Rev. J.J. Derricks, Rev. A.J. Green, Rev. W. Barclift, Sister Bertha Johnson, Her holiness, the Shepherdess Miriam (wife of Athlyi), Her Holiness, the Shepherdmiss Muriel (the daughter of Athlyi), Brother F.L. Redd.
And at Springfield, Massachusetts, USA, Athlyi concretized with water Sister Sylvie Randall, Brother and Sister Eugene Kitchen, Brother and Sister Joseph Rutherford, Rev. R.G. Gaines, Brother J. When, Sister Ellen Frazier, Sister Minnielo Walker, Sister M.A. Bryant, Irene Chambers, E. Dempsey.
Then Athlyi traveled to South America and the West Indies, preaching the law and concretation by water for the sake of God and humanity.

And the Shepherd Athlyi taught the people to assemble once a month on their knees before the altar at Solemnity feast, then shall the parson and ordained cleffs administer to them bread and water, saying 'eat in remembrance of your pledge to God and work for the welfare of your generation and for the rescue of suffering humanity. Drink in remembrance of your baptism when thy sins hath been washed away, bid far the devil and his iniquities; arise and go in the name of one God, His Law and the Holy Ghost.'

There shall be on the 29th day of the seventh month three days of celebration known as the concord in accordance with the celestial and terrestrial concord led by the mighty angel Douglas.

And it came to pass that a newcomer in the Athlican Faith of the Rastafarians asked Athlyi 'What is the principal belief of the religion?' And straight-way the Shepherd Athlyi answered saying, the fundamental belief is justice for all, but hear ye the creed:

The Athlyian's Creed

We believe in one God, maker of all things, Father of Ethiopia and then in His Holy Law as it is written in the book Piby, the sincerity of Angel Douglas and the power of the Holy Ghost. We believe in one Shepherd Athlyi as an anointed apostle of the Lord our God, then in the Afro Athlican Constructive Church unto the most Holy House of Athlyi. We believe in the Freedom of Ethiopia and the maintenance of an efficient government recorded upon the catalog of nations in honor of her posterities and the glory of her God, the establishment of true love and the administration of Justice to all men, the celebration of concord, the virtue of the Solemnity feast and in the form of baptism and concretation as taught by our Shepherd Athlyi.

We believe in the utilization of the power and blessings of God for the good of mankind, the creation of industries, the maintenance of colleges and the unity of people, then in the end when earth toil is over we shall be rewarded a place of rest in the kingdom of Heaven, thereto sing with the saints of Ethiopia, singing Hallelujah, hosanna to the Lord our God forever and ever. Amen.

Amos

And Amos was a man who was striving to conquer evils; and Athlyi spoke unto him saying 'There is no hell for him who believeth in me, for I am not of myself but of God, the Father, who is in me. He that gives himself up to me wholeheartedly, I shall nurse him at my breast and he shall be strong. He that is not clean, industrious and thrifty is not in me, for I am a lover of cleanness, Lord of industry and a builder of commerce, that men, women, and children may be happy in me.

For he that liveth a productive life in me, seeketh and shall obtain heaven terrestrial and heaven eternal. Go ye out upon the earth, gather in the blessings of God and develop them in me that you prove yourself worthy of compensation.
And where there is no love, righteousness, and faith in your transactions the glory of heaven shall vanish and the misery of hell shall occupy the soul.'

And to beggars, Athlyi shall be a light in their darkness and a hop to raise them up.

But Athlyi shall harden his heart against backsliders, hypocrites, liars, and thieves.

And the God of Ethiopia is a god of salvation and a conqueror of evil.

The Athlyian Apostles

The Apostle Marcus Garvey journeyed to Detroit, Michigan, USA to hear apostle Robert Lincoln Poston preaching the word of God; they greeted each other with great joy, and the heart of one was the heart of the other.
And they journeyed to New York City, United States of America, to work for the redemption of Ethiopia and the oppression of her people.
And in 1923CE, Marcus Garvey told his colleagues to go to Ethiopia, Africa, and request then to open the door for the return of thy children to their own land and there to establish a great nation.

THELEMA

1. Aleister Crowley (1875-1946CE) was a prophet of a new age in Egypt in 1904. His wife Rose Edith helped him write The Book of the Law, the Liber Al Vel Legis, after his guardian angel Aiwass (Aiwaz) dictated him to write the book.

The book was written on April 8, 9, and 10, 1904 CE in Cairo, Egypt; at noon each day were written Chapters 1, 2, and 3. The 3 speakers of the book are (1) Nuit (Egyptian Goddess of the Sky and all possibilities), (2) Hadit (Egyptian God of the Sky and the heart of all matters and all possibilities - the center of a circle, the axle of a wheel, the cube in a circle, the flame that burns in every heart or the Holy Ghost, a worshipper's inner self), (3) Ra-Hoor-Khuit or RA (God of the Sun). The scribe of the book, Ankh-af-na Khonsu, the priest of the princes shall not in one letter change the book but lest there be folly, he shall comment thereupon by the wisdom of Ra-Hoor-Khu-it.

Thelemian monks in 1532CE were Dominican monk Francesco Colonna and Franciscan monk Francois Rabelais who included Greek words logistica (reason), thelemia (will or desire) the verse 'Do what thou will' , and the Roman Liberalia Festival (liberation festival to celebrate maturity into adulthood and celebrated with songs, sacrifices, masks, and processions with *toga*, the garment of ancient Rome) in their writings.

Ankh-ef-en-Khonsu i was a priest of the Egyptian god Mentu who lived in Thebes, Egypt during 725BCE. *Ankh* is a symbol meaning 'new life'. There is a wooden stela dedicated to Ankh in Cairo in an Egyptian Museum.

To Thelemians, history can be divided into a series of aeons, each with its own magical and religious expression. The first was the Aeon of Isis, an Egyptian goddess. The second was the Aeon of Osiris, her husband who established patriarchal (male head of household) values. Osiris was the oldest son of the Earth God Geb. The third Aeon was their son, Horus, a time of self-realization.

Egyptian Pharaoh King Tutankhamun is said to have joined Osiris in the constellations when he died around 1324 BCE.

Thelema scriptures derived from Liber Al Vel Legis

CHAPTER 1

Hadit is the manifestation of Nuit, the universe.

The unveiling of the company of Heaven.

Every man and every woman is a star. Each us are stars on our own orbit and our actions must be done by the law of love.

Lord, be thou my Hadit, my secret centre, my heart and my tongue!

Come forth, O children under the stars and take your fill of love!

I am above you and in you. My ecstasy is in yours! My joy is to see your joy.

The chosen priest shall gather my children under his wings and bring the glory of the stars into the hearts of all men and women.

He is forever a sun and she a moon.

I am infinite Stars and Space.

My scribe Ankh-af-na-khonsu shall not change one letter of this book, lest there be folly; he shall comment on by the wisdom of Ra-Hoor-Khunit.

Whoever is called a Thelemite will do no wrong and no sin. Do what thou wilt shall be the whole of the Law. Love is the law, love under will.

The perfect and the perfect are one perfect, not two.

There are no secret keys to the laws of God.

There is a dove and there is a serpent; chose thee well.

My incense is in resinous woods and because of my hair are Trees of Eternity.

All sacred words of all prophets are true.

The Five Pointed Star with a Circle in the Middle, and the Circle is Red. I have a special glory for those who love Me.

To love Me is better than all things.

Invoke me under the stars! The manifestation of Nuit.

CHAPTER 2

In the sphere I am everywhere the centre.

Let evil rituals be cast aside, for Knowledge to go aright.

I am a Magician and an Exorcist. I am the axle of a wheel and the cube in a circle.
I am the flame that burns in the heart of every human and in the core of every star.

I am alone; there is no God where I am.

There is great danger in me for those who do not understand the rule of love; they are fallen into sorrow or a misery of Hell.

Lift thyself up and receive the kisses of the stars and rain upon thy body; thus the Hadit – blessing and worship to the lovely Star!

CHAPTER 3

Abrahadabra, the reward of Ra Hoor Khuit (The Sun God).

Nu is your refuge as Hadit is your light, and I am the strength and force of your arms.

My image is in the East and in the West.

Mix meal and honey and make cakes in olive oil; eat unto Me.

My altar is open brass but burn silver and gold therein to forge metals.

My holy place is invisible and standeth untouched throughout centuries.

Another prophet may arise to bring fresh fervor from the skies.

The prophet sang: The light is mine; its rays consume me. I have made a secret door into the House of Ra. Bid me within thine House to dwell, abide with me Ra-Hoor-Khuit.

Hadit burning in they heart will make thy prayer secure and the writings of thy pen secure.

I despise harlots and those who commit evil.

I will lift to pinnacles of power those who worship Nu and achieve Hadit.

There is no law beyond Do what thou will and love is the law.

There is an end to the word of God enthroned in Ra's seat; to all it will seem beautiful.

I am the Hawk-Headed Lord of Silence and Strength.

There is a splendor in my name hidden and glorious, as the sun of midnight is ever the son.

The ending of the words is the Word Abrahadabra.

The Book of the Law is Written and Concealed. Aum. Ha.

The priest of the princes, Ankh-ef-en-Khonsu.

LIBER OZ

Each person has a right to live in the way one wills to do; to work, play, rest, and die as one will; to think, speak, write, draw, paint, carve, etch, mould, build, and dress as one will; and to love when, where, and with whom one will.

Ordo Templi Orientis

There is duty to do good for your self, others, and humanity, and to use for good purposes all other things and animals.

HINDU

In Hinduism, dharma is to do everything that is
correct, proper, or decent.
Dharma is duty to do the karma the right way.

The Dharma preached by Ashoka the Great (304-232BCE), an Indian emperor explained moral precepts such as: right behavior, kindness,
generosity,
truthfulness,
purity,
gentleness,
goodness,
kindness to prisoners,
respect for animals,
belief in a next world,
welfare for people and animals,
roadside facilities,
water-placing for humans and animals,
officers of the faith.

A guru is a religious leader of Hindu.

A Hindu saint is a sadhu or rishi and are free of desire, adhere to Vedic motto, and are highly desired.

An avatar is a deity that is reincarnated or that appears on earth.

In Hinduism, moksha is when you have achieved a place of balance, when bliss is natural and permanent. The secret of joy is a personal choice – a person must choose heaven over hell – on a daily basis when they first wake up. A person must choose to be happy.
God Mukunda is the giver of moksha or mukti (liberation from cycle of rebirth). Another source said God Vishnu is the giver of Moksha.

In Hinduism, God Vishnu has a meaning of presence everywhere, the Power of the Supreme Being has entered within the Universe and is not limited by space, time, or substance and pervades everything.

God Mahesh also has a meaning of Supreme Lord.
God Shiva means 'abode of joy.'

God Shakti is the Divine Mother of Hinduism, the primordial cosmic energy of the Universe.

The Great Triad in Hinduism is called the Trimurti and consists of 'Brahma-Vishnu-Maheshwara'.
Ten Avatars (incarnation of a Hindu god) of God Vishnu are:
1) Matsya – fish (beginning of life)
2) Kurma – tortoise (beginning of embryo)
3) Varaha –boar (embryo)
4) Narasimha – man-lion (newborn baby)
5) Vamana – young child (dwarf)
6) Parashurama – (adult)
7) Rama – (older adult) Incarnation of Vishnu
8) Balarama – elder brother of Krishna
9) Krishna – Full-incarnation of Vishnu. Radha is Krishna's female consort.
10) Kalki – time & eternity, period of hardship until the end of the world.

A popular deva (personal god, murti) is Ganesha, who has an elephant head. It was said that the God Shani had an evil-eye and looked at baby Ganesha and caused his head to be burned to ashes. So the God Vishnu came to the rescue and gave the baby the head of an elephant. But another account says that Ganesha was created directly by the God Shiva's laughter because Shiva considered Ganesha too alluring so he gave him the head of an elephant so Ganesha would be less popular.

Goddess Parvati was Shiva's wife. Ganesha was Parvati's son; it is said that she fashioned Ganesha from clay. God Skanda is Ganesha's brother.

A Hindu Mantra of Aum (Om) is associated with Ganesha: You are Trinity (Brahma-Vishnu-Maheshwara), You are fire (agni), air (vayu), sun (surya), and moon (chandrama). You are 3 worlds: bhuloka (earth), antariksha-loka (space), and swargaloka (heaven). You are all this. You are Om.

The goddess Durga fulfills your wishes. She has 8 arms and sits on a lion. She is a goddess of time and transformation, cycle of creation, life, death, and rebirth. Navrati is a Nine Day Festival to honor Durga; the nine days represent her 9 avatars.

The goddess Lakshmi is worshipped for wealth.
During the festival of Dewali, her idol is respectfully and prominently displayed.

The goddess Saraswati stands for knowledge and learning.

The goddess Kali is anti-devil. She is the goddess of time and changes.

(Kali Yoga is different from goddess Kali. The world is currently in the time period of Kali Yoga and it will last for almost 500,000 years.)

Caste systems classified humans into jatis or varnas and were hereditary to a person and automatically determined a person's place in society. 4 varnas or castes of Hindu social order: (1) Brahaman or Brahmin are priests (2) Kshatriya are ruling and military elite (3) vaishyas are agriculture, cattle rearers, landowners, traders and money-lenders (4) shudras are lowest class workers serving other castes.

Dussera is a celebration to commemorate victory of the god Rama over the devil Ravana.

Namaste is an Indian way of salutation or greeting which is done by saying 'Namaste' with folded hands or bowing.

In India, the cow is sacred and it is prohibited to kill any cows. Cows and elephants may roam freely and the populations of people exist among the sacred animals.

The 24 spokes of the Hindu Wheel of Dharmacakra are:

1) Love
2) Courage
3) Patience
4) Peacefulness
5) Magnanimity (forgive)
6) Goodness
7) Faithfulness
8) Gentleness
9) Selflessness
10) Self-Control
11) Self Sacrifice

12) Truthfulness
13) Righteousness (dharma)
14) Justice
15) Mercy (forgiveness)
16) Gracefulness (generosity)
17) Humility
18) Empathy
19) Sympathy
20) Spiritual Knowledge
21) Moral Values
22) Spiritual Wisdom
23) The Fear of God
24) Faith or Belief or Hope

Gyaan, Jnana, gnaan are Sanskrit words that mean 'deep knowledge'. A Greek word for knowledge is *gnosis*.

The Four Stages of Life of Vedic religions are (1) we are born and we learn, (2) we live our lives – we work, marry, have children, have personal interests, (3) we withdraw later in life when we retire from active work; we reflect and advise, and (4) we detach or make preparations for our final steps on earth.

The Miracle of Rice Grains

Krishna had a good childhood friend named Sudama. Years went by and Sudama's life ended in poverty but Krishna became an incarnation of the divine. Krishna was born into a royal lineage as an avatar.

Sudama's wife begged him to go to Krishna and ask for help. Sudama wrapped all the rice they had left in a cloth and went to Krishna's palace, where he was welcomed and the two friends sat and talked for hours, recalling memories and eating the rice.

Sudama left on his journey back home, forgetting to ask Krishna for the help like he had intended. When Sudama reached his gate, as dawn broke, he saw that the small hut had been turned into a huge stately home, and his family was waiting to greet him, with baskets spread all around the kitchen filled with food, one for every grain of rice that Krishna had eaten. Krishna had understood what Sudama's need was when he had visited.

It is not the material gift that mattered, but the love that Krishna gave it with, and as Sudama's gift to Krishna became a gift to Sudama, what we give becomes a gift to us. We all have a choice whether to keep our gifts to ourselves or share them with others.

The city of Varanasi, India is the holiest of 7 cities in Hinduism and Jainism. The river Ganges is located at Varanasi and it is considered to be a holy river. People bathe and worship in the river in order to purify themselves. The sick and crippled come hoping that the touch of water will cure their ailments. Some Hindus who believe dying in the Ganges will carry them to Paradise come to die in the river.

Often, the Hindu do surya namaskar at sunrise to pay respect to the sun that is considered the god of energy.

There are many temples, also called 'mandir' on the banks of the Ganges.

Dharmakshetra is the Holy City where the Bhagavad Gita was

preached by Lord Krishna during a war dilemma. Kurushetra is a city where the battle of Mahabharat was fought.

The Tirupati Temple is dedicated to Lord Venkateswara, an incarnation of Vishnu. Millions of pilgrims visit the temple each year.

Hindu Scriptures derived from the ancient Sanskrit Vedas, Upanishads, and the Gita

Rig-Veda

1. They call it Indra the god of Storms, Mitra, Varuna god of Sky, Fire; or again it is the celestial bird Garutmat. What is but one the wise call manifold by many names.

2. The Gayatri Verse: The Brahman's Daily Prayer:

We meditate on the lovely light of the god Savitri; may it stimulate our thoughts!

3. None has attained to thy sovereignty and power,
None to thine undaunted spirit –
None –
Nor swift-winged bird,
Nor restless-moving water,
Nor curbing wind's
impulsive might.

In the abyss, king Varuna the sky god, by the power of his pure will upholds aloft the cosmic tree's high crown. There stand below the branches and above the roots. Within us, may the banners of this light be firmly set!

For the sun hath king Varuna prepared
A broad path that he may roam along it;
For the footless he made feet that he might move;
And he it is who the stricken of heart absolves.

A hundred and a thousand men of healing
Hast thou, O king: how wide, profound thy grace!
Ward off and drive away unjust decay:
From the sin we have incurred deliver us.

The stars of the Bear at night are set on high to see; by day where do they go?
Of the laws of Varuna there's no deceiving:
At night the moon rides forth, herself displaying.

Praising thee with holy prayer (brahman), I beg thee, -
The sacrifice by his oblation begs thee:
O Varuna, be not enraged, - thy words
Are widely heard, so rob us not of life.

By night and by day, the longing of my heart calls upon Varuna, the king, may he release us!

With obeisance, sacrifice, oblations we would pray away thine anger, Varuna:
Wise sovereign (asura), king, make loose our sins, - For thou has power.
Make loose our fetters and we will stand in thy covenant (vrata), sinless before thy mother Aditi (goddess of the infinite sky and mother of the Adityas.)!

4. I now proclaim the manly powers of Vishnu god

Who measured out earth's broad expanses,
Propped up the highest place of meeting;
Three steps he paced, the widely striding!

For his manly power is Vishnu praised,
Like a dread beast he wanders where he will,
Haunting the mountains: in three wide paces
All worlds and beings (bhuvana) dwell.

May this hymn attain to Vishnu and inspire him,
Dwelling in the mountains, widely striding Bull,
Who, one and alone, with but three steps this long
And far-flung place of meeting measured out.

The marks of his three steps are filled with honey;
Unfailing they rejoice each in its own way.
Though one, in threefold wise he has propped up
Heaven and earth, all beings (and all worlds).

Gladly I would reach that well-loved home
Where god-devoted men and women are steeped in joy,
For that is kith and kin of the Wide-strider, -
The honey's source in Vishnu's highest footstep!

To the dwellings of you we would gladly go
Where there are cattle, many-horned
There indeed the widely striding Bull's
Highest footstep, copious and abundant, downward shines.

5. Rudra (forces of human body & soul), may thy grace (sumna) come down:
Do not withhold from us the vision of the sun!
May our warriors on horseback remain unscathed:
Rudra, may we bring forth progeny abounding!

Most healing are the remedies thou givest:
By these for a hundred years I'd live!
Hatred, distress, disease drive far away, Rudra (Siva), dispel them, - away, on every side!

Most glorious in glory, in strength most strong art thou
Of all that's born, O Rudra, wielder of the bolt!
Ferry us in safety to the shore beyond distress;
Fend off from us all assaults of injury and disease.

May we not, Lord Rudra, provoke they wrath. We bow down to thee,
We praising thee and invoke with others asking for healing remedies for the ill.

We offer up praise to Lord Rudra, with songs of praise.

With tough, compelling force
The Bull Rudra
Hath cheered my humble heart,
As shade in torrid heat,
Would I, unhurt, attain
With Rudra's saving grace (sumna).

O, Lord Rudra (Siva), where is thy caressing hand, the hand that heals, the hand that cools,

the hand that beats away god-given hurt?
Great Bull, forbear with me!

Lord of this far-flung world is he:
Rudra is his name.
May never celestial sovereignty (asurya)
part company with him!

Praise the Lord Rudra, widely famed,
Enthroned in his chariot,
Fearful and strong,
Praised by the singer.

As a son bows to a father who esteems him,
So, Rudra, bow I to thee as thou draw'st nigh:
Deep is my prostration,
Thee, giver of much, the lord of truth I praise, -
And praised, thou givest us thy healing remedies.

Pure are your remedies,
Healing they bring,
Gladness they inspire,
Our fathers chose them;
These do I desire
With health and Rudra's blessing.

O, rich in grace (milvat)!
O God, hearken thou the invocation of this assembly devoted to thy worship.

6. What was the primal matter and the beginning? How and what manner of thing was that from which the Maker of All, God Visvakarman, brought forth the earth, and by his might the heavens unfolded?

With eyes on every side, arms on every side, feet on every side-
With arms and wings he together forges heaven and earth, begetting them, God, the One!

What was the wood and the tree from which heaven and earth were fashioned forth? Ask, ye wise in heart, on what did Visvakarman rely on that he should support these worlds?

Teach us thy highest dwelling-places, thy lowest too, thy midmost, Maker of All;
Teach thy friends at the oblation (offering) , O Thou of Great Strength.

Let us today invoke the Lord of Speech, Maker of All, inspirer of the mind,
To help us at the time of sacrifice,
Let him take pleasure in all our invocations,
Bring us all blessing, working good to help us!

Maker of All, exceeding wise, exceeding strong,
Disposer, Ordainer, highest Exemplar (saindrs):
All worlds he knows and all gods he named,
The One only; other beings go to question him.

Singers give of their abundance to the Lord Visvakarman;
So did the ancient seers together offer him wealth; after the sunless and the sunlit spaces had been set down for all beings.

Beyond the heavens, beyond the earth, beyond the gods, beyond the Asuras,

What was the first embryo the waters bore to which all the gods bore witness?

7. The Lord of immortality made primal man (purusa) to encompass the whole universe; all beings (purushas) form a quarter of him, three-quarters are the immortal in heaven.

With three-quarters Man rose up on high,
A quarter of him came to be down again here:
From this he spread in all directions,
Into all that eats and does not eat.

From him (Purusha, Primal Man) was Viraj born,
From Viraj Man again;
Once born, -behind, before,
He reached beyond the earth.

When with Man as their oblation (offering)
The gods performed the sacrifice,
Spring was the melted butter,
Summer the fuel, and autumn the oblation.

From the sacrifice were fashioned horses, cattle, goats, sheep, and birds, creatures of the woods and creatures of the village.

From this sacrifice completely offered were born the Rig-Veda, the Sama-Veda, and the Yajur-Veda.

When they divided primal Man, into how many parts was he divided?

The Brahman was his mouth,
The arms were made the Prince,
His thighs the common people,
And from his feet the serf was born.

From his mind the moon was born, And from his eye the sun,
From his mouth Indra and the fire,
From his breath the wind was born.

From his navel arose the atmosphere, From his head the sky evolved,From his feet the earth, and from his ear,
The cardinal points of the compass:
So did they fashion forth those worlds.

These were the first religious rites (dharma),
To the firmament these powers went up
Where dwell the ancient Sadhya gods.

8. In the beginning the Golden Embryo evolved:
Once born he was the one Lord of every being;
This heaven and earth did he sustain....
What god shall we revere with the oblation?

Giver of life (atman), giver of strength,
Who all must obey,
Who the gods obey,
Whose shadow is immortality,
What god shall we revere with the oblation?

Who by his might has ever been the One King of all that breathes and blinks the eye,
Who rules all creatures that have two feet or four....
What god shall we revere with the oblation?

By whose might the snowy peaks,
By whose might, the sea,
With Rasa, the earth-encircling stream,
By whose might the cardinal directions exist which are his arms,
What god shall we revere with the oblation?

By whom strong heaven and earth are held in place,

By whom the sun is given a firm support,
By whom the firmament, by whom the ether (rajas)
Is measured out within the atmosphere....
What god shall we revere with the oblation?
To whom opposing armies, strengthened by his help,
Look up, though trembling in their hearts,
By whom the risen sun sheds forth its light....
What god shall we revere with the oblation?
When the mighty waters moved, conceived the All as an embryo, giving birth to fire,
Then did he evolve, the One life-force (asu) of the gods....
What god shall we revere with the oblation?
Who looked upon the waters, with power,
As they conceived insight (strength or daksha), brought forth from the sacrifice;
Who, among the gods, was the One God above...
What god shall we revere with the oblation?
May he not harm us, father of the earth,
Who generated heaven, for truth is his law,
Who gave birth to the waters, - shimmering and strong....
What god shall we revere with the oblation?
Prajapati! None other than thou hath comprehended
All these creatures brought to birth.
Whatever desires be ours in offering up, The oblation to thee, may that be ours! May we be lords of riches!

9. In the beginning -
Then neither Being nor Not-being was,
Nor atmosphere, nor firmament, nor what is beyond.
What did it encompass? Where? In whose protection?
What was water, the deep, unfathomable?
Neither death or immortality was there then,
No sign of night or day,
That One breathed, windless, by its own energy (svadha):
Nought else existed then.
In the beginning was darkness swathed in darkness;
All this was but unmanifested water.
Whatever was, that One, coming into being, Hidden by the Void,
Was generated by the power of heat (tapas).
In the beginning this One evolved,
Became desire, first seed of mind,
Wise seers, searching within their hearts,
Found the bond of Being in Not-being.
Their cord was extended athwart:
Was there a below? Was there an above?
Casters of seed there were, and powers
Who knows truly? Who can here declare it?
Whence it was born, whence is this emanation.
By the emanation of this the gods
Only later came to be.

Who then knows whence it has arisen?
Whence this emanation hath arisen,
Whether God disposed it, or whether he did not,
Only he who is its overseer in highest heaven knows
He only knows, or perhaps he does not know.

Atharva-Veda

1. How many gods and which were they who built beast and man?

What gave man form of body and state of mind – consciousness, dream, and sleep? What gave man and beast breathings? Who planted truth and untruth within him?

And who placed in man the many-sided tongue - that dwells within the power of speech?
Within the worlds he roves abroad, dwelling in the waters.
Who can understand it?

What arranges to man pleasings, displeasings,
dream, affliction, weariness, joys and satisfactions? Or wisdom, music, and dance?
Whence comes to Man distress, depression, decay, and mindlessness, and whence comes affluence, success, prosperity, thought, and exaltations?

2. Who spread the waters out, made the day to shine,
kindled the light of dawn,
granted the gift of eventide, and bedecked the earth with mountains and flowing waters?

Through what power does man surpass the mountains and sail the waters?
What keeps the world in being and in many forms, becomes just One?

3. Brahman dwells besides the common people among the gods.
Such is a Brahman's eternal majesty,
By karma, free in the Brahman world,
Every Brahman dwells.
Seek out the track of it!
For knowing Him,
By no evil work wilt thou be defiled.

4. The city of the gods has circles eight and portals nine and is encompassed in radiant yellow and gold round about; in it is a golden treasure-chest, - celestial, suffused with light – In this golden treasure-chest, three-spoked and thrice supported, containing self (atmanvat).

This is what knowers of Brahman know. And in the city is stored glory in all its forms. And thereon together sit the Seven Seers who became this mighty One's protectors.

5. Skambha is the Support;
the first principle which is both the material and efficient cause of the Universe, -
in which of his limbs does the earth abide, and all directions, and all seasons?
from which of his limbs does Matarisvan (the Wind) blow?
Where in him does faith abide and is truth established?

In the limbs of Skambha, wherein are the Vedas, all four of them; the Rig-Veda (hymns), the Sama-Veda (chants), the Yajur-Veda(sacrifice), and the Artharva-Veda(charms) – as seers did come forth.

On whom Prajapati propped up the worlds and brought forth all life – above, below, and in between – With how much of himself did Skambha enter in?

With how much of himself did Skambha enter the past, and how much of him extends into the future?

Wherein in Man (purusa), immortality and death are held together.

Whoso in Man knows the highest Lord, - whoso knows Brahman, Prajapati, and Skambha by analogy.

Whereas in that one limb of Skambha the three and thirty gods.

In the beginning it was the Golden Embryo poured forth by Skambha and filled therin with life by Prajapati (Lord of Creatures).

6. Again and again, name after name, many does a man invoke before the rising of the sun dawn and at sunset of nighttime.

Who holds in place the heaven earth, who supervises all that was and that is yet to be, to whom the sun belongs – in Skambha this whole universe, possessed of self (atmanvat). With a single wheel it turns with many spokes and a thousand syllables; the path it has not traversed some have seen; what it has traversed the higher above see more than the further down below. What moves, what falls, what stands, what breathes, what does not breathe, what blinks, what becomes,

This keeps the world in being, - many are its forms – this, growing together, becomes just One (Unity).

The infinite is extended out in many places; infinite and finite meet at a common edge. The guardian of the firmament moves and discriminates between them, knowing what of it was and what is yet to be.

7. When recently, or in the middle past, or long ago,
Men speak about the man who knows the Veda,
It is the sun of which they one and all do speak,
Of fire as second and of the three fold swan.

For a thousand-day journey the wings of the yellow swan are spread abroad as heavenward it flies:
Gathering all the gods into its bosom, it flies on,
Surveying all the worlds.

By truth he gives heat on high,
By Brahman he looks below;
He breathes obliquely by the breath
In which the Best has found a home.

Who knows the fire-sticks from which, by rubbing, Wealth is won,
He, knowing, ponders on the highest, best:
He knows the mighty Brahman-power.

8. In the beginning he, footless, came to be;
In the beginning he bore the heavenly light;
He acquired footing and became of use;
All enjoyment took he for himself.

Whoso reveres the eternal God who reigns on high,
Then he becomes of use,

And his hunger will be satisfied with God.

Eternal do they call him, and yet even now
Day and night are each from the other born,
each in its different form.

A hundred, a thousand, a myriad, a hundred million, - what is his own, how can it be counted? All belongs to the One as the One looks on.

The One is finer than a hair; the One cannot be seen.
Hence is that deity so dear to me, most fit to be embraced.

9. Thou art woman, thou art man, Thou art lad and maiden,
Thou art the old man and the old woman tottering on the staff (cane):
Once born thou comest to be, thy face turned toward the city of the gods!

10. She, the eternal, was born in right olden times; the great primeval goddess, of all things encompassed.

The deity named 'Helpful' sits encompassed by the law:

Because its hue is such, these trees are green, and green are their garlands.

Near though he is, one cannot leave him;
Near though he is, one cannot see him.
Behold God's wise artistry!
God does not die;
God grows not old.

11. Words uttered by him than whom there's nothing earlier speak of things as they really are: the place the words go to when speaking,
Men call it the city of the gods, of Brahman-power, where the presence of Vishnu sits;
That wherein gods, men and women were set as spokes within the hub of the wheel revolving, wherein the waters' flower by some uncanny power grows, of that I ask thee.

The gods whom impel the wind to blow forth, who cause the points of the compass to converge, these gods who guide the waters, clothe the earth and encompass the atmosphere; One of them, the Disposer, gives the sky, Others protect all the directions. The One of them knows the thread extended, on which all creatures are spun;
Who knows the thread of the thread.

Words to utter:
I know the thread extended on which all creatures and life is spun;
I know the thread of the thread,
Hence the almighty Power of the Highest One.

Free from desire, immortal, wise and self-existent, with its own savour satisfied, and nothing lacking, - whoso knows him, the Self, - wise, ageless, ever-young, -
Of death will have no fear.

12. Homage to the Breath of Life, for this whole universe obeys it, which has become the Lord of all, on which all things are based.

Homage to thee, Breath of Life; homage to thee, Thunder; homage to thee, Lightening.
Homage to thee, O Breath of Life, when thou pourest rain.

When upon the plants the Breath of Life in thunder roars, they then conceive and form the embryo; then manifold are they born.

When upon the plants the Breath of Life, the season come in spring, all things upon the earth rejoice with great rejoicing.

When the Breath of Life this mighty earth with rain
Bedews, then do the cattle too rejoice: 'Great strength will be our portion.'

Rained upon by the Breath of Life, the plants give voice: 'Thou hast prolonged for us ourlife; fragrance hast thou given.'

Homage to thee, O Breath of Life, when thou comest, when thou goest: Homage to thee when standing still; homage to thee when sitting or stretched prostrate before you! Homage to thee, Lord, when breathing in and when breathing out:

O, Lord Vishnu, that form of thine so dear to us,
that which is healing to us,
place it in us that we may live and speak the truth of the highest world.

The Breath of Life is Viraj;
The Breath of Life all things revere;
The Breath of Life is sun and moon;
The Breath of Life they call
Prajapati.

The breathing in and the breathing out is rice and barley, and herbs,
And the oxen is called the Breath of Life too.
Within the womb the man grows from an embryo and when the Breath of Life quickenest him, then he is born again.

The Breath of Life some call the wind and some call the breeze.

Who this of thee knows, O Breath of Life, Bring tribute unto thee,
So too shall they to The One bring tribute from all ends of the earth, to Who hears thee, - thou, so good to hear.

As an embryo the One stirs within the deities;
The One comes to be, has been, and what is yet to be Hath the One entered with divine powers.

Like a swan from the ocean he rises up, withdrawing not a single foot: should a foot be withdrawn, there would not be todays, tomorrows, nights or days; it would never dawn again.

With eight turns of the wheel and a thousand syllables, the One gave birth to the world.

To thee who rules all things and to thee whose bow is swift among the rest, to thee, O Breath of Life, do we give homage!

The Breath of life is ever awake and never sleeps while others sleep.

Utter these words:
I within myself bind my soul (atman)to the Breath of Life, that I may live!

Brihadaranyaka Upanishad

1. In the beginning nothing at all existed here, until the Invisible Self (Brahma, Vishnu, Manesh) brought forth water, fire, heat, and vital life breath by divine mind and divine voice.

The waters churned to make the earth, and the heat generated fire and the sun was born.

He rubbed his hands together backwards and forwards and from his mouth (as from the womb) he brought forth fire. That is why both hands and mouth are hairless on the inside; for the womb too is hairless on the inside.

The first Self said: 'Since nothing else exists other than I, of whom or what am I afraid? I also find no pleasure at all in being alone.'

Now he was of the size of a man and a woman in close embrace. He split (pat-) this Self in two: and from this arose husband (pati) and wife (patni).

Self was the size of a man and a woman in close embrace. He split in two; that is why space is filled up with woman. He copulated with her, and thence were human beings born. The woman was confused that she was generated from man and copulated with her, and she decided to disappear. She became a cow; he became a bull. They copulated and thence cattle were born.
She became a mare; he became a stallion. They copulated and thence single-hoofed animals were born.
She became a she-goat; he became a he-goat. She became a ewe; he became a ram. They copulated and goats and sheep were born.
So did he bring forth all couples that exist, even down to the ants. He himself (the Self of all selfs) is all the gods.
This is the super-emanation of Brahma, who was mortal but brought forth all immortals, who brought forth Soma, which is the food and seed (semen and egg) for the extent of the whole universe. (Soma was later called God of the Moon). Whoso thus knows comes to be in that super-emanation of his, which was a covenant or promise to the extension for all humanity. Even the seer (rsi) Vamadeva realized this and became part of universe, sun, and Self: 'I became Manu and the sun!'

Now at this time the world was undifferentiated. What introduces differentiation is name and form so that we can say 'A thing has this name and this form.'

Thus, the universe is a triad (trinity) - name, form, and work. The Self, though one, is a triad (trinity) - that is the immortal hidden is the real; the Self of the immortal (the breath of life of the immortal) hidden in the name (mind) and form (body) of a person.

All things are incomplete individually, for therein (the One Self) do all things and works become one.

Whoso knows this becomes Brahman and becomes this whole Universe.

Whoso knows this becomes Brahman and becomes this whole Universe with Self;
the Self (Vishnu, Mahesh, Brahma, Shiva) should be revered and held dear; what one holds dear will never perish.

By supreme effort (ati), the One Brought forth a form of the Good (sreyo-rupa), a princely power (ksatra) - and gave it to gods such as Indra, Vanuna, Soma, Rudra, Parjanya, Yama, Isana
so they could be divine helpers.

Pushan is this earth, which by nourished by Prajapati.

And on the natural phenomena of the wind and the light of the fire, sun, and moon, there is this verse:
'From whence the sun arises
To whither it goes down –'
This means that is rises out of the breath of life and sets in the breath of life.
The gods made right and law (dharma)
For today and tomorrow too!
Men and women should follow this observance: they should breathe in and breathe out, saying: 'May not the evil one take possession of me!' And see this through constantly to the end; thereby they will win union (sayujya) with the natural phenomena and will share in its state of being (salokata).

Now, in the end, all beings return to the womb of the Universe of Self (All Existence). So, whoever injures another does violence to his mother's womb.

2. Salt dissolved in water cannot be seen; such is the Invisible Creator to all things and beings.
Salt dissolved in water is in all parts; such is the Invisible Creator in all things and beings.
This is the parable of the salt.
Yajnavalkya, a man who was a householder did tell this parable to Maitreyi and his wife, Katyayani.
Yajnavalkya also said:
'It is not for the love of things and contingent beings that all things and contingent beings are loved; rather it is for the love of the Self (Invisible Creator, Spirit of God)that all things and contingent beings are loved.'

3. The earth and universe and all that is in it is the honey of all beings (bhuta) and all beings are honey for this earth and universe. That radiant, immortal Person who indwells this earth and universe and, in the case of the human self, that radiant, immortal Person who consists of mind and body is indeed that very Self; this is Immortal, this Brahman, this is All.

Cosmic law of righteousness living (dharma) is the honey of all beings and all beings are honey for the law. That radiant, immortal Person who indwells this law and, in the case of the human self, that radiant, immortal Person who consists of duty (dharma), is indeed that very Self; this is the Immortal this Brahman, this is All.

Truth is the honey of all beings and all beings are honey for the truth. That radiant, immortal Person who indwells this truth, and in the case of the human self, that radiant, immortal Person who consists of truthfulness (satya), is indeed that very Self; this is Immortal, this Brahman, this is All.

4. Janaka, who was King of Videha, was sitting on his couch and conversing with his officiating priest, Asvala. They were talking to Yajnavalkya and Jaratkarava Artabbhaga about obscurities and where the vital breaths go when a man (purusa) dies.

Jaratkarava asked: 'When one dies, where do the vital breath depart to?'

Yajnavalkya said: 'When one dies his voice enters the fire, his breath goes to the wind, his body to the earth, and his mind to the sun, and his self to space.'

Jaratkarava asked: 'When one dies what part does not leave that one?'

Yajnavalkya said: 'The name. Infinite is the name. Infinite is the name of All-gods; and infinite is the state of being (loka) that is gained when the soul (atman) transcends to the divine realm (heavens).'
And Jaratkarava Artabbhaga held his peace.

Then they talked about works (karma) , and how by good works (punya) one becomes holy (punya), but becomes evil by evil.

Ushasta Cakrayana then walked up and asked Yajnavalkya: 'Explain to me that Brahman that is evident and not obscure.'

And Yajnavalkya repied: 'It is that Self that indwells all things and is within (is evident) in you (te).'

Ushasta said: 'But which is it that indwells in all things?'

Yajnavlkya said: 'That is the Self that gives the in-breaths, the out-breaths, who breathes along with the diffused breath (vyana), and the upper breath (udana). The Self indwells all things and is the understander of understandings; what is other than this is not it.'

And Ushasta Cakrayana held his peace.

Then Kahola Kaushitakeya came up and questioned Yajnavalkya: 'Now explain that which is Brahman that is evident in me.'

Yajnavalkya replied:'Once a Brahman has come to know the One Self, they rise above their desire for riches and their state of being on the earth; they put aside childish ways and disdain for learning, and they work do good works (dharma) of karma. Then, one will be like a Brahman.'
And Kahola Kaushitakeya held his peace.

Gargi Vacaknavi, a woman, was drawn into the conversation and asked Yajnavlkya: 'If the whole universe is woven together, then what is it woven with? What is the thread that holds it all together?'

To which Yajnavlkya replied: 'On the worlds of the gods, Gargi. Do not question overmuch.'
And Gargi Vacaknavi held her peace.

Then Uddalaka Aruni told Yajnavalkya: 'We were living among the Madras in the house of Patanjala Kapya, whose wife was possessed of a spirit (gandharva) and Kabandaha Atharvana was listening to her. Kabandaha told Patanjala about the thread by which this whole world and the next world and all beings (bhuta) are strung together:

Whoever knows the thread and that Inner Controller will also know the Brahman, all worlds, all gods, Vedas, contingent beings, all animals and vegetation, the Self – everything.

What abides in the wind, is other than the wind,
whom the wind does not know, whose body is the wind, who controls the wind from within – this is the Self of the self within you, the Inner Controller, the Immortal.

What abides in the fire, is other than the fire,
whom the fire does not know, whose body is the fire, who controls the fire from within – this is the Self of the self within you, the Inner Controller, the Immortal.

What abides in the water, is other than the water,
whom the water does not know, whose body is the water, who controls the water from within – this is the Self of the self within you, the Inner Controller, the Immortal.

What abides in the atmosphere, is other than the atmosphere,
whom the atmosphere does not know, whose body is the atmosphere, who controls the atmosphere from within – this is the Self of the self within you, the Inner Controller, the Immortal.

What abides in space, is other than space,
whom the space does not know, whose body is the space, who controls space from within – this is the Self of the self within you, the Inner Controller, the Immortal.

What abides in the moon and stars, is other than the moon and stars, whom the moon and stars do not know, whose body is the moon and stars, who controls the moon and stars from within – this is the Self of the self within you, the Inner Controller, the Immortal.

What abides in the sun, is other than the sun,
whom the sun does not know, whose body is the sun, who controls the sun from within – this is the Self of the self within you, the Inner Controller, the Immortal.

What abides in a human self, is other than the human self,
whom the human self does not know, whose body is the human self, who controls the human self from within – this is the Self of the self within you, the Inner Controller, the Immortal.

What abides in the animal self, is other than the animal self,
whom the animal self does not know, whose body is the animal self, who controls the animal self from within – this is the Self of the self within you, the Inner Controller, the Immortal.

What abides in vegetation, is other than the vegetation,
whom the vegetation does not know, whose body is the vegetation, who controls the vegetation from within – this is the Self of the self within

you, the Inner Controller, the Immortal.

What abides in the life breath, is other than the life breath,
whom the life breath does not know, whose body is the life breath, who controls the life breath from within - this is the Self of the self within you, the Inner Controller, the Immortal.

The Immortal is the unseen seer, the unheard hearer; the unthought thinker; the ununderstood understander;
The Self within you, the Inner Controller, what is other than this, it is not.'

Then did Uddalaka Aruni hold his peace.

Then the woman Gargi Vacaknavi did speak again:
'Vajnavalkya, if everything is woven together, then how is past, present, and future woven together?'

And Vajnavalkya did reply:
'That is what Brahmans call the "Imperishable". It is not coarse or fine, not short or long, not fire or water, it casts no shadow, is not wind or space, it is not attached to anything, it has no taste of smell, it has no "with" or "without", it has no inside or outside, nothing does it consume nor is it consumed by anything, it has not a personal name, it does not age or die, it is not revealed or hidden.

It is the same Immortal that is the unseen seer, the unheard hearer; the unthought thinker; the ununderstood understander;
The Self within you, the Inner Controller, what is other than this, it is not.'

And Gargi Vacaknavi said 'We should count ourselves lucky to have this man , Yajnavalkya, as a Venerable Brahman to teach us.' And Gargi Vacaknavi held her peace.

And Vidagdha Sakalya questioned him, saying: 'How many gods are there, Yajnavalkya?'

And Yajnavalkya answered:
'There is one god but there are 3306 mentioned in the invocatory formula in the hymn to the All-gods.'

'But these are only the attributes of majesty (mahiman). There are only thirty-three gods in this religion, the 8 Vasus, the 11 Rudras, the 12 Adityas, Indra and his wife Viraj, and Prajapati. But
Vishnu, Brahma, Mahesh, Shiva is the Supreme Self.'

The group of Brahmans dispersed and went their separate ways.
King Janaka came down from his couch and spoke to Yajnavalkya:
'Will you further instruct me about the One God? I will give you a thousand cows for your teaching.'
The two men went and stood in front of the fire.

Yajnavalkya said: 'My father always thought that one should not accept gifts without first imparting instruction.'

'I will tell you what others have told me.'

'Jirvan Sailini told me the Brahman is in speech, cognition (prajna), the stories of the Vedas and the secret doctrines of the Upanishads.'

'Udanka Saulbayana told me the Brahman is in the breath of life and should be revered as love.'

'Barku Varshna told me the Brahman is sight and should be revered as truth.'

'Gardabhivipita Bharadvaja told me that Brahma is hearing and should be revered as the essence of the infinite like all points of the compass.'

'Satyakama Jabala told me that Brahma is mind because mind is home.'

'Vidagdha Sakalya told me that Brahman is the heart because of stability.'

'Just as one prepares for a long journey, one must spend time to read scriptures, meditate, or pray to learn to free yourself from the world.'

King Janaka asked next:
'Tell me about the self (person).'

'The Immortal Self is the One God that is found when your soul is free. The self is the essence of the individual who knows 3 states: consciousness in the state of wakefulness, the realm of dreaming, and the state of deep sleep – where does the conscious go in the state of deep sleep?'

'As a fish that skirts both banks of a river, so does a person skirt both realms – the realm of sleep and the realm of wakefulness.'

'As a falcon or another bird, flying around in the sky, tires, folds its wings and glides down to its nest, so does a person hasten to the realm of sleep, where they desire nothing whatsoever.'

'Like Indra and his wife, Viraj, the place where they meet in mutual praise is in the heart. The path they move on together is like an established channel coming up from the heart. They closely embrace each other and are free from desire because they know nothing without each other, this is just as being closely embraced by the Self that consists of wisdom (prajna)where the self is free from all other desire.'

'This is the Highest Path, the highest goal, the highest bliss, the highest prize.'

'Reaching the highest path will be like a caterpillar transforming into a butterfly.'

'Reaching the highest path will be like a goldsmith forging a new and more beautiful form.'

'As a person acts (karma), as a person behaves, so does he become.'

'Whoso does good, becomes good; whoso does evil, becomes evil. By good (punya) works (karma), one becomes holy (punya), and those who knowingly do evil becomes evil.

'To what a person's mind and character are attached;
to that attached a person goes with their works (karma).'

'Whoso knows two thoughts:
"So I have done evil" or "So I have done what is good and fair" knows the law of dharma (righteousness) and
knows the Brahman's eternal majesty;
otherwise,
what one has done or what one has left undone does not torment themself'.

And Yajnavalkya did hold his peace.

Then King Janaka did thank Yajnavalkya for the teaching and said: 'I could give you my whole wealth for your teaching.'

And Yajnavalkya was about to adopt another way of life; he decided to give up his household and retire to the forest to pursue a life of meditation as a wandering friar. So, he made a settlement with his two wives: Maitreyi who like to discuss the Brahman, and Katayayani, who possessed only such knowledge as is proper to a woman.

5. Svetaketu Aruneya went to an assembly and approached
a man named Jaivali Pravahana, who was surrounded by servants.
Looking up, Jaivali addressed Svetaketu as such:
'Young man!'

'Sir', replied Svetaketu.

'Have you been instructed by your father about the Divine?' asked Jaivali.

'Yes, indeed', replied Svetaketu.

'Do you know where the spirit (essence) of creatures go when they depart?' asked Jaivali.

'No', replied Svetaketu.

'Do you know how they come back to the world again (in reincarnation)?'
asked Jaivali.

'No', replied Svetaketu.

'Do you know why it takes some souls a long time to reach nirvana (freedom from karma)?' asked Jaivali.

'No', replied Svetaketu.

'Do you know about the parable of the salt and the water?' asked Jaivali.

'No', replied Svetaketu.

'Do you know how one obtains access to the path of the gods?'

'No', replied Svetaketu, 'But I will readdress my father.'

Jaivali invited Svetaketu to his house for an assembly later that night and told Svetaketu to bring his father if he wished.

When Svetaketu and his father, Gautama, arrived at the house of Jaivali that night, he invited them in, offered them a seat, ordered water to be brought in and gave them customary offerings.

Gautama said to Jaivali: 'Tell me the words you said in the young man's presence and what needs to be said. I come here as a pupil. It is well known that I am busy and have adequate wealth. Please do not measure me out for something extravagant.'

And Jaivali told him: 'I am offering to tell you about
the divine realm as I believe it.'

And Jaivali said before them:
'There are two paths for mortal man, I've heard, the path of the ancestors and the path of the gods; on these all things converge, all things between Father Heaven and Mother Earth.
Now, who are the divine gods? You cannot see salt that is dissolved in water, yet the salt is there; and the essence of God is this same way – God is everywhere, in all things, even though you cannot see God, this is Vishnu. To be One with God, to know that God is within
all things and all universe,
even within a person's own self – this is to know the paths of the mortal and the path of the immortal.
When one dies, the breath of life (soul, atman) leaves the body.
If one practiced dharma (good works of karma), their soul merges into the light (flame) of the universe, reaches the sun and merges into the sun which leads to the Brahman world, the city of the gods, where the soul will find nirvana.
But the soul that did not practice good works or was tarnished with evil is bounced back to earth; that soul is reborn into the light (fire) as men and women again, so they are caught up in the cycle of karma. And those who don't know about the two paths become lesser creatures like animals and insects.'

'I, Jaivali, wanted to instruct Svetaketu to stay in the way of good dharma to avoid the bondage of karma. Practice the essence of yoga and be self-restrained and wise, my good friend, like a good Brahman (buddhi). Svetaketu, stay out of trouble and live a good, long life, my young lad.'

And Gautama did nod graciously to Jaivali, and he bowed to Jaivali, and Gautama and Svetaketu left to go back to their home.

6. This Self is indeed the Lord of all contingent beings. Just as the spokes of a wheel are together fixed on to

the hub and felly, so are all contingent beings, all gods, all worlds, all vital breaths and all these selves together fixed in this Self.

This Self is tens and thousands, many and infinite. This is Brahman, - without an earlier or a later, without inside or outside. This Self is Brahman, - all experiencing (anubhu). Such is the teaching.

7. Driptabalaki was a learned member of the Gargya clan. He offered to tell Ajatasatru, King of Benares, about the Brahma. King Benares was known as a Janaka, who was a generous king. And Ajatasatru replied that he would give a thousand cows for his teaching.

The Gargya said it was the person in the sun whom he revered as Brahma. And Ajatasatru said that he revered him as sovereign Lord, the head and king of all contingent beings and whoso reveres him thus becomes a sovereign Lord, the head and king of all contingent beings.

The Gargya said it was the person in the moon whom he revered as Brahma. And Ajatasatru said that he revered him as the great king Soma, robed in white and whoso reveres him thus, for him is the Soma-juice pressed out day after day and never lacks for food.

The Gargya said it was the person in lightening whom he revered as Brahma. And Ajatasatru said that whoever revered him thus becomes radiant, and radiant in offspring.

The Gargya said it was the person in space whom he revered as Brahma. And
Ajatasatru said that he revered him as full inactive, underdeveloping apravartin, filled with offspring and cattle, with offspring that is never-ending.

The Gargya said it was the person in the wind whom he revered as Brahma. And Ajatasatru said that he revered him as the invincible god Indra, an unconquerable army, and whoso reveres him thus becomes a conqueror, unconquered, conqueror of others.

The Gargya said it was the person in fire whom he revered as Brahma. And Ajatasatru said that he revered him as the all-powerful visasahin, and whoso reveres him thus becomes all-powerful, and all-powerful in his offspring.

The Gargya said it was the person in water whom he revered as Brahma. And
Ajatasatru said that he revered him as the reflection in the water, and whoso reveres him thus is attended by what reflects, not by what does not, and offspring reflecting are born to him.

The Gargya said it was the Person in the mirror whom he revered as the Brahma. And Ajatasatru said he revered him as brilliant and whoso reveres him thus becomes brilliant and brilliant in his offspring. Moreover, he outshines all with whom he comes into contact.

The Gargya said it was the sound that follows after a man as he walks that he revered as Brahma. And Ajatastru said that he revered him as life (asu), and whoever reveres him thus, to him does all the life-force (ayu) in the world accrue, nor does the breath of life leave him before his time.

The Gargya said it was the Person in the points of the compass whom he revered as Brahma. And Ajatasatru said that he revered him as the second that is inseparable from the One, and whoso reveres him thus acquires a 'second'; plurality (gana) is not cut away from him.

The Gargya said it was the Person in the shadow whom he revered as Brahma. And Ajatasatru said that he revered him as death, and whoso revered him thus, to him does all the life-force in the world accrue, nor does death approach before his time.

The Gargya said that it is the Person in the self whom he revered as Brahma. And Ajatasatru said that he revered him as one who possesses a self (atmanvin), and whoso reveres him thus will himself come to possess a self, as well as his offspring.

And the Gargya held his peace.

Ajatasatru said 'Is that all?'

'That is all,' replied the Gargya.

'It is not enough to know Brahma,' said Ajatasatru.

'Then I will be your pupil,' replied the Gargya.

'It goes against the grain that a Brahman should come to a king to ask him to discourse on Brahman. Even so, I shall bring you to know him clearly,' said Ajatasatru.

So, Ajatasatru, who was King of Benares, took the Gargya by the hand and stood up; and the two of them went up to a man who was asleep and addressed him in these words: 'O great King Soma, robed in white!' But he did not get up. Then Ajatasatru rubbed him with his hand and woke him up. He stood up.

Ajatasatru said: 'When this man was asleep, where was the "person" who consists of consciousness (vijnana) then? And from where did he return? But the Gargya did not know.

Ajatasatru said: 'When this man was asleep, the "person" who consists of consciousness, with consciousness, took hold of the consciousness of the senses (prana) and lay down in the space which is within the heart. When he takes hold of them, that means the man is asleep. Then is his breath captive, and- captive too the voice, the eye and ear and mind.

'When he moves around in dream, the worlds are his. It seems to him that he has become a great king or a great Brahman; regions high and low he seems to visit. As a great king, taking his people with him, might move at will within his kingdom, so does "this person" take the senses with him and move at will throughout his own body.

'But when he has fallen into a deep sleep and is conscious (vid-) of nothing at all, then does he slip out from the heart into the pericardium, passing through the seventy-two thousand channels called (hita) which lead from the heart to the pericardium, and there he lies. Just as a youth or a great king or a great Brahman might lie down on reaching the highest peak of bliss, so does he lie.

'As a spider emerges from itself by spinning threads out of its own body, as small sparks rise up from a fire, so too from this Self do all the life-breaths, all the worlds, all the gods, and all contingent beings rise up in all directions. The hidden meaning (Upanisad) of this is the 'Real of the real'. The life-breaths are real, and He is their Real.

Chandogya Upanishad

1. The gods revered the syllable Om in the breaths of life. But the demons who struck at the syllable were smashed to pieces just as a clod of earth would be smashed to pieces upon striking solid stone.

The breath in the mouth and the sun in the sky are the same (samana). This is hot and that is hot; this is called sound (svara) and that is called 'sound and echo' (pratyasvara). That is why the syllable OM and the sun (svar) are revered.

2. Silaka Salavatya asked 'What is the final goal of this world?' and Pravahana answered: 'Space, for all contingent beings did originate from space and to space do they return.'

3. Atidhanvan Saunaka, after expounding about the manifestation of the syllable OM to Udarasandilya, said: "To the extent that this supremely desirable manifestation of the syllable OM (all of Creation) shall be known among your offspring, to the extent will they enjoy a supremely desirable life in this world and an exalted state in the next.

4. Then, as you say chants, say 'Om' at the beginning and say chants to the sun god Savitri, the sky god Varuna, the celestial gods Aadityas that watch over the skies for the 12 months of the year for Varuna, and the Lord of all Creatures, Prajapati.

5. For those who know the secret doctrine (Upanishad) of the Lord, the sun never sets nor does it ever rise at all, alone it shines – and it is always glorious in the heart of those who know this doctrine; such is the teaching of the Brahman.

6. The Gayatri verse - 'We meditate on the lovely light of the god, Savitri: May it stimulate out thoughts!'

The Gayatri verse is the whole universe and all vital breaths and whatever it has come to be. The space that is outside of a man and the space that is inside of a man are the same thing; it is also what the space inside of the heart is.

7. When a man feels the heat from the body of another, or hears the crackling blaze of a fire, he feels and hears the light which shines in the universe; the same light that shines on the back of every single thing. Let all revere it in tranquility, for all works, all desires, all scents, all tastes, and all atman (souls) when they depart shall merge into it.
The sun is the Brahman because the sun is space.

8. And Ghora Angirasa told this to Krishna, son of Devaki: 'When the end of one's life approaches, let one know these thoughts: You are something that can never be destroyed; you are something that can never fall or fail; you are something quickened (samsita) by the breath of life and joined to akasha (universal energy).

9. Let all revere Brahman as mind, self, space, and pleasure.

10. Once upon a time there lived one Janasruti, the great-grandson of Janasruta, a man of faith and generosity, who gave away much in alms and supplied many a cooked meal to his people. He built rest-houses everywhere, hoping that people would thus everywhere benefit from eating good food.

One night some flamingos flew by, and one said to another, 'Look – the light of Janasruti is as extensive as the sky.'

And a teacher of sacred knowledge said to listeners: 'In all regions, the highest throw of the dice is food. Just as a winner in a game of a throw of the dice, so do all the good deeds performed by people go to the Lord of Self (Brahman).

And a ponderer thought about this and retorted:
'The Self, the Highest One of the gods and every creature, is great is majesty and they say: the One is uneaten and devours even what is not food.'

11. The student Satyakama, whose mother was Jabala, learned of the Brahman from the teacher named Haridrumata, who said 'My dear boy, I will tell you of the four quarters of the Brahman' and selected 400 cows for Satyakama to drive to the teacher's home.

On the first night, a bull of the herd spoke to Satyakama as he penned up the cows for the night, saying: 'The One is North, South, East, and West. Whoever knows this knows vastness and will become vast in mind themselves in this world.'

The next night, when sitting around the campfire, the fire spoke to Satyakama and said:
'The One is earth, atmosphere, sky, and sea.
Whoever knows this knows infinity and will become infinite themself in this world.'

On the following day, a flamingo spoke to Satyakama, saying:
'The One is fire, sun, moon, and lightening. Whoever knows this knows radiance and will become radiant themselves in this world.'

At the campsite the following day, a diver-bird flew down and spoke to Satyakama, saying:
'The One is mind, breath,
eye, and ear. Whoever knows this knows existence of being and will win for themselves a state of being.'

Satyakama drove the cattle of Haridrumata home to the house of the teacher and the teacher asked him 'You are radiant as is one who knows Brahman. Now, who has been instructing you?'

'Not human beings', Satyakama replied.' But it is you alone whom I should like to teach me, for I have heard that men like you have great wisdom.'

Then the teacher repeated word for word the words that the bull, fire, flamingo, and diver-bird had spoken – none of it was omitted – nothing was left out.

And Satyakama took a student named Upaklsala Kamalayana as a student of sacred knowledge, and for twelve years he tended his sacred fires.

And the housekeeper's fire did instruct him, ' Earth, fire, food, and sun – the Person who is seen in the sun – that One am I; am I indeed. Whoever thus knows and reveres this fire wards off evil deeds, wins exalted states of being, lives a long and generous life, and lives long and gloriously. I am the Person in the moon, the Person who is seen in the lightening, the water, the points of the compass, the stars and moon, and the breath of life. Whoever thus knows and reveres this wards off evil deeds, winds exalted states of being, lives a long and vigorous life, lives long and gloriously. We are well pleased to serve them in this world and the next.'

12. And the phallus of the man and the velva of the woman are the fuels for a fire, and the ecstasy is their sparks. In this fire the gods offer semen and an egg; from this oblation the embryo comes to be. The embryo lies within the womb for nine months, and is then born. Once born he lives out his allotted span. When the atman (soul) passes, he is carried to the funeral pyre to go back to the place from which he came, from which he arose. And there is a Person who is other than Brahman who leads them on the path to the way of the gods.

13. And in the cycle of reincarnation, those whose conduct on earth has given pleasure can hope to enter again into a pleasant life, but those whose conduct has been evil can expect a lesser life.

14. A man who was making a study of the universal Self did tell his friends about the scriptures, saying the Universal Self was indeed the brilliant sky, the sun, the wind that follows various paths, the waters, the earth, fire, and the universe. His friends were Pracinasala Aupamanyava, Satyayajna Paulushi, Indradyumna Bhallaveya, Jana Sarkarakshya, and Budila Asvatarasvi, all of them owners of stately mansions and greatly learned in the scriptures. And Uddalaka Aruni was the man who made the study and he told his friends 'Whoever reveres this universal Self, the Lord of the Universe, who has the measure of a

span of limitless dimensions, knows all creatures, selves, and foods in all worlds. I thank you for coming to see me for this teaching.'

15. And Svetaketu Aruneya lived the life of a chaste student of sacred knowledge and dharma (life of righteousness and good conduct). And he studied all of the Vedas. But his father also taught him other things about the universe. When water is consumed it becomes part of the body and breath, and part of it is released as sweat or urine.
When food is consumed it becomes part of the body and part of it is released from the bowels. Light and heat, when absorbed, become body and voice.
When a man is sleeping, he is suffused in Being,
when the mind is captive of the breath of life, their resting-place.
When a man dies, his voice is absorbed into the mind, his mind unto breath, breath into light and heat, which leaves into the highest substance, the finest essence – the whole universe. That is Real. That is Self. That is you and what you are, Svetaketu, my dear son!'

And Svetaketu said to his father, 'Good sir, will you kindly instruct me further?'

'As bees make honey by collecting the juices of many trees and reduce it to a single unity, so it is that all Beings in the world, be it tiger or lion, wolf or boar, worm or moth, gnat or fly, that become again as One in the single essence of the Universe. And all waters of the world, be it oceans, rivers, or the sweat of man, become a single essence of the Universe.'

'So you understand it, when the life has gone out of the body, the body dies; but the life does not die. It is in the Akasha of the Universe.'

'When you cut open a fig, you find the smallest of seeds. Can you perceive that this huge fig tree grows from the finest small seed; or like salt that is dissolved in water; it is the same that you are the finest essence of the Universe, Svetaketu.'

'Teach others what you know to help them.'

'When a relative is ill, gather around their bed and ask them what they need to help. Ask them over and over again what their name is and if they recognize you.'

'Show yourself in truth (satya).'

16. Nirada approached Sanatkumara and asked him to teach him. Sanatkumara replied:'Tell me what you know and I will develop your knowledge further.'

Nirada said: 'I know about the Vedas, the language, the funeral rites for the dead, the way to approach disembodied spirits, arithmetic, divination, chronometry, logic, politics, archery, astronomy, the danger of snakes, and the fine arts, but I want to know about the Brahma Self for I have heard from men like you that those who know Self know happiness and I am unhappy, sir. Can you enable me to transcend happiness?"

Sanatkumara said: 'All of these things have names. But there are things greater than names. Speech is greater than the names, for speech enables discussions and knowledge of right and wrong. Revere speech.'

'Mind is greater than speech. Mind is the Self, mind is the whole world, mind is Brahman. Mind enables reasoning. Revere mind.'

'Will is greater than mind. For when a man wills something, then he has it in mind, can possibly utter speech and formulate it in a name. The One willed everything into Existence with sacred formulas, such is will. Revere will.'

'Thought is greater than will. For when a man thinks, then he wills, then he has it in mind, then he utters speech and formulates it a name. For thought is where other faculties meet, so revere thought.'

'Meditation (dhyana) is greater than thought, for whenever men achieve greatness on the earth, they may be said to have received their due portion of the fruits of meditation. Whereas those who are quarrelsome or slanderous gossips are said to be evil-doers, the great may be said to have received great rewards for their due portion of the fruits of meditation. Revere meditation.'

'Understanding (vijnana) is greater than meditation. For understanding of all the Vedas and all subjects that you know, and understanding of heaven and earth, birds and beasts, grasses and trees, animals right down to worms, moths, and ants, right and falsehood, good and evil, pleasant and unpleasant, food and taste, this world and the next. Revere the understanding. Whoso reveres the understanding as Brahman, attains to states of being characterized by understanding and wisdom, and gains freedom of movement in the whole sphere of understanding.'

'Strength is greater than understanding. For one strong man can make a hundred men of understanding tremble. If a man is strong (utthata), he will serve the wise and understanding. It is by strength that the universe and the earth exist. Revere strength.'

'Food is greater than strength. For is a man should abstain and fast for days, he would not be able to see, hear, think, be aware, act or understand. Whoso reveres food as Brahman attains to states of being (loka) rich in food and drink. Revere food.'

'Water is greater than food. If rain is deficient, than food could be scarce, and all animals and plants need water. Revere the whole sphere of water.'

'Heat is greater than water. For heat seizes hold of the wind and warms up space. It is heat that makes lightening and clouds and makes it able to later pour down rainwater. Revere heat.'

'Space is greater than heat. For in space are the sun and the moon, stars and fire. Through space a man calls, through space he hears and answers. In space does a man take his pleasure and receive distress; in space is he born and for space is he born. Revere space.'

'Memory is greater than space. If one had no memory then one would not hear anything. By memory one recognizes one's family and cattle.'

'Hope is greater than memory. For it is only when kindled by hope that memory learns the sacred formulas, performs sacred actions, wishes for family and cattle, wishes for this world and the next. Revere hope.'

'The breath of life is greater than hope. For just as the spokes of the wheel are fixed in the hub, so is everything fixed in this breath of life. By life (prana) does life itself go on. Life gives life. Life is mother. Life is father. Life is brother and sister. Life is teacher. Life is the One.

'For the breath of life is all these things; and the man who hears this is so, has it thus in mind and understands that it is so, becomes a master of logic and debate of dialectics.'

'When one understands, then one speaks the truth.

When one thinks, then one can understand. When one has faith, then one thinks.

When one has faith, then one thinks; otherwise one would not think.

When one has an ideal, then one has faith. When one acts, then one has an ideal.'

'When one is blessed with happiness (sukha), then does one act. Happiness is nothing less than the Infinite (bhuman). There is no happiness in the finite. There is only happiness in the infinite.'

The infinite is the immortal, on its own greatness. Cows, horses, elephants, gold, fields, and dwelling-places are called 'greatness' but this is not the way to talk . The infinite is the whole universe.'

'The man who understands in this way has pleasure in sovereign Self, in freedom of movement until his allotted time is up and his breath of life is joined back to the Universe.'

'If your food is pure, your whole nature will be pure; if your whole nature is pure, your memory will be unfailing; if you have mastered your memory, all the doubt within your heart will be loosened. O such a one from whom all stains have been wiped away the blessed Sanatkumara shows the further shore beyond darkness. He is called 'Skanda', he who leaps from shore to shore – Skanda is he called.'

17. 'In the city of the gods, there is a tiny lotus-flower, within that there is a tiny space. What is within that is what you should seek; that is what you should really want to understand.

As wide as the space around us, so wide is the space with the heart, yet everything is concentrated in this tiny space within the heart.'

If one wills his desires, by a mere act of will may it rise up and be magnified before them. On whatever end a man sets his heart, by a mere act of will that same object will rise up before him, duly magnified. Never on earth can one bring one close to them back from the dead. And some desires will be covered in unreality. Yet, all of it he will find if he will but go to that city of Brahman within the heart, for there it is that his real desires are. Truly, the Self is in the heart. The deep serenity reveals itself from deep within the heart.

The word 'satiyam' means 'Reality and Truth'. 'Sat' means immortal, 'Ti' means mortal, and 'yam' means by this the two are held together. Whoever understands it in this way day in and day out, understands the heavenly world.

18. The Self is a causeway (bridge) that must be crossed to enter the light (sakrt) into full freedom of movement.

19. In the Brahman world there are two seas called Ara and Nya, the lake Airam Madiyam (Refreshment and Ecstasy), the fig-tree (Soma-dripping), the city of Brahman called Aparajita (Unconquered), and the golden palace built by the Lord (prabhuvimita). Those who live a life of dharma and sacred knowledge will find the city. When a man leaves the body behind, he strides on upwards until he reaches the rays of light to meet the sun, ascending to immortality.

20. Prajapati said: 'Look at yourselves in a dish of water, and report anything that you do not understand about yourselves. Tell me, what do you see?'

They said: 'We see our bodies and our gorgeous attire.'

And Prajapati said; "You see the mortal but do you not understand that you cannot see the immortal. When you understand the immortal, then you will understand the Self and the next world.'

21. And Prajapati said to Bountiful (Indra) : 'Now when a man is asleep and is not dreaming (samasta), where does he go – this is the Self, at serenity and immortal peace. When one is conscious of the pain and pleasure of the body, it is in the mortal Self, but when freed from the body to the immortal, pleasure and pain cannot touch it, and he will not return again but become a superman (uttara purusa) of the highest lights.'

And Indra stayed with Prajapati for one hundred and one years as a student of sacred knowledge.

22. When a person is conscious of wanting to say something, it is the Self (that is so conscious); the voice is only the instrument of speech. Let a person understand this, and then they will make their own states of being (loka) and desires to shake off evils, as a horse shakes off hairs, and bring no harm to another living creature (ahimsan), except in sacrifice for food.

(Some people eat animals and some do not; but there is a natural food chain in the world and people have been eating meat for centuries. But many people only eat fruits, nuts, vegetables, dairy products from the cow and goat, and honey from the bees and flowers.)

23. Space is indeed which brings out name and form,
that within which they are,
the names of the gods.

Taittiriya Upanishad

1. Homage to thee, O wind, for thou art manifest of the One of cosmic law (rta).

I shall speak of the truth. May it help me, may it help you. Om. Peace – peace – peace.

(Om means consent.)

May glory come to both of us together. May the spendour of the Lord come to both of us together.

May students of sacred knowledge be at peace!

May the students of sacred knowledge come to the Ordainer (creator, dhatr) from everywhere!

May the One be thy refuge and thy home!

The sacred teaching of this Upanishad is the phrase samhita meaning the great 5 combinations: the earth, the luminaries, the knowledge, offspring, and self.

(1) The earth (rupa) is connected to heavens by space. We are connected to Our Maker.

(2) The earth is connected to the luminaries of the sun and stars, which enables fire and water.

(3) Pupils learn from teachers and teachers learn from pupils (students). Knowledge is found in all the earth and universe if one seeks it. Knowledge is sacred.

(4) Children are a connection between the mother and the father. Biological relatives are family members that are connected genetically.
Relatives by law are those family that are joined by law agreements.

(5) The lower jaw and the upper jaw are connected and work together with the tongue and voice box in the throat to enable speech and eating.

And these are five great combinations to know and realize.

2. Exalted is the Lord, possessor of every form,
May God deliver me by
Your real (satya), true, infinite wisdom!
May I, O God, become a carrier of immortality.
May my body be robust and vigorous
and my tongue sweet!
You are the breath of life (prana) whose joy is mind, immortal, and peace abounding.

You are the shaker of the tree. Your fame is like a mountain's ridge. You surpass pureness, like a goodly nectar in the sun.
You, Lord, are a dazzling treasure, most wise and immortal.

3. A teacher of the Veda will give his pupil these *Vedic Instructions*:

Speak the truth.
Do what is right. (dharma)
Do not neglect study of the Scriptures.
Do not be careless about the truth.
Do not be careless about what is right.
Do not be careless about welfare.
Do not be careless about prosperity.
Do not be careless with safety.
Do not be careless with yourself.
Do not neglect duties to family and employer.
Let your mother be a god to you.
Let your father be a god to you.
Let your teacher be a god to you.
Let a guest be a god to you.

Perform only deeds to
which no blame
attaches, no others.
Respect deeds that have
been well done, no
others.
Offer the comfort seat to
others.
Give with faith.
Give plentifully; give
modestly.
Give with awe.
Give with sympathy.

If you are in doubt about how to act or behave, then behave of good judgement, as if the gods were present. Behave as Brahmans of good judgment and devoted to what is right; this is the rule and the teaching and it should be respected.

May the gods Mitra, Vayu, Varuna, Aryaman (of the Adityas), Indra, Brihaspati, Prajapati, Savitri, Rudra, Brahma, Agni, Yama, and Vishnu all be favorable to you!

Food and water is the elixir of all, for we need food and water to live. But we also need the breath (prana) of life (ayu), which is 'life for all'. We also need shelter from the forces of the rain, clouds, wind, and sun, or lack of sun. These are realities. Whoever has been fortunate to accumulate a large food supply should share with others; whoever knows this is radiant in goodness.

Be not smitten by desires - measure not your bliss on a human scale, but measure your bliss on the divine scale.

A man who chooses good and avoids evil will have less worry; this is a sacred teaching.

The Lord is understanding (vijnana).
The Lord is bliss.(ananda).
These were doctrines (vidya) of Bhrigu, son of Varuna, god of the sky.

Aitareya Upanishad

In the beginning, the Self made water and rays of light fill up the atmosphere.

And when a man and women are intimate and join bodies, each self becomes part of the other self, and they give offspring. They are given to do good deeds for one another.

The Self is the One Whom distinguishes what is sweet from what is not sweet.

The Self is mind,
conscience (samjnana),
perception (ajnana),
discrimination (vijnana),
consciousness (prajnana),
inspiration (medhas), vision,
steadfastness, thought,
thoughtfulness,
impulse, memory, conception (samkalpa),
will (kratu), life (asu),
desire and will power (vasa). All these are but names of consciousness (prajnana). The Lord is the eye of the world and all consciousness.

Kaushitaki Upanishad

Citra Gargyayani was a man who asked about the paths to world of the gods with the priest Aruni, and with Svetaketu the son of Aruni. And Aruni the priest replied: 'Let us go to the assembly where others are studying the Veda, and listen to what others are saying or receive what others are giving. Come, let us go.'

And Citra Gargyayani replied: 'You are fit to receive the sacred word because you do not show pride but seek truth.
Now, it has been said that everyone who departs from this world goes to the moon, for the moon is the gateway to heaven. Then from the moon, they are reborn into life according to their former deeds and knowledge – worms and moths, fish or birds, tigers or lions, boars or rhinoceros, bears or horses, cats and dogs, men or women – or some other animal. And this will continue until one reaches the path of the gods.'

'In the city of the world of the gods, they will meet the fire-god Agni, the wind-god Vayu, the sun-god Varuna,the god king of heaven Indra, the god of creatures Prajapati, and Brahman. There is a lake Ara, the moments Yeshtiha, the river Vijara (ageless),the tree Ilya, the public place Salajya, the residence Aparajita (unconquered), the door-keepers Indra and Prajapati, the palace Vibhu (extensive), the throne Vicakshana (far-seeing), the couch Amitaujas (of boundless strength), the dearly beloved Manasi (mental) and her counterpart Cakshushi (visual) who weave the world of flowers , and the river Ambaya.'

'The Lord is seated at the couch Amitaujas with a pillow and coverlet of prosperity called Udgitha.
The Lord is the Real (satyam), the Self of every being and comprising the whole universe and says - What thou art, so is it. What there is, so is it. '

'And those approach the throne do so humbly to the One.'

And Svetaketu suggested: 'Perhaps when animals are reborn they stay in the animal realm, and when humans are reborn, they stay in the human realm.'
And his father, Aruni the priest did reply: 'Dear boy,
no one is certain. But all of this discussion is knowledge.'

And there continued much discussion in the assembly that day concerning the pathway to the divine world of immortality – until those in temple returned home for dinner.

Indra taught Pratardana Daivodasi sacred knowledge that all parts of the body and the life-breaths were controlled by the brain. With consciousness and no injury to brain or spine, the movements and actions of the organs produce delight (ananda), pleasure (rati), pain, smell, sight, sound, feeling, procreation, speech, locomotion, and thoughts and thinking.
He said: 'Without consciousness the mind would be elsewhere. And this is sacred knowledge of the body and mind.'

And a Brahman, Gargya Balaki, volunteered to reveal the essence of Brahman to King

Ajatasatru and Queen Sonel, who were of different regions – saying: 'In your body, heart, and soul, and in all animals, rocks, waters, plants, stars, moons and suns of the cosmos lives the immortal Self, the Supremacy over all beings - this is sacred knowledge.'

Kena Upanishad

1. By Whom sent forth, by whom impelled soars forth the mind?
By Whom enjoined does the breath go forth, the first?
By Whom impelled do men and women speak?
What god enjoins them?
Ear of the ear, mind of the mind,
Voice of the voice, God too is breath of breath,
Eye of the eye: transcending all, most wise, departing from this world, immortal.
There no eye can penetrate,
No voice, no mind can penetrate:
We do not know, we do not understand
How one should teach it.
Other It is, for sure, than what is known,
Beyond the scope of the unknown too.
So have we heard from men and women of old
Who instructed us therein.
That which cannot be expressed by speech,
By which speech itself is uttered,
That is God –
know thou this –
Not that which is honoured here as such.

That which thinks not by the mind,
By which, they say, the mind is thought,
That is God –
know thou this –
Not that which is
honoured here as such.

That which sees not by the eye,
By which the eyes have sight,
That is God –
know thou this –
Not that which is honoured here as such.

That which hears not by the ear,
By which this ear is heard,
That is God –
know thou this –
Not that which is honoured here as such.

That which breathes not by the breath,
By which breath is drawn in,
That is God –
Know thou this –
Not that which is hounoured here as such.

2. A pupil said 'I think I know It.'

A teacher replied:
'Should thou think, 'I know God well,' now little indeed thou knowest, what of It is thou, what of It is among the gods. Think then upon It seriously.'

I do not think 'I know it well,'
I do not know, 'I do not know';
Those who know It,
know It;
They do not know,

'I know it not.'

God is not understood by
those who understand.
Known by an awakening, God is in our thought,
And so one finds
wisdom, courage, and immortality.
If one has known God, then there is truth.
If one has not known God,
great can be destruction.

Discerning God in each
single contingent being,
Wise men, departing from this
world, become immortal.

3. At one point Brahman was unrecognizable to gods Agni (Fire-god) also called Jatavedas, Vayu (wind-god) also called Matarisvan, and Indra the Bountiful also called Maghavan. The three gods asked a woman of great beauty, Uma, Himavat's daughter who the strange creature might be. She said 'It is Brahman.' There is the description of Brahman as when the lightning flashes and people say 'Ah!' And they understood. So much for the sphere of the gods. Now for the sphere of the individual self. When a thought occurs to the mind and the mind recollects it repeatedly, - this is conceptual thought (samkalpa). Brahman is called tadvanam 'one who desires it' and as such Brahman is to be revered.
The individual self should desire divine knowledge and truth.

The basis of the secret doctrines (Upanishads) is ascetic practice, self-restraint, works (karma), the Vedas and all the treatises that depend on them(vedanga).

Vendanga has 6 parts:

1) Shiksha - phonetics
2) Kalpa - ritual
3) Vyakarana - grammar
4) Nirukta - history of words
5) Chandas - meter
6) Jyotisha - time determination in astrology

Truth is its dwelling place. Whoever knows this doctrine in this way will vanquish evil and find his home in the infinite, unconquerable world of heaven - there will he find his home (Veda's end - vedanta).

Isa Upanishad

1. This whole universe must be pervaded by a Lord, -
Whatever moves in this moving world,
Abandon it, and then enjoy:
Covet not the goods of
anyone at all.
Performing works on earth -
A man or woman may wish to live a hundred years;
They are not defiled by good works, but devilish
ways hurt the self.
Unmoving - One - God -
swifter than thought (manas), -
The lesser gods could not seize hold of It as it sped before them:
Standing, It overtakes all others as they run;

In It the wind incites activity.
It moves. It moves not.
It is far, yet It is near.
It is within the whole universe,
And yet It is without it.
Those who see all beings in the Self, And the Self in all beings
Will never shrink from It.
When once one understands that in oneself
The Self's become all beings.
When once one's seen the unity,
What room is there for sorrow?
What room for perplexity?
God, the wise Sage, all-conquering, self-existent,
Encompassed that which is resplendent, incorporeal (intangible), invulnerable.
Devoid of faults, pure, unpierced by evil;
All things God ordered each according to its nature for years unending.

Discord surrounds those who revere unwisdom (avidya).
But those who know the Self know wisdom and immortality.
Wind of immortal breath,
This body whose end is in ashes,
Om, O mind (kratu) remember; what's done remember.
Lord, lead us along fair paths to riches,
The Lord knows the way
To repel from us the fault that leads astray.
May we compile for the One of Spirit a hymn of homage!
That Person yonder in the sun, the Lord in truth is the One.

O Pushan, single seer, god of roads, O sun, born of Prajapati
Display thy rays, diffuse thy light;
That form of thine which is most fair
That Person yonder, is Me and I am God.

Katha Upanishad

A certain man named Usan, son of Vajasravas, had a son named Naciketas.

And Usan did teach Naciketas about the Brahman. Naciketas did acquire sacred wisdom
saying:

'In paradise there's no such thing as fear;
Thou art not there, nor shrinks one from old age.
Hunger and thirst, these two transcending,
Sorrow surpassing, a man makes merry in paradise.

God, thou understandest the way to paradise;
Declare it to me, for I have faith;
The heavenly worlds partake of immortality;
It is the ground of all hidden secret places.
To know God the adorable transcends both birth and death;
And realizing God is to attain peace and what is absolute.

When man is dead, this doubt remains:
Some say 'He is,' and others say 'He is not.'
How hard it is to know!

No other is there equal to this in any wise.'

And god Yama, the god of death did teach the following:

Live out thy years as many
as thou wilt
May thy sons and grandsons,
daughters and granddaughters live
to be a hundred years,
Thou shouldest think this is a boon
(blessing).
Choose wealth in elephants, cattle,
horses, gold, instruments of music,
land and the power of the senses.
We are granted enjoyment
of all we canst desire!
Whatever we can desire in this
world is hard to win,
an entire life lived is short indeed,
with riches a man can
never be satisfied,
so long as we live as thou for us has
ordained,
this should be the only boon to
claim.
Mortal men seek the immortals, to
know them and meditate on colours,
pleasures, and joys,
finding some comfort in this life
however long.
Whereas mortal men and women
are puzzled by death and exactly
what happens at our great
departing!
One should not accept garlands of
wealth if it will drag one down to
lesser than agreeable.
Wisdom says not to be distracted
by manifold desire!
Be self-wise and receptive to
learning; turn your mind round and
round for wisdom.
Some think they will never
fall from wealth, but this is foolish;
they think this is the only world and
there is no other.
Many never come to hear about
the Holy Spirit;
many hear about the Holy Spirit but
know it not.
the Ideal is subtle so they do not
know unless they are told.
What is called permanent treasure
on earth is not permanent; by things
impermanent we will attain the
Permanent.
Let a wise man think upon God
Vishnu, the Brahman, the Self, Let
him engage in the spiritual exercise
(yoga).
Then the wise man will put behind
him sorrows and fleeting (unstable)
joys, and have dharma (ways of
righteousness).

A word proclaimed in ascetic
practices in Om.
The imperishable Brahman is not
born nor dies;
From nowhere has Brahman sprung
nor has Brahman anyone become;
It is eternal, everlasting,
and was at the beginning.
The Self is hidden in the heart of
creatures,
The Majesty of the Self, by the grace
of the Ordainer who is the Creator of
All.
Those who know peace know
God. Those who are not at peace
cannot grasp It – whose mind dwells
in the uttermost beyond,
so say the seers of Brahman.
There is a bridge that leads to
Brahman, imperishable, supreme,
where there is no fear,

for those seeking to reach the shore beyond the reach of fear.

Know this:
The self is the owner of the chariot,
the chariot is the body,
Soul (atman or buddhi) is
the body's charioteer,
Mind are the reins that curb it.
Senses are the horses.
What, then, is the subject of experience?
'Self, sense, and mind conjoined,' do wise men
reply. (parable of the chariot)
Those who know how to discriminate with mind (controlling one's behaviors) (enabling the Inner Controller) and discipline, - like well-trained horses, -
One who masters fully
controlling the senses by the mind with wisdom (vijnana) – reaches the highest state (pada) of Vishnu's journey.

Higher than the senses are the mind,
Higher than the mind is
the soul (atman or buddhi),
Higher than the soul is
The Self – this is the Greatest
Person, the Goal, the All-Highest
Way that is deep-hidden in all things
and conformed to infinity,
that which gave to all things the breath of life , the firmness of the rocks, or the first all-knowing fire.

This in truth is That.

A wise sage will look inward in search of treasures and immortality, but those who pursue desires outside of themselves may fall onto unstable things.

This in truth is That.

From whence the suns arise, and to whither they go down,
Thereon are all the gods suspended;
None passes beyond this.

This in truth is That.

What we see here is also there beyond;
What there, that too is here;
Death beyond death does
the Lord incur
Who sees in this what seems to be diverse!

Grasp this with your mind:
Herein there's no diversity at all.
Death beyond death is all the lot of the Lord
Who seems in this what
seems to be diverse.

Of the measure of a thumb,
the 'Person' abides within the self,
Lord of what was and what is yet to be;
Resembling a Smokeless Flame,
Lord, of what was and of what is yet to be;
Lord of today and tomorrow.

This in truth is That.

Or, as Rain that falls in
Craggy places loses itself, dispersed throughout the Mountains,
So does the one who sees things as diverse, the one becomes dispersed in their pursuit.

As Water pure into pure water
poured
Becomes even as (tadrg) that pure
water is,
So too becomes the self of him, -
The silent sage who knows.

For those who know dharma (good
ways), they grieve not.

This in truth is That.

As Swan it swells in the pure Sky,
As God Vasu it dwells in the
Atmosphere (water, fire, earth,
universe)
As Priest it dwells by the altar,
As Guest it dwells in the House,
Among Men and Women it dwells, in
vows,
In Cosmic Law and in the
Firmament (Universe) and Heavens,
Of Water born,
Of Rock – all are the same
One – the great Cosmic Law! (rta)!
The One leads the out-breath
upward
And casts the in-breath
downward:
When the embodied soul
whose dwelling is the body
dissolves and from the body is
released,
what then of this remains?

This in truth is That.

Neither by breathing in nor yet by
breathing out lives any mortal man:
By something else they live on
which the two breaths depend.

Lo! I will declare to thee this
mystery of Brahman
Never-failing,
And of what the self becomes when
it comes
to the hour of death.

Some to the womb return,
Embodied souls, to receive
another body;
Others pass into a lifeless stone
(sthanu)
In accordance with their works
(karma)
In accordance with the tradition
they had heard (sruta).

When all things sleep, that
Person (God) is awake, assessing all
desires:
That is the Pure, that
Brahman,
That the immortal, so they say:
In it all the worlds are
established;
Beyond it none can pass.

This in truth is That.

As the one fire ensconced within the
house
Takes on the form of all that's in it,
So the One inmost Self of every
being
Takes on their several forms,
without (remaining the while).
As the one wind, once entered into a
house,
Takes on the forms of all that's in it,
So the One inmost Self of every
being
Takes on their several forms,
without (remaining the while).

Just as the sun, the eye of the world,
Is not defiled by the eye's
outward blemishes,
So the One Inmost Self of every
being
Is not defiled by the suffering of the
world, -
but remains outside of it.

One and all-mastering is the Inmost
Self of every being;
God makes the one form
manifold:

Wise men and women who see God
as subsistent
in their own selves,
Taste Everlasting Joy (sukha).

Permanent among the
impermanents, conscious among the
conscious,
The One among the many,
Disposer of desires:
Wise men and women who see God
as subsistent in their own selves,
Taste of Everlasting Peace.

'That is this', so think the wise
Concerning that all-highest bliss
which none can indicate.
How, then, should I discern it?
Does it shine of itself or but reflect
the brilliance?

There the sun shines not, nor moon
or stars;
The lightning shines not there, nor a
fire.
All things shine with the
shining of this light,
This whole world reflects its
radiance.

With roots above and boughs
beneath
This immortal fig tree;
That is the Pure, that Brahman,
That the Immortal, so men say:
In it all the worlds are established;
Beyond it none can pass.

This in truth is That.

The whole moving world stirs in the
breath of life (prana) deriving from
it;
From it the fire burns bright,
From it the sun gives forth heat,
From it goes storm and wind,
And from it death does fly.

Could one but know it here and now
Before the body's breaking up
Falling from such a state a man is
doomed
To bodily existence in the 'created'
(sarga) worlds.

In the self that one sees in a mirror,
In the world of the ancestors as in a
dream,
In the world of heavenly
minstrels as across the waters,
In the world of Brahman as into
light and shade.
Separately the senses come to be,
Higher than the senses is the mind,
Higher than the mind is the soul,
Higher than the soul is the
Self, the 'Great', the 'Person',
When once a creature knows It, the
creature goes on to immortality.

The form of the Highest Person
cannot be seen;
No one beholds it with the eye;
By heart and mind and soul

Whoso knows this becomes immortal and is at the all-highest Way.

'Yoga' , this is how to think of it –
It means to check the senses firmly, still them;
Then is one free from heedlessness,
For Yoga is origin and end.

This Highest-Self cannot be apprehended
By voice or mind or eye;
How, then, can God be understood,
Unless we say GOD IS?

GOD IS – so must we understand God,
As the true essence of the two (the absolute and the relative):
Once we understand the
Creator of All, the nature
of divine essence is known.

When all desires that shelter in the heart are
cast aside (pramuc-),
Thence to Brahman he attains.

When here and now the knots of doubt are erased from the heart,
Mortal puts on immortality:
Thus far the teaching goes.

Pure and immortal is the Inmost Self, so know It!

So did Naciketas learn this holy science and sacred knowledge, and all the arts of Yoga:
Immaculate, immortal to
Brahman he attained;
And so shall all who know what appertains to Self.

May God bring aid to all of us; May God bring profit to all of us; May we together make a united effort for good thing; May this lesson bring us glory; May we never hate each other. Om. Peace – peace – peace.

Mundaka Upanishad

First of the gods did Brahma come to be,
Maker of all, protector of the world.
To his eldest son, Atharvan, he made known the science of Brahman, of all sciences the base.
Atharvan passed it on to
Angir, and Angir passed it on to
Bharadvaja Satyavaha, who passed it to Angiras.

Then Saunaka, the owner of a handsome property, approached Angiras with due formality and asked: 'Sir, what is it that by knowing it alone one can obtain knowledge of the whole universe?'

To him Angiras answered: 'There are two sciences that must be known, so say those who are well versed in Brahman, a higher and a lower; the lower is the study of the Vedas scriptures and the higher is that by which the Imperishable Invisible can be understood.'

As a spider emits threads
As plants absorb sunlight
As hair grows on the body and of humans and animals
So does everything on earth arise from this
Imperishable Invisible.

By ascetic fervor is Brahman built up;
Therefrom does food rise -
From food rises life, mind,
wisdom and truth,
and all worlds and all
works (karma) and deaths and
deathlessness (reincarnation).

This is the truth:
the path of work well done on earth will be received with greeting at the proper time to where is the one Lord of the gods, the place of immortality. The goal will be won at the all-glorious flame.
Those of faith who are tranquil and wise, and immaculate of soul, will pass on through the doorway of the sun to where the deathless Person dwells, of changeless Self.

When Brahman surveys the world
built up by human effort,
between what is made and what is unmade Brahman is the connection.

This is the truth:
As a thousand sparks from a blazing fire
Leap forth each like the other,
So, friend, from the Imperishable, mode of being (bhava)
Variously spring forth and return again thereto.
For divine and formless is the Person;
What is without and what within are the Person;
Unborn is the Person, - pure, brilliant (subhra),
The Person is beyond the Imperishable.

From this Divine Person springs forth the breath of life, mind, and all senses,
Sky, wind, light, and water, and fire,
And the earth that all sustains.
The Great Abode (pada) has been revealed;
'Hidden and moving in secret places,' is It's name;
This is more to be desired
than what is and what is not, -
Beyond consciousness (vijnana) and far the best!

The Lord is the life (prana)
that shimmers through all
contingent beings who
understand and follow good ways,
follow charity and chastity,
and truthfulness.

This is the path that sages and seers (prophets) tread so that all their desires will be fulfilled,
Leading to the place wherein truth's highest treasure lies –
In the vast heaven.
Those who are resolute and pure of heart, By practicing (yoga) of self-surrender, Make the wisdom of the Veda's end (Vedanta) their goal,
And at their last hour, transcend to the city of the gods.

Those who know Brahma transcend grief and doubt.

All hail to the highest seers (prophets) and holy laws.

Two birds, inseparable companions, sit on the same tree, the one eating the sweet fruit, the other looking on without eating. When jiva, attached to the world, realizes that it is not other than atman, which is in the world but not of it, it leaves the sweet fruit, 'becomes' the other bird, and becomes freed from sorrow.

Prasna Upanishad

Sukesan Bharadvaja, Saibya Satyakama, Sauryayanin Gargya, Kausalya Asvalayana, Bhargava Vaidarbhi and Kabandhin Katyayana, all these persons were intent on Brahman and made Brahman their goal. They approached the Master Pippalada the seer for spiritual lessons.

The seer told them about the universal (vaisvanara) life-breath (prana) which has every possible form – fire, water, earth, wind, all creatures, the sun, moon, and stars.
'It is possessed of every form, all-knowing, the final goal, the single light, it burns:
A thousand rays it has,
One hundredfold revolving,
Life-breath of living creatures it rises up – the sun! It is also in what is not the sun.'

Then Bhargava Vaidarbhi asked the seer, Master Pippladi: 'Master, how many natural phenomena support a creature?'

'The breath of life supports everything.'

'Just as the bees in a hive rise up after their queen when she rises up, all of them settle down when she settles down, even so do the voice and mind follow the Breath of Life of the Holy Spirit'.

'The whole universe and the three heavens are subject to the Breath of Life (Holy Spirit).'

Then Kausalya Asvalayana asked the seer, Master Pippalada: 'Master, whence is this breath of life born? How does it come into this body? How does it correlate itself to the outside world?'

The seer responded; 'Your questions are welcomed. The breath of life is born of self. As his shadow is to man, so in this case there is an extension. It comes into the body with the mind, and the Self is in the soul (atman) and inside of every cell of the body and in every particle of the entire Cosmos of the Universe.'

Then Sauryayanin Gargya asked him: 'Master, what are the elements that sleep in a man (purusa)? What are they that stay awake? Which is the faculty that sees dreams?'

The Master answered; 'Gargya, just as the rays of the sun all become one in the circle of light, when it sets, and shine forth when it rises, so too does everything in the body become one in the highest faculty, the mind, when he is asleep. In sleep, the mind experiences a great expansion (mahiman). All that it has ever known (seen, heard, felt, feared, desired, experienced) is in the mind.

When the mind sees no dreams (susupta), a well-known happiness (prajnana) arises in the body and it is at rest in deep sleep.

Then Saibya Satyakama asked 'What state of being does one win by meditating on the syllable 'Om'?
The Master answered: 'The syllable Om as a firm base attains to the All-Highest, Tranquil, ageless, immortal, free from fear!'

Then Sukesan Bharadvaja asked: 'Who is the person of sixteen parts?'
And the Master answered that person is inside the body:
The breath of life, faith, space, wind, fire, water, earth, sense, mind, food, strength, fervid ascetic practice, sacred formulas, sacred action (karma), the worlds, and the individual.

On this there is the following verse:
'In whom the sixteen parts are firmly fixed
Like the spokes in the hub of a wheel,
God is the person do I know as the 'person' to be known:
So let not death unnerve thee!

Then the six of the inquirers praised the Master, saying 'You are indeed our seer, for you ferry us across to the further shore which is beyond the reach of ignorance.'

Homage to the highest seers!

Mandukya Upanishad

The syllable Om is this whole universe and the interpretation is this:
What was and is and is yet to be.
The Lord of all is the Source of All, for it is both the origin and the end of all things.

Om = A + U + M

A is the awake state of the mind (apti), or obtaining (adimattva) 'what is in the beginning'. Who knows this obtains all his desires and becomes the beginning.

U is the state of dream, composed of light, signifying utkarsa (exaltation) and ubhayatva (partaking of both). Who knows this exalts a continuum of knowledge.

M is the state of deep sleep, the wise, signifying miti (building up). He who knows this builds up or measures the whole universe in very deed and is absorbed into it.

The fourth is beyond all letters: there can be no commerce with it; it is devoid of duality – such is the Om, the Self. Who knows this merges his soul (atman) into It.

Svetasvatara Upanishad

Sages well-practised of yoga in meditation have beheld God's native power deep-hidden by divine attributes.

We understand the Brahman as a wheel, Giving life and livelihood to all, Existing in all things,

Until our souls (atman) pass on to immortality, to enjoy experience once it knows its Highest Brahman, the Eternal Self –
Then there's nothing higher to be known –
the highest teaching
(Upanishad).

Just as the form of fire returns to its source cannot be seen in its subtle form (linga) it is not destroyed for it can be grasped again at its very source; so too can be grasped again by uttering within one's body, the single syllable Om.

Make thy body the lower fire-stick, the syllable Om the upper;
Make use of meditation like the friction of the stick,
Then wilt thou see God, like hidden fire.

As oil in sesame, as butter in cream, as water in river beds, as fire between fire sticks, So is that Self to be grasped within the self,
of one who beholds the Self in very truth – that is the highest teaching (Upanishad).

First harnessing his mind and thoughts to what is real (tattva),
God Savitri discerned the light of fire and brought
it to the earth.

With mind well harnessed we attend to Savitri, the sun-god, with power directed heavenward,
to make a mighty light,
May Savitri urge us on!

Holding the body straight with head, neck, and chest in line,
With senses and the mind withdrawn into the heart,
Let a wise man on Brahman's raft cross over
all the rivers of this life so fraught with peril.
Restraining here his breath, his movements well controlled,
Let a wise man breathe in through his nostrils, his breath reduced;
Free from distraction, let him hold his mind in check
like a chariot to its horses.
Let him meditate in a clean and level place free from pebbles, fire, and gravel,
Pleasing to the mind by reason of soft sounds,
Water and dwelling places, not offensive, a secret spot protected from the wind.

Fog, smoke, sun, fire, and wind, fire-flies, lightning, crystal, the moon, woman, man, child, a dark-blue moth, a green parrot with red eyes –
In Yoga these are the visions (rupa) that anticipate the fuller revelations seen in Brahman.

When the fivefold attributes (guna) of Yoga come to be and grow, -
the attributes of earth, water, fire, wind and space, -
then is there one who has won himself a body of Yogic fire.

Even as a mirror with dirt begrimed
Shines brightly once it is well cleaned,
So too the embodied soul, once it has seen
Self as it really is (tattva),
Becomes one, it goal achieved, free from self;
there is nothing higher.

Siva , the Benign, is God:
Maker of what becomes (bhava) and what does not become:
Siva can be grasped by the mind.

Some sages say 'Inherent Nature'; other sages say 'Time'.
For all the Universe does encompass the work of the Highest Lord Supreme Being.
No one is a higher Master, for this One is the Cause of Nature and all Essences; this One is the Highest Mystery.

Maitri Upanishad

A teacher of sacred knowledge instructs to direct your meditation To the One Who is called the Breath of Life.

King Brihadratha asked Master Sakayanya to teach him about the Self (the Immortal) and the Master replied that it was a difficult question and he wanted to talk about a different topic that day.

But King Brihadratha begged the Master to help him understand about the concept of 'God'; he said to Sakayanya:
'Master, we could talk about how the human body works , disease, hunger and thirst, sorrow and happiness and all human emotions and desires like anger, greed, delusion, fear, depression, envy, what one wants and what one does not want, and love. We could talk about birth and death. We could talk about all the great riches in the world that one cannot take with them when they die. We could talk about ghosts, goblins, ghouls, spirits, and demons. We could talk about forces of nature such as the drying up of mighty oceans, avalanches, earthquakes, lightning storms, and such...but talking about these today will not satisfy my desire. Please, Master, in this existence on earth, which confuses me sometimes, tell me about that thing which is called The Only Way?'

And the Master Sakayanya listened to the King and replied:
'Brihadratha, great king, when you come to know the Self, which is the goal achieved, it is like the name of Marut (the wind) - it is the Breath of Life found in the Self of all individual selfs. It is the immortal and mortal, it is infinite and finite, it is invisible and visible.
Some call it Brahma or Vishnu,
Rudra or Prajapati,
Agni, Varuna, Vayu, Indra,
Kali, the Moon, the Earth, Yama, Siva (Sambhu), Golden Embryo, Ruler, Narayana, the Swan – for thine own sake, for Nature's sake –
The Many subsist in Thee:
The Immortal.
All life and universe is the Immortal Being,
The Lord of all sport and
all delight. It is the most
hidden mystery, the most
peaceful, without beginning or end!'

'The Master Maitri taught that the wisdom of all of the Upanishads is the wisdom of Brahman.'

'The unknown lord is the pure consciousness of all minds and is contained in all parts of Nature and the entire Universe – it is the real Truth (satya).'

'Each of us has an individual self and an immortal self – like a drop of water on a lotus petal. The water is like the immortal.'

'Each of us is like a lump of iron shaped by fire and hammer. The fire is like the immortal.'

'Each of us is subject to mental confusion, fear, depression, sleepiness, fatigue, carelessness, old age, sorrow, hunger and thirst, wretchedness, anger, atheism, ignorance, jealousy, cruelty, stupidity, shamelessness, conceit, unfairness, cravings, loves, passions, greed, wishing others ill, sexual pleasure (rati), hatred, secretiveness, envy, desire, instability, fickleness, distraction, ambition, inquisitiveness, favouritism, reliance on worldy wealth, aversion to objects repellent to the senses, attachment to objects attractive to them, churlish speech, and gluttony – and we were given consciousness (abhimana), will (adhyava-saya), and conception (samkalpa) which is the immortal in us.'

'So when you feel confused, you are thinking of yourself as an individual self and are forgetting that you are also part of the True Self, the Immortal One.'

'The reason we have senses like sight, hearing, touch, taste, smell, sense of intuition, sense of acceleration, sense of temperature, and so forth is that god Prajapati wanted us to be able to enjoy things other than our own self; otherwise, we would be pillars of stone having no feelings.'

'The things of sound and touch and sense that people aspire to, are rather worthless nothingness (anartha):
Clinging to them the individual self forgets his or her
Highest Destiny (pada).'

'Now the individual self has its own power to counteract all confusion and negative passions - and the formula is to stay in good ways – all other rules are chaff.'

'You can't reverse a deed once it is done, just as you can't change the direction of the waves in the sea.'

For Master Maitri also said:

By ascetic practice
comes Goodness
By Goodness mind is
Won
By mind the Self (God)
Becomes known, When Self is gotten,
No more return to earth.
Brahman is unchanging and unlimited, and unlimited bliss (sukha) in the realm of divinity (adhidaivatva). When a charioteer is finally free from all encumbrances that have held him down, then does he attain to union (sayojya) with the Self.'

'The listeners then asked the Master, how should we salute this One? For you say Fire, Wind, the sun,

The Swan, time, the breath of life, food, - Brahma, Rudra, Vishnu: some mediate on one, some mediate on another. Which is the best? Tell us that.'

'To them Maitri replied: The names for the most exalted form is the all-highest, immortal, and intangible; whatever forms is attached in this world will that know. The thing is the whole Universe. You should discard all of the names and raise higher and higher into the states of being – then at the universal place of Unity you will find it. It is both with and without.'

'Maitri also said that every person who rids themselves of evil, keeps themselves aware, who is pure in mind and heart, whose goal and ground is That Unity of Consciousness in the afterlife, knows That of Which we came from and return.'

'The golden Person in the sun exists in the lotus of the heart.
'The universe is the lotus.'

'Maitri also did say that knowledge is of two natures

(1) Knowledge is of dual nature if it is known by the senses (taste, touch, smell, sight, hearing, temperature, acceleration, for examples).
(2) If knowledge transcends cause, effect, and action and is beyond speech, nothing can be likened to it, or one cannot tell of it – this kind of knowledge is impossible to say what it is.'

'Food is necessary for all life. The sun gives out its rays which the plants absorb, and living creatures are refreshed by digesting the food they grow. The Lord Vishnu is known as 'Supporter of All' including the breath of life which is the essence of food, the mind of life, the understanding of mind, the bliss of the understanding. Food is the origin of the universe (yoni). The origin of food is time, and of time the sun. However many divisions of time there be, through all of them does the Brahman move.'

'Who reveres Brahman as time, there are two forms – time and the timeless. Before the universe was timeless. That which began with the universe is time.'

'Some say "Brahman in the Sun" and Maitri also said:

Offerer, recipient, sacred formula, Vishnu, Prajapati, The Lord is everyone who exists, the Witness Who shines in the circle of the sun up there.'

'Inconceivable is this All-Highest, the One that is awake when all things are gone.'

'Maitri talked about the Meditation and Yoga:'

'What is not thought in the midst of thought abiding,
Unthinkable, the highest mystery –
There fix thy thought, there that subtle body (linga) which has

nothing to support it. This is the fourth state beyond the waking state, dream, and dreamless sleep.'

'This is a higher form of concentration when one becomes selfless, the mark of spiritual freedom (moksa):

By stilling (prasada)
thought one stops
Both good and evil deeds;
Self-stilled, abiding in Self,
One wins unalterable
happiness (sukha),'

'Some know Brahman as the syllable Om. Its summit is immortal, unfailing, enduring: Vishnu is Its name, meaning that It is above and beyond everything.'

'Two Brahmans there are which must be known,
Brahman as sound and Brahman as beyond (para).'

Some know Brahman as the Lone Fig Tree whose roots are above and whose branches are space, wind, fire, water, earth, and much besides.

'Maitri also did say: The higher and lower, Whose name is Om, soundless and void of contingency, Fix Om firmly in thy head and heart! The shining Guide whose name is Om knows not sleep or age or death or sorrow.'

'When one integrates the breath and the syllable Om and all things manifold,
This spiritual exercise is known as Yoga.'

'Oneness of breath and mind and all the senses,
Abandonment of all emotive states – this is called Yoga.'

'Pass beyond the elements and senses, rid yourself of self-conceit, confusion, cravings, envy, wickedness, anger, and greed and embark on the boat of Om and cross the space within the heart gradually to the other side where Brahman is waiting in magnificence and tranquility.
Be one solely devoted (bhakta) and possessing only good virtues (guna).'

'Our blessed Lord (bhagavat), the sun up there, is the cause of emanation of heaven and of final emancipation (apavargo).'

'Just as clouds of smoke are issued from a fire, so too this whole universe was breathed forth by that great Being.'

'Just as fire whose fuel has extinguished, the thoughts of the mind that cause anger, confusion, and wickedness can be extinguished in the mind for lack of the thinking-matter – extinguish bad thoughts at the source.'

'The mind itself in man is the cause of bondage and release;
Attached to objects it brings bondage to itself;

Absence of object – that is called release!'

Demons are in desire of a self that is quite different from the good Self.

'It is only a fraction of the glory (tejas) that pervades the sun, - for the moon, and all living beings are also a part of the glory of the Brahman Unity.'

'The all-highest glory (tejas) is of the same essence (svarupa)as that which is hidden within the spiritual firmament of the heart of the human.'

'As a candle stirred by a gentle breeze flickers,
So does the Lord permeate,
Like lightning's brilliance,
Like drops of rain,
So does the Lord permeate.'

'The highest of all homes (dharma) is called Vishnu, who dwells within the constituent of Goodness, unfailing, permanent, united in will, immortal, pure Consciousness (caitanya), all-knowing, shining in magnificence (mahiman). Vishnu's law is truth (satyadharma). It is Yoga's Lord.'

So spoke Sakayanya from the depths of his heart.
Then he bowed to King Brihadratha, and the king bowed back.
The Self (atman) is identical to the ultimate ground of reality (Brahman) which is found by one who realized the liberation thru *moksha* (nirvana) from the cycle of wandering through *samsara* in birth, death, and rebirth. The bhutatman is the elemental self entangled in change, as a bird is caught in a snare.

Maitri Sutt:

This is what should be done by the man who is wise, who seeks the good, and knows the meaning of the place of peace. Let him be strenuous, upright and truly straight, without conceit of self, easily contented and joyous, free of cares; let him not take upon himself the burden of worldly goods; let his senses be controlled...May all beings be happy and at their ease! May they be joyous and live in safety...Even as a mother watches over and protects her child, so with a boundless mind should one cherish all living beings, radiating friendliness over the entire world, above, below, and all around, without limit. So let him cultivate a boundless good-will towards the entire world, uncramped, free from ill-will or enmity. Standing or walking, sitting or lying down, during all waking hours, let him establish this mindfulness of good-will, which men call the highest state! Abandoning vain discussions, having a clear vision, free from sense appetites, he who is made perfect will never again know rebirth.

Bhagavad Gita

1. The Bhagavad Gita means 'The Blessed One' and is a poem of the battle at Mahabharata. The Gita tells

of the story of war between the two clans of a royal family in northern India. One clan is the Pandavas, led by Arjuna and his four brothers. The opposing clan is the Kauravas, their cousins who betrayed them are of King Dhritarashtra. On a battlefield, Arjuna and Krishna go into the open space between the two armies with their chariots to survey the combatants. But Arjuna is overwhelmed by the potential loss of so many lives and drops his weapons and refuses to fight, after Krishna, who is God Vishnu incarnate, begins to preach about life and death, nonattachment to material things, the Self, love, spiritual practice, and the inconceivable depths of reality. The essence of the teaching is to let go of desire and ideas about reality, and focus on Self in freedom, which can be achieved through karma yoga (the path of action), jnana yoga (the path of knowledge or wisdom), raja yoga (the path of meditation), and bhakti yoga (the path of devotion, love, and true worship).

2. King Dhritarashtra said:
'On the field of justice, the Kuru field, My men and the sons of Pandu too stand massed together, intent on war. What Sanjaya, did they do?'

3. Sanjaya, advisor to King Dhritarashtra, said:
'There was a dispute about between the Pandavas and our own Kauravas – the Kauravas told a lie to the Pandavas.
King Duryodhana, surveyed the host of Pandu's sons that are drawn up in ranks and told His Teacher, Drona, that Pandu's son, Drupada, thine own disciple, is wise and skilled. Here are men, brave and mighty archers, equals of Bhima for the Kauravas and Arjuna for the Pandavas in the art of war, - Yuyudhana, Virata, Drupada (the mighty charioteer), Dhrishtaketu, Cekitana, and Kashi's valiant king, Kurujit, Kuntibhoja, and the Shibi's king, foremost of the fighting men, also high-mettled Yudhamanyu, valiant Uttamaujas, Sughadra's son and the sons of Draudapi, all of them mighty charioteers.

This is a list of outstanding leaders on our side of the army, for your information – thyself (Drona), Bhishma, Karna, Kripa, Ashvatthaman, Vikarna, and Somadatta's son as well.
Many another hero will risk their life for me. Various are their arms and weapons, and all of them are skilled at war.
Imperfect are those our forces under Bhishma's guards, but perfect are their forces under Bhima's care. Stand firm in your ranks at your appointed place and guard Bhishma above all others, every one of you!"

4. And Bhishma, the aged grandsire of the Kuru clan, gave cheer with a blow from his conch.

5. Then conches, cymbals, drums, tabors, and kettledrums burst into sudden sound; tumultuous was the sound.

6. Then did Krishna, Madhu's son, and Pandu's third-born, Arjuna, standing erect on their chariot, yoked to white horses, blow their mighty conches.

7. Krishna's conch was called Panchajanya and Arjuna's conch was called Devadatta.
Yudhishthira, the king (Kunti's son) blew the conch called Anantavijaya.
Sughosha and Manipushpaka blew Nakula and Sahadeva.
And Kashi's king, archer supreme, and Shikandin, the great charioteer, Dhrishtadyumna, Virata too, and unconquered Satyaki.
Drupada and the sons of Draupadi, and Subhadrs's strong-armed son, blew each his conch, resounding from every side.

8. Then Aruna gazed upon the ranks of Dhritarashtra's sons and lifted his bow.
To Krishna then these words he spake:
"Halt my chariot between the armies twain, that I may see these men drawn up, spoiling for the fight, that I may see with whom I must do battle in this strife of war waged by Dhritarashtra's son.
Thus, Arjuna and Krishna brought the splendid chariot to a halt between the armies, and in front of them Bhisma and Drona and the assembled kings of the Kurus stood.

9. Krishna was suddenly transformed and took the form of the Unseen, Imperishable, and Immortal Lord Vishnu and said to Arjuna:
"Millions of my divine forms, beings of all kinds and sizes, of every color and shape
The whole universe, all things, animate or inanimate, are gathered here inside my infinite body.
But you cannot see me with mortal eyes
So I will grant you divine sight. Look!"
Then the Lord of Yoga, revealed to Arjuna the majestic, transcendent, limitless form as the infinite Lord, composed of all wonders.

10. The sight of the Lord was brilliant and too marvelous to stare at, composed of the whole universe enfolded, with its countless billions of life-forms, gathered together in the body of all gods.
And Arjuna trembled with awe, he bowed and, joining his palms, spoke these words to the Lord:
"I see all gods in your body and multitudes of beings, Lord, and Brahma on his lotus throne, and the seers, and the shining angels.
I see you everywhere, with billions of arms, eyes, bellies, faces, without end, middle, or beginning, your body the whole universe, Lord. You dazzle my vision. You light the whole universe with radiant splendor as Lord Vishnu fills the universe with brilliance. You alone fill all space."

11. Then the Lord stood before Arjuna in the mild and pleasant form of Krishna, the kind, the beautiful, and said:
"The cosmic vision that you have been granted is difficult to attain.
Not by study or rites

can I be seen in cosmic form as you have just seen me.
Only by single-minded
devotion can I be known
as I truly am.
Folding back in on myself,
I create again and again.
He who acts for my sake,
Loving me, and free of attachment,
and acting
benevolent toward all beings, will come to me in the end."

12. Krishna then said:
"Look at the Kurus gathered here.
What do you see, Arjuna?"

13. And Arjuna looked at fathers, grandsires, venerable teachers, uncles, brothers, sons, grandsons, and comrades who had joined, fathers-in-laws, and friends all arrayed together waiting for the fight.

And Arjuna, the son of Kunti, seeing them, all his kinsmen thus arrayed, was filled with deep compassion and desponding, spake these words: 'Krishna, when these mine own folk I see standing before me, spoiling for the fight, my limbs give way beneath me, my mouth dries up, and trembling takes hold upon my frame, and my body's hairs stand up in dread – my bow, Gandiva, slips from hand, my skin is all ablaze with sweat; I cannot stand, my distraught mind seems to wander. I see bad things to happen. Should I strike down in battle mine own folk, no good therein see I. Krishna, I hanker not for victory, not for the kingdom, nor yet for things of pleasure. What use to us is a kingdom, my friend, what use enjoyment of life itself after a loss of half our family in battle?
Those for whose sake we covet kingdom, delights and things of pleasure, here stand they, arrayed for battle, surrendering both wealth and life. They are our venerable teachers, fathers, sons, grandsires, uncles, fathers-in-law, grandsons, brothers-in-law, kinsmen all. These would I nowise slay though they slay me, my friend, not for dominion over the three wide worlds, how much less for this paltry earth.
And should we slaughter Dhritarashtra's sons?
Krishna, what sweetness then is ours? Evil, and only evil, would come to dwell with us, should we slay them, hate us as they may. Therefore we have no right to kill the sons of Dhritarashtra, our own kinsmen, even though they are filled with greed and have done wrong to our clan. Should we lay low our own folk, Krishna – how could we find joy in killing them? We should be wise enough to turn aside from this evil war.
For the annihilation of a family we know full well - is wickedness, for with it collapses the eternal laws that rule the family. Once law's destroyed, then lawlessness overwhelms all we know as family. If all of our men are killed in battle, then the women and children who are left will be in danger and all confusion will lead to hell, and they may be cheated of their offerings of food and drink and starve, and our own lives will be lost.

What good can we do when we are dead?
These evil ways of war will wreck the family.
Coveting the sweet joys of sovereignty, look at us, all poised to slaughter our own folk! What are we doing? '

14. So saying, Arjuna sat down upon the chariot-seat and let slip his bow and arrows, his mind distraught with grief, his eyes filled with tears. Arjuna said: "Krishna, how can I engage in battle with Bhishma and Drona, raining them with my arrows? Should we kill them, ourselves might be killed. Even though they are ambitious liars, standing there before us, my mind is perplexed concerning right (dharma)and wrong. My grief at killing them would not be dispelled even though I would win an empire, unrivaled, prosperous, or even a lordship over the gods.'

Then Arjuna said to Krishna: 'I will not fight.'
And Arjuna held his peace.

15. And Krishna joined with Arjuna, standing there between the armies, and spoke to Arjuna: 'What you have renounced is of greatness like the great God Vishnu, - Arjuna, for what good will come from such destruction of the battle today? We will fight for the truth and for our rights but we should not kill each other if possible. There will not be a battle today between the two clans of our family. If our nation was in danger it would be our duty to fight, but we should avoid killing if possible.'

16. And Arjuna and Krishna turned their chariots around and gave the signal to disperse the Pandavas of their own clan off the battlefield.

17. The Kauravas were left alone on the battlefield.

18. King Dhritarashtra blew his conch and declared: 'Charioteers of the Kurus, leave the Pandavas be. Do not follow them. Disperse to thine own abodes (houses).'

19. Then King Duryodhana turned his horse to the place on the battlefield where King Dhritarashtr was placed for battle.

20. And Duryodhana, Dhritarashtra, and Sanjaya
spoke among themselves of what to do next in the resolution of the conflict between the Pandavas and the Kauravas.

21. And King Duryodhana, said: 'The Kauravas have done the Pandavas wrong, no doubt. But we can negotiate – in some time - to avoid the loss of lives in battle, because killing each other really will not solve anything.'

22. King Dhritarashtra replied: 'Duryodhana, I agree with you and I will work with you to end this conflict between both sides of the family clan, big as we are.
Both sides need to work together, for we need to think about next

year's food crops, there are at least 50 chariots in need of repair on both sides of the family, the rice is ready to be bagged and shipped, and Sanjaya has advised me that he heard the lion population is out of control in a nearby region so we need to be thinking of some plans to control the lion population.'

23. Duryodhana replied;
'Yay, everyone needs to cooperate if this family and the whole of humanity is to survive the perils.'

24. And Arjuna said: 'What impels people to do evil things? I wish all people could be filled with God's good wisdom. It was by divine help today that we called off the battle – the gracious favor from the All-Highest Mystery. Praise Krishna and Praise the Immortal One! I am so glad that by the grace of God our confusion was destroyed and all of us are alive and well. We have regained a proper way of thinking.'

25. Therewith Krishna was suddenly filled again with the immortal form of Krishna, saying:
'You now know the better part of mortal life,
The way is definite and clear,
Be my disciple and follow me.
Never was there a time when I was not, Nor will there be a time when we shall cease to be, -
All of us hereafter.
Your embodied soul must pass through childhood, youth, adult, and age, and then your soul (atman) will pass to Me where
of what is not there is no becoming and
of what is there is no ceasing to be.
No one at all can bring
destruction to the Indestructible
Immortal in the three heavens.

Many a word that is better left unsaid will one say to another to wish them ill but this is not my essence;

My essence is that by which pleasure and success is achieved.
Surrender attachment to the material world,
Control thy anger,
And mediate on Me.
This wisdom (buddhi)
is instructed to thee
and is to be practiced in yoga.
The essence of the soul
(buddhi) (atman) is will
(vyavasaya) – it is single here on earth but it
is many-branched and infinite in the Universe, for all the Universe is connected together as One Unity.
Whoso is integrated by the Yoga of the soul discards evil works, puts aside desires of self, and embraces the Universe.

Put aside anger and confusion, and hate.
Be self-possessed of serenity (prasada).
Calm your thoughts and your soul will firmly stand.
Be not a desirer of desires but free yourself and live peacefully, as a tortoise might draw in its limbs on every side. Work for the integration of the soul and renounce the fruit that's born of works on earth. Let thy soul pass beyond delusions of

turbid quicksands and then you will learn to hear what you have heard.
This is the fixed, indifferent, still state (sthiti) of Brahman; To Nirvana the embodied soul is joined in Unity,
when one is Intent on Me,
when one is firm-established in wisdom,
whose senses are subdued with self-control and joined with Me.
For with anger comes bewilderment,
For with the wandering of the mind (smrti),
From this comes the destruction of the soul and one is lost.
But one who roves among things of sense, Maintaining calm serenity (prasada),
Free from hate and passion,
With senses of full self-control,
Is not far off from Me.
And as the waters flow to the sea,
So too do all the desires flow into the hearts of men and women,
And such men and women
Who know integration of
Soul of Unity
Win Peace –
Not the desirer of desires.

The Blessed Imperishable One is everywhere;
The Wheel is in motion
with works done and works undone.
This world is bound
by bonds of work.
Not for a moment can a man or a woman
do no work, for men and women are forced to work by the constituents of Nature.
The three constituentsof Nature are: goodness (sattva), passion or energy (rajas), and difficulty (tamas).

Do thou the work that is prescribed for thee,
for to work is better than to do no work at all;
work even to keep your body in good repair to the best of your ability.

Of ancient times, the Lord of Creatures, Prajapati, said when all life was emitted in creation:
"By this shall ye prolong your lineage,
Let this be to you the milk and food of all that ye desire.
With this shall ye sustain one another and ye shall achieve the highest good;
Whoso enjoys these gifts yet give back nothing in return, not even thanks, is a thief, no more nor less."

Let one not take pleasure in works of self alone,
On earth what interest has one?
What interest in all contingent beings does one depend?
Perform the works that
must be done to win through to the Labours on to the Highest.

Like a Brahman, perform
good charitable acts of karma for other creatures.
The world will fall to ruin
unless all people practice good dharma (righteousness).

I am tireless.
The world would fall to ruin if I were not to do My Work, Guiding wise men and women to be concerned about the Welfare of My World.

A wise one will not split the mind, but keep the full self-control of the mind.

In all the senses of passion, love, and hate, let none fall victim to their power.

Practice My Doctrine of Love constantly.

Know the One who is yet the One True Soul of all things.

The Royal Seers and Sages came to know Me. Unborn am I,
Changeless is my Self;
Of all beings and things, I AM!
I consort with all Nature.

Whenever the law of righteousness (dharma) withers away, and lawlessness and wickedness (adharma) raises up, then do I generate Myself on earth.

I come into being, age after age for the setting up of righteousness.

Find your sanctuary in me, I am of pure wisdom and learn the manner of my being; I will guide you if you seek Me.

I am the food of immortality.

I am better than wealth.

Learn the humble reverence of the good servant, for the wise see things as they really are.

As a kindled fire reduces
its fuel to ashes,
so one should rid of evil ways.

As a kindled fire reduces
its fuel to ashes,
so one should remember
that I provide warmth for my creatures.

As the wheel of universal energy is working,
birth after birth in revolving round, remember that all people on earth are working hard to achieve great things.
Appreciate each person's hard work!

Wisdom is to apply knowledge for good dharma (righteousness) – anything else is evil.

Nirvana is the Pleasure Real.

With sense and mind and soul restrained, the Wise Sage who has forever banished fear, anger, hatred, and desire is truly liberated and knows Peace.
Then does one know Me.

Attach thyself to Me;
Integrate thyself with Me,
Nothing possessing on Earth.
Let the Yogin ever integrate
themself with
stillness and peace,
Then will they approach
Nirvana as its end
Which subsists in Me.

As a lamp might stand in a windless place,
unflickering – this likeness we have heard of such Yogins who control their thoughts and practice the integration of the self into the Immortal Self in their minds.

Still your minds with the highest joys, all passions controlled, holding your soul steadfast.

Who sees Me everywhere,
Who sees the All in Me,
For that one I am not lost,
Nor is that one lost for Me.
Who loves and worships Me,
embracing Unity,
As abiding in all things,

That man of Yoga abides in Me.

By analogy of the self who sees the same essence everywhere - that one understands Who I Am.

Fickle is the mind and difficult to curb, but by untiring effort and by transcending passions it can be held in check.

Hard to come by is this self-control (yoga) by one who self is not restrained,
but the one to strives can win it if by dedication.

If you want to crash and perish like storm clouds,
your firm foundation will be lost, so stay on the path of the Brahman.
Krishna and Arjuna saved hundreds of men and that was Perfection – there's nothing higher whatsoever:
On Me the universe is strung like pearls upon a thread.

In water I am the flavor,
In sun and moon I am the light,
In all the Vedas, I am Om the sacred syllable,
In space I am the sound,
Pure fragrance in the earth am I,
The flame of the fire am I,
I am the life of all beings and the eternal seed of all things,
I am reason in the rational,
I am the glory in glorious,
I am the power in Powerful.
I am dharma (righteousness) but I am not desires or passions that are at war with dharma.

My creative powers are divine, hard to transcend, but I welcome
those who put their trust in Me and My Good Ways.

Doers of evil lead a devilish form of life. Desire, anger, and greed are gates to hell and destruction of the self.

But once one is freed from the gates of destruction, then can they work for salvation (sreyas),
Thence tread the highest Way.

Those who love and worship (bhakti) Me –
who strive for gain,
who help others,
who hurt no one - these people are very dear to Me.

At the end of many a birth of reincarnation, the one of wisdom resigns himself to Me.

Arjuna and Krishna were of great soul that is exceedingly hard to find – They are confirmed by Me
In faith and love –
they were not fools of desire and hate. I direct karma; I am the Lord of Karma. the fate of good souls and the bad souls is in My Power.

Know thou imperishable works of good karma and integrated thoughts to find Me.
Think of Me always,
And do not go to war,
Negotiate between yourselves,
I am the Supreme and I do not approve of war.
I am the Ordainer and the Governor of all things.
I am the ancient Seer.
I am a wise Sage.
Meditate on Me and I will instill in you Peace.
Your mind is in My Mind.
Utter not deceit or hatred,
Utter only truths.

A sacred teaching is:
you have a choice to do good or bad.
Arjuna and Krishna chose good merit.
Arjuna, ever be.
Krishna, ever be.
Who has Me in mind unceasingly, thinking of nothing else at all, -
Is a Good Yogin integrated forever.
Coming right nigh to Me, those of great soul, is to be reborn in Me forever and you shall never be reborn again on earth.
For a thousand ages lasts one day of Brahma, And for a thousand ages one such night:
This knowing, one will know what is meant by day and night.
The Spirit of the Highest Person is in the All-Highest Way in the All-Highest Home.
I wrote the law of righteousness (dharma). By Me, the whole Universe was made,
All moving and unmoving things,
I look on and supervise,
I am the Cause and Means
by which the Universe works.
Human form I have assumed yet fools scorn Me; knowing nothing of my higher nature, Great Lord of all.
I am the father and mother of this world, ordainer, grandsire, all that needs to be known. I am a vessel of purity.
I am the Way, sustainer,
Lord, and the Witness True, I am Your Home and Refuge, I am Your Friend, I am the Origin and Dissolution and the In-Between, I am a Treasure-House, The Seed that passes not away.
It is I who pour out heat or cold, hold back the rain and send it forth:
I am birth and death, what is not and that which is.
Meditate on Me, Who do Me honour, ever persevere, I bring attainment and possession of what has been attained.
The worship of all gods with love (bhakta), full filled with faith, do worship ME, though the rites differ between the acts – I am the Recipient Lord of All so do not worry. Know me as I am and do not fall off the good path.
The spirits of worshippers who worshipped the ancient gods, and devotees of the gods all come to Me.
Be it a leaf, or flower, or fruit, or water, or rocks, or a soul, everything is Mine;
these are bonds of Divine Nature and I integrated all things and all energy. The workings of the Universe are Divine Mystery.
Thy sacrifice to Me is loving service, devotion, and prayer.
The ancients sacrificed animals to me, but that was a rite made by men, not Me.
So free thyself from bonds whose rewards are foul, and integrate (yujyate) thyself by renunciation of evil ways and do engage in spiritual exercise, yoga, or prayer, and Free, thous shalt draw night to Me.

In all beings and things the same am I: None do I hate and none do I fondly love
(priya), But those who commune with me in love's devotion (bhakti) abide in Me, and I in them.
Live a good honest livelihood and do no evil acts,

Worship Me with love and serve no other, then you shall be reckoned among the good, for your resolve will be right.
Right soon will his self be filled with righteousness (dharmatma) and win eternal rest (santi),
Arjuna, of this be sure:
None who pays me worship of loyalty and love (bhakti) is ever lost.
For whosoever makes Me their haven,
Theirs it is to tread the Highest Way.
Royal seers who know devoted love (bhakta)
Commune with Me in love!
On Me thy mind, for Me thy loving service (bhakta),
For Me thy thanks, and to Me thy worship;
Let thy self be integrated to Me in self-control and love,
And shalt thou come to Me, thy striving bent on Me.
So give ear to my all-highest wish,
Which I shall speak to thee,
For therein is thy delight and thy good welfare is my wish.
None knows from whence I came,
For I am the Beginning of the gods themselves
Whoso shall know Me as Unborn,
Beginningless, Great Lord of all the worlds,
Shall never know delusion among men and women,
From every evil freed.
I am intellect (buddhi), wisdom, freedom from delusion, truth, restraint,
tranquility, patience, the future, and the past.
I am Refusal to do harm,
Equanimity (samata), content,
Helpful - this is what I desire in all diversity.
The seven mighty seers of old share in My mode of being - they were children of My Mind.
Whoso should know of my far-flung power and how I use it;
Whoso should know me as I really am;
Is truly integrated (yujyate)with Me;
Let it never be Undone.
The Source of all am I;
From Me all things proceed:
This knowing, wise men commune with Me,
Full filled with warm
Affection and
Appreciative of My Diversity.
On Me their thoughts,
And so enlightening each other,
Telling my story constantly,
Those who commune with Me
I give them an integrated Soul
By which they may draw nigh to Me.'

26. Then Arjuna said:
'All-highest Lord, highest-home, highest vessel of Purity,
All seers agree that Thou
Art the eternal and divine.
All this Thou tellest me is true:
So, Krishna, I believe,
Thy manifestation.
to be like Krishna and connect to celestial energy.'

27. Then Krishna in the Immortal form of Krishna said:
'I am the Self established
In the heart of all things
I am the beginning, the middle, and the end.
Among the Adityas, Vishnu am I,

Among lights, the radiant sun,
Among the storm gods of lightning the Maruts,
Among the Maruts, Marici am I,
Among the Vedas, Sama Veda am I,
Among the senses, I am the mind,
Among contingent beings, I am thought,
Among the Rudras, Siva am I,
I am the Lord of Wealth Kuvera,
I am a creator god
Tvashtri,
Among the Vasus of Indra, I am Fire,
Among the mountains, I am Meru,
Among human beings
I am Manu the father,
Among priests I am the chief,
Brihaspati
Among warlords, I am Skanda, god of war,
Among lakes, I am Ocean,
Among utterances, I am
the highest syllable, Om,
Among the highest Self,
I am Brahman,
Among mighty seers, I am Bhrigu,
Among things unmovable, I am the Himalayas,
Among all trees I am the holy fig tree,
Among the celestial seers,
I am Narada,
Among heavenly minstrels,
Among Gandharvas, the male minstrels who before were gods of marriages,
I am Citraratha,
Among perfect beings I am Kapila, the silent sage.
Among horses know that I am Uccaihsravas, Indra's horse from nectar born,
Among princely elephants, Indra's called Airavata.
Of roads, I am Pushan.
I am the thunderbolt,
I am Kandarpa, the god of love who generates seed,
Among serpents, I am Vasuki, the serpent King.
Of water-dwellers, I am Varuna,Of the ancestors I am Aryaman,
Among that which subdues, I am Yama, the god of death,
Among birds, I am Garuda, Vishnu's bird,
Among rivers, I am the Ganges Jahnavi.
In very truth I am imperishable Time,
I am origin and death.
Among feminine nouns,
I am fame, fortune, speech, memory, intelligence, steadfastness, patience.
I am glory of the glorious,
Victory and firm resolve am I,
And the Courage of the Brave.
Among the Vrishni clansmen I am Krishna,
Vasudeva's son,
Among Pandu's sons I am Arjuna,
Among sages I am Vyasa,
Among psalmists, I am the psalmist, Ushanas.
Of those who subdue the rod of chastisement am I,
The very silence of secret things am I, the wisdom of the wise.
What is the seed of all, that too am I.
No being there is, whether moving or unmoving, that could exist apart from Me.
Of these my far-reaching powers divine, there is not end, As much as I have said concerning them must serve as an example.

Whatever being shows good things, prosperity or strength,
Be sure that this derives from but a fragment of my glory.
This whole universe I hold apart and support it as One, with but a fragment of myself, yet I abide unchanging.'

28. Then Sanjaya said:
'So saying, Hari (form) Krishna, The Great Lord of Yogic Power, Revealed to the son of Pritha, Krishna's all-highest forms,
of countless marvelous aspects,
of many divine adornments,
garlands and robes celestial were worn,
fragrance divine was anointed,

Behold this God whose every mark spells wonder,
The infinite, facing every way!
A thousand suns would perhaps resemble the brilliance of that God so great of Self,
You are Brahma Lord enthroned on the lotus-flower. Thou art the eternal Person, I understand!
All gods, angels, minstrels divine, and the hosts of perfected saints and prophets gaze upon Thee,
All utterly amazed.

Monsters who will not find Your Pleasure and Joy scatter in terror in all directions.
See the whole wide
Universe in One converged
there in the body of the God of gods, yet divided out in diversity and multiplicity. Goodness causes a man to cling to joy;
From goodness wisdom springs;
Passion causes work;
Let not pain be the fruit of passion;
Evil stifles wisdom;
Evil causes hatred and greed.

You are the Knower and What Is To Be Known, the
Highest Wisdom.
You are Our Infinite Immortal Final Home, Our Final Goal.
By Vyasa's favor
We did hear this wondrous dialogue between Arjuna and Krishna, a holy dialogue.
I thrill with joy and thrill
With joy again!
How great is my amazement.
Wherever God is - there is good fortune, victory, success, love, and sound policy. I am a
loving devotee (bhakta). Person and Nature are One; God is established everywhere.

This do I believe.

BUDDHIST

Buddhist scriptures derived from Buddha and Veda

The Edicts of Ashoka are a collection of 33 inscriptions made by Emperor Ashoka of the Mauryan Dynasty (269 BCE-232 BCE) around Bangladesh, India, Nepal, and Pakistan and represents the first evidence of Buddhism.
The Dharma preached by Emperor Ashoka explained moral precepts such as good behavior, kindness, generosity, truthfulness, purity, gentleness, goodness, kindness to prisoners, respect for animals, belief in a next world, welfare for humans and animals, roadside facilities and watering-places for humans and animals, and the duties of officers of the Buddhist faith.

A Bhikku or Bhikshu or monk is an ordained male Buddhist.
A female monastic is called a Bhikkhuni or a nun. The life of Bhikkus and Bhikkhunis are governed by rules called patimokkha. The monks and nuns were followers or disciples of the Buddha and practiced his teachings.

The Bodh Gaya is a religious site for Buddhists at the Mahabodi Temple, where Gautama Buddha also known as Siddhartha is said to have obtained enlightenment under a fig tree. Buddha often taught followers meditation and self-control while sitting under trees. To be a wise, fair judging, and cautious person is to be a sage. The sacred syllable is Om.

Gautama Buddha was born in 563BCE in Lumbini, Nepal and died in Kushinager, India. His father was Suddhodana and his mother was Maya. Gautama Buddha was married to Queen Yashdhara and their child was son named Rahula.
Siddhartha Gautama practiced a period of great self-denial while living an asthetic life; he only ate a single leaf or a single nut during an entire day and almost starved himself to death. Then, he realized that he must change his thinking about his serving bowl. He then taught the Middle Way between severe indulgence and severe asceticism. Siddhartha said that every human being has the same wish – to be happy and avoid suffering.

The Jokhang Temple also called the QoiKang Monastery is a sacred Buddhist Temple in Lhasa, Tibet.

Sramana movements were the early ascetic practices of ahimsa (non-violence), vegetarianism, silence. The sramana movements later led to yogi practices as well as samsara (cycle of birth and death of reincarnation) and moksha (liberation of that cycle or reaching nirvana).

Gautama Buddha (Siddhartha Gautama) preached five moral commandments of the Buddhistic gospel:
1) You shall not kill.
2) You shall not steal.
3) You shall not be unchaste but be humble and modest.
4) You shall not tell lies.
5) You shall not drink intoxicating liquors.

The Buddhistic believers became of community of unselfish social service.

Buddhism promotes calmness and self-control, serenity and happiness, and tries to prevent sorrows and mourning. True cosmic self-realization results from identification with cosmic realities of energy, mind, and spirit.

Out of a pure heart shall gladness spring forth to the Infinite; and your being shall be at peace with the supermortal rejoicing. Your soul will be filled with content and peace, trusting with the Infinite, having no fear or anxiety. Make an end to your misery by loathing sin, wickedness, and destruction.

Cheerfulness and gladness are the rewards of deeds well done and for the glory of following the Immortal. A righteous soul is more to be desired than all the sovereignty of all the earth.

Buddhas have a physical body, rupakaya, and a Dharmakaya aspect, which is 'one who has become truth'. You are a dharma when you are a living example of the truth. Dharmakaya is nirvana, or self-truth. Nirvana or moksha is freedom from karma (may be cycle of reincarnation).
Moksha is a concept in Jainism, Hinduism, and Buddhism.

Zen is a school of Mahayana Buddhism which means 'meditative state' and emphasizes attainment of enlightenment. The name was evolved from the Sanskrit word dhyana.

Sutras are Buddhist sacred texts or philosophical doctrines. Many families have a sutra that is treasured by the family in way of learning by heart.

The dharmacakra is a Buddhist dharma wheel with 8 spokes and can have many planes of existence. The hub of the wheel is the essential core of meditation. The rim holds the spokes and the core together.

The 8 spokes of the Noble Eightfold Path (Ariya Magga):
Right Beliefs,
Right Aspirations,
Right Speech,
Right Conduct,
Right Livelihood,
Right Effort,
Right Mindfulness,
Right Meditational Attainment.

(1) The first turning of the wheel is Gautama Buddha's

original teaching. The Four Noble Truths, which are the mechanics of attachment,desire, suffering, and liberation are attained via the Eightfold Path.

(2) The second turning is the Perfection of Wisdom sutra of Mahayana Buddhism of Prajnaparmita.

(3) The third turning is the teaching of the Mahavairocana Sutra of Mahayana Buddhism. But other turnings may include the Abhidharma,
Yogacara, or Tathagata Garbha Sutras.

Love in Buddha's Sanskrit means 'will to the happiness of the beloved' and compassion means 'will to end the suffering of the beloved', and these two loves are the fundamental energy of Universal Love.

A famous sage is Ramana Marhasi, who had no needs for money or possessions, and is dispassionate about himself only but has expanded to embrace all universe, which is to be enlightened.

The great Indian Buddhist sage and saint Shantideva said that if you can do something about a bad situation to improve it, then do it. But if you cannot do anything about a situation, why hurt yourself more by getting angry and frustrated about it? So, remain cheerful and stay free, and enjoy your life until your death.

An arhat is a Buddhist saint that has achieved nirvana; an arhat has a soul at rest. A bodhisattva saint is seeking rest and salvation.
Tulku are 'living saints' on the earth; reincarnations of previous past scholoars and holy men. The Dalai Lamas are tulku.

Tenzin Gyatso, His Holiness the Fourteenth Dalai Lama, wrote in 1998 CE that there are two ways to inner contentment. The first way is to obtain everything you want or desire. The second way, which is more feasible for most people, is not to have everything we want, but appreciate what we have.

When interviewed in 2006 by movie director Rick Ray, the Fourteenth Dalai Lama spoke about issues such as world population control, and economic and environmental responsibilities. The Dalai Lama said he believes the whole world is interconnected and destruction of your enemies is the same as destruction of yourself. The Dalai Lama said that preserving religious traditions is important to cultures because they are comforting to us.

Brahman Immortal
(Buddha)

There are two forms of Brahman, the formed and the unformed, the mortal and the immortal, the static and the moving, the actual and the beyond.

The 'formed' is the mortal sun that gives off heat; this is the essence of the actual, mortal and static.

The 'unformed' is the wind and atmosphere, the breath of life and space within self; this is the immortal, the moving, the beyond.

The form of this immortal Person is like a saffron-colored robe, or like white wool, an inadragopa beetle, a flame of fire, a white lotus, or a sudden flash of lightening.

Like a sudden flash of lightening too is the good fortune of a man who thus knows. Again, it can be named the 'Real of the real'.
The life-breaths are real and this Person is their real.

Scriptures derived from:

The LOTUS SUTRA
By Gautama Buddha 580 BCE

Chapter 1 The Lord's Ray of Light

Thus I have heard. Once upon a time the Lord was staying at Ragagriha on the Gridhrakuta Mountain with an assemblage of monks, 1200 monks, all of them Arhats, stainless, free from depravity, self-controlled, emancipated in thought and knowledge, of noble breed (like unto great elephants), who had reached the utmost perfection in subduing their thoughts and were possessed of the transcendent faculties; eminent disciples such as the venerable Agnata-Kaundinya, the venerable Asvagit, the venerable Vashpa, the venerable Mahanaman, the venerable Bhadrikal, the venerable Maha-Kasyapa, the venerable Kasyapa of Uruvilva, the venerable Kasyapa of Nadi, the venerable Kasyapa of Gaya, the venerable Sariputra, the venerable Maha-Maudgalyayana, the venerable Maha-Katyayana, the venerable Aniruddha, the venerable Revata, the venerable Kapphina, the venerable Gavampati, the venerable Pilindavatsa, the venerable Vakula, the venerable Bharadvaga, the venerable Maha-Kaushthila, the venerable Nanda (alias Mahananda), the venerable Upananda, the venerable Sundara-Nanda, the venerable Purna Maitrayaniputra, the venerable Subhuti, the venerable Rahula; with them yet other great disciples, as the venerable Ananda, still under training, 2000 other monks (some training and some masters), 6000 nuns having at their head Mahapragapati, and the nun Yasodhara, the mother of Rahula, along with her train;with 80,000 Bodhisattvas endowed with supreme, perfect enlightenment, firmly standing in wisdom and moved onward the never deviating wheel of the law; who had propitiated many hundred thousands of Buddhas who had planted roots of goodness and gave charity, able in communicating wisdom of the Tathagatas; such as the Bodhisattva Mahasattva Mangusri, as prince royal; the Bodhisattvas Mahasattvas Avalokitesvara, Mahasthamaprapta, Sarvarthanaman, Nityodyukta,

Anikshiptadhura, Ratnakandra, Bhaishagyaraga, Pradanasura, Ratnakandra, Ratnaprabha, Purnakandra, Mahivikramin, Trailokavikramin, Anantavikramin, Mahapratibhana, Satatasamitabhiyukta, Dharanidhara, Akshayamati, Padmasri, Nakshatraraga, the Bodhisattva Mahasattva Maitreya, the Bodhisattva Mahasattva Simha.

With them were 16 virtuous men: Bhadrapala, Ratnikara, Susarthavaha, Naradatta, Guhagupta, Varunadatta, Indradatta, Uttaramati, Viseshamati, Vardhamanamati, Amoghadarsin, Susamsthita, Suvikrantavikramin, Anupamamati, Suryagarbha, and Dharanidhara.

Further, Sakra who was the ruler of the celestials with 20,000 gods, the god Kandra (the Moon), the god Surya (the Sun), the god Samantagandha (the Wind), the great ruler Virudhaka, the great ruler Virupaksha, the great ruler Dhritarashtra, and the great ruler Vaisravana. Further, the gods Ratnaprabha, Avabhasaprabha, Isvara, Mahesvara. Further, Brahma Sahdmpati and his 12,000 followers, the Brahmakdyika gods, amongst whom Brahma Sikhin and Brahma Gyotishprabha with 12,000 Brahmakdyika gods, devotees, Nagas kings (Nanda, Manasvin, Anavatapta, and utpalaka), the Kinnara kings (Druma, Mahadharma, Sudharma, Dharmadhara), gandharvas (celestial singers), garudas (birds), Garuda chiefs, kinnaras (half-bird and half-human), great serpents, humans and beings not human, governors and ruler of armies, demons and demon chiefs. Buddhas sat cross-legged on the seat of the law. The Lord entered upon His meditation and there fell a great rain of divine flowers. Then the Lord cast a ray of light from His forehead out upon all 4 classes of hearers of the assembly.Then all beings in any of the six states of existence became visible. All Buddhas became visible in all Buddha fields even those who had reached final Nirvana. All Yogins and students of Yoga who had obtained fruition on Paths of Sanctification became visible and those who had not become visible, too.

QUESTION

1. Then rose in the mind of Bodhisattva Mahasattva Maitreya to ask the prince royal Bodhisattva Mahasattva Mangusri this thought: What, O Mangusri, is the cause, what is the reason of this wonderful, prodigious, miraculous shine having produced by the Lord? Look at how these 18,000 Buddha-fields appear as gold-colored columns, why an abundant rain of Mandaravas (lotus flower)?

The gods, overjoyed, let drop Mangushakas (flowers) and let drop sandal powder ground from sandalwood with its divine, fragrant, and delicious scent. Lapis lazulil (blue stones) are seen in Buddha-fields as well as fig trees and fruits.

5. I see the universe as far as Aviki (hell) and the extreme limit of existence all have become visible; whether they are in a happy, unhappy, low, eminent, or intermediate position, all that I see from this place.

7. I see Buddhas, those lions of kings, revealing and showing the essence of the law, comforting many kotis (a big number from ten to a hundred million) of creatures and emitting sweet-sounding voices.

13. I see in many fields Bodhisattvas by many thousands of kotis, like the sands of the Ganges River, who are producing enlightenment according to the degree of their power.

14. There are some who charitably bestow wealth, gold, silver, gold money, pearls, jewels, conch shells, stones, coral, male and female slaves, horses and sheep, or carriages yoked with four horses and furnished with benches, flowers, banners, and flags. They are spending gifts with glad hearts, developing themselves for superior enlightenment, in the hope of gaining the Buddha-vehicle of supreme enlightenment (Nirvana) and conquering the Evil One, they strike the drum of the law.

18. Some give their children or wives; others offer the work of their eyes, hands, and feet. Some give their flesh and blood, cheerfully bestowing their gifts as they aspire to the knowledge of the Tathagatas (another heavenly title for a Buddha).

21. Some betaken themselves to the guides of the world to ask for the most excellent law, for the sake of bliss; they put on reddish-yellow robes and shave their hair and beard.

22. Some Bodhisattvas are like monks who live in the wilderness of forests or deserts or in mountain caves, The monks spend their time reciting and reading, whereby cultivating and meditating on Buddha knowledge (Sariputra) they arrive at its perception. The Bodhisattvas are full of wisdom and constancy.

24. Some have renounced all sensual desires for meditation.

25. Some are standing firm, the feet put together and the hands joined in token of respect towards the leaders, and are praising the king of the leading Ginas in thousands of stanzas.

26. Some are thoughtful, meek, and tranquil, purifying their spheres (minds) and have obtained the five transcendent faculties. Faith and wisdom are one pair that balance the capacities for devotion and comprehension. Energy and concentration are a second pair that balance the capacities for active exertion and calm recollection. Above both pairs is mindfulness, which protects the mind from

extremes and holds all faculties in harmony.

29. I see some sons of the Saguta, humble, calm, and quiet in conduct, living under the command of the Sugutas, honored by men, gods, goblins, and Titans.

31. Some abide in vigor, renouncing sloth, and actively engage in walking, for it is by energy they are striving for supreme enlightenment. Some Bodhisattvas forsake all wanton pleasures, shun unwise companions, and delight in conversation with genteel men (aryas) who are polite and well-mannered in society.

32. Some keep a constant purity and an unbroken morality like precious stones and jewels; by morality do these strive for supreme enlightenment.

33. Some of the sons of the Gina, whose strength consists in forbearance, patiently endure abuse, censure,and threats from proud monks; they try to attain enlightenment by forbearance.

36. Some offer the assemblage of disciples food hard and soft, meat, drink, clothes and garments, medicaments for the sick, in plenty and abundance.

38. Some of the sons of the Ginas and Sugatas have offered to build monasteries; some have offered to build Stupas (a holy dome) for the relics of those who hav met extinction, made of seven precious substances and sandal-wood, furnished with couches, measuring in height no less than 5000 yoganas and 2000 in circumference, adorned with umbrellas, banners, bells, and celestial coral trees in full blossom. Sons and daughters pay honor at the Stupas with flowers, perfume, and music.

41. Some set forth the law of quietness, by many myriads of illustrations and proofs they are tending to supreme enlightenment by science.

42. The sons of the Sugata try to reach enlightenment by wisdom; they understand the law of indifference and avoid acting at the antinomy (of things), unattached like birds in the sky.

ANSWER

56. Whereupon Mangusri, the prince royal, addressed Maitreya in answer (in these words): It is the intention of the Tathagata (Buddha) who are men of good family and it is the intention of Mandaravas (female guru) who are women of good family to give grand discourse of the teaching of the good laws of dharma, to pour the great rain of the law, to make resound the great drum of the law, to raise the great banner of the law, to kindle the great torch of the law, to blow the great conch of the trumpet of the law, and to strike the great tymbal of the law. It is the intention of the Tathagata (Buddha) and the Mandaravas (female guru) to make a grand exposition of the

good laws every day. The Lord desires that grand speeches of the Dharmaparyaya (the 'Lotus of the True Law') be heard everywhere, therefore does he display so great a miracle and this fore-token consisting in the lustre occasioned by the emission of a ray. The Lord expounded the most excellent laws of properness and goodness of the Dharmaparyaya or "The Station of the Great Exposition of Infinity" to the assemblage so that they can achieve enlightenment.

Thousands of eons ago, there was born a Tathagata called Lord Kandrasuryapradipa, an Arhat, a Sugata, endowed with science and good conduct, with great knowledge of the world, an incomparable tamer of men, a teacher (and ruler) of gods and humans, a Buddha and Lord. He showed the law; he revealed the duteous course which is holy at its commencement, holy in it middle, holy at the end, good in substance and form, complete and perfect, correct and pure. He preached to the disciples the four Noble Truths (1. Dukkha or 'suffering' 2. Samudaya or 'there is a reason for suffering' 3. Nirodha or 'people can be free from suffering' and 4. Marga or 'to stop wanting things follow the Eightfold Path.') and starting from the chain of causes and effects, tending to overcome birth, decrepitude, sickness, sorrow, death, and finally leading to Nirvana. To the Bodhisattvas he preached the law connected with the Six Perfections (generosity, morality, patience, energy, meditation, and wisdom), and terminating in the knowledge of the Omniscient, after the attainment of supreme, perfect enlightenment. Lord Kandrasuryapradipa had eight sons who were called Mati, Sumati, Anantamati, Ratnamati, Viseshamati, Vimatisamudghatin, Ghoshamati, and Dharmamati.

59. All eight sons resigned worldly pleasures and became monks after they saw Bodhissattva Varaprabha embrace ascetic life. There fell celestial rain of Mandaravas (flowers) and the drums of heaven resounded. The gods and elves in the sky paid honor to the highest of men. Simultaneously all the fields (of Buddha) began trembling. A wonder it was, a great prodigy.

79. Varaprabha, the son of Gina and a preacher of the law spoke one day to a crowd: "I have manifested the rules of the good laws and have shown the nature of the good laws; now, O monks, it is the time of my Nirvana; this very night, in the middle watch. Be zealous and strong in good persuasions; apply yourselves to my lessons. Be not afraid, O monks; after my Nirvana there shall be another Buddha. The wise Bodhisattva Srigarbha shall reach the highest enlightenment and become a Gina under the name of Vimalagranetra." The many sons of Buddhas were struck with grief and filled with sorrow when they heard the voice of the highest of men announcing that his Nirvana was near at hand. That very night, Varaprabha met complete

extinction, like a lamp when the oil is exhausted.

86. Among the 800 pupils who were taught and educated by the monk and sage Bodhisattva Mahasattva Varaprabha were the eight sons of Lord Kandrasuryapradipa.

90. One of the eight sons of Kandrasuryapradipa was slothful, covetous, greedy of gain and cleverness, excessively desirous of glory, but very fickle, so that the lessons dictated to him and his own reading faded from his memory as soon as lernt. His name was Yasaskama. By the accumulated merit of good actions, he went through his course of duties and saw Buddhas but he shall be the last to reach superior enlightenment and become a Lord known by the family name of Maitreya.

98. The chief of the Ginas, the Lion of the Sakyas is to make a declaration of the fixed law: Be well minded and join your hands; he who is affectionate and merciful to the world will be refreshed with enlightenment.

Chapter 2 Skillfulness

I, Sariputra, am at the present period a Tathagata for the wheel of many humans and am preaching the law of dharma of right paths. I teach about Nirvana. There is no envy in me, no jealousy, no untamed passions or desires. Therefore I am the Buddha because the world follows my teachings.

Chapter 3 Parable of Burning House

Sariputra told his sons that their house was burning. He wanted the sons to go outside quickly so he told them that there were bullock-carts, goat-carts, and deer-carts outside. The boys eagerly ran out of the burning house and asked for the carts, but Sariputra only had bullock-carts to give to each of the boys. The ox-carts were made of seven precious substances with bells, jewels, jewel wreaths, flowers, and benches covered with cloth and silk and yoked with ox, led by men. Sariputra felt guilty of a falsehood by not giving his children the lesser carts as he had promised but gave them all the ox cart which was the finest of all carts.

The venerable Siriputra spoke to Sariputra: He is not a speaker of falsehood because he had been meditating on saving the little boys from the fire and he was prompted by no other motive than the love of his sons.
The Lord said: very well, Sariputra is exempt from misfortune, despondency, calamity, pain, grief; Sariputra has reached the highest perfection of Buddha-knowledge of skillful means, who is most merciful, long-suffering, benevolent, compassionate. Sariputra appears in the triple world, which is like (1) a house that will burn or decay (misery, samsara), (2) the three carts represent Buddhist teachings (fleeing from this world as disciples;

coveting the carts saved the boys because they ran to the donkey, goat and deer carts from the fire), and (3) the ox cart is the true liberation (the one great vehicle led the boys and Sariputra to Nirvana).

Chapter 4
Parable of the Lost Heir

A boy left home and wandered thru life, surviving on low-paying jobs. He wandered into a city and took a job with a wealthy man that he did not know was his own father. The boy performed his jobs to the best of his abilities. On his deathbed, his father revealed his identity to his son. The father is the Buddha, the son is the disciple, the wandering in poverty is samsara, the jobs were the Buddhist teachings and the inheritance is Buddha nature.

Chapter 5 Plants
Parable of Clay Vessels

As a potter makes clay vessels for the quality of the substance put into it, some for sugar, some for milk, ghee or water, humans are a diversity of vehicles; the Buddha-vehicle is the only indisputable one.

The great cloud Kasyapa expands over the entire universe, pouring the same water that is recreated by all grasses, shrubs, herbs, and trees. In like manner, the law preached by the Tathagata Bodhissatvas is of one and the same essence as all who preach dharma.

Chapter 6 Future Destiny

The Lord spoke to the assembly of monks saying: The monk and my disciple Kasyapa, shall respect, honor, and worship the thirty thousand kotis of Buddhas. Kasyapa will become a Buddha at a future epoch. His Buddha-field will be pure, clean, devoid of stones, grit, gravel, pits, or gutters but will be even, pretty, beautiful and pleasant to see, adorned with jewel-trees, gold threads, and flowers.

Chapter 7 Ancient Devotion

The great Brahma-angels and monks celebrate with this seasonable stanza: May the Lord move forward the wheel of the law! Show the law, O Lord, O most high of men. Show the power of thy kindness.

The gods of Paradise (Trayastrimsas) prepared the Lord a magnificent royal throne, a hundred yoganas high. When the Lord occupied the seat, the Brahmakayika gods scattered a rain of flowers around the seat.

Parable of Phantom City

A group of people are led by a guide through the wilderness to find a treasure. After a while, they are discouraged and do not want to continue. The guide tells them that a great city is a short distance ahead. They enter the city but then it disappears. The guide tells them to not give up and to make another effort to find the treasure; the treasure is not like a city or something that can be held in your hand; the true treasure cannot be seen.The guide is the Buddha, the people are the disciples, the journey is the Buddhist teaching, and the treasure is the Buddha Nature.

Chapter 8 Destiny of 500 Monks

The venerable Purna, scion (offspring) son of Maitrayani, was an exceptional monk who was called 'the Disciple.' Purna prostrated himself before the Lord, O Sugata, and said: "It is a difficult thing that the Tathagatas preach the law to all creatures with their many proofs of skillfulness and attachments." Under the mastership of Purna, the 500 Buddhas in this Bhadra-kalpa shall be taught the true law of innumerable Lords and Buddhas. After completing such a Badhisattva-course, they shall reach supreme and perfect enlightenment. They will learn that they are not free from affections and hatred. They shall know no other food but pleasure in the law. No womankind shall be there.

Parable of Hidden Jewel

A man gets drunk (sattva) and is sleeping at the home of a friend. The friend has to leave on business and sews a priceless jewel into the lining of the drunk man's coat. The drunk man wakes up and continues in his life, unaware of the concealed jewel. Later, his friend shows him the jewel and the sattva realizes his wealth. The friend is the Buddha, the drunk man is the sattva consumed by passions, the jewel is the truth about Buddha nature.

Chapter 9 Announcements

The Lord addressed the venerable Ananda in these words: Thou , Ananda, shalt in future become a Tathagata by the name of Sagaravaradharabuddhivikriditabhigna, an Arhat, endowed with science , good conduct, and supreme prefect enlightenment.

Chapter 10 The Preacher

All shall hear the Dharmaparyaya and joyfully accept it, even were it a single stanza, a single thought. Consider Buddha-knowledge as being reborn.

A wise man, owing to the performance of pious work, shall obtain the seat of Brahma, the seat of kings.

Light of the world, the All-sided One, thou knowest all who have flocked to you and know if we speak and live the truth of the sutras of the Dharmaparyaya.

Chapter 11-16
Lord Buddha, the Chief

Wonderful is the law of the Lotus Sutra.
The Lord has established by glorious wisdom the most perfect and excellent organs of hearing, smelling, tasting, seeing, and touching.

The Lord has established the cows, goats, sheep, birds, sandalwood and agallochum, incense, river waters, lamps filled with scented oils, full-blown lotuses, beautiful gardens, and all creatures.

One should present Him with divine flowers, cover Him with fine clothes, and bow the head to salute His feet.

Whoever is the hero that pronounces a single stanza of the Lotus Sutra.

Let a man who is seeking Buddha-knowledge practice perfect virtues and bestow gifts to others. Let him be zealous, without other preoccupation in the mind, and practice meditation.

That spot on earth has been enjoyed by myself; there I have walked myself, and there have I been sitting; where that son of Buddha has stayed, there I am.

Chapter 17 Agita

Agita is the merit which a person, by ranking in the series of the traditions of the wheel, produces by joyfully accepting, were it but a single stanza, a single word, from this Dharmaparyaya. His accumulation of merit shall be everlasting and he shall be established in happiness.

Chapter 18 Ancient Masters

The Ancient Masters of the world preached the Law of the Sutra; the mind of a Bodhisattva is in self-control, lucid, wise, and untroubled. The Bodhisattva hears the holy sound of the law of the Highest One, the Lord Buddha of the Universe. His body becomes pure, clear as if consisting of lapis lazuli (sparkiling blue rock). He who keeps this sublime Sutra is always a pleasant site for all creatures. As on the surface of a mirror an image is seen, so on his body he reflects the kindness and dazzling purity of the Highest One in the dear heavens.

Chapter 19-25 Transformations

These Bodhisattvas Mahasattvas were transformed to enlightenment: Mahasthamaprapta, Sadaparibhuta, Prabhutaratna, Lamba, Vilamba, Kutadanti, Pushpandanti, Makutadanti, Kesini, Akala, Maladhari, Kunti, Sarvasattvogahari, Hariti, Pradanasura, Bhaishagyaraga, Nakshatrarara, Saravasattvapri, Gadgadasvara, Akshayamati, and Avalokitesvara. And Bodhissattva Mahasattva Dharanindhara rose from his seat, put his upper robe upon one shoulder, fixed his right knee against the earth, stretched his hands toward the Lord and said: They are possessed of good roots and possess good virtues, beholding all beings with compassion and kindness, bodhissattvas worthy of adoration, with which nothing else can be compared. The Buddhas made of noise of expectoration and of snapping fingers, calling the attention of the whole world. A Buddha illuminates all around him while roaming the earth in different directions, rousing many Bodhisattvas to piety and enlightenment.

Chapter 26 Samantabhadra

The Lord Sakyamuni said to the monks, nuns, and devotees assembled at the gathering of the Dharmaparyaya of the Lotus of the

Law : young men of good family shall be entrusted to a female if she be possessed of four requisites, to wit: she shall stand under supervision of Lords Buddhas; she shall have planted good roots; she shall keep steadily to disciplinary regulations; she shall have thoughts of supreme and perfect enlightenment to save creatures. Bodhisattva Mahasattva Samantabhadra said to the Lord Sakyamuni: I will protect monks, nuns, and devotees who keep this Satranta and study the Dharmaparyaya, so that no one laying evil snares may surprise them, neither Mara the Evil One nor goblins, ghosts, imps, wizards, spectres laying snares for them. No passionate attachments will hinder their good life, no hatred, no infatuation, no jealousy, no envy, no hypocrisy, no pride, no conceitedness, no mendaciousness. This encouragement of Samantabhadra was expounded to hundred thousands of kotis of Bodhissatvas Mahasattvas, equal to the sands of the river Ganges, acquired to the talismanic spell Avarta (descent or appearance of diety on earth).

Chapter 27 The Period of the Dharmaparyaya

Thereupon the Lord Sakyamuni rose from his pulpit, and joined his hands to the hands of the Bodhissattvas Mahasattvas who joined their hands to other Bodhissattvas Mahasattvas, among them Bodhissattvas Samantabhadra and Bodhissattvas Visishtakaritra. The Lord spoke and restored the Stupa of precious substances of the Lord Prabhutaratna, who was extinct, to its place. And the Lord dismissed them and wished them a happy existence. The Tathagatas who had come from other worlds and were sitting on their thrones surrounded by jewel trees, the innumerable, incalculable Bodhissatvas Mahasattvas, the great disciples, the four classes, the world, including gods, men, demons, and the celestial singers Gandharvas, in ecstasy all applauded the words of the Lord.

SIKH

A Sikh means to be a disciple of the Holy Spirit, to adhere to truthful living, practice remembrance and devotion to God at all times. In Sikhism the lotus flower blossoms forth and eternal peace is obtained as one's light merges into the Supreme Light.
Sikhs are supposed to follow a life of honesty, earning a livelihood through hard work, sincerely practice the institution of marriage and family life, and share blessings with others. *Dastar* turbans are worn by men.

Sikhism teaches that rituals such as fasting, superstitions, and pilgrimages to holy sites are not necessary. Sikhism teaches that all places of worship are holy and it is not necessary to have one mandatory designated place as the one holy place. Sikhism teaches that men and women are fully equal and can equally preach and work upon the earth. The Golden Temple at Amritsar in India is a holy worship site for Sikhs. The Harimandir Sahif is a sacred shrine.

The Sikh Rehat Maryada (code of conduct) is to faithfully believe in One Immortal Being, 10 Gurus, (from Guru Nanak to Guru Gobind Singh), Guru Granth Sahib, the Bani or teachings of the 10 gurus and the baptism bequeathed by the 10th Guru.

Male Sikhs have Singh (Lion) and female Sikhs have Kaur (princess) as their middle name. The Khande-Ki-Pahul is the Sikh initiation ceremony and may be recognized by the Five K's.

Five K's

Kesh – unshorn hair, symbol of saintliness

Kangha – comb for the hair

Kara – a steel bracelet to symbolize restraint from evil deeds

Kachha – the soldier's shorts to symbolize self-restraint

Kirpan – the sword is the emblem of courage and self-defense

Principles of Sikhism:

Nam Japna: Remembering God all the time

Kirat Karni: Make an honest living

Vand Chhakna: Sharing your blessings with others.

GRANTH SAHIB

The Adi Granth (First Book) was compiled by the 5th Sikh Guru Arjan (1563-1606CE). The Adi Granth is ritually opened in the morning in a ceremony called Prakash and wrapped up and put away for the night. The 10th Sikh Guru Gobind Singh (1666-1708CE) added 115 of Guru Tegh Bahadur's hymns or ragas and the holy book became the Granth Sahib. Shabads (scriptures) derived from the holy book Guru Granth Sahib:

Japuji

IK Onkaar: There is only one God

Sat Naam: God's Name is Truth

Karata Purkh: God is Creator

Nir Bhau: God is without Fear

Nir Vair: God is without Enmity (Hatred)

Akaal Moorat: God is beyond Time immortal

Ajooni: God is beyond birth and death

Saibhang: God is self-existent

Gur Parsad: God is realized by Guru's grace

By the Hukam (command) of God, bodies are created and souls come into being. By God's command glory and greatness are obtained.

Everyone is subject to God's commands.

Some sing of God's power.
Some sing of God's gifts.
Some sing of God's virtues.
Some sings of knowledge obtained from God.
Some sing that God fashions the body and then again reduced it to dust.
Some sing that God watches over us, ever-present.

There is no shortage of those who preach and teach about God.

Millions upon millions offer millions of sermons and stories.

The Great Giver keeps on giving.

God The Commander leads us to walk on the good path.

O Nanak, He blossoms forth, carefree and untroubled. True is the Master, True is His Name – speak it with infinite love.

In the Amrit Vaylaa, the ambrosial hours before dawn, chant the True Name and contemplate God's glorious greatness.

By the karma of past actions, the robe of this physical body is obtained. By His grace, the gate of liberation is found.

God is Immaculate and Pure.

Those who serve Him are honored.
Sing, and listen, and
let your mind be filled with love.
Your pain shall be sent far away, and peace shall come to your house.

The Guru's word is the sound-current of the Naad (the essence of all sound which is vibrational harmony with the universe in light, sound, and energy; vibration of the cosmos; cosmic sound).
The Guru's word is the wisdom of the Vedas. The Guru's word is all-pervading.
The Guru is Shiva, Vishnu, and Brahma, Paarvat and Lakhshmi.

Even knowing God, I cannot describe Him, He cannot be described in words.

The Guru has given me this understanding: there is only the One, the Giver of all souls. May I never forget him!

If I am pleasing to Him, then that is my pilgrimage and cleansing bath. Without pleasing Him, what good are ritual cleansings?

I gaze upon all the created beings; without the karma of good actions, what are they given to receive?

Within the mind are gems, jewels, and rubies, if you listen to the Guru's Teachings, even once.

If you could live through the ages and were known on all continents and followed by all, with a good name and reputation, with praise and fame throughout the world – still, if the Lord does not bless you with His Glance of Grace, then who cares? What is the use?

Among worms, you would be considered a lowly worm, and even contemptible sinners would hold you in contempt.

O Nanak, God blesses both the unworthy and the virtuous with virtue. No one can even imagine anyone who can bestow virtue upon us!

Listening – the Siddhas, the spiritual teachers, the heroic warriors, the yogic masters.

Listening – the earth, its support and the akashic ethers.

Listening – the oceans, the lands of this world, and the nether regions of the underworld.

O Nanak, the devotees are forever in bliss.

Listening – pain and sin are erased.
Listening – Shiva, Brahma, and Indra.
Listening – even foul-mouthed people praise God.
Listening – the technology of Yoga and the secrets of the body.
Listening – the Shaastras, the Simritees, and the Vedas.
Listening – pain and sin are erased.

Listening – truth, contentment, and spiritual wisdom.

Listening – reading and reciting – honor is obtained.
Listening – intuitively grasp the essence of meditation.

The state of the faithful cannot be described.

No paper, no pen, no scribe can record the state of the faithful.

Such is the name of the Immaculate Lord.

Only one who has faith comes to know such a state of mind.

The faithful have intuitive awareness and intelligence.

The faithful know about worlds and realms.

The faithful do not have to go with the Messenger of Death.

The path of the faithful shall never be blocked.

The faithful do not follow empty religious rituals but are firmly bound to Dharma (good actions).

Such is the name of the Immaculate Lord.

The faithful find the Door of Liberation.
The faithful uplift and redeem their family and relations.

The faithful are saved and carried across with the Sikhs of the Guru.

The faithful, O Nanak, do not wander around begging.

The chosen ones, the self-elect, are accepted and approved.

The chosen ones are honored in the Court of the Lord.

The chosen ones look beautiful and meditate single-mindedly on the Guru and God.

No matter how much anyone tries to explain and describe them, the actions of the Creator cannot be counted.

The mythical bull Dharma, the son of compassion; this is what patiently hold the earth in place.
One who understands this becomes truthful.
What a great load there is on the bull!

So many worlds beyond this world – so very many!
What power hold them and support their weight!

The names and the colors of the assorted species of beings were all inscribed by the ever-flowing pen of God.
Who knows how to write of this account? Just imagine what a huge scroll it would take!
How can Your creative potency be described?

I cannot even once be a sacrifice to you. Whatever pleases You is the only good done, You, Eternal and Formless One!

Countless devotees contemplate the wisdom, virtues, and works of the Lord.

Countless worship services, countless austere disciplines.

Countless scriptures and ritual recitations of the Vedas.

Countless meditation yogis, whose minds remain detached.

Countless the holy, countless the givers.

Countless the heroic spiritual warriors, who bear the brunt of attack in battle.

Countless the silent sages, vibrating God's love.

How can Your Creative Potency be described?

I cannot even once be a sacrifice to You.

Whatever pleases You is the only good done.

You, Eternal and Formless One!

Countless the thieves and embezzlers.

Countless liars, wandering lost in their lives.

Countless sinners, who keep on sinning.

From the Word comes the Naam (Name); from the word, comes Your Praise.

From the Word, comes spiritual wisdom, singing the songs of Your Glory.

From the Word, comes the written and spoken words and hymns.

From the Word, comes destiny, written on one's forehead.

But the One who wrote these words of destiny – no words are written on His Forehead.

As He ordains, so do we receive.

The created universe is the manifestation of Your Name. Without Your Name, there is no place at all.

How can I describe Your Creative Power?

When the intellect is stained and polluted by sin, it can only be cleansed by the Love of Your Name.

Virtue and vice do not come by mere words; actions repeated over and over again, are engraved on the soul.

You shall harvest what you plant.

O Nanak, by the Hukam of God's Command, we come and go in reincarnation.

Pilgramages, austere discipline, compassion, and charity – these by themselves bring only an iota of merit.

Listening and believing with love and humility in your mind, cleanse yourself with The Name, at the sacred shrine deep within.

All virtues are Yours, Lord. I have none at all.

I bow to the Lord of the World, to His Word, to Brahma the Creator.

He is Beautiful, True, and Eternally Joyful.

What was the exact moment when the universe was created?
The Pandits, the religious scholars, cannot find that time, even if it is written in the Puraanas.
That time is not known to the Qazis, who study the Koran.
The day and the date are not known to the Yogis, nor is the month or season.

The Creator who created this Creation – only He Himself knows.
Great is The Master, Great is His Name.

Whatever happens is according to His Will.

Kings and emperors with mountains of property and oceans of wealth – they are not even equal to an ant, who does not forget God.

Endless are God's praises, endless are those who speak of them.

Endless are God's actions, endless are God's gifts.

Endless is God's vision, endless is God's hearing.

God's limits cannot be perceived.

The limits of the universe cannot be perceived.

The more you say about them, the more there still remains to be said.

Great is The Master, High is His Heavenly Home.

Highest of the High, Above all is His Name.

Only one as Great and High as God, Who has a lofty and exalted state.

Priceless is the divine law of Dharma.
Priceless is God's mercy.
Priceless beyond expression!

Speak of God continually, and remain absorbed in His Love.

The Vedas and the Puraanas speak.

The scholars speak and lecture.

Brahma speaks, Indra speaks.

The Gopis and Krishna speak.

Shiva speaks, the Siddhas speak.

The many created Buddhas speak.

The Yogic Masters speak.

The demons speak, the demi-gods speak.

The spiritual warriors, the heavenly beings, the silent sages, the humble and serviceful speak. Many speak and try to describe God.

O, Nanak, the True Lord knows.

Where is that Gate, and where is that Dwelling, in which you sit and take care of it all?

Countless musicians play on all sorts of instuments there. So many ragas (hymns) and so many musicians, singing there.

The Righteous Judge of Dharma sings at Your Door.

Chitr and Gupt, the angels of the conscious and the subconscious, record actions.

Shiva, Brahma, and the Goddess of Beauty, everadorned, sing.

Indra, seated upon His Throne, sings with the deities at Your Door.

The celestial order of planets, solar systems and galaxies, arranged by Your Hand, all sing.

Your devotees are imbued with the Nectar of Your Essence.

The Lord God is the King of Kings, the Supreme Word, and the Master of Kings.
Guru Nanak remains subject to God's Will.

That the Lord is True, Forever True, and True to His Name.

I bow to God, I humbly bow.

The Primal One, the Pure Light without beginning and without end. Throughout all the ages, God is One and the Same.

The One Divine Mother conceived and gave birth to three dieties: One, the Creator of the World; One, the Sustainer; and One, the Destroyer.

God makes things happen according to the pleasure of His Will, such is His Celestial Order.

God watches over all, but none see Him. How wonderful this is!

I bow to God. I humbly bow.

On world after world are His Seats of Authority and His Storehouses. Whatever was put into them was put there for once and for all.

Having created the Creation, the Creator Lord watches over it.

O Nanak, True is the Creation of the True Lord.

I could repeat, hundreds of thousands of times, the Name of the Lord, the Name of the Universe.

Hearing of etheric realms, even worms long to come back home.

O Nanak, by His Grace God is obtained. False are the boastings of the false.

God alone has the Power in His Hands and watches over all.

Nights, days, weeks, and seasons; winds, waters, fires and the nether regions;

moons and suns, worlds and lands,

- in the midst of these, God established the earth as a home for Dharma (the realm of spiritual wisdom; righteousness).

Upon earth, God placed the various species of beings. Their names are uncounted and endless.

By their deeds and actions, they shall be judged. The ripe and the unripe, the good and the bad shall be judged.

God is True, and True in His Court.

There, in perfect grace and ease, sit the self-elect, the self-realized Saints before the Merciful Lord.

So many intuitive people, so many ways of life, so many languages, so many dynasties of rulers, so many oceans of jewels, so many selfless servants. O Nanak, God's limit has no limit!

In the realm of wisdom, spiritual wisdom reigns supreme.

The sound current of the Naad vibrates there, amidst the sounds and the sights of bliss.
In the realm of Humility, the word is Beauty.

Forms of incomparable beauty are fashioned there.

These things cannot be described.

The intuitive consciousness, intellect and understanding of the mind are shaped there.

In the realm of karma, the Word is Power. The spiritual warriors are heroes imbued with God's Essence.

Neither evil nor deception comes to those within whose minds the Lord abides.
The devotees of many worlds dwell there.

They celebrate; their minds are imbued with the True Lord.

In the realm of Truth, the Formless Lord abides.

If one speaks of planets, solar systems, and galaxies, there is no limit, no end.

There are worlds upon worlds of God's creation.

As God commands, they exist.

To describe this is as hard as steel!

Let self-control be the furnace, and patience the goldsmith.

Let understanding be the anvil, and spiritual wisdom be the tools!

With the Fear of God as the bellows (roaring energy), fan the flames of tapa, the body's inner heat.

In the crucible of love, mint the True Coin which is the Word of God.

Shalok:

Air is the Guru, Water is the Father, and Earth is the Great Mother of All.

Day and Night are the two nurses, in whose lap all the world is at play.

Good deeds and bad deeds – the record is read out in the Presence of the Lord of Dharma.

Those who have meditated on the Naam (Name) of the Lord,
O, Nanak, their faces are radiant in the Court of the Lord, and many are saved along with them.

RAGAS

The 31 Ragas are hymns to the Lord and all begin with the same verse:

One Universal Creator God, By the Grace of the True Guru

Raag 1 Siree

If I had a palace made with pearls and inlaid with jewels, scented with musk, saffron, and sandalwood, a sheer delight to behold, I might go astray and forget You, O God. I consulted my Guru, and now I see that there is no other place at all.

We cannot estimate Your Value or the Greatness of Your Name, o Lord.

As it is pre-ordained, people speak, eat, walk, see, hear, and breathe. Why should I go and ask the scholars about this?

Life and death come to all who are born.

Nanak seeks the company of the lowest; where the lowly are cared for the Blessing of God's Glance of Grace will rain down.

Greed, lies, and cheating are evil.

Slandering others is putting the filth of others into your mouth.

Harsh words bring grief, O foolish mind!

Intoxicating drugs are falsehood.

Serving God, peace is attained and you will go to God's Court with honor.

Tell your troubles to the One who is the Source of All Comfort.

Do not forget the One who created your soul.

Without God, we are impure.

Make the love of the Lord your consciousness.

Eternal peace and everlasting joy are bestowed on the minds attuned to the True Great Name.

Some are born beggars and some hold vast courts. Going to the world hereafter, everyone shall realize that without God, all is useless.

The 36 flavors of ambrosial nectar are in the love of the Lord.

The Naam (Name) of the Lord is my pleasure.

The Guru is the Ladder to the Sacred Shrine. The Guru is the Boat or Raft to sail me across the holy river to the Lord.

Join together with spiritual companions and tell stories about the virtues of the Lord.

Whatever pleases God will come to pass; nothing else can be done.

The Lord makes no mistakes. God is the Great Farmer who plants seeds to spread dharma and the True Name.

One may oil their body with sandalwood and sweeten their breath with betel leaf and camphor but if they are not pleasing to God these things are false trappings and corrupt.

Egotistical pride and possessiveness has plundered everyone.

Those who are protected by the Guru are saved.

By true actions, the True Lord is met, and the Guru's teachings are found. They are not subject to the birth and death of reincarnation. They will not come and go in reincarnation.

They are respected at the Lord's Gate, and they will be robed in honor in the Court of the Lord.

We shall merge into the One from whom we came.

With each and every breath, I dwell upon you and will never forget you; I formed this Universe.

I have given my mind to the True Guru, who will unite me with the Lord.

The Lord is the Cherisher of all beings.

If the mind becomes balanced and detached, and dwells in its own truth, it enjoys the essence of supreme spiritual wisdom.

Do not make love with one who is just a passing show; surrender your body like a bride or bridegroom to a love.

The Name of the Lord is the True Merchandise.

Give up your selfishness and you shall find peace, like water mingling with water.

Those who practice falsehoods will come and go in reincarnation.

Those who chant the Name of the Lord and live a life filled with dharma (good ways) will earn the profits of the Lord.

The flower of youth lasts for a few days and the body becomes old and weary; it withers and fades and will finally die.

The Lord is the bride and the bridegroom.

The Lord is the fisherman, the fish, the water, the net, the bait, and the sinker; the Lord loves in so many ways.

The Lord is the lotus-flower of the day and the water-lily at night.

Let your mind be the farmer and the Lord will sprout in your heart.

The bumblebee is a teacher who continually teaches a lesson like the song of the wind.

Robbers and spies trap others and carry a load of sin; they do not appreciate what You have done for them, O Lord. In attachment to Maya (illusions), they have forgotten their God.

As we plant, so we harvest and eat.

Protect your crops or birds shall descend on your farm.

Let the power of God be the wick for the lamp of Truth.

Everyone belongs to the One who created the Universe.

Those who keep the Lord enshrined on their hearts are true servants of the Lord.

If the Word of the Guru's Shabad abides deep within, you shall not forget the Lord.

Those who unite with a Guru understand and become pure.

The Lord is my Friend and my Companion. God shall be my helper and support in the end.

I will fall at the feet of those who serve the True Guru.

The souls on their spiritual journey chant and meditate with their minds on the True Lord, the Treasure of Excellence.

One who eliminates Wickedness from their mind comes to recognize the All-Pervading Soul of the Lord.

Without the Lord, the manmukhs engrossed in corruption do not find liberation but wander around like lunatics.

I just speak as God makes me speak, when God makes me speak.

God, please save people from a terrifying world of corruption and poison. This is servant Guru Nanak's humble prayer.

The Gurmukhs are my spiritual friends who share good virtues.

I follow in the footsteps of those who enjoy the Love of My Beloved Lord. I have a yearning to meet God!

All things happen according to the Will of the Lord God. No one can erase the preordained Writ of Destiny.

The Word of the True Guru is the Jewel. One who believes in it tastes the Sublime Essence of the Lord.

This Sublime Essence of the Lord is in the forests, in the fields and everywhere, but the unfortunate ones do not taste it.

Without the Sublime Essence of the Lord and the Guru's love, the demon of anger is within them.

The day dawns, and then it ends, and the night passes away. Man's life is diminishing each day and some do not realize how quickly the days pass.

People are entangled in the enjoyment of fine clothes, but gold and silver are only dust.
O my mind, the Lord is the giver of peace.

They acquire beautiful horses and elephants, and ornate carriages of many kinds.

They think of nothing else, and they forget all their relatives.

They ignore their Creator; without the Name, they are impure.

Gathering the wealth of Maya (illusions), you earn an evil reputation.

Masters of wealth and great emperors issue their commands fearlessly, act in pride, and subdue all under their command; but without the Name, they are reduced to dust.

Those who always remember the Naam, the Name of the Lord, are considered to be liberated.

O my mind, praise the Creator.

Your servant begs to serve those who are enjoined to Your service.

The opportunity to work hard serving the Saadh Sangat is obtained, when the Divine Lord is pleased.

The One appears to be my companion; the One is my brother and friend.

The elements and the components are all made by the One; they are held in their order by the One.

When the mind accepts, and is satisfied with God, then the consciousness becomes steady and stable.

Then, one's food is the True Name, one's garments are the True Name, and one's support, O Nanak, is the True Name.

The precious gift of this human life becomes fruitful when one chants the True Word of the Shabad,

When God bestows his Glance of Grace, thousands of pleasures are enjoyed.

Fruitful is that moment, and fruitful is that time, when one is in love with the True Lord.

Embellished and immaculate is that place where the Saints gather together.

Place the hopes of your mind in the One, in whom all have faith.

Give up all your clever tricks, and grasp the feet of the Guru.

24 hours a day, meditate on God, Constantly sing the glories of the Lord of the Universe.

Seek God's shelter, O my mind; there is no other as Great as God.

Forever and ever, work for God, Our True Lord and Master.

The Lord is said to be the Greatest of the Great; God's Kingdom is the Highest of the High.

What good is worldly greatness?

All the pleasure of Maya (illusions) are tasteless and insipid. In the end, they shall all fade away.

Perfectly fulfilled and supremely acclaimed is the one, in whose heart the Lord abides.

The One is the Support of the mind; the One is the Support of the breath of life.

In God's Sanctuary there is eternal peace.

Dwell upon the Perfect Lord each day. Attach yourself to the One Lord.

May I never forget God from my mind; God holds all in the Power of His Hands.

The One is within the home of the self, and the One is outside as well. God is in all places and interspaces. Soul and body all belong to God; whatever pleases His Will comes to pass.

In God's Sanctuary, one is saved.

The Divine Light illuminates my inner being, and I am lovingly absorbed in the One.

Meeting with the Holy Saint, my face is radiant; I have realized my pre-destiny.

I constantly sing the Glories of the Lord of the Universe. Through the True Name, I have become spotlessly pure.

Please grant Your Grace, God, that we may meditate on Your Ambrosial Naam.

In separation, God is not separated from us; God is pervading and permeating amongst all.

Wondrous is the Form of the Immaculate One.

O, Siblings of Destiny, make God your friend.

Cursed is the emotional attachment and love of Maya (illusions); no one is seen to be at peace.

God is Wise, Giving, Tender-Hearted, Pure, Beautiful, and Infinite.

God is Our Companion and Helper, Supremely Great, Lofty and Our Support; His Court is steady and stable.

Thinking of God, our evil inclinations vanish and we become peaceful.

Meditate on the Lord, the Treasure of Excellence, and all doubts of your mind will be dispelled, Be absorbed in the Samaadhi (meditative state of mind) of the Lord's love.

Forever and ever, worship and adore God. Day and night, do not forget God. Always keep the company of the Holy and focus the consciousness like a Guru.

Diseases of the ego will be cast out. Your soul, breath of life, mind and body shall blossom forth in lush profusions; this is the good essence of the scriptures.

God is obtained deep in our hearts and minds. Without God, everything is falsehood.

The Transcendent Lord is imbued in all times and all universes and all things.

When your allotted time is up, your soul must go back to the Lord, so take care of your real home and hearth.

In this world, the only real profit is the Name of the Lord.

If the mind is filled with pollution, the body and tongue is polluted.

People come and go, regretting and repenting, like crows in a deserted house.

Coming and going, people wander through reincarnations; they act according to past actions.

God draws us to His Touchstone.

Without the Name of the Lord, no one can be saved. My soul and my breath belong to God,

Practice bhakti, loving devotional worship.

The Lord fashions the vessels and His Light pervades all. When one holy person meets another holy person, they abide in contentment.

As thirst is quenched with water, and the baby is satisfied with the mother's milk, and as the lotus flower does not exist without water, and as the fish dies without water, so does the Gurmukh live, receiving the Sublime Essence of the Lord, singing Glorious Praises of the Lord.

Nanak offers a prayer to the Unknowable, Inaccessible, All-Powerful and Merciful Creator. If you call God Allah or Ram, it is the same Spirit.

Sky and earth may pass away but God alone is permanent.

The True Guru has instructed me by the Gurubani or Bani (writings of the guru) in the word of the Shabad and the One Lord abides in my mind.

Walk in harmony with the Guru and remain immersed in the Name of the Lord.

The Gurmukh are like God's tree, green and blossoming, blessed with love and peace.

The Lord is the Ambrosial Fruit.

Those who do wicked evil deeds have not embraced the love of the Lord; they have no inner peace.

When you have terrible hardships, and no one offers you any support, and when your friends turn into enemies, and even your relatives have deserted you, and when all support has given away, and all hope is lost, if you then remember the Supreme Lord God, the Lord will give you comfort.

So praise God through the Perfect Word of the Shabad.

When you are under the power of sexual desire, anger, worldly attachment, a greedy miser in love with your wealth, or committing sins and slander; if remember God and return to Dharma (righteous living), you shall be saved.

The worshipper of Bhagaauti practices self-discipline, the Yogi speaks of liberation, the ascetic is absorbed in self-denial, the men of silence observe silence, the Sanyaasees observe celibacy, and the Udaasees abide in detachment, householders keep faith in their household, hermits never leave their house, pilgrams make pilgrimages and take holy baths, fasters go without food – all of these say that they have found the Lord.

Everyone longs for Your Name, O Lord, even the angelic beings and the society of saints.

The discarded soul-bride suffers in agony; she misses her Husband Lord as she wanders in dishonor.

Happy soul-brides obtain the fruit of their pre-destiny. Casting His Glance of Grace, the Husband Lord unites them with Himself.

Those whom God causes to abide by His Will, have the Shabad of His Word abiding deep within.

My God knows everything.

God has made His Glory manifest, and all People celebrate Him.

God has not considered my merits and demerits; this is God's Nature; God hugs me in His Embrace and protects me.

Some people say my demerits will cause a karma of punishment.

Become one with the universe and God. Avoid dualities(extremes) like happy and sad, content and wanting, Shed emotional attachments to Maya and become detached from the things of this world.

The True Guru has shown me the Lord; Has has placed his hand upon my forehead and whispered 'Wahe Guru' (God). I have found the Temple of Truth.
I sought out the Guru's Sikhs and washed their feet, and waved the fan over them. Bowing low, I fell at their feet. The Guru instilled within me the Naam, the Name of the Lord, the goodness and charity and true cleansing.
All of the world is liberated, O Nanak, by embracing upon the Boat of Truth. There is no difference between the Guru, the True Guru, and the Lord and Master.

The Merciful Lord has issued His Command: Let no one chase after and attack anyone else.

Let all abide in peace, under God's Benevolent Rule.

Soft and gently, drop by drop, the Ambrosial Nectar trickles down.

I speak as my Lord and Master causes me to speak.

I place all my faith in You, please accept me.

Your devotees are forever hungry for You.

O Lord, please fulfill my desires.

Grant me the Blessed Vision of Your Darshan (meeting, vision), Giver of Peace. I have not found any other as Great as You, O Lord.

In the first watch of the night, O mortal, you shall be saved by remembering the Lord.

Remember the Lord in the second, third and fourth watches of the night. Do not let the Grim Reaper harvest your field.

From hand to hand, you are passed around, like Krishna in the House of Yashoda.

From hand to hand, you are passed around and your mother says 'This is my son.'

Remember the Name of the Lord and it will release you from the bondage and confusion of Maya

Do not waste your life revelling in riches or intoxicated with youth; live in righteousness and Dharma and make good deeds with friends.

Receive the summons from the Lord of the Universe and your harvest shall be plentiful and the darkness of ignorance shall be dispelled.

Fruitful are the lives of those who have conquered their minds; they have won the game of life.

Joining with the Humble Saints of the Lord, my good actions will bring prosperity, and I have obtained bliss with the Lord.

The Lord is the Truest of the True, and I am a servant of the Lord.

In age after age, those who join with the Lord's family will prosper and increase.

The Almighty Lord never dies or goes away.

O dear beloved mind, my friend, the Lord shall always be with you.

The Lord's Name is the Support of His Devotees and the Support of the Breath of Life.

The Lord is the Greatest Lover.

The Lord is beautiful in all places and is Patron to all souls.

When you meditate on the Lord, your tongue becomes true and your mind becomes true.

The Lord gives shade to all.

You may call yourself good, but this will only be known when your honor is approved in God's Account.

Some think about religious rituals and regulations but without understanding, how can they cross over to the other side?

Let sincere faith be bowing in prayer and the conquest of your mind be the objective in your life.

Those who love God are blended in with God.

Great is the Greatness of the Lord and the Kirtan (Devotional Music) of the Lord's Praises.

When God abides in your mind, you enjoy peace, wear peace, and pass your life in the peace of peace.

Those who do not serve the True Guru and contemplate the Word of the Shabad go through the cycle of 8.4 million reincarnations; they are ruined through death and rebirth.

Devotees have faith in the Lord. The Lord knows everything.

When saved by the Word of the Shabad, the Lord is obtained, and humans will be transformed into angels.
Sinners will be defeated.

I praise the Lord forever and ever.

The Lord knows the swan from the crane and can transform the crow into a swan.

O, Ravi Daas, one who understands that the Lord is equally in all, is rare,

Raag 2 Maajh

The Lord is my mind, body, and breath of life.
I do not know any other than the Lord.
If I could have the fortue to meet a friendly Saint, he might show me the Way to My Lord.

I have searched my mind and have found the path to God at the Sat Sangat Congregation. The Guru told the sermon of the Lord.

Chanting the Naam, the Name of the Lord, I am a poor song-bird in the sanctuary of the Guru.

The Lord is the Treasure of Water and I am a fish in the water. Without the water, I would die.

O, Siblings of Destiny, let us join together to hear the Sermon of the Lord.

My mind is imbued with the love of the Lord.

We chant the Words of the Guru's Bani, putting the Sublime Essence of the Lord into our minds.
The Guru removes egotism and pollution from our minds.
The Perfect Guru has shown me that the Lord is always with me.

There is only one breath; all are made of the same clay; the light within all is the same.

Sweet is the season that I remember You. Sublime is the work that is done for You.
All place their hope in You.
You dwell in each and every heart.

Raag 3 Gauree

Day after day, God cares for His beings; the Great Giver watches over all.

Unto each and every home; into each and every heart; this summons is sent out from God each day that I may merge with my Lord and Master.

Remember in meditation the One who summons us.

Earn the profit of the Lord's Name and dwell in peace.

The wealth of liberation is only obtained by meditating on the Lord.
The world is engrossed in corruption and cynicism.
Only those who know God are saved.
Remain steady in the home of the self, Your Lord.

Through the Guru, the Lord shall dwell in your mind.
Through sincere efforts, the mind is made peaceful and calm.

Within the home of your own inner-being, you shall obtain the Mansion of the Lord's Presence with intuitive ease. You shall not be consigned again to the wheel of reincarnation.

O, Inner-Knower, Searcher of Hearts, O Primal Being, Architect of Destiny, please fulfill this yearning of my mind.

Walking on the Lord's Way, all pains are taken away.

Raag 4 Aasaa

One Universal Creator God. By the Grace of the True Guru: Where is Your Door, Lord? Where is Your Home?

The Sound of the Naad vibrates for You, Lord, and countless musicians play instruments for You.
There are so many ragas and musical harmonies to You; so many minstrels sing hymns to You.

Wind, water, and fire sing to You. The Righteous Judge of Dharma sings at Your Door.

O My Great Lord and Master of Excellence, no one knows the extent or vastness of Your Expanse.
Those who describe You remain immersed and absorbed in You.

The Lord's Provisions and Gifts never run short.

Blessed is the Sat Sangat, the True Congregation, where the Lord's Essence is obtained.

Raag 5 Goojaree

Why, O mind, do you plot and plan, when the Dear Lord provides for your care?
The Lord places nourishment before them.
By Guru's Grace, the supreme status is obtained, and dry wood blossoms forth again with greenery.

The flamingos fly hundreds of miles and who feeds them?

Meditate on the Lord, O Saints; the Lord is the Dispeller of all sorrows.
You are squandering this life uselessly in the love of Maya (illusions).
I have not practiced meditation, self-discipline, self-restraint or righteous living. I have not served the Holy; I have not acknowledged the Lord, my King. Says Nanak, my actions are contemptible!

Raag 6 Devagandhari

Those who become the humble servants of the Lord and Master lovingly focus their minds on Him.

On what path will I find my Beauteous Lord?
I cherish in my heart the Words of my Beloved, this is the best way.

Raag 7 Bihagara

To associate with those indulging in unethical pursuits is to live with poisonous snakes that destroy.
All are travelers who have gathered under the world-tree, and are bound by their many bonds.
Eternal is the Company of the Holy, where the Kirtan of the Lord's Praises are sung.

Mediatate on the Name of the Lord, O my soul. The Lord is dear to my mind.

Raag 8 Vadahans

My mind is cleansed of doubt, only when I praise You, and pray to You. The peacocks are singing sweetly and the rainy season of Saawan has come.

Think of the one Lord, and you shall obtain peace.

Raag 9 Sorath

Death comes to all and all must suffer separation.
Go and ask the clever people whether they shall meet in the world hereafter.
O Nanak, as many as the sins one commits, so many are the chains around his neck.

Going to the world hereafter, those who have no Guru are not accepted,

Make your mind the farmer, good deeds the farm, modesty the water, and your body the field.

By doing deeds of love, the seed shall sprout, and you shall see your home flourish.

The wealth of Maya (illusions) does not go with anyone. Let your trade be listening to scripture.
Let your work be restrained from sin, only then will people call you blessed.

Raag 10 Dhanaasaree

Upon the plate of the sky, the sun and the moon are the lamps.The stars are the pearls.

The fragrance of sandalwood in the air is the temple incense, and the wind is the fan. The places of worship are the flowers at your altar.
What a beautiful aartee, lamp-lit service this is, O Luminous Lord!
You have thousands of eyes, yet you have no eyes. You have thousands of forms, yet you have no form.
Thru the Guru's teachings, Your Light shines forth!
Bestow the Water of Your Mercy upon Nanak, the thirsty song-bird, so that he may come to dwell on Your Name.

Raag 11 Jaitsree

The Jewel of the Lord's Name abides within my heart; the Guru has placed His hand on my forehead.
The sins and pains of past reincarnations have been cast out.
The Guru has blessed me with the Naam, the Name of the Lord, and my debt has been paid off.
To fools, the jewel is not visible.

I am Your child, Lord. Show me your mercy.

Raag 12 Todi

Without the Lord, my mind cannot survive.
The Lord seems so very sweet to my heart, mind and body, upon my face, upon my forehead, my good destiny is inscribed.

Your canopy is so high, Lord, no one else has any power.

O Lord, ocean of mercy, abide in my heart forever.

Raag 13 Bairari

Riches, wisdom, supernatural spiritual powers and peace are obtained by meditating on the Lord God, under Guru's instruction.
Angels and humble servants, and the celestial singers all sing Praises to the Lord.
The Lord directs the evolution of the world and infuses the five senses into it.
The Lord is dwelling near but cannot be seen.

Raag 14 Tilang

I offer this one prayer to You; please listen to it, O Creator Lord.
You are true, great, merciful, and spotless, O Cherisher Lord.
I long for the Blessed Vision of Your Darshan.
I am a beggar at Your Door – please bless me with Your Charity.

Raag 15 Suhi

Let everyone become a servant of the Lord and there will be no confusion or evil in the world.

Raag 16 Bilaval

Please bless me with Your Understanding, that I may sing Your Glorious Praises.

Whatever happens, all comes from You. You are all-knowing.
Your limits cannot be known. O Lord. Your are indescribable.

Deep within my heart, I bathe at the sacred shrine.

Raag 17 Gond

In my mind, I put my hopes in the Lord, the Giver of Peace.
Chant the Lord's Mantra, take the Guru's Teachings; O Saints, this is the only true hope for emancipation.

Raag 18 Ramkali

Some read the Sanskrit scriptures, some read the Puraanas.
I seek your Sanctuary, God.
My soul searches in four directions for my Lord.
Your Light is prevailing everywhere.

Raag 19 Nat Narayam

Who sings the Lord's Praises each and every instant will be cured on incurable diseases.

Shower me with Your Mercy and Grace, O Life of the World; save me, I seek Your Sanctuary.
The Lord's Saint loves the Lord in his mind, like a lotus flower gazing at the moon.
Like the bitter nimm tree, growing near the sandalwood tree, I am permeated with the fragrance of sandalwood. My faults and sins are many.

Namdev, the calico printer, was driven out by evil villians, as he sang Your praises.
Those houses and homes are sanctified, upon which the dust of the feet of the humble settles.

An elephant was caught in the water by a crocodile, but the elephant chanted the Lord's name and was released.

Raag 20 Mali Gaura

Prahlaad, Your humble servant,
Was caught by Harnaakhash, but
You saved him and carried him across.
Meditating on God, the heart blossoms forth.
I am meek; I seek the Sanctuary of the slaves of the Lord's slaves.

The Company of the Holy is like a boat to a drowning man.
It is like oil to a lamp whose flame is going out.
It is like water poured on a burning fire,
It is like milk to a baby,

As with the magic spell of Garuda the eagle upon one's lips, one does not fear the snake, the cat cannot eat the parrot in its cage, and the bird cherishes the eggs in her heart, as the grains are spared, by sticking to the central post in the mill.

Raag 21 Maru

What separation could be worse than separation from the Lord?
Those who have lost their destiny suffer separation from this union.

The union of the mother and the father brings the body into being.

Abandon the tastes of the world and find intuitive peace.

All must abandon their worldly homes; no one remains here forever.

Sin is a stone that does not float.
So, let the Fear of God be the boat to carry your soul across.

Good and bad actions are recorded in the Lord's Book.

Raag 22 Tukhari

According to the karma of their past actions, every person experiences happiness or sorrow, whatever God gives.
Without the Lord, I cannot survive for an instant.
To obey God is the best course of action.
The song-bird sings the Lord's Bani.

Raag 23 Kedara

Abandon your egotistical pride and self-conceit and you shall be saved in the Society of Saints.
The pleasures of wealth, clothing, youth, property, and other comforts will not stay with you.
O Perfect Transcendent Lord, Giver of Peace, please grant Your Grace and save my honor.

Raag 24 Bhairo

You create the creatures, and gazing on them, you know them.
What can I say? I cannot say anything. Whatever exists, is by Your Will. Do not be proud of your social class and status; everyone says there are four castes of social classes but everyone is made from the same clay.

I am joined, body and mind, to my Creator.

Raag 25 Basant

Among the months, blessed is this month, when Spring always comes. Blossom forth, O My Consciousness, contemplating the Lord of the Universe, forever!
Karma is the tree, the Lord's name the branches, Dharmic faith the flowers, and spiritual wisdom the fruit.

Raag 26 Sarang

The kitchen is golden and the cooking pots are golden. The lines marking the cooking square are silver, The water is from the Ganges, and the firewood is sanctified. The food is soft rice, cooked in milk. These things are worthless, if you are not drenched with the Name of the Lord. Preserve and protect the home of your heart, which should be merged with the Lord.

Raag 27 Malhar

Eating, drinking, laughing, and sleeping, the mortal forgets about dying.
Meditate on the Lord.
You shall go to your true home someday with honor. The Lord is the Giver of Souls. The Lord is the life within all living beings.
O Nanak, the Gurmukh is invited to the Mansion of the Lord's Presence; the Lord unites him in His Union.

Raag 28 Kahnra

The mind roams and rambles in all directions. Meeting with the Holy, it is overpowered and brought under control, just as when a fisherman spread his net over the water, he catches and overpowers the fish. Meeting with the humble Saints, filth is washed away, like soap washing dirty clothes.
My mind is the dust of the feet of the Saints.Meeting with the Lord's Saints, I meet with the Lord; this sinner has been sanctified.
The Lord is servant Nanak's companion; the Lord is his sibling, mother, father, relative, and relation.

Raag 29 Kalyan

The Lord, the Beauteous Lord- no one has found His limits.
I am a child – You cherish and sustain me. You are the Great Primal Being, my Mother and my Father.
The Names of the Lord are Countless.
The virtuous and the spiritual leaders have given it great thought, but they have not found even an iota of God's value.
You are the ocean of water and I am your fish.

Raag 30 Prabhati

Your Name carries us across, Your Name brings respect and worship. Your Name embellishes us; it is the object of the awakened mind.
Your Name is my strength and my support.
Your Name brings peace and comfort to mind.

Your Name is the Jewel and Your Grace is the Light.
There is corruption in the world and Your Name is the only cure.
A body becomes miserable that does not praise Your Name.

Raag 31 Jaijavanti

Meditate in remembrance of the Lord.
Remember that the pleasures of the world – youthful beauty, golden earrings, wondrous mansions, decorations and clothes (Maya) are false, they are just an illusion.
You must understand that wealth is just a dream.
Your body shall perish and pass away.
Moment by moment, yesterday passed. Today is passing as well.

Enshrine the praises of God in your heart. Utter the Naam, the Name of the Lord. At the very last moment, this alone shall go along with you.

You speak lies and creative falsehoods. You recite prayers three times a day, The mala is around your neck and the tilak mark is on your forehead, you keep your head covered and wear cloths, If you know God and kharma, then you know that these rituals are useless. The body is false; its power is temporary. The human is only a temporary guest in the home of a body. When I am dying, I am not grieved or separated from Thee.
I want my mind to be pure like the Lord, like a diamond beside the best diamond.
Allah, Ram, Vishnu, Brahm, or God - whatever name you pray, is no woman or man but the One from the beginning and is within everyone's heart to discriminate between right and wrong. The Lord pleases our mind. The Lord is Our Support, the Essence of Reality. I am absorbed in the Lord. O Eternal, Unchanging, Benevolent Lord God, O Sanctuary of the Saints, Nanak humbly bows to You.

ZOROASTRIAN

Ancient Persian Zoroastrianism *Essentials For Living A Good Life*: pure actions, pure words, and pure thoughts. Ideas in humanity should be logical and less ritualistic. Parsi and Iranian Zoroastrians can pray together in unity and peace. A priest teaches good thoughts, good words, and good deeds are the path to salvation, not adherence to rituals. Zoraster taught that people are free and religion should guide them to the Truth and Goodness instead of Evil.

The symbol of the religion is fire and rituals are prayer and meditation before fire. The Navjote Ceremony is held when inducted into the religion. A sudre is a white upper garment worm and the kusti is a thread that is wrapped around the waist.

The Avesta was composed over several centuries by 31 kings beginning around 559BC and began translation in 51AD (51CE) by King Volgash. Some of the Zend texts were lost. Zend was a sister language to Sanskrit.

The Mazdayacnian religion is as old as Judaism; it is believed that Plato and Aristotle mentioned that Zoroaster (Zarathustra) lived 6,000 years earlier.

The Yasna contains 72 sections that are recited in ceremony. Yasna is from a Sanskrit word yajna that means 'worship obligations.'

The Vispered contains prayers to patrons.

The Vendidad contains Fargards that tell of creation, how to avoid evil spirits, how to clean and make pure a body after coming in contact with dead bodies or animals, what is sinful and the punishments, how Angra Mainyu (devil) created evil animals and sickness, The Yashts are 21 hymns.

The Siroza is invocation and enumeration of 30 divinities over the days of the month.

The Khordeh Avesta is the prayer book for general use and contains prayers for the 5 divisions of the day, blessings, and praises.

Parsee priests stand in a circle after a festival and recite the Atas Nyayis.

The Atas Nyayis

In the name of God, Ormazd, the Ruler, the Increaser of great majesty May the Fire Behram increase (the Fire) Adarfra.
Of all my sins, purify me, O God, give me strength through Armaiti.
Holiest, Heavenly Mazda, give me at my prayer in goodness, strong power through Asha, fullness of blessing through Vohu-mano.
To teach afar for joy give me certainty, that from the kingdom, O Ahura, which belongs to the blessings of Vohu-manu. Teach, O Cpenta-armaiti, the law with purity. Zarathustra (Zoroaster) gives as a gift the soul from his body.
Give to him the precedence of a good mind, O Mazda, Purity in deed and word, obedience and rule.

Satisfaction be for Ahura-Mazda.Praise be to thee, fire son of Ahura-Mazda, giver of good, the greatest Yazata! Ashem-vohu.

The Prophet Zoroaster

Zoroaster was a prophet and composed the Gathas, a sacred hymn for his followers. The prophet Zoroaster recognized good, bad, and equivocating angels (in the middle, also called genies). Zoroaster said 'All things come from and belong to the Creator, the Wise One, the God of all good purposes and the protector of the justice of the universe. Praise God by seeking the pleasure of the Wise One, the One who made the waters, plants, animals, the earth, and the heavens. Our God is Lord, most beneficent. God is farthest from us and at the same time nearest to us in that God dwells in our souls. Our God is divine and holy. Lord, teach us how to live this life in the flesh while preparing us for the next life of the spirit. Teach us the good paths, that we may attain union with you.'

Good and evil are opposite forces and it is a person's duty to choose. *Asha* is righteousness and *druj* is the lie.

Ahura Mazda is the one God who represents good, but dualism is embraced.

Angra Mainyu represents evil.

There are three future saviours in the Zoroastrian tradition, one for the end of each 1,000-year period that comprise the last 3,000 years of the world; all three will be born of maidens, conceived while their mothers bathed in a lake that preserved the seed of the prophet Zoroaster himself.

The first will be Hushedar, the second will be Hushedarmah, and the third will be Saoshyant, who will lead humanity in the final battle of falsehood. The Denkard describes the story of Saoshyant's conception at Lake Kansava and early life; his mother is a maiden named Eredat-fedhri who has 'not associated with men' and receives 'victorious knowledge.' Saoshyant will not need nourishment from his mother; his body will be sun-like and the royal glory of Khwarenah will be with him. Then, for 17 years he will eat only vegetables, then only water for 30 years, and then for the final years, Saoshyant will survive on only spiritual food. In the final battle with evil, the Yazatas Airvaman and Atar will 'melt the metal in the hills and mountains' and the righteous (ashavan) will not be harmed; this is said in the Bundahishn. Then, God Ahura Mazda will triumph, and the Saviour Saoshyant will resurrect the dead, whose bodies will be restored to eternal perfection and whose souls will be cleansed and reunited with God. Time will end, and truth and goodness (asha) and immortality will thereafter be everlasting.

There was a struggle for empire power between Greeks and Persians around 490CE yet the Greeks and Persians allowed religious freedom.

The Parsi (Parsee) are Iranians who fled to India after a Muslim Arab conquest in 700CE or 900CE;

the Parsee fled because the Muslims did not allow religious freedom.

The *Qissa-i Sanjan* is a book that is the story of the journey of the Parsis to India after they fled for reasons of religious freedom and were allowed to live in India thanks to a Hindu prince.

The Parsis built a fire temple. The Parsis believe that earth (frashokeret), fire (atar, azar) , and water (apo, aban) are sacred elements that must be kept pure.

They prohibit burial or cremation and bring the bodies of the dead to the Tower of Silence for scavenging birds.

Scriptures derived from the Zoroastrian AVESTA.

Avesta
559 BCE

VENDIDAD

FARGARD 1

Ahura-Mazda spoke to the holy Zarathustra: I created, O holy Zarathustra, a place, a Creation of delight Airyana-vaeja of the good creation, for had I not, the whole corporeal world would have gone after a place not so delightful as the first that I have created; the second is an opposition of the same - one destroying men (that Angra-mainyus created). I created the home place, a creation of pleasantness, not anywhere else where joy, where a man is born there is he brought up, and he accounts that as the fairest place.

Angra-mainyus created oppositions to every good thing I created. Angra-mainyus created a great Serpent and Cold Winter.

The second best of regions that I created is Gau the dwelling place of Sughdha. Then Angra-mainyus, who is full of death, created a wasp which is very death to cattle and fields.

The third best of regions and lands that I, Ahura-Mazda, created is the strong, the pious Mouru.Thereupon Angra-mainyus created war and pillage.

The fourth best of regions and countries that I, Ahura Mazda, created is the happy Bakhdi with the tall banner. Thereupon Angra-mainyus created buzzing insects and poisonous plants.

The fifth best of regions and countries that I, Ahura Mazda, created is Nisai which is between Bakhdi and Mouru. Thereupon Angra-mainyus created the curse of unbeliefs.

The sixth best of regions and countries that I, Ahura Mazda created is Haroyu, the dispenser of water. Thereupon Angra-mainyu, the death-dealing, created in opposition to it hail and poverty.

The seventh best of regions and places I created, I who am Mazda Ahura, is Vaekereta, in which Duzhaka is situated. Thereupon Angra-mainyus created in opposition to it idol worship.

The eighth best of regions and countries I, Ahura Mazda, created is Urva, abounding in rivers and pasture-gro unds.
Thereupon Angra-mainyus created in opposition to it the curse of devastation.

The ninth best of regions and countries I, Ahura Mazda, created is Khnenta in which Vehrkana is situated. Thereupon Angra-mainyus created in opposition to it the evil of inexpiable sins (sins that cannot be attoned or forgiven).

The tenth best of regions and countries I, Ahura Mazda, created is the beautiful and happy Haraqaiti. Thereupon Angra-mainyus created in opposition to it disrespect for the dead.

The eleventh best of regions and countries that I, Ahura Mazda, created Haetumat, the brilliant the shining and wealthy. Thereupon Angra-mainyus created in opposition to it the Yatu sin (murder or a wound that will not heal in 5 days).

The twelfth best of regions and countries that I, Ahura Mazda, created is Ragha with the three tribes. Thereupon Angra-mainyus created in opposition to it unbelief in the Supreme.

The thirteenth best of regions and countries that I, Ahura Mazda, created is Chakhra the strong. Thereupon Angra-mainyus created thievery in opposition.

The fourteenth best of regions and countries that I, Ahura Mazda, created is Varena with the four corners, to him was born Thraetaona, the slayer of the destructive serpent Dahaka. Thereupon Angra-mainyus created in opposition to it painful menses for women and fevers and illnesses for humans.

The fifteenth best of regions and countries that I, Ahura Mazda, created is Hapta Hindu (India) with sapta sindhavas (seven rivers). Thereupon Angra-mainyus created in opposition to it plagues from afar places.

The sixteenth best of regions and countries that I, Ahura Mazda, created is the lands of the sea coast and the lands of those who ride horses. Thereupon Angra-mainyus created in opposition the work of the Daevas and earthquakes.

There are also other regions and countries, places, plains and lands that I have created that are prosperous, happy, and renowned.

FARGARD 2

1. Zoroaster asked of Ahura-Mazda, the Heavenly, the Holy, Creator of the corporeal world, the Pure: Besides me, to whom hast thou taught the law which is derived from Ahura? Then answered Ahura-

Mazda: To Yima, the beautiful, the owner of a good flock. I spoke to him, the first of mankind, 'Obey me, O Yima the fair, Son of Vivanhao, as the recorder and bearer of the law.' But Yima answered 'I am not the creator, nor the teacher, nor the recorder, nor the bearer of the law.' Then Ahura Mazda said to Yima 'If thou wilt not be a recorder or bearer of the law, then enlarge thy world, make my world fruitful, obey me as protector, nourisher, and overseer of the world.'

Then answered Yima: 'I will enlarge thy world and make thy world fruitful. I will obey thee as protector, nourisher, and overseer of the world. During my rule there shall be no cold wind, nor high heat, no disease, and no death.'

Then brought forth I to him the arms of victory, I who am Ahura-Mazda, a golden plough and a spear made of gold for Yima. After that Yima had a kingdom of 300 hundred countries and his earth was full of cattle, beasts of burden, men, dogs, birds, and ruddy burning fires. He cleft the earth with his golden plough and spear saying 'With love, O Cpenta-armaiti, Go forth and go asunder at my prayer, thou supporter (Mother) of the cattle, the beasts of burden and mankind. And the earth cleaved asunder a third greater, than two thirds greater, and then three thirds greater than before.

The Creator, Ahura Mazda, produced a congregation, the heavenly Yazatas, the renowned in Airyana-vaeja, of the good creation.

Then spake Ahura Mazda to Yima: O Yima, let the cattle depart from the tops of mountains and from the valleys to a secure place before the winter snow melts and before the flow waters. Therefore make thou an area of land such as a circle or a square the length of a rice-ground to all four corners for the cows giving milk. Collect the water; there let the birds dwell in the everlasting golden-hued region whose food never fails. Make there dwelling places with floors, pillars, court-yards, and enclosures. Tither bring thou the seed of all men and women, the seed of all kinds of cattle, the seeds of all kinds of trees, the seeds of all foods and best-smelling plants. Make all these in pairs, and inexhaustible, even to the men who are in the circle or square.

Let there be no strife or vexation, no aversion, no enmity, no beggary, no deceit, no poverty, no sickness.

At the upper part of the region mke nine bridges; six in the middle, three at the bottom.

And make a wall about the circle or square, with a window that gave light within with self-created lights, like the lights seen in stars, moon and sun.

Every forty years human beings are born of every two human beings, the pair of a male and a female. And these men led the most delightful life and lived 300 years in the circle (square) that Yima made.

Then Zoroaster asked: Who has spread abroad the Mazdayacian law in the circle (square) that Yima made? Then answered Ahura-

Mazda: The bird Karshipta, O Zoroaster!

FARGARD 3

Zoroaster asked: Creator of the corporeal world, Pure One! Who rejoices this earth with joy? Then answered Ahura Mazda: He who most cultivates the fruits of the field, grass and trees, which yield food, O holy Zoroaster. Or he who provides water for the waterless.
He who cultivates the fruits (foods) of the field cultivates purity and promotes Mazdayacian law. If one buries dead dogs or dead men in the crop field, the punishment will be ten blows with the horse-goad and ten with the Craosho-charana. The same punishment will occur if one drops dead dogs or dead men down a well that is used for drinking or cooking water.
Also does the Mazdayacian law take away all evil thoughts, words and and deeds from a pure man, even as the strong swift wind clears the sky. O Zarathustra (Zoroaster), when one has performed good works, the good Mazdayacian law cuts completely away all punishment. The good law takes away deceit, murder, inexpiable deeds, high debts, sins.

FARGARD 4

Who to a lending man does not pay back the debt is a thief. How many Mithras (contracts) are Ahura-Mazda's? There are Six Mithras that Ahura-Mazda explained to Zoroaster. The first takes place with the word. The second by joining hands. The third
is of the value of a bullock. The fourth of the value of a beast of burden. The fifth of the value of a man. The sixth of the value of a tract of land. There are punishments for breaking a contract. When a man fills up with sins, he fills up his soul with sins. Atonement can be made with gold or by reciting the Manthra-cpents. If a man rise up a weapon in his hand, it is agerepta and the penalty is 5 strikes or blows with the horse-goad. If a man come upon a man to smite or kill him, it is avaoirista and the penalty is 100 strikes with the horse-goad. Peshotanu is the death penalty or payment with one's own body. Through purity and prayer may one understand how purity and prayer may ever remain.

FARGARD 5

Purity is the best thing for humans: He who keeps himself pure by good thoughts, words, and deeds. Fire and water are pure. Burn down the house of a man who has died inside of the house. If a dead man or dog is found in a stream of water, let the water run over for three days and then the water will be pure. Most birds will devour the bodies of humans. If there is a dead body on a pile of wood, do not use that wood for cooking.
A dead body should be placed on a raised place on earth, thirty steps from water or fire or from the Berecma. After women bear children they can have warm milk or

small fruit but must wait three nights before eating meat, corn, and wine. Wash the woman's naked body with cow's urine and water and then she will be clean. When if a limb is broken or
if there is a wound, or when a woman has born a child, wrap the hand in linen or in the sleeve while eating a piece of bread, until you are clean, then you can eat the bread with your hand.

FARGARD 6

If a dead dog or a dead body is found on a land, it cannot be cultivated for one year. When corpses have been taken out of water, lay the bodies on dry ground and let the water flow from the area where the body was found and after that the water may be used by cattle and men. If a body is found in a well, it must rain three times before the water can be used again. If dead dog or dead body is found in the snow than the area around it for 6 paces is unclean. Dead bodies must be taken to high ground where they are most perceived by carnivorous dogs and birds. Lay the carcasses of the dead bodies on their own mat exposed to the light of the Sun.

FARGARD 7

If the garments of the dead are stained with matter, dirt, or vomit, the garments must be buried. If the garments are made of hair, wash them 3 times with cow urine, rub them 3 times with earth, wash them 3 times with water, and let them air dry at the window.
If the garments are made of wool, wash them 6 times with cow urine, rub them 6 times with earth, wash them 6 times with water, and let them air dry at the window.
Purify any eating utensils or vessels that come in contact with the dead; if they are made with gold, wash them once with cow urine, lift them up from the earth once, wash them with water, then they are clean. If they are of silver, do this 6 times. If they are of earth or wood they are unclean forever. If they are copper, tin, lead or brass do this 3 times.
It is unclean and not pure to eat animals that have died!
When the Mazdayacians wish to make themselves physicians, let a physician cure a priest for a pious blessing. Let a physician cure the master of a house for the value of a small beast of burden. Let him cure the ruler of a clan for the value of a middle-sized beast of burden. Let him cure the chief of a tribe for the value of a large beast of burden. Let him cure the ruler of a territory for the value of a chariot with four oxen. If he cures the mistress of a house, then a female donkey is his reward. If he cures the wife of a chief of a clan, then a cow is his reward. If he cures the wife of a chief of a tribe, then a mare is his reward. If he cures the wife of a ruler of a district, then a female camel is his reward. Let him cure a boy from the village for the price of a large beast of burden. Let him cure large beast of burden for the price of a middle-sized beast of burden. Let him cure a

middle-sized beast of burden for the price of a small-sized beast of burden. Let him cure a small-sized beast of burden for the price of small animals, and small animals for the price of food.
When many physicians come together, they have knives, herbs, and holy sayings of incantations. Hot boiling water makes the water purer.

FARGARD 8

A priest may speak the victorious words: I drive back the Daevas-Drukhs (evil); begone O, Drukhs! Ahura-Mazda, defend us from our foes. Our foes shall not destroy the corporeal world of the pure.
Whoever is a Daeva-worshipper, who practices forbidden intercourse, who takes seed away from a man, they are not pure but have become hardened in soul and sinful. The Mazdyacian law takes away all evil thoughts, words, and works of a pure man, as the strong wind clears the sky.
When a man purifies his body, he must first wash his hands with water. Let him sprinkle the top of his head in front. When the good water comes in front on the top of his head, the Drukhs Nacus rushes between the eye-brows, to the back of his head, to his cheek, to his right ear, to his left ear, to his right shoulder, to his left shoulder, to his right arm-pit, to his left arm-pit, to his upper breast, to his back, to his right nipple, to his left nipple, to his right rib, to his left rib, to his right hip, to his left hip, to his abdomen, to this right thigh, to his left thigh, to his right knee, to his left knee, to his right shin, to his left shin, to his right food, to his left foot, to his right ankle, to his left ankle. The Drukhs Nacus is driven under the sole of the foot like the wing of gnat. With toes pressed down, with heels raised up, shalt thou then sprinkle his right sole of his right foot. Then the Drukhs Nacus rushes to the left sole of the left foot. With heels pressed down, with the toes uprised, shalt thou sprinkle his right toes and left toes. Then the Drukhs Nacus flys away and is gone.
Creator! He who brings fire which has burned dead body to its proper place, a fire which is cooking impurity, a fire from dung, a fire from a potter's furnace, from a glass furnace, an ore, where gold or silver or lead is wrought, from a fire out of roads or houses, what is the reward when the body and soul are separated? Then answered Ahura-Mazda: Like as if in the corporeal world he were to bring ten thousand fire-brands to their proper place.

FARGARD 9

When the sinful and unclean praise the holy Craosha three days and three nights in these regions and at the burning fire, with the Berecma bound together with uplifted Haoma (a divine plant), then return to these places again food and fatness, healthfulness and healing remedies, good health, spreading abroad and increase, thriving of corn grain and fodder.

FARGARD 10

Zoroaster asked Ahura-Mazda: O Pure One! How shall I combat the Drukhs Nucas which flies from the evil and defiles the living?
And Ahura-Mazda answered: Speak the words which are called in the Gathas Bishamruta, Thrishamruta, Chathrushamruta.

Speak twice the words of Bishmruta. Ahya yaca humatananm ashahyaat cairi; yatha tui ahura mazda; humaimthwa icem; thwoi ctaotaraccha; usta ahmai yahmai ; cpenta-mainyu; vohu khshathrem; vahista istis.
Then say these wholesome words: I combat Angra-mainyus away from this dwelling and away from this region and all pure humans and creatures.
I combat the Nacus and I combat uncleanness.

Speak thrice the words of Thrishamruta. Ashem vohu ye cevisto; hukhshathrotemai; dujvarenais.
Then say these victorious and salutary words: I combat Indra, I combat Cauru, I combat the Daeva Naonhaiti away from this dwelling, the clan, the tribe, the region.
Speak four times the words of Chathrushamruta. Yatha abu vairyo, mazda at moi, airyema ishyo.
Then say these victorious and salutary words: I combat the Daeva Aeshma, the very evil; I combat the Daeva Akatasha away from my dwelling and this region. I combat torrential winds and rains away.

These are the words that slay Angra-mainyus, that slay the very evil Aeshma, the very evil Daevas, the very evil Drukhs and Nacus.

As to the right purity of one's own body, that is the purification of every one for his own state, when he keeps himself pure by good thoughts, words, and works.

FARGARD 11

Ahura-Mazda told Zoroaster: Thou shalt pronounce the prayer of purification and then will the dwellings be pure. Pure will be the fire, the water, the earth, the cattle, the trees, the pure man, the pure woman, the stars, the moon, the sun, the lights without beginning, and pure all good things which were created by Ahura-Mazda; they have a pure origin.

Five Ahuna-vairyas shalt thou pronounce that protects the body: Yatha ahu vairyo.

This dwelling I purify, saying: At ma.
This fire I purify, saying: Ahya thwa athro.
This water I purify, saying: Apo at yazamaide.
This earth I purify, saying: Imanm aat zanm.
These cattle I purify, saying: Gave adais.
These trees I purify, saying: At aqya asha.

This pure man and this pure woman, I purify, saying: A airyema ishyo.
Vanheus rafedrai mananho. Ashahya yaca.

Speak eight Ahuna-vairyas: Yatha ahu vairyo.
I combat the Aeshma, I combat the Nacus.
I combat uncleanness, direct and indirect.

Speak four Ahuna-vairyas.

So hast thou combatted Aeshma, so hast thou combatted Nacus.
So hast thous combatted uncleanness, the direct and the indirect.

Thous has combatted Angra-mainyus.

Four times shalt thou pronounce the prayer Mazda at moi, and five Ahuna-vairyas.

FARGARD 12

Say prayers when a mother or father dies. Say prayers when a brother or sister dies.

FARGARD 13

He who gives bad food to a dog belonging to a village or inflicts a dangerous wound to a dog belonging to the cattle will receive a hundred blows with the horse-goad.

The dogs descended from the wolf are vicious and deadly, but the dog belonging to the cattle are patient, goes forth like a warrior, eats what is offered to him, and is friendly like a courtesan; house and treasure are chiefest to him as to a courtesan. He sleeps like a child, has a long tongue (cries often) like a child, and runs forward like a child.

FARGARD 14

As atonement for sins, one may bind together ten thousand bundles, give ten thousand
loads of hard wood and soft wood for fire, kill ten thousand snakes, kill ten thousand lizards, kill ten thousand ants, kill ten thousand mice, kill ten thousand gnats, fill up ten thousand holes and level the ground, make bridges, clean dogs from vermin.

Implements of a warrior are a lance, a knife, a club, a bow-string, a bow and iron points,
a hand-sling and thirty slinging stones, a coat of mail, a neck-piece, the Paita-dana, the helmet, thegirdle, the greaves (pants).

Implements for a husband are a tool for sowing corn, a team which is yoked together,
whips or horse-goad to drive the cattle, stones for grinding, a handmill whose upper stone grinds, reins which hold in and are strong.

FARGARD 15

It is a sin to persuade a pure man to another belief and opinion.
It is a sin to harm a pregnant woman or a pregnant animal.

It is a sin to not provide proper nourishment to a child.
It is a sin to give uneatable bones to a dog because bones could get stuck in their throat.
It is a sin to give hot food to a dog because it could burn the dog's tongue.

FARGARD 16

When a woman is affected with signs, marks, and blood of menstruation, she will stay in a dwelling remote from the trees which grow up for fire wood so that wood can be pure for the fire. Even to three steps may one approach who brings food to a woman who is affected with signs, marks, and blood. The woman should drink cow's urine mixed with ashes if she give birth to a stillborn baby and then she will be clean again.

FARGARD 17

After you trim hair, beard or nails, bury them away in a remote area so lice will not destroy corn or clothing.

FARGARD 18

For many men, - thus spake Ahura-Mazda to O pure Zarathustra (Zoroaster), wear a Paiti-dana (Penom) without being girded according to the law. Falsely do they call themselves Athravas. They carry a stick for slaying the vermin without being girded according to law.
Call him an Athrava who the whole night through asks the pure understanding; which makes us to reach the place, the purity, and the goodness of Paradise. Ask me, O pure!
Me, the Creator, the Holiest, Wisest, who willingly gives an answer when he is asked.

Turn yourselves not away from the three best things: good thought, word and work.

Whoso first brings pure fire-wood to the fire (the son) of Ahura-Mazda, with washed hands, Him will the fire bless, contented without hate, and satisfied.

When atonement is given for sins, you come to the place of the pure.
If you come to the place of the wicked; the dark, which springs from darkness, to darkness.

FARGARD 19

Ahura-Mazda said: Praise thou, O Zoroaster, the good Mazdaycian law.
Praise thou,
Zoroaster, thee Amesha-cpentas (which rule) over the earth, consisting of seven Keshvars.
Praise thou, O Zoroaster, the self-created firmment, the infinite time, the air, which works on high.
Praise thou, O Zoroaster,the swift wind, created by Ahura-Mazda; Cpenta-armaiti, the fair daughter of Ahura-Mazda.
Praise thou, O Zoroaster, my Fravashis (Ferver) Ahura-Mazda's.
The greatest, best, fairest, strongest, most understanding, best formed, highest in holiness;

whose soul is the holy word.
Of thyself, praise thou, O Zoroaster, this creation of Ahura-Mazda's.
Zoroaster gave me for answer.
I praise Ahura-Mazda, the creator of the pure creation.
I praise Mithra who has a great territory, the victorious, the most brilliant of the victorious,the most victorious of the victorious.
I praise Craosha, the holy, beautiful, who holds a weapon in his hands against the head of the Daevas (evil).
I praise the holy word, the very brilliant.
I praise the heaven, the self-created, the never-ending time, the air which works above.
I praise the wind, the swift which Ahura-Mazda created.
Praise to the tree, created by the Creator of Good, Ahura-Mazda.
I praise the earth, the sea (Vouru-kasha), the shining heaven, the lights without a beginning, the strong Fravashis of the pure, the Verethraghna (carrier of light), the star Tistar who has the body of bull and golden hoofs.
I praise the Gathas, the holy, who rule the times, the pure.
I praise the Gatha Ahuna-vaiti, Usta-vaiti, Cpenta-mainyus; Vohu-khshathrem,
Vahistoistois.
I praise the Karshvare Arezahe Cavahe, Fradadafshu Vidadhafshu, Vouru-barsti,
Qaniratha-bami.
I praise Haetumat, the beaming, the shining.
I praise Ashi-vanuhi; I praise the right wisdom.
I praise the brightness of the Aryan regions; I praise Yima-khshaeta, possessing good herds.
Bring Zaothra for the fire, bring woods for the fire. Praise the fire Vazista, which smites
the Daeva Cpen-jaghrn.

To the bridge Chinvat created by Ahura-Mazda where they interrogate the consciousness and the Fravashis (soul of the born and unborn) regarding conduct.
The pure souls go contented,
To the golden thrones of Ahura-Mazda, of the Amesh-cpentas (the other pure);
to Garo-nemana (Heaven), the dwelling of Ahura-Mazda.

FARGARD 20

Zarathustra (Zoroaster) asked Ahura-Mazda: Heavenly Holiest, Creator of the corporeal world, O Pure One! Who is the first of the men skilled and successful in medicine? Then answered Mazda-Ahura: Thrita was the first of men, O holy Zoroaster, of the able, successful, brilliant, strong men to keep back sickness and death, who kept backVazemno-acti, the best of the fire from the body of men.
Thrita desired a means as a favour from Khshathra-vairya to withstand sickness, death, pain, and fever-heat.
I, Ahura-Mazda, brought forth to the earth healing trees. All praise we.
Sickness I curse thee. We smite the Druj. I combat sickness, death, suffering, and fever.
I combat the wicked (Daevas).
Hither may the joy for Vohu-mano;

may he grant the reward to be desired after the law. I wish the good purity of the pure for the men and women of Zarathustra (Zoroaster). Great be Ahura-Mazda. May Airyema, the desirable, smite every sickness, death and wickedness.

FARGARD 21

Praise be to the, O holy bull in the stars, praise to thee, well-created cow, who multiplies. The clouds gather up water and rains on dry land to freshen water, earth, and trees as a fresh remedy.
As the sea Vouru-kasha is the meeting of the waters, lift thyself up and arise, thou for the sake of whose birth and increase Ahura-Mazda has created the air; from air to earth and from earth to air. Go up, O shining Sun, and illumine the creatures. Go up, O Moon, thou who containest the seed of the cattle. Then spake the Holy Word before that Manthra-cpenta: I will purify thy birth and thy growth, I will purify thy body and strength, I will make thee rich in children and rich in milk, activity, fatness, and prosperity for men, women, and children. Go up, Stars, and illumine the creatures; Ahura-Mazda has created the rising.

FARGARD 22

Ahura-Mazda spake to holy Zoroaster: I who am Ahura-Mazda am a Giver of Good when I created this abode. I give thee good healings, a thousand camels, a thousand horses, brilliance, lands, air, water, fire, and all creatures. In opposition, Angra-mainyus created a serpent, sicknesses, and wickedness.
I, God Ahura-Mazda, praise thee O Caoka, the good, created by Ahura-Mazda, pure.
Therefore do thou heal me, O desirable Airyama.
I bless thee with fair, pious blessings, with dear pious blessings.

VISPERED (liturgy)

I invite (invoke) and announce (celebrate) to:
the Lord of the Heaven, Purity, and those under the Heaven - Ahura-Mazda,
the Lord of the Water-creatures - Khar-mahi the fish,
the Lord of the Earth – Zoroaster,
the Lord of the Winged - the bird Karshipta,
the Lord of the Wide-stepping Cattle - Maidhyairya,
the Lord of the beasts – Ermine.

I invite and announce to: the 6 yearly feasts of God Ahura-Mazda who created the world in one year.
(1) Maidhyozaremaya to celebrate creation of Heaven
(2) Maidhyoshema to celebrate creation of waters
(3) Paitis-hahya to celebrate creation of Earth
(4) Ayathrema to celebrate trees and birds of the trees
(5) Maidhyairya to celebrate the creation of cattle
(6) Hamacpathmaedaya for the creation of man

I invite and announce to the future of the world.
I invite and announce to prayers and the praiseworthy.
I invite and announce to men, women, and children.
I invite and announce to pure holy water Zaothra.
I invite and announce to holy writings in the memory of man, woman or child.
I invite and announce to prosperity and pious blessings.
I invite and announce to fodder for cattle and food for men, women, and children.

May those brought up by Vohu-mano, grown up in purity as the best and
most beautiful creatures. Be serviceable as stone or iron mortars, placed upright, as belonging to this clan, this line, this tribe, and this region. For us, the Mazdayacians, who bring offerings with wood, sweet-smelling incense, and prayers, as pure we praise Ahura-Mazda, the Lord of Purity.

YACNA (Prayer sacrifices or offerings)

I invite (invoke) and announce (celebrate) to: the Creator God Ahura-Mazda, the Brilliant, Majestic, Greatest, Best, Most Beautiful, the Strongest, Most Intellectual, of the best body, the Highest through holiness.

I invite and announce to: all lords or Genii of purity: Vohu-mano, Ashavahista, Kshathra-vairya, Cpenta-armaiti, Haurvat, Havani, Cavanhi Vicza, Mithra, Rapithwina, Fradat-fshu,
Uzayeirina, Daqyuma, Aiwicruthrema Aibigaya, Ushahina, Craosha.

Vohu-mano is the Bahman, the protector of all living creatures.
Ashavahista's function is to keep mankind joyful and cheerful.
Kshathra-vairya protects metals.
Cpenta-armaiti is a female genius of wisdom and speech.
Yazata is highest in wisdom.
Haurvat is a lord of waters.
Ameretat is a lord of trees.
Havani is the lord of mornings.
Cavanhi Vicza (Vicya) is an assistant of Havani.
Mithra is the lord of light.
Rama-qactra is the genius thru whom we enjoy our food.
Fradat-fshu is the genius who increases cattle.
Daqyuma is the head of whole province or region.
The navel of the waters is Ahura-Mazda by which the glosses understand and appreciate the mountain Arburj (Alburj).
Vicpanm-hujyaiti is good health.
Zarathustrotema is a high piriest.
Craosha watches over the world.
Tistrya is Sirius the star.
Ushi-darena is the mountain Hoshdstar from which kings descended, endowed with a brightness from Heaven.
Athravas and Herbeds have imperishable majesty obtained through wisdom.
Neriosengh explains the strong mighty genius of an oath.
Berejya watches over the growth of corn.
Fravashis of the pure is of my own soul.
Veretragna is victory created by Ahura-Mazda.
Rashnu is the justest.
Arstat promotes and extends the world.
Haoma and Soma are plant offerings.

The fire Vazista is the son of Ahura-Mazda.
The good waters were created by Mazda.
The New Moon is the Mistress of Purity.
Vishaptatha is the Full Moon.
Yima was a pure man who became a sinner and Mazda abandoned him.

I invite and announce to all lords of purity: if I have sinned and have pained thee, be it with my thoughts, words, or works (actions), be it willingly or against my will,I praise thee now and therefore and with purity offer praise, confession, and atonement. May our foes be conquered, driven away by Cpenta-mainyus. With purity I desire and devote myself to be under the authority of God Ahura-Mazda for all eternity; we praise thee. Then we shall make known good thoughts, words, and deeds (works).

I invite and announce the recitation of the Gathas, written by Zoroaster. Zoroaster was born in Pourushacpa on Mount Zebar, created against the Daevus, devoted to Ahura the renowned in Airyana-vaejo. Zoroaster recited the Ahuna-vairya, which spreads itself fourfold (must be recited four times). I worship the holiness and the Fravashi (souls born and unborn) of the holy Zoroaster, who is pure in this world.

I invite and announce to adversary against the Daevus (evil).
I slay the Daevus by reciting the prayers of the Avesta.

I am a Mazdayacian, a follower of Zoroaster. To Ahura-Mazda, I offer every good.

I invoke Ahura-Mazda, the Lord of the head of the house, of the clan, of the tribe, of the chief of the tribe, the Lord over the lord of the regions.

O Praise and honor to Mazda, the angels, the cattle, the best purity (Asha-vahista), fire, water, and earth. We pray that we belong to the best among the works of men in what we think, say and do. May pleasantness and fodder (food) be distributed.

The GATHAS

I desire with prayer and I draw near to You, O Ahura-Mazda, with good-mindedness.
I praise ye first.
I have entrusted my soul to Heaven.
So long as I can I will teach according to the wish of the pure.
Thou art the Fashioner of the Cow, trees, birds, water, fire, earth, Sun, Moon, Stars, man, woman, and children.
Reciting to You these Perfections, we teach the good words against those who destroy the world of purity with the teaching of the Daevus Drujas.
When Thou, Mazda, first created the world for us and the holy laws, and the understanding through spirit, when Thou clothed the vital powers with bodies,
and created deeds and teachings to satisfy the world,
tither came the wise and unwise in his heart and his soul.
But these I ask Thee, Lord, what there is and what will yet come;
what debt do they pay for judgment of the pure or sinners.
Teach us the tokens of good mindedness.
Mazda-Ahura created immortality and perfection of purity.
What is evil is wicked.

With all good thought, all good words, all good works, we pray and draw to Thee.
Thou art the holiest of the same fire that bears the name Vazista.
This is Thy Body, the greatest among the great lights, that which they call The Sun.

Hymns, reverential adoration and praise to God Ahura-Mazda and Asha-Vahista
we will make known.
The abode of the waters and lands, the separating and the meeting of the ways, praise we. The mountains, youths on horses, the strong wind, the souls of the pure, the sea Vouru-kasha, the Haoma the golden great plant, all Amesha-cpentas praise we.
May Ahura-Mazda rule after his own wish.
May power and strength come to me according to Mazda.
May I be able to maintain purity, give me that, Armaiti, blessings, and the life of Vohu-mano.
To a man full of brightness may the brightness which is best of all be given the Heavenly Holiest blessing of the Lord, the best purity.
That I will ask Thee, tell me the right, O Ahura!
Who, working good, sleeping or working, by dawn, the noons, and the nights.
Who furthers me continually in the world in perfect wisdom of words and deeds.
I shall maintain for myself the pure laws.
That I will ask Thee, tell me right, Lord Ahura-Mazda.
The wish of my words is for your completion that I will speak the truth.That I will be serviceable wise through the holiness of the spirit, O Ahura.
That your brightness give us strength and a mind of good desire.
Everyone is wise through the purity of Armaiti.
This wisdom, Dejamacpa-Hvo-gva, the brightness of the wish.
Teach me the secrets through Vohu-mano and Khshathra.
The words of the Manthra.
The good men and women of the world of purity, praise I. The good men and women of the world bring remedies for the water, the cattle, the trees, food and fodder, praise I.
We praise the lights of the fire, stars, moon and the Sun.
We praise the Ctaota-Yacnya, the creations of the first world.
All right-spoken words and saying praise we.
Praise the victory created by Ahura over the Daevus Drujas.
Our own souls the Fravashis praise we.
May there flow to us the greatest and fairest blessings.
Praise all of creation, from beginning to end.

KHORDAH-AVESTA (Sacred Prayers)

1. ASHEM-VOHU
Purity is the best good.
Happiness, happiness is to him.
Namely, to the best pure in purity.

2. YATHA AHU VAIRYO (Ahuna-vairya)

As is the will of the Lord, so is the Lord the Ruler out of purity. From Vohu-mano will one receive the gifts for the works which one does in the world for God Mazda. And the kingdom we give to Ahura-Mazda when we afford succour to the poor by alms giving to charity.

3. PRAYER TO COMBAT EVIL (Nirang Kucti)

Broken be Satan Ahriman, whose deeds and works are accursed. May the works of Satan Ahriman and Angra-mainyus not attain to us. May the three and thirty Amshaspands and God Ormazd (Ahura-Mazda) be victorious and pure. Ashem-vohu. (3) (Repeat Ashem-vohu 3 times.)

4. CROS VAJ

In the name of God Ormazd, the Lord, the Increaser, the Lord of Majesty, the Pure and strong, I confess that I am a Mazdayacnian, a disciple of Zoroaster (Zarathustra), an opponent of daevas, a worshipper of Mazda Ahura who is holy lord of purity, praise, prayer, contentment, and land. As the will of God is, let God say it to me. Praise shall be to all good things of wisdom. Ashem vohu. A thousand healing-remedies wish I. Ashem vohu. Come to my help, O God, the God who is the stroke from above and who appoints the birds and other creatures from above, to the Ruler of Time of long period.

13. VICPA HUMATA

All good thoughts, words, and works are done with knowledge. All evil thoughts, words, and works are not done with knowledge.

All good thoughts, words, and works lead to Paradise. All bad thoughts, words, and workd lead to hell.

To all good thoughts, words, and works belongs – so is it manifest to the pure. Ashem vohu.

FRAGMENT on DEATH (translations were lost of many ancient Zend writings)

Zoroaster asked Ahura-Mazda: When a pure man dies, where does his soul go during this night? Then answered Mazda: Near his head it sits itself down, reciting the Gatha, praying happiness for itself. The soul sees as much joyness as the whole living world possesses. The second night it sits itself again. The third night it sits itself again. When the lapse of the third night sees daylight, then the soul goes forward and recollects itself at the perfume of plants. A wind goes to meet it at mid-day. In the wind the soul meets a beautiful shining maiden, a fair creature. The pure man arrives in Paradise Humata. The soul takes a second step and arrives at Paradise Hukhta, a third step and arrives at Paradise Hvarsta, the fourth step is the Eternal Lights.

SIROZAH

1. Ormazd. Praise to Ahura-Mazda, the Shining and Majestic.
2. Bahman. To Vohu-mano, to the victorious Peace, which is placed over other animals; to Heavenly

understanding, created by Mazda-Ahura.
3. Ardibehesht. To Asha-vahista, the fairest; to Airyama-ishya, the good Strength, created by Mazda.
4. Shahrevar. To Khshathra-vairya, to Metal, to the charity that feeds the poor.
5. Cpendarmat. To the good Cpenta-armaiti, to the good Liberality, gifted with far-seeing.
6. Khordat. To Haurvatat, the lord. To the yearly good dwelling.
7. Amerdat. To Ameretat, the lord. To the fullness which concerns the herds, corn, and fruits.
8. Dai-pa-Adar. To the Creator Ahura-Mazda, the Shining, Majestic, to the Amesha-cpentas.
9. Adar. To the fire, Yazata, the son of Ahura-Mazda.
10. Aban. To the good waters created by Mazda. To the Water Ardvi-cura, the spotless and pure. To Zaothra, the holy water of prayers.
11. Qarshet. To the Sun, the immortal shining.
12. Mah. To the Moon, which contains the seed of cattle, to the Bull of many kinds.
13. Tistar. To the star Tistar (Sirius). The stars contains the seeds of water, earth and trees. To the star Vanant and Hapto-iringa, the brilliant and health-bringing.
14. Gosh. To the body of the Bull, to the soul of the Bull; to Drvacpa, the strong, created by Mazda.
15. Dai-pa-Mihr. To the Creator Ahura-Mazda, the Shining, Majestic, to the Amesha-cpentas.
16. Mihr. To Mithra, who possesses wide pastures, has a thousand ears, ten thousand eyes, a renowned name, the praiseworthy; to Rama-qactra.
17. Crosh. To Craosha the holy, strong, who has the Manthra as a body, the Ahurian, with strong weapons.
18. Rashnu. To Rashnu, the justest, and Arstat, who furthers the world, increases the world; to the true-spoken word which furthers the world.
19. Farvardin. To the Fravashis (souls) of the pure.
20. Behram. To well-formed, beautiful strength.
21. Ram. To Rama-qactra, to the Air which works on high, which is set over the other creatures, which belongs to Cpenta-mainyus. To the Space of Heaven which follows its own law. To the Unbounded Time, to the Time, the Mistress of the Long Period.
22. Vat. To the Wind, the well-created, which is below and above, before and behind, which blows away impurity. To the manly watchfulness.
23. Dai-pa-din. To the Creator Ahura-Mazda, the Shining, Majestic, to the Amesha-cpentas.
24. Din. To the highest wisdom created by Ahura-Mazda.
25. Asheshing. To Ashis-vanuhi, to the good wisdom, to the good-righting, to the brightness, to the profit
created by Ahura-Mazda,To the Parendi with light chariot (moving from one place to another), to the brightness of Zoroaster created by Mazda,
26. Actat. To Arstat (truthfulness) who furthers the world, to the

mountain Ushi-darena, created by Mazda.
27. Acman. To the Heaven, the great, the strong, the best place for the pure, shining, very brilliant.
28. Zemyat. To the earth, the well-created Yazata (fire), to the mountain Ushi-darena, to places and localities of brightness and purity.
29. Mancer-cpant. To Manthra-cpenta, the pure, efficacious (effective); the wisdom of Manthra-cpenta, to heavenly understanding of Mazdayacian law.
30. Aneran. To the lights without a beginning which follow their own law; to the shining Garo-nemana (the dwelling of Mazda), to the bridge Chinvat created by Mazda which leads to Heaven. To the Navel of the Waters, Ahura-Mazda. To Haoma who has a pure origin, to the pious good blessing, to the strong, highest in wisdom; to all the pure Yazatas (fire) heavenly as earthly; to the pure spirit Yazat, to the Fravashis (souls) of the pure.

PATET (Confession)
Yatha ahu vairyo. (Ahuna-vairya) I repent of all sins and wicked thoughts and actions. I will atone for my bad deeds and make thing right. I praise all good thoughts and actions.

Ashem vohu. I praise the best purity.

May Ormazd bestow gifts of reward on those who thinks, speaks, and does much good.

May good come to those who do good. So may it happen I pray.

PATET of Mazdayacians (Confession of Faith)
The good, righteous, right Religion which the Lord has sent to the creatures is that which Zoroaster has brought. The religion is the religion of Zartusht, the religion of Ormazd, given to Zartusht.
Ahem-vohu.

YARSAN

The Yarsan Religion

Yarsan means Ahl-e Haqq or 'People of Truth'.

The Yarsan religion rejects caste, class, and accepts the idea of reincarnation. The Kalam-e Saranam is the sacred text of Yarsan. The Yarsan religion was started by Sultan Sahak around 1300BCE, who was given birth by Rezbar, a Kurdish woman; Rezbar was sleeping under a pomegranate tree and a kernel of fruit fell into her mouth after being pecked by a bird, and divine conception led to the birth of the (Saviour) Saoshyant.
One should always believe in good people and not stray from the right path. The Divine Essence has successive manifestations in humans.
The outer world humans are aware of is zahir but humans are governed by the inner world of batini.

Seven archangels are: Benjamin who is an incarnation of archangel Gabriel, Dawud or David who is an incarnation of archangel Michael, Mustafa who is an incarnation of archangel Azrael, Pir Musi who is an incarnation of the recording angel, Shah Husain, Baba Yadesar, and Khatun-e-Rezbar who is the mother of Sultan Sahak.
Zoroastrian Mithra was a savior and son of God born out of a rock wearing a Phrygian cap which signifies freedom and liberty.

YAZIDI

The Yazidi Religion

The Yazidi are ancient Persian people. The Yazidi religion of the Kurdish people combines aspects from Zoroastrian, Islam, Christian, and Judaism.

In the Yazidism (Yezidi) religion, God created the earth, stars, and heaven from a pearl that broke into pieces but left it in the care of a heptad of 7 holy beings or angels. The most prominent angel is Melek Taus (Kurdish: Tawuse Melek), the Peacock Angel, God's representative on earth. Melek breathed a soul into Adam in the Garden of Eden. God ordered the angels to bow to His creations, but Melek Taus refuxed and he was thrown into Hell, until his tears quenched the fires of hell and then Melek Taus became reconciled to God. Then Melek Taus was manifested in the form of a peacock which represents resurrection and immortalilty. Yazidis believe in the periodic reincarnation of the seven holy beings in human form. Their holiest shrine and the tomb of the faith's founder Sheikh Adi ibn Musafir, a Sufi preacher, is located in Lalish, in northern Iraq.

Yazidi holy day is Wednesday and Saturday is their day of rest.

Yazidis pray facing the sun at sunrise, noon, and sunset.
The faithful make an annual pilgrammage to the holiest shrine of Yazidi, the tomb of Sheikh Musafir. The holiday of Jema'yye is the Feast of the Seven Days.

There is a caste system of murids, sheikhs, and pirs.

Some Yazidis believe that God breathed a soul into both Adam and Eve.

A basic belief is that all human beings on earth who are doing good things are appreciated.

DRUZE

The Druze (1000CE) is a small sect in Lebanon, Syria, and Israel; it is a sect from Ismailism. Drueze highlights the role of the human mind and truthfulness, elements from Abrahamic religions of Islam, Judaism, and Christianity, Gnosticism, Neoplatoism, Pythagoreanism, Hinduism,and promotes ideas of unity. Neoplatoism was influenced by ideas of Plato; developing the soul through Henosis, which is union with the One, the Source, the Monad which is a circle with a dot in the middle (God), The Absolute. The soul is united with the Cosmic Mind.

The religion takes its name from Muhammad bin Ismail Nashtakin ad-Darazi, an early preacher. Jethro of Midian is the prophet of the Druze. Many Druze communities exist near Jabal al-Druze, a volcanic mountain in southern Syria and Mount Lebanon in the Chouf Mountains of Lebanon.

JAINISM

Jainism (550BCE) prescribes a path of non-violence for all living beings and was originated by the teacher Mahavira (599-527BCE).
Jainism is one of the oldest religions in the world and began parallel to the Oldest Vedic religion in India.

The word Jainism is derived from the Sanskrit verb *jin* which means 'to conquer' – to battle passions of mind and body.

The two main sects of Jainism are Digambara and Svetambara.

The Suduanists of Jainism taught that those who commit sin will not ascend high to heaven.

Those who attain good spiritual nature experience victory over self – the conquest of anger, pride, deceit, and greed.

Self is man's own invincible foe.

When a person looks to God for forgiveness, they are delivered from fear.

A person should treat others as they would like to be treated.

The three main principles of Jainism are nonviolence, non-absolutism (anekantavada) which means people have different viewpoints, and non-possessiveness or non-greediness (aparigraha).

Followers take 5 vows: non-violence, not lying, not stealing (asteya), chastity, and non-attachment.

Dana is the virtue of generosity, charity, or giving alms.

Jains do not eat garlic or onions or potatoes because vegetables that grow underground are host to bacteria and Jains believe it is violent to cause harm to the microorganisms.

Some Jains wear a white mask so bugs cannot fly into their mouth.

CONFUCIAN

Asian Scriptures derived from the Shiki, Liki, and Analects books of Confucianism.

Confucius (551-479BCE) was a man who was born to a poor and common family in the town of Tsou, state of Lu, in country of Ch'angping which is now Shantung.

Shuliang Ho was his father and Yen Chentsai was his mother.

Yen prayed at the hill of Nich'iu and begat Confucious in answer to a prayer.

'Confucius' means 'K'ung the Master'. His name was Chungni K'ung. He was 9 feet six inches tall.

Confucius loved historic learning and became a philosopher.

His parents died within a short time of each other and he buried them both at Fangshan.

Confucius was put in charge of the granary of the house of Baron Chi and Confucius was noted for the fairness of his measures. He was also made to keep charge of cattle and sheep. He was promoted to minister of public works.

He had disciples study under him who were called Yen Huei (Yen Yun), Tselu, Tsekung, Tsehsia, Tseyu, Tsengtse (Tseng Ts'an).

Confucius taught poetry, history, ceremonies, and music to 3,000 pupils of whom 72 mastered the Six Arts. The Six Arts are Math, Calligraphy, Literature, Equestrianism and Chariot Racing, Archery, Music & Rites. The Eastern Six Arts are equivalent to the Western Renaissance Intellect.

Confucius taught about literature, human conduct, being ones's true self, and honesty in social relationships. He liked to sing along to music with friends.

Five Confuci teachings were:
(1) government and society should have good morals and good purposes,
(2) individuals should have good morals and good conduct which is *li*,
(3) Humanism is an important aspect of life - benevolence and *shu* (forgiveness) should be shown to family and others.
Being a good son and a good younger brother provides already the basis for being a true man (*jen*).
The measure of a man is man.
One should follow an ethical approach with a responsibility toward one's fellow beings with a humanist attitude, brushing aside mysticism, immortality, and spirits.
Look to human nature and not to the perfection of a divine ideal.
(4) personal cultivation is the basis for a good world foundation. A nation of good people makes a peaceful nation.
Acquire habits of love and respect for family and others.
Teach young children to love family and friends and to be respectful in order to have a superior foundation for the next generation of citizens.

(5) The moral intellectual upper class of society sets good examples for others.
Baron Kang Chi and Chik'angtse were officials who told Confucius they were concerned about the thieves and robbers; Confucius replied 'Don't love money yourself and the thieves won't take it.'

He took ceremonial baths before religious worship, war,
and in sickness.
He made sacrifices to ancestors and felt their presence. He made sacrifices to gods and felt their presence.
He liked the music of Hsiao in Ch'i and sang along with others, saying 'Wake yourself up with poetry and music.'
He was eloquent in public, but careful with his words.
At courts, he bowed respectfully. If a king's messenger came, he would leave at once and not wait for a carriage.
He said 'I never take a walk in the company of three persons, without finding out that one of them has something to teach me.'
Confucius did not like the sound of thunder.
Confucius died when he was 73. He was buried in Lu on the River Sze in the north of the city.
For generations, sacrifices were laid at the Temple of Confucius.
Confucius begat Li, alias Poyu, who died before Confucius at the age of 50; Poyu begat Ch'i, alias Tsesze, who died at 62;
Tsesze begat Po, alias Tseshang, who died at 47; Tseshang begat Ch'iu, alias Tsechia, who died at 45; Tsechia begat Ch'i, alias Tseching, who died at 46; Tseching begat Ch'uan, alias Tsekao, who died at 51; Tsekao begat Tseshen, who died at 57; Tseshen begat Fu, who died at 57.
All people in China who discuss the six arts, from the emperors, kings, and princes down, regard the Master Confucius as the final authority.

Wisdom of Confucius

A bird can choose a tree for its habitation, but a tree cannot choose the bird.

Raise the righteous men into power and let them serve as the measure for the unrighteous; then the unrighteous will return to righteousness.

There is nothing more evident than that which cannot be seen by the eyes and nothing more palpable than that which cannot be perceived by the senses. Wherefore the moral man watches diligently over his secret thoughts.

When our passions of joy, anger, grief, and pleasure have not awakened; that is our central self or moral being (chung). When the passions are awakened and attain due measure and degree, that is harmony, or the moral order (ho). When our central self and harmony are realized, the universe then becomes a cosmos and all things attain their full growth and development.

There are truly moral men who unconsciously live a life in entire harmony with the universal moral order and who live unknown to the world and unnoticed of men without any concern. It is only men of holy, divine natures who are capable of this.
The power of spiritual forces in the Universe – how active it is everywhere! Invisible to the eyes, and impalpable to the senses, it is inherent in all things, and nothing can escape its operation.

For God in giving life to all created things is surely bountiful to them according to their qualities. Hence the tree that is full of life. He fosters and sustains, while that which is ready to fall, he cuts off and destroys.

To gather in the same places where our fathers before us have gathered; to perform the same ceremonies which they before us have performed; to play the same music which they before us have played; to pay respect to those whom they honored; to love those who were dear to them – in fact, to serve those now dead as if they were living, and now departed as if they were still with us; this is the highest achievement of true filial piety.

The conduct of government depends upon the men. The right men are cultivated by moral law (*tao*). To cultivate moral law, a ruler must use moral sense (*jen*, principles of true manhood). The sense of justice (*yi* or propriety) is the recognition of what is right and proper. *Li* is the principles of social order.

To be true to oneself is the law of God. To try to be true to oneself is the law of man.

He who is his true self has understanding, and he who has understanding finds his true self.

Whatever good thing you learn or think, you must never give up until you have mastered it. It matters not what you inquire into, but when you inquire into, you must never give up until have understood it. If another man succeeds by one effort, you will use a hundred efforts. If another man succeeds by ten efforts, you will use a thousand efforts.
Let a man proceed in this manner, and though dull, he will surely become intelligent; though weak, he will surely become strong.
In order to climb high, one must start from lower ground. In order to reach a distant land, one must take a step.
I haven't yet seen people who love virtue as they love beauty.
It is my ambition that the old people should be able to live in peace, all friends should be loyal and all young people should love their elders.

Time may change me, but I cannot change the times.

TAOISM

Asian Scriptures derived from Taoism, Buddhism, and Confucianism.

Zen Buddhists are concerned with the transformation of consciousness, using one's senses to attain bodhi, or enlightenment; we wake up to see the truth of present, the reality of time; a transformation of awareness in which an individual becomes a part of universe (from egocentric to the universal mode of awareness). We yield to our true nature which connects with all nature. Zen Buddhism came from Taoism.

'Zen' is derived from the Japanese pronunciation of Middle Chinese *dzjen* , which is in turn derived from the Sanskrit word *dhyana* which means absorption or meditative state.

Zen wisdom gives a person a cosmic understanding that is expressed when they cut firewood, look at a tree or flower, smell the rain, eat or drink foods, or chant mantras.

The Paradox of the Spear and The Shield

There is a Chinese folk tale about a blacksmith who was a great craftsman. He said that he had made a spear that could pierce anything. He said that he had made a shield that could deflect anything. When a young boy asked him if the spear could pierce the shield, the blacksmith realized that he could not answer the question. Such is the paradox of the spear and the shield.

TAO means the way of nature, the process of the universe. TAO is a way of life, a way of living in accordance with nature, a path, a route, a doctrine or principle.

Taoism and Buddhism have spiritual and mystical aspects. The Confucian way of life or Indian mandala mostly represent conventions and wisdom acceptable for community and social way of life.

The 4 principles of tea are harmony (wa), respect (kei),
purity (sei), tranquility (jaku).

Li is patterns in flowing water, the order in a group of clouds, the marking in jade, the outlines of trees; *li* is the order of things in nature, an ungraspable and indefinable principled order of things, a certain element of the uncontrolled.

Taoist philosophy contains *wu wei* (not to force things).

A day in our life is *li* (many actions) among *wu wei* (we can't impose on a natural day); it is harmony of man and nature.

Tzuran is that which is so of itself, or that which comes naturally; what we do that is second-nature and we don't really think about it as we do it.

Budji is a mysterious quality that means 'nothing special' or 'no business'. It doesn't mean modest. It means that if someone knows they do something well, they just say they can; because if they explain the method the element of surprise is gone. It is like making someone laugh when they are surprised; you cannot premeditate being surprised. *Budji* is also experienced when an archer is aiming at a target; if he hesitates too long, he may miss. This may be why beginners have good luck.

Yugen is a Japanese quality of aesthetics that is made up of two Chinese characters, meaning the mysterious. It is like looking at the ocean sky and your spirit knows there is no place for a bird to land.

Wabi-sabi is beauty among imperfections caused by time, such as cracks in wood, dried-out leaves, liver spots on skin, or rust on metal.

Wabi means harmony, peace, tranquil, balance, satisfied with who you are and what you have.

Sabi is natural progression, a blossom of time, tarnish, rust, growing old.

Aware (a-war-e) is a nostalgic feeling, like watching the flight of the last bird who migrated to a warmer climate for the winter.

Tsukaeru is to be of service to another.

Ci is benevolence, like the love of a mother or father for their child.

Learn to 'let go'. When eating, try not to think about extraneous matters. When
sleeping, don't let dreams interfere.

Yin is the shaded side of the mountain and feminine force; *yang* is the sunny side and male force; neither is complete without the other.

Taoist priests offer cinnamon sticks as offerings to Chen-wu and the Jade Emperor.

The New Year or Spring Festival is the most important holiday, for beginnings and family reunions.

There is a shrine in the Huang Shan Mountain range in Eastern China where the Yellow Emperor is said to have ascended to immortality.

Lao-tzu (Laozi) (or Li Erh) was a Great Master who wrote the Tao Te Ching. 'Lao Tzu' means Old Master. The sacred text was written on bamboo slats tied together with rope. Tao (Reality) and Te (Power) is a classic piece of Zen wisdom. The Chinese scholar Ssu-ma Ch'ien (145 – 86 BCE) wrote in the Shih Chi (Records of the Historian) that it mentioned in the archives that Lao

Tzu met Confucius sometime between 518 and 511 BCE. Ch'ien reported that at an advanced age, Lao Tzu departed for the western wilderness of China and when he passed through the last gate, the gatekeeper, who had been advised in dream of Lao Tzu's coming, asked him to write down what he knew; what he wrote down the proverbial wisdom that became the Tao Te Ching. After he passed through the gate he was heard from no more. *Tao* means the way or the path. *Te* means your human integrity; Te is the power of Tao in each creature and every form of energy that can be used to stay in harmony with its source or diverge from it.

Scriptures derived from thousands of pages of Tao Te Ching

Tao Te Ching
722BCE

Tao (Reality)
Tao Virtue 1

The tao that can be described is not the Constant Tao.
The name that can be named is not the Constant Name.

Something-without-a-name is the beginning of Heaven and Earth.

Something without a name is the mother of all the ten-thousand things.

Being without desire, you can behold the subtleties.
Having desire, you can behold the manifestations.

These are two things.
They issue forth from the Sameness but have different names.
This Sameness is called 'Profound, the Profundity of the Profound, the Gate of the Collective Subtlety.'

How the Great Te appears follows exclusively from the Tao.

Tao, when being like a substance, appears nebulous and hazy.

Hazy and nebulous, within it are images.

Nebulous and hazy, within it are substances.

Obscure and vague, within it are essences.

These essences are very real.
Within this Tao is something you can believe in!

From ancient times to the present, its name has not been forgotten. Use it to
understand the common origin.

How do I know the nature of the common origin? By this!

Therefore, follow Tao
and be one with Tao.
Follow Te
and be one with Te.
Follow loss

and be one with loss.

Tao Virtue 2

Humans are conditioned by Earth.
Earth is conditioned by
Heaven.
Heaven is conditioned by
Tao.
Tao is conditioned by its own
nature.

In the midst of our world there are these four great things.

Each and every thing returns to its root. Returning to the root is called 'Tranquility.'
This is known as the cycle of life.
This cycle of life is called 'Constant.'
To understand Constant is 'Insight.'
To know Constant is to know
tolerance.
Tolerance leads to impartiality.
Impartiality leads to completeness.
Completeness leads to a natural
state,
a natural state to the Tao.

Not to know this Constant leads to rash, foolish, and ill-fated actions.

No self – no danger.

Tao Virtue 3

The sage is good at saving people so no one is left out.
He is good at saving things so
nothing is wasted.
This is called 'holding to the light.'
This is called the 'essential mystery.'

Tao Virtue 4

Know purity.
Be a model for the world.
If you are a model for the world,
your constant Te
will never deviate
and you will return to the state of
Being Without
Bounds.

Therefore the sage
avoids the extremes,
avoids the extravagant,
and avoids the excessive.

Good people achieve their purpose but do not brag.

Tao Virtue 5

There are those who want to control the world by action.
But I see that they cannot
it is to lose it.

Fine weapons are not auspicious tools. The world hates them.
Therefore succeed.
The world is a sacred vessel.
It should not be interfered with.
To interfere is to spoil it.
To grasp those with Tao do not like to deal with them.
He only uses them if he cannot avoid them.
Do not boast in victory, to boast of such things means to delight in the slaughter of men.Those who delight in the slaughter of men cannot expect to thrive in this world.

Tao Virtue 6

Tao is constantly without a name. It is characterized by simplicity.
In the beginning, names appeared.
Once names appear, you should know it is time to stop.
Knowing when to stop, you can avoid danger.

Tao is to the world as rivers and seas are to valley streams.
None in the world can make it serve them.
If rulers could hold to Tao, all things would behave as guests.

Tao Virtue 7

To understand human beings is wisdom.
To understand your self is insight.

To overcome human beings requires force.
To overcome your self requires strength.

To know when you have enough is true wealth.
To act with strength requires determination.
Not to lose your place is long-lasting.
To die, and not yet perish, is longevity.

Tao Virtue 8

The Great Tao flows everywhere, like an inundation that reaches far to the left and far to the right.
All things depend on it for life but it is never depleted.
It clothes and feeds all things, but it does not act like it is their master.
All things return to it, but it does not act like their master.
It can be called 'Great'.
It never acts as if it were great even when it expresses itself to the fullest extent.
Therefore, it can fulfill its greatness.

Tao Virtue 9

Hold fast to the Great Form and the world will follow you.
It will follow without harm.
Then absolute tranquility and calm will prevail.
There will be joy and good food and passing travelers will stop.
The Tao, when spoken of with the mouth, is like the taste in water.
Looked for – it cannot be fully seen.
Listened for – it cannot be fully heard.
Used – it cannot be fully depleted.

Tao Virtue 10

The Tao constantly acts by not-doing, yet there is nothing that is not accomplished.

If nobles and kings could hold to Tao, all things would transform themselves.
If, after this transformation, desires continued to arise,
I would calm them with Nameless Simplicity.
Nameless Simplicity means being without desire.
Being without desire leads to tranquility.

The world will then become
peaceful by itself.

Te (Power)
Te Virtue 1

Superior Te never shows its Te and therefore has Te.
Inferior Te never neglects its Te and therefore is without Te.
Superior Te follows not-doing, and nothing is forced.
Inferior Te acts, and it resorts to force.
Superior kindheartedness acts, and nothing is forced.
Prophetic knowledge is the ornament of Tao.

Te Virtue 2

From ancient times, these have attained Oneness:

Heaven attained Oneness and became clear.
Earth attained Oneness and became tranquil.
The gods attained Oneness and became potent.
Valleys attained Oneness and became full.
All things attained Oneness and became alive.
Nobles and kings attained Oneness and became rulers in the world.
Thus did all these arise.

Therefore the superior has the inferior as its root.
The high has the low as its foundation.
Don't desire to be shiny like ornamental jade.
Just be an ordinary rock.

Returning is how Tao moves.
Yielding is how Tao functions.

All things in the world are born from Fullness.
Fullness is born from Emptiness.

Te Virtue 3

Tao gave birth to the One.
The One gave birth to the Two.
The Two gave birth to the Three.
The Three gave birth to the ten-thousand things.

The ten-thousand things carry yin on their backs and embrace yang in their arms.
Made whole by natural breathing, they achieve harmony.

People hate to be orphaned, widowed, or without grain, but nobles and kings call themselves by these names.

Therefore, things can be diminished when augmented and augmented when diminished.

I teach what others teach:
Powerful and violent people
do not get a good death.

I make this the father of my teaching.

Te Virtue 4

The softest thing in the world overwhelms the hardest thing in the world.

The teaching without words can only rarely be found in the world.

What matters more - your reputation or your self?
What is more important - your self or your possessions?
Which is worse - getting or losing?

Knowing what is enough - no disgrace.
Knowing when to stop - no danger.
Then you can last for a long time.
Therefore, to know the contentment of contentment is to be constantly content.

Te Virtue 5

Great completeness seems incomplete.
Its usefulness is not limited!

Great fullness seems empty.
Its usefulness is not exhausted!

Great straightness seems crooked.
Great skill seems clumsy.
Great eloquence seems tongue-tied.

True words seem paradoxical.

In the world, simplicity and stillness are the model.

Te Virtue 6

To good people, I am good.
To not-good people, I am also good.
Te is good.

The sage remains at one with the world.
He breathes in its air and, for the sake of the world, lets his mind remain universal.
The people all fix their ears and eyes on him.
The sage treats them all as his children.

Te Virtue 7

The well-built is not destroyed. The firmly-embraced is not lost.
So children and grandchildren offer ancestral sacrifices without ceasing.
Cultivate your self, and its Te will be genuine.
Cultivate your family, and its Te will be plentiful.
Cultivate your community, and it Te will endure.
Cultivate your country, and its Te will be abundant.
Cultivate the world, and its Te will be universal.

Te Virtue 8

Those who know do not speak.
Those who speak do not know.
Be at one with the dust of the world.
This is called the 'Profound Identification'.
Therefore it is valued by the world.

Te Virtue 9

Use uprighteous to govern the state.

When laws and decrees are promulgated, more thieves and robbers arise.

When the people have many weapons, the state becomes chaotic.
In a world with many taboos and prohibitions, the people become poorer.

There the sage has a method that does not overpower.
He is honest but not offensive.
He is direct but not excessively so.
He is bright but not dazzling.

Te Virtue 10

In ruling people and serving Heaven, nothing is like frugality; knowing the limit and overcoming anything.
Being like a mother in possessing the state, you can long endure.
This is called 'being deeply rooted and firmly based.'
By living a long life, you can catch sight of the Tao.
All creatures follow the law of reversal which leads to the Great Harmony.

Profound Te is far-reaching.

KOREAN

In ancient Korean traditional religion, Mudang (female priest) and Baksu (male priest) are intermediaries between the first God, gods of nature, and humanity. Sungmo 'Holy Mother', Daemo 'Great Mother', Jamo 'Benevolent Mother', Sinmo 'Divine Mother', and Nogo 'Ancient Lady' are names for Goddess and the origin of a mother goddess is linked to a mountain.

Dangun is the name of the Sandlewood King, the heavenly king and initiator of the Korean nation. Dangun is also called Sansin 'God of the Mountain'.

Dangun's grandfather Hwanin and 3,000 followers established Shinshi (the City of God) on Paektu Mountain.

The mu is an ancient word meaning magician, medicine man, mystic, and poet. Kangshinmu are chosen priests and seseummu are hereditary priests who have obtained the position through families.

A *shaman* is an intermediary or messenger between the human world and the spirit world. The shaman can enter the supernatural realm or dimension to obtain solutions to problems afflicting individuals or community. The shaman in ancient times were monks in North Asia or Korea, or Natives of America or Africa who could spend time in a dangerous forest and spend a lot of time hunting for food and connecting to the spiritual world.

In South Korean culture and some North Korean cultures, Buddhism and Confucian practices are followed by many. Catholic and Christian Protestant churches exist. Some religious beliefs are:
1. God created the Universe.
2. Humans should follow good ethics.
3. It is important to honor mother, father, elders, spouse, and family.
4. Students should honor teachers.
5. It is kind to help others who need help.
6. Honesty and hard work are good virtues.

North Korea and South Korea have been split since after WWII in 1945.

CAO DAI

Vietnam gained its independence from Imperial China in 938 CE.

1. *Buddhism, Confucianism, and Taoism*

Most Vietnamese people follow a practice of Three Teachings - Mahayana Buddhism, Confucianism, and Taoism.

2. *Cao Dai 1926 CE*

In Vietnam in 1920 CE, a civil servant named Ngo Van Chieu stated that during a séance he was contacted by a Supreme Being informing him to tell the world to unite all religions into one. God told Ngo that his name was Cao Dai (Supreme Palace or Altar) and his message had been revealed previously through prophets and Ngo had been chosen to also tell the people to unite in God's name. 'Cao Dai' is also the Highest Venerable Lord.

Caodaism was established in the city of Tay Ninh and the Holy See Temple is the center of the religion.

Spiritual power includes Divine Beings directed by Duc Cao Dai; the Divine Beings are Buddha, Lao Tze, Confucius, Jesus Christ, and Jiang Ziya (a Chinese military strategist).

CaoDai is a universal religion with the principle that all religions are one and of one origin. CaoDai finds an easy alliance with Baha'i, Theosophy, Unitarian Universalism, Unity Church, and The Oomoto Foundation of Japan. Many New Age teachings would agree that there is one Truth and many paths to this Truth. The Hindu Vedas put it this way: Truth is One, but sages have given it different names.
Dai Dao Tam Ky Pho Do means The Third Revelation of the Tao; it encompasses CaoDai and means the Great Way, the way of all religions.
The history of religion can be divided into 3 major periods of revelation. In the first two, selected individuals received God's instruction and served humanity by developing Humanism, Shintoism, The Way of the Saints (Judaism, Christianity, and Islam), The Way of the Immortals (Taoism), and The Way of the Buddhas (Hinduism, Buddhism).
In the first era, King Phuc Hi founded Humanism. Moses founded Judaism. Thai Thuong Dao Quan (Lao Tse) founded The Way of the Immortals in Taoism, and Nhien Dang Co Phat (a Buddha) founded The Way of the Buddhas.
In the second era, Confucius developed Confucianism and Zoroaster founded Zoroasterianism. Khuong Thai Cong developed Shintoism. Jesus Christ thru Christianity and Mohammed thru Islam taught The Way of the Saints.

Lao Tse fostered The Way of the Immortals. Sakya Muni (Gautama Buddha) originated The Way of the Buddhas.
The revelations given by these messengers were Truth, but the messages were not completely followed because the messages were somewhat time and culture bound.
In the third era of revelation, God (Cao Dai) deigned to the world unique integrative faiths which teaches the world the unity of all religions and paths of self-cultivation leading to the reunification with the Supreme Being. Victor Hugo was a French poet (1802-1885) who became the spiritual head of the CaoDai Foreign Mission.
Spiritism or spiritualism involves receiving communication from the spiritual realm.
To be able to reunify with Origin, which is the Supreme Being, one must transcend a karmic cycle by physical and spiritual purification and cultivation. CaoDai teachings support humanity to progress and to find understanding and oneness with The All That is.

CAO DAI COSMOLOGY

After creating the universe, I divided My spirit and with it made all creatures, plants, and materials. Everything in this universe comes from My spirit and therefore has a life. Where there is life, there is Myself, even in materials and plants. I am each of you and you are Me.

All religions are one, created by the Supreme Being at different times and places.

As the divine law is love and justice, this law is the golden rule for the spirit to follow in order to progress. Justice means to treat others as you wish to be treated. True love and justice and self-cultivation all lead to harmony on earth.

The main directive of Cao Dai is to promote unity and religious tolerance. God is love. Put nothing before God; put nothing before love.

Duc Cao Dai and Duc Phat Mau represent the Yin and the Yang.

The Five Vows

We pray that the wisdom the Great Tao (Great Way) be widely spread on Earth,
May peaceful existence manifest for all creatures of Nature's birth.
May all humanity be redeemed and our whole world know peace.
And may the places we meet to worship You be granted safety's lease.

Prayer Before Sleep

All material desires consume me by day,
Leading my mind and my actions astray,
Holy One, I am prostrating here to pray
That your lovingness will cause my mind to stay
Focused and clear on Your Divinity,
Taking no actions toward infidelity.

During my sleep, when my soul is at rest,
Superior Spirits, please guide me to what is best.
Toward my home in your Sacred Nirvana I yearn.
So teach me what I need to learn.

Entering Divine Realms

Though arduous it may be to entre Divine realms,
Hesitate not to surpass your human kin,
Keep a peaceful heart to turn negative to positive and keep a plain mindset as your place to begin.
Keep practicing your miracles, and slowly, day by day,
Your tireless devotion will keep you from the fray.
The wicked flaunt their wickedness but the pure remain pure,
Practicing triple cultivation to assure their spirit's cure.

Cultivate Heart

As the moon shines brightly in the clear night,
In cultivating self, child, keep your heart and mind aright.
Be completely patient with your hardships year by year,
The blessing of your growth shall wipe clean your fears.
Child, you were taught to have compassion and blessed for your sincerity of cultivation, The Huyen Quan Khieu (Crown Chakra) will open through the clarity of your heart, Which has been replete with My blessings from the start.

Tending your virtues and having mind toward cultivation,
Willing to pray to Superior Spirits in your comtemplation,
They bless and grant you vision to their emanations bright,
Your name will be sanctified as a gentle being's birthright.
Being conscientious of the test of the Flower Convention Day,
You'll be elated to discover where your predestiny has lain,
But, for now, focus only on the growth of mind and virtue
Thereby your home in the divine abode will be well reserved for you.

Give deep thought to all that I have said, Let your conscience give your reply, Meanwhile My blessings all flow out to you
as you are held in My own eye (Thien Nhan).

CAO DAI

I am the father of love. Love has created the universe and given birth to all of you. You come from love and are the body (physical manifestation) of love. Love is the cause of the existence of the universe. With love, all living beings can be at peace and the universe calm. With peace, there would be no mutual hatred, no mutual destruction and subsequently there would be maintenance of life and evolvement. Evil is against life and evolvement. I am life and Evil is like death. Evil wants to harm you by inducing you into hatred, because hatred would lead to mutual

destruction and death.
Therefore, if you can't love each other, I forbid you to hate each other.

LOVE

Promote religious tolerance in the world: that is the main directive of CaoDai. In championing unity and tolerance of diversity, CaoDai fulfills its role as a bridge between religions. CaoDaists seek out similarities and parallels between religions so that humankind may realize love, which in all religions is the paramount law.
There are two supreme motivations which serve to guide the Thoughts and actions of all CaoDaists, whether they be of the esoteric or exoteric persuasion: Love and Justice. Love, of course, reigns supreme in CaoDai as it does in other religions. In the Bible it is written: God is Love. CaoDaists believe one should put nothing before God, therefore they would put nothing before Love.

DEATH

To a CaoDaist, death is the gateway to another life with continuing spiritual progression. Depending on one's level of spiritual evolution, a human spirit may return, reincarnating on earth to learn more, or it may progress on to other dimensions. As the divine law is love and justice, this law is the golden rule for the spirit to follow in order to progress. Justice on the personal, behavioral level simply involves treating others as you would wish to be treated.
The rule of justice involves karma. The results of one's actions, wise and kind or nasty and ignoble, take on karmic meaning. The Bible teaches
it this way: As ye sow, so shall ye reap. Karma helps explain why perfectly wonderful humans on this earth may sustain great
suffering: they may be reaping the result of misdeeds, unfavorable actions, sins, not from this life but from previous lives. Or, perhaps they haven't yet acquired the inner instinct or knowledge to move
out of the way and will, at any rate, gain knowledge and
development from the experience.
Two ways to detach from suffering is to practice love and justice with others and practice self-cultivation. CaoDai's diverse spiritual teachings allow all persons in all spiritual states to find refuge.

HEAVEN

There are twelve heavens or dimensions or spiritual levels which one may pass through after death. The levels of heavens depend on the proportion of good and bad emotions. The level with positive emotions are closer to GOD. The way to
cultivate positive emotions and the higher self is to return
to the inner self to find the quietness and peace which are naturally in the heart. Then one finds Nirvana.

The first nine heavens are called Cuu thien. The Mother

Goddess is in charge of these nine heavens. Each heaven
is controlled by Superior Spirits that help the souls navigate in the afterlife according to Karmic law.
The soul may progress upward to higher dimensions of heaven or reincarnate back to lower dimensions to continue their self-cultivation.
Prayers help direct the soul through the afterlife dimensions
but cannot change Karmic law.

3. *Hoa Hao*

Hoahaoism was founded in 1939 CE by the prophet Huynh Phu So. It is a sect of Buddhism that believes in living Buddhas that save humans from suffering and protect the country of Vietnam.
Followers also practice ancestor worship.
Simple brown cloths serve as altars for a family to offer prayers. Water, flowers, and incense may adorn the altar.
A believer prays while facing west to India to Buddha.

JAPANESE

1. Shinto, or Shintoism, is the native religion of Japan, a system of nature and ancestor worship and the way of the Gods, but some regard Shinto as a way of life. 'Shinto' means 'way of the gods'. A kamidana is a home shrine that is a sacred place for the spirit. Kami is sacred energies.

KOJIKI (711 CE)

By O no Yasumaru

The creation myth of Shinto is recorded in the Kojiki and depicts events leading up to and including the Japanese islands. A myriad of gods including the god Kunitokotachi ordered Izanagi-no-Mikoto (male) and Izanami-no-Mikoto (female) to create Japan. They were given a spear to stir up the waters, and when removed, water dripped from the end, creating the islands. The Japanese islands were specifically created as a paradise for the Japanese people.

The three children of Izanagi and Izanami were:
1) Amaterasu (goddess of sun and universe),
2) Susanoo (god of storm and sea)
3) Tsukuyomi (god of moon)

The Emperor of Japan in 680 CE was a direct descendant of Amaterasu so the peasants bowed to him.

It is forbidden to step in a Japanese emperor's shadow.
Around 1950CE, Emperor Hirohito (Showa) renounced his status as a god and a descendant of Amaterasu.

In Shintoism, the *Kind of Life You Live* determines the type of saint you become – good or bad.

The Ryomin caste system (600CE) designated people as kanjin (government officers), komin (citizen), shinabe (high merchant), and zakko (miscellaneous household). The senmin were the lower class castes. The burakumin were the poorest castes. The Ryomin caste system fell into disuse in 900CE.
Sukumabikona is a saint of rice-brewing beverages.

In both the beauties of nature and the virtues of humans does God reveal to show forth divine existence. The Maker rules over the sun,the moon, all stars, all creatures, all land, and all seas.

Pride and anxiety obscure God; such natures are a step away from the leading spirit of the heart, which should be God.

Tanabata is the July 7 star festival to celebrate the dieties Orihime and Hikobushi (for starts Vega and Altair). The Milky Way separates the 2 lovers and they are only to meet of the 7th day of the 7th lunar month.

2. The Tenrikyo religion was started by a Japanese peasant woman named Nakayama Miki (Oyasama), following revelations to her from Tenri-O-no-Mikoto, God the Parent, during a Buddhist ritual in 1838. The Ofudesaki book was a divine revelation from God to Oyasama and contains 1,711 worship poems that are intended to return the human mind to original pristine condition, a mind like clear water, a mind that is appropriate to time, place, and spiritual maturity of all human beings.
'Ofudesaki' means 'Tip of the Writing Brush'. Tenrikyo followers believe in a benevolent God, who wishes humans to find happiness on the earth. Oyasama is ever-living.

The *Ofudesaki Eight Dusts* (hokori) need to be swept away by Otsutome services:
1) oshii (miserliness)
2) huoshii (covetousness)
3) nikui (hatred)
4) kawai (self-love)
5) urami (grudge-bearing)
6) haradachi (anger)
7) yoku (greed)
8) koman (arrogance)

Calming your mind is *shizumeru.*

Caring is *oteire.*

Hinokishin is the practice of voluntary effort to wipe away mental dusts. Tenrikyans give thanks to Tenro-O-no-Mikoto for allowing believers to borrow their bodies in a cycle of reincarnation based on the notion of kashimono-karimono (a thing lent, a thing borrowed). The Kagura ritual is performed around the Kanrodai pillar called the Jiba, which will bring salvation to all human beings. A pilgrimage to the Jiba is interpreted as a return to one's origin. Reincarnation is in the form of denaoshi or 'passing away for rebirth.' God has 3 natures: Kami (everyday God), Tsukihi (Moon, Sun, and creator of nature), and Oya (Parent of human beings), The Besseki is the lectures of Words of the Path given by chosen lecturers. A *kyoto* is a missionary. A *kyokai* is a church. A *kyokaicho* is the head minister. *Tanno* is joyous acceptance. *Yoki-gurashi* is a joyous life. Universal brotherhood is *ichiretsu kyodai.*
The Proof Amulet is a piece of red clothes that the ever-living Oyasama has worn and is granted as proof of returning to the Jiba. The Proof Amulet protects the mind and body from evils.

Oyasama Maegawa had a son named Shuji. Shuji had a son named Otojira by a common-law wife Ochie and a daughter named Oshu by his wife Matsue Kohigashi. Oshu died when she was 18. Tamae Nakayama was also a daughter of Shuji.

The Tenrikyo religion was discouraged by the police; in 1882 the Kanrodai was confiscated at one point and Oyasama's followers were discouraged from following Tenrikyo.

OFUDESAKI

The Tip of the Writing Brush

PART I

From the 1st month in the 2nd year of Meiji, the year of the Serpent

An old woman of 72 years

Looking all over the world and through the ages, I find no one who has understood My heart. 1

So should it be, for I have never taught it to you. It is natural that you know nothing. 2

At this time, I, God reveal Myself and teach the truth of all things in detail. 3

You call the place the Jiba, the Residence of God, in Yamato, but you may not know the origin. 4

When you learn of this origin in full, a great yearning will come over you, whoever you may be. 5

If you wish to know and will come to Me, I shall teach you the original cause of all things. 6

As God is revealed and teaches the truth of all things in detail,
the minds of all in the world will become spirited. 7

As your minds become spirited step by step, there shall be rich harvests and prosperity everywhere. 9

I shall teach you the hand movements of the Kagura Service and wait for all to assemble and perform it. 10

When all are assembled and quickly do the Service, as those close to Me become spirited, God also, will be spirited. 11

When the mind of God is depressed over everything, the growth of all crops will be depressed, too. 12

The mind that causes depressed crops is pitiful. Quickly become spirited so that the crops are not depressed. 13

If you wish that the crops grow spiritedly, first do the Teodori Dance and then the Kagura Service. 14

Speaking of the sign and miracles, they are not yet seen. When the day arrives, you will understand clearly. 16

When the day arrives and understanding comes, whoever you may be, you will all be filled with admiration. 17

To teach of things after they appear is the way of the world. I teach of things before they appear. 18

I desire that those in high places gradually calm their minds and make peace. 19

This peace may seem difficult to attain, but it will come step by step through God's protection. 20

This is a world constructed on reason. So I shall press upon you everything with the reason in verse.

21

I shall press, though not by force or word of mouth. I shall press by the tip of My writing brush. 22

Obey the words of God and remove all wrongdoings. 26

The illness in your leg may be caused by the anger of God. 32

You close to Me may question what I do. This is because you do not know the future. 40

When the day arrives and things are seen, you close to Me will know that God's words never err. 41

Among the words of God, who began this world, there is not even a single mistake in a thousand. 43

Looking all over the world and through all ages, I see various paths of life. 45

Over steep mountains, through tangles of thorns, along narrow ledges, and through brandished swords, if you come, 47

Yet ahead through a sea of flames and a deep abyss, you will arrive at a narrow path. 48

After following the narrow path step by step, you will come to a broad path. This is the trustworthy main path. 49

This talk is not someone else's concern. It is a matter of your own and your single-heartednesswith God. 50

Looking all over the world and through the ages, I find no one who is evil. 52

Among all humankind, there is no one who is evil. It is only a bit of dust stuck on. 53

Hereafter, calm your minds and ponder. Make sure you will not be remorseful later. 54

From now on, I shall teach you about the long journey of humankind. 57

You say you want to train the child for two or three more years. But she is no longer in the hands of God. 60

Ponder well: however dear she may be to you, her parent, you can do nothing if she is out of the hands of God. 61

This has always been the world of God, but it is the first time that I act as a go-between. 70

People will think this is odd. But however much they may laugh, it is of prime importance. 71

But the laughter of people is God's delight. 72

The self-centered mind will not do. The mind of God differs entirely. 73

I bring you together according to the causality (innen) of your previous lives and protect you. This settles the matter for all time. 74

PART II

From the 3rd month in the 2nd year of Meiji, the year of the Serpent

An old woman of 72 years

From now, I shall begin to open a broad path. I shall make all minds in the world spirited. 1

Those in high places will come at any moment, spirited in mind. The appointed time has arrived. 2

After the tea is picked and the plants are trimmed, the Joyous Service will follow. 3

Step by step, the providence (shugo) of God will bring about every new and marvelous working. 5

Day after day, the mind of God hastens. What are all of you thinking of it? 6

Illness and pain of whatever kind do not exist. They are none other than the hastening and guidance of God. 7

The reason for My hastening, if you should ask, is that I desire performers for the Service. 8

What do you think this Service is? It is none other than the means to universal salvation. 9

Do not think this salvation is for the present time alone. It will be the Divine Record for eternity. 10

When this path can be seen, even a little, all minds in the world will become spirited. 17

When the dust is completely swept away, nothing will remain but universal salvation. 20

Though it is springwater that fills the pond in the high mountains, yet at its spout, it is mixed with mud. 25

When you calm your mind step by step and ponder (shizumeru), it will change into clear water. 26

I shall go into the water in the mountains and make it clear, whatever kind of water it may be. 27

You who are devoting yourselves day after day, settle the heart. Then a promising future will be yours. 28

Step by step, I am preparing to save Nihon (those who use their mind for God's intention). God will deal with those of Kara (those who need improvement of mind for God's intention) as God wishes. 33

Marvelous is the Kanrodai of this world's beginning. 39

Everything has been arranged for your happiness. Look forward to it! 42

If you indulge in extreme greed, the anger of God will begin to appear. 43

PART III

From January in the 7th year of Meiji, the year of the Dog

An old woman of 77 years

At this time, set about quickly to clear away the structure from within the gate. 1

When you have completed the sweeping, please rope off the ground plan quickly. 2

After you have truly finished the sweeping, your mind will be spirited by being single-hearted with God. 3

When the minds of the world are spirited step by step, peace will come to the world. 4

Until now, you have understood nothing, but from now on you will see wondrous signs. 5

I do not force you to come along if you do not wish to, but if you should, you will be blessed forever. 6

From now on I shall speak in the metaphor of water. Be enlightened by the words 'clear' and 'muddy.' 7

Truly, the hastening in the mind of God is to put in the central pillar quickly. 8

Though I desire to put in the pillar quickly, I cannot find where to put it because of the muddy water. 9

Arrange to clear this water quickly. Purify it by using a filter and sand.
10

Do not wonder where this filter can be found. Your heart and mouth are the sand and filter. 11

If you quickly understand this talk, I shall put in the central pillar at once.
12

If only the pillar is firmly established, the whole world will truly settle. 13

This talk requires only your enlightenment. With enlightenment will come tested proof. 14

I am God of Origin, who began the human beings of this world. Yet there may be no one who knows Me.
15

I teach single-hearted salvation (tasuke-ichijo), beginning once more that which never existed.
17

Day after day, the words of God pile up mountainously, stuck in My throat, I cannot speak them, though I so desire. 19

There is nothing I cannot teach, but there is no one who listens with a purified mind. 20

If you quickly purify your mind and listen, I shall give you all of My teachings on everything. 21

I have put them to a test of certainty in this world. Be convinced that there is no error. 22

I shall teach you on any and every matter. Never take it to be false, whatever I may say. 24

It may be difficult to understand the sayings and workings of God, whom you cannot see. 25

If you have borrowed something from another, you will need to pay interest. Return it quickly with a word of thanks. 28

You are mistaking your child's cry at night. It is not a child's cry, it is God's persuasion. 29

As God desires to inform you quickly, you must understand whatever occurs. 30

Lest there be any error in the minds of you parents, you had better ponder quickly. 31

If you are truly of a mind to save others, there is no need for the persuasion of God. 32

Take delight in the main path of God. 37

If you are truly of a mind to save others single-heartedly, I shall firmly accept you, even if you say nothing. 38

This universe is the body of God. 40

All human bodies are things lent by God. With what thought are you using them? 41

Sweeping the innermost heart of everyone in the world, God is hastening to show the central pillar. 51

Throughout the world, God is the broom for the sweeping of the innermost heart. Watch and ponder carefully. 52

When God accomplishes the sweeping of all humankind, you will be spirited and full of joy. 54

At this time, after purifying the water, I desire quickly to take in the Shinbashira (Administrative Leader of Tenrikyo), who is to settle matters within. 56

This power cannot be thought of as being human strength. It is the power of God, which nothing can match. 91

The paths of miserliness, covetousness, self-love, greed, and arrogance are dusts. 96

All human beings in this world are the children of God. Listen and understand well the words of God! 97

If only the dusts are cleanly swept away, then I shall work marvelous salvation. 98

Working miracles one after another, the mind of God hastens for your salvation. 104

Listen and ponder step by step over the words and works of God, who is invisible to your eyes. 119

Just a word: the hastening in the mind of God is solely to prepare to assemble the useful timber. 128

Though there are many and varied trees, perhaps no one knows which will become useful timber. 129

Of these timbers, it is not to be just a few. I desire a great number of timbers. 130

Day by day, I shall tend those trees which are to become My useful timber, and others that I shall let fall as they are. 132

My intent is single-hearted salvation in all matters; I desire to cut off the root of rebellion and evil quickly. 144

The present path is covered with dust. Take up a broom and do the sweeping. 145

The path thereafter will be broad and clear. Take along with you as many others as you wish. 146

After listening to the sermons of those on high mountains, listen to the teachings of God in Truth and ponder. 148

Day after day, listen to the teachings of God step by step and enjoy them. It is the Divine Record. 149

PART IV

April in the 7th year of the Meiji

An old woman of 77 years

The present path: what kind of path do you think it is? Though it seems to you to be unclear, 1

I already see a broad path ahead. 2

A thanksgiving pilgrimage will begin. Look for it. 4

I shall hasten the construction step by step, and it will become busy in all matters. 6

Watch this marvelous path. There will be a mountain of stories about it from now on. 11

How delightful it will be! So many people will assemble, coming to ask for the gifts of heaven. 12

Day after day, I desire to make the mind of God quickly known to the minds of all human beings. 15

Day after day, the mind of God impatiently awaits those who have dusts in their mind to replace their minds entirely. 17

Everything depends on the hearts of each of you. 48

Truly be spirited and ponder (think and seek the truth). 49

I will distinguish between good and evil, step by step. 58

To God, people throughout the world are My Children.
All of you equally, know that I am Your Parent! 79

The Service is for the path of salvation for the entire world. 91

When this path is clearly seen, the root of illness will be cut off entirely. 94

Until now the high mountains have been boastful while the low valleys withered. 120

From now on, I shall teach both the high mountains and the low valleys about the beginnings of the origin. 121

Watch the workings of God given in return! No one will be able to imitate Me, whoever one may be. 129

PART V

May in the 7th year of Meiji

An old woman of 77 years

Until now, there has been much talk of rebirth as oxen or horses, but there has been no one who knows his past or future. 1

Among those living in the same residence, know that there are both god and buddha. 5

Even between parent and child, husband and wife, and brothers and sisters; their minds all differ from one another. 8

Indicating no one in the world in particular, I say to you: dust in the mind causes disorders of the body. 9

It does not matter how difficult your condition may be, for God desires to reveal free and unlimited workings quickly. 11

If God accepts your mind of sincerity, I shall work freely and unlimitedly in any matter. 14

You close to Me quickly become enlightened in this teaching of the truth of God. 15

I hasten you to the broad path. 17

I appeal to you repeatedly out of My deep love for you. 21

Think of you humans admonishing your children. The anger, too, comes from love. 23

Ponder and come follow Me with firm resolve. There is a path of hope in the future. 24

When you have come onto this path, this will be the Divine Record forever in Nihon. 31

Then I shall show you God's free and unlimited workings in all matters. 48

When God in Truth begins to work, the minds of all in the world will be purified. 49

Whether you speak good or think evil, I shall give returns for both. 53

Do not think of anything in worldly terms, there is a new and marvelous path for you. 61

There is no one who knows the way to dig up the root, the truth of this world. 65

If you have but truly dug up this root, this path will become truly promising. 66

I desire to teach the whole world about all matters. The intention of God is deep. 70

From now on, please quickly make preparations truly to purify your innermost heart. 74

When the mind is made pure and open to reason, the truth will be seen of its own accord. 77

There may be no one at all who knows the true working of God day after day. 78

Whatever marvels you may see, they are none other than the workings of God. 80

Listen carefully: whatever you may say or think, or wherever you may say or think, 87

I shall give a return just as you deserve. Beware, all of you, for God may withdraw! 88

PART VI

From December in the 7th year of Meiji

An old woman of 77 years

All of you, please calm your minds and listen. 1

I shall never cause trouble to you who are close to Me. 2

Know that the distinction between fire and water will be made by the performance of the Joyous Service at this place. 6

I shall do marvelous things, the same as My beginning of this world. 7

I shall begin a Service which has never existed since I began this world, and assuredly settle the world. 8

There may be no one at all who knows the truth of the mind ofTsukihi of this universe. 9

The origin is represented by Izanagi and Izanami who were taught the providence of how to begin human beings. 31

Izanagi and Izanami are the prime instruments and the basis of the Grand Meiji Shrine of Teshoko. 52

Until now, since I kept Myself behind a bamboo screen, nothing was able to be seen. 61

This time, as I have come out into brightness, everything will be seen quickly. 62

What do you think of these red clothes? Tsukihi dwells within. 63

Whatever I may say or write by the tip of my brush, it is none other than directions from the mind of Tsukihi. 68

The true Parent of this universe is Tsukihi. It is I who protect you in everything. 102

No matter how serious the illness may be, I shall save you by the truth of Breath. 108

Tsukihi will grant you every protection. 109
Your newborns shall be free from smallpox and measles. 110

Listen carefully; whatever free and unlimited workings I may do, it is all from the mind of Tsukihi (God). 111

Though I appeal to you in sorrow over and over, I shall save you if you become of a sincere mind. 118

Great blessings are intended by Tsukihi (God). 126

The conception of a baby is by Tsukihi. The giving birth to it, also, is by the work of Tsukihi. 131

PART VII

February in the 8th year of Meiji

An old mother of 78 years

Just as you humans worry about your children, I worry over your dreadful and dangerous path. 9

Tsukihi will enter your bodies and show you free and unlimited workings in all things. 27

I shall not refuse any prayer, for I am hastening to save you. 47

Whatever I say, it is not from a human mind but from the mind of Tsukihi (God). 52

Never take it to be an ordinary matter. The intention of God is profound. 66

Of whatever salvation you are assured, because your true Parent lives. 101

Tsukihi (God the Parent or Moon-Sun) will teach on every kind of thing, Things never known since I began in this world. 106

Tsukihi will teach about every matter to all humankind equally, and the world will be filled with joy. 108

PART VIII

May in the 8th year of Meiji

An old woman of 78 years

The innermost heart of everyone in the world is all reflected to Tsukihi. 12

Hereafter, I shall teach you everything about the true path step by step. 14

This Parent, who began human beings, lives. This is the truth. 37

Watching each and every one of you, Tsukihi will discern the good and evil. 52

If you wonder why Tsukihi is so persistent, it is because I pity you when evil appears. 53

If you let your debts pile up, a path of oxen and horses will appear. 54

Each one of you is a child of Mine. I am filled with love for you. 60

But the innermost heart of every one of you is covered with piles of dust. 61

Unless this dust is cleanly swept away,
The deep concern of Tsukihi will be to naught. 62

Though My thoughts for you are filled with love, Tsukihi is anxious about your dreadful and dangerous course.
Yet none of you are aware. 63

Thereafter, I shall need only to proceed with the means to save all of you, whoever you may be. 68

PART IX

June in the 8th year of Meiji

An old woman of 78 years

Prepare your minds for the place of the Jiba where the first 2 humans were conceived, the place where the Kanrodai pillar is to be set up. 19

I shall teach you the family recipe and ingredients for assured salvation. 34, 35

I shall teach you clearly about the preparations for the Kanrodai. 46

Make the base of this Stand three shaku across and six-sided with a mortise at its center, 47

Watch! Tsukihi will surely bestow the Gift, the Food of Heaven, without fail. 55

This Stand is to be made one block atop another. The uppermost is to be two shaku and four sun.
59

Place a flat vessel on top, and I shall surely bestow the Food of Heaven.
60

PART X

June in the 8th year of Meiji

An old woman of 78 years

Never take it as a trivial matter.The intention of Heaven is profound. 2

I desire as many as 36 people for the Kagura Service, including those for musical instruments. 26

If only the Service is done without error,
The Gift of Heaven, also will be given without fail. 34

This path is a path of true sincerity and is difficult to follow.
Everyone must ponder well. 35

This time, returning to the origin, Tsukihi will clearly reveal the whole root of the tree. 46

There is perhaps no one anywhere who clearly knows the origin of this world. 47

The earth and heaven of this world is your real Parent.
Out of this, human beings were born. 54

Those who follow the path of sincerity truly understand and are purified in mind; they lean on God in all matters. 102

PART XI

June in the 8th year of Meiji
An old woman of 78 years

Tsukihi (God) clearly sees what kind of mind you have and will at this time make the distinction in all. 7

When understanding comes to all, God will assuredly save you. 15

Your unawareness of the splendid path of God has led to your remorse. 39

Hear Me clearly on the present work of Tsukihi. I shall do nothing evil 51

I began the work because I desired to teach you marvelous salvation by all means. 52

Firmly replace the mind you have had until now and become of the mind filled with joy. 53

Tsukihi sees everything. Whatever I say, you must comply with it. 58

From this year forward, if you, husband and wife, live on for seventy more years, there can perhaps be no greater happiness. 59

The very beginning of this world was at Shoyashiki Village of Yamabe County in Yamato Province. 69

There, at the place known as the Nakayama Residence, appeared the instruments of Izanagi, Izanami, Kunisazuchi, and Tsukiyomi. 70

Whenever you return, never think that it is caused by your individual minds, but the mind of Tsukihi (God). 78

Everyone will return, no one can resist the mind of Tsukihi (God). 80

PART XII

I shall manifest all of the mind of each of you. 2

I shall manifest all things whatever. 5

About My useful timber: I do not indicate anyone in particular. From one trunk, there are eight branches. 15

If one branch of this tree is securely grafted, the others will all quickly settle. 17

The truth recorded by My writing brush: lo, it is seen!
Your minds will be spirited. 44

The intention of God is good and great. 48

God will take all matters in hand and desires for you a life full of joy everlasting. 57

Do not think I have a human mind. 65

If you come on the path of God, I will save you and you will be spirited. 82, 94

Another salvation I desire to teach: an equally abundant harvest everywhere at all times. 96
I do not discriminate among any of you in the world. Please ponder, each of you. 98

If you speak falsely, you yourself will become false. 112

God will withdraw if your mind is not sincere. 113

I desire to teach you everything that has been unknown since I began this world. 138

If the heart and the mouth differ in any matter, never will it accord with the mind of God.133
Whatever is said and done, is done by God. 160

Whatever you may dream, it is all by Tsukihi. The reality seen, also, is all by Tsukihi. 163

PART XIII

If only the blessings are seen, thereafter will be the Kanrodai for all time. 12

You human beings must love your children. From this,
please think of God. 27

If all the world comes to help one another, Tsukihi will accept all your minds. 38

God desires to end the wars between those on the high mountains. 50

I, God, truly give you My firm assurance and shall work. 54

What Tsukihi sas once said will never become false through all time. 65

If your mind is truly sincere, there will never be a failure in any salvation. 71

Let there be no failure in fertilizer or water for the barley crops. Say a prayer for rain. 72

Your bodies are things lent by Tsukihi and you are all children of Mine. 79

Never bear a grudge against others. 108

Another salvation: I desire quickly to give you the Proof Amulet that protects you from illness, death, and weakening. 115

PART XIV

From June in the 12th year of Meiji

Whatever you may dream, it is by Tsuksihi. Whatever you say, it is also by Tsukshihi. 1

Never think that curses, demons, or evil spirits exist in this world. 16

If each of you keeps silent, the Parent will enter you and make you begin to speak out. 71

PART XV

January in the 123h year of Meiji

This Service is the beginning of this world. 29

The path does not discriminate between those within and the others. It is to sweep the heart of everyone in the world. 47

From now on, however high the mountains may be, they will never be able to do as they please to the low valleys. 58

I see many useful timbers ahead, appearing in the low valleys step by step. 59

Whatever I do, do not worry. Any and everything is assured by the Parent. 62

On this matter, you on the highest mountains as well as in the low valleys, set your mind so as not to be unaware. 71

Quickly begin to bring out the musical instruments at least. I am hastening soley for the Kagura Service and the Teodori. 90

PART XVI

From April in the 14th year of Meiji

What is called the Kagura this time is the Parent who began human beings. 4

The origin is the venerable Kunitokotachi and Omotari. 12

I shall work in the high mountains and in the low valleys, throughout the world. 62

Now ponder! From now you must replace your mind. It will not do, not to ponder and resolve! 79

PART XVII

At this time, I truly wish to teach everything about this origin to the world. 5

This origin is exactly the center of the bodies of Izanogi and izanami. 6

There at the Jiba which was made of Japanese cypress, I began all the human beings in this world. 7

The Jiba at Nihon is the native place of all people in the world. 8

As proof of My beginning of human beings, I shall put the Kanrodai into place. 9

If only this Stand comes to completion, there will be nothing that cannot be realized. 10

The heart of everyone throughout the world must be swept clean. 11

In this sweeping, there will be no discrimination. Know that Tsukihi is discerning you. 12
To Tsukihi, all of you in the world are My children. 16

I request that you ponder over these teachings and sweep the dust from your mind. 75

OSASHIZU

The Osashizu are writings of revelations given to a man named Izo Iburi who was a carpenter after Oyasama died in 1887, Izo Iburi is considered to be the first Honseki (the Main Seat position of revealing the Divine Directions of God the Parent in Oyasama's place.) Osashizu is considered to be secondary to the Ofudesaki.

SAZUKE

The Sazuke is the prayer that Tenrikyo followers say to petition God for divine intervention.
The Service and the Sazuke are the two main components for the path of salvation.

AFRICAN

Yoruba Religion

1. In Southwestern Nigeria and parts of Benin, Togo, Brazil, Cuba, Puerto Rico, and Trinidad, the religious practice is Yoruba.

Yoruba is part of Itan, which is the total complexity of songs, histories, songs, and culture of Yoruba society.

In the Yoruba religion, all humans have Ayanmo (destiny, fate) and will eventually become one in Spirit with Olodumare (Olorun, the Divine Creator and Source of All Energy).

Each person in Aye (physical realm) interacts with all living things and the earth.

A physical body is ara. A soul is ori. This ori in each of us is animated by the same sacred power that animate the orishas (Divine Beings). Priests and diviners, known as babalawos (men) and iyalawos (women) practice IFA divination to channel energy between orishas and a human being. The divining practice may be chants, the casting of palm nuts, and the use of divining techniques or divining chains that have ashe (which means power).

It is in this tradition of communication that diviners communicate with the orishahs to help human beings.

The diviners are helping the human being to be brought back to their original selves, to recover the destinies that we chose for ourselves before this life began.

'Ashe' is a sacred force or superhuman energy or spiritual electricity, what the Chinese called *qi*.

The *oba* is the Yoruba religious ruler of a town.

The Supreme God has three manifestations: Olodumare - The Creator, Olorun - Ruler of Heavens, and Olofi – conduit between Heaven and Earth.

Each person attempts to achieve transcendence and find their destiny in Orun-Rere (the spiritual realm of those who do good and beneficial things).

Each person's spiritual conscience in the physical realm, the Ori-Iru, must grow in order to consummate with one's Iponri (spiritual self);
I want to gain Iponri in Orun-Rere.
If one stops growing spiritually, they are destined for Orun-Apadi, and invisibile realm of potsherds (pottery fragments).

Iwapele (well-balanced) meditative recitation and sincere veneration (high respect) is sufficient to strengthen the Ori-Iru.

Ori (to know oneself) is balanced character and spiritual intuition of the human essence; when you obtain it, you have inner peace. A Yoruba proverb 'Ori la ba bo, a ba forisa sile' means 'It is the inner self we ought to venerate, and let divinity be.'

The prayer or *Petition For Divine Support* is called adura.

Important orishas are Oya, the storm diety, who brings abundance of irrigation and devastation of floods. The Supreme Being is Olodumare, also known as Olorun, who rules the cosmos from on high, the supreme power. Orunmila delivers messages from heaven to earth to humans. Eshu is also known as Elegbara or Legba; every day a little sacrifice such as palm oil or tobacco must be given to him so he will have the energy to do your bidding to heaven. Eshu is associated with crossroads, because as the holder of ashe, he has the power to take almost any situation in whatever direction he pleases. The cross roads is the meeting of the natural and the supernatural, the visible and the invisible, the known and the unknown. Here two roads diverge, and we determine our destinies by choosing the road less or more traveled. As for the guardian of the crossroads, Eshu clears the way for those who attend to him and puts up roadblocks for those who neglect him.
So Eshu can be an ambiguous troublemaker, similar to what Christians call the devil.
Eshu is associated with change. Also, for example, if you hit the curb with your car, it is attributed to Eshu.

Orunmila is the mastermind behind Ifa divination and is also called Orula or Orunla.
Some believe that Orunmila, the orisha of wisdom, and Ifa, the orisha of destiny, are the same sage. Orunmila represents the cornerstone of the Yoruba religion, metaphysics, and spirituality. Orunmila is considered to be known as a spoken word and not seen.

Oshun is the orisha of rivers and sweet water, particularly of Nigeria's Osun River.
In West Africa, she is an orisha of fertility and childbearing, and a goddess of love. Oshun is a great beauty and is called the 'Yoruba Venus' and a Shakti.

Obatala or Orishanla is the god of human creation who first fashioned clay into human form. Oshun is credited with conception but Obatala (Oxala in Brazil) fashions the stuff of the embryo into a human being. Followers of Obatala dress in white and wear lead bangles. Temples dedicated to Obatala have whitewashed walls, white fruits, white yams, white birds (especially doves), white rice, and white coconut. Obatala got drunk while drinking palm wine when he was creating the world, so Oduduwa took over. Oduduwa used a chicken that spread sand over the water in all direction with it claws.
Ogun is an orisha of iron. (Ogun is known as Ogum in Brazil and Ogou in Haiti.)
He is the god of creativity and technology as well as the god of the first tool. Ogun is the orisha god behind the invention of the locomotive, automobile, trucks, and airplanes. Some believe if you are injured in an accident involving tools or vehicles, it was because you have offended orisha Ogun.
Ogun is also worshipped as St. Peter, St. Anthony, and St. George.

After the world and humans were created, the orishas tried to reconnect with the humans on the earth. Ogun fashioned a tool out of iron ore and found his way across the abyss, clearing a path for the other orishas to descend to earth behind him.

Ogun has been associated with violence, but like the Hindu goddess Kali, he is also a god of justice who uses pathbreaking abilities to overcome oppression.

By kissing a block of iron, Ogun swore to protect orphans and the homeless.

Shango (also Xango and Chango) is the god of thunder and lightning, electricity, virility, and male sexuality.

Oya (also Iansa) is the goddess of the Niger River, guardian of cemetaries,and owner of the wind. Oya is married to Shango. She sends winds in advance of her husband's storms.

It is said that Oya and Shango need each other, because she sends the winds and he creates the storms.

Shopona (also Babaluaye, 'Father, Lord of the World', and Obaluaye) is the god of contagious diseases and the god of healing.

Yemoja (also Yemaja and Yemanja) is the goddess of the ocean and of motherhood; her dancing causes the tides.

Osanyin is a one-legged, one-eyed, one armed god of healing herbs who graces bontanica signs across the world.

Dogon Religion

2. The Dogon people live in a plateau region of Mali in western Africa. There is a mighty sandstone cliff in the region and the Niger River is near. The Dogon religion embraces many aspects of nature. A Sigui ceremony takes place every 60 years and can last for several years.

The ancient Dogon people had astronomical knowledge about the stars Sirius (Star of the Sigui) *sigi tolo*, and 2 companion stars: Digitaria *po tolo* and Sorghum *emme ya tolo*. The orbit cycle of the 2 companion stars is 50 years.

Sects of the Dogon religion are:

(1) The Amma sect worships the Creator God Amma.

A celebration once a years consists of offering boiled millet on an Amma altar

(2) The Lebe sect worships Lebe Serou, the first mortal being, who was transformed into a snake.

(3) The Binou sect uses totems; common totems for the village and individual totems for the priests. A totem animal such as a buffalo, panther, or crocodile, is worshipped on an altar. It is believed that one will not be harmed by and one cannot eat the animal of their totem.

(4)The twin sect believes that twin births are good luck.

(5) The mono sect have altars at the entrance of each village. Oncea year unmarried men carry fire torches around the altar while singing and chanting.

The *dama* is a masquerade ritual of dancing and rites by wearing masks that will lead the soul of a departed loved one to their final resting place.

The 4 masks are the Yana Gulay mask, the Satimbe mask, the Sirigie mask, and the Kanaga mask. The Yana Gulay mask impersonates a woman of the Fulani pastoral nomad people; the mask is made of cotton cloth and shells. The Satimbe mask represents women ancestors who discovered the guiding purpose of the masks for departed souls. The Sirigie mask is a tall mask that is used in funerals for men that were alive during the Sigui ceremony. The Kanaga mask dance and sit next to a bundkamba that represents the deceased. Rituals performed include yingim ritual (sacrifice of cows or other animals to chase the spirit or *nyama* from the deceased's body) and danyim ritual (masqueraders dance every morning and evening for up to 6 days depending on which village performs the ritual; the masqueraders dance on the deceased's rooftops, throughout the village, and in the fields around the village. Until the rituals are completed, any misfortunes are blamed on the remaining spirit until it is completed guided to its final place. A gourd is smashed over the deceased's wooden bowl to signify the entrance of the masks into the ceremony.

Igbo Religion

3. The Igbo people of Nigeria include music, masking, and abstract conceptions of bronze art as part of the culture. Glass beads from Egypt, Venice and India are among the castings of bronze. The Nsude Pyramids in Abaja in northern Igboland are ten pyramids built of clay of mud, temples for the God Ala / Uto. The ancient Igbo religion is known as Odinani and the god is Chuckwu. Supernatural forces are Alusi; Mmuo are spirits, UWA is the world. The New Yam Festival is held when it is time to harvest yams (iwaji). A Yam festival is held in early August. Many Igbo people are Christians, Catholic, Jews and Muslims. Excavators in Igbo-Ukwu, Nigeria have found artifacts of bronze of a ram, manila (money), jewelry, and ceramics.

FAMOUS AFRICAN HYMNS

Kumbaya 1920 We join hands in agreement

This Little Light of Mine (African Spiritual)

Hosana, Aja Kwa Jina La Yesu by Manaseh G. Mutsoli of Kenya

Mwamba ni Yesu

Utukufu Mbinguni Juu by Abaluyia People of Kenya

Wimba Wa Shukrani Hymn of Thanks (Psalm 136) by Glenn T. Boyd, a Baptist missionary in Tanzania based on a Kihaya tune.

SPIRITUAL / UNITY

1. The Druze (1000CE) is a small sect of people in Lebanon, Syria, and Israel; it is a sect from Ismailism. Drueze highlights the role of the human mind and truthfulness, elements from Abrahamic religions of Islam, Judaism, and Christianity, Gnosticism, Neoplatoism, Pythagoreanism, Hinduism,and promotes ideas of unity.

2. The Cao Dai religion began in Vietnam in 1920, a civil servant named Ngo Van Chieu stated that a Surpreme Being said to unite all religions.

3. The New Thought Movement begun by Phineas Quimby (1802-1866CE), an American clockmaker, inventor and philosopher who lived in New Hampshire but moved to Maine taught that infinite intelligence (God) is everywhere and divinity dwells within each person. It has a holistic view of the cosmos with an emphasis on self-spirituality and motivational self-help. The New Age Movement is infused with influences from the zodiac, wisdom from philosophers,

4. The *Unitarian Universalist Association of Congregations* began in 1825CE and has seven principles to affirm and promote:
(1) The inherent worth and dignity of every person;
(2) Justice, equity and compassion in human relations;
(3) Acceptance of one another and encouragement to spiritual growth in our congregations;
(4) A free and responsible search for truth and meaning;
(5) The right of conscience and the use of the democratic process with the Unitarian congregations and in society at large;
(6) The goal of world community with peace, liberty, and justice for all;
(7) Respect for the interdependent web of all existence of which we are a part.

5. In 1863CE Baha'ullah which means 'Glory of God' or the 'Promised One' claimed he was a messiah messenger and a fulfiller of prophecies just as Moses, Buddha, Jesus, Krishna, and Mohammad. Baha'ullah taught unification for humanity in global society. Baha'i Faith followers believe in the progression of divine leaders from the beginning of time.

9. There were spiritual shamans in Native American Indian, Norse, Korean, African, and Australian aborigine peoples thousands of years ago.

10. Kabalarian Philosophy is the study of who we are, healthful living, harmonious talking, spiritual ideas, personal growth, and logic, reason and fact. It was started by Alfred J. Parker in 1930 in Canada.

SCIENTOLOGY

Scientology was founded by Ron Hubbard (1911-1986), a nuclear physicist and philosopher who lived in Nebraska, USA.

1. We believe in God and in good ethics.

2. SELF-ANALYSIS: Learn to know yourself – not just a shadow of yourself. Self analysis takes you through your past, through your potentials, your life. Two auditing commands: (1) Find some things you cannot do. (2)Find some things you can do. The second is correct.

3. Walk around a room and touch objects in the room. Then you will know the room differently.

4. Realize what you can do and what you cannot do.

5. Three Rules of Processing: toward truth, ability, and for a good life.

6. A person can become so dependent upon others that they have no efficiency.
If you become self-sufficient you will have more confidence and options.

7. Be aware of how you talk to people and appreciate the value of conversations and discussions. Great discussions have led to much progress in the world.

8. Exhaustion can cloud your thinking.

9. Try to get along with others. Discuss conflicts reasonably and avoid extremes.

10. Work is an important stability. New work may have to be created in changing economies.

11. Men who detest their job should try to find a new job.

12. Control addictions. Work on recovery and relapses.

13. Warfare is madness.

14. Knowledge, clear communication, good organization, financial security can reduce confusion or worry.

15. The past does not equal the future.

REQUESTS

Scriptures inspired by the Family Prayer Book of the Anglican Book of Common Prayer. The English Church that became the Church of England was formed in 1246. The Anglican Book of Common Prayer also contained verses from the Jewish Torah and the Christian Gospels.

Prayers for Guidance

Lord Jesus, we seek your truth with great and earnest desire as the foremost necessity of our lives. We see many things, O Lord, but help us to observe and apprehend their true meaning. Teach us what we do not see. God be in our hearts, our minds, and in our understanding. Amen.

Listen to Your people, Lord, and heed our prayers. Heed the request of your loyal servants. We ask you, Lord, to be attentive to our prayers offered to You. Alleluia.

We bring our causes to you, O Lord. Show us the way and the work we must do. We are valiant in seeking your will. Hosanna in the Highest.

Lord, make me an instrument of Thy Peace; Where there is hatred, let me sow love; Where there is injury, pardon; where there is doubt, faith; where there is despair, hope; where there is darkness, light; and where there is sadness, joy. Shalom.

Prayers for Forgiveness

Dear Lord, I admit that I am a sinner. I invite You to come live into my heart and be the Lord of my life. Please help me to live for You. Keep me in Your loving ways.

Serenity Prayer

God grant me the serenity to accept the things I cannot change; the courage to change the things I can; and the wisdom to know the difference.

Prayer for Peace of Mind

Make me patient when I worry
Make me calm where there is strife
Make me loving when my heart is hard
Make me forgiving when I have been wronged
Make me charitable where there is need
Make me hopeful when I am lost
Make me strong when I am weak
Make me faithful when I am tempted.

Prayer for the Deceased

We are sojourners; we are temporary residents on the Earth. No human has power over God, who gives us the breath of life and takes us back in death. As you came forth from your mother's womb, naked, so you will go again. For all of your labors on Earth, you will take nothing with you in your hands when you die, except your soul. We are dust and unto dust we shall return; we are of thee. Our souls belong to the Lord. Our days on Earth are numbered. A person comes forth like a flower and withers; a person's days are determined by God and they cannot pass the bounds of their allotted time. We are but a shadow upon the Earth. Guide us in our journey of life here on Earth, O Lord, until you take us back as saints into your glorious heaven. We pray for the soul of our deceased loved one today, O Lord, and feel the contentment of knowing that our loved one has been united with You in the Heaven of Righteousness. May the precious memories that we share of our dearly deceased loved one give us strength and comfort in the times to come.

Almighty God, we remember our deceased loved one, we pray that you have opened to him the gates of larger life, and have received him into thy joyful service, that our loved one is living an eternal victory in Your Favour with other servants. Thank you for the everlasting memories of our loved one, whom we sorely miss. Our loved one fought the good fight, finished the race, kept the faith, and now there is in store for them the crown of righteousness in the glorious realm of the Creator.

We are gathered together today to say goodbye to our loved one (insert name) who lived (insert age) years.
We are next, for death is certain. Death is a part of life.We're all headed in the same direction step by step to our final resting place, where we'll meet our loved ones on the other side. The Lord is preparing a place for us. When the Lord is ready, and all things are ready , and you have done everything you are supposed to do in this life according to the will of the Holy Spirit, then God will take you. We are like a ship without a sail without God; how lost we would be without God, for God is making plans for all of us. Today we are left with a void, for our loved one has passed on. But our loved one and the name they left behind still lives on in our hearts.

Earth to earth,
Ashes to ashes,
Dust to dust,
In sure and certain hope and belief
of the resurrection unto
eternal life.
Rest in peace.
Amen.

Prayer for Memorial Days

Almighty God, in whose hands are the living and the dead, we give thanks and commemoration for the civil servants who laid down their lives in service to their country. Grant them mercy and the light of Your Presence. And bless their families who are left with only memories of their deceased heroes.

Prayer for Lives Stopped

Forgive us for stopping a life that was given by you, Lord, be it animal, plant, human, or embryo. We are struggling in a difficult world. Guide us to better times when these difficult decisions will be no more.

Prayers for a Spiritual Dedication

Behold, (insert name of person):
for God will make all things new in you;
a new mind, a new heart, a new spirit.
Commit your life to God and be anointed by this
(insert word: Dedication, Christening, Baptism)
for the Holy Spirit be with you forevermore.
Refresh yourself into a righteous life with God. May the Lord guide and bless you all the days of your life.
Dedicate yourself to the Lord.
Teach all nations of the goodness of the Lord
Who created the world and universe.
Anoint yourselves for the holy work of the Lord. We pray that the Lord will save our souls. We call on the name of the Lord and begin new lives. We pray for God the Spirit to be with us.

Pray for Unity of God's People

O Gracious Inventor of Peace, give us strength to lay aside our differences of unhappy hearts. Take away all hatred and prejudice, and whatever hinders us from godly union and concord. Keep us united in one holy bond of truth and peace, of faith and charity, and with one mind and one mouth to glorify you, O Divine Creator of all the Universe.

Prayer for A Wedding

O, Lord, these two bright orbs are wedding in Thy Love, conjoined in servitude to Thy Holy Threshold, united in
ministering to Thy Cause. Make Thou this marriage to be as threading lights of Thine Abounding Grace and as luminous
rays of Thy Bestowals, that there may branch out from this great tree boughs that will grow green and flourishing through the gifts that rain

down from Thy Grace. Verily thou art the Generous, the Almighty, and the Ever-Loving.

Marriage Vows

Officiant says: 'Today we are gathered together as friends to witness the marriage of (name) and (name) (in the presence of God) – or - (with Divine assistance). There may be religious readings. Officiant may ask each partner: 'Do you promise to take (name) to be your (wife/husband) and live
together (with the promise of a lifetime –or- under the
covenant of marriage) ? Do you promise to love her/him, comfort her/him, honor and help her/him, forsaking all
others, to be faithful unto her/him as long as you both shall live?'

Each partner may say 'I, (name), take thee, (partner's name), to be my lawfully wedded wife/husband, to have and to hold, from this day forward, for better, for worse, for richer, for poorer, in sickness and in health, to love and to cherish, as long as we both shall live, until death do us part, thereto I pledge thee my faith. Let us acquire knowledge, happiness, and harmony by mutual love, discussion, and trust. Let us become true companions and lifelong partners by this wedlock/marriage. I will love and honor you all the days of my life. This is my solemn vow.'

Each partner may put a ring on the other partner's hand and say: '(name), I give you this ring as a symbol of my vow, to love you and honor you in this marriage all the days of my life.'

Prayer for Children

Lord, guide and protect my child always and keep them safe from all harm. Open my child's spiritual sight and place within their heart passionate commitment to Your Good Ways. Almighty God, be the Ultimate Guardian for my child, protect them from all corruption, and place them under your divine guidance and wisdom.

Prayer for a Peace Treaty

The Lord of all humankind hath fashioned an earthly paradise for the human realm. It must find its way to harmony and peace; it is a place of manifold blessings and unending delights, yet violence and war rage in the world – this world would become another world if humankind would take heed and cease from fighting and violence!
May God grant the promise of peace and enable this distinguished assemblage to conclude a fair treaty and establish a just agreement (covenant) to bless all humankind forever, across the unborn reaches of time.

Prayer for Safety

Dear Heavenly Creator, we pray to thee for thy mercy and to defend us from all perils and dangers of this day and night that we may encounter, known and unknown. Be merciful to those whose work or duties are difficult, burdensome, or dangerous and comfort the workers concerning their toil. Let us remind each other to Be Safe.

Shield all people from bodily accident or harm or emotional turmoil. Keep us safe in Your Loving Arms that we may know that we are Your People. Protect us from all harm with the stronghold of Your Holy Spirit.

Prayer for Thanks

Lord, thank you for all good people and for all that we have.

Prayer for the Kidnapped

Condemn the evil ones who kidnapped innocent lives and bring the taken home.

Prayer for Accord

Be merciful to and protect the efforts of sober and honest industry; incline the hearts of all people toward mutual respect, fair negotiation and non-dissension answers. Give the spirit of goodwill and fair governance to places of authority. Be with your people - the loyal followers of your good ways. Fill all people with charity, peace, and thankfulness.

PROVERBS

1. Where love is, there God is.
2. With God, nothing shall be impossible.
3. Whoever wishes to be great among
   you must be a servant.
4. Every human has a need to be forgiven.
5. If you want to put the world right, start with yourself.
6. The worship of money is a root of evil.
7. Think first and speak afterwards.
8. Be the true human you seek.
9. Whatever we need, there are some who need more.
10. Anger is a wind that blows out the lamp of the mind.
11. To admit I have been in the wrong is but saying that
    I am wiser today than I was yesterday.
12. There is only one person with whom you should
    compare yourself; you in yesterday.
13. Every person I meet is in some way my
    superior; in that I can learn from them.
14. Put yourself in your brother's shoes
    before you judge him.
15. A mistake is evidence that someone
    tried to do something.
16. The kindly word that falls today may
    bear its fruit tomorrow.
17. Speech may sometimes do harm; but so may silence
    when a word expected is withheld and not spoken.
18. The world is slowly learning that because two
    people think differently neither need be wicked.
19. The flowers of tomorrow are the seeds of today.
20. All people smile in the same language.
21. The cost of a smile is nothing; it is given free.
22. Habit is a one's best friend or worst enemy.
23. Children need good role models more than critics.
24. When I was a child, I talked like a child,
    I thought like a child, I reasoned like a child;
    now that I have become an adult, I am done
    with childish ways and have put them aside.
25. It is better to give than to receive.
26. Be good in thoughts, words, and actions.
27. The past cannot be changed; the
    future is still in your power.
28. Where your treasure is, there will your

heart be also.

29. Many plans are in a person's mind, but it is the Lord's purpose for them that will stand.
30. Be imitators of God, as well-behaved children.
31. Do not waste time; live life purposefully.
32. Wisdom consists in knowing what to do with knowledge.
33. An end can be a beginning.
34. Build your house on rock, not sand, for you need a strong foundation.
35. Conscience is God's presence in humans.
36. Love cannot be wasted. It makes no difference where it is bestowed; love always has big returns.
37. A great fault is to be conscience of none.
38. Whoever commits and practices sin is the slave of sin.
39. If at first you don't succeed, try and try again.
40. It is better to have loved and lost than never to have loved at all.
41. The more you know, the more you know you don't know.
42. Be cheerful. Cheer someone up. Attitude is a little thing that can make a great difference.
43. If we fill our hearts with regrets over failures of yesterday, and with worries over the problems of tomorrow, we have no today in which to be thankful.
44. If it is the will of the Lord,
    if you keep knocking, a door will be opened;
    if you keep asking, you will receive;
    if you keep seeking; you will find.
45. Whoever tends the fig tree shall eat its fruit;
    and whoever patiently and faithfully
    heeds their master shall be honored.
46. Life is not the destination; it is the journey.
47. Today is the tomorrow you worried about yesterday.
48. Do all the good you can
    By all the means you can
    In all the ways you can
    In all the places you can
    At all the times you can
    To all the people you can
    As long as you can.
49. People believe what they want to believe despite all evidence to the contrary.

50. He who loses money loses much;
He who loses a friend loses more;
But he who loses faith, loses all.
51. When young, consider that one day you will be old and when old, remember you were once young.
52. Out of the mouths of babes comes perfect praise and wonderment.
53. Wise men are not always silent, but know when to be.
54. Tact is the unsaid part of what you think.
55. Once a word is spoken, it cannot be taken back.
56. Do you act or react?
57. Your body is for use, not abuse.
58. Laughter is cheap medicine.
59. Happiness can be found in the darkest of times if one only remembers to turn on the light.
60. In a cloud, look for a silver lining.
61. Obstacles are what you see when you take your eyes off of the goal.
62. Make life the best it can be.
63. Is the glass half-empty or half-full?
64. I used to complain about my food until I remembered the starving people of the world.
65. Narrow is the gate to heaven, but wide is the gate for error.
66. As iron sharpens iron, so one person sharpens another.
67. To get what we've never had, we must do what we've never done.
68. Today is the first day of the rest of your life.
69. Money does not grow on trees. Money cannot make you happy but money can give you more options.
70. One person's weed is another person's rose.
71. God turns broken pieces into masterpieces.
72. Freedom is free for some but costly for others.
73. A journey of a thousand miles begins with a single step.
74. Honor is better than honors.
75. Children are tomorrow's future.
76. Put a little love in your heart.
77. Talk less about the love of power; talk more about the power of love.
78. Do not put your happiness in the hands of someone else; instead, be happy in your heart.
79. In all the senses of passion, love, and hate, let none fall victim to their power.
80. Counting time is not as important as making time count.
81. Give a man a fish, he eats for a day; teach a man to fish and he eats for a lifetime.
82. Not knowing God is like a fish out of water.
83. Boats are safe in the harbor, but that's not what

boats are made for. A smooth sea never made a skillful sailor.

84. To err is human; to forgive is divine.
85. God is the gift that keeps on giving.
86. Safety is no accident.
87. Each human life is irreplaceable.
88. Actions should follow beliefs.
89. Love God in good times and bad times.
90. Humans plan. God laughs.
91. If you put the cart before the horse, it is wrong.
92. I am older than dirt, but younger than dust.
93. Cat hair or dog hair just complete the outfit.
94. All people smile in the same language.
95. Not all who wander are lost.
96. Let go of those who bring you down or people who do bad things and want to bring out the worst in you. Surround yourself with good people who bring out the best in you.
97. Resiliency is an important factor in living. The winds of life may bend us, but if we have resiliency of spirit, they cannot break us.
98. Enjoy your life, the precious moments you have.
99. Don't forget where you hid the money.
100. Fog is a cloud on the ground.
101. A chain is only as strong as its weakest link.
102. A sea refuses no river.
103. Don't believe everything a parrot says.
104. If you change the way you look at things, things change.
105. Thought is free.
106. The sooner begun, the sooner done.
107. Where there's bees, there's honey.
108. Variety is a spice of life.
109. Honesty is the best policy.
110. Imitation is the sincerest form of flattery.
111. Thrift is a great revenue.
112. He who dances should pay the fiddler.
113. If a snake is dead, some think it is disrespectful to keep beating it.
114. Don't jump to conclusions until you know facts.
115. Hate not a person; hate their bad behavior.
116. Tame the dragon inside your self to sweet emotions.
117. It takes both rain and sunshine to make a rainbow.
118. Those who think they know everything, do not.
     Two people think better together than one.
119. War is hell.
120. I have a million excuses; which one do you want?
121. Our foundation is our trust in the Lord, the God of All Comforts
     Who comforts us. God is to be trusted even in the hardest of times.
     To thee we'll ever be faithful, O Lord, Honest to God.

122. God will give wisdom, courage, and strength to all people.
123. No person, country, human race, organization, computer company, or religion should try to take over the world.
124. There's no place like home.
125. It is morning somewhere and it is night somewhere.
126. Enjoy today because it could be your last day on earth.
127. Our Creator God is an unending truth in a changing world.
128. Man can predict the weather but only God can make it happen.
129. Pray, wait, trust.
130. One world. Many faiths.
131. Rhetoric without substance is just rhetoric.
132. It is best to be silent and thought a fool then it is to open one's mouth and remove all doubt.
133. Slandering another human is the work of the devil.
134. An early bird gets a worm.
135. A tree planted by water is content.
136. Be a problem solver, not a creator of problems.
137. Words are easy but actions matter.
138. The universe is like an interconnected hologram of information about energy, matter, space, and time.
139. Don't waste time trying to reinvent the wheel.
140. Much of our life is what we make of it and our attitude. Let go of anguish and lighten your heart.
141. Look around you and see examples and proof of the Living God.
142. Every person has a story to tell and a wound to heal.
143. It is better to be poor and honest than rich and corrupt.
144. Home is where the heart is.
145. Life is not a rose garden all the time.
146. If you do not paddle your own canoe, you do not move.
147. The highest reward for a person's work is not what he gets for it, but what he gains in character.
148. Do not sail into a hurricane.
149. Are we humans having a spiritual experience or are we spiritual beings having a human experience?
150. Age is not guarantee of maturity.
151. Streams had stepping stones before bridges were built.
152. Vicious words hurt the soul and can damage your health.
153. A rolling stone gathers no moss.
154. If the trumpet gives an uncertain sound, who will come?
155. Look at someone with your heart, not with your eyes.
156. They who know not, know not that they know not.
157. Birds of a feather fly together.
158. Those who think they know everything annoy us that do.
159. The big picture is made up of little pictures.
160. Lord, we can't do it alone. We need help from heaven.

WORSHIP

1. Mighty is our God, mighty is the Spirit;
Mighty is our Lord, Ruler of everything;
Glory to our God, glory to our Creator;
God's name is higher, higher than any
other name;
God's power is greater, for God
created everything.
Come into God's presence with
thanksgiving in your heart;
And give God praise, give God the highest
praise.
Come into God's presence with gladness
in your heart;
Your voices raised, your voices gladly
raised.
Give glory and honor and power unto God,
Our Holy Creator, the name above all names.

2. It is the cry of my heart to follow You.
It is the cry of my heart to be close to You.
It is the cry of my heart to follow You all
the days of my life.
Teach me Your holy ways, O Lord,
so I can walk in Your truth.
Teach me Your holy ways, O Lord,
and make me wholly devoted to You.

Lovely Lord, you are all to me.
Lovely Lord, full of majesty,
You are the Creator and You rule the land.
Lovely Lord, I'm at your command.

You make me want to shout
Hallelujah, Thank you, Lord!
You are worthy of my praise;
All the glory, all the honor, all the praise
Is delivered to you, O Lord.

3. I will worship You with all of my heart,
I will praise You with all of my strength.
I will seek You all of my days,

And I will follow, follow all of Your ways.

I will give You all my worship,
I will give You all my praise.
You alone I long to worship,
You alone are worthy of my praise.
Lord God, lover of my soul, I will
never let You go;
You've taken me from clay;
You are the potter.
You've set my feet upon rock
and now I know;
I love You, I need You, though my
world will fall,
I'll never let you go;
my savior, my closest Friend,
I will worship You each day of my life.

My soul longs and even faints for You.
My heart is satisfied with Your presence.
I sing beneath the shadow of Your wings.
You make broken hearts renewed.
Better is one day worshipping the Lord
than thousands of days elsewhere.
One thing I ask and I would seek:
to see Your beauty,
To find You in the place Your glory dwells.
My eyes look to the heavens for You.
My heart and flesh cry out for You,
the living God.
Your Spirit is water to my soul.
I will draw near to You.
For holy, holy is the Lord.

4. Walk in the light to praise our Sacred Lord.
Walk with the Holy Spirit.
Put all your faith in the Glorified God.
Do not let anyone dissuade you
from believing in God.
God is watching over us.
God is a fisher for followers.
God is Our Shepherd and we are God's sheep.
Receive the Holy Spirit into your hearts.
Break free from the evil powers.

Hear the message of the Lord.
Turn your life over to the Lord.
The blessings of God are
overflowing to all people.
Open your hearts to receive the Lord.
Focus your expectations on God.
God in the Heavens is watching over us.
No one knows God's plan except God.
There's your plan and there's God's plan.
God's plan is the best plan.
Make up your mind to walk in the
path of righteousness.
This will be your greatest season of
restoration and revival
if you step into the supernatural of God.
Leave behind negativity, fears, and
doubts;
Put all your faith in God
and the Good Books of the Lord.
The Holy Spirit is the breath of life.
The Universal One is the empirical Self;
We are united with God
when we have self-control of
thoughts and actions;
and open our hearts to receive God.
Let the Divine Spirit work through you.
Deny the power of Satan who is our enemy.
The devil's water is not sweet.
But the water of the Lord is sweet.
Live in the supernatural arena of holiness.
Power, Glory, and Honor to you, O Lord,
Our Blessed Redeemer.
Hosanna in the Highest!

5. Reach out to someone and tell them about the Lord.
God's authority rules the Universe. God is in our midst.
Divine Lord, we are delighted and overwhelmed
by Your Goodness!
Don't give up on your faith.
When you are experiencing sorrows
turn your heart to God in prayer for answers.
Humans have to deal with God on God's time.
Pray: Be my healer, my comfort, my peace;
Be my everything, I am so lost, O Lord.

O Lord, I need you now, be my strength.

God will carry you through hard times.
Carry each other and comfort one another.
What God has in store for each of us
is too big to comprehend.
The Lord is changing the universe by microseconds!
The Lord is creating over and over again
in the huge energy field called the universe.
The Lord is directing angels to do divine
work and bring divine knowledge.
So do not be discouraged.

6. We are all on a life's journey.
We learn more each day.
Request God's presence in your life.
Pray as you go. Pray continually.
All things are possible with God
Trust in Our Heavenly Creator.
God's Word will accomplish where it is sent.
Raise your faith together in hope.
Receive the Holy Spirit in your heart.
Meditate and find your yogi Self that is one
with the Lord.
Find your Self that is in control of
your Thoughts and Actions -
Repel Satan!
Keep your testimony with the Lord!

7. We bask in the glory of God's love.
We are overjoyed with God's Goodness.
We are enthralled by God's Power.
Our God is an Awesome God!

We have perfect faith in the Lord.
We will keep our attention on the Lord.
We ask for divine guidance.
Our God is an Awesome God!

8. Lord, I want to thank you.
You've made the way for me.

Lord, I want to praise you.
You've been good to me.

Lord, I want to glorify you.
You've set me free.

Lord, I want to honor you.
You've saved my soul.

Lord, I want to worship you.
You've been my mentor.

Lord, where you lead, I will follow
You are my blessed assurance.

9. Behold, God will make all things new in you;
A new mind, a new heart, a new spirit.
Commit your life to God.
Start a new life today with God.
We call on the name of the Lord to
begin a new life. Forgive our offenses.
Let the words of our hearts be holy.
Our hope is renewed.
Carry God in your heart every day.

10. Help a friend or family today.
We are humble servants to each other.
Pray for each other.
Pray for God's presence in our hearts.
God will never leave our side.
All souls are mine, says the Lord.
Have faith that humans will find answers.
God will lead us with Divine Intellect.
Deliver us from Destruction, O Lord.
Fill us with good matters of the heart.
You are the Ultimate Healer.
There are no limits to what God can do.
Expand yourself to the world.
Be a follower of the Lord; declare it and do it.
Love is the law! Do it for the love of God.
Where we are weak, God is strong.
Let God be your leader.
Whatever presence Satan has in your
life must be removed.
Your life will never be the same
after you let God control your life.

Let there be peace in the valley and mountains.
The earth belongs to God – not people.
Look at the blue skies and the white clouds -
Look at the nighttime stars –
God already has a Plan in action. O My Stars!
Time and time again we seek refuge
in God from our storms.
Share the revelations and testimonies
of divine works.

11. Come together in prayer. God is listening.
God is worthy of all honor and praise.
Pray for something to change.
Say it to declare a change of energy.
Replace negative energy with positive energy.
God will receive your prayer.
Come together in praise and prayer
in the name of the Lord.
Lord, we are amazed by You.
We imagine your Glory Divine.
Help us to do what it is for us to do;
we pray this in your Great Names.
God is the way, the truth, and the light.
Every praise is to Our God.
God is the fragrance after a rain.
God is one of a kind.
The Lord's character is the ultimate truth.
In the arms of Your mercy we find rest.
In the glory of Your love we find hope.

12. Surrender to God's peace
which transcends all understanding.
If we cannot agree in harmony or
If we cannot meet in the middle
let us go our separate ways.
For the Earth is huge and there is room for all.
If you believe in God, then you believe in Peace.
Stay away from trouble.
Don't be a wild tempest in a teapot;
Control anger, jealousy, impatience,
addictions and fanaticisms.
Your life consists of many things
so seek the balance.
Make today the best it can be.

13. Lord, where You lead I will follow.
    I have a hope and longing for the Lord.
    I know that what You've got planned
        for me is more than I can see.
    Your voice is calling out to me.
    I hear your love calling.
    Make our hearts good like Yours.
    Let us be angels by Your side.
    We are part of your divine plan
        called the Universe.
    You know the number of stars in the Universe
        and everyone and everything by name.
    God is the Master Planner of the Universe.
    Share your passion for the Lord with all people.
    God is always one step ahead of you.

14. Guide us to live in harmony
        in this imperfect world.
    We are all struggling.
    Save us from ourselves!
    To be before you, O Lord, is a great honor.
    Help us with the stresses of life.
    Make all our moments calm and bright.
    Carry us through our day's business.
    Our hope is in You all day long.
    Lord, the very thought of thee
        fills us with sweetness.
    All the world reveres the Lord.

15. God looks upon everyone the same.
    God carries us in Holy Arms.
    Every man, woman, and child
        is beautiful to God.
    Every animal and plant
        is beautiful to God.
    Every person is handsome, gifted,
        capable of higher intelligence,
        capable of achieving great things,
        loved & respected,
        worthy of happiness,
        worthy of basic good standards of living,
        worthy of freedom from living in fear.
    Lord, You are the way, the truth, and the life.

God is our Home.

16. When the weight of the world seems to be
upon your shoulders,
When you feel all hope is gone,
When hope turns to disappointment,
When you feel forgotten,
You are not alone.
God has not forgotten your name
So don't give up.
When you cannot face another day
You will find a way. The Lord is with us.
Divine love will renew us.
Our promise is with the Lord.

17. Tell others the good news, how God
makes people right and saves us.
Trust in God's grace to save us.
Our mistakes remind us to do better.
We may need to refocus or get some sleep.
Let our essential energy *qi* be for good purposes.
We beg for forgiveness for our wrongdoings.
You are the strong and mighty.
You are the Creator of Glory.
You are ultimately Unique.
You are the Origin of Love.
With God is the fountain of life.
God's love is like a waterfall.
With God we have hope.
We are nothing without God.
God is the reason we are here.
We give praise and thanks to You.
You bless us with harvest and jubilee.
Your wondrous works declare Your Names.
Blessed be the name of the Lord forever.
This is the day which the Lord has made; let us
rejoice and be glad in it!
You are Our Everlasting God!
Your Great Names Endure Forever!

18. We lift up Your Name
We find Your Glory divine
God is for us and with us
God is a friend to the lost

God is there for the hopeless
We bask in the Glory of Our Creator;
the Parent of the Universe.
Make us good sons and daughters.

19. Practice humanism and help each other.
Food pantries can be shared.
Clothing closets can be shared.
Homes can be built for all so all are sheltered.
Water wells can be built so all have clean water.
Dangerous smog in the air can be reduced.
Recycle plastics, metals, glass, paper, and foam.
Energy and resources can be conserved.
Unite to help each other.
We all want good lives.
Praise God!
Nothing compares to God's embrace.

20. All the Earth is Holy to the Lord.
The Spirit is the center of all religions.
The Divine has no boundaries.
Our Creator is known by many names.
Be like a dove in spiritualism.
Help each other and lift each other up.
Humans can make choices to change things.
Unite and make the world a better place.
What we become is in our command, in our hands.
The God in me beholds the God in you.
We are loved by ones we hold dear.
When our family needs us we will be there.
Let us lift up each other in prayer.
We will provide sacred service to Our Lord!
We are all beautiful. We are all God's people.
Join hands and form a circle for peace.
We are all of one and the same universe.
Believe this with all your heart, mind, and strength.
God is the desire of all ages.

LIFE

Chapter 1

Human Lives

1. No one asked to be born; we are forced into the gift of life. We are born into our lives totally innocent, naked, without the knowledge of how to communicate with others or how to care for ourselves, wrapped in a swaddling blanket and kept warm and cradled with loving arms. Babies are born sinless. In infancy we totally rely on others for our well-being. As time progresses, as our brains and bodies grow, we become more aware of what is happening around us and we learn to interact with our environment and are educated. Humans need the human touch to thrive which is what hugs and handshakes offer. In the stages of human life, babies progress from infancy into children and then into teenagers, young adults, middle-aged adults, older adults and finally senior citizens. There is no fountain of perpetual life to drink from. We come from universal energy and go back to it.

The first five years are especially important to children because it is their formative years, the foundation of their lives. It is not necessary to spank babies and small children if you do not understand why they are crying; hitting them will not solve the problem. Is the child hungry, thirsty, cold or hot, tired, teething, wanting to be held, bored? Some think an infant could be cranky because of a pinched nerve caused by childbirth. It is thought that infants can hear sounds outside of the womb and see images with bold contrasts in the weeks after they are born; infants may enjoy hearing cooing and musical sounds or grasping items safe for infants like rattles and soft plush toys. Babies will grasp your finger with their tiny hand if you let them. If you need help with an infant, ask for help; do not hurt the baby or a small child. Always support an infant's neck. Diaper rash ointment can be applied to a baby's bottom to prevent or soothe diaper rash. Test a few drops from a bottle of warm milk on your own wrist before giving the bottle to a baby to make sure the liquid is not too hot. It is believed that a mother who breast feeds her infant for a few months is giving her child important antibodies. Never shake a baby or anyone.

Young children are eager to learn and must be taught many things. Children may ask many questions over and over again as they learn new things everyday. Children may mimic their parents or adults who are caring for them. Children need a stable, supportive adult to care for them and be a good role models. A safe environment helps children to grow healthy emotionally, socially, physically, mentally, and spiritually to lead productive lives.

It may be helpful to put names on school items so they will not get lost.

Spend quality time with children and teenagers, who need love, guidance, education, nutrition, proper sleep, physical exercise, and encouragement.

If a child is misbehaving, try to find out why the child is misbehaving. The child may need a hug, may not be feeling well, may be hungry, scared, have to use the bathroom, or need a sip of water. The child may need guidance to engage their interest in a book, a toy, a project or task to keep their mind busy. The adult in charge can read a book to the child.

Never shake a baby or a child. Never lock a human or animal in a closet.

When caring for children, adults may remember that others cared for them when they were young.

Enjoy your children because they will only be in the nest for a short time before they go out into the world.

Teenagers are in between the days of innocent childhood and the life realities and responsibility of adulthood. Young people are full of hopes and dreams but may not be aware of consequences of their actions due to their lack of experience. Teenagers may remember the first job they had and what they did with their first paycheck.

Teenagers can make great achievements. If a teen is uncertain what they want to do with their life, joining the military for 2 or 4 years is a great way to serve your country and could lead to a great career path. Armies with diversity may be needed to defend nations with diversity.

The age of adulthood varies in countries in the world to marry, have sex, vote, and hold office. The body quits growing between the ages of 18-24.

Teenagers and adults may feel they have to follow advertising trends, the trends or buzz words of their peers, or believe rumors, but they should make decisions based on their own beliefs and needs.

A buzz word of the 1990s and 2000s is that it is good to be *awesome* or *magnificent*.

There is no need for sibling rivalry or rivalry between neighbors; each person is living their own individual life that the Lord gave them. You and your sibling are two different people. You and your neighbor are two different people. It has been said that the only person you should actually compete with is yourself, to try to improve yourself. God gave us unique lives. Only God could know the purpose of every atom in the universe.

A person's individual self-worth or self-image should not be based strictly on only their birth location, wealth, family, profession, gender; you are your own individual self with other people in your life.

We have different roles in life. A man can be a son, a father, a brother, a friend, and the craft of his profession at the same time. A woman can be a daughter, a mother, a sister, a friend, and the craft of her profession at the same time.

There are many roads for traveling souls, and many count their blessings instead of their years. At some point in life, we all pass on to eternity.

After many years of living, older adults often say 'I wish I knew then what I know now.'
Seniors have experiences of many years. Senior years have been called reflective golden years. Senior citizens may move more slowly due to the physical aging of their body. Loss of hormones cause changes to the body, such as loss of bone mass and increased facial hair. Gray hair may turn to white hair. Even though seniors have snow colored hair, they still have warmth in the furnace of their heart and mind. Senior living communities may offer meal plans, medical assistance, physical activities like ping pong and bus tours, and entertainment like movie nights and prom nights with music and dancing.

Seniors who once cared for the younger often need help in their senior years.

Families should take care of each other through the seasons of our lives from infancy to senior years.

2. Goals can be set and dreams can be achieved. Humans make great achievements at all ages.

Failures are evidence that you tried to do something.

Be a responsible adult and be accountable for your actions. Admit your mistakes and make corrections.

Some people know exactly how they want their life to go and what they want to do. Others have no particular plan in life and just want to experience life as it occurs.

Daily routines or plans for the day can help us to focus on what we need to do to accomplish work and fulfill obligations, to help other human beings, and to include some free time for relaxation and enjoyment in our lives.

Some record details of their lives with diaries, photos, biographies, or momentos.

What kind of person do you want to be in this lifetime?
How would people describe you?
What motivates you?
How do you handle stress?
What type of work would you like to do if you need to work to earn money? Who are some people that you admire and why? Do you procrastinate until the last minute or do you accomplish

what needs to be done on schedule? What are your values, what is important to you and why?

In many countries, people work in an occupation of their choice and they offer professional services and products to other human beings through business commerce and business connections. Some people may choose to change their professions several times in their life, but some will want to spend their entire career doing the same work.

Many people who are employed often keep an updated resume prepared and even go to career networking to meet other professionals to discuss new opportunities or trends.

3. The Lord made each human being unique. There is no one exactly like you, just as no two snowflakes are alike. Every person has a unique handwriting, fingerprints, retinal pattern, core values, and defining moments that give us unique personalities, thoughts, opinions, preferences, and styles.
Everyone is beautiful in their own way. We all have gifts that were given to us by God to make us each uniquely special. Each person may have different needs. We each have a unique life and a unique spirit. Every person should have self-awareness and learn the nature of their own spirit and self-desires. We are all special and not special at the same time; there are many people on the planet.

Personalities can be described as steady and reliable, meek, modest, eager to learn, self-sufficient, too-confident and arrogant, easy-going, crack the whip driver, inpatient, patient, kind, selfish, perfectionist, formal, informal, curious, intrusive, fidgety, vulnerable, obsessive, narcissistic, naive, complainer, condescending to others, accusatory, cranky, helpful, reserved, timid, energetic, empathetic, compassionate, happy, unhappy, blessed, encouraging, nervous and anxious, cold, hot, lost, greedy, frugal, focused, rule-breaker, and more. What kind of household you are raised in (peaceful, volatile, threatening) can shape your personality and beliefs.

4. Each person matters to God.

5. A person is a product of all of life's experiences and all of the people that we have known in our life.

6. You only live once. Enjoy your life and make it the best it can be. A human life is relatively short in the great scheme of time.

7. Try to fit everything you want to do in *the course of a lifetime*; you don't have to do everything at once.

8. For the human species to survive and not go extinct, repopulation is needed; a new baby needs to replace each human that exists or the number

of humans on the earth will dwindle.

Chapter 2

Happiness

1. Happiness is the cause and effect of many circumstances such as a strong marriage, good friends, good health, success, more energy, better self-control, a longer life.
2. Cultivate a happiness in your mind that you can envision. Start a project or a new hobby to keep you busy.
3. Consider all that you see is made by God or human ingenuity.

Appreciate the efforts of humans who are creating good things and doing good things.

4. Humans enjoy favorite hobbies, interests, and vacations to fill times when we are not working in the professions that earn us money. Having interests that delight us and cause us happiness can make our lives more fulfilling.
5. Sports, recreation, and physical exercise should provide enjoyment without causing harm to our bodies.

Chapter 3

Changes & Realities

1. The seasons change and the periods and needs of our lives will change. Life dynamics will give us happiness, excitement, stress, changes, unknowns, and sorrow.

It has been said that it is best to have an open-mind and not have definite expectations about our lives, because changes may occur that we cannot control.

2. You can lose everything in life, but you still have your soul and the spirit of who you are. Sometimes sorrow hurts so bad that life goes on but you do not feel much. Some try to get through life one day at a time.
3. If you want something to change, you have to do something different.

We all have our own comfort zones; sometimes we may have to think out of our comfort zone to do something different.

4. A reality or realities become apparent when facts, clues, logic, instinct, and experience come together to indicate what is actually happening.

Become aware of realities; when you have realizations then you must come to understand the realizations.

Then you can consciously make plans to take control of your life to make the changes or goals you desire.

5. Beliefs may change in the course of a lifetime. Humans laughed when other humans tried to invent airplanes, yet they believed it after airplanes were invented.
6. If we blow each other up with military precision, it could mean chaos or the end of existence for life on Earth.
7. If we do not care about the ecology of the Earth, it could mean the end of existence for all life on Earth.

8. Live within your financial means. Establish a budget and know how you are spending money.
9. It is a reality that no one knows when the end of time will be. Some think God, a messiah (savior), a messenger of God, or an angel will come back to earth at the end of time. Some think when the sun goes out, that it will be the end of time. Some think if the moon drifts away from the earth, the tilt of the earth will be lost and the seasons will be lost which will lead to the end of time. Some think the universe might revert to a Big Crunch or a Big Rip and all existence will be lost as we know it. At the center of the galaxy is a black hole that emanates 511 keV gamma rays; the black hole totally annihilates incoming particles and nothing is left.

Some think unfriendly bacteria that can eat humans will eradicate the human race.
Survival requires cooperation by all humans.

10. Some people believe there is a chance for and a possibility of life elsewhere in the universe besides our solar system, or that it is possible for humans to establish colonies on another planet.
If we inhabit another planet, what foliage and animal life will be brought to the new planet?

Chapter 4
Problems

1. Human problems may be finances, physical addictions, confusion, psychological fanaticisms or obsessions, lack of will power, losses, conflicts in relationships, lack of education, sickness, untimely pregnancy, loneliness, disabilities, enemies, lack of time, too much responsibility, lack of support, anxiety, depression, irrational anger, world problems, and more. Some think there could be spiritual warfare that we cannot see.

The level of problems can be personal, family, work, local community, global world, and universe.

2. You are not alone; there are people and organizations that offer to help with problems.
A friend can listen and offer advice. If you know someone that needs help, try to give help.

Sometimes we all get stuck or in a rut or a pit, but get help and keep moving forward.

Family support, friendship, volunteerism, military support, economic support, and life support are types of support systems.

3. If you can remain calm and keep the faith during tense times of crisis, it is beneficial.

Try to break a problem down into small manageable parts.

During emergencies, a triage center at a hospital establishes the first most critical patients, the second most critical, and then the third.

4. Stress may cause the medulla in our brainstem to produce a hormone called adrenaline. Adrenaline causes increase in heart rate, blood pressure, blood circulation, expands air passages in the lungs, alters metabolism maximizing glucose, and causes a decrease in pain which is why in an emergency people's bodies may do remarkable things.

Chapter 5

Charity

1. If you offer help, be ready, willing and able to provide actual help. Volunteering to help others is commendable and good.
2. If a person asks for help but is denied, a person should accept a refusal.
3. The person who is asking for help should make a commitment to receive the help and initiate changes that will remedy their situation.
4. Reciprocal agreements are agreements to help each other.

Chapter 6

Priorities

1. A person should have good priorities; for example, you should pay your bills first before spending money for things you do not really need at the moment. Some think it is honorable to sit down and eat a meal with friends or family at least once a week. Some make a list of priorities.
2. Sacrifices are things that are voluntarily given up in times of need or when forced to prioritize, such as: unselfish giving or putting other people's needs before our own, when relaxation and sleep are sacrificed for work, when people put aside personal interests to serve their nation, when quality is sacrificed for quantity, time, or money or vice versa. Sometimes words are sacrificed and not spoken for the cause of peace.
3. Time management, resource management and being organized, emotion management, physical health and fitness, financial management, self-awareness and knowing our abilities and goals are valuable tools to help us have better lives and give us a sense of security, peace, and direction for our life. Having a will and instructions for last wishes prepared gives loved ones information on how to handle your estate after your death.

Chapter 7

Perfection

1. If you blame yourself continually for not doing everything perfectly, you are engaging in energy-draining behavior.

You may say to yourself 'I said too much' or 'I didn't say enough' but do not upset yourself because nobody is perfect.

2. Perfection has it place. Some works in engineering and surgeries may require perfection.
3. Do the best with what you have at the moment. If you wait for perfection or perfect conditions, nothing may ever get done. There are times to be satisfied

with *good enough* and be thankful for what you have.

Chapter 8

People

1. The world of human beings around you contains strangers, acquaintances, special loved ones and family, coworkers, employers, and professionals.
2. When you meet a stranger, that stranger becomes an acquaintance. Be aware of how you treat a stranger, for they could be an angel to you or a villain. Conversation with strangers usually involve everyday topics and normal talk like current events and trends, foods, and common business. Do not ask 'How much money is in your bank account?' unless you have a valid reason to ask.
That acquaintance may or may not become a friend.
Friendship is a mutual gift between two people.
When a stranger becomes a friend, then issues are shared that are more personal.
3. To have a friend is a gift from Providence.
Friends are people who treat you good. Friends are not people who influence you in a bad way. Friends keep friends out of trouble. Friends treat you with respect and in a fair manner. Friends will listen to you in good times and bad times and offer good advice; it does not mean that they can offer to give or loan money and resources all of the time because they have their own lives and problems.
Friends can often finish each others' sentences before they are spoken because friends often know what the other friend will say. Comfortable silences can be shared between friends; talking is not always necessary.
There are spaces in togetherness; all people may need to spend some time alone to do things as an individual.
4. Soul mates are people that feel like they were destined to be together, that they made an instant connection when they met, like 2 peas in a pod or like milk and sugar. Soul mates miss each other when separated and wonder how long it will be before they can be together again.
It is interesting to hear stories of how friends met each other.
5. When people share love with a special loved one, they often think that everything will fall into place and life will be perfect; but all relationships may require discussions and compromises because there will be disagreements. Having a marital spouse or a loved one to share life's experiences with and to rely on gives you a special bond and feeling of warmth and security. Holding hands is plenty for dating teenagers.
It is interesting to hear how married couples met. Some felt like it was fate that brought them together. Love, respect, and trust go together in a relationship. Some refer to married couples as

lovebirds, like the small affectionate parrots.

Some relationships will last a lifetime and some will not. When some people divorce or break up from a relationship, they remain friends; in some cases they become enemies or move on and never speak to each other again. Do not hurt people. Do not stalk people. There will be more people to meet and good times in your lives. You can go to the next street and see a whole new world. Many times after a relationship ends, a person can find a new hobby or interest to fill their time.

Love has been described as first love, cuddly love, unreturned or unrequited love, love that goes through difficulties, physical love, false love, platonic or friendship love, true love, universal love, and godly agape love.

6. Employees should do the best job they can for their employers. Employers should give their employees adequate breaks and fair pay. If an employee needs to concentrate on their work, try not to disturb them.

7. The world does not exist for a single person; instead a person is a small part of a big world. The thinking that the world revolves around you as a center point is egocentricity. Everyone is egocentric in that we are all concerned about our lives. *Realize that you are only one of many.*

8. *Narcissism* is when you are too fond of yourself and think your needs and opinions always prevail.

9. Try to speak to others with patience and in a nice tone of voice. There will be disagreements, but talk things out and debate fairly. With everything being said, try to shake hands.

10. We should recommit ourselves to our family, loved ones, and friends, and be thankful for our jobs. Often we take our everyday lives for granted. We should recount our blessings each day. We should make affirmations each day. Be a living angel, a saint, or as solid as a rock to your family and friends. Be good to your employer or employees.

11. The people in your life and the country you live in can influence your thoughts and help determine your faith, actions, and goals.

Chapter 9

Opinions

1. People have different opinions about favorite colors, numbers, music, art, seasons, vacation spots, sports, politics, food, clothing, pets, furniture, easy chairs, spirituality, humors, hobbies, interests, vehicles, occupations and everything else.

Some people like to travel and go places; some people prefer to stay home and not travel. Some people love to go places; some people just love to sit on their porch.

People have different interests like reading, painting, restoring furniture, cars, machinery, clothing, sewing, cooking, cleaning, gardening, quilting, knitting or crocheting or fine needle-point, sports like tennis or golf or billiards or others, education, volunteering, social groups, community groups, politics, science adventures, space exploration, electronics and computers, communication, cards and games, gambling, recycling and green projects that are good for the earth, religious rituals, and more.

Some people devote their entire life to their work professions.

People enjoy different types of music such as classical, opera, jazz, big band, rock band, alternative rock, country, hip-hop, rap, reggae, mainstream pop, rhythm and blues, blues, fado, folk, acoustic, unplugged, ballads, polka, waltz, mariachi, children's music, movie themes, instrumental, religious hymns, religious pop, religious rock, natural earth sounds, national and school anthems, singers at an assisted living community.

Compositions of music reflect harmony of musical instruments and may include voice accompaniment.

Music can be cultural, such as Western, Middle-Eastern, Oriental, Hispanic, African, Celtic, and more; some music is blended.

The music in the electromagnetic spectrum is a harmonic connection between everything in the universe, even the stars. It is in the laws of physics.

People have favorite instruments or combinations of instruments such as harpsichord, keyboard, piano, organ, drums, tambourine, guitar, violin, viola, fiddle, dulcimer, mandolin, banjo, harp, cello, saxophone, trumpet, recorder, clarinet, flute, piccolo, trombone, oboe, bassoons, tuba, bells, accordian, balalaika, harmonica, temur komuz (lute), morsing (mukharshanku), Jew's harp, Chinese 21-string guzheng, Chinese 7-string guqin, Australian didgeridoo.

Visual arts can be landscapes, portraits, still lifes, abstracts, photos, computer graphics, statues, figurines, and more.

2. We can listen and learn from each other; it may change our opinions or not.

Some people form opinions about others in one moment and it is unfair to analyze a person in one moment's time.

Extreme Thoughts

The following statements are examples of extreme subjective (personal) opinions that a person might think in one moment of time:

'This person is a bad person because they do not have my religious viewpoint.'

'I don't like them because they are too different from me.'

'They are evil. They raised their voice.'

'They are on a highway to hell. Listen to what they said.'

'This person is a moron who cannot do anything right.'

'I don't understand how anyone could like this person.'

'They don't care about anything.'

'I'm never going to talk to this person ever again.'

'This person is stupid because they do not have any money.'

'You are young and do not know anything.'

'You are old and do not know anything.'

'You only expect perfection from others.'

'That person is weird because they will not try orange juice with pulp and it is my favorite so I must be right and they must be wrong.'

'My family and friends are better than theirs.'

'You never finish a project that you have started.'

'I only like them when they are sleeping.'

'All you want to do is go fishing and tell of the legends of the waters.'

'You are in your own little world and that's okay. But you need to be more aware of the bigger picture and know what's going on in the real world.'

'You love your guitar more than you love me.'

'You never have time for me.'

'You are emotionally unavailable to me and will never listen to me.'

'They are like a bull in a porcelain shop, a real klutz.'

'You are acting childish.'

'They always try to break the rules.'

'They have a perfect life.'

'They are always complaining. They are not grateful for anything.'

'They strut their feathers like a peacock.'

'They always give me weird looks.'

The reality should be: to not form opinions of a person for what they are doing in one moment of time, because you do not know everything that person has lived through, is going through and the thoughts of their mind, their health issues, their dreams, their potential, spirituality, or God's plan for that person.
Objective opinions are when you base an opinion on facts and not strictly on your own personal feelings and preferences.

Learn how to have calm and honest discussions with others in order to improve relationships.

If you see something in a person that you think needs help, ask the person if you could have a discussion with them, and you might want to reassess your own thoughts, habits and goals also.

Encourage each other. Give someone a compliment.

You do not have to be friends with everyone but you can at least respect their individual life.

Most everyone on the planet wants the same things; we all want friends, family, love, food & water, shelter, opportunities for work and fun, and peace; most of us want good lives.

Snacks & Goodies

For snacks, some prefer fresh fruits like apples, pears, oranges, tangerines, bananas, blueberries, cherries, strawberries, peaches, pineapple, green grapes, red grapes, raspberries, quinces, pomegranates, watermelon, cantaloupe, mango, papaya, persimmons and more.

Some like fresh salads and vegetable snacks like lettuce, celery, carrots, parsnips, tomatoes, cucumbers, avocados, radishes, olives, broccoli, cauliflower, green bean, onions, squash and red, yellow, orange, and green pepper slices to go along with croutons and lemon, orange, balsamic, cranberry, or raspberry vinaigrette, ranch, French, Thousand Island, chipotle, jalapeno, curry, honey mustard, honey Dijon, bleu cheese, mayonnaise, and other dressings.

Others prefer potato chips, corn chips, corn curls, corn balls, popcorn, pretzels, all types of fancy crackers, sunflower seeds, raisins, yogurt, ice cream, cheese wedges, pickles, cottage cheese, sausages, meat slices, peanut butter, pizza rolls, tuna salad, egg salad, pickled herring, quiche, sandwiches, omelets, soup, pastries, cakes, jello, pudding, cold macaroni salad, cold potato salad, cole slaw, carrot salad, cookies and biscotti, Chinese fortune cookies, Girl Scout cookies. Some like drink beverages for snacks.

People like different numbers of chocolate chips in their cookies. Some people want 12-15 chocolate chips in each cookie, some people want 6-8, and some people want only 1-3. You can add almond flavor to the cookies instead of vanilla for a new taste. And, some people do not like chocolate chip cookies at all.

Some like square ice cubes, some like circular ice cubes, some like crushed ice, and some do not like ice cubes at all.

Some people have food allergies or diet restrictions to certain foods.

An essential balance of water, nutrients, proteins, fats, and sugars is needed for good health.

The foods that are eaten in different cultures around the world are becoming more familiar in all parts of the world as the world is becoming a more interconnected society, woven like a beautiful quilt.

People have opinions about favorite interior designs.

A study was done and it was determined that some people

have preferences, passions, or spiritual feelings about geometric shapes such triangles, circles, squares, or other forms or patterns that are filled with various colors, shapes, or patterns.

People can be monochromatic at times and polychromatic at other times. The colors of visible light in the electromagnetic spectrum of the rainbow prism are red, orange, yellow, green, blue and violet.

It has been said that the prism is a symbol for the way God works differently in all of our lives.

People have favorite colors and color combinations.

Aqua and turquoise are greenish-blue colors, also the name of minerals.

Chartreuse is yellow-green.

Fuschia is a bluish-pink.

Violet is a reddish-blue color, like the flower.

Amber is a reddish-yellowish-brown color, also the name of a mineral. Ocher is also an earthly yellow-orange-red. Raisin is purple-brown.

Coral is an orange pink, like some of the sea coral.

Periwinkle is a light blue-violet color, also the name of a flower. Indigo is a deep violet blue or a dark grayish blue. Mauve is a pale purple.

Safflower is orange-reddish color, also the name of a flower.

Saffron is yellow-brownish color with a hint of orange, also the name of a spice.

Salmon is a yellowish-pink, also the name of a fish.

Rose is a pinkish red, also the name of a flower.

Buttercup is a creamy yellow, like the flower.

Ginger is an orangey-brown, also the name of a spice plant.

Charcoal is a textured dark gray-black color, also the name of a mineral.

Slate is a dark smooth gray-black color, named after the mineral.

Mint green is a whitish light green with pale blue and pale pink highlights, and also the name of the herb that has a light sparkly taste that is used in candy, mint gum, toothpaste, and food dishes.

Olive green is a yellow-green with a hint of brown color, also the name of the oval fruit of the olive tree.

Forest green is a dark green color, named after forests.

Have you ever noticed how many shades of green exist in nature?

Standard green is a color like the green grasses.

Standard orange is color that is like the orange of
the round orange fruit of the orange tree.

Tangerine is a pinkish-reddish orange named after the smaller mandarin oranges which are not rounded like oranges but more flattened on top.

Lemon is the yellow color like that of the oval fruit of the lemon tree.

Standard blue is usually based on the reflection of blue that humans see from the skies and waters.

Sienna brown is a brown with an orange tint.

Ecru is a grey-yellow beige.

People pick color combinations for flags, clothing, blankets, quilts, and decorating, such as:

Red and Yellow,

White and Blue and Gold,

Purple, Red, and Blue,

Black and Yellow,

Orange and White,

Brown, Purple, Orange, and White,

Green and Pink,

Beige, Brown, Red, Mustard, Blue,

Silver and Black,

and there are lots of more combinations of colors together.

Colors can be bright, pastels, muted, neons, and reflective.

Unless you want to mix colors, do not put a yellow paintbrush into a blue paint pot or the paint will turn green. Do not put a red paintbrush into a blue paint pot or the paint will turn purple.

There are 143,000 registered colors, but 34,000 are used, an amazing fact.

Light can change the way a color looks.

Many people will have the same favorite colors their whole life, but many will change their favorite colors or color combinations.

Some people cannot see certain colors because of retinal differences of the eye.

Yellow tulips contain molecules with waves that are anti-bonding (hostile), but purple tulips contain molecules with waves that are nonbonding (indifferent).

Some people have passions or spiritual feelings about geography – some love the mountains and the valleys, some love just the mountains or just the valleys, some love the outer banks, the shores, some love the plains.

The human mind can be very complex and it has been said that no two people think exactly alike. It can be a fascinating to discuss with another person why they are thinking what they are thinking and why you are thinking what you are thinking. Sometimes a person's logic and reasoning can be stored somewhere in their consciousness or unconsciousness for reasons known or unknown, and the person cannot explain to you why they are feeling what they are feeling or doing what they are doing.

You can't please all of the people all of the time.

3. Personality assessments and first impressions are just opinions. Some people make good first impressions but others may have nervous anxieties or some reason why they did not make a good first impression.

4. Handwriting analysis and jury decisions are opinions.

Chapter 10

Choices and Decisions

1. Life is different for everyone and everyone has both easy and difficult choices to make. If everyone had all of the resources they needed, decisions might be easier. *Analysis* means to consider all possibilities of actions and outcomes.

2. There are times to put others first, and there are times to put yourself first.

3. Choose good ways and avoid trouble. Choose to be in control of mind, body, and spirit. Control your mouth, what you say and what you eat.

4. You can choose what you think about and the words you speak. Once you speak words, they cannot be taken back. If you give an evil eye or hateful look, they cannot be taken back.

5. Our actions can make things better or worse, so we should not be careless in our actions.

6. Sometimes you may have to make a decision very quickly. Sometimes you may be able to go to sleep and get a good rest before making a decision. Some think you should postpone making major decisions if you are in the middle of a personal crisis.

Chapter 11

Ethics

1. It is not right to take advantage of people or businesses.

Do not take advantage of anyone lacking in knowledge about a situation.

Do not take advantage of a person who is drunk.

Do not take advantage of someone's well-being because you have more resources and have clout with powerful people to destroy other people's good lives.

Customers should not try to cheat businesses by returning items with the wrong receipts or stealing items. Wear underwear when trying on bathing suits and clothing.

Customers should not take items from hotel rooms like towels and pillows.

Doctors should not order tests or perform procedures that are unnecessary, just to make money. Doctors should keep patient information confidential.

Genetic scientists should not change human genes or genes of a developing embryo inside a womb without permission.

A doctor should not steal a woman's egg.

Lawyers who charge by the hour should not postpone work just to bill another hour.

Police officers should not plant evidence at crime scenes or steal goods from crime scenes.

People should not try to sneak in behind someone to enter into a building or past a gate.

Bus or cab drivers should not disclose information about passengers to other passengers when offered bribes.

Car mechanics should not tamper with car parts other than what it specified in the contract agreement that is to be fixed.

Fisherman should use turtle excluder devices in their shrimping nets so turtles will not get caught and drown.

Most people think animal fighting contests are wrong because it is cruel to the animals.

It is wrong to trick a person to a bad consequence.

It is wrong to serve someone bad food or water.

Do not let a person keep drinking alcohol if they are drunk. Call them a cab or find their designated driver.

Do not use someone's toothbrush without their knowledge.

Do not go through someone's belongings while they are sleeping.

Do not violate a person's privacy by reading their private personal diary or going through their hope chest or treasure chest.

Do not spit on a human being.

2. Nobody should lie.

Patients should not lie to medical professionals who are trying to help them.

Clients should not lie to lawyers who are trying to help them.

Victims of injustice should not lie to law enforcement who are trying to help them.

Criminals should tell the truth if they are arrested or things could get worse.

Don't lie to yourself but be truthful to yourself.

Saying 'I will just charge this item and pay it off in 2 months' is a lie if it will not fit into your budget.

Do not say 'I can easily climb to the top of Mount Everest' because it is not easy.

3. Nobody should vandalize another's property.

Do not damage public property with graffiti or chewing gum.

Do not throw trash onto streets; put it in trash bins.

Do not scrape the whipped topping or icing from an entire cake so that the next person cannot enjoy it.

4. Idle gossip about others should not be shared; rumors could start.

5. It is wrong to intimidate, bully, torment or harass a person by saying mean things to them, or call them crazy if they are not bothering you.

6. Customers should not bring filth or trash into any public venue, taxi, or public transportation system.

Visitors should not bring open drinks or foods into public venues that prohibit it.

Construction workers or anyone with mud on their shoes should try to scrap the mud off before entering businesses, restaurants, public libraries, museums, or religious institutions.

Customers should wash hands before eating in restaurants.

Ideally, if you touch your eyes, nose, mouth, ears, hair, skin, or a skin lesion, dirty items like car keys or cell phones, you should wash your hands or use hand sanitizer to avoid passing germs to anyone else, especially when touching things that a lot of people touch, like door handles or utensils at food buffets.

In public, try to cover your mouth with your hand or a napkin when coughing to avoid passing germs to others.

Do not pee on a public toilet seat so the next person will not have to sit on your pee. Put paper down on the seat before you sit down on it.

Discard trash in proper receptables.

Visitors should wash hands and wear clean clothing if possible when visiting a hospital.

7. Medical professionals in hospitals should wash hands before tasks and surgeries. Make sure the correct body part is operated on. Never perform medical procedures while under the influence of alcohol or drugs.

8. Restaurant professionals should follow food safety practices and wash hands often. Cooks, food servers, baristas, and bartenders should not cough or sneeze over the foods and drinks they are preparing; they should never dip glasses into ice bins to fill the glass with ice because glass or plastic fragments could break off into the ice.

9. People should not go tramping through flower beds that a gardener or landscaper worked hard to plant and that someone provided money for.

10. Employees should try to do good, honest work for their employers. Employers should treat their workers fairly by giving them rest breaks and fair pay.

Do not disturb a coworker who is doing important work.

11. Computer hackers should not hack. Some think ethical hacking is justified.

If computer hackers continue to hack into the wireless components of car engines, medical implants, laptops, and security cameras and systems, it may be necessary to revert to car engines, medical implants, and cell phones with no computer, internet, or radio technology parts.

Computer hackers can run cars off the road, cause misfunctions in medical implants to kill people, change the time in your clock radio, and steal creative ideas and personal information from personal laptops and cellphones.

Jammers are devices that block cell signals for a fifty-yard radius, rendering cell phones or garage doors useless. When someone has you on their radar, they are following you.

Computer hackers can also change and plant false information on any computer devices. Messages of terrorists were found hidden in pixels of pictures that they were sharing.

If you don't want to be tracked with GPS or overheard, don't carry your cell phone with you or take out the battery.

GPS chips are tiny and can be put in things like business cards, clothing, or handbags.

People can place hidden cameras in housing without the knowledge of the resident, and most people do not want total strangers watching their personal living habits. If you want to see if there are hidden cameras or listening devices in your house, RF detectors may help locate them.

Hidden cameras can be placed by the resident to allow visual security to see predators like burglars.

If the spies that are spying on us are righteous, there is nothing to worry; however, evil spies have been known to set innocent people up in crimes that they did not commit because it is easy to plant DNA evidence at crime sites, plant illegal drugs in a person's car or home, plant fingerprints, wear plastic face masks that look like another person, manipulate electronic data in phones, appliances, and computers. Photos and videos can be altered. Even security cameras videos can be altered.

Some think the internet should be optional, but manufacturers seem to be forcing everyone onto the internet.

There are pros and cons to the internet.

If everyone is forced onto the internet, it may be necessary for the public to know who is spying on them and if they do not like the company spying on them, they could move to another city or switch surveillance companies. With the current internet technology, people could start disappearing from their homes, people could be easily manipulated and robbed by spies.

A good thing about the internet is that less paper is being used for mail so trees are saved. But more cardboard is being used for shipping.

12. Shred important documents before putting into the trash or recycle bin.

13. Some controversial topics are genetic engineering, birth-control, abortion, selling human body parts, cosmetic surgery, sexual orientation, the internet, spying, pulling weeds, killing animals that are on the extinct list, eating meat, wanting what your neighbor has, declaring war, promoting sex as glamorous, and more. Consider all options before abortion. The sex of a fetus is determined when the egg cell and

sperm cell are joined but the sex organs develop in a fetus around 18-20 weeks. The heartbeat can be detected approximately in 8-12 weeks. Women who are raped may consider an abortion because they were a victim of violence. Protestors of abortions can offer a pregnant woman options such as housing, food, money to raise the child, a good job, medical care, adoptive parents with visitation rights and more. Many believe it is unethical for scientists to study the growth of human embryos and then destroy the embryos; has science gone too far?

14. Some think it is wrong to withhold the identity of biological parents if the child wants the information.

15. If you find something, try to return it to its owner.

16. If you borrow something, return it to its owner.

17. Some think it is impolite to look into another person's shopping cart to see what they are buying, or to look into the windows of another person's car or house. Many think it is impolite to stare at someone.

18. Some do not like it if you show up at their home or a function uninvited. If you are a guest in someone's home, do not wander through their house or go through their personal belongings without their permission.

19. Don't spend more than an hour a day before a mirror and getting dressed. Women do not have to wear makeup every day just because it was a custom started centuries ago.

20. Don't stress over photographs being perfect. God doesn't need a photo of anyone or anything.

21. Malingerers are people who fake or shirk an illness to avoid work or responsibility.

22. Translators should translate accurately.

23. Do not take someone's sunshine away. If someone is happy, lucky, or prosperous, do not interfere. Do not ruin someone's life or prosperity.

24. Torture to animals or humans is wrong.

25. Some think it is wrong to take another's picture if they do not know they are being photographed. In some countries, it is against the law for visitors to take any photographs.

26. If you see a piece of broken glass or a small object on the ground that could be harmful to a child, put it in a trash can out of harm's way.

27. Some are bothered by others who are very coercive or forceful, such as making a person jump off cliffs into waters, eating foods they don't want to eat, riding rides at theme parks that they don't want to ride, watching movies that they don't want to see, or taking drugs or alcohol. If a person is being forceful to you and you don't want to do something, just say NO.

28. Do not be impatient with someone who cannot find

something in their wallet or purse; give them a moment to find it.

29. If you live in a household with hot water and have to take a warm shower, leave some hot water for the next person.

30. Do not tamper with solar panels that supply energy for public use.

31. Turn down loud music in cars and at road intersections so drivers can hear the sirens of emergency vehicles or bad weather sirens.

32. Follow noise ordinances in apartment complexes.

33. Pilots of airplanes, helicopters (choppers), and boats should follow noise ordinances in airports and along rivers.

34. Some people consider other people guilty without even considering their innocence first.

35. It has been said that sometimes people don't remember the good things a person did; they only remember what the person didn't do or the mistakes the person made.

36. Some people will never trust a person again if their trust has been broken once; others will give another a second chance and rekindle a relationship.

37. If you are sitting next to someone on public transportation, do not bother them if they want to relax and not talk.

38. If you touch your eyes, nose, mouth, or ears, try to wash your hands or use hand sanitizer to avoid passing on germs to anyone else, especially when touching things that a lot of people touch, like door handles or utensils at food buffets.

39. If you have to cough, cover your mouth with your hand or with a napkin, then wash your hands.

40. It is good to try to substantiate all facts and truths of a matter.

Chapter 12

Pets

1. Pets are special companions for humans. A pet is special because pets have heard you sing and have never once laughed. All your loyal pet cares about is that you take care of them and love them. A pet can be a soul mate. It has been said that pets can have proud looks on their faces when out in public with their masters. Some consider pets to be family members. Some blind, or deaf persons or persons with other ailments have service dogs that have been specially trained to assist them.

2. In times of stress, you can think about your pet and it might help to calm you. You could think about your cat making endless figure-eight loops around your ankles or about your dog looking at you with smiling eyes and a wagging tail that moves back and forth like a windshield wiper or makes thumps on the floor. Many dogs bark at fax machines, landscapers using leaf blowers or chain saws, roofers putting on roof tiles or nailing on roof

shingles, ice makers, the sound of the rain on the roof, and can alert you to danger. Dogs, cats, and birds can be attentive listeners and nod their heads at you. Most dogs like to ride in cars and trucks, but cats do not like it. Dogs will put their head out of the window and bark at other cars. Some dogs do not like other dogs. Some cats do not like other cats. Some dogs and cats that grow up together in the same house will be peaceful to each other.

Many enjoy horses, camels, fish, ferrets, hamsters, reptiles, chimps, dragons.

Thinking about dolphins jumping in the oceans is a pleasure, a nice thing to think about.

3. Never release pets into the wild if you cannot care for them; call animal rescue.
4. Care for pets may include grooming, keeping food supplies, Dogs usually need baths. keeping travel papers and veterinarian visits up to date, excercising and playing with your pet. Neutering your pet prevents unplanned pregnancies.
5. Dogs have been trained to assist humans, such as companion dogs for the disabled, and bomb and drug- sniffing dogs for the police.
6. Do not leave children alone with pets, who may harm a small child.
7. Parents with children who are having pajama parties where other children spend the night should check with other parents to make sure their children are not afraid of pets.
8. When walking a dog or riding a horse, hold firmly onto the leash or the reins; the animal could suddenly bolt forward and the leash or reins could get tangled on your hands and throw you to the ground.
9. Virtual and robotic pets have been invented.
10. Pippa was a dog in Australia that would wait for the post master each day and would carry the mail to his master in his mouth. One day there was no mail to be delivered, but Pippa did not understand and would not stop barking at the postman. The next time there was no mail, the postman put a plain piece of paper in Pippa's mouth to satisfy the dog who happily wagged his tail each time.
11. Never give alcohol or bad food to a pet. If food smells bad, throw it away.

Chapter 13

Energy

1. Always do your best in life. You will have less to worry about and less regret if you put forth good effort and do the right things.
2. Use your personal energy to improve your mind and your body. Fill your brain with good information; throw out all evil, jealous, and foolish thoughts from your brain. Restrain from physical violence. Let your head rule the emotions and passions of your heart for good things. Use

your physical and mental energy to live a good life and do good things.
3. Feng shui is the energy balance of our surroundings. Sometimes things may not seem in balance; we may be left mystified and confused and cannot find answers other than our instincts telling us that something is wrong or right.
4. God gave us instincts to follow as part of our innate nature that will give us a sense of safety or harm. We must also use good common sense and logical reasoning and think with our minds as well as with our hearts.
5. Everyone has individual gifts that God gave them.
6. Time and the energy of the moment can be used wisely.
7. Like the wind, love is powerful energy that you can feel around you and within you always. Consider the power of love that is contained in a smile or given through a loving touch or loving deed.
Love each other like there's no tomorrow.
8. Acknowledge the sun, for without the sun, there would be no organic life on our planet. Only the Lord knows how long the sun will shine or how long the earth will keep spinning. Thank the stars!
9. Acknowledge the earth's water, minerals, vegetation, life forms, atmosphere, and tilt of the moon that sustain all life and matter.
10. Scientists study ways to harnass and use energy sources such as the winds, waters, sun, biofuels, fossil fuels, geothermal energy beneath the earth, nuclear energy, fussion energy, hydrogen energy.
Strip mining excavates mountaintops or earth while traditional mining involves humans going into the earth. Scientists think that some pyramids could have been formed from excavation of a mountain instead of being built up from the ground.

Chapter 14
Globalism

1. There is a global energy between all people to unite together and achieve great things upon the planet. Join minds and hearts to make improvements on the planet so life can be good for all.
2. *Survival requires cooperation by all*; asteroids could hit the earth so they must be destroyed; flesh-eating bacteria and flesh-eating amoebae must be eradicated. Flavivirus or yellow fever and West Nile virus caused by mosquitos have caused epidemics in some areas of the globe. HIV is pandemic which means it has spread globally.
Good governments may give aid to the needy, but people should learn to be ready for catastrophies by learning survival skills and having emergency supplies on hand such as water, food, candles and matches, blankets, generators, and sterno because there are so

many people that the governments cannot help everyone all of the time. Some governments claim their purpose is only to secure the borders and safety of their country.

The citizens of small communities and the citizens of the global world can work together to be well-connected for most aspects and needs of life such as food, medical attention, education, clothing, transportation, entertainment and recreation, charitable sharing, etc.

3. Universal traffic signals are: Green means GO. Red means STOP.

4. The International Date Line which designates a new revolution of the earth and thus a new day is 180 ^{0} longitude but deviates to go around some territories and island groups in the Pacific Ocean.

International time zone standards are being used by the whole world which make traveling and communicating much easier than in the past.

A travel journey can be as short as next door or as long as 14 or 20 hours by airplane, bus, car, train, or ship. Journeys can be made by walking, bicycle, horse and buggy, horse and covered wagon, camel caravan.

Travelers should check currency exchange rates before leaving to go on a trip. Keep passports in a safe place so they cannot be lost or stolen.

5. On the planet, people are doing many things – some are leaders, some are followers. There are givers, takers, producers, critics, and more. Some people try to make things better while some people are making things worse. Some people are encouraging while others are destructive.

6. If you were the Creator, wouldn't you want the best for everyone?

Chapter 15

Work and Progress

1. Appreciate the progress that humans have made in the world such as explorations to new lands which helped to populate the earth, and inventions that humans created to make lives better and work easier; many believe such progress was divinely inspired. When you thank the Lord for the material things in your life, you are also thanking other human beings for their hard work and generosity. Most everything around you is the effort and energy of many human beings. We should not take each other or our hard work for granted and forget the great things that humans have achieved individually and in teamwork. We should not be inappropriately cynical or critical about good things that other humans are trying to accomplish.

2. A cup of clean water is not just a cup of clean water; many humans and the efforts of their hard work resulted in your being able to use clean water for drinking, cooking, bathing, and swimming.

A cup of coffee, tea, juice or warm broth is not just a cup of coffee, tea, juice or warm broth. Humans got up from their sleep and put forth energy to work and produce coffee, tea, juice, cups, foods, clothing, soaps, and other items for human consumption.

Sipping hot coffee and hot tea from mugs begins with coffee and tea that may have journeyed over a span of several continents.

The earliest people had to invent elevator-like buckets that were lowered into wells by cables to bring up the water, which may or may not have been safe to drink.

3. There was a time when the earliest humans lived in caves or even treehouses. The early humans learned to rub sticks together to build fires; they invented the wheel, the spinning wheel and the loom to weave sheep's hair into woolen garments, and the dock at the edge of waters for easier access to boats. People had to make their own clothes and they spent a lot of time finding food supplies. Humans used the bathroom in a hole in the ground or in an old pot until toilets were invented around 1596 and modern plumbing in 1890.

4. Later homes were built with sticks or logs from trees with mud or twine to hold them together; thatched reeds served as roofs. Mats covered dirt floors and linens woven from cotton served as curtains and doors.

Nails were invented to hold hewn wood strips together.

Hinges enabled doors to be connected to a doorframe

by nails. Stairs were invented.

5. There was a time when all roads were dirt paths, then brick roads were laid, then paved concrete roads and black-top roads were invented. The autobahn road system (interstate) was invented in Germany circa 1920 CE. Some roads, bridges, and big holes in the world are dangerous.

6. Oil lamps and candles lit dwellings for thousands of years until electricity was harnassed around 1800CE.

7. Windmills were created to harnass winds to create energy to pump water up from water wells.

8. Waterwheels were created to harnass the waterfalls of rivers to create energy that was used to grind wheat or corn into flour.

9. Then humans harnassed electricity which led to the inventions of light bulbs, telephones, ovens, factories, televisions, radios, computers, heaters and air conditioners. Pleated paper fans kept people cool before air conditioners.

10. Gears were invented that controlled energy and speed.

11. Pockets were added to robes.

12. There was a time when there was much sickness and humans and animals died easily from bacterial infections and viruses, and many women died in childbirth, then new medical and scientific knowledge was learned and people are now living longer and healthier lives.

13. It is believed that 30,000 years ago unleavened bread cakes were made from flour pounded with rocks from grains and baked over fires; then leavenings like yeast or fermented grape juice were added.

14. Packaged sliced breads were invented in the early 1900's CE.

15. Paperweights were often made from glass; they held down stacks of paper before staples, binding, clips, and tape were invented.

16. The first saws were carved from metal and were hand-held saws. Later on, power chain-saws that run on petrol and oil and table saws that run on electricity were invented.

Chapter 16
Sleep

1. Proper sleep is important to one's well-being and the well-being of a person's family and employer.

If you are not getting proper sleep, remind yourself to monitor your emotions and actions. If you get frustrated because you are fatigued, tell yourself that you will feel better after you get some rest. After a nap you can feel like a new person. In Spain and Mexico it is customary to take an afternoon nap called a siesta.

If you are sleeping too much, you may not accomplish everything that needs to be done.

2. Each person's sleep pattern may be different. Many adults sleep about 8 hours after being awake for 16 hours. Infants and children need more sleep.

3. Sleep researchers have actually lived in caves for months at a time trying to study sleep patterns called circadian rhythms. Melatonin is the chemical involved in sleep cycles. REM is rapid eye movement.

When your eyes are exposed to the light of the sun or electrical devices such as TVs which contain blue lightwaves, the brain does not produce melatonin which helps sleep occur.

Campfires, lanterns, and candles do not have blue lightwaves.

4. Fatigue can result in impulses such as overeating, verbal outbursts, physical outbursts, despair, agitation, and crying.

Fatigue can cause one to make mistakes, be grumpy, be confused, have memory problems, say things they don't really mean or do things they didn't intend to do. When a person is fatigued their mind may be fuzzy and they are not thinking clearly.

5. Sleep problems may be caused by: eating before sleeping, wearing tight clothing, sleeping too close to cell phones or radios, drinking too much liquid before sleeping, too much brain stimulation before sleeping, being too overtired before sleeping or staying up too late, medications, not exposing your brain to daylight upon awakening, work schedules, being too cold or too hot when sleeping, being awakened by spouses, children, pets, loud neighbors, or alarms, a mattress that is not comfortable to your likeness, and sleep-walking.

6. Lack of sleep can cause serious problems. Do not drive vehicles, boats, helicopters or airplanes, or operate machinery when very fatigued. Sleep deprivation is believed to cause dreaming while being awake which may cause psychotic episodes.

7. If you are a caregiver to infants or children, or adults and you are fatigued, ask for someone to help you so you can get some rest to catch up on your sleep.

8. If you are college student who has a busy schedule and has been studying way into the night, you need to set time aside to sleep.

9. If you travel a lot between time zones, your sleep schedule may get crazy.

10. Each person has their favorite way to wake up from sleep. Some wake up by an alarm, some want someone to gently nudge them on their shoulder and whisper their name. Some children could be awakened by tickling their cheek with their favorite stuffed animal.

11. To make sure you wake up on time, if you rest while traveling on public transportation, set your alarm on your watch or cell phone so you will not fall asleep and miss your stop or your next flight.

12. Hotels offer telephone wake-up calls.

13. You could ask several friends to call you and wake you up so you do not miss an important event.
14. It is very dangerous to fall asleep in public places because it makes you vulnerable to thieves, predators, and kidnappers.
15. Sometimes it is a relief to find out that a dream was only a dream and not true.

Chapter 17

Acceptable Behavior

1. Virtues are highly esteemed good qualities found in people such as peacefulness, honesty, patience, wisdom, chastity, perseverance, love, charity, respect, empathy, compassion, tact, self-awareness, good self-conduct, keeping promises, apologizing when due, thoughtful speech.

In ancient cultures, birth order was a virtue, as the first-born was awarded important inheritance such as family title and wealth.

2. Peacefulness is not showing violent conduct, not trying to manipulate others, hurt them, or make them angry.

Taking walks, looking at the sky and clouds, listening to the sounds of birds, owls, crickets, cicadas, rain, thunder, the rolling surf of the ocean, human voices, the laughter of children, smelling aromas of foods or earth oils, enjoying meals, reading books, creating art or music, and working can be peaceful activites.

Art can evoke a sense of mystery to give you something to think about. Art, music, cooking, and working can take you to another world.

If someone asks you to please be quiet so they can enjoy a concert or a movie, do not annoy them. A peaceful heart finds joy in life's simple pleasures.

Conflicts

When anger is justified, try to find help or compromise for a solution; do not hurt anyone or destroy things that will cause more trouble and loss. Some think that angry people are lacking comfort in their life for something they want.

Do not say things that you do not mean; think before you speak. How you talk to another person is important; speak to others respectfully.

Apologize to another when due because the lack of an apology truly hurts the deserving one who incurred an injustice.

It has been thought by some mental health professionals that some people may enjoy hurting or provoking other people or being mad or violent, but most people do not enjoy feeling that way.

Some people believe in giving a child a timeout in an area by themselves for a few minutes if the child is behaving badly or stressed out. This is true for adults also; take a few minutes to calm down if you need to.

Do not force food on children if they do not like the taste of a particular food. Taste buds are acquired over a lifetime.

Thank God for taste buds, sounds, sights, feelings, people, and the seasons.

3. Honesty is to conduct affairs in truthfulness and sincerity, honorable in principles, intentions, and actions. It has been said that a person of integrity does the right things even when they know that no one is watching them.

The real and actual truth *is* the truth, the whole truth and nothing but the truth. Some put their hand over their heart or swear on a holy book that they will speak truths.

A partial truth is a slight lie.

A complete lie is the absence of any truth.

Everybody makes mistakes.

Some think that *fibbing or joking* is not telling the truth for a good reason that is not harmful. Be careful with humor, for some might be offended with hurt feelings and an awkward situation might result.

If you cheat while playing a card game, it is said that you played a dirty hand.

A frenemy is a person that you are not sure whether they are your friend or your enemy.

Many think that Our Maker would like for us to love and trust each other and work for each other's benefit.

When someone is found out to be a liar, consider all facts. Sometimes people will give the liar a second chance to come clean and change their ways.

3 Way Clean

Humans should be clean physically, emotionally, and spiritually to be a bonafide believer in the Lord.

4. Patience is being slow to anger, persevering, diligent, having tolerance to annoyances, delays, and provocation, to control your emotions when you are annoyed at another.

5. Wisdom is to have knowledge and to know how to use knowledge, to use knowledge to apply judgment as to action, to have sagacity, discernment, and insight. Wisdom is a deep understanding and realization of people, things, events, or situations, resulting in the ability to apply perceptions, judgments, and actions in keeping with this understanding. It often requires control of one's emotional reactions and passions so that universal principles, reason, and knowledge prevail to determine one's actions.

There can be wisdom in paradoxes which are things that seem contradictory but may contain truths; such as 'It is admirable to have pride and to not have pride.' 'A poor man of great wealth' is a paradox because it seems contradictory at first but if you realize that the meaning of wealth is spiritual wealth, the paradox disappears.

To carefully consider your actions is wise. Impulsive behavior when you act on a whim may lead to bad consequences.

6. Chastity is to be moderate.

7. Perseverance is to never give up, to maintain a purpose in spite of difficult obstacles, or discouragement, to continue steadfastly, to bolder, to sustain, to uphold.
It is a reality that sometimes a plan, hope, or dream will have to be abandoned, that success was not reached and that it is time to move on. When do you give up?
8. Love is to give benevolent affection and friendliness to others, the divine love Our Creator has for all of creation, the reverent love for the Lord from all people. Love is tenderness, fondness, warmth, passion, adoration, and charity for others. Being joyful expresses the love of your spirit. Love is the answer.

Where love is, there God is.

Love is service and giving to others.

The power of love is so strong that it cannot be understood.

A smile is a curve that sets everything straight.

Love should be given unconditionally, expecting nothing in return.
Love is profound, and of all the things love teaches, love always teaches the heart.

Scientists have noticed changes in the structure of water molecules when the water was subjected to positive energy.

Caregiving can be part-time or 24 hours and include daily hygiene, bathing and toilet, meal planning and preparation, housekeeping, shopping and errands, companionship, medication and appointment reminders, mobility assistance, and more.
9. Charity is the generous work or actions for others to aid the poor, ill, helpless, or needy. Charity can be leniency in judging others, or forbearance. Practicing goodness and kindness to others.
10. Respect is to give homage or reverence to acknowledge or consider the worth of another or something, to pay tribute or devotion to. Self-respect is to have dignity of one's own character.
11. Empathy is the ability to relate to another person's feelings, volitions, and ideas.
12. Compassion is feeling selfless tenderness toward another's misery or sorrow.
13. Tact is the skill for showing sensitive mental perception, a keen sense of what to do or say in a difficult or delicate situation or matter in order to maintain good relations and avoid offense. Tact is to be diplomatic, considerate of others' feelings, to have poise.
14. Self-awareness is to know your mind, body, and temperament of spirit all at the same time, taking charge of actions and words, and mental and physical and spiritual health, knowing 'Who you are' versus 'who you want to be'.

15. Good self-conduct is to exhibit good control of your emotions and actions.
16. To keep a promise is a strong thing; it is to do as you said you would. A promise is a commitment, a pledge, to give someone your word.
17. People generally do not appreciate the behavior of others when they exhibit angry outbursts, dishonesty, hurtful sarcasm, selfish demands, or too many controlling demands but everyone has bad moments. Emotions and misunderstandings happen; the best thing to do is to communicate with each other and talk things out.

If you have bad table manners or exhibit rowdy behavior in public, your friends or family may not want to go places with you.

Wipe the slate clean and start over, or if you cannot get along with another person, move on to other things in life.

18. We should not be ashamed or embarrassed by body odors that are natural or caused by hormones but we should follow good hygiene. Emitting digestive gases is natural but should be checked out if excessive. Digestive gas is natural science and has nothing to do with your personality or dignity.
19. Some people are bothered by strong perfume or cologne.
20. Some people are bothered by people who talk too much or too little, or by people who talk too loudly or only in whispers. Some say the same line twice such as 'I understand. I understand.' which may be left and right brain.

Chapter 18

Communication

1. Communication means talking and listening. Talk 'to' each other instead of 'at' each other. One person says something, then pauses and lets the other person say something, and so on. If one person rattles on and doesn't let the other person talk, then it isn't a conversation but a speech by one person. 'Say what you mean and mean what you say' is a popular proverb.
2. Be good listeners to each other. To be a good listener means you give a person your undivided attention with no distractions and you could possibly repeat back to the person what they told you to insure the person that you correctly understood what they told you.
3. Listening to what other people say can give you ideas about what you would like to say to others.
4. Good communication and understanding between people is very important for clarity and to avoid misunderstandings that can hurt feelings and cause arguments. Mumbo jumbo is meaningless talk.
5. Conflict does not have to turn out bad; talking things out can often lead to wonderful resolutions; if not, have an open mind that peace may be obtained in the future. Some good news is that there are ways to negotiate almost anything.

6. Everyone has a story to tell, praises to share, sorrows to heal.
7. There is power behind words, so be careful what you speak. When speaking, choose your words carefully.
8. Some people will say everything that is on their mind at once; others will be more reserved and take time to think about things, leaving some things to be said at another time.
9. It may be helpful to possibly plan what you want to say to someone in advance and have some ideas ready so you will be ready for a conversation. Many people greet each other when they see other, saying 'Hello, how are you today?'

In some cases, you may want to wait until someone is in a good mood to speak with them.

10. If other people are having a conversation and you need to interrupt, say 'Excuse me, may I interrupt?'
11. Saying *please* when making a request and *thank you* in gratitude are good manners. Many who hurt another person's feelings say 'I am sorry' as an apology.
12. When something is repeated to another person who repeats it to another as in a grapevine, the actual truth may become slanted and false rumors may start as the translations become different. It is important to substantiate truthful facts before affirming (confirming) personal beliefs; this will keep emotions (passions) from getting out of control and will keep false rumors from getting started.
13. If you cry 'WOLF' too many times for help like Peter in Aesop's fable and it is not true, or if you lie all the time, people will stop believing in you.

Chapter 19

Education

1. Humans learn new things every day and improve ourselves with time. We can acquire new skills, education, employment, attitudes, opinions, habits, friends, knowledge about everyday living.
2. People's brains work at different speeds and may be stronger in certain parts of their brains, and people learn differently and retain information differently.

Chapter 20

Physical and Mental Health

1. Mental exercises can be done to improve cognitive brain performance such as memory and problem-solving exercises. Reading, solving crossword puzzles, listening and watching, memorizing and reciting can all increase alertness, speed, memory, attention and all cognitive functions of the brain.

A person is a sum total of all their life experiences in the memory in their brains. It is said that some cannot remember or do not want to remember earlier parts of their lives while others want to remember every part of their life. Scientists have said that memory is what has allowed languages and cognitive functions to evolve.

2. Some humans may have special needs and special education needs.

3. Physical exercises can be done to strengthen muscles in arms, torso, legs, toes, and build brain cells.

Isometric exercises can be done to strengthen abdominal muscles for a stronger back and better posture, muscles to regulate the flow of urine, and facial muscles. Sometimes when you are peeing, if you stop the flow of urine, it will strengthen these muscles.

Walking backwards exercises lesser used muscles.

Standing barefoot on the earth infuses your body with earth neutrons.

4. A wise course of action is to eat healthy food, lower the intake of fat, sugar, salt, caffeine, and alcohol. Include fiber and water in your diet. Try to exercise. Get proper sleep. Live, laugh, love, and work hard. Think positively and do the best you can.

The *rule of moderation* and nothing excessive is thought by many to be wise. To be moderate is to be chaste. Take care of yourself and be safe.

5. Too much caffeine can cause nervousness, insomnia, and headaches. A little caffeine can improve alertness.

Drinking caffeine before bed can interfere with sleep.

Caffeine can make small children hyper-active.

6. Sipping water can prevent dehydration which can cause headaches. Drinking too much water or too little water can harm or kill you because it disturbs the balance of sodium, sugar and other minerals in your body.

7. Consult with your doctor, a knowledgeable person, or reference materials for answers.

8. Get moving. Research shows that moving your body increases your circulation and metabolism and could lower your sugar and cholesterol so your body will be healthy.

9. Vaccines have protected humans from many dangerous bacterias. Many vaccines are given in early childhood, for situations where people live in close quarters such as when teenagers go to college, for people working or eating in restaurants, or when traveling to a different country.

Flesh-eating bacteria and flesh-eating amoebae have been found in certain outdoor waters so humans should avoid these waters. Do not let outdoor waters of lakes and rivers get into your mouth, nose, ears, and eyes.

10. Moderate or refrain from harmful habits or obsessive addictions that can cause you financial ruin, cause you to get in trouble, or cause you mental or physical distress.

Emotional intelligence is being aware of your emotions and controlling your actions.

IQ is having abilities such as reading comprehension,

deciphering information, and math skills.

Addictions, anger, desires, love, sorrow are *passions* of the heart, mind, and body.

Controlling emotions is an intelligence that must be learned just as intelligence is learned that gives one the ability to discern and apply information in math, science, languages, arts, and social studies.

Be in control of yourself, body and mind.

It is said the human mind creates a complex ego to protect the self.

Consolidate errands and assess shopping needs to save time, money and stress. Spend within your financial budget.

When planning driving trips plan the route to save time, money, gas and reduce stress. Planning ahead can improve efficiency and increase chances of success.

Know what your stressors are and learn to handle them.

If a person spends time in mental, physical, or behavior rehabilitation, they should make an effort for recovery and others should be patient and try to help them.

Some people think that addictions may be a temporary fix that let people escape from reality and feelings into a fog of unreality.

Drugs or alcohol can damage your brain cells and your liver. Being an alcoholic or a drug addict can ruin your life because accidents can happen if you are not sober, you may say or do inappropriate things, you may embarrass others by inappropriate actions, you may end up in financial ruin for supplying your habit, etc.

Being a shopaholic can ruin your life by running up your bills and you constantly feel the need for more.

Being a sex addict can ruin your life for many reasons. You may lose your focus on other important areas of your life like family, self-respect, and work. You may contract an STD, a sexually transmitted disease; some STD's can be cured and some cannot be cured. You may be involved in violent situations between jealous lovers or illegal situations involving pornography, drugs, and alcohol which could lead to a police arrest or death.

Being a gambling addict can cause financial ruin.

Being a workaholic or perfectionist in a hobby may not give you enough time for other things in your life, like family and friends or pets.

Eating disorders may harm your health and can be fatal.

Accumulating too many souvenirs or items of a collection is harmless but it may take up too much space in your house and accumulate dust mites and clutter.

Obsessive cleaning or working may make you exhausted. Take a break.

Obsessive perfection may cause you distress, which can drain you of energy that you could be using to do something else.

People suffering from addictions should remember the Boundary Of Balances that God has set such as day and night, the seasons and the Tao symbol of Yin & Yang. There is a time for yes and a time for no. An example of tough love is keeping a loved one from alcohol who is trying to be rehabilitated from alcohol dependence.

Evil thinking causes people to kill, rape, steal, lie, and oppress others.

Logical thinking can prevent intellectual servitude for the underprivileged and it can free the highly educated from the habit of presuming every claim true until proven false.

Wishful thinking can cause significant errors if facts are misinterpreted.

Egotistical thinking is when we think we are always right and this can cause problems.

Counter-intuitive thinking can cause errors if we deny our instincts; our instincts can give us power in our logical thinking but facts must be considered.

Passive thinking can be detrimental when people have all of their needs met; they may be less prone to make further achievements in education or improving their health.

Progressive thinking is when you recognize changes in thinking that are improvements. For example, old thinking believed that the world was flat. New thinking believed that the earth was round. 'What if' questions have led to much progress in the world. 'What if' questions can broaden knowledge and change life circumstances. The idea of 'What if man could create fire' led to fires being started by rubbing sticks together. Or maybe fire was discovered when ancient people rubbed sticks together to make pointed sticks for hunting and a spark occurred.

Old thinking is 'That person is a bad person.' New thinking is 'That person is exhibiting some bad behavior.'

Old thinking is 'I need many possessions to be happy.' New thinking is 'Happiness is a state of mind.'

Old thinking is 'That person cannot do anything right.'
New thinking is 'That person made a mistake.'

Convergent thinking is when people do research or have discussions and they share similar or the same beliefs.

Divergent thinking is when you dare to think differently from the normal standards of society or out of your comfort zone.

Thinking out loud is when you say something and you don't realize that you said it.

Naive thinking is when you don't have enough knowledge about something and may not make the best decisions or when you think that someone has good intentions when they do not.

Idealistic thinking is when you think how things could be perfect or the best they could be for a situation.

Cynical thinking is when you question things and have a hard time believing.

Analytical thinking is when you consider all facts and possibilities and consider the various outcomes that could happen, why things happened the way they did in the past, or how to make improvements.

'Thinking in reverse' is thinking about what has happened in the past and what you could have done differently, if at all. Maybe you wouldn't have changed a thing,

You might change your mind about something for various reasons.

Love and compassionate thinking can sometimes defy logical thinking.

Fantastical thinking can include characters, actions and outcomes that are not realistic.

Day dreaming is fantasizing about possibilities.

Altruistic thinking is hoping for the best for everyone and having unselfish concern for others.

Positive thinking is having hope and wishing for a good outcome.

Negative thinking is focusing on the bad points of a matter.

In times of crisis, detach your emotions and focus your thinking on what needs to be done to survive.

Chapter 21

Home

1. Let everyone live their lives in good ways, and the whole world will be happy.
2. Let us make our home a place of comfort, rest, and tranquility. Our home should be a safe haven.
3. Many have reunions with members of family, schools, associations, or religious entities.
4. Many people consider their workplace or work cubicle as a part of their home because it is an important part of their life; it is how they earn money to live or it is their passion and they may spend a substantial amount of time at work.

Chapter 22

Communities

1. Communities are places where humans work together to promote good living for all. Food may be sold at local farmers market that was grown on local farms or in community gardens. A water reservoir may be shared. Community magazines may be printed that contain information about businesses, education, recreation, spirituality, and government in the local region.
2. Some think that sitting in a circle in some group settings can make everyone feel included, a circle of support in an endless circle of love.

Chapter 23

Spirituality

1. Make a pledge to live on a good pathway, to live together in civil harmony, fellowship, agreement, closely knit, united in efforts for a good world for all people.
2. Remedy the people to rid their hearts of hatred and spite; to be truthful and honest, conciliatory, loving, transformed to all good ways, and to strive for universal peace; deliver this joyous message to all people.
3. Listen to and be good to each other. If possible, help each other.
4. Revitalize your *soul* (also called *spirit, atman, conscience*) with hope and love, become a part of the soul of the world that billions of humans call home.
5. Your conscience is the *soul* or *atman* that is your connection to God.

Some think the soul goes to a place called heaven on Resurrection Day or the Day of Judgement or Day of Accountabiliy. Some think souls can be in limbo (Purgatory). Some think evil souls go to hell which is a bad place or God will extinguish the energy of their soul. Some believe that the soul or spirit is reincarnated into another human, animal, or plant life. Some believe our spirits are ended in death.

6. The soul is the core of who you are. What kind of spirit are you?

Describe yourself. Knowing your own personality is having self-awareness. Most think core values versus loose talk is who we really are.

Chapter 24

Affirmations

1. Reaffirm each day your love for your family.
2. Reaffirm your faith and goals.
3. Tell your friends, employees, and employer how much you appreciate them and their efforts. It takes teamwork to get things done and make achievements.

Some believe in magic formulas or charms (mojo) for success.

Chapter 25

Continuum of Time

1. Tomorrow is a new day and you don't know what tomorrow may bring. Rejoice in the hope of tomorrow.
2. Now is the only time you actually have. Yesterday is gone. Tomorrow is the future. Live, love, and work today. Enjoy the moment.
3. Trust in the Lord's Timing.

SAFETY

Chapter 1

Practical wisdom is to remove safety hazards in homes, businesses, and transport.

1. Never shake a baby.
2. Do not let babies or toddlers put small items into their mouths or they could choke. Fasten buckle of seat belt in high chair so child cannot climb out.
3. Wipe up spills to avoid falling.
4. Remove clutter from stairs and walkways so people will not trip and fall.
5. Be careful when climbing or descending stairs. Hold on to the railing if there is one.
6. Be careful on slippery floors. Wipe up spills if possible so no one will fall.
7. Secure long cords so lamps and coffee pots will not fall on people.
8. Secure cords on window blinds so children cannot strangulate.
9. Secure plastic bags so children cannot suffocate.

Secure heavy bookshelves or furniture that could fall over and harm someone.

10. Remove or secure heavy items on bookshelves , fireplace mantles, or window sills that could fall and hurt someone.
11. If you have to pick something up from under a table or shelf, do not bump your head when you come up.
12. Don't accidentally walk into a glass door.
13. Keep children away from dangers like hot ovens, matches, candles, fires, fireplaces, chemicals, and toothpicks. Do not leave a child unattended in a bathtub of water.
14. Do not cook with long sleeves that may get caught on the handles of pots and pans.
15. Point handles of pots and pans toward the back of the stove so the pots will not get knocked off.
16. Wash vegetables and fruits before eating.
17. Be careful with knives.
18. Sanitize cooking items and surfaces that have touched raw meats, eggs, cheeses, or unwashed veggies and fruits.
19. The tops of spice jars and the insides of flour containers may have to be sanitized after many uses.
20. Toothbrushes may be sanitized with boiling water or replaced with new ones. Germs left toothbrushes after a sore throat can reinfect a human.
21. Door knobs, keys, cell phones, the bottoms of purses, brief cases, and satchels that have touched floors, sinks, tubs, toilets, light switches, computer keyboards may have to be occasionally sanitized.
22. Keep sink and tubs drains covered so bugs cannot crawl up in search of water.
23. Do not leave electrical applicances on or leave food cooking or water boiling on the stove without being in attendance; you could forget about it or leave home and a fire could result or the pipes behind the washing machines could burst and cause flooding.

24. Do not leave water running in a sink or bathtub and walk away; the water could spill over and cause a flood.
25. Never leave a backyard grill unattended around people or pets.
26. Never put electrical appliances into water.
27. Do not put metal into microwave ovens.
28. Operate appliances, electronics, and machinery safely, read the manuals, and make sure they are in good working order.
29. If there is a cut in an electrical cord, do not touch it because you can get electrocuted; replace the cord or wrap it with black electrical tape.
30. If you have to remove a light bulb, unplug the lamp or appliance first; never place your finger into the socket that the bulb is screwed into or you can get electrocuted.
31. Stagnant water can breed bugs.
32. Keep children away from open windows or screens so they don't fall out.
33. Do not let children play alone in streets. Do not let young children out of your site.
34. Make sure small children cannot open doors from inside a house by themselves as they could wander out alone.
35. Keep doors closed so flies do not get in.
36. Stock emergency supplies like candles, matches, batteries, hand-crank world radios, bottled water, canned foods, can-opener, medicines, pet foods.
37. Make sure cigarette butts, matches, or barbeque skewers are totally extinguished before throwing them into a trash can. Never smoke in bed; you could fall asleep and the bed could catch on fire. Do not throw cigarette butts out of a car window.
38. Turn on a battery-powered flashlight occasionally to keep it active.
39. Fire detectors, carbon-monoxide detectors can detect fire or build-up of dangerous carbon monoxide gas.
40. In a fireplace, the flue should be opened to let dangerous toxic fumes of carbon monoxide gas escape. Keep pets and kids away from fireplaces and candles.
41. Emergency evacuation plans should be devised and rehearsed by family and guests of a home and by employees at a business location. Rope ladders can be used to lower humans to the ground from a second-story of a house. Many buildings have special fire escapes.
42. Know where fire extinguishers are.
43. Do not put water on a grease fire because it could cause the grease to splatter; turn off the stove or the circuit breaker to the fire. You could cover the fire with a lid or fire blanket.
44. Do not fall asleep with food, gum, or tobacco in your mouth to avoid choking. Also, the item could fall out of your mouth and get all over your pillow or couch.
45. Do not eat food that has been dropped onto a dirty floor; the 5-second rule is a myth.
46. Do not open your door to strangers. Ask who is knocking.

Giving telemarketers or interviewers personal information can be risky.

47. Secure patio furniture and close windows of house and car before a storm.

48. Burning plastics or mixing certain household chemicals can produce toxic fumes that can be fatal when breathed. Open windows when using chemicals to ventilate the rooms. Use pesticides safely. Make sure all containers are labeled with chemical names. Add water to concentrates when directed.

49. Use separate sponges for cleaning the bathroom and the kitchen.

50. Certain medications cannot be mixed and can be fatal.

51. Before doing laundry, remove items from pockets of clothing to prevent loss and zip up zippers to prevent snagging other items being washed. Clothing can be turned inside out to protect fabrics. Count pairs of socks at beginning of laundry and pairs of socks at end of laundry; socks can get lost.

52. Mattresses and bed covers that are more than 5 years old may contain dust mites.

53. Watch your drink in a bar so a villain will not slip a drug into your drink.

54. A designated driver is a person who vows to not drink so they can be a safe driver to drive others home.

55. Women's high-heeled shoes can cause ankle injuries and stress on knee joints.

56. Mold problems should be addressed to avoid health problems.

57. Slip-resistant mats can prevent falls in the bathtub, especially for senior citizens.

58. Keep firearms and guns secure and operate firearms safely.

59. Never shoot a gun in celebratory gesture. Shooting a gun into the air can result in the bullet coming down on a human being somewhere else.

60. When you come home, you could check all closets and under the beds (with a big stick in hand) to make sure that nobody is in your home.

61. Humans who live in sewers should find other shelter; sometimes sewers are fumigated with pesticides to kill rodents which may also be fatal to humans.

62. If you have to do heavy lifting, learn proper lifting techniques so you do not strain your back or hurt your knees.

63. If a house or building is built in the northern hemisphere of the world, the north side of a structure is the side that usually does not get enough sunlight and is subject to mold or moss.

64. Decks should be supported well with support beams underneath and not just brackets to avoid collapsing from the weight of many people on the deck. Decks can be waterproofed to avoid wood rot.

65. If you leave windows or doors open, lizards, snakes, wasps, bees, spiders, or mosquitoes could come in without your knowledge. Squirrels or birds may get into your attic.

66. Window and door screens should be intact to keep small creatures out.

67. If you are trying to catch a mouse, studies have shown that mice prefer bacon and peanut butter more than cheese wedges. Ants do not like vinegar.
Mosquitoes may be deterred by camphor oil.

68. Recycle large cardboard boxes; do not leave them at the curb of your home for thieves to know what you have recently purchased.

69. If a urine sample cannot be frozen immediately, preservatives may be added at the time of collection. Human blood, tissues, and organs can be packed in dry ice which is frozen carbon dioxide or CO_2.

70. Humans have devised air, ground, and water shipping guidelines and packaging requirements for:
(1) non-fatal biological samples, (2) infectious pathogens and biological samples that can cause fatalities,
(3) dead humans or their remains or dead animals or their remains,
(3) corrosives and oxidizers, (4) flammables, compressed gases, and dry ice.
(5) magnetized materials, (6) wildlife, (6) alcohol and drugs, (7) poisons, (8) liquids, perishables and fragile goods, (9) medical, hazardous, and nuclear wastes, (10) asbestos, lithium batteries, and light bulbs that contain mercury or other elements.

71. Never throw batteries into a fire because they could explode.

Chapter 2
Operate vehicles safely

1. Never leave a child, pet, or adult alone in a car when it is extremely hot or cold.

2. If a child is asleep in the back seat, you could put a toy in the front seat with the driver to remind them the child is in the back seat.

3. It is wrong to operate machinery, cars, boats, motorcycles, golf carts, lawnmowers, or aircraft while under the influence of drugs or alcohol, texting, fatigued, having a medical condition that advises against it, having road rage, or doing anything that takes away your concentration of the operation of the vehicle, as it could hurt or kill people by causing an accident.

4. Do not put a vehicle in reverse without making sure no one is behind the vehicle.
Do not drive forward without making sure no one is in front of the vehicle.

5. If you put something on top of your roof while getting in, do not forget to retrieve the item before you drive off.

6. Watch for bicycles and motorcycles, and joggers.

7. Do not block intersections or pedestrian crosswalks.

8. Do not drive too fast around curves or in bad weather.

9. Do not follow another vehicle too closely; it could suddenly stop and you could crash into it.

10. Driving with your headlights on at dusk, dawn, and in rain or fog can make your vehicle more visible.

11. Make sure vehicles are in good working order including good tires inflated to proper level, good spare tire, car jack, lug nut wrench, oil changed and fluids checked, no cracks in windshield, seat belts in working order and being used, jumper cables available, mototcycle helmets in good repair.

Learn to use jumper cables safely to start a car battery: Raise the hood of the car with the dead battery. Park a car having a good battery with the engine as close as possible to the engine of the stranded car and raise the hood of the car. In the car that has the engine running attach both clips at one end of the cable to the battery, attaching the positive cable clip to the positive post of the battery and the negative cable clip to the negative post of the battery. Then attach both clips at the other end of the cable to the battery in the car that needs to be started, attaching the positive clip to the positive post and the negative clip to the negative post, being careful to not let any metal clips touch each other while you are holding them.

12. Cars that have engines running but are not moving when enclosed in garages or stuck in snow need to have ventilation to release dangerous carbon monoxide gas. Open garage doors or garage window if car is parked in a garage. Open car window and make opening in snow to sky if trapped in snow to allow carbon monoxide gas to be released.

13. Do not drive with arms tangled in the steering wheel; if you are in an accident you could damage your arms.
It is best to drive with your hands at the 10AM and 2PM positions of the steering wheel for best steering control of the vehicle.

14. The front seat passenger should not ride with their legs upon the dashboard because if there is a wreck and the air bag deploys, their legs could be thrown up into the windshield and cause major injuries to their feet or legs.

15. When driving, it is not wise to pick up hitchhikers.

16. Keep doors locked to prevent car jackings.

17. Always glance into the back seat of your car before you get in to make sure there is not a predator in the car.

18. If you are being picked up by another, always look inside the car to make sure the driver is the correct person; some people have gotten into the wrong car.

19. If it is an emergency in the middle of the night and you are on your way to a hospital,
if the light is red and there is no traffic in a remote area, many think it is ok to drive through the red light to get to the hospital.

20. Let someone know your travel route.

21. If a power line falls on top of your car, stay in the car until help arrives.

22. Close windows of car when parking near bushes or under trees because spiders and bugs can crawl into a car.

23. If law enforcement stops you, try to find a well-lit public area

before pulling over if it is late at night. You could also call someone on a cell phone to have a witness on the phone when the police officer confronts you. Most law enforcement officers are good cops, but if you have reason to be afraid, avoid trouble. Some innocent people have been sent to jail or shot by cops.
If the cop is questioning you for a valid reason, the best thing to do is to cooperate. You could check the police officer's credentials.

24. If you dent someone's car in a parking lot and do not know who owns the car, it is very nice to leave your name and phone number and to make amends.

25. Do not leave items in your cars that thieves can see; store items in the trunk.

26. Wear car seat belts.

27. Pedestrians should cross streets at crosswalks.

28. Do not drive the wrong way on a one-way street.

29. Workplaces where work involves the use of chemicals or danger of carbon monoxide should have proper ventilation. Nuclear facilities should follow safety guidelines.

Chapter 3
Personal Safety

1. Do not let children wander alone in public places.

2. Hold tightly onto a child's hand when crossing a street.

3. Remove doors or locks from doors of old refrigerators so children cannot get locked inside.

4. If you are at a park or large venue, plan a time and plan to regather with your group in case someone gets lost.

5. Never punch a human being in the stomach because there is a major artery which could rupture and kill the person.

6. Do not let shoes or shoelaces, satchels, scarves, or hair get caught in escalator stairs, elevator doors, or hottub drains.

7. Stay away from railings and ledges in buildings, stadiums, and on ships to avoid falling.

8. Never dive into a shallow body of water or a swimming pool until you know the depth of it.
Do not swim too far out into the ocean to avoid rip tides.
Do not swim in river with strong currents.

9. Wear life vest in boats. Do not rev up the engine throttle too quickly in a smaller boat because the boat could capsize and the propellars could injure people in the water.

10. Do not swim in the ocean or rivers at night; since it is dark you cannot know which way is up and some have swam towards the bottom and have drowned.

11. Be careful on slippery ski slopes.

12. Sledders and skiers should not crash into trees.

13. Never walk on top of a frozen pond unless you are sure it is frozen.

14. Never walk on, play around, or stop a vehicle on railroad tracks. Shoes could get stuck in the tracks.

15. Food-eating contests are not healthy.

16. People on ladders should have a spotter, which is someone at the bottom to keep the ladder steady.

17. Some people are allergic to nuts, dairy products, latex plastics, soaps, or other things and it is toxic or allergenic for them to touch or ingest these certain substances or foods. Mulberries are listed as toxic.

18. Do not touch downed power lines.

19. Do not fly kites if it is rainy or near power lines.

20. Do not let children play near metal electrical boxes that are above ground.

21. Stay away from storm drains. People have been swept down into them during rainstorms.

22. If you hear thunder, get out of a swimming pool or get off the lake or ocean because when you hear thunder, lightning is near.

23. When camping in the wild, use the bathroom in a safe place; people have been biten by snakes when using the bathroom in the dark.

24. Always let someone know where you are going and when you will be back.

25. Do not fall asleep in strange places.
Do not fall asleep alone in a public place like a beach or park or on public transportation because you could get kidnapped.

26. Do not meet strangers in remote places or go anywhere with strangers. Do not go alone to remote areas.

27. If you are out walking and a stranger asks for directions, stand several feet away from them or their car.

28. Joggers, bicyclists, and motorcyclists can wear reflective clothing to be seen. Joggers should beware of banana peels or slick surfaces, curbs, holes in the ground to avoid falling.

29. Mace or a heavy stick can be a weapon.

30. Options for computer security are change passwords, email addresses, credit card numbers, phone numbers, cars, physical address, use nicknames instead of real names, use biometric recognition systems that read retinas, palms, or voice pattern, take battery out of cell phone.

31. If you go bowling, do not drop the ball on your foot. Do not put your hand into the ball return; it could get smashed.

32. Don't leave a cup on the roof of your car and drive off.

33. Do not leave keys in doors.

34. Report unauthorized drones.

35. Crematories, military bases, electrical grids, water sources like reservoirs with dams and water towers, water filtering and sewage pumps, major food sources, hospitals, and laboratories with pathogen samples should be kept secured and guarded 24 hours each day in shifts if needed and with security systems and weapons on-site to defend community resources.

36. Know the customs of a foreign country before entering it. Do not take a picture in a foreign country unless it is ok to take pictures; you could be accused of being a spy.

37. Never accept a large amount of money from anyone unless you have paperwork that it is a loan;

otherwise you could be arrested for money laundering.

38. For the safety, respect, and comfort of all, many public restrooms are being converted to single bathrooms where one person uses it at a time.

39. Make sure food is given in small bites to children so they will not choke. Do not give children round hard candy or marshmallows which can get lodged in their throats.

40. Never fire a gun with a cracked muzzle (open end of the barrel) or a cracked barrel because the gun could explode in your face.
The Glock 17 designed in the 1980s by Gaston Glock of Austria is made of advanced synthetic polymer plastics; the Glock became popular because it was lighter than metal guns but the barrel can crack under extreme pressures.

41. People who have had neck injuries should avoid riding roller coasters.

42. Do not sunbathe on a driveway where a vehicle could run over you.

Chapter 4
Survival Skills

1. Hand-crank radios, bottled water, flashlight and batteries, candles, food supplies, pet foods, medicines, pocketknife, can opener should be stocked for emergencies.

2. Take food and water with you if you are going on a long hike or expedition. Eat healthy and well before you embark on the hike. Drink water before you leave so you will be hydrated.

3. If you have medical conditions, check with your doctor before leaving and bring medications if needed. Some medications should not be taken if the body is exposed to sunlight.

4. Do not drink seawater, urine, coffee, tea, or alcohol; they dehydrate the body. Instead drink rainwater, dew, ice and snow. But melt ice and snow so you do not lower your body temperature.
To reduce water loss from the body, eat less because water is used to digest food. Boil any water used from a river for 15 minutes.

5. Reflective mirrors can be used to reflect sunlight that can be seen by aircraft miles away. Also, bring flares with you. Or, build a pile of stones or something that could attract attention from the sky or road. A paper message can be put into a bottle and tossed into the sea.

6. Breath through the nose instead of the mouth; less moisture will escape.

7. Wear clothes that will protect you from the sun and wind; both cause water to evaporate from the skin.

8. Huddle close together for body warmth. Take blankets or jackets on your trip.

9. Learn to build a campfire pit so that the fire cannot spead. If you are very cold, don't warm yourself too close to a fire; surface blood vessels will open and send icy blood straight to vital organs.

10. Tie a bright colored cloth to the top of your car if stuck in snow and seek a rescue.

11. If a vehicle is stuck in snow, make sure the tailpipe is not clogged with snow and is open to sky

because dangerous carbon monoxide could build up inside the car if engine is on.

12. If you are in an avalance of snow, cover your nose and mouth with your hands to create a pocket of air and to prevent choking on snow.

13. Keep to the sheltered side of a ridge instead of the top for less wind and exposure.

14. When walking on streets covered with snow, remember that there are curbs, uneven concrete, and storm drains under the snow so walk carefully. You could carry a stick or an umbrella to poke around as you walk.

15. If you start to sink in mud in a marsh or swamp, don't panic and try to move your legs because it might make you sink further. Try to discard anything heavy that you are carrying and try to swim to the side keeping your head above the surface; try to spread your body over a wide surface area.

16. If you are in a riverbed and it starts to rain heavily, get out immediately and go to higher ground.

17. Dust devils or whirlwinds in the desert sweep sand and grit around at great speed; take shelter immediately or cover your face, eyes, ears.

18. Leave water pipes dripping in freezing weather so the water will not freeze.
Cover fruit and flower plants from cold frosts.

19. If you smell gas in your house, never light a match or a fire could erupt. Check if a pilot light has gone out. If needed, call the authorities or gas company for help.

20. Know how to turn off the main electrical supply and the main water supply to your building.

21. Never use electrical appliances near water to avoid shock to human or animal.

22. If a person grabs you from behind around your neck, reach for their little fingers and jerk them outwards or twist them; it will cause them pain.
If they grab you around your waist, kick them with your legs.

If a person grabs you from the front, forcefully move your arms outward to try to break their hold; you can also try to kick them in the knees, hit them in the throat, or poke them in the eyes.

If an attacker grabs your wrist, move your hand against their thumb to weaken their grip.

23. Learn how to use the sun and a stick to tell direction if you don't have a compass. Push a long straight stick into the ground and mark where the shadow is. The shadow points north if you are in the northern hemisphere. The shadow points south if you are in the southern hemisphere. Wait 15 minutes. The shadow will move around the stick. Mark the spot of the new shadow. Draw a line between the two points of the shadows; it will be the west-east line in the northern hemisphere (the first marked shadow is west and the second is east) and the east-west line in the southern hemisphere (the first marked shadow is east and the second is west). North and south

would be at right angles to the east and west line that you drew.

24. If someone is on fire or if you are on fire, stop, drop and roll to put out the flames.

25. A pocketknife could be useful to cut branches that could be used to build shelter or clear a pathway. It can be dangerous to eat wild plants that could be poisonous.

26. A shelter can be make with a waterproof tarp and one tall, straight stick that is stuck into the ground. Drape the tarp over the top and spread out the tarp, securing the tarp in place by putting stones or something heavy to hold the tarp in place. Shelters can be made from tarps using four sticks and five sticks. To make a tent with five sticks, secure two sticks in an X formation with twine. Secure two more sticks in an X formation with twine. Place the first pair into the ground in an upright formation. Place the second pair into the ground a few feet away in an upright formation. Place a fifth stick that is as long as the width of the two pairs horizontally between the tops of the X's. Then drape a tarp over the top; the slant will allow any rain to fall off the tent.

27. Water can be collected from a solar still. First dig a hole in the ground and place a container on the ground in the center of the hole. Cover the hole with plastic and secure around with stones to keep the plastic in place. Put a few stones in the middle of the plastic that is stretched over the hole. If the sky is sunny, water that is in the dirt of the earth will condense on the bottom of the plastic and drip into the container. The water should only be consumed if the tarp is clean and there are no bugs in the collected water.

28. Cotton fabrics absorb water from the skin. Fabrics can be worn for cold outdoor activities that will allow water to escape so the fabrics will not freeze.

29. If someone has fallen out of a canoe, try to row to shore with the person hanging on in tow. If the person tries to get back in, the canoe could overturn (capsize) and both people would be in the water.

30. Don't dive into unknown waters. Don't swim in the dark. Don't swim near boats and buoys: Propellors and anchoring chains are dangerous. Make sure lifejackets are stocked on the boat. Learn how to tread water. Don't fall off the dock.

31. To escape from a second level of a house, curtains can be torn and tied together in a chain using square knots. Tie one end of the chain to a heavy piece of furniture using a square knot. Drop the free end of the chain out of the window and lower yourself to the ground. Rope ladders can hang from window ledges.

32. A fire can turn insects away. Do not light a fire at the base of a tree because the tree could start on fire.

If the ground is waterlogged, you might have to build a platform for the fire with rocks and earth or even a platform built with four upright sticks and horizontal sticks laid crosswise and then with rocks and earth. Be careful: some rocks can explode and spit fragments.

33. In times of a major economic crisis, assets can be sold to raise cash. Family

members and friends may live together and share resources in order to survive. To save money anytime, a gift can be wrapped in newspaper or magazine pages.

34. Stay out of alligator, crocodile, snake, stingray, and shark infested waters.

Large crocodiles can overturn boats in shallow waters. Stay away from the edges of lagoons and lakes where an alligator can snatch a human in its mouth in a second. Take caution so that a large bird or animal does not carry off a baby.

35. Beware of and remove stray rodents or reptiles from imports and exports on inbound and outbound cargo ships.

36. Do not panic if you are in quicksand. Try to throw off any heavy items that you might have, like a backpack. Try to lean back and let body float to the top. Try to swim on your back. Try to reach for something to pull you out of the sand.

37. A stretcher to carry a patient on can be made in the wilderness by using tree limbs as poles. Stick the poles through the arms of shirts on both sides or use other fabrics to create a stretcher.

38. In a country having many diverse cultures, it is beneficial for the country if the government and the military consists of people from many different races and cultures to avoid a coup by one group of people having their own agenda.

39. Do not surf or go surfing on the oceans in the fog when the weather is foggy. You could get lost and not know the direction to the shore.

Chapter 5
War Tactics

1. The enemy could starve you, so you might have to hide food and supplies like blankets and water.
2. Trenches could be built or roads destroyed to prevent tanks from driving into your area.
3. Signposts and maps could be destroyed so the enemy is confused.
4. Underground bomb shelters could be built.
5. Blackout curtains hides light at night.
6. Civilians like doctors, nurses, and other citizens might have to be asked to help by working in military positions.
7. Civilians might have to share their own house with the military guarding their country or with the enemy.
8. The enemy could throw you out of your house onto the street, or kill you.
9. If an enemy invades your territory, you could escape to another region.
10. Metals from clothes hangers, pots & pans, or appliances may be needed by the military to produce trucks and aircraft.
11. Care packages and letters could be sent to soldiers. Many say 'I'll wait for you' and don't break marriage vows.

REMINDERS

1. For best results, sweep the floor before mopping.
2. Do not forget to look at calendar for upcoming events, appointments, or phone calls.
3. Do not forget to pick someone up or meet them.
4. Prepare food for upcoming meals; clean out refrigerator.
5. Wash the laundry. Try to ration laundry detergent to match the number of recommended loads listed on the container. Many detergents are concentrated so you only need to use a small amount.
6. Copies of important keys and documents can be given friends and family or put in a safe vault.
Extra keys can be kept in case of lockouts. Keep keys in same place each day for ease in finding. Do not leave keys in doors or items outside that you meant to bring inside.
7. To prevent identity theft, do not give important information to random strangers. You can even give a fake name.
Some people tape a small piece of paper over their selfie camera lens to prevent hackers from randomly spying on them to see what they look like. Some people think that people can watch tv viewers through the TV units that have computer parts. Is someone watching us? Does the tv have a receiver and a transmitter?
8. Don't leave items on the roof of your car and drive off.
9. Cut food into bite-sized pieces and do not talk with food in your mouth.
10. Wear shoes in public places to avoid stepping on broken glass.
Stand barefoot in grass to get beneficial earth neutrons. Take shoes off when you enter your home to avoid tracking in germs.
11. Recaulk around the tiles in the bathtub when the caulking has worn away and cracks appear, or mold will get behind the tiles and the tiles will fall off the wall.
12. Shoes and expecially shoes with rubber soles are very slippery on slick floors and on walkways with ice. Walk slowly so you will not fall.
13. Customers who linger in restaurants for a long time may be holding up tables for other customers who are hungry.
14. Trying to reuse and recycle items can save stress, money, resources, and save the planet.
15. Humans can make conscious decisions for their actions.
16. Even when on vacation, you can attend a worship service.
17. You may have to leave for a trip early in the morning at 4am or late at night at 11pm to avoid much traffic.
18. Always let someone know where you are going and when you will return.
It is risky to venture to remote areas alone. Many people disappear from remote areas, even of state parks.
For some group outings, people will matching tee shirts so that it is easy to find others in your group.

There may be dangerous animals in remote areas.
19. Clean vacuum, air conditioning, heater, and clothes dryer filters.
20. Water or fertilize plants. Leave water for pets.
21. Turn off lights that are not needed to save electricity.
22. Some wash their hair before getting a hair cut in a salon; some pay for a shampoo at the salon.
23. If you are going to be part of a crowd of people, do not use too much perfume because many people are bothered by the smell of strong perfume.
24. Some people are bothered by people who only speak in whispers or speak too loud.
25. Do not take for granted pictures of the earth that were taken from space, because humans worked hard for years to make space technology.
26. Do not take for granted clean water, electrical power, clean food, or a warm shower or bath, because humans have worked very hard to provide these things.
27. If your electricity goes off and there is an electrical power outage, report it to your power company. Be patient, for the crews are working very hard to restore power.
28. Organizations that adopt out animals should make sure the animals are healthy and do not have diseases.
29. Helpful hint: You might be able to undo a knot in a shoelace by sticking the prong of a fork into the knot to loosen it.
30. If you are serving in the military and are visiting in a foreign country, do not get drunk or go off with strangers who could make false accusations against you to cause trouble. Stay safe.
31. A woman giving birth at a hospital may have witnesses to the birth so no one kidnaps her baby. Friends and relatives should stay with or help patients in hospitals. There have been instances of corruption in hospitals where patients have been harmed by insiders or outsiders.
32. Be nice to humans who are trying hard to do good things.
33. Thank people for their time and good efforts.

ELEMENTS

CHAPTER 1
Periodic Table

The elements are all balanced by the Lord. The philosopher John Leslie pointed out most things in the world could be stamped MADE BY GOD.

All known elements are cataloged in the periodic table. An element is an atom that cannot be broken down or taken apart into something simpler. An element is defined by its atomic number, the number of positively charged protons in the nucleus of every atom of that atom. The positive protons are equally matched by negatively charged electrons outside the nucleus. Some electrons may stay close to the nucleus while some electrons may tend to stay farther out in shell orbitals. Chemists refer to electrons as having no specific actual locations but possibilities. The electrons give the elements their unique characteristics. All nuclei except ^{1}H have neutrons in the nucleus also. The spinning of the electrons creates different types of waves; the figure-eight loop wave is only found in atoms.

Frederick Soddy of Scotland discovered that it's possiblefor atoms of the same element to have different masses because of varying number of neutrons in the nucleus of an atom. All nuclei except ^{1}H contains neutrons in addition to protons. Isotopes of an element have the same number of protons but a different number of neutrons. Nuclei without a suitable number of neutrons tend to be unstable and eventually fly apart into radioactive decay. When atoms disintegrate it is called fission and thermal energy is released; the molecules fidget and move around; the reactions make the molecules turn into something else – this is the basis for nuclear energy and bombs. After humans made nuclear bombs, Frederick Soddy turned away from nuclear science and began warning people about the dangers of continued research into the nucleus.

The periodic table was established by Dimitri Mendeleev in 1869. But another chemist named John Newlands had began classifying the elements three years prior; Newlands grouped the elements by weight and he noticed that they repeated certain properties along the scale. But Mendeleev grouped the elements vertically that have similar properties, and horizontally in ascending order by the number of protons in their nuclei, which is their atomic number.

There are 118 known elements; 92 of them are naturally occurring and the rest have to be produced in nuclear reactors. One source said 120 or more elements.

The elements are the substances that cannot be separated further into a simpler substance. Compounds consists of two or more elements whose chemical composition is constant.

Elements in the first column of the periodic table are known as the alkali metals earth (1,3,11,19,37,55,87). The alkali metals are highly reactive to water, exploding to release hydrogen gas.

Elements in the second column are known as the alkali earth metals (4,12,20,38,56,88) which are reactive to water and release hydrogen gas but are tamer.

Elements in the wide central block of the periodic table are known as the transition metals, most of which are stable and oxidize slowly. They are elements 21, 22, 23, 24, 25, 26, 27, 28, 29, 30, 39, 40, 41, 42, 43, 44, 45, 46, 47, 48, 72, 73, 74, 75, 76, 77, 78, 79, 80, 104, 105, 106,107, 108, 109, 110, 111, 112.

Elements in the two rows across the bottom of the periodic table are the rare earths. Elements 57-71are called lanthanides which are chemically similar to each other. Elements 89-103 are the actinides which are all radioactive.

The two rightmost columns are the halogen and noble gases. Elements 9, 17, 35, 53, 85, and 117 are highly reactive and smelly. Elements 2, 10, 18, 36, 54, 86, and 118 are inert and non-reactive; they are often used as shielding elements against other volatile elements.

Elements 6, 7, 8, 15, 16, and 34 form a triangle known as nonmetals that are electrical insulators. Elements 13, 31, 49, 50, 81, 82, 83, 113, 114, 115, and 116 form a triangle known as ordinary metals which conduct electricity. The elements between the two triangles are 5, 14, 32, 33, 51, 52, and 84 are the metalloids which are somewhat like metal and somewhat not like metal.

Many naturally-occurring pure elements are acutely harmful or fatal to life such as Chlorine(17) gas, Arsenic(33), Selenium(34), Cadmium(48), Mercury(80), Thallium(81), Lead(82), and radioactive elements such as Polonium(84), Radon (86), Radium(88), Thorium(90), and Uranium(92).

Combinations of elements can be poisonous or non-poisonous; for example, sodium chloride is used as table salt, but sodium hydroxide is known as lye, a drain opener for plumbing and poisonous if consumed. Fluorine(9) is the most reactive of all elements and can even make glass burn, yet it is used as a compound in toothpaste. Potassium chloride, rubidium chloride, and cesium chloride have been used as salt substitutes. Some elements are fatal to humans if consumed in large doses but harmless and necessary for good health if consumed in small doses.

Spontaneous combustion is when a substance self-heats or self-combusts. The substance begins to self-heat by oxidation or bacterial fermentation generates heat, the temperatures rises and combustion begins. Spontaneous combustion has occurred in manure piles, compost piles, piles of oil seeds and oil-seed products. Huge piles of pistachio nuts have been known to be highly flammable and self-combustible.

Humans have been studying and experimenting with the elements for hundreds of years to acquire knowledge of and about the elements, and many people have died in the process. For example, in the 1920s CE, people worked in factories to create watches and clocks that had luminous numbers and dials that were painted with zinc (30) sulfide and radium paint; people were licking the tips of paintbrushes to keep the tips of the paintbrushes firm and soon the workers began to die which finally convinced people that something had to be done and the process was stopped. Also, some children died who had been eating paint chips that chipped off walls and toys and the paint contained lead so finally lead was taken out of paint. Arsenic was used to create green pigments for paint, but people died from inhaling fumes from molds that grew on wallpaper that had been painted with paint that contained arsenic green pigment. Uranium is in the glaze of paints of tiles and plates and bowls made prior to 1942CE, especially those that have orange paint; it is not a good idea to eat from these plates and bowls because uranium is a heavy metal poison like lead that can leach out of the glaze on contact with acidic foods.

A Geiger counter is a tool that can detect radiation.

The 92 known naturally-occurring elements are:

1) Hydrogen – Hydrogen is the lightest of all gases. Combined with carbon(6), nitrogen(7), and oxygen(8), it bonds together the blood and body of all living things. It is one of the most abundant elements. The sun works by turning hydrogen into helium.
2) Helium – Helium is an inert gas that does not interact. The helium on the earth was created over time by the radioactive decay of uranium and thorium. Helium turns pale peach by an electric current.
3) Lithium – Lithium is a soft light metal that is reactive and melts at low temperature. Lithium will react with water to release hydrogen. Lithium is widely used in consumer products such as batteries and a medicine to control mood swings.
4) Beryllium – Beryllium is a light metal that is strong, melts at high temperature, and is resistant to corrosion. Melted-down, it has been used to make parts for missiles and spacecraft. It has been alloyed with copper to make golf clubs. It is transparent to x-rays, so it is used in the windows of x-ray tubes. It is toxic.
5) Boron –Combine boron with nitrogen and you get crystals similar to carbon, meaning that boron is very hard and heat resistant. Boron is used to make tools for cutting hardened steel. Boron by itself is brittle.
6) Carbon – Carbon is the element of organic compounds and is the most important element of life. It is the spiral backbone of DNA and in the rings and streamers of steroids and proteins. Carbon also forms diamond, which is the hardest known substance, except maybe boron under certain conditions but this is being studied. If

you burn a diamond, it turns into carbon dioxide gas. The lead in pencils is graphite, a form of carbon. Carbon has been boycotted before by people who mine for diamonds because they do not want diamonds to be artificially created; lives have been lost due to wars over diamonds and carbon even though diamonds are just rocks. Carbon is in sugars. Carbon-12 has 6 protons, 6 neutrons, 6 electons.

7) Nitrogen – Nitrogen makes up 78 percent of the atmosphere, the rest mostly oxygen. Nitrogen combined with hydrogen makes ammonia, which is used in nitrogen fertilizers. Combined with silicon, silicon nitride is so hard it is used to make cutting tools. Nitrogen is also part of nitroglycerine pills for angina (C3,H5,N3,O9). Liquid nitrogen is used as a cooling liquid. The boiling point of liquid nitrogen is -196^0 Celsius.

8) Oxygen - Oxygen reacts with organic compounds as an oxidizer, or fuel. Combustion with oxygen drives furnaces and motors that use fuel. At $-183\ ^0$ Celsius oxygen is a pale blue liquid. Oxygen is one of The most abundant elements on earth because it is even in the compound of mineral rocks.

9) Fluorine – Fluorine is a pale yellow gas that is the most reactive of all the elements. A fluorine compound isused in a non-stick frying pan. Fluorine is used in fluoride toothpaste.

10) Neon –Neon is an invisible gas. Neon orange-red lights are made with low-pressure neon gas that is charged with a high-voltage electric discharge. Neon is non-reactive.

11) Sodium – Sodium is explosive. If you throw sodium into water, it makes hydrogen gas and ignites with a bang, throwing flaming sodium in all directions. Combined with chlorine, it forms table salt. Combined with hydroxide, it forms lye, which is sold as a drain cleaner and is poisonous to humans if ingested and can severely burn the skin. When sodium(11) is sold, it is sold in a container sealed with argon(18)

12) Magnesium –Magnesium is a metal that is strong, light, easy to machine, and flammable. It has been used in race cars, airplanes, and bicycles. Chestnuts have magnesium.

13) Aluminum –Aluminum is light and strong and does not rust. Instead of rust, the hard substance corundum oxidizes on the surface. Aluminum cookware has good thermal conductivity.

14) Silicon – White silica sand (silicon dioxide) is silicon and oxygen and is an oxide of silicon. Silicon dioxide is used in computer chips. Quartz is SiO4. Some sea sponges grow bones of silica glass. Most of the earth's soil, clay, sand, and rocks contain some silicate minerals.

15) Phosphorus – Phosphorus can be deadly because it is ignitable. It is what is on the tips of matches that you strike to get the match to burn. Phosphate fertilizer made from phosphate rocks help replenish soil so crops can grow. Human bones are calcium phosphate.

16) Sulfur – Sulfur occurs around volcanoes and geothermal vents and has a strong odor. Foods like eggs, garlic, and onions, give off gases from sulfur compounds.

17) Chlorine – Chlorine gas has a pale yellow color and is poisonous. Chlorine is used in bleach cleaning solution. Common table salt is

sodium chloride (NaCl). The main component of stomach acid is hydrochloric acid (HCl). Calcium chloride pellets melt snow and ice.

18) Argon -Argon is a nonreactive inert gas which turns blue with electric current. Argon and nitrogen is used in light bulbs. Krypton (36), xenon(54), and halogen gases are also used in light bulbs. Argon is in the atmosphere. Argon can be produced as a by-product of the production of liquid oxygen(8) and liquid nitrogen(7). Argon has been used to top off bottles of wine to preserve the wine. When sodium(11) is sold, it is sold in a container sealed with argon.

19) Potassium – Potassium is a metal that oxidizes quickly when exposed to air and turns black. Potassium bursts into violet flames when it is thrown into water. Potassium contains some radioactive isotopes. Bananas contain potassium. The human body needs potassium for nerve transmission. Potassium is used to make fertilizers. Potassium chloride can be used instead of sodium chloride to season food.

20) Calcium – Calcium is a shiny metal, similar in appearance to aluminum. It is unstable in air, decomposing into calcium hydroxide and calcium carbonate, which are chalky white. Calcium produces hydrogen gas when it is thrown in water. Chalk is made of gypsum, which is calcium sulfate. Mammal bones are a rigid hydroxyapatite foam, a form of hydrated calcium phosphate. In humans, calcium is constantly moving in and out of cells, mediating the actions of nerves and muscles, so calcium is needed in substantial quantities. Seashells are made of calcium carbonate.

21) Scandium – Scandium is a metal that is not concentrated anywhere on earth but scattered all over the earth, which makes it expensive. It is used to make metal halide lights and parts for fighter jets, baseball bats, and bicycles.

22) Titanium – Titanium is a metal of great strength that does not rust so it is used for jet engines, tools, rockets, artificial hip joints, dental implants, jewelry, hammers, electric razor blades. It is considered to be non-allergenic. Titanium dioxide is the white in paint.

23) Vanadium – Vanadium is added to steel to make tools such as socket wrenches, drill and router bits, and pliers. Vanadium steel is harder than Titanium steel. Green emeralds can be vanadium with impurities but green emeralds can also be crystals of beryllium aluminum silicate.

24) Chromium -Chromium is a shiny non-corrosive metal that is used to make chromium stainless steel silverware and chrome car bumpers of the 1950s and 1960sCE. If chromium is oxidized, it produces a green pigment that is used in paints and glazes

25) Manganese – Manganese is a metal used to make steel alloys. Manganese can make a sharp edge such as the blades of razors. Manganese oxide pigments are black and have been found in cave drawings dated 15,000 BCE. Manganese carbonate crystals are reddish in color and are called rhodochrosites. Hazelnuts have manganese.

26) Iron - Iron is a metal. The first humans made tools out of stone during the stone age, then humans began making tools out of copper(29) and tin(50) during the bronze age. Next, the iron age followed and iron is widely used to make steel alloys. Stoves, cooking skillets, coins of

currency, wrenches, weights, horseshoes, and nails were once made from only iron before steel compounds were produced. Iron nails became obsolete when steel nails were invented that did not corrode. Iron balls were once shot out of canons as weapons. Steel cables, steel beams, steel chain gloves, steel milling bits are all made with iron. Iron transports oxygen in the blood of human bodies. For plants, magnesium(12) transports chlorophyll. Copper(29) is an important metal enzyme for spiders and horseshoe crabs with blue blood. For vitamin B12, the core is cobalt(27).

27) Cobalt – Cobalt is a metal that is used as a component in steel alloys used to make drills and milling bits. Added in trace amounts to glass, cobalt compounds gives the glass a blue tint.
Cobalt-aluminum oxide is used as a purple pigment.

28) Nickel – Nickel is a metal that is often plated over iron to prevent the corrosion of iron. It is used in the alloys used to make jet engines because the alloys can maintain strength at high temperatures.
Nickel and chrome are used to plate automobile bumpers.

29) Copper – Copper is a metal that is soft enough that it is used to make jewelry, chains, and statues. Copper is blended with tin(50) to make bronze, and blended with zinc(30) to make brass. Copper has electrical conductivity and is used for wiring. Acidic foods stored in copper containers may contain traces of copper. Copper doorknobs may have antimicrobial properties. Coins of currency have been made from pure copper, but later coins were made from copper alloys or the coins were only copper plated on the outside and the inside consisted of a cheaper metal so that the total cost of making the coin was cheaper than the intended worth of the coin.

30) Zinc – Zinc is a metal of lower strength that is used in coins, in batteries, some bolts, and to plate steel structures to prevent corrosion of iron(26). The mineral smithsonite is zinc carbonate.

31) Gallium – Gallium, mercury(80), and cesium(55) are soft metals. Gallium can melt at room temperature. Gallium is used in alloys used make computer chips, gallium nitride laser diodes, and thermometers.

32) Germanium – Germanium is a metalloid, somewhat like metal and somewhat not like metal. Metalloid elements are Boron(5), Silicon(14), Germanium(32), Arsenic(33), Antimony(51), Tellurium(52), and Polonium(84). Germanium has been used to make semiconductors, diodes, transistors, fiber optics, and infrared optics. Germanium is opaque in visible light but transparent in infrared light.

33) Arsenic – Arsenic is a metalloid poisonous to humans but research is being done to see if human bodies need it at small levels; it is being fed to chickens and seems to benefit the growth of chickens but it is unclear the affect this may have on humans who eat the chicken. Arsenic was used in green pigments on green wallpaper, and when mold grew on the wallpaper, arsenic gas could kill everyone in the room. The same arsenic in arsenic green pigment is rat poison.

34) Selenium – Selenium is a non-metal. It is an electrical insulator in the dark but a conductor when exposed to light. It is used in xerographic photocopiers and laser printers. Selenium was used in diodes before

silicon and germanium. Selenium is a nutrient to the human body in small amounts but toxic in big amounts. Brazil nuts contain selenium. Red pigments have been made from selenium.

35) Bromine - Bromine is a halogen as Fluorine(9), Chlorine(17), Iodine(53) are in the halogen column of the periodic table. These elements are highly reactive. Bromine atoms are added to citrus oil as an emulsifier in citrus drinks so the oil will remain suspended in water. Bromine tablets are added to hot tubs as a disinfectant in the way that chlorine is the disinfectant of cool-water swimming pools. Bromine can evaporate at room temperature as a reddish purple vapor. Mercury also evaporates so it is an insidious poison. Bromine is also used in making flame retardants for synthetic fabrics, such as pajamas. If pajamas are made from cotton, they are not required to be treated with flame retardants.

36) Krypton - Krypton is a noble gas in the same column of the periodic table as Helium(2), Neon(10), Argon(18), Xenon(54), Radon(86), and the unnamed element (118). Krypton will not bond or react with other elements. Krypton has a bluish tint when an electric current is ran through it. It has been used in light bulbs.

37) Rubidium - Rubidium is a soft silvery metal with a low melting point. It has been used in fireworks to create a purplish light. It is an alkali metal which means it is highly reactive. Rubidium has been used in atomic clocks.

38) Strontium - Strontium is an alkali earth metal that has been used in bright paints that glow in the dark. The glow comes from light that is absorbed and then slowly released. Strontium is used in sensitive toothpaste. Strontium titanate is a gem that looks like a golden diamond and was developed before cubic zirconia.

39) Yttrium - Yttrium is a transition metal. Yttrium barium copper oxide turns into a superconductor when cooled by liquid nitrogen. A magnet would float about a quarter of an inch above the superconductor. Yttrium aluminum garnet crystals are used in pulsed lasers to bounce beams of light; the beams have even been bounced off the moon by reflectors put there by astronauts and cosmonauts. Scientists have been studying the moon for decades and have calculated that the moon is moving away from the earth each year at a rate of about 38 mm (1.4972 inches) each year.

40) Zirconium - Zirconium is a transition metal that is used to make the tubes for the fuel pellets in nuclear reactors, laboratory crucibles, bombs, sandpaper lapping wheels for grinding down welds on oil rigs, giant earth-moving equipment, and dirt bikes. Zirconium dioxide in crystal form is a cubic zirconia which looks like a diamond.

41) Niobium - Niobium is a transition metal that has been used in alloys to make rocket nozzles because they resist corrosion even at high temperatures. Niobium has been used to make jewelry and coins because it can be anodized to show colors. Coils of niobium-titanium wire are superconducting and are used to create the huge magnetic fields inside MRI (magnetic

resonance imaging) machines in the medical field.

42) Molybdenum – Molybdenum is a transition metal used in steel alloys where it gives great strength and heat resistance. Molybdenum is used as a high-pressure lubricant. It is also used in a device to decay into Technetium, which is used in creating medical images.

43) Technetium – Technetium is radioactive and is used to create gamma ray images of bones. It is stored in containers shielded by lead or tungsten. It is found in small amounts in some ores but it was the first non-naturally occurring element to be created. It exists only through technology.

44) Ruthenium – Ruthenium is called a precious metal. It is very expensive. It shares properties with element platinum. It is highly resistant to corrosion and has been used in superalloys to make turbine blades. It is used as a catalyst and an alloying agent. Ruthenium chloride is red. Ruthenium has been used to make jewelry and solar cells.

45) Rhodium – Rhodium is minor part of platinum(78) ore. Rhodium has a shiny shine. It has been used to make jewelry, as a catalyst in automobile catalytic converters, and on electrical contacts in reed switches.

46) Palladium – Palladium is used in automobile catalytic converters which reduce smog by burningup residues of unburned fuel in the exhaust and converting it to carbon dioxide and water. Palladium metal will absorb hydrogen gas.

47) Silver – Silver tarnishes. Silver has been used in coins for thousands of Years. Coins dated 261BCE have been found. Silver is the most reflective element and is used to make mirrors. Silver is the best electrical conductor of all the elements but copper is used more because it is cheaper and tarnishes more slowly. Gold electrical contacts do not tarnish at all. Silver is used in compunds to improve heat conductivity.

48) Cadmium – Cadmium is toxic to the environment and humans as it accumulates in the body as does lead(82), and mercury(80). Nickel-cadmium rechargeable batteries should be taken recycling points instead of being thrown into the garbage. Cadmium has been used to make bolts and brake rotors because it does not rust or cause corrosion. Cadmium foil was intended for radiation shielding. Cadmium sulfide is a yellow pigment.

49) Indium – Indium is a soft metal that you can dent with your fingernails. It is one of very few metals that can wet glass so it is used as a gasket in high-vacuum applications. Indium in the form of indium tin(50) oxide is a transparent conductor of electricity that is used in display pixels in LCD screens.

50) Tin – Tin is non-magnetic. It is not used to make coins because over time in cold weather it will turn almost into a dark gray powder because the cold changes its crystal structure.

51) Antimony – Antimony is a metal that was alloyed with lead(82), and tin(50) for over 500 years from about 1500 CE to 2000 CE in an invention called movable type that was used in printing presses. Johann Gutenberg was

the inventor. Antimony is also alloyed in metals to produce gun bullets. An element collector named Theodore Gray reported that as ingots of cast antimony are cooling they emit beautiful melodic pinging noises that sound like Tibetan chimes. Antimony was used to make incense burners.

52) Tellurium – Tellurium is a metalloid that has an odor like garlic. Tellurium has been used to make DVD rewritable discs. Bismuth telluride has been used in thermoelectric coolers in one-can-of-soda machines. It is a rare element.

53) Iodine – Iodine is halogen gas that is more mellow than the gases above it in the halogen column of the periodic table, which are fluorine(9), chlorine(17), and bromine(35). Iodine has been mixed with alcohol and used as a disinfectant for the skin. It has been used to kill fungus on the hooves of horses. Iodine is consumed by humans to avoid goiter, which is the enlargement of the thyroid gland in the neck area under the throat. Iodine has been used as a contrasting agent in CT scans. Iodine was combined with chewing gum, then it was put in table salt. Iodine is a solid at room temperature.

54) Xenon – Xenon is a noble gas and was thought to be inert and non-reactive, but is was observed in 1962 that xenon actually formed compounds with another element, like with the halogen gas fluorine(9). When lit by an electric current it produces a pale-violet glow. Xenon is used in producing lightbulbs for cinema projectors where a long beam of light has to be bounced off of a mirror.n Xenon has been used in headlights for cars to produce a bright dazzling light.

55) Cesium – Cesium is an alkali metal that explodes when you throw it into water like sodium. Cesium is used in atomic clocks to keep time of day. Cesium is used to clear oxygen and water from vacuum chambers. Cesium would melt if you held it in your hand but it would catch on fire if it broke and reacted with the moisture on your skin.

56) Barium – Barium is less dense than titanium(22) but barium compounds can be heavy. Barium sulfate is opaque to x-rays, so it is swallowed to make images of the digestive tract. Barium is used to remove oxygen from lamps and vacuum tubes. Barium is used in yttrium barium copper oxide (YBCO) superconductors.

57) Lanthanum - Lanthanumis a rare earth metal that is used in lighter flints to make sparks. Rare earth oxides are heat-resistant and glow brightly when hot; for example, lanthanum oxide glows brightly in camping lantern mantles. Rare earth metals are not really rare; they used to be hard to isolate them in pure form, but extraction methods were improved and now they are available for scientists to study pplications for them.

58) Cerium – Cerium oxide is used as an abrasive to polish glass and for lighter flints as it sparks when scratched.

59) Praseodymium – Praseodymium is a rare earth metal combined with neodymium(60) and to make didymium eyelenses for glassblowers to filter out yellow light.

60) Neodymium – Neodymium is a rare earth metal used to make strong magnets; the magnets can jump at each other from a foot away and can cause bodily injury. Neodymium has been used in making bracelets, earrings, and miniature motors.

61) Promethium – Promethium used to be used to make luminous dials for diving watches as radium(88) were both were replaced by tritium which is an isotope of hydrogen (1). The isotope of Promethium used to make diving watches only lasted 2.6 years. Promethium can help keep the gas ionized inside of fluorescent light bulbs. Promethium and technetium(43) are the two exceptions to the rule that rare earth element below bismuth(83) are stable.

62) Samarium – Samarium-cobalt magnets can operate at highter temperatures where neodymium-iron-boron magnets would lose their magnetism. Samarium-cobalt magnets are used in guitar picks. Samarium has been used to make medicines.

63) Europium – Europium's applications involve paints that can glow brightly for many minutes or dimly for many hours. It is also used in the phosphors of compact fluorescent light bulbs. Europium is also used in cathode-ray tube monitors and color television sets. CRT's are becoming scarce.

64) Gadolinium – Gadolinium compounds are paramagnetic and are used as a contrast for MRI scans in medicine the way barium(56) is used as a contrast to image the gastrointestinal system.

66) Dysprosium- Dysprosium is used in the form of dysprosium iodide and dysprosium bromide salts to impart spectral lines to the red color range in high intensity discharge lighting.

67) Holmium – Holmium is used in magnetic applications of MRI imaging and laser surgery. Holmium chloride is used in high intensity discharge lights, where holmium's spectrum is useful.

If you have done any welding or metalwork, do not agree to MRI imaging until you have had your eyes x-rayed for metal fragments; any metal fragments must be removed before MRI imaging because metal pieces can damage your eyes by the magnets of the MRI; also, bones that have metal pins can be damaged.

MRI radiology imaging machines contain magnets that have magnetic fields of strengths that are 60,000 times that of the Earth's. Do not have an MRI If you have metal in your body.

68) Erbium – Erbium has been used in fiber optics and lasers to make a pulse of light stronger.

69) Thulium – Thulium bromide is the form of thulium that is used in high-intensity discharge lights. Thulium could be used as a lighter flint like Lanthanum(57) and Cerium(58). Thulium is one of the rare earth metals that are not actually rare – it took scientists a long time over decades to enable a method of extracting and

separating elements that are combined together in rocks so that the elements could be used in pure forms, kind of like separating oil and water that are mixed together.

70) Ytterbium – Ytterbium is used as a doping agent in lasers. To understand how lasers work, you would have to study calculus and physics for several years; scientists have said that math is the secret to understanding the entire universe.

71) Lutetium – Lutetium has been used in high-intensity discharge lights.

72) Hafnium – Hafnium is used in plasma torches to cut steel. Hafnium is highly resistant corrosion at high temperatures and has a high melting point.

73) Tantalum – Tantalum is used to make high-capacity adaptors which absorb and dampen noise spikes in digital circuits that generate a lot of electrical noise. Tantalum has been boycotted because it is mined where endangered gorillas live; gorillas have died just because people were fighting overtantalum.

74) Tungsten – Tungsten is more durable than diamond and harder than steel. Tungsten is dense and has been used to make fishing sinkers, darts, and shot puts. Rings have been made for fingers from tungsten, but if they get stuck on your finger, they are hard to cut off because the metal is so strong. Tungsten filament incandescent light bulbs converts only 10 percent of electricity into lightand the rest is released as heat and infrared radiation. Compact fluorescent bulbs are more efficient than tungsten filament incandescent light bulbs.

75) Rhenium – Rhenium is used to make super alloys for the turbine blades in fighter-jet engines. It has been used in x-ray tubes and in mass spectrometers.

76) Osmium – Osmium is the densest element. It is the hardest metal element. It has a bluish tint in the right light. Osmium found with iridium(77) in nature has been used to make phonograph needles and fountain pen nibs. Finely powdered osmium oxidizes in air and forms osmium tetroxide which is volatile and extremely toxic.

77) Iridium – Iridium is extremely hard to melt. It has been used to make spark plugs. Iridium may have been introduced to the earth from an asteroid that wiped out the dinosaurs.

78) Platinum – Platinum is resistant to corrosion and can withstand high temperatures. It is used in catalytic converters to oxidize unburned hydrocarbon fragments into carbon dioxide and water, Platinum has been used to make spark plugs for cars and laboratory equipment.

79) Gold – Gold is rare and never loses its shine. It is a good conductor of electricity and has been used to make gold-plated electrical connectors and circuit boards.

80) Mercury – Mercury is toxic. It is dense. It has been used in thermostat switches.

81) Thallium – Thallium is toxic.

82) Lead – Lead is toxic. It is dense yet soft enough to be easily molded into piping and bullets. Old lead piping is being replaced with iron, copper, and plastic piping. Lead has been removed from paint and gasoline.

Leaded glass is transparent but the lead increases the index of refraction which makes leaded glass sparkly. Lead sulfide crystals have been used in radios. Lead containers have been used to hold radioactive materials. Lead was used a long time ago in linotype printing before antimony(51) was added to make it stronger.

83) Bismuth – Bismuth is the active ingredient in bismuth subsalicylate, which is a medicine for the stomach. If a human consumes too much bismuth salts, their gums may turn black, but this is a rare side effect.

84) Polonium – Polonium is radioactive and fatal to humans. Polonium(84) and Radium(88) was discovered by Marie and Pierre Curie. Marie Curie was born in 1867CE. Pierre experienced signs of radiation sickness such as dull aches in his bones and malaise, but he was killed by a carriage while crossing a street in Paris. Marie died of leukemia in 1934 CE. Even today in 2015CE her notebooks and cookbooks are kept in lead-lined boxes and people who wish to read her notes must wear protective clothing. Polonium was used between sheets of gold and silver in anti-static brushes that were used on phonograph records and film negatives. The half-life is only 138 days.

85) Astatine – Astatine is a radioactive decay of uranium(92) and thorium(90). Only about an ounce of it is present in the entire earth at one time, and because its half-life is only 8.3 hours, it is never the same ounce day to day.

86) Radon – Radon gas is a radioactive decay of uranium(92) and thorium(90) that exist in granite bedrock. Some people want to get rid of the gas, while others breathe in the air containing radon, believing it to be healthy, such as near hot springs of water that are naturally warm due to radiation.

87) Francium – Francium is radioactive and has a 22-minute half-life. Francium is like sodium; it is an alkali metal that would explode if you threw it into a lake. It is hard to find francium; for example the mineral thorite might contain an atom of francium, and if you could put together a lump of francium, it would evaporate itself violently by the heat of its own radioactivity.

88) Radium – Radium is radioactive. It is added to zinc(30) sulfide paint to make it luminous. When the zinc sulfide breaks down, the paint will not glow anymore, but the radium is still radioactive, because the half-life of radium is 1,602 years. Workers in factories about 1920 often licked the tips of their paintbrushes to keep the tips pointed as they painted the numbers and dials of watches; when the workers began to die, people finally realized the dangers of radium and the practice was stopped.

89) Actinium – Actinium has a half-life of 21.8 years and is so radioactive that it glows on its own, unlike radium(88) that needs zinc(30) sulfide to show off its glow. Very little of it is found in nature, but it can be produced in a nuclear reactor. It occurs naturally in uranium ore or the mineral vicanite as an atom or two.

90) Thorium – Thorium is radioactive and is more abundant. Before humans realized radioactivity can kill humans, some humans put thorium in tubes of toothpaste and bottles of radioactive drinking

water. At one time research was done to see if thorium-based nuclear power reactors were possible but the idea was abandoned.

91) Protactinium – Protactinium is radioactive and has a half-life of 32,788 years. An isotope of protactinium has a half-life of 1.17 minutes.

92) Uranium – Uranium was put in the glaze of tiles, plates, and bowls prior to 1942. Geiger counters in 2009CE can still detect radioactivity in such tiles, plates and bowls, especially those with orange-colored pigments. Green glass and red ceramics made with uranium is radioactive. Uranium was used to build a nuclear bomb in the United States of America, and sadly, for all humanity, the bomb was dropped on Japan in 1945CE at the end of WW II.
Uranium bombs involve making lumps of uranium collide with other lumps of uranium; the nuclei of the atoms split, and neutrons and energy is released. The neutrons strike and split other atoms, releasing more neutrons and energy and so on, exponentially. Albert Einstein and Leo Szilard were scientists who realized the danger of nuclear fission. Enrico Fermi was a scientist who discovered that neutrons could be 'moderated' in a controlled way in order to continue a chain reaction. Glenn Seaborg and many other scientists discovered elements.

93) Neptunium – Neptunium was discovered in 1940CE. Neptunium is a side reaction triggered by uranium's decay. Uranium was discovered in 1789 but humans had no idea uranium was radioactive.

94) Plutonium – Plutonium was used in the past in pacemakers but was replaced by lithium batteries. All plutonium is regulated by laws in countries.

95) Americium – Americium is used inside of smoke alarms to detect smoke particles from fires. As Polonium(84) is used between silver and gold for anti-static brushes, americium is put between gold. Scientists have actually swallowed a button of radioactive americium protected by a layer of gold; the gold button simply passed through the human body and was excreted, the gold was unharmed by the acids of the digestive system.

96) Curium – Curium's only applications involve its radioactivity, the heat of which is used to power things that need long-term energy, such as space probes.

97) Berkelium – Berkelium has no practical applications. The longest-lived isotope of berkelium has a half-life of 1,379 years which means that a pound of berkelium would weigh one-half pound after 1,379 years. And there would only be one-quarter pound left after another 1,379 years. The berkelium decays into other elements such as americium(95), neptunium(93), Plutonium(94), and others.

98) Californium – Californium is a powerful neutron emitter. Neutrons have no positive or negative charge, so they are not repelled by negatively charged electrons or positively charged protons, so neutrons can pass through solid matter; such neutrons will convert other elements into radioactive isotopes - humans could become radioactive with a half-life of 15 hours primarily from a sodium isotope. This type of neutron activation analysis has enabled instruments to be manufactured that can see through solid steel, can

detect gold in the middle of a rock, and can detect oil in the bottom of a well.

Elements 99-118 are all radioactive with no practical applications.

99) Einsteinium
100) Fermium
101) Mendelevium
102) Nobelium
103) Lawrencium
104) Rutherfordium
105) Dubnium
106) Seaborgium
107) Bohrium
108) Hassium
109) Meitnerium
110) Darmstadium
111) Roentgenium
112) Copernicium
113) Ununtrium
114) Ununquadium
115) Ununpentium
116) Ununhexium
117) Ununseptium
118) Ununoctium

Anti-matter is identical to matter except that it is composed of particles whose electric charges are opposite to those found in normal matter. There is an asymmetry of matter and antimatter in the visible universe and it is called baryogenesis; this is a great unsolved problem in physics. Anti-matter is the most powerful energy source known to humans; it creates no pollution or radiation and a drop of it could power a large city for a day, but it is highly unstable and ignites when it comes into contact with anything, even air.

Scientists are looking for a higgsino particle and a Higgs boson particle which will be a monumental discovery in particle physics; it is named after Peter Higgs.

An asteroid could hit the earth and wipe out life on earth; humans must find a way to eliminate them before impact.

Golf balls that have been passed through electron beam accelerators have a 5% average increase in bounce.

Magnetometers measure magnetization of ferrous (having iron) metals. Metal detectors detect metals.

To understand how lasers work, you would have to study calculus and physics for several years; scientists have said that math is the secret to understanding the universe.

The earth spins toward the east and the 'sunrise' starts our day as the sun appears in the horizon. In both the northern and southern hemispheres, cyclones (called hurricanes in the west and typhoons in the east) spin in the direction of the earth's rotation, but appear to spin differently in the northern hemisphere and southern hemisphere – this is called the Coriolis effect as explained by engineer Gustave Coriolis (1792-1843) of Paris, France. The cyclones spin in the same direction as the earth's rotation but appear to rotate differently due to the viewer perspective.

The effect of the vortex and spin of water draining from sinks and tubs in the northern and southern hemispheres has been debated. In the Northern Hemisphere, water may go down the drain in a clockwise motion as in a clock with numbers 1 to 12 go around the right side of the clock; in the Southern Hemisphere water may down the drain in a counter-clockwise motion as in a clock with numbers 1 to 12 going around the right side of the clock, but some have documentated that water goes down counter-clockwise in the northern hemisphere and goes down clockwise in the southern hemisphere. Near the equator, water may go down in either direction because the effect is stronger toward the poles.

The principles put forth by Coriolis are important in calculating time and distance for airplanes needing to consider the earth's curvature, rotation, and wind patterns. An example is to imagine that you are standing on the north pole and throw a ball to a person on the equator - you need to throw the ball to the left of the person because the earth is rotating east and rotates faster at the equator so you have to throw the ball where the person will be when the ball reaches the equator. These principles are used for shooting bullets at some targets.

Clocks with the numbers 1 to 12 going around the right side of the clock corresponded to the shadows counted by ancient sundials in the Northern Hemisphere. But some clocks show numbers going from 1 to 12 around the left side of the clock and this corresponds to the way the planet spins; the numbers go in ascending order like the time zones. For example, where it is 8PM in New York, it is 5PM in a location to the west like Los Angelos or Vancouver, 2PM further west in Samoa, it is 11PM in Rio de Janeiro, and 2AM (next day) in locations to the east in France and 9AM (next day) in Hong Kong.

Ernest Shackleton took an expedition to Antarctica South Pole in 1901 CE. William Edward Parry went to the Arctic North Pole in 1827 CE. From Antarctica, water flows north.

There are no two snowflakes exactly alike. Hexagonal snowflakes are crystalline formations of ice which fall through the Earth's atmosphere. Snowflakes have intrigued people throughout history, even 2,300 years ago or around 300BCE, artists, philosophers, and scientists wondered at their shape, recorded them by hand or in photographs, or attempted to recreate them.

It is fun to use your imagination and look for shapesand images in clouds, wood markings, or floor tiles.

Water boils at different temperatures depending on the barometric pressure, or elevation. Water covers 70% of the Earth. Water can be a liquid, vapor, or solid. Water is essential for all life.

Boiling point is the temperature at which a liquid boils, equal to 212 F (100 C) for water at sea level.

The bonds that hold the one oxygen and two hydrogen molecules of water together are so strong that the water molecule would need to be heated to about 3632∘ (2000∘) in a special furnace in order to break the bonds.

Absolute zero is the theoretical temperature in thermodynamic equilibrium at which entropy reaches itsminimum value. It is 0 Kelvin,-273.15 Celsius, -459.67 F, and 0 Rankine.

Triple point of water in thermodynamic equilibrium is 273.16K and 0.01 C. The triple point of a substance is the temperature and pressure at which the three phases (gas, liquid, solid) of it coexists in thermodynamic equilibrium.

Three mediums for the internet are copper, fiber optics, and radio.

CHAPTER 2
Electromagnetic Radiation

Sunlight takes about 8 minutes to reach Earth; moonlight takes 1.3 seconds to reach Earth. It takes sunlight 5.5 years to reach Pluto.

The speed of light is 186,282 miles per second or 300,000 kilometers per second. The speed of light is the maximum speed at which all energy and matter in the universe can travel. The speed of light in a vacuum as a universal physical constant is denoted as **c** and is 299792458 meters per second or $3.00 \text{ X } 10^8$ m/s.

The speed of sound depends on the medium the waves pass through.

The Lord gave us the diversity of colors to see that are the visible range of lightwaves of electromagnetic radiation.

Rainbows are translucent concentric arcs of colored bands that are visible in the air when rain or mist is present in the air and the Sun is at the observer's back. When the sunlight enters the raindrops, it is bent like in a prism. The reflected light emerges from the raindrop at different angles for each color; red light emerges at 42 ^{0}from the incoming beam and violet light emerges at 40 ^{0}. Light from different raindrops enters the observer's eyes.

Twilight is the zone of light that exists when the sun is not more than 12°below the horizon.

People have favorite colors and color combinations. The sunrises, sunsets, and auroras at the poles show breathtaking, amazing colors.

Looking at the sun for too long may damage your eyes.

The Lord gave human beings sounds to hear in certain frequencies of sound waves, and the Lord gave animals and insects sounds to hear in certain frequencies of sound waves. For example, there are dog whistles that dogs can hear but human beings cannot hear.

Dogs can smell 100,000 times stronger than humans.

Some scientists believe that the spirits of the supernatural may be trying to communicate with live humans. There have been recordings made in places where it was thought that spirits, ghosts, or apparitions, have dwelled and recordings showed sound waves that mediums can hear.

Radio waves, microwaves, infrared radiation, visible light, ultraviolet radiation, X-Rays, and gamma rays are the waves of the electromagnetic spectrum.

A telescope named ALMA in Chile, South America is designed to sense longer waves of electromagnetic radiation, where the microwave and infrared bands meet, enabling scientists to see deep space gas clouds and dark areas usually veiled to optical instruments. ALMA is a joint venture of America, Europe, Japan, and Chile.

A spectrometer measures properties of light over a specific portion of the electromagnetic spectrum of radiation, typically used in spectroscopic analysis to identify materials. Early spectroscopes were prisms.
Joseph von Fraunhofer was a German optician (1787-1826CE) in Bavaria who developed the first spectrometer.

Sound waves are mechanical waves. Sonic pertains to the speed of a sound in air at the same height above sea level.

Thermography, which is the science of infrared imaging, measures the amount of radiation emitted by an object which allows one to see something without illumination and allows one to see objects in the dark or through smoke. Thermography has enabled firefighters to find people through smoke and find the hottest part of a fire, building construction workers to find leaks in thermal insulation, rescue workers to find people in snowstorms, militaries to develop weapons that can be used in darkness or low-visibility conditions, and medical technicians and doctors to study the human body and save human lives.

CHAPTER 3
Genetic Evolution

God, the Commander of Evolution, created all living organisms in the Universe. Humans have debated whether God created human beings in a single instant, or if humans evolved; no one knows the correct answer about our beginnings except God. Humans are a mammal in the animal charts that humans have recorded to organize life forms. Placental mammal females carry their young inside of their uterus, most give birth to live babies through a vaginal canal, and the the babies can suckle milk from a breast. All life on Earth is the result of genetic reproduction of nature that has evolved through millenniums of time.

Scientists think it is a possibility that the first organism was in the ocean and evolved to be a land creature. Scientists think humans have evolved from an ape hominid in Africa 4 million years ago and spread to northern latitudes, where the skin lightened to allow the body to produce more Vitamin D. The darker skins are a genetic sunscreen against ultraviolet radiatin. Homo erectus is the earliest ancestor of homo sapiens in the Homo genus and lived 1.3 million to 1.8 million years ago during the Pleistocene Age. Homo neanderthalensis is another species of evolutionary humans larger in size that existed about 200,000 years ago; some scientists believe Neanderthal DNA is mixed in with Homo Sapien DNA. Cro Magnon (Homo Sapiens Sapiens) evolved about 40,000 years ago. The study of humans is the scientific discipline of anthropology. Humans could have evolved from many species mixing; there is something primitive in all humans such as shared DNA with chimpanzees, bananas, and lettuce. Our ancestors were electrically grounded to the earth because they did not wear shoes but were barefoot on the ground. Some think it is possible that another alien life form came from outer space and landed on the earth; the aliens could have mixed with life forms on earth. A gigantic spaceship that was reported to be an alien mothership was seen in Manipur, India in 2015. Other alien spaceship sightings were in California 2017, New Jersey 1952. Some think aliens could be kidnapping humans to create alien hybrids.

Chemicals and vitamin deficiencies in pregnant women have caused genetic changes to occur in babies growing inside a woman's uterus, so pregnant women should not ingest drugs or certain medicines, or alcohol. Pregnant women should alert an X-ray technician if she is pregnant.

Pregnant women should avoid trampolines, skiing, sky-diving, hot baths, horseback riding, x-rays, alcohol, drugs, high-heels, soft cheese, deli meats, sushi, eggnog that has not been pasteurized, and limit the use of caffeine so babies can have a good chance to be healthy.

It is a general rule that when a baby is being born, when the head is coming out of the birth canal, do not push on the head to push it back up the birth canal to postpone delivery because it can physically injure the baby or the mother or cause fatalities.

Scientists have classified humans as mammals in the animalia kingdom, in the subphylum cordata meaning animals that have vertebrates. Scientists believe the appendix is a genetic remnant leftover from thousands of years ago; Charles Darwin proposed that humans millions of years ago may have used the appendix to help digest great amounts of foliage that the early humans ate. Human wisdom teeth are molars that may be remnants.

Blood is about twice as thick as water, thanks to all the cells and other particles floating in it. It takes roughly 20 to 60 seconds for a drop of blood to travel away from the heart and back again. Blood makes up 10 percent of your body weight. To find out how many pints your body contains, weigh yourself and divide your weight by 12. Adults usually have roughly 10 to 15 pints. A newborn baby has about one half pint or one cup of blood.

Scientists have been studying blood types and chromosomes since the early 1900s CE. There are 33 human blood group systems that are internationally recognized but most humans fit into the ABO category with A, B, AB, O being the blood type with a + or – after the blood type for the RH factor. The other categories involve the presence of antigens on different chromosomes and much more. Type O Negative is a universal blood donor; any human can receive Type O Negative. Type AB is a universal recipient and can receive any blood type. Compatibility for receiving plasma and platelets is different.

Blood, plasma, and platelets are needed around the globe to save lives and to continue research.

45% of humans have Blood Type O (from 40,000 years ago when humans were mostly hunters and meat eaters). 40% of humans have Blood Type A (from 25,000-15,000 years ago when Caucasian cultivators ate meats and whole grains). 11% of humans have Blood Type B (from 15,000-10,000 years ago when Mongolians of the Himalayan steppes ate meat and dairy). Less than 5% of human have Blood Type AB.

Crabs and spiders have blue blood. Their blood contains copper instead of iron. Earthworms and leeches have green blood – the green comes from an iron substance called chlorocruorin. Many invertebrates, such as starfish, have clear or yellowish blood. Ladybugs have orange blood. For plants, magnesium is an important metal ion for the chlorophyll molecules.

All races of people are beautiful, with various skin tones, with various eye colors and hair textures. No one race of people is superior over another but all are equal. The Caucasian race of humans with blonde or red hair, blue or green eyes, and light skin are in danger of extinction because of recessive genes.

Scientists think the increasing number of Cesarean births, which are infants delivered by surgery through the mother's abdomen, is a result of genetic mixing of different cultures where smaller-sized women are mating with bigger-sized males, causing bigger babies.

Some humans choose to live in a traditional family lifestyle, having one spouse and babies. Be faithful to your mate and keep your bodies pure for each other. Other humans choose to live a single life or may just want to have different partners throughout life.

People participating in multiple sex partners, or surrogate motherhood or fatherhood should consider the details of the pregnancies because most children want to know the identities of their biological mother and father.

Cloning humans and chimera genetics raises concerns for many people.

CHAPTER 4 *Human Body*

Almost 99% of the mass of the human body is made up of the six elements oxygen, carbon, hydrogen, nitrogen, calcium, and phosphorus. About .85% is composed of only the five elements potassium, sulfur, sodium, chlorine, magnesium. All are necessary for life.

The remaining elements are trace elements, of which more than a dozen are thought to be necessary for life or play an active role in health; for example, fluorine, which hardens enamel but seems to have no other function. The human body is 10% human and 90% bacteria, fungi, and microorganisms. At one time, there is 6 septillion (6 followed by 24 zeros) processes going on in the human body that is estimated to have 100 trillion cells.

The human body contains cells. There are 46 chromosomes in 23 pairs. One pair of chromosomes determines gender; XX is female and XY is male. All human gametes begin as XX and some turn into XY.

A scientist named Robert Hooke was the first to describe a cell.

Many cells grouped together form tissue. The tissues make up the organs such as heart, lungs, kidneys, digestive system. There are 2.5 million blood cells in a human body at one time.One scientist wrote that there is six feet of DNA in every cell. Every cell in your body is constantly working and never stops. Even when you are resting, every cell in your body is working. Some cells can be replaced.

Human Body Systems

The human body has two eyes, two ears, one nose, one mouth, and one anus for waste removal. Females have a vaginal canal to give live birth to babies. The male is born with a natural condom.

The skeletal system contains 206 bones. The bones produce blood. The ribs protect the heart. The skull protects the brain. Vertebrae of the spinal column protect the spinal cord which is connected to the brain.

The muscular system consists of 600 muscles that keep the skeletal system moving. You move the muscles in the legs, arms, and neck. But heart, stomach, and lung muscles move by themselves. There are large muscles in the legs and arms, and small muscles around the eyes.

The heart is a pump with 4 chambers and 4 valves that handles about 2,000 gallons (7570 liters) of blood daily. The heart beats about 108,000 times a day and about 2.5 billion times in a lifetime.

The digestive system processes food to break it down into a size the cells can handle in order for the cells to get energy and nutrients. First, teeth and saliva tear food apart and grind food into mush. When swallowed, the food goes down a long muscular tube into the stomach. Even if you were upside down on your head and swallowed food, it would travel up to your stomach because of muscles. Inside the stomach the food is digested into a soupy liquid and travels into coiled tubes called intestines where your food will be released into the blood system as nutrients

through the walls of your intestines. Then, cells all over your body will get some food.
Humans have two sets of teeth: baby teeth which fall out and then adult teeth come in.

The respiratory system gets the oxygen we need into our bodies. When air is breathed through our noses and mouths, the air goes down the trachea into smaller tubes that go into the lungs. The oxygen gets picked up by the blood. Every single cell of the body needs oxygen to stay alive and work properly. The lungs also allow carbon dioxide to be released from the body when we breathe out, which is part of the excretory system.

The circulatory system is the delivery system for the things our bodies need. The stomach is not the end of the line for food. The lungs are not the end of the line for oxygen. Cells need oxygen and nutrients to live, and it is the job of the circulatory system to deliver the oxygen and nutrients. There are about 100,000 miles (160900 kilometers) of vessels in the circulatory system.

The 3 main parts of the circulatory system are the blood, the heart muscle, and the blood vessels. The blood contains the oxygen and nutrients. The heart pumps the blood. The blood vessels are the tubes that reach every part of your body. Some tubes are so narrow that cells have to line up single-file in order to travel down the tube. If all of the tubes in your body were lined up, the length would go around the world twice.
White blood cells are germ fighters and help to keep the body warm. Blood is a liquid organ.

The body contains electricity. Standing barefoot or in leather soles on soil, sand, or grass infuses the body with neutrons which can thin the blood, reduce inflammation in cells with a positive charge, and serve as antioxidants and free-radical electron busters. The neutrons cannot pass through rubber soles but can pass through leather soles.

Some are concerned that there are great fields of electromagnetic radiation that are caused naturally or are man-made that could have harmful effects on humans. Places inside and around the outside of your home may have EMF radiation. A pink nose may indicate that your nose is getting radiation from a microwave oven. Do not keep cell phones near your body when sleeping.

The excretory system is the system that gets rid of the waste in the body. When we breathe out, we exhale carbon dioxide. Our digestive system allows us to release the remains of food that the body does not need. Blood passes through kidneys to get rid of water, salt, and other wastes. The kidneys clean and filter the blood. Urine is stored in the bladder until it can be released from the body. Skin helps to remove body waste like water and salt through sweat and tears, and also helps keep you cool. Sweat contains protein that reacts with aluminum in anti-perspirant that reacts with protein in cotton to create a yellow-brownish stain in the armpits.

Kidneys contain approximately 145 miles of tiny tubes and filter 50 gallons of blood each day, extracting up to 2 quarts of water and impurities.

Lungs are part 2 body systems; respiratory and excretory.

Blood is part of 2 body systems; circulatory and excretory.

Bones are part of 2 body systems; circulatory and skeletal.

The immune system helps fight germs such as bacteria and viruses. The immune system is constantly on guard to keep you safe from sickness and infection.

The skin is part of the immune system and is the first line of defense against germs. The skin keeps germs outside of the body. Saliva, mucous, tears, and ear wax help prevent germs from entering the body. White cells destroy germs.

The circulatory system helps the immune system by having white cells on guard for you if you get a cut by helping to prevent infection.

The endocrine system affects every system in our body and controls how our bodies grow and develop with a collection of chemicals called hormones. Hormones affect all body systems, help us grow, burn sugar for energy, help us recover from injuries, digest foods, affect moods, and prepare our bodies to handle stress.

The nervous system is made up of the brain, spinal cord, and nerves. Millions of nerve cells carry messages from the brain to other nerve endings in every part of our body through the spinal cord. The brain is the command center for all of the other parts of our body. Muscles are controlled by nerves. Skin contains nerve endings which allow us to feel the sensations of cold, hot, sharp, soft, and hot. The nerve endings send the sensation to your brain via the spinal cord. Senses that help our brain determine our balance and reaction include sight, sound, taste, touch, smell, need to go to the bathroom. Normally a human has two legs to stand on for balance. Try standing on one leg, lifting the other one out. Your body will naturally have a shaky reaction as your brain tries to compensate and get rebalanced.

The brain and nervous system keep all your body systems working every minute of every day. Every cell in your body is constantly working and never stops. Some cells are replaced.

Spinal pain can be caused by repetitive motions and other things. Wearing different types of shoes may cause pressure points on knees, ankles, feet, or spine and tailbone. Carrying heavy shoulder bags or backpacks may cause pain in the neck area of the spine.

The left brain processes from parts to whole, arranging things in logical sequence, and then draws conclusions. The left brain deals with reality. Left-brained people have no problem making lists, daily planning, and getting things done. Left-brain people can express themselves cleary in words when giving directions such as 'Go 2 miles and take a left at Green Street'.

The right brain processes from whole to parts. Right-brained people need an overview at the beginning in order to understand the parts. They might need to read an overview of a lecture before actually listening to the lecture or they might have difficulty understanding the parts. Right-brained people may be more emotional or deal with the imagination. Right-brained people may skip from task to task so they might need to focus more to finish a task. Right-brained people may have difficulty expressing themselves in words and they may give more visual directions such as 'Go 2 miles and then you'll see a library on the right and then take a left at the street when you see the fire station'.

Language may be processed in the left brain and visual arts in the right brain. Scientists say we speak from the left brain but sing from the right brain.

If a person is very emotional, they may be stuck in their right brain – they should do some math problems, read a book, play a music instrument, or do a task that involves sequencing like playing a card game of solitaire to invoke their left brain processes. The left brain pays attention to spelling and punctuation, but the right brain pays attention to coherence and meaning, so use both of your brains.

Doctor Guyatri Devi is a neurologist who studied the brain for 23 years and said in 2017 that the aging of the brain varies with each individual and there is a spectrum of hope as to how long seniors will retain their cognizance and awareness.

Massage therapy can help relieve stress. Reflexology is massaging reflex points of the hands, feet, and head. If you massage your thumbs, it is believed to relieve headaches. Daily exercises and stretching is healthy.

Some human senses are hearing, seeing, smelling, tasting, touching, instinct, sense of acceleration, feeling pressure, sense of time, feeling hot and cold, itches, sexual urge and release which can be done alone or with a partner.

In the act of sexual reproduction, after the rod of the male is joined with the velva of the female and the male or female gyrate and move their hips, a baby will come in about 9 full moons. Once a month, the female's womb will be emptied of life-giving substances of an egg and blood that will be refreshed the next month with a fresh egg and a fresh layer of blood to nourish a developing embryo.

In sex for pleasure, it has been said that one should not make the other responsible for the climax because each person must learn to relax and achieve it themself. It is helpful if a male can retain the rod for a few minutes so the female can gyrate herself on the rod. The female and male can move their hips to locate their focal points. The female can take the man's rod in her hand and rub it on her velva for pleasure.

If a woman's menstrual cycles are regular, it may be assumed that the only time the woman could have unprotected sex without getting pregnant would be during the few days after her menstrual cycle has ended. Protected sex avoids pregnancy and sexually transmitted diseases.

Some think it is best to not get pregnant at older age or right before a menstrual cycle, because right before a menstrual cycle, the egg composition starts breaking down. The egg is at its best when ovulation first occurs, about 14 days after the beginning of the last menstrual period.

If a loved one falls asleep in the middle of intimacy, do not let this be an upset, for the loved one is tired.

Since it take one male and one female to create a new human, most think that 2 is a divine number for a marriage. Heterosexual means a man and a woman in a sexual relationship.

Some humans engage in a same-sex love relationship or change their gender. Monogamous sex is being with one person. Just because two friends are the same sex, do not assume that they are homosexual.

Do not be a sexual predator on any human or animal. The sexual urge is just like an itch or a sneeze and can be released by masturbation massage. Sexual urge is natural and we should not be embarrassed or disgusted by sexual urge. Sex and porn is for adults only. Many think that sex should be a private affair and not highlighted in the media.

Some animals like spiders do not connect together to reproduce. The male spider sprays his sperm on a web and then the female spider lays her eggs on top of the sperm to fertilize the eggs.

Some fish are all male upon birth but the largest fish will evolve into a female to lay eggs.

In plants and trees, flowers and pine cones are the sex organs. Some pine cones are female and some pine cones are male.

Plant, Animal and Human life are fragile

Many plants like the tentree and animals like the dodo bird, saber-toothed tiger, and woolly mammoth have become extinct in past centuries. In 1809CE a man named Darwin from England suggested a theory of natural selection and evolution and survival of the fittest. Carl Linne classified plants and animals in Sweden in 1707CE. John Hogg from Scotland, R H Whittaker, Carl Woese of Illinois, Kevin Kelley, T H Huxley, and George Mendel from Czech Republic in 1822CE were biologists or researchers who studied genes.

Ernst Haeckel, who was a man, suggested bacteria should be in their own classification. A geochemist named Victoria Bennett, who was a woman, said stromatolites created oxygen 3.5 billion years ago; then scientists believed that oxygen was not present in the atmosphere when the earth was first formed. Later, scientists theorized that life forms of vertebrates could have evolved from the oceans. A small wormlike being called Pikaia Gracilens has a primitive spinal column and is the earliest known ancestor of vertebrates, including possibly humans.

Some scientists say survival of the human species is not guaranteed. Humans must cooperate and work together in order to survive; there is harmful bacteria on the earth that could wipe out the human race. The human mind can be as fragile as the body, so we should treat each other with respect.

Henry J. Heimlich (b. 2-3-1920) an American Jewish Thoracic surgeon, of Wilmington, Delaware, is known for inventing the Heimlich maneuver to aid choking victims.The Heimlich maneuver has also been used on animals such as a dog who was choking on a tennis ball.

CPR or Cardio-Pulmonary Resuscitation to save a human life to open airway and return breathing with head tilting and mouth-to-mouth resuscitation and blood circulation with chest cardiac massage was invented by Austrian Surgeon Peter Safar (b. 4-12-1924).

If a human faints, lay them down and elevate their legs so blood can flow back to their brain.

Analogies

People often refer to earth elements to describe humans such as saying a person is acting like a tornado, she is a delightful buttercup, he is as strong as a lion, they are laughing like a hyena, they are as smart as an owl, have skin as smooth as silk, eyes sparkle like stars, they are sweeter than honey, have a heart of gold. A kiss can leave us 'breathless.'

The elements have also been used to name electrical appliances such as a hurricane blender, which is blender that will make fruit and vegetable smoothies, purees, juices, and other beverages.

Vehicles have been named after animals such as mustang, lynx, jaguar, cougar and more, to honor the speedy animals. A fin has been put on a car roof to mimic a shark fin.

People have given names to towns after animals such as a place where lizards would sunbathe on top of fence posts, so they called the town 'Lizard Lick'. Another place was called 'Horseshoe Bend' because there were many horse farms.

A 'sundress' allows sun to shine on a woman's shoulders.

People 'surf' TV and radio frequencies as well as surf the waves of the oceans.

'In a nutshell' is a saying that means to sum something up in a concise, short way.

Life events can be like flowing 'water under the bridge', the time of past history.

To 'sleep with one eye open' means to be alert 24 hours each day by 7 days each week.

If you are in La La Land, it means you are not paying attention.
Insurance coverage can 'cover you like the dew'.

People say they caught someone doing something 'hook, line, and sinker' as an analogy to fishing for fish.

If you are 'going around in circles' it means that you are not getting anywhere.

When a person wakes up from sleeping, their hair may look like a 'bird's nest.'

'A bird's eye view' is being able to see a big picture of things. A 'cow lick' is a place where your hair does strange things.

If you 'ruffle someone's feathers' or 'stir the waters' you make them feel uneasy and not calm.

If a person has bad breath, they have 'dog breath' or 'hog breath.'

People can be as happy as two clams in their shells.

'Chicken scratch' describes handwriting like chickens leaving scratch marks in the dirt.

Asking 'Can you wrap your mind around it?' means can you imagine it or believe it.

TV antennae have been called 'rabbit ears.'

'Cursing a blue streak' means that someone is very mad.

Critics give stars to hotels, movies, and restaurants.

Like the dawn, a human may have an enlightening or a realization.

A birthday may be described as 'another trip around the sun'.

A person can be lost in their thoughts like being lost in the woods or in a fog.

Opportunity knocks.

Someone may take to something 'like a duck takes to water.'

People who hardly get to spend time together are like 'ships passing in the night.'

A life event can be described as being a 'bittersweet synchronicity.'

'Too many irons in the fire' means a person is involved in a lot of things.

'Too many cooks in the kitchen' means confusion.

'Telephone tag' is when 2 people keep leaving messages for each other but cannot seem to connect at the same time to have a conversation.

'Jaws of life' describes hydraulic tools that are used to save passengers from vehicles that have been in accidents.

To say 'I have roots there' means you lived in a certain land.

If one is 'in tune with the world' then they are aware of what is going on.

If something is 'off the charts' or 'off the chain' it is unusual from the norm.

Engines knock.

An 'open door policy' means that issues may be discussed in peace.

People say 'my ship came in' if they finally got something they needed.

A 'late bloomer' is when something is achieved later in the season of things.

A 'empty nest' is a home that all the children have grown and left.

If someone is as 'stubborn as a mule', it is hard to sway their opinion.

If 'a cloud is hanging over you', you have the blues or trouble in your life.

A 'godsend' is a friend or someone who saves you at a critical moment.

If you tell someone to 'get back on their horse and take the reins', you want them to recover from a loss.
If you are 'on the road to recovery' you are getting better after an illness.

If someone went back into their shell like a turtle or a clam, they are being withdrawn socially from the world.
If they came out of their shell, they are feeling better and more socially interactive.

If you know something by heart, you know it well.

If you are 'sleeping like a baby' you are sleeping well.

If you go against the flow or walk to the beat of a different drummer, you are doing something different than what others are currently doing.

If a son is like his father some say the apple does not fall far from the tree or the son is like a chip off the block of wood.

If something is difficult to find, some say it is like finding a needle in a haystack.

Seniors have 'salt and pepper' hair or hair as 'white as snow.'

Many countries have a newspaper with 'the daily sun' as the title.

The birds and the bees is a story used to tell kids about mating when kids ask 'Where do babies come from'? and another story is telling kids that the flying stork brought the new baby to the family.

Hermetically sealed windows are windows that may have two panes and are airtight in between the panes. The word *hermetic* is derived from the Greek god Hermes who was the god of transitions and boundaries and was a messenger for the gods. Hermes' signs were the herma, rooster, tortoise, purse or pouch, winged sandals, and a herald's staff.

Chapter 5
Protecting Your Body From Elements

People wear clothing because it has become customary around the entire globe and clothing protects against the elements, but some people believe in nudity.

Your skin needs to be taken care of. Use sunscreen or zinc oxide to protect your skin from harmful radiation from the sun. A scarf, hat, and clothing can also protect your skin. Some do not put soap on all of their skin everyday because it may erode the natural bacteria that protects the skin. It is not necessary to wash your hair every day.

Drink water to rehydrate.

Do not over brush your teeth or brush your teeth too hard or you can hurt the enamel of your teeth, your gums, or disrupt the natural flora of bacteria inside your mouth. It only takes a small drop of toothpaste on your toothbrush to brush your teeth. Gentle flossing helps to remove food particles from between your teeth. Swishing with water after eating can help prevent cavities.

Do not over clean your ears. Ear wax was designed by the Lord to catch dust from entering into the ear canal.

Women should not use too much harsh soap on their velva because it needs its natural oils.

Women who use too much lipstick or lip balm can swallow a pound a year. Lipstick may contain lead or other metals. Let your toenails air out to avoid fungus growth.

Your body reacts to anything you put into your body. Cigarette smoke and coal mining will cause black soot to build up in your lungs, which is not healthy. Asbestos ceiling tile fibers contain silicate minerals that are carcinogenic.

Scientists have determined that chemicals such as household cleaners can enter the body through the skin or inhalation and interfere with the normal hormonal functions of the body and affect a person's well-being.

Certain household cleaners cannot be mixed or dangerous gases will result which can be harmful or kill you. Houses should be aired out if you are cleaning with chemicals.

Make sure the fireplace flue is open to avoid death from carbon monoxide poisoning. Never burn charcoal in an indoor fireplace to avoid carbon monoxide poisoning.

Some people are allergic to poison-ivy and some people are not allergic to poison-ivy. Some people are allergic to nuts or chemicals which are toxic to these people.

Scientists are working hard to improve our understanding of the way the human body works, which is good for the world. It is unethical for scientists to experiment on a human being without the human's approval.

Any type of repetitive motions can cause irritations to the body in muscles, joints, bones, ears, eyes, teeth, etc. Many people get eye strain from reading too long. People in certain professions have to wear ear muffs. Others work in professions in which the hands or legs are used all day. Some have to do heavy-lifting. Employers should have concern for the emotional and physical well-being of their employees.

There are ways to lift properly and reach for things to minimize the possibility that you will hurt your back.

Sitting on firm chairs and sleeping on firm mattresses can give your back good support.

Pillows can be placed between you and your mate's head on the same bed in order to block the sound waves of snoring.

Air mattresses have been invented that allow one to adjust the firmness of the mattress.

The study of designing devices for the requirements of humans is called ergonomics.

Historians have said that the conveniences of modern civilization is causing obesity (being very overweight) because humans are not expending as much physical energy to survive as we once did. All of the hard work, human ingenuity, human energy and prayer that has been put forth to bring civilization to where we are currently allows us more time to relax, some people use the popular term 'couch potatoes', because we can lounge on nice furniture and do things like watch news, entertainment, and fun apps on electronics like TVs, computers, and smart phones; conduct business, read books, enjoy knitting or crocheting, or eat meals all while sitting comfortably. Scientists feel that humans are sitting too much and not getting enough exercise. Circulation is important for the human body to function healthily. Some experts say that for every hour that you are sitting in a chair or sitting in a car or airplane, do some type of exercise to get your blood circulating; try to move your arms, wiggle your hands or toes, move your legs, take a short walk, etc. Don't leave a toddler sitting in a highchair too long without letting them down to crawl around and get exercise.

Animals also protect themselves from the heat and harsh sunlight. When it gets too hot, many animals burrow under big rocks or logs where temperatures may be several degrees cooler than the surface. Snakes and other reptiles may crawl underground to keep cool. Many animals such as birds lose feathers in warm seasons. Many animals only come out at night when it is cooler. The ears of deer, rabbit, foxes and other animals are engorged with blood vessels that help radiate heat from their bodies into the air. Bats, birds, and vultures stretch out their wings to release heat. Dogs pant to increase the volume of air moving in and out of their bodies to cool off.

It is wise to shake out clothing, shoes, handbags, luggage, or blankets, as poisonous bugs and spiders have been known to invade closets, attics, cars, and a person could be harmed if bitten. Bugs and spiders have been known to camouflage themselves on brown cardboard boxes, dark bedding linens and furniture.

Anytime you go outdoors, you might come in contact with outdoor creatures. When you take out the trash at night, go camping, go running or walking at night, be careful of spider webs also called cobwebs, spiders, mosquitoes, coyotes, bears, bats, snakes, and turtles. Even while working in your garden during the day or mowing grass, beware of spiders, snakes, mosquitoes, and poison ivy. Venomous spiders can lurk around mailboxes, furniture, boxes filled with paraphernalia of your stuff. If you check an outdoor mailbox at night, you may want to bring a flashlight with you and check for spiders.

Many love the smell of freshly cut grass or flowers, wild onions, woodsmoke, or the smell in the air after a rain.

If you live in an area with deer, be especially careful when driving because deer are known to stop in their tracks and look at car headlights or cross the road while cars are driving by, causing many accidents and deer fatalities.

Scientists gave a spider some hallucinogenic drugs to see what kind of web the spider would weave; while under the influence of drugs the spider did not weave a perfect web. A spider spins a web to catch an insect for dinner.

There are certain plants that are poisonous and fatal to humans, such as the spikey and striped oleander leaf, the strychnine tree, and the castor bean plant.

The pheromones of plants and the venoms of animals and insects have been studied to create medicines and poisons. Pheromones are the signaling chemicals that animals and plants use for communication; the invisible language of nature. Scientists believe that plants send signals to protect themselves just as animals do. Millipedes produce cyanide. The oleander leaf, strychnine tree, and castor bean plant have been studied for their poisons.

Spider silk is as strong as steel and has been used in manufacturing electronics, except a drawback is that spider sill is biodegradable and doesn't last too long.

The world needs insects because insects pollinate the plants on the earth for continued vegetation and also because insects are a part of the natural animal food chain. Bees and butterflies are prolific pollinators. The birds and the bees mate in the spring. Fungi and microorganisms sustain the soil. There are method's in the Lord's works.

Animal activists debate about whether humans should kill animals just to make leather, when modern times enable synthetic leathers to be manufactured. In times long ago, native tribes were respectful when an animal was killed for food; all remaining parts of the animals were used if possible; animals skins were dried and tanned over heat and used to
make clothing, blankets, and even strung together to make tents, baskets, and satchels.

CHAPTER 6 *Chemistry*

Water is two elements: 2 hydrogen molecules and 1 oxygen molecule. Water is essential for all life. Your body is 70% water.

Water and air has been recycled about the earth for millions of years.
You might be breathing the same air particles that a dinosaur breathed millions of years ago.

Salt is two elements: sodium and chloride. Chloride and sodium are needed by all known living creatures. Salt helps regulate the water
content in the body.

Gargling with warm water mixed with a little salt can clear up some
mild throat and tooth irritations. Also, a same mild saline solution can be used as nose drops to clear up some mild sinus irritations. Do not overuse nose drops or gargle solution. Your body has a natural chemistry and a natural flora of bacteria that you don't want to mess up. Liquor has been used as an antiseptic on a tooth or wound. Alcohol can kill tissues. Heat therapy such as sitting in a hot car or sauna is

used in some countries to try to kill infections because it is said the body cannot tell the difference between a fever and a heat-induced state.

Antibiotics kill bacteria. Antibiotics should not be overused.

Vaccines are available that have helped to eradicate many diseases. Tetanus shots might be needed in case of puncture wounds. People working in restaurants and hospitals might benefit from Hepatitis vaccinations. Anyone traveling to a different country from their own may need to be immunized. Children are usually vaccinated as infants against diseases that were once very prevalent in the world. Teenagers living in close quarters in colleges may need to get the vaccine for meningitis. Flu shots can prevent serious illness.

Employees that have been diagnosed or exposed to pathogens such as: Norovirus, Hepatitis A Virus, Shigella species, or Enterohemorrhagic or Shiga toxin producing E. Coli, or Typhoid Fever (Salmonella Typhi) should not report to work but stay home until cleared by a doctor. Employees should not report to work if they have: lesions with pus draining, coughing and sneezing or discharge from eyes and nose, diarrhea, vomiting, jaundice (dark urine or yellow eyes), sore throat with fever.

Washing or rinsing hands after touching eyes, nose, ears, and mouth can avoid passing germs to others.

Your body produces Vitamin D from sunlight, so brief exposures to the sun are beneficial. Lack of sunlight can cause seasonal affective disorder (SAD) which is gloominess. Sunlight can clear up some cases of psoriasis.

The process of photosynthesis is sustained by sunlight. Plants use sunlight, carbon dioxide, and water to produce simple sugars in photosynthesis, which supports the existence of nearly all life on Earth.

The art of making modern perfume fragrances began in the South of France in the 1600s CE. One perfume that used jasmine flowers in its formula required 1,000 jasmine petals for one ounce. It is believed that perfume was invented due to the tanning of animal skins that were used as leather; the fragrances were used to infuse scent into the leather. But
incense is mentioned in ancient religious scriptures.

CHAPTER 7 *Sugar*

Sugar is food for the body cells. All food eaten is converted to sugar.

Sugars are found in the tissues of most plants but only present in sufficient concentrations for efficient extraction in sugar cane and sugar beet. Sugar production and trade changed human history in many ways such as the formation of human colonies, the perpetuation of slavery, the transition to indentured labor, the migration of peoples, and wars between 19th century sugar trade controlling nations.

The world produced 168 million tons of sugar in 2011.

One of the earliest references to sugar is in 8th century BC (BCE) Chinese manuscripts that refer to the knowledge that sugar cane was derived in India in 500 BC or 500 BCE. Residents of India began making sugar syrup and cooling it in large flat bowls to make crystals that were easier to store and transport than the sugar cane itself. The crystals were called khanda, which is the source of the word candy. At first the crystals were called 'sweet salt'. The sugar became popular and spread to regions of the world.

Eating too much sugar is linked to obesity, diabetes, tooth decay, cardiovascular disease, dementia, and macular eye degeneration.

Sugars can cause gastrointestinal side effects such as bloating, flatulence, and diarrhea. Smoking, chewing gum, eating too much or too frequently, eating too many sweet, salty or spicy foods, and other things can mess up your taste buds. Don't burn your tongue on food that is too hot or let your tongue get frozen onto a frozen surface. Most men need 2,500 calories each day and most women need 2,000 calories each day for their body to perform effectively. Use willpower to stay within the boundary of daily caloric needs. My body is a temple, do I want to put too much salt, sugar and fat into it?

Honey is a natural sweet substance made by bees using nectar from flowers. In Russia bees produced white honey from feeding on certain flowers. In France bees produced blue or red honey after feeding on candies from a candy factory. Never give honey or corn syrup to infants or small children, according to food safety guidelines.

Andreas Marggraf was German chemist who discovered glucose in 1747CE. Emil Fishcher (German), Jacobus Henricus van't Hoff (Netherlands), and Joseph Achille Le Bel (French) were chemists (circa 1900CE) who worked on the synthesis of glucose and the tetrahedron of molecules.

Many fruit juices are concentrated (pure juice having a high sugar content and not diluted with water) so they may cause a spike in your blood sugar which will actually leave you feeling more hungry than before; so drink a smaller amount.

Eating high-carb foods like breads, pastas, cupcakes, and crackers made with refined flours may cause spikes in your blood sugar. Some athletes load up on carbs before races.

The pancreas in the torso area of your body releases a hormone called insulin; insulin allows cells to use the sugars which are broken down into glucose as energy (glycolysis). The glucose that the body cannot use is stored as fat. Eating much sugar or starches like wheat, corn, rice, oats, and malted grain can cause the cells to become *insulin-resistant* which can result in fatigue and sluggishness because the cells are not getting the energy needed from sugar. Nutritionists think it is better to eat less carbohydrates at one time and eat more balanced meals or snacks (combinations of carbs, veggies, fruits, proteins, fats, dairy) in order to keep your blood sugar and insulin steady to help *maintain a healthy weight*. When liver glycogen stores are depleted, the liver releases ketone bodies in the blood that are used for energy (ketosis) to burn fat.

In the Regions of Jericho and Gilgal near the Lower Jordan Valley, researchers have studied fig fossils carbon-dated to 11,000 years ago, found with stone-cut tools left behind by early humans.

If you eat too many carbohydrates at once, the body uses only glucose for energy but if you eat less carbohydrates, the body will begin burning fat after using up the glucose reserves.

The brain primarily uses glucose for energy, so prolonged fasting or starvation may affect psychological reasoning. But after a few days, the brain starts burning ketones to get energy from fat.

Glucose (and dextrose which is found in fruits and plants), fructose, and galactose are 3 simple sugars (monosaccharides) occurring in fruits and honey. Glucose has calories.

Sucrose is a combination of glucose and fructose (disaccharide); it is the commonly used sugar known as table sugar, derived from sugar cane. Sucrose has calories.

Polysaccharides contain more than ten monosaccharide units; they are complex carbohydrates like starches and dietary fiber.

Maltodextrin is a polysaccharide that is produced from starch and is used as a food additive; it is moderately sweet. It is used to enhance the flavor and the appearance of sodas, candy, and a variety of processed foods.

Some bulk natural sugar substitutes are sorbitol, xylitol, and stevia.

Sorbitol is made from a reduction of glucose; it is known as a sugar alcohol, the body metabolizes it slowly, and it does not cause tooth decay. Sorbitol is made from apples, pears, peaches, prunes, and corn syrup.

Xylitol is made from a reduction of xylose; it is also known as a sugar alcohol, has less calories than sucrose, and does not cause tooth decay. Xylitol is made from corn husks, berries, oats, mushrooms, and sugar cane bagasse (the fibrous matter that is leftover after sugar cane has been crushed to extract the juice; it is used to make biofuels like ethanol and even paper products).

Stevia is from the family of herbs and shrubs from the sunflower family. It was used widely in Japan as a sweetener before it was used in other parts of the world. Stevia has negligible calories.

Zero-calories sweeteners that are called 'artificial sweeteners' are aspartame, sucralose, neotame, acesulfame potassium, alitame, cyclamate, and saccharin; the majority are artificially-synthesized compounds. A baby may have their heeled pricked within a day after being born to be tested for PKU, a condition where their body cannot process phenyalanine and causing toxicity. Robert Guthrie (1916-1995), a microbiologist from Missosuri, USA developed the PKU test. Phenylketonurics are components in many artificial sweeteners and foods.

Lead shavings once were used as a sweetener until people realized they were fatal.

Drinking too much alcohol can cause a person to have liver damage or alcohol poisoning, which can be fatal.

Chapter 8 *Nutrients*

Scientists have been studying vitamins for over 200 years and there is still more information to be learned. In the early 1700's CE, it was discovered that sailors at sea suffered from scurvy due to the lack of fresh fruit and vitamins, which led to the discovery of Vitamin C.

Today, there are 13 known vitamins to the human body.

Vitamins A,D,E,K are fat-soluble and are absorbed in the intestine with the help of lipid fats. The fat-soluble vitamins may be stored in the body.

The 8 B-Vitamins and Vitamin C are water-soluble. Water-soluble vitamins dissolve in water and are excreted in urine.Water-soluble vitamins are not stored, so humans need more intake of these vitamins in order to avoid a deficiency.

Taking too much of a vitamin or mineral can be toxic (poison).

Overeating one kind of food can induce an apparent deficiency or surplus of another vitamin or mineral. For example, Vitamin C enhances the absorption of iron. But eating too much dairy can decrease the absorption of iron. Your stomach is the size of a fist, so eat a portion of food the size of fist so the food can be digested properly.

Some vitamins act like hormones in that they are metabolizers. Some vitamins act like anti-oxidants to fight free radicals that cause cell damage.

Cellular activity causes chemical reactions called oxidation, which produces free radicals. Free radicals damage cells.
Anti-oxidants are molecules that inhibit the chain reactions caused by free radicals. Anti-oxidants do this by being oxidized themselves and are reducing agents such as thiols, ascorbic acid, or polyphenols. Antioxidants are classified depending on whether they are soluble in water (hydrophilic) or soluble in lipid fats (hydrophobic).

Oxidation reactions are crucial for life but are also naturally damaging; plants and animals maintain complex antioxidants such as vitamins and enzymes to avoid oxidative stress.

There is still much more to learn about nutrition. Many people and animals in the past have lost their lives in nutrition research. For example, several people died who were only given rice to eat and nothing else. Several mice died who were only given sugar to eat and nothing else.

Pasteurized foods and irradiated foods have been processed to destroy pathogenic organisms which can cause diseases. Louis Pasteur was a French chemist who invented pasteurization.

Chlorinated water was invented around 1846 in Vienna, Austria by Dr. Ignaz Semmelweis who instructed physicians to wash their hands with soap and chlorinated water to reduce germs. In 1846 water chlorination began in Hamburg, Germany and Maidstone, England and scientists noticed a reduction in chlorea, dysentery, and typhoid. Vincent Nesfield was a British officer in the Indian Medical Service who advocated chlorinated water in 1903. In New Jersey, U.S.A., John L. Leal and George Warren Fuller invented a public chlorination water plant. In 1854 John Snow instructed a water pump in London to be disinfected due to cholera outbreak. Some bacteria are becoming chlorine-resistant.

Some food facts:

Vitamin A is essential for normal vision. It is found in orange and ripe yellow fruits and leafy vegetables, carrots, pumpkin, squash, spinach, green beans, sweet potatoes, vegetable eggroll, and liver.

Vitamin B complex is essential for nervous system health, sugar energy metabolism, strong nails, skin and hair, healthy cell growth, heart health, memory, and pregnant women.

Vitamin B1 Thiamin
Vitamin B2 Riboflavin
Vitamin B3 Niacin
Vitamin B5 Pantothenic acid
Vitamin B6 Pyrodoxine
Vitamin B7 Biotin (Healthy nails and hair)
Vitamin B9 Folic acid
Vitamin B12 Cobalamin (Memory)

Foods rich in vitamin B are oatmeal, brown rice, potatoes, Liver, eggs, dairy products, bananas, popcorn, asparagus, Broccoli, avocados, cucumbers, peanuts, mushrooms, legumes such as Kidney beans, soy beans, pinto beans, navy beans, white beans, black beans, green beans, black-eyed peas, green peas, and lentils. Beans contain starch, protein, iron, and zinc.

Uncooked beans may contain a poisonous toxin called phytohaemagglutinin, a lectin, which is why kidney beans should be soaked and boiled for at least 10 minutes and the water discarded. Poisonous cyanogenic glycosides can be found in the seeds and cores of apples, peaches, apricots, cherries, almonds, and lima beans.

Vitamin C enhances iron absorption when eaten with iron-rich foods.
Vitamin C aids in the formation of collagen which is the support structure for bones, teeth, skin and tendons. Vitamin C is an antioxidant that fights cell-damaging free radicals. Vitamin C helps the immune system.
Foods rich in Vitamin C are citrus fruits and juices such as kiwi, cantaloupe, strawberries, oranges, grapefruits, mangos, watermelons, green or red or yellow peppers, vegetables, green beans, sweet potatoes and white potatoes, tomatoes, broccoli, tomatoes, tomato juice, broccoli, raw cabbage, apricots, squash, cauliflower, vegetable eggroll.

Raw or cold vegetables have resistant starch, which means less sugar is absorbed in your body when eating them.

Apples have a low sugar content. Grapes and pineapples have a high sugar content.

Vitamin D helps the overall immune function. Foods rich in Vitamin D are fish, eggs, liver, and mushrooms.

Vitamin E is called Tocopherol and promotes heart health, and circulatory function. Vitamin E is an effective fat-soluble antioxidant, helps immune system. Foods rich in Vitamin E are fruits and vegetables and hazelnuts.

Vitamin K helps joint health and blood clotting. Vitamin K1 is called Phylloquinone and helps form prothrombin, for blood clotting.
Vitamin K2 is also called Menaquinone.
Vitamin K is found in collard greens, spinach, kale, egg yolks, cucumbers, and liver.

Beta-Carotene converts Vitamin A in your body when needed.

Calcium and magnesium are for bone and muscle structure.
Calcium is found in milk, yogurt, cheese, meat, fish, eggs, sesame seeds, and other foods. Calcium citrate is a form of calcium that is easier for the body to absorb.
Yogurt contains probiotics such as S. thermophilus, L. bulgaricus, L. acidophilus, Bifudus, and L. Casei which are beneficial bacteria that help digest foods.

French chemist and Nobel Prize nominee Louis Kervran (1983) postulated that supplemental silicon may improve calcium uptake.

Choline is needed for liver and heart health, and nervous system health.
Chromium plays a role in the release of energy from cells, supports carbohydrate, fat, and protein metabolism, and maintains healthy blood sugar levels that were already in a normal range.

Ellasic acid, believed to enable wrinkle reduction, is found in pomegranates.

Iodine is an essential component of the thyroid hormone that plays a role in growth, development, and metabolic processes.

Iron is for normal red blood cell production and energy metabolism. Hemoglobin and myoglobin carry oxygen in the blood.

Lutein is for healthy eyes and is not made in the body.
Collard greens, broccoli, turnip greens, kale, swiss chard, basil, parsley, cayenne pepper, and spinach contain lutein.

Lycopene is an antioxidant and for healthy immune, heart, and prostrate health and is found in tomatoes.

Mercury, which is toxic to humans, has been found in fish and sprayed on golf courses.

Omega-3 is alpha-linolenic acid.

Omega-6 is linoleic acid.

Omega-7 is palmitoleic, vaccenic and paullinic acid.

Omega-9 is oleic acid.

Omega-3 fatty acids help assist normal cell growth. Flax seed oil, fish oil, and walnuts are sources of omega-3.

Omega-3 and Omega-6 are a polyunsaturated fats.

Dietary sources of omega-6 fatty acids include poultry, eggs, avocado, nuts, cereals, durum wheat, whole-grain breads, most vegetable oils, evening primrose oil, borage oil, black currant seed oil, flax/linseed oil, rapeseed or canola oil, hemp oil, soybean oil, cottonseed oil, sunflower seed oil, corn oil, safflower oil, pumpkin seeds, acai berry, cashews, pecans, pine nuts, walnuts, spirulina, coconut.

Omega-7 is found is macadamia nut oil and sea buckthorn oil and is a monounsaturated fat.

Omega-9 oils are monounsaturated fats found in sunflower and canola oils that help to eliminate trans and saturated fats from diets.

Eating seaweed or algae from the ocean may contain omega oils and be very healthy for humans instead of eating fish which may contain mercury.

Hickory nuts have low saturated fat.

Phosphorous plays a role in biological molecules such as DNA and RNA and to transport cellular energy.

Potassium works with sodium to regulate water balance, muscle function, and maintain mineral balance of the blood.

Selenium is an antioxidant, helps thyroid function, and prostrate health.

Taurine is an amino acid for healthy muscles.

Zinc is for healthy bones, vision, skin and for male reproductive health. Zinc helps new collagen to form in skin. Collard greens, kale, and spinach contain zinc.

Raisins are dried grapes. Craisins are dried cranberries. Prunes are dried plums. There are also dried apricots, apples, kiwi, and more.

Coffee, tea, blueberries, strawberries, muscadine grapes, olive oil, and beets have antioxidants to fight free radicals. Coffee grinds, used tea bags, egg shells, raw eggs can be placed in flower beds or buried to enrich soil.

If you gobble your food down, there is a danger of choking or constipation. If you nibble at your food, it may help digestion and control your diet.

Do not swallow chewing gum; the body cannot digest it.

Eating is very personal and each person has unique eating preferences or needs.

Breakfast is an important meal even if it is just a bite or two because you haven't eaten in 8 or 12 hours and you need to give your body some energy.

Blind persons may eat their food with silverware, but some blind persons may prefer to eat their food by picking up food from their plates with their hands while wearing plastic gloves.

Four tastes are sweet for sugar, salty for salt, sour for acids, bitter for bases. Eight olfactory receptors for our noses help us taste mint, hot pepper, natural veggie, ugami (protein), fishy, buttery, fatty.

The Egyptian papyrus called Ebers Papyrus written in 1550 BCE lists poppy seeds as a sedative.

Table salt is sodium chloride but table salt consisting of sodium and potassium has been used in some countries. A long time ago, only the rich could afford to buy salt. The Romans sometimes paid the wages of their soldiers in salt. Egyptians burned salt to scare away evil spirits before embarking on a journey. In Buddhism and Shintoism salt was used as a purifier. In Africa, salt baths healed the body. Tossing salt in the corners of your dwelling is folklore myth to scare away negative energy or witches.

Carbonated water which dissolves carbon dioxide in water was invented by Britain Joseph Priestley in 1767. Lemonades were believed to exist in ancient Egypt. Lemon water, lime water, and cucumber water are popular all over the world. Drinking through a straw causes less tooth decay on the front teeth.

Oil and vinegar will not mix. Milk and sugar will mix.

Chapter 9 *Food Safety*

Vegetables and fruits should be washed before eating, as they could contain bacteria from bugs and the soil, or chemicals from fertilizers or food processing.

Preservatives are added to extend shelf life of foods.

Hands, surfaces, and utensils that touch food, especially uncooked meats, should be sanitized and kept sanitized.

Plastic cutting boards are better than wooden cutting boards because wooden cutting boards are porous and bacteria from raw meat can get trapped in the pores of the wood. Some people use green plastic cutting boards for vegetables, fruits, and breads, and red plastic cutting boards for meats. Do not use the same knife that you used to cut raw meat with to cut raw vegetables or bread without first sanitizing the knife! Sanitize utensils and cloths.

Food poisoning can caused by drinking dirty water. Water should be boiled if there is any question the water is unsafe. When boiling water, If you put a lid on a pot of water, it will boil faster. Wearing a hat keeps in body heat.

The 5-second rule is a myth: never eat any food that has dropped on the ground unless it can be washed off or cooked at a high temperature to kill any germs (bacteria or viruses).

Do not eat food that smells bad and may have spoiled. Throw it away.

Meats should be heated to the proper temperatures to kill bacteria. People have died from eating raw shellfish, such as oysters.

Uncooked meats should be stored on the bottom shelf of a refrigerator. If meats are stored on the higher shelves, the juices can drip down onto other foods and contaminate them.

Recommended minimum temperature for cooking meats:

pork, beef, veal, and lamb	145^0 F ($62.8\ ^0$C)
ground meats	160^0 F (71.1^0C)
poultry	165^0 F (73.9^0C)
eggs	160^0 F (71.1^0C)
leftovers or casseroles	165^0 F (73.9^0C).

Hot foods should be kept hot (over 140 ^{0} Fahrenheit) and cold foods should be kept cold (under 40 ^{0} Fahrenheit) on open food bars, such as buffets and smorgasbords, brunch spreads, and school lunch-lines. Prepared foods that are served in bulk quantities at parties, picnics, and family gatherings are in danger if the foods are sitting out for more than 3-4 hours because bacteria can begin to grow on certain foods when the temperature of the foods falls between 40 ^{0} F and 140 ^{0} F. Foods should be reheated to above 140 ^{0} F (165 ^{0} F is recommended) before eating if the food has been sitting out too long to kill bacteria that might have begun to grow, especially foods containing proteins. Cold foods such as macaroni, chicken, tuna and egg salads that were made with mayonnaise or cream-filled pastries should not be eaten and thrown away if they have been sitting out more than 4 hours at room temperature.

Parchment paper is for baking. Wax paper is not for baking but for stacking foods on wax sheets so they don't stick together. Aluminum foil can be used for baking, freezing, and fireside meals. Plastic wrap and plastic bags are used for storing, freezing but some plastic bags may be used for boiling or baking.

Do not store opened canned goods in the refrigerator but transfer the food to a glass or plastic container before refrigerating. Do not cook canned goods in the cans they were packaged in. Dangerous chemicals in the can liners and metals of the cans can leak into the foods.

Flying insects and human factors such as sneezing and dirty hands can all adversely affect food safety.

Store dangerous household chemicals, cleaning supplies, pesticides, medicines, perfumes, sewing and building tacks away from human or pet food supplies so they do not accidentally get mixed into the food.

Honey, corn syrup, and home-canned goods should not be given to infants and small children.

Wash your hands often when working with food or before eating food, especially after touching door handles, cell phones, car keys, or touching any animal.

If you find a hair in food and the food was prepared by good clean humans, it doesn't mean the entire plate of food is bad or the entire restaurant is dirty. We all breathe the same air. Be grateful you have good food to eat.

'Double-dipping' may spread germs; an example is when a person dips a chip in a dip, takes a bite, and then puts the chip back into the dip that is shared with others.

When you have a common cold, soup can be good for the soul, like it has a secret ingredient. You can put an ice cube in a bowl of soup to cool it off if it is too hot and you are in a hurry to eat. When using a tissue to wipe your runny nose, dab or gently rub the tissue beneath the nose so you do not irritate the skin beneath the nose. Babies, children, and adults may lose their appetites when they have a cold or they may lose their taste buds and may not be able to taste the food. Decongestants and analgesics have been made from essential oils such at camphor, menthol, eucalyptus, cedarleaf, nutmeg, and turpentine that can be inhaled or rubbed on the skin and give a cool minty sensation.

Many people object to cows being given rBGH synthetic version of bovine somatotropin (BST) to stimulate milk production. Also, cows that give too much milk may suffer abuse such as sore udders and infection from overmilking. Chickens should not be given poultry feed that contains arsenic-based chemicals that causes the chickens to gain weight. Pork, beef, and fish should not be given ractopamine chemicals to make them gain weight. Citrus-based soft drinks may contain brominated vegetable oil, which contains a flame retardant chemical. Some bread and pastry dough is made with potassium bromate which make the dough elastic.

Chapter 10 *Numbers*

Numerals 0,1,2,3,4,5,6,7,8, and 9 were invented in India. Math has many concepts such as Basic Math, Algebra, Geometry, Trigonometry, Statistics, Calculus, Series, Theorems, rational numbers, irrational numbers, prime numbers, complex numbers, perfect numbers, fractions, fractals, equations, Wonders of Math, music, sports ratios and much more. Origami paper art involves numbers.

Numbers in statistical analysis can mean the number of occurrences that something will happen. For example, if you place a red ball and a blue ball in a box, the odds or the chance that you will retrieve a red ball will be 50% or ½. If you place two green balls and two yellow balls in the box, there is a 25% or ¼ that you will retrieve two yellow balls. This is because there are only four combinations that will be retrieved: one green ball and one yellow ball, one yellow ball and one green ball, two green balls, or two yellow balls.

If a pair of dice is rolled, there is a 1/36 chance of statistical probability that both dice will show one dot.

Deductive and logical reasoning can help figure out problems. For example, there are 3 light switches at the end of a hall and you have to figure out which switch lights up which light bulb with the least number of trips down the hall to the room that contains the three light bulbs, assuming all three light bulbs are working. This can be accomplished with one trip to the room. First, turn on the first switch and wait a minute; then turn the switch off. Second, turn on the second switch. Third, go down the hall to the room. The light bulb attached to the the first switch will be warm. The light bulb that is lit is attached to the second switch. The light bulb that is not warm or lit belongs to the third switch.

A series of Fiobonacci Numbers can be found in nature in branches of trees, leaves on stems, fruit sprouts of pineapples, flowering of artichokes, ferns and pinecones.

Phi is said to be a Golden Ratio and such calculations can be found or closely found in the human body, solar system, DNA, nature, animals, and music. Phi is 1.61803...

Pi is 3.14159...and has been studied since 2000 BCE and is used to calculate the area and circumference of a circle.

It is rare that droppings from a bird will land on the top of a human head, but it happens.

It was estimated in 2000 CE that there were 7 billion people on the Earth in 267 countries.

If all 7 billion people on Earth were to gather together for a picture taken with a camera and each person was to stand on a piece of ground 2 X 2 feet, the group would cover an area of less than 100 square miles, the size of a large city. Before cameras, artists painted portraits or made ink drawings of people on canvases.

About 230,000 marine species have been identified in the five main oceans called the Pacific, Atlantic, Indian, Arctic and Antarctic Oceans. The average depth of the oceans is 3,790 meters, or 12,430 feet. The world's oceans cover about 60 percent of the Northern Hemisphere and more than 80 percent of the Southern Hemisphere.

Earth's mass is 6.6 sextillion tons. Its equatorial circumference is 24,902 miles; polar circumference is 24,860 miles. The total surface area is 196,940,000 square miles (29%land, 71% saline water). The distance from the Earth's surface to the middle is 3,959 miles.

The highest mountain on Earth is Mount Everest. The higher you climb, the farther you can see to the horizon. The lowest point on Earth is the Dead Sea. Mount Chimborazo is the farthest point from the center of the Earth.

There are 10,000 species of grass on the Earth and this family of plants is the most abundant on Earth.

Scientists have identified Earth is part of a Solar System that has a sun, 8 planets, and 5 dwarf-planets. The planets in order from the sun are Mercury, Venus, Earth,

Mars, Jupiter, Saturn, Uranus, and Neptune. The five outer dwarf planets are Ceres, Pluto, Haumea, Makemake, and Eris.

On April 12, 1961, The first human in space was Yuri Gagarin (b. 3-9-1934) of Russia on the VOSTOK 1. Yuri died in a test plane crash in 1968. The first satellite to be put into space was the Russian Sputnik 1. Sputnik 2 was launched carrying a dog named Laika. Sergei Korolev was the leading engineer and rocket expert who headed the Soviet Space Program.

In May 1961, Alan Shepard from the United States of America flew the Freedom 7 as it orbited the earth. A USA satellite called Ranger IV was launched in 1962CE to impact the moon. It was launched on April 23, 1962 at 3:50 P.M. and impacted the moon on April 26, 1962 at 7:49A.M. after traveling 229,541 miles.

Soviet Union LUNA Programme reached the moon with Unmanned spacecraft in 1959CE. The first woman into space was Valentina Tereshkova from Russia in 1963.

USA NASA Apollo 11 Astronauts Neil Armstrong and Buzz Aldrin landed on the moon on July 20, 1969CE on a location called the Sea of Tranquility while Michael Collins orbited around the moon.

'Escape velocity' is the minimum speed an object must have to free itself from the gravitational pull of a celestial body.

Japan, China, India, USA, and the European Space Agency sent lunar orbiters and rover missions to the moon.

The ISRO (Indian Space Research Organisation) and NASA (National Aeronautics and Space Administration - USA) both launched spacecraft to the planet Mars in November of 2013 and both spacecraft reached the orbit of Mars in Sept. 2014. The Soviet Space Program and the European Space Agency also have sent missions to Mars.

Edwin Powell Hubble (1889-1953CE) was an American astronomer who established the field of extragalactic astronomy. There is a telescope on earth and a telescope in space that is named after Hubble.

Austrian physicist Christian Doppler proposed in 1842CE mathematical equations for frequency of waves.

There is no atmosphere on the moon; that is why if you are standing on the moon you can see directly into space. The atmosphere on earth deflects the sunlight through the hydrogen and oxygen that surrounds the earth – that is why we see blue skies that some call azure. Scientists have labeled 5 layers of atmosphere that exist around the earth. The lowest layer is the troposphere and extends from 0-12 km, or 0-7 miles; the lowest 5.6 km or 18,000 feet of atmosphere mostly contains 78%nitrogen and 21% oxygen. The second layer is called the stratosphere and extends from 12-50km, or 7-31 miles. The third layer is the mesosphere and extends from 50-80 km or 31-50 mi les; meteors entering the mesosphere would burn up and the mesosphere is too high for aircraft. The fourth layer is the thermosphere which extends from 80-700km or 50-440 miles; the thermosphere is the layer of atmosphere where the International Space Station orbits above the earth. The fifth layer is called the exosphere and extends from 700km or 440 mi to about 10,000km or 6,200 miles; it is where most of the satellites orbiting the earth have been placed.

A pulse of light travels from earth to moon in 1.26 seconds. The moon is approx. 2160 miles (3476.089km) in diameter and 234,000 miles (376576 km) away from Earth and is moving away from earth each year at a rate of about 38 mm (1.4972 inches) each year. Seismometers left on the moon indicate that moonquakes have occurred. The moon is in synchronous rotation with the earth; it rotates about its axis in about the time it takes to orbit the earth – this results in its nearly always keeping the same face turned towards earth.

An astronaut 100 miles above the Earth spoke by radio to an aquanaut 205 feet beneath the Pacific Ocean in 1965.

As of 2013, scientists want to place a space station in one of the magnetic LaGrange points around the moon and earth for more space study.

As of 2013 there are more than 50 electronic satellites in space to enable global world communication. As of 2017, 450 people from 37 countries have gone into space.

Around 1910CE, Ejnar Hertzsprung (1873-1967CE) and Henry Norris Russell (1877-1957CE) worked together around 1910CE to establish a chart that classified stars according to brightness and color (temperature); the stars are classified into super giant stars, red giant stars, and yellow, blue, brown, white dwarfs, and more, all according to the light spectrum indicating their elemental gaseous combinations. Black holes are indicated. Stephen Hawking (b. 1942CE) a physicist and cosmologist from Oxford, England is noted for his research involving radiation that is emitted from black holes. Jeff Steinhauer simulated a sonic black hole in his laboratory in Haifa, Israel.

The Sun of our earth's solar system is made up of hydrogen, helium, oxygen, carbon, neon, iron, and other elements. The Sun is three-quarters hydrogen. A yellow-dwarf sun indicates the energy is generated by nuclear fusion of hydrogen to helium. The earth is 93,000,000,000 miles (93 million miles) from the sun. One source said that scientists believe our sun is 4.6 billion years old and will become a red giant in 5 billion years.

The slowest rifle bullets fly 1000 mph (1600 kph) and the fastest rifle bullets fly 2700 mph (4300kph). With binoculars and mathematical equations, snipers can kill targets over a mile away.

Spaceships need propulsion systems that would enable the spacecraft to travel about 150 times the speed of bullets in order to make space travel to other planets feasible. But there is the problem of deaccelerating the spacecraft that needs to be considered. The gravitational pull and orbits of the planets help astrologists figure out the travel trajectory paths for spacecraft.

A BOEING 737 aircraft can lift off with 16 tons or 14 metric tons of weight aboard.

CUISINE

1. At a meal, many people ask for a volunteer to say a blessing or say a blessing silently, giving thanks to God and good human beings who produce or provide food and wash the dishes. Some remember the lives of animals sacrificed in human need.

2. All over the world, fresh vegetables are washed and eaten raw, or boiled or steamed with onions, lemons, limes, oranges, pomegranate juice, herbs, oil or butter; they are low-in-fat and high in fiber. Canned and frozen vegetables are also delicious. Just add water to dehydrated vegetables. Fresh vegetables and fruits may be unavailable when out of season.

Breakfast foods can be cereals with milk, eggs, potatoes, breads, pastries and turnovers, cinnamon rolls, donuts, fruits, yogurt, bacon, sausage, meat or fish, stir-fry noodles, tea, coffee, juices, water, smoothies, waffles, pancakes, French Toast, Oatmeal, Kasha porridge and more.

Tea, coffee, fruit juices, carrot juice, soft drinks, smoothies, milkshakes, champagne, wines, beer and liquor are enjoyed in many countries.

Meals can be homemade, (home made, home-made, home-cooked). Meals can be microwaved or baked from premade frozen foods. Meals can also be bought at stores, fast-food chains, and dine-in restaurants.
Food budgets may cause meals to be simple or rationed.

POPULAR FOODS

French Potatoes Au Gratin is potatoes in a creamy sauce topped with buttered breadcrumbs and grated cheese that is browned and may be infused with onions and peas or broccoli; this dish contains Vitamin A, C, Calcium, Iron, Fat, Cholesterol, Sodium, and Carbohydrates. French foods: wine, cheese, French bread, liver pate, salmon croquettes, duck, pastry, croissant, quiches, soufflé, coffee. Coq au vin is chicken cooked with wine, mushrooms, and lardons (pork fat). A soufflé is an egg dish. Omelettes originated in France and are an egg dish with Cheddar or Gruyere cheese, ham or bacon, and spinach or other vegetables. Lobster bisque and consommé are soups. Five sauces are White bechamel, Broth veloute, Brown espagnole, Sauce Tomat, and Hollandaise.

Spanish Paelia is white rice seasoned with saffron, green olives, onions, rosemary, and lemon; it may contain chicken, fish or ham. Spanish Gazpacho is a cold soup made with pureed tomatoes, cucumber, bell pepper, onion, garlic, olive oil, salt. Spanish omelettes are egg dishes with cheese, potatoes, onions, and ham or bacon.

Italian Lasagna contains Vitamin A, Vitamin C, Calcium, and iron. Lasagna contains fat, cholesterol, sodium, protein, carbohydrates, dietary fiber, and sugars. The package container contains the nutrition information as well as recipe ideas, the manufacturer, and possibly coupons. Italian foods: pasta like baked ziti, fettuccine alfredo, breads, cappuccino, espresso, salami, squash, cabbage, ham, polenta (porridge of barley and lentils), Genoa pesto (olive oil, basil, and pine nuts), chicken parmesan with eggplant, tiramishu, biscotti, spumoni, cannoli. Vegetable lasagna with tomato sauce and 4-cheese pasta with spinach have no meat. Caprese salad is mozzarella, tomatoes, and basil. A fritata is a fried egg dish. Scampi is seasoned shrimp and pasta. Risotto is a rice dish. Fettuccine Alfredo is pasta with white cream sauce. White sauces originated in northern Italy while the red sauces originated in southern Italy. Fettuccine noodles are wider and thinner than linguine noodles. Spaghetti noodles made from durham wheat flour were invented in Italy, but cyclindrical noodles made from rice flour may have been brought by Italian merchant traveler Marco Polo to Venice from Peking, China. Ravioli, tortellini,and gnocchi are pasta. Polenta is made from cornmeal.

Indian Chole Pindi is curried and marinated chick peas, tomatoes, onions, water, potatoes, butter, corn oil, chili, coriander leaves, coriander, salt, cumin, ginger, garlic, cinnamon, cloves, black pepper, and asafetida. Chole Pindi contains vitamin A, C, calcium, iron, carbohydrates, protein, fiber, sodium, sugar, and fat. Garam masala spray is a spice mixture of black pepper, cumin, cinnamon, cardamom, cloves, and nutmeg. Indian potatoes may be red potatoes seasoned with garam masala spray, black mustard seed, dried red chiles, minced peeled fresh Ginger, cloves, jalapeno, salt, turmeric, cilantro, mint, and lime. Mattar paneer is paneer cheese, green peas, and tomato sauce. Dudhi chana is squash and lentils.

Chinese dinners include Chow Mein, Lo Mein, Egg Foo Young, Wonton Soup, Fried rice, egg rolls (cabbage, carrots, bok choy, celery, water chestnuts, bamboo shoots, or seaweed wrapped in a crust of flour, eggs, oil and fried in vegetable oil and served with sweet chili sauce made of water, sugar, chili pepper, salt, vinegar, and garlic), rangoon, noodle soup, General Tso Chicken, Sweet & Sour Chicken, Szechuan Chicken, Mandarin Sauce,Vegetable Stir-Fry, Vegetable Delight, soy sauce, Sizzling Rice Soup, Dragon Rolls, Triple Delight, Pepper Steak, Snow Peas, Lobster Sauce, Chinese fortune cookies, mandarin oranges, hot tea.

Vietnamese, Cambodian, and Thai food also include a delicious variety of rice dishes, pho soup, and vegetable rolls, Chicken Teriyaki, Chicken Wings, Beef Spare Ribs, Shrimp Rolls, Scallops, Chicken Dumplings, Black Bean Sauce. GA

XAO GUNG is white meat chicken in ginger-honey sauce with bell peppers & onions. GA XAO SA OT is sautéed white meat chicken with bell pepper & onion in lemon grass and chili sauce, iced tea and hot tea.

Japan Food: Hibachi vegetables, miso soup contains tofu (soy bean curd), scallions, and wakame (seaweed). Wagashi is red bean paste made from azuki beans, sugar, and honey. Vegetables cooked in broth and pickled vegetables are popular. Sushi is a fish delicacy but vegetable sushi is available. Teriyaki sauce is a glaze of soy sauce, mirin (rice wine) and sugar. Wasabi is a green paste made from the wasabi plant, horseradish, and green food coloring. Green tea daifuku consists of green tea, soy powder, and bean paste, wrapped in sticky rice. Bonito flakes are fish. Tempura is fish fried in batter. Kembu is seaweed. Scrambled eggs with pea pods or tomato, soy sauce, and fish, beef, or ham with a side dish of rice is tamago (omelette). Carrot-tofu dish is seasoned with sesame seeds and soy sauce with side of eggplant or rice noodle, hot tea.

In Indonesia, the sate is skewered grilled meat that is served with a sauce; similar to the yakitori in Japan, shish kebab in Turkey and Middle-East, shashlik from the Caucasus Mountains near Europe and Asia, chuanr from China, and sosatie from South Africa, hot tea.

In Malaysia, dodol is a sweet confection made with coconut milk, jaggery (sugar), and rice flour, hot tea.

Canadian foods: smoked meat, vegetables, butter tart, maple syrup, poutine (French fries, gravy, and cheese topping), Nanaimo (dessert with custard between two layers of chocolate; chocolate may be mint, peanut butter, coconut, or mocha).

U.S.A. North American foods: potatoes, vegetables, beef, chicken, chicken livers and gizzards, pork, Heinz 57 sauce, fish and tartar sauce, pasta, pizza, chili, hamburgers, hot dog with mustard, relish and may have onions, ketchup or chili cheese dog or coleslaw dog, sandwiches, mayonnaise, cheeses, apples, oranges, fruits, cereal grains, salads, coffee, hot tea, apple pie, pumpkin pie, key lime pie, banana bread, jello, green bean casserole, squash casserole, broccoli casserole, souffle, tomato ketchup, yellow mustard, pickles, pastries, cakes, pies with flour crust, cheesecake with graham cracker crust, and ice cream. Sweet iced tea, cornbread, collards, yams, cabbage, rutabaga, peach cobbler, and grits are popular in the Southern USA. In the southeastern USA a soul food is chitlins or chitterlings which is pork fat or pork intestines that is often used to flavor collard greens. Ambrosia is a fruit salad with pineapple, coconut, pecans, mandarin oranges or cherries, marshmallows, and sour cream or whipped cream. Boston crème cake is Bavarian crème cake with chocolate icing. New England white cream based clam chowder was invented in Rhode Island. Manhattan clam chowder is tomato based. Salisbury steak is hamburger steak covered in a brown gravy; the Japanese version is Hanbagu; the Russian version is Cutlet. The steak is served with mashed potatoes or macaroni and cheese. Shepherd's Pie is made with leftovers of meat, potatoes, and cheese. Some like a cold piece of chicken or meat loaf sandwich from leftovers that were promptly refrigerated. Caramel candy was invented in America. Reuben sandwiches have corned beef, sauerkraut, Swiss cheese, and Russian dressing on rye toast and was invented by a Jewish Lithuanian grocer in Omaha, Nebraska. In Southwestern USA, black bean cakes infused with roasted corn and green peppers are popular. Creole cooking in Louisiana, USA blends French, Spanish, Portuguese, Italian, Native American, and African recipes. Cajun food consists of jambalaya rice(which may have sausage, ham, chicken, shrimp, oysters, tomatoes, cumin, pepper, and oregano), crab cakes with roasted vegetables and tangy butter sauce, sausage or seafood which may include garlic, carrots, parsley, bay leaf, green onions (scallions), cayenne pepper, and black pepper. The holy trinity of bell pepper, onion, and celery is used in both Cajun and Creole cooking. Shrimp etouffee or crawfish etouffee is shellfish served over rice and may include vegetables. Native American Indian foods include cornbread, acorn bread, Piki bread of the Hopi is made with blue corn, dried meats like jerky (pemmican) and salmon strips, turkey, muscadines, blackberries, raspberries, hominy, corn (maize), beans, succotash (beans & corn mixed), potatoes, squash, pumpkin, venison, wojape (pudding made from berries), tiswin (corn or fruit beer) of the Apache. Taro (also called kalo) is a classic vegetable dish in Hawaii.

Mexican dinners: Tacos, Chalupas, Enchiladas, Burritos, Fajitas, Quesadillas, Avocado, Salsa, Pico de gallo, Chile con queso, Refried Beans, Queso Cheese Dip, White Queso Cheese Dip.

Caribbean foods: Jamaican Jerk Spice(Blackened Chicken), Black Beans, Fu-Fu, Rice and Peas, Plantains, Goat stew, vegetables seasoned with cilantro (coriander), marjoram, rosemary, tarragon, thyme, cassava.

South American foods: Feijoada stew (white or kidney beans, beef or port, tomatoes, carrots, cabbage), potatoes, seafood, lamb, venison, bananas, coffee. In Argentina and Brazil and other Latin American countries, Churrasco (beef) is often marinated with Nicaraguan chimichurri sauce (parsley, garlic, olive oil, white wine vinegar, water, salt, pepper), quinoa flour, dulce de leche sauce. Empanada is Columbia.

Australian foods: beer, wine, cheese, mushroom truffles, seafood.

New Zealand foods: rewena (Maori bread), pork, seafood, potatoes, vegetables, white cabbage, figs, dumplings, kumara (sweet potatoes), pavlova (meringue-based desert with strawberries, passionfruit, kiwifruit, and cream topping).

Russian foods: borscht (cabbage soup with beets), shashlik or shish kebabs (marinated in a mixture of bay leaves, pepper, apple cider vinegar, oregano, lemon juice and served with tomatoes, mushrooms, cucumbers, zucchini, onions, or potatoes), fish, poultry, salad, potatoes, pasta, caviar, smoked salmon, salted herring, cake, chocolate, kvass (fermented rye beverage), brown rye bread, hot tea, mushrooms, honey, vodka. Russian custom is for families to eat dinner together each night.

Polish foods include kielbasa sausages with mustard, kotlet schabowy (breaded meat cutlets) served with home fries or mashed potatoes, and boiled cabbage or cole slaw. Roulade is meat rolled aound a filling before slicing. Slavic cooking around the regions of Balarus, Ukraine, and Russia were influenced by German, Austrian, and Hungarian cuisines and Jewish, French, and Italian culinary traditions. Ghoulash is a Hungarian stew. A Jewish bagel is a ring of bread.

German foods: sauerkraut, potatoes, bratwurst sausage, braunschweiger or liverwurst, asparagus, lamb, poultry, Bavarian crème cake, Potato pancakes are popular in Germany, Austria, and many other countries. Keilbasa is a sausage of Poland and Ukraine. Stuffed cabbages are boiled cabbage leaves filled with beef, onions, rice, tomato and sauerkraut may be added into the pot. Austrian schnitzel is a meat that may be breaded and is fried in oil or fat.

Swedish foods: lingonberry jam, Swedish meatballs, pickled gherkins, potatoes, pork.
Danish foods: meatballs, roast pork, seasonings of black pepper, cinnamon, cardamom, pickled gherkins, beer, cod with mustard, boiled potatoes, carmelized potatoes, cauliflower. Russian red beet salad and Italian salad (carrots, asparagus, green peas, mayonnaise) are popular in Denmark.

Norway foods: Lefse is Norwegian potato flatbread. It can be topped with sugar and butter. Salmon, herring, trout, codfish, cheese, and bread are popular foods.

Finnish foods are fish, meat, vegetables, grains, pastries

Belgian foods are chocolates, cheese, fruits, breads, ice cream, beers, Brussels sprouts, French fries, beef stew, fish stew, speculoos (shortbread cookies).

Swiss foods: Chocolate, Gruyere cheese, fondues, Rosti potatoes (grated hash brown potatoes seasoned with bacon, cheese, apples, and herbs), sausages, tarts.

Chocolates may contain nuts and fruits. A box of assorted chocolates has a delightful variety. Butterscotch was invented in Scotland. Toffee with rum was derived in India and Britain.
Scones were invented in Scotland.

Irish foods: Crème de menthe, potatoes, rashers (bacon), bangers (sausages), grilled tomato, black pudding (pork and oatmeal sausage), white pudding (oatmeal sausage seasoned with black pepper, cumin, basic, and garlic), baked beans, mushrooms, brown soda bread, Irish stew, soda bread, corned beef hash and eggs.

Britain foods: hot tea, crumpets and marmalade jam, roast beef, roast potatoes, vegetables, Yorkshire pudding, steak and kidney pie, shepherd's pie, fish and chips, chicken tikka masala (chicken marinated in yogurt and spices and cooked with tomatoes, coriander, cream or coconut cream, turmeric, or paprika), oxtail soup, mushroom ketchup, worchestershire sauce, cucumber sandwiches, egg salad sandwiches. A1 sauce was invented in 1824 by Henderson William Brand, a chef for King George IV of the U.K.

Greek foods: zucchini, yogurt, eggplant with tomatoes and onions, olives, cheese, lamb, poultry, pork, gyros with tzatziki sauce, apple pie, beef or chicken pot pie, cheesecake.

Middle-eastern foods: grape leaves, pita bread, rice, figs, saffron, cinnamon, parsley, baklava pastry, falafel (fava beans or chick peas), hummus (chick peas, garlic, olive oil, lemon, salt), samosas, shakshouka (eggs, tomatoes, chili peppers, onions, cumin), zaatar (herbs, thyme, sesame seeds, dried sumac, and spices). Kabsah is a dish popular in Jordan and Saudi Arabia that is made with meat, rice, black pepper, cloves, cardamom, saffron, cinnamon, black lime, bay leaves, and nutmeg. Challah is a bread of Israel made with eggs, white flour, water, yeast, sugar or honey or molasses, and sprinkled with sesame seeds. Palestinian food: lentils, chili peppers, laffa bread (taboon bread), musakhan (roasted chicken seasoned with onions, sumac, allspice, and saffron). Lebanese foods include kafta which is beef kebabs. Ashure is Noah's pudding, an Islamic dessert served on 10th day of Muharram. Oman kahwa coffee has cardamom powder and saltah is meat stew. Yemen flatbread is filled with rice, potatoes, scrambled eggs, vegetables and lamb or chicken. Couscous are Maghrebi Arabic pasta balls. Baklava and borek pastries made with phyllo dough can be made differently in different countries such as Iran, Albania, Syria, Israel, Iraq, Greece, and Azerbaijan, filled with fruits, cheeses, meats, and vegetables.
Marzipan is a sweet concoction made with sugar or honey, ground almonds, and almond oil, and is used to make sweets and icings for cakes. It is believed to have originated in Persia (Iran), China,

Hungary, or Italy. Sheer pira is an Afghanistan sweet milk fudge with sugar and almonds.

North Africa (near Morocco, Algeria, Egypt, and Saudi Arabia): couscous with vegetables and chick peas, (may be seasoned with saffron, nutmeg, cinnamon, ginger, olives, olives oil), pastries, tajine (egg/omelette/quiche dish served with honey, cinnamon, almonds), potatoes, zucchini, tomatoes, chilies. Ful medames is an Egyptian dish containing fava beans and may be seasoned with vegetable oil, cumin, lemon juice, onion, parsley, garlic, and hot peppers; this dish is served with eggs and vegetables.
Horn of Africa (area near Ethiopia) foods: tsebhis (stew), injera (flatbread), hilbet (paste made from lentils or faba beans), couscous, vegetables, chick peas, kitcha fit-fit (seasoned unleavened bread served with yogurt and berbere spice), Xalwo (confection made with sugar, cornstarch, cardamom, nutmeg and ghee (seasoned butter), basmati rice, wat (vegetable stew). Pieces of injera are used instead of a fork to pick up wat. Samosa is a fried or baked pastry filled with savory spices, potatoes, onions, peas, lentils, or meat; these pastries are also made in Central Asia, India, and Mediterranean areas.
Central African stew (chicken, okra, ginger), Spinach stew (tomato, peppers, chilis, onions, and peanut butter), fu-fu (starchy food made from flour of the cassava plant which is dipped into soup or sauce). Bambara is a porridge of rice, peanut butter and sugar.
East Africa foods: Rice in the Persian-style seasoned with saffron, cloves, cinnamon, and pomegranate juice, Barbeque Beef, pork, coffee, Ugali (starch food made from corn maize and eaten with cabbage or kale), pineapples, lentil soup, pickles. In Uganda, steamed green bananas is a popular dish.
South African Stew: Potijekos (a stew that contains meat and vegetables; beer or wine may be added), seafood, apples, grapes, mangoes, bananas, papayas, avocado, oranges, peaches, apricots, cereal grains.
West Africa Stew: Maafe is meat (lamb, beef, or chicken), tomatoes, onions, garlic, cabbage, vegetables, and peanuts if desired; served with rice, couscous, fu-fu, or yams (sweet potatoes). Vegetables can be okra, corn, carrots, sweet potatoes, cocoyams, beans. Spices can be cinnamon, hot peppers, paprika, black pepper, turmeric. Klouikloui is fried rings of peanut butter. Joliof rice is rice seasoned with tomatoes, onion, salt, and may contain nutmeg, ginger, cumin, chili pepper, pepper, garlic, or curry. 'Kiburi' means 'pride' in Swahili and there is a Kiburi coffee in Kenya.

3. Farmers, food manufacturers and transporters, and food providers should ensure that food is grown, processed, transported, and prepared safely for human consumption. Food labels should list all ingredients. Import and export

trade agreements between countries should be fair.

4. It is a busy world, but many families try to eat meals together once a day or once a week. Some people may prefer to eat alone and watch tv or read. A pot luck dinner is a dinner when each person brings a dish to share with the others.

5. If you are at dinner, it may bother someone sitting next to you if you talk the entire way through the meal because they may want to relax.

6. An apron can be worn over clothes while cooking to avoid stains.

7. Babies, toddlers, and children may wear bibs to protect their clothing from food stains. Children may use small child-size cups, forks, spoons, and knives that enable them to eat more easily. Children may need bland food, not too spicy. When babies are teething, their gums in their mouths may hurt. Babies may need extra TLC then. Orajel is a topical numbing ointment benzocaine that may be rubbed on the baby's gums to help soothe the pain.

8. If you rinse your mouth with water after you finishing eating, it may help remove sugar and food from your teeth that may help prevent tooth decay.

9. Many family and social events are centered around meal or foods. But events do not always have to be centered around eating. Events can be centered around trips to museums, music, art & crafts shows, walks, watching movies, playing cards, ping pong or badminton.

10. Don't get distracted and forget that you left a pot boiling on the stove or something cooking inside the oven.

11. Don't go grocery shopping when you are hungry because people tend to buy more than they need when they are hungry.

12. An empty cookie jar can be refilled with raisins or dried figs or apricots.

HOME

CHAPTER 1

1. Our real home is with the Lord. Our home on Earth is only temporary until we reach our ultimate destiny.
It has been said that home is where your heart is. As followers, Our hearts are with the Lord.

2. We should take care of earthly and universal home, reduce pollution and conserve our resources. We should recycle and reuse what we can, and reduce the amount of trash.

3. The whole Earth is a home for all organisms including humans. The vegetation, soil, air, oceans, lakes and streams, lagoons and marshes, sun, and moon support all plant and animal life on the earth.

CHAPTER 2

Home Sweet Home

1. Home on earth is a special place because it is a place where we go for comfort, food, and rest, a place to lay our head. Home can be viewed as a foundation of safety, a safe haven. When it is raining and thundering outside, we usually feel safe and cozy inside of our homes.

Some people have lived in one home or one place their whole lives, often leaving the property to heirs, while other people have lived in many places and dwellings, and even all over the world. Many think home is anywhere as long as your heart and life are peaceful and fulfilled.

On earth, people live on flatlands, on mountains, on the coast, on waterways.

2. At times many people have lost their homes due to unfortunate circumstances, causing much sorrow. But remember, just as we were born into the world with nothing, we can take nothing with us when we leave, so pray for the Lord to lead you to a new home where you will find comfort.

3. And most people think the important things in a home are loved ones, pets, and things of sentimental value because most other things can be replaced if lost, but if a life is lost then there are only special memories left.

4. Many people have parties, dinners with suitable table-talk, get-togethers, worship, after-worship dinners, and meetings in their homes or as lawn or street parties.

5. Home is a place to rest and relax, do chores, and enjoy activities like recreation, entertainment, hobbies, cook meals, bathe, restore mental and physical health, exercise, sleep, listen to music, experience aromatherapy, engage in conversations, make plans, cuddle with the loved ones, copulate, create everlasting memories of love and good cheer.

The laundry, the floors and sinks, the linens, the dishes and glasses, cooking utensils, the baseboards, the windowsills, the window seats, the drawers, the storage areas, and the porches need to be cleaned and dusted. The fire pit may need cleaning.
The surrounding grass and foliage need to be trimmed.

6. Some people have offices, work-spaces, or music studios in their home in which they earn income.

7. Most people agree that there is no place like home.

8. Many people in the world are homeless and have nowhere to go, but many charities and good organizations are trying to find ways so that everyone on the planet Earth can have a special and comfortable place to call home. All people on Earth deserve a decent life with clean water and food, shelter, employment, and opportunities for growth.

9. It is believed that the first homes were caves, then, as humans progressed, shelters were improved.

By human effort, which many believe is guided by the Goodness of God, electricity and indoor plumbing with clean running water were invented and included in shelters.

In the earliest homes, kitchens and laundries were outside in the courtyard because food was cooked on wood-burning stoves and water pails were carried from outdoor wells to laundry basins. Butter was churned daily outside in the courtyard.The earliest homes had no plumbing; outhouses were constructed in back yards that had a hole in the ground for humans to release the waste movement from the body and water was lifted from water wells for cooking, bathing, cleaning, and drinking. Toilets, sinks, bathtubs, and plumbing were great inventions.The earliest homes had no closets; clothing was hung in pieces of furniture called armoires or wardrobes. The earliest homes had dirt driveways or paths, then the paved ones became popular. Some think that there is too much pavement on the earth now, which is preventing the rainwater from seeping into the ground more evenly, so many are constructing the driveways consisting of grids of grass and pavement to allow the water to permeate more evenly to the earth; then, when you wash your car, all of the water will not be directed down the city sewer to the city water supply but the water can filter through the earth beneath the car as you are washing it. Also, use less soap and try to use organic citrus-based cleaner to wash your vehicle.

Many builders are including miniature tree gardens in the middle of parking lots, which is good thing, because trees take in carbon dioxide and release oxygen, whereas humans breathe in oxygen and release carbon dioxide. Trees and plants are vital in the environment to maintain an atmosphere that can support human life.

A long time ago, there was no organized mail service.
Humans have worked hard to establish mail and emergency help systems upon the earth, and people mark the address of their homes with numbers and street names so the postman would know where to deliver letters, bills, and packages; some people display the name of the family upon the house.
Now, you can have a hot pizza, hoagie sandwich, grilled cheese sandwich, salad, Chinese food, groceries, internet orders, and more - delivered to your address.

Some prefer privacy and do not have anything delivered to their home; they use post office boxes to receive all of their correspondence.

There are humanitarian and government organizations that have been established for the cause of helping people who have lost their homes in times of major disasters like earthquakes, mudslides, fires, or hurricanes. Temporary homes, businesses, and worship sites have been constructed of recyclable materials like cardboard.

10. Homes can be *detached dwellings* such as single, cluster, floating, mobile, tents, teepees or tipi, tree houses, log cabins, mountain chalets, beach huts, vehicles, campers, cardboard structures.

Homes can be in *one dwelling with multiple units* such as apartment homes, lofts, condominiums, and much more.

The exterior of the dwelling may be brick and mortar, wood, stacked stone, stucco, plastic, glass, metal, vinyl, cardboard, glass bricks, or combinations of materials.

Walkways and streets can be made of dirt, cobblestone, bricks, tarmac, or cement.

People have lived in workspaces such as offices, units over stores, storage units, trucks, cars, and caves.

Humans live in many spaces to survive. Many people struggle to keep a roof over their head because they are unable to improve their financial situation.

Many people can live together under one roof in a group home and share the space for companionship and financial reasons.

If your home can be located near your work location, many problems can be reduced such as commute time, commute cost (fuel and car depreciation and car maintenance), and air pollution.

Some have both winter and summer homes.

Homes need maintenance which costs money. Rental property should be treated with respect and should not be trashed.

11. Homes can include: family, friends, and cherished possessions,

kitchens with island counters and kitchen appliances, windows and skylights, cabinets, dishwashers, refrigerators, coffee makers, ovens, microwave ovens, recessed lighting, tables, floors consisting of tiles, linoleum, laminated hard-wood, trash cans, trash cans with lids, knives and sharpeners, can openers, bars and bar stools, ice bucket.

family rooms with irreplaceable family items, entertainment centers, big-screen TVs, couches, footstool, swivel glider chair, recliner chair, benches, bean bags, rugs, bookcases, fireplaces, billiards, dart boards, table-tennis or ping-pong, miniature golf-putting courses, music systems, fake plastic or fabric plants and flowers

sunrooms or porches with a lot of windows, screens, and ceiling fans

al fresco or outdoor dining

bedrooms with luxurious furniture and mattresses, vanities, over-sized walk-in closets filled with beautiful clothing, shoes and other accessories, reading nooks, chaise lounges, soft lighting, twinkling light strands, mirrors, big-screen TVs, entertainment centers, multiplex workout gyms

offices or libraries with the latest state-of-the-art technology and workspaces

restrooms or bathrooms with luxurious toiletries, bathtubs, sinks, wallpapers, mirrors, trash baskets, small trash cans with lids

front porches, front patios, lanterns, welcome mats, courtyards, wrap-around porches, back-yard decks, and garden patios for outdoor enjoyment, mailboxes, outdoor firepits, screened-in porches, cabanas, gazebos, hammocks, Adirondack chairs, papsan chairs, an item or plant that is the belle of the garden

windows that open or are hermetically sealed, window shutters and curtains

black-out curtains, embroidered linens, quilts, comforters, soft plush blankets

rock and water gardens
gazing balls
wind chimes
flower gardens
vegetable and herb gardens
bird feeders or bird baths

fences surrounding the property or parts of the property built of wood, chain links, ornamental iron, vinyl, or shrubbery

foyers to greet guests in, doors, screen doors, door bell, docks at lake houses formal living rooms and dining rooms with vaulted ceilings, crown moldings and chair railings, hand-hewn beams, fine furniture and fixtures

floors of hardwood, ceramic tiles, linoleum, limestone

roofs with ceramic tiles, tin, or shingles

garages to park vehicles in or to store yard equipment or recreational equipment like bike, kites, boats, jet skis, kayaks, hiking equipment, roller skates, camping equipment

driveway or carport with awning

panic rooms with special safety, food, medicine, and communication provisions

hobby rooms to explore personal creativity like art, ceramics, basket weaving, collections, music, sewing, furniture construction or welding

guest room

mudrooms to store shoes, umbrellas, and raincoats in

laundry rooms with washers and dryers, ironing boards, lint rollers

wheelchair access, low countertops, low cabinets, low shelves in closets, accessible shower

stairs and banisters, escape ladder or rope from second floors

basements for storage, entertainment, or for safety in times of bad weather, wine cellar

utility closets or rooms for electrical circuit breakers, water heaters, furnaces, power storage for solar energy.

12. Apartment homes or loft and condominium unit homes can provide elegant amenities and services such as: pools, clubhouses, executive business centers, resort-style swimming pools and fitness centers, tennis courts, grill and picnic areas, games, clothes-care centers, cabanas, car-care centers, pet parks, valet trash and recycling centers, storage and garage units, restaurants, and chauffer services.

13. When you live somewhere, you get very familiar with the space.
You may learn detailed knowledge like the noises of your dwelling, such as creaks in the floorboards, rattling of window panes, leaks in the roof, sounds of the refrigerator, air conditioning and heater. Empty rooms are louder than rooms filled with items. Rooms with carpets and drapes are quieter than rooms with bare floors.

A house is said to be haunted if it is believed that spirits of the deceased live there.

You may determine the topography of your yard, such as how rainfall flows on the soil. Problems like sink holes or unstable trees should be addressed. When doing yardwork be careful of insects, snakes, poisonous vines; wear protective gloves. When mowing grass, beware of rocks that could be thrown from the mower and hit you.

Having a home and a place to enjoy also involves home maintenance like cleaning, inspecting for pests, mold, structural integrity, painting, and possible property taxes.

If you live in the northern hemisphere of the world, the north side of a structure is the side that usually does not get enough sunlight and is subject to mold or moss.

Many people construct homes and other buildings based on the way the sunlight will shine on the dwelling.

Decks should be supported well with support beams underneath and not just brackets to avoid collapsing from the weight of many people on the deck.

Decks can be waterproofed to avoid wood rot.

The first windows were invented by Russians who used sheets of muscovite mica as translucent window panes.

Hermetically sealed windows are windows that may have two panes and are airtight in between the panes. The word *hermetic* is derived from the Greek god Hermes who was the god of transitions and boundaries and was a messenger for the gods. Hermes' signs were the herma, rooster, tortoise, purse or pouch, winged sandals, and a herald's staff.

Bullet-proof glass panes protect from bullets.

If you leave windows or doors open, lizards, snakes, wasps, bees, spiders, or mosquitoes could come in without your knowledge. Squirrels or birds may get into your attic. Window and door screens should be intact to keep small creatures out.

If you are trying to catch a mouse, studies have shown that mice prefer bacon and peanut butter more than cheese wedges.

Small spaces around windows and doors can be sealed to keep out weather elements and small critters. Moths can make holes in cashmere or wool clothing.

Pudding and desserts can be put in wineglasses.

14. Is your house clean and organized? Do you need to do laundry? Are you dinner ready or have you made plans for dinner? What about food and other supplies for the week? Does your house need to exterminated for bugs? Do you have some non-perishable items on hand such as bottled water or canned goods in case of emergencies like power outages or bad weather? Do you have candles and matches in case of power outages? Some people go to a relative's or friend's home, or motels or hotels during a power outage. Do you need to clean out closets or redecorate rooms? Can you donate clothing, furniture, decorative items, or cars to charities? Are you aware of any birthdays coming up for people in the household or for other family, friends or pets? Are you ready with a kind word, a smile, a hug, a word of encouragement for a loved one or for a roommate? Do you need to take a quiet moment to reflect and thank the Lord for all you have or make a request to the Lord?

15. You may want tomato vines or blueberry bushes, flags, statues, boats, broken cars in your front yard, but your neighborhood association may not want such things in your front yard, saying *not in my neighborhood*. The best thing to do is negotiate.

There are junk collectors that will come to your house for free and take your junk away; some charge a fee.

16. Many people advocate for personal or community gardens so food could be shared in case of national food crises and to enjoy locally grown organic fruits and vegetables. Community gardens can be maintained by many volunteers.

17. When a guest leaves your home, it is nice to make sure they get safely to their car or transportation hub. It is nice for the guest to notify the friends he left that he arrived safely back at his home or destination.

CHAPTER 3 *Animal Habitats*

1. Humans have taken all kinds of animals as pets: avian pets like canaries, parakeets, and parrots; aquatic pets like tropical fish and frogs; arthropods like tarantulas and hermit crabs; reptiles like turtles, lizards and snakes; monkeys, horses, pigs, guinea pigs, rabbits, ferrets, gerbils, hamsters, chinchillas, rats.

Virtual and robotic pets have been invented for human enjoyment.

Pets live in dog houses, aquariums, terrariums, bird houses, horse stalls, or in owner's personal homes.

Pets can travel domestically and internationally by airplane, train, and ship in animal carriers with travel papers and immunization requirements. Animals can be subject to the time lags incurred while travelling. Some animals may enjoy traveling, and some may not.

Animal shelters provide homes for homeless dogs and cats.

2. Milk from cows and goats is consumed in many parts of the world. A Guernsey cow can give 20 gallons (75.5 liters) of milk a day.

3. Butterfly domes, zoos, aquariums, sea world theme parks, national parks, wildlife habitats are homes to many animals.

4. In some countries, animals are allowed to roam wild. In some countries, animals only roam wild in designated natural habitats.

Many cities and countries have enacted lease laws and other animal restriction laws in order to create more healthy living environments for the citizens.

Hunters and fisherman are allowed to hunt certain wild animals, reptiles, and fish in certain areas to keep animal populations from getting out of control where it could be harmful to humans.

5. The forest, woods, mountains and fields are home to owls, snakes, birds, pudu, deer, moose, bears, coyotes, buffalo, foxes, elk, sheep, goats, chipmunks, woodchucks, squirrels, porcupines, turtles, monkeys, raccoons, skunks, jackals, wolves, ostriches, horses, rabbits, pigs, chickens, cows, mice, cats, groundhog, crickets, spiders, ants, centipedes, frogs, cicadas, snails, chameleons, beetles, lightening bugs, bats, worms, caterpillar, peacocks, bison, yaks, and many others. Hens with white ear lobes lay white eggs while hens with red or blue ear lobes lay brown eggs.

Virgin lands are lands that have never been disturbed from their natural formations.

Hawks, eagles, doves, pigeons, redbirds, blue jays, blackbirds, finches, hummingbirds, butterflies, wasps, crossbills, cuckoos, nutcrackers, bumblebees, and other birds fly the skies and woods.

Some northern forests consist of only conifer trees, the needles of which cannot be digested by animals, so the floor of these forests is bare except for specialized fungi which can digest the needles. The conifer forest has been called a green desert. Some northern forests contain tigers, leopards, wolverines.

Some of the oldest, tallest trees are sequoia, bristlecone, and redwood.

Grand Teton National Park in the valley of Jackson Hole, Wyoming, USA, offers hiking, fishing, and camping.

There are deer, squirrels, and black bear in Shenandoah National Park in Shenandoah Valley, Virginia, USA. Adirondack Park in New York is the largest park in the USA. Baniff National Park and Jasper National Park are near Alberta Canada.

Some ocean-foraging seabirds that hide their eggs on high cliffs may also hide their eggs in branches of treetops of nearby forests.

Some forests contain the cicada insect, which submerges itself for 17 years and then a trillion cicadas will come out in an emergence year, mate during a ten-day period, and then all of the adults will die. The nymph cicadas that hatch from the eggs on the leaves drop to the ground and bury themselves until the next 17 year emergence.

Underneath the earth are millions of millipedes, centipedes, slugs, snails, and tinier creatures.

Monkeys in some forests eat fruit and insects and swing in the trees by tree limbs. Some monkeys eat plants and bark so they have adapted to live in groups of about 30 during winters when food is scarce but live in groups of about 600 during the summer.

The nutcracker bird will use its bill to open the cones of the white bark pine tree and remove an average of 30,000 nuts each year, and stash them in about 5000 places, but only use about 75% of the caches. Squirrels only cache their nuts in few larders. Scientists are not sure why birds cache the nuts in so many places but one explanation has been so that bears would not smell a large cache of nuts.

6. The highest mountain on earth is Mount Everest in the Himalaya which range across Afghanistan, Pakistan, India, Nepal, Bhutan, and China.

Giant panda bears live in the Himalaya Mountains of China.
Baby panda bears are 900 times smaller than the mother; baby panda bears weigh less than a pound (less than .454 kilograms) and therefore less than a human infant; such is the wonder of the miracles in all of God's creation.

The Ethiopian Highlands are in Africa are homes for goats, wolves, and geladas. There is volcanic activity in the Danakil Depression of Ethiopia.

The longest mountain chain on earth is the Andes is South America which stretch across Chile, Ecuador, and Bolivia. Llamas, guanacos, and pumas live in the Andes. There is volcanic activity in the Andes and in other parts of the world.

The Rockies are in North America are homes for mountain goats, and grizzly bears. Hybernation is the winter sleep of bears and is one of the holy laws.

The Middle West has fertile farm lands. The ladybug is a farmer's friend because it eats tiny aphids. Hens have a pecking order of importance.

Volcanic activity occurred in mountains of Northwest America.

The Alps and Pyrenees are the high mountains of Europe. The Matterhorn is a mountain with a top that looks like a hook and is between Switzerland and Italy, The Urals are the high mountains of western Russia. The Amur region are high mountains of parts of China and Japan.

7. The tundra is above the tree line, which is about 65 degrees north of the equator. The tundra near the north pole is home to the Arctic fox and musk ox. Above the tree line no trees will grow. The tundra is also home to the wolf packs, caribou herds, flocks of snow geese, flies and mosquitoes. The fjords of Newfoundland were cut by ancient glaciers.

8. It is cold at the poles of the earth with practically no carbon activity. The temperature is around -55 ^{0} C or -67 ^{0} F. The South Pole of Antarctica is colder than the North Arctic Pole.

Antarctica has higher elevation than the Arctic.
There is 6 months of sunlight and then 6 months of darkness at both of the poles.

The period of darkness at the South Pole is from late March to late September, while at the same time it is the period of sunlight at the North Pole. Then around September 21 the periods change, with 6 months of sunlight at the South Pole and 6 months of darkness at the North Pole. The sun's radiation is reflected back by the surface, one reason why it remains frozen.

The frozen north pole is home to about 40 animals including oxen, lemming, seals, polar bears, walrus.
Bats, rodents, polar bears all may lay dormant, or hibernate (sleep) for days months in cold weather.

There are 90 flowering plants at the Arctic as far north as 82 degrees.

The frozen south pole is home to the penguin bird and the mammal seal.
The only thing that grows at the south pole are some lichens on top of a few

mountains that raise above the ice and 2 flowering plants on the entire continent of Antarctica.

In the south, fewer than 20 bird species will visit south of 70 degrees toward Antarctica, while in the north at least 100 bird species will visit as far north as 82 degrees toward the Arctic. Conditions in Antarctica are much harsher than in the Arctic.

Birds called Arctic terns have been tracked to migrate 9,300 miles (15,000km) to Antarctica to join Antarctic terns during the sunlit season. Then, the Antarctic terns will migrate with Arctic terns to the Arctic for the Arctic sunlit season.

Thridarangar lighthouse built in 1939 in Iceland is a step cliff with a heliport.

9. The safari and savannah of the plains of Africa contain elephants, giraffes, hyenas, lions, tigers, rhinoceros, hippopotamus, monkeys, gorillas, zebras, pumas, leopards, cheetahs, cougars, jaguars, aardvark, black mamba snake. The Sahara Desert is north of the safari and savannah. The roar of a lion can be heard 5 miles away. Sometimes animals will reject their young after being born.

There is a great Tibetan plateau on one side of the Himalayan Mountains, and a plateau called Gangetic Plains to the south, the Taklamakan Desert to the north. Herds of yaks exist in the region.

10. The freshwater rivers, lakes, and streams, marshes and swamps may contain bass, trout, catfish, snakes, ducks, swans, beavers, otters, lizards, flies, mosquitoes, crocodiles, alligators, and more. Swans, beavers, gibbon monkeys, wolves, barn owls, bald eagles, skinks, and some angel fish, worms, and birds mate for life.

Lake Baikal in Siberia, Russia, is the largest body of fresh water in the world and it is also the world's oldest lake. It is the home of the world's only freshwater seal, which is thought to have emigrated to the lake 22 million years ago from the Arctic, the adjoining rivers have long since disappeared.

At the bottom of the lake divers (aquanauts) also found a hydrothermal vent which were once thought to only occur in deep oceans. Around the heated vents live sponges, snails, fish, and transparent shrimps, and flatworms.

Three of the world's largest freshwater lakes are in East Africa and are called Malawi, Tanganyika, and Victoria. The lakes contain the cichlids which is unique to the lakes. If the parent cichlid senses a predator, the parent cichlid will signal for its babies to swim into its own cavernous mouth for protection until the predator passes.

Some lakes are man-made.

Giant salamanders, the world's largest amphibian, live in the mountain rivers of China and Japan.

Each spring salmon fish from the sea make a journey upstream and even jump up waterfalls and rapids along the coasts of North America, Europe, and Korea to make their way back to spawning grounds where they were spawned before they swam out to sea. The salmon change color from silver to bright red in fresh water.

The worlds giant rivers are the Amazon, Congo, Orinoco, Yangtze, Parana, Brahmaputra, Yellow, Yenisei, Ganges, and Mississippi. The Nile river in Africa is the world's longest river and has crocodiles.

Botos are pink river dolphins that live in the Amazon. The Amazon flows through the Andes mountains of South America.

The flowing waters contain stories of times past, present, and possibly the future. Life is like a river in that the water passes a particular point only once and is gone forever, just like the moments of our lives. Stratum in the layers of rock, fossils, and cave markings also tell about the history of the area.

Large freshwater fishes like sturgeons and stingrays can weigh more than 1,105 pounds (500kg).

11. The saltwater oceans and seas are home to whales, sharks, porpoise, dolphins, tuna, salmon, mahi mahi, seals, yellowtail, shrimp, seahorses, manatee, walruses, pelicans, puffins, heron, seagull, cranes, eels, stingrays, clams, oysters, crabs, scallops, seahorses, corral, sea urchins, jellyfish, octopuses, squid, sea turtles, lobsters, and many others.

Scientists say that porpoises and dolphins have a sonar that sends out high-intensity and high-frequency ultrasonic pulses to detect potential prey and other objects. White sharks and orca whales are enemies of porpoises and dolphins. Old dolphns and baby dolphins are at highest risk of being attacked by white sharks and orca whales.

The orca whale has no enemies. Marine biologists say that no animal hunts orca whales.

Scientists are studying to see if there is DNA in animals and humans that direct aggression, or territorial, and passive behaviors.

The blue whale is the biggest marine mammal on earth.

Lobsters in the Bahamas line up physically, each lobster physically touching the next in line, and migrate to deeper waters during storm season.

The fastest fishes in the oceans are the tuna, and the blue marlin and sailfish of the billfish. They can swim from 40 miles (65km) a day.

Their speed can be as high as 68mph (110kph). Tuna and marlins have been tagged as swimming from Japan to Mexico and California.

The largest marine animal is the whale and can weigh 100-tons. Whales can have barnacles growing on them.

Beluga whales at the arctic can bash their heads through ice to make breathing holes. Humpback whales have been tracked as migrating from Antarctica to the Caribbean coast of Colombia 8330km (5175 miles), from Tonga to Antarctica 6000km (3720 miles), and from Hawaii to the Arctic.

The top 100m (340 feet) of sunlit shallow waters contains 90 percent of life in the oceans.

There are several huge coral reefs in the oceans. Coral can only establish itself in shallow, sunlit waters.

The Great Coral Reef of Australia covers 86,875 square miles (225,000 sq km) and can be seen from space; it consists of coral reefs, sandy cays, and islands. There is also a huge reef near Belize in the Caribbean. Near New Guinea, there is a marine habitat of great biodiversity in coral, fish, and sea snakes. There are coral reefs in Hawaii, Marshall Islands, and Easter Island.

Underneath the waters are millions of types of small creatures and organisms, many which create their own light of bioluminescence. Communities of marine life exist around hot thermal vents in some places.

Humans have built piers that extend out into the oceans from the shorelines and docks that extend out into freshwater lakes.

12. The tropical rainforests, and rivers around the equators in Panama, Cost Rica, and Brazil of South America, Borneo, Malaya and Indonesia have the most plant abundance because of the warm year-round temperatures and are believed to have more than 50 percent of all animal and plant species. Birds like toucans, hornbills, and hoatzins, butterflies, jaguars, bats, monkeys, parrots, birds of paradise, hummingbirds, spiders, and ants are some animals that thrive in the very humid rainforest jungles.

A glasswing butterfly uses transparent wings to camouflage itself as it rests on flowering plants.

A young caterpillar is transformed into an adult butterfly in a silk-like cocoon made by a larva through a process known as metamorphosis. A tadpole is transformed into a frog. A maggot is transformed into a fly.

Figs are a prevalent fruit food for many animals in the rainforest.

The monsoon rainforests in Asia have periods of heavy rain and then periods of dry months. Talking myna birds are native to southern Asia and India, but have been introduced to North America, Australia, South Africa, Fiji, and New Zealand.

Tropical rainforests along the river basins of the Amazon and Zaire rivers, Central America, West Africa, and Southeast Asia all contain huge canopies of trees that have been cut down by loggers.

Mount Kilimanjaro in Tanzania is the highest mountain in Africa. The Darien Gap in Panama has no roads because of the rainforest jungle.

There are monkeys, oxen, pythons near the giant rain forest and in the mountains of South America.

There is a giant iguana in Ecuador.

13. The deserts may have the camels, lizards, solifugids (relative of spiders), scorpions, snakes, toads, oryx, lions, elephants, and birds like roadrunners, larks, coursers, and budgerigars.

The camels have thick eye lashes and tightly closing nostrils to keep out the dust.

The eggs of some locusts can be dormant and survive for 20 years until they hatch, and then there can be a swarm of locusts with 500 billion locusts. The swarm can travel at 80 miles a day, eating all of the vegetation and returning the desert back to wasteland.

Vegetation in the deserts are the cactus, flowering poppies, desert lilies, desert verbena, desert bluebells, roots, bushes. Some cacti can grow to heights of 15m (50 feet) tall and weigh more than 15 tons.

There is not much vegetation, water, or animal life in the deserts so the carbon activity rate is low. Deserts can get as low as 2 inches (50mm) of rain a year.

Deserts temperatures can be over 38°C (100°F) in the day and at night can drop more than 30 degrees in just a few hours. Most deserts are hot all year around while some in high altitudes can reach -21° C (-5°F) in winter.

The hottest desert is the Sahara in Africa; air temperature can be 50°C (122°F) while sand and rock temperature can be 75°C (167°F). The coldest is the Gobi in Asia which can be covered in two inches of snow in the winter where temperatures drop to -40°C (-40°F).

There are also extensive deserts are on the Arabian Peninsula, the Simpson desert and the Great Sandy Desert in Australia, the Mojave desert in North America, the Sonora on the Baja California peninsula, the Namib in southwest Africa, the Kalahari desert in south Africa, the Atacama in Peru of South America, the Patagonia near the Andes Mountains in Argentina.

The kangaroo, koala bear, and cattlefish exist in Australia. A domesticated koala bear in Australia ate from a spoon. Koala bears like to eat eucalyptus leaves.

14. There are extensive cave systems on the earth. In New Mexico, USA, Lechuguilla Cave has beautiful underground crystals and other rock formations.

Krubera Cave in the Arabika massif, Abkhazia, on the edge of the Black Sea is considered to be the deepest cave in the world; explorers have dropped down 2km (1.2 miles).

In Borneo, birds called cave swiflets live in Gomantong Cave and bats live in Deer Cave.

The cave at Sarawak Chamber, Borneo, is big enough to hold 40 huge airplanes.

The Cave of Swallows in Mexico could hold a skyscraper with 80 floors.

The Mammoth Cave in Kentucky, USA is over 350 miles long (563km).
Mangawhatikau Cave in New Zealand contain luminous cave glow-worms.
Treefrogs and bats live in Bat Cleft Cave in Queensland, Australia.
There are gigantic caves in Vietnam and Madagascar formed out of limestone.
15. There are varieties of all flowers such as alstroemaria, alyssum, aster, azalea, begonia, buttercup, camellia, carnation, chrysanthemum, daffodil, daisy, delphinium, freesia, Gabriel's trumpet, gardenia, geranium, gladiola, hisbiscus, hydrangea, iris, lavender, lily, linum, pansy, peony, petunia, phylox, poppy, primrose, rhododendron, ranunculus, rose, snapdragon, sunflower, tulip, verbena, violet, zinnia, pentas.
16. Some varieties of trees are: pine, oak, chestnut, ash, beech, ghada, dogwood, maple, crape myrtle, fir, ginkgo, eucalyptus, cyprus, cedar, magnolia, sycamore, acacia, redwood, juniper, Japanese cherry, pecan, walnut, hickory, hazelnut, almond, brazil nut, persimmon, mulberry, holly, willow, palm, orange, apple, pear, banana, lemon, kumquat, wild olive, fig (ficus), coconut, peach, angel trumpet. Carrots, pineapples, and potatoes grow underground.
17. There are many varieties of grasses and many animals eat grass as their main food source. Unlike trees, bushes, and flowers, the leaves of grass grow continuously from the base, regenerating from below even as they are being grazed at from the top or even if the leaf if damaged from the top. Grasses are survivors.
Some vines such as kudzu can grow at startling rates such as several feet a day.
18. There are many varieties of vines such as ivy, kudzu, aspers, creepers.
19. There are varieties of plants that produce carrots, green beans, spinach, collards, squash, beans, corn, peas, okra, cabbage, red onions, yellow onions, white onions, green onions, leeks, green peppers, red peppers, yellow peppers, hot peppers, eggplant, zucchini, celery, cucumbers, tomatoes, lettuce, asparagus, potatoes, sweet potatoes, rutabagas, olives, turnips, radishes, mushrooms.
There are varieties of herbal plants that produce seasonings for foods. Medical herbalism is the belief that some herbal plants like aloe vera, black cumin, cinnamon, garlic, bay laurel, basil, turmeric, propolis, and fish oil can be natural remedies for inflammation, to lower blood sugar, or to lower blood pressure and the herbs are used instead of synthetic drugs.
20. There are carnivorous plants that eat small insects, rodents, frogs, and reptiles. Some of these plants are found in Australia and Borneo and are called Nepenthes, Heliamphora, Drosera glanduligera, and Triphyophyllum. Some of these plants look like a jar and the 'jar' is filled with a digestive liquid that digests the prey.
21. Anaerobic bacteria have been found on earth that do not breathe air but exist on sulfide and iron.

CHAPTER 4

Coexist with Neighbors For a Good Life

1. Most believe that God is everywhere upon the earth, so God can be in all homes and places upon the earth. There will always be different races, languages, opinions, religions, sexual orientations, electric voltages, currencies and countries so the best thing to do is to coexist in peace.
2. Don't be envious or jealous of what your neighbors have. Live your own life and make it the best it can be.
3. Many believe that if populations of snakes, rats, lions, or other animals become a threat to human life, these populations must be controlled.

WORLD COUNTRIES BY CONTINENT

AFRICA

Algeria
Angola
Benin
Botswana
Burkina Faso
Burundi
Cabo Verde
Cameroon
Central African Republic
Chad
Comoros
Congo-Kinshasa, Democratic Republic of
Congo-Brazzaville, Republic of
Cote d'Ivoire (Ivory Coast)
Djibouti
Egypt
Equatorial Guinea
Eritrea
Ethiopia
Gabon
Gambia, Republic of
Ghana
Guinea
Guinea-Bissau
Kenya and Mombasa Island
Lesotho
Liberia
Libya
Madagascar
Malawi
Mali
Mauritania
Mauritius
Mayotte (France)
Morocco
Mozambique
Namibia
Niger
Nigeria
Reunion (France)
Rwanda
Saint Helena (U.K.)
Sao Tome & Principe
Senegal
Seychelles
Sierra Leone
Somalia
South Africa
South Sudan
Sudan
Swaziland
Tanzania
Togo
Tunisia
Uganda
Western Sahara
Zambia
Zimbabwe

ASIA

Afghanistan
Armenia
Azerbaijan
Bahrain
Bangladesh
Bhutan
Brunei
Cambodia
China, People's Republic, Tibet, Hong Kong
China, Republic of Taiwan
Cyprus
Georgia
India (Andaman, Nicobar Islands)
Indonesia (Sumatra)
Lebanon
Macau
Malaysia
Maldives
Mongolia
Myanmar (Burma) & Rohingya
Nepal
Oman
Pakistan
Palestine
Philippines
Qatar
Saudi Arabia
Singapore

Iran
Iraq
Israel
Japan
Jordan
Kazakhstan
Korea, Republic of South
Korea, Democratic Peoples's Republic of North
Kuwait
Kyrgyzstan
Laos
Sri Lanka
Syria
Tajikistan
Thailand
Timor-Leste (East Timor)
Turkey
Turkmenistan
United Arab Emirates
Uzbekistan
Vietnam
Yemen

There is a natural boundary between Europe and Asia formed by the Caucasus Mountains, the Caspian Sean, the Ural River and the Ural Mountains. Therefore, many sources list the countries of Russia, Kazakhstan, Azerbaijan, Georgia, and Turkey as both in Europe and Asia.

The equator passes through 11 countries and the atolls of 2 countries. Africa: Sao Tome & Principe, Gabon, Republic of Congo, Democratic Republic of Congo, Uganda, Kenya, and Somalia. Asia: Indonesia, Maldives atolls, Kiribati atolls. South America: Ecuador, Colombia, Brazil. The River Zaire crosses the equator twice.

ASIAN ISLANDS in DISPUTE
Kuril Islands (Japan, Russia, Ainu People)
Spratly Islands (China, Philippines)

EUROPE
Albania
Andorra
Armenia
Belarus
Belgium
Bosnia and Herzegovina
Bulgaria
Croatia
Czech Republic (Czechia)
Denmark & Faroe Islands
Estonia
Finland
France & Corsica
Germany
Gilbraltar
Greece (Crete)
Guernsey
Hungary
Iceland
Liechtenstein
Lithuania
Luxembourg
Former Yugoslav Republic of Macedonia
Malta
Moldova
Monaco
Montenegro
Netherlands (Holland)
Norway
Poland
Portugal and Azores
Romania
Russia and Arctic Islands
San Marino
Serbia
Slovakia
Slovenia
Spain (Canary Islands)

Ireland
Italy (Sicily, Sardinia)
Isle of Man (U.K.)
Jersey (U.K.)
Kosovo
Latvia
Basque, Catalonia
Sweden
Switzerland
Ukraine
United Kingdom (Great Britain)
Vatican City (Holy See)

NORTH AMERICA & CARIBBEAN

Anguilla (U.K.)
Antigua and Barbuda
Aruba (Netherland Islands)
Bahamas
Barbados
Belize
Bermuda (U.K.)
Bonaire Islands
British Virgin Island
Canada
Cayman Islands (U.K.)
Clipperton Isle (France)
Costa Rica
Curacao
Cuba
Dominica
Dominican Republic
El Salvador
Faroe Islands (Denmark)
Greenland (Denmark)
Grenada
Guadeloupe (France)
Guatemala
Haiti
Honduras
Jamaica
Martinique (France)
Mexico & Guadalupe Island
Montserrat (U.K.)
Navassa Island (U.S.)
Nicaragua
Panama
Puerto Rico (U.S.)
Saba
Saint Barthelemy (France)
Saint Kitts and Nevis
Saint Lucia
Saint Martin (France)
Saint Pierre and Miquelon (France)
Saint Vincent and the Grenadines
Sint Eustatius (Netherlands)
Sint Maarten (Netherlands)
Trinidad &Tobago
Turks & Caicos Island (U.K.)
United States
U.S. Virgin Islands

SOUTH AMERICA

Argentina
Bolivia
Brazil
Chile
Colombia
Ecuador (Galapagos Island)
French Guiana
Guyana
Paraguay
Peru
Suriname
Uruguay
Venezuela
Falkland Islands (U.K.)

PACIFIC OCEANIA

Australia (Norfolk Island, Christmas Island, Cocos Koeling Island)

French Polynesia (Tahiti and 1000 isles)

Polynesia (Tuvalu, Tokelau, Samoa, Society, Marquesus, Tudmotu, Mangareva, Tonga, American Samoa, Easter Island (Rapa Nui, Chile))

Melanesia (Fiji, Soloman Isle, Santa Cruz, Bismarck, Vanuatu, New Caledonia)

Micronesia (Guam (U.S.), Mariana Island, Marshall Island, Kiribati, Nauru, Palau, Wake Island)

Jarvis Island and Kingman Reef
New Zealand & Cook Island
Niue
Papua New Guinea (shares a border with West New Guinea of Indonesia)
Pitcairn Islands (U.K.)
Midway, Palmyra, Johnston Atoll (U.S.)
Baker and Howard Island (U.S.
Wallis and Futuna (France)

<u>ANTARCTICA</u>
South Georgia and S. Sandwich Islands (U.K)
Bouver Island (Norway)
French Southern Territory
Heard and McDonald Islands (Australia)

WORK / LEISURE

1. Most human beings that are born onto the Earth will have to work for a living. Very few persons are born into wealth.

2. Your profession is only a part of who you are. You are also a person outside of what you do to get money. You have family, friends, hobbies, spiritual beliefs. You may have pets. You may do volunteer work. You may have dreams that you are working on. Also, everyone was born into this world naked and into different circumstances - you are not entirely your clothes, the car you drive or the house you live in - your material possessions are only a part of who you are. The most important part of who you are is your soul.

3. You may or may not get along with all of your coworkers. If you cannot get along with someone you work with, you can find a new job or follow company procedures to handle and settle disputes.

If a person has the ability to get along with others, communicate with others, negotiate with others, and plan - these are great abilities that will enable a successful work career.

Do not have a romantic relationship with a coworker and ruin your personal life with a love of a marriage vow. In some cultures, men and women have been separated in religious and work settings, perhaps to save marriages. In modern cultures, men and women often work together. Many think it is evil for anyone to interfere in a love relationship or a marriage.

4. Be a good employee. Ask your boss what you can do to help.

5. Employers should treat employees with respect and employees should treat employers with respect. Employees should know their job description. Most people believe employees should be paid for their work, have provisions for snack or lunch breaks, vacation, sick leave, and time off for births and deaths, and possibly profit sharing or bonuses, and workers' compensation for job-related injuries.
Many employers also offer benefits like life insurance, medical and dental insurance, food refreshments, adequate parking. Employers may keep a list of special needs their employees may have and emergency contact information. Employees may wear medical id bracelets with special alerts in case that employee has a medical emergency at work.

An employer may require a doctor's excuse if the employee is out for many days.

Regarding shift work, some people prefer to work during 1st shift of the day, some prefer to work 2nd or 3rd shift. It would be ideal if employers could let employees rotate off day or night shifts after 4 months if they wanted to. Rotating after 4 or 8 months or 1 year gives the employee time to work and enjoy life during night and day over the course of the years.

6. Some people will stay in the same profession all of their lives. Some people will switch careers several times during their lifetimes.
Children sometimes follow the professions of their parents or other family members, and children sometimes will not follow the same career paths of their family.

7. A few signs that may indicate a job is not suitable for you:

1) You are always late, or you don't like your job, or you don't appreciate your job.

2) You make a lot of excuses and the number of times you cannot perform the work exceeds the times you successfully complete the work.

3) You complain about unexpected assignments.

4) There are personality issues such as: You are convinced you are the smartest and best employee; you do not believe in teamwork. Or, you are too sensitive and are too easily offended by things. Or your personality and the personality of another employee differs and it makes working together difficult much of the time.

5) You don't believe in your company's mission.

6) You are noticeably less productive than your coworkers

8. There are famous skilled humans in all areas of life such as writers, poets, physicists, astronomers, astronauts, chefs, teachers, philosophers, engineers, inventors, craftsmen, politicians, preachers, artists, musicians, doctors and more.

9. Each country on earth has a long history of its music, art, literature, political system, religious traditions, clothing and jewelry, business economy, technology, education system, food, architecture, medical care, work and leisure activities, and transportation. In some countries that were ruled by dictators or communists at certain times of world history, art and music, religions, news media and internet were not allowed or were regulated by the government.

10. People have tried to record history by grouping music, art, political systems, plants and animal evolution, and many other things into classifications or genres.

11. The divine work of the Creator Spirit is unknown and mysterious. God is always on the job. Many believe that divine angels help with tasks as instructed by God by direct actions of human, miracles and unexplained occurrences.

12. Lord, as your followers, we humbly and truly believe in your divine work. Show us Your Will to achieve great things in Your Honor. Help us to stay in good ways. Let our work be for good causes. The lists in the pages of this book are not all inclusive and are only partial lists.

Work Classifications

accounting,
actor or actress,
adoption agencies,
adult day-care,
advertising,
alarm systems,
alterations,
air conditioning & heating,
air purification for high-rise and
 air-tight buildings,
air-duct cleaner,
airplanes,
airline industry, airports,
air traffic controller,
allergist,
amusement park,
analyst,
 banking,
 business,
 computer,
 conflict management & resolution,
 crisis,
 disaster,
 financial,
 government,
 medical,
 mental,
 news,
 operations,
 political,
 security,
 situation,
 weather,
animal care and sitters,
animal control,
animal shelter,
animal hospital,
animal rescue,
animal trainer,
apartment (flat) industry,
appliances,
appraising,
aquanaut & scuba diving,
aquarium,

aquatic center,
arborist (trees),
architecture & drafting,
arson investigator,
art framing,
arts & crafts retail,
art gallery,
artist in graphic computer arts,
artist in music,
artist in visual arts,
astronomy,
astronaut, cosmonaut, vyomanaut, spationaut, takionaut (taikong yuhang yuan)
auction houses,
audiologist,
auditing,
automobile,
awards & plaques,
bakery,
bail bondsmen,
balloons,
balloon art,
banking, & finance,
barber,
bars & lounges,
bartender,
bathrooms, public restroom,
bed linens,
beverage bottlers -
beer, juice, milk,
soda, water, wine, liquor
bikes,
billboards,
blood banks,
boats and marinas,
body piercing and tattoo,
bounty hunter,
brewery,
bridges,
broadcasting (radio, tv, internet),
broker,
bubblegum and kid trinket machines,
builder,
bus driver,
bus industry,
buyer,
cab driver,
cable,
candle-maker,
candy-maker & chewing gum,
car designer,
car detailing,
car repair,
car sales,
car title pawn,
car wash,
caregiver,
carpentry,
carpet,
carnival,
cashier,
casino,
cellular telephone industry,
cemeteries and memorial parks,
charitable organizations,
cheese maker,
chef,
chemicals,
chemist,
chickens,
child-care & preschool education,
children's home,
chiropractor,
choreographer,
cigarettes and cigars, e cig vaporizer
circus,
civic organizations in society,
clothes cleaning,
clothing industry,
clubs,
coach– animal, business, personal, sports
coast guard,
colleges,
comedian,
commercial truck driver,
commodities and stocks,
communications,
community service,
community resources,
competitions (contests)-
computers,
concert & symphony,
concierge,
concrete contractors,
consultant,
consumer advocate,
consumer education,

construction,
cook,
copywriter (advertising ads),
coroner,
cosmetics,
cosmetologist,
cosmologist,
costumes,
counseling,
coupons, groupon for large group
court system,
cows,
credit agency,
credit analyst,
credit counselor,
creditor,
crematory/funeral home,
criminal justice,
critic/critique,
crops,
crossword puzzles,
cryobiology industry,
culinary,
curator,
currency,
customer service,
dairy industry,
dancer,
debt collectors,
debt consolidators,
debt relief,
decks,
decorator or designer for interiors,
degreasers,
delivery service truck,
- bread
- Chinese food
- dry-cleaning
- flowers
- groceries
- meals on wheels
- medical supplies
- Mexican food
- office supplies
- packages
- pizza
- potato chips
- sandwich delivery

demolition expert,
dental care
dentist,
dental assistant,
designer –
- advertising
- cars
- clothes
- electronics
- fabric
- furniture
- hair
- housewares
- interior
- media
- packaging
- recycled matrials
- toys

detective,
disaster relief,
disaster recovery - computers,
disaster recovery - storm or water damage,
dishwasher,
distillery,
disk jockey,
diving,
docks,
doorman,
doors,
driver, driving school,
drug store,
dry-cleaning,
earth exploration,
ecig, e cig vaporizer,
editor,
education and teaching,
electrician,
electricity,
electronics,
emergency assistance services,
emergency shelter,
emissions inspectors,
employment agency,
energy -
- biofuels industry
- coal mining
-electricity industry
- fusion industry
- geothermal

- hydrogen industry
- natural gas
- nuclear industry
- oil industry
- sea water industry
- solar industry
- water hydro
- wind power industry

engineering -
- aeronautical,
- architectural,
- automation,
- civil,
- computer,
- consumer products,
- construction,
- electrical,
- environmental,
- fire protection,
- food,
- forensic,
- genetic,
- geotechnical,
- industrial,
- mechanical,
- nuclear,
- structural,
- traffic

entertainment arts,
entrepreneur,
environmental disasters,
environmental planning,
equipment, (all kinds)
- art
- baby,
- camping and hiking,
- cleaning,
- construction,
- farming,
- medical,
- music
- senior

essential vitamins and essential oils,
explorer,
event & party planning,
facility management,
farm equipment,
farmer, farming,
farmers market,
fast food,
fasteners,
fences,
fertilizers,
festival,
finance and banking,
firefighter,
fireplace cleaner,
fireworks,
fishing,
flight attendant,
flight instructor,
flight safety,
flight tester,
florist/flowers,
food and beverage industry,
food server,
forensic science
fragrances,
fruit,
funeral home/crematory,
furniture,
gambling,
garbage and junk removal,
gas and diesel-fuel station,
gemologist,
genealogy,
genetics,
geological sciences,
gerontology,
glass artist,
government systems and elected officials,
grader (land),
grease trap collection/processing,
grocery store,
guard,
gym,
handicapped assistance,
hair care,
hair salon,
hardware suppliers,
hazmat (hazardous materials and classifications),
health fitness,
health store,
heating and air conditioning,
helicopters,
historian,

holistic medicine,
homebuilder or remodeler,
homemaker,
home goods,
homeless shelter,
horticulture,
horse jockey,
horses,
hospitals,
hospices,
hospitality industry
and extended-stay lodge,
hotels & motels, bed & breakfast,
houses,
house and office cleaning,
housekeeper, housekeeping,
house sitter,
human nature and cultures,
human resources,
hypnotist,
ice cream, yogurt, glacee,
ice machine, ice makers,
ice resurfacing,
identity theft investigation and
protection,
incense and perfume,
inspector,
insurance,
insurance adjuster,
intelligence network,
international imports and exports,
internet computers,
internet web site design,
internet - advertising,
retail, news, video,
social apps, security
interpreters,
inventory counters,
inventor,
investigator,
investment portfolio, investor,
irrigation systems,
jails and prison systems,
jet ski,
jewelry,
job banks, job recruiting,
journalism, news media,
newspaper, magazine, tabloid,
judge,
junk collector,
junk and garbage removal,
junk yards,
justice system,
kennel for animals,
kitchens and kitchenware,
laboratories,
lab technician,
land clearing and grading,
landscape architecture, landscaper,
languages (linguistics),
lasers,
laundry,
law enforcement,
law maker,
lawyer, (attorney)
legal assistant,
legal field,
lender,
libraries,
lifeguard,
lighthouses,
lighting,
limosine,
linen maker,
linens, (bed, curtains, table)
linguistics,
lip balm,
loan officer,
locally grown fresh produce,
locksmith,
logistics,
loss prevention,
lost & found,
lottery,
lounges and bars,
machinist, machinery,
make-up artist,
maid,
mail carrier,
mailing & shipping,
management,
manufacturing,
marketing and retail,
marina,
marine animals,
massage therapy,
mathematics,
mattresses,

meat industry,
medic, medical assistant,
medical alerts, bracelets, necklaces,
medical billing,
medical doctor, nurse, or technician,
anesthesiology,
bariatrics,
cosmetic,
dermatologist,
endocrinologist,
eye,
ears, nose, & throat,
family,
heart,
mental health,
oncologist,
obstetrics,
orthopedics,
neurologist,
pediatrics,
phlebotomy,
podiatry,
pulmonary,
surgeon,
urology
x-ray.
medical equipment,
medical examiner,
medical field,
mental health,
milliner, (hat maker),
military (army, air force, navy, marines, special forces, coast guard, reserves, national guard, naval security force, air force police, veteran),
military band,
military cook,
military hospital,
military librarian,
military plumber,
military – civilian support organization, contractor
miner,
ministries, (local, foreign, prison)
motels & hotels, and extended stay lodge
motorcycles,
movers,
movie industry,
museum, (art, music, wax, car, science, aviation, train)
music,
music industry,
musical instruments,
music teacher,
nail salon,
national security,
natural resources conservation,
nature center,
non-profits,
novelist,
nursing and nursing assistant,
nutritional expert,
oceanography,
off-shore work such as fishing, drilling, patroling,
oil,
oranges,
organic foods,
origami paper art,
orphanage,
optometrist and optical,
outdoor patio furniture and fireplaces, arbors, and patios,
packaging & printing,
paints and painting,
paper,
paralegal, (assistant to lawyer)
paramedic emergency,
parking and parking meters,
parks and nature,
parole officer,
pawn shop,
perfume and fragrant oils,
personal assistant or butler,
personal fitness,
personal life coach,
personal assistant,
personal shopper or errand runner,
pest control,
petroleum,
pet grooming,
pet sitter, petsitter, dogsitter, catsitter,
pet trainer,
pharmaceutical,
pharmacist,
photography,
physical therapy,

physician or physician assistant,
physicist,
picnic equipment (individuals, family, corporate, religious),
piers,
pilot,
pinball machines,
planner,
playgrounds,
plumber,
plumbing,
police (also called peace officer),
politics and government,
pork,
potter,
poultry,
printing & packaging,
prisons and jails,
private investigator,
process improvement,
proof reader,
property manager,
psychic science,
public transportation,
publishers,
race car driver,
radio,
railroad industry,
real estate
- advertising
- appraising-
- commercial sales
- government
- residential sales
- loans & mortgage
- development
- management
- security systems
- vacation

record keeper,
recreation
recycling industry,
rehab,
referee,
referrals,
refrigeration,
religion,
rentals,
repossessions,
restaurants,
retirement home and assisted living,
research & development,
retail stores,
roads, highways, and interstate, (safety lanes, runaway lanes)
rock carver,
roof gutters,
roofer, roofing,
salesperson,
satellites,
schools (private, public, trade, college, university),
science and technology,
sculptor,
seamstress,
security alarm systems,
security guard,
secretary,
self-help groups,
senior citizen center,
septic and sewer, sewage pumps,
sewing machines,
shelves (residential, commercial),
sheriff,
ships,
shipping,
shoe repair shop,
shoes,
shredding documents,
shrimper,
signs and banners,
singer, backup singer.
sirens for emergencies and bad weather,
skin care,
sleep science,
snake and reptile eliminator,
sommelier (wine steward),
space exploration,
space science,
sports agent,
sports commentator,
sports referee,
sports industry,
spy shop,
staffing agency,
state fair,
statues,
stevedore,

stocker,
stocks & commodities,
storage containers,
storage industry, self-storage,
street cleaner,
subways,
support groups,
surgeon,
surgical assistant,
surveyor,
tailor,
talent agent,
talent scout,
tattoos & body art,
taxes,
taxicabs and shuttles,
taxidermy,
teacher (all kinds),
team leader,
technician,
- automotive,
- cabinets,
- cameras,
- computer,
- dental,
- electronics,
- floors,
- heating & air,
- installer,
- lights,
- landscape,
- medical,
- nails and hair,
- pools & spas,
-pressure wash
- remodel,
- washer & dryer,
- windows
telescopes and binoculars,
television,
theatre & plays,
theme parks (amusement, water),
theft & loss protection,
timekeeper,
tires and alignments,
tobacco industry,
tools,
towing,
toys,
trains,
translator,
transportation and trucking,
trash pick-up,
travel - work,vacation, see people,
tree & vine removal (arborist),
trolley,
truck driver,
tutor,
typist,
upholstery,
utility locator,
vacation,
valet,
vein center,
vegetables,
vending machines,
venues -amphitheatre, arena, music hall, stadium, special event, exhibits, theatre
veterinarian, veterinary science,
vineyard,
vintage antiques,
visitor's center,
volunteerism,
waste removal,
water purification,
- distilled
- deionization (demineralization),
- microfiltration,
- ultrafiltration,
- nanofiltration,
- reverse osmosis (hyperfiltration),
- ultraviolet oxidation,
- electrodeionization
water works and
infrastructure,
weatherman, weather tracker,
weddings & formal events,
welder,
wheelchairs,
windows,
window cleaner,
window treatments, window blinds, shutters, shades, and tinting,
winery,
winter holiday greeting cards,
wood carver,
work zone design & setup.
writer,

zoning and planning,
zoos,
zoo fund raiser,
any category not listed above.

Leisure & Recreation

- amusement parks,
- arcade games
- artifacts
- arts & crafts
- badminton
- baking
- basket-weaving
- bicycling
- billiards
- bird watching
- board games like Monopoly, CLUE, Mastermind, Trivial Pursuit
- boating
- bowling
- camping
- candy-making
- card games
- carpentry
- ceramics
- charades
- Chinese mahjong,
- coins
- collections
- computer applications
- cooking
- dancing
- darts / roulette
- diving
- fly aircraft
- flying disc
- fishing
- French croquet
- garage sales
- gardening
- gymnastics
- hang-gliding
- hiking
- history
- horseback riding
- horseshoe toss
- hunting
- Indian / British cricket
- inventions
- kayaking
- knitting and crocheting
- martial arts / karate, taijutsu, jujutsu, taekwondo
- mountain biking
- movies
- museum
- music
- painting
- personal fitness / gym workout
- ping-pong
- puzzles
- racquetball
- reading
- rock-collecting
- rock-climbing
- scouting
- sewing
- shopping
- singing
- skating
- skiing
- sky-diving
- scuba diving and snorkeling
- snow globes
- softball
- speedway racing, motor sports
- swimming
- symphony
- tennis
- theatre
- traveling
- volleyball
- volunteering
- water sports
- windsurfing
- white water rafting
- writing
- raja and sahaja yoga, zen yoga
- zip-lining

Sports/Competition/Contest

- archery,
- art,
- bakeoffs,
- basketball,
- baseball, wiffle ball,
- baton twirler,
- beautiful personality contest,

- best movie, tv show or video,
- best novel or book or writing
- billiards (pool ball),
- bowling,
- card games like poker, blackjack, solitaire, bridge, craps, rummy, canasta, UNO
- car racing,
- cat show,
- checkers
- chess,
- comedy,
- computer application contest,
- cooking & recipes,
- cricket,
- debates,
- essays,
- disc thrower,
- dog show,
- fastest texter contest,
- fighting,
- football,
- gardening,
- golf,
- gooney golf, (miniature golf)
- gymnastics,
- hair design contest,
- horse racing,
- ice hockey,
- ice skating,
- interior design contest,
- javelin,
- kickball,
- lacrosse,
- laughing,
- music, singing, and dancing,
- pageants (glitz, glamour),
- pet contest,
- ping-pong (table tennis)
- pole-vaulting,
- roller derby,
- rugby,
- running,
- science fair,
- shuffleboard
- skateboarding,
- skeet shooting (clay pigeons),
- skiing and ice sports,
- soccer,
- spelling bee,
- swimming and diving sports,
- squash,
- talent contest,
- table tennis (ping-pong),
- tennis,
- triathlon,
- volleyball,
- weight-loss contest,
- wrestling.

FINE ARTS

Asian Art may be grouped by political dynasties or by Chinese, Japanese, Indian, and Korean influence.

Western and European Art may be grouped as:

1. **Stone Age Cave drawings**
2. **Roman, Byzantine, Greek, Persian, Egyptian, and Norse Art 1000 BCE**
3. **Fresco and Altar art of the 1000s**

The paintings were done with oil paints or tempera (pigments mixed with egg yolk, gum, Arabic or animal glue.

4. **Middle Ages or Medieval Period**

From 400 – 1400. Marked by the fall of the Western Roman Empire of the Middle-Eastern Mediterranean due to invaders of other empires, civil wars, famine, and plagues. Around 1054, a Great Schism occurred in the Roman Empire and it divided into East and West. The Western Roman Empire of the Middle-Eastern Mediterranean region was ruled from Rome as the Roman Catholic Church. The Eastern Empire was ruled by Greeks from the city of Constantinople as the Eastern Orthodox Church.

5. **Renaissance Art of the 1300 – 1700**
6. **Age of Discovery and Exploration when ships sailed the world** 1400-1600
7. **English Victorian Art 1845**
8. **French Impressionist Monet of the 1800s**
   Oil paintings with a lot of color and mostly outdoor scenes and portraits.
   Art Noveau of the 1800s
   Art Nouveau was started by German artist Les Vingt in Paris. Japanese woodcarving art with simple lines was incorporated into European art. Simple Ink etchings became popular.
9. **Modern Contemporary Art**
   Later etchings (drawings) and paintings were done by artists with colored pencils, chalks, translucent watercolors (pigments binded in natural gum Arabic or synthetic glycol), giclee digital prints, encaustic wax paints, gouache opaque watercolors.

Famous Ancient Visual Artists

- Pierre-Auguste Renior of France 1841
- Vincent Van Gogh of Denmark 1853
- Leonardo da Vinci of Italy 1452
- Pable Picasso of Spain 1881
- Michelangelo of Italy 1475
- Sandra Botticelli of Italy 1455
- Donatello of Italy 1836
- Claude Monet of France 1840
- Rembrandt of Denmark 1606
- Raphael of Italy 1485
- Anton Losenko of Ukraine 1737
- Alexei Venetsianov of Russia 1780
- Alexander Ivanov of Russia 1806
- Hokusai of Japan 1760
- Yoshitoshi of Japan 1839
- Harunobu Suzuki of Japan 1724
- Fan Kuan of China 990
- Mi Fu of China 1051
- Li Cheng of China 919
- Bada Shanren of China 1626
- Albrecht Durer of Germany 1471
- Edvard Munch of Norway 1863
- Gustav Klimt of Austria 1862
- Edgar Degas of France 1834
- Paul Klee of Switzerland 1879
- Piet Mondrian of Denmark 1872
- Wassily Kandinsky of Russia 1866
- Utagawa Hiroshige of Japan 1797
- Camille Pissarro U.S. Virgin Isle 1830
- Henri de Toulouse-Lautrec of France1864
- Paul Cezanne of France 1839
- Teodoro Ardemans of Spain 1651
- Isidoro Arredondo of Spain 1653
- Jose de Cieza of Spain 1656
- Michel Ange Houasse of Spain 1675
- Frida Kahlo of Mexico 1907
- Hans von Aachen of Germany 1552
- Andreas Achenback of Germany 1815
- John James Audubon of U.S.A. 1800
- Otto Dix of Germany 1891
- Karl Abt of Germnay 1899
- Francois Belleflamme Belgium 1891
- Norman Rockwell of U.S.A. 1894
- Yannis Tsarouchis of Greece 1910
- Jewad Selim of Iraq 1919
- Fred Williams of Australia 1927
- Mohamed Ghani Hikmat of Iraq 1929
- Ismail Fattah of Iraq 1938
- Akaine Kramarik of U.S.A. 1904
- Fabrice de Villeneuve of France 1954
- Kathy Rennell Forbes of U.S.A. 1960
- Frank Mechau of Kansas 1904

LOCAL ARTISTS

Every community has local music and visual artists that like to share their music compositions, paintings, sculptures, and crafts with others. Gregory and Katherine were local artists in Georgia that painted murals on public buildings. Gregory traveled to Jordan with his employer to paint a mural of a desert, palm trees, and camels on a public building. Taylor Kinzel Gallery in Roswell featured paintings, sculptures, and other art by local artists such as Patrick Taylor, Ali Leja, Ann Wren Nye, Barbara Rheingrover, Bob Ichter, Bob Snider, Brenda Griffith, Carol Christie, Carol Roddenberry, Craig Griffin, David

Swanagh, Doug Pisik, Greg Osterhaus, Hought Wahl, Inky Hwang, Jo Fassnact, Lorrie Lane, Joan Carew, Judy Shreve, Julie Simon, and Kerry Brook.

Many artists are poor. Some stand on street corners playing musical instruments, singing requested songs, painting or drawing pictures to earn money.

Famous Photographers

- Dorothea Lange 1895 of California USA. She took pictures documenting the economic Great Depression in the U.S.A. which went global 1929-1941 and during WW II 1939-1945
- Pierre Lamy Petit of France 1832
- Ansel Adams 1902 of California, USA
- Yousuf Karsh 1908 of Armenia & Canada.
- Enrique Meneses of Spain 1929
- Annie Leibovitz 1949 of Connecticut USA
- Robert Capa 1913 of Hungary
- Dmitry Kostyukev 1984 of Russia
- Gyula Kalasz 1984 also known as Brassai from Hungary and France
- Omar Victor Diop 1980 of Senegal
- George Osodi 1974 of Nigeria
- Aisha Augie-Kuta 1980 of Nigeria
- Getty Images since 1995

A panoroma is a 360 degree image invented by Robert Barker in 1787.

Famous Ancient Musicians

- Wolfgang Amadeus Mozart of Austria 1756
- Ludwig van Beethoven of Germany 1770
- Frederic Chopin of Poland 1810
- Johann Pachelbel of Germany 1653
- Johann Sebastian Bach of Germany 1685
- George Frideric Handel of Germany 1759
- Johannes Brahms of Germany 1833
- Antonio Vivaldi of Italy 1678
- Camille Saint-Saens of France 1835
- Felix Mendelssohn of Germany 1840
- Richard Wagner Lohengrin of Germany 1850
- Antonin Kraft, Antonin Vranicky of Czech Republic 1752
- Richard Strauss of Germany 1864
- Franz Schubert of Austria 1797
- Franz Liszt of Hungary 1811
- Joseph Haydn of Austria 1732
- Franz Schubert of Austria 1797
- Pyotr Ilyich Tchaikovsky of Russia 1840
- Manuel de Zumaya of Mexico 1678
- Guan Pinghu of China 1871
- Chou Wen-Chung, a Chinese American 1923
- Chen Yi of China 1953

Some famous music compositions by the ancient musicians:

Mozart:

Syphony No. 40 in G minor, Symphony No. 25 in G minor,
Symphony No. 38 in D,
Symphony 36 in C,
Einekleine Nachtmusik,
Requiem,
Magic Flute,
Violin Sonata No. 26 in B-Flat major,
Piano Concerto No. 21 in C Major,
Clarinet Concerto in A Major,
Flute Concerto No. 2 in D Major,

Beethoven:

Ode to joy, part of Symphony No. 9 in C sharp minor
Septet Op. 20
Moonlight Sonata No. 14 Op. 27 no. 2
Symphony No. 3, No. 4, No. 5
Air
Violin Sonata No. 9
Fur Elise
A melody of Tears & Silence
Adagio

Chopin:

Nocturne No,2, No. 20 in C Sharp
Nocturne Op. 9 No. 2
Waltz Op. 64

Marche Funbre
Prelude No. 4
Fantasie Impromptu

Pachelbel:
Canon in D

Bach:
Toccota and Fugue in D Minor

Handel:
Hallelujah Chorus , Messiah

Brahms:
Lullaby

Vivaldi:
Four Seasons (1723CE)

Saint-Saens:
Rondo Capriccioso, Second Piano Concerto, First Cello Concerto, Danse Macabre, Samson and Delilah, Third Organ Symphony, Carnival of The Animals

Mendelssohn:
Violin Concerto E Minor OP.64

Richard Wagner:
Ride of the Valkyries (Took Wagner 26 years to complete it. Based on Odin's daughter in Norse mythology.)

Richard Strauss:
Spring, Four Last Songs.

Schubert: 600 Leider (Songs)
Symphony No. 5 in B-flat major
Der Erlkonig D328 (1815CE)
Nacht und Traume D827 (1875CE)
Serenade

Tchaikovsky:
Waltz of the Flowers
Swan Lake

Antonin Dvorak:
Song to the Moon

Carl Orft:
O Fortuna

Josef Szalai:
Csardas-Vittori Monti:

Claude DeBussy:
Claire de Lune

Edvard Grieg:
Peace of the Woods

Johann Strauss:
The Blue Danube

Gioachino Rossini:
4-part overture with finale

King Henry VIII of England 1500:
Greensleeves

Salzburg Festival is an opera and music festival held in Austria each year. In 2014, an 8-year old violinist named Ko So-hyun from South Korea was invited to play Mozart's violin. Opera and symphony attendees wear formal attire.

Phonograph, Radio, TV, Movies, and Computers

Thomas Edison invented a phonograph machine in 1877 that enabled recordings to be made of human voices. Oberlin Smith invented magnetic recording in 1888. Valderman Poulsen invented a magnetic wire recorder. Music was recorded from 1890 onward. Silent films with no sound were invented in the 1920s. In silent films, Gloria Swanson was a female singer and an actress, Charlie Chaplin was an actor, and The Three Stooges were comedians. The first sounds that were synchronized to visual films began in France, but the first very successful film that was fully music and lip sound synchronized was The Jazz Singer in 1927 in the U.S.A. Movies and TV were shown in black and white color until color became economically feasible in the 1950s and 1960s. Guglielmo Marconi of Italy invented the radio in 1895 and many songs and news was broadcast over radios. Paphlets and newspapers printed in bulk are a primary source of news and existed in 1400 in Germany and in 1832 in England. Vaudeville was variety entertainment in theatres from 1880-1930 with singing, dancing, skits, puppets, magicians, jugglers, and poets. Symphony orchestra and theatre have remained popular throughout the centuries. Johnny Mercer and Buddy DeSylva founded Capital Records in 1942.

Vinyl Albums

In 1877 Thomas Alva Edison invented the gramophone with needle. Songs and comedy were analog recordings on vinyl albums with grooves and played on gramophones and record players.

Good music was described as 'groovy hits' because of the grooves on the vinyl discs.

Small vinyl records with 7" 1 hit song on Side A and another song on Side B were 45 RPM.

Large vinyl records with several songs that comprised the album were 33 1/3 RPM were 10" or 12" (25 cm or 30 cm).

Magnetic Tape

In the 1970s-90s, songs and movies were recorded mostly on 8-track tapes and VHS which are magnetic media. In the 1990s, songs were recored on tape cassettes.

Some tape players offered the capability to skip ahead on the tapes or rewind them.

'Slow motion' is the effect in a movie when everything in time moves slower.

Microfiche film

Archived newspapers were stored on microfiche film.

Digital Music

In the 1980s computer data was stored on hard drives and on floppy disks in mini-computers.

In the 1990s, songs were recorded on CDs and Apple IPODs and music lovers could create their own playlists and even wear ear buds in quiet places to listen to music. Movies were recorded on DVDs which are read by lasers. Around 2000, songs, movies, literary works such as newspapers, books, food recipes, science articles, medical information, historical documentations, retail sites, and language translators were digitalized and put into computer data bases on worldwide computer networks and portable USB. Computer users can access data bases through web pages called search engines such as AOL, BAIDU, YAHOO, BING, GOOGLE, MSN, Yandex and ASK. The search engines are computer software programs offered by huge computer corporations around the world. By 2010 there were many computer hackers sabotaging information on computers, even posting fake news. Many people changed their ideas about the reliability of information found on computers; some people went back to reading news in newspapers. There were debates about having computers in TVs and car engines.

There are millions of famous songs and chord sheets recorded from the 1890 and movies produced from the 1920s or 1930s until modern times that have been put in computer data bases. Jingles are songs in TV commericals for consumer goods. Elevator music is pleasant music in elevator lifts. When digital music and visual art became popular, artists made less money than they could make by selling individual paper copies or vinyl copies of their work because of the free dounloads from computers. Many artists had to rely on live music concerts, art exhibits, or selling trademark art in order to make money for their work and creativity. If a concert goer is drunken and disorderly, they may be evicted from a concert and may embarrass his or her friends. Earplugs can be worn at really loud concerts.

There are thousands of music bands and solo artists, movies, TV shows, magicians, animal trainers, talent acts, comedians, historical shows,news documentaries, sports games, and reality shows; it is impossible to list them all here in this book. There is much good music, visual art, and literary works but much of it is unknown by all because perhaps the artists did not get a lucky break to be famous on the top 100 Billboard or New York Times or the London Review of books, but some artists do not desire fame and they practice their art for simple enjoyment.

Some artists desire to be a world celebrity while some desire to be a local celebrity.

Songs, literary works, and movies have been kept alive for decades as new artists re-sing and sing old songs and produce remakes of old art. Karaoke is a Japanese invention where amateur singers could easily sing along with popular songs by reading and singing the correct original lyrics. Before karaoke was invented, many times listeners would sing wrong lyrics if they did not know the correct lyrics and this would cause other people to laugh at them. Many people have impersonated Elvis Presley, Rod Stewart, Barbara Streisand, Lucille Ball, Mick Jagger and other celebrities. A caricature is a humorous illustration of a celebrity. Reruns of old movies and TV shows remain popular as viewers watch tv alone or watch tv and snuggle with a loved one.

The ART WORLD

Producers, directors, set crew, artists, advertisers, and financiers continue to produce new art. Art has often helped to shape the ideas and moral code in world communities. Art evokes the imagination and can bring us into a different world. Producing art or enjoying art can be something we do to pass the time.

Be careful before you sign an entertainment contract because some unknown people may be ruthless and may instigate unusual situations to create new art and sell newspapers just to make money. Most movie producers are nice, honest, caring people but some could be ruthless.

In 2017, Hollywood, California and Bollywood, India are major movie hubs in the world. Senoia, Georgia is a big movie and music hub. Zambia, Southern Africa is a new movie hub.

Actress Marilyn Monroe was found dead from a drug overdose in 1962 at age 36.

Heath Ledger was found dead from a drug overdose in 2008 at age 29.

In 1993 actor Brandon Lee, son of actor Bruce Lee, was accidentally killed by a gun that contained a real bullet while filming the movie The Crow.

In 2006, Steve Irwin of Australia was killed when he was stung by a stingray while filming Ocean's Deadliest.

In 2011, British rocker Amy Winehouse died from alcohol overdose.

Wynonna Judd had an addiction problem and was in rehab for depression after her father died; she never had an opportunity to meet her biological father. Actor Robert Downey, Jr. and Lindsay Lohan also went to rehab. It is commendable to get help, pick up the pieces, and move on with your life.

Teamwork to Produce Movies

There are many movie producers, directors, actors, actresses, artists, IT information technology experts, advertisers, restaurants, musicians, bank financiers, religious leaders, politicians, doctors, airline pilots, professors and teachers in education systems, sports figures, volunteers, researchers, scientists and many more humans who come together to work and produce art, movies, and events for the benefit of all humanity and world peace. No humans or animals should be hurt or abused in the process of making TV or movies.

In movies and TV shows, there are good characters and bad characters in scripts. Some thespians may not want to play the role of the bad characters, but they may have to in order to earn money.

TOP 100 BILLBOARD HITS U.S.A./U.K.

'He's Got The Whole World In His Hands' 1927 was sung by Laurie London of England and became an international hit. In 1929 Tiptoe Through the Tulips by Al Dubin (lyrics), Joe Burke (music), and Nick Lucas (Guitar). The song was also released in 1968 by Tiny Tim. Ray Charles sang Georgia On My Mind in 1930.

In 1934 Richard Rodgers and Lorenz Hart released Blue Moon, based on the phenomenon when the moon looks blue because of particles in the atmosphere. In 1935 Fred Astaire and Ginger Rogers sang Cheek to Cheek in the movie Top Hat. In 1939 the Andrew Sisters sang Beer Barrel Polka which was also called Roll Out the Barrel in Britain. The song was popular during WW II. The World Will Sing Again was another British song that help Brits through WW II.

Jimmie Davis and Charles Mitchell sang You Are My Sunshine in 1939 and the song melody was popular for a hundred years and sung by many music artists. In 1951 Hank Williams sang Hey, Good Lookin.

In 1952, Rock Around the Clock was a song written in 1952 by Max C. Freeman and James E. Myers in the 12-bar blues format. The most popular rendition was by Bill Haley and His Comets in 1954. The song was liked in England and other countries.

In 1956 Elvis Presley sang Love Me Tender. Elvis had a daughter named Lisa Marie Presley who sang Over Me in 2013. Elvis had a grand daughter named Riley Keough who was an actress. Elvis was a Caucasian white man. In 1957 Danny and the Juniors sang At the Hop, a doo-wop song. Some other songs:

Save the Last Dance for Me by The Drifters 1960. Louie Louie by The Kingsmen 1960.

Ferry 'Cross the Mersey by Gerry & The Pacemakers 1964 a hit in the U.K. and the U.S.A.

Light My Fire and Riders on the Storm by Jim Morrison & The Doors 1965. Wild Thing by The Troggs of the U.K.. written by Chip Taylor of the U.S.A.1966. Born to Be Wild and A Magic Carpet Ride by Steppenwolf 1969. The House of the Rising Sun by The Animals 1964.

Baby, I'm Yours was written by Van McCoy and sung by Barbara Lewis in 1965. A Rainy Night in Georgia was written by Tony Joe White in 1962 and sung by vocalist Brook Benton in 1970. By the time I get to Phoenix was written in 1965 by Jimmy Webb and it has been recorded by many vocalists.

California Dreamin' by Mama & the Papas in 1965.

'Please Release Me' by Engelbert Humperdinck 1966.

What A Wonderful World by Louis Armstrong in 1967.

In 1965, Burt Bacharach and Hal David wrote a song called What the World Needs Now is Love sung by Jackie DeShannon. In 1964 Barbra Streisand was a Jewish singer who sang People and the song says that people who need people are lucky.

In 1964 the Beatles of England released "I Wanna Hold Your Hand' and 'In My Life' 1965 about memories of people and places.

'I Heard It Thru The Grapevine' was a Motown hit in 1966 by Marvin Gaye and 1967 by Gladys Knight & The Pips. The Bee Gees sang I Started A Joke in 1968.

Otis Redding released The Dock of the Bay in 1967 with guitarist Steve Cooper. In 1969 the Beatles released 'Here Comes the Sun' about springtime.

In 1969 the Rolling Stones released 'You Can't Always Get What You Want.'

In 1967 Procol Harem of England released A Whiter Shade of Pale.

In 1968 Marvin Gaye and Tammi Terrell sang Ain't Nothing Like the Real Thing. Raindrops Keep Falling On My Head by BJ Thomas in 1969 and written for the movie Butch Cassidy and the Sundance Kid. "Proud Mary' 1969 by Creedence Clearwater Revival was originally meant to be about a maid working for rich people but later on it was switched to the idea of a riverboat.

In 1970 Ray Stevens wrote a song called Everything is Beautiful in its Own Way. In 1970 Cat Stevens released Morning Has Broken, Jesus, King of Trees, and Lady D'arbanville. Donna Summer

released Last Dance and On the Radio in the 1970s. Elton John and Bernie Taupin wrote released Harmony and Rocket Man in 1971. Ain't She A Honey by Don McLean 1971.
In 1971 John Lennon who played with the Beatles released a song called Imagine describing what life would be like if all people lived in peace and Strawberry Fields about a children's home in Liverpool, England. There is a section of Central Park in New York City that is dedicated to the memory of John Lennon called Strawberry Fields. His 2nd wife, Yoko Ono, is still living across the street from Central Park in the building she lived in with John Lennon until he was shot to death outside of his home in 1980. She is 85 years old and relies on a wheelchair to get around because she is frail. Yoko Ono produced solo songs by herself as well as collaborative efforts with John Lennon.

Debby Boone sang You Light Up My Life. 'Stairway to Heaven' 1971 by Led Zepplin is about materialism.
'Ain't No Sunshine' and "Lean On Me' 1971 by Bill Withers. Diary by David Gates & Bread 1972. Donny Osmond released Puppy Love in 1972.
Wildflower by Skylark 1972.
The Reverend Al Green sung Let's Stay Together in 1972.
Before the Next Teardrop Falls by Freddy Fender 1974. I Wanna Rock and Roll All Night by KISS 1975. Landslide by Stevie Nicks and Fleetwood Mac 1975.
Bohemian Rhapsody by Queen 1975.
Baby, I Love Your Way by Peter Frampton 1975. Electric Light Orchestra released a song called 'Evil Woman' in 1975.
Eric Carmen released 'All By Myself' in 1975.
In 1976 the Greek Orchestra Emmetron released Zorba The Greek Dance. In 1976, James Taylor sang a song 'Shower The People' you love with love, Up On The Roof written with Carole King, and You've Got A Friend.

The Arrows sang a song I Love Rock n Roll in 1979 in the U.K. Joan Jett & The BlackHearts released the same song I Love Rock n Roll in the U.S.A. in 1981.
Queen sang 'Another One Bites the Dust' in 1980.
In the 1980's Stevie Ray Vaughn sang blues like Texas Flood and Oreo Cookie Blues. Let It Go by Def Leppard in 1981.
In 1981 Hall & Oates sang Private Eyes saying they are watching your every move.
Endless Love and Upside Down by Diana Ross 1982.
Eclipse of the Heart by Bonnie Tyler 1983. True by Spandau Ballet 1983.
'If I Could Turn Back Time' by Cher 1983.
'Missing You.' by John Waite of Britain 1984.'
'We are the World' by Michael Jackson was a song compilation sung by many popular worldwide music artists in 1984.
Stevie Wonder who is blind wrote a song about the planet Saturn and a song called 'I just called to say I Love You' in 1984.
"I wanna know what love is' by Foreigner 1984.
In 1985 Tears for Fears released Everybody Wants to Rule the World. Tears for Fears also recorded a song called Mad World that was written by Ronald Orzabal. Janet Jackson sang Escapade about cashing a paycheck after a workweek and relaxing on an escapade which meant to have a good time.
In 1985 Falco of Austria sang Rock Me Amadeus about Mozart the musician.
'Livin' On A Prayer' 1985 and You Give Love A Bad Name by Bon Jovi tells about relying on faith to get by.
In 1986 the Bangles sang Walk Like An Egyptian. Only Human by Human League 1986.
Bruce Springsteen sang 'One Step Up' in 1987 about one step up and two steps back. Johnny Hates Jazz sang 'Shattered Dreams' in 1987 about an empty heart.

Journey released the love ballad 'Faithfully' in 1988.
In 1989 Phil Collins sang 'Another Day in Paradise' about the homeless.
In 1990 From a Distance sung by Bette Midler and written by Julie Gold is a song telling us that God is watching us. Natalie Cole sang I've Got Love on my Mind. Natalie Cole was Nat King Cole's daughter. Wilson Phillips sang 'Hold On' in 1990 saying that things can change tomorrow.
Axel Rose of Guns N Roses sang 'November Rain' in 1991 saying everybody needs some time on their own.
Because You Loved Me by Celine Dion 1996 written by Diane Warren.
B52s sang Summer of Love and Love Shack in 1986.
Eric Clapton wrote a song called No More Tears in Heaven 1992 for the movie Rush 1991 but it reminded him of his son who fell to death after falling out a window of a New York apartment building.
In 1991 Bonnie Raitt sang I Can't Make You Love Me.
Sade sang No Ordinary Love and Kiss of Life in 1992 and said an angel was by her side because something heavenly led her to you.
In 1993 Rick Astley from England sang 'Together Forever' and 'Never Gonna Give You Up.'
In 1995 Tracy Chapman sang a song Give Me One Reason about getting out of a homeless shelter.
Everything I Do I Do It For You by Bryan Adams 1996.
In 1994, Joan Osborne released 'One of Us' asking questions about God. In 1994 Soundgarden sang 'Black Hole Sun.'
In 1994 Melissa Etheridge sang 'Come To My Window'. Melissa Etheridge was also an environmental and activist for individuals with homosexual or transsexual lifestyles.
Only Wanna Be With You by Hootie & The Blowfish 1994.
You Gotta Be by Des'ree 1994.
Kiss From A Rose by Seal 1994.
Lightning Crashes 1994 by Live.
In 1995 Alanis Morisette sang the song 'Ironic' and 'You Oughta Know' about a broken love relationship. Bryan Adams sang Summer of 69 in 1996.
'I Am Barely Breathing' 1996 was released by Duncan Sheik.
Toni Braxton sang There's No Me Without You in 1996.
I'm Your Angel by R. Kelly and Celine Dion 1996. I Believe I Can Fly by R. Kelly.
In 1997 British alternative rock band The Verve released Bittersweet Symphony.
In 1997 the Back Street Boys released Quit Playing Games With My Heart.
I Knew I Loved You by Darren Hayes & Savage Garden 1999. Lee Ann Womack sang an inspirational song called "I Hope You'll Dance' in 1999 saying to not lose your wonder for all that life offers.
Steven Tyler sang I Don't Want to Miss a Thing in 1998. Michael Bolton sang That's What Love is All About.
'My Hero' by Foo Fighters 1998.
I'll Be 1998 by Edwin McCain and Misguided Roses.
In 1999, Christina Aguilera released Genie in a Bottle.
I Try by Macy Gray 1999.
In 2000 Nelly Furtado of Canada sang I'm Like A Bird.
In 2000, Irish rock band U2 released a song called It's A Beautiful Day. U2 also released a song called 'In the Name of Love' about civil resistance in the United States that led to social change for the betterment of all people. U2 also released Where the Streets Have No Name about taking shelter from the poison rain.
'Here Without You' 2001 and 'Love Me When I'm Gone' 2003 by 3 Doors Down describes how much he misses his girlfriend. In 2001 Train released Drops of Jupiter.

This Year 2002 is a song about having an incredibly good year with the planets lined up for you and it was written by Leah Andreon, Martin Frederiksen, and Billy E. Steinberg who also wrote a song called True Colors about determination and surviving unhappiness sung by Cyndi Lauper in 1986.
Hard to Handle by the Black Crowes 1990. Hybrid Theory by Linkin Park 2000.
Fleetwood Mac released 'What's the World Coming To?' in 2003 questioning why people tell lies.
In 2003 Britney Spears sang Toxic. British singer James Blunt released 'You're Beautiful" in 2004 about seeing a beautiful woman on a train that he will probably never see again.
Coldplay sang Speed of Sound in 2005. Hey There Delilah 2006 by Plain White T's. 'Apologise' was released by Timbaland in 2006 about troubles in a relationship. 'No Air' by Jordin Sparks and Chris Brown in 2007. Bleeding Love by Leona Lewis 2007.
Kenye West sang 'Heartless' in 2008 about an evil woman. Beyonce sang Halo in 2008. Akon is a musician from Senegal, Africa who released Right Now (Na Na Na) in 2008. Matt Nathanson sang Come On Get Higher in 2008 saying I miss the sound of your voice.
Duffy sang Mercy in 2008. 'Everlong' by Foo Fighters 2009.
John Mayer sang Heartbreak Warfare in 2009. Firework 2010 Katy Perry.
The A Team 2011 Ed Sheeran.
Radioacitve by Imagine Dragons 2011.
In 2012 Jason Mraz released 'I Won't Give Up'. Mirrors by Justin Timberlake 2013. All of Me by John Legend 2013. Animals 2014 by Maroon 5. All About That Bass by Meghan Trainor 1014. Rihanna sang Love on the Brain in 2015. What Do You Mean? 2015 Justin Beiber. Julia Michaels sang Issues in 2017 saying do not judge me and I won't judge you because we both have issues so let us listen to each other and try to solve the issues. In 2017 Lady Gaga released Born This Way saying God makes no mistakes. 'What About Us?' 2017 by Pink. Feel It Still by Portugal The Man 2017.
Songs with the theme of support saying I'll Be There For You such as Rembrandts in 1994 for the sitcom FRIENDS and the Week End in 2017 an R&B version.

Some songs with the word CRAZY: Patsy Cline Crazy 1962, Madonna Crazy For You 1985, SEAL Crazy 1991, Bobbie Eakes and Big Trouble Crazy1987, Aerosmith 1993, Gnarls Barkley Crazy 2006.

Some songs about money are: Money, money, money by the Swedish Group ABBA, For the Love of Money by the O'Jays, and Money by Pink Floyd.

Some songs about saying HELLO: Hello, Goodbye by the Beatles 1967, Harmony by Elton John and Bernie Taupin 1973, Hello, It's Me by Todd Rundgren 1972, Hello, Hello by Mitch Allan and Tomorrow Band 2002,

Some songs about Time: As Time Goes By 1931 by Herman Hupfeld, Colour My World 1970 by Chicago.

Some songs about Love: Can't Help Falling In Love by Elvis Presley 1961. I Can't Stop Loving You by Ray Charles 1962. I Got You I Feel Good by James Brown 1964, Ain't No Mountain High Enough by Diana Ross and the Supremes 1966. Hooked On A Feeling by BJ Thomas 1969. Help Me Make It Through The Night by Sammi Smith and Kris Kristofferson 1970. Feelings by Morris Albert, Andy Williams 1975. Come and Get Your Love by Redbone 1974. Feel Like Makin Love by Bad Company 1975. Tonight's the Night by Rod Stewart 1977. Count On Me by Jefferson Starship 1978. By The Time I Get to Phoenix sung by Isaac Hayes or Glen Campbell. Bruce Springsteen released Tunnel of Love in 1987. In 1974 Dolly Parton released 'I

Will Always Love You' and Whitney Houston sang it in 1992. Lovesong by The Cure 1989. More Than Words by Extreme 1990. Before You Walk Out My Life by Monica 1995. Love Song by Sara Bareilles 2007. 'Only Love.' by Wynonna Judd 1993. Take It To Heart by Michael McDonald 1990, That's What Love is All About by Michael Bolton 1987. Tainted Love by Soft Cell in 1981 which was a remake from Ed Cobb 1964. Anniversary by Tony Toni Tone 1993. Nobody Knows by Tony Rich and Kenny Edmonds Babyface 1996. That's My Girl by Usher 1997. I Could Not Love You More 1996 by the Bee Gees. I'll Be There For You. Home Life by John Mayer 2003. Closer by The Chainsmokers 2016.

Some songs about Happiness: No Stress by DJ Laurent Wolfe 2008, Happy by Pharrell Williams 2013, Don't Worry Be Happy by Bobby McFerrin 1988, Happiness by Need to Breathe 2016.

Some songs about MUSIC: I Believe in Music by Mac Davis 1971. Music by Madonna 2000.

Some songs about dancing: Save the Last Dance For Me by The Drifters 1960. Last Dance by Donna Summer 1978. I Wanna Dance With Somebody by Whitney Houston 1987. Can't Stop the Feeling by Justin Timberlake 2016.

Some songs about rain: A Rainy Night in Georgia sung by vocalist Brook Benton in 1970. Raindrops Keep Fallin on My Head by BJ Thomas. Georgia Rain by Trisha Yearwood. Purple Rain by Prince.

Genres of Music

There are many genres of music and art besides the classical artists from the 1700-1800s. Some names from the 1800s were George W. Johnson who sang The Whistling Coon in 1891, George W. Johnson who sang The Laughing Song in 1898, Arthur Collins who sang Hello Ma Baby in 1899. In 1912 WC Handy sang Memphis Blues.

In the 1920s-1930s, big bands called jazz and swing bands and jazz solo artists were popular in the USA. Benny Goodman, Duke Ellington, Artie Shaw, Glenn Miller, and Louis Armstrong were popular. In the U.S.A. in the 1920s, Billie Holliday was a female jazz singer and Lana Turner was a famous female actress and singer. Marlene Dietrich was a famous German singer and actress in the 1920s. Claude Gordon 1916 was a famous trumpeter from Helena, Montana. Harry Fox from California was a vaudeville actor who invented a ballroom dance in 4/4 times called the Foxtrot that is similar to the waltz. Harry Fox appeared in the silent films Beatrice Fairfax and the biopic The Dolly Sisters. A biopic or biography is a movie that is based on a true story.

Arthur Murray started a dance studio in the 1920s in the U.S.A. and began teaching dancing lessons. He had a contract with Colombia Gramophone Company to produce vinyl records about dancing. He took business courses at Georgia School of Technology in Atlanta, Georgia (Georgia Tech). He organized the world's first radio dance. The Georgia Tech school band played 'Ramblin' Wreck From Ga. Tech' the school's alma mater and some other songs that were broadcast by radio to 150 dancers that danced on top of the roof of the Capital City Country Club. Arthur Murray had over 200 dance studios.

In the 1940s-1960s, some popular singers in the USA were Eddy Arnold, Bing Crosby, Andy Williams, Frank Sinatra, Doris Day, Patsy Cline, Ray Charles, Connie Francis, Bobby Darin, Lulu, Tony Bennett, Frankie Valli and the Four Seasons, and Johnny Mathis. Around the 1930s, movie productions and song recordings happened all around the world in many countries besides the U.S.A. such as Brazil, Japan, Spain, Portugal, Great Britain, Germany-Austria, Australia, India, Denmark,

Sweden, France, Italy, and Mexico. In the 2000s movies were produced in the middle-east country of Afghanistan and Pakistan.

There are thousands of music bands, solo artists, and backup singers and it is impossible to list them all here in this book. There is much good music, visual art, and literary works but much of it is unknown by all because perhaps the artists or writers did not get a lucky break to be famous on the top music 100 Billboard or book review lists of New York Times, London Review, Yomiuri Shimbun of Tokyo, Valor of Brazil, Shanghai Daily in China, Times of India, or Dainik Jagran in India. Some artists do not desire fame and they practice their art for simple enjoyment.

Liberace was a famous pianist in the U.S.A. in the 1950-1960s. His parents were Polish immigrants to the U.S.A.

COUNTRY MUSIC

A main venue for country, bluegrass, or folk music is at the Grand Ole Opry House in Nashville, Tennessee. Famous singers are: Fiddlin' John Carson in 1923, Jimmie Rodgers, Ray Price, Vernon Dalhart, Dave Macon, George Jones, Hank Williams, Hank Williams, Jr. his son, George Strait, Jimmy Dean, Loretta Lynn, Johnny Cash, Lynn Anderson, Tammy Wynette, Buck Owens, Merle Haggard, Roy Rogers and Gail Davis, Naomi and Wynona Judd, Willie Nelson, Waylon Jennings, John Denver, Glen Campbell, Ronnie Millsap, Dolly Parton, Kenny Rogers, Emmy Lou Harris, Linda Ronstadt, Tim McGraw, Alan Jackson, Garth Brooks, Randy Travis, Vince Gill, Amy Grant, Shania Twain, the Eagles, Carrie Underwood, Keith Urban, Charley Pride, Reba McEntire, Faith Hill, Kenny Chesney, Keith Urban from Australia, Martina McBride, Taylor Swift, Jason Aldean, Lady Antebellum, Mark Wills, Scotty McGreery, Maren Morris, Pam Tillis, Nate Fortner. Some country songs:
I Walk the Line by Johnny Cash 1956.
Your Tattoo by Sammy Kershaw 1958.
Mustang Sally by Wilson Pickett 1965.
Do I Ever Cross Your Mind by Randy Travis 1990.
Thunder Rolls by Garth Brooks 1990.
Love Can Build a Bridge by Naomi and Wynonna Judd 1990. Go Rest High On That Mountain by Vince Gill 1994.
Strawberry Wine by Deana Carter 1996.
You're Still the One by Shania Twain 1997. She's Got It All by Kenny Chesney 1997.
This Kiss by Faith Hill 1998.
Remember When by Alan Jackson 2003.
How Do I Live? By LeAnn Rimes 2003.
God's Will by Martina McBride 2003.
Trisha Yearwood 'Georgia Rain' in 2006.
All Summer Long by Kid Rock 2008.
Lady Antebellum 'Need you Now' 2010.
Like A Back Road 2017 Sam Hunt U.S.A.
Nothing Like This by Rascal Flats 2010.
Colder Weather by Zac Brown Band 2010.
Remind Me by Brad Paisley and Carrie Underwood 2011.
Lee Brice 'I Drive Your Truck' 2012.
Burnin' It Down by Jason ALdean 2014.
Yeah by Joe Nichols 2014. Most People Are Good by Luke Bryan 2017.

Humble and Kind by Tim McGraw 2015.
I Lived It by Blake Shelton 2017.

BLUEGRASS

Remington Ryde, Deer Creek Boys, and Old Crow Medicine Show are bluegrass bands.

SOUTHERN ROCK

Southern rock bands were Allman Brothers, Charlie Daniels, Marshall Tucker, Lynyrd Skynyrd, Atlanta Rhythm Section. Duane Allman played a slide guitar. Tres Hombres was a small local band in Warner Robins, Georgia that played at a Mexican eatery.

SOUTHERN CALIFORNIA ROCK

Chris Anderson band played in Long Beach, California.

ACAPELLA QUARTETS

The Big Chicken Chorus is a men's quartet in Atlanta, Georgia.

Rock N Roll

Rock and roll music originated the USA in the 1950s from African American rhythm and blues, gospel, country, bluegrass, swing bands, and tin pan alley piano players. The Apollo Theater in Harlem, New York is a famous venue for African American entertainers.

American musician rockers in the 1950s and 1960s were Everly Brothers, Iggy Pop, Elvis Presley, Little Richard, Otis Redding, Buddy Holly, Chuck Berry, Carl Perkins, Robert Johnson, Muddy Waters, Howlin Wolf, Bill Haley and His Comets, The Hollies, The Turtles, The Grateful Dead, The Cascades, The Boys Next Door from Chicago, Illionois, The Upsetters a college band at the University of Georgia in 1968, The Monkees, David Cassidy, Mamas & the Papas, Blue Oyster Cult, The Ventures, Roy Orbison, Neil Diamond, and Jimmy Hendrix who was a famous guitarist. The Ed Sullivan Show in New York ran on CBS TV channel from 1948-1971 and featured live performances with variety music, magic acts, sketch comedy and comedians, and jugglers, and acts with animal trainers. Steve Allen was also another big show that Elvis Presley, the Beatles, and other acts appeared on.

At diners, you could put a nickel into a jukebox and hear your favorite songs.

The lyricists and musicians best know the meaning of their songs, but people may have their own individual interpretation of songs. Music lovers love opening notes, chord progressions, hooks, closing notes, vocals and harmony, and music videos.

MOTOWN R&B

American Motown started in Detroit, Michigan by African American Berry Gordy in 1959 and featured rhythm and blues also called R&B, doo-wop, soul, pop, and disco of African Americans. Motown musicians or R&B musicians of other record labels were Duke Ellington, Nat King Cole, B.B. King, Ella Fitzgerald, Isaac Hayes, Aretha Franklin, Stylistics, O'Jays with Eddie Levert, Walter Williams, William Powell, Bobby Massey, and Bill Isles, Diana Ross and the Supremes, Jackson Five, James Brown, Stevie Wonder, Four Tops, Smokey Robinson and the Miracles, The Temptations, Curits Mayfield, Isley Brothers, Dionne Warwick, Roberta Flack, Jimi Hendrix, Funkadelic, Herbie Hancock, Boys II Men, Toni Braxton, Babyface also called Kenny Edmonds, Gerald and Sean Levert, Usher.

Some R&B hits not listed above in HIT SONGS: Will You Still Love Me Tomorrow? By the Shirelles 1961. All Along the Watchtower by Jimi Hendrix 1968. Isn't She Lovely? By Stevie Wonder 1976. She's a Brickhouse by Lionel Richie and the Commodores 1977. Heaven is a Place on Earth by Belinda Carlisle 1987. I Wanna Know by Joe 2000. Nobody by Keith Sweat 1996. Come Back To Me and Let's Wait Awhile by Janet Jackson 1986.

Michael Jackson released Beat It and Billie Jean in 1982 and Man In The Mirror in 1987.

Purple Rain, When Doves Fly, and The Most Beautiful Girl In The World by Prince and The Revolution 1984.

Sexual Healing by Marvin Gaye 1982.

All My Life by K-Ci & JoJo 2010.

When Can I See You by Babyface 1993.

Count on Me by Whitney Houston & CeCe Winans 1996.

On Bended Knee, A Song for Mama by Boyz II Men 1995.

One Sweet Day by Mariah Carey 1995.

Do I Ever Cross Your Mind? By Brian McKnight 1997.

American Woman by Lenny Kravitz 1998.

This Woman's Work by Maxwell 1997.

Differences by Ginuwine 2001.

Wishing on a Star by Rose Royce 1996.

Sittin' Up in My Room and Have You Ever by Brandy 1995.
Waterfalls by TLC 1994.
Can We Talk? By Tevin Campbell 1993.
Walking Away and 7 Days by Craig David 2001.
Angel of Mine by Monica 1998.
I Swear by All-4-One 1998.
We're Not Making Love No More by Dru Hill 1997.
Yeah! Ft. Lil Jon, Ludacris by Usher 2004.
How You Gonna Act Like That by Tyrese 2002.Heartless by Kanye West 2008.
Over and Over by Nelly 2004.

Some TOP 100 BILLBOARD Names

Some top ten pop solo artists and groups in the 1970s-2000s in the USA were Janis Joplin, Barbara Streisand, Barbara Streisnad and Kris Kristofferson duet, Billy Joel, Peter Simon & Art Garfunkel, Bob Dylan, Don Mclean, Dan Fogelberg, Rod Stewart, John Cougar Mellencamp, Barry Manilow, Cher, Stevie Ray Vaughn who was a famous guitarist, James Taylor, Carole King, Carpenters, Captain & Tenille, Beach Boys, the Bee Gees, BJ Thomas, Al Green, Bill Withers, Bread, Three Dog Night, Jimmy Buffett and the Coral Reefers Band, Steely Dan, Michael McDonald and the Doobie Brothers, the GoGos, the Doors, Peter Frampton, Kenny G who played the saxophone, Sade, Bruce Springsteen, Sean Lennon, Julian Lennon, Chris Isaak, Michael Jackson who was very famous of the Jackson Five and his sister Janet Jackson, Selena from Texas, Celine Dion & Adrea Bocelli duet, Celine Deon & R. Kelly duet, Mariah Carey, Whitney Houston, Luther Van Dross, Tevin Campbell, Elton John who was from England, Madonna who was a Catholic female singer and used an icon from her church as her singing name, Michael Bolton, Phil Collins and Genesis Band, Cat Stevens, Joan Jett, Tom Petty, Annie Lennox and the Eurethmics, George Michael, Bryan Adams, Seal, Black Crowes, Dave Matthews, Widespread Panic, Alanis Morisette, John Mayer, James Blunt, Sheryl Crow, Jewel, Darren Hayes & Savage Garden, Melissa Etheridge, Gloria Estefan, Meatloaf, Stevie Nicks and Fleetwood Mac, Richard Marx, Blondie, Cyndi Lauper, Paula Abdul, Kenny Loggins, TLC, Brandy, Chris De Burgh, Sam Smith, Justin Timberlake, Christina Aguilera, Brittney Spears, Jessica Simpson, Norah Jones, Adele, Justin Beiber, Walter Murphy, Joel McNeely, Bruno Mars from Hawaii, Katy Perry, Kelly Clarkston who won the first American Idol singing contest on TV, Jordin Sparks, Chris Brown, Maroon 5, Sara Bareilles, Lady Gaga, Crowded House, Rihanna from Barbados in the Caribbean Islands, Beyonce Knowles and Destiny's Child, Maxwell, Lenny Kravitz, Jason Mraz, John Legend, Ellie Goulding, Steady Commons, Sandra Eakes and San Rah Lees, Kayla Taylor who sang to jazz music, Dominic Gaudious who played guitar and didgeridoo. Joe Bonamassa is a blues guitarist who opened for B.B. King.

Some USA Rock bands in the 1970s-2000s: Led Zeppelin, Ted Nugent and Amboy Dukes, Bon Jovi, Pink Floyd, Steven Tyler and Aerosmith, Guns N Roses and Axel Rose, Foreigner, Boston, REM and Michael Stipe, Todd Rundgren & Utopia, Queen, Grand Funk Railroad, Poison, New York Dolls, Kiss, U2, Coldplay, Kings of Leon, Trans-Siberian Orchestra, Humble Pie, Scorpions.

ALTERNATIVE ROCK

In the USA, a genre of music called alternative played band music that was not considered to be 1970's rock such as like the Rolling Stones who sang 'Beast of Burden' or Aerosmith who sand 'Dream On'. A new alternative sound was like the bands of Smashing Pumpkins, Foo Fighters, Red Hot Chili Peppers, Nirvana,The Cure, REM and Michael Stipe a college band that started at University of Georgia, The B52s a college band that started at the University of

Georgia, the Fray, Jane's Addiction, Nine Inch Nails, Third Eye Blind, Blind Melon, Godsmack, Live, Collective Soul, The Wallflowers, Oasis, Beck, Green Day, The Naked and the Famous, Tomorrow, Perfect Circle, Circle from Finland, Jet from Australia, Bastille from England.

Some alternative music was also called funk or punk. Some famous funk bands were the Ramones, Patti Smith, Stooges and Iggy Pop, Matchbox Twenty, Ben Folds Five, Pistols, Pere Uber, Flowers of Romance, Raincoats, Pink, Slits, Clash, Chain Smokers, Bad Brains, Everlast, Spin Doctors, and Trash Talk. Some of these bands played in New York, Los Angeles, and Washington D. C.
Some famous alternative songs: '1979' and Tonight, Tonight by Smashing Pumpkins released in 1996.
Everlong and Monkey Wrench by Foo Fighters 1997. Enter Sandman by Metallica 1991. In Bloom, Come As You Are by Nirvana 1991. Definitely Maybe by Oasis 1994. Hemorrhage (In My Hands) by Fuel 2000. How's It Gonna Be by third Eye Blind 1996. December by Collective Soul 1995. One Headlight by Jakob Dylan and The Wallflowers 1996. Jakob Dylan is Bob Dylan's son. Found Out About You by Gin Blossoms 1996. By the Way by Red Hot Chili Peppers 2002, Runaway Train by Soul Asylum 1992. Brick by Ben Folds Five 1997. Loser by Beck 1994. It's Been Awhile by Staind 2001. So Far Away by Nickelback 2005.

HEAVY METAL ROCK

Heavy metal bands were AC/DC, Metallica, Alice Cooper, Black Sabbath, Pearl Jam, Alice in Chains, and more. 'Tom Sawyer' by Rush 1981.
Alice in Chains released the song Rooster in 1992. AC/DC released Hells Bells and Highway to Hell in 1994.

CANADA

In Canada, Anvil is a heavy metal band. Sarah McLaughlin sang ballads. Neil Young from Toronto was also a movie producer and screenwriter. Isabelle Boulay sang 'Parle Moi'. Nelly Furtado of Canada sang I'm Like A Bird.

ENGLAND

British rockers in the 1950s-2000s were Tommy Steele, Wee Willie Harris, Cliff Richard and the Shadows, Teddy Boy, Lonnie Donegan, The Vipers, Skiffle Group, Ken Colyer, Chas McDevitt, Marty Wilde, Adam Faith, Bill Fury, Joe Brown, Johnny Kidd and the Pirates, Alex Korner, The Troggs, Cyril Davies, the Quarryman who became the Beatles, the Animals, the Rolling Stones with Mick Jagger and guitarist Keith Richards, the Yardbirds, Jethro Tull. Roger Daltrey and the Who, Badfinger who were the first band signed to the Beatles' Apple Records Label. XTC, Freddie and the Dreamers, Wayne Fontana and the Mindbenders, Herman's Hermits, Yes, Engelbert Humperdinck, Tom Jones, Dave Clark Five, Elvis Costello, Def Leppard, Elton John, Amy Winehouse, Leona Lewis, Des'ree, Ed Sheeran, Liam Gallagher and Noel Gallagher, Oasis, Spandau Ballet. Music was recorded in Liverpool, Manchester, Birmingham, and London. The four Beatles were Paul McCartney, John Lennon, George Harrison, and Ringo Starr and they were very famous. George Harrison sang My Sweet Lord in 1970.
The End of the World and Bring Me Sunshine were written by Arthur Kent and Sylvia Dee. Bring Me Sunshine became the anthem (signature tune) of the comedy duo Morecambe & Wise of BBC in the U.K. Soul II Soul is a British R&B band that released Back to Life in 1989.

GERMANY

La Bouche was a German and American dance duo based in Germany in 1994. Apparat is a German electronic musician. Milli Vanilli were a German R&B duo in 1988.

IRELAND

Some famous Irish rock bands were U2 1976 and The Cranberries 1989, Enya.

Snow Patrol released the song Chasing Cars in 2006.

RUSSIA

Sonic Speed Monkeys is a Russia band that also plays in India and England. Dmitri Hvorostovsky is a Russian operatic baritone. Anna Netrebko is a Russian operatic soprano who lives in Russia, Austria, and New York City.

FRANCE

In France, Christophe sang Aline in 1965. Lara Fabian sang 'Je T'Aime'. Lara Fabian and Patrick Fiori sang 'L'Hymne a L'Amour' together. Lara Fabian also sang a duet with Dmitri Hvorostovsky the Russian opera singer. Edith Piaf was a famous French singer who became an international star in the 1930s.

HIP HOP

In Chile, Ana Tijoux of Makiza is a hip-hop artist.

Hip-hop music started in Bronx, New York. Hip-hop is rhyming lyrics to music and may include break-dancing. Some lyrics are angry. Some famous hip-hop or rap artists called rappers are Ice-T, Aaliya, R. Kelly, Eminem, Kidd Rock, Snoop Dogg, Ludacris, P. Diddy, Felicia Pearson, Cassidy, Kendrick Lamar, Kanye West, LL Cool J also called James Todd Smith, Jay Z, Drake and Queen Latifah. Ahmad Balshe also known as Belly is a hip-hop artist born in West Bank, Palestine and raised in Canada. Ayo & Teo are rappers from Ann Arbor, Michigan.

Jude Abaga also known as M.I. Abaga is a Nigerian hip-hop producer.

Some hip hop songs: Hey Ya! by Outkast 2003. U Can't Touch This by MC Hammer 1990. Play That Funky Music by Vanilla Ice 1990. Not Afraid by Eminem 2010.

REGGAE

Jamaican reggae musicians are Bob Marley, Toots and the Maytals. Reggae includes offbeat lyrics and staccato chords. Bob Marley sang Is This Love? in 1978.

Cuban music artists are Camila Cabelo, and Gloria Estefan. Jencarlos Canela is a Cuban American singer and actor.

Puerto Rico musicians are Roselyn Sanchez and Residente also called Rene Juan Perez.

Australian music included Men At Work, INXS, Crowded House, Johnny O'Keefe, Keith Urban, a country singer. Jet, an alternative rock band. AC/DC a heavy metal band, and Empire of the Sun. Split Enz is a goup from New Zealand.

Manfred Mann was a band from South Africa who sang Blinded By the Light, a remake of Bruce Springsteen's song.

DISCO

Disco or discotheque music is a type of dancing music as in the U.S.A. movies Saturday Night Fever with John Travolta and Karen Lynn Gorney and Grease with John Travolta and Olivia Newton John, the music of Chaka Khan, Donna Summer, KC & The Sunshine Band, Yvonne Elliman, Gloria Gaynor, Bee Gees, and Prince. The Bump and the Hustler were popular dance moves to disco music.

Laura Wright and AnthonyPadilla were dancers who performed in las Vegas. Anthony Padilla was also a comedian.

Rumba is a Cuban dance that became famous in the 1930s.

Zumba is a dance designed for body workouts for cardio fitness, weight loss, and weight management.

Electronic music is played on keyboards that have computer parts. The keyboards can recreate the sounds of guitars, drums, trumpets, and pianos all by playing a keyboard. Christopher Cross produced a CD called Sailing with electronic music.

In Cambodia, Sin Sisamouth and Ros Sereysothea were musicians in 1970.

In Thailand, The Impossibles were musicians in 1970.

In Vietnam, Trinh Cong Sow was a male musician and Khanh Ly was a woman musician.

In the Philippines, Wally Gonzales and the Juan De La Cruz Band were popular.

In South Korea, Shin Jung-hyeon was a male musician in the 1960s - 1970s.

In Japan, Chiemi Eri was a woman who recorded Rock Around the Clock in 1955. Keijiro Yamashita was a male musician and Michiko Hamamura was a woman musician. Carol and the Cools, the Black Cats, Peppermint Jam, Guitar Wolf, and Akiko Urae and Take Blue Angle were popular musicians. Anthem and BOW WOW were heavy metal bands.

SPANISH MUSIC

Ranchero classic mexican music may include accordion, bajo sexton, bass, drums, and saxophone. Manuela Vargas was a dancer that performed on the Ed Sullivan Show in 1966.

Mexican singer Danna Paola sang a song called Mundo de Caramelo about candy. Danny Flores played Mexican music.

Other popular artists are Sergio Santos Mendes and Brazil, Los Rockets, Los Crazy Boys, Jose Feliciano, Carlos Santana, Enrique Iglesias, the Refrescos, Pistones, Emilio Sancho & Los Nikis, Ivete Sangalo, Selena Gomez, Luan Santana, Jorge & Mateus, Bruno & Marrone, Roberto Carlos, Joao Neto & Frederico, Joel Marques, Los Tigres Del Norte, Pesado, Nuevo Leon, Ramon Ayala, Intocable, Los Cadetes de Linares, Los Alegres de Teran, Los Tucanesde Tijuana, Los Rieleros del Norte, Los Huracanes del Norte, Los Angeles Azules, Remmy Valenzuela, Ulices Chaidez y Sus Plebes, Los Corceles De Linares, La Septima Banda, Edwin Luna y La Trakalosa de Monterry, Christian Nodal, Regulo Caro, Banda Carnaval, Gerardo Ortiz, Romeo Sautos, Marc Anthony, Calibre 50, Banda los Recoditos, Romeo Santos.

Lani Hall was a woman who married A&M records founder Herb Alpert of Los Angeles who had a band called the Tijuana Brass and Herb Alpert and Brazil. Janis Hansen of the United States sang with Herb Alpert also. The band had a Latino jazz sound.

Maluma also named Juan Luis Londono Arias was a music artist from Columbia who signed with Sony Music.

La Ley is a famous band in Chile formed in 1987 that included Beto Cuevas, Andres Bobe, Rodrigo Aboitiz, Luciano Rojas, and Mauricio Claveria. Some of their famous songs: Desiertos, Tejedores de Ilusion, Prisioneros de la Piel, and Aqui for Warner Music Mexico.

La Movida Madrilena was a music clubhouse for bands after the death of dictator Francisco Franco in Spain in 1975.

EASY LISTENING MUSIC

Tubular Bells by Michael Gordon Oldfield of U.K.

Tangerine Dream and Edgar Froese of Germany 1967.

Secret Garden of Ireland and Norway 1996.

Kenny G of U.S.A. 1986.

Bonne Nuit French Lullabies by Jane Woodruff and Jana Minter 1995.

Where I Stand by guitarist Nick Gaudious 1996.

Enchantment by Charlotte Church of U.K. 2001.

Passion: The Love Album by Placido Domingo. 2011.

RELIGIOUS MUSIC

Some Jewish music artists in the 2000s were Six13 and Max Stern. Max Stern Song of Moses Ha'azinu was 32 minutes long.

From the 1980s and into the 2000s there were many Christian music artists that produced rock and contemporary music including Brandon Heath, Kari Jobe, Casting Crowns, Mercy Me, Tenth Avenue North, Aaron Shust, Newsboys, Jeremy Camp, Chris Tomlin,

TobyMac, Steven Curtis Chapman, Mary Mary, Yolanda Adams, Patti Labelle, CeCe Winans, Kirk Franklin, Judy Jacobs, Muzeel Fairley, Jars of Clay, Josh Grogan, Northpoint InsideOut Band, Mandisa, Nichole Nordeman, Natalie Grant, Petra, Switchfoot, Big Daddy Weave, Francesca Battistelli, Phillips, Craig & Dean, Hillsong Worship, Selah, Oak Ridge Boys, Paul Cardell, Matthew West, Laura Story, Third Day, Christy Nockels, Nathan Pacheco, Chris and Conrad, Rich Mullins, Johnny Diaz, Michael W. Smith, Nate Fortner, Lighthouse, and more. Some songs: Brandon Heath 'Give Me Your Eyes' 1997. Chris Tomlin 'God of this City' 2008. Kari Jobe "I Am Not Alone' 2013. Mercy Me 'I Can Only Imagine' 2000. Amy Grant 'Better Than A Hallelujah' in 2010. Natalie Grant 'Your Great Name' in 2010, Plumb 'Need You Now' in 2013. Sara Groves 'Tent in the Center of Town' about Christian tent revivals. Jon Thurlow 'Jesus You're Beautiful' in 2010. John Stringer s'That's Love' in 2015. Sanctus Real 'Lead Me' 2010. Josh Groban 'You Raise Me Up' 2003.

The Booth Brothers, The Three Bridges, The Browders, Soul'd Out Quartet, and Collinsworth were famous Christian gospel acts. Gospel acts could be a capello (acapello) quartets sung in harmony with no musical instruments or with music.

Cat Stevens (Yusuf Islam) was a Muslim musician who wrote a song called A is for Allah as it is spelled in the English language. Allah means God in the Arabic and Farsi languages. Gott means God in German. Dieu means God in French. Elohim means God in Hebrew.

Cat Stevens was drowning in the ocean off the coast of England and prayed to God to save him and he would devote his life to God. When he was recovering in the hospital, his brother gave him a copy of the Quran and that is when he was became Muslim.

Pandit Jaitly, Aparat, Jagjit and Chitra Singh offer Hindu music.

Apsaras offer Thai and Japanese music.

Demis Roussos was born in Egypt to a Greek family. Demis Roussos and his band Aphrodite's Child created an album entitled 666 based on the Book of Revelation in the King James Bible. Other bandmates were Loukas Sideras, Silver Koulouris. Other contributors to the album were Michael Ripoche, John Forst, Daniel Koplowitz, Yanni Tsarouchis, and actress Irene Papas. Vangelis is another Greek composer.

There was a talent show at Christ United Methodist Church in Roswell, Ga. Adults, teenagers, and children who attended the church participated in the event which followed a BBQ dinner. Acts included piano players, a saxophone and horn duet, dancers, a singer, and storyteller. The event was free with a donation box.

Juju is music of the Yoruba religion with guitars and drums.

CHILDREN'S MUSIC

Famous children's music artists were Pete Seeger 1919, Captain Kangaroo 1950-1960, Mister Rogers and Sesame Street 1980, Raffi of Canada, Egypt, and Armenia 1948, and Ziggy Marley of Jamaica 1968. Some famous children's songs are Twinkle, Twinkle Little Star, The Wheels on the Bus, Three Little Monkeys Jumping on the Bed, Itsy Bitsy Spider, This Old Man, If You're Happy And You Know It Clap Your Hands, The Chipmunks are animated music for kids and also included Christmas songs.

Many music artists have also worked in visual arts, literary arts, or movies & tv.

WORLD LITERATURE / LITERARY ARTS

Etchings were on cave walls and on stone tablets in 3500 BCE. Words and symbols written on paper scrolls in 2400 BCE. In 600BCE people in Europe wrote on parchment from left to right, while in the middle east people wrote from right to left in Hebrew and Arabic. In 200BCE wax tablets were used to record words. In 100 Current Era leafs of paper and block printing were a revolution in China. In 1400, moveable type was invented by Johannes Gutenberg in Germany and he printed 180 copies of the Gutenberg Bible. In 1500, the printing revolution began across Europe as newspapers and books were mass-produced.

It is impossible to list all authors and poets of great world literature in the pages of this book.

Librarians and book publishers around the world work hard to catalog the titles of thousands of books that are written each year. Some say Don't give away the surprise ending; let them read it themself.' It is a tradition to be quiet in a library, so quiet that you can hear a pin drop. Don't judge a book by its cover.

Famous Ancient Literature

Geographia by Ptolemy of Egypt 100.
The Republic by Plato of Greece 380 BCE.
The Tale of Genji by Murasaki Shikibu of Japan in 1008.
Canterbury Tales by Geoffrey Chaucer of England 1300.
Divine Comedy by Dante Alighieir of Italy 1308.
The Prince by Miccolo Machiavelli of Italy 1513.
Complete Works of Shakespeare of England 1600.
Christopher Marlow of England 1500.
Don Quixote by Miguelde Cervantes of Spain 1615.
Philosophae Naturalis Principia Mathematica by Isaac Newton of United Kingdom 1687.
Voltaire of France 1700,
Guy de Manpassant of France 1850.
The Communist Manifesto by Karl Marx and Friedrich Engels of Germany 1818.
The Rights of Man by Thomas Paine of France 1791.
Commen Sense by Thomas Paine of United States 1776.
Democracy in America by Alexis de Tocqueville of France 1805.
Jane Eyre by Charlotte Bronte of England 1816.
Crime and Punishment by Fyodor Dostoyevsky of Russia 1866.
Faust by Johann Wolfgang von Goethe of Germany 1808.
On the Origin of the Species by Charles Darwin of the United Kingdom 1859.
Uncle Tom's Cabin by Harriet Beecher Stowe in 1852.
War and Peace and Anna Karenina by Leo Tolstoy of Russia in 1867.
Wuthering Heights Emily Bronte 1845.
Treasure Island Robert L. Stevenson 1883.
The Jungle by Upton Sinclair of California in 1906.
The Diary of Anne Frank 1947 published in Denmark.
The Torah.
The King James Bible 1611.
The Holy Qur'an.
The Analects of C.onfucious.
Rigveda.
The Mahabharata and The Ramayana.
Bhagavad Gita.
Kojiki.
Avesta.
Kitabi-Aqdas.
Ofudesaki
Adi Granth.
The Red Record, The Wal.lum Odom
Tao Te Ching.
The Lotus Sutra.
The Book of Mormon.

Famous Modern Contemporary Literature

The Hobbit and The Lord of the Rings Trilogy, by J.R.R. Tolkien 1892.
Book of Common Prayer, 1928, by English Anglican Church.
I Know Why The Caged Bird Sings by Maya Angelou 1928.

The Road Less Traveled by Morgan Scott Peck 1936.
To Kill A Mockingbird by Harper Lee 1960.
The Great Divorce by C.S. Lewis of Ireland 1898.
What if the World had Two Moons? By Neil F. Comins. 2010.
Selections from the writings of Abdul-Baha 1978 The Universal House of Justice Bahai World.
Left Brain, Right Brain by Sally P. Springerr 1981.
Prayer Language of the Soul by Peter Lorie 1997.
Mother Theresa, The Joy of Living, 1996.
Marvels of the Molecule 1987 by Lionel Salem.
Peace is the Way by Deepak Chopra 2005.
The Art of Happiness 1998 by Tenzin Gyatso, His Holiness the Fourteenth Dalai Lama.
The Divine Matrix by Greg Braden.
When Bad Things Happen to Good People 1981 by Harold S. Kushner.
The World Through the Eyes of Angels by Mahmoud Saeed of Iran in the U.S.A. 2011.
There are Seven Homes on My Street by Ron Flowers and Anise Flowers 2014.
Step Out, Step Up by Mark E. Green 1964.
The DNA of Achievers by Mathew Knowles 2015 who was Beyonce the singer's father.

Famous Plays at Theatres: Phantom of the Opera, Les Miserables, Oklahoma, The Fantasticks, Oh Calcutta, Cats, Fiddler on the Roof, Plaza Suite, Rent

Famous Poets: E.E.Cumming, Walt Whitman, Emily Dickinson

There are millions of books, magazines, newspapers, and other written materials in libraries, stores, museums, and homes. Many books are made into movies. Screenwriters write movie scripts which are lines the actors and actresses recite. Book illustrators design covers and add drawings, pictures, and graphics.

Fiction is material that is written from the creative imagination of the author such as novels, short stories, children's books, suspense thrillers, horror, fantasy, science fiction, romance, mystery, satire.

Nonfiction writings are about truth and actual happenings such as biographies of a person's life, gardening, cooking, automotive, science, history, and documentaries of news items.

An **autobiography** is an account of life memories written by the author themself.
It is a sin to steal another artist's or inventor's creative idea and pitch is as your own.

Authors of Adult NonFiction
Natural Gardening in Small Spaces by Noel Kingsbury of Britain 1960.
Plenty by Yotam Ottolenghi of Britain, Israel, and Australia 1968.
The Joy of Cooking by Irma S. Rombauer of Missouri U.S.A. 1877.
Mastering the Art of French Cooking by Louisette Bertholle of France 1905.
The Taste of Country Cooking by Edna Lewis 1916.
The Greens Cookbook by Deborah Madison 1987.
Glorious Needlepoint by Kaffe Fassett 1937.
Ceramics for Beginners 2010 by Emily Reason.
Terry A. Anderson of U.S.A. 1947 Den of Lions a story about being held hostage by Islamic Jihad from 1985-1991.
Brian Keener of Ireland An Evil Cradling about being kidnapped in Beirut, Lebanon in 1985.
Alia Malek 1974 The Home That Was Our Country: A Memoir of Syria.
Bury My Heart At Wounded Knee by Dee Brown 1970.

Authors of Adult Fiction Recent Years

Karen Abbott of U.S.A. 1973 Liar Temptress Soldier Spy
Chinua Achebe of Nigeria 1930 Things Fall Apart.
Boris Akunin of Russia 1953 The Death of Achilles.
Wang Anyi of China 1954 The Song of Everlasting Sorrows.
Jeffrey Archer of U.K. 1960 Be Careful What You Wish For.
David Baldacci of U.S.A. 1960 King & Maxwell.
M.C. Beaton (Marion Chesney) of Scotland 1936 Hamish MacBeth mysteries.
Chetan Bhagat of India 1974 Making India Awesome.
Terri Blackstock of U.S.A. 1957 Distortion.
Barbara Taylor Bradford of U.S.A. 1933 Woman of Substance.
Geraldine Brooks of Australia 1955 The Secret Chord.
Dan Brown of U.S.A 1964 The Da Vinci Code.
Pearl S. Buck of U.S.A. 1932 The Good Earth.
Sandra Brown of U.S.A. 1948 Mirror Image.
James Lee Burke of U.S.A. 1936 The Neon Rain.
Peter Carey of Australia 1943 Oscar and Lucinda.
Barbara Cartland of Britain 1901 Romance of Food.
Lee Child of Britain 1954 Night School.
Tom Clancy of U.S.A. 1947 Red Storm Rising.
Michael Connelly of U.S.A. 1956 The Wrong Side of Goodbye.
Catherine Cookson of U.K. 1906 A Dinner of Herbs.
Jackie Collins of U.K. 1937 The World is Full of Divorced Women.
Robin Cook of U.S.A. 1940 Coma.
Michael Crichton of U,S,A. 1942 Jurassic Park.
Clive Cussler of U.S.A. 1931 Arctic Drift.
Patricia Cornwell of U.S.A.1946 Scarpetta.
Bei Dao of China 1949 The August Sleepwalker.
Jeffrey Deaver of U.S.A. 1950 Twelfth Card.
Nelson Demille of Jamaica 1943 Radiant Angel.
Jude Deveraux of U.S.A. 1947 A Knight in Shining Armor.
Sue Duffy of U.S.A. 1955 Red Dawn Rising.
Dorothy Eden of New Zealand 1912 Bride by Candlelight.
Jennifer Egan of U.S.A. 1962 A Visit from the Goon Squad.
Janet Evanovich of U.S.A. 1943 One For The Money.
Nicholas Evans of Worchestershire, U.K. 1950 The Horse Whisperer.
Richard Flanagan of Australia 1961 The Great Australian.
Vince Flynn of U.S.A. 1966 Consent to Kill.
Ken Follett of U.K. 1949 The Pillars of the Earth.
William R. Forstchen of U.S.A. 1950 One Second After
Julia Franck of Germany 1970 The Blindness of the Heart.
Lisa Gardner of U.S.A. 1971 The Perfect Husband.
Helen Garner of Australia 1942 Our Man Elsewhere.
Mark Greaney of U.S.A. 1968 Gunmetal Gray.
Kate Grenville of Australia 1950 The Secret River.
John Grisham of U.S.A. 1955 The Firm.
Charlene Harris of U.S.A.1951 Dead to Worse.
Elin Hildebrand of U.S.A. 1960 The Island.
Tony Hillerman of U.S.A. 1925 The Fallen Man.
Takashi Hiraide of Japan 1950 The Guest Cat.
Mary Higgins Clark of U.S.A. 1927 Every Breath You Take.
Yu Hua of China 1960 Brothers.
Kazuo Ishiguro of U.K. 1989 The Remains of the Day. JA Jance 1944 Judgement Call.

Grant Jeffrey of Canada 1948 The Signature of God.
Muriel Jensen of Vancouver 1945 Mommy and Me, a Harlequin novel.
Iris Johansen of U.S.A. 1938 Mind Game.
Joan Johnston of U.S.A. 1948 The Price about a lawyer.
Brenda Joyce of U.S.A. 1968 The Prize.
Stieg Larsson of Sweden 1954 The Girl With The Dragon Tatoo.
Mitsuyo Kakuta of Japan 1967 Sagashimono.
Jan Karon 1937 Come Rain or Shine
Stephen King of U.S.A. 1947 Cujo.
Dean Koontz of U.S.A. 1945 Innocence.
Judith Krantz a Jewish American 1928 Spring Collection.
Tim La Haye of U.S.A. 1926 Left Behind.
Louis L'Amour of U.S.A. 1908 Big Country.
Yan Lianke of China 1958 Dream of Ding Village.
Johanna Lindsey of U.S.A. 1952 Until Forever, a Romance
Robert Ludlum of U.S.A. 1927 The Bourne Identity.
Debbie Macomber of U.S.A. 1948 Cedar Cove.
Henning Mankell of Sweden 1948 After the Fire.
Brad Meltzer of U.S.A. 1970 The Zero Game.
Claire Messud of USA in Germany 1966 Relentless.
Fern Michaels of U.S.A. 1945 Final Justice.
Linda Lael Miller of U.S.A. 1949 Springwater.
Anchee Min of China 1957 Wild Ginger.
Kenzaburo Oe of Japan 1935 A Personal Matter.
Ben Okri of Nigeria 1959 An African Elegy.
James Patterson of U.S.A. 1947 Alex Cross.
Victor Pelevin of Russia 1956 Omon Ra.
Ann Rice of U.S.A. 1941 Interview with A Vampire. Nora Roberts 1950 Come Sundown.
Arundhati Roy of India 1961 The God of Small Things.
Jennifer Ryan of U.K. 1960 The Chilbury Ladies Choir (set in WW II).
Salman Rushdie of India 1947 The Ground Beneath Her Feet.
Carl Sagan of U.S.A. 1934 COSMOS.
John Sanford of U.S.A. 1944 Rules of Prey.
Lisa Scottoline of U.S.A. 1955 Exposed.
Vikram Seth of India 1952 A Suitable Boy.
Han Shaogong of China 1953 Pa Pa Pa.
Sidney Sheldon of U.S.A. 1917 The Other Side of Midnight.
Anita Shreve of U.S.A. 1946 The Pilot's WIfe
Frank G. Slaughter of U.S.A. 1908 Convention, M.D.
Nicholas Sparks of U.S.A.1965 The Notebook.
Danielle Steel of U.S.A. 1947 A Perfect Life.
Amy Tan of China 1952 The Joy Luck Club.
Corin Tellado of Spain 1927 My Friend's Lover.
Ross Thomas of U.S.A. 1926 Out on the Rim.
Uwe Timm of Germany 1940 Morenga.
Lyudmila Ulitskaya of Russia 1943 The Big Green Tent.
Susan Wiggs of U.S.A. Family Tree 1987.
Virginia Woolf of Britain 1882 Mrs. Dalloway.
Xue Xinran of China 1958 The Good Women of China.
Mo Yan of China 1955 The Republic of Wine.
Hong Ying of China 1962 Good Children of the Flower.
Banana Yoshimato of Japan 1964 Kitchen.
Kathy Zebert of U.S.A. 1960 Incredulity.
Juli Zeh of Germany 1974 In Free Fall.

Authors of Teenager or Children's Books

Jacob and Wilhelm Grimm of Germany 1812 Rapunzel, Cinderella, Snow White and the 7 Dwarfs, Hansel & Gretel.
Hans Christian Anderson of Denmark 1805 Thumbelina, The Ugly Duckling, The Princess and the Pea, The Emperor's New Clothes.

Robert Southey 1837 Goldilocks and The Three Bears.
Peter Christen Asbjornsen 1841 The Three Billy Goats Gruff.
James Orchard Halliwell 1849 The Three Little Pigs.
Watty Piper 1930 The Little Engine That Could.
Mark Twain of U.S.A. 1835 The Adventures of Tom Sawyer and Huckleberry Finn.
Stan & Jan Berenstain of U.S.A. 1946 The Spooky Old Tree.
Judy Blume of U.S.A.1938 Tales of a Fourth Grade.
Enid Blyton of U.K. 1897 The Famous Five On A Treasure.
Michael Bond of U.K. 1958 A Bear Called Paddington.
Beverly Cleary of U.S.A. 1916 The Mouse and the Motorcycle.
Roald Dahl of U.K. 1916 Charlie and the Chocolate Factory.
Franklin Dixon 1902 The Haunted Fort.
P.D. Eastman 1909 Go, Dog, Go!.
Paul Goble of England 1933 Star Boy.
Beatrix Potter of England 1866 The Tale of Peter Rabbit.
Dr. Seuss was a German-American 1904 The Cat in the Hat.
Madonna Louise Ciccone of U.S.A. 1958 The English Roses.
David Baldacci of U.S.A. 1960 Freddy and the French Fries.
Carolyn Keene 1905 Nancy Drew.
Robert Lopshire 1927 Put Me in The Zoo
Brad Meltzer of U.S.A. 1970 I am Sacagawea.
A.A. Milne & Walt Disney 1882 Winnie the Pooh and Eeyore.
James Patterson of U.S.A. 1947 Word of Mouse.
R.L.Stine of U.S.A. 1943 Goosebumps.
Tim Winton of Australia 1960 My Magic Mirror.
Ludwig Bemelmans of Austria, USA 1898 Madeline.
Margret & H.A.Rey of Germany,USA 1939 Curious George.
Malala Yousafzai 1997 Malala's Magic Pencil.
Priscilla & Otto Friedrich 1961 The Marshmallow Ghosts a Halloween story.
The Caboose Who Got Loose 1971 Bill Peet.
Javaka Steptoe 2010 The Jones Family.
E.B. White 1899 Charlotte's Web.
Kevin Henkes 1960 Chrysanthemum.
Nancy Springer 1948 The Case of the Left Handed Lady.
Pete the Cat by James Dean 1957.
Boy of the Pyramids 1958 by Ruth Fosdick Jones.
The Night Before the Tooth Fairy by Natasha King 2003.
Silverlicious by Victoria Kann 2011.
Splash! A Penguin Counting Book by Jonathan Chester.
Danny the Caterpillar by Dawn Brooks and Angela Simonovska.

Children's Book Illustrator

Saul Bass was a graphic designer and filmmaker who also illustrated the book Henri's Walk to Paris 1974 by author Lenore Klein

Authors of Christian Christmas Books

Clement Clarke Moore, Dr. Seuss, Charles Dickens with the character Ebenezer Scrooge in A Christmas Carol, Nancy Tillman, Jan Berenstain, Laura Numeroff, Anna Dewdney, Nolo Buck and Felicia Bond, Lee Smith, Glenn Beck, Karen Kingsbury, Jim Stovall, Carol Higgins Clark, W. Bruce Cameron, Richard Paul Evans, Anne Perry, Celestine Sibley, Max Lucado, Linda Lael Miller, Sherryl Woods, Garrison Keillor, Kristin Hannah, Jimmy Carter, Philip Gulley, Jacquelyn Mitchard, Fern Michaels, Elin Hildebrand

Author of Christian Book: Joyce Meyer 1943– Living Beyond Your Feelings, Elise Ballard, Chicken Soup for the Soul 1993 Amy Newmart

Authors of Jewish Hanukkah Books

Eric Kimmel, Amanda Peet and Andrea Troyer, Ellen Kushner, Lauren Graham, David Martin, Gloria Koster, Greg Wolfe, Isaac Bushevis Singer, Fran Manushkin

Authors of Muslim Ramaden Books

Sylvia Whitman, Karen Katz, H.A. Ray and Hena Khan, Reza Jalali, Taherah Mafi, Yasmeen Bahim, R.J. Bailey

Authors of India Hindu Diwali Books

Shuchi Mehta, Bhakti Mather, Ajanta Chakraborty and Vivek Kumar, Richard Sebra, Shweta Chopra and Shuchi Mehta, Johnny Zucker and Jan Berger Cohen

Authors of China Duanwu Books

Sanmu Tang, Arlene Chan, Qu Yuan, Ni Hao and Kai-Lan, Lisa Spillane

Authors of Africa Kwanzaa Books

Karen Katz, Albert Whitman Prairie, Deborah M. Newton, Deborah Chocolate

Book about Rastafari Judah Square Festival: Book Ethiopia Holy Land

Authors of Buddha Vesak Books

Vajirarama, Dharmakosajarn, Zara Saeed, Clive Erricker, George E. Shibata, Dhammasaavaka, Vesak Nanayakkara

Authors of Japan Tanbata Books

Sara Fujimara, Betty Reynolds

Authors of Bahai Ridvan Books

Belgesel Kitaplar, Wendi Momen

Authors of Zoroastrian Sadeh Books

Jesse Russell, Isarela Louis

There are too many radio announcers, music DJs, Tv new broadcasters, weather trackers, and talk show hosts to list in these pages.

Famous Radio Announcers in 1920 - 1040s:

Britian radio BBC: William Joyce, Alvar Lidell, Winston Churchill who was Prime Minister of the United Kingdom from 1940-1945 and 1951-1955

Australia radio: Conrad Charlton, Queenie Aston, Ethel Lang, Grace Gibson, William Henry Bragg, Joseph Lyon who was Prime Minister of Australia 1932-1939

U.S.A. radio: Graham McNamee, Red Barber, Brain Belanger, Harold Arlin, Tommy Cowan, Andrew White, Milton Cross, Vin Scully (radio sportscaster for 67 seasons for L.A. Dodgers baseball team), Jack Burk (sportscaster for St. Louis Cardinals baseball team), Curt Gowdy (sportscaster for Boston Red Sox baseball team), Franklin Delano Roosevelt 32nd President of the U.S.A. Famous broadcasts in the U.S.A.: 1937 Herbert Morrison's broadcast of Crash of the Hindenburg, a German Zeppelin that transported passengers from Europe to America that had a crash landing in New Jersey. 1938 Orson Welles' broadcast of 'The War of the Worlds' a Halloween broadcast about aliens invading the world and scared many people.

German radio: Albert Einstein who put forth the theory of relativity at the Opening of the Radio Show in 1930 in Berlin, Joseph Goebbels, William Joyce, Adolph Hitler who was Chancellor of Germany 1933-1945, Paul Ferdonnet, Robert Henry Best, Duncan Newmarch

France radio: Philippe Henriot

WW II radio announcers: Tokyo Rose (name given to Japanese female radio announcer in the South Pacific islands who said negative propaganda to demoralize U.S.A. troops), Axis Sally (from U.S.A. and broadcasted in Italy and North Africa. Axis Sally was employed by the Third Reich in Nazi Germany and was captured and convicted of treason in 1949 in the U.S.A.), Frederick Wilhelm Kaltenbach,

India radio: Ameen Sayani, Zulfiqari Ali Bokhari (British India and Pakistan)

China radio: Mai Feng and Hara Kiyoshit of Zinhua New China Radio

Japan radio: Shigeru Nakamura NHK radio

Some radio shows:

Dave Ramsey, finance, Brentwood, Tenn. 1510 WLAC, IHeart Radio, 585 stations /

Rush Limbaugh, Conservative, Florida 590 Am WOR-AM / Larry King, radio announcer / Sports & Politics Talk Show, Florida / Herman Cain Show Politics/ Frank & Wanda V103.3 R&B Atlanta / Kiss 104.1 R&B Atlanta / Q100 Top 100 Billboard Atlanta / B98.5 Mixture of 80s, 90s, and Now with Steve, Vikki, Charly, Madison / 106.7 News Radio Atlanta / 95.5 News Radio Atlanta / Rock 100.5 with Baily, Southside, Brandi, and Nate / 91.9 JAZZ / 99X Alternative Rock / 105.7 Alternative Rock / 94.9 The Bull Country Radio / 107.5 Spanish Radio Pedro Gonzalez, Music & News, California / 107.9 Hip Hop with DJ Amanda

Gwyneth Williams, current affairs, U.K.
BBC Radio 4

BBC continuity announcers Jasmine Bligh, Elizabeth Cowell, Leslie Mitchell, Jennifer Gray, Andy Crane, Andi Peters, Phillip Schofield, Fritz Spiegl

Russia: Radio Maximun, Echo Moscow

Arabic Language Radio: Voice of Iraq,
Voice of Malaysia, Al-Nour

Australia: Conrad Charlton

China: Rick O'Shea an American in China
3000 radio stations in China

Japan: NHK Fm
Nigeria : Domi

Some Comedians/TV Talk Show Hosts

Merv Griffin of U.S.A. 1925
Sammy Davis Jr. of U.S.A. 1925
Larry King of U.S.A. 1933
Louis C.K. of Mexico 1967
George Carlin of U.S.A. 1937
Jerry Seinfeld of U.S.A. 1954
Chris Rock of U.S.A. 1954
Eddie Murphy of U.S.A. 1961
Robin Williams of U.S.A. 1951
Jim Carrey of Canada 1962
Rosie O'Donnell of U.S.A. 1962
Adam Sandler of U.S.A. 1966
Jimmy Kimmel of U.S.A. 1967
Jimmy Fallon of U.S.A. 1974
Rufus Hound of England 1979
Sarah Silverman of U.S.A. 1970
Joan Rivers of U.S.A. 1933
Richard Pryor of U.S.A. 1940
Ellen DeGeneres of U.S.A. 1958
Steve Martin of U.S.A. 1945
Rodney Dangerfield of U.S.A.1921
Jerry Lewis of U.S.A. 1926
Lucille Ball of U.S.A. 1911
David Letterman of U.S.A. 1947
Meredith Vieira of U.S.A. 1953
Margaret Cho of U.S.A. 1980
Carol Burnett of U.S.A. 1933
Conan O'Brien of U.S.A. 1963
Gabriel Iglesias of Mexico 1976
Michel Denisot of France 1945
Jay Leno of U.S.A. 1950
Johnny Carson of U.S.A. 1925
Anu Hasan of India 1970
Hamid Mir of Pakistan 1966
Oprah Winfrey of U.S.A. 1954
Dr. Phil MacGraw of U.S.A. 1950
Lily Allen of England 1985
Bryant Gumbel 1948
Katie Couric of U.S.A. 1954
Donald Glover 1983
Aziz Ansari 1983
Tetsuko Kuroyanagi of Japan 1933
Mona el-Shazly of Egypt 1973
Jo Soares of Brazil 1938
Rabi Lamichhane of Nepal
Faisal al-Qassem of Syria 1961
Jon Almaas of Norway 1967
Delilah Rene of U.S.A. 1960
Simon Cowell of U.K. 1959

Some Music DJs:

DJ Cream spinned at Teak on the Hudson in Hoboken, New Jersey.
Gina Turner was a guest DJ in New York in dance clubs. Gina was also a yoga instructor.

Jay the DJ is popular in Gunnedah, Australia.
DJ Keelez is a wedding and special events DJ in Los Angeles, California.
DJ Rizey, DJ Abbs, DJ Nomi were DJ employed by Desipride in London, England and DJ'd for many Asian and Indian events held in London.
DJ Jmoney Lovvorn worked party gigs in Memphis, Tennessee.
DJ Africa Oratilwe Hlongwane was a young DJ in Johannesburg, South Africa.
Discohire, Gigmaster, and Party DJ are companies that provide DJ and entertainment
for weddings, special events, and corporate events.

Countries have popular newspapers, tabloids, magazines, News Reports, Weather Team Reports, TV shows and movie guides, cookbooks, comic strips and travel guides printed on paper and online internet.
The newspapers contain news items that happen at the local, state, national, and world levels, weather reports, cartoons and comics, crossword puzzles, Sudoku, word search games, classified ads and employment ads, advertisements, stock prices, sports news, and more.
Vietnam: BAO, Tuoi Tre, Thanh Nien
Africa: Ilanga, Iangesonto, Isolezwe NgeSonto, Confidential, Africa News
South Korea: Chosun Ilbo, Dong-a Ilbo, Hankook Ilbo, Joong Ang Ilbo
Saudi Arabia: Al Eqtisadiah, Al Jazirah, Al Madina, Al Riyadh
Russia: Rossiyskaya Gazeta, Izvestia, Konsomolskaya Pravda, Argumeuty i Fakty, RBK Moscow
Malaysia: Star, Sun Express, Borneo Post
Australia: The Australian, The Age, The Daily Telegraph, Sydney Morning Herald, Herald Sun
Japan: Yomiuri Shimbun, Asahi Shimbun, Mainichi Shimbun, Sankei Shimbun, Nikkei Shimbun, Nihon Keizai Shimbun
U.S.A.: The New York Times, The Wall Street Journal, USA Today, Los Angeles Times, Chicago Tribune, Atlanta Journal & Constitution, Cox Meida, CNN, FOX News, Time Magazine, People Magazine, Elle, Vogue, Better Homes & Gardens, Coastal Living, Mountain Living, Forbes, U.S. News & World Report, TV Guide, Farmer's Almanac, Reader's Digest, Family Circle, Newsmax, MTV Music Television, The Today Show
India: Dainik Jagran (Hindi language), Daily Thanthi (Tamil language), The Times of India (English language), Malayala Manorama (Malayalam language)
Germany: Suddeutsche Zeitung, Die Zeit, BILD, faz.net
Spain: El Nuevo Dia, El Bravado
Sweden: Dagens-Nyheter, Expressen, Metro
France: Le Monde, Le Figaro, Liberation, le Parisien, Metro, L'Equipe
China: Xinhua, People's Daily, China Daily, Guangming Daily, Enlightenment Daily
England: The Daily Telegraph, The Guardian

The paparazzi are photographers who follow celebrities. The paparazzi and tabloids should not publish private photographs, lies, or information about celebrities without their consent.

Big Tent Acts

The Flying Wallendas Acrobats 1905
Barnum & Bailey Ringling Circus 1919.
In 1902, Barnum's Animal Crackers in a box became famous cookies. Animal cookies remain a popular cookie for children.

Animal Life

Children like to learn to mimic animal sounds:
A dog goes 'Ruff Ruff' or 'Bow Wow'.
A cat goes 'Meow'.
A bird goes 'Tweet Tweet'.

A duck goes 'Quack quack quack'.
A cow goes 'Moo'.
A lion goes 'RRRRRRRR'.
A donkey goes 'Hee Haa'.
A horse goes 'Neigh neigh'.
A pig goes 'Oink oink'.
A rooster goes "Cockadoodledoo' or 'Er Er Er Er Er'.
A hen goes 'cluck cluck'.
A sheep goes 'Baa Baa'.
A Tyrannasauras Rex goes 'ROAR'.

Through milleniums of time, animals have helped humanity to survive. Humans drink the milk of goats and cows, eat eggs from hens and fish, and eat meat from cows, sheep, chickens, fish, and more. Animal skin and furs have protected humans from the elements of nature. Oxen helped man to plow the fields to plant crops. Horses provided transportation by horseback or by pulling chariots, carriages, stagecoaches,and wagons. Scientists have studied animal in their natural habitats and made inventions for humanity such as airplanes from watching birds fly and painting white stripes on black tarmac and concrete like the stripes on a zebra. Pets provide comfort and amusement. Animal activists promote respect for all animals and demand that no animals should be treated with cruelty. Many countries set aside habitats for animals. The ostrich is the fastest two-legged creature on earth and can run 48 mph or 77 kph. The earth contains some very dangerous animal species of snakes, reptiles, spiders, viruses and bacteria. Scientists, educators, and journalists and many more are needed to preserve humanity and the global environment.

Famous Magicians

David Copperfield of U.S.A. 1956
Harry Houdini of Hungary 1926
Dynamo of U.S.A. 1952
Cyril Takayama of Japanese, Morocco, and France 1973
Steven Hatfield also known as Cowboy Hank of U.S.A. Hank played 10 instruments with the Hank band 2015.

Famous Jugglers

Jason Garfield of U.S.A. 1974
Anthony Gatto of U.S.A. 1973
Francis Brunn of Germany 1922
Thomas Dietz of Germany 1982
Stefan Sing of Germany 1980
Toby Walker of Wales 1989
Alexander Koblikov of Russia 1987

Famous Puppeteers/Ventriloquists

Frank OZ of U.K
Jason Jordan Segel of USA
Jim Henson of USA
Brad Garrett of USA
Kermit Love of USA
Ronnie Burkett of Canada
Patrick Marber of England
Kevin Clash of USA
Ramdas Padhye of India

Theme Parks / Nature Parks / Casinos

Walt Disney / Disneyworld 1901
Six Flags Amusement Parks 1961
White Water Rides 1980
Aquariums
River Boat Tours
African Safari Tours
Telescopes
Casinos (Roulette Wheel, Slot machines)

Some advertisers say you will have 'Twice the Fun' or you will 'Double Your Fun' at their entertainment venue.

Shows / Exhibits

Cirque du Soleil of Canada 1984
Shen Yun Chinese Dance Company 2006
Music concert
Art Exhibit or Museum Exhibit
Cooking Shows
Fashion Shows
Horse Show
Dog & Cat Show
Flower Show
Gem & Rock Show
Car Show
Japan 3D Exhibits
Science Exhibition

Dinosaur Exhibit
Human Body Exhibit
The Science of Spying Exhibits
Fireworks Show
Botanical Gardens

Events

Taste of the Town Restaurant Sampler
Rocket and Satellite Launch
Military Event
Movie Premiere or Art Debut
International Film Festival
Music CD or book promotion
Building Opening, Dedication, or Demolition
Gala Public Event
Soiree Private Event
Fundraiser
Insurance Open enrollment Seminar
School Graduation and Diploma Award
Birthday Party
Retirement Party
Engagement Party, Wedding, Honeymoon
Bridal Gift Shower
Baby Gift Shower
Space / Sky Watch Event
International Exhibit
News Conference
Important Business Meeting / Convention
5 K Run or Walk for Charity

Political leader, important dignitaries, and diplomats are often invited to events.
At many events, special amenities are provided for disabled or handicapped individuals.
Some events require high security.
Always watch your children and watch for their safety, especially at crowded events or around bodies of water.

MOVIES/TV SHOWS

It is impossible to list all movies, tv shows, thespians (actresses, actors), producers, directors, set designers, set crews, movie promoters, costume designers, makeup artists, or scriptwriters in this book.

Parents can preview books, TV shows, and movies to decide if the content is appropriate for their children. Many people believe that materials containing sex or violence is only appropriate for mature adult audiences.

Documentary about World History
Andrew Marrs BBC History In the World

Movie about Napoleonic War in 1813: Robert Louis Stevenson's St. Ives, 1998.

Movies about WW I and WW II: Hell's Angels 1930 by Howard Hughes, The Best Years of Our Lives 1946 by Samuel Goldwyn,
Casablanca 1942 with Humphrey Bogart and Ingrid Bergman,
African Queen 1952 with Humphrey Bogart, Katherine Hepburn, Paul Henreid, Claude Rain, and Conrad Veidt. The song As Time Goes By 1931 by Herman Hupfeld was featured in Casablanca. Night and Fog 1955 by Alain Resnais a French film, The Sound of Music 1959 by Robert Wise with a song "My Favorite Things' written by Rodgers & Hammerstein,
Das Boot based on the German novel by Lothar Gunthor Buchheim,
The Guns of Navarone 1961 with Irene Papas, Anthony Quinn, Gregory Peck, David Nevin, Anthony Quayle.
Battle of Britain 1969 by Guy Hamilton.
Salon Kitty 1976. The Remains of the Day 1993 with Anthony Hopkins.
The Good Shephard 2006 by Robert De Niro. Enigma 2001 produced by Mick Jagger and Lorne Michaels,
Snuf De Hond in Oorlogstijd 2008 from the Netherlands.
Schlinder's List 1993,
Letters from Iwo Jima 2006 by Clint Eastwood, The Boy in the Striped Pajamas 2008, An American in Paris 1951 by Vincente Minnelli
Green Zone 2010 based in Iraq starring Matt Damon. Green Day is based on the story by Rajiv Chandrusekaran (b.1973) who is an American journalist. The movie grossed $94.9 million U.S. dollars, The Debt 2007 a German film, Protektor

2009 by Marek Najbrt, Beyond the Steppes by Vanja D'alcantara when Russia invaded Poland, In Darkness 2011 when German Nazis occupied the city of Lvov, Poland, The English Patient with Ralph Fiennes 1995. The Grand Budapest Hotel 2014 set in Hungary between the wars, Rangoon 2017.

Movie about cold war between Soviet-bloc countries and US-led western countries from 1945-1990 regarding political, economic, and ideological differences: Jet Pilot 1957 with John Wayne and Janet Leigh

Movie about Vietnam War: Good Morning, Vietnam 1987 with Robin Williams, Rambo with Sylvester Stallone, war veteran

Movies about Korean War: Go-ji-jeon 2011, The Bridges at Toko-ri 2001, The Frontline 2011 by Jang Hoon with Shin Ha-Kyun

Movie about life in or after leaving the Army: Blue Hawaii 1961 with Elvis Presley, GI Blues 1960 with Elvis

Movies about Arab-Israeli Conflicts: Tears of GAZA 2010 a Norway film, Lemon Tree 2008, Paradise Now 2005, Hanna K 1983, The Years War Israel and The Arabs 1999, Against All Odds: In Search of a Miracle 2005, Zero Motivation 2014 by Talya Lavie, Waltz with Bashir 2008, Patriot's Day by Peter Berg 2016 about Boston Marathon bombing by an Islamic terrorist.

Movies about Egyptian Prince: The Prince of Egypt 1999

Movies about slavery of the Roman Republic Empire: Gladiator 2000, Spartacus 1960

Movies about white slavery during the Muslim Ottoman Empire: The Ottomans Europe's Muslim Emperors

Movies about African Middle-Eastern slavery: Santa Fe Teail 1940, Roots 1988, Beloved 1998, Ashanti 1979, Django Unchained 2012, Lincoln 2012.

Movies about wars in U.S.A.: Gone With The Wind starring Clark Gable & Vivien Leigh, The Patriot starring Mel Gibson, Washington the Warrior Documentary by Robert M. Wise, Rough Crossings by Simon Schama about African slaves who fought on Britain's side of the American Revolutionary War, Glory 1989 with Matthew Broderick. Bury My Heart At Wounded Knee with Chevez Ezaneh and August Schellenber 2007.

Movies about fictional wars in the U.S.A: Red Dawn 1984, 2012

Movies about anger: Anger Management 2003 with Adam Sandler and Jack Nicholson featuring Jimmy Buffett's song 'Margaritaville.'

Movies about 1920s /1930s in the U.S.A:

The Great Gatsby 2013 version starring Leonardo DiCaprio directed by Baz Lurhmann version based on the 1925 novel by F. Scott Fitzgerald set during the alcohol prohibition in the U.S.A. from 1920-1933. The Great Gatsby 1974 version starred Robert Redford, The Artist 2011, Water for Elephants 2011

Movies about oil wells in Texas: Giant 1956 with Rock Hudson and Elizabeth Taylor

Movies about mafia, crimes, or computer corruption: The Godfather starring Marlon Brando and Al Pacino, Rocky starring Sylvester Stallone, The Net with Sandra Bullock, Enemy of State starring Gene Hackman and Will Smith, Flash of Genius by Marc Abraham which is about the invention of the intermittent windshield wiper was stolen, Eraser with Arnold Schwarzenegger and Vanessa Williams, Goodfellas 1990. Arnold Schwarzenegger became a governor of California. Vanessa Williams won a Miss America talent pageant before she became an actress.

Movies about singers: Lady Sings the Blues 1972 starring Diana Ross who portrays Billie Holliday. The movie has a scene in which the band bus drives through a KKK white-supremist group rally during a time of racial riots in the U.S.A. during the 1950s. The Black Panthers is a black supremist group. The NAACP is the National Association for the Advancement of Colored People. The NAAWP is the National Association for the Advancement of White People. Walk the Line 2005 about Johnny Cash. The Beatles: Eight Days A Week. The Touring Years 2016 by Ron Howard.

Movies about pets: Why We Love Cats and Dogs by Ellen Goosenberg Kent a PBS Nature production

Movies about swimming the English Channel between England and France: Dangerous When Wet, 1953
On A Clear Day 2005 United Kingdom

Britain movies: To The Lighthouse 1983 based on a novel by author Virginia Woolf, How the Earth Changed History The Incredible Story of the Natural Forces That Have Shaped Our History 2 DVD Disc set BBC.

Britain children's movie based on the novel by Frank Cottrell Boyce that was an international bestseller: Millions 2004.

South Korean movie: Marriage Blue 2013 a comedy.

Japan movies: Seven Samurai, Tokoyo Story, Antarctica, The Pirates of Bubuan 1972 by Shohei Imamura about pirates on a Philippine island, Outlaw 1973 about a Japanese soldier who returns homes after war, The Hidden Fortress 1958 Kakushi toride nu san akunin by Akira Kurosawa, Kagemusha The Shadow Warrior 1980 by Akira Kurosawa, 13 Assassins 2010 by Takashi Miike about revenge on an evil ruler.

Chinese Movies: Crouching Tiger, Hidden Dragon by Ang Lee with Chow Yun-Fat and Michelle Yeoh, King Fu by Stephen Chow from Hong Kong, Dim Sum Funeral 2008, Snow Flower and the Secret Fan 2011 by Wayne Wang, Curse of the Golden Flower 2006 by Zhang Yimou which grossed $78.57 million, Memoirs of a Geisha 2005 by Rob Marshall, Crouching Tiger, Hidden Dragon 2000 by Ang Lee, Shaolin 2011 a martial arts film with Andy Lau, Nicholas Tse, Jackie Chan, Fan Bingbing, and Shaoqun Yu about a lord who take refuge with monks, Detective Dee and the Mystery of the Phantom Flame 2010 by Tsui Hark a murder mystery

Sweden movie:
The Girl With the Dragon Tatoo 2011 a crime movie, Sommarlek (Summer Interlude) 1951 by Ingmer Bergman, Sound of Noise 2010 a comedy, Wallander by Henning Mankell about a chief inspector who investigates crimes

Czech Movie: The Country Teacher 2008 by Bohdan Slama, Protektor

Poland Movie: IDA 2013 by Pawel Pawlikowski about an orphan in a convent planning to become a nun

Pakistan Movie:
Zero Bridge by Tariq Tapa about daily life

Turkish Movie: The Ottoman Republic Osmanli Cumnuriyeti by Gani Mujde

Jordan Movie: When I Saw You 2012 by Annemarie Jacir about refugees from Palestime,

Movie about Iran: The Stoning of Soraya M. 2009 based on a true story with Jim Caviezel & Shohreh Aghdashloo

France Movies: La Vie En Rose - The Extraordinary Life of Edith Piaf 2007, Cache (Hidden) by Michael Haneke starring Daniel Auteuil, Juliette Binoche, Maurice Benichou, Annie Girardot, Bernard Le Coq, Elle 2016, Coco Before Chanel 2009, Children of Paradise by Marcel Carne, The French Lieutenant's Woman 1981 by Karel Reisz, Vigo 1999 by Julien Temple about French filmmaker Jean Vigo, who died of tuberculosis at age 29. A propos de Nice 1930 by Jean Vigo and Russian filmmaker Boris Kaufman, Zero de Conduite (Zero for Conduct) 1933 by Jean Vigo, L'Atalante 1934 by Jean Vigo.

Germany Movies: Into Great SIlence a film about Carthusian monastery in

France by Philip Groning, The Bitter Tears of Petra Von Lant 1972 and Ali: Fear Eats the Soul by Rainer Werner Fassbinder about a beauty who wants to be a model. It was said that Fear Eats the Soul is similar to All That Heaven Allows by Douglas Sirk 1955 with Jane Wyman and Rock Hudson.

India Hindi Movies: Shaadi Ke Baad 1972 by L.V. Prasad with Jeetendra, Shaadi Ke 2014, Like Stars on Earth with Taare Zameen Par 2007 by Aamir Khan, Paa 2009 about a boy with a genetic defect that causes accelerated aging. Railroad Children 2016 by Prithvi Konanur

Jewish Hebrew Movies: Sallah 1964 starring Topol, Newland 1994 by Chaim Sharir, A Matter of Size 2009 by Sharon Maymon

Italy Movies: Angela 2002 by Roberta Torre with Donatella Finacchiaro, Light of My Eyes 2001 by Giuseppe Piccioni, Il Postino The Postman 1994 by Massiimo Troisi and Michael Radford, Otello The Royal Opera by Giuseppe Verd 1887 Based on Shakeseare, Wolfgang Amadeus Mozart 1984 by Milos Forman, The Story of the Jews with Simon Schama 2013 by BBC

Rwanda movie: Munyurangabo 2007 by Lee Isaac Chung about 2 boys who are supposed to be enemies but are friends.

Uganda movie: War Dance 2007 by Sean Fine and Andrea Nix Fine about children who suffered horror yet remained in strong spirit

Spain Movies: Flowers 2014 by Jon Garano & Jose Mari Goenaga Basque romance, Instructions not Included 2013 by Egenio Derbez about a father raising his baby alone, Ilona arrives with the Rain 1996 by Sergio Cabrera about a prisoner who is released from prison, Keiko en Peligro 1990 by Rene Cardona III directed by Hugo Stiglitz about an extraterrestrial whale, Marshland (La Isla Minima) 2014 about two girls who go missing in Andalusia, Spain, Pulling Strings with Laura Ramsey, Jaime Camil, and Omar Chaparro who play hardworking mariachi singers, Me, Too 2009 by Alvaro Pastor and Antonio Naharro, Sugar 2009 by Anna boden about a baseball pitcher in the Dominican Republic, Talk to Her 2002, Como Reproducir Plantas

Portugal Movie: The Middle of the World (O Caminho das Nuvens) 2003 by Vincente Amorim about a family of 7 who bicycle 2000 miles across Brazil in search of a job.

Russian Movie: Elena 2011 by Andrey Zvyagintsev about an older couple in Moscow, Russia.

Movie about Russia: Dr. Zhivago with Omar Sharif 1965.

Brazil Movie: Elena 2012 by Petra Costa about a Brazilian woman who moves to New York

Fantasy/Science fiction movies: Mad Monster Party 1967 by Jules Bass. 2001: A Space Odyssey a 1969 film by Stanley Kubrick that had a famous movie soundtrack, Close Encounters 1977, King Kong in 1933, Star Wars with Jedi and lightsabers produced and created by George Lucas in 1977 starring Mark Hamill and Carrie Fisher. Star Wars had a 13 million dollar budget and grossed $178,119,600 U.S. dollars. Carrie Fisher was the daughter of Eddie Fisher and Debbie Reynolds, both were thespians. Todd Fisher is her brother. Joely Fisher and Tricia Leigh Fisher are half-sisters by their mother Connie Stevens. Aladdin 1986 with Bud Spencer about a genie in a bottle, Excalibur 1988 about King Arthur who defended Britain from Saxon invaders, Lancelot, and Tintagel Castle, Buffy the Vampire Slayer, The Return of Jafar 1994, E.T. and Jurassic Park produced by Steven Spielberg, RoboCop 1987, Jumanji 1995 & 2017, Star Trek 2002, 2009, The Abyss 1989, Avatar 2009 directed by James Cameron, Aliens starring Sigourney Weaver, Flatliners 1990 and 2017, Interview with a Vampire starring Tom Cruise, Ghostbusters 2016, Hugo 2011, The Space Movie 1980. Men in Black 1997, The Hobbit 2012, The Lord of the Rings 2001, Kazaam 1996 with Shaquille O'Neal a basketball player, Phase IV a film by Saul Bass 1974 about desert ants who wage war, The Hills Have Eyes by Alexandre Aja a 2006 French film about cannibalism and a remake of the 1977 film, Odd Thomas 2013 with Anton Yeldin who was the son of Irina Korina and Viktor Yelchin who were Russian figure skaters for the Leningrad Ice Ballet. Anton Yeldin died in an auto accident when he was 27 years old when his car went into reverse and he was pinned against a tree. Guardians of the Galaxy by James Gunn 2014.

Space movies: Apollo 11 about the U.S.A. moon landing, Apollo 13, Apollo 18, The Martian 2015 starring Matt Damon, Gravity 2013 with Sandra Bullock and George Clooney.

Russian Space Movies: Pilot Prix's Inquest 1978 a Russian movie about a voyage to Saturn, The Grand Space Voyage 1974, Aelita 1924 by Yakov Protazanov, Cosmic Voyage 1935 by Vasily Zhuravlev, Solaris 1972.

Pirate Movies: The Pirate Movie 1948 with Gene Kelly, The Pirate Movie 1982 with Christopher Atkins

Movies with spiritual or religious themes, ghosts or ideas:
It's A Wonderful Life with Jimmy Stewart and Donna Reed 1944, Lillies of the Field 1963 with Sidney Poitier, The Ten Commandments starring Charlton Heston, Ben-Hur starring Charlton Heston, Oh, God with George Burns 1977, Raiders of the Lost Ark 1981, Armageddon starring Bruce Willis, Ghost starring Demi Moore. Poltergeist 1982, Apocalypse Now, The Passion of Christ starring Mel Gibson, Tribulation 2000 with Gary Busey, Peter 7 Paul Lalonde, and Mariam Carvell, Left Behind: World at War 2005, and 2014, Saving God 2008, Gandhi starring Ben Kingsley, The Ballad of Narayama a Japanese movie by Keisuke Kinoshita, The Trouble with Angels and Where Angels Go, Trouble Follows about a Catholic school, Love Finds You in Sugarcreek, Ohio 2014 about the Amish, Fly Wheel 2003 by Alex Kendrick, about a used car salesman, The Bucket List 2007 about making a list of things you want to accomplish before you die, A Little Piece of Heaven by Mimi Leder 2000, Miracles from Heaven 2016 by Patricia Riggen, Sins of the Preacher by John Stimpson 2013, 10 Questions for the Dalai Lama by Rick Ray 2006, Dharm 2007 a Hindi film by Bhavna Talwar, The Leopard 1963 an Italian epic period (historical) drama, Silence 2016 by Martin Scorsese, The 12 Biggest Lies by Andre van Heerden. The Drop Box by Brian Ivie 2014, Angel House with Toni Collette.

Movie about lives lost in fires:
Ladder 49, (2004)

Movies about car racing: Champion 2017 by Judd Brannon, Viva Las Vegas 1964 and Speedway 1968 with Elvis, Rush 2013 about Formula 1 racing, Lucky Logan 2017

Movie about clothes fashion: The September Issue 2009 by R.J. Cutler, The Eye Has to Travel 2012 by Diana Vreeland about Harper's Bazaar magazine

Movies about Seniors: Bucket List 2007, Grumpy Old Men 1993, On Golden Pond 1981, Driving Miss Daisy 1989,

Comedy Movies: Boy Did I Get The Wrong Number 1966 with Bob Hope and Phyllis Diller, Arthur 1981 with Dudley Moore and Liza Minelli who was the daughter of Judy Garland, Arthur was remade in 2008. Trading Places with Eddie Murphy, Tootsie 1982 with Dustin Hoffman, My Cousin Vinny starring Joe Pesci, Beetlejuice 1988 about a haunted house, Meet the Browns by Tyler Perry. Meet the Browns was also a TV show.

Mrs. Doubtfire starring Robin Williams with the song Jump Around by House of Pain, Tyler Perry's Madea, Yes Man with Jim Carey, Airplane 1980, Dumb and Dumber 1994, Monty Python and the Holy Grail 1975, The Odd Couple 1968, Harold & Kumar Go To White Castle with John Cho (2nd generation Korean American) and Kal Penn (2nd generation Indian American), Anchorman: The Legend of Ron Burgundy, Stealing Harvard with Tom Green, Jason Lee, Megan Mullally, Dennis Farina 2002. 13 Going On 30 with Jennifer Garner.

Comedy / Action Movie: Hot Shots! With Charlie Sheen and Valeria Golino 1993, Wrongfully Accused with Leslie Nielsen 1998 with Richard Crenna, Kelly LeBrock.

Comedy / Drama Movie: Diary of a Mad Housewife 1970 by Frank Perry, Lady Bird 2017, Middle Men 2010 by George Gallo. The Three Musketeers. Little Red Wagon by David Anspaugh about a young boy concerned with homeless families.

Comedy /or Romance Movie: The Man in the Moon 1991 with Sam Waterston and Reese Witherspoon, Clueless 1985 by Amy Heckering.

Movies that are Musicals: Singin in the Rain 1952 with Gene Kelly who was an actor, singer, dancer, choreographer, director, and producer. Gene Kelly was married to Patricia Ward who was a literary author.
Mamma Mia 2008 by Phyllida Lloyd

Movie about a ballerina: The Red Shoes 1948

Movie about a woman who invented a mop: Joy 2015 with Jennifer Lawrence

Movie about a paralyzed man who communicated by blinking his left eye and was based on a true story of Jean-Dominique Bauby of France 1997: The Diving Bell and the Butterfly 2007

Movies about Sports:
Take Me Out to the Ballgame 1949 with Gene Kelly by Busby Berkeley, Rocky 1976, Creed 2015, Ice Castles 1978 about a blind ice skater.
Invictus by Clint Eastwood 2009 about rugby in South Africa,
Bull Durham 1988 with Kevin Costner by Ron Shelton about a minor league,
Draft Day 2014, For Love of the Game 1999 by Sam Raimi and Dana Stevens

Movies with Martial Arts:
Kung Fu Yoga 2017 with Jackie Khan

Movies with horses: Black Stallion 1979, Seabiscuit 2003, Flicka 2006

Western Movies with cowboys: 1971 Big Jake with John Wayne, 1969 True Grit, 1967 El Dorado, Bronco Billy 1980 with Clint Eastwood, Unforgiven 1992, Two Mules for Sister 1970, The Paleface 1948 with Jane Russell as Calamity Jane, The Texan 1930 with Gary Cooper, StageCoach with Bing Crosby, Ann Margaret.

Thrillers/Adventure/Drama/ Controversial/ or Smash Hit Movies
The Day of the Dolphins 1973 with George C. Scott about communicating with dolphins. Walking Tall 1973 and 2004, Rain Main with Dustin Hoffman and Tom Cruise 1988.
Silkwood 1983 about alleged murder at a plutonium processing plant starring Kurt Russell, Cher, and Meryl Streep.
Out of Africa 1985 starring Robert Redford and Meryl Streep about a coffee plantation in Kenya, Africa. Die Hard 1988 starring Bruce Willis.
Home Alone 1990. Switched At Birth 1991.
It Could Happen to You starring Nicholas Cage about a winning lottery ticket.
The Fugitive with Harrison Ford, Space Cowboy starring Tommy Lee Jones, Double Jeopardy with Tommy Lee Jones and Ashley Judd 1999.
The Pelican Brief starring Julia Roberts, Jaws starring Richard Dreyfuss and Robert Shaw,
Deep Impact starring Morgan Freeman, Top Gun with Tom Cruise,

The 100-foot Journey with Om Puri and Manash Dayal,
James Bond Agent 007 series movies that were played by 7 different actors, the 1st was Sean Connery;
Batman movies that were played by 10 actors, the first one was Bruce Wayne in 1966,
Spiderman movies, Superman movies, Wonderwoman movies, Mickey Mouse, Cookie Monster and Big Bird Muppet movies, Iron Man 2008,
Kindergarten Cop 1990 by Ivan Reitman,
Panic Room 2002 by David Fincher starring Jodie Foster,
Titanic about the oceanliner that sank in 1912 in the Atlantic Ocean,
Smilla's Sense of Snow 1997, a Danish-British-American thriller.
Paying It Forward 2000 is about doing a favor with a possible hope of repayment of a favor in the future.
O Brother, Where Art Thou? 2000 by Ethan and Joel Coen with George Clooney.
Bourne Supremacy in which an assassin played by Matt Damon apologizes for killing,
Slumdog Millionaire 2008 starring Dev Patel.
The Deep End of the Ocean with Michelle Pfeiffer about a kidnapping,
Lorenzo's Oil by George Miller and starring Susan Sarandon about parents determined to help a needy child.
A Beautiful Mind by Ron Howard starring Russel Crowe, includes a character diagnosed with mental illness
John Q. 2002 with Denzel Washington who takes hostages in a hospital as insurance denied coverage for his child.
Copying Beethoven 2006 by Agnieszka Holland,
Men of Honor 2006 with Cuba Gooding
The Blind Side 2009 starring Sandra Bullock about a family who helps a homeless teenager who plays football.
King Arthur: Legend of the Sword 2004 believed to be based on a real person who lived centuries ago.
The Accountant 2016 Ben Affleck
Outbreak 1995 starring Rene Russo, Dustin Hoffman, and Morgan Freeman about a lethal virus epidemic
Ondine 2010 a Denmark film by Neil Jordan about a woman caught in a f ishing net.
2012 with John Cusak (2009) about a family trying to keep alive amidst global catastrophes.
Facing Darkness 2017 by Samaritan's Purse about Ebola Virus.
Mama Mia starring Meryl Streep, filmed in Greece.
The Women 1939 starring Joan Crawford and the remake dated 2008.
Salmon Fishing in the Yemen 2012 a British movie by Lasse Holstrom with Kristin Scott Thomas and Amr Waked
Coma by Michael Crichton 1978
The Kite Runner 2007 about a kite flying tournament in Afghanistan. The Great Debaters with Denzel Washington 2007.
The Help 2009 based on the novel by Kathryn Stockett
Breaking Bad 2017 based on the TV Series about a science teacher who begins to manufacture drugs and it ruins his life and his family's life. Atlas Shrugged 2011 about a railroad.

Movie about mathematicians: Travelling Salesman 2012

Movie about teacher who inspires his students: Stand and Deliver 1988, Mona Lisa Smile with Julia Roberts 2003.

Movies about revenge: Cape Fear 1991 with Nick Nolte

Movies about Crime Drama: Married to the Mob starring Alec Baldwin 1988,The Call starring Halle Berry, The Hateful Eight by director Quentin Tarantino with Tim Roth, Jennifer Jason Leigh, Samuel L. Jackson, Walton Goggins about a bounty hunter and his prisoner in Montana. Big Trouble 2002. Looper with Bruce Willis.

Movies with several themes:
Rachel Getting Married 2008,
All About My Mother 1999 by Almodovar, a Spanish film.

Movies about addiction or rehabilitation:
Rachel Getting Married 2008,
Clean and Sober 1988 with Michael Keaton and directed by Glenn Gordon Caron with screenplay by Tod Carroll
28 days 2000
The Man with the Golden Arm 1955
Permanent Midnight 1998
Gridlock'd 1997

Movies about mental hospital or psychiatric ward or crazy:
It's Kind of a Funny Story 2010
12 Monkeys 1995
One Flew Over the Cuckoo's Nest 1975
Shutter Island 2010, Stonehurst Asylum 2014, Zela! 2010, MadHouse 2005, Just Crazy Enough 2012.

Movies about prison:
Jailhouse Rock 1957 with Elvis Presley, The Shawshank Redemption 1994 by Frank Darabont and story by Stephen King, Alcatraz 1962, Papillon 1973, 'R' 2010 a Danish film, A Prophet 2009 by Jacques Audiard, Le Trou 1960 a French film, The Great Escape 1963, A Man Escaped 1956, The Stanford Prisoner Experiment 2015, Bronson 2008, Brubaker 1980 with Robert Redford, Brute Force 1947, Cook Hand Luke 1967, From Alcatraz 1977, The Experiment 2001 a German film.

Movies with storms: Avalanche 1978, The Perfect Storm 2000 by Wolfgang Peterson starring George Clooney. The Guardian starring Kevin Costner 2006. Twister starring Bill Paxton Helen Hunt 1996, Hurricane Katrina. The Impossible about the tsunami in Indonesia.

Movie about a mother who dies in childbirth and the family: Jersey Girl with Jennifer Lopez and Ben Affleck

Movies with Romance or Love Themes: Pillow Talk with Rock Hudson and Doris Day 1959,
The Three Musketeers 1948 and 2011 directed by Paul W. S. Anderson,
Love Story with Ryan O'Neal and Ali McGraw 1970, The Bodyguard with Whitney Houston and Kevin Costner 1992, Where the Boys Are 1960, Clambake 1967 with Elvis Presley, Serendipity with John Cusak and Kate Beckinsale 2001, Nights in Rodanthe with Richard Gere and Diane Lane, Romeo & Julkiet 1968 and 1996,
An Officer and A Gentleman with Richard Gere & Debra Winger 1982,
The Vow 2012 with Rachel McAdams and Channing Tatum about a married couple who are in a car wreck and amnesia caused by brain injury impacts their marriage,

Movie about a child in an orphanage who finds romance in adulthood:
Jane Eyre 1971 with George C. Scott and Susannah York

Thriller / Romance Movie:
To Catch A Thief by Alfred Hitchcock 1955 with Cary Grant and Grace Kelly. Grace Patricia Kelly became the Princess of Monaco after marrying Prince Rainer III in 1956, Naked Gun 1988.

Movie about divorce and love:
Kramer vs. Kramer, Are We There Yet? 2005, Mrs. Doubtfire 1993, The Tempest with Molly Ringwald 1982 filmed in New York and Greece

Movie about a husband living a double life in a marriage: The Pilot's Wife 2002.

Movie about STDs (sexually transmitted disease):
Calliope 1971

Movie about a divorce and a psychopath killer: Gone Girl by David Fincher 2014. A psychopath is a person who lacks empathy for others.

Movie about problems in a marriage: Unfaithful with Richard Gere and Diane Lane, Deceived 1991 by Damian Harris with Goldie Hawn and John Heard, Secrets 1971, Plaza Suite 1971

Shakespeare movie: The Tempest 2010 by Julie Taymor based on the play in 1611 by William Shakespeare. Romeo & Juliet 2010

Mystery Movies

Alfred Hitchcock / Agatha Christie, Get Smart with Secret Agent 23 and Secret Agent 99, Pink Panther and Inspector Clouseau, Sherlock Holmes.

Family and Children's Movies:

Looney Tunes 1930-1969 by Warner Brothers that included characters Buddy, Bosko, Bugs Bunny, Daffy Duck, Foghorn Leghorn, Elmer Fudd, Porky Pig, Yosemite Sam, Speedy Gonzales, Pepe le Pew, Tasmanian Devil, Tweety, Sylvester, Marvin the Martian, Petunia Pig, Witch Hazel, Beans, Barnyard Dog, Henery Hawk, Beaky Buzzard, Granny, and more. Mickey Mouse 1927 (and his friends Minnie Mouse, Pluto, Goofy, Donald Duck, and his nemesis Pete), Snow White & The Seven Dwarfs 1937, Peculiar Penguins by Walt Disney 1934, Peter Pan and Tinkerbell by Walt Disney 1935, Mary Poppins and her flying umbrella 1964, The Wizard of Oz with a flying witch and a wizard starring Judy Garland and her dog named Toto 1939. Here Comes Peter Cottontail 1971 by Rankin/Bass Productions based on the 1957 novel The Easter Bunny That Overslept by Priscilla and Otto Friedrich, Ferdinand. Happily Ever After 1990, 2004, 2005 a trilogy.

Home Alone, The Lion King, Under the Sea. The Little Mermaid, Happy Feet, Grumpy Old Men, Toy Story, The Lego Movie, Beethoven's 5th, Smurfs, C.H.O.M.P.S. 1979 about a robot dog, Ferris Bueller's Day Off 1986, Kindergarten Cop 1990 by Ivan Reitman, The Castaways on Gilligan's Island, Rescue from Gilligan's Island 1978. Alice Looking Through the Glass 1987. Gilligan's Island was a TV show, Pinnochio, Harry Potter, The Family Man with Nicolas Cage, Madagascar movies, Beauty & The Beast, Moana, Trolls, Up, Rio, Frozen, Pippi Longstocking, Aladdin 1992, Dennis the Menace 1993. Motocross Kids 2004 with a chimp, Alice in Wonderland and Chesire Cat 2010, Cars 2006 by Pixar, Alvin and the Chipmunks 2007, UP 2009 about a balloon salesman, Paddington Bear 2014 and 2017.

Sesame Street movies: Follow That Bird (1985) and The Adventures of Elmo in Grouchland (1999) with the Sesame Street Muppets: Elmo, Big Bird, Cookie Monster, Mr. Snuffleupagus, Bert, Ernie, Grover, Oscar the Grouch, Susan, Bob, Maria, Muppet, Gordon, Hoots the Owl, Grundgetta, Guy Smiley, Prairie Dawn, Baby Natasha, Sam the Robot, Count von Count.

Casper's Scary School 2006.

Cinderella 2015 which grossed $544 million in the U.S.A, The Secret Life of Pets 2016 by Chris Renaud. Boss Baby with Alec Baldwin 2017.

Movies about Mining for Gold:

Blood Diamond, Dreams of Dust 2007 by director Laurent Salgues a French film

Native American Movie Themes:

Smoke Signals, with Chris Eyre, Dances with Wolves with Kevin Costner, The Last of the Mohicians with Russell Means.

Movies about obsessions. Obsessions are not necessarily bad except when they hurt people.

Fatal Attraction starring Glenn Close and Michael Douglas 1987 about jealousy and obsession. Unfaithful with Richard Gere and Diane Lane about infidelity, murder, and obsession.

Irresistible starring Susan Sarandon and Sam Neill, 2006 about mental fixation and beliefs.

Obsession 1949, Obsession 1976, Obsession 1997, Obsessed 2009
The Silence of the Lambs a Jonathan Demme film 1991 and Hannibal 2001 about a cannibal killer.
House of Sand and Fog with Ben Kinsley 2003, Irrestible by Ann Turner with Sam Neill, Susan Sarandon, and Emily Blunt.
Movie with a support group: Cake with Jennifer Aniston 2014.
Movie about being trapped: Trapped 2007 about being trapped in your own mind, Trapped 2007 about human kidnappings and human trafficking.
Movies about people hiding in attics or houses:
Hider in the House 1989,
4closed 2013 with Marlee Matin who is a deaf actress and directed by Nick Lyon about a man who spies on a family with computers and hacks their teenager's cell phone with evil intention.
Wakefield 1989
Within 2015
Inside 2007 a French horror film
Kidnapped 2011 a Spanish film by Miguel Angel Vivas
Horror Movies Frankenstein 1931, It 2017 based on the novel by Stephen King. The Texas Chainsaw Massacre 1974, The Amityville Horror 1979, Monsters by Gareth Edwards 2010, Zombies by Hamid Torabpour 2017, Misery 1990 tarring Kathy Bates and James Caan, Bram Stoker's Dracula 1992 by Framcis Ford Cappola based on the 1897 novel by Bram Stoker. Day of the Dead 1985 by George A. Romero with Joseph Pilato, Lori Cadille, and Terry Alexander. Dawn of the Dead 2004 by Zack Snyder. From Hell 2001 about Jack the Ripper a serial killer in London in 1888.
Movies about Time Travel:
Back to the Future 1985 starring Michael Fox, Kate & Leopold 2001 starring Meg Ryan and Hugh Jackmann, Déjà Vu 2006 with Denzel Washington

Movies about computers or cyber crimes:
Hackers 1985, The Net 1995,
23 produced in1998 about German hackers, Pirates of Silicon Valley 1999 about Bill Gates and Steve Jobs,
The Social Network 2010 about Facebook and Mark Zuckerberg, Jobs 2013 Steve Jobs Apple founder, Grandma's Boy 2006 video game creator, War Games 1983, Sneakers 1992, Swordfish 2001, Antitrust 2001, Takedown 2000, Untraceable 2008, Eagle Eye 2008, Killswitch 2014, Firewall 2006, Snowden 2016
Movies with radio: Private Parts by Ivan Reitman and Betty Thomas about a radio on-air personality with Howard Stern who was a radio announcer on Sirius XM satellite radio, Sleepless in Seattle (1998) with Tom Hanks
Movies about airplanes:
Airport 1975 with George Kennedy, Charlton Heston, and Karen Black, The Concord 1979 with Alain Delon and Susan Blakely and Robert Wagner, Airplane 1980 a comedy wit Robert Hays, Julie Hagerty, and Lloyd Bridges, Snakes on a Plane 2006 with Samuel L. Jackson,
Amelia 2009, The Wright Brothers 1997, Kitty Hawk 2003, Julianna Margulies, and Nathan Phillips, Sully 2016 about a passenger plane landing on the Hudson River in New York.
Movies about Cooking:
Julie & Julia 2009 by Nora Ephron starring Amy Adams based on a true story about a woman who cooked every recipe in Julia Child's Cookbook. Julia Child helped write the screenplay along with Julie Powell and Alex Prud'homme.
Chocolat a French movie 2000.
The Best Exotic Marigold Hotel with Judi Dench 2012 filmed in India.
Movies about hair styling: Hairspray 1988, 2007, Shampoo 1975, Vidal Sassoon 2010, Good Hair by Chris Rock

2009 about dangerous chemicals being put on hair and scalp.
Movies about deaf persons:
The Miracle Worker 1962 by Arthur Penn about Helen Keller who was blind and deaf after a fever as a baby, Love is Never Silent 1985 by Joseph Sargent, In the Land of the Deaf 1992 by Nicolas Philibert, Bridge to Silence 1989 by Karen Arthur, If I Knew What You Said 2001(Dinig-Sana-Kita in Philippines), Lake Windfall 2013 by Roger Vass, No Ordinary Hero: The Super Deafy Movie 2013 by Troy Kotsur
Movies about blind persons: A Patch of Blue 1965 with Sidney Poitier and Elizabeth Hartman, Scent of a Woman 1992 with Al Pacino by Martin Brest, At First Sight 1999 with Val Kilmer,

Actresses: Bette Davis, Elizabeth Taylor, Sophia Loren, Zsa Zsa Gabor, Marilyn Monroe, Bridgette Bardot, Goldie Hawn, Kate Hudson who was the daughter of Goldie Hawn and Kurt Russell, Jodie Foster, Halle Berry, Angelina Jolie, Zhang Ziyi, Fan Bingbing, Berrak Tuzunatac, Asli Tandogan, Shilpa Shinde, Penelope Cruz, Paz Vega, Salma Hayek, Anjelica Huston, Scarlet Johansson, Irene Papas. Bridget Bardot was a French actress who became an animal rights activist. Angelina Jolie was married to actor Brad Pit and they received awards for Global Citizen and humanitarian causes.
Actors: Cary Grant, Paul Newman, Anthony Hopkins, Tom Cruise, Kurt Russell, Sean Connery, Denzel Washington, Manash Dayal, Jackie Chan, Jet Li, Paulo Pascoal, Tunde Adebimpe, Aleksey Chadov, Salman Khan, Hiten Tejwani, Raul Julia, Will Smith, Antonio Banderas, Javier Bardem, Jordi Molla, Pedro Almodovar, Fabio Lanzoni, John Cho.
Child Stars: Shirley Temple 1935, Jay North 1951, Christina Ricci, Macauley Culkin 1990, Drew Barrymore 1982, Gary Coleman 1978, Michael Jackson 1972.
Movie Atmosphere It is customary in many countries to eat popcorn, candies, and sip on colas while watching movies. Some movie taverns serve coffee, alcohol, and small meals. Movies were primarily watched inside of theatres until DVDs were invented in the late 1990s, then it became popular to watch movies in your home. In the 1950s-1960s it was popular to watch movies while sitting in your car at a drive-in theatre or while sitting on a blanket on a lawn. Movies budgets can be low budget or in the millions.

Watching movies and TV shows can be educational, entertaining, and sometimes be intensely emotional and can evoke memories or create hysteria. If you are affected by media, you may need to monitor your exposure.

TV Broadcasting

The earliest TV channels offered news broadcasts and weather reports on major channels, commercials from advertisers, variety shows with acts from entertainers and inventors, sitcom comedies, dramas, and movie nights. Cable channels were available in 1948. Satellite TV was available in 1962. TV that was received by picking up signals with an antenna went off the air at midnight and the broadcaster would say good night to the audience and then the screen would be filled with static.
Emergency broadcasting is indicated with a loud signal to interrupt regular programming. In 1991, BBC began broadcasting 24 hours a day. Big screen TVs with computers in them became popular in the early 2000s and offered close caption which allowed languages to be shown on the screen translating what was being spoken with scripts, if the TV show offered close caption. There is also computer

applications to watch TV online.

TV in the U.S.A.

In the U.S.A the first major networks were ABC, CBS, and NBC. New broadcasts were early in the morning, at noon, in the evening, and before midnight. Walter Cronkite was a TV news anchor for CBS. Brian Williams for NBC, and Peter Jennings for ABC. Glenn Burns and Karen Minton were weather trackers for ABC. Joy Bauer was a nutritionist on The Today Show at NBC. Matt Lauer, Katie Kouric, and Houda Kotb were a few of the hosts of The Today Show.

Soap Opera Day Shows

At noon and through mid-afternoon, dramas called soap operas aired on radios that were sponsored by soap manufacturers because daytime viewers were often cleaning or doing laundry. The shows were televised after TVs were invented. The Guiding Light began in 1952 and aired until 2009. Other soap operas were General Hospital, Another World, As The World Turns, Days of Our Lives, The Young and the Restless, All My Children, The Bold and The Beautiful, The Edge of Night, One Life to Live, Santa Barbara, Ryan's Hope, Search for Tomorrow.
The even lighting on the sets of the soap operas makes it easy for cameras to focus on actors from all different positions and is one reason why soap operas look different from other TV shows.

Some popular late afternoon and evening shows in the U.S.A. in the 1950s-70s:

Ozzie and Harriet with singer Ricky Nelson, The Donna Reed Show, Father Knows Best, My Three Sons, Voyage to the Bottom of the Sea, Lost In Space where ROBOT says Danger Will Robinson!, Mr. Ed the Talking Horse, The Twilight Zone, Dick Van Dyke where Rob and Laura sleep in twin beds in a nice home, a son and a good income, Daniel Boone, Honeymooners, Sea Hunt (with Lloyd Bridges, Beau Bridges, and Jeff Bridges), Mannix, Cannon, Baretta, Marcus Welby M.D., The Brady Bunch, Waltons, Gilligan's Island, Flipper, McHales's Navy about WW II, I Dream of Jeannie about an astronaut and a genie in a bottle, Bewitched, Dark Shadows, Andy Griffith, Lassie, Gomer Pyle, Bonanza, The Big Valley, Hawaii Five-O, The Lucy Show, Charlie's Angels by Aaron Spelling, The A Team, Mission Impossible, Knight Rider about a talking car, That Girl, Mary Tyler Moore, That Girl, Barney Miller, Fantasy Island, Gunsmoke, The Beverly Hillbillies at the end they say Y'all Come Back, Little House on the Prairie, Get Smart, Happy Days with the Fonz, Cheers, Leave It to Beaver, All In The Family, Sanford and Son, Magnum PI, Dallas & The Ewing Mansion, One Day at a Time about a divorced mother and her 2 daughters, Golden Girls, Lorne Michael's Saturday Night Live. Star Trek was created in 1966. Willian Shatner was the captain of the Starfleet USS Enterprise. Crew members said Beam me up, Scottie to be transported to another place in time. The Star Trek Crew ventured forth for the quest for the unknown, to go where no man has gone before.

TV shows in the U.S.A. with spiritual or religious themes or ideas:

The Flying Nun about a nun in a convent in Puerto Rico, Touched by An Angel, The Ghost Whisperer, Homeland about fighting terrorism, Carrier - a PBS documentary about an aircraft carrier with a crew of over 5,000 dedicated navy personnel and 85 aircraft. The 700 Club with Pat Robertson.Atlanta WATC Channel 57 Community TV Broadcasting religious programmes with Jack Van Impe, Oral Roberts, Babbie's House with Babbie Mason, Frank Santora, Joseph Prince. Seniors Today with Betty Cornett and Pat Mathis features programs for senior citizens.

TV Shows about Santa Claus & Christmas:

The Scrooge, Charlie Brown Christmas, Grandma Got Run Over by a Reindeer

TV shows in the USA in the 1990s-2000s: Blue Bloods, 24,CSI Miami, CSI New York, CSI Las Vegas, CSI Los Angeles, NYPD Blue, Law and Order Criminal Intent, Law and Order Special Victim's Unit, NCIS, NCIS Los Angeles, NCIS New Orleans, Criminal Minds, House, E.R. for Emergency Room, Station 19 Seattle Fire Rescue, Seinfeld, Friends, Will & Grace, The Big Bang Theory, The 70s Show, Frazier,

Beverly Hills 90210, Two and a Half Men about a divorced man, Spin City, Psych, Medium about psychic intuition, Madmen about advertising and cigarettes in the 1950s, Shameless with Jimmy Steve, The Walking Dead filmed in Atlanta, Haven based on a Stephen King novel, Breaking Bad about a chemistry teacher who becomes involved in making meth and it ruins his and his family's life, Grey's Anatomy by Shonda Rhimes, The Real Housewives of Beverly Hills, The Real Housewives of Dallas, Impractical Jokers 2011 on TruTV network, Amish Mafia 2012, Duck Dynasty 2012, Community 2001 a sitcom, Chrisley Knows Best, The Hateful Eight with Walton Goggins as Sheriff Chris Mannix, One Tree Hill by Mark Schwahn, Hart of Dixie with Rachel Bilson,Cress Williams, Scott Porter, Jaime King. Hap & Leonard Sundance TV, Mr. Robot

Reality Shows: The Doctors a show about real doctors and how they helped patients, The Bachelor and The Bachelorette about singles looking for a marriage mate, Home Makeovers, Survivor, Hell's Kitchen, American Idol, The Voice, Dancing With The Stars, Blue Collar Millionaires, Shark Tank produced by Mark Burnett with Kevin Harrington, Trapped 2007 a National Geographic documentary about people being trapped at various places.

Cartoons: Dennis the Menace 1959, The Jetsons, Scooby Doo, The Flintstones, Felix the Cat, Popeye, Brutus, and Olive Oil, Woody Woodpecker by Walter Lantz animation studio at Universal, Hong Kong Phooey, Garfield The Cat, Bugs Bunny a Looney Tunes Cartoon, Road Runner, Rug Rats, Sponge Bob, Ren & Stimpy. The Peanuts comic series featured Charlie Brown, Snoopy dog, Peppermint Patty, Lucy van Pelt, Linus van Pelt, and Sally Brown.

Animated TV shows: The Simpsons, Family Guy, Rick and Morty, Rockmo

Disney Channel: Girl Meets World with actress Sabrina Carpenter, Mickey Mouse Clubhouse, Puppy Dog Pals, Muppet Babies, Vampirina, Stuck in the Middle, Jesse, Bunk'd, Ant Farm, Sneaky Pete

Game Shows: Let's Make a Deal, Jeopardy, Family Feud, Wheel of Fortune, The Price is Right, Deal or No Deal

Shopping Channels: QVC, HSN, LC, EVINE

TV movies created and budgeted for television: Cinderella 1957 by Rodgers & Hammerstein. The Thorn Birds with Richard Chamberlain and Rachel Ward 1983 about a priest who falls in love with a woman.

Crawlspace, 1972. Ice Bound: A Woman's Survival at the South Pole, 2003, 9/11 about the attack on the World Trade Center Twin Towers in New York on 9/11/2001 by Islamic terrorist Bin Laden, Miracle on the Hudson 2014, Firestorm: 72 Hours in Oakland 1993, A Maiden's Grave 1995 an HBo movie based on a novel by Jeffrey Deaver who was a lawyer, actor, journalist, and singer. Jeffrey Deaver appeared on the soap opera As The World Turns as a corrupt reporter. Bone Collector with Denzel Washington and Angelina Jolie 1999.

TV in Great Britain:

Some popular shows in the 2000s: Downton Abbey, Mr. Selfridge with Jeremy Pivan, Happy Valley, X Factor, Luther, Black Mirror, Line of Duty, Red Dwarf, Sherlock

Holmes, Wallander based on the Swedish series, The Crown, The Inbetweeners, House of Cards, East Enders, Jonathan Creek, The Dark, Inspector Lynley, Prime Suspect, Doctor Who, Bramwell, Agatha Christie's Marple

Children's Animated TV show in Great Britain: Bob the Builder, Ben and Holly Little Kingdom

TV In Canada: Murdoch Mysteries since 2005, Trailer Park Boys, Degrassi: The Next Generation, Orphan Black, The Friendly Giant, The X-Files, Saving Hope, Degrassi Junior High 1987-1989, Heartland, Continuum, Bitten, Lost Girl
Children's Animated TV show: Xcalibur

TV in Australia: How to Stay Married a comedy, The Gates of Hell a drama, Bluey is an animated show.

Game Show in Australia: Pick A Box 1950

TV series in Sweden:
Henning Mankell's Wallander, Real Humans, The Bridge, Solsidan, Modus includes a child with autism

TV in Israel
Mossad 101 with Yehuda Levi, Fauda, Prisoners of War, Srugim

TV in India on Desi/Colours networks:
Big Boss 11, Laado, Tu Aashiqui, Ishq Mein Marjawan

TV in North Korea:
It's So Funny 1970, Waiting for Father 2014

TV in South Korea:
OnDemandKorea dramas:
Suspicious Partner 2017 with Ji Chang Wook and Nam Ji hyun.
Because This is My First Life,
While You Were Sleeping,
My Golden Life

TV in Japan: Pokemon anime series, Bayside Shakedown, FNS Music Festival, Sasuke, Downtown no Gaki no Tsukai, Panel Quiz Attack 25.

TV in Mexico: Por Siempre mi amor by Ejecutivo by Ignacio Sada for TV with Susan Gonzalez and Guy Ecker.

TV in Indonesia:
Cinta Fitri 2007-2011, Love in the Sky of the Taj 2015, Roro Janggrang 2016, Extravaganza 2004-2009, Opera Van Java Claudya Fritska won Indonesia's Got Talent

TV in Russia: Evening Urgant since 2012, Kitchen 2012-2106, My Fair Nanny, Catherine, Interns, Silver Spoon, Brigada, Poor Nastya, Voroniny
Children's Animated Shows: Kikioriki, Masha and the Bear since 2009

FASHIONS/ Clothing /Uniforms/
It would impossible to list all clothing designers, manufacturers, designers of accessories such as jewelry, handbags, scarves, hats, shoes, or retailers in the pages of this book.

Real beauty is not in an external image, but within your heart, thoughts, and good actions.

Clothing can be ready to wear and sold in bulk, haute couture made and tailored just for you, uniforms for work, or clothing bought at thrift stores, garage sales, and hand-me-downs. Camoflauge material blends with nature.

Take pride in your creations and the names you have picked for them. Designer labels are proudly attached to the clothing by designers and manufacturers to identify garments in case the garments need to be returned or exchanged at stores.

The Invention of the Sewing Machine

The sewing machine was invented by the efforts of several inventors from 1755 until 1819. Some names are Charles Weisenthal of Germany 1755, Josef Madersperger of Austria 1768, Barthelemy Thimonnier of Framce 1793, Walter Hunt of New York 1796, Elias Howe of Massachusetts 1819, Henry Lye of Philadelphia 1826, John Fisher of England 1844, Benjamin Wilson of Massachusetts 1949, and Isaac Merritt Singer of New York 1851.

Levi Strauss invented denim in 1829 and blue jeans have remained popular.

Women Fashion Models: Twiggy (she was too thin), Cheryl Tiegs, Heidi Klum, Kate Moss, Naomi Campbell, Cindy Crawford, China Machado, Vanessa Lorenzo, Miriam Giovanelli, Liu Wen, Ming Xi, Sui He, Fei Fei Sun, Almudena Fernandez, Stella Angelova, Evgeniya Radilova.

It was reported in the news that models Anna Carolina Reston of Brazil and Bethaney Wallace of Britain starved themselves to death because of pressures in the media that they needed to be thinner. Russina model Vlada Dzyuba worked herself to death from sheer exhaustion and chronic meningitis; Vlada had a modeling contract that did not include medical insurance and she did not seek medical treatment.

Men Fashion Models: Jon Kortajarena, Sean O'Pry, Brad Kroenig, Rick Mora, Ashton Kucher, Tyson Beckford, Zhao Lei, Yon Gonzalez, Yogi Cameron Alborzian, Ivan Andonov

Famous Fashion Designers & Brands
Coco Chanel of Paris, Calvin Klein, Anne Klein, Diane von Furstenberg, Karl Lagerfield, Donna Karan of New York, Ralph Lauren, Alexander McQueen, Givenchy, Ann Taylor, Michael Kors, Liz Claiborne, Tommy Hilfiger, Oscar de la Renta, Giovanni Gianni Versace, Donnatella Versace, Louis Vuitton, Christian Dior, Jaclyn Smith for K-Mart, Bobbie Brooks, Yves Saint Laurent, Vera Wang, Burberry, Giorgio Armani, Will Smith, Jaden Smith, Stella McCartney, Sean John, Southern Charm, Tommy Bahama, Salt Life, Naeem Khan, Derek Lam, Elie Saab, Christian Siriano, Couture, Monique Lhuillier, Luella, Jason Wu, Prabol Gurung, Peter Pilotto, Priyanka Chopra, Thakoon Panichgul, Giambattista Valli, Victoria Beckham, Phillip Lim, Joseph Altuzarra, Missoni, Danskin, North Face, Nike, Fila, Adidas, Reebok, Puma, Asics, And1, Skechers, New Balance, K-Swiss, Umbro, Speedo, Titleist, Wilson, Jordan, Vineyard Vine, Ashworth Clothing, Under Armour, Slazenger, Hibbett, Bio 5, Spalding, Converse, Greg Norman Golf Attire, Vans, Kappa, Baden, Saucony, Le Coq, La Coste, Vonev, Ellesse, Molten, Izod, Dockers, CATO Fashions, Danny Bear, OshKosh B'Gosh, Carter's Baby, Gerber Baby, Aeropostale, Knox Rose & Exhilaration at Target, Hello Molly,
Faded Glory & White Stag at Walmart, Rocky Mountain Clothing, Toil Zazzle, Rasta Empire Jamaican Clothing,
G.H. Bass since 1876, Oakley Sunglasses, OGI EyeglassesRay-Ban Eyeglasses, Ray-Ban Sunglasses, Isotoner, Tapestry Coach, Nicole Miller, Ebags, XinXin China, Franco Sarto Purses, Borghese, Hermes Birkin, Fossil Wallet, Champion, Pacific Trail, White Tail Deer, Nautica, Viper, Beach Cabana, Dockside, Lee, Levi, Merona, Studio I, Briggs of NY, GAP, Hanes, Fruit of the Loom, Catalina, Zulily, Wrangler, Rafaella, Everlast, Red Sail Clothing, The Limited, Polartec, Patagonia, Misook, Zulily, Winwin China, Cheongsam China dress, Hitojki Kimono Japan dress, Kimono Yukata, Native American Indian shawl & poncho, CINTAS Uniforms, SCRUBS, KOI Scrubs, Carhartt Fire Resistant Clothing, Winwear Professional Aprons.

Famous Clothing Retailers and

Department Stores: Sears, Macy's, JC Penney, Belk, Saks Fifth Avenue, Nordstrom, Harrods, Selfridges, The Limited, Old Navy, Banana Republic, Dillard, TJ Maxx, Marshall's, Ross, Bloomingdale's, Victoria's Secret, Kohl's, Kmart, Walmart, Target, Abercrombie & Fitch, G.H. Bass since 1876, Dress Barn, Goodwill Stores, It's About Time, Les Galeries Lafayette, Au Bon Marche, Bazarde l'Hotel de Ville, Nordiska Kompaniet, GUM Russia, El Corte Ingles, Tiger, Super Bazar Naixiao, Ludwig Beck, Danny Bear Malaysia, Buy Buy Baby, OshKosh B'Gosh, Carter's Baby, Gerber, Faizal Tumin Enterprises, Bukit Rambai, Babies R Us, Boscovs, FredMeyer, Meijer, Fashion Bug, Catherines, Ocean Walk, Lane Bryant, DSW, Nine West Shoes, Steve Madden, Payless Shoes, Shoeland, Shoe Carnival, Ugg Boots, Fashion Ten

Outdoor Gear Retailers: Eddie Bauer, RCI Outfitters, RAK Outfitters, TEK Gear, Big5, Champs, L L Bean, Cabelas, Eddie Bauer, Mossy Oak, Realtree Outfitters, APALACH Outfitters, Coleman, Columbia, American Eagle Outfitter, Browning, J. Crew, Aussie Outback Australia, One Planet Australia, Costa, Chinook Canada, Dunlop Sport Britain, PEAK Performance Sweden, Zajo Slovakia, Chiruca Spain, BASK Russia, Berg Outdoor Portugal, Verge Sport Poland, Icepeak Finland, Peak69 Bangladesh, Naturehike China, Gaya Iran, Descente Japan, Consina Indonesia, Redback Australia, Sandugo Sandals Philippines, Prime Time Crusader RV Camper, Airstream Xcella Camper, Keystone Laredo Camper, Tiffin Phaeton Motorhome, Winnebago

New shoes are stiff. Wear new shoes a few times before they are comfortable.

Sometimes broken shoes can be repaired by a shoe repair specialist.

If you buy a pair of shoes from a thrift store, look at the soles before you buy them because the previous owner may have a different walking pattern than you. People have sprained their ankles or tripped from wearing previously used shoes.

Always let someone know your hiking route and never venture alone. In 2003, Aron Ralston was an outdoorsman who had to amputate his right forearm when he was trapped by a rock in a canyon in Utah, U.S.A.

SOME CLOTHING FABRICS

Ancient artifacts that were unearthed or found in some tombs showed that the earliest humans wore tunics made from animal skins, fur, and bird feathers.

Modern clothing labels show the content of fibers in the fabrics and the care needed to clean the garment such as if the garment can be dry cleaned, needs to lay flat to dry, line dry or if it can be put into a clothes dryer powered by natural gas or electricity, and to know the content of fibers in the clothing.

100% cotton from cotton plants.
Cotton fibers absorb sweat. Flannel is a fabric that is usually 100% cotton or wool and is great for making warm pajamas. Cotton wrinkles a lot.
Some people like no wrinkles, but some people like the wrinkled-look.

Plaid desgins originated in Scotland.
Madras is colorful summer plaid originated in India. Burberry plaids are plaids originated in Britain.

100% linen from flax plants.
Linen wrinkles a lot.

100% wool from sheep.
Cashmere wool are fibers from around the neck region of the sheep.

Egypt and India are famous for 100% cotton and linen fabrics which are fabrics of ancient times even found in tombs.

100% silk from silkworms.

Silk is made from boiling silkworm larvae and then creating silk fibers which have an illustrious sheen. The silkworms are killed in the process so some animal activists protest silk.

Never put silk into a hot dryer or lay it in the hot sun or the illustrious shine might be destroyed.

Some other famous fabrics are velvet, taffeta, organza, chiffon, satin, brocade, corduroy, muslin, voile, damask, poplin, tartan, fleece, denim, tweed, hessian, wool, flannel, felt. Monogrammed clothing or items show a person's name or initials.

Invention of Spandex

Spandex added stretch to 100% cotton shirts and jeans to make the garments more comfortable.

Some fabrics blends with spandex:

98% cotton, 2% spandex.

88% cotton, 8% polyester, 4% spandex.

60% polyester, 35% rayon, 5% spandex.

Spandex also called elastane and lycra was invented by Joseph Shivers in 1958. Shivers was a chemist at Dupont. Spandex revolutionized the fabric industry because fabrics with more stretch in them were created which were great for athletes because the fabrics were more comfortable, gave the body more ease and were easy to move in. But spandex and fabrics with a polyester base do not absorb sweat so skin could chaff. Nylon, rayon, viscose, and acrylic are popular synthetic polymer fibers. Polyester fabrics are synthetic which means artificially created.

Fleece is a polyester that is used to make many soft plush blankets and jackets.

Different types of liners also called inner layer can be attached to the inside of fabrics to create the effect that is needed.

Some fabrics may shrink when washed.

Clothes can be mended by sewing on or applying a patch with a hot iron.

People try different things to remove stains. Talcum powder can remove grease and tomato spots sometimes. It is okay to wear clothing with stains and holes.

People keep some of their favorite clothing and jewelry for as long as 20 or 30 years or more.

Clothing is manufactured in many countries in the world, such as:

Made in China, Philippines, Vietnam, Mexico, U.S.A., Indonesia, Guatemala, Qatar, Bangladesh, Sri Lanka, Egypt, India, Honduras, Thailand, Northern Mariana Islands, Jordan, Cambodia, Taiwan, Pakistan, LeSotho, Nicaragua, and many more.

Clothing can also be hand-made, sewn at home on sewing machines, or by knitting or crochet.

Civvies is a nickname for clothes worn by non-military citizens.

Military uniforms are worn by soldiers.

Jewelers

Tiffany of New York, Nektar De Stagnir of New York and Miami, Hermes of Paris, Helzberg Diamonds, Art Jewelers, Signet Jewelers of US, UK, Canada - Kay, Jared, Zales, Shane of U.S., Faberge of Russia - Alchemia, Markin, Gourji, Axenoff, Yana Raskovalova, Nihaojewelry of China, Kingold of China, Wish of China, Wallace Chan, Anna Hu, Michelle Ong of China, Satomi Kawakita of New York & Japan, Niwaka of Japan, STAR of Japan, Mikimoto of Japan, Wako of Japan, Okachimachi of Japan, TOUS of Spain, Damascene of Spain, Eleonora di Toledo of Spain, John Greed of England,

Rachel Boston of England, Rosa del la Cruz of London, Daniella Draper of England, Gee Woods of England, Lily Kamper of England, Katrine Kristensen from Denmark, Alison Lou of New York Estelle Deve of France, Australia, Seven Arrows American Indian Jewelry & Art, Gavilan's of California, Rudi Fine Jewelry of Georgia U.S.A., Marie Zimmermann of New York, Rolex, Timex, Hamilton Watch, Grandfather Clocks, German Cuckoo Clocks, Armitron Watch, IZOD watch, Apple watch that works in sync with IPHONE, Seiko, Orient, Swatch, Tissot, Citizen, Casio, Bulova, Longines, Rado, Tag Heuer, Fossil, Invicta, ETA SA, Breitling, Skagen, Victorinox, Movado, IWC International Watch Company.

Gems: Diamond, Ruby or Siam, Garnet, Topaz, Amethyst, Turquoise, Sapphire, Aquamarine, Crystal, Emerald, Peridot, Rose, Zirconia, Opal, Onyx, Tiger's Eye

Metals: Gold, Silver, Titanium, Platinum, Copper, Palladium, Rhodium, Tungsten, Niobium

A Few of Many Famous Perfumes:

Ladies: Eau de Gucci (1906), Chanel No. 5 (1921), Dana Tabu (1932), Jovan Musk (1973) Diane Von Furstenberg Tatiana (1975), Faberge Tigress (1970), Nina Ricci LiAir du Temps (1978), Guerlain Shalimar (1925), Yves Saint Laurent Opium (1977), Ombre Rose by Jean Charles Brosseau 1981, Kenzo Par Fums Flower (2000), Estee Lauder White Linen, Estee Lauder Pleasure(1990), Sung by Alfred Sung (2010), Rapture by Victoria Secret (2000), Avon Timeless Perfume (1980), Christian Dior Poison (1990), Calvin Klein Obesession (1985), Mary Kay Acapella, Elizabeth Taylor White Diamonds, Prada Candy, Yves Rocher Voile D'Ambre, Ralph Lauren Lauren, Ralph Lauren Safari, Champs Elysee by Guerlain (1996), Il Bacio by Marcello Borghese (1993), Oscar de la Renta (1977), Desnuda by Ungaro (2001), Versace Bright Crystal.

Men: Old Spice (1938), Giorgio Armani Acqua di Gio, Hollister Guys, Polo by Ralph Lauren (1978), Aramis, Drakkar Noir by Guy Laroche (1982), 1 Million Cologne by Paco Rabanne (2008), Azzaro (1978) by Azzaro, Versace Man by Gianni Versace

Levels of Perfume Concentrations

1) Perfume 2) Eau de Parfum

3) Eau de toilette spray 4) Cologne

Perfumes may contain essential oils, aroma compounds, fixents, or solvents. Ambergris is sometimes found on beaches; ambergris is a substance ejected from the whale of a stomach that is added to perfumes.

RETAIL STORES / Cash & Carry

U.S.A. Safeway, Woolworths, Dollar Store, Kroger, Publix, Trader Joe's, Walmart, Target, Aldi, Whole Foods, Sprouts, Blalock Seafood,
Nam Dae Mun Asian Farmers Market

Mexico: Bodega Aurrera

Britain: Sainsbury, ASDA

Germany: Aldi, Metro AG, REWE Group, Lidl

Austria: Billa

France: Auchan, Carrefour

Denmark: Koninklijke, Spar

Finland: Kesko

Switzerland: COOP

Chile: Cencosud

Belgium: Delhaize

Romania: Selgros

Russia: Sedmoi Kontinent, Lenta, Magnit, Dixy, Azbuka Vkusa

Belarus: Sedmoi Kontinent

Africa: Devland Metro, Shoprite, Woolworths

FAMOUS CONSUMER BRANDS

It is impossible to list all consumer goods in the pages of this book.

The variety of goods that are offered to consumers is astounding. People are working hard to produce items for other people to use in daily life. Customers should be grateful for all of the offers that are available to them.

People can 'fall in love' with a product, fabric, food, color, or song and it will be a favorite for them.

In modern times, proprietors are painting the backs of stores or shopping center walls and putting in lighting to make the areas more safe and pleasant areas. These isolated areas were once and still are dangerous places so it is not good safety practice to linger behind stores or shopping centers.

Hair Care: Prell Shampoo, Pantene, Herbal Essences, Head & Shoulders Dandruff Shampoo, Kerastase, Suave, VO5, Garnier, Neutrogena, TRESemme, L'Oreal, Sunsilk

Skin Cream: Noxema contains eucalyptus oil.

Baby Shampoo: Johnson & Johnson Baby Shampoo, Comfort, Aveeno, Baby Infant, Dove Baby, Sheamoisture, Equate, Dumex French Baby Food

Cosmetics: Revlon, Cover Girl, Maybelline, Clinique, Physicians, Elizabeth Arden, Avon, Mary Kay, Lancome, Neutrogena, Bare Minerals, Shiseido, Colourpop, NYX, Sephora, Jordana, Bath and Body Works, Alba Botanical, Bed, Bath & Beyond

Sports & Workout / Recreational Equipment: Hampton Gym Equipment, Matrix Gym Equipment, Joola Table Tennis, DUOL air dome, LA Fitness, Gold's Gym, Suvidha International of India, Schwinn Bicycle, Firebird Bicycle, Gibson Firebird Guitar, England Piano, Steinway Grand Piano, Fazioli Grand Piano, Yamaha Keyboard, Yamaha Guitar, Wilson Tennis Rackets, Wilson Football, Asics, Prince, Brunswick Bowling Ball, OTB Russia Bowling Ball, Gilbert, Adidas, Mitre, Puma Soccer Ball

Therapy: Daily Massage Neck Back Arms & Shoulder $10 for Ten Minutes, Challise & Company full service Salon & Spa, Lenox Spa Luxury Resort, Five Star Destination Luxury Spa & Boutique Hotel, Angel Psychic Healing, Tarot Cards & Palm Reading,
Divorce Support Group, Cancer Support Group, Grief Support Group, A Hobby or Music therapy

Emergency, Medical Equipment & Wheelchairs: NOVA, Best Friend (Germany), Karma Europe, Karman, Sunrise, Medline, Hugo Walker, Drive Wheelchairs, Freedom Prosthetics, China Prosthetic Limb, Mueller Back Brace, Morningstar Ambulance, Pierce Firetruck, Ameriglide, Band-Aid

Batteries: Duracell, Energizer, Panasonic, Philips, Rayovac of U.S.A., Joyetech, Senec and Sonnen of Germany, Yuasa of Japan, VARTA, Montana Tech, Spectrum, Johnson Controls.

Food Brands: P.F. Chang Egg Rolls, Stouffer's Lasagna, Hebrew National Kosher Hot Dogs, Ezekiel Bread, Essene Bread, Falafel Bread, Kings Hawaiian Bread, Grandma's Blackberry Lemon Poppy Seed Muffins, Borden Milk, Mayfield Milk, Lays Potato Chips, Fritos Corn Chips, Takis Tortillas, Stacy's Pita Chips, Sun Chips, Smartfood, Natural Intentions, Sensible Portions Vegetable Chips, Terra Original Vegetable Chips, Pepperidge Farm Goldfish Crackers, Smithfield Bacon, Jimmy Dean Sausage (named after the country singer), Gerber Baby Food, Hunt's Canned Tomatoes, Tip Top Tomatoes, Jolly Green Giant Cut Green Beans, Del Monte Whole Kernel Golden Sweet Corn, Goya, Dole Pineapple, V8 Juice, Juicy Juice, Soon's Orchards, Berry Patch, Bolthouse Farms, Ocean Spray, Frooti, Ceres, Tropicana, Simply Orange, Langers, Minute Maid, Capri Sun, Kool-Aid, Mission Pride Fruit, Fresh Express Salads, Vietti Beef Stew, Double Q Pink Salmon, Jiffy Peanut Butter, Boost Protein Drink, Ensure Protein Drink, Vitamin Water,

Tandoor Chef Aloo Gobi (Potatoes, Cauliflower and Curry), Ashoka Paneer Cheese, Bombay Kitchen Mateer Paneer, Weight Watchers, Nutrisystems, Hostess Twinkie, Famous Amos cookies, Little Debbie Pecan Spinwheels, Murray Sugar-Free Cookies, Nabisco Fig Newtons, Nabisco Oreos, McCormick Spices, Tone's Spices, Crisco Shortening made from vegetable oil, Arm & Hammer Baking Powder, Argo & Kingsford Corn Starch, Runford Baking Powder, Morton Salt, Tabasco, Texas Pete, Cholula Hot Sauce, Huy Fong Chili Sauce, El Yucateco Hot Sauce, Chiquita Banana. Kellogg's Pop Tarts, United Egg Producers, Morristown Tennessee's Best Tomatoes, Russian Alibaba Stanichnye Sunflower Seeds, Amera Melt Cheese
Food Wrap: Reynolds Aluminum Foil, Glad, Ziploc, Hefty Plastic Bags, Anchor Purity
Pet food: Purina, Beneful Petfood, Blue Buffalo, Fancy Feast, Orijen, Royal Canin Veterinary, Taste of the Wild Pacific, TetraMin Fish Flakes, Zoo Med Turtle Food
Bird Seed: Wagner's Classic, Pennington Select Ultra Fruit & Seed, Audubon Park Wild Bird
Seeds: Burpee, American Seed, Monsanto, Dupont, Land O'Lakes, DOW USA, Syngenta Switzerland, Groupe Limagrain France, KWS Germany, Bayer Germany, Sakata Japan, DLF-Trifolium Denmark. The largest seed in the world is coco de mer or the Seychelles Island Palm the Maldive coconut. The smallest seeds are believed to be the orchid seeds.

Tea Brands:
U.S.A.: Luzianne, Celestial Seasonings, Salada, Bigelow
Canada Tea: TAZO
Britian Tea: Lipton, Twinings
China Tea Brands: Da Hong Pao, Lapsang Souchong, Huangshan Maofeng, Dianhong, Tieguanyin, Longjing, Bai Mudan (White Peony), Oolong (Green & Black), Red Tea (black tea roasted), Yellow Tea, Flower Tea, Pu'er tea (fermented dark tea), Long-Jing (Dragon Well) green tea from Xi Hu in Zhejiang Province, Bi Luo Chu (Spring Snail) green tea from taitlu in Jiangsu Province, Tie Guan Yin (Iron goddess) oolong from Anxi in Fujian Province, Mao Feng (Fur Peak) green tea from Huang Shan in Anhui Province
Japan Tea: Shincha, Sencha, Gyokuro, Matcha, Bancha, Hojicha, Genmaicha, Fukujuen (since 1790), Suntory Lyemon (bottled green tea), Yuzu Sencha (citrus flavored), IPPODO (since 1846), Giontsujin (since 1860), Aikokuseicha (since 1933), Itohkynemon (since 1832) uji tea (not too bitter)

Coffee Brands: Paulig Presidentti (Russia), Melitta (German), Tchibo (German), Andronicus (Greece), Vittoria (Italy), Kenya AA, Ehtiopian Yirgacheffe, Ethiopian Harrar, Tanzanian Peaberry, Uganda Good African Coffee, Madagascar Excellence Roasted Coffee, Burundi AA Kirimiro, Cameroon Arabica Coffee, Rwanda Gaseke, Nicaragua El Penon, Panama Finca La Mula, Gold Peak, Maxwell House (U.S.A.), Seattles Best, Folgers (U.S.A.), Starbucks, Dunkin Donuts, McCafe, Café Bustelo (J.M. Smucher U.S.A.,
Panorama Coffee (Thailand),
Panorama Coffee (Vancouver, B.C.),
Panorama Coffee (Sydney, Australia),
Groove Korea Coffee

Guns: Colt 45, Ruger, Glock, Sig Sauer, Beretta, Smith & Wesson, Winchester, Dan Wesson, Ithaca,
Remington (U.S.A. and China),
Lider (Europe), Bersa (Argentina),
Jenson (Turkey), Norinco (China), Baikal Izhmekh (Russia), Benelli (Italy)

Guns may have laser pointers or silencers.
Other Weapons: Sling Shot, Bow & Arrow,

Canon, Hand Grenade, Hand Club, Brass Knuckles, Taser, Ballistic Missle, Nuclear Missle, Knives, Biological Warfare,
Lies, Harsh Words, Evil Looks, Evil tactics.
Stop the Violence.
Why is killing other humans necessary?

In the early 2000s, Massoud Hussuni and his brother Mahmud who were from Afghanistan and moved to Denmark developed airborne devices that eradicate land mines. One of the Mine Kafon designs looks like a giant tumbleweed blowing across the land. The brothers demonstrated the land mine blasters to Queen Maxima of Netherlands.

Paper Products like diapers, toilet tissue, and personal hygiene products that promote wellness: Georgia Pacific (U.S.A.), Kimberly-Clark (U.S.A), Brighton USA, Kapstone (U.S.A), Weyerhaeuser (U.S.A), HD Supply (U.S.A), Sikes Paper, Stora Enso (Finland), UPM (Finland), Nipppoon Unipac (Japan), OJI Paper (Japan), Dongguan Xing Yao (China), Zhejiang Jindong (China)
Cleaning Supplies: Clorox Bleach, Brillo Pads, Libman Mop, Swiffer Mop, Lysol, Pine-Sol, Comet Powdered Cleaner (an abrasive), Tide Laundry Detergent, Scotchbrite sponges, Ocelo Sponges, Finish Power Ball Quantum Ultimate Clean & Shine, GOJO Fast Wipes, Krud Kutter, Mr. Clean, Meyer's Clean Day, Seventh Generation Clean, Liquid Plumr, Pledge Furniture Polish, Murphy's Oil, Old English, Fantastik, Fabuloso, Woolite, Mop & Glo, Super Tech Windshield Wiper Fluid for automobiles.

Some say to run a washing machine for a cycle with only bleach water or vinegar water to sanitize it.
Office Supplies: Scotch Tape, Bic, Staples, Office Depot, Office Xpress, CDW, Fed Ex, UPS, Shaheen Office Supply (U.S.A.) Flair (India), Burnham, Cartier, Zebra (U.K.), Hangzhou Ownseas China Pen (China), Russian Post, Komus (Russia)
Beach Attire & Equipment: Ron Jon Surf Shop, King Crab Beach Chairs, Panama Surf, Emerald Surf Water (Florida),
Patagonia Inc. (Argentina and Chile), Brazilian Beach, Maui Clothing Hawaii, China Beach, Cronulla Beach Australia

SOME FAST FOOD CHAINS / Restaurants
Sandwiches and hoagie rolls: Schlotsky's , Subway, Firehouse, Jimmy John's, Jason's Deli, Albert's Deli & Bagels, Philly Connection, Jersey Mike's Subs, Dallmayr Germany

Hamburgers, French Fries, French Fried Onion Rings, Salads, Milkshakes, Colas: McDonald's, Burger King, Burger Chef, Wendy's, Five Guys, Hardees, Checkers, Cheddars, Sonic Drive-in, Jack in the Box, In-N-Out Burger, Carl's Jr., Krystal, White Castle, Cheeseburger Bobby's, Martin's, Steak n Shake, Varsity, Coach's Cuts Jasper, Georgia

Pizza and Pasta: Pizza Hut, Little Caesar's, Papa John's Pizza, Domino's Pizza, Peace Love & Pizza, Mellow Mushroom, Marco's, Hunt Brothers Pizza, Johnny's New York Style Pizza, Rosa's, Gondoliers, Your Pie, Shakey's Pizza, Lucia's, Carrabba's Frankie's Italian Restaurant, Vingenzo's, Capozzi, Chuck E Cheese, Monkey Joe's

Roast Beef and Chicken: Arby's
Chicken: KFC Kentucky Fried Chicken, Chick-fil-A, Bojangles, Zaxby's, Pollo Loco, Polla Tropical, Qdoba, Wild Wings,
Wing Stop, Popeyes Louisiana Kitchen, Chicken Salad Chick (founded by a woman Auburn University Alabama graduate), Beasley's Chicken & Honey (Releigh, North Carolina), Gus's World Famous Hot & Spicy Fried Chicken (Memphis, Tennessee)

Seafood: Captain D's Seafood, Red Lobster, Sizzlehouse, Marietta Fish Market, Reel, Pappadeux Seafood Kitchen, Pier 213, Crawfish Shack, C&S Chowder House, Flora-Bama Lounge & Oyster Bar

Asian: CNHLS (Chinese fast food), Chin Chin, Mr. Wonton, Peking & Tokyo Buffet, Tokyo Boat Hibachi & Sushi, Panda Express, Kani House, Thai Taste, Hana Japanese Steakhouse, Fujihana Japanese Steakhouse, KYU Miami (Korean), Saigon Thai & Vietnamese Food

Mexican: Taco Bell, del Taco, El Ranchero, Cancun Mexican Grill, Mi Casa Mexican Moe's Southwest Grill & Catering, Los Bravos, Little Donkey, Pure Taqueria, Fiesta Café Mechanicsville, Maryland

Brazil: Fogo de Chao Brazilian Steakhouse

Mediterranean: Ameer's Mediterranean Grill, Basil Gyro & Mediterranean Grill, Pita Mediterranean

Jamaican: Tortuga Beach Jamaican Seafood Grill & Bar, The Island Spot, Jamaican Cabana Restaurant, Bob Marley Café Jamaican Grill

Cuban: Cuban Libre Café Pork Sandwiches

Scandanavia (Norway, Sweden, Finland, and Denmark) Hok-elanto liiketoiminta

India Food: Maharaja Indian Restaurant, Malgudi Garden, Moon Indian Restaurant

Indonesia: Ku De Ta Beach Club, Potato Head Beach Club

Irish: O'Malley Irish Pub

French: La Madeleine

Variety Restaurants: Boston Market, Panera Bread, Chili's, Cheesecake Factory, O'Charley's, TGI Friday, Ruby Tuesday, 1950 Jukebox American City Diner, Honeybaked Ham, Hard Rock Café, IHOP, Waffle House, Cracker Barrel, Folks, Golden Corral, Taco Mac, Friday's, Shoney's, Mary Mac's Tea Room (Atlanta, Georgia), Busy Bee Café (Atlanta, Georgia), Canyon Room at Grand Canyon, Olive Garden, Buffalo's Café, Hooters, River Dock Café at Staton Island Ferry, Nantucket Grill and Bar, Mulligan's Food & Spirits, Leon's (Charlestion South Carolina), Moody's Diner of Waldoboro Maine, Salty Dog Café (Hilton Head, S.C. U.S.A.), Kings Hawaiian Bakery & Restaurant of Torrance California, Brookwood Grill, Zoes, Fisher's at Orange Beach Marina, Sunset Garden Restaurant, Paia Fish Market & Restaurant in Maui, Hawaii, Wagon Wheel Grille (Gill, Massachusetts, U.S.A), 1761 Old Mill Restaurant (Westminster, Massachusetts, U.S.A.), Fried Green Tomato Café, Johnboy's All You Can Eat Buffet, S & S Cafeteria, Picadilly Cafeteria, Family Tradition, The Brunch Club, Malibu Café California U.S.A., Gramma's Marine Pub at Gibsons, British Columbia, Masada Café at the United House of Prayer for All People (Savannah, Georgia), Café Procope of Paris France, River Café & Terrace in Bangkok Thailand, University of Zurich Switzerland Restaurant, Java Moon Café in Port Royal Jamaica, Red Dog Saloon in Juneau, Alaska.

Sports Bars: Marlow's Tavern, Keegan's Irish Pub, Donovan's Irish Pub, Izakaya Japanese Bar, Paper Tiger Chinese Bar, Good Luck Chinese Bar, Sidelines Grille

Some customers who ate at Main Street Diner: Pete Petree and Houston Kelly are centurians. Pete is 104 years old and Houston is 102 years old. They both still drive cars and do housework at home. Wes is a truck driver for Fed Ex who was offered a transfer with Fed Ex to Myrtle Beach,

South Carolina with an option to return to Atlanta. He lived in Myrtle Beach for 2 years and then returned to Atlanta. John and David drove for UPS Freight and stopped in for lunch or dinner. Dave Langley was a radio broadcaster from Reading, Pennsylvania at WEEU 830 AM who was passing through Atlanta on the way to Florida who stopped to eat a meal. Ginger Abbott was a native Atlantan who ate there often because she was in her 80's and did not have the energy to cook each day. Ginger knew all of the wait staff and managers. She told them that she had lost her husband last year. Then she lost both of her brothers who both died the same week within a few days of each other. For awhile, she lost her appetite and had trouble eating any food at all. Another customer was named Mike who worked for Georgia Pacific. He said he had been transferred from Georgia to Texas then to Portland, Oregon and then back to Georgia when he took a job with another company. A young man named Tyler ate with his grandparents at the restaurant in between the games of a baseball tournament. His team had played 2 games that day and had 1 more game to play. It was called a triple-header because it was 3 consecutive games. The first customers to walk in the doors when the diner opened was Cecil and his wife Peggy and they ate there on and off for 15 years. A few customers were artists. Samantha was a dancer and a sculptor who traveled from the USA to Spain to teach sculpting classes. Her husband was also a dancer. Rob was a visual artist. The wait staff appreciated tips from the customers. The diner closed in 2012.

Restaurant Safety: Caution signs should be visible to warn of slick floors. Dishes and foods should be covered when the restaurant is sprayed with any chemicals, pesticides, or paints.

Food safety inspection grades given by restaurant inspector authority can be displayed for customers to see that it is safe-certified.

FOOD DELIVERY: GrubHub, Uber, Just Eat, Door Dash, Seamless, Target, Kroger, Publix, Lyft

Coffee, Tea, & Snacks: Starbucks Coffee, Caribou Coffee, Scooter's Coffee, Tim Hortons (Canadian coffee), Groove Korea Coffee, Dancing Goats Coffee, Tchibo (German), Tea Leaves & Thyme Tea Room

How much do you have to sell a sandwich for if you sell 250 sandwiches in order to make $ 500? 500 divided by 250 sandwiches equals $ 2.

Sweets and Breakfast: Dunkin Donuts, Krispy Kreme Donuts, Cupcake Café, Cupcakelicious, Piece of Cake, Cakes by Darcy, Cinnabon

Ice Cream / Yogurt / Smoothies: Dairy Queen, Brusters, Baskin-Robbins Ice Cream, Cold Stone Creamery, Orange Julius, Smoothie King, Yogli Mogli Yogurt, Pelican SnoBalls

ICE CREAM FLAVORS

Vanilla, Chocolate, Strawberry, Neopolitan (box with vanilla, chocolate, strawberry side by side in 3 parts), Chocolate Chip, Mint Chocolate Chip, Cherry, Creamy Peach, Rocky Road with chocolate, nuts, and marshmallows, Butter Pecan, Butter Brickle, Tiger Tail (Orange with Licorice ribbon), Blue Moon (Smurf blue with Fruity Candy Flavor), Superman ice cream (blue, red, and yellow), Cookies & cream, Green Tea, Bastani Sonnati, Raspberry Ripple, Stracciatella.

Some restaurants offer menus in Braille for the blind or picture menus for the deaf.

An 'early bird special' is lower, special pricing that may be offered in off-peak hours.

It was heard that a restaurant proprietor required a customer who could not pay his bill to help wash dishes to cover the cost of the meal he ate.

Some restaurants advertise 'We are the best thing that could happen to a potato or a bag of rice because we know how to cook it right!' But people have different opinions about the foods they like to eat.

The Invention of Soda Pop Joseph Priestly of England invented carbonated water in 1767 by suspending a bowl of water over a vat of fermenting beer. Then, carbonated waters were mostly used by pharmacists who recommended them for illnesses. In 1835 bottled soda was offered to consumers in the U.S.

Some soft drink labels:
Coca-Cola, Sprite, Barq's Root Beer, Mr. Pibb, Fanta, Hi-C Fruit Punch, Hi-C Lemonade, Dr. Pepper, Pepsi, Mtn. Dew, RC Royal Crown Cola, Steaz Green Tea Beverages(U.S.A), Gold Spot, Citra, Maaza, Gold Spot CoCo Rico (India), Kirks (Australia), Sparletta (Africa), Hi Orange (China), Bubble Man (Japan), Barr Cream Soda (Britian), Guarana Antarctic (South America), Canada Dry Club Soda, Ginger Ale

Store Brand soft drink labels:
Big K Cola (Kroger Store Brand), Sam's Cola (Walmart Store Brand), Publix Cola (Publix Store Brand)

Companies also offer soft drinks made with sugar substitutes that have less calories such as: Diet Coke, Diet Sprite, Diet Pepsi, Diet Ginger Ale.

People have debated whether or not colas are good for your body. Some people drink the colas to settle an upset stomach. Some think drinking too much acid could be bad for your bones.

Energy Drinks such as Red Bull, Full Throttle, Rock Star, B2, and Monster offer a lot of caffeine. Limit the intake because too much caffeine has caused heart attacks in some people.

Some bottled water labels: Nestle Pure Life (U.S.A. and Canada), Dasani, Perrier, Le Croix, Aquafina (Pepsi), Poland Spring, S. Pellegrino, Aqua Panna (Italy), Ice Mountain, Zephyrhills, Contrex, Mey Eden, Panama Blue, Valpre (South Africa), Badoit (Brazil), Ein Gedi, Ades (Indonesia), Ty Nant, Ciel, Danone, Evian (France), Kinley (Coca-Cola), Highland Spring (Scotland), Wenlock Spring Water (Britain), Bisleri (India), Kingfisher, Parle Agro Bailley, Himalayas, Tingyi (China), Nongu Springs, Hangshou Wahaha Group, Arukari (Japan), Asahi, ASO, Aqua Clara, Cool Ridge (Australia), Mount Franklin, Qatrat (Saudi Arabia), Fiji, Panda, Dala, Safa, Hana (Saudi Arabia).

ALCOHOLIC BEVERAGES

It is controversial whether alcoholic drinks are good for human consumption. Drinking alcohol can impair judgment and make a person physically sick. It is best to keep consumption of alcohol to a minimum. Many companies offer wines, sparkling wines, and beers that are low-alcohol or non-alcohol.

Some red wines: Merlot, Cabernet Sauvignon, Rose, Port, Zinfandel, Syrah or Shiraz, Marsala Dry or Sweet.

Some white wines: Pinot Grigio, Chardonnay, Riesling, Moscato.

Champagne was invented in France and is wine with a second fermentation to create carbonation.

Some wine brands: Kendall Jackson, Sutter Home, Taylor, Woodbridge, Barefot, Arbor Mist, Ecco Domani (Italian), Snoma, Closdu Bois, Napa Valley, Sangria (Spain), Perrin & Fils Vacqueyras (France), Robert Mondavi (U.S.A.),
Alamos (Argentina), Vendage, Apothic, 14 Hands, Little Penguin, Penfolds (Australia), Schmitt Sohne (German), Mateus Rose Wine since 1942, Cumvee Blanc Indian..

Wine is made from fermented red or white grapes.
Some wines are topped with Argon gas to protect the wine.
Proper training and education is needed to make alcoholic beverages.
Do not drink alcohol if you are taking medications or are pregnant.
Never give alcohol to minor children.
Do not operate vehicles or machinery while under the influence of alcohol or drugs. Designate a sober person to drive a car from a party.
Alcohol kills brain cells, may cause liver damage, and may cause damage to an unborn baby.

Some Liquors:

Crown Royal Canadian Whisky since 1939, Canadian Mist, Johnnie Walker Scotch Whisky since 1820, Smirnoff Russian Vodka since 1864, Jim Beam Kentucky Bourbon since 1795, Jack Daniels Tennessee Whiskey since 1956, Bombay Gin since 1761 India, Martini Italian Vermouth, French Brandy since 1313, Napolean Cognac since 1549, Plantation Barbados Rum and El Dorado Rum since 1627, Jose Cuervo Tequila, Jagermeifter herbal liqueur (A German digestif) since 1935, Glenlivet Scotch Whiskey since 1922 Scotland. Skol Vodka since 1949 by J.A. Dougherty. Tito's Vodka of Austin, Texas, Casmus Cognac, Italian Grappa is a digestif.

Some Beers:

Some beers are made from brewer's yeast, malted wheat or barley and hops. Some beers are made with rice, corn, with or without sugar:
Jever, Becks, Erdinger, Samuel Adams, Holsten (German), Pabst Blue Ribbon, Colt 45, Miller, Budweiser, Coors, Blue Moon, Fiji Bitter (U.S.A.),
Asahi, Yebisu, Sapporo (Japan),
Bario, Moussy, Prostel non-alcoholic (Saudi Arabia), Heineken (Denmark), Guinness (Ireland), Blue Moon (Belgium), San Miguel (Philippines)

Cigarette Brands: Marlboro, Winston, Camel, Virginia Slims, Carlton, Benson & Hedges, Pall Mall, Newport, Merit, Talon, Phillies. (Cigarette smoking causes lung cancer. Secondary smoke causes lung cancer. Only smoke 2 cigarettes a year, one in the summer and one in the winter.)
Do not drink or smoke too much. Say 'Satan, Be Gone'. Ask God, Jesus, and Buddha to fill your Spirit with self-control. Find something good to do.

Building Design Exteriors & Interiors/ Architects /Builders /Renters/Movers

It is impossible to list all designers and producers of consumer goods in the pages of this book.
Martha Stewart, Lauren Conrad, Verde, Wayfair, Fieldcrest Linens, Home Depot, ACE Hardware, Lowe's, Cindy Crawford, Stefan Antoni Olmesdahl Truen, African Eleganza, Obokun African Fabric, Sprezzatura Interiors, Nicespace, Lushome, Elizabeth Metcalfe, Alexander Interiors, John Wieland Homes, Horton Development, Invitation Homes, Pulte Builders, Callaway Homes and Golf Course, Edward Andrews Homes, Red Barn Realty, Tin Roof Realty,
Buffalo Construction,
Sungwon Design Builder Construction,
R W Mechanical and Construction,
Ethan Allen, Rooms To Go, Ashley Furniture, Badcock, Haverty, Houzz Furniture, Studio Crystal, Sevres Porcelain Manufactory of France, Kuhn & Rikon Cookware of Switzerland, Frank Lloyd Wright 1867, Zillow Real Estate, Mario Batali Dutch Oven, John Boos & Co. Butcher Block, Crock-Pot Slow Cooker, Corningware, Correlle Dinnerware, Pyrex, Oneida Flatware (knives, forks, spoons, cake knife, soup ladle), Winco High Chairs for toddlers, Rubbermaid Trash Can, Cutlery and More, Mikasa Silverware, Pfaltzgraff Silverware, Wusthof Knives, J. A. Henckel Knives,

Farberware Cookware, Le Creuset Cookware, Mr. Coffee, Keurig, Alibaba, Bunn Coffee Maker, Curtis Ice Tea Maker, Sunbeam Blankets, Original Mattress Factory, Select Comfort Sleep Number Bed, Dream Bed, California Closets, Liberty Pro Organizers, Hancock Fabrics, Fabric and Fringe Warehouse, Apollo Home Improvement, Mike Karp Kitchens & Cabinets, J.R. Bush Plumbing, Florida Floor Décor, Sunniva Chairs, Williams & Sonoma, Pike's Plant Nursery, Pottery Warehouse, Pottery Barn, Mainstay Curtain Rods, Sunflex Window Blinds, Swish Cordless Venetian Blinds, Castleberry Wooden Window Shutters, Roman Shades Hunter Douglas, Uhaul Trucks, Penske Trucks, Budget Rental Truck, Enterprise Rental Truck, PODS Portable On Demand Storage, Mister Sparky Electricians, Staton Mechanical Heating & Air, Reliable Heating & Air Conditioning, Carrier Heating & Air Conditioning, Cheapest Freon Air Conditioning, Premier Indoor Comfort Systems, Casteel Heating, Cooling, Plumbing, and Electrical, Atlanta Iron Design, Victa Lawn Mower of Australia, Black & Decker Tools, Snap-On Tools, Big Lots, Brandsmart, Parkway Used Appliances, Bosch Appliances, Sears Appliances, GE Appliances, Glidden Paint, Sherwin-Williams Paint, PPG Paint, Benjamin Moore Paints, Fifth Generation Contracting, Merry Maids Cleaning Service, Spotless Cleaners, PRO Janitorial Services, Mohawk Flooring, Shaw Industries Floors, Southeastern Flooring, Woodlands Office Park, Samson & Delilah Antiques, Cobb Antique Mall, Glaber Upholstery, Bob's Upholstery We Pick Up Your Furniture, Bell Industrial Park, Platinum Realty, Deer Run Neighborhood Homes, Cherokee Forest Homes Nestled in the Pines, Eagle Watch Mountain Cabins, Twin Cedars Shopping Mall, Oak City Landscaping, Five-Star Landscaping, Unlimited Lawn Care, Salomon's Tree Service Experts, Arrow Pest Control, Public Storage, Weather Guard Basement Waterproofer, Sundry Foundation Repair, Belden Brick, Brampton Brick, Wienerberger, Melbourne Brick (Australia), Gladstone Brick, Ocon Brick, Allbrick, Gongyi Machinery, Glen-Gery, China Brick, Cherokee Brick & Tile of Macon Georgia U.S.A, Maudlin & Cook Fence Company, Cedar Living Fences, Neuffer Windows & Doors (Germany), Fakro Windows & Doors (Poland), Andersn Windows & Doors (U.S.A), Pella Windows & Doors, Jeldwen, Marvin Windows & Doors, Harloc Door Knobs & Levers, Wesloc Door Knobs, Moen Faucets, American Standard Plebe, Mansfield Toilet, TOTO toilet Japan, Kohler Toilet, Metpar Bathroom Partitions, Bradley Bathroom Partitions, Dixie Plywood, Super Sod, NG Turf, Top Turf Lawn Car, Michaels Arts & Crafts, Pamlico Swimming Pools of Georgia, Leslie's Pools, Limplex of Brazil, Ambiental Piscinas Americana of Brazil, Kubota of Japan, Hitachi Graders and Tools of Japan, John Deere Graders, Caterpillar Graders of U.S.A., Walker Tractor, Ogden Forklift, Brent US Bulldozer, Gear Wrench Adaptor, ABC Recycling, ABC Doors, United Rentals Equipment, USIC Underground Utility Locator, Excalibur Containers, Irwin Tools, Armstrong Industrial Hand Tools, Ken-Tool, Knipex German Tools, E Z Red Specialty Tools, Dial Tools, Rocket Mortgage, State Farm Homeowners or Renters Insurance, Founder's Insurance, Toltec Lighting, Petco Animal Supplies, Petsmart, Decorating Mart, Holson Burnes Group Photo Albums, Premier Staffing Agency, Aladdin Home Decorating, The Pruning Guru, Sergio's

Carpentry & Painting, Jose Painting, Waste Management Trash Pickup, TruGreen Lawn Care, Computer Crusher Recycling, Master Recycling of Texas, Glammed Funk Rethunk Junk Paints, Yellow Ribbon Tree Expert, Pike Electric, Atlanta Gas Company, Mayberry Electric, Affordable Pet Sitting, Restoration Water and Fire Damage, Dover Elevator, Otis Elevator, All Four Seasons Garage Doors, Pinestraw Specialties, Best Pawn Shop, AWP Area Wide Protective Work Zone Protection (Safety Starts Here is our slogan), WacKeys Locksmith, Roger's Firewood Delivery Available, Peaceful Gardens Senior Living Community, Saint George Retirement Villas, Sansom Shag Rugs, Hahn Oriental Rugs, Reza Persian Rugs, Safavieh Carpet, Stanley Steemer Carpet Cleaner, Hydrospec Erosion Control, Pateco Services We Clean Parking Lots & Grounds.

Construction crews can inadvertently leave behind tacks, nails, or buckets so be careful when walking or driving near construction areas.

Construction crews should wear a mask to avoid inhaling sheetrock, sawdust, or chemical fumes, wear sunblock lotion on the face to avoid sunburn, wear gloves when working with chemicals that should not be absorbed into the body through the skin, keep dangerous chemicals in check, wear a hard hat or protective eye gear when necessary.

Use a certified electrician when having electrical work done to make sure the wiring and circuits are hooked up correctly. Coolant R410A is replacing R22 freon in air conditioners because it is more environmentally safe.

DOGS

Smaller dogs:
Chihuahua, Yorkie, Pekingese, Beagle, Pomeranian, Terrier, Dachshund, Maltese, Schnauser, Toy Poodle, Shih Tzu, Pug

Larger Dogs: Doberman Pincher, German Shephard, Belgian Malinois, Greyhound, Poodle, Norwegian Lundehund, Great Dane, Bloodhound, Collie, Border Collie, Golden Retriever, Labrador, Bulldog, Pit Bull, Siberian Husky, French Briard, Basset Hound, Mixed Breed

CATS

Short-hair Tabby, Bengal, Siamese, British short hair, Turkish Angora, Abyssinian, Persian, Norwegian Forest, Ragdoll, Birman, Siberian, Mixed Breed

Dog Kennel Clubs, Cat Associations, and Horse Associations keep records or pedigrees of bloodlines and names of dogs, cats, and horses for people who want ancestor history.

SECURITY SYSTEMS

ADT Home Security, Ackerman Security, Stanley Security, Securitas, Loud, Cintas Fire Protection, Brinks Armored Transport, Dunbar Armored Transport, G4S, PSA Security, Alarm Tek, Liberty Security, BerkOne, Kaspersky, Australia Security, Security Systems Canada, Dion, RAP, Ntcctv Security, Beijing Andisheng Security Systems, Nico Security of Malaysia, Nawakara Security of Indonesia.

Furniture Exporters

China, Germany, Italy, Vietnam, Poland, Malaysia

ADVERTISING COMPANIES / COPYWRITERS

Leo Burnett, Bernice Bowles Fitz-Gibbon, David Abbott, William Bernbach, Drayton Bird, Jo Foxworth, Fairfox Cone, Stan Freberg, Joanna Wiebe, Bernadette Jiwa, Lester Wunderman, and many more.

The middle men buy from producers and sell to retailers and consumers.

Many companies advertise their products and services in magazines, newspapers, on TV, radio, and internet, on billboards, and in bulk mailouts. Many times consumers are overwhelmed by receiving so much mail from marketers or do not have time to read all of the mailouts and this mail ends up in a stack of mail called junk mail. An advertisement should not be placed on another company's sign post without permission or they will take it down. Window shoppers are like star gazers; window shoppers look at merchandise but do not buy.

CONSULTANTS

Pivotal Performance Group is a project management consulting team that helps retailers and suppliers reduce process defects, offer data-analysis and effective solutions, get products to market faster, increase customer safisfaction, and implement and optimizes call center operations.

The supply chain is the sequence of processes involved in the distribution of a commodity.

Consumers demand truth in lending, truth in advertising, and quality goods.

Consumers should address professional help by their title such as 'Dr.' and should cancel appointments well in advance so the professional can schedule another consumer in the cancelled spot.

REFERENCE Wikipedia online encyclopedia is world information translated in major world languages. Wikimedia is a non-profit company and relies on donations and volunteers.
World Book of Chicago, Illinois,
Britannica International,
Baidu Baike of China,
Columbia of England,
Encarta of Microsoft are encyclopedias offering information.

National Geographic, BBC Earth, Jacque Cousteau Ocean Society with Jacques and Philippe Cousteau, World Atlases, and Maps offer earth maps, and geographic information such as highest mountain peak, largest lake, longest river, etc.

Dictionaries explain meanings of words.

Investopedia is a website offering information about finances and money.

CHILDREN TOY MANUFACTURERS

Maisto International (Hong Kong)
Tonka Trucks
Mattel (U.S.A) Hot Wheels
Lego (Denmark)
Barbie
Fisher-Price
Barnes & Noble
Agglo
Applied Minds
Levitation
Bandai (Japan)
Banpresto (Japan)
BRIO (Sweden)
Coleco
Atari (French and U.S.A)
Nintendo (Japan)
XBOX (U.S.A.)
Hasbro (U.S.A) Nerf
Milton Bradley (U.S.A)
SEGA
Parker Brothers (U.S.A)
Estrela (Brazil)
Leapfrog
Milton & Goose Play Kitchen
Global Sources Sandbox
Swingset Company
First Playground of China
Little Tikes Play House
Alibaba (China)
Keter (Israel)
Cedar Works Playhouse

Famous Toy Retailers: F.A.O. Schwartz of New York U.S.A., Dinosaur Farm of California U.S.A., Toys R Us of New Jersey U.S.A., Hamley's Toys of London, England,
RCS Toys and Poona Toys of India,
Toy Land of Hyderabad, India,
Eloyza Toys of Malaysia,
Toy Kingdom of Africa,
Hurley Burley of Australia,
Mr. Toys Toyworld of Australia,
Estrela of Brazil, Alibaba of China,
Hakuhinkan of Japan,
Detsky Mir of Russia,

Steiff Shop and Uncle Philip's of Germany,

CAR BRANDS

Alfa Romeo 1910 Italy
Aston Martin 1913 England
Audi 1909 Germany
Bentley 1919 England
BMW (Mini Cooper) 1916 Germany
Bugatti 1998 France
Chevrolet (Corvette) 1911 U.S.A
Chrysler (Jeep) 1941 U.S.A
Dodge (Charger) 1900 U.S.A
Ferrari 1947 Italy
Fiat Abarth 1899 Italy
Ford (Mustang) 1903 U.S.A
GMC (Cadillac, Buick) 1911 U.S.A.
Honda (Acura) 1948 Japan
Hyundai 1947 South Korea
KIA 1944 South Korea
Lamborghini 1963 Italy
Land Rover (Jaguar) 1948 England
Lincoln 1917 U.S.A.
Maserati 1914 Italy
Mazda 1920 Japan
Mercedes 1926 Germany
Mitsubishi 1870 Japan
Nissan (Infinity) 1933 Japan
Porsche 1931 Germany
Renault 1899 France
Rolls Royce 1904 England
Saab 1945 Sweden
Smart 1994 Germany
Subaru 1954 Japan
Suzuki 1909 Japan
Tesla 2003 U.S.A.
Toyota (Lexus) 1937 Japan
Volkswagen 1937 Germany
Volvo 1927 Sweden

Plymouth was a brand of Chrysler from 1920-2001. LaSalle was a division of GMC Cadillac from 1927-1940, Pontiac of GMC from 1926-2010, Hummer of GMC from 1992-2010. Edsel, DeSoto, and Mercury were brands of Ford in the 1920s-1050s. Studebaker was a brand of cars in the U.S.A. from 1852-1967. American Motors was a merger of Nash-Kelvinator and Hudson Motor from 1954-1988. Saturn was a division of GMC from 1985-2010. Troller of Brazil 1995 is a subsidiary of Ford.

Invention of the Automobile

The first car was invented in 1886 by Karl Benz in Germany. Karl Benz and Gottlieb Daimler produced the Mercedes automobile in 1901. The Volkswagen Beetle was an economy car produced in Germany by Ferdinand Porsche under German leader Adolf Hitler.
Henry Ford (1863-1947) of America helped created the first assembly line to mass produce cars. The first car engines were very loud until mufflers were invented. The first cars had no seatbelts, until people died in car wrecks and then seatbelts were invented. Charles Goodyear of Connecticut, USA is credited with developing a pliable rubber for tires by treating rubber with sulfur in the late 1800's. Dayton Tires in Ohio produced rubber airless tires. Robert Thomson and John Boyd Dunlop of Sweden; and Eduardo Michelin of France are credited with developing usable pneumatic tires that were inflated with air. Michelin also developed wheels for trains. Giovanni Pirelli of Italy, Harvey Firestone of Tennessee, USA; Nitto Tires, Hitto Tires, Continental Tire of Germany; Bridgestone Tire of Japan; Fountain Tire of Canada; Cooper of Ohio; Yokohama of Japan; JK Tyre of India; Petroshina of Russia; Shanghai Tyre of China were the earliest major tire manufacturers. If you look at tires or at the bottoms of your shoes you can see the wear patterns of how the tread or leather is being worn down. Rubber is made from rubber trees or petroleum products.

When you buy a car, you may want to consider the cost to fuel it and the cost to insure it.

Engine power is described as being compared to horsepower or the power of a horse. Horse and oxen power helped humans to survive on the planet.

Motorcycles/3 and 4-Wheel ATV All Terrain Vehicles

Aeon 1970 Taiwan
BMW 1916 Germany
Ducati
Harley-Davidson
Honda
Kawasaki 1966 U.S.A.
KTM 1992 Austria
Piaggio 1884 Italy
Polaris, Indian, Victory ATV
Suzuki
Yamaha

TRUCKS, EQUIPMENT, & TOOLS

There are hundreds of truck manufacturers, companies, industrial designers and engineers that make equipment and tools.

Bill Moggridge is an industrial engineer who designed the first laptop computer and a camping trailer that can be attached to a car bumper.

Some freight companies: SAIA, Tribe which is owned by a Native American woman, Holland regional, Fleet, Werner Enterprises, Mayflower, CRST Expedited, EPES of North Carolina, HSM of Florida, Trans Am Trucking, R&L Trucking, Old Dominion, Swift Transportation, Danny Herman Trucking, Maersk Group of Denmark Kenfreight of Africa, Logistics Australia, MSC Tracking Mediterranean Shipping, Yamato Holdings of Japan, XPO Logistics of Europe, DHL Freight, Dachser, TNT, LKW Walter, Kuehne + Nagel, Estes, Crete, Yellow, Abmere, Blakely, JB Hunt, Stevens, Marten, Lasalle Bristol, Simon's,Evergreen Trucking, Tote Maritime Shipping & Trucking, Benore Logistics, Spoerl Trucking, Hapag-Lloyd of Germany, Schneider

Vehicle and Engine Maintenance

Oil change, engine coolant filled if applicable, Brake fluid filled, Tires filled with air, balanced, and rotated, Transmission flushed, Spark plugs and battery in good condition, All lights working. Clean windshield and windows. Windshield wipers in good condition. Spare tire and jumper cables in trunk.

If you have the correct size windshield wipers on, the wipers will glide quietly across the windshield during a rain.

Make sure driver's license and car insurance premiums are up to date. You may have to take a driver's exam to get your license. Truck drivers take the CDL exam to get a commercial driver's license.

Many countries have different classifications of licenses for trucks versus automobiles because trucks require more training in order to operate the trucks.

Drive the speed limit to avoid getting a ticket by the police or state patrol.

Always wear seat belts when driving and make sure children are in their car seats.

When you are driving, get out of the way and pull off the road to the side of the road to allow emergency vehicles like ambulances and firetrucks to pass.

You can buy emergency roadside assistance in case you have car trouble and are left stranded. The roadside assistance companies will come to you.

Drive slow in ice and snow. Ice forms on bridges before it forms on the roads.

You may want to use the restroom before embarking on a trip, keep goodies, water, medicine, or blankets in the vehicle, or preplan stopping points. Some keep a big jar in their vehicle in case of a traffic jam which could be used as a toilet.

In 2012 there was a 140 car pileup on an interstate in Texas during a fog.

Blast cool air onto your windshield to defog.

Make sure you are not driving down the road with your blinker on, as this can be confusing to other drivers. There is a blind spot to the side that a driver cannot see.

CAR REPOSSESSIONS

If you do not make car payments on a financed car or truck, the vehicle may be repossessed. You will then have to make arrangements to get the car back or the

repossession will be reported to a credit bureau.
When the principal amount of the car is paid off, there might be some late fees that are due if any of your car payments have been late. You must pay the late fees in order to get the title of ownership to your car. Some car financiers will repossess your car in the middle of the night and leave you stranded without a car until you pay the late fees. Many think this is an unethical practice because the buyer should be able to pay the late fees without having the car repossessed.

ROADS & BRIDGES: No potholes, Traffic Signals and Road Signs Correct & Visible, Safe structures. Some highways have express lanes and mile markers.

LUXURIES in 2010 THAT HUMANS DID NOT HAVE 100 YEARS AGO

Clean water, appliances powered by natural gas and electricity, cars, trucks, airplanes, Polyester jackets with fleece linings with zippers and pockets, vinyl rain jackets, suntan lotion to protect the skin from ultraviolet rays, antibiotics, soft toilet tissue, disposable baby diapers, computers, communication by telephones to hear human voices, frozen or canned foods, sliced bread, refrigerators, modern tools, shoes with rubber soles, bottled water.

Some wooden bridges may be over 100 years old. Wooden bridges only last about 15-20 years because they rot out.

Bicycles were invented in 1817-1860 with wooden wheels.

Modern Tools:

Stainless steel eating utensils: fork, knife, spoon, spoon ladle, spatula or turner, cake icer, vegetable peeler, garlic press, cheese grater, salad tongs, bread tongs, can opener, nut cracker, microwave oven, ice bucket, ice crusher,
scissors, hammer & stainless steel nails, screwdriver and stainless steel nails, pliers, dust pan & broom, wheelbarrow, multi-cutter titanium steel cutter that cuts nails, wood, steel cables, and tree limbs.

INTERNATIONAL COMPANIES 2017

McDonalds, State Grid Corporation of China, China National Petroleum, Sinopec Petroleum, Delta Airlines, Emirates Airlines, Air China, British Airways, Egypt Air, Air India, Pepsi, Royal Dutch Shell, Exxon, Valero Energy, Mobil, BP Oil, Chevron, Citgo, Amoco, Racetrac, QT, Total, Volkswagen Group, Toyota, Apple, Intel, Walmart, Home Depot, 3M Science innovations, Quintiles Healthcare, Accenture, Atento Brazil Call Center, Novo Nordish Pharmaceuticals, Roche Pharmaceuticals, Warner-Lambert, PfizerMars Chocolate, Facebook, Google, Marriott, Kimberly Clark, Fed Ex Express, UPS, Adidas, Bicardi, Fujitsu, Sony, Nestle, Nokia, Oracle, Whirlpool, Sears, Toshiba, Procter & Gamble, Red Bull, Siemens, SAS, NetApp, Medtronic, International House of Pancakes IHOP, J. Christopher, Waffle House, General Electric, Scana Energy, JAT Energy of Chattanooga Tennessee, Atlanta Fuel Company, AAA Travel International Club, Amazon, Masonic Regalia International, Genentech Biotech, WUXI Genomics, deCode Genetics, Proctor and Gamble, GermX Hand Sanitizer, Birla Carbon, En Plas Injection Molding, Canada, Anchor Hocking Company since 1905.

98 countries produce oil. Russia, Saudi Arabia, U.S.A, Iran, Iraq, China, Canada, U.A.E., Kuwait, Brazil, Venezuela, Mexico, Nigeria, Angola, Norway, Kazakhstan, Qatar, Algeria, Oman, U.K., Colombia, Indonesia, Azerbaijan, India, Malaysia, Ecuador, Atgentina, Egypt, Libya, Congo Republic of, Vietnam, Australia, Thailand, Sudan and South Sudan, Turkmenistan and many more. The first oil rush was in Titusville, Pennsylvania, U.S.A. in 1959 discovered by Edwin L. Drake.

FIRE and CARBON MONOXIDE DETECTOR Manufacturers

Kidde, First-Alert, Universal Security Instrument, BRK, Asante, System Sensor, Roost, Gogogu, Halo, Nest Protect, Lennox.

In 2013 19 firefighters were killed when they were accidentally trapped while trying to extinguish a wildfire on Granite Mountain in Arizona, U.S.A.

In 2017 a family was killed while sleeping in a condo they rented while on vacation in Cancun Mexico by inhaling propane gas from a water heater that had rusted pipes.

INVESTMENTS / FINANCE/ BANKS

Examples of STOCK MARKETS

DOW
S&P 500
NY Stock Exchange
NASDAQ NY
London Stock Exchange
Euronext EU
TMX Group of Canada
National Stock Exchange of India
Japan Exchange Group Tokoyo
Shanghai Stock Exchange
Hong Kong Stock Exchange
Deutsche Borse Germany
Korea Exchange
Six Swiss Exchange
Nasdaq Nordic Stockholm
Australian Securities Exchange
JSE Limited South Africa
Taiwan Stock Exchange
BM&F Bovespa Brazil
BME Spain
Saudi Stock Exchange

Usually bondholders get paid returns before stockholders and taxes may apply. Corporations and cities issue bonds to raise money for financial goals.

Jamal was a Hindu investor who was born in Kenya but lived in Germany, India, Great Britain, and the U.S.A. Jamal played the stock market and lost $300,000 in March 2009 but he regained it back 8 years laters and tripled his losses. $300,000 U.S. At the time he invested, $300,000 U.S. dollars equaled 30,410,700 Kenya shillings.

He searched his soul and his soul told him to stay put and hang in there. He learned a valuable lesson from this episode. He realized that he needed a reserve fund to cover living expenses for use during bad times. That was his primary focus and withing 3 years he was able to maintain a reserve fund to carry him through for 2 years in bad times.

It is a well known saying from ancient times that man does not live by bread alone.

A question in the world that many ask is: What is a fair profit?

PLASTIC CARDS:

Credit cards such as:

Mastercard, Visa, Discover, Emerald, American Express, Capital One, Barclaycard, Chase, Citi, Care Credit affiliated with banks.

Interest rates can vary from 5% to 25% on credit cards.

Prepaid gift cards or reloadable money cards available to make purchases at retail stores, on-line purchases, or to pay bills. Walmart and Target offer reloadable money cards. Greendot is a prepaid money card.

Debit cards associated with your checking account where you bank.

Financial planners, wealth management advisors, investment advisors, capital investors, banks, and credit unions can help individuals and corporations meet their goals by investing money and hoping to receive a monetary increase on the investments.

A reverse mortgage draws money from the equity a person has in a property.

The exchange rates of currencies between countries is decided by the traders and may be decided on such factors as the
stability of a country's economy and citizens, reserves,liabilities, and more.

If a country is war-torn and the streets have no name and militia are roaming the streets and causing violence, investors may not want to help develop a country's communication, energy, water infrastructure, or fortification of grain storage.
It is impossible to list all financial corporations and the CEOs of corporations and advisors in the pages of this book.

Some names of wealth management Advisors, banks, mortage brokers, finance planners are:
Merrill Lynch, Morgan Stanley, Fidelity Investments, Charles Schwab, Goldman Sachs, The Vanguard Group, UBS Wealth Management, JP Morgan Chase, Edward Jones Investments, TD Ameritrade, Citigroup, Lehman Brothers, E-Trade, Bank of America, Wells Fargo, Raymond James Financial, Suntrust Bank, Northern Trust, Renasant Bank, Hamilton Bank, Thrivent, BNY Mellon Wealth Management, Bank of the Ozarks, RBC Wealth Management, Bessemer Trust, Confidence Banco Brazil, Berstein Private Wealth Management, PNC Wealth Management, U.S.Bank, Stifel, Robert W. Bird, First Republic, Wilmington Trust, Neuberger, Fifth Third, BB&T, Silvercrest, William Blair, Glenmede, ALPHA-Bank (Russia), Sberbank of Russia, Credit Suisse, Scottrade, Bear Stearns, Deutsche Bank, Prudential, Sun life, Manulife, Motley Fool, Tidewater Finance, Charter Bank, Capital Mortgage, GoBank, Peoples Financial of Georgia, Horizon Bank, Captial One, BBVA Compass, Vystar Credit Union, Teacher's Credit Union, Key Bank, Cornerstone Bank, Heuberger and Andes, Juniper Bank, Iberia Bank, Woodforest Bank, United Community Bank, Diebold Nixdorf, Entegra, Comerica, World Bank.

Compound interest is interest made on interest. As an example, compound interest is good for an investor when gaining money in a mutual fund.
But, another example is that compound interest is bad for a debtor who is accumulating huge amounts of interest owed on credit cards.

Reconcile your checking account balance with the bank's balance often so no debits or withdrawals will bounce.
'Playing the float' means that you do not have enough money in your account to cover the
withdrawals on your account but you plan to make a deposit before the withdrawals hit your account. Consider the risk factor of the bounce fees before you play the float.

Interest rates, real estate values, retail prices are based on many factors studied by marketers, economists, investors, and others who study fair market values, consumer demand, commodities (bulk shipments of corn, oil, oranges,
pork bellies), and politics locally and across the globe. Investments have risk values and humans have to decide what level of risk they are willing to take when investing.
Sometimes investors will lose money in their portfolio investments or business.
Some countries allow financial restructuring and bankruptcy.
If you lose all of your money and go broke, remember that some people lose their life in the line of duty of their job, to their country in military service, or due to illness or unfortunate circumstances.
Money is not everything.

Examples of COMMODITIES / Mercantiles / Metals EXCHANGES Raw Materials such as wheat, barley, sugar, maize (corn), cotton, cocoa, rubber, coffee, milk, gold, pork, oil, metals, gold, energy

AfMX Nairobi, Africa
NCDEX India
NMCE India
MCX Manila Phillippines
EGYCOMEX Cairo, Egypt
JSE Sandton, South Africa
ECX Addis Ababa, Ethiopia
BMF Sao Paulo, Brazil
NYMEX New York, USA
MGEX Minneapolis, USA
MATba Buenos Aires, Argentina
CMEX Phnom Penh, Cambodia
DCE Dalian, China
KANEX Osaka, Japan
TGE Tokyo, Japan
NSE Kathmandu, Nepal
PMEX Pakistan
SICOM Singapore
CZCE Zhengzhou, China
VNX Ho Chi Minh City, Vietnam
MCE Ulaanbaatar City, Mongolia
DEE Lagos State, Nigeria

ACCOUNTING PRINCIPLES

4 Accounting Measurements:
Assets (property you own), Liabilities (what you owe to others), Income (Money Earned), and Expenses (Costs of Doing Business and Expenditures).

5 Major Accounting Reports:
Income Statement, Balance Sheet,
Statement of Cash Flow,
Statement of Retained Earnings,
Notes to Financial Reports.

IFRS is an acronym for International Financial Reporting Standards. Agencies have tried to set some global standards for financial reporting because trade and stock options have become international. Disclosure of information must reflect the true and fair value of an enterprise to satisfy the needs and gain the trust of investors, employees, and stakeholders such as customers, contractors, creditors, and suppliers.

Business people need to gather as much information they can in order to decide if they will take a chance on a person or a business entity.

INSURANCE

Car insurance may include liability (coverage if you hurt another driver or their car), collision (coverage to repair your own car damaged in an accident), comprehensive (coverages from theft, fire, flood, and vandalism), uninsured motorist (coverage for damages when the other driver is uninsured). Roadside assistance coverage can be purchased for roadside emergencies.

After your vehicle is paid off and you receive the title to your car, some people drop the collision insurance so the premiums will be lower, but it depends on the value of the car and a person's financial situation.

A decuctible is the monetary amount that you are willing to pay before the insurance pays. Higher deductibles mean lower premium payments.

Other types of insurance are home owners, renters, health, dental, life, and mortgage insurance.

A whole life insurance policy accumulates cash value. A term insurance policy does not accumulate cash value.

Some countries may offer worker's compensation insurance in case an employee gets injured on the job. And cannot work for a time. Worker's Compensation insurance could pay the employee's bills until the employee can work again.

Some large insurance companies:
Assicurazioni Generali (Italy 1831)
AXA (Paris)
Zurich Insurance Group (Switzerland)
China Life Insurance (1949)
Bershire Hathaway (U.S.A. 1889)
Mountain Lakes Insurance (U.S.A.2000)
Prudential (U.S.A. 1848)

United Health Group
Munich Re Group (Germany 1880)
Japan Post Holding
Allianz SE (Germany 1890)
AIA Group (Hong Kong)
ING
Ping An Insurance of China
MetLife (MET)
Manulife Financial Corp (MFC)
AIG
Aviva (Britain)
Aetna Foundation (U.S.A.)
Blue Cross Blue Shield (U.S.A.)
CIGNA (1792 Philadelphia, U.S.A)
GEICO (U.S.A.)
Express Scripts
Assurance
Progressive
Humana (U.S.A)

WORLD's Largest Food Companies

Russia: Russky Produkt OAO, Yekaterinburg Meat, Baltika Breweries

Denmark: Carlsberg Group

U.S.A.: General Mills,Haagen Dazs, Mondelez, Mars, Coca-Cola, Con Agra, PepsiCo, Frito-Lay, Kellogg, Eggland Eggs, Wrigley, Oceanspray, Tropicana, Welch's, SunMaid, Tyson, Anheuser-Busch, Phoenix Foods, Mott's, Smithfield, Conagra, Sysco, Monarch, Treehouse Foods, Dupont, US Foods, Imcol Distribution (Hispanic Foods), Bakkal International Foods, Suvidha International Foods, Huy Fong Foods, Sutherland's Foodservice since 1947, Seaboard, Performance Foods, TAMA, Jelly Belly since 1898, Mars since 1911, Hershey since 1894, Ferrara since 1908

Brazil: JBS SA Brazil

Peru: Agricola Pampa Baja Grapes

China: WH Group of China, Shenzhey

India: Food Corporation of India

Japan: JFC International

South Africa: Tiger Brands

Saudi Arabia: Almarai Dairy Riyadh

France: Danone

U.K. Britain: Cadbury, Unilever (Denmark and Britain), Swizzels since 1928, Rowntree's since 1862, Smith & Company (Altoids Breath Mints)

Scandanavia (Norway, Sweden, Finland, and Denmark): Fazer Foods

Sweden: Wasabrod

Switzerland: COOP Group, Lindt since 1845, Nestle since 1905

Denmark: Arla Dairy

Denmark and Italy: Perfetti Van Melle since 2001

Italy: Parmalat Dairy, Perugina since 1907

Spain: Chupa Chups since 1958

Germany: Dr. Oetker since 1891, Storck since 1903

Australia: Fonterra, Lion Nathan, Bursaria Fine Foods, Bulla Dairy

New Zealand: Fonterra

Consumers should read labels of goods to educate themselves as to the contents. Chef Boyardee is a canned brand of Chef Hector Boiardi tomato sauce and pasta that has been sold since 1924 by ConAgra in Omaha, Nebraska, U.S.A. The Chef Boyardee has no artificial preservatives, no

artificial colors, and has no BPA epoxy liner in the can. BPA liners were intended to prevent acids in foods from causing aluminum metals of cans to leak into foods but BPA liners contain bisphenol A chemicals which are artificial estrogens that can interfere with human endocrine system.
Some people think that canned food, canned soda, or foods in plastic containers should only be consumed once a week. Many people advocate for organic foods. Boxed prepared caked mixes were invented in 1947 and included powdered dehydrated eggs and milk in the mix. Around 1970 the mixes became popular when dehydrated eggs and milk were left out requiring fresh eggs and fresh milk to be added to the mixes. Charlotte Cramer Sachs, a German immigrant living in New York, and John P. Duff of Pittsburgh, Pennsylvania both made boxed mixes.
In 1953 frozen dinners were introduced by Carl A. Swanson, a Swedish immigrant living in Nebraska who moved to New Jersey. Pinnacle Foods currently provides the Swanson brand and Campbell Soup took over the Swanson broth.

Boxed breakfast cereals were invented in 1863 by James Caleb Jackson in New York. Varieties of cold cereals include toasted oat rings, puffed rice, corn flakes, granola with nuts and fruits, and square chex of rice, wheat, and corn. There are also hot cereal varieties of oatmeal and wheat.

Cranberry bogs are pollinated by bees. Bees are reducing in population and scientists think one cause may be wireless technology radiation.

Names of cheeses: Swiss,
Gruyere (Switzerland), Mozzarrella,
Parmesan, Provolone, Ricotta,
Asiago (Italy), Paneer, Khoya (India),
Feta (Greece),
Cheddar, Port Wine (England),
Camembert, Muenster (France),
Havarti (Denmark), Gouda (Netherlands),
Jarlsberg, Norvegia (Norway),
Aura Blue Cheese (Finland),
Jibneh Baida or Arabic White Cheese,
Nabulsi (Palestine), Jibin White Cheese
(Lebanon), Colby-Jack, Velveeta, American
White, Yellow, or White Cheese (United
States),
Cotija, Oaxaca (Mexico), Manchego
(Spain), Domiati (Egypt),
Ayibe (Ethiopia), Carivane (Mauritania),
Chhena (Bangladesh),
Chura Kampo, Rushan (China),
Dangke (Indonesia), Lighvan, Mahali (Iran),
Sakura (Japan), Byaslag (Mongolia), Flower
of Rajya (Nepal), Kesong puti (Philippines),
Imsil (South Korea), Chechil (Armenia),
Bergkase, Mondseer (Austria),
Brussels, Passendale (Belgium), Bryndza,
Circassian (Russia), Telemea,
Cas (Romania), Castelo Branco (Portugal),
Gbejna (Malta), Jani (Latvia),
Hofoingi (Iceland),
Orda, Trappista (Hungary),
Urda (Moldova), Urda (Macedonia),
Sulguni (Georgia),
Atleet, Kadaka, Eesti Juust (Estonia),
Abertam (Czech Republic),
Paski sir, Dimsi (Croatia),
Akkawi (Cyprus), Sirene,
Kashkaval (Bulgaria), Livno,
Travnicki (Bosnia, Herzegovina)

POPULAR SOUPS

Vegetable with Barley
Potato / Potato with Bacon
Green Split Pea and Ham
Tomato
Kale
Chicken with Rice, Noodle, or Dumpling
Cream of Celery, Cream of Broccoli
Cream of Mushroom
Fish Soup
Maruchan
French Onion w Gruyere cheese & Bread
French Vichyssoise
French Lobster or Shrimp Bisque

French Bouillabaisse
Japanese Miso or Maruchan
Chinese Won Ton
Chinese Sweet & Sour
Chinese Egg Drop
Thai Coconut Chicken
Thai Curry Vegetable
Italian Minestrone
Middle-Eastern Lentil
Moroccan Squash and Carrot
Spanish Gazpacho or Salmorejo
Russian Borscht or Ukha or Solyanka
New England Clam Chowder
Manhattan Clam Chowder
African Pepper
West African Peanut Soup
Swedish Yellow Split Pea
Swedish Spinach, Swedish Meatball
Chili

Tea Flavors

Orange Pekoe Black, Green Pekoe, Mint or Spearmint Peppermint Combo, Peach Mango, Chamomile, Lemon, Honey, Blackberry, Blueberry, Earl Gray, Chai. Some add a little milk or cream and a few drops of honey or sugar to their hot tea. Some drink plain hot water with lemon.

Coffee Flavors

Plain Coffee, Hazelnut, Vanilla, Irish Crème de menthe, Salty caramel, dulce de caramel, maple, cinnamon vanilla, white Chocolate raspberry, pumpkin, peppermint Mocha (Chocolate), Italian crème, toffee, amaretto, espresso. Brewed coffee in a pot on a burner is only good for about an hour. Cappucino is double espresso with steamed milk foam. Americano is espresso with added hot water.

Coffee labels may say: Arabian, Colombian, Guatamalen, Hawaiian, Kenyan, Ethiopian, Tanzanian, Madagascan, Barundi, Sumatra, Cameroon, Seattle to indicate the type of coffee plants from different parts of the world.

The chemical composition of caffeine is C8 H10 N4 O2 and is a stimulant to the body. Consuming too much caffeine can be fatal so limit the tea, coffee, and energy drinks such as Monster, Full Throttle, Red Bull, Boost, B2, and Rock Star energy drinks.

Coffee is a common luxury taken for granted in that coffee is not served in most jails.

Hot Cocoa Flavors

Creamy hot cocoa with marshmallows or whipped cream on top and made with real milk, Mint, Dark Chocolate, Malted Milk Chocolate, Salted Caramel, Gingerbread

Juices

Orange, apple, cranberry, tomato, carrot, tropical juice blends with mango, kiwi, pineapple, berries, aloe vera. Homemade lemonade can be made with water, lemons, and a sweetener such as sugar.

Some **HOTEL CHAINS**

InterContinental Hotels Group, Holiday Inn, Hilton Worldwide, AccorHotels of France, Marriott International, Vienna Hotels, Plateno Hotels (China), China Lodging, Grand Metropark (Hong Kong), Traveler Inn (Hong Kong), Shangrila Hotels, Jinling, New Century (East China), Green Tree (Shanghai), Azimut Moscow, Radisson, Sheraton, Lonrho (South Africa), Ibis Styles, Hyatt, Mercure, Swiss Spirits, Golden Tulip, Choice, Best Western, Starwood, Novotel, Okamura (Japan), APA Always Pleasant Amenity (Japan), Comfort Inn, Wingate Hotels, Trident, Lalit, ITC, and Taj Mahal of India, Sheraton Princess Kaiulani Hotel (Hawaii), Claridges Hotel (London), Four Seasons Hotel (New York, London, Atlanta), Ritz Carlton, Mark Twain Hotel (Chicago), Motel 6, Red Roof Inn, Quality Inn, Sleep inn, Fairfield Inn, Rodeway Inn, Howard

Johnson Hotels, Excalibur Hotel & Casino (Las Vegas, Nevada, U.S.A.), Hard Rock Hotel & Casino (Biloxi, Mississippi), Wild Goose Lodge (Oregon, U.S.A.), Kakslauttanen Arctic Resort (Finland).

Housekeeping Tasks: Floors Cleaned & Vacuumed, Linens Changed, Bathrooms cleaned & stocked, Kitchen Appliances cleaned, Trash emptied, Windows cleaned, Laundry Done, No mildew or mold present on cabinets, carpets, sheetrock, windows, vents, or ducts. It is not necessary to bleach inside an oven or microwave because high heats sanitize. Degreasers are effective on stoves. If you boil a cup of water for 3 minutes inside a microwave, the inside will be steamy and you can wipe the inside with a wet cloth. If a person cleans wells, they have the Midas touch.

World's Largest TELECOM

China Mobile, Vodafone Group, Telefonica, AmericaMovil, Telenor Group, Deutsche Telecom, China Unicom, Telia Sonera, France Telecom, Bharti Airtel, MTN Group, Mobile Telesystems, Reliance Commnications, Orascom Telecom, Svyaznoy Russia & Belarus, Russia MegaFon, Russia Euroset, ACE Australia, U.S.A. AT&T, Verizon, Sprint, TMobile, MCI, Intel, EMC, Symantec, Cisco
An emergency beep signal may indicate severe weather or a kidnapping child alert. 3-Way Calling means that 3 people can speak together on one phone call.

COMPUTER, ELECTRONICS & TECH

Apple, Samsung, Hewlett Packard, IBM, Foxconn, Panasonic, Toshiba, Microsoft. Sony, Dell, NEC, Philips, Radio Shack, Canon (USA), Digi-Key, Lenova, Epson, Neumann USA (microphones and amplifiers), Media Markt (Germany), m.video (Russia), High Fidelity, Kingston, Konica Minolta of Japan, Rubycon, Nichicon (Japan), Acer (Taiwan), Asus Tek (Taiwan), Datong Electronics (England), Verifone Credit Card Machine, Ingenico Credit Card Machine, Comcast Xfinity Internet, AT&T DirecTV, Dish HD satellite Asia,Pro-Tech Cabling, Halo Electronics, Emerson, Samsung, RCA, Sceptre, Magnavox, Mitsubishi, Hitachi, Lucent, Westinghouse, insignia, Vizio, LG, Coby, Sharp, Sanyo, Hisense, Element, CISCO, Polaroid, JVC, Sylvania, Apex, Funai, Motorola, Pioneer, Akai, Zenith, Viacom, Fujitsu, General Electric GE, Amano, SanDisk, Transcend, MIS Medical Imaging Solutions, Siemens Hearing Aids, Insource Solutions.

SEARCH ENGINES

Google, Bing, Yahoo, Ask, AOL, Baidu, Juno, Yandex, Wolframalpha, DuckDuckGo, Mozilla Fox, MSN, Firefox, Chrome.

You can click on button icons such as Web,Images, Videos, Shopping, or News to pull up different types of information such as articles with written words, pictures, videos, news articles, shopping ads.

You may have to type in words several different ways in order to find web pages on the topics you are researching because the words that you type into the box have to match the words that are stored in the web pages. For example, if you are looking for 'homemade meals', the words could be entered as homemade, home -made, or home made.

Some words to include in your search along with other search words that could help to locate articles: original, history, since, list, author, movie, today, what is, year released.

SEO means search engine optimizer that computer programmers use to display web pages from data bases. IP address is a unique string of numbers separated by periods that identifies each computer using internet protocol to communicate over a network.

Google apps have a feature that allows web pages to be translated into the language of your choice.

Siri is a computer program that allows a person to speak into the microphone of their cell phone and ask a question and Siri will talk back to you with an answer.

Modern computers and cellphones have made communication on earth between humans almost instantaneous whereas communication was slow before. The new technologies allow for more people to be able to be witnesses to live events.

Cardio EKG computer apps can allow a patient to transmit their cardio rhythm to their doctor over the internet.

Lifealert.com allows a person to press a button on a necklace to cry for help in an instant.

A problem with computers is that hackers can create false computer news,data, and take over a person's identity.

Many computer apps can be downloaded for free to enjoy.

Some social media or computer apps:
Facebook (Directory for anyone who wants to post a personal profile. Facebook had over 2 billion users in 2017, making it one of the top ten biggest websites Facebook also allows messages to be sent to friends privately and allows users to post information on blogs for all to see.) Mark Zuckerberg is the CEO of Facebook Year 2015. Other founders are Eduardo Saverin, Dustin Moskovitz, Andrew McCollum, and Chris Hughes. Facebook started as an online app for Harvard University students in Massachusetts. Mark married Priscilla Chan, a pediatrician from Boston.
Microsoft MSN Network:
CEO Satya Nadella 2017.
Google: Sundar Pichai an Indian American CEO of GOOGLE Year 2017.
Yahoo: Marissa Mayer is a woman CEO Year 2017.
LinkedIn (Directory for work professionals to search for jobs and post information.)
Skype (Communicate with another person by looking at each other in computer monitors).
Twitter, Messenger (send messages)
YouTube (Users post their own videos made with cellphones, tablets, and computers.)
Pinterest (post photos)
Kik (Messenger for video calls and chat)
Viber (Japanese instant messenger and voice)
Video sharing: YouTube, Baidu Video, Google Video, Yahoo Video, AOL Video, Crackle, DailyMotion, MetaCafe, Fujitsu, Vimeo
Shazam music
Spotify music
Match.com (singles match dating site)
Kindle.com ebooks
Scribd.com ebooks
Computer game apps:
Candy Crush, Toy Blast, Solitaire, Slot Machines, Super Mario Brothers, Space Invaders, Geometry Dash, Jumanji Dash, Train Simulator, Space Simulator, Airplane Simulator, Car Races, Build a Meal Game App for Kids, Bake a Cake App for Kids, Fruit Ninja, Balloon Pop, Peppa Pig
Adult design apps:
Design a Room with Furniture App.
Document Editors: Microsoft Office, Kingsoft Office, Google Docs, Apple iWork Pages
Computer Virus Protection: Norton Antivirus, McAfee, Avira, Kaspersky, Bitdefender, Avast
Maps: Google Earth, Google Maps
Website Builders: Wordpress, Wix, Soverse, Weebly, Blazonco

Most laptops or cell phones run on Microsoft Windows Platform, Apple Mac OS Platform, Linux, or Android.

Modern laptops may offer a C Drive connected to the Cloud. Many programmers want old computers like in the 1980s where the C Hard Drive is not connected to the Internet or the Cloud.

Computer apps allow the brightness to be turned off after a specified time to save battery power and the apps describe it as putting your device to sleep.

Microsoft XBOX games: Call of Duty, Lego World, Fighter Z, Dragonball, Super Heroes, Overwatch, Minecraft, Cars, Need for Speed, Peggle, Barbie and her sisters, Overcooked
Nintendo games: Super Mario Bros, Tetris, The Legend of Zelda, Splatoon, Red Racer, Excite Bike, Bill Elliott's NASCAR Challenge, Cooking Mama, Animal Crossing
Nintendo Gameboy; Tetris
LeapFrog LeapPad children's educational games

ECOMMERCE or E-Commerce

FORBES and The Economist are some magazines reporting that 52 billion U.S. dollars was generated through internet purchases in 2014, 107 billion was generated in 2015, and 200 billion was generated in 2017.
5 billion people clicked on the internet each day in 2017.
LAW ENFORCEMENT AGENCIES such as: FBI, INTERPOL, SLEDCOM Police are working hard to catch criminals such as thieves, cyber criminals, human traffickers, and more. Forensic experts study the details of crime scenes in order to understand what happened and find information that will lead to the culprit or culprit.

AFIS is a fingerprint database.

In 2016 in Oswego, New York a man tried to steal an ATM by connecting the ATM with a chain to his truck, hoping to pull the ATM out of the concrete. The police caught him.

Report suspicious activity to the police.

Some people who are victims of crimes hire private investigators to assist in solving crimes.

COURTS and JUDGES

Many countries have a court system in which criminals, civilians, corporations, or work professionals are brought before judges and/or a jury to be judged for:
(1) criminal issues such as murder, robbery, theft, vehicle hit and runs, vandalism, criminal negligence, marijuana raids
(2) civil issues such as divorces, tax evasion, breach of contracft, civil negligence, traffic violations such as parking violations, and more.
In some countries, illegal parking on a street is a crime.
(3) juvenile issues committed by youth who are not condidered to be adults
Judges, jury members, and lawyers take an oath to offer a fair trial for the accused and to uphold the laws of the country or region. Judges and jurors should not take bribes to deliver a judgement but should be impartial investigators and offer a fair judgement based on evidence presented and proved.

Probate courts may administer marriage licenses, weapons carrying licenses, fishing licenses, building permits, and more.

Archaeologists and excavators believe from studying ancient relics that men and women in ancient Egypt and Europe both stood equal in the eyes of the law, because there were both kings and queens that ruled the lands.

The Magna Carta Libertatum was a charter signed by King John of England at Runnymeade on June 15, 1215 to improve relations between King John and baron rebels on his lands. The Magna Carta provided for church rights, protected the barons from illegal prisonment, access to swift and fair justice, and limits on feudal payments to Crown of England.

A notary is a person who is authorized to verify a person's signature on important official legal documents.

A divorce should be avoided, but some say: This is not the same person that I married and I cannot live with them. It is said that a news reporter wants to get a story right and accurate and a lawyer wants to get the story right for the side he is representing.

There was a story about a trucker named Joe who got a speeding ticket while crossing the plains of Texas. The trucker argued with the cop that there was no speed limit on the desert roads. The trucker was thrown in jail for arguing and the trucker could not find his lawyer or a judge he knew so he had to spend a few nights in a small jail. The judge had been playing golf and the lawyer was on a cruise. The situation was finally resolved when his lawyer called back form the port of Miami and Joe was let go.

World's Busiest Airports

Hartsfield-Jackson Atlanta, Ga. USA
Beijing Capital, China
Dubai, United Arab Emirates
O'Hare, Chicago, Illinois, USA
London Heathrow, England

AIRCRAFT

ICAO is the International Civil Aviation Organization that keeps a list of aircraft manufacturers. It is an agency of the United Nations formed in 1947. It codifies principles of international aviation.

Airlines and travel agencies offer assistance in making travel plans and reservations for your trip. Discounts and special deals may be offered. Some offer help booking hotels, rental cars, travel guides, and more.

Many airports offer passengers moving walkways that work on electricity, escalators in addition to stairs, food and gift shops, lounges & restrooms, and waiting areas with chairs.

Handcuffs may be necessary on aircraft to detain a rowdy passenger.

Many medics and firefighters use aircraft, helicopters, and heliports.

Many hospitals & buildings have heliports for politicians, dignitaries, or patients. Traffic helicopters survey and report traffic from the skies.

If you miss a plane, train, or bus and your luggage gets lost, many companies will deliver your luggage the next day to you by taxi or courier. Some put a loving note inside of luggage for a traveler to find.

SHIPPING TERMS

FOB free on board means the supplier will pay to place goods on the ship of departure

CNF CFR C&F seller pays cost and freight to nearest delivery port

CIF m seller pays cost, insurance, and freight

CIF buyer pays cost, insurance, and freight

Many retailers will not ship until payment or partial payment is received first.
Some companies can ship an item to most places in the world within 24-48-72 hours.

World's Busiest Cargo Ports

Yangshan Port of Shanghai, China
Keppel Container Terminal of Singapore
Tsuen Wan Port of Hong Kong, China
Busan, South Korea
Jebel Ali, Dubai, United Arab Emirates
Rotterdam, Netherlands
Port Kiang, Malaysia
Antwerp, Belgium
Hamburg, Germany
Los Angeles, California, U.S.A.
Keihin Ports, Japan
Laem Chabang, Thailand
Ho Chi Minh, Vietnam
Tanjung Priok Jakarta, Indonesia
Colombo, Sri Lanka
Valencia, Spain
Jawaharlal, India
Manila, Phillippines
Jeddah, Saudi Arabia
Felixstowe, U.K.
Santos, Brazil
New York, New Jersey Ports, U.S.A.
Port Said East, Egypt

Colon, Panama
Piraeus, Greece
Ambarli, Turkey
Marsaxlokk, Malta
Vancouver, Canada

Many ships, yachts, speedboats, and sailboats have unique names painted on them by the owner to identify the boat.

In 2018 it was estimated that there are about 19,800 lighthouses in the world.

Some ships have jail cells for rowdy passengers who may have to be detained until port. Some ships have a morgue in case a passenger dies enroute to port.

Princess, Viking, and Royal Caribbean are some famous cruise lines.

World's Busiest Passenger Ship Ports
Port of Dover, U.K. (passengers)
Port of Miami, Florida, U.S.A. (cruises)

Large Railroad Train Hubs Gare du Nord in Paris,New York Grand Central Station, Japan Nagoya Station.

Some railways: Qinghai-Tibet Railway, Indian Railways, East Japan Railway, JR Sanyo West Pass Japan, MTR Hong Kong, Norfolk Southern USA, CSX USA, Amtrak, Canadian Pacific Railway USA, Daqin Railway China, Peru Rail, Cusco Line, Machu Picchu Line, Atlantic Rainforest Train Brazil, Devil's Nose Equador, Rail South America, Tren Crucero Equador, Deutsche Bahn Germany.

From 2004-2014 Africa borrowed money from China Export Import Bank (EXIM) for railway projects. In 2015 China was helping to build railways in South America.

Large Bus Hubs: Penn Station in New York, Port Authority Bus Terminal in New York & New Jersey, Kamppi Center in Finland. Blue Diamond is a tour bus company.

Physical SPORTS LEAGUES

There are millions of famous athletes, even before paper was invented and records were written down. It is impossible to list all great athletes in this book.

Youth sports leagues are for small children. School leagues offer sports to students who attend the schools. Some cities and non-profits have public recreation leagues. Professional leagues are for adults who may make a career of playing the sport.

There are many good athletes at all age levels. Christi Cahill was a high school athlete who broke Canadian records as a sprinter and pole-vaulter. James Brooks was a high school football player who played for Auburn Tigers and then pro ball with the San Diego Chargers, Cincinnati Bengals, Cleveland Browns, and Tampa Bay Buccaneers.

Draft season is the time in some professional sports leagues when players are selected and offered contracts. A rookie is a player in their first year.

Many sports leagues keep souvenirs or record-breaking statistics in a Hall of Fame Museum. Some leagues offer season tickets or entire sections of seats to rent. Sports teams may wear the same color uniform so they can identify their teammates. Big numbers on the backs of jerseys identify the players so statistics may be kept and plays can be identified.

If a ball goes out of bounds, it may be called a dead ball. Many games are monitored and scored by a referee also called umpire who may blow a whistle, use hand signals, or throw a flag on a bad play.

A tailgate party is when spectators gather in the parking lot before the game and have a picnic that is set up in the back of their truck or on the hood of their car.

Bad sportsmanship is doing things such as saying curse words to a referee or an opponent, throwing down a tennis racket onto the court in anger, tripping an opponent so they will fall, or intentionally causing another sports car to wreck.

Some teams may say a prayer before a game for guidance, for safety of all players, and for a good time to be had by all in spirit of friendship and fun.

Winning sports takes teamwork. Athletes have died in or after sports games. Lily Partridge was a 22-year old rugby player who died in Britain in 2015 after a head crash during a match. Ronan Costello was a 17-year old rugby player who lost his balance and died of a head injury in 2016. Ray Chapman was a 29-year old shortstop for the baseball team Cleveland Indians who died 12 hours after being hit in the head by Yankees pitcher Carl Mays in 1920. Robert Grays was a College football player in Texas who died from a serious neck injury during a game.Sarah Burke was an Olympic ice freestlye skater who died after crashing during a practice.

BASEBALL Baseball is played by hitting a hard fist-sized ball with a bat and running around a grid of 3 bases and scoring a run point by reaching the 4th homeplate. Baseball was invented in Cooperstown, New York in 1939. Softball is played with a softer ball. Some famous baseball players were Babe Ruth 1895 for New York Yankees, Boston Red Sox, Atlanta Braves, Yogi Berra 1925 for New York Yankees, Hank Aaron 1934 for Milwaukee Braves, Jackie Robinson 1919 for the Brooklyn Dodgers, Lou Gehrig 1903 New York Yankees, Mickey Mantle, Joe DiMaggio, Ty Cobb, Derek Jeter, Willie Mays, Cal Ripken, Pete Rose, and Barry Bonds 1964 for the Pittsburgh Pirates and San Francisco Giants. MLB is Major League Baseball in the USA began in 1876. There are two leagues the NL for National League and the AL for American League. Canada is included. The World Series is the championship game. The PCL is a minor baseball league in the west and Midwest USA.Baseball in Japan is the NPB league for Nippon Professional Baseball.
KBO is Korean Baseball Organization.
CPBL is the Chinese Professional Baseball League, founded in 2002.
Softball is a version of baseball that is played with a softer ball.

CRICKET Cricket is similar to baseball. It is played in India, South Africa, West Indies, Great Britain, Australia, New Zealand, New Guinea, and Ireland. The ICC Cricket World Cup is a championship game. Some famous players are Sachin Tendulkan from India, Viv Richards from West Indies, Sir Donald George Bradman from Australia, Adam Gilchrist from Australia, and Chris Gayle from Jamaica.

CHEERLEADING / MASCOTS/ HALF-TIME ENTERTAINMENT Cheering on the sidelines and promotions to initiate enthusiasm for your team.

BASKETBALL The NBA is the National Basketball Association in North America for men's professional basketball. The NBB is Novo Basquete Brazil. CBA is Chinese Basketball Association. FIBA Asia is the Champion's Cup.FIBA EuroBasket is an International championship. The NBL is the Oceania League for Australia, New Zealand, and New Guinea.

Some famous basketball players are Michael Jordan 1963 of the Chicago Bulls, Shaquille O'Neal of the Orlando Magic 1992, Larry Bird 1956 of the Boston Celtics, Kobe Bryant 1978 of the L.A. Lakers, Suleiman Ali Nashnush 1943 of Libya, Sun Mingming 1983 of China, Kareem Abdul-Jabbar 1947 of the Milwaukee Bucks and Los Angeles Lakers. The Harlem Globetrotters from New York (1926) is an exhibition team that travels to promote basketball skills and comedy.

USA AMERICAN FOOTBALL The NFL is the National Football League played by tossing a gridiron oblong ball.Face helmets and knee pads are worn. The Super Bowl is the championship game.
Some famous football players were Tom Brady 1979 of the New England Patriots, Joe Montana 1956 of the San Francisco 49ers, Joe Namath 1943 of the New York Jets. **NCAA** The National Collegiate Athletic

Association is a non-profit that manages college sports competitions in the US and Canada. The Final Four are the four final teams in a playoff.

BBC FOOTBALL British football league played like soccer kicking a soft round ball. Famous players are George Best, Bobby Charlton, Bobby Moore, Kenny Dalglish, Gordon Banks, Steven Gerrard.

BRITISH INVICTUS GAMES
Invictus Games for soldiers who incurred injuries was founded by Prince Harry of England in 2015.

IRISH GAELIC FOOTBALL Gaelic football is like soccer.There is a men's league and a women's league. Famous men: Aidan O'Mahony (Kerry), Paul Gavin (Finuge), Jonny Cooper (Dublin), David Clarke(Mayo), John Small(Dublin)
Famous ladies: Cora Staunton (Mayo, Juliet Murphy (cork), Marina Barry (Kerry), Brenda McAnespie (Monaghan), Angela Downey (Kilkeany), Kate Kelly (Wexford), Deirdre Hughes (Tipperay), Fiona O'Driscoll (Cork)

AUSTRALIAN FOOTBALL LEAGUE
AFL Australian football is like soccer. Famous players are Johnny Warren, Tim Cahill, Harry Kewell, mark Schwarzer, mark Viduka, Mark Milligan.

GOLF Championships for men are The Masters, The U.S. Open, The British Open, The PGA Championship, The Saint-Omer Open, The French Open. **Some Men golfers**: Jack Nicklaus, Tiger Woods, Ben Hogan, Bobby Jones, Arnold Palmer, Sam Snead, Tom Watson, Gary Player, Byron Nelson, and Phil Mickelson.
The Ladies European Tour is the Evian Masters and the French Open.
The Ryder Cup is the championship for men between the U.S. and Europe. The Solheim Cup is the championship for women. **Some Lady golfers**: Annika Sorenstam, Mildred Zaharias, Kathy Whitworth, Mickey Wright, Nancy Lopez.

ICE HOCKEY IIHF is the international ice hockey foundation and lists 76 countries that participate in competitions. Famous players were Tom Lysiak, Wayne Gretzky, Bobby Orr, Mario Lemieux, Gordie Howe, Jaromir Jagr.

RACQUETBALL Racquetball is played inside of a room, which is why it is not a sport in the Olympic Games. Famous men: Bud Muehleisen, Charlie Brunfield, Freddy Ramirez, Robert Sostre, Daniel De la Rosa, Jason Mannino, Cliff Swain

JAI-ALAI is like racquetball and is played in Brazil, Phillippines, Italy, Indonesia, China, and Egypt. Famous players are Victor Valcarce, Goikoetxea, Irastorza, Aritz, Lopez

FIFA SOCCER / FIFA FOOTBALL FIFA is managed in Switzerland. There are men's leagues and women's leagues and the FIFA WORLD CUP is fhe championship game.
Famous men: Pele (Brazil), Zinedine Zidane (France), Diego Maradona (Argentina), Zlatan Ibrahimovic (Sweden), Franz Beckenbauer (Germany), Johan Cruyff (Netherlands), Gerd Muller (Germany), Fabien Barthez (France), Carlos Tevez (Argentina), Hans Krankl (Austria), Lothar Matthaus (Germany), Franck Ribery (France),Lionel Messi (a forward for Argentina and F.C. Barcelona), Cristiano Ronaldo (a forward for Real Madrid and Manchester United), Luis Suarez (a forward for Uruguray and Barcelona), Neymar (A forward for Brazil and F.C. Barcelona), Manuel Neuer (a goalkeeper for Germany), Gareth Bale (a midfield and forward for Wales and a forward for Real Madrid), Arjen Robben (a forward for Holland and a midfielder for Bayern Munich)
Famous women: Christine Sinclair (Canada and Olympics), Carli Lloyd (U.S.A. and Olympics), Alex Morgan (U.S.A. and Olympics), Marta (Brazil and Sweden), Dzsenifer Marozsan (German), Lotta Schelin (Sweden), Kim Little (Scotland and

Australia), Sydney Leroux (Canada), Hope Solo (U.S.A. and Olympics), Amandine Henry (France).

UEFA Champions League is the Union of European Football Associations which determine the continental champion of Europe. (This sport is also called soccer.) Games similar to soccer:

Handball: originated in Denmark and is also played in Czech Republic, Ukraine, Germany, Norway, Sweden, and Russia.

Lacrosse: originated in Native America and Canada.

JAPANESE SOCCER The J League is soccer in Japan. **Famous men**: Hidetoshi Nakata, Shinji Kagawa, Keisuke Honda, Shunsuke Nakamura, Shinji Okazaki, Makoto Hasebe, Shinji Ono, Yasuhito Endo. Famous women: Aya Miyama, Kozue Ando, Mana Iwobuchi, Saki Kumagai, Rumi Utsugi, Aya Sameshina, Shinobu Ohno, Mizuho Sakaguchi, Emi Nakajima, Yuki Nagasoto

RUGBY A rugby ball is oblong and similar to a USA American football. It is played in 95 countries including New Zealand, South Africa, France, Australia, Italy, England, Scotland, Wales, and Finland. **Some famous rugby players** are David Pocock 1988 of Australia, Pierre Spies 1985 of S. Africa, Martin Johnson 1970 of U.K., and Keven Mealamy 1979 of New Zealand.

SNOOKER / BILLIARDS Played in China, England, India. Snooker is regulated by the World Professional Billiards and Snooker Association in the United Kingdom. The UPA is the United States Professional Poolplayers Association regulates pocket billiards in the United States. Some games are 8-ball and 9-ball. BILLIARDS: Famous men: Earl Strickland (U.S.A.), Francisco Bustamante (Philippines), Allen Hopkins (U.S.A.),Chezka Centeno (Philippines). Famous women: Pan Xiaoting (China), Jasmin Ouschan (Austria), Kim Ga-Young (S. Korea).

SWIMMING Popular in many countries. **Famous men**: Aleksandr Vladimirovich Popov (Russia) Olympic gold freestyle sprinter, Mark Spitz (U.S.A.) 16 Olympic gold medals and broke 33 world records, Michael Phelps 18 Olympic gold medals, Ian Thorpe (Australia) 5 Olympic gold medals and 11 World Championships, Pieter van den Hoogenband (Denmark) triple Olympic champion, Johnny Weissmuller (Austria-Hungry) 5 Olympic gold medals, Grant Hackett (Australian) Olympic gold and 10 World Championships distance swimmer, Matt Biondi (U.S.A.) 7 Olympic gold medals and set 7 records. **Famous women:** Krisztina Egerszegi (Hungary) 5 Olympic gold medals, Debbie Meyer (U.S.A.) 3 Olympic gold medals, Kristin Otto (Germany) 6 Olympic gold medals

TABLE TENNIS / PING PONG

Two to four players hit a small lightweight ball back and forth on a table that has a net in the middle. A small paddle bat is used to hit the ball. The biggest leagues are in China, Germany, Russia, France, Austria, and Sweden but table tennis is played in many countries. Famous men players: Ma Long (China), Timo Boll (Germany), Ma Lin (China), Xu Xin (China), Wang Hao (China), Liu Guoliang (China), Dimitrij Ovtcharov (Ukraine), Mikael Appelgren (Sweden), JOrg Robkopf (Germany), Tim Boggan (U.S.A.) Famous women players: Deng Yaping (China), Zhang Yining (China), Kasumi Ishikawa (Japan), Wu Yue (U.S.A.), Lily Zhang (U.S.A.), Erica Wu (U.S.A.), Ariel Hsing (U.S.A.), Jha Prachi (U.S.A.)

TENNIS The major tournaments are the Grand Slam Tournaments of Wimbledon, US Open, Australian Open, and French Roland Garros Open. **Men**: Roger Federer (Switzerland), Rafael Nadad (Spain), Bjorn Berg (Sweden), Ivan Lendl (Czech Rep), Jimmy Connors (U.S.A.), William Renshaw (U.K.), Andre Agassi (U.S.A.). **Ladies**: Billie Jean King (U.S.A.), Christ Evert (U.S.A.), Maria Sharapova (Russia), Venus and

Serena Williams who are sisters (U.S.A.), Margaret Court (Australia), Monica Seles (Serbia), Martina Hingis (Slovakia), Steffi Graf (Germany).

Some players who threw their tennis rackets down in anger were male players John McEnroe (U.S.A.), Nick Kyrgios (Australia), Fabio Fognini (Italy) and women players Serena Williams (U.S.A.), Andrea Petkovic (German).

Tai Chi Practitioners Bruce Lee, Liang Zipeng, Jackie Chan. Allen Ginsberg is a poet, a Buddhist, and Tai Chi practitioner. Other famous Tai Chi practitioners: Mel Gibson, Oprah Winfrey, Michelle Obama, Will Smith, Catherine Zeta-Jones, Robert De Niro, Steven Tyler of Aerosmith Band.

BOWLING QubicaAMF Bowling World Cup Ten-Pin Bowling Championship WBT World Bowling Tour. **Famous men bowlers** in U.S.A.: Earl Anthony, Walter Ray Williams, Pete Weber, son of Dick Weber. Norm Duke. **Famous women bowlers** in U.S.A.: Donna Adamek, Kim Adler, Lynda Barnes, Leanne Barrette, Carolyn Dorin-Ballard. Helen Duval of Denmark.

VOLLEYBALL is similar to tennis. A volleyball is hit over a net with the hands and not with a racquet. There are men's and women's volleyball leagues all over the world. Men: Karch Kiraly (U.S.A.), Gilberto Giba (Brazil), Ivan Miljkovia (Serbia), Andrea Giani (Italy), Maxim Mikhaylov (Russia), Bartosz Kurek (Poland) Ladies: Kerri Walsh (U.S.A.), Gabrielle Reece (U.S.A.), Yumilka Ruiz Luaces (Cuba), Helia Souza Fafoa (Brazil), Nikolic Jelena (Serbia), Yang Hao (China).

CYCLING The Tour De France is a popular bicycle race. Cycling is a popular sport in European countries such as France, Germany, Italy, Spain, England, and the Netherlands. **Famous men**: Marshall taylor (U.S.A.), Tom Simpson (Britian), Pedro Delgado (Spain), Viatcheslav Ekimov (Russia), Miguel Indurain (Spain), Lance Armstrong (U.S.A.). **Famous women**: Anne-Caroline Chausson (France), Nicole Cooke (U.K.), Dede Berry (U.S.A.), Annie Londonderry (Latvia), Kristin Armstrong (U.S.A), Nikki Butterfield (Australia), Seiko Hashimoto (Japan)

OLYMPICS IOC is the International Olympic Committee that regulates the games.

The Winter Olympics are held every fours years. The seven games are skiing, skating, curling, ice hockey, bobsled, luge, and biathlon. The most recent games were held in Vancouver Canada 2010, Sochi Russia 2014, Pyeongchang South Korea 2018, Beijjing China 2022.

The Summer Olympics are held every four years. The games are swimming, synchronized swimming, water polo, diving, equestrian, gymnastics, cycling, volleyball, wrestling, boxing, canoeing and more. The most recent games were held in London England 2012, Rio de Janeiro Brazil 2016, Tokyo Japan 2020, and Paris France 2024.

The Paralympic Games are for athletes with physical disabilities.

In 1986, professional athletes were allowed to compete in the Olympics as well as professional leagues.

Special Olympics are held in some cities for athletes with intellectual challenges.

It is impossible to list all Olympic athletes in the pages of this book.

Some famous Olympic athletes: Michael Phelps (U.S.A. 2008 male swimmer), Carl Lewis (U.S.A. 1979 male track & field), Usain Bolt (Jamaica 2001 male sprinter), Mark Spitz (U.S.A. 1972 male swimmer), Jesse Owens (U.S.A. 1936 male tract & field), Nadia Comaneci (Romania 1980 female gymnast), Jackie Joyner-Kersee (U.S.A. 1988 female long jump & heptathlon), Greg Louganis (U.S.A. 1982 male springboard diver), Mary Lou Retton (U.S.A. 1984 female gymnast), Muhammed Ali (U.S.A. 1960 male boxing), Larisa

Latynina (Ukraine 1956 female gymnast), Jan Ingemar Stenmark (Sweden 1980 male alpine race skier), Sawao Kato (Japan 1968 male gymnast), Kerri Walsh Jennings (U.S.A. 2000 female volleyball), Natalie Coughlin (U.S.A. 2004 female swimmer), Steve Redgrave (Britain 1984 male rower), Jim Thorpe (U.S.A. of the SAC and FOX Nation 1912 male pentathlon and decathlon), Ferdinand Bie (Norway 1912 male pentathlon, Wilma Rudolph (U.S.A. 1956 female sprinter), Birgit Fischer (German 1988 female kayaker), Fanny Blankers-Koen (Denmanrk 1948 track & field), Ian Thorpe (Australia 2000 male swimmer), Mia Hamm (U.S.A. 1996 female soccer), Lasse Viren (Finland 1972 male long-distance runner), Reiner Klimke (German 1960 male equestrian), Babe Didrikson Zaharis (U.S.A. 1932 golf, basketball, baseball, track & field), Bonnie Blair and Nancy Kerrigan (U.S.A. 1994 female ice figure skater), Bonnie Blair (U.S.A. 1992 female ice speed skater), Sonja Henie (Norway 1928 female ice figure skater who was also an actress and film star), Carolina Kostner (Italy 2014 ice figure skater), Yulia Lipnitskaya (Russia 2014 ice figure skater), Ekaterina Gordeeva and her husband Jergei Grinkov (Russia 1988 ice pair skaters), Zhao Hongbe and his wife Shen Xue (China 2010 ice pair skaters), Scott Hamilton (U.S.A. 1984 male ice figure skater), Tessa Virtue (Canada 2010 female ice dancer), Benjamin Agosto 2006 male ice dancer), Ashley Wagner (U.S.A. 2016 ice figure skater who is also an internet web designer).Elfie Willemsen and Eva Willemarck (Belgium 2010 female bobsleigh), Charles Green (Britain 1930 male bobsleigh), Anton Paz and Fernando Echavarri (Spain 2008-9 male sailor in Volvo Ocean Race), Laurie Hernandez (U.S.A. 2016 female gymnast), Chad le Clos (South Africa 2012 male swimmer), Gabby Douglas (U.S.A. 2012 gymnast).

Biathlon is cross-country skiing and rifle shooting.Triathlon is 3 events.
Pentathlon is 5 events: long jump, javelin throw, discus throw, stadion run, wrestling.
Heptathlon is 7 events and is different for men and women competitions.
Decathlon is 10 events.

Some famous Paralympic Athletes are:
Tomas Hjert (Sweden) 2011 wheel chair rugby. Tomas Hjert formerly played ice hockey but was paralyzed from the chest down from a game injury.
Jessica Long (Russia-U.S.A.) swimmer.
Anjali Forber-Pratt (India-U.S.A.) wheelchair races, Paul Nitz (U.S.A.) Track & Field, Tanni Grey-Thompson (Britain) wheelchair racer who was alsp a parliamentarian and a TV presenter,
Rajinder Singh Rahelu (India) weightlifter,
Ali Jawad (Lebanon) powerlifter,
Randy Snow (U.S.A.) wheelchair basketball,
Erin Popovich (U.S.A.) swimmer,
Liesl Tesch (Australia) wheelchair basketball

MILITARY WORLD GAMES founded in Brussels, Belgium since 1995 by CISM Conseil International du Sport Militaire or IMSC International Miliatary Sports Council is for military sportspeople. Marvin Chobowski (Poland) participated in the games as a runner. Frank Workman (USA) and Aydin Polatci (Turkey) participated as wrestlers. The first female to head a sport committee was in Canada for sailing events.

MOTORSPORTS Daytona 500, Indy 500, Winston Cup, NASCAR Cup, Formula 1 World Championship and Grand Prix are races. **Famous men race car drivers**: Jeff Gordon, Dale Earnhardt, Dale Earnhardt son of Dale Earnhardt and grandson of Ralph Earnhardt, Jimmie Johnson, Richard Petty, Mario Andretti, Tony Stewart, Michael Schumacher, Juan Pablo Montoya, Matt Kenseth, Mark Martin, Kurt Busch, Ryan Newman, Carl Edwards, Robby Gordon, Darrell Waltrip and Michael

Waltrip who were brothers. Charles Ng (Hong Kong, China), Kunimitsu Takahasi (Japan), John Bowe (Australia), Jack Perkins (Australia), James Hunt (Britian)

Lady race car drivers: Ann Bunselmeyer (New York, U.S.A.),Danica Patrick (U.S.A.), Madalena Antas (Portugal – U.S.A.), Maryeve Dufault (Canada) who was also a Miss Hawaiian Tropic International, Milka Duno (Venezuela), Janet Guthier (U.S.A.), Katherine Legge (Britain), Genevra Delphine Mudge (U.S.A.), Leilani Munter (U.S.A.), Susie WSolff (Scotland), Ashley Force Hood and her sister Courtney Force (U.S.A.), Shannon McIntosh (U.S.A., Cyndie Allemann (Switzerland), Nur Ali (Asian-American), Keiki Ihara (Japan).

In 1974, Evel Knievel from Montana, U.S.A. was a international daredevil stuntperformer on a motorcycle.

Monster Jam Events since 1992 showcase stunts with big-wheeled trucks.

WRESTLING: Some Championship belts are NWA, WWE, UFC, TNA, RAW WORLD, and NCAA. WWF is the World Wrestling Foundation. **Famous men wrestlers**: Hulk Hogan (U.S.A.), Bret Hart (U.S.A.), Randy Savage (U.S.A.), The Undertaker Mark Calaway (U.S.A.), Shawn Michaels (U.S.A.), Steve Austin (U.S.A.), Eddie & Chavo Guerrero (Mexico, Japan, and U.S.A.), Dwayne Johnson who was also an actor (U.S.A.), Curt Henning who was also a sports commentator (U.S.A.). Hashem Akbarian (Iran), Hassan Yazdani (Iran), Rasoul Khadem (Iran), Gholamreza Takhti (Iran).

Famous women wrestlers: Chyna, Sable, Lita, Trish Stratus (Canada), Mae Young, The Fabulous Moolah, Mickie James (U.S.A.), Torrie Wilson, Stacy Keibler, Sensational Sherri Martel, Molly Holly, Kellie Kellie, Paige (Britain), Lisa Marie Varon, Christy Hemme, Sasha Banks (U.S.A. WWE wrestler) who is rapper Snoop Dogg's cousin.

HORSE RACES Some different breeds of horses are: Thoroughbred, Mustang, Clydesdale, Arabian, Purebred. Not all breeds of horses are trained to race. Some names of famous races: Kentucky Derby, The Preakness Stakes, Belmont Stakes in U.S.A., Prix de l'Arc de Triomphe in France, The Royal Ascot in England,

Dubai World Cup in United Arab Emirates, Grand National in England Melbourne Cup in Australia, Cheltenham Festival in U.K., Japan Cup.**Famous men horse jockeys**: Bill Shoemaker (U.S.A.) John Red Pollard (Canada), Russell Blaze (Canada), Javier Castellano (Venezuela), Jerry Bailey (U.S.A), Lester Piggott (U.K.), Laffiot Pincay (Panama). **Famous lady horse jockeys:** Clare Balding (U.K.), Chantal Sutherland (Canada), Julie Krone (U.S.A).

DOG RACES are popular.

SCOUTING 216 countries have scouting for girls & boys to teach outdoor survival skills, physical, mental, and moral growth. It would be impossible to list all names for scouting in this book.

In India, the program is called Bharat Scouts & Guides.

In U.S.A. there is Boy Scouts and Girl Scouts of America founded by Juliette Gordon Low in 1897, 4H Club, Campfire Girls, American Heritage Girls, American Camping Association.

In Russia, the Young Cavalrymen and Skautskoye are names for boy scouts. The Russian Association of Girl Scouts is the organization for girls.

Scouts South Africa is the name of the boy scouts in South Africa.

BOY SCOUTS / CAMPING

Eagle Scout is the highest award for U.S.A.boy scouts. Queen's Scout is the highest award in Britain.

Famous boy scouts: Steven Speilberg (movie producer), Michael Moore (filmmaker), Jamie Oliver (British celebrity chef and media personality), Walter Cronkite (CBS News TV broadcaster and journalist), Donald Rumsfeld (politician), Alfred Kinsey (biologist), Nolan Ryan (baseball player for Texas rangers), Michael Jordan (basketball player for Chicago Bulls), Neil Armstrong (first astronaut on the moon), Buzz Aldrin (astronaut), Martin Luther King, Jr. (U.S.A. civil rights activist), Bill Gates (businessman and IT entrepreneur), Sam Walton (Walmart corporation), Ron Hubbard (Scientology founder), Herbert William Garnet de la Hunt (Chief Scout of South Africa), Girija Shankar Bajpai (Chief Justice and Minister of Justice of Jaipur State in India), Dharma Vira (Governor of Punjab, West Bengal, and Karnataka and Cabinet Secretary for the Government of India).**Male Actors who were scouts**: Ozzie Nelson, Andy Griffith, John Wayne, Harrison Ford, James Stewart, George Takei (Star Trek), John Travolta.

Male Musicians who were scouts: Paul McCartney (Beatles), Keith Richards (Rolling Stones), Jimmy Buffett (Coral Reefers Band), George Strait (Ace in the Hole Band).

Male Political Leaders: John F. Kennedy (35th President of the U.S.A), Gerald R. Ford (38th President of the U.S.A.), Bill Clinton (42nd President of the U.S.A.), George W. Bush (43rd President of the U.S.A.), Barack Obama (44th President of the U.S.A.), Dr. Rajendra Prasad of India, Shri Rameshwar Thakur of India, **Male Advertising and cartoonist:** Victor J. Clapham (South Africa)

GIRL SCOUTS / CAMPING

In some countries,a fundraiser for Girl Scouts is selling boxed Girl Scout cookies.

Famous Girl Scouts/ Girl Guides: Queen Elizabeth II of England (B. 1926), Martha Stewart (business magnate), Sandra Day O'Connor (U.S. Supreme Court Judge), Elizabeth Dole (politician and author), Laura Bush (librarian and U.S.A. First lady married to George W. Bush, Jr. 43rd President of the U.S.A.), Nancy Reagan (U.S.A. First lady married to Ronald W. Reagan 40th President of the U.S.A.), Joyce Brothers (psychologist and author), Chelsea Clinton (Daughter of William J. Clinton 42nd President of U.S.A.), Rosalyn Carter (U.S.A. First lady married to James earl Carter 39th President of the U.S.A.), Sally Ride (astronaut), Gloria Steinem (magazine editor and journalist).

Women Journalists who were scouts: Barbara Walters, Katie Couric, Lisa Ling, Star Jones (Talk show host and journalist).

Women Singers who were scouts: Celine Dion (pop singer), Jesse Norman (opera singer). **Women Actresses who were scouts:** Susan Lucci, Shirley Temple, Candice Bergen (TV producer and actress), Grace Patricia Kelly, Mary Tyler Moore, Bette Davis, Marlo Thomas, Abigail Breslin.

Women Athletes who were scouts: Venus Williams (tennis player), Dorothy Hamill (ice skater), Blythe Danner (environmentalist and actress), Florence Griffith joyner (field & track athlete and actress)

MIND SPORTS

There are international card games, word games, and more.

CHESS: Famous men chess players: Sergey Karjakin (Russia), Bobby Fischer (U.S.A.), Garry Kasparov (Azerbaijan), Magnus Carlsen (Norway), Anatoly Karpov (Russia), Jose Raul Capablanca (Havana, Cuba).

Famous women chess players: Judit Plogar (Hungary), Hou Yifan (Chinese), Anna Muzychuk (Ukraine), Alexandra Kostegluk (Russia), Natalia Pogonina (Russia), Harika Dronavalli (India).

POKER: Famous men poker players: Daniel Negreana (Canada), Phil Ivey (California, U.S.A.), Phil Hellmuth (Wisconsin, U.S.A.), Chris Ferguson (California, U.S.A.), Doyle Brunson (Texas, U.S.A.), Jaime Staples (Alberta, Canada), Johnny Chan (China).

Famous women poker players: Vanessa Selbst (U.S.A.), Liv Boeree (Kent, England).

HOSPITALS and MEDICAL CARE

Hospitals may have as many as 100 to 3400 beds, depending on the size of the city. A hospital with 3400 beds may employ as many as 6700 employees of hospital staff, and perform 25,000 surgeries each year. Some services offered in hospitals are: surgeries, radiology and X-RAY, adult services, children services, emergency rooms and trauma care, psychiatric ward, orthopaedic center, vascular surgery, cardio-thoracic care, neurology, women's gynecology center, cosmetic care and plastic surgery, cancer treatment, maternity delivery and newborn care.

Hospitals may have gift shops and cafeterias. Volunteers in hospitals often do tasks like offering books and magazines to patients or passing out and collectioning meal choice cards for Patient Meals.

Xanitos is a company that offers housekeeping and laundry services for hospitals. Electrostatic disinfectant processes are used in many hospitals and childcare centers.

HUMAN VITAL SIGNS

Blood pressure is recorded as a fraction with systolic pressure as the top number and diastolic pressure as the bottom number. Systolic is the pressure inside your blood vessels at the moment your heart beats. Diastolic is the pressure in your blood vessels between heartbeats. .
In infants normal blood pressure is 64/41. Childern ages 1-5 normal blood pressure ranges can be 80/50 to 110/80. Children ages 6-12 normal ranges can be 85/55 to 120/80. In humans age 13 or older, normal blood pressures ranges from 95/60 to 140/90.

Normal temperature of humans in 98.6 but varies between 97.4 and 99.6.

Heartbeat of a newborn infant is 100-160 beats per minute.

Children ages 1-2 is 80-130 beats per minute. Adults 60-100 beats per minute.

Respirations: infants is 25-50 breaths per minute, child 15-30 breaths per minute, Adult 12-20 breaths per minute.

Some Signs of Human Distress

Dizziness, Feeling faint, heart palpitations, blurred vision, cold & clammy skin, hot skin, nausea, vomiting, numbness, crying, rapid breathing or no breathing, lack of concentration, fatigue, confusion, emaciation, obesity, toothache, earache, discoloration of eye whites, irrational unjustified anger,panic or phobias, obsessions, addictions.

Adrenaline is a hormone secreted by glands in times of stress and causes an Increase in heartrate and blood circulation, breathing, and carbohydrate metabolism.

Some people are grateful to have a cool damp cloth to put on their forehead or neck when they are not feeling well.

HEALTHCARE

It would be impossible to list all of the advances made by healthcare experts.

In 1852, Adolphe Chatin from France postulated that iodine is needed in the human diet to avoid goiter of the thyroid. Seafood contains iodine.

In 1818, Louis Jacque Thenard discovered hydrogen peroxide H_2O_2. Hydrogen Peroxide is a pale blue liquid that has been used as a disinfectant for small wounds, a mouth rinse, nail whitener, and used as an ingredient in a concentrated form as a rocket propellant. Hydrogen peroxide and vinegar have both been used on toenails to fight toenail fungus.

Petroleum jelly can be put on your hands to help heal dry skin or a small wound. Vaseline Petroleum Jelly is a famous brand for the lubricant.

Aspirin, acetaminophen, ibuprofen are analgesics for pain and headache relief.

Guaifenesin is a drug that is an expectorant to thin mucus and cough it up. Pseudoephedrine is a decongestant to relieve sinus pressure. Mucinex, Sudafed,

Nyquil, Dayquil, Dimetapp, Zicam, Claritin, and Coricidin are some other brands of sinus and cold medicines.

Vicks VapoRub has the smell of menthol and is often rubbed on the chest to help relieve congestion and stuffy n oses associated with colds. Vicks VapoRub contains camphor and eucalyptus oil.

A few minutes of a neckrub or a backrub may help relax a person.

A little amount of table salt can be mixed into warm water and gargled with to help cure a sort throat. Salt has also been applied to superficial wounds to cure infections.

Alcohol has been used by many people over the centuries to treat infections by pouring it over superficial wounds or toothaches.

Anesthesia revolutionized healthcare when it was invented in 1846 by William T. G. Morton (1819-1968). The first patient that ether anesthesia for surgery was performed on was Edward Gilbert Abbott at Massachusetts General Hospital in the U.S.A.

Dr. Ludwig Rehn of Frankfurt, Germany performed heart surgery on Sept. 7, 1896 and successfully repaired a stab wound to the heart. Doctors studying heart surgery included Henry Souttar (1925CE), Horace Smith (1914-1948CE), Dwight Harken, Charles Bailey (1910-1993CE), Russell Brock (1948), Thomas Holmes Sellors (1947), Wilfred G. Bigelow (Canada), John Heysham Gibbom (1953), Russell M. Nelson, John W. Kirklin, C. Walton Lillehei, F. John Lewis, Nazih Zuhdi. A Soviet scientist named Sergei Brukhonendo designed a heart-lung machine in 1926CE. John Heysham Gibbon developed a heart-lung machine in 1953CE that was used during open-heart surgery. Clarence Dennis, Russell M. Nelson, Forest Dewey Dodrill, and Robert Hooke also worked in this area of medical research. Terry Gene Nix, age 7, was a heart patient who was operated on in Oklahoma, USA on Feb. 25, 1960 by Doctors Zuhdi, Carey, and Greer. In 1953, Soviet surgeon Aleksandr Aleksandrovich Vishnevskiy performed a heart surgery in which the heart was exposed and the blood was bypassed so the heart could be operated on. From 1949E until 1981CE, doctors invented artificial hearts and implanted them in dogs, bulls, and calves. On Dec. 12, 1957, a dog lived for 90 minutes after receiving an artificial heart.

Doctors who worked on inventing an artificial heart for humans included Domingo Liotta (who worked in France and Argentina), Adrian Kantrowitz (American), Alain F. Carpenter (French). Robert Jarvik, M.D. who was also a physicist, and William DeVries, a cardiovascular surgeon, successfully implanted a Jarvik-7 artificial heart into a patient on Dec. 2, 1982. Barney Clark, a dentist, was the patient. Barney lived for 112 days after the operation. The Phoenix-7 Total Artificial Heart was manufactured in The Republic of China (Taiwan) and implanted in Mr. Yao St by surgeon Jeng Wei in June 1996. Mr. Yao St was still alive in March 2013. The Phoenix-7 was manufactured by Kelvin K. Cheng (a dentist), T. M. Kao (a Chinese physician), and colleagues at a Taiwan research center. In Dec. 2013 in France, Dr. Alain F. Carpenter implanted a CARMAT artificial heart in a patient who lived for 75 days after receiving the heart.

Robotic surgery is enabling improvements in many areas of surgery including colon/rectal, cardiothoracic, gastrointestinal, gynecological, neurosurgery, and orthopedics.

In 1943CE, Willem Koff was a Dutch physician who constructed the first working dialyzer for kidney patients in the Netherlands. Over the next 2 years, 16 patients were treated but results were not highly successful. In 1945CE, a comatose woman regained consciousness after 11 hours of hemodialysis and she lived for another 7 years.

Mercury fillings for teeth were invented in 1819 by British Chemist Bell but they were banned in 1840 because of mercury poisoning. Then fillings with tin, silver, copper, and a small amount of mercury were invented. Composite while fillings were invented in the 1980s.Novocaine was invented by German chemist Alfred Einhorn that numbed a patient's gums to prevent pain while the patient could remain conscious. Lidocaine is also a local anesthetic.

Dental implant technology with titanium dental implants was invented in 1957 by Professor Per-Ingvar Branemark who was an orthopedic surgeon in Gothenburg, Sweden.

Cerec 3D dental crowns were developed by W. Mormann and M. Brandestini at the University of Zurich in Switzerland 1980.

Spectacles or eyeglasses were invented around 1285 in Italy. Salvino Darmate is believed to have been one inventor. Contact lenses for eyes were invented by Otto Wichterle 1913 of Austria-Hungary now Czech Republic.

Dr. Gholam A. Peyman (b. 1937) of Shiraz, Iran invented Lasik Eye Surgery in the 1990s where laser surgery could correct vision so a patient no longer needed eye glasses with corrective lenses. The invention revolutionized eye vision care.

Scientists are working hard to create anti-venoms and antibiotics. Many think that the overuse of oral antibiotics or external antibiotics creams, soaps, and lotions are causing bacteria to become resistant.

The spider bite from a brown recluse can be serious if left untreated. Some people have squeezed the puss and venom from a spider bite over a period of several days in order to try to expel all of the venom from the bitten area, even peeling back the small scab that forms over the bite so that more puss and venom can be expelled. Salt has been put on the spider bite to help prevent infection. Activated charcoal has been put on the spider bite to remove toxins. It was reported on the internet that an anti-venom was developed for black-widow bites.

It is recommended to squeeze the venom and puss out of snake bites.

Spiders can have 6 to 8 eyes. Scientists have reported that spiders do not like peppermint oil.

People can be bitten by jellyfish, bluebottle jellyfish physalia, stingrays, sharks, fire ants, sea urchin, ticks, fleas, lice.

Pets can get bitten by insects such as ticks and spiders.

Technicians and dermatologists are finding ways to remove tattoos or other skin conditions with micro dermabrasian techniques or with lasers.

Some people try holistic natural techniques and substances to cure ailments before turning to manufactured drugs and surgery.

Adele Wang is a spiritual energy healer in metro Atlanta, Georgia at Safe Haven Healing who helps women and men reduce stress and overwhelming anxieties by teaching them to focus on their natural energy as a healing technique called Reiki . She has helped people suffering from insomnia, OCD, arthritis, fibromyalgia, stress, anxiety, digestive issues, and migraine headaches. She believed in communicating with others in person instead of only with cell phones and computers.

Terry H. Wright is a homeopath nutritionist helping people to restore their health.

SCIENCES

It would be impossible to list all of the advances made by scientists.

Over 2400 years, the work of philosophers, naturalists, scientists, and chemists led to the discovery and harnessment of electricity. Thales of Miletus of Greece studied static electricity in 600BCE. It is believed that gold and silver plated pottery could have been used as batteries in tunnels in Persia (what is now Baghdad, Iraq) in 275BCE. William Gilbert (1544-1600CE), Thomas Browne (1646CE), and Stephen Gray (1666-1736CE) from England, Otto von Guericke (1686CE) from Germany, Robert Boyle (1627-1691CE) from Ireland, C.F. du Fay (1698-1739CE) from France, and Benjamin Franklin (1785-1788CE) from America worked to invent ways to harness electricity.

It took 22 inventors over a period of 75 years to make a long-lasting light bulb. In 1879CE, Thomas A. Edison invented a bulb that could last 13.5 hours with a carbon-filament. Eventually the bulb was improved to last 1200 hours.

Nikola Tesla (b. July 1856) was a Serbian Austrian-American from the area that is now Croatia. Tesla invented the alternating current AC electrical generation which used 240 volts as opposed to Thomas Edison who used 110 volts in direct current DC. 50 or 60 HZ are common frequencies.

Scientist Albert Michelson in 1929 CE worked to measure the velocity of light. A Belgian Catholic priest-scholar with a Ph.D. from MIT named Georges Lemaitre suggested the universe began from one geometrical point which established the idea of the Big Bang Theory.

In the 1960s CE at Princeton University, Robert Dicke lectured about the Big Bang Theory, and Alan Guth put forth the idea of inflation theory in the first moments of the formation of the universe. At the same time Arno Penzias and Robert Wilson heard background noise from a large communications antenna that was believed to be radiation leftover from a big bang, which had been postulated by Russian astrophysicist George Gamow in the 1940s.

The physicist Richard Feynman (1918-1988CE) made scientific history with his statement that all things are made of atoms.

There were many great physicists – some other names were Leonhard Euler (1707-1783) from Switzerland, John Dalton (1766-1844) from England, William Rowan Hamilton (1833) from Ireland, Joseph Louis Lagrange (1788) from Italy, Jean Baptiste Perrin (1870-1942) from France, Robert Brown (1827) from Scotland, Max Born (1882-1970) from Germany, Vladimir Fock (1898-1974) from the Soviet Union, Wendell Furry (1907-1984) from USA, Robert Oppenheimer (1904-1967) from USA, Ernst Stueckelberg (1905-1984) from Switzerland, Owen Chamberlain (1920-2006) from USA, Erwin Schrodinger (1926) from Austria, Enrico Fermi (1901-1954) from Italy, Paul Dirac (1932) from Great Britain, Carl David Anderson (1905-1991) from USA, Emilio Gino Segre (1905-1989) from Italy, Ludwig Boltzman (1844-1906) from Austria-Hungary, James Clerk Maxwell (1831-1879) from Scotland. Great atom-smasher physicists were Rolf Wideroe (1902-1996) from Norway, Gustav Ising (1883-1960) from Sweden, Leo Szilard (1898-1964) from Austria-Hungary, Donald William Kerst (1911-1993) from USA, Ernest Lawrence (1901-1958) from USA.

On May 21, 1927 aviator Charles Lindbergh made the first solo airplant flight across the Atlantic Ocean from Long Island, NY to Paris, France.

Martin Rees, (b. 1942) a British astronomer, believes there may be different universes with different attributes. The way that hydrogen is converted to helium is at the same precise manner – at seven one-thousandths of its mass to energy. If the value varied from 0.007 percent, the universe would not exist as we know it.

Stephen Hawking (b. 1942CE) a physicist and cosmologist from Oxford, England is noted for his research involving radiation that is emitted from black holes.

In 1748, William Cullen of the University of Glasgow in Scotland, who studied chemistry and medicine, invented the first artificial refrigeration system by boiling ether. In 1805, U.S.A. inventor Oliver Evans invented a practical refrigerator by using a vapor to cool.

Teflon on fry pans was invented in 1938 by Dupont Company. Teflon was invented for NASA for liquid-cooled space suits and space clothing worn by astronauts, for heat shields on space stations, for breathing systems for firefighters, for cargo hold liners in ships.

Velcro was invented in 1941 in the U.K. by Swiss engineer George de Mestral after wondering why burdock seeds clung to his coat after a walk in the woods.

George Washington Carver (1864-1943) was an American from Africa who invented 125 products derived from peanuts.

Wood-burning cast iron stoves to cook on were designed in Germany in 1728. An electric stove was invented in 1892 by Thomas Ahearn of Canada. In 1946, American engineer Percy Spencer invented the microwave oven from radar technology developed during WW II.

Biologists modified star-tracking algorithms of the Hubble Telescope to track fish and polar bears on earth.

Norman Orentreich of New York was a dermatologist and founder of Estee Lauder Company's Clinique cosmetics. Orentreich invented a way to transplant hair follicles revolutionizing hair transplants.

Bees are diminishing in population numbers. Some scientists say it could be due to genetically modified plants and crops. Evil people could be producing genetically modified insects that are killing the good insects.

Some people believe that the white Caucasian race will become obsolete due to interfacial mixing, because most genes in the race are recessive. If all the races mix, all humans will look the same and there will be less distinction. Many people are concernted about genetic cloning of humans.

Massage therapy may help to reduce stress or headaches. If a person is really stressing, even a minute or two of a neck and shoulder massage could help.

Toenail fungus thrives on moisture. Some remedies that people have used are vinegar or vinegar water on the toenail, natural sunlight, and more. Antifungal creams are available at pharmacies. Wearing the same pair of socks all day long may contribute to toenail fungus, so change your socks halfway through the day and see if wearing dry socks helps. Let your toenails dry out after work hours.

Johnny Gruelle was an American artist who created the children's characters Raggedy Ann and Raggedy in memory of his daughter who received a smallpox vaccine and died shortly afterwards.

Pollen is the yellow powdery microscopic substance that are grains emitted from the male parts of plants which are then transmitted by wind, bees, or insects to fertilize female parts of plants. Pollen season can cause allergy symptoms to flare in some humans. Some say that eating local honey can alleviate allergy symptoms but some say it does not.

Science matters and our actions affect the future.

Manufacturing & Engineering

The zipper was invented in 1890 by Whitcomb Judson, a salesman, mechanical engineer, and inventor from Chicago Illinois who worked for Earle Manufacturing Company. Judson envisioned a 'clasp locker' for high button shoes to replace the buttons. Other uses for the clasp locker would be for garments such as corsets, gloves, and mail bags. Judson invented a street railway system that ran on compressed air but it was not successful and replaced by electric street cars. The invention was introduced at a debut at the World's Fair in Chicago in 1893 without success. Judson founded Universal Fastener Company which moved from Chicago to Ohio to Pennsylvania to Hoboken, New Jersey. Judson applied for patents for his zipper. In 1913, Gideon Sunback a Swedish-American and Catharina Kuhn-Moos who worked for Universal Fastener Company applied for more patents for a zipper. YKK, Inc. is Universal Fastener Company.

BIG MINING HOLES or SINKHOLES

Chuquicamater in Chile, Udachnaya in Russia, Guatemale Sinkhole, Diavik Mine in Canada, Mirny Diamond Mine in Siberia, Great Blue Hole underwater sinkhole in Belize, Bingham Canyon Mine in Utah, Monticello Dam in California, Kimberley Diamond Mine in South Africa, Darvaza Gas Crater in Turkmenistan.

In 1987 in Midland, Texas, U.S.A. a young toddler named Jessica fell down a 22 foot well. Dedicated rescuers used a diamond drill bit to help rescue her after 58 hours.

In 1992 8 miners were killed after a mine explosion on Scuta Mountain in Virginia.

In 2010 33 miners were trapped for 69 days in Chile after a mine explosion.

Government / Politics / Diplomacy

In many countries, through centuries of time - politicians, county commissioners, city managers, human right activists, educators, and military forces have fought and negotiated for freedoms so people can travel, enjoy arts & lilterature, own businesses, vote, own land and houses.

Spies may have to change walk routes, cars, airplanes, clothing and disguises in order to complete an espionage mission and retain a low profile. Spies should only do work that is good for the entire world and cause no harm to anyone. A dossier is a secret file someone has made about you, your information, your personality, and possibly your photo.

IMPERFECTIONS

In manufacturing, production, and cooking there are bound to be mistakes in clothing, cars, foods. Irregulars clothing can be sold at a discount, cars can be recalled and fixed, food can be thrown into compost piles or trash. If a little piece of plastic from food packaging or a small bug is found in food, do not assume the restaurant is bad. Bugs invade everywhere. Food preparers should do the best they can to produce fine quality food. Try to rinse all vegetables before cooking or eating them raw. Boiling or cooking at high temperatures destroys good and bad bacteria.

HOME & HOUSEHOLD

Homemakers direct the household, care for family members and themselves, make sure homes are clean, help schedules run as smoothly as possible, make plans for healthy and delicious meals. The designated homemaker can be a single person living alone, a parent, or all of the people living under the same roof sharing responsibilities.

A parent who is financially able to stay home and raise their children is fortunate. Children also benefit by having interaction with people outside of the home.

In some parts of the world it is necessary for both parents to work to earn money, so children must attend day school.

If you are a parent and bring a child into the world, it is your responsibility to care for your child and help them to have the best life possible. Children are forever hurt by parents who abandon them. What kind of home and community do you want to live in?

Some CHARITABLE ORGANIZATIONS

Salvation Army	England, U.K	1865
Save the Children	U.K.	1919
Action Aid	U.K.	1972
Charities Aid Foundation	U.K.	1974
Oxfam	U.K.	2013
Plan	U.K. and Spain	1937

UNHCR UN Refugee Agency Geneva 1950
World Food Programme Italy 1961
SOS Children's Village Austria 1949
CARE Switzerland 1945
UNICEF New York, U.S.A. 1946
Mercy Corps Oregon U.S.A.1979
Medecins sans Frontieres France & Switzerland 1971 Doctors Without Borders
Habitat for Humanity Georgia, U.S.A. 1976
World Vision Intl California, U.S.A. 1950
Samaritan's Purse F. Graham U.S.A. 1970
Ronald McDonald House RMHC U.S.A.1974
Chick Fil A Winshape Georgia U.S.A. 1984
Goonj Delhi, India 1999
Akshaya Patra Foundation India 2000
HelpAge Elderly India 1978
Sevalaya India 1988
Smile Foundation India
St. Jude India
Railway Children India, E. Africa, U.K.
SOS Child Villages Canada 1949
Tenrikyo Disaster Relief Japan 1923
Southern Baptist Disaster Relief U.S.A.1967
Islamic Relief of U.K. 1984
United Methodist Committee on Relief U.S.A. 1940
Missions of Charity Mother Theresa 1950
Catholic Relief Services U.S.A. 1943
Ghandi Foundation
Affordable Housing Inititative
Everyday Angels
Giving Children Hope
Christian Foundation for Children
Compassion International
Colorado U.S.A. 1952
Veterans Fund for wounded soldiers
Human Organ Funds
Heart Association
St. Jude's Children's Hospital U.S.A. 1942
Shriners Children Hospital U.S.A. 1922
The Campaign for Mayo Clinic U.S.A. 1819
St. Mary's Good Samaritan Hospital Georgia, U.S.A. 1906
MercyShips.org
Frank Lloyd Wright Foundation of Scottsdale Arizona, U.S.A. 1940
WWF World Wildlife Fund 1972
Africa Wildlife Federation 1961
Cancer Research Foundations
African Drought Relief
Hurricane Relief
American Red Cross
Red Crescent, Red Lion, Red Star of David, Red Crystal
Unbound of Kansas City U.S.A. 1981
Greenpeace Canada 1971
Cherokee Child Advocacy Council working with Anna Crawford Children's Center (child abuse response and prevention) Woodstock, Ga. U.S.A. 1989
Hope Center Pregnancy Care Center, Woodstock, Ga. U.S.A.
International Justice Mission Gary Haugen U.S.A. 1997
Elton John Aids Foundation 1992
Darrell and Sandy Blatchley Family Circus Children's Ministry, Philippines 1993
Helping Hands Georgia, U.S.A. 2002
Palaba De Vida (Word of Life) Bolivia.
Next Step Ministries Wisconsin 2003.
There's Hope For The Hungry U.S.A. 2003
Spirit of Harmony Foundation Todd Rundgren, Chicago Illinois 2013
Cultural Initiatives Foundation Mikhail Prokhorov Russia 2004
Hand of Hope Joyce Meyer U.S.A. 2005
Make A Wish America, Arizona 1980
Feed the Children Oklahoma, U.S.A.1979
Food for the Poor Florida, U.S.A. 1982
Firehouse Subs Public Safety Foundation Chris & Robin Sorenson Florida U.S.A. 2005
Gideon's Promise 2007 Legal Aid
Meals on Wheels
Suicide Prevention Support

Some people make small donations to friends or beggars. Some people will buy another person's meal at a restaurant.

SUPPORT EDUCATION and Teachers

You can make donations to most schools and universities to support education for children and adults.

It has been said that parents and family are the first educators of a child with teachers focusing on academics.

Many think that life skills learning, arts, and physical education should be offered to students as well as math, science, history, and languages.

Many believe that teachers should not get romantically involved with students.

Children and teens should not skip school (truancy) to engage in activities with others that could lead to trouble.

In many countries it is standard for a child to have 12 years of education and get their high school diploma.

If you can read this, thank a teacher !

COMPETITION

In our daily lives, it is not necessary to compete in our business, sports, or artistic dealings so fiercely that we ruin each other's good efforts, health, confidence, happiness, and profits.

Share the happiness! Share the world!

Be proud of what you have achieved or tried to invent or improve.

Be proud of what others have accomplished and thank them for their diligent and creative efforts.

WORLD, WORK and HOME LIFE

It is evil to interfere in a person's love relationship. In your daily lives, stick to your work plan for the day and remember your loved ones or your marriage partner who is waiting at home for you. If you have a family and have brought children into this world, your family should take priority over your work life. It is necessary to work to make the money needed to sustain your life but do not destroy your home life.

There are lots of ways for single persons to meet other singles if they are interested in dating.

Speed dating is often held at coffee bars and enables singles to meet a lot of other singles in a short amount of time because each person gets a chance to speak with another person for a few minutes and then move on to meet another person. Contact information can be exchanged. One should always be careful when meeting and exchanging information with strangers; some feel that too much information should not be given. You could meet a person several times in a public place until trust is established between the persons.

Some people date people that other people know or are familiar with.

HARMONY & BALANCE

The spirit of God is real. The spirit in each of us should harmonize the spirit of God, in our lives and in the work we do. We should exist in peaceful harmony.

Some say a balance exists in all things. Try to balance time for work, home, family & friends, enjoyment, rest, God and charitable causes. Live a genuine life devoted to God.

Accept God's blessings, the rain and the sun, the warm weather and the cold weather, the days and the nights. God is the lover of all. Accept God's loving acceptance of all people, God's forgiveness, God's good guidance.

Our human world runs on harmony, energy, synergy, synchronization, changes, cooperation, negotiation, tolerance, creativity, perseverance, information, governments, education, volunteers, charity, donations, sacrifices, supplements, helping each other, faith, luck, friendships, love, work, sleep and rest, nutrition, clean water, clean air, and some think divine forces. Hatred, violence, and wars do not help.

BUDGET

1. Rent or Mortgage (Property Taxes, Maintenance, Pest Control, Security)
   Utilities (Water, Electricity, Gas, Trash Pick-Up)
   Communication (Cable, Satellite, Internet, Phone)
   Transportation Costs or Investment (Vehicle Payment, Maintenance, Insurance)
   Homeowner or Renter Insurance Premium
   Medical & Dental Insurance Premium and out-of-pocket costs
   Life Insurance Premium
   Credit Card Payments
   Checking Account Fees
   Food
   Clothing
   Pets (Food, Veterinarian Visits, Toys, Grooming)
   Entertainment and Personal Allowances
   Club Fees (Condo, Homeowner, Fitness Center, Social Club,
   Marina Fee, Professional Organization)
   Lawyer Premium or Retainer Fee, Accountant Fee, Mechanic Fee
   Landscaping & Road Maintenance
   Maid & Laundry Fee
   Long-term retirement savings & investments)
   Short-term savings (Vacation, Emergencies, Goals)
   Charitable Donations & Tithes
2. Money does not grow on trees so people should not take money for granted or waste money. Sometimes it is okay to splurge on treats, but splurges should be budgeted into your finances. Money is hard to come by, and people work hard for their money. The bills cannot pay themselves, so do not run up the bills unless there is money to pay the bills. When people have no money; the budget is rationing donations, using assets, and bartering (trading goods and services). Money cannot make you happy but money can give you more options.
3. Taxes are collected from people to fund: firefighters, police officers, law enforcement, government employees, government programs, military defense, road construction and road maintenance, aid for poor and disabled persons, new development, and more.
4. Some people think too much greediness of business people is causing high costs of living; many wonder what the definition of a fair profit is; in ancient Judaism it was sinful to charge interest on money loaned to relatives; in ancient Christianity it was sinful to be rich; in ancient Islam charity is important; in ancient Hinduism and Buddhism there is wealth in teachings, wisdom and honor; in ancient Confucianism there is wealth in truth and honor. Some think wages are too low. Some governments allow people to keep profits of their own work; some governments own everything and all profits. Some people believe poor people should be entitled to benefits from a government but some people think it should be left to the citizens (private sector) to help the poor. Good governments have offered to help the needy, since there may not be help from the private sector citizens.
5. Human rights activists are advocating very hard to make clean water, electricity, affordable food and shelter, affordable health care, affordable insurance premiums, individual career choices, religious freedoms, affordable public transportation and communication systems, and a decent working wage available to every human being on Earth, for the well-being and progress of all peoples.

Progress means that advancements and improvements have been made; then new things, more opportunities and options (choices) are available. Progress is a good thing. Progress can begin with a simple idea; then plans are made; maybe a budget will be needed. Progress could happen in a minute. A miracle could occur; a prayer could be answered; someone could say something or do something which could lead to instant progress. Sometimes humans make what they think is progress, but then pitfalls occur and the project has to be re-evaluated, restarted or scrapped.

6. In a household, it is very common for both partners in a relationship to have jobs and contribute to the income of the household. The budget in a household is the concern of both partners. It is wrong for either partner to lie about spending, go on a spending rampage and run up credit cards, make large purchases unbeknownst to their marriage partner, or to save money in a private account without the knowledge of the other partner. Money problems can destroy marriages, friendships, and business relationships.

7. Businesses and countries also have budgets.

8. Religious organizations also have budgets; bills that need to be paid are mortgage or rent, utilities, salaries of staff members and musicians, fees paid to guest speakers and artists, fees paid to police officers or parking attendants, and expenses such as advertising mailouts and supplies.

Most think that God wouldn't want anyone to go into spiritual debt by giving monetary or worldly possessions to religious or charitable entities that you cannot afford. When you go to spiritual assemblies, give a money gift if you can afford to give, but you shouldn't exceed your budget when giving spiritual gifts.

9. The subject of gift-giving can invoke discussion. For example, some think you should not give gifts that you know a person would not like; some are offended if you do not want to receive a gift or do not like a particular item that was given to you; some try to analyze the person who gave the gift or the gift if it was personal or impersonal; some people spend megabucks on gifts and others spend wisely within in their budget. Most think that others give a gift with good intentions, so just say *thank you*, If you cannot use a gift that was given to you, give it away or take it back to a store and exchange it. Gift-givers should not be offended if the gift that was given could not be used. The best gift to each other is friendship.

10. A balanced budget means there is an equal amount of money going into the budget and going out of the budget.

11. Use coupons and discounts, buy in bulk if needed, look for bargains, or buy resales to save money. It is okay to use a coupon when on a romantic date because saving money anytime is wise. A perk is an incentive to buy or do something.

12. Let us all look for ways to help each other. If a person can be helped to reduce their liabilities and improve or increase their assets or life, that person will become stronger financially or possibly have a better life; better people leads to better and stronger neighborhoods and cities; better neighborhoods and cities leads to better countries; better countries will lead to a better and stronger world! Many people are working hard and doing good things. There are more good peaceful people on earth than bad violent people.

13. A person's wealth does not determine the worth of a person's soul.

TIME

1. Only God has perfect timing.
2. Everyone receives an equal amount of time every day. You spend it even if you accomplish nothing. Use your precious time wisely.
A human lives about 36,500 days upon the Earth, or about 100 years. Parrots and sea turtles can live to be 100 years old.
A study was done where people in their 20s and 30s supplied a current photo to an interviewer who ran an age-progression computer application on the photos. The result of the study made people think more about their future.
If you put your car or home keys, purse, and wallet in the same place every day, you will find them and it will save you time.
Being organized and knowing where things are will help save time. Put your bills and mail in one place. File away all warranty information in the same place. Know where your will and last instructions are kept. Know where your address book and your phone book are kept. Organize your kitchen cabinets and drawers, clothes closets, bathroom cabinets, desk, and garage.
It helps to make lists of tasks and errands and to consolidate them.
It helps to have Plan A as the primary plan and Plan B as a back-up plan.
Some people set small-term goals and long-term goals.
You can save time by doing things right the first time so you do not have to do it all over again.
3. At different times in your life, you will have different needs.
When you are younger, you might need a bigger house or apartment to live in because there might be people living with you, you might need space for collections, work, or hobbies, or you might buy a property for investment.
When you get older, people often want smaller areas to live in with less furniture and possessions so utility bills are smaller, it is easier to get around and there is less dusting to do.
4. You should thank someone when they give you their time because their time is valuable. You should appreciate each other's' time.
5. Time can be defined as indefinite, finite, against time, ahead of time, airtime, at one time, at the same time, at times, beat someone's time, behind the times, best time, divide the time, for the time being, from time to time, gain time, in good time, in no time, keep time, kill time, make time, make time with, many a time, mark time, 'me' time, military time, on one's time, on time, out of time, pass the time of day, one's time, saved time, time after time, time and time again, time for adults, time for kids, time of life, time of one's life, time and a half, time will tell, time zones, now is the time, in God's time, with God's perfect timing. There is also time for reckoning (time to decide) like a crossroads. Some think they are or aren't meant to cross paths with another twice in this life. Marriage

is a crossroads; a joining of two lives.

Stealing time means that time may have been allotted for a purpose but a factor took the time away from the purpose.

'When hell freezes over' means that something may not happen.

We are all in the same boat, riding the waves of time. We all harbor under the same umbrella. Time does not stand still. Time can heal.

6. Time has been described as eras of time; for example, the dinosaurs existed for 135 million years in the Mesozoic Era, then 70 million years after that came the Cenozoic Era, which is the current era of science. Pre-historic or stone-age times were when modern Homo Sapiens or humans started creating tools and making fires and occurred 200,000 years ago. Anthropologists believe that the humans who migrated north from Africa created inventions in order to survive cold weather; it changed the DNA in their bodies and thought patterns in their brains in order to survive.

Humans realized the Earth was round instead of flat, and they studied time in relation to the phases of the moon, the seasons and the time it took for the Earth to revolve around the Sun, and invented calendars.

The Seasons and Tilt of the Earth

7. Seasons are the result of the tilt of the Earth on its axis by 23.4 degrees. As the Earth orbits the Sun, different parts of the world receive different amounts of direct sunlight. In July, the Northern Hemisphere is tilted towards the Sun and summer happens, while the Southern Hemisphere is having winter.

In January, the Northern Hemisphere is tilted away from the sun and winter happens, while the Southern Hemisphere is having summer. The seasons are reversed in the Northern and Southern Hemispheres.

During the June solstice (around June 20) in the Northern Hemisphere, the longest period of daylight occurs, except in polar regions where daylight is continuous from a few days to 6 months. But in the Southern Hemisphere, it is the shortest period of daylite.

During the December solstice the effect is opposite in both hemispheres.

The word solstice is derived from Latin words meaning 'sun-standing'.

Equinox occurs twice a year, around March 20 and September 22, when daytime and nighttime are approximately equal in duration. The word equinox is derived from Latin words meaning 'equal night'.

Each season is glorious in its own beauty, a beauty of its own.

Day and Night

8. God gave humans day and night. Man used to plow and reap by the full Harvest Moon which occurred at night because the farmer wanted to make full use of his time and the most profit from his crops; now improvements in farm methods and electricity allow man to not have to rely on a Harvest Moon.

In the current era many jobs require humans to work all schedules of both day and night, with schedules involving all 7 days of the week.

Shift work and travel between time zones can affect a human's spirit so set aside extra time for sleep or rest.

Humans started keeping track of time by putting marks on cave walls, then with shadows of the invention of sun dials, sand in hourglasses and then by the gears and hands clocks, and then numerals in digital clocks.

Humans realized day and night, the lunar cycle of the moon around the Earth, and the cycle of the Earth around the Sun. The Gregorian solar calendar or Current Era Calendar was invented in 1582 by Aloysius Lilius also called Luigi and is currently used by many countries. The earth rotates around the sun in 365.256 days so an extra day was added in every 4 years in the Julian calendar of Julius Caesar of the year 45. The Gregorian calendar removed leap years from turn of the century 00 years that were not divisible by 400.

It has been said that some view time as circular. It has also been said that some view time as linear and simply moving on indefinitely (infinity).

9. Time is past, present, and future.

<u>God's Minute</u>
I have only just a minute.
Only 60 seconds in it,
Forced upon me, I can't
refuse it.
Didn't seek it,
Didn't choose it,
But it's up to me to use it.
I must suffer if I lose it.
Give account if I abuse it.
Just a tiny little minute –
But eternity is in it.

60 seconds could be spent in a sweet minute of prayer.

10. Scientists have determined that the Earth was formed between 4.3-4.6 billion years ago. The constant rate of decay of radioactive isotopes (nuclei of the same element with different amounts of neutron in the nucleus) was used to date minerals and rocks.

Scientists believe the solar system was formed between 4.5 and 5 billion years ago.

Scientists have found trees on the earth that are believed to have been at least 5,000 years old, based on the number of circles of rings in the trunk of the tree. Scientists have dated some trees to be older than the Egyptian pyramids.

An asteroid impact is believed to have changed weather conditions upon the planet and caused the extinction of the dinosaurs that dominated the planet for 135 million years during the Mesozoic Era. It is believed that the impact of a six-mile (or 10-km) wide meteorite with the Yucatan Peninsula is now thought to have caused the extinction event. The impact of the meteorite instantly formed a fireball 1,240 miles (or 2,000 km) across the planet, followed by tsunami hundreds of meters tall. The dust thrown out of the crater left by the impact caused the world to turn to darkness and freezing temperatures for years because there was no sunlight, hindering photosynthesis and severely disrupting the Earth's biosphere. When the dust settled years later, huge amounts of carbon dioxide caused intense global warming. Scientists believe that 65 percent of all species went extinct during this period of weather conditions on the planet. The word 'dinosaur' comes from the Latin or Greek words 'deino' for terrible and 'sauros' for lizard.

One theory scientists have is that the moon could have been a large asteroid that hit the earth, bounced off of the earth, and landed in the orbit of the earth. Perhaps the asteroid brought the first living organism which evolved into all life.

Scientists believe there was only one giant land mass at Antarctica 600 million years ago and they refer to it as Rodinia. Rodinia existed for 400 million years until a large chunk broke off which scientists call the supercontinent of Pangaea which broke up into the current 7 continents.

After the asteroid-impact weather conditions, some birds survived and are believed to be dinosaur descendants.

The Cenozoic Era, which is the current science era, began 70 million years ago after the Mesozoic Era ended with the extinction event. Mammals diverged into terrestrial, marine, and flying animals in the Cenozoic Era.

Scientists think it is a possibility that the first organism was in the ocean and evolved to be a land creature. Scientists think humans have evolved from an ape hominid in Africa 4 million years ago and spread to northern latitudes, where the skin lightened to allow the body to produce more Vitamin D. The darker skins are a genetic sunscreen against ultraviolet radiatin. Homo erectus is the earliest ancestor of homo sapiens in the Homo genus and lived 1.3 million to 1.8 million years ago during the Pleistocene Age. Homo neanderthalensis is another species of evolutionary humans larger in size that existed about 200,000 years ago; some scientists believe Neanderthal DNA is mixed in with Homo Sapien DNA. Cro Magnon (Homo Sapiens Sapiens) evolved about 40,000 years ago. The study of humans is the scientific discipline of anthropology. Many fossils are lost due to the shifting of gigantic earth plates. Some scientists argue that there are not enough old fossils to substantiate the processes of evolution, but skeletons have been found called Homo Ergaster for humans who lived in Africa from about two million to one and a half million years ago. These erectus humans were transitional between Homo Habilis and the later human species called Homo Erectus. Finding the Homo Ergaster skeleton was an important link in human evolution and proved that the human brain kept increasing in size as time passed.

Dinosaurs walked this planet for 135 million years but modern humans have only walked the planet for about than 50,000 years.

The majority of animals on Earth are insects with at least 6 legs,

Our Creator created all living organisms in the Universe.
Man has debated whether God created human beings in a single instant, or if man evolved; no one knows the correct answer except for God. Humans are the highest mammal in the animal charts that humans have recorded according to human intellectual thinking.

Early peoples thought that fiery streaks in the sky were omens of ill fortune or evil power. Now humans know that comets and asteroids are small to nearly planet-sized celestial bodies that are orbiting the Sun. A wide asteroid belt 250-million-miles (400-million km)wide exists between the orbits of Mars and Jupiter. There are at least a million asteroids that are stony or metallic in the asteroid belt, and some of these occasionally get knocked out of their regular orbit and placed into an Earth-crossing orbit. Some asteroids also lie in the same orbit as Jupiter. More than 2,000 asteroids that are larger than a kilometer wide are in Earth-crossing orbits. When an asteroid enters the Earth's atmosphere, their outer surface burns up and creates the fiery streak moving across the sky. Asteroids that enter the Earth are known as meteorites. Small asteroids burn up completely before hitting the Earth but larger asteroids and comets may impact the Earth.

11. Humans have learned a lot from studying nature.
God gave us rainbows, and humans learned many things related to the electromagnetic radiation spectrum of wavelengths which is radio, microwave, and infrared wavelengths, visible light, ultraviolet light, X-rays, and gamma rays. Humans know certain frequencies are heard by the human ear and certain frequencies are heard by animal ears. Some people think rainbows are a symbol of luck. In Irish folklore, it was said there was a leprechaun sitting at the end of the rainbow with a pot of gold, but it was tricky to catch the leprechaun to share in the good fortune. You can see a rainbow in a drop of spilt engine oil on the ground if viewed at a certain angle.

12. God gave lightning bolts ending in fire and humans discovered that they could make fire which led to inventions like fireplaces, cooking, branding, symbols, and sterilization techniques.

13. God gave birds and now humans can fly in gliders, zeppelins, balloons, and airplanes because of human ingenuity, inventions, and hard work. Kites were invented in China. Then hot-air balloons were invented. Louis Paulhan of France (1883-1963CE) and Frederick W. Baldwin of USA (1882-1948CE) were balloon pilots. Orville Wright (1871-1948CE) and Wilbur Wright (1867-1912CE) were brothers in the USA (but whoses ancestors were

German, Dutch, English and Swiss) and are credited with inventing the 3-dimension or 3-axis control (pitch, roll, and yaw) for aircraft to fly. Other aviator inventors were Charlie Taylor (1868-1956CE) who also had a bicycle shop, Thomas E. Selfridge (1882-1908CE) who died while testing an airplane with Orville Wright, Thomas S. Baldwin (1854-1923CE) all of USA, and Alexander G. Bell (1847-1922E) who was from Scotland. Alexander Graham Bell is also credited with inventing the telephone in the USA.
Charles Lindbergh (1902-1974CE) was the first man to fly solo across the Atlantic Ocean. Amelia Earhart (1897-1937CE) was the first woman to fly solo across the Atlantic Ocean.

14. At one time, humans used carrier pigeons as messengers that flew carrying actual scrolls of parchment. Eventually, a global mail system was established with human mail carriers delivering mail on foot, on horseback or with vehicles. Now text messages are sent in an instant with cell phones.

15. God's chameleons change color with time. Now eyeglass lenses and fabric paints can change color with time.

16. Scientists are manufacturing biodegradable trash bags and food containers that will decompose with time.

17. Some say you can be at the right place at the right time, or the right place at the wrong time. Or the wrong place at the right time, or the wrong place at the wrong time.

18. A law of physics is that every action causes another action. For example, it is believed that the action of a butterfly fluttering its wings in one spot on earth could cause a thunderstorm to occur far away at another place on earth; this is called the *ripple effect* and it involves subatomic particles. If you think about this in terms of time – the butterfly fly was in the exact spot at the exact time needed to make the thunderstorm happen. Some physicists think there is a divine matrix connecting everything in the universe, like a blanket.

19. As of the year 2015 CE, scientists have studied the aerodynamics of bumbees and cannot find the answer as to why the bumblebee flies. Many times birds fly in V formation or in varying flight patterns.

20. When baby eagles are learning to fly in the air with their mother, if the baby eagle falters in the air the mother will dip down under the baby eagle and lift it up. The mother will do it time and time again until the baby eagle learns to fly.

21. A golden moment is a time for one to shine. Glory days are good.

22. There is a time to wake up from sleep: to alarm clocks, pets licking our hand, the sound of cracking or rolling thunder, heavy or drizzling rain, or a loved one nudging us.

23. You cannot stop time. It keeps on going.

24. There is a time to stop behavior or actions.

25. As time has progressed, boats have become more varied from the ancient fishing or sailing vessels like the Spanish galleons or Chinese

junks; there are tour boats, ferry, submarines, cruise ships, freighters, patrol boats, barges, aircraft carriers, ski boats, racing boats, pontoon boats, paddle boats.

26. As time has progressed, vehicles have become more varied from handcarts or carriages with wooden wheels. Some early vehicles were 2-wheel bike and 3-wheeler rickshaw (tuk-tuk) or (bajaj) or (tricycle); then the 4-wheel car and 2-wheel scooter and motorcycle. A unicycle has one wheel. Next inventions were the 4-wheeler or 6-wheeler truck with a short bed or a long bed that may also have the ability to tow a boat, tool or horse trailer. Other trucks are huge 18-wheeler tractor rigs that carry cargos like household goods, building materials, chemicals, raw materials, and more in closed or open trailers. Refrigerated trucks carry flowers, milk, frozen foods, and ice cream. Catering trucks keep foods hot. Other trucks are dump trucks, transporter trucks that carry cars and vehicles, wreckers, ambulances, animal control trucks, bucket sky-lift trucks, moving vans, tow trucks, waste management trucks, mail trucks, delivery trucks, fire trucks, concrete trucks, lumber trucks, hoe, plow, steam-rollers, asphalt painter, buses, double-decker buses, armored money truck, fuel and gas carriers, forklifts, crane and wrecking ball, pipe lifter, sprayers, and mulcher. In most engines, a person can switch gears to adjust the speed. Luxury cars offer high standards. Convertible cars have removeable roofs. Roof racks and trailer hitches can be added to vehicles. A school bus carries children to school. Buses transport many passengers to a destination. Both local and long distance. Some buses are double-decker. Railroad trains transport people long distances. The moon buggy was for the moon.

Frederick Simms from Britain invented a steel bumper for cars which U.S. automakers attached to cars in 1915. In 1968 Chevrolet attached plastic bumpers to cars. In the late 1970's, Shahid Khan from Pakistan invented a one-piece bumper for cars. Now some people want to put steel bumpers back on.

27. When analyzing a situation in time, five questions that can be considered are: (1) who, (2) what, (3) where, (4) when, and (5) why.

28. *Taking things for granted* means we are so busy and caught up in our minutes, hours and days that we forget to stop and appreciate what we have.

29. You cannot please all of the people all of the time. Life is not a bed or roses; there are thorns along the way. God is listening to our prayers so open your mind to God.

30. Every day draws closer to our ending and the way seems clearer to that land of perfect day when we will reach at last the home of Our Maker, our soul's true abode. Have your soul ready. Take a moment and choose love divine, how happy you will be; it is a grand and glorious feeling, to make your pathway brighter, to be walking with God, walking closer each day until we are inside the home gate, where friends

and family will be waiting and we will know God. No one knows if or when the end of time will be. Many believe the Lord is always one step ahead of us, leading the way. The beginning of the end is a time to start preparing to go back to God.

The Meeting in the Air

I will go there someday to meet my sweet Lord. It will be glorious, I do declare, at the meeting in the air. When God calls, I'll fly away, in the Lord's light, all hopes renewed in the sweet forever.

Eternity

31. Even before the beginning of all time, the Spirit was and is still the source of all origin and creation. Our time on Earth will perish and pass away, but the divine will not perish or pass away. God will guide our souls home, but of that day or hour not a single person knows, not even all the angels in Heaven, but only God.
The unseen Lord is with us all the days to the close and consummation of our lives on this earth.
32. With united hearts and one voice, we praise and glorify God. May the Spirit so fill your heart today with joy and peace in believing that by the power of the divine you may be filled with hope, love and peace. Love each other, as the Messiahs, Prophets, Messengers, Avatars, and Brahman told you. The Unseen Spirit is the Alpha and the Omega, the Beginning and the End, as it was in the beginning, is now, and ever shall be without end. God Bless our Earth, all lands and people. Peace and love for all the earth.

MEASUREMENT CONVERSIONS

Length and Distance

To convert	Into	Multiply by
centimeters	inches	0.3937
centimeters	feet	0.0328
centimeters	meters	0.01
centimeters	millimeters	10
millimeters	inches	.0394
inches	centimeters	2.5400
inches	feet	0.0833
inches	meters	0.0254
inches	yards	0.0278
meters	feet	3.2808
meters	inches	39.37
meters	miles	0.0006214
meters	millimeters	1000
meters	centimeters	100
meters	kilometers	0.001
meters	yards	1.0936
feet	meters	0.3048
feet	inches	12
feet	miles	0.0001894
feet	yards	0.3333
kilometers	miles	.6214
kilometers	feet	3281
kilometers	yards	1093
kilometers	meters	1000
miles	kilometers	1.6093
miles	feet	5280
miles	yards	1760
yards	meters	0.9144
yards	inches	36
yards	feet	3
yards	miles	.0005682

Surface or Area

To convert	Into	Multiply by
square feet	square meters	.0929
square yards	square meters	.8361
square miles	square kilometers	2.5900
square kilometers	square miles	.3861
hectares	acres	2.4710

Volume and Capacity

To convert	Into	Multiply by
pints (U.S.)	liters	.4732
quarts (U.S.)	liters	.9463
gallons (U.S.)	liters	3.7853
liters	cups	4.226
liters	pints (U.S.)	2.1134
liters	quarts (U.S.)	1.0567
liters	gallons (U.S.)	.2642
liters	milliliters	1000
gallons (U.S.)	pints	8
gallons (U.S.)	quarts	4
gallons	ounces	128
quarts	pints	2.0
quarts	gallons	.25
pints	cups	2

Weight and Mass

To convert	Into	Multiply by
ounces	grams	28.3495
ounces	pounds	0.0625
ounces	kilograms	0.028
pounds	kilograms	.4536
pounds	ounces	16
pounds	grams	453.59
short tons	metric tons	.9072
kilograms	pounds	2.2046
kilograms	ounces	35.274
kilograms	grams	1000
metric tons	short tons	1.1023

METRIC SYSTEM OF MEASURE
LINEAR MEASURE

10 millimeters............... 1 centimeter
10 centimeters............. 1 decimeter
10 decimeters.............. 1 meter
10 meters............... .... 1 dekameter
10 dekameters.............. 1 hectometer
10 hectometers............. 1 kilometer

1 meter (m) = 100 cm = 1000 mm
1 millimeter (mm) = .001 m
1 centimeter (cm) = .01 m
1 decimeter (dm) = .1 m

1 dekameter (dkm)	=	10 m
1 hectometer (hm)	=	100 m
1 kilometer (km)	=	1000 m

AREA MEASURE

100 sq millimeters......... 1 sq centimeter
10,000 sq centimeter..... 1 sq meter
1,000,000 sq millimeter... 1 sq meter
100 sq meters.............. 1 are (a)
100 ares...................... 1 hectare (ha)
100 hectares............... 1 sq kilometer
1,000,000 sq meters....... 1 sq kilometer

VOLUME MEASURE

1 liter........................... 0.001 cubic meter
10 milliliters................... 1 centiliter
10 centiliters................. 1 deciliter
10 deciliters.................. 1 liter
10 liters......................... 1 dekaliter
10 dekaliters................. 1 hectoliter
10 hectoliters................ 1 kiloliter

1 liter (l) = 100 cl	=	1000 ml
1 milliliter (ml)	=	.001 liter
1 centiliter (cl)	=	.01 liter
1 deciliter (dl)	=	.1 liter
1 dekaliter (dkl)	=	10 liter
1 hectoliter (hl)	=	100 liter
1 kiloliter (kl)	=	1000 liter

WEIGHT

10 milligrams...............1 centigram
10 centigrams............ 1 decigram
10 decigrams............ 1 gram
10 grams.......... .... 1 dekagram
10 dekagrams........... 1 hectogram
10 hectograms.......... 1 kilogram
1000 kilograms......... 1 metric ton

1 gram (g) = 100 cg	=	1000 mg
1 milligram (mg)	=	.001 g
1 centigram (cg)	=	.01 g
1 decigram (dg)	=	.1 g
1 dekagram (dkg)	=	10 g
1 hectogram (hg)	=	100 g

1 kilogram (kg) = 1000 g

US CUSTOMARY MEASUREMENT

LINEAR MEASURE

12 inches.................. 1 foot
3 feet....................... 1 yard
5 ½ yards................ 1 rod
40 rods..................... 1 furlong
8 furlongs.................. 1 mile
5280 feet................... 1 mile
3 land miles............... 1 league

AREA MEASURE

144 sq inches............. 1 sq foot
9 sq feet.................... 1 sq yard
30 ¼ sq yards............. 1 sq rod
160 square rods.......... 1 acre
640 acres.................. 1 sq mile
1 sq mile.................... 1 section
36 sections................. 1 township

VOLUME MEASURE

4 gills (2 cups)............. 1 pint
2 pints....................... 1 quart
4 quarts..................... 1 gallon
3 tsp..........................1 tbsp
4 tbsp........................ ¼ cup
5 1/3 tbsp.................. 1/3 cup
16 tbsp....................... 1 cup
2 cups....................... 1 pint
4 cups....................... 1 quart

DRY MEASURE

2 pints............................ 1 quart
8 quarts.......................... 1 peck
4 pecks.......................... 1 bushel

WEIGHT

27-11/32 grains................. 1 dram
16 drams......................... 1 ounce
16 ounces....................... 1 pound
100 pounds..................... 1 hundredweight
20 hundredweights............ 1 ton

COMPUTER MEASURE

Bit – unit or measure of storage that can be transmitted
Byte – unit of measure for storage capacity
8 bits in a byte
1024 bytes in a kilobyte (Kbyte or KB)
1024 kilobytes in a megabyte (Mbyte or MB)
1024 megabytes in a gigabyte (Gbyte or GB)
1024 gigabytes in a terabyte (Tbyte or TB)

TEMPERATURE CONVERSIONS

To convert Celsius (C°) to Fahrenheit (F°): multiply by 9, divide by 5 and then add 32.
To convert Fahrenheit (F°) to Celsius (C°): subtract 32, multiply by 5, and then divide by 9.

Fraction Conversions

FRACTION	DECIMAL	PERCENT
1/1000	0.001	0.1%
1/100	0.01	1.0%
1/16	0.0625	6.25%
1/8	0.125	12.5%
3/16	0.1875	18.75%
1/4	0.25	25.0%
5/16	0.3125	31.25%
1/3	0.3333	33.33%
3/8	0.375	37.5%
1/2	0.5	50.0%
9/16	0.5625	56.25%
5/8	0.625	62.5%
2/3	0.6666	66.66%
3/4	0.75	75.0%
13/16	0.8125	81.25%
7/8	0.875	87.5%
1	1.0	100.0%

MATH

Arabic Counting Numbers

0 ZERO

1, 2, 3, 4, 5, 6, 7, 8, 9, 10,
11, 12, 13, 14, 15, 16, 17, 18, 19, 20,
21, 22, 23, 24, 25, 26, 27, 28, 29, 30,
31, 32, 33, 34, 35, 36, 37, 38, 39, 40,
41, 42, 43, 44, 45, 46, 47, 48, 49, 50,
51, 52, 53, 54, 55, 56, 57, 58, 59, 60,
61, 62, 63, 64, 65, 66, 67, 68, 69, 70,
71, 72, 73, 74, 75, 76, 77, 78, 79, 80,
81, 82, 83, 84, 85, 86, 87, 88, 89, 90,
91, 92, 93, 94, 95, 96, 97, 98, 99, 100

101, 102, 103, 104, 105, 106, 107, 108, 109, 110,
111, 112, 113, 114, 115, 116, 117, 118, 119, 120,
121, 122, 123, 124, 125, 126, 127, 128, 129, 130,
131, 132, 133, 134, 135, 136, 137, 138, 139, 140,
141, 142, 143, 144, 145, 146, 147, 148, 149, 150,
151, 152, 153, 154, 155, 156, 157, 158, 159, 160,
161, 162, 163, 164, 165, 166, 167, 168, 169, 170,
171, 172, 173, 174, 175, 176, 177, 178, 179, 180,
181, 182, 183, 184, 185, 186, 187, 188, 189, 190,
191, 192, 193, 194, 195, 196, 197, 198, 199, 200

201, 202, 203, 204, 205, 206, 207, 208, 209, 210,
211, 212, 213, 214, 215, 216, 217, 218, 219, 220,
221, 222, 223, 224, 225, 226, 227, 228, 229, 230,
231, 232, 233, 234, 235, 236, 237, 238, 239, 240,
241, 242, 243, 244, 245, 246, 247, 248, 249, 250,
251, 252, 253, 254, 255, 256, 257, 258, 259, 260,
261, 262, 263, 264, 265, 266, 267, 268, 269, 270,
271, 272, 273, 274, 275, 276, 277, 278, 279, 280,
281, 282, 283, 284, 285, 286, 287, 288, 289, 290,
291, 292, 293, 294, 295, 296, 297, 298, 299, 300

301, 302, 303, 304, 305, 306, 307, 308, 309, 310,
311, 312, 313, 314, 315, 316, 317, 318, 319, 320,
321, 322, 323, 324, 325, 326, 327, 328, 329, 330,
331, 332, 333, 334, 335, 336, 337, 338, 339, 340,
341, 342, 343, 344, 345, 346, 347, 348, 349, 350,
351, 352, 353, 354, 355, 356, 357, 358, 359, 360,
361, 362, 363, 364, 365, 366, 367, 368, 369, 370,
371, 372, 373, 374, 375, 376, 377, 378, 379, 380,
381, 382, 383, 384, 385, 386, 387, 388, 389, 390,
391, 392, 393, 394, 395, 396, 397, 398, 399, 400

401, 402, 403, 404, 405, 406, 407, 408, 409, 410,
411, 412, 413, 414, 415, 416, 417, 418, 419, 420,
421, 422, 423, 424, 425, 426, 427, 428, 429, 430,
431, 432, 433, 434, 435, 436, 437, 438, 439, 440,
441, 442, 443, 444, 445, 446, 447, 448, 449, 450,
451, 452, 453, 454, 455, 456, 457, 458, 459, 460,
461, 462, 463, 464, 465, 466, 467, 468, 469, 470,
471, 472, 473, 474, 475, 476, 477, 478, 479, 480,
481, 482, 483, 484, 485, 486, 487, 488, 489, 490,
491, 492, 493, 494, 495, 496, 497, 498, 499, 500

501, 502, 503, 504, 505, 506, 507, 508, 509, 510,
511, 512, 513, 514, 515, 516, 517, 518, 519, 520,
521, 522, 523, 524, 525, 526, 527, 528, 529, 530,
531, 532, 533, 534, 535, 536, 537, 538, 539, 540,
541, 542, 543, 544, 545, 546, 547, 548, 549, 550,
551, 552, 553, 554, 555, 556, 557, 558, 559, 560,
561, 562, 563, 564, 565, 566, 567, 568, 569, 570,
571, 572, 573, 574, 575, 576, 577, 578, 579, 580,
581, 582, 583, 584, 585, 586, 587, 588, 589, 590,
591, 592, 593, 594, 595, 596, 597, 598, 599, 600

601, 602, 603, 604, 605, 606, 607, 608, 609, 610,
611, 612, 613, 614, 615, 616, 617, 618, 619, 620,
621, 622, 623, 624, 625, 626, 627, 628, 629, 630,
631, 632, 633, 634, 635, 636, 637, 638, 639, 640,
641, 642, 643, 644, 645, 646, 647, 648, 649, 650,
651, 652, 653, 654, 655, 656, 657, 658, 659, 660,
661, 662, 663, 664, 665, 666, 667, 668, 669, 670,
671, 672, 673, 674, 675, 676, 677, 678, 679, 680,
681, 682, 683, 684, 685, 686, 687, 688, 689, 690,
691, 692, 693, 694, 695, 696, 697, 698, 699, 700

701, 702, 703, 704, 705, 706, 707, 708, 709, 710,
711, 712, 713, 714, 715, 716, 717, 718, 719, 720,
721, 722, 723, 724, 725, 726, 727, 728, 729, 730,
731, 732, 733, 734, 735, 736, 737, 738, 739, 740,
741, 742, 743, 744, 745, 746, 747, 748, 749, 750,
751, 752, 753, 754, 755, 756, 757, 758, 759, 760,
761, 762, 763, 764, 765, 766, 767, 768, 769, 770,
771, 772, 773, 774, 775, 776, 777, 778, 779, 780,
781, 782, 783, 784, 785, 786, 787, 788, 789, 790,
791, 792, 793, 794, 795, 796, 797, 798, 799, 800

801, 802, 803, 804, 805, 806, 807, 808, 809, 810,
811, 812, 813, 814, 815, 816, 817, 818, 819, 820,
821, 822, 823, 824, 825, 826, 827, 828, 829, 830,
831, 832, 833, 834, 835, 836, 837, 838, 839, 840,
841, 842, 843, 844, 845, 846, 847, 848, 849, 850,

851, 852, 853, 854, 855, 856, 857, 858, 859, 860,
861, 862, 863, 864, 865, 866, 867, 868, 869, 870,
871, 872, 873, 874, 875, 876, 877, 878, 879, 880,
881, 882, 883, 884, 885, 886, 887, 888, 889, 890,
891, 892, 893, 894, 895, 896, 897, 898, 899, 900

901, 902, 903, 904, 905, 906, 907, 908, 909, 910,
911, 912, 913, 914, 915, 916, 917, 918, 919, 920,
921, 922, 923, 924, 925, 926, 927, 928, 929, 930,
931, 932, 933, 934, 935, 936, 937, 938, 939, 940,
941, 942, 943, 944, 945, 946, 947, 948, 949, 950,
951, 952, 953, 954, 955, 956, 957, 958, 959, 960,
961, 962, 963, 964, 965, 966, 967, 968, 969, 970,
971, 972, 973, 974, 975, 976, 977, 978, 979, 980,
981, 982, 983, 984, 985, 986, 987, 988, 989, 990,
991, 992, 993, 994, 995, 996, 997, 998, 999, 1000.

Addition

1 + 1 = 2
9 + 1 = 10
25 + 2 = 27
99 + 1 = 100
100 + 3 = 103
114 + 89 = 203
4 + 0 = 4
40,500 + 700 = 41,200
100,013 + 906,000 = 1,006,013
1,000,400,020 + 300,001 = 1,000,700,021

Subtraction

4 – 0 = 4
17 – 2 = 15
100 – 40 = 60
55 – 55 = 0
20 – 9 = 11
947 – 298 = 649
746 – 52 = 694

Multiplication Table

	1	2	3	4	5	6	7	8	9	10	11	12
1	1	2	3	4	5	6	7	8	9	10	11	12
2	2	4	6	8	10	12	14	16	18	20	22	24
3	3	6	9	12	15	18	21	24	27	30	33	36
4	4	8	12	16	20	24	28	32	36	40	44	48
5	5	10	15	20	25	30	35	40	45	50	55	60
6	6	12	18	24	30	36	42	48	54	60	66	72
7	7	14	21	28	35	42	49	56	63	70	77	84
8	8	16	24	32	40	48	56	64	72	80	88	96
9	9	18	27	36	45	54	63	72	81	90	99	108
10	10	20	30	40	50	60	70	80	90	100	110	120
11	11	22	33	44	55	66	77	88	99	110	121	132
12	12	24	36	48	60	72	84	96	108	120	132	144

Division

Numbers can be divided equally by an integer.

10 ÷ 2 = 5   33 ÷ 11 = 3   7 ÷ 7 = 1
10 ÷ 5 = 2   24 ÷ 3 = 8   7 ÷ 1 = 7

10 ÷ 3 = 3.3333 repeating so 3 is not an integer of 10.

A number cannot be divided by 0.

FRACTIONS

The numerator is the top number.
The denominator is the bottom number.

To add or subtract fractions, first find the common denominator. Then add the numerators across. Then add the denominators across. Reduce fraction if possible by a common denominator.

1/3 + 2/5 = 5/15 + 6/15 = 11/15

To multiply, multiply numerators across then denominators across:

1/3 X 2/5 = 2/15

To divide, multiply the first fraction with the reciprocal of the second fraction:

2/3 ÷ 1/6 = 2/3 X 6/1 = 12/3 = 4

Decimals and Percent

To write a decimal for a percent, move the decimal point two places to the left or divide by 100. Omit the percent sign.

15% = .15 = 0.15
15 / 100 = .15

22.6% = .226 = 0.226
22.6 / 100 = .226

To write a percent for a decimal, move the decimal point two places to the right or multiply by 100. Add the percent sign.

0.15 = 15.0 = 15 %
.15 x 100 = 15 %

0.226 = 22.6 = 22.6 %
.226 x 100 = 22.6 %

To find the percentage for a fraction you have to cross multiply across the equal sign and then divide by the common denominator to find x. Add the percent sign.

3 / 4 = x / 100

300 = 4 x

300 / 4 = 4 x / 4

75 = 1 x

75 / 1 = 1 x / 1

75 = x

75%

To convert a percentage to a fraction, omit the percent sign. Make the percent the numerator and 100 the denominator. Reduce by a common denominator.

25% = 25/100 ÷ 25/25 = 1/4

31.25% = 31.25/100 ÷ 6.25/6.25 = 5/16

ORDER OF ALGEBRAIC EXPRESSIONS

1. Do all operations inside of parentheses or brackets,
2. Do any exponents or roots.
3. Working left to right, do all multiplication and division.
4. Working left to right, do all addition and subtraction.

12 / 6 x 3 / 2
12 / 6 = 2
2 x 3 = 6
6 / 2 = 3

$7 + (6 \times 5^2 + 3)$
7 + (6 x 25 + 3)
7 + (150 + 3)
7 + (153)
160

CHOKING VICTIM HELP

Baby – 1 year

Conscious

1. Have someone call 911 or a local emergency number.
2. Lay baby on its stomach on your lap with head slanting downwards and give 5 back blows.
3. If object remains lodged, turn baby on back and give 5 chest compressions: use 2 fingers and depress sternum ½ to 1 inch for each thrust.

Unconscious

1. Look for and remove foreign object seen in mouth.
2. Give 1 rescue breath covering both baby's nose and mouth with your mouth. If air does not go in...
3. Give 5 chest compressions.

Children and Adults

Conscious

1. Have someone call 911 or a local emergency number.
2. Get behind the victim and use a fist to make abdominal thrusts in the area above the belly button and under the diaphragm (Heimlich maneuver). (This compresses the lungs and exerts pressure on any object lodged in the trachea, hopefully expelling it. It amounts to an artificial cough.)

A person can also be thrust against a fixed object such as a railing or the back of a chair to apply pressure where a rescuer's hands would normally do so.

A person can perform abdominal thrusts on themselves by throwing themself against a fixed object such as a railing or the back of a chair to apply pressure where a rescuer's hands would normally do so. As with other forms of the procedure, it is possible that internal injuries may result to the abdomen or ribs.

For pregnant or obese patients, the rescuer places their hand in the center of the chest to compress, rather than in the abdomen.

Many protocols now advocate the use of hard blows with the heel of the hand on the upper back of the victim between the shoulder blades. Some have said this could cause the object to fall lower into the windpipe. It could help if the choking victim could slant their body in a downward position before the back blows were given.

3. Continue until the object is forced out or until victim becomes unconscious.

Unconscious

1. Look for and remove any foreign object seen in mouth.
2. Give 2 rescue breaths. If air does not go in...
3. Give 15 chest compressions. For children 1 to 8 years old, give 1 rescue breath and 5 chest compressions.

Repeat steps until successful or help arrives.

CPR HELP

Cardiopulmonary resuscitation (CPR) involves a rescuer performing chest compressions and artificial respiration (rescue breaths) on an unconscious heart attack victim.

Chest compressions are at least 5cm (2 inches) deep except for infants 4 cm (1.6 inches) and at a rate of at least 100 per minute in an effort to create artificial blood circulation by manually pumping blood through the heart and thus the body. The rescuer may also provide rescue breaths by either exhaling into the subject's mouth or nose or using a device that pushes air into the subject's lungs.
The recommended order of interventions is chest compressions, check airway, rescue breaths but some recommend check airway, breaths, and compressions for children.

Use 30 compressions and then 2 rescue breaths for adults.
Use 15 compressions and then 2 rescue breaths for children.
For infants, use 3 compressions and then 1 rescue breath.

In adults, rescuers should use two hands for the chest compressions, while in children they should use one hand, and with infants two fingers (index and middle fingers).

It can be difficult to determine the presence or absence of a pulse.
If an advanced airway such as an endotracheal tube or laryngeal mask airway is in place, artificial ventilation should occur without pauses in compressions at a rate of 8-10 per minute.

MAIN BLOOD TYPES

Blood Type	Antibodies	Antigens	Who can receive it
O+	A, B	none	O+, A+, B+, AB+
O-	A, B	none	All blood types
A+	B	A	A+, AB+
A-	B	A	A+, A-, AB+, AB-
B+	A	B	B+, AB+
B-	A	B	B+, B-, AB+, AB-
AB+	none	A, B	AB+
AB-	none	A, B	AB+, AB-

Rh factor is an antigen indicated by positive + or negative -.
Usually, Rh – blood is given to Rh – patients, and Rh+
and Rh- may be given to Rh + patients.

Blood type and what that blood type can receive

O+ can receive O+, O-
O- can receive O-
A+ can receive A+, A-, O+, O-
A- can receive A-, O-
B+ can receive B+,B-,O+,O-
B- can receive B-, O-
AB+ can receive AB+, AB-, B+,B-, A+,A-,O+,O-
AB- can receive AB-, B-, A-, O-

COMPATIBLE BLOOD PLASMA TYPES

O can receive O, A, B, AB
A can receive A, AB
B can receive B, AB
AB can receive AB

Pat Bean
678 216 2126